The Routledge International Handbook of Globalization Studies

The Routledge International Handbook of Globalization Studies offers students clear and informed chapters on the history of globalization and key theories that have considered the causes and consequences of the globalization process. There are substantive sections looking at demographic, economic, technological, social and cultural changes in globalization. The Handbook examines many negative aspects – new wars, slavery, illegal migration, pollution and inequality – but concludes with an examination of responses to these problems through human rights organizations, international labour law and the growth of cosmopolitanism. There is a strong emphasis on interdisciplinary approaches with essays covering sociology, demography, economics, politics, anthropology and history.

The Handbook, written in a clear and direct style, will appeal to a wide audience. The extensive references and sources will direct students to areas of further study.

Bryan S. Turner was Professor of Sociology at the University of Cambridge (1998–2005) and at the National University of Singapore (2005–2009). He is currently the Alona Evans Distinguished Visiting Professor of Sociology at Wellesley College, USA, and the Director of the Centre for the Study of Contemporary Muslim Societies, University of Western Sydney, Australia. He has published The New Medical Sociology (2004) and The Body and Society (2008).

'Bryan Turner is one of today's most creative social scientists and it is a treat for the reader that he now has turned his attention also to globalization. The topics that are discussed in this work are all extremely well chosen and cover everything from economics, internet and politics to the climate, Human Rights and the spread of infectious diseases. *The Routledge International Handbook of Globalization Studies* is a must for everybody who wants to better understand the contemporary world as well as for every library that wants to serve and educate its visitors.'
Professor Richard Swedberg, Cornell University, USA

'This volume provides a valuable overview of contemporary discussions of globalization and what exactly the term means. Bryan Turner's introduction surveys the relevant debates with breadth and sobriety, calling into question some of the reigning shibboleths about this much-discussed but little-understood buzzword of our times. The volume will be useful to the specialist and the student alike.'
Professor John Torpey, City University of New York Graduate Center, USA

'*The Routledge International Handbook of Globalization Studies* makes a significant contribution to the widely discussed theme of globalization. Bryan Turner has skilfully brought together a variety of scholars from a broad range of social science disciplines, and the reader will be impressed by the rich and insightful arguments that emerge from this diverse range of perspectives.'
Professor Mohamed Cherkaoui, CNRS and University of Paris Sorbonne

The Routledge International Handbook of Globalization Studies

Edited by Bryan S. Turner

Routledge
Taylor & Francis Group

LONDON AND NEW YORK

First published 2010
by Routledge

Paperback edition published in 2011
2 Park Square, Milton Park, Abingdon, Oxon, OX14 4RN

Simultaneously published in the USA and Canada
by Routledge
711 Third Avenue, New York, NY 10017

Routledge is an imprint of the Taylor & Francis Group, an informa business

British Library Cataloguing in Publication Data
A catalogue record for this book is available from the British Library

Library of Congress Cataloging in Publication Data
The Routledge international handbook of globalization studies / edited by Bryan
S. Turner.
    p. cm.
    1. Globalization–History. I. Turner, Bryan S.
    HF1365.R68 2011
    303.48′2–dc23
        2011018175

ISBN 13: 978-0-415-45808-5 hbk
ISBN 13: 978-0-415-68608-2 pbk
ISBN 13: 978-0-203-87000-6 ebk

Typeset in Bembo
by Taylor & Francis Books

Printed and bound in Great Britain by
CPI Antony Rowe, Chippenham, Wiltshire

Contents

Figures

Tables

Contributors

Kadambari Anantram is a graduate student at the University of California, Riverside. She received a BA in Economics from Stella Maris College, Chennai, India, an MSc in Environmental Economics from the University of York, UK and an MA in Environment, Development and Policy from the University of Sussex, Brighton, UK. Her research interests include the application of neo-classical techniques in addressing environmental problems, political economy of the environment and issues of rural development, especially within India. She is author of 'Adaptation to Climate Change in the Context of Sustainable Development' (written for the 2006 UNDESA conference on Climate Change and Sustainable Development Conference in New Delhi), *Atlas of the Sustainability of Food Security* (2004, a report for the Swaminathan Research Foundation and the World Food Programme), 'Climate Change' (2003), co-author of 'Mapping Climate Vulnerability and Poverty in Africa' (2006, a Report to the Department for International Development, ILRI), *Financing Adaptation* (2005, written for the Conference of Parties in Montreal) and *The Geography Teachers, India* 8(3): 20–26. She is currently doing research with Christopher Chase-Dunn and Ellen Reese on global civil society and social forum participation. Her next research project will examine the development of rural farmer households' indebtedness nexus in India.

Patrik Aspers is currently a researcher at the Max Planck Institute for the Study of Societies in Cologne and Associate Professor at Stockholm University. He holds a PhD in Sociology from Stockholm University (2001), where he also finished his undergraduate studies. He has been guest researcher, among other places, at Harvard University, Columbia University and the London School of Economics. He has been the chair of the economic sociology research network of the European Sociological Association, and is the chair of the economic sociology section of the Swedish Sociological Association. At the Max Planck Institute for the Study of Societies he is part of the research group that studies markets. He is author of *Markets in Fashion: A Phenomenological Approach* (2nd edn 2005). In addition to studies on virtues and sociological theory, he has published texts on classical economists such as Alfred Marshall and Vilfredo Pareto and on the sociology of Friedrich Nietzsche. He is currently researching two books, one on the economic sociology of markets and the other on the fashion garment industry.

Ulrich Beck is Professor of Sociology at the University of Munich, and the *British Journal of Sociology* Visiting Centennial Professor at the London School of Economics and Political Sciences since 1997. He is editor of *Soziale Welt* and *Second Modernity* at Suhrkamp (Frankfurt am Main). His interests focus on 'risk society', 'globalization', 'individualization', 'reflexive modernization' and 'cosmopolitanism'. He is founding director of the research centre Reflexive Modernization at the University of Munich (in cooperation with four other universities in the area), financed since 1999 by the DFG (German Research Society). Among his books are: *Risk Society* (1992); *Reflexive Modernization* (1994, with Anthony Giddens and Scott Lash); *The Reinvention of Politics* (1997); *Power in the Gobal Age* (2005); *The Cosmopolitan Vision* (2006); *The Cosmopolitan Europe* (2007, with Edgar Grande); *World Risk Society* (2008); *World at Risk* (2008). His books have been translated into 35 languages.

Peter Beyer is Professor of Religious Studies (Sociology of Religion) at the University of Ottawa. He obtained his PhD in 1981 at the University of St. Michael's College in Toronto, and completed postdoctoral studies at the Université du Québec à Montréal between 1981 and 1983. He taught at the University of Toronto between 1983 and 1995, whereupon he took up his current position in Ottawa. In the early part of his career his research focused on issues in the nineteenth- and twentieth-century religious history of Canada, particularly French Canadian Roman Catholicism. Currently, his major areas of expertise include religion and globalization, sociological theory of religion, religion and migration, and religion in contemporary Canada, especially as concerns the religious diversity that has resulted from post-1970 immigration. He has had a lifelong interest in the sociological theories of Niklas Luhmann, and published an English translation of some of his work on religion in 1984. Beside this, his publications include *Religion and Globalization* (1994), *Religion in the Process of Globalization* (ed., 2001) and *Religions in Global Society* (2006), *Religion, Globalization, and Culture* (ed. with Lori Beaman, 2007), *Religious and Diversity in Canada* (ed. with Lori Beaman, 2008), as well as around 50 articles and chapters in scholarly journals and edited volumes. He is currently completing two major research projects on the religious expression of locally born or raised youth and young adults of recent immigrant background in Canada.

Robin Blackburn is Professor of Sociology at Essex University, and a Distinguished Visiting Professor of Historical Studies at the New School for Social Research in New York. He was editor of the *New Left Review* from 1981 to 1999. Educated at Oxford and the London School of Economics, he was a member of the International Marxist Group. He has written a number of influential historical works such as *The Overthrow of Colonial Society 1776–1848* (1988), and his most recent publications include *Banking on Death or Investing in Life* (2002) and *Age Shock and Pension Power* (2007).

Christopher Chase-Dunn is Distinguished Professor of Sociology and Director of the Institute for Research on World-Systems at the University of California-Riverside and founding editor of the *Journal of World-Systems Research*. His research focuses on the causes of human socio-cultural evolution, global state formation and the democratization of global governance.

Daniele Conversi is Senior Lecturer at the European Policy Research Centre, University of Lincoln. He received his PhD at the London School of Economics and then taught at Cornell and Syracuse Universities, as well as at the Central European University, Budapest. His books include *The Basques, the Catalans, and Spain* (http://easyweb.easynet. co.uk/conversi/book.html) and the edited volume *Ethnonationalism in the Contemporary World* (http://easyweb.easynet.co.uk/conversi/ethnonat). Among his recent articles, 'Art, Nationalism and War: Political Futurism in Italy (1909–1944)', *Sociology Compass*, 2009, is part of a British Academy-funded project on Italian Futurism, war and state-making. His fields of teaching and research include theories of nationalism, ethnic conflict resolution, globalization, comparative politics and political sociology. His current research explores the role of culture in the process of state-building from 1789 to the present, particularly the relationship between nationalism and culture.

Thomas Cushman is Professor of Sociology and Chair of the Sociology Department at Wellesley College, MA. He is the founding editor and editor-at-large of the *Journal of Human Rights* and the editor of the *Routledge International Handbook of Human Rights*. In 2009 he edited with Thomas Brudholm *The Religious in Responses to Mass Atrocity*. He is an Honorary Professor in the Social Sciences at the University of Witwatersrand and he has been Visiting Professor at Brandeis University and Birkbeck College, University of London.

Julio Pérez Díaz is a research fellow in the demography department of the Spanish Council for Scientific Research (CSIC) in Madrid. He studied Philosophy and Education Science at the Universities of Barcelona and the National Distance Learning University (Spanish equivalent of the Open University). From 1991 to 2007 he was a research fellow at the Centre d'Estudis Demogràfics, Universitat Autònoma de Barcelona where he completed his PhD thesis (2001) 'Socio-demographic transformations in routes towards maturity: the Spanish generations of 1906 to 1945'. He specializes in the history of demography, population policies and demographic ageing, and is a member of the International Union for the Scientific Study of Population. He edits a portal on the internet on such issues (http://www.ced.uab.es/jperez) and advises the Colegio de Médicos de Barcelona on the subject. Recent publications include the book *La Madurez de Masas* [*Mass Maturity*] (2005) which received a Fundació La Caixa Research Prize, and a forthcoming monograph with John MacInnes *The Reproductive Revolution*. Additional recent collaborations are publications in *International Sociological Review*, and papers with John MacInnes: 'La tercera revolución de la modernidad: la reproductiva' in *Revista Española de Investigaciones Sociológicas* (2008); 'Low fertility and population replacement in Scotland' in *Population, Space and Place* (2007); 'Demography' in Bryan S. Turner (ed.) *The New Blackwell Companion to Social Theory* (2009); and 'Valoración social del incremento de la violencia doméstica' in Guillermo Barrios and Pilar Rivas (eds) *Violencia de Género: Perspectiva Multidisciplinar y Práctica Forense* (2007).

Peter Dickens is Visiting Professor of Sociology at the University of Brighton. He is also Associate Lecturer in Sociology, Faculty of Social and Political Sciences, University of Cambridge. Between 1973 and 1999 he was a Lecturer, Reader and Head of the Department of Sociology, University of Sussex. In 2000 he was made Fellow and Director of Studies in Social and Political Sciences, Fitzwilliam College, Cambridge. Originally trained as an architect, he designed public-sector housing for the London

County Council during the late 1960s. Since the early 1970s he has published ten books and a large number of papers linking social theory, psychoanalysis and the natural sciences within a critical realist perspective. His 2004 book *Society and Nature: Changing Our Environment, Changing Ourselves* was given an Outstanding Publication Award by the American Sociological Association. In 2007 he published (with James Ormrod) *Cosmic Society: Towards a Sociology of the Universe.* He continues to work on the sociology of outer-space humanization and the changing relationships between cosmologies, societies and human subjectivity.

Lior Gelernter is a doctoral candidate at the department of Sociology and Anthropology in Bar-Ilan University in Israel. His main research interests are sociology of internet and culture. He wrote his MA dissertation on social capital formation in the internet and its effects on the field of science-fiction fandom in Israel. He is currently conducting research on the epistemic culture emerging in Wikipedia, the online encyclopedia, for his doctoral thesis, under the supervision of Dr. Ilana Friedrich-Silber.

Carlos Gigoux is a PhD candidate in Sociology at the University of Essex. His thesis examines the production of ethnic representations concerning the Indigenous peoples of the Archipelago of Tierra del Fuego and its relationship with their genocide. His research interests are mainly concerned with the relationship between the modern world and Indigenous peoples, particularly looking at topics such as globalization, social and cultural identity, colonial violence and politics of representations. He also works as a Teaching Assistant at the Department of Sociology for the courses of American Society: Ethnic Encounters in the Making of the United States, Sociology and the Modern World, and Continuity and Controversy in Sociology.

Chris Hudson is a Senior Lecturer in the School of Applied Communication, Royal Melbourne Institute of Technology University in Melbourne. She has an eclectic academic background with studies in literature, politics, gender studies and urban geography of Southeast Asia. Her doctoral dissertation at the University of Melbourne was a study of textual strategies in the discourses of gender and nation in Singapore. Her current research interests include gender and cultural politics in Southeast Asia, cultural and social change in response to urban development and infrastructure change in Asia, and global mobilities and identity in Asia. She is a Chief Investigator on a research project funded by the Australian Research Council entitled 'Theatre in the Asia-Pacific: Regional Culture in a Modern Global Context'. She is a member of the Globalization and Culture programme and the Art and Urbanism programme of the Global Cities Institute at RMIT. She is also the leader of a team investigating global ideology, urban infrastructure and the transformation of public space in Chongqing, China. Her focus is on spatial mobilities and cultural change in Chongqing. Recent publications include book chapters and journal articles on Asian cyberfeminism, the politics of the family in Singapore, SARS and the public discourse in Singapore. Forthcoming publications include articles on global mobilities and place-making in Delhi, and tourist mobilities and national identity in Thailand.

David Inglis is Professor of Sociology at the University of Aberdeen. He holds degrees from the University of Cambridge and the University of York. He is an Academician of the UK Academy of the Social Sciences. He has written widely in the areas of the history of social thought, the sociologies of culture, art and aesthetics, and the cultural sociology of globalization and globality. He has particular interests in the sociological historiography of modes of consciousness, with especial reference to ancient Greece and Rome. He is currently working on a project which reinterprets classical social thought in light of contemporary concerns to do with globaization and globality. His books include *The Globalization of Food* (2009), *Art and Aesthetics: Critical Concepts in the Social Sciences*, 4 vols (2009), *Food and Society: Critical Concepts in the Social Sciences*, 4 vols (2007), *The Sociology of Art: Ways of Seeing* (2005), *Nature: Critical Concepts in the Social Sciences*, 4 vols (2005), *Culture and Everyday Life* (2005) and *Confronting Culture: Sociological Vistas* (2003). Recent papers include '*Culture Agonistes*: Social Differentiation, Cultural Policy and Cultural Olympiads', *International Journal of Cultural Policy*, 2008; 'The Elementary Forms of Globality: Durkheim and the Emergence and Nature of Global Life', *Journal of Classical Sociology*, 2008 (with Roland Robertson); and 'The Warring Twins: Sociology, Cultural Studies, Alterity and Sameness', *History of the Human Sciences*, 2007. He is also editor of the journal *Cultural Sociology*, published by Sage, a journal of the British Sociological Association.

Humeira Iqtidar is a research fellow at the Centre of South Asian Studies, and King's College, University of Cambridge. Previously educated at Quaid-e-Azam University, Pakistan and McGill University, Canada, she completed her PhD from the University of Cambridge. Her larger interests lie in exploring aspects of political theory through a focus on contemporary Muslim life. Her doctoral research involved an ethnographic engagement with two Islamists parties in Pakistan: Jamaat-e-Islami and Jamaat-ud-Dawa. She has published several papers based on this research, and is currently working on a book manuscript. Her new project involves an exploration of the concept of the 'market' through a focus on pietist Muslim groups, such as the Tablighi Jamaat, both in the UK and in Pakistan.

Habibul Khondker is Professor of Sociology in the at Zayed University, Abu Dhabi, United Arab Emirates. He gained his PhD from the University of Pittsburgh in 1985. He has taught at the National University of Singapore and held visiting research appointments at the University of Pittsburgh, Institute of Social Studies, the Hague, Columbia University, and Cornell University. He has given talks at seminars at the University of Tokyo, Sophia University, Tokyo and Tsukuba University. Born in Bangladesh, he was educated in Bangladesh, Canada and the US. His research interests cover fields from theoretical issues of globalization, science and technology, gender sociology to disasters and democratization. He has co-authored with Bryan S. Turner *Globalization: East/West* (forthcoming) and co-edited with Goran Therborn *Asia and Europe in Globalization: Continents, Regions, and Nations* (2006). He is on the editorial board of *Globalizations* (Routledge), *Journal of Global Studies* (University of Illinois), *Journal of Classical Sociology* (Sage) and *Encounters* (Zayed University). His articles on globalization, state, civil society, democracy, famine, internet, science and gender issues have been published in journals such as *International Sociology*, *British Journal of Sociology*, *Current Sociology*, *International Migration*, *City*, *Contemporary Sociology*, *Globalizations*, *Armed Forces and Society*, *International Journal of Sociology and Social Policy*, *International Journal of Contemporary Sociology*, *International Journal of Mass Emergencies*, *Asian Journal of Social Science*, *South Asia*, *Bulletin of Science, Technology and Society*, *Economic and Political Weekly*. He also writes columns for newspapers in Bangladesh.

Susan Kippax is Professorial Research Fellow at the National Centre in HIV Social Research (NCHSR) in the Faculty of Arts and Social Sciences at the University of New South Wales, having retired from the position of Director (1995–2007). She has a BA (Hons) in Psychology and a PhD in Social Psychology (University of Sydney). She is a Fellow of the Academy of the Social Sciences of Australia and was a Yale Visiting Fellow at the Centre for the Study of AIDS, Pretoria, South Africa, 2003. Her research in HIV/AIDS social research is internationally regarded and she has published extensively – over 200 refereed social science papers, chapters and monographs. She is joint Editor-in-Chief of the *Journal of the International AIDS Society*, a founding Editor of *Culture, Health and Sexuality: An International Journal* and has been on the editorial boards of a number of journals, including *AIDS* (2005–8), *AIDS Education & Prevention* and *Sexualities*. Through her research, teaching and policy advisory roles she has played an integral role in the framing of Australia's response to HIV/AIDS. In her role as Director (NCHSR), she was instrumental in developing strong partnership links with government and non-government organisations; partnerships that have proved important to the successful responses of communities to the threat of HIV and, more recently, hepatitis C. She has served on numerous international committees, including the Global HIV Prevention Working Group, and the UNAIDS prevention reference group, and has spoken at a large number of international and national conferences and workshops.

Peadar Kirby is Professor of International Politics and Public Policy at the Department of Politics and Public Administration, University of Limerick. He holds a PhD from the London School of Economics. He is author of 'Explaining Ireland's Development: Economic Growth with Weakening Welfare', Social Policy and Development Paper No. 37 published in 2008 by the United Nations Research Institute for Social Development (UNRISD) as part of its research project on Poverty Reduction and Policy Regimes. He has published extensively on international development and globalization, especially in Ireland and Latin America. Among his books are *Contesting the State: Lessons from the Irish Case,* co-edited with Maura Adshead and Michelle Millar (2008), *Taming the Tiger: Social Exclusion in a Globalised Ireland,* co-edited with David Jacobson and Deiric Ó Broin (2006), *Vulnerability and Violence: The Impact of Globalisation* (2006), *Introduction to Latin America: Twenty-First Century Challenges* (2003), *The Celtic Tiger in Distress: Growth with Inequality* (2002), *Reinventing Ireland: Culture, Society and the Global Economy*, co-edited with Luke Gibbons and Michael Cronin (2002) and *Poverty Amid Plenty: World and Irish Development Reconsidered* (1997). He has two books forthcoming in 2009: *Power, Dissent and Democracy: Civil Society and the State in Ireland,* co-edited with Deiric Ó Broin and *Transforming Ireland: Challenges, Critiques and Resources,* co-edited with Debbie Ging and Michael Cronin.

Sebastian Kohl works at the Max Planck Institute for the Study of Societies in Cologne, and is currently studying sociology, economics, philosophy, political science and French literature. He is mainly interested in the philosophy of the social sciences and the intersection of economic, philosophical and sociological issues. In association with Patrik Aspers he has published three issues of the European Economic Sociological Newsletter that surveyed social science disciplines that are adjacent to and of interest to economic sociology.

Ronnie D. Lipschutz is Professor of Politics and Co-Director of the Center for Global, International and Regional Studies at the University of California, Santa Cruz. Lipschutz received his PhD in Energy and Resources from UC-Berkeley in 1987 and an SM in Physics from MIT in 1978. He has been a faculty member at UCSC since 1990. His primary areas of research and teaching include international politics, global environmental affairs, US foreign policy, empire and religion, globalization, international regulation, technology and public policy, and film, fiction and politics. He has published and lectured widely on these topics. His books include *The Constitution of Imperium* (2008), *Civil Societies and Social Movements* (edited, 2006). *Globalization, Governmentality and Global Politics: Regulation for the Rest of Us?* (2005), *Global Politics as if People Mattered* (with Mary Ann Tétreault, 2005), *Global Environmental Politics: Power, Perspectives and Practice* (2004), *Cold War Fantasies—Film, Fiction and Foreign Policy* (2001), *After Authority—War, Peace and Global Politics in the 21st Century* (2000) and *Global Civil Society and Global Environmental Politics* (1996).

John MacInnes holds a personal chair in the Sociology of European Society at the University of Edinburgh and is an honorary research fellow at the Centre d'Estudis Demogràfics, Universitat Autònoma de Barcelona, Spain. He has also worked at or been a visiting fellow at the Universities of Glasgow, Sussex, Pompeu Fabra (Spain) and Lyon II (France), and was recently appointed Strategic Advisor to the UK Economic and Social Research Council on the undergraduate teaching of quantitative methods. He has been researching the labour market, families, demography and social change for thirty years, holding grants from the UK, Spanish and Catalan governments, the European Union, the UK Economic and Social Research Council, the Centre National de Rechèrche Scientifique (France), Leverhulme Trust (UK) and Royal Society of Edinburgh (UK). He has published widely on such issues as gender and labour market change, work–life balance, 'low fertility', the relationship between sociology and demography, and the uses and abuses of the concept of 'identity' in sociology and demography. His books include *Thatcherism at Work* (1987) and *The End of Masculinity* (1998) and the forthcoming *The Reproductive Revolution* (with Julio Pérez). Recent articles include 'The Reproductive Revolution' (*Sociological Review*, 2009) with Julio Pérez; 'Time Stress, Well-being and the Double Burden' in *Family Formation and Family Dilemmas in Contemporary Europe* (ed. Gøsta Esping-Andersen, 2007) with Tizianna Nazio; and 'Castells' Catalan Routes: nationalism and the sociology of identity' (*British Journal of Sociology*, 2006).

Adam McKeown is an Associate Professor of the History of the United States and East Asia at Columbia University, where he teaches courses on world migration, the history of globalization and the history of drugs. He received his PhD from the University of Chicago in 1997. He wrote *Melancholy Order: Asian Migration and the Globalization of Borders* (2008), *Chinese Migrant Networks and Cultural Change: Peru, Chicago, Hawaii, 1900–1936* (2001) and 'Periodizing Globalization', *History Workshop Journal* 63 (2007): 218–30. He is now working on a Foucauldian history of globalization since 1760 based on graphs.

Stephen Mennell is Professor of Sociology at University College Dublin. He read Economics at St Catharine's College, Cambridge, and then spent a year as Frank Knox Fellow in the Department of Social Relations at Harvard (1966–67). After teaching for many years at the University of Exeter, he became Professor of Sociology at Monash University, Australia (1990–93). He was Fellow of the Netherlands Institute for Advanced Study, Wassenaar (1987–88). In Ireland, he was founding chairman of UCD Press (1995–2006), founding Director of the Institute for the Study of Social Change (not the Geary Institute) at UCD and a founding member of the Irish Research Council for the Humanities and Social Sciences (2000–02). He is a leading exponent of the sociology of Norbert Elias, and is a member of the board of the Norbert Elias Foundation, Amsterdam, as well as General Editor of the Collected Works of Norbert Elias, now in the course of publication in 18 volumes by UCD Press. His books include *Sociological Theory: Uses and Unities* (1974, 1980), *All Manners of Food: Eating and Taste in England and France from the Middle Ages to the Present* (1985), *Norbert Elias: Civilization and the Human Self-Image* (1989, paperback *Norbert Elias: An Introduction*, 1992, 1998) and *The American Civilizing Process* (2007). He holds the degrees of Doctor in de Sociale Wetenschappen (Amsterdam) and Doctor of Letters (Cambridge), and is a member of the Royal Netherlands Academy of Arts and Sciences.

Tom Mertes is the Administrator of the Center for Social Theory and Comparative History at UCLA and teaches US history courses for UCLA Extension. He is the editor of, and a contributor to, *A Movement of Movements: Is Another World Really Possible?* (2004), which grew out of his work as an editor at the *New Left Review*.

James S. Ormrod is Lecturer in Sociology, University of Brighton, and teaches at the University Centre, Hastings. His doctoral research, conducted at the University of Essex, was an ethnographic study of the pro-space movement – activists campaigning in support of human activity in outer space. He remained a teaching fellow in the Department of Sociology at the University of Essex until moving to Brighton in 2007 to join the Psychosocial Studies research group in the School of Applied Social Science. Theoretically, his work has been heavily influenced by psychoanalysis, writing for *Psychoanalysis, Culture and Society*. He has also made ongoing contributions to social movement theory, which he teaches at the University of Brighton, with work recently appearing in *Social Movement Studies*. With Peter Dickens, he began to bring his own research into social issues regarding outer space into dialogue with literature on the philosophy

Jan Pakulski is Professor of Sociology at the University of Tasmania, Hobart. He gained his MA from Warsaw University and PhD from Australian National University. He is a Fellow of the Academy of the Social Sciences in Australia and of the Center for the Study of Poverty and Inequality at Stanford University. His publications include *Elite Recruitment in Australia* (1980), *Social Movements* (1991), *Postmodernization: Change in Advanced Society* (1992; with S. Crook and M. Waters), *The Death of Class* (1996; with M. Waters), *Postcommunist Elites and Democracy in Eastern Europe* (edited in 1998 with J. Higley and W.Wesolowski), *Globalizing Inequalities* (2004), as well as about 100 articles and chapters in scholarly books. His current research interests focus on elites, democratization and globalization, post-communism, social movements and social inequality.

Felicia Allegra Peck is a PhD student in the Department of Politics at the University of California Santa Cruz. She graduated from Beloit College with a BA in Political

Science. Felicia holds a MA in Political Science, with concentrations in environmental politics and policy and political theory, from Colorado State University. She participates in the Environmental Political Theory workshop at the Western Political Science Association annual meeting, and presented papers in the Environmental Political Theory section of the WPSA conference in 2007, 2008 and 2009. She is involved with the interdisciplinary Science and Social Justice working group at UCSC. Her current research considers the interplay between science, politics and the public, focusing on the extent to which 'what is to be done' about the environment is a scientific matter, and to what extent it is a political one.

Michael G. Peletz is Professor of Anthropology at Emory University. He was born and raised in the San Francisco area; and attended the University of California, Berkeley (BA 1973) and the University of Michigan (PhD 1983). His specialities include social and cultural theory, gender, sexuality, kinship, law, religion (especially Islam) and modernity, particularly in Malaysia, Indonesia and other parts of Southeast Asia and the Pacific Rim. His books include *Gender Pluralism: Southeast Asia Since Early Modern Times* (2009); *Gender, Sexuality, and Body Politics in Modern Asia* (2007); *Islamic Modern: Religious Courts and Cultural Politics in Malaysia* (2002); *Reason and Passion: Representations of Gender in a Malay Society* (1996); and *A Share of the Harvest: Kinship, Property, and Social History among the Malays of Rembau* (1988). In addition to being the editor (with Aihwa Ong) of *Bewitching Women, Pious Men: Gender and Body Politics in Southeast Asia* (1995), Peletz is the recipient of fellowships and grants from the Institute for Advanced Study in Princeton, the National Endowment for the Humanities, the National Humanities Center, the Social Science Research Council, the Wenner-Gren Foundation for Anthropological Research and the National Science Foundation.

Jan Nederveen Pieterse is the Mellichamp Professor of Global Studies and Sociology University of California at Santa Barbara. Specilaizing in globalization, development and cultural studies, his recent publications include *Is there Hope for Uncle Sam? Beyond the American Bubble* (2008), *Ethnicities and Global Multiculture. Pants for an Octopus* (2007), *Globalization or Empire?* (2004), *Globalization and Culture. Global Melange* (second edition 2009) and *Development Theory: Deconstructions/Reconstructions* (second edition 2009).

Smitha Radhakrishnan is an Assistant Professor of Sociology at Wellesley College. Previously she was a Global Fellow at UCLA's International Institute. She received her PhD from UC Berkeley in 2006. Her research interests lie at the intersection of gender, globalization and nationalism. She has studied meanings of race, ethnicity and femininity amongst South African Indians in Durban (South Africa), and gender and development in Rajasthan and Kerala (India). Her recent publications have appeared in *Gender and Society*, *Theory and Society* and *Journal of Intercultural Studies*, among others. Her most recent project examines the transnational class culture of Indian information technology (IT) professionals in India, the Silicon Valley and South Africa for a book manuscript entitled *A Certain Background: Gender and Culture in India's Transnational Press*.

Ellen Reese is an Associate Professor of Sociology at the University of California, Riverside and chair of the Labor Studies programme. She is a graduate of Reed College and received her PhD from the University of California, Los Angeles. Her research focuses on the politics of welfare in the United States and on social movements. She is author of *Backlash Against Welfare Mothers: Past and Present* (2005), co-author of *The World Social Forums and the Challenges of Global Democracy* (2008) and co-editor of *The Wages of Empire: Globalization, State Transformation, and Women's Poverty* (2007). She is currently writing a new book on the contemporary welfare rights movement. With Christopher Chase-Dunn and a team of graduate students, she is completing a research project on the World Social Forum and the US Social Forum. She is also co-editing, with Jackie Smith, a special issue of *Mobilization* and an edited volume focusing on the involvement of social movements in the social forum process.

Motti Regev is Associate Professor of Sociology at The Open University of Israel and a sociologist of culture and art, whose major research interest is in popular music studies. He is the author of *Popular Music and National Culture in Israel* (2004, co-authored with Edwin Seroussi), *Rock: Music and Culture* (1994, in Hebrew) and *Úd and Guitar: The Musical Culture of the Arabs in Israel* (1993, in Hebrew). He edited (with Jason Toynbee) a special issue of *Popular Music* (25/1, 2006) on canonization. Recent articles include: 'Ethno-National Pop-Rock Music: Aesthetic Cosmopolitanism Made From Within' (*Cultural Sociology* 1: 317–41, 2007) and 'Cultural Uniqueness and Aesthetic Cosmopolitanism' (*European Journal of Social Theory* 10: 123–38, 2007).

Mark B. Salter is an Associate Professor at the School of Political Studies, University of Ottawa. In autumn 2008, he was Visiting Fellow at the Centre for Research in the Arts, Social Sciences, and Humanities, Wolfson College, and Visiting Scholar at the Centre of International Studies at the University of Cambridge. In 2007, he was the recipient of the National Capital Educator's Award and the Excellence in Education Prize at the University of Ottawa. He is author of *Rights of Passage: The Passport in International Relations* and *Barbarians and Civilization in International Relations* (2002, also published in Chinese), as well as editor of *Politics at the Airport* (2008) and co-editor with Elia Zureik of *Global Surveillance and Policing: Borders, Security Identity* (2005). Recent research appears in *Geopolitics, Citizenship Studies, International Political Sociology, Alternatives, Security Dialogue*, the *Journal of Air Transport Management* and the *Journal of Transportation Security*. He is currently writing a manuscript on 'Politics of the Spaces In-between' that connects the theoretical work on states of exception with empirical research on interstitial sites in global politics.

Colin Samson is a sociologist and Director of the Humanities Programme at the University of Essex. He has been working with the Innu peoples of the Labrador-Quebec peninsula since 1994. Much of his research has sought to understand the health impacts and human rights implications of forced changes to the Innu way of life. His book *A Way of Life that Does Not Exist: Canada and the Extinguishment of the Innu* (2003) won the International Council for Canadian Studies' Pierre Savard Award in 2006. He is currently writing a book on the health, psychological and environmental benefits of cultural continuity for Indigenous peoples globally. Recently he has published articles on the role of anthropology and colonialism in Indigenous rights conflicts, and the continuing impact of the *terra nullius* doctrine on the rights of Indigenous peoples. In March 2009 he will embark upon a British Academy-sponsored collaborative film project with the Innu community of Natuashish and the photographer Sarah Sandring.

Cornel Sandvoss is Senior Lecturer in the Department of Sociology at the University of Surrey and co-editor (with C. Lee Harrington and Jonathan Gray) of *Popular Communication: The International Journal of Media and Culture*. He has studied fans and audiences of popular culture and spectator sport in transnational contexts. His publications include two monographs on this subject, *A Game of Two Halves: Football, Television and Globalisation* (2003) and *Fans: The Mirror of Consumption* (2005), and the anthology *Fandom: Identities and Communities in a Mediated World* (2007).

Martin Shaw is Research Professor and Co-Director of the Justice and Violence Research Centre at the University of Sussex, where he held the Chair of International Relations and Politics from 1995 to 2008. He was born in Yorkshire in 1947, graduated in Sociology from the London School of Economics and Political Science in 1968 and later gained his PhD in the Sociology of International Relations and War from the University of Hull. He was a Lecturer in Sociology at the University of Durham (1970–72), and then Lecturer, Senior Lecturer, Reader and Professor of Sociology at the University of Hull (1972–95). His work has focused on the sociology of global politics, war and genocide. His books include *Marxism and Social Science: The Roots of Social Knowledge* (1975); *Dialectics of War: An Essay on the Social Theory of War and Peace* (1988); *Post-Military Society: Militarism, Demilitarization and War at the End of the Twentieth Century* (1991); *Global Society and International Relations: Sociological Concepts and Political Perspectives* (1994); *Civil Society and Media in Global Crises: Representing Distant Violence* (1996); *Theory of the Global State: Globality as Unfinished Revolution* (2000); *War and Genocide: Organized Killing in Modern Society*, (2003); *The New Western Way of War: Risk-Transfer War and Its Crisis in Iraq* (2005); and *What is Genocide?* (2007). His personal website is www.martinshaw.org and he is a regular contributor to www.opendemocracy.net.

Niamh Stephenson is a Senior Lecturer in Social Science in the School of Public Health and Community Medicine at the University of New South Wales, Sydney, Australia. She has a PhD in social psychology. Her research interests include the role of experience on socio-political change, as examined in *Analysing Everyday Experience: Social Research and Political Change* (co-authored with Dimitris Papadopoulos, 2006). More recently, *Escape Routes! Power and Revolt in the 21st Century* (co-authored with Dimitris Papadopoulos and Vassilis Tsianos, 2008) interrogates how postliberal regimes of control are impacting on the politics of experience in the fields of health, labour and migration.

Natan Sznaider is Professor for Sociology at the Academic College of Tel-Aviv in Israel. He is also a guest professor at the University of Munich in Germany. His interests are in the study of the collective memory of the Holocaust. In addition he works on the cosmopolitanization of the ethics of victimhood and the sociology of human rights. In 2006, with Ulrich Beck, he co-edited a special issue on 'Cosmopolitan Sociology' for the *British Journal of Sociology*. His books include *Gedächtnisraum Europa: Kosmopolitismus: Jüdische Erfahrung und Europäische Vision* [The Memory Space of Europe: Cosmopolitanism, Jewish Experience and European Vision], transcript in 2008 and (with Daniel Levy) *Memory and Human Rights*, forthcoming.

Stephen Teo is Associate Professor in the Wee Kim Wee School of Communication and Information Nanyang Technological University Singapore. Previously he was a research fellow at the Asia Research Institute at the National University of Singapore (2005–8). With extensive work experience with the Hong Kong International Film Festival and the Yamagata International Documentary Film Festival in Japan, he has published *Hong Kong Cinema: The Extra Dimensions* (1997), *Wong Karwai* (2005), *A Touch of Zen* (2007), *Director in Action: Johnnie To and the Hong Kong Action Cinema* (2007) and *The Chinese Martial Arts Cinema: The Wuxia Tradition* (forthcoming).

Frank Trentmann is Professor of History at Birkbeck College, University of London. He was director of the £5 million Cultures of Consumption research programme, and has taught at Bielefeld University and Princeton University. His work has focused on consumption, civil society and political culture. Recent publications include *Free Trade Nation* (2008); *Food and Globalization*, edited with Alexander Nützenadel (2008); *Citizenship and Consumption* (edited with Kate Soper, 2007); *Consuming Cultures: Global Perspectives* (edited with John Brewer, 2006); and *Civil Society: A Reader in History, Theory and Global Politics* (edited with John A. Hall, 2005). He is currently working on the book *The Consuming Passion: How Things Came to Seduce, Enriche, and Define our Lives*.

Bryan S. Turner is Alona Evans Distinguished Visiting Professor of Sociology at Wellesley College, MA and Professor of Social and Political Thought at the University of Western Sydney. He was Professor of Sociology at the University of Cambridge (1998–2005) and at the National University of Singapore (2005–9). He is the founding editor of the *Journal of Classical Sociology* (with John O'Neill) and *Citizenship Studies*. He recent books include *Vulnerability and Human Rights* (2006), *Rights and Virtues* (2008) and (as editor) *New Blackwell Companion to Social Theory* (2009).

Robert Winslow is a Professor Emeritus at San Diego State University. He received his PhD in Sociology from the University of California at Los Angeles (UCLA). During the years 2000–2007, he developed a website which contains criminal justice information for all countries of the world (http://www-rohan.sdsu.edu/faculty/rwinslow/index.html). Based upon this website, he wrote (with Sheldon X. Zhang) *Criminology: A Global Perspective* (2008). His other textbooks include *Society in Transition: A Social Approach to Deviancy* (1970); *The Emergence of Deviant Minorities* (1972); *Juvenile Delinquency in a Free Society* (1976); *Crime in a Free Society* (1977); *Deviant Reality* (1981); *Crime and Society* (1998); *Police, Courts, and Corrections*; and *Juvenile Delinquency: An Adolescent Subcultural Approach* (1998).

Virginia Winslow is a writer who received her Master's Degree and California Teacher's Credential from California State University at Long Beach, with a double major in sociology and journalism. She was the Editor-in-Chief of the *Long Beach Daily News*, and has worked as a magazine writer and syndicated columnist. She collaborated with her husband, Robert Winslow, on numerous writing projects, including nine textbooks, and co-authored the book *Deviant Reality: Alternative World Views* (1974). The term 'deviant reality', which she originated for that text, is now frequently used in criminological literature.

Anthony Woodiwiss is Distinguished Professor of Sociology at Seoul National University. Previously he had been Dean of the School of Social Sciences at City University in London and Head of the Department of Sociology at Essex University. In addition he has been a Visiting Professor at various universities in the US, China, Japan, Australia and Mexico. He has published many articles and nine books, most of which are concerned with theoretical and substantive issues in the area of human rights, including *Human Rights* (2005); *Scoping the Social: An Introduction to the Practice of Social Theory* (2005); *Making Human Rights Work Globally* (2003); *Globalisation, Human Rights, and Labour Law in Pacific Asia* (1998); *Law, Labour and Society in Japan: from Repression to Reluctant Recognition* (1993); *Rights v. Conspiracy: a Sociological Essay on the Development of Labour Law in the United States* (1990); *Social Theory after Postmodernism: Rethinking Production, Law and Class* (1990).

Part I

Theories and definitions

Theories of globalization

Issues and origins

Bryan S. Turner

Introduction: precursors, paradigms, and problems

The theme of globalization has in the last two or three decades become established as the key topic of the social sciences. Various aspects of globalization such as transnational corporations, financial deregulation and the credit crunch of 2008–9 are now understood to influence every aspect of human life in every corner of the planet. Nevertheless globalization is probably more feared than understood. Unsurprisingly there are now a large number of major handbooks, companions and textbooks on the subject such as Frank Lechner and John Boli's *The Globalization Reader* (2004), Jan Nederveen Pieterse's *Global Future* (2000), Robert Holton's *Making Globalization* (2005) and George Ritzer's *The Blackwell Companion to Globalization* (2007). In addition, there has been much sociological interest in the social instability caused by globalization in, for example, Ulrich Beck's *World Risk Society* (1999).

This *Handbook of Globalization Studies*, however, has a somewhat different focus, being not only an analysis of globalization as such, but also an overview and critical assessment of globalization as a field of study within the social sciences. The aim therefore is to provide an assessment of the analysis of globalization processes in political science, demography, cultural studies, film studies, sociology and so forth. In addition this *Handbook* examines certain fields such as global population movements and global migration, which are often neglected, and also considers new areas of development such as the global politics of space exploration and the various cultures of sexual life in Asia. It also attempts to take a balanced view of both the negative dimensions – global crime and environmental pollution – and the positive side – the spread of human rights and international law – of contemporary globalization.

While globalization studies have become in the twenty-first century a major field of inquiry, recognition of globalization started much earlier. For example, one legacy of Marxist sociology was recognition of the importance of international trade, economic imperialism, transnational corporations and capitalism as a world system of exploitation and production. Awareness of such global economic institutions produced a number of schools and approaches whose research examined the structure of economic exploitation between the core and the periphery of capitalism. This focus eventually gave rise to the notion of 'underdevelopment' as a key feature of capitalist economic growth; that is Marxist economic sociology rejected the simple distinction between 'tradition' and 'modernity' in modernization theory and argued that capitalist growth at the core underdeveloped the periphery (or semi-periphery) through a network of exploitative relationships (Baran, 1957). This perspective was originally applied to the developmental problems of Latin America (Frank, 1971) and more recently to the Orient more generally (Frank, 1998). In more specific terms, this Marxist legacy underpinned a major academic development in understanding the global world around the work of Immanuel Wallerstein (1974) who developed 'world systems theory', initially on the basis of his research in Africa. Wallerstein's theory simply postulates that it is impossible to study the modern world successfully without recognizing the multiple connections between societies and the global processes that shape them, but the world systems approach has also emphasized the historical depth of these processes. Furthermore it has recognized that de-globalization can also take place in conjunction with major periods of recession and economic decline, and hence this approach is especially relevant today (Chase-Dunn, 2006).

While there were important developments in theories of economic globalization, there were equally significant developments in the study of the cultural and political dimensions of globalization. To some extent, the analysis of the cultural and social dimensions of globalization was a reaction against the predominance of political economy in the social sciences. Although the study of globalization has been growing in importance since the 1990s, perhaps the key intervention in the popular literature came in the 1960s with the growth of communication research. In the study of communication and media, Marshall McLuhan (1964) made 'understanding the media' a major topic and developed the popular idea of a 'global village'. Research on communications and the media has ever since occupied a dominant position in the field (Castells, 1996). In comparative religious studies, growing awareness of global processes added weight to the conventional debate about religious fundamentalism. These cultural studies often painted a picture of the world in terms of major binary contrasts such as East and West. The struggle to understand the Orient also has a long history. In the late 1970s Orientalism as a largely implicit paradigm for western research came under increasing critical scrutiny, giving way to greater awareness of the interconnectedness of human societies and their cultures (Said, 1978; Turner, 1978 and 1994). In historical research writers like Marshall G. S. Hodgson began to invent 'world history' as an alternative framework for the study of Islam in terms not of specific societies but by reference to Islam as a global movement. He came to see Islam as part of world history and from an ecumenical standpoint as a world cultural system. Political globalization has also been addressed by some influential studies of the consequences of globalization for democracy and civil society (Held, 1995; Keane, 2003). Political globalization involves the study of the institutionalization of international political structures and the evolution of the European interstate system has given rise to 'both an increasingly consensual international normative order and a set of international political structures that regulate all sorts of interactions' (Chase-Dunn, 2006: 85). This development has been labelled simply the growth of 'global governance' (Murphy, 1994).

In retrospect, it can be suggested in broad terms that globalization theory has gone through three stages of development from an early emphasis on the economic system, through a focus on culture and finally a concentration on its political dimensions, giving rise to debates about world governance and cosmopolitanism. These economic, political and cultural themes were outlined early on by Barrie Axford in *The Global System* (1995) which examined the axial features of globalization in terms of the world economic order, the world political order, the global military order and cosmopolitan cultures. Axford's observation in 1995 that, while there has been much intellectual excitement about the concept of globalization, there has been little reliable or systematic empirical research on its core components and consequences, remains valid. By its very nature, globalization is often difficult to study empirically. Comparative and historical research often stands in the place of genuinely global empirical studies. In addition, it is to some extent easier to measure economic globalization such as the growth of international trade or the size of multinational corporations than cultural globalization. While economists can examine the flow of commodities, it is often difficult to identify appropriate measures of cultural globalization. There are some important exceptions such as George Ritzer's work in *The McDonaldization of Society* (1993) which does provide both qualitative and quantitative measures of cultural standardization.

In addition, while globalization studies have flourished, there is still little agreement about the nature of globalization and its overall direction. Although there has been much dispute over the definition of globalization, we need not concern ourselves too deeply over definitional disagreements at this stage. The problem of defining 'money' satisfactorily has not stopped the progress of economics any more than the absence of a wholly coherent notion of 'power' has inconvenienced the development of political science. There is, however, some consensus that globalization involves the compression of time and space, the increased interconnectivity of human groups, the increased volume of the exchange of commodities, people and ideas, and finally the emergence of various forms of global consciousness which, for the sake of brevity, we may simply call 'cosmopolitanism'.

There has also been much dispute about the historical origins of the notion of globalization, but it is clear that at least in sociology the early driving force in the development of globalization theories was dissatisfaction with the economic assumptions of world-systems theory, especially as this approach had been constructed by Wallerstein and his school. In economic terms, globalization had often been treated as simply another phase of the emergence of a capitalist world system, the principal causal mechanisms of which were the economic requirements of global trade and transnational corporations. Sociological theories of globalization attempted to establish the independent development of social and cultural forces contributing to the emergence of the world as a single place. The foundations of a specifically sociological approach to globalization had been established by a series of influential articles by Roland Robertson, but these were not finally published as a collection until 1992. At the same time, there was equal frustration with the unidimensional aspects of modernization theory and with the theoretical difficulties of so-called civilizational analysis.

Early formulations of globalization theory in the 1980s often assumed either that the process was equivalent to the inevitable enforcement of cultural standardization or that this form of global standardization in fact involved processes which were merely Americanization. In early sociological versions of globalization theory, as Tony Spybey notes in *Globalization and World Society* (1996: 48–52), the convergence thesis suggested that the world was moving towards a single model of industrial society and that model was indubitably American. George Ritzer (1993) had successfully employed Max Weber's notion of a general process of rationalization to write about McDonald's as a general process of global standardization in his *McDonaldization*. The world development of Starbucks,

McDonald's and KFC outlets was compelling evidence of American influence over popular culture and lifestyles. Clearly the United States has played a pivotal role in modern globalization, but it is too simplistic to describe the whole process of globalization as merely Americanization. The impact of Japan on management systems, car manufacture, cuisine, fashion and films would be one simple example of the influence of Asia on the rest of the world.

The development of globalization studies has also been characterized by either extreme pessimism or naïve optimism. With the final collapse of the Soviet system between 1989 and 1992, many social scientists welcomed the potential development of a peace dividend, the end of the Cold War and the prospect of global co-operation over trade, security and cultural exchange. Globalization was welcomed as the flowering of human rights and global peace, and political philosophers looked back towards the Enlightenment and Immanuel Kant's aspiration for world government and perpetual peace as a model of a future global civil society. The globalization of a rights regime offered the prospect of a more just world (Wasserstrom et al., 2000). However, an alternative voice also became influential at the time in international relations theory. In particular Samuel Huntington's 'clash of cultures' article and later book sparked off a furious debate about the possibility of new conflicts around ethnicity and religion (Huntington, 1993 and 1996). After 9/11, the bombings in London, Madrid and Bali, and more recent terrorist attacks in Mumbai in 2008, globalization studies took a more critical and pessimistic turn, with much more emphasis on the state, political borders and security. It is recognized that globalization also brings with it the globalization of violence, low-intensity conflicts, international crime and trafficking in people. Warfare has played a critical role in the process of globalization, but this issue rarely surfaces in debates about the origins and character of global violence (Hirst, 2001). While optimistic visions of globalization had talked about mobility across borders as a key feature of a global world, the porous nature of societies and the possible decline of the nation state, the security crisis produced a renewed interest in state activities in controlling migration and patrolling borders. It was clear that globalization could also result in the 'enclave society' (Turner, 2007a).

We need to avoid simple dichotomies between optimism and pessimism, and also avoid simple assumptions that suggest globalization is only Americanization or that globalization is a recent historical phenomenon. More sophisticated discussions of the cultural dimensions of globalization have recognized the complexities of the process, emphasizing the interaction between local and regional politics and the broader social movements towards global integration, giving rising to a new dynamic between the local and the global. There has been a more general awareness of the importance of 'glocalization' or the interaction and merger between local cultures and global processes. Contemporary cultural theories recognize that standardization is a very unlikely (and certainly an unpromising) outcome of the global system, because the global/local dynamic will tend to produce a fluid and unstable hybridization of cultures. Anthropological research in particular has explored the cultural complexities of hybridity, glocalism (or 'global localization'), post-colonial cultures and continuing cultural imperialism without adopting either utopian expectations or a pessimistic nostalgia for a more traditional world (Wilson and Dissanayake, 1996).

Globalization also brings, often implicitly, into the foreground the role of religion in the politics of global identity. From the point of view of cultural politics, globalization theory has somewhat neglected the obvious fact 'the world religions' have been globalizing forces long before the modern period. In the early modern period, Islam, mainly through the development of trade, developed into a world culture. The same is true for Christianity, which spread through missionary activity and often in tandem with western colonial expansion in Africa and parts of Asia. Generally speaking, globalization theory, apart from the work of Roland Robertson (1992) and Peter Beyer (1994), has neglected the interaction between world religions and globalization, and the consequences of this cultural dynamic for global politics. Other exceptions include *The Oxford Handbook of Global Religions* (Juergensmeyer, 2006). James Beckford's *Social Theory & Religion* (2003) also made an important contribution to the field, providing an entire chapter on 'Globalisation and Religion', and in the introduction to *The Sage Handbook of Sociology of Religion* he correctly observed that since the mid-1980s religion 'presents major challenges and opportunities to social scientific explorations of globalisation' (Beckford and Demerath, 2007: 7). The growth of a global Muslim *ummah* or world-wide community through migration and the internet is a further example of contemporary religious globalization (Mandaville, 2001).

Against a background of economic and cultural analysis of globalization, there has been since 1995 a steady stream of publications on the political consequences and dilemmas of globalization. These political issues include the alleged erosion of or threat to national sovereignty and the decline of the nation state, the implications of internet communication for democracy, the possibilities of cosmopolitan democracy, and finally the growth of reactive nationalist and ethnic politics in response to global development. One prominent question in political globalization is the tension between nation-state patterns of citizenship and the global impact of human rights legislation.

There is a consensus in contemporary political science that, as a result of globalization, the nation-state has *not* lost its significance (Calhoun, 2008), but it is equally clear that the nature of modern politics has changed irrevocably. The changing nature of the nation state has obvious implications for democracy and citizenship. For many political analysts, conventional approaches to citizenship cannot capture either the dangers or the opportunities made possible by the rise of a global system. Aihwa Ong has in a variety of publications argued that new and more flexible forms of citizenship that address the needs of transnational communities can be detected and has examined the cultural logics of transnational movements (Ong, 1999; Ong and Collier, 2004; Ong and Nonini, 1997). Ambiguities of and conflicts about identity arise from ethnic complexity in the global labour market, but, following Daniel Archibugi, David Held and Martin Kohler in *Re-imagining Political Community*, there is greater conscious of the possibilities of a cosmopolitan democracy.

David Held has over a number of years attempted to analyse and understand the impact of globalization on democratic governance. His *Democracy and the Global Order* (1995) was an early and systematic attempt to conceptualize the impact of globalization on conventional patterns of democratic rule. For Held, there is a clear need to expand the sway of democracy through a new model of cosmopolitan governance to regulate the world order in favour of democratic accountability. With Archibugi and Kohler, he explored the principles of cosmopolitan democracy through a range of debates on universal rights, European unification, human rights, refugees and citizenship. The political programme of cosmopolitan democracy has become a major aspect of globalization studies and obviously central to overcoming the limitations of national citizenship.

The rise of cosmopolitanism – in part through the growth of cosmopolitan city, diasporic global cultures, global migration patterns and ensuing multiculturalism – has also taken place in a context of resurgent nationalism, ethnic cleansing, and the anti-migration policies of right-wing political parties and movements. The migration policies of modern

7

nation-states often reflect a nationalistic rhetoric which defines identity in terms of particularistic criteria, such as descent by (imputed) blood relationships. The conflict over
citizenship entitlement with respect to descent versus residence has been a major policy
issue in contemporary Europe. Rainer Baubock has, over a number of years, made an
important contribution to our understanding of the dilemmas and issues surrounding
citizenship, political membership and migration. In his *Transnational Citizenship* he
developed a political analysis of the challenge to traditional definitions of citizenship from
mass migration, the growth of transnational organizations and regional integration. As a
concept 'transnational citizenship' identifies three key issues in the expansion of social
citizenship beyond the national framework: the tension between the normative principles
of liberal democracy and the exclusionary practices of nation-states; the emergence of interstate citizenship (such as the European Union); and finally the development of human
rights as an element of international law, albeit with fairly limited powers of enforcement.
We need to consider the ways in which states might become more open and liberal in
accepting migrants as citizens through naturalization, the extension of citizenship rights
to non-citizens, and the admission of immigrants.

These issues of entry, membership and participation raise basic questions about identity, loyalty and obligation (Axtman, 1996).When and under what circumstances would
cosmopolitan citizens identify with communities, states or global associations? Although
there has been much talk about universal citizenship and cosmopolitan democracy, postmodern and feminist political theory has attacked abstract notions of universal justice
within the conventional paradigm of liberal political theory. Whereas the politics of universalism has sought the equalization of rights, the politics of difference seeks to recognize
the unique identity of actual social groups and individuals. For postmodern philosophers,
universalism undermines or contradicts the possibility of local or grounded authenticity.
The argument in favour of recognizing fundamental differences between individuals has
been articulated as a defence of group-differentiated rights in the context of feminist and
multicultural politics. These criticisms of the legacy of the Enlightenment are somewhat
without foundation and Chase-Dunn's counter-argument looks highly reasonable when
he says that Enlightenment ideas have 'never been a major cause of exploitation and
domination. Rather, it was the military and economic power generated by capitalism
that made European hegemony possible' (Chase-Dunn, 2006: 96–97).

Behind the issue about globalization, there is therefore a debate about the history and
moral standing of modernity and progress. For some sociologists such as Niklas Luhmann
(1990), globalization is the (accidental) consequence of the structural differentiation of western society that is a consequence of structural modernization and 'institutional upgrading'
(to use the language of Talcott Parsons). The implication is that the pattern of globalization is general and relatively uniform. The arguments of sociologists like Robertson
have by contrast both denied that globalization comes after modernization and emphasized
the uneven quality of 'globality' (through the tensions between the local and global) in
the notion of 'glocalization'. Perhaps the core issue in the debate (which in turn impacts
on questions of identity, loyalty and commitment) is whether globalization produces
cultural standardization in terms of a single and uniform global village or whether globalization, through the processes of adaptation and simulation, results in cultural hybridity. In this respect, the conclusions of Albrow (1996: 149) are plausible in suggesting that
'the multiplication and diversification of worlds rather than the homogenization and
hybridization better express the dominant forms of cultural relations under globalized
conditions'. In turn this multiplication of life-worlds raises a question about the capacity

of political systems to recognize, embrace and ultimately manage such global diversity within a political framework which requires a certain level of loyalty and obligation to match the rights and immunities of modern citizens. The danger is that global forms of political and religious fundamentalism will develop to counter-act, and possibly nullify, the possibility of cosmopolitan diversity. Perhaps this prospect is the real peril of the clash of civilizations. Axford (1995: 190–94), building on the work of Robertson, articulates this relationship between fundamentalism and cosmopolitanism as a response to the post-Cold War pessimism of Huntington's version of international relations theory with its focus on 'the dynamics of fault line wars' (1996: 266–98). Again the issue is whether modernization produced a greater need for specific political identities (through a process of 'essentialization') in the form of the national citizen or whether globalization goes beyond modernity to create new cosmopolitan identities which are not grounded in national grand narratives. The pessimistic view is that modernization went along with the creation of ethnic minorities in a process of 'minoritization' (Mufti, 2007). The optimistic view is that globalization creates opportunities for a cosmopolitan imagination (Beck, 2006). These questions in various critical but productive ways take the debate about citizenship well beyond the traditional framework of social citizenship in a national framework of ethnic homogeneity.

Defining globalization

Many of the problems of definition are discussed in the modern sociological literature such as Ulrich Beck's (2000) *What Is Globalization?* Although definitions of globalization are contested, the following points must be taken into account. Internationalization and transnationalization are not the equivalent of globalization. There were major changes in the 1970s (in finance, computing and economics), in the 1980s (the fall of organized communism and the end of the Cold War) and in the early twenty-first century (the terrorist attacks on the Twin Towers, the London underground and Mumbai) that intensified the process of globalization, but it is important to be sensitive to other historical events such as the Treaty of Westphalia or the discovery of America in shaping globalization. It is important to look beyond merely economic causes of globalization in order to examine and include the impact of world religions. It is probably also valuable to remain sceptical as to the actual degree of economic globalization (Hirst and Thompson, 1996). While economic internationalization has certainly taken place, these developments do not necessarily constitute economic globalization and very few transnational corporations operate at a genuinely global level. In defining globalization, we must avoid other forms of crude reductionism in treating globalization as a uniform process or by treating it as simply an aspect of hegemonic Americanization and finally we should recognize that anti-globalization is ironically also an expression of globalization. We must also look beyond modernization theory in our accounts of the global world. Martin Albrow in *The Global Age* recognized the difficulties in providing a precise and convincing definition of globalization, but warned against the nostalgic view that conventional notions of modernity are sufficient to capture the changes taking place in globalization.

Although there is no accepted definition of globalization, we can, following James Beckford (2003: 119) define some of its main contours: (1) the growing frequency, volume and interrelatedness of cultures, commodities, information, and peoples across both time and space; (2) the increasing capacity of information technologies to reduce and compress time and space (giving rise to notions such as the global village); (3) the diffusion of routine practices and protocols for processing global flows of information, money, commodities and people; and (4) the emergence of institutions and social movements to promote, regulate, oversee or reject globalization; and (5) the emergence of new types of global consciousness or ideologies of globalism that give some expression to this social interconnectedness such as cosmopolitanism.

In terms of these various definitions of globalization, there is some justification in claiming that some approaches have overstated the economic nature of globalization (in terms of free trade, neo-liberalism, financial deregulation, integrated production and management systems) to the neglect of its social, cultural, and political characteristics. From a socio-logical perspective, we need to examine globalization as the interconnectedness of the world as a whole and the corresponding increase in reflexive, global consciousness. Concepts like 'globalism' and 'globality' can usefully refer to the cultural conditions of globalization. As we have already observed, sociologists have claimed that globalization produces a complex interaction between the local and the global. These interactions or glocalization often result in complex hybrid cultures. There is also controversy in defin-ing the field as to the consequences of globalization – either standardization such as McDonaldization versus cultural and social hybridity. There are consequently two highly contradictory views of globalization between Ritzer's view of global culture (McDonald's is a world without surprises) and Beck's account of risk society (a world of contingency and complexity). We also need to attend to the various dimensions of globalization and their causal priority: economic and technological (global markets); informational and cultural (global knowledge); legal and political (human rights and globalization of democratic institutions); and the globalization of health and illness.

Before 9/11, the mood of much sociology towards this emerging world was optimistic. More recent writing has begun to emphasize militarism, war, terrorism, slavery, drugs and crime as equally important dimensions of global processes (Turner, 2007b). There is also recognition of the extent of global slavery in the modern world economy (Bales, 1999). The economic crisis of 2008–9, the credit crunch, and the growth of global recession have also forced social scientists to re-assess the shape and development of globalization. In contemporary globalization literature, there is therefore an important division between utopian versions of globalization that perceive important opportunities for global justice, human rights and cosmopolitanism, dystopian versions that emphasize the destruction of local cultures, the dominance of consumerism, and the growth of international terrorism and crime; and revolutionary conclusions such as Hardt and Negri's *Empire*. Global consumerism has also been criticized by George Ritzer. In his early work on McDonaldization, he had examined the negative force of rationalization on a variety of modern institutions, but he has gone further in *The Globalization of Nothing* (2003) to argue that globalization empties out culture and that global cultures are devoid of value; globalization offers us nothing. We might think of this development as a process of global gouging in which deeply rooted cultures and traditions are disembedded and devalued.

Risk, modernity, and global consciousness

Some key issues around the question of modernity emerge repeatedly in the analysis of global society: what if anything has changed decisively with globalization and can con-ventional forms of sociology adequately conceptualize these changes? Is the concept of 'late modernity' sufficient to describe these developments? Ulrich Beck and Anthony Giddens have both in different ways influenced the sociology of globalization which they understand in terms of a theory of reflexive modernization. It is often difficult to distinguish between their theories and there is in general considerable overlap between their publications. Beck published *Risk Society* in Germany in 1986 and the English translation appeared in 1992. Giddens's principal contribution to globalization theory was originally *The Consequences of Modernity* (1990) which developed theoretical ideas from *The Nation State and Violence* (1985). These early publications were followed by attempts to address globalization directly such as his *Runaway World* (1999). Emotions and subjectivity are also influenced by processes of globalization. Giddens followed Beck and Beck-Gernsheim's *The Normal Chaos of Love* (1990), which was eventually translated in 1995, in his *The Transformation of Intimacy* (Giddens, 1992).

What does their work have in common? Neither Giddens nor Beck subscribed to the idea of 'postmodernity' as an account of the contemporary world and instead they developed ideas about late or high modernity in which global modernity is defined as a more radical version of modernity. Globalization deepens and intensifies modernity. Both are concerned to describe the experience of globalization at the level of the individual and also to analyse large-scale structural changes. Risk society is the modernization of modernity that is a radicalization and intensification of modernity's key characteristics. Risk is seen to be endemic to modernization and this risky environment consequently places a special emphasis on the importance of expert systems. Indeed Beck argues that risk creates a new type of reflexivity, which is an ongoing process of scrutiny, assessment and evaluation.

Beck's work was based on his earlier industrial sociology and on environmental debates in Germany (such as pollution in the Black Forest). Criticisms of this early work included the claim that: (1) he tends to confuse risk and hazard, and in fact does not define risk; (2) he does not clearly demonstrate its late modern features; and (3) he fails to analyse the complex interaction between risk, regulation and surveillance. We can note the growth of surveillance systems in response to risk and indeed the rise of an audit society appears to be a necessary consequence of increased risk (Power, 1997). Systems of verification and accounting appear to be inevitable consequences of an auditing culture. In support of Beck's position, it is based on real empirical research rather than theoretical speculation. It clearly identifies the negative and indeed catastrophic features of globalization and his theories are very relevant to environmental politics. Finally, he has a programme of political action not being content merely to describe the problems of risk society. More recently he has developed his understanding of globalization by developing the idea of cosmopolitanism as a progressive culture of global society (Beck, 2006, 2008 and 2009; Beck and Grande, 2007).

Giddens defines globalization (1990: 64) as 'the intensification of worldwide social relations which link distant localities in such a way that local happenings are shaped by events occurring many miles away and vice versa'. More complexly, he describes the dynamic of globalization in terms of three processes: time–space distantiation, disembedding and reflexivity. His theory of globalization depends on a juxtaposition between four elements – the economic production of commodities, the surveillance and control mechanisms, the organization of violence and the extraction of resources from the environment. As a result, he describes four key institutions of modernization – capitalism, surveillance, military power and industrialism (transformation of the environment). These are in turn used to describe four dimensions of globalization – the world capitalist economy, nation-state systems, world military order and the international division of labour. Four

11

high-risk consequences of global modernity flow from this analysis – the collapse of economic growth mechanisms, the growth of totalitarian power, nuclear conflict and finally
ecological disaster.

These assumptions can be criticized on the grounds that we need a more complex
periodization of globalization that takes into account long-term changes. World-system
theorists, such as Wallerstein and Chase-Dunn, argue that some processes of globalization
are relatively recent, but they also claim correctly that some aspects of globalization have
been in the making for almost six hundred years. Trade during the Spanish Empire from
the fifteenth century clearly made a contribution to the foundations of globalization by
for example creating trading ports and introducing new commodities into Europe. The
rise and fall of empires and nation-states provides an important historical backdrop to
contemporary globalization (Kennedy, 1988).

In addition, Giddens has had relatively little to say about cultural aspects of globalization such as world religions. It is also not clear whether reflexivity refers to individuals or
systems or both. In the approach adopted by Beck and Giddens, traditional society is,
implicitly at least, non-western, and furthermore these traditional societies are not
reflexive – would this judgement do justice to Confucian China, medieval Islamic Spain,
or classical Greece? In short, in Giddens's sociology his 'undifferentiated account of the
experience of modernity is based on a universalisation of the western experience' (Loyal
2003: 127) and consequently he fails to engage genuinely with what Pierre Bourdieu
calls 'reflexive sociology' which is constantly critical of the institutional position on
which it stands (Bourdieu, 1990; Bourdieu and Wacquant, 1992; Shusterman, 1999).

If we compare Beck and Giddens with Bourdieu, the latter has a much stronger sense
of what I would call the ethnography of the global–local encounter and a clear sense of
the human miseries created by the global labour market, especially in terms of migrant
experiences. Bourdieu (1999) had a better grasp of the problem of a global sociology
from the perspective of marginal, dispossessed communities. Because Giddens and Beck
have a weak sense of the anthropology of globalization, their work contains nothing
about the ongoing destruction of aboriginal communities (for example in South America) and the resulting destruction of natural habitat that appears to be an inevitable outcome of globalization, and in general they do not engage effectively with the developing
world. They have little to say about the place of Asia in the debate about emerging global
cultures. Bourdieu became a profound critic of neo-liberalism because of its negative
effects on public life and defended an alternative internationalism. Giddens's arguments
contributed to the emergence of third-way politics, but these ideas became compromised
eventually by the disappointments surrounding the legacy of the British Prime Minister
Tony Blair. Bourdieu remained relatively sceptical about the possible reform of mainstream
political life and exhibited a fairly intense dislike for the United States and condemned
the use of the media to promote the popularity of political figures.

Media and the information revolution

There are many theories about the causation of globalization. However, perhaps the most
influential has been concerned to understand the spread of information technology, especially
the internet and its impact on finance, economic development, education and the military.
As we have already noted, Marshall McLuhan in the 1960s anticipated contemporary
debates in his *Understanding Media* (1964). He argued that electronic systems of information

delivery would abolish time and space; hence we are all living in a village. What are the implications of global knowledge for the economy, social networks and higher education? What the implications of new forms of pedagogy for technologies of the self?

The principal issue in the debate about the globalization of the media and information concerns their implications for a global civil society and democracy. The implications of global communication are contradictory. There are at least two contradictions. On the one hand, it creates expanded opportunities for the growth of civil society, and at the same time it creates commercial opportunities for trivialization and standardization. The aim of the commercial global media is largely to entertain rather than educate the public. It creates mass audiences in which the lowest common denominator determines the quality of production. The mass media are consistent with passive rather than active citizenship, because news broadcasting in particular is rarely critical or comprehensive. The second contradiction is that such media systems democratize communication, because they can overcome the issue of access (despite the digital divide), but they also corrode and contaminate the conditions by which communications can be made valuable, worthwhile and authoritative. Democratic politics have not been served adequately by the commercial media since the education of the citizen is not regarded as a priority of such broadcasting (Crick, 2000).

As we have seen, Giddens and Beck treat globalization as a recent development that was associated with the growth of the internet and as the 'modernization of modernity' or 'reflexive modernity'. My argument is that the causes of globalization are much older and deeper, and the theoretical sources for understanding it are consequently much richer. Because the computerization of knowledge and the growth of the media are crucial developments, let us consider three social theorists in more detail who have explored information technology, the knowledge society, computerization and their effects on power/knowledge. In this regard, Marshall McLuhan (1911–80) is in fact a much neglected social theorist. Influenced by Wyndham Lewis's manifesto in 1911 called *Blast*, McLuhan set up the Centre for Culture and Technology in Toronto to study the social effects of new technologies. Because his works were popular and much quoted in the popular press, they were often dismissed by academic sociologists like Daniel Bell for allegedly trivializing the issues. His catch-phrases – the medium is the message and the global village – offered an imaginative understanding of the social implications of print and electronic media as modes of communication, and he came to be regarded as the father of the electronic age. His media theory and the idea of the global village imaginatively captured important technological changes and their implications for teaching in universities and for education in general. He insisted that text-based knowledge required pedagogic techniques that had become obsolete in the electronic era of global communication. Technologies he argued are extensions of the body. If the book is an extension of the eye, then information media are an extension of the nervous system. We can plausibly develop a Foucauldian framework for McLuhan by asking what forms of 'technologies of the self' are produced by different media of knowledge and information? Media globalization for McLuhan brings to an end the linear time of modernity and creates new possibilities of time and space through information technology. The metaphor of the web to describe electronic communication illustrates perfectly well how the linear reality of the book gives way to the multiple possibilities of the web.

Daniel Bell developed the idea of post-industrialism in the 1960s and published this theory in his *The Coming of Post-Industrial Society* (1974) to describe a society in which the 'axial principle' involved the production of theoretical knowledge, the dominance of the service sector over manufacturing, the pre-eminent role of the research university in organizing and developing scientific innovations for industry, the growth of a new and powerful managerial class, and the centrality of professional and technological occupations in the economy and occupational structure. Bell's work anticipated the debate about the globalization of knowledge and the dominance of IKE (information and knowledge economy) in the globalization of production. Universities are increasingly combined into global consortia that compete for science investment, postgraduate markets and international recognition. Most universities now have a globalization strategy or 'mission statement' in which they proclaim their desire to compete globally, to recruit staff and students world-wide, and to create an image, ethos and reputation that are global. The globalization of management degrees, especially the MBA, and accountancy courses illustrates the competition for status and dominance in the accreditation of business professionals. The globalization of knowledge has, however, created serious problems for those universities who saw their mission predominantly in terms of serving the local community. Research design and investment are often no longer part of a national strategy, because research professorships for example are often sponsored by large corporations which are not primarily concerned with the local relevance of knowledge. In conjunction with these changes, the relationship between universities, states and society is also changing. At least 60 per cent of fundamental research now takes place outside the university system through research institutions that are housed in the corporate sector. Much research is conducted in association with private companies and this relationship can often seriously influence the way in which research results are published and developed. As state funding of universities declines, university faculties become increasingly dependent on (often short-term) funding from industry. The credit crunch has consequently had a damaging economic impact on those private universities such as Harvard which are heavily dependent on private investments, donations and alumni support. Universities are also increasingly subject to globalized management systems that demand detailed accounting, transparency and surveillance. Even the architecture of the academic workplace can be influenced by these developments such as the use of shared spaces ('hot desks' and open-plan offices) in academic departments. With the globalization of neo-liberal ideas and values, the student is often seen as a customer and faculties are divisions that are subject to compliance audits.

J.-F. Lyotard (1924–98) was influential in the development of the idea of the post-modernization of knowledge which he deployed to describe the impact of computerization on knowledge and authority in the university. New systems of knowledge would be reflexive, fragmentary and post-disciplinary. Lyotard used Bell's notion of post-industrialism to take the argument one step further. How could knowledge be effectively legitimized in a computerized society? Lyotard's postmodern questioning of legitimate knowledge (such as scepticism about what he called 'grand narratives' such as democracy and Enlightenment) raised questions about the forms of authority that a knowledge society will require. Linearity was the main organizing principle of the age of print. Print requires linear learning techniques, separate disciplines, and a clear hierarchy of authority. Professorial authority is a decisive example of such a system in which professors closely guarded the authority of their respective disciplines. The idea of queuing is a further illustration of linearity in the print age. Learning often involved an apprenticeship system in which young scholars queued to work their way through a master's programme to become accredited scholars. In contrast webs and nets are principles of organization in global knowledge societies, in which access and exit can have many different points in the net. There are no linear or necessary principles of pedagogy – no accumulation, hierarchy or structure. Students are encouraged to mix and match. Plagiarism and simulation can no longer be easily or seriously monitored and authorship is often difficult to determine. Hence these educational systems in the contemporary knowledge society are typically post-disciplinary (Turner, 2003). Postmodern global classification would appear to be characterized by its incompleteness and instability, because categories are fluid and unstable. Knowledge is endlessly self-referential and randomness is present insofar as entry and exit points are arbitrary.

Web knowledge creates critical problems of authority – how to protect knowledge sites from theft, vandalism, fraud and force. Hence there are serious problems about the feasibility of global knowledge parks in new information systems. As we move from book cultures to a paperless global economy, how can the authenticity of knowledge be secured and underpinned? New systems that are not based on print knowledge will require new types of social systems and innovative technologies of the self. Despite these problems, there is also an argument that globalization helps to democratize knowledge. For example, Google is currently digitalizing millions of books from the collections of many major research libraries and these volumes will be available to download for free. While it is consistent with Enlightenment principles to make books available within the public domain, how can we protect the interests of authors? One measure is contained in the Sonny Bono Copyright Term Extension Act of 1998 which supports copyright for the life of the author plus 70 years. However, most books published in the twentieth century have not yet come into the public domain and 1 January 1923 is the date when most books are subject to copyright. While Google's aims are laudatory – making knowledge accessible to the public – these legal settlements will give Google considerable power and will limit the scope of competition.

The globalization of knowledge is driven by the contradictions and competition by the conflicting interests of three elites: military, business and academics (Castells, 1996, 1997, 1998). Some of the major developments in this field include: the emergence of ubiquitous mobile telecommunications and computing links; the consolidation of electronically integrated, global financial markets; the expansion of an interlinked, cohesive capitalist economy; the shift in the labour force from primary and manufacturing industries to knowledge, information and communication industries; and the emergence of 'real virtuality' in the hyper-texting of cultural and economic relations (Turner and Rojek, 2001). Network society was created by the competition between the elites who sought to control the new communication systems: military, business and academic. Business elites wanted to keep websites open and free in the interests of the free expansion of business and academics wanted free access to information for research reasons. While military and government elites would prefer some regulation of networks, business and academic pressure groups for very different reasons want open access. While the net creates opportunities for heterogeneous movements from global Nazi sites to women's co-operatives, Castells argues optimistically that the net embraces two values, horizontal free communication and self-directed networking.

America and empire

One persistent criticism of the theory of globalization is that globalization is in essence Americanization. This counter-argument has in recent years taken a more interesting turn, namely a debate about the existence and nature of the American empire. This perspective has taken on a more urgent aspect as a consequence of the American intervention into Afghanistan and Iraq. What is the nature of empire in the modern world? Let us consider another analysis of America in Michael Mann's *Incoherent Empire*. He claims that, especially after the end of the Cold War in the late 1980s, America has become an imperial power, and possibly the only viable global power. For Mann, the American empire is not threatened by the rise of another power or by the classical problem of over-stretched and over-extended resources. The new empire is challenged by uneven, ineffective and inappropriate power resources resulting in imperial incoherence and a failure of foreign policy. The unresolved problems of Afghanistan, Iraq, Iran, and North Korea are the legacy of the Bush administration's aggressive but less than successful international strategy.

Let us examine these four sources of power that form the analytical framework of Mann's approach. In military terms, no power has the capacity to challenge or confront American superiority. After the end of the Vietnam War in 1975, the Powell doctrine said that America should intervene overseas with overwhelming military force and minimal US casualties. The Iraq and Afghan invasions were based on this doctrine, but Mann notes that rogue states, terrorist attacks and guerrilla wars pose military problems for which American technical superiority has few relevant answers. The casualties of modern conflict are civilian not military, and nuclear shields are no defence against 9/11 strikes or Madrid bombings. American military casualties in Iraq may be unacceptable to the American public, but they are dwarfed by civilian Iraqi casualties. Paradoxically America does not have an enemy that is sufficiently sophisticated in technical terms with which it could appropriately engage. In the economic sphere, Mann argues that the neo-liberal revolution to free global trade has clearly worked in favour of US interests. While America has championed free trade as the mechanism for economic growth, no society has in fact ever achieved economic success on the basis of today's neo-liberal strategies. From the perspective of economic history, liberal strategies only work after a country has grown economically through protectionism by successfully taxing imports and subsidising exports – Germany and Japan being the primary examples. While America has reaped rewards from these global neo-liberal policies, it was not able directly to regulate the competing economies of the European Union, Japan or China. Worse still, the poverty and inequality produced by neo-liberalism create social conditions in which oppression, resistance and terrorism flourish. Neo-liberalism is the cause not the cure, to use Joseph Stiglitz's (2002) expression, of 'globalization and its discontents'. The economic crisis of 2008–9 has in any case raised serious questions about the underlying philosophy of de-regulation and it appears to be the case that the major economies are now to experience a return to Keynesian strategies in which the state will return to regulating the market. There is a strong inclination to see President Obama's stimulus package as a repeat of President Roosevelt's response to the recession of the 1930s in his famous first hundred days in office (Alter, 2009; Badger, 2009).

In terms of political power, America has failed in foreign-policy terms, because it cannot effectively secure the loyalty of its client states. For example, Ariel Sharon, the former Prime Minister of Israel, operated independently, often undermining the 'road map' for peace which America regarded as a necessary step towards solving the Middle East crisis. Many of the political leaders of 'old Europe', especially the French government before the election of President Nicolas Sarkozy, remained recalcitrant. The wars in Afghanistan and Iraq have so far given America and its allies tentative political control over Kabul and

Baghdad, but it is often difficult to get the full co-operation of Pakistan. Finally, it is difficult for America to win an ideological war, because modern forms of communication, such as the global Net, are deregulated and devolved. The UN remained unconvinced by arguments regarding Iraqi WMD and the legality of intervention. The American liberal press may well have been originally uncritical of the Iraq war, but global information sources about the war remained open. Furthermore, newspapers such as al-Jazeera and al-Quds ensured that what Chalmers Johnson (2000), borrowing from CIA jargon, called the 'blowback effects' of American policy have been well publicized. Modern democracies find it difficult to fight sustained wars, because the body-bag count will sooner rather than later undermine public confidence. The global growth of political Islam and radical fundamentalism is in part the unintended consequence of the imperial incoherence of modern America.

The argument that globalization is simply Americanization can therefore assume a more interesting form. If America were to suffer a rapid economic downturn, the effects on the global economy would be very profound. The credit crunch of 2008–9 demonstrated that the crisis of the American economy would indeed have far-reaching consequences for the global system. The financial crisis in the Icelandic banking system was devastating, demonstrating the interconnectivity of the modern world. The British economy, in which the City of London has been a dominant element, was also severely compromised by these global problems. We have seen that, while the Chinese economy has suffered significantly from the decline in American demand, it may be that by increasing its own consumer market China could continue to grow despite the problems in the American economy. In a similar fashion, the Japanese government has been encouraging its citizens, especially the elderly, to spend and consume rather than save and hoard.

The crisis of the American housing market brought home the global impact of any weakness in the American economy. But it also brought into view the prospect that China and India may well be strong competitors with America, and that they may eventually replace America as the dominant societies of the twenty-first century. At present it is unclear how the credit crunch will finally play itself out. It is unclear whether the American economy will implode, or whether the recession will be deep and short, or shallow and long. We shall return to this issue in the final chapter of this *Handbook*, but in the meantime let us consider some recent interpretations of the problems facing American society.

Many interpretations of America as a global power draw on Marxist theories of imperialism to understand the post-communist and postcolonial world. However, early Marxist theories of 'unequal development' that emphasized core–periphery differences and explained the lack of development in the South in terms of the extraction of a surplus to the North have become increasingly untenable. The main problem for underdeveloped societies is that they have no surplus to be extracted, or have conditions that cannot be exploited productively. While underdevelopment theory might have made some sense of the economic plight of societies such as Burma and Bangladesh, it does not provide a useful framework to understand the success of Singapore, South Korea and Japan. Export-driven industrialization by many Asian societies appears to be a successful strategy, while Latin America remained in economic terms relatively stagnant through much of the second half of the twentieth century. With the credit crunch and the global economic crisis, there is now a strong temptation to interpret the present in terms of the destructive nature of the capitalist system and the inevitable business crises of over-production and under-consumption. Because the western capitalist economies became dependent on investment in China, it became necessary to sustain high levels of consumption in the West. The boom in the housing market in the United States and United Kingdom in particular sustained this relationship in the boom years of the late twentieth century.

Over a number of decades the West, and America in particular, has become increasingly economically dependent on Chinese economic growth and a domestic consumer boom in the West has been fuelled by cheap money, low interest rates and easy credit. One consequence has been the slow decline of industrial manufacturing, low domestic investment, and an inflated housing market founded on cheap mortgages. At an individual level, there has been the creation of a credit-card culture that has in turn given rise to widespread personal indebtedness (Pieterse, 2008). The social changes that have accompanied these macro-structural transformations of the capitalist economies as the USA moved from a society based on competitive capitalist production to a consumer society driven by consumerism, credit and advertising include growing social inequality, the rise of a permanent underclass, child poverty and wholly inadequate health insurance for some 47 million Americans. In 2005 America ranked 27th nation among 163 societies on the Index of Social Progress and male life expectancy in the US is now lower than in Costa Rica.

Contemporary analyses of the social and economic dilemmas of the West are in some respects built on the foundation of Bell's brilliant *The Cultural Contradictions of Capitalism* of 1976 in which he studied the tensions between the traditional asceticism required by capitalist economic production and the new hedonism that appeared to be required by modern consumerism. America in the Greenspan era enjoyed falling personal taxation, a flow of easy credit and inflated real estate values. However, America's economic prosperity was not based on real gains in personal income, increases in labour productivity, growing domestic investment or technological improvements but on a strategy of borrowing against the future. There was a growing gap between the financial sector and what economists have come to call 'the real economy'. The underlying American inflation rate was partly hidden by cheap imports from China, but the sudden rise in commodity prices, especially oil in 2008, the collapse of house values, falling demand from American consumers and changes within the Chinese economy itself eventually broke this relationship between the American and the Chinese economies. The relationship was radically challenged by the credit crunch as rising unemployment in the US economy indicated that the boost to the economy from the incoming Obama administration would probably be too late and too limited to pull the American economy out of recession. The economic crisis of 2008–9 clearly demonstrated the interconnectivity of the world economy and showed that there was no possibility of insulating societies from the specific difficulties of the American housing market.

The economic crisis has also brought into question the capacity of America to continue to exercise the largely unchallenged predatory hegemony that America had imposed in the second half of the twentieth century. Historians such as Niall Ferguson (2004) had argued in his *Colossus* that the world system needs a global policeman. With the eventual collapse of the British Empire around the time of the First World War, America emerged at the end of the Cold War as the hegemonic guardian of the international order. For some political scientists hegemonic America is capable of reform and repair, but hegemonic stability cannot be sustained indefinitely and in any case it produces a concentration of power that eventually prevents a clear and intelligent analysis of contemporary difficulties. Economic and global decline can produce an opportunism that is too ready to engage in risky imperial adventures and it can bring about a serious erosion of accountability. These aspects of decline were all too clearly illustrated by the Pentagon papers, the Iran–Contra episode, Watergate and the intelligence debacles in the preparation for the Iraq invasion. It is difficult to predict whether the credit crunch and the decline of American economic power will be translated into declining global political leadership.

Conclusion: cosmopolitan sociology

There has been much discussion of a borderless world and of the decline of the nation-state (Urry, 2000). In association with these arguments, there has been as we have seen a sustained interest in the prospects of cosmopolitanism (Beck, 2006 and 2008). What little research we have suggests people have very strong subjective ties with their local town, city or region, but they do not exhibit strong cosmopolitanism (Savage et al., 2005) and with the current crisis around global terrorism there is an increasing emphasis on the regulation of migration and the management of political borders. In the United States, the credit crunch has given rise to calls for greater regulation of immigration and especially illegal immigration.

In recent research therefore on democracy and territory, arguments against the general notion of increasing or unrestricted mobility have emerged in the literature on globalization. In particular as a consequence of 9/11 and the acts of terrorism in Bali, Madrid, London, Istanbul and Mumbai, governments have begun to reconsider their policies towards visa restrictions and open borders. Globalization theory has given greater recognition to the fact that 'territory and re-territorialization' are a major form of social organization and ordering (Newman, 2006: 183). The causes of re-territorialization include the development of policies of securitization, the global terrorist threat to civil society, the re-emergence of racialism and nationalist hostility towards migrants and foreign workers, the fear of an epidemic of infectious disease and mounting hostility towards multiculturalism and cosmopolitan values. Racism in Europe and elsewhere remains a significant aspect of public life and there is a general sense that multiculturalism as a liberal policy is in trouble. Public opinion continues to associate immigrants with crime, poverty, prostitution, disease and lawlessness. Low trust in any society produces a general sense of the offensive character of juvenile crime and vandalism. This image of incivility is generally associated with migrant communities, especially with the young men who are dislodged and alienated from the host society. By the late 1980s one-third of the prisoners in Belgium, Switzerland and France were recruited from foreign and ethnic minority communities. As a result, the demand for new policies to control migration has become a common feature of European politics.

In the contemporary world, societies that are in the grip of such anxieties are evolving new forms of social enclosure. There is emerging in these low-trust societies a 'paradigm of suspicion' (Shamir, 2005) in which a variety of persons are thought to be dangerous and disruptive, and hence their movements need to be contained and regulated. Sociologists need to re-conceptualize globalization not as a system of endless and uncontrolled liquid mobility but as a system that also produces 'closure, entrapment and containment' (Shamir, 2005: 199). These new risk-management systems have global consequences. Freedom of movement is a resource, and the rights and capacities for mobility are unequally distributed in society. Hence there is a 'mobility gap' that is parallel to the 'information gap' and the 'digital divide'. Finally, there has been some evolution of these

19

systems from their basic forms (walls, dykes and fences) to more complex and sophisticated systems (involving the use of forensic medicine and bio-profiling) (Turner, 2007a). But what is perhaps more remarkable is the persistence of these traditional forms of 'immurialization' into the modern period including, for example, Guantanamo Bay, which perfectly illustrates the issues of political sovereignty and 'bare life' in an emergency (Butler, 2006). Given the problems of security and terror, the growing political emphasis on securitization will throw a dark shadow over the aspiration to cultivate a cosmopolitan consciousness and may in turn limit the prospects of further democratization. I shall return to these problems in the final chapter of this collection.

References

Albrow, Martin (1996) *The Global Age: State and Society beyond Modernity*, Cambridge: Polity Press.

Alter, Jonathan (2009) *The Defining Moment: FDR's Hundred Days and the Triumph of Hope*, New York: Simon and Schuster.

Appaduri, Arjun (ed.) (2003) *Globalization*, Durham: Duke University Press.

Archibugi, Daniel, David Held and Martin Kohler (eds) (1998) *Re-Imagining Political Community: Studies in Cosmopolitan Citizenship*, Cambridge: Polity.

Axford, Barrie (1995) *The Global System: Economics, Politics and Culture*, Cambridge: Polity Press.

Axtman, Roland (1996) *Liberal Democracy into the Twenty-first Century: Globalization, Integration and the Nation-state*, Manchester: Manchester University Press.

Badger, Anthony (2009) *FDR: The First Hundred Days*, New York: Hill and Wang.

Bales, Keith (1999) *Disposable People*, Berkeley: University of California Press.

Baran, Paul (1957) *The Political Economy of Growth*, New York: Monthly Review Press.

Barber, Benjamin (2001) *Jihad versus McWorld*, New York: Ballantine Books.

Baubock, Rainer (1994) *Transnational Citizenship: Membership Rights in International Migration*, Aldershot: Edward Elgar.

Beck, Ulrich (1992) *Risk Society*, London: Sage.

——(1999) *World Risk Society*, Cambridge: Polity Press.

——(2000) *What Is Globalization?* Cambridge: Polity Press.

——(2006) *The Cosmopolitan Vision*, Cambridge: Polity Press.

——(2008) *World at Risk*, Cambridge: Polity Press.

——(2009) *A God of Its Own*, Cambridge: Polity Press.

Beck, Ulrich and Beck-Gernsheim, Elizabeth (1990) *The Normal Chaos of Love*, Cambridge: Polity.

Beck, Ulrich and Grande, Edgar (2007) *The Cosmopolitan Europe*, Cambridge: Polity Press.

Beckford, James (2003) *Social Theory & Religion*, Cambridge: Cambridge University Press.

Beckford, James A. and Demerath III, N.J. (eds) (2007) *The Sage Handbook of Sociology of Religion*, London: Sage.

Bell, Daniel (1974) *The Coming of Post-Industrial Society*, New York: Basic Books.

Beyer, Peter (1994) *Religion and Globalization*, London: Sage.

Bourdieu, Pierre (1990) *In Other Words: Essays Towards a Reflexive Sociology*, Cambridge: Polity Press.

Bourdieu, Pierre (ed.) (1999) *The Weight of the World: Social Suffering in Contemporary Society*, Cambridge: Polity

Bourdieu, Pierre and Loïc J. D. Wacquant (1992) *An Invitation to Reflexive Sociology*, Cambridge: Polity Press.

Brah, Avtar, Hickman, M. J. and M. Mac an Ghaill (eds) (1999) *Global Futures: Migration, Environment and Globalization*, Houndmills: Macmillan.

Brysk, Alison (ed.) (2002) *Globalization and Human Rights*, Berkeley: University of California Press.

Butler, Judith (2006) *Precarious Life: The Powers of Mourning and Violence*, London: Verso.

Calhoun, Craig (2008) *Nations Matter: Culture, History and the Cosmopolitan Dream* London: Routledge.

Castells, Manuel (1996) *The Rise of Network Society*, Cambridge: Polity Press.

——(1997) *The Role of Identity*, Oxford: Blackwell.

——(1998) *The End of the Millennium*, Oxford: Blackwell.

——(2001) *The Internet Galaxy*, Oxford: Oxford University Press.

Chase-Dunn, Christopher (2006) 'Globalization: A World Systems Perspective' in Christopher Chase-Dunn and Salvatore J. Babones (eds) *Global Social Change*, Baltimore: Johns Hopkins University Press, pp. 79–108.

Collins, Randall (1999) *Macro History: Essays in Sociology of the Long Run*, Stanford: Stanford University Press.

Crick, Bernard (2000) *Essays on Citizenship*, London: Continuum.

Ferguson, Niall (2004) *Colossus: The Rise and Fall of the American Empire*, London: Allen Lane.

Frank, Andre Gunder (1971) *Sociology of Development and Underdevelopment of Sociology*, London: Pluto Press.

——(1998) *ReOrient: Global Economy in the Asian Age*, London and Los Angeles: University of California Press.

Giddens, Anthony (1985) *The Nation State and Violence*, Cambridge: Polity Press.

——(1990) *The Consequences of Modernity*, Cambridge: Polity Press.

——(1992) *The Transformation of Intimacy*, Cambridge: Polity Press.

——(1999) *Runaway World: How Globalization is Changing our Lives*, London: Profile.

Hardt, Michael and Negri, Antonio (2000) *Empire*, Cambridge: Harvard University Press.

Held, David (1995) *Democracy and the Global Order: From the Modern State to Cosmopiltan Governance*, Cambridge: Polity Press.

Hirst, Paul (2001) *War and Power in the 21st Century*, Cambridge: Polity Press.

Hirst, Paul and Thompson, Graeme (1996) *Globalization in Question: The International Economy and the Possibilities of Governance*, Cambridge: Polity Press.

Holton, Robert J. (2005) *Making Globalization*, Basingstoke: Palgrave Macmillan.

Huntington, S. P. (1993) 'The Clash of Civilizations', *Foreign Affairs* 72(3): 22–48.

——(1996) *The Clash of Civilizations and the Remaking of World Order*, New York: Simon & Schuster.

Johnson, Chalmers (2000) *Blowback: The Costs and Consequences of American Empire*, New York: Henry Holt.

Juergensmeyer, Mark (2006) *The Oxford Handbook of Global Religions*, New York: Oxford University Press.

Keane, John (2003) *Global Civil Society?* Cambridge: Cambridge University Press.

Kennedy, Paul (1988) *The Rise and Fall of the Great Powers*, London: Unwin Hyman.

Lash, Scott (2002) *Critique of Information*, London: Sage.

Lechner, F. and Boli, J. (eds) (2004) *The Globalization Reader*, Oxford: Blackwell.

Loyal, Steven (2003) *The Sociology of Anthony Giddens*, London: Pluto.

Luhmann, Niklas (1990) 'The World Society as a Social System' in *Essays on Self-Reference*, New York: Columbia University Press.

Lyotard, Jean-François. (1984) *The Postmodern Condition*, Manchester: Manchester University Press.

Mandaville, Peter (2001) *Transnational Muslim Politics*, London: Routledge.

Mann, Michael (2003) *Incoherent Empire*, London: Verso.

McLuhan, Marshall (1962) *The Gutenberg Galaxy: The Making of Typographic Man*, Toronto: Toronto University Press.

——(1964) *Understanding Media: The Extensions of Man*, London: Routledge & Kegan Paul.

——(1967) *The Medium is the Message*, San Francisco: Hardwired.

——(1969) *Counter-Blast*, New York: Harcourt, Brace & World.

Moore, W. E. (1966) 'Global Sociology:the World as a Singular System', *American Journal of Sociology* 71: 475–82.

Mufti, Aamir R. (2007) *Enlightenment in the Colony: The Jewish Question and the Crisis of Postcolonial Culture*, Princeton and Oxford: Princeton University Press.

Murphy, Craig (1994) *International Organization and Industrial Change: Global Governance since 1850*, New York: Oxford University Press.

Newman, David (2006) 'Borders and Bordering:Towards an Interdisciplinary Dialogue', *European Journal of Social Theory* 9(2): 171–86.

Ong, Aiwha (1999) *Flexible Citizenship: The Cultural Logics of Transnationality*, Durham: Duke University Press.

Ong, Aihwa and Collier, Stephen (2004) *Global Assemblages: Technology, Politics and Ethics as Anthropological Problems*, Oxford: Blackwell.

Ong, Aihwa and Nonini, Donald (eds) (1997) *Ungrounded Empires: The Cultural Politucs of Modern Chinese Transnationalism*, New York: Routledge.

Pieterse, Jan Nederveen (ed.) (2000) *Global Futures: Shaping Globalization*, London: Zed Books.

Pieterse, Jan Nederveen (2004) *Globalization or Empire?* New York: Routledge.

——(2008) *Is There Hope for Uncle Sam?Beyond the American Bubble*, London and New York: Zed Books.

Power, Michael (1997) *The Audit Society: Rituals of Verification*, Oxford: Oxford University Press.

Ritzer, George (1993) *The McDonaldization of Society*, London: Sage.

——(2003) *The Globalization of Nothing*, London: Sage.

Ritzer, George (ed.) (2007) *The Blackwell Companion to Globalization*, Oxford: Blackwell.

Robertson, Roland. (1992) *Globalization: Social Theory and Global Culture*, London: Sage.

Said, Edward (1978) *Orientalism*, London: Routledge & Kegan Paul.

Savage, Mike, Bagnall, G. and Longhurst, Brian (2005) *Globalization & Belonging*, London: Sage.

Schudson, Michael (2003) *The Sociology of News*, New York :Norton.

Shusterman, Richard (ed.) (1999) *Bourdieu: A Critical Reader*, Oxford: Blackwell.

Shamir, Ronen (2005) 'Without Borders? Notes on Globalization as a Mobility Regime', *Sociological Theory* 23(2): 197–217.

Spybey, Anthony (1996) *Globalization and World Society*, Cambridge: Polity.

Stiglitz, Joseph (2002) *Globalization and its Discontents*, New York: W.W. Norton.

Turner, Bryan S. (1978) *Marx and the End of Orientalism*, London: Allen & Unwin.

——(1994) *Orientalism, Postmodernism and Globalism*, London: Routledge.

——(2003) 'McDonaldization: Linearity and Liquidity in Consumer Cultures', *American Behavioral Scientist* 47(2): 137–53.

——(2007a) 'The Enclave Society: Towards a Sociology of Immobility', *European Journal of Social Theory* 10(2): 287–303.

——(2007b) 'The Futures of Globalization', in George Ritzer (ed.) *The Blackwell Companion to Globalization*, Oxford: Blackwell, pp. 675–92.

Turner, Bryan S. and Rojek, Chris (2001) *Society & Culture*, London: Sage.

Urry, John (2000) *Sociology Beyond Societies: Mobilities for the Twenty First Century*, London: Routledge.

Wallerstein, Immanuel (1974) *The Modern World System*, New York: Academic Press.

Wasserstrom, Jeffrey N., Hunt, Lynn, and Young, Marilyn B. (eds) (2000) *Human Rights and Revolutions*, Lanham: Rowman and Littlefield.

Wilson, Rob and Dissanayake, Wimal (eds) (1996) *Global/Local: Cultural Production and the Transnational Imaginary*, Durham, NC and London: Duke University Press.

Zaret, David (2000) *Origins of Democratic Culture: Printing, Petitions and the Public Sphere in Early-modern England*, Princeton, NJ: Princeton University Press.

2

Limiting theory

Rethinking approaches to cultures of globalization

Smitha Radhakrishnan

In the last two decades, sociologists, anthropologists, and human geographers have wrestled with the vague and all-encompassing task of theorizing the cultural dimensions of globalization. This has proven to be even more complicated and problematic than theorizing the economics of globalization. Although most scholars of globalization accept that the spatial stretching of production lines and the expansion of capital and free markets comprise a central component of globalization, it has been much more difficult to establish the social and cultural implications of these seemingly self-evident shifts in political economy. To a large extent, globalization has raised issues that fundamentally challenge the presumptions built into our social scientific toolkits for studying culture. *Where* is culture located? *How* can seemingly endless processes of cultural change be tracked and studied? Or, more directly, "*What* about modernity?" While previously, a specific evolutionary script of modernity allowed "us" to "go" to faraway locations and track cultural change just by being there, something that we call globalization has forced us to forsake such easy answers, to examine the relations of power inherent in the production of knowledge about culture, and finally, to leave us without our usual theoretical hangers on which we might drape the coats of our empirical and analytical studies.

Yet, new hangers abound. Efforts to create just such theoretical hangers to fill the void have generated a powerful discourse surrounding globalization's cultural effects, bringing to the academic forefront such themes and keywords as hybridity, deterritorialization, and cosmopolitanism, to name just a few. These interdisciplinary debates have generated a vast, sophisticated, and complex literature on this topic, yet this literature presents a puzzling trend: despite its ostensible imperative to theorize rapidly changing empirical realities, cultural theories of globalization have remained largely separate from, and indeed at times irrelevant to, sustained empirical studies of those phenomena these theories are meant to describe. As students of globalization, how do we understand this disjuncture? What is the critique that this disjuncture offers us, not only in terms of the concept of globalization, but also in terms of our scholastic procedure of theory construction more generally?

Here, I aim to provide an overview of some of the major theoretical approaches to the culture of globalization, while attempting to analyze the unifying themes and accomplishments of this literature as it relates to sociology, as well as key recurring issues and the implications of these issues. Diverse characterizations of the cultural dimensions of globalization are unified by a few key convictions. Most obviously, theorists of the cultural dimensions of globalization tend to implicitly or explicitly reject older anthropological notions of culture as a bounded system located in a specific place. Indeed, it is the apparently (new?) inability to locate and define culture and the realm of the social that informs and underpins new theories. In an age of transnational migration, freely traveling consumer goods, and satellite television, no longer can we assume, if ever we could in the first place, a thoroughgoing coincidence between territory and community, place, and identity. The recognition of this displacement has produced a heightened concern with the social construction of space and spatiality, often operating through the micro/macro lens of economics (i.e. local/global). This critical attention on the part of sociologists and anthropologists to questions of location and culture has forced scholars to rethink the nation as a source of identity and belonging and reframe the question of culture in terms that acknowledge the continued importance of nations with also recognizing new sources of meaning and belonging—from professional or workplace identifications to affiliations and commitments to transnational causes. To what extent can the nation be a source of belonging and cultural identification in a world that seems to de-link individuals from their national contexts? And more vexingly, how can we study such a thing meaningfully?

Since the task of theorizing culture must necessarily be embedded in an historical context, however broad, theorists of the cultural dimensions of globalization must grapple with some version of the most compelling historical narrative of all: the modernization narrative. For some, world-systems theory forms the systemic economic base upon which to construct and think through new cultural shifts and flows, while for others, a progressive narrative of social and political modernity, though not necessarily defined by an economic system, prevails. In any of its forms, these theorists reveal to us the extent to which the paradigm of modernity, one-way progress and/or development is embedded into social scientific knowledge production about culture. Yet, the complicated theoretical tumble with modernity in this literature ends up neither returning to nor rejecting modernist ideals of progress and development. Rather, we find compromises of various hues, in which hybrid conceptions of culture and identity take center stage.

At the heart of the endeavor to theorize the cultural dimensions of globalization stand classic social scientific dilemmas that seem to loom larger and more befuddling than ever: the relationship between the universal and the particular, continuity and change, the individual and the collective. Indeed, I would suggest that these theoretical innovations are more centrally concerned with mapping these philosophical dilemmas onto the contemporary phenomenon of globalization than about explaining and understanding cultural change as it is experienced in the lives of individuals or even in the historical scripts of societies. How might cultural theory shift when rooted in sustained empirical studies? Why might it be that the task of theorizing the cultural dimensions of globalization is so separate from the profusion of empirical work on globalization?

To answer these questions, I turn to a selected literature of ethnographic studies to examine the implications of these studies for a larger theory of culture in an interconnected, globalized world. Empirical studies of the cultural dimensions of globalization tend to broadly cluster around a few key strategies. One strategy is to follow the movement of people or groups of people. Transnational studies of international migration have provided us with a rich body of work detailing the lives and dilemmas of people who move (Mahler, 1995; Levitt, 2001; Parreñas, 2001). Another strategy is to follow capital investment. Since the 1980s, feminist ethnographers in particular have provided rich insights into the lives of women whose lives are transformed by new factory and service occupations that crop up in their local environments (Ong, 1987; Wolf, 1992; Salzinger, 2003; Lynch, 2007). A third strategy has been to follow products and ideas, often by examining consumer or activist practices as they traverse the globe (Appadurai, 1986; Thayer, 2001; Mazzarella, 2003; Davis, 2007). Here, I examine one example of each of these types of studies to highlight the ways in which these empirical treatments complicate our theoretical paradigms, perhaps to the point of obviating them.

Empirical studies of the culture of globalization reveal layers of cultural process that go far beyond even the most complex and nuanced of theories that attempt to locate (or disembed) culture in a global world. Perhaps the most important intervention that empirical studies can offer theory is that such studies can render the modernization narrative moot. Systemic economic explanations seem to continue to have some explanatory value and traction, allowing us to find common threads between disparate social and cultural experiences. Yet a linear narrative of modernization, with all of the binaries and presumptions that come with it, does not seem to stand up to sustained empirical inquiry; the status of the "center" comes into question, and class position becomes more indicative of socio-economic standing in the world than national or global location. Similarly, empirical studies draw into question the concept of the nation, so important for social scientific research on belonging and identity. Theorists of globalization and nationalism clash on the extent to which the nation is an abiding source of identification in a "global" cultural landscape, while theorists of deterritorialization and diaspora reconceptualize the nation as one disconnected from a physical territory (Appadurai, 1996; Castells, 1997; Puri, 2004). Yet, much of this theoretical literature maps onto grounded ethnographic studies unevenly and without much analytical traction. As with the terms "local" and "global," "traditional" and "modern," which have all become so overburdened with analytical responsibility that they have taken on lives of their own, the nation faces new theoretical challenges in a rapidly shifting global cultural landscape.

I conclude with a set of reflections that attempt to emerge from the quagmire of theoretical and empirical dilemmas by suggesting a shift away from efforts to theorize the cultural dimensions of existing paradigms. This is not to argue for a world of fragments or disjuncture (which itself contains within it a narrative theory), but to continue to make connections between global capitalism and cultural change in various parts of the world on the one hand, and on the other hand, to approach cultural change in a partial way, adopting lessons from feminist epistemology. Such an approach would be able to rely more heavily on empirical accounts by sacrificing totalizing theories for limiting (rather than fragmented) ones, thus responding appropriately to the lessons that the empirical realities of globalization offer the discipline of sociology and the social sciences more generally.

Local/global: the culture of the world system and beyond

With the opening of borders and the rise of free market ideology in the 1980s, a riveting set of cultural phenomena began to emerge that have now become commonplace icons of globalization's new landscape. While the stretching of capitalist lines of production drew millions of mostly women into waged work, technological advances in travel and communication transformed large cities into ever intensified nodes of economic activity (Harvey, 1989; Sassen, 1994; Ward and Pyle, 1995). Expansions in capital and media capacity also meant that consumer goods traveled the world more freely than before, bringing Western products and cable television to previously far-flung locations (Appadurai, 1996). These shifts seemed to signal cultural change on an unprecedented scale, and produced a range of theoretical responses. Did these changes articulate new aspects of an existing world-system, or did these changes signal the emergence of new forms of global social organization? Or, did these changes signal the breakdown of previously existing systems, leaving us only to think about disconnected cultural fragments? In thinking through such questions, scholars sought to develop a new vocabulary through which to reflect upon the age-old dilemma of the relationship between the particular and the universal, this time in terms of spatial metaphors: the local and the global. As "local" came to stand in for the particular, and "global" for the universal, an overloaded binary embedded in exiting theories of development became a dominant language with which to frame theoretical analyses.

By the 1990s, theorists of the economic, political, and spatial dimensions of globalization noted trends that seemed to signal the emergence of a distinctive "global" ethos: the (much contested) decline of the nation-state as a coherent entity, the stretching of global production lines and social relationships, and the compression of time through technology (Harvey, 1989; Appadurai, 1996; Castells, 2000). These trends suggested the emergence of denser, more intensified modes of human interaction that destabilized older anthropological notions of localized culture. This newfound "global" ethos appeared to be a threat to "local" cultures, which seemed vulnerable in this new environment. Poststructural development theorists of the early 1990s proposed a *return* to "local" culture and knowledge as a much-needed reaction against the ostensible "global forces" of development and globalization associated with the spread of capitalism. Such efforts aimed at valorizing the local, which seemed to be at risk (Escobar, 1995). Other theorists emerged with more complex formulations, seeing the local and global as intermeshed and co-constitutive, emphasizing the ways in which cultures were being remade anew, not being destroyed, in the context of globalization (Friedman, 1994).

The local/global opposition underpinning this theorizing was not, however, a purely cultural argument, but also an economic one that enhanced world-systems theory by linking it to cultural formations (King and State University of New York at Binghamton, Dept. of Art and Art History, 1991). Immanuel Wallerstein's enormously influential conception of the world system proposed that the world was structured primarily by the economic relationships between states in the core, periphery, and semi-periphery. This conceptualization formed a critical part of the attack on theories of modernization and autonomous growth championed most famously in sociology by Talcott Parsons (Robertson and Turner, 1991). Wallerstein and other world-systems theorists argued that core/periphery locations were based on exploitative capitalist relationships in which the core (namely, the US and Europe) extracts resources and goods from the periphery (the so-called "developing" or "third" world) in an interdependent exchange that keeps the periphery poor and the core wealthy, while the semi-periphery, a buffer group, ensures political stability in the system. The rapid spread of particularly American corporate products and services in the late 1980s and 1990s led scholars to extend Wallerstein's conceptualization from the economic to the cultural realm, with significant elaboration and detail. These cultural theories growing out of world-systems theory went well beyond cultural imperialism to examine the ways in which the local and the global constitute one another, acknowledging the extent to which globalization is constituted by new cultural forms that come into being through a vast network of economic and cultural interconnections (King and State University of New York at Binghamton, Dept. of Art and Art History, 1991; Friedman, 1994). Although connected to the global dynamics of capital as conceptualized in world systems theory, such studies have moved away from pitting "the local" and "the global" as culturally oppositional, making a break from both modernization theory as well as attempts to romanticize the local as an unspoiled location in need of protection.

Despite sophisticated efforts to distance cultural theorizing from a zero-sum game between the local and the global, the preoccupation with the idea of a dominant "global force" raining down on a "local culture," with all its attendant spatial and political metaphors, remains a dominant theme throughout a major body of this literature. The opposition between the local and global takes various forms, but theoretically speaking, continues to grapple with this dichotomy at its core, despite variation in conceptualization and theme. Even theories of hybrid culture that reject the binary rely upon the opposition between the local and global at heart. Roland Robertson's very detailed and sophisticated treatment of "glocalization" epitomizes this tendency:

> The global is not in and of itself counterposed to the local. Rather, what is often referred to as the local is essentially included within the global. In this respect, globalization, defined in its most general sense as the compression of the world as a whole, involves the linking of localities. But it also involves the "invention" of locality, in the same general sense of the idea of the invention of tradition.
>
> (Robertson, 1992: 35)

In this passage, we are confronted with the dilemmas of theorizing a phenomenon that contains at once a spatial component (indicated not only by the local/global framework in the first place, but also in the notions of "compression" and "linking of localities"), but also a temporal one, as Robertson inevitably comes to the (contemporary?) "invention" of both spatial and temporal (tradition-al) cultural components. Yet, in this as in other similar attempts to reconcile the local and the global in a coherent theory of cultural globalization, the opposition (with the spatial and temporal implication attendant upon it) persists. How are "local" and "global" cultures to be identified as analytically separate if they are completely enmeshed in one another, as the same theories claim? Is it possible to take space and location completely out of a metaphor that is essentially spatial and still have it be useful? In Robertson's statement as in statements of other similar theorists, concerns with the particular and the universal are translated into a spatial metaphor—one that packs in temporal metaphors as well—losing analytical leverage in the transformation.

Other theorists proposed that the dramatic cultural changes accompanying economic globalization were constituted through an altogether different kind of system. Forsaking the structured economic interdependency of world systems theory, sociologists such as Manuel Castells and Saskia Sassen conceptualized a network system (Castells, 2000; Sassen, 2001). A network approach focused on the interconnections and exchanges between locations or nodes in different parts of the globe. Thus, nodes of power *and* powerlessness could be located either in the "center" or in the "periphery." The network metaphor allowed for geographic location and material location to be analytically distinct in some sense. Still, "the global" comprises a coherent economic and cultural system, despite the unevenness of the system's landscape. In Castells's notion of the

27

network society, actors connected through electronic information networks replace social networks to constitute a global society. Those who cannot participate in those networks, due either to geographic or material location, are left out of the system and marginalized. Similarly, for Sassen, economic and financial ties cross borders, but come together in the intensified nodes of global cities. Here too, material and geographic location holds the key to accessing the global economic system; the majority of the world's population is marginal to it. Although similar to world-systems conceptions of culture because of the primary place afforded economics, network theories gave rise to new kinds of questions for the cultural dimensions of globalization that moved away from economics: might cultural networks exist independently of financial and electronic ones? Are cultural networks always simply overlaid on economic ones?

Still other theorists found that the rapid cultural change of globalization indicated no system at all, but rather indicated the fragmentation of culture, wherein identities and locations no longer resided together. Arjun Appadurai conceptualized the culture of globalization in terms of fragments, disjunctures, flows, and "scapes," presenting a dramatic break from other approaches to the culture of globalization that pivoted around primarily the economic dimensions of globalization, with culture following (Appadurai, 1996). Appadurai's approach instead focuses on the movement of culture across geographic locations. Global capital, then, is just one more moving scape or flow among many. Through Appadurai's framework, then, we can trace, at a relatively broad level of generality, everything from diasporic nationalism to the proliferation of ideas about democracy all over the world. In this sense, Appadurai is not as embedded in the local/global formulations as others mentioned above. Yet, the local/global tension appears at the heart of his focus on movement; indeed, the movement of identities, goods, ideas, and capital serves as a way in which to trace and interpret local/global interactions, often coded as the interaction between the national and the global. In some sense, then, Appadurai's conception offers us a reinvigorated, dynamic view of particularity, while conceiving of the universal only in the broadest of terms.

Finally, the rapidly growing literature around global ethnography, led by the work of Michael Burawoy, offers a distinct approach to cultural theories of globalization by focusing very specifically on the ways in which "the local" constitutes "the global," defined not as a singular ethos, but as a phenomenon viewed alternately as forces, connections, and imaginations (Burawoy et al., 2000; Burawoy, 2001). Scholars associated with global ethnography do not posit an overarching theory or framework for thinking about the cultural dimensions of globalization, but instead focus on the ways in which globalization forces ethnographers to rethink the ethnographic site itself. The location of global ethnography might be singular, as in Seán Ó Riain''s examination of Irish technologists or Teresa Gowan's examination of homeless recyclers in San Francisco (Gowan, 2000; O'Riain, 2004). It might also be multi-sited, however, as in Sheba George's work on Indian migrant nurses (George, 2005). Such a diversity of methods explodes the local/global dichotomy to some extent, acting on the conviction that the global is not intelligible outside its local articulation and expression. More specifically, with regard to culture, scholars of global ethnography do not necessarily look to the ethnographic site as the source of culture, but rather use traditional ethnographic tools to examine specific phenomena, which might include a cultural component. Studies that share the tools and theoretical presumptions of global ethnography tend to ground their analyses in the empirical, thus setting this body of work apart from other cultural theorists. In this sense, although still embedded within the search for the local and the global that is still not quite examining space per se, global ethnography tends to refrain from drawing conclusions about the culture of globalization in general, a point I will return to later as I further consider the role of the empirical in cultural theories.

The disparate group of theories I have examined here are similar in that they all regard in some way the local/global metaphor as a critical lens through which to examine the cultural changes wrought by globalization all over the world. I have suggested that often the spatial metaphor belies the profoundly aspatial approach to theorizing cultural phenomena, and becomes a way in which to embed sociological inquiries about the relationship between the universal and the particular within the rubric of "globalization." Some approaches are systemic, while others forsake a systemic core, yet all of these theories grow out of a critique of modernization theory, aiming to de-center the West in the study of globalization. By taking into account cultural phenomena in the global South as well as in the industrialized world, and looking at the interconnectedness of these locations, these theories are linked to critiques of a postwar development paradigm for which unidirectional modernization was imperative.

Yet, not all theorists of globalization were focused on the kinds of cultural changes framed by divisions in power and geography. For many important sociological thinkers, globalization was constituted centrally by the social and political, rather than by the economic. In this view, the industrialized world comprises the starting point of cultural change by offering a glimpse into a future for the rest of the world, or at least a potential trajectory of social reconfiguration and change. In these theories, the postwar development project of modernization in the global South is far away, yet a narrative of progress located in the industrialized world underpins their theorization of culture.

Tradition/modernity: the logics of individuality and culture

For many, the significance of the 1980s and 1990s was not the expansion of capital markets or the movement of factories overseas, but rather the disintegration of the Soviet Union. That is, a new global *political* landscape, marked by the ostensible triumph of liberal capitalist democracy, provided the key catalyst of global cultural change (Beck et al., 1994). The collapse of the Berlin Wall in 1989 was seen as being linked to other kinds of social collapses: the shift away from collective identification, and eventually, the collapse of the state as the primary provider of social services. Theorists focusing on these shifts rather than purely economic shifts gave rise to a parallel strand of theorizing, largely separate from the local/global debates, and centered primarily on the industrialized world. Rather than focusing on themes of cultural hybridity and accommodation, these theories have tended to emphasize the ways in which countries in the global North have been culturally reconstituted as their economies and societies have shifted in response to global trends. This body of theory is centrally concerned with individual and societal responses to the scaled-back state emerging from neoliberal economic regimes, and views globalization as constituted importantly through modernity as constituted through the experience of the West. In this literature, globalization is defined as a new phase of modernity—often a hyper- or postmodernity—thus privileging a temporal mode of interpreting culture over a spatial one (Giddens, 1990; Beck, 1999). Concomitantly, these theorists provide explanations for cultural change that stem from shifts in social logics and rationalities, rather than from systems, thus providing an altogether distinct exploration of the cultural dynamics of globalization.

Unlike the local/global literature, tradition and modernity are less concerned with specific issues of the nation that stem from a preoccupation with space and territory. Instead, a temporal focus that looks for changing logics and rationalities examines processes of individualization, wherein "new" modes of being and interconnection in a world disrupt and replace "old" modes of social connection and belonging. Power is no longer defined within a global economic system, but rather within an often unspecified society, either drawing from Foucauldian concepts of knowledge and power or a more Weberian focus on state power (Barry et al., 1996). More recently, ethnographers working primarily in the global South have adopted these ideas to explain the changes that global capital has brought to parts of Asia, reconstituting ideas of the nation through the notion of "alternative modernities" (Ong, 1999; Gaonkar, 2001). This latter variation of this type of theory moves towards expanding the scope of these ideas by grounding the temporal in specific national histories. In practice, however, the traditional and the modern are difficult to identify as analytically distinct, limiting the empirical traction we can get from it in lived settings and reinforcing a progressive narrative of modernity in which the experience of the West remains the implicit reference.

In contrast with those theorists focused on linking a changing culture to spatial and systemic dimensions of globalization, these thinkers examine shifts in the organizational logics of society as the role of the individual is heightened and the responsibility of the state declines. Anthony Giddens and Ulrich Beck both explain globalization in terms of modernity. Rejecting claims towards postmodernity, these theorists propose instead hyper-modernity or radical modernization, in which a new form of modernity has displaced an older one. Specifically, a "risk society" emerges from the success and subsequent obsolescence of modern industrial society (Giddens, 1990; Beck, 1999; Beck et al., 1994). In a modification of Marx's progressive model of history, risk society is then a new stage of modernity, centered around the threats presented by industrial modernity. A new kind of modernization, "reflexive modernization," displaces the old industrial modernity, arriving "on cats" paws, as it were," rather than on the heels of revolt or upheaval, to signal the transition from an industrial society to a risk society (Beck et al., 1994).

This transformation has particular implications for the notion of the individual, which becomes the focal point of examination for many cultural theorists of modernity and post-modernity. For Giddens, individuals are "disembedded" from their local contexts and attachments; social relations are "restructured across indefinite time-space." For Beck, the central implication of reflexive modernization and risk society is the reconstitution of the individual as the most important manager of risks, displacing the importance of the family group and social class, which previously absorbed widespread risk. This "individualization," as Beck calls it, is not a reference to fragmentation and isolation, but rather to a new social form in which "individuals must produce, stage, and cobble together their biographies themselves" (13). The implications of this shift are decidedly political. Indeed, Beck argues that the 1980s has given rise to a renaissance of political subjectivity, evidenced by the new political power of citizen groups.

Although approaching modernity from a completely different set of theoretical presumptions, Nikolas Rose's Foucauldian approach to modernity, also focused on the logics of individuals, has dovetailed with the work of Beck and Giddens to influence an altogether new type of globalization theory. Rose's analyses focus largely on what he calls "advanced liberal societies," such as the US and Britain. These post-industrial societies are undergoing dramatic changes in their political, social, and economic conditions, especially in response to neoliberalism as a political and economic philosophy (Rose, 1999). Following Foucault, Rose views freedom as a technique through which individuals are governed, rather than as an absence of government. The "political rationality" of freedom enables, supports, and pushes forward the dominance of the free market in every aspect of social life, while in parallel, state-sponsored programs and works are dramatically scaled back. These trends radically shift the ways in which individuals relate to their societies, as they rely increasing upon themselves for calculation, thought, and planning. Rose argues that individuals in advanced liberal societies develop individualized expertise that helps them to make decisions without the help of trained experts, but at the same time, forms of legitimate authority proliferate. Beyond the expectation of the isolated, independent individual emblematic of liberalism, these political subjects govern themselves through a culture of the self that is pervasive in social and political realms. Whether through confessional talk shows or niche marketing, every aspect of personal and political life becomes shaped to fit an individual focused on the development and actualization of herself, thus fundamentally transforming meanings of citizenship, community, and autonomy. Rose connects these specific patterns to the de-legitimization of the welfare state and the rise of new technologies of expertise.

In relation to other theorists of tradition and modernity, Rose's framework similarly emphasizes the temporal over the spatial, while focusing his analysis more explicitly on the ways in which a new social and political temporality brings with it a new orientation between the individual and society. In this way, Rose's analysis engages with classic social scientific questions while not necessarily making broad statements about globalization per se, although the trends he describes in Britain and the US are an important part of the cultural phenomenon of globalization as it is examined by other scholars. Rose does not seem to make claims about the post-colonial world nor about a generalized global condition. Yet, Rose's Foucauldian approach, especially as it links with the work of such scholars as Beck and Giddens, has given rise to a new focus within globalization studies that uses the lens of individualization and cultural logic to examine new cultural phenomena.

Stephen Collier and Aihwa Ong's important edited volume *Global Assemblages* offered a new framework for thinking through new cultures of globalization by focusing on technologies of the self in multiple locations (Ong and Collier, 2005). In many ways, the specific anthropological approaches advocated in this volume attempt to straddle the attention to the spatial privileged in the local/global literature while also attending to temporal aspects of the tradition/modernity literature. Collier and Ong's definition of "global assemblage" (of which each of the various topics explored in the book is an example) bridges the gap between the general, transferable, abstract aspects of globalization's cultures on one hand, and the grounded, specific, rooted aspects of these cultures on the other hand. Indeed, they purposely highlight the inherent tensions these two dimensions in any given object of study. Such a framework allows for an empirically grounded anthropological examination of new objects of cultural analysis: stem cell research, the global organ trade, financial markets, and urban planning, to name a few. These objects of analysis are similar in that they are governed by the neoliberal political rationality that Rose describes; Collier and Ong's approach highlights these common (albeit abstract) logics that underpin global objects.

Collier and Ong's approach certainly enables us to examine new objects of study through a cultural lens tooled to interpret a landscape constituted through the slipperiness of transnational flows and shifting subjectivities. Unlike other theories, "global assemblage" appears to offer an analytic language that can connect meaningfully to empirical

31

settings. Despite these advantages, "global assemblage" as an approach seems to rely upon the same local/global, traditional/modern binaries that other theorists have battled with, albeit with a more clearly specified and demarcated language. Moreover, by privileging neoliberal political rationality—a logic meant to explain conditions in post-industrial societies like the US and Europe—the concept of global assemblage seems to presume the ubiquity of this logic rather than investigating the possibility of that ubiquity. While the authors seem to have neither an explicitly systemic theory of culture here, nor a linear narrative of modernity, their formulation is already embedded in all of these theoretical ancestors. Still, global assemblage, like global ethnography, offers the advantage of a specified theoretical language that could be used to interpret a wide range of new cultural phenomena.

In grounded empirical studies, then, how are theories of cultural globalization engaged and how are they kept at a distance? What can we learn from these interactions?

Partial theory: emerging from the empirical

Following the people: cultures of migration

Although the international migration literature in sociology has historically been focused on questions of assimilation or lack thereof, a new disciplinary focus on globalization has transformed the field, making it less US-centered and more multi-sited in its approach. Transnational studies of migration focus on groups of migrants in multiple places; due to advances in travel and communication, migration seldom means that migrant groups sever their ties to their home country. Unlike the theories of globalization discussed above, studies of migration tend to be focused on the empirical details and realities of the people whose lives they are engaged in; its implications for a broad theory of culture of globalization are seldom examined (Waters, 1990; Mahler, 1995).

Peggy Levitt's landmark book *The Transnational Villagers* examines the rich transnational exchanges that take place through the lives of migrants between Miraflores, a small village in the Dominican Republic, and Jamaica Plain, an area just outside of Boston where many Dominican migrants live. Her study begins from the premise that these transnational villagers maintain such close ties with family and friends in their home village that "it is as if village life takes place in two settings" (2). Responding to the inadequacy of conventional assimilation paradigms in the migration literature, Levitt examines the sharing of ideas, fashions, products, and money between Dominican migrants in the US and their friends and family in their home village of Miraflores. In her rich ethnographic analysis that draws from interviews and fieldwork both in Boston and the Dominican Republic, Levitt details the various aspects of these transnational lifestyles, explaining how ideas and information are shared, how economics shapes their everyday lives in the US and in the Dominican Republic, and the various practices through which the transnational villagers she analyzes maintain a sense of belonging to two locations, constructing a circuit of goods, ideas, and information that moves easily between these locations.

Levitt's work directly engages questions of globalization's cultural impact. By following people who have the opportunity to move away from their home countries for work from their home to their host country and back again, Levitt captures key empirical realities based on the everyday experiences of those individuals who are on the front lines of globalization and cultural change. Her key theoretical innovation coalesces around the idea of "social remittances": normative structures, systems of practice, and social capital that move between Boston and the Dominican Republic. By using this approach to specify those cultural facets that travel, Levitt develops a tool with which to think through similar kinds of transnational exchanges in other communities with similar migration patterns. In her approach, Levitt builds her theoretical apparatus carefully to analyze the wealth of empirical evidence she brings to bear. Avoiding the macro-language of local/global cultural change, she instead asserts that social remittances are evidence of a kind of cultural globalization that is occurring through communities on an everyday basis, rather than through political or economic institutions.

Although clearly a rich illustration of the very processes of globalization that cultural theories of globalization are meant to theorize, it is difficult to employ the conceptual framework of these theories to analyze the evidence she provides. Although she does hint at notions of progress and modernity in her use of the term "social evolution" to describe the changes that migrants experience, it is difficult to specify or identify the elements of "global" culture or "local" culture in her story without making a number of conceptual leaps that are not borne out by the empirical evidence. Indeed, by linking two locations (Miraflores and Jamaica Plain), all of the processes she describes are simultaneously local and trans-local; yet it is these "local" processes that come to define globalization. The economic dynamics of the world system are certainly at play here; it is the continued economic dominance of the US and the relative lack of economic opportunity in the Dominican Republic that draws Dominican migrants away from their homes in the first place. Her analysis also could be interpreted as revealing perhaps a corresponding hegemony of American behaviors, attitudes, and fashions, all of which get transplanted and adopted on the island. Yet, such an analytic frame would belie the give-and-take relationship that engages people in each of these locations. Even with regard to questions of nation, identity, and belonging, Levitt's empirical evidence demonstrates a dual sense of belonging, wherein both the US and the Dominican Republic are meaningful homes. It is not that the nation has been "deterritorialized," nor is this a straightforward type of hybridity, although it might be interpreted as such. Levitt finds that migrants pick and choose the attitudes, cultural goods, and identifications that are meaningful to them in both homes, denying easy categorization. Thus, Levitt stays away from either the local/global or modernity/tradition, opting instead for a language of transnationalism that specifies the borders being crossed and the mechanisms of the crossing.

Cultural theories of globalization can have explanatory traction only when they can be mapped convincingly onto an appropriate empirical object; Levitt's study provides an important example of the limitations of these theories in this regard. When we study the everyday experience of globalization, how do we decide, analytically speaking, what is to be categorized as "global" and "local" or "traditional" and "modern" without simply reinforcing folk categories? Is the preservation of Dominican home arrangements in Boston, for example, to be considered "local" or "global" and why? The messiness of the empirical world does not provide guidelines for these questions, yet our theory takes our ability to identify these categories for granted, sending us down a slippery analytical slope. In a study like Levitt's, then, theory stays close to the ground, and stops short of making large claims about the nature of globalization in general, opting instead for limited claims about the changing nature of citizenship, belonging, and assimilation in America.

Follow the money: new cultures of work

Apart from migration, a key feature of globalization has been the rapid expansion of global capital, as production lines stretch across borders, always in search of cheaper labor. The transfer of manufacturing from the industrialized world to the developing world has brought into being a new workforce participating in the global capitalist production chain. In each place, industrialization has brought with it new cultures of work that have formed an important area of inquiry for scholars of globalization. The gender and globalization literature has been particularly attentive to these changes. In-depth empirical studies of women workers in locations as diverse as Malaysia, Mexico, London, Sri Lanka, and the Caribbean have provided rich insight into the formation of new subjectivities produced by the dynamics of globalization. In rural industrial settings, women workers not only participate in globalized processes of production, but also help to constitute new discourses about ideal workers, while becoming new consumers of capitalist goods (Ong, 1987; Wolf, 1992; Lynch, 2007). In urban factory towns, these workers are the drivers of the local economy, even as their entitlements as workers continue to diminish (Fernández-Kelly, 1983; Freeman, 2000; Salzinger, 2003). These studies illuminate a constitutive facet of the culture of globalization, as they capture in detail the tensions that arise in societies facing dramatic social and economic changes. As local communities confronted with the brutalities of global capital, these changes might be framed within the language of transition from tradition to modernity, but the stories that emerge on the ground make it difficult to map such binaries onto the empirical realities of these places and people. Instead, nuanced theories concerning gender, capitalism, discipline, and consumerism emerge, and these theories bear little resonance with the large body of literature on globalization.

Leslie Salzinger's study of Mexican maquiladoras in the border town of Cuidad Juarez serves as an important example of the kinds of theoretical innovations that can only come from sustained empirical work. Her book *Genders in Production* argues that gender itself is made on the shop floors of factories, and that even within the same town at the same place, multiple gender regimes can operate. The gendered subjectivities produced in each factory depended upon the setup of the factory (often dictated more by the product itself than the management; for example, assembling gowns is a very different factory process than assembling televisions), the pay arrangements (per item or per hour), and the relationships established between the workers and the managers. For example, in the factory she calls Panoptimex, Salzinger finds "icons of paradigmatic femininity": seductively dressed and made up women working in "detail" work, monitored by male managers, while men on the production line deal with the "heavy" work. Production is managed through relentless watching. Salzinger details the ways in which production in the Panoptimex factory is set up to make paradigmatic femininity, which becomes a malleable resource on the shop floor. However, not all factories fit this easily recognizable prototype of feminized labor. At Andromex, another factory she examines, we find a masculinized workforce in which the work is not categorized as women's work. Cloaking gender becomes the key strategy that allows the factory to be successful, even to the point of covering up gendered bodies while sewing the hospital garments they make. This result emerged from a worker-led struggle with the management that had the effect of transforming Andromex's workforce "from feminine assembly to masculine manufacturing," constructing the work as difficult work for breadwinners, and giving workers greater autonomy through the piece-rate scale (104–5).

By examining the various tropes of the ideal worker and how factories condition the women (and men) to be docile, malleable workers—constructions that can be made and unmade as circumstances require—Salzinger unsettles conventional gender and globalization theories that take the feminization of work and the category of women as a fixed given. Instead, Salzinger shows both the possibilities and the limitations of firms that seek out and produce "the transnationally elaborated image of productive femininity," enforcing appropriate femininity and cheap productivity at the same time (89). Because these femininities and masculinities look so dramatically different in the different factories she studies, Salzinger's study raises questions about the kinds of claims we as scholars can make about how globalization transforms social and cultural worlds. Yet, this is not simply a question of local/global or of the empirical versus the theoretical. Rather, Salzinger's work uses detailed ethnographic data to illuminate global trends and ideas. Her research investigates the transnational prototype of the woman worker's role in the global production line and traces the extent to which these meanings become real in the everyday lives of the places she studies. It is not that the image fits only uneasily upon the realities she finds; it is that the image of the cheap, docile, woman worker helps to *produce* the realities she finds. Managers and workers alike *make* gender productive on the shop floor—productive of good workers who are also desirable women. Gender is malleable, and comprises an important set of discursive resources that can be drawn upon to make spatially stretched production lines successful. This insight offers two lessons for cultural theories of globalization: first, this goes far beyond the idea that the "global" is in some way constituted through the "local," as many sophisticated theories suggest, and indeed befuddles any type of a modernization narrative, melding traditional Mexican gender roles with the demands of capitalist production in ways that shift from moment to moment, from factory to factory. Rather, Salzinger's study suggests that "the global" is in itself a powerful set of discourses that get translated into the capitalist production system in the most concrete of ways. In this sense, "the global" is no longer an analytical term, but a descriptive one, used by managers and corporations as a set of guidelines for creating new production sites. Similarly, "the local" becomes a site that must be produced in order to conform to the notions of a "local labor market." Salzinger invites us to examine these terms associated with globalization as powerful discursive tropes to be analyzed, and not to be deployed analytically.

Secondly, Salzinger's book joins other books on gender and globalization in its focus on the subjectivities of workers and managers. Such an approach grows out of feminist ethnographic techniques that place the positionality of the researcher at the center of the production of knowledge of those that the author studies. It is not just that her study is empirical, then, that makes it stand apart from theoretical approaches to globalization. Rather, her engagement with the empirical is self-consciously reflective of her theoretical commitment to feminist ethnography; she never claims to stand outside or above the object of her analysis. Yet, that position yields broader theoretical insights than macro-level positions that claim either "a view from nowhere" or "a view from everywhere." In this sense, studies like Salzinger's bring into sharp view the role of analysts of globalization in proliferating the very discourses about globalization that we intend to analyze. Is the object of our theoretical analyses discourses about globalization or the phenomena that constitute globalization? And in attempting to do the latter, do we simply unreflexively produce more of the former?

Follow the thing/idea: traveling discourses

Levitt's study followed migration of people while Salzinger studied the movement of capital. What of the movement of ideas and discourses? Sociologists in particular have been extremely attentive to the ways in which globalization has led to a kind of global consensus on a number of key ethical, social, and cultural practices, ranging from the organization and presentation of nations to the definition and defense of human rights, violence against women, and the environment (Meyer et al., 1997; Keck and Sikkink, 1998). In particular, the work of Meyer and Boli (1997) and Keck and Sikkink (1998) have offered accounts of this kind of global consensus around key issues, and have convincingly explained the mechanisms through which these changes take place. Both these studies operate at a macro-level of generality, but the explanations and accounts they engage bring to bear specific empirical cases. While these studies have been extremely influential in the field of sociology, helping to fuel new literatures in sociology, here, I turn to an approach towards traveling discourses that is less visible in the field. Kathy Davis's recent book *The Making of Our Bodies, Ourselves* provides a detailed account of the genesis and worldwide travel of the classic feminist text *Our Bodies, Ourselves* [*OBOS*]. *OBOS* fueled the formation of an imagined feminist community that crossed cultural, moral, and ideological barriers, offering women around the world accurate and culturally relevant information about their bodies and life course in its many translations. Davis's study—a book about a book—provides a fresh insight specifically into the issues of translation and community that haunt other studies of cultural globalization, while providing a powerful commentary on the limitations of globalization theory.

OBOS came into being among a group of white, middle-class, college-educated women meeting to discuss women's health in the early 1970s—a time when women's health was ignored by the medical establishment and was a taboo subject in popular discourse. Published first as an underground pamphlet on newsprint, the book turned into an international best-seller that was later translated into dozens of languages and country-specific adaptations, and sold around the world. Davis's book traces the history of this classic book and the people who produced it, the book's status within feminist scholarship, and the complexities and challenges that the various authors of the texts faced in translating the text to make it relevant to the lives of women in different material and geographic locations from the women who began writing it all those years ago. In this sense, the book deals directly with issues surrounding location, thus engaging with one of the key concerns of cultural globalization theories.

Davis uses a feminist theoretical toolkit to ask how this task helped to produce feminist subjectivities ready to engage in political action. Was the book simply a US export, one more product of American cultural hegemony popularized through print media? Davis offers convincing evidence to the contrary. By focusing on the formation of feminist subjectivities in a transnational nexus, Davis moves away from the treatment of subjectivity, belonging, and politics that pervades globalization theorizing that is focused on neoliberal subjectivities when approaching the individual. Instead, Davis shows that the interactions between the text and women in various parts of the globe makes these women both feel a part of something bigger than themselves, and feel ownership of the book. As a part of this feeling of ownership and collaboration, feminists outside the US asserted their own authority and ability to recreate the meaning of the text for themselves. In reflecting upon a meeting of OBOS translators in 2001 and retelling the story of the original collective that gave rise to the book, Davis notes:

> This story "belonged" to them. In re-creating *OBOS* in their specific historical and geographic locations, they were appropriating more than a book. They were also becoming part of the (mythical) feminist community that had made *OBOS* an icon not only for US feminism, but for transnational feminism as well.
>
> (Davis, 2007: 174)

The simultaneous sense of belonging that Davis identifies among *OBOS*'s translators as well as the authority they feel in rewriting and re-creating the text to suit their particular cultural settings challenges cultural theories of globalization in many ways. The new subjectivities being formed in reading *OBOS* are not quite the generalized neoliberal subjects that emerge from Foucauldian treatments of modernity and globalization. At the same time, the range of available "glocal" approaches, blending the local and global, do not fit either. In this case, the text of *OBOS* takes on a life of its own, but unlike other kinds of consumer products that acquire lives of their own in a global sphere, this text spurs the formation of a political subjectivity that is relevant across borders. This political subjectivity is at once tied to particular nationalities, cultures, and spaces, but is realized only in conversation with other feminists and health activists living in other parts of the world. The story of *OBOS* and its "travels," then, is one that is at once national and transnational, at once embodied, political, and transcendent.

Davis joins Levitt and Salzinger in analyzing cultures of globalization by bringing to life subjectivities that are formed when new kinds of movements occur, be they through migration, the movement of capital, or the movement of discourses or ideas. What distinguishes these approaches to cultures of globalization from the kinds of purely theoretical approaches explored in the earlier part of this essay is not just the fact that these are primarily empirical studies; it is that their empirical approach gives rise to different kinds of theory. Indeed, each of these authors, like the globalization theorists, are mapping sociological concerns with the particular and the universal, continuity and change, onto the theoretical and empirical worlds they are exploring. Each of these authors makes a set of broad claims about culture and globalization; yet, these claims are fundamentally distinct in logic, form, and language from the more popular kinds of macro-theory that have entered mainstream academic discourse on globalization. What are the broader lessons that these studies offer us, not only in terms of their incompatibility with the theoretical toolkit we should be able to use in our studies, but also in terms of the new kinds of insights that such studies yield? To what extent is cultural globalization theory in particular and sociological theory more generally reshaped and reframed by these grounded studies?

Looking ahead: situated knowledges and global cultural change

Theories of cultural globalization challenge us as scholars to re-examine some of our most fundamental methods, convictions, and concerns. To what extent is it appropriate to continue to privilege "high theory" that is divorced from empirical realities? How do such theories help to develop our analytical toolkits and to what extent do they hinder them, reproducing and proliferating a discourse of globalization that we must critique?

Feminist theorizing has remained almost entirely outside the realm of macro-level cultural theory about globalization. While feminist thought has greatly influenced postcolonial theory and cultural studies more generally, the insights of feminist thinking have remained at the margins of theories of globalization widely accepted in the social sciences, especially in sociology. This oversight is not something that can be easily attributed to some kind of thoroughgoing denial of the importance of gender or feminist methods, nor does it imply that such approaches are in some way inappropriate or irrelevant to globalization. Rather, it seems that some of the deepest analytical insights of feminist theory and methodology fundamentally threaten the transcendent status of high theory, forcing us to make more careful claims and generalizations and ground them more firmly in lived human experiences. Feminist methods and epistemology hinge upon a detailed, reflexive approach that highlights the situatedness of knowledge, and a diversity of human practices, experiences, and logics. These principles can lead to new kinds of theory, placing limits on high theory while at the same time deepening it and making it more relevant to empirical work.

Innovations in transnational feminist theory and in the gender and globalization literature have the potential to reformulate cultural theories of globalization in three critical ways: (1) by contextualizing theoretical claims within the position of the author and the methods used in making those claims, (2) by examining interconnections between times and spaces without dependence upon conventional binary hierarchies, such as local/global, traditional/modern (and carefully placing them within an analytical context when such terms are deployed), and (3) by refusing to subordinate difference to generality and the particular to the universal, but rather viewing difference and particularity in themselves as comprising a broader set of lessons and themes that can be useful for analyzing empirical realities. These principles acknowledge the extent to which globalization has transformed the place of theory in the social sciences. Using these insights as a springboard for future theoretical and empirical work moves us away from the search for the location of culture, focusing instead on the economic, social, and political interconnections that constitute culture as it comes into being and moves through national and transnational circuits. These principles also distance themselves from modernization narratives to explain culture, while still acknowledging the powerful role that discourses of modernization have played historically and continue to play in diverse cultural phenomena.

The gender and globalization literature, of which Salzinger's work is emblematic, is primarily an empirically-grounded literature, but contains within it important lessons for potential futures in theorizing the cultural dimensions of globalization. Because this literature tends to be deeply ethnographic, conducted over long periods of time, the position of the ethnographer is central to the account of cultural change that is provided. Salzinger, for example, situates herself within the study reflexively, constantly acknowledging the tiers of power and privilege that she encounters and traverses during her research. Feminist methodology has historically been particularly reflexive, emphasizing power relations between the researcher and the researched and questioning at every step the representation of the objects of study. While these principles are of course important for any social scientific study, they become even more important when studying rapid cultural change as the researcher is an integral part of the cultural change underway. Theories of the cultural dimensions of globalization that adopt a view from nowhere lose analytical traction because of the impossibility of equating one scholar's view of culture to another's. Adopting a fundamentally situated perspective forces us to make more measured claims that can further our engagement with our empirical realities. Gender and globalization also draws attention to individual subjectivities when trying to define and understand culture. Unlike tradition/modernity that is focused on the logic of individuality, individuals are seen as snapshot composites of the social worlds they occupy. Culture, then, is located not in a geographic place, per se, but takes shape in the experiences, attitudes, and beliefs of individuals reflecting complex social realities.

Transnational feminist theory, in contrast with the gender and globalization literature, is seldom focused on empirical studies. Although much of the work of transnational feminists deals directly with issues related directly to the politics of feminism and its relevance, translation, and movement across borders, transnational feminists have also been an important analytical voice in highlighting the relationships between global capital, national and religious identities, and everyday lives, and it is this latter accomplishment that I wish to focus on here. Caren Kaplan and Inderpal Grewal's edited volume *Scattered Hegemonies* signaled the emergence of transnational feminism as a critical perspective within feminist theory and globalization. Emphasizing the persistence and revitalization of national and religious identities alongside an increasingly de-centered, transnational world, the essays in the volume drew attention to multiplicities of local/ global meanings while anchoring analyses to questions of method, power, language, and inequality. While many have subsequently used the analytic tools this volume proposes, Chandra Mohanty's 2003 book *Feminism without Borders* was important in taking the perspective forward. Mohanty establishes linkages between the politics of feminist solidarity and difference on one hand, and the spread of capitalism and the proliferation of inequality on the other. She argues for a critical perspective on globalization that recognizes the proliferation of difference while also forging new kinds of solidarity across common interests. Mohanty's emphasis on difference of all kinds is instructive for theorists of cultural globalization; she and other transnational feminists highlight particularity and difference as constitutive of culture. Yet, this is not simply a postmodern recommendation to see the proliferation of difference without end; rather this type of theory looks for connections among difference, both for political and analytical ends. The result is not a type of theory that is governed by a singular logic or narrative, but rather a partial type of theory that wishes at once to generalize and to examine the production of culture in a most grounded fashion.

If these lessons became integrated into mainstream theorizing about cultures of globalization, it would distance us somewhat from some of our most basic social scientific presumptions about how culture is constituted and how we come to know and understand culture at some level of generality. But such a shift responds appropriately to a global landscape for which our current toolkits are inadequate. A shift in our discipline's approach to the cultural dimensions of globalization could allow for the construction of a limited kind of theory—limited in the sense of being clearly demarcated—rather than theories that attempt to explain all cultural phenomena everywhere. Yet, in forsaking the former to some degree, we constructively build upon our theoretical ancestors to forge a new set of analytical tools.

References

Appadurai, A. (1986) *The social life of things: commodities in cultural perspective*, Cambridge and New York, Cambridge University Press.

——(1996) *Modernity at large: cultural dimensions of globalization*, Minneapolis, University of Minnesota Press.

Barry, A., Osborne, T. and Rose, N. S. (1996) *Foucault and political reason: liberalism, neo-liberalism, and rationalities of government*, Chicago, University of Chicago Press.

Beck, U. (1999) *World risk society*, Cambridge Malden, MA, Polity Press; Blackwell.

Beck, U., Giddens, A. and Lash, S. (1994) *Reflexive modernization: politics, tradition and aesthetics in the modern social order*, Cambridge, Polity Press.

Burawoy, M. (2001) "Manufacturing the global," *Ethnography*, 2.

Burawoy, M., Blum, J. A., George, S., Gille, Z., Gowan, T., Haney, L., Klawiter, M., Lopez, S. H., Riain, S. Ó. and Thayer, M. (2000) *Global Ethnography: forces, connections, and imaginations in a postmodern world*, Berkeley, CA, University of California Press.

Castells, M. (1997) *The power of identity*, Malden, MA, Blackwell.

——(2000) *The rise of the network society*, Oxford, Blackwell Publishers.

Davis, K. (2007) *The making of* Our Bodies, Ourselves: *how feminism travels across borders*, Durham, NC, Duke University Press.

Escobar, A. (1995) *Encountering development: the making and unmaking of the Third World*, Princeton, NJ, Princeton University Press.

Fernández-Kelly, M. P. (1983) *For we are sold, I and my people: women and industry in Mexico's frontier*, Albany, N. State University of New York Press.

Freeman, C. (2000) *High tech and high heels in the global economy: women, work, and pink collar identities in the Caribbean*, Durham, NC, Duke University Press.

Friedman, J. (1994) *Cultural identity and global process*, London; Thousand Oaks, CA, Sage Publications.

Gaonkar, D. P. (2001) *Alternative modernities*, Durham, NC, Duke University Press.

George, S. M. (2005) *When women come first: gender and class in transnational migration*, Berkeley, CA, University of California Press.

Giddens, A. (1990) *The consequences of modernity*, Stanford, CA, Stanford University Press.

Gowan, T. (2000) "Excavating globalization from street level: homeless men recycle their pasts," in Burawoy, M. et al. (ed.) *Global ethnography: forces, connections and imaginations in a postmodern world*. Berkeley, CA, University of California Press.

Harvey, D. (1989) *The condition of postmodernity: an enquiry into the origins of cultural change*, Oxford and New York, Blackwell.

Keck, M. E. and Sikkink, K. (1998) *Activists beyond borders: advocacy networks in international politics*, Ithaca, NY, Cornell University Press.

King, A. D. and State University of New York at Binghamton, Dept. of Art and Art History. (1991) *Culture, globalization, and the world-system: contemporary conditions for the representation of identity*, Binghamton, Dept. of Art and Art History, State University of New York at Binghamton.

Levitt, P. (2001) *The transnational villagers*, Berkeley, CA, University of California Press.

Lynch, C. (2007) *Juki girls, good girls: gender and cultural politics in Sri Lanka's global garment industry*, Ithaca, NY, ILR Press/Cornell University Press.

Mahler, S. J. (1995) *American dreaming: immigrant life on the margins*, Princeton, NJ, Princeton University Press.

Mazzarella, W. (2003) *Shoveling smoke: advertising and globalization in contemporary India*, Durham, NC, Duke University Press.

Meyer, J. W., Bolt, J., Thomas, G. and Ramirez, F. (1997) "World society and the nation state," *American Journal of Sociology*, 103, 144–91.

O'Riain, S. (2004) *The politics of high-tech growth*, Cambridge, Cambridge University Press.

Ong, A. (1987) *Spirits of resistance and capitalist discipline: factory women in Malaysia*, Albany, NY, State University of New York Press.

——(1999) *Flexible citizenship: the cultural logics of transnationality*, Durham, NC and London, Duke University Press.

Ong, A. and Collier, S. J. (2005) "Global assemblages, anthropological problems." in Collier, S. J. and Ong, A. (eds.) *Global assemblages: technology, politics, and ethics as anthropoligical problems*, Malden, MA, Oxford and Victoria, Blackwell Publishing Ltd.

Parreñas, R. S. (2001) *Servants of globalization: women, migration and domestic work*, Stanford, CA, Stanford University Press.

Puri, J. (2004) *Encountering nationalism*, Malden, MA, Blackwell.

Robertson, R. (1992) *Globalization: social theory and global culture*, London, Sage.

Robertson, R. and Turner, B. S. (1991) "An introduction to Talcott Parsons: theory, politics, and humanity," in Robertson, R. and Turner, B. S. (eds.) *Talcott Parsons: theorist of modernity*, London, Sage Publications.

Rose, N. (1999) *Powers of freedom: reframing political thought*, Cambridge, UK, Cambridge University Press.

Salzinger, L. (2003) *Genders in production:making workers in Mexico's global factories*, Berkeley, CA, University of California Press.

Sassen, S. (1994) *Cities in a world economy*, Thousand Oaks, CA, Pine Forge Press.

——(2001) *The global city*, Princeton, NJ, Princeton University Press.

Thayer, M. (2001) "Transnational feminism: reading Joan Scott in the Brazilian Sertao," *Ethnography*, 2, 243–71.

Ward, K. B. and Pyle, J. L. (1995) "Gender, industrialization, transnational corporations, and development: an overview of trends and patterns," in Bose, C. E. and Acosta-Belen, E. (eds.) *Women in the Latin American Development Process*. Philadelphia, PA, Temple University Press.

Waters, M. C. (1990) *Ethnic options: choosing identities in America*, Berkeley, CA, University of California Press.

Wolf, D. (1992) *Factory daughter: gender, household dynamics, and rural industrialization in Java*, Berkeley, CA, University of California Press.

3

Economic theories of globalization

Patrik Aspers and Sebastian Kohl

Introduction

This chapter will show how the notions of globalization, capitalism, and markets can be used for analyzing economic globalization. We will look at the globalization of markets, from the local market that offers fruit from all over the world to contemporary financial markets that operate around the clock due to shift work by traders around the globe. This will take us to analyses of global interdependency patterns, but this can only be done if one takes the theories that people have developed to understand the economy into account.

Globalization is often seen as a form of convergence of associated production systems, cultures, and even political processes. The neoclassical economic model presents the idea of convergence of prices and products all over the world, as a result of arbitrage and the clearing of markets. Convergence of cultures is sometimes linked with a critique of "Western hegemony," wherein the democratic polity is even referred to as the end of history. We show that a simple scheme of divergence–convergence cannot fully grasp diverse matters such as international consumption patterns, organizational structures, and national policies. Therefore, we do not claim that the world is moving in one direction; we limit our discussion to economic cases for analyzing divergence and convergence.

This chapter addresses a number of concrete questions. How has the view of trading with others and of being dependent on them changed over time? What normative standpoints can be identified in the discussion of economic "globalization"? What can be said about efficiency and inequality? What markets today are global? Throughout the text we relate the theoretical discussion to empirical examples. This framework is also used to understand the first financial crisis of the third millennium.

We discuss these questions in the light of the large amount of literature on economic globalization. The discussion emphasizes markets and capitalism, and has a historical perspective, which means that we will look at economic and sociological theories that discuss aspects of economic internationalization and globalization. The discussion can only make a few stops on the journey into the history of economic ideas from Aristotle to today. We first try to give some flesh to discussions of economic globalization. The chapter then briefly discusses and defines capitalism. The next section deals with and defines markets. The third section covers globalization. These three concepts will be used in the remaining sections to analyze the co-evolution of global economic processes and economic ideas about globalization. It should be said that these three notions are only tools to highlight what we think are the most central aspects, whereas others, as a consequence, are downplayed.

Glimpses from the global economy

What is a global market? Let us look at a few examples. By the proliferation of the internet and the emergence of market places like eBay it is possible to access products of all kinds from all over the world. In this global market place it is easy to compare the prices of products, both for buyers and sellers. Tramp shipping, to take another example, is an industry with a very long history of being global; ships were, and still are, central for making contact and transporting goods between people all around the globe. This industry is made up of ship owners, agents, shipbrokers, and in the ends those who trade commodities. These actors operate in several interconnected markets all over the world. The tramp shipping market is part of the international shipping industry, and a certain market segment, in which vessels that operate do not trade regularly between certain fixed ports. Instead they take cargoes from any port to the port required by the customer. Prices in this market can be extremely volatile, about twice as volatile as the S&P index that includes the largest stocks on the New York Stock Exchange. Volatility depends on oil prices, wars, and much more that boils down to market prices. This market has for a very long time been operated by actors across the world. Today about 150 nations have vessels operating on the seven oceans. The industry has a labor force of people from many different nations who work together on the ships, which means that there is also a global labor market for sailors. Let us look at a third global market case. The market for foreign exchange is the largest market in the world in terms of turnover. In the same way as it is necessary to trade British pounds for euros when going from London to Paris for a weekend holiday, large firms and central banks, as well as financial speculators, must trade with different currencies to pay for the goods they buy. The financial market is highly globalized and traders are located all over the world.

These three cases can of course be seen as different and independent cases. But let us look a bit closer to see how they may be connected. When a student sits in her dormitory in Austin, Texas she can compare prices and objects from virtually every corner of the world. Let us assume that she is looking for a used and rare Gibson guitar, and she decides to go for one that is for sale in Germany. She orders the Gibson guitar from Trier in Germany, for which she will pay with her debit card in US dollars. The retired rock musician in Trier, who has put out this guitar for sale, will soon see that the money he required in euros is registered on his account. This single transaction can only take place given that there is a market for foreign exchange. But neither of them must directly take part in this financial market, though their banks will have to do it. When the rock musician sends the guitar to the US, he may send it by air, but since this is more expensive, the two have agreed that he shall send it by surface mail. This means that the guitar will go perhaps by car and train, but certainly by ship, before she can play it in Austin, US. Thus, this economic relation ties these two persons with different interests together because one has an item for sale that the other is willing to pay for. But since they never meet and directly hand over the money for the guitar, it is still not clear how this works.

To understand this one must begin to look at economic dependency patterns that involve a number of actors, operating in different markets. How do these myriad actions, interests, goods, and money hang together? What, in other words, makes the system tick? Let us first clarify a few things. The internet was not developed by Google; it was developed with tax-payers' money to facilitate information within the military. This suggests that the state has played a role in this market. The state may also force actors who transact to pay taxes or custom for the goods. We have also mentioned the motives of the buyer and seller. In between them several transactions may have taken place. But they did not take place because the private companies that take care of the transport of the guitar within Germany are so enthusiastic about music, nor is it because the sailors on board of the vessel who take it across the Atlantic like their tin can so much that they stay away from home three months, so that the guitar successfully can make this journey. In their eyes, it is not the guitar as such that has been traded. These firms, and those employed by these firms, have made sure that the package, quite regardless of its content, gets to the right address in Austin. Many actors and institutions are involved in the process of taking the guitar in one direction and money in the other. However, in the global economy money travels only as accounts, that is, only as registration of numbers, and never as actual physical money.

Though neither the guitar player in the US nor the seller in Germany has had as their primary interest to make profit on this trade, they may both have looked at different alternatives to get a better deal. The actors, the middlemen, who made this deal possible are motivated by profit, and may compete with each other. This extremely complicated transaction, which in reality is much more complicated than what has been indicated here, is made possible by people who are organized in firms in order to make money. In addition to the motives, the knowledge of where and how to transact, and to know the rules of the market-game, are important components for trade to take place. These examples show interdependence in the global economy. To speak of global markets cannot be done unless one also refers to local markets. In the examples, it moreover becomes evident that one cannot reduce these global economic dependency patterns to technology, nor to individual motives alone. In fact, it is possible to identify these patterns in old societies, long before there were computers. People have been trading for thousands of years, and there have been future markets in shipping for hundreds of years. The human desire to explore, learn, and acquire objects that make life easier and more pleasurable has contributed to human journeys and trade, and we have, as a result, increasingly become dependent on one another. This is, of course, only a necessary condition which does not lead to trade in the absence of specific historical constellations or even geographical factors. Having said this, the change, which cannot only be reduced to economic factors, has taken place over the last decades means that the globe has become smaller in more than one way.

The examples, moreover, indicate that there are global markets in the contemporary economy. One could, in fact, talk of a completely global economy if all markets were global, i.e., if there was an oligopolistic structure in all markets, where everyone takes all other market actors' actions into account and in which most of the trade volume is international (Fligstein, 2001). This, of course, is not the case, and one may talk of economic globalization also in other respects, such as when local garment producers in Vietnam compete with producers in China to get an order of skirts for a European

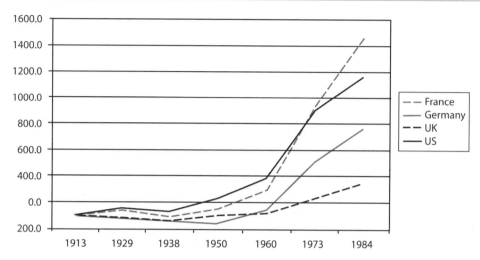

Figure 3.1 Relative volume of export, 1913–84, standardized by year 1913 (100).
Source: Adapted from Hirst and Thompson (1996: 21).

fashion brand. This suggests that people – who live under wide economic, cultural, political, and social conditions, are involved, and tied together, in a global economy through systems of markets. However, there is not a global labor market, and to gain labor and many other services these firms are deeply embedded in their respective local economy. Furthermore, in both China and Vietnam people buy groceries that are largely of local origin, and they find and pay their housing under conditions that one can only understand if one sees how the economy is embedded in the local culture and formal institutions. Economic globalization, more generally, refers to increased international trade (see Figure 3.1).

The examples we have taken, and the discussion so far, suggest that one cannot speak of one global economy, because many people are almost or even completely outside of the economy, and some markets are still local. One must therefore have analytical tools to understand and be able to penetrate the rhetoric of politicians and discourses in the press about globalization and interpretation of facts. We now turn to the first central concept, capitalism, then we will discuss markets, and finally globalization.

Capitalism and its origin

The etymological origin of the word capitalism is "head," and it refers to the time when wealth was measured in the number of heads of cattle a person owned. The word also means "interest," and a capitalist, in the late eighteenth century in France, was a person who aimed for high interest, or was simply a wealthy person. Capitalism as a phenomenon has existed for a long time, but the notion is much younger. Scientists have identified the phenomenon even in Ancient Greece. When one speaks of capitalism today, it is usually rational capitalism that emerged in the sixteenth century which one refers to. Capitalists should be separated from capitalism. Capitalism refers to the social system and its corresponding values. Usually, a capitalist is seen as someone who has accumulated

45

capital, and who reinvests this capital according to a rational logic to increase profit. The capitalist system is driven by competition among capitalists to gain profit. Though competition is crucial to a "well-functioning" capitalistic market economy, the individual capitalist usually strives to be the sole actor, as everyone who has played Monopoly knows. This means that the actor, either a person or a firm, tries to get rid of her competitors and to become a monopolist (one seller) or a monopsonist (one buyer), to be able to set the price in the market and thereby maximize the profit. Whereas some scholars view this tendency as an inherent destabilizing force within capitalism, others view individual striving for monopolistic profits as canalized by a benevolent competition in favor of all.

To get a better understanding of the emergence of modern rational capitalism, we turn to those who had this new development in front of their eyes and who were stunned by this inexplicable cultural phenomenon. Early nineteenth-century capitalism in Great Britain, for example, caused turmoil in society, as cities grew when people moved in from the countryside, starting to work in factories. This change in society produced incredible wealth for some people, but it also generated the first wave of modern mass unemployment and poverty (see, e.g., Polanyi, 1954). This caused many to question the cohesion and order of society. The change was highly visible. Also the social consequences were visible. In his largely empirical report about *The Condition of the Working Class in England in 1844* Engels reports about the unseen, stunningly new phenomenon:

> The condition of the working-class is the condition of the vast majority of the English people. The question: What is to become of those destitute millions, who consume to-day what they earned yesterday; who have created the greatness of England by their inventions and their toil; who become with every passing day more conscious of their might, and demand, with daily increasing urgency, their share of the advantages of society?

Social theorists tried to understand what they observed with the tools they had at their disposal, but they realized that new ideas must be formed to account for the change. According to the traditional ethical doctrine a poor person was either unable to support himself, and in need of charity, or they were lazy, for which they should be condemned. Another observation that did not go well with the contemporary normative ideas was that the most egoistic traders seemed to be more successful than those who held the more traditional virtues. Thus, daily problems were one reason for seeking new explanatory patterns that centered on a notion of the economy as an independently functioning realm.

But how is one to explain the great transformation of society in which rational capitalism played a key role? There are several theories about the origin of capitalism. The first theory of capitalism was developed by the precursor of sociology Karl Marx (1818–83), though he never used the word capitalism himself. Marx transformed a totally idealistic German philosophy into a so-called "historical materialism," arguing that historical development could not be explained without taking into account material technological processes and real human beings. His scientific predictions about how capitalism would develop and ultimately lead to its demise were empirically falsified. On these and other grounds one may conclude that the scientific value of his theory of capitalism is limited. Marx, however, foresaw a global capitalism, and the influence of his theories in society is unparalleled. He was also the first to address the inequality and social turmoil that is associated with capitalism.

The German sociologist Max Weber (1864–1920) developed the best-known scientific theory of capitalism. Also Weber stresses the social process that eventually leads to rational capitalism. Weber acknowledges that various types of capitalism had existed long before the Western rationalistic type emerged, for example in China, India, and mediaeval Europe. Thus, Weber (1978: 164–66) distinguishes between several forms of capitalisms, such as political, authoritative, and predatory, each with a different form of profit opportunities. Weber defines a (rational) capitalistic action, "as one which rests on the expectation of profit by the utilization of opportunities for exchange, that is on (formally) peaceful chances of profit" (1968: 17). One important aspect of capitalistic actions is the market, which is a precondition for rational calculations.

As Weber himself pointed out, stability is a condition for calculability, which is vital to rational capitalism (1978: 296). Weber's analysis suggests that money, which is the primary means of calculation, became an end in itself, and this fundamentally changed the values of society. This analysis, and the role of money in modern society was carried out in great detail by another German sociologist, Georg Simmel, in his work *The Philosophy of Money* (1978). A further consequence of capitalism is that people not only made some money, and then settled down, or used the money for social display. Capitalism rather means, according to Weber, that people accumulate money where it was profitable, and reinvest it in industries, which lead to a growth in the economy.

Weber argues that rational industrial capitalism only emerged in the Western world. But what sets the Western rational capitalism and its spirit apart from other forms of capitalism? It is not "The impulse to acquisition, pursuit of gain, of money" according to Weber (1968: 17), since this is common also in non-capitalistic societies. Weber identifies, in contrast to Marx, the capitalistic spirit in certain specific values that came to be seen as virtues. It is the consequences of the virtuous actions that generated the dominating form of capitalism in the West. Weber, to be specific, argues that Calvinism in particular is an example of a religious belief that is correlated to how one does business in a capitalistic fashion. Calvinistic ideas, Weber says, promoted, more than others, the spirit of capitalism. Weber makes the point that the interpretation of the religious virtues provided an ethical foundation for "capitalistic actions." When people, later, became socialized into these economic virtues, they may accept them without their religious undertones. Weber has established a link which indicates the way the religious virtues affect the economy. In fact, he explains how the economy could become an autonomous sphere, separated from the "original" sphere of religion.

Though it is clear that there are different theories about the emergence of capitalism, there is at least some agreement about what it means. Capitalism is defined as "accumulation of wealth," and this implies making profit. Profit is predominantly generated in markets. All in all, these ideas suggest that capitalism gave the impetus to the ever increasing wish for accumulation of wealth, which means that national markets were not enough. As a consequence, economic actors and the corresponding market relations soon stretched beyond the European nation states with the ambition to further increase profit.

Markets

Markets are the central institution of the contemporary capitalistic economy. There is also a second reason for stressing the role of markets. By the development of a global economy, the role of states as regulators or triggers of markets must be analyzed. Furthermore, it is not primarily trade between states (as organizational units) that has increased, but the trade between firms across the globe, though these of course reside in countries. The unit of analysis is the market, not the nation, if one wants to take economic globalization seriously. Ever more companies, however, grow and are best described as multinational or global actors. This development, in other words, cannot be understood unless the role of the globalization of markets is considered.

What is a market? In a way we all know what a market is, since we take part in "markets" almost on a daily basis. When we decide to make our tea at home in the morning, or decide to buy a take away from one of those who offer this "in the market" on the way from your home to the university, we are "in" the market. A market, in short, is a social structure for exchange of rights, which enables people, firms, and products to be evaluated and priced (Aspers, 2006). Let us elaborate on this definition. This means that at least three actors are needed for a market to exist; at least one actor, on the one side of the market, who is aware of at least two actors on the other side whose offerings can be evaluated in relation to each other. The social structure consists of roles (buyer and seller, and consumer and producer), divided on the two sides of the market interface. Actors take part in markets to become better off. Different interests or goals characterize these two roles: the one wants to sell for a good profit, the other to purchase for as little as possible. Property rights, often embedded in trust, are conventional in a market, which makes market interaction peaceful. Exchange implies that something, for example money, is traded for something else, such as a commodity. What is traded in a market is usually what gives it a name, for example "the market for clothes." That there is a stable social structure made up of roles implies that the market is extended over time. Though the notion of market is used to refer to a specific place, the proposed definition does not imply a location in space. A market may, in other words, exist "in several" places over time, this is the case of the "market for foreign currencies." Trade in this market is an around-the-clock activity. That a market is defined as existing over time usually means that a specific market has its own "market culture." Culture is defined as beliefs, "tools," and behaviors, e.g., discourse and practice, which are appropriate to the market. This refers, for example, to how one interacts in the stores, how products are priced and much more. Each market may not necessarily have a unique culture, the culture in the market for clothes and the market for shoes may not be so different. In fact, both are today essentially markets of fashion. More generally, many markets may have similar cultures, and people today are socialized into a general "market culture" that may not differ much, for example, between different consumer markets. What we have just described is a minimal definition, and it assumes institutions, i.e., rules and regulations that govern behavior with sanctions, that may be used also outside the market.

It is important to keep in mind that many markets have been organized by the state, and towards the end we will get back to this issue and discuss how states in the form of state-capitalism today operate in global markets. The state provides, of course, the legal system that aims at "law and order." It is, however, also involved in the creation and governance of many individual markets, as has been shown by the sociologist Neil Fligstein (2001). But does not the development of a large number of global markets diminish the role of the state? So far we have assumed that we know what a globalized market means. But to address this question we need to look at what "global" and "globalization" mean. Only then is it possible for us to say something about global capitalism and the markets that make it up.

Globalization

The notion of globalization catches how culture, economy, and politics, as well as other fields, are transformed in terms of dependency patterns. People depend on each other and what used to be segmented on a local, regional, or national level is increasingly turned into a global dependency. The increased number of contacts, including business contacts, correlated with a greater flow of commodities and services around the globe, manifests the process of globalization in the economic sphere. There is both a quantitative increase, but one can also speak of qualitative new relations, such as when large firms come together and organize markets without the states.

Though most researchers would agree that the increase of dependency patterns that reach across the globe constitute the core of globalization, different social sciences have stressed different aspects. Sociologists ever since Immanuel Wallerstein (1974), and with later followers like Gary Gereffi (2005), whose works have had an impact also on economic geography and political economy, have stressed the global inequality. Relations between wealthy nations, often located in the northern hemisphere, and poor countries, often located in the southern hemisphere, is a dependency relation because they need each other to flourish. It is, however, a relation which is characterized by asymmetry, as most of the wealth has ended up in the already rich countries. Though few have denied that economic growth has also taken place in poor countries as a result of globalization, the initial idea of the Marxist-influenced world system theory of Wallerstein emphasizes that the very inequality between developmental and industrial regions is a precondition for the wealth of the latter.

Anthropologists were among the first to notice globalization. This is because they, in contrast to sociologists and economists, ground much of their research in their "fields," which are often made up of villages, towns, and associations in developing countries. It was also in these settings, rather than in the developed world, that one at first, and more directly, could observe how activities in one part of the world were connected to activities in another part of the world. In other words, the relative change is much larger in areas that until quite recently have hardly seen any development at all. Anthropologists tend to focus on the notion of culture and they have therefore studied how culture in one place is changed as a consequence of its relation to other cultures. Economic activities mediated through global supply chains that are organized to meet the demand of final consumers have increasingly penetrated the local cultures and caused traditional commodities, such as pottery, to be molded in a way that they are sellable in the shops in Tokyo or Detroit. Also vegetables have been modified to suit the final consumers. Moreover, vegetables exist in stores in, for example, Nordic countries, in larger quantities but above all in greater variety than they did 30 years. These are examples of how dependency patterns change over time and have consequences on both ends of the economic chain of transaction.

Globalization has, of course, a spatial dimension, which economic geographers have been quick to notice. Economic relations, which used to exist in the village, the clan, and later in the country or the region, are today reaching all over the globe. Outsourcing, not only to other firms within the same country, but to firms in other countries and parts of the world, is common. This we see in traditional industries such as the textile industry and the auto industry, but also in modern service industries as is shown by the outsourcing of call centers to other continents. Economic geographers have particularly shown how industrial networks within firms, but also across markets, connect places across the globe. Finally, as we will see later, economists have also discussed globalization. Some, like Paul

Krugman (1991), argue that there are decreasing marginal costs that result from economies of scale, as well as agglomeration effects. A consequence is that one may talk of imperfect competition and the existence of clustering effects.

Globalization has been addressed in most social sciences, and in the rest of the chapter we will take a closer look at various theories and ideas that address "globalization" in a broad sense, using the concepts that so far have been discussed and defined: capitalism, market, and globalization. We suggest that globalization can only be understood in relation to a discussion of capitalist markets, and this of course implies that one takes a historical perspective. One can in addition speak of three modern economic theory positions: mercantilism, liberalism, and socialism.

Economic dependence in early societies

We said that globalization must be understood in terms of dependence on a global scale. However, economic dependency must not be global. Though we cannot discuss the entire history of economics, we will make a few stops on the journey to rational capitalism, and the global tendencies that one sees with increased international trade. This will give a background to the economic phase that is increasingly characterized by a global economy and that some may even take for granted.

Though many of us today are accustomed to markets and to capitalism, this has not always been the case. To address the question of economic globalization, one should remember that there are still economies that are only integrated in the global economy to a small extent. Economic issues in the widest sense, i.e., of production, distribution, and consumption of scarce goods have been solved in all social formations. One form is the household, or "oikos," which was described by Aristotle. There is no trade within the household; economic transactions only take place between the household and its environment. The household ("oikos") can be seen as a form of hierarchy that is organized to the benefit and good life of the master. Those who know each other well and who may even be part of the same household do not trade. This, however, does not exclude the trading of surpluses between households. For the first trade to take place – and that might have happened in agricultural Mesopotamia around 3,500 B.C.E. – a surplus production is naturally a necessary condition (Swedberg, 2003). In Greece, there were some nobles of one polis who joined forces in order to organize long-distance trade with nobles of other polises. One could say, however, that these exchanges were mainly based on the autarky principle and were performed for the goods themselves – mostly luxury goods – and not primarily for profits.

The market was seen as the opposition to the autarky of the household, as it creates interdependence between actors and opens up the possible profit motive. Thus, the market is in this view the arena that threatens the household. It is not surprising that trade, in the Greek tradition, corresponds with foreigners. Trading for the sake of profits (chrematistic) appeared, however, more and more frequently among the Athenians themselves in the fourth century B.C.E. and was largely perceived as a decadent phenomenon by Aristotle and others. Making money for its own sake, decoupled from the agrarian basis, was morally condemned. However, autarky was the inherent telos of the polis and the oikoi and trade, especially in grains, was strongly necessary. Insofar as the polis could be considered an analogy to the oikos one could even speak of an early international trade regime – regulated by the Athenian-dominated Attic Sea Alliance. In his "Poroi"

Xenophon considers how an increase of trade and the according tariffs on it as well as an engagement of the polis itself in slave-leasing could be a way to secure revenues for the growing inhabitants of Athens.

This brief account of the household as the center of ancient economic life largely covers other forms of organizing the economy. Clan societies, various forms of small groups and of course hierarchical social-economic formations have also been in contact with other tribes or clans to trade. This suggests that economic dependency, between one group and another, is reproduced in history. Though trade was not global, actors were not rational, and though early social formations were by and large able to sustain themselves, trade was an integrated part of life. Later with further division of labor, between different societies, actors also came to see products that they could not produce themselves as "essential," which increased the dependence between groups of people located in different places. The history of economic development cannot be separated from the history of trade and the web of commerce helped to create a civilization as Fernand Braudel has discussed in his three-volume work *Civilization and Capitalism*. We leap forward to the period in which nations, in a modern sense were developed in relation to each other, and in struggle with each other, to the period in economic history called mercantilism.

Early modern theories of economics – mercantilism

Contrary to its name – *mercatus* means trade – mercantilism as an economic doctrine did not favor international trade. It is, in contrast, associated with a trade policy of nations to create national markets, a restraining development and independence of local markets, export monopolism and exchange controls in favor of a positive balance of trade. This doctrine was most popular between 1500 and 1750. The unifying name and homogenization of a pool of different ideas are mainly a result of the liberal classics' reception and opposition to their preceding doctrine. The central political unit of the time in Europe was the emergent nation state and all economic thought was practically devised to enhance one nation relative to another, or in the words of Schumpeter: "The resulting economy was a Planned Economy; and it was planned, primarily, with a view to war" (1954: 147). If trade could establish interdependences, it was only during the time when war – which was always a latent possibility on the continent – did not rage. Both internal and foreign markets could develop as long as they were perceived to serve the final purpose – the nation state, which was regarded as a purpose in itself. The newly constructed nation and the constant necessity of resources in war times led to the development of general taxation systems. In this way, something like the economy of a country had to be represented for example in the early tables of Quesnay. He described how the household of the state developed and one can see how the autarky principle associated with the oikos and polis in Greece was transferred to the national level, at which the degree of autarky could be measured in precious metals by precursors of trading balances. On the one hand, the idea was to make the nation subsistent and independent of foreign supplies while at the same time gaining from the export of its own surpluses; these were the "conditions of trade." Great Britain or the Netherlands subsidized monopolistic foreign trade companies ("East India") not only financially but if necessary with military force. On the other hand, the early manufactures and merchants with a profit-maximizing mentality tried to change medieval structures such as craft guilds and their idea that a monopolistic production was favorable to all.

Economic literature of the time reflects its scholastic heritage. Economics was one part of a general ethic which considered natural development as inherently good. Especially the physiocrats (1760–80) – the dominant economic doctrine in France – considered natural resources and foremost agriculture as the source of all wealth. In their view, only land generated a surplus and thus physiocratic arguments could be used to further agricultural class interests. Quesnay, however, was already a proponent of free trade under the guidance of state activity. Of course, it is difficult to apply the term "capitalism" to mainly agricultural countries which today we would consider as developing. It is however possible to see the development of capitalism in relation to the development of nations and both these developments have affected economic reasoning.

Modern theories of the market economy

Out of a critique of mercantilism, which was voiced in Great Britain already at the end of seventeenth century and the physiocratic tradition, grew the discipline of modern economics represented by Adam Smith and later David Ricardo. They set out the liberal theory that was to accompany the upcoming industrialization, increasing world trade and nation building in Europe. At that time the connection between moral philosophy and economics was still strong. Adam Smith, for example, had a chair in moral philosophy and taught classes ranging from astronomy to ethics. Whereas Smith still thought of economic life being integrated in the natural order of a cosmic whole, the nineteenth-century representations of economics turned to naturalistic laws governing a separable realm of the society. This idea has prevailed until today. In the introductory words of a standard textbook on international economics (Krugman and Obstfeld, 1994) the extent of a country's international trade is considered in terms of Newton's law of gravity, i.e., depending on distance and size. The basic tenets of liberalism can be summarized as the proposition of competition on all markets, especially the newly created labor market, the free trade amongst all nations and – later on – the gold standard (Polanyi, 1954: 141ff.). These conditions, within a certain legal and political framework are seen to guarantee, the transformation of divergent individual interests to a harmonious optimal order. The idea of the bees – each of whom concentrates on one thing according to the principle of the division of labor and contributes to the good of society – without being an explicit goal became a popular metaphor that in fact could be applied for how society should be organized. This "invisible hand" argument allowed for the individualistic explanation of a macro-phenomenon via recurring wholly on the unintended consequences of intentional actions.

Adam Smith (1976) has already dealt with globalization – on the one hand he considers both the geographical spread of markets and the improvement of transportation as the prerequisite of further division of labor, which he claims to be the major source of the wealth of nations. The explanation of the mysterious abundance of goods was thus shifted from land into labor power. Adam Smith is a major proponent of free trade and competition between nations – only through the surpluses on foreign markets can the wealth-generating division of labor prosper. On the other hand, he explicitly deals with foreign trade questions such as the dependence on colonial resources or the disturbance of market expansion by protectionist measures. In fact, the controversy of free trade versus protectionism stems from the class conflict between agricultural versus trading interests (Polanyi, 1954) in which Smith and Ricardo were strongly involved. The first coherent theoretical consideration of the international trade phenomenon is ascribed to Hume and his "Of the Balance of Trade." A first major explanation of why free trade happens and why it should happen was furnished by Ricardo (1970) when he explained the international division of labor via the differences in labor productivity. If a country is able to produce a good more efficiently than another country, it shall specialize in this activity. This argument about the absolute-cost advantage was proposed by Smith against Mercantilism and it relies on the idea that international trade is a constant-sum game. But even if one country produces two goods with higher efficiency, each country should specialize in making the product it can do best, expressed in terms of relative comparative advantages. As a consequence, Ricardo claims that even developing countries should enter in the international trade system to the benefit of all. Ricardo was the first thinker who rigorously separated the economy as a self-organizing system from the social whole and thus put a wrench in between different social sciences, also separating them from general ethics. His argument about the comparative advantage of trading is still the major anti-protectionist argument in current debates.

When, however, it became evident that social disruption, mass poverty, and dependency on a seemingly uncontrollable economic system accompanied the supposedly orderly wealth-generating processes, antagonistic socialist, utopist, and nationalist ideas emerged, out of which the most lasting were those proposed by Karl Marx (1818–83). Raised in the Hegelian tradition he took over the idea that modern life is characterized by deep bifurcations which are to be overcome to reach a true whole. These bifurcations were not mere logical contradictions, such as the lack of a consistent theory of truth, but could be witnessed on a daily basis in the modern economy: capital has the tendency to cover the whole world with markets in order to maintain the necessary profits to survive, but the movement of market expansion will find its natural limit. Capital moves beyond the nation state, even undermines it, but still relies in part on its existence (Engels and Marx, 1969: 30). Furthermore, the exploited labor as a source of profit is constantly reduced by the ferocious competition, impoverishment, and upcoming automation, and as a consequence it diminishes the surplus value of production value and consumer demand in home markets.

In his *Communist Manifesto* of 1848 Marx anticipated essential features of globalization process:

> The need of a constantly expanding market for its products chases the bourgeoisie over the entire surface of the globe. It must nestle everywhere, settle everywhere, establish connections everywhere. The bourgeoisie has, through its exploitation of the world market, given a cosmopolitan character to production and consumption in every country. To the great chagrin of reactionaries, it has drawn from under the feet of industry the national ground on which it stood. All old-established national industries have been destroyed or are daily being destroyed. They are dislodged by new industries, whose introduction becomes a life and death question for all civilized nations, by industries that no longer work up Indigenous raw material, but raw material drawn from the remotest zones; industries whose products are consumed, not only at home, but in every quarter of the globe. In place of the old wants, satisfied by the production of the country, we find new wants, requiring for their satisfaction the products of distant lands and climes. In place of the old local and national seclusion and self-sufficiency, we have intercourse in every direction, universal inter-dependence of nations. And as in material, so also in intellectual production. The intellectual creations of individual nations become common property.

> National one-sidedness and narrow-mindedness become more and more impossible, and from the numerous national and local literatures, there arises a world literature.
>
> (Marx, 1978: 476–7)

Marx's main œuvre *Das Kapital* was intended to be completed by a tome on the world market as the final and therefore most evidently contradictory stage of economic theory and reality. The first economic world crisis in 1857 in which large amounts of accumulated wealth were destroyed and the fact that the New York Stock Market became suddenly relevant to workers in Manchester's manufacturers and the Ruhr's coal mines give a plausible underpinning to Marx's idea that even the dullest consciousness would be awakened. The fact that while the capitalist system becomes richer while the proletarian becomes poorer, less able to realize its human capacities and thus alienated, must at a certain point strike the proletarian consciousness as a human-made fact that can be overcome only by concerted human action.

Marx deals with themes of international trade, though mainly in an unsystematic way, in newspaper articles from the 1850s onward. Subsequent Marxist theorists were to systematize these texts, adding much of their own thoughts. Lenin, for example, considered the international system as imperialistic and anticipated a rise of the peripheral economies that could only be prevented by the capitalist core countries through wars. Marx's ideas, as is known, became an important component of economic life itself – to be reckoned with by later economists, social theorists, and activists, as well as politicians.

But also within economic theory proper the classic models about world trade did not remain unchallenged. One major point of critique is the assumption that wealth and different specializations within the world economy would hinge solely upon the unique factor of labor. In contrast to these ideas, the Swedish economists Heckscher and Ohlin considered the actual amount of different production factors such as land, labor, and capital as major causes of international trade. If a production requires, for example, much labor input and if accidentally a country is well equipped with labor, it will specialize in that production. Whereas in Ricardo's model all benefit directly from trading, in the Heckscher–Ohlin model more trade involves more competition with imports and relative losses for those scarce factors in a country which do not profit from more exports. In another more recent model (Krugman and Obstfeld, 1994), the standard trade model put forth in different elements of the two preceding models have been combined. This is to say that demand and supply are mediated by the relative terms of trade, quoted in the ratio of export and import prices. Export growth and subventions of exports reduce the terms of trade in this model and lead to diminishing wealth. This can be seen as a refinement of the original liberal Ricardian ideas.

Although the first wars of protectionism began during the 1870s, world trade still grew within the system of the gold standard until 1914. Schumpeter says that in the 1870s many "predicted confidently that universal and perfect free trade would prevail before the century was out" (1954: 766). Each new leading industry – railway, coal and iron, engineering, electronics and communication, the chemical and pharmaceutical industries – did not only propel the national economies, but furthered international trade as well. Another major economic factor was the ongoing colonialization, guaranteeing a supply of raw material and sales markets at the same time. With the First World War, however, the trading system broke down, the requirements of the gold standard were loosened or abandoned and during the 1920s the international trading regime could not be re-established. The US and also Germany had meanwhile overtaken the Commonwealth as the world's biggest traders – while the US home market remained highly protected by tariffs – and the US had become the world's greatest creditor at the end of the war.

When the 1929 crash eliminated the fortunes and savings of millions within a month, resulting in the Great Depression, the classical ideas about the merits of self-regulated markets and uncontrolled exchange were put in question. How could one trust an abstract mechanism that eliminates one's life-time savings, which shuts down companies via uncontrolled interest rates on loans, and which creates the paradox of food destruction while simultaneously famishing people in the Midwest? And how could one claim that economic theories that had allegedly contributed to the clash were true?

The most lasting intellectual and political-practical critique of the classic theoretical view was put forward by the Cambridge economist John Maynard Keynes. In his early years, he followed his teachers in advocating the advantages of free trade, but he revised this view in his *General Theory* (Keynes, 1967: 333ff.), and argued for governmental interventions to stabilize the economy and gain a positive balance of trade. In his argument he supposes an economy with a currency tied to gold, relatively rigid wages, liquidity preferences and banking conventions. As follows, the only factor influencing the interest rate is the amount of gold that depends on the trade balance (more imports lead to less gold implying a falling interest rate). Thus, the only way to influence a factor that is important for the national economy is to have an active trade policy. Keynes did not hold a protectionist view, as he clearly acknowledges some advantages of free trade. Nevertheless, in his consideration of the economy as an economic-political whole, he theoretically criticized classical ideas about a naturally self-adjusting rate of interest. The *General Theory* can be called the first coherent work in which the national economy is represented as a self-contained system – not only a somewhat separated realm – functioning according to mechanical laws. This representation was additionally backed by the macroeconomic econometric constructions that soon came to be a fact of their own, connecting economic activities and the comprehension and interpretations of these activities. After the decline of the economically rather dispersed empires, one could more easily associate the nation state with an economic system.

In the era following the Second World War the consensus position could be described as trust in free-market forces if institutionally regulated. The Bretton Woods System – that to some extent built on Keynes's ideas – was to give the international trade an institutional underpinning: relatively fixed exchange rates, an anti-protectionist regime, and transnational finance institutions such as the International Monetary Fund and the World Bank. These institutions were designed to grant financial and knowledge-based aid to developing countries and were meant as a stabilizing mechanism. The 1970s oil shocks, free-floating currencies, debt crises, and the rise of huge multinational companies changed, however, the economic conditions.

The neoliberal ideas of a free market, especially in the UK and the US, but also in traditional welfare countries like Sweden, must be seen in the light of the strong state and strong influence by unions in many Western European countries. In some countries it was, and still is, an explicit goal by some unions to socialize the economy, for example §2 of the German IG-Metall-constitution. Free trade and less regulation were seen as essential components to increase wealth, but also to keep control of the economy. At the end of 1980, with the collapse of the communist system, the global liberal economy expanded into the virgin land of Eastern Europe.

While the 1980s was the time when classical ideas reappeared in the form of neo-liberal and neo-classical theories, new forms of intra-economic critique emerged. Whereas all previous classic economic models explain the advantages of trade through the differences in countries and the subsequent gain they have when cooperating. The New Trade Theory was developed in the 1980s as an explanation for increasing returns in production. Mass production in some countries, often times initiated by contingent historical events, can offer goods at a much lower price than dispersed production in many countries. One interesting feature of this theory is its connection with a monopolistic market structure. These economists argue, in a way that resembles Smith's argument, that the initial protection of a growth industry via the state is favorable in the long run. Krugman (1991) as one of the theory's main proponents linked its ideas with classical themes in economic geography such as agglomeration effects and transportation costs.

Almost contrary to the views of the economic theories that do not imply one totally free market, the European Union began to deregulate and at least to construct a European telecommunication market in the 1980s. This project would be accomplished in 1998, despite the obstacles of technological compatibility problems and the specific national interest in providing telecommunication access. But as a result of a political struggle within EU policy, the technical standards could be harmonized and in the 1990s all major state-owned telecommunication companies could be privatized. Although this does not imply that the old major companies were driven out of competition, nor that states ceased to play a role in the market play, new technologies could be adopted and especially the market for mobile phones was entered into a considerable number of new private companies. This development is accompanied by further delegation of competences to the European level – market-making is in this case at least partially accompanied by further state-building at the European level.

Global capitalism

Since the 1990s, the notion of "the global market" has become common, not only in academic economics, but also in newspapers and in everyday gossip. The rising food prices due to increased demand for grain in the world market do not need further explanation when mentioned. Moreover, Russian energy politics influence the calculation of European households. At the same time, some formerly nation-based multi-national firms have become true transnationals, whereas the political integration or a cosmopolitan identity construction among the "economic subjects" within the trading zones usually lags behind. The representation of economic globalization in discourse, however, is highly ambivalent and not especially clarified by its excessive use even in everyday conversations.

Throughout history, capitalism has been criticized – from Aristotle and onwards – by the nobilities, who looked down on capitalists and merchants. Later on, during the period of industrialization and large factory production, capitalism became associated with an immanently destructive and alienated form of society, as argued by Karl Marx. In Marx's version the rivalry is not between the nobility and capitalism, nor between various types of capitalists, but between workers and capitalists. Marx eventually saw a global struggle coming with capitalists on the one side, and the internationally unified proletarian army on the other. Though the original class concept is hardly to be maintained in today's circumstances, the idea of international social movements as expressed in international boycotts of polluting oil firms or donations for catastrophes can be observed today.

Capitalism has been seen as the road poor and less developed countries should travel in order to flourish. Free trade in markets, rather than protectionism, is the remedy that global economical-political bodies, such as the International Monetary Fund, propose. The shock therapy proposed by the international finance institutions, which use the neoclassical model to predict outcomes without considering the cultural and historical contexts of the different "cases," have often lead to disastrous consequences on the environment and local communities. Nonetheless, there is empirical evidence supporting the view that many countries, especially in Asia, have seen great improvements in their living conditions from the 1970s and onwards due to increasing international trade, though this may have little to do with trade *theory*.

At the same time as many people have seen improvements, due to increased international trade and global competition, others have not. In some countries there is a gulf between those who have and those who lack economic resources. In other words, global capitalism is the most superior economic system of increasing the total amount of wealth, but it may also create wealth gaps between countries and also among people within the same nation.

The critique of capitalism is not only directed to these effects, but it is also argued that it is ecologically unsustainable. Though capitalism *per se* perhaps cannot be blamed for pollution and other effects of industrial development, it has become the target of critique. It may be because there is no global organization capable of fulfilling the role of protecting and policing the global arena. Legislation and politics is at the dawn of the twenty-first century still essentially national, though markets and the economy at large are becoming increasingly global. This may cause tensions.

One of the more academic but equally fervent and popular critiques of neoclassical versions of globalization stems from Stiglitz (2002), the 2001 Nobel Price winner and economics' "enfant terrible." His arguments are quite forceful, because his theoretical critique of the efficient market model, based on his economics of information, is accompanied by his first-hand empirical accounts of the model's failure in developing countries and the ideological involvement of the IMF in generating these failures. If markets within more developed countries with a long capitalistic tradition tend to lead to inefficient results in cases of small information imperfections, it is no surprise if a shock-therapy implementation of the market system in Russia or Latin America does not function as intended. Stiglitz concludes that for free trade to have favorable effects it needs to be regulated. Moreover, the institutions governing world-trade regulation today – the WTO, World Bank, and the IMF – need to act more transparently and be open for institutional peculiarities of countries. Whereas Stiglitz's critique is still directed to enhancing existing imperfections within the market system, there is an amount of left-wing opposition such as ATTAC or rising socialist thought in Latin America who consider the market system itself as the core problem. One constant point of critique is the dimension and impact of speculative international finance markets in which a day's trading exceeds the annual trading in real goods. In the 1970s James Tobin suggested applying an international tax of only a few per mill in order to avoid major fluctuations.

The critique is nourished by the observations of the most recent economic crisis, which erupted in 2008. It had its epicenter in the American financial system, initiated a worldwide economic downturn, and has been described as the most severe crisis since the Great Depression of the 1930s. This crisis, first, showed that even local markets are affected by the global finance markets. Second, and independently from historically specific conditions, financial markets seem to follow a certain pattern of destructive development that suddenly makes globally unpredictable events locally relevant. Finally, it shows that, like in the first global crisis in 1857, purely financial events have repercussions on the real economy through the credit market within the global market system. Below we take a closer look at these three points to get a better understanding of this crisis and to demonstrate the interconnection of markets.

(1) In the aftermath of the technological bubble after the turn of the last millennium, the local American housing market – an asset that is national and immobile – was made globally relevant through the creation and dispersion of sophisticated financial instruments. The low interest rates set by the US's Federal Reserve made it easy and cheap to borrow, which meant that markets were flooded with credit. Low interest rates, in addition to the expectation of continuously rising house prices, furthered the demand for credit in the US. The rising housing prices meant that people could borrow more money as the worth of their homes increased, with their houses as an underlying asset; money that could be used for renovating the house, but also for consumption and speculation. The so-called subprime loans are loans primarily given in the US to people who normally would not be seen as credit-worthy. The loans financial institutions had given, which included more than subprime loans, were transformed into investment products known as collateralized debt obligations that could offer high interest returns to international capital from, for example, Asia or the oil producing countries. The speculative moment of the investments were multiplied through hedging instruments making huge wins and losses possible with only a limited amount of capital. When it became evident that many homeowners could not pay their debts, when the ever-rising house prices came to an end, and when even well-known and established financial institutions had subprime loans in their portfolios, international capital demanded much higher interest rates or simply stopped offering money in the credit market. As a result, not only high-risk investors found it hard to obtain money. Banks were, because of the so-called credit-crunch, thus pressured from two sides: from the one side by the problem of finding capital as their capital bases decreased with the lowered value of their stock of credit, and from the other by customers who increasingly were unable to pay their mortgages. Several banks and investment banks in the US, the UK, and many other countries had to be rescued by the state. The connection between local mortgage markets and the global level is a clear indication of a global economy, in which markets are tied together.

(2) Is the current crisis an expression of a general cyclical phenomenon inherent in market economies or is it a historical contingency? Without giving a clear answer to this question, we here take a position in between, pointing at the weaknesses of the two approaches. The argument of economic historians is quite strong: from 1618 onwards, one can discern at least 38 crises which where all characterized by a self-disequilibrating financial market due to self-enforcing expectations, the inability to learn of the actors involved and a knowledge divide between insiders and outsiders with massive financial redistributions to the former (Aliber and Kindleberger, 2005). These general characteristics can be found also in the most recent crisis: the FED's low interest rates, American and international actors in the financial markets mutually fueled positive expectations of continuously rising prices; the abstracting force of the financial instruments created an even smaller community of insiders who at least had some knowledge of what was offered, which left out even major American bank experts. At the same time, pointing to the general characteristics does not allow us to answer the question of who were the concrete actors of the general trajectory and why the crisis finally erupted at a certain point in time. It is, in this respect, necessary to consider variables such as the economic bubble of 2001, and the FED's low-interest

response, the collapse of Bear Stearns, Lehman Brothers, and others that triggered what were the first signs, the business worldview of "shareholder-value" which makes the financial representation of business more important than, for example, its business-to-business image. However, this universalistic approach does not account for the fact that two economic crises are not independent events: historical actors associate a certain meaning with a crisis, which often becomes entrenched in financial institutions that emerged in reaction to the crisis or even in stories and gossip about the crisis that circulate among traders. Thus, even in the recent events former crises played a constituting role: the governmental responses to the crises in 1929 or 1987 were an implicit part of the institutional environment in which the recent crisis took place. If one accepts the idea that these regulations have also an enabling effect, one could claim that institution-building by governments did not only guarantee a longer period of stability, but also a more severe crash to take place, because financial traders could never before put that much (over-)confidence in the stability of the system. Another point proving the dependence on former crises are the stories remembered and told by the market actors – the constant comparison with the 1929 crash might well have been an accelerating moment to the disruptive market movements. Thus, in the recent crisis comparisons with the 1929 crash became a constituent part of the debate about the stock market crash.

(3) The up-and-downs on the financial market are connected to the real economy, as the latter depends on the stability of prices, exchange, and interest rates in order to make the necessary profits. If the stability is lacking and production slows down and massive deployment strategies are announced, the economy enters almost inevitably into a spiral of negative expectations. Max Weber observed this in his treaty on the stock exchange as early as 1894:

> The long series of numbers at the back of the newspapers, which even readers who are neither capitalists nor businessmen cannot fail to notice, are not only of importance to capitalists and businessmen. Rather, the manner in which the dry numbers listed there change in the course of a year signifies the flourishing and decline of whole branches of production, upon whose situation hangs the happiness or misery of thousands.
>
> (Weber, 2000: 326)

The stock exchange is often considered the epitome of the market model and the source of inspiration for the market theorists. Economists usually point to the financial market, in addition to the stock exchange, as the most empirically developed version of their abstract market model. It is therefore surprising that this market seems to require massive institutional interventions for its stability to be maintained, though this is not a recent finding: "[…] central banking and the management of the monetary system were needed to keep manufactures and other productive enterprises safe from the harm involved in the commodity fiction as applied to money" (Polanyi, 1954: 138). The recent crisis has caused a massive state intervention, which quickly put much of the former liberalization politics in question. In contrast to previous crises, national governments coordinated their intervention plans, with the public, politicians, and media in one country, often times at the same time as other national governments to intervene. Intensified competition and expansion of self-regulated markets at the global level seems to require new, and perhaps, more rules and the creation of transnational institutions to stabilize the market system.

The recent crisis has been less virulent in some economies such as Russia or China, in which a certain kind of state-capitalism contradicts the globalization logic that is often presented as inevitable. Both these countries are centralized and governed by politicians who actively promote economic interests using an economic-political framework. Russia has regained some of its strength due to export of natural resources and China has grown as a result of its capacity to produce and export goods for the world market. This development in the global economy emphasizes the role of the state in the global economy. As a result, some countries have begun to protect their economies from state-run companies and investment funds that operate outside of its borders. Will this lead to yet a new form of capitalism, such as global state-capitalism?

Conclusion

From an economic perspective, our globe has become smaller. Economic dependency patterns that used to be within the clan, between clans in the form of long-distance trade, between economic actors who could not produce everything, today include most people of the world, directly or indirectly. Relations today are more complex and above all more indirect. Technologies, for example the internet and a great number of mediators and a differentiation of markets, have contributed to making the global market more difficult to understand. We may only, at the best, have a vague idea of how the parts of our computer, including the programs, have been produced, compiled, and sold; we are unlikely to know who took part in the large number of steps of development, testing, and production operation that made it what it is.

We have stressed how the forms of dependency have changed over the last two thousand years (Durkheim, 1984), focusing on the last 500 years. In this chapter, we have argued that to understand economic globalization and the theories that are relevant both for explaining this change as well as for actually generating some of the changes, one must—besides the theories—take markets, capitalism, and globalization into account. Today we see some industries, like the garment industry, as practically impossible to operate in the way they do, were it not for the global opportunities and division of labor. The ambition of firms for profit and the fact that people wish to buy the garments, all of which is coordinated via markets, mean that competition between actors, sometimes all over the world, may result in a global market capitalism, when many markets (all of which are driven by profit motives) are interconnected. These market relations imply that actors operating in markets in which quite different capitalistic modes dominate can also be connected. From a more general sociological point of view, the global interconnections make it problematic to speak of kinds of societies, as notions like "consumer society" or "knowledge society" suggest. Markets are the central coordinating form in the economy and we suggest that the degree of globalization and the kind of capitalism should be connected to the level of markets.

References

Aliber, R. and Kindleberger, C. P. (2005) *Manias, Panics and Crashes: A History of Financial Crises*, Hoboken: Wiley.

Aspers, P. (2006) 'Markets, Sociology of', In Beckert, J. and Zafirovski, M. (eds.) *International Encyclopedia of Economic Sociology*. London: Routledge.

Braudel, F. (1992) *Civilization and Capitalism 15th–18th Century*, 3 vols, London: Fontana Press.

Durkheim, É. (1984) *The Division of Labour in Society*, London: Macmillan.

Engels, F. (1845/1887) *The Condition of the Working Class in England in 1844*, http://www.marxists.org/archive/marx/works/download/Engles_Condition_of_the_Working_Class_in_England.pdf

Engels, F. and Marx, K. (1969) Die deutsche Ideologie, *MEW 3*. Berlin: Dietz Verlag.

Fligstein, N. (2001) *The Architecture of Markets: An Economic Sociology for the Twenty-First Century Capitalist Societies*, Princeton: Princeton University Press.

Gereffi, G., Humphrey, J. and Sturgeon, T. (2005) 'The Governance of Global Value Chains', *Review of International Political Economy*, 12: 78–104.

Hirst, P. and Thompson, G. (1996) *Globalization in Question*, Cambridge: Polity Press.

Keynes, J. M. (1967) *The General Theory of Employment, Interest and Money*, London: Macmillan.

Krugman, P. (1991) 'Increasing Returns and Economic Geography', *Journal of Political Economy*, 99: 483–99.

Krugman, P. R. and Obstfeld, M. (1994) *International Economics*, New York: HarperCollins.

Marx, K. (1978) 'Manifesto of the Communist Party', in *The Marx Engels Reader*, edited by R. Tucker, New York: W. W. Norton & Company, pp. 469–500.

Polanyi, K. (1954) *The Great Transformation*, Boston: Beacon.

Ricardo, D. (1970) *On the Principles of Political Economy and Taxation*, Cambridge: Cambridge University Press.

Schumpeter, J. A. (1954) *History of Economic Analysis*, New York: Oxford University Press.

Simmel, G. (1978) *The Philosophy of Money*, London: Routledge.

Smith, A. (1976) *An Inquiry into the Nature and Causes of the Wealth of Nations*, Oxford: Clarendon Press.

Stiglitz, J. E. (2002) *Globalization and its Discontents*, New York: W.W. Norton & Company.

Swedberg, R. (2003) *Principles of Economic Sociology*, Princeton: University Press.

Wallerstein, I. (1974) *The Modern World-System, vol. I: Capitalist Agriculture and the Origins of the European World-Economy in the Sixteenth Century*, New York/London: Academic Press.

Weber, M. (1968) *The Protestant Ethic and the Spirit of Capitalism*, London: Unwin University Books.

——(1978) *Economy and Society: An Outline of Interpretive Sociology*, Berkeley: University of California Press.

——(2000) 'Stock and Commodity Exchanges', *Theory and Society*, 29, 305–38.

4

Internet and globalization

Lior Gelernter and Motti Regev

Introduction and overview

In April 2007, Estonia's decision to move a Soviet World War II memorial from its place in central Tallinn resulted in what was described in the *New York Times* as "the first war in cyberspace." Coordinated web traffic flooding, commonly known as distributed denial of service (DDoS) attacks, brought down its government network, e-mail servers, and the websites of banks, universities, and newspapers. Even with international aid, it was weeks before internet activity returned to normal. Though critical infrastructure such as electricity or water supply remained unharmed, the world took notice: NATO, various governments and private security companies promptly began analyzing the methods of the attack, to prepare for the next time. The internet has become so intertwined in our lives and societies that severe damage to it might create a communication catastrophe. In an increasingly interconnected world, no one can risk the internet breaking down.

But the *New York Times*'s attempt to explain this event by invoking the image of war between nation-states may be misleading. Estonia blamed Russia for the attacks, but no proof was presented to counter Russia's angry denial. Experts disagree on the Russian government involvement, but it is certain that much of the attack was the result of mass mobilization by ethnic Russian volunteers from all over the world—including Estonia itself. This well-orchestrated collective action was coordinated through messages posted in Russian-language websites and mailing lists, rather than by political or military chain of command. This is only one demonstration of how inadequate our old categories are in explaining the complex dynamics of politics, culture, and social structure in the contemporary digital world. This story also demonstrates the crucial role that the internet is playing in these dynamics, as it allows collective identity and collective action to manifest itself across great geographical distances.

From a humble beginning as a textual communication medium used by a small elite of computer experts, the internet has become a universal medium, connecting people and distributing diverse content around the world. Based on standards and protocols which allow information to flow through it without a central switchboard, it cancels out the traditional dichotomies of private vs. mass media and synchronous vs. a-synchronous communication. New forms of expression such as e-mails, blogs, Wikis, and social networks are now a part of everyday life for a large and growing part of world population. While its decentralized structure makes it particularly adaptive to cultural innovation, the internet still tends to foster a unique cultural logic. As Manuel Castells (2001: 200) notes, "it is open source, free posting, decentralized broadcasting, serendipitous interaction, purpose oriented communication, and shared creation that find their expression on the internet."

Spreading rapidly during the last decade, internet infrastructure now extends to every continent, accessible in even the remotest of places. The deployment of this infrastructure is extremely uneven, with more than 55 percent of users coming from high-income countries (which hold less than 16 percent of global population). There is a strong and continuous trend towards shrinking this global digital divide: in 2005, low- and lower-middle-income countries accounted for 30 percent of internet users worldwide, rising from merely 5 percent in 1997. A significant gap still exists in access to broadband connections which enable users to access multimedia materials. Even more important, there is still a wide global disparity in the frequency and ways people around the world use the internet, as well as in the composition of user population, which tend to be more elite in less connected regions (Chen et al., 2002; ITU, 2007). As its web is continuously spreading around the world, the internet is playing a major role in the growth of worldwide interconnectedness.

In the twenty-odd years since the internet began to emerge into public awareness, the concept of globalization came to the forefront of academic research and became a household term. The internet itself is at least partially responsible for this development, as the ability to instantly reach people and content around the world captured the imagination and encouraged the perception of the world as one global village. While both the extent and the novelty of globalization are still highly contested, there is a general consensus that social, political, cultural, and economic processes are increasingly acquiring global dimensions. For the purpose of this chapter, we will describe globalization as a process by which networks of interaction spread around the world—especially across national borders—connecting diverse people, institutions, ideas, and representations in increasingly complex patterns of interdependence. This does not mean, however, that locality loses its importance, or that the nation-state is disappearing. As the Estonian example shows, the global and the local are always tightly intertwined, and nation-states play a crucial part in mediating their relations.

The next three sections of this chapter discuss the extension of social, cultural, and political global networks into the internet, while the following section is devoted to the attempts made by nation-states to influence, control, and regulate it. In the first section, we explore the globalization of social structures via information and communication technologies, concentrating on the writings of Manuel Castells and Karin Knorr-Cetina. In the second section, we describe the internet's effects on the relations between local and global culture, illustrating them through the examples of global popular culture and transnational diasporas. In the third section, we show how the internet is used as an assembling space for transnational advocacy networks. In the fourth section, we explain how efforts of nation-states to govern the internet—both by individual states and through international regimes—foster the creation of multifarious global networks. We conclude with a discussion of the implications of these phenomena, and point out some theoretical implications.

The globalization of social structures

With the spread of information and communication technologies (ICT) in the last decades of the twentieth century, a growing number of social researchers attempted to conceptualize the ways these networks take part in the redeployment of social structures on a global scale, and the ways they change the nature of these structures. The growing social importance of ICT networks may be best demonstrated by the fact that many of these attempts use the network itself as a central organizing metaphor, abandoning holistic conceptions of societies as stable entities contained within national territorial borders in favor of this more flexible view. In this section we present two theories that provide useful conceptual tools for tracing the new social structures that follow the contours of ICT networks beyond the borders of the nation-state: Manuel Castells (2000, 2001, 2003) offers the most comprehensive attempt to use the networks frame for understanding the emergent global information society; Knorr-Cetina (1999, 2005; Knorr-Cetina and Brugger, 2000), on the other hand, attempts to go beyond the network metaphor to explain the new global social structures and their effect through micro-level theory and analysis, moving the emphasis from their form to content.

Network society and the internet galaxy

In his wide-ranging *Information Age* trilogy and in *The Internet Galaxy*, Castells presents an impressive attempt to lay down the theoretical and empirical foundations for assessing the social implications of the internet. Heavily influenced by Harold Innis and Marshall McLuhan (1962), Castells describes the internet as the core of a technological communication revolution which brings about a new, post-industrial "information age." In this new configuration, society is gradually being restructured around digital communication networks and the flows of information that run through them, turning into "network society." While not the cause of this transformation, the internet provides the material support needed to sustain and spread it. This is characteristic of Castells' thinking about the internet, as he suggests that it tends to intensify existing social and cultural trends rather than create new ones.

At the center of Castells' theory lies the idea that the development of new communication technologies has transformed the basic organizational structures of society. The heart of this change is the rise of the network itself as a form of social organization. Networks, which are sets of interconnected nodes with no inherent internal hierarchy, are hardly a new form of social organization. However, large and complex networks are usually hard to maintain, and are inferior to hierarchical organizations when required to allocate resources, coordinate action and perform tasks on a large scale. Therefore, networks were usually restricted to the private sphere, while hierarchical organizations historically dominated the fields of power and large-scale production.

The incredible growth of communication networks in the last decades provided a material basis on which very large networks could flourish for the first time. As the "network of networks," the internet emerges as a global medium facilitating and connecting the various networks that increasingly make up society. This infrastructure enables such networks to manage complexities of unprecedented scale, to the extent that it is gradually replacing old organizational structures of the industrial age. The unique qualities of these networks—their fractal structure, their elasticity, the compression of distance between their nodes, and the barriers raised between those within and those beyond them—become the basis for the character of contemporary societies. This is evident not only from the expansion and use statistics of the internet noted above, but mainly from the fact that local and global activities alike are being structured by networks that are connected through it, to the extent that exclusion from them is exclusion from crucial domains of the social.

Castells uses network structures to outline new social phenomena which relate to ICT on various scales, often with conflicting outcomes. Thus, he notes that older patterns of sociability, which were based on geographical proximity and shared values, are gradually being replaced by a new "networked individualism" (Wellman et al., 2003) based on individual choices and strategies. By enabling individuals to create and maintain social ties, both weak and strong, over very large distances, the internet is essential for the growth of "communities of choice," which enable greater individual freedom and capacity for social inclusion. At the same time, however, the networks' capacity to immediately link to new sources of value and sever their links to nodes which no longer produce value is the basis for social exclusion on an unprecedented scale, as the reorganization of global economy in a new networked structure causes an intensification of inequality both between and within countries, regions and cities.

Global microstructures

Unlike the macro-sociological analysis characteristic to theories that link networks and globalization, Karin Knorr-Cetina developed a research program that relies on micro-sociological theory and qualitative methods in order to interpret phenomena of global scale and effects. At the heart of this research program lies the concept of *global microstructures*, which are "forms of connectivity and coordination that combine global reach with microstructural mechanisms that instantiate self-organizing principles and patterns" (Knorr-Cetina 2005). While partly congruent with the concept of the network, it diverges from it in important aspects, namely the displacement of focus from spatial aspects to time and synchronization. The internet is increasingly becoming the primary means for the maintenance and growth of these micro-structures, as it allows people around the world to transcend their immediate environment and create the mediated intersubjectivity that they require.

Much like Castells' networks, global microstructures are conceptually opposed to formal organization, as they are based on features characteristic of face-to-face interactions such as trust and acquaintance, rather than on clear structure and hierarchy. Lacking formal organizations' rational structuring of social relations, they are inherently unstable and unpredictable. Despite this semi-chaotic character, these structures tend to be highly effective and sustainable thanks to extensive use of *strategies of amplification and augmentation*. These strategies allow them to mediate conflicting goals and magnify the outcomes of a given effort. This is done both by using technological resources, such as computers or digital communication, and by using social mechanisms, such as outsourcing certain functions to the external environment, thus remaining structurally "light" and more adaptable.

The conceptualization of microstructures, while close to that of networks, diverges from it on several crucial points: (a) the content which flows through them is often more important in explaining their stability then their structure; (b) they utilize multiple and overlapping forms of coordination, networks being just one of them; (c) their durability is not associated with the stability of their nodes and the strength of their ties; it may even be the result of inherent instability, as a constant degeneration and restructuring facilitates their adaptation to external environment; and finally (d) focusing on the network is taken to underplay important structural and "textural" differences between different global microstructures. Thus, as a complementary method to network analysis, Knorr-Cetina advocates the use of micro-sociological theories and qualitative methods to trace the unique characteristics of global microstructures. In her empirical studies, encompassing diverse topics such as high-energy physics, financial markets and terrorist networks, she focuses on the use of information technologies for social coordination, and the temporal aspects of this coordination.

Despite their differences, both Castells and Knorr-Cetina share a similar understanding of the connections between the new ICTs and globalization, as they reject the view of globalization as a process of worldwide homogenization. The stretching of forms of sociality which were formerly restricted to face-to-face interaction on a global scale indicate that globalization is not a top-bottom process, but one in which individuals take active and vital roles. For both of them, ICTs erode the older structures of industrial society and re-shape social relations on a global scale, but at the same time support the plurality and particularity of these relations. This process involves a re-definition of locality, as social distance becomes ever more detached from geographical distance and solidarity is increasingly built over great distances. As the geographies of belonging take on a global and mediated quality they draw closer to geographies of culture, on which they are increasingly based. In the next section, we further explore this connection.

The globalization of culture

While the attempts to account for the globalization of networked social structures are paving a way through new territories, theories concerning the globalization of culture predate the internet. Cultural imperialism and reception theories were both developed in the era of broadcasting, and are based on the division between the broadcasting center and the receiving periphery: the first stresses the center's ability to exert cultural dominance over global audience; the latter stresses this audience's ability to resist such dominance and preserve local culture. Though both have contemporary adaptations which deal with the internet, a third model has come to dominate much of the research in recent years. The networks or flows model views globalization as a process in which cultural goods move throughout the globe in increasingly complex and unexpected trajectories and their meaning is produced through a process of hybridization and convergence (cf. Appadurai, 1996). Rejecting the view of globalization as a zero-sum game between local and global, universal and particular, it regards them as mutually constitutive. In this section we explore these dynamics through two phenomena: active participation in popular culture and transnational diasporas.

Popular culture

In recent decades, popular culture—media events, sporting events, music, movies, and TV shows—has become integrated into the texture of experience in everyday life, juxtaposing the local and the global in new and complex ways. The relations between the local and the global in popular culture are shaped by two opposing and complementary processes: on the side of production, popular culture is increasingly concentrated in the hands of a few multinational corporations whose profits are dependent on globalization. On the side of consumption, audiences are taking on new roles in processes of production, distribution and reception, thus further undermining the traditional structure of the cultural industries. The internet is a central mediator in this process, as it allows global access to popular culture materials, enables fans to create and maintain social and cultural ties, and spreads new participatory cultural forms.

Over the last decade, the internet has become a global storehouse for a wealth of popular culture materials, owing to digital technologies which allow consumers to freely store, share, and edit content of all sorts. Through file-sharing software such as bittorrent and websites such as YouTube, an abundance of works can be accessed globally and freely. Along with the original works, the internet contains ample information about these materials as well as edited and "mashed up" versions created by active consumers. The cultural industries' attempts to defend their copyrights are not successful at the moment, as new services rapidly replace the ones shut down. While the cultural industries are struggling to cope with this new empowerment of consumers and to find new revenue-generating strategies, some cultural producers decided to leave the system altogether—the rock band Radiohead, for example, distributed their album *In Rainbows* through their website, relinquishing traditional distribution and allowing the downloaders to choose how much to pay—if at all.

But the internet is more than a cheap media-center: it enables the active consumers of popular culture, commonly known as fans, to build and maintain transnational identities based on global popular culture materials. The immediacy and anonymity of the internet allowed the thinly spread and often stigmatized fans of specific genres, authors or works to communicate with each other and construct specialized communities of taste. Often, these virtual communities serve as a basis for the construction of offline communities and organizations which help push the fandom object into local societies. In other cases, fans interact across national boundaries, whether to access resources created and gathered by fans in other countries, or to specifically create transnational fan networks and communities (cf. Jenkins, 2006: 152–72). In both cases, fan communities exemplify "the ways that transcultural flows of popular culture inspires new forms of global consciousness and cultural competency," which Jenkins (2006: 156) defines as "pop cosmopolitanism."

Beyond its role in transforming the dynamics surrounding established genres of popular culture, the internet also introduces new genres, which tend to be global in form, local in content and participatory in essence. These new genres—such as blogs, Wikis, and social-networking sites—are easily copied or localized, thus making them global. However, they are utilized differently in different localities or social contexts: blogs, for example, tend to exist in relatively distinct networks (known as "blogospheres") which differ in languages, populations, writing conventions, and audiences. The same is true for multi-language websites: each language version of Wikipedia, the popular online encyclopedia, has a different community of users with different preferences and conventions. The meaning of localization in this context is not self-evident, though. In an ironic demonstration of the growing globalization of the cultural particularity, Wikipedia in Chinese is written almost exclusively by diaspora members living outside mainland China. Indeed, as we shall see in the next part, the use of the internet in transnational diasporas generates ample examples for the tense relations between the local and the global.

Diasporas

Diasporas are "transnations" (Appadurai, 1996), transnational imagined communities perceived as primordial and (usually) connected to some sort of shared homeland.

Through global migration and refugee movements, they have become an integral part of the contemporary global landscape. Braced by the spread of transnational communication, which supports their social ties and particularistic identities, they are increasingly assuming important position roles in culture and politics. Old homelands, new homelands and the mediated networks between them thus create a new ethnoscape (Appadurai 1996) in which identity, politics, and distance become entangled and problematized. The internet now plays a central role in shaping these ethnoscapes, as it supports ubiquitous diasporic networks, offers a space in which identities and hierarchies are negotiated and allows for their political mobilization.

The low cost and immediacy of person-to-person communication on the internet enables diaspora members—mainly in developed countries—to maintain and strengthen their reciprocal connections, enhancing their autonomy and strength relative both to their localities and to their homelands. Furthermore, websites provide a cheap and easy publishing venue, making diaspora news and information easily accessible (Georgiou, 2005). Usually bilingual, these sites typically include news and information about local community life, news about the old homeland, and interactive sections (forums or chatrooms). Transcending the dichotomy between person to person and broadcast, these interactive sections connect a multitude of active participants in conversation with each other. This new type of "many-to-many" communication enables active participations in shaping and negotiating diasporic communities, and change the way transnational diasporas are being imagined (Karim, 2003).

Though old media, like newspapers, radio, and satellite TV (usually connected to the homelands' nation-states) help maintain a collective identity among diasporas, they also tend to enforce a pre-packed notion of diasporic identity through a top-down process. Usenet groups, mailing lists and forums, on the other hand, create public spaces in which diaspora members can interact and negotiate freely, with relative disregard for exogenous hierarchies and prepackaged definitions of identity. Within the confine of these global commons (Silverstone, 2002), diasporic identity can be negotiated and redeployed in ways that challenge existing notions of belonging. For example, after the spread of rumors about ethnic cleansing of Chinese minorities in Indonesia in 1998, a transnational group of Chinese descendents—mainly high-tech workers in the west—built and maintained a protest website based on a novel racial construction of Chinese identity, competing with older political and cultural notions of Chineseness which were mainly mediated through nation-states (Ong, 2006).

The internet is also a venue which enables political entrepreneurs to mobilize on the basis of diasporic identities, as the same example shows. The above-mentioned website quickly became the basis for a transnational movement which orchestrated a synchronized transnational protest in order to attract media attention to the events in Indonesia. In an interesting twist, however, this project was opposed by Chinese activists from Indonesia itself, who preferred to define themselves as Indonesian citizens and base their struggle on human rights rather than racial discourse. Stressing the suffering of various groups and minorities in Indonesia, they tried linking themselves to the nation rather than to a transnational ethnicity. As Ong comments, on line activism has its dark sides, as it may serve to further polarization in local conflicts and escalate them.

As the dynamics of global popular culture and diasporas show, the internet allows individuals and collectives to shape their identity around transnationally circulated cultural goods. This process challenges the traditional order of nation-states, which assumed congruence between nation, territory, culture, and political action. Worn down by global culture and particularistic identities, national cultures worldwide gradually lose their monopolistic status. The result of this erosion is an intensification of cosmopolitanism, both as an aesthetic experience and as a growing awareness of the intensifying mixing of cultures on a global level (Beck and Sznaider, 2006). While this does not mean that nation-states are losing their relevance in any way, it does change considerably the playground in which they operate in ways we are already beginning to see. However, this cultural transformation is just one of many challenges which nation-states must endure in the age of the internet. Another important challenge facing the nation-state is the growing use of the internet as a means for transnational political activism, which is the subject of the next section.

The globalization of political activism

In the second half of the 1990s, it became commonplace to see the internet as a basis for a radical globalization of political discourse and activism. This process was often depicted as the emergence of a global public sphere and a corresponding global civil society which will transcend—and ultimately replace—national politics. In the beginning of the current decade, however, and at least partially due to the effect of the 9/11 attacks, this view was replaced by a more skeptical outlook, which doubted the internet's ability to radically change the basic structures of politics and political activism. Indeed, as the primary and presidential election campaigns in the US in 2004 and 2008 have shown, in some respects the internet becomes increasingly integrated in national political campaigns rather than transcending it.

Though it seems that a global public sphere is more of a vision than a reality (Goldsmith and Wu, 2006), the internet does seem to contribute to the globalization of political action in some cases. Transnational collective action utilizing the internet is on the rise, and while it may still be the exception rather than the rule, it often challenges the traditional connection between politics and the nation-state. In this section, we focus on the role of the internet in the emergence of transnational advocacy networks (cf. Keck and Sikkink, 1998), and in particular the opposition to neo-liberal policies in the late 1990s and the 2003 war in Iraq.

Transnational political action is not a new phenomenon, and there were several important movements with transnational ties as early as the nineteenth century, including the anti-slavery movement and the socialist movement, with its famous "Workers of the world unite!" slogan. Nonetheless, the internet changed both the intensity and the structure of transnational political activism, making it less hierarchical and consistent, more culturally oriented and network structured—bridging various levels of activity, and enabling ad hoc connections and decentralized organization.

Chadwick (2006) outlines several important changes the internet introduces into the field of political activism, most of which contribute directly or indirectly to the development of global political activism: (a) the internet *fosters the creation of permanent networks* between political movements and organizations, both within and across national borders; (b) it *reduces the impact of ideological fragmentation*, and enables common mobilization of ideologically divergent groups around common goals or action; (c) the internet *increases organizational flexibility*, fostering network structures which are better adapted to rapid response to shifting conditions; (d) it *provides access to mainstream media* for grassroots and fringe political activists, often enabling local initiatives to gain global recognition and

69

support; (e) it *fuses together politics and culture*, as political movements who increasingly rely on the cheap and easy exposure the internet offers focus on creating cultural products rather than recruiting people; and finally (f) the internet *reduces the problems inherent to collective action*, especially action over distance and across national borders.

The most notable cases in which the use of the internet has facilitated the growth and consolidation of transnational advocacy networks are those of the global opposition to neo-liberal policies in the late 1990s and to the 2003 war in Iraq. These networks, which brought together various political movements and organizations, coordinated synchronized contentious politics on a global level on several occasions, creating what we may term "global macrostructure." Following these networks, one can discern a succession of online campaigns dating as early as the 1994 Zapatista uprising, growing through the so-called "anti-globalization movement" of the late 1990s and the early twenty-first century, and culminating with the protests against the war in Iraq. These campaigns, which were based on growing and overlapping social networks, are the source for many of the practices which are now a standard part of the toolbox for online political activists in various contexts, as well as for many resources which are still available for online activists.

It is commonplace to pinpoint the emergence of effective online transnational political activism to the Zapatista uprising in 1994. The EZLN, a movement supporting the rights of Indigenous people led an uprising in the state of Chiapas which was triggered by the Mexican government's decision to abolish communal ownership of agricultural land. Though militarily inferior, this "first informational guerilla movement's" (Castells, 2003: 82) success in reframing a local struggle into a much larger framework of neo-liberalism and global trade agreements enabled the rapid construction of an "international solidarity network" (Olesen, 2005), mainly through mailing lists, Usenet discussion boards, and websites. Their cause was aided by various groups of programmers and computer hackers which participated in various incidents of "electronic civil disobedience" against Mexican government websites. Ultimately, the use of internet technology enabled the EZLN to achieve instant global media exposure which helped force the government to declare a ceasefire and open negotiations with them.

Apart from the emergence of a cultural tool box of practices for online activism, the Zapatista insurgence's main contribution is the creation of communication networks which became the basis for the so-called anti-globalization movements. This massive and geographically widespread political struggle against neo-liberalism rose to fame in the late 1990s, when the net became a central tool for mobilization of masses to sites of major economic conferences such as Seattle in 1999 and Genoa in 2001. These networks and practices were used again in the global protests against the war in Iraq, primarily during 2003–4, and were an important factor in enabling the collaboration between diverse groups and organizations which led to massive globally synchronized protests against the war which occurred on several occasions (most notably the ones on February 2003, which included several millions of protesters in hundreds of cities throughout the world, and in March 2006, marking the third anniversary of the invasion).

These movements, which utilized the internet as the basis for coordination and activity on an unprecedented scale, are global both practically and reflexively, as their goals and identity formation transcend the political framework of the nation-state. The internet actively shapes the organizational logic which allows them to function: they are decentralized, with overlapping local and global networks, and link innovative organizations and modes of action with older, more established ones. These new modes of action are based more on digital media activism than on member recruitment, institution building, and gaining electoral support. Media activism, whether in the form of creating alternative media websites or in the form of subversion of mainstream media, challenges the prevalent political and economic powers by building new "cultural practices and political imaginaries for a digital age" (Juris, 2008). However, as we see in the next section, these powers are not staying still: they promote and implement their own political imaginaries for the digital age, as they engage in increasing efforts to govern and tame the "electronic frontier" (Rheingold, 1994) of the internet.

The challenges of internet governance

As demonstrated above, the internet is now a major factor in contemporary global economy and media ecology, a venue for political fundraising, a tool in transnational identity formation, and a medium for coordination of offline political activities. In other words, it had become a global political issue: a public resource which nation-states and other economic and political actors attempt to achieve a measure of authority over. These efforts can be broadly divided into two categories: the effort of particular nation-states to control internet use within their borders, and the ongoing attempts to create an international regime which will govern and regulate internet activity on a global scale. As we shall see in this section, these attempts, while only partially successful, are themselves part of the process of globalization.

State control mechanisms

When the internet emerged into public view in the 1990s it was conceived as—and by and large was—free from extraneous political interference, as its technical and organizational administration was mainly informal, based on mutual trust between users. This aspect of the net was so dominant that it was considered as an essentially autonomous space, the basis of a post-national global society. In recent years, however, as states and other political institutions are involved in efforts to supervise and control it, this perception of the internet is rapidly giving way to a more realistic one.

To understand the complexities of internet governance, it is important to bear in mind that the internet was not planned or invented: it evolved. Though key players and initiatives were financed by the American government, the internet in its early years was gradually developed by users, a loose community of computer experts and students who moved between academic, corporate, the public sector, and military organizations (Hafner and Lyon, 1996). Standards, protocols, and code were distributed freely, to be fitted and fixed until there was a "rough consensus" over their adequacy. In the institutional vacuum which surrounded the net, organizational bodies—which had no formal or legal status—were formed in a similar fashion, and anyone interested could partake in them, including non-Americans.

Following its rapid spread in the 1990s, the internet's history of autonomy and its global extent created an influential view of the net as a new "electronic frontier" (Rheingold, 1994) which transcends borders and renders obsolete the division of the world into nation-states. According to its advocates, the net should not—and in fact, *can* not—be regulated or supervised. It has no sovereign but its "netizens," which will develop and govern it based on participatory logic and mechanisms. The most influential manifestation of this belief was probably the "Declaration of the Independence of Cyberspace," published in

1996 by John Perry Barlow, which proclaimed, in the name of web surfers, that governments "have no sovereignty where we gather […] no moral right to rule us nor […] any methods of enforcement we have true reason to fear." This declaration was premature: though up until the end of the 1990s the internet was considered inherently immune to censorship, the last decade had seen a growing number of states employ surveillance, filtering, and censorship techniques, with varying degrees of pervasiveness and success.

As of 2008, at least 40 states are actively engaged in some sort of filtering or censorship of content. Typically, content is filtered in critical points such as the international gateway connecting states to the outer net or by the internet service providers. In other cases, censorship is based on legal rather than technological mechanisms—in Egypt, for example, bloggers have been charged and arrested for political and religious postings. While banned content varies from state to state, censorship generally tends to involve one of four general issues: (a) political struggles, such as suppressing internal political content in South Korea; (b) social norms and morality issues, such as the blocking of pornography websites in the United Arab Emirates; (c) security concerns, such as Bahrain's block of Google's map services; and (d) intellectual property rights, such as Italy's block on the torrent tracker site Pirate Bay (Deibert et al., 2008).

The best-known and most far-reaching case of state control over the internet is that of China. While as late as 1998, American President Bill Clinton equated China's attempts to crack down on the internet to "nailing jell-O to a wall" (Goldsmith and Wu, 2006: 90), it is now agreed that it's doing a very good job at it. China exerts multiple means to monitor and filter internet content within its borders. As information comes in or out of China through one of its very few internet access providers, the internet routers directing it filter out packets arriving from banned sites based on a comprehensive list which includes IP addresses, URLs, and specific words in URLs. As a result, the users seeking such information receive a technical error message, which prevents differentiating between censorship and malfunction. However, this kind of censorship is relatively redundant, as Chinese internet traffic tends to stay within the confines of the Chinese net. Thus, China has a second, internal, layer of filtering: through technical and human means, content providers are filtered according to state policy, relying both on keyword lists and on meaning.

While these processes are putting a damper on the hopes that the internet will become the basis for a global liberal democracy over which states have no hold, they do not necessarily create roadblocks on the path of globalization. If globalization is taken as a growing interconnectedness of heterogeneous actors around the world, then attempts of states to supervise the internet often foster these in new and paradoxical ways. For example, the internet routers that China uses to filter out unwanted content are manufactured by Cisco, an American-based multinational company. Even more interesting is the case of western internet content providers such as Yahoo!, which are required by law to censor "harmful" materials: this demand, which forces them to act as a de facto state regulatory body of the Chinese government is also a part of the growing interconnectedness between states, citizens, and corporations on a global scale. This point becomes more obvious when considering that alongside attempts of state control, a global governance regime for the internet is emerging, bringing together multiple stakeholders in a global arena.

A new international regime?

Much of the literature which deals with questions of internet governance is centered on the concept of *international regimes*, "implicit or explicit principles, norms, rules and decision-making procedures around which actors' expectations converge in a given area of international relations" (Krasner, 1982, in Mueller, 2002). These are usually erected by states in order to regulate the access to resources that do not fall under clear sovereignty (like radio frequencies or Antarctica), or to deal with transnational problems (like greenhouse gas emissions or piracy). The growth of international regimes, as well as the convergences between them, can be used as a parameter for the spread of globalization, testifying to socio-political structures which bind actors on a global scale. This is especially true for the emerging internet governance regime, which is being constructed by various stakeholders who are creating networks and coalitions based on shared values, interests and visions of connectivity on a global scale.

A focal issue for this process was the disputes about the allocation of domain names, a function which was traditionally controlled by Jon Postel, a well-known and trusted web developer. In the mid-1990s, as the net's economic potential became clearer, a host of controversies around domain names emerged, mainly around "cybersquatters" who registered domains using registered trademarks. Thus began a complicated process of coalition building and negotiations aimed at creating an international regime, which multiple stakeholders tried to shape. Among these were diverse actors such as the internet technical community, intellectual property owners, hi-tech corporations, internet service providers, civil society organizations, intergovernmental organizations, and national governments (Mueller, 2002, 166–67).

The result of these efforts was the creation by the US government—which still held a formal authority over the net—of ICANN (Internet Corporation for Assigned Names and Numbers), a private nonprofit corporation which serves as the cornerstone for the internet governance regime. However, its power should not be exaggerated. Its mission, assigning of IP addresses and domain names, is quite modest; the ultimate authority and the computers storing the database still lie in the hands of the US government, despite international demands; and it receives endless criticism from experts and reporters. ICANN's importance lies mainly in the precedence it sets: its innovative inception, which was made possible by a coalition forged by a global network of governments, business corporations, NGOs, and individual experts; its unclear legal status, blurring the borders between intergovernmental and private-sector regulation bodies; its attempt to hold global democratic elections to appoint "at large," and its transnational aspirations, which will play a significant part in the future development of internet governance (Mueller, 2002).

The formation of ICANN serves as a precedent for current efforts to develop an internet governance regime, which take place through various summits, working groups, and organizations. The most notable is the World Summit on the Information Society (WSIS), which was spearheaded by the UN an its affiliate ITU and took place in two phases, the first in 2003 in Geneva and the second in 2005 in Tunisia. Formally, it was an intergovernmental process and only government delegations could vote in it, but in fact a multitude of UN bodies, international organizations, non-governmental organizations, civil-society and private-sector entities took part in it—the full list of participants is over 200 pages long. The final resolution called for the creation of an Internet Governance Forum (IGF), which is a multi-stakeholder body including governments, private corporations, civil-society organizations and academic and technical communities—all of which participate equally, at least in principle. Spanning such diverse issues as technological infrastructure, security standards and universal access, these discussions are ambitious attempts at creating a policy structure for the emerging global information society. Although attempts to create global political structures around the internet are in their

73

infancy, the multifarious networks which they generate offer us a glimpse at what may become the global mode of governance.

As this section shows, the governance of the internet is an extremely complicated issue. The somewhat naïve expectations prevalent in the 1990s that the internet will simply and easily create a new and better global politics based on participatory democracy and abolish the nation-state politics did not age well. As the internet becomes more pervasive and important, it becomes increasingly entangled with states and other political actors which will probably prevent it from fulfilling the hopes and promises it helped wake up. At the moment, it seems that the only realistic move in this direction is its role in transnational civil mobilizations whose concrete political effects—as the case of the war in Iraq demonstrates—are quite negligible. However, from a different point of view it seems that the internet has an important role in the globalization of politics, as the same attempts to control it are contributing to the establishment of new multilevel transnational relations between actors of various scales and interests.

Conclusion

As the internet is integrating with the structures of human societies on a global scale, it is having profound effects on many aspects of social life. Social structures extend beyond the confines of the geographical and political proximity, changing their nature in the process; culture and identity become ever more hybrid, mixing local and global elements in intricate and contingent patterns; political goals are sought beyond the confines of the nation-state, with the aid of new means of coordination, organization, and action; finally, political and economic institutions change established patterns of action and connect to each other in new ways as they attempt to get a hold on these processes. Other significant changes, not reviewed here due to lack of space, happen in the realms of organizational behavior, economic activity, the use of language, the meaning of knowledge and expertise, and countless other realms.

Research on the relations between internet and globalization is only beginning, as data collection is still in its preliminary stages, and theories and methods are still being debated. This process is complicated by the need to overcome disciplinary boundaries, which are proving inadequate as technology, society, culture, and politics interact in new and complex ways. Another major difficulty stems from the extremely dynamic nature of both subject matters. As the growing outdatedness of much of the literature written just a decade ago indicates, claims regarding the connections between internet and society tend to be temporary and contingent. We must accept that much of what is written today may be obsolete in the very near future, and be very careful in drawing far-reaching conclusions—a habit that is sadly prevalent in writing on these subjects.

However, as we hope this chapter has shown, there is a growing body of works which trace the connections between the internet and globalization. It is interesting to note that the most common organizing metaphor in these works, as in many other works about globalization, is that of the network. This metaphor, whose popularity probably owes much to the spread of the internet, has important theoretical implications. It encourages replacing the holistic view characteristic to methodological nationalism (Beck and Sznaider, 2006) with a thinner interpretation of the social, rather than trying to stretch the former to fit a global scale. Another important aspect of this metaphor is the de-emphasizing of distinctions prevalent in earlier models, such as those between base and super-structure or center and periphery. This relative "flatness," which makes the assertion of predetermined relations of causality less important, allows more space for contingency in explanation.

As the relations between internet and society are still in their early stages, it is probably better to refrain from pursuing a theoretization which will explain their general dynamics. Simple deterministic explanations, in which the logic of technology unproblematically extends itself to transform older social structures, or vice versa, tend to miss out on much of what is actually going on. The connection between societies and technologies changes both of them in unexpected ways, as each takes on some of the forms and features of the other. For example, the demand for music and entertainment in media saturated societies results in profound changes to internet structure, protocols, and traffic, and these in turn cause profound changes to the structure of the entertainment industry—which again triggers changes in net traffic and protocols. There will be time enough for drawing broader generalizations about these interrelations when internet technology stabilizes—if it ever will. The task at hand is to describe rather than explain. There is still very sparse information on the composition and structure of the transnational networks which are connected through the internet. The challenge of developing and implementing methods for tracing these networks and assessing their effects in various locales will be a worthy challenge for social research in the following years.

Acknowledgments

The authors would like to thank Iddo Tavory, Stav Raviv-Kaufman, and Noah Efron for helpful comments on earlier drafts.

References

Appadurai, A. (1996). *Modernity at Large: Cultural Dimensions of Globalization*, Minneapolis, MN: University of Minnesota Press.

Beck, U. and N. Sznaider (2006). "Unpacking Cosmopolitanism for the Social Sciences." *BJS*, 57(1): 1–23.

Castells, M. (2000). *The Rise of the Network Society*. Cambridge: Blackwell Publishers.

——(2001). *The Internet Galaxy*. Oxford: Oxford University Press.

——(2003). *The Power of Identity*. Cambridge: Blackwell Publishers.

Chadwick, A. (2006). *Internet Politics*. Oxford: Oxford University Press.

Chen, W., J. Boase, and B. Wellman (2002). "The Global Villagers: Comparing Internet Users and Uses Around the World." In Wellman, B. and C. Haythornthwaite (eds.), *The Internet in Everyday Life* (pp. 74–113). Oxford: Blackwell.

Deibert, R., Palfrey, J., Rohozinski, R. and Zittrain, J. (2008). *Access Denied: The Practice and Policy of Global Internet Filtering*. Cambridge, MA: MIT Press.

Georgiou, M. (2005). "Mapping Diasporic Media Cultures: A Transnational Cultural Approach to Exclusion." In Silverstone, R. (ed.) *From Information to Communication: Media, Technology and Everyday Life in Europe*. London: Ashgate.

Goldsmith, J. and Wu, T. (2006). *Who Controls the Internet?* Oxford: Oxford University Press.

Hafner, K. and Lyon, M. (1996). *Where Wizards Stay up Late*. New York: Simon & Schuster.

International Telecommunication Union (2007). *Measuring The Information Society 2007: ICT Opportunity Index and World Telecommunication/ICT Indicators*. Geneva: ITU.

Jenkins, H. (2006). *Fans, Bloggers, and Gamers*. New York: New York University Press.

Juris, J. S. (2008). "The New Digital Media and Activist Networking within Anti-Corporate Globalization Movements." In Jonathan Xavier Inda and Renato Rosaldo (eds.) *The Anthropology of Globalization*, second edition. Malden, MA: Blackwell.

Karim, H. K. (2003). "Mapping Diasporic Media." In Karim, H. K. (ed.) *The Media of Diaspora*. New York: Routledge.

Keck, M. E. and K. Sikkink (1998). *Activists beyond Borders: Advocacy Networks in International Politics*. Ithaca, NY: Cornell University Press.

Knorr-Cetina, K. (1999). *Epistemic Cultures*. Cambridge, MA: Harvard University Press.

——(2005). "Complex Micro Structures: the New Terrorist Societies." *TCS*, 22 (5): 213–34

Knorr-Cetina, K. and Brugger, U. (2000). "The Market as an Object of Attachment: Exploring Postsocial Relations in Financial Markets." *Canadian Journal of Sociology*, 25(2): 141–68.

Mcluhan, M. (1962). *The Gutenberg Galaxy*. London: Routledge & Kegan Paul.

Mueller, M. (2002). *Ruling the Root*. Cambridge, MA: MIT Press.

Olesen, T. (2005). *International Zapatismo: The Construction of Solidarity in the Age of Globalization*. London: ZED books.

Ong, A. (2006). *Neoliberalism as Exception*. Durham, NC: Duke University Press.

Regev, M. (2007). "Cultural Uniqueness and Aesthetic Cosmopolitanism," *European Journal of Social Theory*, 10: 123–38.

Rheingold, H. (1994). *The Virtual Community*. New York: HarperPerennial.

Silverstone, R. (2001). "Finding a Voice: Media, Minorities and the Global Commons," *Emergences*, 11 (1): 3–27.

Wellman, B., A. Quan-Hasse, J. Boase, W. Chen, K. Hampton, I.I. de Diaz, and K. Miyata (2003). "The Social Affordances of the Internet for Networked Individualism." *Journal of Computer-Mediated Communication*, 8(3): http://jcmc.indiana.edu/vol8/issue3/wellman.html.

5

Anti-globalization movements

From critiques to alternatives

Tom Mertes

"Anti-globalization movement" is a misnomer for the wide-ranging and, at times, splintered social movements that principally grew in response to the imposition of neo-liberal economic policies beginning in the late 1970s. Most scholars of the movements prefer more precise labels such as the "global justice movement," "global social movements," "global solidarity movement" or "alter-globalization movement." The term "anti-globalization" began to appear in the English language in the mid-1990s but did not gain currency until the last years of the decade. It was deployed early on to discredit opposition to economic restructuring and trade liberalization as being merely anachronistic. *New York Times* editorialist Thomas Friedman complained that "the anti-globalization movement, led by Pat Buchanan [sic!], is still with us, arguing that free trade and global integration cause stagnating wages" (Friedman 1997). Most of the movements' activists do not identify with the label because they do not necessarily oppose other forms of globalization such as commodity trading, cultural exchanges, social solidarities, free movements of peoples, and knowledge transfers. The new social movements have hoisted their sails to the winds of planetary solidarity, non-violence, true sustainable development, and radical democratization. For the purposes of this chapter, this movement of movements will be referred to as the global justice movement (GJM).

The GJM has had numerous historical parallels. Transnational activism has a long history reaching back at least as far as the International Workingmen's Association, "First International," in 1866. As the twentieth century unfolded transnationalism flourished in a variety of areas from Marcus Garvey's Pan-Africanism to anti-colonial struggles to women's rights movements. What sets GJM apart from earlier movements that served as a foundation for the late twentieth century are the scale of activities, the reach of the movements from rural to urban and especially across borders, and the bundling of local concerns with international problems. Moreover, the international institutional and technological context in which the movements operate has changed significantly. International institutions have been important both as a catalyst for action but also as a forum for domestic movement activists to oppose their nation's policies. Advances in telecommunications and transportation have also created greater openings for activists, organizers and researchers to communicate, facilitate solidarities, educate and plan actions with greater speed and clarity.

The GJM rose out of the stagflation and lower rates of profit experienced in the Global North by the late 1970s. The 1979 recession in the US and record oil prices combined to create an economic crisis across much of the Global South. The International Monetary Fund (IMF) and the World Bank (WB), as lenders of last resort, offered many crisis-ridden states debt relief but with conditions attached to their loans. As the name implies, these creditor demands were understood as "structural adjustment programs" (SAPs). These macro-economic policies included austerity measures such as radical cuts in governmental subsidies for food and energy. Societies already troubled by hyper-inflation were then devastated by the new cuts giving rise to "IMF riots" which were the precursors to the "anti-globalization" movement. SAPs typically also included fire sales of state-owned enterprises, national mineral-resource privatization, weakened labor unions (euphemistically praised as "flexible labor markets"), capital market liberalization, lowered tariffs and deregulation. The policies were significant for enabling the process of global economic integration but they also caused tremendous social dislocations.

The critiques of neo-liberal globalization multiplied on a number of fronts. In brief, besides the rising inequalities within and between nations, activists and some academics note that it "privatized profits and socialized the risk," national resource endowments were sold at the expense of the citizenry, it put workers in a weaker position (decline of unions, lower wages, more employment insecurity), it enabled quick exit for foreign capital and firms, and international bodies now adjudicate domestic economic, environmental, and social disputes. Environmentally, deregulation allowed for rapid exploitation of natural resources without much regard for the long-term impact of extraction processes. Easy exit made it more difficult for states to hold corporations accountable for damages incurred in resource extraction.

States have also increasingly lost their ability to guarantee food sovereignty or even prohibit the production of genetically modified crops. Trade agreements and IMF/World Bank policies also endangered Indigenous lands through resource exploration and exploitation. Many feminists argue that economic globalization and its effects reinforce patriarchy shifting more work onto women as men become redundant or underemployed due to the new economic orientation. Cuts in state programs and protections often make women's lives more burdensome and diminish their ability to resist further oppressions. Many critics of neo-liberal globalization also document decreases in social provisions even as police and military budgets remain high to respond to domestic unrest and border disputes often created by SAPs or competition over resources. Finally, many GJM activists consider this form of economic globalization as imperialistic because of the imposition of policies from above with little democratic input from below, because it perpetuates the cleavage between developed and less developed nations, because of the opaque decision-making structure of the WTO/IMF/WB, and because it imposes Western values and models onto the Global South.

Opposition to SAPs was spasmodic at first but political parties, movements, and organizations soon rose at the local and national levels to put pressure on respective states to ameliorate the decline in economic rights and increasing deprivation. In general, linkages between national movements were very weak until after the mid-1990s when a number of factors combined to deepen the linkages, raise abilities for coordination, and build stronger solidarities between movements. One of the most powerful factors is that multinational corporations have penetrated more open markets. Local activists target the multinationals and discovered that people are fighting the same struggles and corporations elsewhere creating the grounds for networks and solidarities for collective action against companies such as Monsanto, Pfizer, Nike, Vivendi, Occidental Petroleum, Chevron, Wal-Mart, and Coca-Cola.

During the 1994 General Agreement on Tariffs and Trade (GATT) Uruguay Round, the World Trade Organization (WTO) was established. Instead of the GATT's loose and negative regulatory institution for trade agreements, a positive and proactive institution began to oversee trade. While the WTO did give developing nations a timetable for implementation of liberalized trade in manufactures, it also put in place stricter protections for other areas of trade including intellectual property to the advantage of the developed nations. The Uruguay Round and the WTO failed to reach substantive agreements on agriculture because of the power of domestic agribusiness, farmers, and peasants to limit their governments' designs. Their opposition began to take on a transnational character as early as 1992 when farmers from Latin America, Europe, and Asia protested at Geneva and Strasbourg against the GATT talks (Edelman, 2003).

In the same year that the WTO was established, the North American Free Trade Agreement (NAFTA) went into effect. The new trade regime, like other neo-liberal policies, created significant opposition. Arguably, the origins of the GJM lay in the transitional Zapatistas (*Ejército Zapatista de Liberación Nacional* or EZLN). They opposed the regional deployment of neo-liberal policy in their strident criticism of NAFTA. The agreement threatened multinational exploitation of Chiapas and the lives and culture of its Indigenous people. More to the point, the Zapatistas called for a meeting of international activists in the Lacandón Forest (Chiapas) for the foundation of a larger web of resistance. In 1996 the First International Encounter for Humanity and against Neo-liberalism agreed that another "*encuentro*" should meet in Andalucia where the participants initiated the Peoples' Global Action (PGA) that would be formally established in Geneva early in 1998. The Italian *Ya Basta!* was another spin-off from the *encuentros* and it, in turn, gave birth to the *Tute Bianche* whose English cousins were the Wombles.[1] All of these movements had several commonalities that differed from earlier social movements. They opposed neo-liberalism and fought against it both within their own borders and, more importantly, on a transnational level. They sought to pressure their own governments but also international institutions of economic management. They also tended to appropriate new telecommunications technology to build networks to share information, tactics, strategies of opposition, and alternative economic practices.

In parallel fashion, peasants and farmers were also constructing mutual aid and resistance networks. The most prominent and powerful of these is Via Campesina. This network of farmers and peasants from all over the world started in the same year as the *EZLN*. It now has over 200 million agricultural producers under its umbrella. It too opposes neo-liberal policies as well as WTO-protected genetically modified seeds and trade subsidies that support corporate farming. As with most other GJM entities, it has alternatives to offer including a platform for food sovereignty, seed banks, land reform, as well as organic and intensive production methods (rather than extensive industrial agricultural). Finally in 1994, on the fiftieth anniversary of the World Bank and the IMF, a number of groups including Development Gap for Alternative Policies, International Rivers Network, Global Exchange, Oxfam America, Colombian Justice and Peace Office, and the Maryknoll Office for Global Concerns founded the 50 Years is Enough campaign. Most of these organizations had been working on various aspects of World Bank and IMF policies. They decided that they would be much stronger working together and, thus, argued for reform of these 1944 Bretton Woods Conference inspired institutions.

The promise of coordinated action was reinforced by a series of financial ruptures ending in the 1997 Asian Financial Crisis. It was becoming clearer that the IMF/World Bank were not providing solutions but rather promoting policies for the benefit of large investors, corporations, and the international financial system. The legitimacy of these institutions began to be questioned by more than just the subject populations but also many mainstream economists and policy-makers including the US Congress. Still in the midst of the Asian crisis, the first flowering of international mass mobilizations began against institution-driven economic globalization. During 1998, regional conferences were held in India to protest the WTO; in Canada workers and activists marched against the Organization of Economic Co-operation and Development's Multilateral Agreements on Investments; the *Movimento dos Trabalhadores Rurais Sem Terra* (MST—Landless Workers Movement) held a 50,000 strong march on Brazilia; and in Geneva thousands protested at the headquarters of the WTO. The PGA estimated that over a million people had participated in some form of opposition to the WTO in the first weeks of May. A little over a year later it organized "carnivals against capitalism" in most of the world's financial centers to coincide with the meeting of the G8. The critical mass of popular forces that would shut down the Seattle WTO was picking up steam.

One example of this momentum was the formation of United Students Against Sweatshops in the US less than one month after the first PGA demonstrations. This US organization of college or university chapters campaigns individually by campus on a host of issues. They have been at the forefront in targeting multinational corporations for exploitative labor practices as well as educating and mobilizing students. At almost the same moment, on the other side of the Atlantic, *Association pour la Taxe Tobin pour l'Aide aux Citoyens* (ATTAC) was formed in opposition to the ongoing liberalization of capital markets by the IMF.[2] In response to the bombing of Serbia, European activists including *Ya Basta!* organized a number of marches and a caravan on the continent to oppose the Yugoslav wars as well as the prisons for migrants to Europe who had been pushed off the land by economic globalization and drought. In Asia a group of Korean activists organized the "People Challenging the IMF: Neo-liberalism, the IMF and International Solidarity" conference in Seoul for September 1998. Early in the summer of 1999 the Jubilee 2000 (a solidarity network of over 75 organizations from 40 countries) created a human chain around the US Treasury calling on it to push for the cancellation of Global South debts owed to the IMF and World Bank. At the G8 Summit in Cologne activists formed another human chain and solidarity rallies were held in London, Latin America, and Africa.

By the fall of 1999 José Bové led his comrades from the Confédéracion Paysanne in the dismantling of a McDonald's in Millau, France to highlight a WTO-sanctioned US surcharge on Roquefort cheese produced in the town. However, the movement's iconic moment was beginning to take shape. Central to organizing the Seattle protests against the WTO was the Direct Action Network, Earth First!, Rainforest Action Network, and the Ruckus Society who trained a good number of the activists in non-violent direct action techniques. The "Battle of Seattle" helped convince delegates from the Global South that the WTO was detrimental to their people but also did not have the solid support of people in North America. Seattle was a crucial success for GJM because it demonstrated the possibility of mass mobilizations to alter the best-laid plans of corporations and governments. The WTO, the Seattle police, the Secret Service, and broad swaths of the press fabricated an argument that the activists were violent because a small segment of the groups damaged a bit of *property*. The activists pointed out that the WTO et al. were violent against *people* both as a consequence of their policies but also as the police used tear-gas, pepper-spray, truncheons, and rubber bullets to clear the streets. Despite clear intentions of non-violence by activists, the forces of the status quo increased their militarization and internationalized their techniques. As with other global actions, the Seattle protest was not confined to one location: 75,000 marched in various French cities, protests were also registered in Manila, Bangalore, Berlin, and all over the British Isles. Seattle confirmed the convergence of many networks, non-governmental organizations (NGOs), and even some labor unions. This power was extended to many of the delegations from the South who used it as leverage in negotiations and refused to agree to another round of WTO protocols.

Yet, even in the face of a clampdown, the new millennium carried forward the momentum of GJM. The next large demonstration was "A16" (April 16), in Washington, DC as the IMF and World Bank held talks. Even prior to the actions the police and fire departments invaded convergence centers and shut down workshops where potential weapons of mass distraction were being crafted: paper-mâché puppets, protest signs, banners, and the like. A month later Quebec hosted elite discussions for a hemispheric free trade zone for the Americas (FTAA). While opposition had grown exponentially, the forces of corporate capital and neo-liberalism were undaunted. Canadian authorities in preparation for mass demonstrations built a mini-fortress of chain-link fences, turned activists back at the Canadian–US border, adorned full-combat gear, and suspended civil liberties. Police riots followed where over 4,500 people were tear-gassed with chemicals that police would later admit were experimental. In solidarity actions, 1,800 protested in Sao Paulo. They too suffered from police repression.

Two months later, the Swedish police not satisfied with the Canadian model used live ammunition to beat back demonstrators at the EU summit. The increased state violence of Quebec and Gothenburg (Sweden) raised the apparent ante for Italian police. They drew on the tradition of Mussolini in their designs for the G8 meeting in Genoa. In this very large demonstration of more than 200,000 demonstrators from all over Europe, walls were again constructed to eliminate the potential for democratic input. The *carabinieri* (military police) used *agent provocateurs* dressed as Black Blockers to smash banks, and make crowds seem more menacing. The *carabinieri* also drove marches into dead-end streets, invaded independent media centers, and even arrested their own elected officials. They detained GJM activists with no charges, used humiliation, intimidation, and torture. In sum at least 600 protesters were injured and, unfortunately, a young *carabinieri* murdered another young Italian protestor. International meetings of financial and political elites were now cordoned off with chain-link fences or held in remote areas from Evian to Doha to Kananaskis. Governments cooperated on repressing broad democratic expressions. For example, in preparation for Evian 2003, the Swiss government invited both German and French police to join them in Geneva. International economic institutions also adjusted their public pronouncements but have not, as yet, reformed many of their policies.

The actions in the developed nations had parallels in the rest of the world. Bolivia exploded as the Banzer government extended World Bank proscriptions to privatize the economy including water services. In Cochabamba the sole bid for a water works was from a subsidiary of Bechtel Corporation who promptly raised rates by 35 percent. The exorbitant rate sparked massive protests organized by the *La Coordinara* (Coalition in Defense of Water and Life) that led to a violent repression. As an international outcry spread, the Bolivian government was forced to roll back charges only to be sued by

Bechtel for lost profits. Elsewhere in South America, in Quito, and various other places in Ecuador, people took to the streets in January 2001 against IMF austerity measures implemented by Gustavo Noboa. CONAIE (Confederation of Indigenous Nationalities of Ecuador) was at the head of the protests that echoed the previous year's demonstrations that deposed the Jamil Mahuad government with the aid of the military. Noboa was forced to make significant adjustments to austerity measures but stayed in power with military backing. Likewise, South Africans organized against the privatization of electricity with the Soweto Electricity Crisis Committee, and a month later the Anti-Privatization Forum formed in response to Igoli 2002, an African National Congress program informed by neo-liberal inspired IMF and World Bank policies.

As popular oppositions gained strength, activists and intellectuals sought an arena to articulate and promote the positive and constructive agenda of the GJM that was often left out of media reports. Further, they sought an outlet to expose the misconception that "there is no alternative" to neo-liberal economic globalization. Rather they showcased debates on the many alternatives. The First World Social Forum (WSF) held in 2001 chose the motto that indeed "Another World is Possible." The subsequent forums have brought together activists, NGOs, intellectuals, and social movement representatives to debate alternatives, share strategies, build coalitions, and deepen solidarities. The Forum has grown exponentially both at its annual meetings and in the proliferation of national and local forums. The WSF has become quite large, almost unwieldy. It has generated a great deal of criticism and debate over its course, its procedures, and its ability to serve as an activist body (see below).

The US "war on terror" in response to the crime of September 11 stalled many GJM mobilizations as the networks debated the proper response even as the Bush administration went into high gear in planning a roll back of civil rights in the United States. One exception was the UN World Summit on Sustainable Development in August 2002 in Johannesburg. While corporations tried to carry their agenda for "public–private" development plans inside the conference, activists who wanted alternatives to privatizations marched in the streets in the tens of thousands and revealed to the international press through interviews and meetings the terrible conditions of poverty, lack of clean water, sanitation, health care, electricity, and other necessaries of life. Since September 11, US troops have killed foreign nationals in at least four countries: Iraq, Afghanistan, Syria, Colombia, and probably in the Philippines and Pakistan. While activists chose not to protest in September 2001, they began to formulate plans for stopping large-scale US military operations. The GJM was significantly altered, possibly distracted, but also strategically fortified. It had successfully removed the façade of multilateral action by the US and many world leaders now had to fear for the sovereignty of their nations. The rising use of US military power depleted its soft power including its leadership in international institutions.

Despite the focus on war, global justice activists continue to apply pressure at international meetings including the G8 meeting at places like the very exclusive Evian but more importantly local struggles also continue including the MST, South African squatters, Indian *Narmada Bachao Andolan* (NBA—Save Narmada Movement) damn site occupations, pro-immigrant rights demonstrations, Nigerian strikes against the oil industry and government, and a host of other critiques of ongoing neo-liberal policies across the world. Activists aside, the biggest challenge facing multilateral institutions is the unilateral and aggressive approach of the US in world affairs.

In 2003 the opposition to neo-liberalism had become more powerful. Yet, the Global North had not reformed in response. Their own economic policies especially in the area of large farm subsidies persisted in being hypocritical. Hence, WTO meetings at Cancun were troubled from the start as many nations from the Global South refused to budge on the agenda presented by the North. Added to the intramural divisions was a large manifestation that was precluded from confronting and dialoguing with delegates who were safely cocooned by fences, private security forces and the Mexican military. Some infiltrators did make it into the meetings and protesters breached the wall only to sit down for a moment of silence in remembrance of the South Korean agronomist Lee Kyung Hae who took his own life at the head of a march of over 15,000 farmers from all over the world in the previous days.

The ministerial talks ended in failure as a number of delegates walked out and no consensus was achieved. The WTO has made little or no headway in securing any new agreements. Moreover, high commodity prices and fiscal austerity have increased current account surpluses in many countries in the Global South. In part, they have been insuring themselves against future attacks on their currency but also from IMF conditionalities. In effect, the IMF has lost much of its legitimacy. Talks continue on how it might be reformed and the possibility that it might sell some of its gold stock to make its payroll because its revenues have declined significantly. The appointment of Paul Wolfowitz, one of the architects of the Iraq War, as president of the World Bank, further undermined the credibility of the institution and its appointment process. Wolfowitz tried to increase the anti-corruption policies of the Bank but found himself involved in a personal corruption scandal and was eventually forced to resign. In his place, Robert Zoellick, the former free-trade crusader as the US Trade Representative, was appointed to the vacated seat.

The delegitimation of the international financial institutions (IFI—WTO, IMF, and World Bank) has changed the focus of GJM but it has not been its undoing. Social movements and NGOs have gained considerable leverage in domestic politics across the globe. They have a greater ability to influence their governments because they have forced open the political process and have international allies on whom they can draw support. In some cases they have pressed their governments hard but have been unable to stop what they have considered inimical state policies or actions. For example, in Guatemala opponents of the Central American Free Trade Agreement were able to shut down their Congress for several days in 2005 before the military was sent in to crush the demonstrators. During the 2006 Mexican presidential elections, Lopez Obrador nearly defeated Felipe Calderon running on an explicit rejection of much of the NAFTA accords. In other countries, huge demonstrations have attempted to sway governments from agreeing to bilateral and regional free trade agreements including: Peru (2006, 2008—four farmers killed), Panama (2006), Colombia (2006), South Korea (2006–8), Philippines (2007–8), Japan (2007), and Mexico (2008). In 2008 50,000 Senegalese turned out to oppose the Economic Partnership Agreement with the EU. Several thousand in Ougadougou (Burkina Faso) joined them and African activists are planning mobilizations for Bamako and Mauritania.

In some states the explicit opponents of neo-liberal policies, aligned with GJM activists, have been voted into office. Nestor Kirchner was elected president of Argentina in 2003 with less than 30 percent of the vote. His popularity skyrocketed to over 85 percent when he refused to repay IMF loans and was able to have them reduced to about 25 percent of their face value. His wife has succeeded him in office. Bolivia's president, Evo Morales was an Indigenous activist who participated in campaigns for farmers to grow their traditional crop of coca and against the privatization of water before becoming the executive in 2005. In Ecuador Raphael Correa was elected president in 2006 on a platform rejecting free trade agreements. In Venezuela Hugo Chávez is well known for his opposition to international financial institutions and has been re-elected president twice. Daniel Ortega ran on an anti-free trade platform though he has since given his support to CAFTA. These governments as well as Brazil, Uruguay, and Paraguay have agreed to fund an alternative to the World Bank and IMF, the Banco del Sur, in 2007.

Activists and analysts

The GJM has an incredible number of ideological tendencies and organizational forms. This disparate group of activists, academics, intellectuals, scientists, doctors, workers, farmers, and politicos hold to a wide spectrum of ideologies and practical alternatives to neo-liberal globalization mostly on the left including, environmentalists, feminists, gay and Indigenous-rights activists, anarchists, libertarians, socialists, communitarians, communists, and autonomists. Key contributors stretch across these ideologies as well as the globe. Obviously, Subcommandante Marcos, a spokesperson for the Zapatistas, is one of the most quoted alter-globalization activists but he is joined by a host of other thinkers and activists. Some of the most read intellectuals within the movements include Walden Bello, prolific author and Senior Analyst and co-founder of Focus on the Global South; Arundhati Roy, Booker Prize winner and author of *Power Politics* (2001); Naomi Klein, journalist and author of *No Logo* (2000) and *The Shock Doctrine* (2007); Noam Chomsky, world renowned anti-imperialist academic; Susan George, author of numerous books including *The Lugano Report* (1999), Vice-President of ATTAC France for six years, and chair of the Planning Committee at the Transnational Institute; Ignacio Ramonet, an editor of *Le Monde Diplomatique* and co-founder of ATTAC; Michael Hardt and Antonio Negri, authors of the influential and foundational *Empire* (2000); Anuradha Mittal, author and Executive Director of The Oakland Institute; Robert Weisman and Russell Mohhiber, editors of *Multinational Monitor* and STOP-IMF listserv; Patrick Bond, prolific author, activist, and Director of the Centre for Civil Society at University of KwaZulu-Natal; Vandana Shiva, physicist, activist, and author of numerous books including the influential *Water Wars: Privatization, Pollution, and Profit* (2002); Emir Sader, a leading Brazilian intellectual and the author of over 50 books; David Graeber, anthropologist, author, and activist; Michel Albert, activist, author, and founder of *Z* magazine and a co-editor of Znet. Most recently, Mark Engler has produced an important intervention on new ideas and strategies for activists in his *How to Rule the World* (2008).

Intellectual critiques are only potent when they have the power of a block of citizens legitimizing their arguments with their life-histories and willingness to put their bodies as a stop sign to more of the same. A list of key activists would not do justice to the movements that are mass-based or their brave actions but a few noteworthy include: José Bové, who led the toppling of a McDonald's in France and is a spokesperson for Via Campesina; Oscar Olivera, a Bolivian spokesperson for anti-water privatization; Maude Barlow, a founder of Council of Canadians; Njoki Njehu, former director of 50 Years is Enough; Lee Kyung-hae, Korean agronomist who sacrificed his life at Cancún; Mehta Patkar and Chittaroopa Palit, leaders in the *Narmada Bachao Andolan*; Nila Ardhianie of the Indonesian Forum on Globalization, a water-rights spokesperson; João Pedro Stedile, a founder of the Brazilian MST; Martin Khor, director of the Third World Network; Starhawk, US activist and author; John Sellers, former director of the Ruckus Society; Trevor Ngwane, a founder of the Anti-Privatization Forum in South Africa; Ann

Pettifor, former director of the Debt Crisis Network and one of the founders of the Jubliee 2000; Vittioro Agnoletto, doctor, HIV-AIDS activist, and politician; Au Loong Yu, a founder of the Hong Kong *Globalization Monitor* and labor organizer.

More important than key activists and leaders are the movements and more radical NGOs themselves. They are the "critical mass" that has achieved some victories and continue to be vigilant against ongoing economic, ecological, and social threats. Besides the above-mentioned movements and organizations, there are many others that deserve attention and this list only scratches the surface: Cochabambinos, who were able to halt water privatization in Bolivia; fisherfolk in India, Pakistan, and Philippines; Development Alternatives for Women in a New Era; Notes from Nowhere, a British anarchist collective and authors of the groundbreaking *We are Everywhere* (2003), and also in the UK the autonomous Trapeze Collective who have edited *Do It Yourself: A Handbook for Changing Our World* (2007); Hong Kong's People's Alliance which organized the WTO manifestations in 2005; Reclaim the Streets, formerly a British squatting festival that created temporary commons; Our World Is Not for Sale, a "hub" organization for opposing corporate domination through trade agreements; Third World Network, a Malaysia-based research organization dedicated to collecting and distributing perspectives from the Global South; Korean People's Action Against FTA and WTO, a network of 50 organizations dedicated to direct action; Jubliee 2000, a network of organizations that called for the cancellation of debt for the poorest countries by 2000—after the millennium, it split off into a number of smaller activist networks including Jubliee USA and Jubliee South,[3] which is now a network of 85 groups from 40 countries in the Global South campaigning for debt-relief including: social movements, people's organizations, communities, NGOs, and political formations; Maryknoll Office for Global Concerns, a Catholic organization that provides information and lobbies governments for the poor; Oxfam and Christian Aid—UK, aid and advocacy organizations; Globalise Resistance, a UK-based activist organization closely connected with the Socialist Workers' Party; World Development Movement, a UK-based research and campaigning organization especially on water issues; Food First, a San Francisco-based information gathering and disseminating organization; Friends of the Earth, US-based environmental NGO, Action Aid, an anti-poverty agency; Africa Action, a US-based political lobbying organization; Frente Indígena de Organizaciones Binacionales (Binational Front of Indigenous Organizations), a political action organization uniting families and communities in Mexico and the US; Karnataka State Farmers' Association, a "Gandhian" movement of approximately 10 million people seeking social and economic transformation nationally and internationally; International Forum on Globalization, a collective of scholars and activists who link and broker movement activities as well as produce analytical frames that create a wide and inclusive program for actions and movements; Indymedia, a locally-based activists' collectives, unpaid journalists, and media organizations that post unedited news stories on the web; Yesmen, a group of imposters who parody corporate and IFI policies; Bayan, a Filipino social and economic rights movement; Gabriela Network, a Filipino–US network for social transformation. Moreover, examples of local movements and actions including anti-eviction squatters (land, electricity, water, etc.), anarchists, and Indigenous groups who have struggled to create alternatives and survive on what little they have are too numerous to list.

The potency and power of movements, NGOs, activists, and actions have made them worthy objects of research and reflection. The academic study of the GJM is a burgeoning field of inquiry. Sidney Tarrow, author most recently of *The New Transnational Activism*

(2005), might correctly be called the dean of sociological studies of the "global social movements." He argues that without internationalization of institutional structures, NGOs and movements would not have been able to build across borders to oppose the IFIs. Moreover, he finds that most of the movements are geared more towards domestic struggles than fighting on the global level. Movements are most salient at the grass-roots level. He is joined by a number of other scholars including Jackie Smith, who is the editor of numerous books and author of *Social Movements for Global Democracy* (2008) and *Global Democracy and World Social Forums* (with Marina Karides, 2007). Smith's work is focused on the transnational nature of social movements and their effects on international organizations. Donatella della Porta is the author and editor of numerous books on social movements including *Social Movements in a Globalizing World* (1999), *Transnational Protest and Global Activism* (editor with Sidney Tarrow, 2005) and *Globalization from Below: Transnational Activists and Protest Networks* (with Massimiliano Andretta, 2006). Her work focuses primarily on European movements and especially the relationship between activists and the state. Ruth Reitan brings a multi-disciplinary approach to exploring four key "networks of networks" in her *Global Activism* (2007). Another widely read author-activist is Boaventura de Sousa Santos, a prolific scholar whose work includes *Law and Globalization from Below* (2005) and *The Rise of the Global Left* (2006). Anthropologist Jeffrey Juris has recently published an ethnography of the alter-globalization movements in *Networking Futures: The Movements Against Corporate Globalization* (2008). Amory Starr's *Global Revolt* (2005) is perhaps the single most detailed and comprehensive primer on the movements and was preceded by her germinal *Naming the Enemy: Anti-Corporate Movements Confront Globalization* (2000).

In addition to academic study of the GJM, there is a considerable literature critiquing neoliberal globalization but, more importantly, offering alternative policies and economic practices. David Korten's *When Corporations Ruled the World* (1995) was one of the most important works for the North American movements. He has since published *The Post-Corporate World* (2000) and *The Great Turning from Empire to Earth Community* (2007). Also from a pro-market perspective, Paul Hawken's *Blessed Unrest* (2007) argues for a more environmentally aware and community-centered future. Another early but influential work, much more critical of markets, is *The Case Against the Global Economy and the Turn Toward the Local* (1997) that was edited by Jerry Mander and Edward Goldsmith. Peter Waterman is a long-time activist and academic whose many works take a left-laborist perspective. John Cavanagh, the Director of the Institute for Policy Studies in Washington, DC, is an editor of the path-breaking *Alternatives to Economic Globalization: A Better World is Possible* (2002). The text is the product of an ongoing debate begun in 1994 by the International Forum on Globalization that is an alliance of NGOs from over 25 countries. Many of the co-authors of the book have written separately as well, including Walden Bello, *DeGlobalization: Ideas for a New Economy* (2002) and Robin Broad, *Global Backlash: Citizen Initiatives for a Just World Economy* (2002). Leslie Sklair, author of *Globalization, Capitalism and its Alternatives*, and William Robinson, author of *Transnational Conflicts: Central America, Social Change, and Globalization* (2003), assert that a transnational capitalist class has become increasingly salient and powerful, undermining democracy at the local level. Economic geographer David Harvey has produced two works that are particularly incisive and widely read: *A Brief History of Neoliberalism* (2005) and *The New Imperialism* (2005). *Global Village, Global Pillage* (1998) and *Globalization from Below* (2000), coauthored by Jeremy Brecher and Tim Costello, were early interventions that have resonated since in activist communities and academic debates.

World Social Forum

In the above narrative I have mentioned some of the signal contributions to the alter-globalization movements but one of the most important and ongoing symbols and convergences of the GJM is the World Social Forum. It is an "open space" for dialogues and debates among activists, academics, politicians, and NGOs. In January of 2001 the first World Social Forum was held. It was the brainchild of Bernhard Cassen, Chico Whitaker, and Oded Grajew. They outlined an alternative to the World Economic Forum at Davos to be held in the largely working class Porto Alegre. It has a participatory budget[4] and was at that time under a PT (*Partido dos Trabalhadores*—a left-leaning workers' party) administration. The WSF kicked off with a debate between two very different gatherings. The WSF was recognized by the global elite when financier George Soros, Bjorn Edlund (ABB Communications) and two UN functionaries teledebated Cassen, Walden Bello, Njoki Njehu, and Trevor Ngwane. Thus, on the one hand there were some of the richest men in the world and their lieutenants calling from one of the world's most exclusive resorts, while, on the other, were activists and thinkers from Porto Alegre, an industrial city in the heart of Latin America. The publicity for the debate, dominated by Global Southerners, created a great deal of reporting and helped to put the forum on the map. The first forum had between 12–15,000 participants, mostly from the Global South and Europe. From these origins the forum grew exponentially in the coming years. It has generated criticism and debate over its course, its procedures, its ability to serve as an activist body, its lack of ideological clarity, and strategic vacuity. The criticisms of the WSF are echoed throughout the movements, academia, and the press.

When WSF met for the second time in January 2002, only two months after the WTO Doha Round, Argentina had essentially declared itself bankrupt and the De la Rúa government fell on December 20, 2001. The flashpoint that ended the presidency was the failure of the IMF to renew its loans to Argentina because it had failed to cut state spending far enough and it stuck to dollarization. The nation had been a model for IMF prescriptions in the latter half of the 1990s. The political and economic legacies of Juan Perón and SAPs had wrought ruin and the first to bolt were middle-income groups who began a run on the nation's banks and chaos ensued. The legitimacy of the IMF/World Bank policy had taken another body-blow; a cough of reform followed and little or no alteration in theoretical orientation. As the WSF II met, *piqueteros* (protestors who obstructed roads) were still in the streets of Buenos Aires and the 50–60,000 delegates at Porto Alegre marched in solidarity. The march also opposed imperialism especially because the US had recently begun its perpetual war against "terrorism" by invading Afghanistan. Likewise, the Free Trade Area of the Americas figured prominently in the marches.

As the US re-invasion of Iraq loomed large, activists throughout the world began to focus intently on stopping yet another aggressive action by the world's hegemon. In European elections and polls, one point unified most Europeans and that was rejection of the impending war on Iraq. The European Social Forum (ESF, a spin-off from World Social Forum paralleled by other regional forums) at Florence galvanized this sentiment into an anti-war march. Planners expected 200,000 but by November 9, 2002 over 500,000 activists marched. Some estimates were as high as a million in a city of 500,000. Unlike Genoa, the police chose not to challenge the protesters and, thus the demonstration went peacefully. Approximately 100,000 people participated in the third WSF in Puerto Alegre. It too took up the question of war and condemned it but did not officially organize a campaign against it. However, the activists at the WSF and the ESF did the early planning for perhaps the largest call for peace in world history. The worldwide marches and demonstrations on February 15, 2003 against the possible invasion of Iraq marked a renewed and reinvigorated mobilization with global justice advocates at the forefront. Estimates of the turnout range from ten to twelve million people in most of the world's major cities. This outpouring was unprecedented since 1968.

To widen the scope of the WSF, its international coordinating body decided to hold the 2004 Forum in India. This was done for a number of reasons including the fact that it made it more possible for local activists in Asia to attend the meeting. It was held in Bombay, January 16–21. Over 75,000 people attended the meeting. It was notable for having the first counter-World Social Forum held by Maoists near the Forum. They pointed out that it was ineffectual and NGO-driven. Cultural diversity and women's rights were cast as central themes of the WSF. The question of state power, whether movements should morph into political parties or stay aloof from the corruptions of power, was also debated but, again, the WSF is seen as an open space for dialogue and debate and no official position was taken.

In 2005, Porto Alegre again hosted the WSF. 155,000 participants appeared at the Forum. Brazil, Argentina, the United States, Uruguay, and France were the most represented nations. One outcome of the proceedings was the "Porto Alegre Manifesto" that was compiled by a number of left-wing intellectuals and reflects widely-held positions. Rather than being formally adopted by the Forum, it was greeted with a good deal of criticism from a variety of perspectives. The provisions included:

1 Cancellation of the external national debts of the Global South.
2 A Tobin tax on international financial transactions the proceeds to be used for combating major epidemics (like AIDS), provision of clean water, housing, energy, health services and medication, education, and other social services.
3 Elimination of tax havens and offshore banking.
4 Right to work, social provision, and equal rights on an international and national level.
5 "Fair trade" and the "upward equalization of social and environmental norms on the production of goods and services as defined by International Labor Organization."
6 Food sovereignty and the national protections to outlaw the importation or production of genetically modified organisms for consumption.
7 Outlaw the patenting of living organisms and making "common goods for humanity, particularly water."
8 Create protection for minorities whether based on sex, religion, race, place of origin, and full legal rights for Indigenous peoples.
9 Urgently implement alternative development models, based on energy efficiency, and "democratic control of natural resources, most notably potable water, on a global scale" to protect the environment and reverse climate change.
10 Tear down all foreign military bases and withdraw foreign troops from all countries, "except when operating under explicit mandate of the United Nations."
11 Liberate the media from corporate concentration, encourage the not-for-profit press, Indymedia, and information networks.
12 Democratize the IFIs by placing them under the UN and hold them responsible to the Universal Declaration of Human Rights.

Surveys conducted by UC Riverside researchers reveal that the majority of the participants in the WSF 2005 onward are mainly drawn from NGOs/academics and are not particularly ideologically radical. While there are a number of problems with the surveys and they are still preliminary in their findings, they do give a snapshot of the domination of the forums by white-collar professionals who have little incentive to truly engage in praxis or to see through the agenda of social movements that stray far from the center-left of political discourse.

The international organizing committee thought that it was critical to promote local dialogues and again overcome the problems of geography for poor people and therefore chose a "polycentric" approach to the WSF for 2006. By far the most successful was the Caracas forum where 52,000 participants gathered. Here again, the theme of state power was central to debates. In 2007 Nairobi hosted a World Social Forum and over 50,000 people attended. The forum was controversial on several levels. In a desperately poor nation, much of the food for sale at the forum was well beyond the means of most Kenyans, entrance fees were imposed, and water was not free. Participation at the world forums has leveled-off and is uneven at the regional forum level. The recently held ESF in Athens was not particularly well attended (3–5,000) nor was the Asian Social Forum in Karachi as big as expected though 35,000 people from 59 countries attended it. The policies of the organizing committee have come under strong attack from many sides. The WSF international organizing committee declared that rather than holding a forum, a "day of action" organized locally would take its place in 2008. The intention was for activists to organize local events that addressed global problems and report back to the WSF 2008 website (see: http://www.wsf2008.net/). The 2009 World Social Forum will be held in Belem, Brazil.

The forum remains a vibrant point of solidarity and hope within the movements but it has become the focus of contention and criticism. Many activists consider it to be dominated by NGOs and to be "star-driven." Politicians have increasingly used the Forum for their agendas or to promote their parties. The expense of the forums is seen as limiting the input of the very people the attendees claim to represent. Poverty-stricken movements do not have the time or resources to have their voices heard in the discussions at the forum. Many of the social movement activists and smaller NGOs argue that the funds used for flying, food, and miscellaneous expenses would be better spent on the local level. Finally, many critics think that there is too much talking and not enough organizing for actions and long-term struggles.

The critics

The GJM is the subject of a great deal of controversy at many levels. *New York Times* columnist Thomas Friedman is probably the most glib critic of the "anti-globalization" movement but he is almost certainly the most widely read. His *The Lexis and the Olive Tree* (2000) was a best-seller. Friedman argues that there is no alternative to globalization. Rather than fight against it, people should find the "solutions and opportunities" that globalization creates. He does point out that processes of globalization do harm some people, but its rewards far outweigh its dislocations. Friedman discounts the ability of alter-globalizers to reach any consensus, much less achieve political power because economic globalization has helped so many people. Jagdish Bhagwati is another of the most persuasive critics of "anti-globalization" activists. He is a renowned economist whose views on "free trade" are respected worldwide. His *In Defense of Globalization* (2004) is sometimes quoted as the definitive rebuttal of the global justice movement. He argues that open-trade regimes increase economic growth and thus improve GDP, facilitate technology transfers, and reduce poverty. He attempts to decouple free trade from finance arguing that open capital markets are the real culprits in financial meltdowns like the Asian Crisis. He also correctly maintains that while international financial institutions do impose conditionalities, they are rarely enforced to the letter. He also maintains that the WTO has not yet been successful in reducing further tariffs on many of goods and services. While he discusses IFIs critically, he does not address how they coordinate demands for open capital markets, impose basically the same programs no matter the nation, and reinforce the status quo between the developed and developing worlds.

William Easterly is also a particularly cogent critic of alter-globalization movements, especially the anti–capitalist wing that he dismisses out of hand. Easterly is effective because he notes the limitations of the arguments and proscriptions of orthodox econo-mists as being incomprehensible to the common reader. He opposes shock therapy (a radical form of SAPs) in favor of more piecemeal policy changes that take into account local conditions. Moreover, he cautions that IFIs inflate potential positive results from conditionalities preparing the ground for opposition to neo-liberal programs. In contrast, he thinks that sensible policies that promote more open economies in the long run do produce economic growth and diminish inequalities. Most other academic critics of the GJM fall within this broad spectrum of critiques.

Institutional and governmental criticism of the GJM runs the gamut from the praise-worthy cooptation of slogans and ideas to vituperative name-calling. At the World Bank in July 2001 President George W. Bush had this to say about protesters against neo-liberal globalization: "make no mistake, those who protest free trade are no friends of the poor. Those who protest free trade seek to deny them their best hope for escaping poverty" (Bush, 2001). Former President Zedillo of Mexico claimed that activists "seem strangely determined to save the developing world from development" (Ibid.). Less than two weeks after 9/11 US Trade Representative Robert Zoellick laid the groundwork for a new McCarthyism aimed at GJM dissidents: "Terrorists hate the ideas America has championed around the world. ... it is inevitable that people will wonder if there are intellectual connections with others who have turned to violence to attack international finance, globalization, and the United States. ... " (Zoellick, 2001).

The US National Intelligence Assessment 2006 report warned: "Anti-US and anti-globalization sentiment is on the rise and fueling other radical ideologies. This could prompt some leftist, nationalist, or separatist groups to adopt terrorist methods to attack US interests." South African President Thabo Mbeki claimed that protesters at the World Summit on Sustainable Development were "anti-poor."[5] World Bank Director James Wolfensohn (1999–2003) argued that public services inevitably led to waste, and maintained that countries like Bolivia need to have a "a proper system of charging" for water or it will be wasted. The former Wall Street financier claimed bank-backed pri-vatization of the Cochabamba water system was by no means directed against the poor. In La Paz, Bolivia, protest leader Oscar Olivera responded: "In Mr. Wolfensohn's view, requiring families who earn $100 per month to pay $20 for water may be 'a proper system of charging'" (Schultz, 2000), but the thousands of people who filled the streets and shut down Cochabamba last week apparently felt otherwise.

More substantive critiques also argue that the empirical evidence undermines the arguments of the GJM. They often deploy a wide-range of statistics that show poverty has declined globally and that overall growth has been strong. Critics give globalization most of the credit for these positive developments. According to some data sets, the number of people surviving on less than a $1 per day has been reduced by half in the last two decades. Since World War II, child mortality has declined as life expectancy has increased. Per capita food supply has risen significantly and access to clean water, technology and education have also ticked upward. However, these statistics are not definitive for a variety of reasons, including the dates of analysis. Specifically, the start date of "economic globalization" is debatable (see especially Wesibrot et al., 2005). If the start date of 1945 or 1960 is used then growth rates are definitively higher but if 1980 is used they go down with the exception of China and India. These two countries also create problems in arguments from various vantage points because they constitute a large percentage of the world population, they are relatively closed economies (not as neo-liberalized as other states), and they started at a low level (meaning high growth numbers are easier to achieve). It is difficult to create data sets that are comparable on an international scale because there is no general agreement on measures of currency whether they are measured in current dollars, purchasing price parity, or some other yardstick. Finally, what can be attributed to neo-liberal policies and what to advances in the sciences, technology, and more democratically-responsive governments is difficult to disentangle.

On other fronts, the GJM is faulted for not actually creating alternatives, especially a one-size-fits-all model. It is considered to be "violent" because the Black Bloc and other groups have engaged in vandalism, rock throwing, and property destruction. Anarchists respond to this criticism by noting that they may commit property damage but states and IFI policies are violent towards humans, animals, and the ecosystem. Not surprisingly, many GJM NGOs side with the forces of order and increase the fragmentation within the movements. Some critics also argue that the GJM is "anti-American" because of its fierce opposition to war and imperialism as well as "anti-Semitic" because a segment of the movement is pro-Palestinian and highly critical of the Israeli government.

Within the GJM itself there are very vital debates and critiques. The lack of an ideological coherence is a weakness on a variety of fronts because it creates the impression that there is not one alternative[6] that is being pursued and, thus, no strategy for replacing the status quo. In response to this criticism, some activists argue that the movements are inherently reinventing democracy through new organizational forms from land squats to intentional autonomous spaces. In determining actions and strategy, new forms of organization have sprung forth: "spokescouncils, affinity groups, facilitation tools, breakouts, fishbowls, blocking concerns, vibe-watching and so on. ... " (Graeber, 2004). Despite the new forms, critics note there is no central manifesto, no "official spokespersons," and no party representation at national levels, making it difficult to shape and direct movement activities or present a consistent face to the mass media. This is particularly poignant given the fact that the GJM cannot even agree on whether they want to reform, destroy or transform IFIs. Local movements also have a difficult time persisting especially if they are single-issue campaigns and thus, splinter or collapse in the face of immediate successes or failures. Additionally, networks are generally weaker than hierarchical institutions especially in long-term campaigns. Furthermore, many movement activists chafe in the face of some well-funded NGOs who have little knowledge of local conditions, needs or even diversity of opinions. Rather than promote local interests, they have come to serve as "shock-absorbers" for IFIs, national governments, and the Global North. NGOs are eyed with some suspicion because philanthropies, religious groups, and governments with their own agendas typically fund them. Some have also been co-opted into public–private partnerships. Finally, they often lack transparency and their hierarchical structure is seen as being less than democratic.

World order and legitimation

Despite the criticisms raised above, it has become clear that global problems have increased significantly from the neo-liberals' halcyon days of the 1990s. The GJM has to meet the problems with critiques of how they arose but also how to ameliorate or solve their effects. While the US remains the dominant military power, its economy is no longer seen as a model for the rest of world nor can it resolve the problems of world economy as it attempted to do with the Bretton Woods institutions. The implosion of housing prices has reverberated across many economies because investors and bankers have had to swallow the losses. As financial risks rise, incentives for loans and investing decline, slowing economic growth. As the US Federal Reserve continues to keep inter-est rates low (increasing the potential for inflation), capitalists look to commodities to shore up their portfolios driving up prices in oil, food, minerals, and other raw materials on a world market that was much less protected from the 1980s onward.

The US economy has come to this precarious position as a result of both short and long-term causes. In the long term the financial sector has crowded out the manu-facturing base.[7] Manufacturing jobs historically paid better, were more unionized, and thus political resistance slowed the worst effects of "liberalization." The effects have been manifold because consumption now drives so much of the US economy. The Federal Reserve and deregulation allowed for two successive bubbles (technology and housing) to inflate in the US that allowed demand to increase, sustaining the GDP (two-thirds is consumption) and helping immensely for the rest of the world to grow at least at the macro-economic level. Yet, much of the growth was perverse because producers of exports to the US were also lending to the US in order to continue to sell consumer goods and meet US government expenditures. The world is now awash in dollar-denominated debt with little prospect of the US paying it back because its manufacturing base has shrunk and new capital investment in plant has been very low—almost all of it to replace old capital goods (Brenner 2006: pp. 338–39). The result is that the world no longer has a consumer of last resort.

In the short term, the real estate bubble is also part and parcel of financialization. Its bursting has obviously had ripple effects that will continue to emanate because new financial instruments and vehicles have been sold off in various tranches of mortgages bundled together and sold to investors all over the world. Formerly banks and other savings institutions carried much of this localized risk. Losses in one section of the country rarely caused decline in other regions though the Savings and Loan Crisis of the late 1980s certainly foreshadowed the worst to come. With even less regulation than in the 1980s, low interest rates, new types of loans and financial instruments, across the board misinformation, and the distribution of these risks to foreign investors, the unsus-tainable housing market began to crumble early in 2007 and has yet to reach a bottom. US banks and other financial institutions have been hit hard. Bankruptcies have increased including brand name firms like Bear Stearns, many of the largest banks have had to be recapitalized by foreign investors, and even Freddie Mac and Fannie Mae[8] are now in the hands of the US Treasury Department. European banks have also been affected. Northern Rock in the UK had to be rescued by the Bank of England. Switzerland's

UBS has lost $18.7 billion on subprime loans and received new capital from Singapore and the Middle East to bolster its balance sheet. Japan's Mizuho Financial recorded losses of $6 billion. In the short term, banks have access to cheap capital but are afraid to lend. The IMF has already reduced its projections for world growth. The policies that have affected the poor of the world have come home to roost in the heart of the financial system.

While bankers may lose a little sleep, they will not go home hungry. In contrast, many of the nations that have instituted SAPs are now experiencing resource protests and riots in the face of scarce food, high energy prices, and lower subsidies. Countries throughout Asia, Latin America, the Caribbean, and Africa have devoted much of their best land and financial incentives for cash crops including cotton, coffee, tea, tobacco, cocoa, and flowers with the intention of supplying the world market. For example, Kenya is growing flowers for the European market that is highly dependent on large supplies of water. This dries up water supplies and Kenyans produce less food. Likewise, Vietnam is now growing coffee for export instead of rice for consumption. Exports are used to offset debts incurred just prior to or during the period of economic globalization and to enrich the elites in the Global South. US-induced inflation, greater demand from China and India, biofuels, speculation in commodities including food, global warming, and petroleum-based agricultural practices have already contributed to high food prices. The market signals so cherished by the IFIs have distorted food production to the point that people are driven into the streets to demand sustenance. Similarly, most biofuels are grown through the use of petroleum that they are attempting to replace, driving up the price and taking up land that could be yielding food crops. All of these problems have been predicted by the GJM and they have consistently offered alternatives—see, for example, Via Campesina's recently published critique "An Answer to the Global Food Crisis: Peasants and Small Farmers Can Feed the World!" (La Via Campesina, 2008).

Economies that have not followed the Washington Consensus seem to undermine the legitimacy of its ideas but have their own structural problems. China and India's economies have grown rapidly in the recent decade. However, they have not implemented many of the structures of a neo-liberal economy. Their capital markets are comparatively closed. China has been very strategic about importing high technology, obtaining foreign direct investment, and has been able to exploit its labor to very great degree, in part, putting huge pressures on its agricultural sector. Yet, China will not likely be able to sustain the level of growth that has taken place so far because the US can no longer afford to purchase as much from it nor is its industrial system sustainable environmentally or socially. India has been able to develop from the Bangalore tech sector, outsourcing for the service sector (English-speakers that other developing nations do not have), and a more fully developed internal market that is part and parcel of its large population. It too has low labor costs and is sacrificing its agricultural sector in favor of growth. Russia is not particularly liberalized and would not have much growth without its oil. In all of these cases, rapid economic growth has been bad for the environment but this is historically the case no matter what the economic model. The GJM is particularly strong in India but not in China and Russia not because they are illiberal but more likely because of their authoritarian states.

The Global Justice Movement remains a vital force in local, national, regional, and international politics. Rising food prices, environmental destruction, global warming, an international credit crisis, and war continue to be intractable problems. Many people across the world have no other choice but to express dissent, riot, protest, and organize if their state, economy, and society have failed to nourish and protect them. The WTO rounds have been brought to a standstill with little hope of forward momentum. The

IMF has recently seen a massive wave of buyouts, doubling the projected number of employee departures signaling the lack of legitimacy and optimism in the organization. As noted previously, the World Bank has largely lost credibility. The ideas that have animated these institutions no longer seem to capture the imagination of political elites, at least, in the much of the Global South where nations have accumulated large current account balances to ward off any future impositions of conditionalities. The GJM, in contrast, has predicted much of the problems raised above, though perhaps not persuasively. They have an embarrassment of alternative models to address all of these problems. The strength of many of these movements appears to be increasing, especially at the local level. However, it remains to be seen whether they can unite, or whether they can and will take state power.

Notes

1 After Genoa, the *Tute Bianche* began to call themselves *Disobedienti*.
2 ATTAC grew out of a call by *Le Monde Diplomatique* for a Tobin Tax on all currency exchange transactions. While it began in France, national chapters sprang up quick in Europe after 1998. ATTAC addresses a broad range of issues and now has chapters in forty countries.
3 The groups split for various reasons. For example, in Jubliee South, the people actually experiencing the problems of debt and SAPs, argued that the G8 Gleneagles pledge of debt reduction for the poorest countries did not go far enough and had conditionalities along the lines of previous SAPs. Rather they demanded reductions if not reparations for past colonization and excessive debt payments. The northern Jubliees felt the pledges were a step forward.
4 A participatory budget is one in which citizens have a much larger influence on decisions, i.e., the budget is submitted to local councils and communities who are given specific powers to insert and veto parts of the budget as well as set priorities.
5 Most of the 20,000+ marchers in the protest on the final day of the summit were themselves poor. Mbeki's ANC counter-march was barely able to muster 3,000.
6 In fact, many in GJM do not advocate one solution but many autonomous approaches based on local conditions and history. This is reduced in one slogan to "One No, Many Yeses" (No to neo-liberal globalization and Yeses to variation in alternative model).
7 Finance, insurance and real-estate sector surpassed manufacturing in terms of value added to the GDP in 1987 and has increased since.
8 Freddie Mac and Fannie Mae are government-sponsored enterprises that were privatized in 1969. It guarantees or owns roughly half of all household mortgages in the US, worth about five trillion dollars. Foreign governments in Asia and Europe hold much of their debt but domestic governments as well. The US government was compelled to socialize this risk or the credibility of the US dollar and bonds would have been drastically undermined.

References

Bhagwati, J. (2004) *In Defense of Globalization*, New York: Oxford University Press.
Bello, W. (2002) *Deglobalization: Ideas for a New Economy*, London: Zed Books.
Bush, G. W. (2001) "Remarks by the President to the World Bank," World Bank, Washington, DC, July 17.
Brenner, R. (2006) *Economics of Global Turbulence*, London: Verso.
Cavanaugh, J. and Mander, J. (eds.) (2004) *Alternatives to Economic Globalization: A Better World is Possible*, San Francisco: International Forum on Globalization.
Edelman, M. (2003) "Transnational Peasant and Farmer Movements and Networks," in Kaldor, M., Anheier, H. and Glasius, M. (eds.) *Global Civil Society 2003*, New York: Oxford University Press, pp. 185–219.

Engler, M. (2008) *How To Rule the World: The Coming Battle Over the Global Economy*, New York: Nation Books.

Friedman, T. (1997) "Gephardt Vs. Gore," *New York Times*, April 3, p. A21.

——(1999) *The Lexus and Olive Tree*, New York: Farrar, Straus & Giroux.

Graeber, D. (2004) "The New Anarchists," in Mertes, T. (ed.) *A Movement of Movements: Is Another World Really Possible?* London: Verso.

La Via Campesina (2008) "An Answer to the Global Food Crisis: Peasants and small farmers can feed the world!" [online] Available at: http://www.viacampesina.org/main_en/index.php?option=com_content &task=view&id=525&Itemid=38 [Accessed September 1, 2008].

Notes from Nowhere (eds.) (2003) *We are Everywhere: The Irresistible Rise of Global Anticapitalism*, London: Verso.

Reitan, R. (2007) *Global Activism*, New York: Routledge.

Schultz, J. (2000) "Bolivian Protest Leader Heads To Washington," The Democracy Center, Cochabamba, April 13.

Starr, A. (2005) *Global Revolt: A Guide to the Movements Against Globalization*, London: Zed Books.

Weisbrot, M., Baker, D. and Rosnick, D. (2005) *Scorecard on Development: 25 Years of Diminished Progress* Washington, DC: Center for Economic and Policy Studies.

Zoellick, R. (2001) "American Trade Leadership: What is at Stake," speech presented at the Institute of International Economics, Washington, DC, September 24.

6

History and hegemony

The United States and twenty-first century globalization

Jan Nederveen Pieterse

The twenty-first century global landscape is that of a multipolar, multi-currency world. The United States, Europe, and Japan rode the previous wave of globalization during 1980–2000, but their lead in manufacturing, trade, finance, and international politics has been slipping. This shift is largest for the United States, the erstwhile hegemon and driver of the world economy. All advanced countries have become postindustrial economies that face increasing competition in the maelstrom of accelerated globalization, but only in the American case has this been combined with a mammoth trade deficit and foreign debt.

The twenty-first century represents a trend break. Patterns that defined late twentieth-century globalization are now fading, with American hegemony in decline, American capitalism teetering from its excesses and financial crisis undermining western financial institutions.

This discussion is a critical history of contemporary globalization through the lens of American hegemony, organized in three sections: empire, globalization, and the afterlife of hegemony.[1]

The first section discusses the upsurge of the idea of empire particularly during the rule of the neoconservatives in the George W. Bush administration. During this period the idea of empire loomed large, although the actual role of empire was limited and brief (in Afghanistan and Iraq).

The second section turns to the relationship between the United States and contemporary globalization. Through the 'American century' the US was the 'driver' of globalization, in two major phases, the postwar boom and the 1980–2000 period. In the twenty-first century, the American lead has been slipping away and this section takes up how American discourse and policy respond to this situation.

The third section probes specific questions about the decline and endgame of American hegemony. Will the United States be able to hold on to its financial lead, as did previous hegemons? Will the United States be able to use its vast military resources to prolong its hegemony? Will American decline reshuffle elites and thus be a source of hope that brings the United States back on a more balanced course?

Table 6.1 Phases of unequal power relations

1400 >	European reconnaissance and expansion
1600–mid-20C	Colonialism, imperialism, neocolonialism
1960s >	Contemporary accelerated globalization
1980–2000	Neoliberal globalization
2001 >	War on terrorism, preventive war

Table 6.2 International unequal relations of power

Empire	The political control by one polity over the internal and external policy of another
Imperialism	The pursuit of empire
Hegemony	The control of one polity over the foreign policy of another political entity
	In a Gramscian sense: international leadership based on legitimacy (agreed upon rules and fair procedures)
Dependency	Reliance of a state on economic and political support of a more powerful state, without formal control over internal or foreign policy

Empire as a metaphor

In the wake of the terrorist attacks of 9/11, the language and conduct of American politics changed markedly. A stream of articles and books referred to and at times recommended imperialism, for instance: 'the logic of neoimperialism is too compelling for the Bush administration to resist … a new imperial moment has arrived' (Mallaby 2002: 3). Robert Kaplan (2002) called for *Warrior Politics* and for militant foreign policy (Kaplan 2002). Michael Ignatieff (2002) deemed American imperialism necessary. Robert Cooper, a senior British diplomat, argued that in addition to 'voluntary imperialism' through the IMF and World Bank, 'what is needed is a new kind of imperialism, one compatible with human rights and cosmopolitan values', which he generously referred to as the 'export of stability' (Cooper 2002; see also Boot 2001). Until recently imperialism was a left-wing term, but now empire has become a mainstream theme and entered everyday language. In this climate, past empires were revisited and whitewashed, too (e.g. Ferguson 2002).

What is the difference between contemporary globalization and empire? This question could be waved away as academic hairsplitting or on the argument that contemporary globalization, no matter how it is packaged or phrased, is a form of domination. Yet, how it is phrased *does* matter in how and to what ends unequal power is exercised and in the agenda of social movements. If globalization equals empire all along, then what is different about the imperial turn?

The basic question is simple. Contemporary globalization, although it is multidimensional, has been primarily economically driven. From the 1980s the dominant project has been neoliberal globalization, so empire would mean a profound break, a U-turn that places state and political strategic interests rather than corporate interests in the forefront. Neoliberal ideology preaches lean and cheap government (though the US government was always a military-industrial complex and a strong security and law and order state) and empire means big government. Neoliberal globalization hinges on economics and finance whereas empire prioritizes geopolitics and military and political power. Neoliberal globalization and hegemony are intrusive, but empire is intrusive to a much greater degree.

Note an ordinary American newspaper report of August 2003:

As one of the 24 senior advisors with the Coalition Provisional Authority, the United States-led civilian administration of postwar Iraq, Dr Erdmann is charged with getting the higher education system back on its feet. While American policy puts the future of Iraqi academia in its own hands, the 20 universities and 43 technical schools must turn to Dr Erdmann for everything from rebuilding looted lecture halls to releasing their budgets. … Dr Erdmann, 36, has little experience in university administration …

(Asquith 2003)

And so forth. This is empire in action, and a bridge further than merely globalization or hegemony. Along with the stark innocence of the report's title, 'Righting Iraq's Universities', this illustrates the nitty-gritty of empire in action.

The brief periodization in Table 6.1 sets the stage historically and explains my use of terms. Definitions of basic terms – I deliberately opt for conventional definitions – set the stage analytically (Table 6.2).

From some points of view, the difference between globalization and empire is a non-question to begin with. Let me highlight four such perspectives on the relationship between capitalism and imperialism, which all use empire in a metaphorical sense: imperial corporations; economic imperialism; economics imperialism; and empire in the sense of Hardt and Negri. I then turn to the differences between imperialism and contemporary globalization.

Imperial corporations

This refers to transnational corporations that 'run the world' (e.g. Barnet and Cavanagh 1994; Korten 1995). The argument is that the turnover of large transnational corporations exceeds the GNP of most states and their operations range widely and across state borders. Joint operations of states and corporations, on the model of the East India Company, were part of the capitalist infrastructure of imperialism. Energy and mineral sectors in particular show long-standing patterns of joint state and corporate crossborder intervention, as in the case of the oil majors before World War Two and the postwar cooperation between metropolitan states, mineral conglomerates and arms industries (Aramco, Alcoa, Bechtel, Rio Tinto, etc.). Agribusiness, telecommunications, and banks have all been involved in strategic tie-ups of corporate and metropolitan designs.[2] International finance trails international development like a shadow.

The triad of governments, intergovernmental organizations, and corporations takes new shape in the United Nations' Global Compact, but in fact goes back to colonial regimes and the postwar development era (George 1977). Agribusiness has long been involved in international food policies, from American food aid to the Green Revolution. New technologies such as bioengineering give corporations a stake in WTO patenting regulations and intellectual property rights. The 'revolving door' between US government officials and major corporations and consultancy firms suggests a commonality of interests. The relative retreat of state regulation has been made up for by a role expansion of corporations – in the form of corporate self-regulation (an interesting model is Enron) and in the polite form of corporate citizenship and responsibility.

Yet, for all these interlocking interests, the idea of 'corporate imperialism' is a step too far and a contradiction in terms, for it implies nonstate actors undertaking political (not just economic) projects. Political control of the kind implied by empire is of little

economic significance and counterproductive in view of the responsibility and accountability it entails. Most transnational corporations can achieve their objectives without
control over sovereignty; economic influence of the type provided by the IMF, World
Bank, and WTO regulations suffices, along with lobbying and sponsoring political actors.
The interests of most corporations (such as financial services, advertising, pharmaceuticals,
software, and telecommunications) are of a non-territorial nature and those with territorial stakes (energy, mining, construction, weapons) are relatively few. Most foreign
direct investment is concentrated in North America, Europe, and Japan and a major
preoccupation of developing countries is to attract foreign investment. Countries that are
in high demand by investors can exact their conditions on investor entry and exit. While
corporations come and go, witness the Fortune 500, geopolitics requires a different type
of actor and project. The 'imperial CEO' is a figure of speech that refers to executives
who expand rather than manage their firms. To ascribe imperialism to corporations is to
trivialize the term, while disregarding the role of corporations and viewing it solely in
economic, apolitical terms is naïve.

Economic imperialism

A common view, almost a collective cliché in the Global South during past decades, is
that contemporary globalization is imperialism, recolonization or dependency by another
name.[3] Debt, conditionalities of the international financial institutions, and McDonaldization in the cultural sphere, all point in this direction. Domination is now exercised
through financial and economic regimes. Sanctions on Cuba, Plan Colombia and the
occasional invasion and bombing are outliers in this pattern.

Over time the shadow of empire has been gradually lengthening. Some of the literature on neoliberal globalization since the 1990s reinvokes empire, which usually involves
redefining empire in a looser sense. Thus, for Chalmers Johnson imperialism refers not
to 'the extension of one state's legal dominion over another' but to 'imposing one's
own social system' by various means. According to Michael Parenti, 'By "imperialism"
I mean the process whereby the dominant politico-economic interests of one nation
expropriate for their own enrichment the land, labor, raw materials, and markets of
another people'. In this treatment, the actor is 'politico-economic interests of one nation'
(not even transnational corporations) and the target is a people (not a state) (Johnson 2000:
19–20; Parenti 1995: 1; cf. Petras and Morley 1995; Petras and Veltmeyer 2001; Furedi
1994).

This builds on a body of literature that dates back to the Vietnam War and analyses
American hegemony and the cold war as imperialism. It typically takes us back to Manifest
Destiny and draws a picture of a more or less continuously aggressive and warlike role of
the United States, as in the work of William Appleman Williams and Noam Chomsky
(Williams 1962 and 1980; Chomsky 1993; see also Lefever 1999). Thus, according to
Howard Zinn, 'aggressive expansion was a constant of national ideology and politics'
(2001: 153). Cultural and postcolonial studies of a historical and interpretive nature have
also renewed the interest in imperialism (e.g. Said 1993).

These accounts are welcome antidotes to chauvinism, but they are not analytically
precise; they are pertinent, but not through the whole period. This approach homo-
genizes national ideology, ignores isolationist currents, and refers to dispositions rather
than outcomes. These views don't usually distinguish between economic regimes and
formal political control. In Nye's words, 'they mistake the politics of primacy for those of

Table 6.3 Empire as metaphor

Corporate imperialism	Transnational corporations
Economic imperialism	International financial institutions
Economics imperialism	Economism dominates policy
Empire (Hardt and Negri)	Metaphysics of power

empire' (2003: 70). Control exercised by the Wall Street IMF complex means control of *part* of domestic policy and not foreign policy, and thus falls short of empire. It is true, of course, that the line between economic and political control is fine. In shaping developing countries' economic policy, structural reforms wield incisive political influence; IMF conditionalities involve political components. Yet this is short of empire and quite different in terms of the *scope* of political influence, its legal *status* and ideological *justification*. These accounts overlook the multilateral framework and rules in which the US operated; neoliberal globalization is a rules-based order. By overusing imperialism, these accounts are short of words and reasons if empire *does* occur (as in the instances of Iraq and Afghanistan).

Economics imperialism

This refers first, in the words of the economist Ben Fine, to 'the colonisation of the other social sciences by economics' (2002). I think this claim is counterfactual because the influence of economics in social science has been limited (with rational choice in the United States as a major exception). Economics does dominate policy, but the blanket metaphor 'imperialism' is more hindrance than help. The charge of *economism* is more appropriate and effective. Hazel Henderson, among others, has long argued against economism and notes that 'The economism paradigm sees economics as the primary focus of public policy as well as individual and public choices'. In her view, 'economics, far from a science, is simply politics in disguise' (1996: 581, 582).

Empire

According to Michael Hardt and Antonio Negri, imperialism ended in the 1970s and was followed by a new constellation they call Empire and describe as follows:

> The concept of Empire is characterized by lack of boundaries: Empire's rule has no limits ... Second, the concept of Empire presents itself not as a historical regime originating in conquest, but rather as an order that effectively suspends history and thereby fixes the existing state of affairs for eternity. ... Third, the rule of Empire operates on all registers of the social order extending down to the depth of the social world ... The object of its rule is social life in its entirety.
>
> (2000: xiv–xv)

Conceptualizing globalization as Empire stretches the meaning of empire to the point of defining it *in contrast to* imperialism, which is confusing. This exercise combines features of Foucault (power is everywhere), Fukuyama (end of history) and Marcuse (hope lies with the multitude). Encompassing all space and existing outside history, Empire becomes a metaphysics of power, which is countered by a metaphysics of transcendence (by the multitude). If Empire is everywhere, it is nowhere. Even if one would follow this metaphysics, Hardt and Negri's account of the Empire of globalization as a 'smooth space' is as misplaced and misleading as Thomas Friedman's *Flat World*. Hardt and Negri's Empire is not an analytic but a poetic invocation that has attracted attention because of the trendiness of imperialism.

To sum up, Table 6.3 identifies several uses of empire as a metaphor. In these instances, 'empire' is used metaphorically, just as Habermas describing capitalist commodification and bureaucratization as the 'colonization of the life-world' uses colonization as a metaphor. As a metaphor, 'imperial' means domineering, aggressive, and expansive. 'Imperialism' is a fighting word that serves mobilizing purposes, but the question remains what fight, against what and how? Analytical and political clarity go together. These perspectives reflect two main strands: using empire as a metaphor and equating capitalism and imperialism.

In the latter view, differences between imperialism and contemporary globalization fade essentially because of reasoning by similes (capitalism = imperialism and capitalism = globalization, therefore globalization = imperialism). The equation capitalism = imperialism tells us little because circa 500 years of capitalism have not coincided with 500 years of imperialism – or, they have but only according to the crudest reading of history that skips over the non-imperial episodes. Lenin's definition of imperialism casts a long shadow. Lenin's classic definition, according to which the highest stage of capitalism (= monopoly capitalism) = imperialism, involves fundamental problems.[4] The assumption that empire is undertaken for the sake of and yields economic gain is simplistic and counterfactual (e. g. Fieldhouse 1973). While economic gain has been a propaganda point in defence of imperialism, it has often been disputed by business interests and political forces. Equating capitalism = imperialism = globalization = neoliberal globalization creates a transhistorical soup in which nothing essentially changes over, well, two to five hundred years.[5] If nothing really changes, then why bother to analyze at all?

Dispositional definitions of empire, as Michael Doyle points out, fail to explain if the outcome (empire) does *not* come about (1986). The bouillabaisse approach, viewing history as a stew with everything mixed in, and the failure to use precise terms, make it impossible to identify different periods, designs, and configurations. If the new imperialism of the late-nineteenth century, the cold war, neoliberal globalization and present times are all empire, in what then resides the difference between these periods? At minimum we would have to define different *types* of empire, at which point we are back to square one.

If there were concertation among diverse actors, contemporary globalization might yield a new imperialism, but in view of the diversity of actors this is unlikely. This is the point of conventional arguments against new empire; as Richard Haass, the former director of policy planning at the State Department points out, the contemporary diffusion of power and resistance, covert and overt, is too great (2001). Moreover, a Washington cliché during the Clinton administration was that the cost of major war exceeds its benefits: 'war may have become a luxury that only the poor peoples of the world can afford' (Brzezinski 1997: 213). During the George W. Bush administration, the era of the neoconservatives, this view apparently changed.

Social movements of the 1990s, local and transnational, targeted neoliberal globalization, not empire; though they occasionally use the imperialism metaphor their aims and methods are fundamentally different from the decolonization movements. Examples are the Zapatistas and the World Social Forum. Contemporary globalization, according to the Jamaican economist Clive Thomas, represents a paradigm shift. Analyzing neo-liberal globalization *without* invoking imperialism is more effective analytically and politically (Thomas 2000).[6] This targets unequal relations of power exercised through economic regimes and ideologies – coinciding with shifts in technology, production, and politics, implemented through international institutions and short of political control over sovereignty.

I think the blanket equation contemporary globalization = imperialism is confusing, not because imperialism is 'directional', while globalization is not. Globalization, too, is directional; it is multi-directional since it involves many actors, each with diverse projects. I reject it not because, as Anthony Giddens argues, imperialism refers to an intentional and systematic endeavour, whereas globalization is more complex: 'a dialectical process because ... local happenings may move in obverse direction' (1990: 64). Imperialism too was dialectical and local processes moved in multiple directions; thus in the *pericentric* theory of imperialism, the turbulent periphery plays a central role (Fieldhouse 1965) and real imperialism has a web-like and multi-centric character. Both imperialism and contemporary globalization are intentional and involve multiple actors. Yet contemporary globalization is marked by a greater diffusion of power, including international institutions and NGOs.

A further argument for rejecting globalization = imperialism is that globalization is plural: *globalizations*; i.e. there are multiple globalization projects and designs – from corporate globalism to feminist and human rights globalization, etc. – so generalizations based on just one mode of globalization are not tenable. In addition, from taking a historical angle on globalization it follows that empire is a *phase* of globalization (as is decolonization). Contemporary globalization means not just Westernization but also Easternization, as in the influence of Japanese and East Asian forms of capitalism. Besides, 'the West' is not unified.

In sum, empire is primarily of a political nature, state-centered, and territorial and involves central authority, while late-twentieth-century accelerated globalization is intrinsically multidimensional, involves multiple actors and is in significant respects decentered and deterritorial, involving multiple and diverse jurisdictions. Imperialism often sought (unsuccessfully) to impose a clear division between colonizer and colonized; in contemporary globalization, the lines of inclusion and exclusion are blurred.

The United States and globalization

> Globalization was something the rich countries did to the rest of the world – for the good of all, of course. Now it is beginning to feel like something someone else is doing to them.
>
> (Philip Stephens, 2007)

We can distinguish two main periods in the relation between the United States and contemporary globalization. In phase one, broadly from 1945 to 2000, the US drives globalization. Globalization seems to be a synonym for westernization and Americanization, with familiar shorthand such as Coca Colonization and McDonaldization. In phase two, the US is no longer in charge and the post-American world has begun to unfold.

What is the relationship between phase one and phase two? This question matters because explanation informs policy. Let's consider American perspectives on globalization before and after. This discussion takes up shifts in discourse and then turns to policy, where variation, so far, is much narrower. In considering this we should place the US alongside other advanced regions, Europe and Japan.

American hegemony has been in decline for some time. This has been a phased process, from a 'signal' decline in the 1970s (marked by the end of the Bretton Woods system, stagflation, and defeat in Vietnam) to a terminal decline in the twenty-first century, as Giovanni Arrighi argues (2007). Conservative overreach, giving free rein to neoconservatives, culminating in the wars of Iraq and Afghanistan, has hastened the passing of American power. This overreach itself stems from 35 years of backlash political culture, the kind of conservatism that I characterize as Dixie politics (Nederveen Pieterse 2008b).

When the Cold War ended, the USSR was gone and the 'unipolar moment' set in, American superpower and military confidence went into overdrive and so did American capitalism. American 'free enterprise' capitalism shaped the period of neoliberal globalization from 1980 to 2000. During this period the United States was the main driver and beneficiary of globalization and led the way in the liberalization of trade and capital markets via the WTO, Nafta, and the structural adjustment policies of the IMF and World Bank. The United States promoted the hyper-mobility of capital that led to the diagnosis of casino capitalism; it promoted the liberalization of capital markets and the intellectual property rights regimes that benefited the outward investment strategies of American multinationals, institutionalized in the WTO, Nafta, and bilateral trade agreements. The financial crises that came with the liberalization of capital markets and the opening of economies were used to discipline emerging markets.

During the 1990s the American economy seemed to defy gravity; its long-sustained boom made Anglo-American neoliberalism the global economic standard, the dollar the world currency and the Washington consensus the arbiter of economic orthodoxy. In the 1990s the American economy was sheltered from crisis by the new economy boom – which bust by 2000; it was sheltered by Wall Street financial engineering – which produced the Enron and Anderson scandals in 2001; it was buffered and sheltered by the easy credit regime of Alan Greenspan's Federal Reserve – which produced the housing and credit bubble that burst in August 2007. The financial crisis of 2007–8 marks the end of an era.

In the early years of the twenty-first century the American leads slipped away one by one and the 2007–8 financial crisis reveals that the American performance was all along sustained by a series of 'fixes' that merely postponed, and eventually deepened, the reckoning to come. The financial crisis marks the end of an era – the long American boom; the end of a doctrine – neoliberalism; and the end of an economic and political hegemony.

Now 'the rest' comes to the rescue. It is almost a reversal of the pattern of the 1990s – then financial crises in emerging markets and the IMF imposing its rules and conditions to discipline 'crony capitalism'. Then the IMF and World Bank imposed structural adjustment, now they undergo structural adjustment. Strapped for funds, the IMF stays afloat by letting go 590 staff (2008). Now the crisis is in the US and Europe, exposing crony capitalism in banking and emerging markets are safe havens and their sovereign wealth funds come to the rescue.

In the Global South, American-led globalization elicited cautious and defensive responses of selective or strategic globalization or deglobalization (e.g. Bello 2003). Now gradually the tide has been turning in the United States.

A recent opinion poll showed that 58 percent of Americans think globalization is bad for the US and just 28 percent think it has helped America. Ten years ago there was a narrow majority in favour of globalization. … Democratic presidential candidates are taking an increasingly sceptical line against free trade. Republicans rail against illegal immigration.

(Rachman 2008)

With this come populist responses – Lou Dobbs and 'Dobbsism' or blaming immigrants for taking American jobs; blaming the Chinese currency; and blaming 'free trade' and globalization. American protest at rising energy and food prices, pain at the pump and at the supermarket, reflects a situation where median income has barely risen in decades, although prices have been rising steadily, particularly for health care and education. Thus, arguably, much of the disquiet is a response to steeply rising social inequality in the United States – which has little or nothing to do with 'globalization' per se.

Richard Longworth's study of how globalization has affected the American Midwest (2007) highlights deindustrialization, the decline of manufacturing exports and its effects in Detroit and Flint, Michigan and Gary, Indiana. The Midwest has benefited from the rise of agro-industry and agro exports, but since this mostly concerns large-scale farming, most small towns in the Midwest have been suffering and declining as much as the old industrial centers do.

Technology plays a key part in accounts such as Friedman's *The World is Flat* and in global political economic accounts in which technological change produces skills differentials which lead, in turn, to inequality. Thus, according to Jagdish Bhagwati (2007), 'technology, not globalization, is driving wages down'. Technology changes the relationship between capital and labour to the advantage of capital. Technological change is no doubt a contributing factor to the 'rise of the rest', but can it explain the decline of the United States? Germany, Scandinavia, and Japan have fared well with technological change and prospered. South Korea, China, and India have benefited tremendously from technological change. There is no reason *per se* why this should be different in the case of the United States.

Free trade, too, is often mentioned as a major reason why the US has lost in globalization. In this argument free trade has facilitated foreign competition from low wage economies and cost the US jobs, lowered wages, and worsened labour conditions. However, that the US has become import dependent is not due to free trade. Trade liberalization has, allegedly, brought development and prosperity to several developing countries, especially in East and Southeast Asia. The problem of the US is deindustrialization, not trade policies.

At times immigration is mentioned as a variable. Renewal of the American labour market through immigration has been the envy of Europe and the world and a factor in the vitality of the US economy. It has prompted recurrent nativism, but does it make sense to explain the transition from phase one to phase two to immigration? The argument that immigrants lower wages for American workers has been disproved too (Borjas 2005).

2007–8 brings 'the worst market crisis in sixty years'. According to George Soros, 'what former US president Ronald Reagan called the magic of the market place … I call market fundamentalism' (2008: 6). The new refrain is that 'the market cannot heal itself', 'The market no longer has all the answers', The 'global adjustment will be long and painful' (Skapinker 2008; Münchau 2008).

Tackling the crisis requires large-scale action. The turning point was the $29 billion bailout of Bear Stearns. In the words of Martin Wolf, 'Remember Friday, March 14 2008: it was the day the dream of global free market capitalism died. For three decades we have moved towards market-driven financial systems. … (Now) Deregulation has reached its limits'. The tide has turned in favour of regulation. Martin Wolf – senior economist at the *Financial Times* and an advocate of free market globalization – now argues that 'financial regulation is both difficult and essential' and speaks of 'seven habits that finance regulators must acquire'. The starting point, according to Wolf, is 'recognising that even the recent past is a foreign country' (2008). What is at issue is 'the fall of a financial model'. According to Barney Frank, chairman of the House financial services committee, 'the results are in on America's 30-year experiment with radical economic deregulation … it is clear that market forces have produced too much inequality and government has not adequately used its capacity to mitigate the impact of these forces' (2008).

According to a *Wall Street Journal* headline, 'Political pendulum swings toward stricter regulation'. 'The idea that less regulation is better for the economy has held sway in Washington since the Reagan administration. Now that consensus is crumbling' (Williamson 2008). In international finance, the talk is to rectify the shortcomings of the Basel I capital regime adopted in 1988, in a Basel II that will 'enhance capital regulation, supervision, risk management and market transparency' (Wellink 2008). Köhler, the former director of the IMF and now president of Germany, calls the banking sector a 'monster' (ibid.).

According to Michael Lind, in the US and throughout the western world the center of political gravity has moved left. 'The decline of libertarianism and the revival of populism are already reshaping politics in the US and similar societies. What formerly was the left – welfare state liberalism – is once again the centre. To its left (in economic, not social terms) is protectionist populism; to its right, neoliberalism … Now the line is: in order to save free-market globalism from populists preying on middle-class economic anxieties, we must expand the middle class welfare state' (Lind 2007).

Arguably this is what Lawrence Summers, the former US Treasury secretary, seeks to do in two articles in the *Financial Times*. 'In a world where Americans can legitimately doubt whether the success of the global economy is good for them' the challenge is to devise a new internationalism. The focus, according to Summers, must shift 'to designing an internationalism that more successfully aligns the interests of working people and the middle class in rich countries with the success of the global economy' (2008a). 'A strategy to promote healthy globalization' involves domestic efforts to reduce inequality and an international approach that balances the priorities of global corporations with 'the interests of working people in all countries'. This entails global cooperation in the international tax arena, combating tax havens and international cooperation to prevent harmful regulatory competition and working towards raising standards, i.e. environmental and labour standards (2008b).

Indian economists criticize Summers' approach. They argue, first, 'The problem Mr Summers identifies, the hyper-mobility of capital was an outcome that he and the US actively promoted'. Second, 'That globalization needs appropriate regulation is hardly in doubt. But blaming globalization preponderantly for the ills of American workers runs the risk of providing an alibi for the sins of omission in domestic policy that have had a much bigger impact'. Third, he 'presents the rise of the poorer parts of the world … more as a threat than an opportunity to the US. In effect, globalisation is justified only when it serves American interests' (Kapur et al. 2008).

This is an interesting point: globalization is cast as the scapegoat of unruly capitalism. But is the issue globalization, or *how* globalization is being used? In retrospect it was American companies' foreign direct investment strategies that caused the tide to turn. American outward investment meant, conversely, *underinvestment in the US*. This is probably the most problematic part of the American equation. The usual allegation is public neglect ('private wealth, public squalor') which is the definition of laissez-faire; but actually the issue is not just public neglect but *private neglect*, through decades of under-investment in American productivity, technology, and new plants and products at a time when corporate profits were rising steadily and steeply – but increasingly from overseas investments. This, too, precipitated the American current account crisis – because American exports became imports, the trade deficit deepened, and the external deficit multiplied, eventually to unsustainable levels. The issue then is not just what but *how*. How have American institutions and American corporations utilized and deployed the American lead in globalization and its extraordinary advantages, especially during 1980–2000? Outward investment in low wage countries has been ordinary, also for companies in Europe and Japan. Yet Europe and Japan show that globalization can be combined with domestic, inward investment in new plants and new products and technological innovation. The United States differs from the other advanced economies in, at least, these respects: a vast trade deficit, a vast current account deficit, a low savings rate, and a gigantic hegemonic apparatus.

Outsourcing increasingly involves middle management jobs. Offshoring and outsourcing have been general trends in the US, Europe, and Japan. But there are major differences between American and European and Japanese approaches. Many European and Japanese producers have *also* continued to invest in new production technologies and plants at home, so German, Scandinavian, and Japanese firms continue their industrial exports. Hence European and Japanese trade balances are not as negative as the American, also because there is less emphasis on consumption and credit. Domestic savings in the euro zone have been 12 per cent of disposable income and in the US about 2 per cent (Clark 2004) until in 2005 personal savings turned negative for the first time since the Depression.

'Globalization' is a lightning rod – to divert attention from social problems; globalization is a scapegoat – channelling energies to remote targets; globalization is a smokescreen – the real problem is how corporations and governments use the opportunities that globaliza-tion affords. Accordingly, we need to shift the problem: the problem is not globalization; globalization simply refers to growing worldwide interconnectedness. The problem is why in some countries globalization comes with decreasing inequality and in others with increasing inequality. The issue is not what, but how, i.e. the political economy scripts and in the subtext of globalization. This kind of analysis brings politics back in.

The problem then is not globalization but neoliberal globalization or laissez-faire capitalism. Deregulation and fewer rules for corporations, the retreat of the state or a smaller role for government in mitigating the social impact of globalization and its failure to play a role in coordinating the labour market, economic change, and industrial policy and educational policies; all these have created conditions in which it has been easy for American corporations to have abrogated their social responsibility. As Milton Friedman argued, the only responsibility of corporations is to make money. Now it is clear that we might add: and it doesn't matter where.

The afterlife of hegemony

> Above all, we cannot stop long-term shifts in the economic and strategic balances, because by our economic and social policies we ourselves are the very artificers of these futures changes; we can no more stop the rise of Asia than we can stop the winter snows and the summer heat.
>
> (Paul Kennedy, 2001: 78)

Well into the twenty-first century, the idea that American hegemony is declining is no longer controversial in the United States. This awareness has entered common sense, is commented on in mainstream magazines and is the theme of mainstream books. Fareed Zakaria refers to the 'post-American world' and to 'the rise of the rest' (2008). American decline poses several questions: does it usher in hegemonic rivalry or a transition toward a new hegemon? As a fading hegemon can the US hold on to its financial lead, as did the United Provinces and Britain, and can it sustain its military supremacy?

Will American decline lead to a new era of hegemonic rivalry and wars of succession, as in 1870–1945, or is an altogether different configuration in the making? Complex interdependence and interweaving of economies, technologies, and polities across the world is now so extensive that a retreat to national economies or regional blocs is much less viable than it was in the early twentieth century or in George Orwell's *1984* (with Oceania, Eurasia, and Eastasia). Complex interdependence, high-density globalization and, on the other hand, hegemonic rivalry between nations or regional blocs are not compatible.

This does not imply that what lies ahead is, for instance, a cohesive global Davos elite, as in the thesis of the transnational capitalist class. A transnational Davos elite could come with a straightforward global rift between the World Economic Forum and the World Social Forum. Local, national, and regional interests, however, are deeply anchored; a case in point is the Chinese business elite that has not taken up a 'Davos outlook' (Yan 2008). So more realistic are in-between configurations in which national and regional interests and policies matter, interspersed with technological interweaving, transnational corporate links and civil society networks; complex, layered patterns of competition and cooperation, and cooperation through competition.

Will the United States be able to hold on to its financial lead, as did previous hegemons? The United States faces major drains on its financial resources: because of rapid deindustrialization it has become an importer on a vast scale (unlike twentieth-century Britain), owes interest on a massive debt (unlike the United Provinces) and spends most of its treasury on the military (like sixteenth- and seventeenth-century Spain). The United States has experienced rapid erosion of its reserves; even after a weaker dollar makes its exports more competitive, it lacks the production capacity for recouping this massive drain. Although the declining dollar whittles away the United States debt, it is unlikely that the bulk of the debt will ever be repaid. The United States has been waging war on credit, like twentieth-century Britain, and, as in Britain's case, financial vulnerability augurs decline.

Will the United States be able to use its vast military resources to undertake 'accumulation by dispossession' and thus prolong its hegemony? Timothy Garton Ash notes, 'When the next recession comes along, it will be no use sending for the marines' (2005). The quagmires of Iraq and Afghanistan illustrate the limited utility of military force and the limitations of American armed forces in ground warfare.[7] In Michael Lind's words, 'The US remains the only country capable of projecting military power throughout the world. But unipolarity in the military sphere, narrowly defined, is not preventing the rapid development of multipolarity in the geopolitical and economic arenas – far from it. And the other great powers are content to let the US waste blood and treasure on its doomed attempt to recreate the post-World War One British imperium in the Middle East' (2005).

Whether American military might is an asset or a liability is not a straightforward question. It may be both, in different arenas. American military specialization has its price –

institutionally, in tilting government and government spending toward the security apparatus; economically, by converting private enterprises into government military contractors; ideologically, by sustaining the superpower syndrome; and culturally, by sustaining a brawny garrison state culture. Military force is a temptation; if you have a hammer every problem looks like a nail. American military specialization and deindustrialization are to a certain extent correlated and have precipitated the rise of other forces. Germany and Japan experienced 'economic miracles' once they let go of their military-industrial specialization. In Japan's case it was recruited as an industrial supply platform in the American cold war network, beginning with the Korean War. The United States has been experiencing the reverse. American deindustrialization has been correlated with Asian industrialization. By promoting export-oriented growth and relocating garment, electronics, and high-tech plants in the Asian tiger economies, American multinationals reaped super profits, acquired cheap consumer products, and boosted Asian industrialization. As a corollary American corporations neglected inward investment and the United States gradually yielded its share of global manufacturing to Asia and in the process jacked up its trade deficit. This Pacific Rim symbiosis is now at the point that American trade and current account deficits have become unsustainable and for Asian vendors the risks of holding surplus dollars have begun to outweigh the benefits. American decline, then, is an unintended side effect and by product of American hegemony. The economies of Europe and Japan are more balanced; here companies did not enjoy the perks of hegemony – with Washington institutions paving the way for overseas investments, IMF and World Bank policies backing the Commerce department, and Pentagon contracts shielding their back, along with the dollar as world reserve currency.

American geopolitics and attempts to prolong the unipolar moment have reinforced this shift. 'America's military bark is louder than its economic bite' (Varzi 2007). The preoccupation with strategic primacy leaves the terrain to industrial newcomers and leaves space for industrial development in emerging economies, just as in the early twentieth century when Argentina, Brazil, and other countries industrialized because the great powers were distracted by rivalry and war. Likewise: 'If and when the US finally lifts its gaze from the Middle East, it will find itself facing a much better placed and more formidable China' (Rachman 2007). China emerges as the beneficiary of globalization and as the real winner of the war on terrorism (Arrighi 2007: 295, 301). This makes sense if we add, beyond the Iraq war, the Asian crisis. What is at issue in the twenty-first century turn to the east is the failure of both neoliberalism and neoconservatism – the two faces of American hegemony.

All advanced countries have been navigating the transition to a postindustrial economy and face increasing competition brought about by accelerated globalization. But only in the American case has this been combined with laissez-faire (i.e. no national economic policy), Dixie capitalism (low taxes, low services, no unions), military specialization (brawn over brain), a vast trade deficit and gargantuan debt – all factors that weaken the US' long-term position.

The global picture is mixed. Some countries have an interest in continuing American hegemony of a kind; Asian exporters continue to depend on the American market and continue their vendor financing while others continue to view American military specialization as a savings on their defence budgets; yet the overall trend is away from US influence. The instability that the US has been creating is gradually producing a 'dispensable nation'.[8] The multipolar, multi-currency world that has been taking shape involves a shift in the global scenery in which the background becomes foreground, and vice versa. American dramas that used to be influential in the course of the American century are becoming less salient.

The walkout by developing countries of the WTO ministerial meeting in Cancún in 2003 followed by the failure of the Free Association of the Americas talks in 2004 illustrates the changing climate. The emergence of a new grouping of developing countries – the G22 led by Brazil, South Africa, China, and India – indicates growing clout, as if resuming the momentum of the Movement of Non-Aligned countries, at least in trade talks. At the international climate talks in Bali in December 2007, the message of delegates to the United States was blunt: provide leadership, or follow, or else get out of the way (Fuller and Revkin 2007: 1).

How will the US deal with decline? Can the US recover and climb back? John Gapper notes, 'At times I wonder whether the world's biggest economy has the will to solve its challenges or will end up wandering self-indulgently into the minor economic leagues. I expect it will get serious when the crisis is too blatant to ignore, but it has not done so yet' (2008).

It is not just a matter of redirecting government spending from military expenditure to infrastructure, education, and innovation – although that is essential. There are deeper problems. One is a prima donna mindset and a number one status complex. The US is a de facto dependent economy – dependent on imports, on energy, and on foreign lenders. John Zogby has devoted surveys to the 'downsizing of the American dream' and finds that Americans are recognizing that there are limits to how much they can or should consume, to how much their economy can grow, and to American power in the world. 'My surveying shows that we are in the middle of a fundamental reorientation of the American character away from wanton consumption and toward a new global citizenry in an age of limited resources. Beneath the surface, I have found, millions of us live in quiet acceptance of the new boundaries that have been placed on us' (Zogby 2008, quoted in Berfield 2008). This already deals with the next phase: how are Americans coming to terms with no longer being number one?

The financial crisis of 2008 brings American dilemmas into sharp focus and poses several problems. Initially in September 2008, the talk focused on the bailout of American banks, but this soon changed to the financial crisis spreading and more serious interventions on the agenda, possibly including reorganizing the system of international finance.

Karl Kraus described psychoanalysis as a symptom of the disease that it claims to be the remedy of. This also applies to the bailout and financial crisis management. The bailout of banks in the US and beyond is, first, a symptom of financialization of economies, or the financial sector crowding out the main street economy. During the past twenty years financial rents garnered an ever larger share of profits and revenues at the expense of wages and salaries. Infusing another $1 trillion (and counting) into the American financial sector adds to the ongoing financialization. Second, financial fixes have papered over American economic problems at least since the 1970s (beginning with the decoupling of the dollar and gold in 1971). Most fixes have cheapened credit and provided easy money by lowering interest rates or other maneuvers, particularly during Alan Greenspan's tenure at the Federal Reserve. In turn this built the American bubble, layer by layer. Subprime mortgages were the latest layer, until the bailout became the most recent pyramid scheme annex.

Third, each financial fix set the stage for the next economic problem. Interest rate cuts papered over the dotcom bust, but easy money generated the real estate bubble, and the housing bubble paved the way for the subprime mortgage crisis, and so forth. Fourth, the assumption is that as the problem is financial, fixing finance will fix the economy, which, again, mistakes the symptom for the remedy. Fifth, the attention focused on the $700 billion bailout (of AIG) is overblown. Just a week before the bailout, in September 2008, Congress approved $680 billion for the Pentagon; just a routine allocation, barely mentioned and not discussed in the media. This excludes spending for wars in Iraq and Afghanistan which are dealt with in supplemental budgets. This indicates fundamental misallocations in government spending.

Skipping details, the key problems of the American economy are threefold. The main problem is underinvestment: lack of investment in new plants and technologies has been a major cause of job loss and of the vast trade deficit and hence the massive and growing foreign debt; this is a pattern that has been built up over almost three decades. Rather than investing in industries at home, many American corporations have preferred to invest in low wage zones and have enjoyed the perks of hegemony, with supportive Treasury, IMF and World Bank policies, the dollar as world reserve currency, and so forth. A major reason why European and Japanese companies have, by and large, maintained a balance between outward and inward investment is that they have had neither the advantages nor the temptations of hegemony. The second major American problem is lack of a national economic policy. Or, more precisely, the (partly hidden) link between the Pentagon and Wall Street was the default national economic policy, but it was crony capitalism and a tad inefficient. The third problem is deregulation, in effect easing the way for crony capitalism.

This implies a sequence and priorities. You can re-regulate, but that doesn't amount to a national economic policy. You can have a national economic policy but that, per se, won't fix private sector underinvestment. Comments note the ironies of the bailout: 'Remarkably, the country that prides itself on being the beacon of free enterprise finds itself with a financial system that needs government money to finance the most important asset most Americans will ever own' (Norris 2008: C1) and 'The de facto nationalization of Fannie Mae and Freddie Mac by a pro-market Republican administration is a U-turn of huge proportions' (Plender 2008: 22). Yet this is merely financial fixing. Merely fixing finance risks aggravating a symptom of economic malaise, while leaving the problems of the economy untouched and thus setting the stage for the next crisis. An underlying problem is that 'money without policies is a waste'. This is how the managing director of the IMF comments on US policies (while sternly noting that 'conditionality is part of our business') (Strauss-Kahn 2008).

Thomas Friedman notes, 'the point is, we don't just need a bailout. We need a build-up. We need to get back to making stuff, based on real engineering not just financial engineering' (Friedman 2008: WK11). The American picture is composite and confused, uneven and in flux. The 'church of free trade' is no more (Greider 2007: 12). In one domain neoliberal globalization is repudiated and its demise is noted whereas in another, 'economic freedom' continues to be celebrated – as in the annual Index of Economic Freedom, the ratings guide released by the Heritage Foundation in cooperation with the *Wall Street Journal*.

The 2008 elections have been part of the reassessment. Normally, elections are transactional politics rather than transformational politics. But these are exceptional times. Conservative and neoconservative overreach have brought the country, and the world, to the brink of disaster. Course corrections and an economic stimulus are in the cards, though financial crisis narrows the margins of manoeuvre. Bringing the American economy back to life however requires much deeper interventions and a fundamental overhaul of perspectives and policies. The larger problem is to redirect private investment, which touches on the central nervous system of American capitalism, according to which corporate self interest is an invisible hand that guides the economy. However, since corporate self interest leads to the shores of the Pearl River Delta, the research parks of Bangalore and the offshore havens of the Caribbean, this is no longer valid, or it is, but no longer in the sense that 'what is good for GM is good for America'.

As noted before, what is at issue at the turn of the twenty-first century turn is the failure of both neoliberalism and neoconservatism – the two faces of American hegemony. Thus, in sum, the turn of the twenty-first century brings the end of a financial model – the model of financialization and new financial instruments without appropriate insight and oversight; the end of an economic model – neoliberalism or the idea that the market knows best and knows better than institutions; and the end of American hegemony – giving way to an era of multipolarity.

Notes

1 This treatment draws on several related publications. The section 'Empire as a metaphor' draws on Chapter 3 of my book *Globalization or Empire?* The sections 'The United States and globalization' and 'Afterlife of hegemony' draw on my book *Is There Hope for Uncle Sam?* (2008b) and other recent work (Nederveen Pieterse 2008a; Nederveen Pieterse and Rehbein 2009).
2 Examples are the role of ITT with the CIA in the overthrow of the Allende government in Chile, the United Fruit Company and US exploits in Central America, and so forth (cf. Horowitz 1969).
3 An example is Mohammadi and Absan 2002. Some consider development policies as recolonization since they are externally imposed. According to Edward Goldsmith, what Marxists refer to as 'imperialism' and what western governments today call 'development' amount to much the same thing (2002). A rejoinder is that development is not merely externally imposed but owned as much by the Global South.
4 A detailed discussion is Nederveen Pieterse 1989: chapter 1.
5 If we add radical anti-development perspectives, the equation widens and reads modernization = Westernization = capitalism = globalization = imperialism.
6 This kind of literature is much more common (e.g. Falk, Chossudovsky, MacEwan, and many others).
7 On the limited utility of military force see British Rtd Gen. Rupert Smith 2007.
8 A new world order is indeed emerging—but its architecture is being drafted in Asia and Europe, at meetings to which Americans have not been invited. ... Today the evidence of foreign co-operation to reduce American primacy is everywhere—from the increasing importance of regional trade blocs that exclude the United States to international space projects and military exercises in which the United States is conspicuous by its absence.

(Lind 2005)

References

Arrighi, G. (2007) *Adam Smith in Beijing*. London: Verso.
Ash, T. G. (2005) 'In the path of the storm', *Guardian Weekly*, October 7–13: 5.
Asquith, C. (2003) 'Righting Iraq's universities', *New York Times Education Life*, August 3.
Barnet, R.J. and Cavanagh, J. (1994) *Global Dreams: Imperial Corporations and the New World Order*. New York: Simon & Schuster.
Bello, W. (2003) *Deglobalization: Ideas for a New World Economy*. London: Zed.
Berfield, S. (2008) 'The American dream, downsized', *Business Week*, September 8: 92.
Bhagwati, J. (2007) 'Technology, not globalisation, is driving wages down', *Financial Times*, April 1.

111

Boot, M. (2001) 'The case for American empire', *Weekly Standard*, October 15.

Borjas, G. J. (2005) 'Globalization and immigration', in M. M. Weinstein (ed.) *Globalization: What's New?* New York: Columbia University Press, 77–96.

Brzezinksi, Z. (1997) *The Grand Chess Game: American Primacy and its Geostrategic Imperatives.* New York: Basic Books.

Chomsky, N. (1993) *Year 501: The Conquest Continues.* Cambridge, MA: South End Press.

Clark, N. (2004) 'The struggle to get Europeans to do their duty and spend', *International Herald Tribune*, July 22.

Cooper, R. A. (2002) 'Why we still need empires', *Observer*, April 7.

Doyle, M. (1986) *Empires.* Ithaca, NY: Cornell University Press.

Ferguson, N. (2002) *Empire: The Rise and Demise of the British World Order and the Lessons for Global Power.* New York: Basic Books.

Fieldhouse, D. K. (1965) *The Colonial Empires.* New York: Delacorte.

——(1973) *Economics and Empire 1830–1914.* London: Weidenfeld and Nicolson.

Fine, B. (2002) 'Economics Imperialism and the New Development Economics as Kuhnian Paradigm Shift?', *World Development*, 30, 12: 2057–70.

Frank, B. (2008) 'Why America needs a little less laissez-faire', *Financial Times*, January 14.

Friedman, T. L. (2000) *The Lexus and the Olive Tree: Understanding Globalization.* New York: Anchor Books. 2nd edn.

——(2005) *The World is Flat.* New York: Farrar, Straus, and Giroux.

——(2008) 'Green the bailout', *New York Times*, September 28: WK11.

Fuller, T. and Revkin, A. C. (2007) 'Climate plan looks beyond Bush's tenure', *New York Times*, December 16: 1.

Furedi, F. (1994) *The New Ideology of Imperialism.* London: Pluto.

Gapper, J. (2008) 'On the pot-holed highway to hell', *Financial Times*, May 8: 11.

George, S. (1977) *How the Other Half Dies: The Real Reasons for World Hunger.* Harmondsworth: Penguin, 2nd edn.

Giddens, A. (1990) *The Consequences of Modernity.* Stanford, CA: Stanford University Press.

Goldsmith, E. (2002) 'Development as colonialism,' *World Affairs*, 6, 2: 18–37.

Greider, W. (2007) 'The establishment rethinks globalization', *Nation*, April 30: 11–14.

Gross, D., et al. (2008) 'Is America losing at globalization?', *Newsweek*, September 8: 66.

Haass, R. N. (2001) 'What to do with American primacy?', in C. W. Kegley Jr. and E. R. Wittkopf (eds) *The Global Agenda: Issues and Perspectives.* New York: McGraw-Hill, 6th edn, pp. 147–57.

Hardt, M. and A. Negri (2000) *Empire.* Cambridge, MA: Harvard University Press.

Henderson, H. (1996) 'Fighting economism', *Futures*, 28, 6–7: 580–83.

Horowitz, D. (ed.) (1969) *Corporations and the Cold War.* New York: Monthly Review Press.

Ignatieff, M. (2002) 'Nation-building lite', *New York Times Magazine*, July 28.

Johnson, C. (2000) *Blowback: The Costs and Consequences of American Empire.* New York: Henry Holt.

Kaplan, R. D. (2002) *Warrior Politics: Why Leadership Demands a Pagan Ethos.* New York: Random House.

Kapur, D., Metha, P. and Subramanian, A. (2008) 'Is Larry Summers the canary in the mine?', *Financial Times*, May 15: 9.

Kennedy, P. (2001) 'Maintaining American power: from injury to recovery', in S. Talbott and N. Chanda (eds) *The Age of Terror: America and the World after September 11.* New York: Basic Books, 53–80.

Korten, D. C. (1995) *When Corporations Rule the World.* London: Earthscan.

Lefever, E. W. (1999) *America's Imperial Burden: Is the Past Prologue?* Boulder, CO: Westview.

Lind, M. (2005) 'How the U.S. became the world's dispensable nation', *Financial Times,* January 26.

——(2007) 'The centre-ground's shift to the left', *Financial Times*, November 28: 11.

Longworth, R. (2007) *Caught in the Middle: America's Heartland in an Age of Globalism.* New York: Bloomsbury.

Mallaby, S. (2002) 'The reluctant imperialist', *Foreign Affairs*, 81, 2: 2–7.

Mohammadi, A. and Absan, M. (2002) *Globalisation or Recolonization? The Muslim World in the 21st Century.* London: Ta-Ha Publishers.

Münchau, W. (2008) 'Global adjustment will be long and painful', *Financial Times*, April 28.

Nederveen Pieterse, J. (1989) *Empire and Emancipation: Power and Liberation on a World Scale*. New York: Praeger.

——(2004) *Globalization or Empire?* New York: Routledge.

——(2008a) 'Globalization the next round: sociological perspectives', *Futures*, 40, 8: 707–20.

——(2008b) *Is There Hope for Uncle Sam? Beyond the American Bubble*. London: Zed.

——(2009) 'Globalization is braided: East–West osmosis', in *Globalization and Culture: Global Mélange*. Lanham, MD, Rowman & Littlefield, second rev. edn.

Nederveen Pieterse, J. and Rehbein, B. (eds) (2009) *Globalization and Emerging Societies: Development and Inequality*. London: Palgrave Macmillan.

Norris, F. (2008) 'The dilemma of Fannie and Freddie', *New York Times*, September 8: C1.

Nye, J. S., Jr. (2003) 'U.S. power and strategy after Iraq', *Foreign Affairs*, 82, 4: 60–73.

Parenti, M. (1995) *Against Empire*. San Francisco: City Lights Books.

Petras, J. and Veltmeyer, H. (2001) *Globalization Unmasked: Imperialism in the 21st Century*. London: Zed.

Petras, J. and Morley, M. H. (1995) *Empire or Republic? American Global Power and Domestic Decay*. New York: Routledge.

Plender, J. (2008) 'US mortgage U-turn may not be enough but it is a start', *Financial Times*, September 10: 22.

Rachman, G. (2007) 'As America looks the other way, China's rise accelerates', *Financial Times*, February 2: 13.

——(2008) 'The political threats to globalization', *Financial Times*, April 8: 11.

Said, E. W. (1993) *Culture and Imperialism*. New York: Knopf.

Skapinker, M. (2008) 'The market no longer has all the answers', *Financial Times*, March 25: 13.

Smith, R. (2007) *The Utility of Force: The Art of War in the Modern World*. New York: Knopf.

Soros, G. (2008) *The New Paradigm for Financial Markets: The Credit Crisis of 2008 and What It Means*. New York: Public Affairs.

Steil, B. (2006) 'Dobbsism, unintelligently designed for our times', *Financial Times*, March 27: 13.

Stephens, P. (2007) 'A global response is needed to the shifting world order', *Financial Times*, November 30: 11.

Strauss-Kahn, D. (2008) *Financial Times*, October 17.

Summers, L. (2008a) 'America needs to make a new case for trade', *Financial Times*, 28 April.

——(2008b) 'A strategy to promote healthy globalization', *Financial Times*, May 5.

Thomas, C. (2000) 'Globalisation as paradigm shift: response from the South', in D. Benn and K. Hall (eds) *Globalisation, a Calculus of Inequality: Perspectives from the South*. Kingston: Ian Randle, 8–22.

Varzi, H. (2007) 'A debt culture gone awry', *International Herald Tribune*, August 17.

Wellink, N. (2008) 'Basel II is sophisticated and sorely needed', *Financial Times*, April 10.

Williams, W. A. (1980) *Empire as a Way of Life*. New York: Oxford University Press.

——(1962) *The Tragedy of American Diplomacy*. New York, Delta

Williamson, E. (2008) 'Political pendulum swings toward stricter regulation', *Wall Street Journal*, March 24.

Wolf, M. (2008) 'The rescue of Bear Stearns marks liberalisation's limit', *Financial Times*, March 26.

Yan, Y. (2008) 'Managing cultural conflicts: state power and alternative globalization in China', *Art Today*, 15: 131–44.

Zakaria, F. (2008) *The post-American World*. New York: Norton.

Zinn, H. (2001) *On War*. New York: Seven Stories Press.

7

Vulnerability and globalization

The social impact of globalization

Peadar Kirby

> Globalization evokes a range of reactions from anger to pride, and from enthusiasm to fear. Both the word itself and the realities that it is taken to represent provoke strong opinions and powerful emotions.
>
> (Holton 2005: 3)

> Social science can only react to the challenge of globalization adequately if it manages to overcome methodological nationalism, and if it manages to raise empirically and theoretically fundamental questions within specialized fields of research and to thus elaborate the foundations of a cosmopolitan social and political science.
>
> (Beck 2002: 52)

Introduction

If the concept of globalization has fast become 'the leitmotif of our age' (Held and McGrew 2000: 1), what is unusual about this is that it remains a highly contested concept, not only in intellectual debate but in practical politics. Indeed, it can be argued that globalization has become the principal site of political struggle at an international level today, motivating not just an array of social movements in various parts of the world but also influencing the voting options of electors as in the *Non* vote on the European Constitution in France in May 2005 and, somewhat more indirectly, the No vote on the EU Lisbon Treaty in Ireland in June 2008.[1] Central to both the intellectual debates on globalization and to the political struggles it is spurring is the key question of its impact on society; in other words, is globalization having a largely positive or a largely negative impact on social conditions, on citizens' quality of life, on poverty and inequality?

This chapter seeks to develop a more promising and insightful approach towards answering this key question through proposing the concept of vulnerability to capture the distinctive impacts that globalization is having on society around the world, and thus make a contribution to developing the foundations of a renewed social and political science. The chapter begins by defining the two central concepts of globalization and vulnerability. The following section surveys some of the more important manifestations of vulnerability evident in today's global order and argues that globalization is implicated in deepening and intensifying them. The chapter then surveys some of the key concepts being used in the social scientific literature on globalization to capture its impacts on society, surveying in turn the distributional categories of poverty and inequality, the category of risk, and the category of human insecurity. This section identifies why vulnerability is a more promising interpretative concept to help understand the distinctive ways in which globalization impacts on society.

Defining terms

While the term globalization has been described as 'an elastic concept that has been stretched in many directions' (Boli et al. 2004: 410), its use in the social sciences centres on intensifying processes of transnational interconnectedness across a range of spheres such as the economic, the social, the political, the cultural and the communicational. Attempts to give a more precise definition, such as Scholte's dismissal of internationalization, liberalization, modernization or westernization in favour of what he calls supraterritoriality, run the risk of eliding much of what we mean by globalization in favour of precision and parsimony (see Scholte 2000). Held et al. offer of more inclusive definition of globalization as 'a process (or set of processes) which embodies a transformation in the spatial organization of social relations and transactions – assessed in terms of their extensity, intensity, velocity, and impact – generating transcontinental or interregional flows and networks of activity, interaction, and the exercise of power' (Held et al. 1999: 16). This has the value of identifying both the transformation of social relations being caused by the process of intensifying transnational interconnectedness and its characteristics of extensity, intensity, velocity, and impact. Both of these dimensions are important to the subject of this chapter. However, its levels of abstraction and generality require that it be applied for its meaning to be clear.

The origins of the application of the concept of vulnerability to international relations go back to the work of Keohane and Nye who introduced it as part of their concept of 'complex interdependence' to challenge the dominance of the state in realist theory (Keohane and Nye 2001). In analyzing the costs involved in interdependence, they introduced the dimensions of sensitivity and vulnerability (2001: 10–12). The first refers to economic or political threats faced by a country whereas the latter refers to whether a country has the ability to implement policies that minimize the costs arising from such threats; public policy can therefore help to avoid the threatened vulnerability. To illustrate their point, Keohane and Nye take the issue of rising oil prices: two countries might be equally exposed but if country A manages to reduce consumption or if it discovers domestic sources of oil, then it is less vulnerable than country B if the latter remains in the same position as before. While this introduction of the concept illustrates its utility, the main problem with the way Keohane and Nye use it is that they presuppose state capacity to address vulnerability, displaying the methodological nationalism that Beck, in the quote with which this chapter opens, identifies as an obstacle to the social scientific study of globalization.

More recently, a number of intergovernmental organizations have begun to employ the concept in discussing the impacts of globalization. The World Bank, in its 2000–2001 *World Development Report* on poverty (World Bank 2000–2001), the International

Monetary Fund (IMF) in its financial vulnerability indicators (IMF 2008), the United Nations Development Programme (UNDP) in its annual *Human Development Report* (see UNDP 2003), the UN Economic Commission for Latin America and the Caribbean (ECLAC) in its annual *Social Panorama of Latin America* report (see ECLAC 2000) and the European Union with its Ageing Vulnerability Index (Jackson and Howe 2003) have all employed the concept of vulnerability. An extensive analysis of the social impact of globalization, centrally employing the concept of vulnerability, was the UN Department of Economic and Social Affairs 2003 *Report on the World Social Situation* (UN 2003). This identified groups that are especially vulnerable such as the young, the elderly, people with disabilities, migrants and Indigenous peoples, but the report emphasizes that vulnerability is not limited to such groups and 'exists at all levels and dimensions of society and forms an integral part of the human condition, affecting both individuals and society as a whole' (UN 2003: 14). The report defines vulnerability as 'a state of high exposure to certain risks and uncertainties, in combination with a reduced ability to protect or defend oneself against those risks and uncertainties and cope with their negative consequences' (ibid.). This definition, which pays equal attention to the exposure to risks and to the weakening of coping mechanisms, is the definition adopted for this chapter.

Finally, what is meant by the social impact of globalization? The attempt here is to focus analytical (as distinct from merely descriptive) attention on the ways in which the processes of intensifying transnational interconnectedness affect the life experience of individuals and communities (from local level up to nation states), and the social, economic and political structures through which their lives are lived and structured. Particular attention is paid to how such transnational processes affect livelihoods and well-being at an individual and at a collective level. Employing vulnerability as a concept focuses analytical attention on the two dimensions of risks or threats and of coping mechanisms; it thus offers the prospect of identifying more precisely how processes of transnational interconnectedness impact on society. The next section undertakes this task of identification.

A more vulnerable world?

In his more extensive analysis of globalization and vulnerability on which this account is based, Kirby (2006) surveys risks in the financial, economic, social, political, environmental, and personal spheres of the life of society around the world today and then analyzes what is happening to four forms of coping mechanisms – personal, human, social, and environmental assets. The account here focuses on the heightened awareness of the threats posed by developments in a number of these spheres over recent years and of the weakening of coping mechanisms, taking care throughout to link these to the transformation of social relations being caused by the process of intensifying transnational interconnectedness and its characteristics of extensity, intensity, velocity, and impact.

With the exception of the environment, it is in the financial sphere that developments over recent years have been most dramatic, particularly the crisis in the international financial system that struck with a sudden intensity in the autumn of 2008. The subprime mortgage crisis in the United States and its knock-on effects on global liquidity have illustrated the interconnectedness of the global financial system in dramatic fashion as governments in the US and Europe have had to step in to guarantee bank deposits and nationalize some of their leading banks. The willingness of the US government to allow the Lehman Brothers collapse in September 2008 sent shock waves through the US banking system. Despite hundreds of billions of public monies being committed to deposit guarantee schemes and spent on injecting liquidity into the banking system, stock markets worldwide showed extreme volatility. *The Economist* described the autumn of 2008 as marking 'the end of an era' as governments had to step in to rescue the market. 'As well as partial nationalisation, the price will doubtless be stricter regulation of the financial industry. To invert Karl Marx, investment bankers may have nothing to gain but their chains,' wrote the magazine (18 October 2008: 75). Two issues emphasize just how serious this is for livelihoods and well-being in the global economy. The first derives from the generalized crisis of confidence in the global banking system. With leading banks declaring spectacular losses, normal lending flows were being hit as bankers feared for the financial health of their rivals. This restriction on global liquidity hit access to credit and therefore economic growth in many leading economies; in the jargon of financial journalists, the crisis in the financial system has spilled over into the real economy. This translates into sluggish trade, credit crunches, bursting housing bubbles, and volatile stock markets (Roubini 2008: 46–47).

The second issue is even more serious as it relates to the cause of these problems. If they only derived from banks lending too much to poorly secured borrowers, then they could be seen as conjunctural problems that will pass; however, the origins of this crisis lie in the liberalization of the financial system since the 1980s and the resultant weakening of public regulation. The first, one of the principal drivers of the present phase of globalization, resulted in the spawning of a vast array of new financial instruments known as derivatives, such as futures, options, and swaps, and an array of new actors trading in these instruments, such as hedge funds and new forms of investment banks. For example, de Goede has detailed how the US energy corporation Enron, which collapsed in December 2001, had become an underwriter and trader of complex financial products, 'including weather derivatives (allowing companies to hedge against, or simply speculate on, changes in the weather), credit default swaps (allowing financial institutions to resell the risk of a borrower default) and advertising risk management (allowing companies to hedge against fluctuating prices of advertising space)'. Indeed, he quotes one Enron manager describing the goal of the company as 'the commoditisation of everything' (de Goede 2004: 198). Not being a bank, it was exempt from the regulations applying to financial institutions. Moreover, the growth of such complex financial instruments has made it much more difficult for public authorities to regulate because of their complexity and lack of transparency. As a result, since the mid 1990s the Basel Committee on Banking Supervision, a leading international supervisory body, has relied on banks' own internal risk assessment models (de Goede 2004: 199). All of this was done in the name of spreading risk but in doing this it also intensified it. As the chairman of the US Federal Reserve from 1987 to 2006, Alan Greenspan, admitted to the US Congress, the crisis of autumn 2008 had 'found a flaw' in this thinking: 'I made a mistake in presuming that the self-interest of organisations, specifically banks and others, was such that they were best capable of protecting their own shareholders,' he said (*Financial Times*, 24 October 2008: 6). Thus, the very structural features of the globalized financial system, arguably the core driver of today's globalization, intensify risk and transmit it across the globe (by late 2008 countries in every region of the world were reporting a slowdown in economic growth and the drying up of investment as a result of the financial crisis). But they also weaken many people's physical assets as they have stimulated credit and housing booms based on low interest rates that are unsustainable and when these booms burst they turn what should be assets (ownership of a home and goods) into liabilities (heavy debts) for many.

Turning to the economic system, the transnational interconnectedness of today's globalized world has intensified the competitive nature of economic life with damaging effects on the livelihoods and well-being of many. Two examples will be analyzed to illustrate this: first, the offloading of risk on to the weakest as a structural feature of today's economic system and, second, the growth of the criminal economy taking advantage of the opportunities opened by transnational interconnections. Amoore has analyzed the way in which embracing risk has become a theme in the advice of management consultants who see it as instilling practices of entrepreneurship among workers. She writes: 'The manufacture of specific kinds of uncertainty is central to neo-liberal programmes of the restructuring of labour and working practices' which are presented, by bodies like the World Bank and the British government, as the unavoidable outcomes of globalization (Amoore 2004: 175–77). Analyzing such central features of today's global economy as downsizing and contingency, total quality management (TQM), and outsourcing, Amoore concludes that these practices work as ways of disciplining and atomizing workers while occluding the unequal power relations that lie behind them, the winners and losers from these practices. Also, she adds, 'the people whose working lives are transformed by the consultants' interventions remain relatively invisible in this celebration of uncertainty – and, hence, the concrete displacement of risk into homes, sweatshops, supply-chain workshops, and other ad hoc and unprotected sites is obscured' (ibid.: 188). Ultimately, it is the weakest who suffer most and bear the brunt of risk:

> The garment industry, electronics and assembly sectors, together with services such as catering and cleaning, have found their way into homes. Put simply, the firm that "thrives on uncertainty" may do so on the back of the acute uncertainties of low-paid and unprotected piecework undertaken predominantly by women and children.
>
> (Ibid.: 189)

If risk is purposely generalized in today's business practices, one result of this is to weaken the collective bodies, usually trade unions, that in the past offered some protection to workers and instilled a sense of collective identity. In this way, a major social asset that acted as a coping mechanism for workers has been severely eroded under the conditions of today's globalization. The result is increased vulnerability for many.

The second economic example, intimately related to the conditions of globalization, is the growth of the criminal economy. Seen by Castells as 'an essential feature of the new global economy' (Castells 1998: 167), it has burgeoned into a multi-billion dollar trade in drugs, arms, counterfeit money, cigarettes, diamonds, cybercrime, and sex slaves. As surveyed by Glenny, it involves extensive global networks, far better resourced and more technologically sophisticated than law enforcement agencies, adept at bribing public authorities, and drawing young well-educated people with few economic opportunities in countries all over the world into lucrative alternative but criminal livelihoods. Offering an example of the vast resources at their disposal, he quotes an estimate that the Cali cartel in Colombia make profits of between $4bn and $8bn a year and had such sophisticated surveillance capacity that a computer seized by the US Drugs Enforcement Administration in Cali in 1996 contained logs detailing all calls from US agents in Colombia to their contacts in Cali (Glenny 2008: 248–49).

In his account, Glinny directly links the growth of the criminal economy to the end of the Cold War and the emergence of today's globalization. He draws attention to two dimensions often missed by more academic analysts: first, the collapse of client states of the two superpowers in Africa, Southeast Asia, and Latin America generated huge instability that criminal networks were able to exploit, often in close alliance with local police forces; and, second, the new market opportunities for trade in illicit goods and services opened by the intensification of transnational connections. As economic theory predicts, supply followed demand. So the huge demand for weaponry in the Balkans, the Caucasus, central Asia, the Middle East, and Africa was met from the privatized arsenals of former communist countries while cultural globalization stimulated new markets for drugs in Japan, Thailand, South America, Israel, and Russia met by the growth of supply from traditional producers such as Afghanistan and Colombia. As Glinny emphasizes, this burgeoning criminal economy may be hidden from public view but its social impacts are all too visible in rising levels of violent crime, in the misery of lives destroyed by drug addiction and sex slavery, in the fuelling of corruption among public and political authorities, in the ruthless control of communities by criminal gangs and in the vulnerability of all those who use computers and electronic banking systems in the face of technically sophisticated global cyber criminals. As these risks become evident in almost all countries around the world, the traditional coping mechanisms to which people instinctively turn for some protection, namely police forces and public servants, have been systematically undermined in many countries by the sheer scale and resources of the criminal entrepreneurs.

Social vulnerability has been exacerbated for many of the world's people by the dramatic rise in food prices, especially of staple crops such as wheat and rice that more than doubled in price in the mid-2000s. This caused violent reactions undermining the political stability of dozens of countries, particularly in Africa. The causes are manifold but they again illustrate the intersection of the transnational interconnectedness and market pressures associated with globalization. For a major part of this crisis resulted from the increase in global demand for foodstuffs, partly the result of the economic growth in China and India and partly the new use to which food is being put as a biofuel, thus diverting it from human consumption. As a result, the growth in demand was fast outstripping supply. But market speculation also pushed up prices as commodities, including food, became a growth sector for investors (though one result of the financial crisis of late 2008 was to see a fall in these prices). Added to these factors of interconnectedness and market pressures is the impact of climate change, as drought, desertification, and changing rainfall patterns in places like Australia, China and Sub-Saharan Africa are having a significant impact on agricultural production. Furthermore, the rising price of oil, as demand again outstrips supply, is adding to food costs both through its contribution to rising fertilizer costs and to rising transport costs. Experts were therefore predicting that the era of cheap food was over and that the world was entering a new era of volatility and rising prices (OECD/FAO 2008).

The impact of rising food prices on global inequality is given less attention but it runs the risk of exacerbating an already alarming situation. For example, Pogge reminds us:

Each day, some 50,000 human beings – mostly children, mostly female, and mostly people of colour – die from starvation, diarrhea, pneumonia, tuberculosis, malaria, measles, perinatal, and maternal conditions and other poverty-related causes. This continuous global death toll matches that of the December 2004 tsunami every few days, and it matches, every three years, the entire death toll of World War II, concentration camps and gulags included.

(Pogge 2007: 30)

Furthermore, he calculates, based on World Bank figures, that the per capita Gross National Income (based on Purchasing Power Parity or PPP) in the high-income countries rose 52.6 per cent in real terms over the 1990–2001 globalization period and gives the following list of how the poorer half of humankind have fared over the same period:

+20.4% for the 50th percentile (median)
+21.0% for the 45th percentile
+21.1% for the 40th percentile
+20.0% for the 35th percentile
+18.7% for the 30th percentile
+17.2% for the 25th percentile
+15.9% for the 20th percentile
+14.4% for the 15th percentile
+12.9% for the 10th percentile
+11.9% for the 7th percentile
+10.4% for the 5th percentile
+6.6% for the 3rd percentile
+1.05% for the 2nd percentile
-7.3% for the 1st (bottom) percentile

He concludes:

There is a clear pattern. As trend data about malnutrition and poverty also confirm, the global poor are not participating proportionately in global economic growth. And as they fall further and further behind, they become even more marginalized, with their interests ignored in both national and international decision-making.

(ibid.: 36)

The recent increase in food prices is expected to further worsen this situation as it hits the poor hardest, affecting worst the staple foods that constitute a central part of their diet. Furthermore, and somewhat perversely, the food-producing countries that will benefit from the rise in prices, such as the US, Australia, Canada, Brazil, and Argentina, are already either high-income or middle-income countries, whereas those food importers worst hit are among the world's poorer countries in regions like North and Sub-Saharan Africa, Central America and Andean countries in South America, Haiti and Asian countries like Bangladesh, Iraq, and Mongolia. Not only do rising food prices exacerbate poverty and inequality but also, through the effects of malnutrition, they weaken people's health, an essential asset or coping mechanism.

Turning to political vulnerability, undoubtedly the greatest threat being identified by some of the world's leading countries is that of terrorist violence, following such attacks as 9/11 in New York and Washington, DC in 2001, 11/3 in Madrid in 2004 and 7/7 in London in 2005 (and let it be said the almost daily attacks that citizens of Baghdad have had to endure for years following the Western invasion). These are another consequence of growing global interconnectedness, not just at the level of the state but also at that of civil society. Undoubtedly, this has created a climate of unease for citizens and their governments. However, the response of governments also constitutes a growing threat to citizens' civil liberties and constitutes another form of political vulnerability. According to Amoore and De Goede, 'risk assessment is emerging as the most important way in which terrorist danger is made measurable and manageable' (Amoore and de Goede 2005: 149) and is applied to the protection of borders, to international financial flows, in airport security and in daily financial transactions. It involves what has come to be called data-veillance, namely the proactive surveillance of what become suspect populations to identify risky groups (ibid.: 151) and it tends to target migrants, students, and the unemployed. This unprecedented and extensive surveillance of the civilian population uses mathematical models to identify correlations of behaviour that are regarded as suspicious; all is done secretly, lacks independent oversight and involves no mechanisms of appeal. The authors conclude:

> Risk management via targeted governance, then, rests upon the representation of two worlds of globalization: one populated by legitimate and civilized groups whose normalized patterns of financial, tourist and business behaviour are to be secured; and another populated by illegitimate and uncivilized persons whose suspicious patterns of behaviour are to be targeted and apprehended.

(Ibid.: 168)

This runs the risk of undermining such fundamental assets as notions of equality before the law and presumption of innocence, bedrocks of the Western legal system and fundamental to the basic rights of citizens.

However, perhaps the sphere in which the greatest and most urgent manifestation of vulnerability has emerged in recent years is the environmental. After lengthy debates about the causes and consequences of global warming and climate change, the four reports of the Intergovernmental Panel on Climate Change (IPCC) in 2007 have helped underpin a consensus that climate change is largely caused by human activities that release growing quantities of greenhouse gases (carbon dioxide: 63 per cent; methane: 24 per cent; nitrous oxide: 10 per cent; others: 3 per cent) into the atmosphere and that this is having severely damaging effects on ecosystems, soils, oceans, and climatic conditions. As a result, the United Nations Development Programme (UNDP) could describe climate change as 'the greatest challenge that humankind has ever faced' with the very survival or our children's and their children's generations 'hanging in the balance' (UNDP 2007: 6). Furthermore, its gravity results directly from the extensity, intensity, velocity, and impact of the transformation of social relations worldwide as a model of industrial society ever more dependent on the intense use of fossil fuels, particularly oil, is globalized at an accelerating pace. Climate change is therefore both a result of globalization and also a challenge to the intense transnational interconnectedness of our global economy today as we become aware of the extent of carbon emissions generated by international trade, not least by the food and drink products on which the lifestyle of the world's wealthy depend.

The IPCC reports have also generated a consensus that an increase of over 2 degrees Celsius over pre-industrial average temperatures would risk catastrophic climatic changes and that concentrations of no more than 450ppm (parts per million) of greenhouse gases is the outside limit; 550ppm would increase temperatures to more than 2 degrees (though it must be noted that the British government's Stern report in 2006 issued its calculation on the basis that preventing dangerous levels of climate change would cost only 1 per cent of global GDP on the 550ppm level (see Monbiot 2007: xi)). Were the global community to fail to make the drastic cutbacks in greenhouse gas emissions that will limit global warming to 2 degrees Celsius, then the world faces mass starvation due to widespread crop failures, huge displacement of populations, the severe weakening of economic and political systems and the collapse of the carbon cycle so that the world gets locked into a vicious cycle in which more and more greenhouse gases get released. Yet, meeting this ambitious target will require determined political will and fundamental changes to the lifestyles particularly of the world's wealthy and developed countries (the nature of which are examined in Monbiot, 2007), that have been little evident to date. A separate but interrelated issue that has been forced to the attention of consumers in 2007–8 is the rising price of oil, breaching the $100 a barrel psychological barrier in early 2008 and rising so constantly that by mid-2008 it was being predicted that $200 a barrel would be reached before too long (though it fell again in late 2008 as the financial crisis took its toll). While experts disagree as to whether this indicates that we have reached peak oil after which known stocks of oil begin to decline and the extraction of those remaining becomes more difficult and costly, the rising cost of oil and its impact on a range of other consumer prices is at last forcing an awareness of the need to wean our societies off their dependence on fossil fuels and to diversify to more renewable sources of energy. The twin threats of climate change and exhaustible oil supplies have therefore suddenly come to the top of the agenda of global politics and the negotiation of a successor to the ill-fated Kyoto Protocol to be finalized at a summit in Copenhagen in late 2009 has become a priority for intergovernmental action, with stakes higher than those ever faced before by the world's politicians and diplomats. The environment therefore presents major risks to the survival of the human race. As we discover that such fundamental assets for survival as air, water, soil, and the oceans are also under severe strain in various parts of the world, we can identify in today's environmental crisis a situation of extreme vulnerability.

The brief survey has highlighted some of the principal manifestations of vulnerability and the speed of their emergence in the first decade of the twenty-first century. However, while each of these on its own presents a grave threat to human livelihood and well-being, the full extent of this threat requires attention to their cumulative and interconnected nature. In other words, even if some social sectors or some parts of the world are less vulnerable than others to each of these various threats, ultimately what is at stake is human civilization itself and no social sector or no part of the world can completely escape such a scenario. Therefore, limiting vulnerability to a problem that affects the poor only, as the World Bank does in its 2000–2001 report on poverty, is dangerously selective and myopic. There is nothing new about such apocalyptic predictions of civilizational collapse; Gray traces the tradition back to the origins of Christianity and beyond, shows how it was a persistent strain of belief throughout the medieval era and argues that it has manifested itself through revolutionary utopianism over the past two centuries (Gray 2007: 3–14). However, he firmly places it in the realm of belief, a belief that, for him, is 'a type of thinking that has lost any sense of reality' (ibid.: 21). What he fails to acknowledge is the recent emergence of predictions about civilizational collapse not based on political or religious beliefs but on cutting-edge science.

In his best-selling book *Collapse* (Diamond, 2006), the US biologist, physiologist, and geographer Jared Diamond has shown how most of the major problems our world now faces were faced at other times in history by societies such as Easter Island, the Anasazi and Cahokia within the boundaries of the modern US, the Mayans of Central America, the Pitcairn and Henderson Islands and the Norse in Greenland. All of these societies collapsed and died out because they did not resolve the problems of deforestation and habitat destruction, soil problems such as erosion, salinization and soil-fertility losses, water-management problems, overhunting and overfishing, human population growth and the increased per capita impact of people. He sets himself the task of learning why these societies collapsed while others which faced similarly grave problems, such as Japan, Iceland, New Guinea, and the island of Tikopia, managed to save themselves through taking drastic measures. He acknowledges that he found in the course of his study that collapse was never due just to environmental factors but also to factors such as trading links and friendly or hostile neighbours and that finding adequate responses to the grave problems being faced depended on the sorts of political, economic, and social institutions and on the cultural values that societies possessed. Diamond concludes by listing 12 problems, eight of which faced past societies (natural resource losses, freshwater ceilings, alien species, and population growth) and four additional problems we face (toxic chemicals, atmospheric changes, photosynthetic ceiling, and energy). He writes:

> Our world society is presently on a non-sustainable course, and any of our 12 problems of non-sustainability ... would suffice to limit our lifestyle within the next several decades. They are like time bombs with fuses of less than 50 years. ... [A]ny of the dozen problems if unsolved would do us grave harm, and because they all interact with each other. If we solved 11 of the problems, but not the 12th, we would still be in trouble whichever was the problem that remain unsolved. ... [T]he world's environmental problems will get resolved, in one way or another, within the lifetimes of the children and young adults alive today. The only question is whether they will become resolved in pleasant ways of our own choice, or in unpleasant ways not of our choice, such as warfare, genocide, starvation, disease epidemics, and collapses of societies.
>
> (Diamond 2006: 498)

At the end of his book, Diamond professes himself a cautious optimist as he sees signs that humankind is beginning to wake up to the scale of the challenges facing it and take action. Other scientists are not so optimistic as they locate the source of the problem in the very complexity of modern society. As reported by Debora MacKenzie in *New Scientist*, a number of scientists identify the interconnectedness of modern society as the major source of its vulnerability to collapse. Yaneer Bar-Yam, head of the New England Complex Systems Institute in Cambridge, Massachusetts, argues that 'complexity leads to higher vulnerability in some ways' since as networks become ever tighter they begin to transmit shocks rather than absorb them. Thomas Homer-Dixon, a political scientist at the University of Toronto, offers an example: 'The intricate networks that tightly connect us together – and move people, materials, information, money and energy – amplify and transmit any shock. A financial crisis, a terrorist attack or a disease outbreak has almost instant destabilizing effects, from one side of the world to the other.' The ever more intense interconnectedness being driven by globalization is undermining the resilience of the global system, says Homer-Dixon: 'We need to be more selective about increasing the connectivity and speed of our critical systems. Sometimes the costs outweigh the benefits.' He doubts that we can stave off collapse completely and points to what he calls 'tectonic' stresses that will shove our rigid, tightly coupled system over the edge, such as population growth, the growing divide between the world's rich and poor, financial instability, weapons proliferation, disappearing forests and fisheries, and climate change. Charles Perrow of Yale University, an authority on industrial accidents, states that interconnectedness in the global production system has now reached the point where 'a breakdown anywhere increasingly means a breakdown everywhere', especially in the world's financial systems where the coupling is very tight. This understanding of complex systems echoes the insights of ecologist Buzz Holling of the University of Florida, Gainesville. His work highlights how some ecosystems become steadily more complex over time: as a patch of new forest grows and matures, specialist species may replace more generalist species, biomass builds up and the trees, beetles, and bacteria form an increasingly rigid and ever more tightly coupled system. But unusual conditions such as insect outbreak, fire or drought can trigger dramatic changes as the impact cascades through the system; the end result may be the collapse of the old system and its replacement by a newer and simpler one. For some, such as Lester Brown of the Earth Policy Institute in Washington, DC, the situation is extremely urgent. 'It's now a race between tipping points', he states. 'Which will come first, a switch to sustainable technology, or collapse?' (MacKenzie 2008: 32–35).

One of the trigger points for such a collapse could be a disease pandemic (such as the swine flu outbreak of 2009), argue some scientists. The management practices that have driven globalization, such as just-in-time inventories, mean that stocks of everything from aspirins to coal rely on rapid and regular deliveries. Cities typically have only three days supply of food while hospitals rely on daily deliveries of drugs, blood, and gases. So anything that hits the supply chain, such as a major pandemic, could cripple society in just a few days, not just cutting food and water supplies but electricity generation and oil. Furthermore with most medical equipment and 85 per cent of pharmaceuticals used in the US coming from abroad, any severe disruption to the supply chain would soon lead to a breakdown of the health system. Public health specialist Michael Osterholm of the University of Minnesota in Minneapolis, argues that 'no one in pandemic planning thinks enough about supply chains. They are long and thin, and they can break.' Estimates of how serious a pandemic could be are based on the great flu pandemic of 1918; repeated today it would cause 142 million deaths worldwide and wipe out 12.6 per cent of global GDP. This assumes that 3 per cent of those who fall ill would die. However, of all the people known to have caught H5N1 bird flu so far, 63 per cent have died. So it is very much within the bounds of possibility that the death rate could be far higher if the pandemic was caused by a deadly virus other than flu (MacKenzie 2008: 28–31).

The purpose of this reporting of scientific views is to illustrate that the very interconnectedness made ever more intense by processes of globalization is itself a source of major vulnerability for our world society today. It is the interaction of the various forms of vulnerability, and their swift transmission throughout the complex system that is modern society, that means no one and no part of the world can be immune. Paradoxically, as Bar-Yam puts it in one of the articles cited, those most vulnerable are those most integrated into global networks, particularly modern city dwellers; those most resilient in the face to the vulnerabilities of today's globalization are those least integrated, namely the world's subsistence farmers (MacKenzie 2008: 35). This highlights then a final theme emerging in the literature on vulnerability, namely the vulnerable subject. Fineman (2008) argues that 'understanding the significance, universality, and constancy of vulnerability' challenges the understanding of the human subject as defined in the liberal tradition (the autonomous, self-sufficient, and resourceful individual) and which informs Western legal and political theories. She argues that vulnerability analysis suggests 'that the vulnerable subject is a more accurate and complete universal figure to place at the heart of social policy' (Fineman 2008: 11):

> Constant and variable throughout life, individual vulnerability encompasses not only damage that has been done in the past and speculative harms of the distant future, but also the possibility of immediate harm. We are beings who live with the ever-present possibility that our needs and circumstances will change. On an individual level, the concept of vulnerability (unlike that of liberal autonomy) captures this present potential for each of us to become dependent based upon our persistent susceptibility to misfortune and catastrophe.
>
> (Ibid.: 12)

In a similar way, Turner bases his theory of human rights on 'the idea of our vulnerable human nature' (Turner 2006: 1). He writes:

> There is a foundation to human rights – namely, our common vulnerability. Human beings experience pain and humiliation because they are vulnerable. While humans may not share a common culture, they are bound together by the risks and per-turbations that arise from their vulnerability. Because we have a common ontolo-gical condition as vulnerable, intelligent beings, human happiness is diverse, but misery is common and uniform. This need for ontological security provides a strong moral argument against cultural relativism and offers an endorsement of rights claims for protection from suffering and indignity.
>
> (Ibid.: 9)

Theorizing the vulnerable subject applies the concept of vulnerability to the individual, drawing out its implications for society and the state.[2] As Turner puts it, 'our vulnerability forces us into social dependency and social connectedness' (Turner, 2006: 10) while Fineman uses the concept of the vulnerable subject as the basis for making more robust demands upon the state.

This section has illustrated the explanatory potential of the concept of vulnerability to analyze the social impacts of today's globalization (entailing a heightening of risk and a weakening of coping mechanisms) and ended by making brief allusion to the theoretical potential of the concept, a topic which will be returned to below. While lacking the more systematic treatment in Kirby (2006), it serves to emphasize the concept's relevance to explaining a range of topics of major contemporary concern. Yet, the value of pro-moting a relatively new concept to analyze and explain these topics needs to be justified. In other words, what value does the concept of vulnerability add to more mainstream and established ways of explaining the social impact of globalization. This is the subject of the next section.

Why vulnerability?

In its 2003 report on vulnerability, the UN Department of Economic and Social Affairs recognized that 'use of the words "vulnerability" and "vulnerable" has been quite loose in policy contexts and has entailed neither the theoretical rigour nor the degree of elaboration that one finds in analytical works' (UN 2003: 14). Works cited above (Kirby 2006; Turner 2006; Fineman 2008) help address the weakness correctly identified in the UN report. But this development of the concept begs the question of its utility – what value does it add to existing approaches towards analyzing the social impact of globalization? To answer the question, this section surveys three mainstream and influential approaches that are drawn on in debates on globalization: distributional concepts (poverty and inequality), the concept of risk (particularly risk society) and the concept of human insecurity. Each is surveyed in turn and then, in the light of these, the added value offered by vulnerability is identified.

Poverty and inequality

Debates about the impact of globalization on poverty and inequality have been the predominant way in which the benefits of globalization for society have been debated. For example, the World Bank refers to evidence that poverty is falling in what it calls 'the new globalizers' (countries like China, India, Brazil, and Mexico which have recently liberalized their economies) while it is rising in the rest of the developing world, to justify its claim that the present form of globalization is socially beneficial, reducing both poverty and inequality (World Bank 2002: 7). Other leading 'pro-globalizers', Jagdish Bhagwati and Martin Wolf, argue a similar case, though the latter takes more care to engage with the mixed evidence about globalization's distributional impacts. Bhagwati is scathing of those who attach significance to evidence that inequality at a global level has grown (namely the gap between the richest and the poorest in the world) on the grounds that it makes no sense to compare a household in Mongolia with one in Chile, a household in Bangladesh with one in the United States (Bhagwati 2005: 67) and his claim that globalization has reduced poverty is based on selecting a set of evidence about which others have raised methodological questions (see below for details) (ibid.: 60–66). Wolf accepts that evidence about globalization's impact on poverty and inequality is more mixed and inconclusive but he concludes that on balance 'the proportion of humanity living in desperate misery is declining. The problem of the poorest is not that they are exploited, but that they are almost entirely unexploited: they live outside the world economy' (Wolf 2005: 172).

The main problem with basing conclusions about globalization's social impact on distributional evidence is twofold. First, the fact that the empirical evidence is very mixed and depends to a large extent on how poverty and inequality are defined and measured (relative versus absolute poverty; inequality between the mean incomes of each country or inequality between individuals at a global level regardless of country?). Second, conclusions about what such evidence may tell us about globalization are inevitably based on interpretation and do little to resolve the disagreements. Let us deal with each difficulty in turn.

In his survey of patterns of poverty that have emerged in the most recent era of globalization, Kaplinsky seeks to account for the wide differences and contradictory trends that exist in measures of global poverty, particularly in the most recent era. Differences exist due to the sources of data (national income accounts or household budget surveys), on what is measured (income or consumption), and on how actual buying power is estimated (the use of PPP measures). On balance, he concludes that World Bank estimates of those living in absolute poverty are an underestimate (Kaplinsky 2005: 30–37).

In a similar exercise, Wade asks whether the number of people living in extreme poverty (less than $1 a day measured in terms of PPP) has fallen substantially in the past 25 years reversing the long-term trend. He finds that the fall identified by the World Bank depends entirely on China; 'remove China and the number rises between 1981 and 2001'. Raising the poverty line to $2 a day, and the numbers in poverty increase though the proportion of the world's population in poverty falls. However, Wade adds that 'the World Bank poverty numbers are of very uncertain reliability, but the World Bank virtually never acknowledges the wide margins of error' (Wade 2007: 109–10). Turning to inequality, there is more agreement based substantially on the work of Milanovic. Yet, this is not to say that there is agreement since different measures of inequality show different trends. Essentially, Milanovic's data show that unweighted international inequality (between the mean incomes of countries) has risen since 1850, especially since 1978–80, whereas when countries are weighted according to population, inequality reaches a plateau in 1950 and remains essentially stable since (though it recently shows a slight decline but this effect is entirely due to China's recent growth). His final measure is one of global inequality showing how the gap between the richest and the poorest in the world has evolved and here he finds, based on much more partial data, 'that inequality among people in the world today is extremely high, though its direction of change is unclear' (Milanovic 2007: 32).

Ultimately, then, perceptions of globalization's impact on inequality depend on observers' assessment of what measure matters most. This takes us to the second difficulty mentioned above, namely that of interpretation. For example, almost as if he is replying to Bhagwati's claim that it is 'lunacy' to compare households in low-income countries with those in middle- or high-income countries (Bhagwati 2005: 67), Milanovic asks if globalization itself is resulting in just such comparisons:

> The very process of globalization might influence our perception and our satisfaction with a given level of income. This is a crucial point: as the process of globalization enfolds how much will it influence our perception of our own position in it? If it does, maintaining large inter-country income differences becomes more and more difficult.

> (Milanovic 2007: 44)

Overall, then, the use of distributional categories to argue whether globalization is having a positive or a negative social impact fails to get us very far. Those on both sides of the debate tend to use evidence selectively not always attending to the definitional and methodological difficulties involved while, even if these are acknowledged, the conclusions drawn ultimately rest on interpretations that go beyond the evidence. Perhaps the most that can be drawn from evidence about poverty and inequality is that concluded by Rosenzweig in his assessment of evidence from urban and rural India:

> The examples from India ... show that opening an economy has complex and sometimes conflicting effects on short-run and long-run poverty reduction. Such effects depend both on *what* an economy opens itself to – capital, technical change, new product demands – and on *how* these elements affect unskilled workers' wages and their incentives to upgrade their skills. India's experience also suggests that the responsiveness of poverty to the forces of openness also depends on Indigenous institutions, and will differ across countries and historical periods.

> (Rosenzweig 2008: 175–76; emphases in original)

This shows the futility of drawing any firm conclusions from the correlation of globalization with trends in poverty and inequality as it misses the intervening variables that are the determining factors in the outcomes achieved.

Risk

Beck introduced the concept of 'risk society' (1992, 2000) and more recently he has extended this to speak of 'world risk society' (2002). He defines the latter as follows:

> The speeding up of modernization has produced a gulf between the world of non-quantifiable risk in which we think and act, and the world of non-quantifiable insecurities that we are creating. Past decisions about nuclear energy and present decisions about the use of gene technology, human genetics, nanotechnology, etc. are unleashing unpredictable, uncontrollable and ultimately incommunicable consequences that might ultimately endanger all life on earth.
>
> (Beck 2002: 40)

While Beck's focus from the beginning has been on forms of risk associated not so much with globalization as with modernization and with developments in science and technology, these are consistent with and to an extent included within the concept of globalization. This is clear from Beck's focus on three particular risks, all of them central expressions of the threats associated with contemporary globalization – financial crises, ecological conflicts and global terror networks. While calculating risks was part of 'the master narrative of first modernity' and resulted in the welfare state and the insurance industry as coping mechanisms against risks, what is new about world risk society in Beck's terms is that 'we enter a world of uncontrollable risk'; this, he agrees is a contradiction in terms (since the modern concept 'risk' presumes the ability to calculate the threats involved) but he writes that 'it is the only apt description for the second-order, *un*natural, human-made, manufactured uncertainties and hazards beyond boundaries we are confronted with' (ibid.: 41; emphasis in original). World risk society results not from the fact that everyday life has generally become more dangerous but rather from the 'debounding' of uncontrollable risks in three ways: spatially (since risks like global warming have no boundaries); temporally (since the dangers of nuclear waste or genetically modified foods have a long latency period); and socially (as it is difficult to know who has caused it and not possible for the nation-state to control). He concludes: 'So the hidden central issue in world risk society is *how to feign control over the uncontrollable* – in politics, law, science, technology, economy and everyday life' (ibid.: 41; emphasis in original).

The concept of world risk society obviously parallels that of vulnerability very closely in that it identifies and describes some of the major threats to human well-being and livelihood that arise from structural features of today's global order. The major difference is the tension between structure and agency that debates on the concept of 'risk' reveal. Beck's formulation of risk society seems very deterministic as he acknowledges himself when he writes that 'uncontrollable risk is now irredeemable and deeply engineered into all the processes that sustain life in advanced societies. Pessimism then seems to be the only rational stance' (ibid.: 46). Yet, he immediately pulls back from this deterministic position offering six grounds for optimism, namely 'opportunities opened up by today's threats' (ibid.: 46). These rest on the globalization of politics in that national security now requires transnational cooperation and that neo-liberalism's shortcomings have been revealed by 9/11. Interdependence and cooperation to 'revitalize and transform the state in a cosmopolitan state' (ibid.: 50) thus become the grounds for hope. However, this seems fatally to undermine his earlier claim that risk has become uncontrollable in today's world risk society, since it implies that cooperation by national political authorities to create a cosmopolitan state holds the promise of offering security to citizens from these risks – if not, it does not offer grounds for hope. Beck's highly deterministic account of world risk society therefore yields to a hopeful basis for agency without the seeming contradictions being acknowledged, examined or resolved by Beck.

The tensions inherent in the use of the term 'risk' are further highlighted through reference to the established literature on risk assessment and management which, as Beck acknowledged, has been a central part of capitalism for over a century. For example, O'Malley makes the distinction between risk ('the statistically calculable or predictive model that is descended from positivism') and uncertainty ('the non-statistically calculable model that is relevant to the creative activity of the entrepreneur') (O'Malley 2000: 462). Tracing different relationships between the risk-management practices of government and the risk-enhancing practices of entrepreneurs roughly corresponding to broad historical variants of classical, welfare, and neo-liberal versions of capitalism, he concludes that while there is every reason to expect the expansion of government through statistically calculable risk, 'this is unlikely to result in the formation of a "risk society"' (ibid.: 480). Similarly, Amoore draws attention to the fact that much risk in today's enterprise culture is 'a manufactured uncertainty' as 'the manufacture of specific kinds of uncertainty is central to neo-liberal programmes of the restructuring of labour and working practices' (Amoore 2004: 175). This literature, then, is based on a very different balance between structure and agency as risk is seen as deriving from the practices of enterprise culture and attempts by the state to minimize its impact. If Beck's view of the risk society has the tendency to overdetermine structure, theorists of risk management tend to exaggerate the potential of agency, seeing risk as a discursive device used by entrepreneurs rather than as a structural feature of today's global order. This makes the concept of risk too ill-defined a concept through which to theorize the social impacts of globalization.

Human insecurity

Human insecurity as a concept for understanding the impact of globalization derives from the term 'human security' which emerged in the early 1990s as a way of making the human person rather than the state the central referent of security discourse. It is employed by a number of theorists to undertake what Scholte calls 'a normative evaluation of globalization' (Scholte 2000: 207; see also Bakker and Gill 2003 and Harriss-White 2002). Since its introduction in the 1994 Human Development Report of the UNDP, the concept of human security has been taken up by the United Nations and a group of states in the human security network; Kofi Annan as UN Secretary General established a Human Security Commission to examine the concept which published its report in 2003 (HSC 2003) while more recently a *Human Security Report* has been published (Human Security Centre 2005). Yet, despite the academic and policy debates generated by this activity, the concept of human security remains problematic; furthermore, its use by theorists to evaluate globalization tends to neglect its definitional difficulties and apply the concept in an ill-defined way. For example, though Scholte undertakes a broad assessment of the state of human well-being in the era of globalization under headings such as peace, ecological integrity, subsistence, financial stability, employment,

129

working conditions, identity, and knowledge (Scholte 2000: 208–31), he nowhere defines what the term human security means nor how the reforms he outlines might help enhance it. Similarly, Harriss-White describes various aspects of insecurity generated by processes associated with globalization but leaves the concept loose and undeveloped (Harriss-White 2002: 3). The most satisfying use of the concept is by Bakker and Gill but they see no difficulty in using the term security with different qualifiers (national security, human security, the security of capital) to mean very different things (Bakker and Gill 2003: 9–12).

This imprecision in the use of the term echoes the definitional difficulties that have plagued the term since its inception. In introducing it in 1994, the UNDP defined human security as follows:

> Human security can be said to have two main aspects. It means, first, safety from such chronic threats as hunger, disease and repression. And second, it means protection from sudden and hurtful disruptions in the patterns of daily life – whether in homes, in jobs or in communities. Such threats can exist at all levels of national income and development.
>
> (UNDP 1994: 23)

However, in 2003 *Human Security Now* defined it as: 'To protect the vital core of all human lives in ways that enhance human freedoms and human fulfilment' (HSC 2003: 4). By 2005, the first *Human Security Report* argued that human security could be interpreted in a broad or a narrow way and limited its definition to 'the protection of communities and individuals from internal violence' (Human Security Centre 2005: viii). These difficulties mirror the ambiguities of the term 'security' itself as identified by McSweeney. He writes that 'Security is a slippery term indeed, rooted in a fundamental human emotion which takes on different forms and emphases as it expresses itself at different levels of community' (McSweeney 1999: 199). Thus security can apply to protecting individuals and communities against threats to their livelihood and well-being, as seemed to be the intent of the 1994 and 2003 definitions, but security can also mean securing oneself against others even by violent means. These two very different meanings express what McSweeney calls security as a relationship (the former meaning) and security as a commodity (the latter one). These show the perils of using the concept as a basis for assessing the social impacts of globalization since it runs the risk that analysts can assign it the meaning that suits their normative preferences thereby evacuating it of useful analytical content as has tended to be the case in the ways the concept has been employed in practice (see Burgess and Taylor 2004).

Vulnerability

This critical survey of three central concepts used for assessing the social impact of globalization now permits a return to the concept of vulnerability to identify more precisely its analytical value for this purpose. Five dimensions can be identified:

(a) Definitional precision: As is clear from the survey above, vulnerability offers the value of a precise definition, centred on increased risks and reduced coping mechanisms.

(b) Analytical focus and reach: As illustrated by the analysis of the vulnerabilities associated with globalization undertaken in this chapter, the concept has analytical power to identify key ways in which globalization affects wellbeing and livelihoods.

It therefore is able to combine two important tasks: focus and reach. The first refers to the ability to identify with precision and clarity core threats to society from processes associated with globalization while at the same time not overly narrowing its ability to range widely over the broad field of such threats as can be the case with distributional concepts. Furthermore, the concept of vulnerability allows a more subtle theorizing of structure and agency than does the concept of risk or human insecurity as its double focus of attention (risks and coping mechanisms) attends to what is happening both to structure and to agency.

(c) Clear pointer to policy prescriptions: The concept of vulnerability implies policy prescriptions, namely the minimization of risk and the strengthening of coping mechanisms. By contrast, both risk and human insecurity lack clarity and are even ambiguous in what they imply by way of policy prescriptions. The central means to address vulnerability can be identified as strengthening resilience. Using Kirby's approach, this can be conceived of as strengthening assets – physical, human, social, and environmental.[3] Another useful way of conceiving of it is developed by ECLAC. In outlining its work on a social vulnerability index for the Caribbbean, ECLAC views resilience as being 'tantamount to an ability that is based on enti-tlement, enfranchisement, empowerment and capabilities' (ECLAC 2003: 25). Each of these dimensions requires the strengthening of social rights, both by public authorities and by social collectivities, and the ability to ensure that people can enjoy them (Beck's emphasis on constructing a cosmopolitan state carries some echoes of such a prescription). Furthermore, vulnerability offers a far clearer and less ambiguous answer to what is perhaps the central political question about glo-balization (see Kaplinsky 2005: 48–51): do we need a deepening and extending of our present form of globalization to resolve social problems or a different form of globalization (what in French is called *altermondialisation*)? Vulnerability, with its emphasis on the need to build resilience, offers a useful pointer to what such an alternative version of globalization requires.

(d) Situation in social theory: As outlined in Kirby (2006: 129–50), the concept of vulnerability gives expression to the central theoretical insights of Karl Polanyi on the damage to individuals and society of the imposition of free market mechanisms on society (Polanyi 2001). More than the alternative concepts surveyed, it captures core elements of Polanyian theorizing such as the nature of poverty, the role of the state, the dangers of the 'market mentality' and the commodification of land, labour and capital.

(e) Theorizing the subject: Unlike the other concepts surveyed, vulnerability is sti-mulating theorizing about the 'vulnerable subject' as a more accurate and adequate understanding of the nature of the human person and the basis for demands upon public authority (see Fineman 2008, Turner 2006).[4] Again, this dimension of the concept of vulnerability makes a rich contribution to achieving a more nuanced and empowering relationship between structure and agency, so important for political contestation of the power of market actors in contemporary globalization.

In these ways, therefore, vulnerability adds analytical value to existing approaches towards theorizing the social impact of globalization, a value that has direct political implications for both contesting real existing globalization and for elaborating public policy responses. Furthermore, the concept of vulnerability opens a rich terrain of interdisciplinary research possibilities with major implications for public policy.[5]

Conclusions

This chapter set itself the task of developing and applying the concept of vulnerability to analyze the social impact of globalization. This it has done both theoretically and empirically. Theoretically, it has defined the term and identified the value of using it as against distributional terms, risk, and human insecurity. It has empirically surveyed some major impacts of globalization over recent years, illustrating the utility of the concept of vulnerability to understand them. Finally, it has surveyed uses of vulnerability by scholars in other disciplinary fields in ways that complement and extend the concept as used in this chapter. It is therefore hoped that, in reference to the quote by Beck with which the chapter opens, the task undertaken here is a contribution to raising empirically and theoretically fundamental questions, thereby contributing to the elaboration of a renewed social and political science more adequate to uncovering the stresses and strains of our globalized world.

Notes

1 See, for example, the comment on the Irish vote in June 2008 by Paul Gillespie, the well-regarded foreign-affairs commentator of the *Irish Times*:

> While the Government's eye was off the developing economic crisis during the campaign, it is not surprising that its portents should have affected ordinary voters, many of whom have rational fears about exposure to globalisation and insufficient reason to believe the EU will protect them.
>
> (Gillespie 2008: 13)

2 While Fineman and Turner develop the concept of vulnerability with different objectives than those of this chapter, the concept as developed by them and its use in this chapter are entirely consistent and complementary. As Turner states, we need to understand the vulnerability of the human subject, physical, psychological, moral and spiritual, 'against a background of global risks that in turn draw attention to the precarious nature of human institutions' (Turner 2006: 36). For Fineman, the concept of vulnerability is valuable 'in constructing critical perspectives on political and social institutions, including law. Vulnerability raises new issues, poses different questions, and opens up new avenues for critical exploration' (Fineman 2008: 9). The use of vulnerability as a conceptual tool to analyze the social impact of globalization is an example of this point.

3 This us usefully discussed and expanded upon in Fineman (2008: 13–15; see especially note 42).

4 Beck echoes this ontology when he writes that risk society contradicts the images of *homo economicus* as an autarkic human being and of the individual as a decider and risk taker. Indeed, he argues that the principle of private insurance is partly being replaced by the principle of state insurance as the world of individual risk is challenged by a world of systemic risk 'which contradicts the logic of economic risk calculation' (Beck 2002: 44).

5 A series of discussions on the concept of vulnerability hosted by Emory University Law School in Atlanta, Georgia, in April 2008 decided to establish an international network of vulnerability studies with regular conferences, a PhD programme and plans to publish a volume mapping the field. For more details see: http://www.law.emory.edu/research-scholarship/feminism-legal-theory/vulnerable-populations.html.

References

Amoore, Louise (2004) 'Risk, reward and discipline at work', *Economy and Society*, 33 (2): 174–96.

Amoore, Louise and de Goede, Marieke (2005) 'Governance, risk and dataveillance in the war on terror', *Crime, Law and Social Change*, 43: 149–73.

Bakker, Isabella and Gill, Stephen (eds) (2003) *Power, Production and Social Reproduction*, Basingstoke: Palgrave Macmillan.

Beck, Ulrich (1992) *Risk Society*, London: Sage Publications.

——(2000) 'Risk Society Revisited: Theory, Politics and Research Programmes', in Barbara Adam, Beck, Ulrich and van Loon, Joost (eds) *The Risk Society and Beyond: Critical Issues for Social Theory*, London: Sage Publications, pp. 211–29.

——(2002) 'The Terrorist Threat: World Risk Society Revisited', *Theory, Culture and Society*, 19 (4): 39–55.

Bhagwati, Jagdish (2005) *In Defense of Globalization*, New York: Oxford University Press.

Boli, John, Elliott, Michael A. and Bieri, Franziska (2004) 'Globalization', in George Ritzer (ed.) *Handbook of Social Problems: A Comparative International Perspective*, Thousand Oaks, CA: Sage Publications, pp. 389–415.

Burgess, J. Peter and Taylor, Owen (eds) (2004) 'Special Section: What is "Human Security"?', *Security Dialogue*, 35 (3): 345–87.

Castells, Manuel (1998) *End of Millennium*, Oxford: Blackwell.

de Goede, Marieke (2004) 'Repoliticizing financial risk', *Economy and Society*, 33 (2): 197–217.

Diamond, Jared (2006) *Collapse: How Societies Choose to Fail or Survive*, London: Penguin.

ECLAC (2000) *Social Panorama of Latin America 1999–2000*, Santiago: ECLAC.

——(2003) *Towards a Social Vulnerability Index in the Caribbean*, Port of Spain: ECLAC.

Fineman, Martha Albertson (2008) 'The Vulnerable Subject: Anchoring Equality in the Human Condition', *Yale Journal of Law and Feminism*, 20 (1): 1–23.

Gillespie, Paul (2008) 'Paying the Price for a Weak and Incompetent Lisbon Campaign', *Irish Times*, 12 July: 13.

Glenny, Misha (2008) *McMafia: A Journey through the Global Criminal Underworld*, New York: Alfred A. Knopf.

Gray, John (2007) *Black Mass: Apocalyptic Religion and the Death of Utopia*, London: Allen Lane.

Harriss-White, Barbara (ed.) (2002) *Globalization and Insecurity: Political, Economic and Physical Challenges*, Basingstoke: Palgrave.

Held, David and McGrew, Anthony (2000) *The Global Transformations Reader*, Cambridge: Polity Press.

Held, David, McGrew, Anthony, Goldblatt, David, and Perraton, Jonathan (1999) *Global Transformations: Politics, Economics and Culture*, Cambridge: Polity Press.

Holton, Robert J. (2005) *Making Globalization*, Basingstoke: Palgrave Macmillan.

Human Security Centre (2005) *Human Security Report*, Vancouver: Human Security Centre, University of British Columbia.

Human Security Commission (2003) *Human Security Now*, New York: United Nations.

IMF (2008) 'Vulnerability Indicators: A Factsheet', downloaded from http://www.imf.org/external/np/exr/facts/vul.htm (July 2008).

Jackson, Richard and Howe, Neil (2003) *The 2003 Aging Vulnerability Index*, Washington, DC: The Center for Strategic and International Studies.

Kaplinsky, Raphael (2005) *Globalization, Poverty and Inequality*, Cambridge: Polity Press.

Keohane, Robert O. and Nye, Joseph S. (2001) *Power and Interdependence*, New York: Longman, third edition [First edition: 1977].

Kirby, Peadar (2006) *Vulnerability and Violence: The Impact of Globalization*, London: Pluto Press.

MacKenzie, Debora (2008) 'Are we Doomed?', *New Scientist*, 5 April: 32–35.

——(2008) 'The End of Civilisation', *New Scientist*, 5 April: 28–31.

McSweeney, Bill (1999) *Security, Identity and Interests: A Sociology of International Relations*, Cambridge: Cambridge University Press.

Milanovic, Branko (2007) 'Globalization and Inequality', in David Held and Ayse Kaya (eds) *Global Income Inequality*, Cambridge: Polity Press, pp. 26–49.

Monbiot, George (2007) *Heat: How We Can Stop the Planet Burning*, London: Penguin.

O'Malley, Pat (2000) 'Uncertain Subjects: Risks, Liberalism and Contract', *Economy and Society*, 29 (4): 460–84.

OECD/FAO (2008) 'Agricultural Outlook', downloaded from http://www.fao.org/newsroom/en/news/2008/1000849/index.html (July 2008).

Pogge, Thomas (2007) 'Severe Poverty as a Human Rights Violation', in Thomas Pogge (ed.) *Freedom from Poverty as a Human Right: Who Owes What to the Very Poor?* Oxford: Oxford University Press, and Paris: UNESCO, pp. 11–53.

Polanyi, Karl (2001) *The Great Transformation*, Boston: Beacon Books [Original edition: 1944].

Rosenzweig, Mark (2008) 'Openness and Poverty Reduction: Short and long-run', in Ernesto Zedillo (ed.) *The Future of Globalization: Explorations in Light of Recent Turbulence*, London: Routledge, pp. 163–77.

Roubini, Nouriel (2008) 'The Coming Financial Pandemic', *Foreign Policy*, March/April: 44–48.

Scholte, Jan Aart (2000) *Globalization: A Critical Introduction*, Basingstoke: Palgrave.

Turner, Bryan S. (2006) *Vulnerability and Human Rights*, Pennsylvania: The Pennsylvania State University Press.

UN (2003) *Report on the World Social Situation: Social Vulnerability: Sources and Challenges*, New York: United Nations Department of Economic and Social Affairs.

UNDP (1994) *Human Development Report 1994*, New York: Oxford University Press.

——(2003) *Human Development Report 2003*, New York: Oxford University Press.

——(2007) *Human Development Report 2007/2008: Fighting Climate Change: Human Solidarity in a Divided World*, Basingstoke: Palgrave Macmillan for the UNDP.

Wade, Robert H. (2007) 'Should We Worry about Income Inequality?', in David Held and Ayse Kaya (eds) *Global Income Inequality*, Cambridge: Polity Press, pp. 104–31.

Wolf, Martin (2005) *Why Globalization Works: The Case for the Global Market Economy*, New Haven and London: Yale University Press.

World Bank (2000) *World Development Report 2000–01: Attacking Poverty*, New York: Oxford University Press.

——(2002) *Globalization, Growth, and Poverty: Building an Inclusive World Economy*, New York: Oxford University Press with the World Bank.

Part II

Substantive issues

8

Transformations of the world's population

The demographic revolution

John MacInnes and Julio Pérez Díaz

The institutional origins of global demography

Until about ten thousand years ago, when the agricultural revolution began, the global population of human beings probably numbered a few million. Settled agriculture allowed population to start rising steadily, but very slowly, so that by AD 1 it probably numbered 200–300 million. It reached one billion around 1800, and two billion some time before the outbreak of the Second World War. The four billion mark was reached in 1960 and global population is currently around 6.7 billion (Livi-Bacci 2001).[1] It has perhaps always been possible to imagine a global population of human beings, to describe it, albeit in such rudimentary terms, and even attribute different qualities and behaviour to it. The concept of the human species is a very old one, of course, and one which contemporary biology gives an ever more specific understanding and meaning to. However a specifically *demographic* understanding of the global human population, understood as an integrated population system, has until very recently never been more than a strictly theoretical proposition.

For a start, it was simply not possible to study global population, as there were no good sources of data about it. The figures cited above are intelligent guesswork based on extrapolation from limited sources. Moreover, until the efforts of the United Nations (UN) began at the end of the 1940s, there had been little interest in it. Demography is a relatively recent science born out of the information and surveillance needs of the modern nation-state. Being a statistical discipline in the true sense of the word (MacKenzie 1981) it only developed with the appearance and consolidation of national statistical systems in the most advanced states towards the end of the nineteenth century (Dupâqier and Dupâqier 1985). Accordingly, as a discipline, its concept of population has almost always been banally nationalist (Billig 1995) in the strongest possible sense. It treated each state as comprising a population in its own right, and thus to the twin basic components of the 'demographic equation' – fertility (births) and mortality (deaths) were added those of in- and out-migration defined in terms of state boundaries.

Until the issue of global population growth first became a concern in the late 1940s, virtually the entire corpus of scientific literature addressed national state interests, or the application of such interests to lower level territorial administrative units – cities, counties, provinces, and so on. This continues to be true. Indeed it is the territorial unit within which people live that has become demography's object of study, rather than population as a reproductive system. One result of this theoretical weakness, combined with its institutional dependence on the state, has been a tendency for demography to be driven by the prevailing fears and obsessions of the governing classes, concentrating on the proximate causes of any alarming trend in demographic phenomena (Foucault 1989; Teitelbaum and Winter 1985). There has rarely been any shortage of these.

Its birth as a modern discipline was closely bound up with eugenics (MacKenzie 1976; Soloway 1990) and in the early decades of the twentieth century many national demographies joined in the battle for higher fertility in the professional or 'fitter' classes, or for stronger population growth than that of rival states (Szreter 1996). There has also been a tendency to understand demographic behaviour in moral terms, resulting either in variants of catastophism, a tradition well established by Malthus's original *Essay* (1970), continued by Spengler's *Decline of the West* (1926) and culminating in Ehrlich's predictions of mass global famine in *The Population Bomb* (1968).

The establishment of what might be thought of as global demography both continued and challenged this tradition. Reliable statistical knowledge about global population had to wait until the creation of the United Nations in the aftermath of the Second World War, and the development of censuses across the entire planet by its Population Division (UNPD) established in 1946 (Caldwell and Caldwell 1986), although what was to become the International Union for the Scientific Study of Population (IUSSP) held its first world conference in 1927, and the Milbank Memorial Fund had later established the Office of Population Research at Princeton. The United Nations' activities can be seen as the institutional embryo of a global demography, but originally in a highly ambiguous way. Its origin and early fortunes lay less in the material globalization of population processes than in the world superpower status of the post-war United States of America, and the apprehension of its governing class over the geopolitical consequences of population growth in the developing 'Third World'. In part via the United Nations, but also through the activities of the Ford and Rockefeller Foundations and the US State Department, global demography became a Cold War weapon. The early statistical work of the UN suggested that population growth in the Third World was much faster than had been expected (in turn the early data itself proved to be an underestimate). Not only was such global population growth seen as unsustainable, and likely to impede economic, political and social development, but in the context of the Cold War it was also seen as likely to create, literally, a breeding ground for the spread of communism. This was the backdrop to the publication of *The Population Bomb* in which Ehrlich asserted that global overpopulation was about to make Malthus' prediction a reality: '[t]he battle to feed all of humanity is over … In the 1970s the world will undergo famines – hundreds of millions of people are going to starve to death' (1968: xi). The fact that Ehrlich was a biologist rather than a demographer did not stop his views having a substantial impact.

The answer was seen to lie in encouraging family planning and access to cheap contraception with the UN's role shifting from one of data collection and analysis to policy intervention to support family planning programmes under the auspices of the UN Population Fund (UNFPA) established in 1967 with million-dollar funding from the United States. As Demeny (2003: 13) notes, from the 1960s to 1980s 'population policy in the developing world became essentially synonymous with family planning programs'. The UN established a series of World Population conferences which became intergovernmental conferences from the time of the 1974 Bucharest meeting as demography became more relevant to states' geopolitical interests.

Demographic transition theory

The academic paradigm used to analyze demographic change was demographic transition theory. In the first decades of the century demographers on both sides of the Atlantic (Willcox 1916; Carr-Saunders 1922; Thompson 1929; Landry 1934) had all suggested that economic and social modernization was eventually accompanied by a steep decline in both mortality and fertility, with a relatively short period in which fertility falls might lag behind mortality falls, producing a rapid but temporary expansion of population. At the time of its original development this theory attracted little attention (Szreter 1993) since European demographers were more interested in what Glass (1936) called *The Struggle for Population*: the problem of what was thought (wrongly) to be below-replacement levels of fertility in 1930s Europe and whether modern industrial society and the family were compatible (Davis 1937).[2] However, in the context of a global Cold War, what was originally a theory developed from studying *industrialized* countries and framed in terms of demographic *consequences* that had their *origins* in social, economic, and political change became recast as a theory of how policies aimed at directly changing demographic behaviour (principally fertility) might, on the contrary, *cause* desirable social, economic and political *consequences* in *non-industrialised* countries (Hodgson 1988; Szreter 1993). Population control was argued to be fundamental to economic development, and informed a great deal of policy and intervention in developing countries. Meanwhile, demographic transition theory became virtually the only analytical framework for academic demography, helped on its way by its formulation in economic terms by the Household Economics of Becker (1991) and (Robinson 1997).

This approach eventually suffered two fundamental reverses. At the 1974 Bucharest population conference many Third World countries rejected the UN's draft *World Population Plan* because of its background assumption that demographic change was more a cause than result of underdevelopment. Alarmed at threats to their state sovereignty implied by a global population initiative and frustrated at any progress on the UN's part in challenging global economic inequality they declared that 'Economic development is the best contraceptive'. At Mexico ten years later, bowing to pressure from the religious right, rather than any recognition of changed development priorities, the US delegation announced, to the astonishment of others, that population growth was a 'neutral phenomenon' in relation to economic development (Finkle and McIntosh 2002). By the time of what was to be the last such conference, in Cairo in 1994, the development perspective of population policy was dropped altogether and the rationale became, instead 'that the programs satisfy important health needs and help people exercise a fundamental human right. … even though the name of the conference for the first time included a reference to development, scant attention was paid to that concept. Family planning programs were redefined, instead, as reproductive health programs' (Demeny 2003: 15). Five years earlier the fall of the Berlin Wall removed much of the original rationale for the United States' strategic interest in demography, rendering the return to dominance of a religious moral conservative discourse much less relevant than it might otherwise have been.

Meanwhile demographic transition theory continued to be a plausible general empirical *description* of demographic history, but fell apart as a body of work capable of generating testable hypotheses or predicting the future course of demographic trends. In the original model 'the whole process of modernisation' (trade, technological innovation, specialization, a widening division of labour, the rise of labour and product markets, industrialization, urbanization, formal education, growth of scientific and medical knowledge) first lowered mortality, then gave people a new interest in lowering fertility and finally recognition of this interest. 'Natural' fertility control, the virtual absence of any widespread family limitation and 'a surprising lack of knowledge' (Cleland and Wilson 1987: 13) of contraception given almost universal understanding of procreation, was argued to give way to parity-specific, conscious, birth-control.[3] The professional classes were usually the most rapidly affected, but others soon followed. In some versions of the theory this was because industrial capitalism reversed the previously positive material and political impact of having children. However, one of the largest empirical social-science research projects ever mounted, the Princeton study on the fall of fertility in Europe, singularly failed to produce evidence consistent with the theory's original postulates and struggled to identify any cross national or regional correlation between the 'whole process of modernisation' and fertility fall (Coale and Watkins 1986). The variety of pre-transition fertility behaviour could hardly be subsumed under a single 'natural' variant. Moving beyond Europe it became clear that although fertility falls were virtually universal by the start of the twenty-first century, they occurred under all kinds of different social, political, economic and even demographic conditions. As Cleland (2001: 62) noted 'in the last 40 years the onset of fertility transition has occurred in settings where infant mortality is 150 per thousand live births and survival at older ages is correspondingly low. In other settings, birth rates have remained unchanged until infant mortality dropped to 50 per thousand.' Conversely, it was far from clear just how effective 'family planning' campaigns in developing countries inspired by diffusion theory had been. However, in a classic example of Kuhn's theory of the evolution of scientific thought (Kuhn 1962) transition theory continued unchallenged as the discipline's paradigm even as the empirical dimensions of its shortcomings became ever more apparent.

Because of this institutional and theoretical background, demography has until recently shown less interest in the theory of globalization than other social sciences, such as economics, political science or sociology, although it has certainly been in the business of producing data about the demographic 'aspects' of globalization. By the latter we understand the progressive integration of the diverse systems that form human relations into one general system (in areas such as politics, finance, history, production, commerce, ideology, and so on). However, it is perhaps no accident that reliable information about the population of the world has become available, through the efforts of the United Nations, just at the point when, as we argue below, a genuinely global population system has first emerged as a material reality and when the pace of demographic change has been greater than ever before in human history, and probably greater than it ever will be again.

Population as a reproductive system

In order to understand population dynamics in global terms, it is first of all necessary to distinguish two quite different uses of the term population: that between population as a *stock* and as a *flow*. As a stock, population is an accounting term. A population is simply a group of objects sharing one or more common characteristics at a point in time, including a group of people defined in this way, usually in terms of residence within a territory. With this definition it is possible, at most, to study the exchanges, mixing, and displacements between diverse 'stocks', in other words, migration patterns. Included in such movements would be ethnic movements on a grand scale, such as the Germanic invasions of the declining Roman Empire, or the Spanish and Portuguese conquests of the Americas, as well as all manner of other ways in which more or less isolated 'populations' have managed their contact with those beyond their territorial or ethnic boundaries. However this does not bring us any closer to the idea of a global population system and its analysis.

As we have argued elsewhere (MacInnes and Pérez 2009a), the key tool of demography is to define populations not as stocks but as *flows*: as reproductive systems which continue over time, as opposed to their mortal individual human components. This allows us to examine, for example, the 'efficiency' of a population, taking into account the very diverse combinations of existing structural conditions and individual behaviours, and the 'input' (in terms of births and associated reproductive work needed to convert infants into adults themselves capable of carrying on such work), given such conditions, needed to maintain a population over time. If we understand populations as a flow in this way, it also becomes possible to think of globalization in properly demographic terms, and to examine the extent to which the population system itself has become global. We try to do both below, in order to argue that existing diverse population systems are rapidly fusing into one global population system, whose outlines can be sketched. This newly emerging system comprises a quite new mode of reproduction characterized, on the one hand, by an unprecedented and unrepeatable transformation in the system's efficiency (one might even think in terms of the forces of reproduction) and, on the other hand, by the transformation of its social relations such that power and decision-making relating to fertility becomes, for the first time, individual and private rather than collective and public. However, to understand what follows, a short but necessary methodological argument must be made.

Demography has its own special terminology and as an overwhelmingly quantitative discipline, it own indicators and measurements. Understanding the subtleties of two of these makes a critical appreciation of contemporary population change much more readily accessible to non-demographers. Since population is a flow, and demographic events occur across the life course, a population's characteristics at any point in time cannot fully be grasped by 'period' or transversal measures, since they have no way of distinguishing how far age-dependent variables (which naturally form the essence of demographic analysis) reveal attitudes or behaviour that is rooted in change *across* successive generations, or cohorts, or changes across the life course *within* such generations, or some mixture of both. In addition, 'crude' measures, which express demographic events (such as births, deaths, marriages or divorces) as proportions of or rates within the population for a given time period can be misleading since different populations have very different age structures, and most demographic events are highly dependent on age. For example, a population with a high proportion of young people may have a lower crude death rate compared to another population with a low proportion of young people, even though life expectancy in the former population is much lower, for the simple reason that deaths, by definition, occur at the end of people's lives. When demographic change is rapid, as it surely has been across most of the world over the last century, cohort-based measures, which study the entire reproductive life course of a generation, may give a fuller account of change, but with the grave drawback that they can only be completed in retrospect. In practice 'complete' can be taken to mean women's reproductive behaviour up to the age of forty, since very few women (and surprisingly few men, despite their longer fecundity) become biological parents after this age. However this still means that in the year 2010, we can only have reasonably complete fertility information about women born as early as 1970. With mortality the problem is clearly greater. We may not know the actual life expectancy of those born in 1970 for another ninety years or so.

Clearly it is impossible to obtain future knowledge. However, it is possible to produce 'synthetic' measures that capture something of the dynamics of population, albeit from a transversal perspective. Two of these are important for our analysis here, the *total fertility rate* and *life expectancy at birth*. Crude birth rates depend upon the age structure of a population at a point in time. Other things being equal, a population with a high proportion of women in fertile ages (conventionally taken as 15 to 45, or 49) will have a higher crude birth rate. *Age-specific* fertility rates can be calculated for each year or five-year age group, and these facilitate comparison across populations with different age structures. Making many such comparisons would often be a laborious exercise, so that a *total fertility rate* (TFR) is calculated which gives the fertility rate that would result were each woman to experience *across her lifespan* the age-specific fertility rates for all women for *that calendar year*. This measure is synthetic because it represents what must be a longitudinal process as a transversal one. It inevitably makes assumptions about the 'future' behaviour of younger members of the population in terms of current evidence of the behaviour of older members. This can lead to significant distortions when behaviour is changing over time. Such distortions are inevitable: we cannot know the future. However, we can be aware of these distortions and do our best to interpret such synthetic evidence in the light of what we know about change. A second, and easily overlooked, limitation of the TFR is that it takes no account of mortality. This becomes important when we consider population trends over time and population replacement. Other things being equal, a population with substantial early mortality will need a much higher TFR to reproduce itself. This is because many births will be partly or wholly 'wasted' from the perspective of reproducing the population if female children die before reaching the end of their fertile years. Moreover, a population with higher mortality will need a correspondingly higher fertility rate to maintain a given volume of population. In fact this will vary directly with mean life expectancy. If people live twice as long, the same fertility rate will deliver twice the volume of population (Henry 1965).

Life expectancy at birth (e_0) is a similar synthetic measure calculating the mean years of life that would be achieved by someone born in a population today who experienced the age-specific mortality rates prevailing today in that population across their life course. Life expectancy clearly suffers the same drawback as total fertility. We might expect that the trend reduction in mortality rates will continue (although it would be foolish to discount the possibility of some new epidemiological challenge) in which case the actual life expectancy of those born today will almost certainly be significantly higher. Again this arises because we only know the real life expectancy of the already dead, and predominantly older, members of the population at the current point in time. However, life expectancy at birth has one further shortcoming for the unwary. It is an average measure but one that is often highly skewed and has a wide dispersion, particularly in countries with low life expectancies. This is because for many populations the risk of death may actually be highest in the earliest years of life. In most of the world until the second half of this century up to one quarter or more of infants born died before their first birthday.

Famines or epidemics might double this number for short periods. Such mortality reduces life expectancy dramatically, so that for most of human history it has probably been around 25 to 30 for most populations most of the time. However, this does not mean that most people died at thirty. It means rather that their chances of survival to older ages were modest. A quarter might be dead before reaching five years of age, further similar proportions by their fifteenth and fiftieth birthdays, while a lucky few might live on into their eighties or nineties.

The prehistory of population

In history it is usually misleading to refer in general terms to 'the past', as if it were some coagulated, unchanging mass. However, in demography it has rather more justification than usual because the magnitude and speed of recent change is indeed not only unprecedented but also logically impossible to repeat. What dominated the past was premature death. If populations comprise human groups with both continuity over time and their own diverse ways of achieving such continuity, such diversity was almost universally rigidly conditioned until the eighteenth century (and for many areas of the world until much more recently) by low life expectancy and the very high risk of an early death. In what Omran (1971: 512) called 'the age of pestilence and famine … life expectancy was short and human misery was assured'. Data are scanty and require painstaking effort to reconstruct, but it appears that crude mortality rates oscillated erratically with epidemics, famine or warfare between a range of around 20 to 50 per 1,000 (but with occasional much higher peaks) while mean life expectancy at birth ranged from around twenty to the low thirties (Omran 1971; Coale and Watkins 1986; Livi-Bacci 2001; Riley 2001). A poor harvest, adverse weather, warfare, brigandage or epidemics easily severed what was always a tenuous hold on life for most ordinary people and intermittently sent mortality rates heavenward. Less than a half of most female populations might expect to live through their entire reproductive years if we define these as ending at 45. Such factors did not directly impose the details of whatever survival strategy a population might choose, but they did impose the need to control fertility, subject to two conflicting pressures. Fertility had to be kept high enough to balance the ravages of a high and volatile mortality rate, but too high a rate of fertility might, if it led to too many mouths to feed, drive mortality up on its own account.

Within this stage we can find many quite distinct demographic systems, each of which tried to maintain such fertility as was necessary to secure the reproduction of population in the long run, along with checks to avoid fertility levels that might expand the population beyond a level that available resources and technology could support. In many parts of Asia the early and widespread marriage of women was combined with infanticide in adverse times (Lee and Feng 1999). In Western Europe (Hajnal 1965) it was marriage that was controlled, rather than fertility within it, with marriage ages increasing, and fertility rates decreasing, when times were hard. Indeed Laslett (2000) suggests that England's demographic system not only vanquished famine as a significant contributor to mortality as early as the sixteenth century, but can plausibly be seen as an important precondition of the worlds first industrial revolution.

Elites more concerned with their descendants' inheritance of their wealth and power sometimes practised fertility control (Henry 1956). To their (somewhat) better survival rates and life expectancy was added the concern to avoid 'diluting' their estate, offset by their need to secure an heir. Both social elite and particular territorial areas (such as governing cities) had mechanisms to 'adopt' the produce of other populations to the goal of their own survival. However, logically, these were not strategies that could be extended to the entire population so that even in Western Europe the norm was levels of fertility far above our current experience, with completed fertilities (that is the mean number of children a cohort of women would have in their lifetimes) no lower than four (Laslett's minimum estimate for England) and often nearer five or six. Since averages take no account of the significant proportion of women who never married, and include women dying before reaching the end of their reproductive years, this translated every-where into very large family sizes. Laslett reports 21 births as the maximum encountered for any one woman in the historical reconstruction of English demography. The diverse demographic systems in operation had one common feature, namely the intense regula-tion of the means of reproduction, women's bodies, principally through the institutions of church and state, the norms surrounding sexual activity and sex roles, illegitimacy, marriage, family and kinship obligations and property law. Patriarchy might have taken many forms, but we have no good empirical evidence of any hitherto existing society without it.

The decline of mortality

From around the middle of the eighteenth century, although possibly earlier in England, mortality was slowly conquered by improvements in nutrition, medical knowledge, public health, sanitation, and economic progress. Figure 8.1 shows just how gradual this change was, using the data for Sweden that allow us to track changes in cohort life expectancy at birth (rather than its more widely available period equivalent) from an

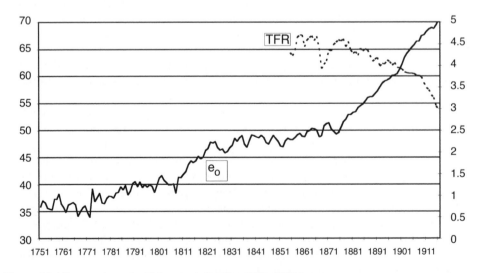

Figure 8.1 Life expectancy by birth cohort, Sweden 1751–1916.
Source: Human Mortality Database: University of California, Berkeley (USA) and Max Planck Institute for Demographic Research (Germany). Available at www.mortality.org or www.humanmortality.de (data downloaded on 4 January 2009).

unusually early date. Note how progress in the struggle against mortality is fitful until the final quarter of the nineteenth century; however, by the end of that century victory is well established, such that mean life expectancy reached 70 for those born in 1916.

As we have seen, demography eventually came to understand this fall as part of the demographic transition, but the initial reaction to falling mortality and fertility was more often the fear that low fertility might lead to a stationary or even declining population (Teitelbaum and Winter 1985). It was in this context that eugenicist alarms were sounded about the prospect of 'race suicide' driven by 'neo-Malthusian' family limitation by within the 'fittest' (i.e. wealthiest) strata of the population. Feminism came in for particular criticism, being blamed for diverting women from their naturally determined and inexorable maternal vocation and threatening 'sex extinction' (Kenealy 1920). One exception to this reaction was the work of Alva Myrdal, who almost alone amongst early theorists of demographic change argued in *Nation and Family* (1939) that greater gender equality and the collectivization of the costs of rearing children through fiscal transfers and public provision of services would sustain fertility. Myrdal's work can be seen as the intellectual genesis of what was to become the Scandinavian welfare state. This current in demographic thought weakened with the post-war baby boom (which actually had its origins in the 1930s) and, as we have seen above, once the focus became the populations of the developing world, the demographic transition model, originally developed to explain the experience of northwest Europe, was now used to make the case that high, not low, fertility was the problem. However, it never disappeared entirely, continuing to underpin French demography's fusion of nationalism and natalism as exemplified in the work of Sauvy (1959) or Dumont (2008) and subject to withering criticism by Le Bras (1991, 1998), so that when fertility rates resumed their downward trend in Europe in the 1970s and 1980s, it promptly re-emerged (MacInnes and Pérez 2007).

The rise of mass maturity

The development of the world's population over the last half-century can perhaps best be illustrated with a single fact. By 2000, the majority of those who had comprised the world's population in 1950 were dead. Fifty years from now, however, most of those alive today will still be around, despite the fact that the average age of the world's inhabitants is now higher than it was in 1950 (a median of 29 years compared to 24). This is because the biggest social change of the twentieth century was the defeat, across almost all of the world, and for the first time in human history, of premature death. In 1950, seven out of ten of the world's women lived in countries with female life expectancy at birth under 65 years. Life expectancy was well below this threshold throughout Africa and Asia, where it was generally in the low 40s, and Latin America and the Caribbean, in the low 50s. Only in Europe, North America, Australia and New Zealand, Israel, Cyprus, Armenia and, by a whisker, Japan, could women expect to reach old age, thus defined. Even within Europe most of the Balkans, Romania, Spain, and Portugal still fell below this threshold. Country averages conceal differences by region, class or ethnicity within states so that although white women in the US comfortably exceeded the threshold in 1950, black or African American women did not pass it for almost another ten years. By the first decade of the new millennium, however, except in sub-Saharan Africa, and a handful of countries beyond (Bangladesh, Haiti, Cambodia, Laos, Ethiopia and Eritrea), women could be confident of reaching their 65th birthday.

What became evident as the twentieth century progressed was that mortality declines which had developed over some centuries in Europe could be achieved much more rapidly in developing countries, thanks to their ability to take advantage of improvements in medical knowledge, especially in combating infectious diseases and recognition of the importance of public health and education. Of course, economic progress also played a part through rising nutrition levels and living standards (Riley 2001). Figure 8.2 shows the fall in infant mortality in Sweden, Spain, Chile, and Egypt. An achievement that had taken well over a century in Sweden was achieved by Spain in half that time and by developing countries elsewhere still more rapidly.

Table 8.1 compares the under-five mortality rates (the number of children per 1,000 live births who die before their fifth birthday) in 1970 and 2005 for a range of countries, as well as the percentage of each cohort born around 2005 that would reach their 40th birthday given current mortality rates. As recently as 1970 these mortality rates were often up to ten times those of affluent countries. However, by the start of the new millennium, most developing countries had largely closed this gap, and many had over-taken the Russian Federation in terms of life expectancy. The exceptions were to be found mostly in sub-Saharan Africa.

Such mortality falls were usually followed rapidly by corresponding falls in fertility, resulting in the great rise in the efficiency of global population reproduction. At first, and for a relatively short period, the result of this improvement was the rapid expansion of the global population which expanded faster in absolute terms than it had ever done

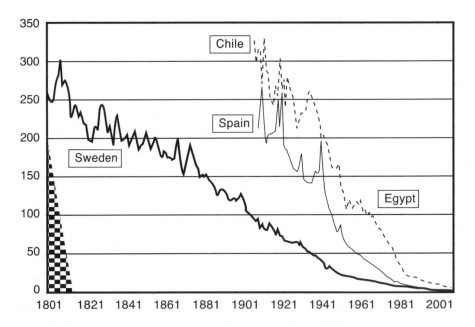

Figure 8.2 Infant mortality (‰): Sweden, Spain, Chile and Egypt, 1801–2005.
Source: Human Mortality Database: University of California, Berkeley (USA) and Max Planck Institute for Demographic Research (Germany). Available at www.mortality.org or www.humanmortality.de (data downloaded on 24 June 2008); Chesnais (1986: Annexe 5.3); *Child Mortality since the 1960s: A Database for Developing Countries*, United Nations Department of Economic and Social Development, NY: 1962; *Anuario De Estadísticas Vitales 2005*, Santiago de Chile: Instituto Nacional d'Estadistica.

Table 8.1 Under-5 mortality and probability of reaching age 40, 1970 and 2005.

Country	Under-5 mortality ‰		Survival to age 40 (2005)
	1970	2005	
US	26	7	96.5
Russian Federation	36	18	89.3
China	120	27	93.2
Turkey	201	29	93.5
Brazil	135	33	90.8
Egypt	235	33	92.5
Iran	191	36	92.2
Bangladesh	239	73	83.6
India	202	74	83.2
Pakistan	181	99	84.6
Myanmar	179	105	79.0
Ethiopia	239	164	67.7
Nigeria	265	194	61.0
Dem. Rep. of the Congo	245	205	58.9

before, and, in all likelihood, will ever do again, rising from around two and a half billion in 1950 to around 6.7 billion in 2009. This expansion is now coming to an end, although population momentum will probably carry the global population above 9 billion by the middle of this century. However, the more enduring effect has been the fall in the proportion of social effort devoted to fertility, through the greatly reduced volume of births needed to sustain a population. This fundamental shift has precipitated an even greater social revolution, which is spreading around the planet: the rise of personal autonomy in fertility decision-making, the consequent erosion of patriarchy (to the point of collapse in much of the North) and the rise of gender quality (MacInnes and Pérez 2009b).

Figure 8.3 shows the general outline of this process for the world as a whole. The annual volume of births, which in 1950 stood at just under 100 million, grew by around one third by 2005. The volume of population more than doubled however, from 2.5 to 6.7 billion, as these births have given rise to longer lives. The increase in the volume of births stayed modest even though the global population of women of fertile age almost trebled, because fertility rates fell rapidly.

Figure 8.4 shows the details of this process for the world, divided into three major regions: the more developed countries, less developed and the least developed.[4] It plots the fertility (TFR) for each of these areas against life expectancy at birth (e_0) for each five-year period from 1950 to 2005, representing each area in proportion to its population in each period. The figure illustrates four aspects of change across this half century. First, rises in life expectancy quickly became associated with falls in fertility: the circles move rapidly leftwards within a few years of shifting upwards. Second, change has been greatest in the less developed countries, which have achieved levels of fertility and life expectancy previously reached only by industrialized states. Third, progress in the least developed countries stalled after the 1970s: fertility continued to fall, but gains in life expectancy halted. Finally, the dramatic convergence between the more and less developed countries means that for the first time we can analyze a truly global population system.

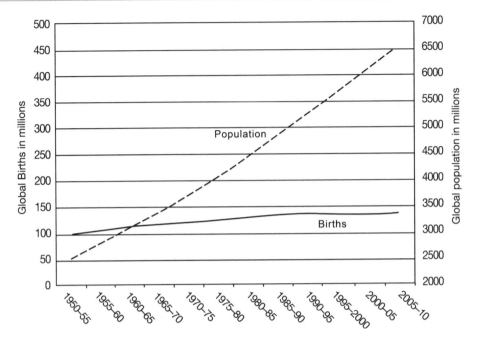

Figure 8.3 World births and population, 1950–2005.

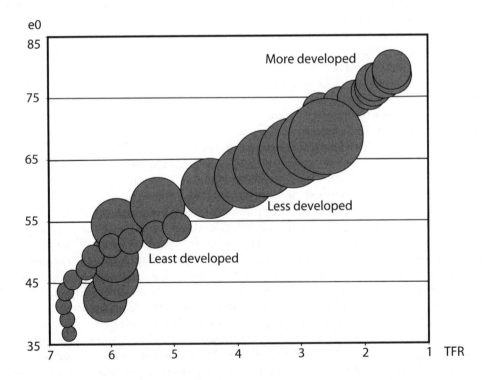

Figure 8.4 Life expectancy at birth, fertility and population size at five-year intervals for more, less and least developed countries, 1950–2005.

Of course, the emergence of a global population system has taken place in a world structured by great inequalities of material affluence. The relationship between fertility, life expectancy and the standard of living as measured by individual or state-wide income or wealth has been a favourite and controversial field of investigation, above all by economists (e.g. Lee 1981; Schultz 1985; Becker 1991). Without entering into the detail of the debate, we can note two points relevant to our argument here. It is clear that the reproductive revolution can begin even with a modest level of development. Many countries with levels of GDP well below that of the richest countries nevertheless manage to approach their life expectancy rates, chiefly by reducing murderous levels of infant mortality. However, underdevelopment, especially when compounded by political disorder, civil and ethnic warfare and the effect of HIV, can also reverse progression on mortality: the experience of much of Sub-Saharan Africa. Second, economic development itself does not erase inequalities in life expectancy, either between states or within them. In most less developed countries, infant mortality rates for the poorest quintile of the population are two to four times higher than for the richest quintile. A recent study in Scotland examining the spatial distribution of mortality found an inner city area of Glasgow, characterized by poverty, unemployment, and drug abuse, where male life expectancy was 54: the level for some of the world's poorest countries. In an affluent suburb nearby it was no less than thirty years higher.

Around 2008 about 10 per cent of the world's people lived in states where GDP per capita was $1,500 or less. Conversely their counterparts in Europe and North America lived in states with economies that were over twenty times richer, and as we shall see below, this disparity maps directly onto wages and living standards. Perhaps it is because of the magnitude of this difference, one that makes it hard to think in global terms when the everyday conditions of life vary so much across areas of the world, that less notice than one might have expected has been taken not only of demographic progress, in the sense of longer, healthier lives, but of demographic convergence, in the sense of the patterns of population reproduction and the particular form the latter have taken. Demographic progress has also been overlooked because one large area of the world has not only missed out on it but has been deteriorating. Life expectancy in parts of Sub-Saharan Africa has been falling and fertility falls there have mostly stalled (Bongaarts 2008). Finally the fragile state of theory within demography as a discipline, dominated by the demographic transition paradigm, has often obscured the wider significance of such convergence.

The last half-century of world population history has been about the rise in cohort life expectancy: the inexorable increase in the proportions of successive generations reaching older age points. Although the precise mechanisms of the linkage may be heterogeneous, wherever they have taken place such improvements have been associated with the rapid arrival not just of lower fertility but fertility levels previously only ever experienced in affluent countries before and after the baby boom, in the 1930s, and since the 1960s. The world is very rapidly becoming one in which most women who do have children will have only one or two. The result of this is what has come to be known as 'population ageing': an increase in each country in the proportion of older cohorts and corresponding decrease in the proportion of younger cohorts. Its precise form and impact varies a good deal across countries, but it is a thoroughly global phenomenon. In affluent societies it has usually been seen as a challenging or threatening development. On the contrary, we argue below that this democratization of longevity, for that is what it is, has been the twentieth century's greatest achievement.

149

The decline of fertility

In the early 1950s, if we looked beyond Europe, North America, Australasia, and Japan, just a handful of countries, accounting for less that 2 per cent of the world's population, had total fertility rates under-five. The only states of any size with fertility levels below this were Argentina (at 3.2) and North Korea (3.4). In the rest of the world, accounting for over three-fifths of its population, the fertility rate was over six. In countries as diverse as Mexico, Turkey, Algeria, Nigeria, Ethiopia, Iran or the Philippines, it was around seven. It must be borne in mind that fertility rates of this magnitude, given the proportion of women who never married, were infertile or who died before reaching the end of their fertile years, implied a much greater numbers of births for most mothers. This was especially so because beyond the industrialized states, life expectancy at birth was almost universally low: around 40 for both Asia and Africa, and a little over ten years more in Latin America and the Caribbean (Table 8.2).

Fifty years later, less than the span of a couple of generations, we find a picture that is utterly transformed for all but that tenth of the world's population condemned to live in Sub-Saharan Africa. Elsewhere, only four countries in the world now have a fertility rate above five: Afghanistan, Yemen, Oman, and the Occupied Territory of the Gaza strip. *Half* the world's population now live in countries with fertility rates near or below what demographers sometimes refer to as 'replacement level' (roughly speaking the fertility level needed to replace the current population, assuming that no women die before reaching the end of their reproductive years). Among the countries with 'below replacement fertility' are not only such well-known cases as China, Singapore or South Korea, but less publicized examples such as Algeria, Iran, Vietnam, Sri Lanka, Myanmar, Thailand or Turkey. Indeed, as Figure 8.6 suggests, despite the publicity its 'one child' policy has received, the fertility drop in China has been no greater than that in many other rapidly developing countries. Fertility rates pay little attention to either the

Table 8.2 Fertility, life expectancy at birth and infant mortality (‰) by major world regions, 1950–5 and 2000–5.

	1950–5			2000–5		
	Fertility rate (TFR)	Life expectancy at birth (e₀) (both sexes)	Infant mortality (‰)	Fertility rate (TFR)	Life expectancy at birth (e₀) (both sexes)	Infant mortality (‰)
N. Africa	6.9	41.8	189	2.9	68.2	41
Sub-Saharan Africa	6.8	37.6	177	5.2	51.0	80
Asia	5.9	41.0	176	2.4	70.8	30
Europe	2.7	65.6	72	1.5	75.2	7
Latin America & Caribbean	5.9	51.4	–	2.4	73.1	22
N. America	3.5	72.0	29	2.0	78.4	6
Oceania	3.7	66.7	61	2.3	77.8	13
World	5.1	46.4	153	2.6	69.5	32

Source: 1950–55: Population Division of the Department of Economic and Social Affairs of the United Nations Secretariat, *World Population Prospects: The 2006 Revision* and *World Urbanization Prospects: The 2005 Revision*, http://esa.un.org/unpp, 4 January 2009; 2008: Central Intelligence Agency, *The 2008 World Factbook*, https://www.cia.gov/library/publications/the-world-factbook/index.html, 4 January 2009.

ideology of the regime in power or religion. The United States now has a higher fertility rate than either Vietnam, governed by the Vietnamese Communist Party, or Iran, officially a Shia Muslim Theocracy.

While world fertility has almost halved since 1950, life expectancy at birth has increased by one half, rising at around five years per decade. Fifty years ago, in most of the world, around one in six or one in seven babies died before their first birthday. Today in Sub-Saharan Africa almost one in twelve still die. Elsewhere, almost half the world's people live in countries where infant mortality is 25 per thousand or below: rates similar to those of the United States or the UK in the early 1960s.

Figure 8.5 shows the very high relationship between fertility and life expectancy for the largest 25 countries in the world, which account for about three-quarters of world population, comparing their position in 1950 and now. The light grey circles represent countries around 2005, and the black ones those same countries around 1950–55. It can be seen that fifty years ago two quite distinct demographic regimes existed. A few countries – the USA, UK, France Germany, Italy, Japan, Russia, and the Ukraine, represented by the cluster of eight black circles at the top right hand side of the graph – enjoyed relatively long life expectancies and had lower fertility rates than countries elsewhere. All the other largest countries were clustered at the lower left-hand side of the graph with high mortality and correspondingly high fertility. Fifty years on, and it can readily be seen that with a few exceptions, the cluster from the bottom left of the graph has joined those at the top right, although the latter have continued to develop still lower rates of fertility and longer life expectancies.

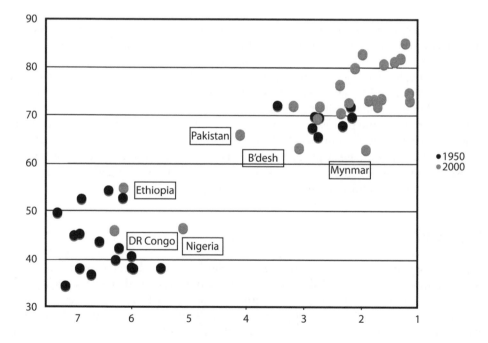

Figure 8.5 Total fertility and life expectancy at birth, 1950–5 and 2000–5.

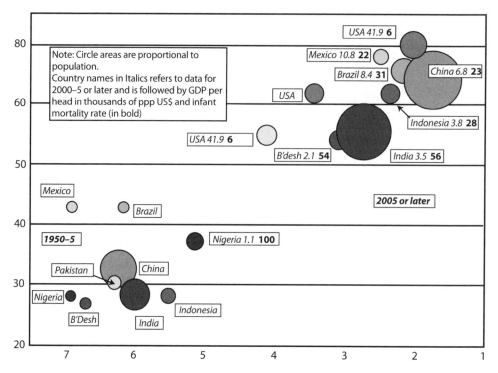

Figure 8.6 Total fertility, life expectancy at birth, GDP and infant mortality, 1950–5 and 2000–5.

There is also a remarkable absence of countries from the middle of the graph. We find this effect too if we repeat the graph for all countries. This is because when fertility and mortality fall they neither drift down gradually nor do they appear to arrive at other end points, although, as the experience of Sub-Saharan Africa shows, such development is not automatic. It is here we find virtually the only countries where the shift to a new demographic regime has 'stalled' (Bongaarts 2008).

Figure 8.6 shows the process in rather more detail for the eight largest countries of the world (which account for just over half its population). In addition to the data contained in Figure 8.2 countries are depicted proportional to the size of their population in each of the two time periods, and current GDP per capita (in US$ ppp) and infant mortality rates (per 1,000 live births) are shown for the later period.

Migration

The development of a global demographic regime has also changed migration. It has often been assumed that globalization has caused unprecedented spatial mobility (e.g. Urry 2000), especially across national frontiers, but as we shall see, states' determination to police such mobility has kept migration *below* the levels reached before the First World War. Almost the entire cost of this is borne by the world's poor. Indeed, states spend about one third as much on maintaining migration controls as they do on all development aid (Pritchett 2006). It is often forgotten that the world's most powerful state was not only founded by migrants, but continues to derive its demographic momentum from them. It was only at the beginning of the twentieth century that most states either developed much interest in controlling migration across their frontiers, or the means to do so (Torpey 1999). Indeed whether they ever have or ever will be able to do so effectively is doubtful. Despite spending billions of dollars attempting to control its border with Mexico, using unmanned drones, seismic sensors, and some 36,000 border guards (*Economist*, 3 January 2008) more than half a million migrants are estimated to enter the US unlawfully each year, on top of the million who enter as official permanent residents, and a third of a million granted temporary entry. Some do not make it. 453 people died attempting to cross this border in 2005: about twice the number of those killed trying to cross the Berlin Wall in its 27-year history. The US thus dominates contemporary global migration.

Emigration to the colonies was not only substantial from the seventeenth century onwards; it was associated with the mass destruction and genocide of Indigenous peoples in North and South America, the Caribbean, Australia, and elsewhere. An estimated 15 million slaves were taken to the Americas by 1850 (when world population was less than one quarter of today's total). Potts (1990) estimates that up to 37 million indentured labourers were used in the nineteenth and early twentieth centuries in systems analogous to slavery. Around 55 million Europeans emigrated to the colonies between 1850 and 1914 mostly to the United States. This 'raised the New World labour force by a third, and decreased the Old World labour force by an eighth' (Hatton and Williamson 1998: 4). Industrialization also drove international migration within Europe, of Irish and Jews to Britain, of Poles, Italians, Belgians, and Dutch to Germany, and of many different countries to France. Polanyi (1944) argues that the free movement of labour was one of the key elements of the capitalist order that fell apart after the First World War.

It is often forgotten that the world's 'huddled masses' who emigrated to the United States, both then and now, did so not only because of political exile or economic oppression, important though these were, but also because of economic opportunity. Hatton and Williamson (1998: 35) estimate wages in the receiving countries in the 1870s at 50 per cent higher than those prevailing in Great Britain, around double those in Germany, and between two and three times those in Ireland, Norway, Sweden, and Italy.

Just as states responded to the economic depression of the interwar period with protectionist policies, they began to restrict immigration. The United States started to regulate immigration from the 1880s onwards, on racial grounds, first barring Chinese and Asians, and under the influence of eugenic ideas, Southern Europeans and Latin Americans in 1920 (Mosisa 2002). An exception to the general picture was France, where the vast loss of men in the First World War, combined with a long-established low fertility rate, led to the inflow of some two million immigrants in the 1920s, many of whom were promptly sacked and deported as the 1930s depression took hold (Castles and Miller 2003).

The long global capitalist boom that followed from the end of the Second World War to the oil shock of the 1970s also stimulated migration, such as that from the Commonwealth countries to the UK, or the 'guest-worker' system in Germany that drew in some two million Turks. By the end of the boom between 6 and 8 per cent of the populations of most European countries comprised foreign-born immigrants. While immigration to the United States did not feature in the long boom (instead this was characterized by the mass migration of blacks from the southern states) the reform of its immigration legislation in 1965 led to a steady increase in immigration until it reached its current volume.

By 2005 the UN estimated that 190 million people were international migrants, almost 3 per cent of the world's population, rather more than double the volume of thirty years ago. Of these some 13 million were refugees. However accurate data on migration in general and refugees in particular are difficult to collect since much immigration is clandestine, in some countries the status of refugees is contested, and in the poorer countries of Sub-Saharan Africa, ravaged by civil and ethnic warfare, estimates of the numbers involved is a question of enlightened guesswork. International migration today is dominated by flows of people towards richer economies in search of work, whether in formal or informal employment, that is usually precarious, badly paid or with poor or unsafe conditions of work that make it unattractive to the resident established population. However many migrants are relatively highly skilled: a World Bank survey in 2000 of OECD economies estimated that over one-third have college educations. The single country with the largest migrant stock is the United States, with 38 million migrants, 13 per cent of its population. Europe, excluding the former Soviet bloc countries, has some 42 million while the Russian Federation, Ukraine, and Belarus have about half that number, although here many 'migrants' are people who have become so as a result of changes in borders and citizenship definitions, rather than by any movement of population. The rich Gulf states of Saudi Arabia, Bahrain, Kuwait, Oman, Qatar, and the Emirates hold another 13 million migrants, accounting for over one-third of their populations. One investigation found construction workers in Dubai earning 400–500 dirhams a month ($90–110) for working 60 hours a week or more. Housed in labour camps they had no access to healthcare or civil or political rights, such as the right to form unions, while the employment agency held their passports (*Guardian*, 8 October 2008). For illegal workers without papers, conditions were much worse.

Singapore and Hong Kong hold 5 million migrants, just over two-fifths of their population, while Australia and New Zealand account for another 5 million migrants, around one-fifth of their populations. However, not all richer countries depend on migration. Japan has only 2 million migrants, less than 2 per cent of its population. The proportion in South Korea, and Thailand is similar, whereas Vietnam claims to have just twenty thousand migrants in a population of 84 million.

However, although these volumes of migration at first sight appear to be high, they are well below the levels of movement across the Atlantic in the forty years before 1914, despite the fact that several forces encouraging migration have become much stronger since then (Pritchett 2006). Technological change has revolutionized both travel and communications not only making migration cheaper, faster, safer, and easier but also by facilitating that social support networks that are often vital to it. Economic and cultural globalization, sustained by new communications technology such as satellite broadcasting and the web, together with the end of the Cold War and increased fluidity in geopolitics, has probably reduced the cultural and symbolic distance between people in different parts of the world. Increases in absolute standards of living almost everywhere beyond sub-Saharan Africa, together with the great increase in urbanization, mean that more of the world's poor than ever before have the minimum resources necessary to put the desire to migrate into practice. There is now, for probably the first time in history a genuinely global proletariat, whose size is growing rapidly. Finally, and most importantly, income differentials between rich and poor countries are far higher than those between the old and new worlds at the end of the nineteenth century. The last two points deserve more detailed attention.

As Table 8.3 shows, since 1980, the global workforce has increased by more than half, from 1.9 to 3.1 billion, and almost all of that increase has been in the less developed countries, and associated with urbanization, as shown in Table 8.4. However, this comparison understates the degree of change, since until around the fall of the Berlin Wall, much of the economic activity in the Soviet bloc, India, and China was only very weakly integrated into the global capitalist market. Freeman (2005) thus suggests that the global proletariat probably doubled in size during the 1980s and 1990s, and most importantly, brought a vast army of increasingly well-qualified workers paid a fraction of the wages typical of older industrialized countries into the global marketplace.

International comparisons of wages are bedevilled by the need to find units of comparison across vastly different social and economic contexts, but Ashenfelter and Jurajda (2004) have proposed an ingenious answer to this problem by analyzing the wages paid for the almost identical jobs done by McDonald's restaurant food preparation staff in capital cities in different countries. The Japanese 'McWage' is no less than 27 times its Indian counterpart. Adjusted for 'Big Macs per hour' (the number of another virtually identical *product* that can be purchased with an hour of the McWage) the differential falls to about 13, and adjusted for purchasing power parity using the World Bank's world development indicators, it is six.

It thus seems clear that wage differentials between developed and developing states now are three to seven times as large as those between the old and new worlds in the previous age of mass migration. Moreover, *within* developed OECD countries, McWages differ little. This paradox is easily explained by immigration controls. McDonald's employees in India, China or Colombia cannot enter Japan, the EU or USA, while migration between advanced states is much easier. They must continue to work three or four hours to earn enough for the same Big Mac that their counterparts in developed countries achieve in a little over twenty minutes.

Debate over the significance of migration often hinges on comparing the impact upon developing countries of the 'brain drain' represented by such immigration, compared to

Table 8.3 Economically active population (15+), 1980–2006.

	2006	1980	Increase	% Increase
More developed countries	608	516	92	18
Less developed countries:	2477	1387	1091	79
Africa	366	172	194	113
Asia	1912	1142	769	67
Latin America & the Caribbean	263	126	136	108
World	3085	1903	1183	62

Source: International Labour Organization estimates and projections of the economically active population: 1980–2020 (fifth edition, August 2008), available at http://laborsta.ilo.org, data downloaded 19 January 2009.

Table 8.4 Urban population as percentage of total population, 1950–2010.

Year	More developed	Less developed	Least developed	World
1950	52.5	19.4	7.3	29.1
1970	64.6	26.9	13.1	36.0
1990	71.2	37.2	21.0	43.0
2000	73.1	42.6	24.8	46.6
2010	75.0	48.1	29.4	50.6

the benefits it may offer them, especially in terms of the remittances sent by migrants, which at up to half a trillion dollars annually represent by far the biggest flow of resources from richer to developing countries. Also important are what have been called 'social remittances': the diffusion of new ideas, attitudes, behaviours, products, information, and technology facilitated by migration. However, as Pritchett (2006) has argued, it has been rich states ability to *prevent* the kind of migration that established the New World in the decades up to 1914 that locks most of the global proletariat out of equal participation in contemporary world capitalist development in what he terms 'everything but labour' globalization. Estimates of the economic impact of liberalizing labour migration depend upon too many assumptions to be precise, but even marginal changes, enough to increase rich states' labour forces by 3 per cent, would bring estimated annual benefits of at least one-third of a trillion dollars to workers from poor countries.

The McWage in developed countries is so high relative to others, not only because most of the global proletariat are excluded, but because post-industrial economies generate not only highly skilled employment, but what Baumol (1967) termed 'technologically non-progressive activities': service work that can neither be automated nor, typically, performed remotely from the site of its consumption because it requires the physical presence of the person providing it rendering it 'non-tradable' (e.g. cleaning). As Marx (1976) described in his General Law of Capitalist Accumulation, as technological innovation displaces labour, it flows to sectors where such innovation is not possible. Someone must be there to hand over your Big Mac, while bank teller operations can be undertaken by a cash-dispensing machine, or call centres located anywhere in the globe. Such non-tradable service activities are concentrated in personal care, or reproduction, which takes us back to the starting point of this chapter.

The global reproductive revolution

Stand outside a school in Barcelona and you will see large numbers of mothers from Peru, Mexico, Ecuador, and other Latin American countries taking the children to school. However, it is not their own children they bring; the latter are usually still in Latin America. They are 'Canguros': childminders. Others care for the elderly or work in such occupations such as cleaning, retailing or catering. Spain stands out since illegal migration there from Latin America is facilitated by the low risk of deportation, the high chance of regularization, and a common language, while the dearth of public services for either child or elder care increases the private demand for such reproductive work. According to the Labour Force Survey (which may well undercount undocumented workers) over a million such women have arrived there since 2000, three-quarters of them aged from 16 to 54.

Both such migration and the changes in mortality and fertility we have considered earlier can be seen as part of the final, global stages of the general reproductive revolution which has accompanied the rise of modernity. Migration within states is linked to international migration, insofar as the move to urban centres may be the first stage in international migration, and both are driven by the development of the global market. The expansion of the latter, in turn is bound up with the shift of resources from the reproduction of people to the production of commodities made possible by the reproductive revolution. Meanwhile the expansion of population made possible by the latter in its early stages has produced what can be seen as a global workforce. Domestic and international migration can be seen as the result of the ability of capital to draw the surplus population released by this process into both the production of goods and reproduction of people.

Zelinsky (1971) outlined a theory of what he called 'the mobility transition'. Social and spatial mobility is first stimulated by uneven economic development, such as the concentration of industry in urban centres, or the process of colonization of 'virgin' territories by the imperial powers. As the demographic transition advances, lowering the increase in surplus population, the focus of mobility shifts towards the redistribution of the population within the economically more developed areas, so that for example, population declines in inner city areas, suburban sprawl develops, rural depopulation comes to an end, until ultimately mobility becomes predominantly a function of the rise and decline of different sectors of the economy and the relative attractiveness of different spatial locations in a world with little surplus population to be drawn into the system, since the latter has become global: what he called 'the super-advanced society of the future'.

In a sense Zelinsky was only filling in some of the empirical detail to Marx and Engel's precocious portrait, over a century earlier, of the creation of a global capitalist system which was subjecting the country to the rule of the towns and drawing barbarian nations into civilization, using raw materials 'drawn from the remotest zones' for products to be consumed, 'in every quarter of the globe' and smashing all 'fixed, fast-frozen relations, with their train of ancient and venerable prejudices and opinions' (Marx and Engels 1976: 486–89). However Zelinsky's theory draws greater attention than their simpler formulation to the relationship between reproduction and production. A further step in such theorization was the work of Cabré (1999) on the demographic history of Catalonia, which showed how the reproduction of population in this region of Spain had from an early stage depended heavily on in-migration. In this sense the earlier demographic history of Catalonia serves as a precursor to what has become the emergence of a new global pattern to the reproduction of population: with one exception. Just as towns usually drew no barriers around themselves to migration (although at times this was attempted in Russia and China) there was no frontier between Catalonia and the destitute agrarian Spanish hinterland on which it drew.

The global fall of fertility, and rise in life expectancy can be seen as perhaps the most revolutionary shift of all, since it at once undermines one of the most important roots of patriarchy, while at the same time liberating a tremendous proportion of social effort previously devoted to reproduction for use in production, analogous to the way in which the revolution in agricultural productivity released labour from the countryside for work in industry, or de-industrialization enabled the growth of the service sector (MacInnes and Pérez 2009b). The way in which this revolution produced a period of rapid global population growth, made possible the creation of a truly global market system and expanding world proletariat in the final two decades of the last century. For a few decades to come this new system will continue to be characterized by the both domestic and international migration flows as the surplus population created by the early stages of the reproductive revolution is drawn towards the centres of economic development.

However, as fertility continues to fall, and the economies of Asia and Latin America continue to expand, the size of this surplus population, and the migration flows associated with it, will reduce rapidly. Meanwhile, both the male breadwinner system, and other forms of gender inequality in production and reproduction, will continue to be undermined, first by the declining relevance of the social regulation of fertility, and later by the declining weight of specifically reproductive work in society as a whole. At the same time, as life spans continue to increase, and the years of healthy life available after retirement rise steadily, issues of intergenerational equity will become more important. In the longer term, the global capitalist system will at some point in the future run out of surplus population for the first time in its history. Henceforth its ability to generate such a surplus will indeed depend upon its ability to slough off labour from established sectors of production faster than it can be absorbed by newly emerging ones. The probable considerable tightening of the global labour supply might augur well for further social progress.

Of course the actual course of such development will depend on all manner of unpredictable empirical change. Much will depend on whether a way is found to liberate Africa from its political, economic, and demographic prison, and on whether the institutions of global trade and commerce manage the shift in economic power from the North to the East without either collapsing or veering towards some post cold war system of economic blocks.

The population of Europe is already dependent on immigration to continue rising, and it looks as if the world population itself will likely soon reach a maximum at around 9 billion (Lutz 2004). Mortality will continue to fall, but it is far from clear where its limits lie (Olshansky et al. 1990; Wilmoth 1997; Wilmoth et al. 1999, 2000). Already more than half of the world's population of those over 65 live outside more developed countries. The proportion of what are sometimes called the 'oldest old', those over 80, will grow rapidly, so that on current projections, the world will have over 400 million octogenarians by 2050, three-quarters of whom will live in what are today classed as less or least developed countries. However, it is unclear what extra demand, if any, this will place on health and welfare systems. As long as *healthy* life expectancy (something intrinsically more difficult to measure than the span of life itself) continues to increase with life expectancy, and morbidity continues to be concentrated in the final years of life, then there may be little extra demand. Conversely, to the extent that new interventions become possible to combat the very different patterns of mortality and morbidity found in populations with longer life spans, and to the extent that older people demand higher standards of healthy living made possible by new treatments and technologies, then demand may increase greatly.

Nor is the future course of fertility clear. In contrast to the fears expressed by many demographers that fertility might have no lower limit, and that rapid population decline be in prospect for many countries in Europe or elsewhere, few have noticed that since before the turn of the century, fertility has been rising almost everywhere in Europe, and in other affluent countries too. However, the course of history will be shaped by the development for the first time of a global reproductive system with no surplus population to colonize. This might further increase the pressure towards gender equality, made possible by the reproductive revolution, analogous to the way in which the long boom of 1945 to 1973 eroded the foundations of the male breadwinner system in North America and Europe. Insofar as it does so, humankind will leave behind what we might think of as the pre-history of reproduction and with it the greatest of all 'ancient and venerable prejudices'.

Notes

1 Unless otherwise stated the sources for data quoted in the text is the United Nations Population Division, *World Population Prospects 2006 revision Population Database*, available at http://esa.un.org/unpp. More recent estimates, where available, have also been used.

2 Replacement level fertility is a term used by demographers to refer to that level of fertility necessary in a population to maintain its current volume in the long term. Frequently this level is stated to be a total fertiltiy rate (see below) of 2.1 children per woman. This is a misnomer, however. It applies only in populations where all women survive to the end of their fertile years, and takes no account of falling mortality or of migration, both of which may push the level of replacement fertility well below the 2.1 mark.

3 Demographers use the term 'parity' to refer to the number and order of births. Thus parity specific control refers to control aimed at producing a specific final desired number of children.

4 We use the United Nations definitions: the more developed countries comprise all of Europe and Northern America, Australia, New Zealand, and Japan. The less developed regions comprise all regions of Africa, Asia (excluding Japan), Latin America and the Caribbean, Melanesia, Micronesia, and Polynesia, excluding the least developed countries as defined by the United Nations General Assembly in December 2003: Afghanistan, Angola, Bangladesh, Benin, Bhutan, Burkina Faso, Burundi, Cambodia, Cape Verde, Central African Republic, Chad, Comoros, Democratic Republic of Timor-Leste, Democratic Republic of the Congo, Djibouti, Equatorial Guinea, Eritrea, Ethiopia, Gambia, Guinea, Guinea-Bissau, Haiti, Kiribati, Lao People's Democratic Republic, Lesotho, Liberia, Madagascar, Malawi, Maldives, Mali, Mauritania, Mozambique, Myanmar, Nepal, Niger, Rwanda, Samoa, Sao Tome and Principe, Senegal, Sierra Leone, Solomon Islands, Somalia, Sudan, Togo, Tuvalu, Uganda, the United Republic of Tanzania, Vanuatu, Yemen, and Zambia.

References

Ashenfelter, O and Jurajda, S. 2004. 'Cross-Country Comparisons of Wage Rates: The Big Mac Index', unpublished manuscript, University of Princeton. Available at www.cerge.cuni.cz/news/data/McWage%20Index.pdf.

Baumol, W. J. 1967. 'Macroeconomics of Unbalanced Growth: The Anatomy of Urban Crisis', *American Economic Review*, 157: 415–426.

Becker, G. S. 1991. *A Treatise on the Family*. Cambridge, MA: Harvard University Press.

Billig, M. 1995. *Banal Nationalism*. London: Sage.

Bongaarts, J. 2008. 'Fertility Transitions in Developing Countries: Progress or Stagnation?', *Studies In Family Planning*, 39(2): 105–10.

Caldwell, J. C. and Caldwell, P. 1986. *Limiting Population Growth and the Ford Foundation Contribution*. London: Frances Pinter.

Cabré i Pla, A. 1999. *El sistema català de reproducció. Cent anys de singularitat demogràfica*. Barcelona: Edicions Proa.

Carr-Saunders, A. M. 1922. *The Population Problem: A Study in Human Evolution*. Clarendon: Oxford.

Castles, S. and Miller, J. 2003. *The Age of Migration*, 3rd edn. Basingstoke: Palgrave.

Chesnais, J.-C. 1992. *The Demographic Transition: Stages, Patterns and Implications* (trans. Elizabeth and Philip Kraeger). Oxford: Clarendon Press.

Cleland, J. and Wilson, C. 1987. 'Demand Theories of the Fertility Transition: an Iconoclastic View', *Population Studies*, 41(1): 5–30.

Cleland, J. 2001. 'The Effects of Improved Survival on Fertility: A Reassessment', *Population and Development Review*, Supplement: Global Fertility Transition, 27: 60–92.

Coale, A. J. and Watkins, S. C. (eds) 1986. *The Decline of Fertility in Europe*. Princeton: Princeton University Press.

Davis, K. (1937), 'Reproductive Institutions and the Pressure for Population', *The Sociological Review*, XXIX: 284–306.

Demeny, P. 2003. *Population Policy: A Concise Summary*. Population Council Policy Research Division Working Paper no. 173.

Dumont, G. F. 2008. 'Les conséquences géopolitiques de L'hiver démographique en Europe', *Geéostratégiques*, 20: 29–46.

Dupâquier, J. and Dupâquier, M. 1985. *Histoire de la démographie*. Paris: Librairie Academique Perrin.

Ehrlich, P. 1968. *The Population Bomb*. New York: Ballantine.

Finkle, J. L. and McIntosh, A. C. 2002. 'United Nations Population Conferences: Shaping the Policy Agenda for the Twenty-first Century', *Studies in Family Planning*, 33(1) 11–23.

Freeman, R. 2005, 'What Really Ails Europe (and America): The Doubling of the Global Workforce', *The Globalist*, 3 June.

Foucault, M. 1989. *Sécurité, territoire et population. Résumé des cours*. París: Julliard.

Gilbert, G. 2005. *World Population*, 2nd edn. Oxford: ABC-CLIO.

Glass, D. V. 1936. *The Struggle for Population*. Oxford: Clarendon Press.

Hajnal, J. 1965. 'European Marriage Patterns in Perspective', in D. V. Glass and E. C. Eversley (eds) *Population in History*. London: Edward Arnold, 101–43.

Hatton, T. and Williamson, J. 1998. *The Age of Mass Migration: Causes and Economic Impact*. Oxford: Oxford University Press.

Henry, L. 1956. *Anciennes familles Genevoises*. Paris: INED.

——1965. 'Réflexions sur les taux de reproduction', *Population (French Edition)*, 1: 53–76.

Hodgson, D. 1983. 'Demography as Social Science and Policy Science', *Population and Development Review*, 9: 1–34.

——1988. 'Orthodoxy and revisionism in American demography', *Population and Development Review*, 14: 541–69.

Kenealy, A. 1920. *Feminism and Sex Extinction*. London: T. Fisher Unwin

Kuhn, T. S. 1962. *The Structure of Scientific Revolutions*. Chicago: University of Chicago Press.

Landry, A. 1934. *La révolution démographique*. Paris: Sirey.

Laslett, P. 2000. *The World We Have Lost: Further Explored*. London: Routledge.

Le Bras, H. 1991. *Marianne et les Lapins: l'obsession démographique*. Paris: O. Orban.

——1998. *Le Démon des Origines*. Paris: Éditions de l'Aube.

Lee, R. 1981. 'Short Term Variation: Vital Rates, Prices, and Weather', in J. A. Wrigley and R. S. Schofield (eds) *The Population History of England, 1541–1871*. Cambridge, MA: Harvard University Press.

Lee, J. and Feng, W. 1999. 'Malthusian Models and Chinese Realities: The Chinese Demographic System 1700–2000', *Population and Development Review*, 25(1): 33–65.

Livi-Bacci, M. 2001, *A Concise History of World Population*, 3rd edn. Oxford: Blackwell.

MacInnes, J. and Pérez, J. 2007. 'Low Fertility and Population Replacement in Scotland', *Population Space and Place*, 13(1): 3–21.

——2009a. 'Demography', in B. S. Turner (ed). *The New Blackwell Companion to Social Theory*. Oxford: Blackwell.

——2009b. 'The Reproductive Revolution', *Sociological Review*, 57(2): 262–84.

MacKenzie, D. 1976. 'Eugenics in Britain', *Social Studies of Science*: 499–532.

——1981. *Statistics in Britain 1865 – 1930: The Social Construction of Scientific Knowledge*. Edinburgh: Edinburgh University Press.

Malthus, D. 1970. *An Essay on the Principle of Population* (ed. Anthony Flew). Harmondsworth: Pelican Books.

Marx, K. and Engels, F. 1976. '*Manifesto of the Communist Party*' [1848] in K. Marx and F. Engels, *Collected Works*, Vol. 6. London: Lawrence and Wishart.

Marx, K. 1976. *Capital*, Vol. 1. Harmondsworth: Penguin.

Mosisa, A. I. 2002. 'The Role of Foreign-born Workers in the U.S. Economy', *Monthly Labor Review*, May, 3–15.

Myrdal, A. (1968 [1939]). *Nation and Family*. Cambridge, MA: MIT Press.

Olshansky, S. J., Carnes, B. A. and Cassel, C. 1990. 'In Search of Methuselah: Estimating the Upper Limits to Human Longevity', *Science*, 250: 634–40.

Omran, A. R. 1971. 'The Epidemiologic Transition: A Theory of the Epidemiology of Population Change', *The Milbank Memorial Fund Quarterly*, 49: 509–38. Reprinted in *The Milbank Quarterly*, 83: 731–57 (2005).

Polanyi, K. 1944. *The Great Transformation*. Boston, MA: Beacon Press.

Potts, L. 1990. *The World Labour Market: A History of Migration*. London: Zed Books.

Pritchett, L. 2006. *Let Their People Come*. Washington: Center for Global Development.

Riley, J. C. 2001. *Rising Life Expectancy: A Global History*. Cambridge: Cambridge Uuniversity Press.

Robinson, W. C. 1997. 'The Economic Theory of Fertility Decline Over Three Decades', *Population Studies*, 51: 63–74.

Ryder, N. B. 1964. 'Notes On The Concept Of A Population', *American Journal of Sociology*, 69(5): 447–63.

Sauvy, A. 1959. *La montée des jeunes*. Paris: Calmann-Lévy.

Schultz, T. P. 1985. 'Changing World Prices, Women's Wages, and the Fertility Transition', *Journal of Political Economy*, 93: 1126–54.

Soloway, R. A. 1990. *Demography and Degeneration: Eugenics and the Declining Birthrate in Twentieth-Century Britain*. Chapel Hill, NC: University of North Carolina Press.

Spengler, O. 1926. *The Decline of the West*. London: Allen and Unwin.

Szreter, S. 1993. 'The Idea of Demographic Transition and the Study of Fertility Change', *Population and Development Review*, 19: 659–702.

——1996. *Fertility, Class and Gender in Britain, 1860–1940*. Cambridge: Cambridge University Press.

Teitelbaum, M. S. and Winter, J. 1985. *The Fear of Population Decline*. London: Academic Press.

Thompson, W. 1929. 'Population', *American Journal of Sociology*, 34: 959–75.

Torpey, J. 1999. *The Invention of the Passport*. Cambridge: Cambridge University Press.

Urry, J. 2000. *Sociology Beyond Societies: Mobilities for the Twenty-first Century*. London: Routledge.

Willcox, W. F. 1916. 'The Nature and Significance of the Changes in the Birth and Death Rates in Recent Years', *American Statistical Association. New Series*, No. 113, March.

Wilmoth, J. R. 1997. 'In Search of Limits', in K.W. Wachter and C.E. Finch (eds) *Between Zeus and the Salmon: The Biodemography of Longevity*. Washington, DC: National Academy Press.

Wilmoth, J. R. and Horiuchi, S. 1999. 'Rectangularization Revisted: Variability of Age of Death Within Human Populations', *Demography*, 36(4): 475–96.

Wilmoth, J. R., Deegan, L. J., Lundstrom, H. and Horiuchi, S. 2000. 'Increase of Maximum Life-span in Sweden, 1861–1999', *Science*, 289: 2366–68.

Zelinsky, W. 1971. 'The Hypothesis of the Mobility Transition', *The Geographical Review*, 2: 219–49.

161

9

All that is molten freezes again

Migration history, globalization, and the politics of newness

Adam McKeown

Few people doubt that migration has a history. Many deny that globalization has one. Most analyses of globalization are deeply invested in assertions of its newness. Even accounts that do believe in a history of globalization before the 1970s can rarely agree on when it started, what it looks like, or if that history is relevant at all. But there is a majority consensus on one significant point, even if only a consensus of common omission and indifference. It is that we need not look beyond Western Europe and the North Atlantic to find the history of globalization (Hart and Negri 2001, Held *et al.* 1999, O'Rourke and Williamson 1996, Robertson 1992, Sassen 2006). The many histories of mass migration that claim up to 90 percent of world migration moved across the Atlantic from the 1840s to 1914 are often used to support this narrow geography of the "global" (Castles and Miller 2003, Emmer 1992, Glazier and De Rosa 1986, Hatton and Williamson 1998, Sassen 2000). Thus, even the histories offer little challenge to the idea that at least the "global" part of globalization is new. Belief in the spatial isolation of the West and the temporal break of "newness" are mutually reinforcing.

But if we try to search out the global antecedents of globalization and migration (to take the example for which I have done the legwork), the picture begins to look much different. Merely by putting together information long known by area specialists, we find that by the 1850s, if not earlier, migrants from Africa, Europe, and western and eastern Asia were meeting in places as distant as the Caribbean, Australia, and the steppes of Central Asia. From the islands of Polynesia to the mountains of Norway, and from the Alaskan gold fields to the Mekong Delta rice paddies, no part of the world was untouched by migration. Peak migration rates from China, India, the South Pacific, and the Middle East were easily as dense as peak migration rates from Europe, and movements into the frontiers of southeast and northeast Asia were as numerically significant as those into the Americas. And for most destinations other than the United States, it lasted well beyond the usual cut-off date 1914, until the Great Depression or longer.

The first wave of modern mass migration in the industrial era was a truly global phenomenon, part and parcel of the expanding global industrial economy. Migrants who traveled long and short distances to the factories of Chicago, Manchester, and Tokyo were dependent on resources produced by those who traveled to the tin mines and rubber plantations of Malaya, the sheep ranches of Australia, and the iron and coal mines of Manchuria. All of these ate food produced by migrants who opened the cattle and wheat fields North America, the rice paddies of Southeast Asia, and the soy bean fields of Manchuria, not to mention those recruited to work the sugar plantations of Cuba, the tea plantations of Assam and Sri Lanka, and the coffee plantations of Brazil. These raw materials and manufactures were gathered, transported, and sold by yet more migrants who carried goods and money up and down distant rivers, into and out of dense forests, setting up shop in dusty rural towns and crowded urban ghettos. Many of these goods were used for the creation of an ever-expanding transportation infrastructure of roads, railroads and steamships that generated more migrant labor for construction and operation, who in turn facilitated the movement of yet more migrants, resources and manufactures to more destinations. It was a snowballing process that caused world migration rates to grow even faster than world population (McKeown 2004: 167).

But something funny happened on the road to global integration. Even as global trade and migration intensified in the late nineteenth and early twentieth centuries, and even as the organization and cycles of migration grew increasingly similar around the world, the patterns and destinations became increasingly segregated. More Africans moved only to Africa, Indians and southern Chinese to Southeast Asia, and Japanese, Koreans, and north Chinese to northeast Asia. Only the Europeans retained much of their earlier globe-spanning mobility, although the great bulk still moved to the Americas. Global integration grew hand in hand with the globalization of borders. These included not only the national borders that were increasingly sites of regulation and migration control, but also those macro-borders between East and West, civilized and uncivilized, First and Third Worlds, or white, black and yellow races that, while much less concrete than the national borders have had even more potent effects on the social and cultural organization of the world.

These macro-borders have shaped our histories of globalization and global migration. The segregation of migration into regions makes it easier to obscure those migrations beyond the Atlantic, to imagine those regions as having been outside of globalization rather than as the products of globalization. This is not only a case of bad memory and research. The very ideas and institutions that created this segregation also produced this memory. Indenture, empire, exclusionary migration laws, images of the coolie, contrasts between tropical and temperate regions and international law rooted in discourses of "civilization" are among the many processes that produced ideas of Asians as an ignorant, impoverished, distant, earthbound and tradition-bound peasantry residing in economically and culturally backwards areas that were isolated from the interactions, progress, and dislocations of modernity that shaped the North Atlantic. This spatial segregation makes it possible for globalization history to reside in that timeless epoch of the "new." By obscuring the interactions of the past, the historical institutions and reach of globalization can be restricted to narrow geographical space of the North Atlantic, from which it is always expanding to embrace a virgin world (McKeown 2007).

The rhetoric of newness has inspired sparkling and evocative globalization prose at least since Marx and Engels proclaimed that "All fixed, fast-frozen relations, with their train of venerable prejudices and opinions are swept away. All that is solid melts into air ... [as] the bourgeoisie, by the rapid improvement of all instruments of production, by the immensely facilitated means of communication, draws all, even the most barbarian nations into civilization" (Marx and Engels 2001 (1848): 13–14). Whether the effects of globalization are seen as positive or negative, they are usually depicted as an unprecedented transformation, transcending borders and differences that have never been transcended before (if not for the North Atlantic, then at least for the world). The rhetoric of newness is a key foundation of the politics of globalization, repeated with every generation over the past century and a half. It insists that new institutions and reforms are needed to meet these new challenges. It denies the extent to which the world as we know it was created through earlier global interactions. It obscures the extent to which the reforms and institutions proposed to deal with these challenges are often just intensifications of the very same institutions that over at least the past two centuries have created the world of differences and intercourse in which we now live.

Migration and globalization to 1930

During the first wave of modern mass migrations from the 1830s to the 1930s, over 160 million long distance migrants traveled to the frontiers of the world. They moved from the world's major centers of population in China, South Asia, and Europe towards less populated regions in the Americas, Southeast Asia, and northern Asia. The bulk of these long distance migrants can be divided into three major systems that are roughly equal in number: over 55 million migrants moved from Europe and the Middle East to the Americas, along with another 3 million from East Asia and India; over 50 million migrants from South Asia and South China moved to Southeast Asia, Australia, and islands throughout the Indian and Pacific Oceans, along with another 5 million people from the Middle East and Europe; and over 48 million migrants traveled from China, Russia, Korea, and Japan to Central Asia, Siberia, and Manchuria (sources for all quantitative estimates in this section are listed in McKeown 2004: 186–89).

These numbers only include the migrants who can be counted, that is those who traveled by ship or, as in the case of Russian migrants to Siberia, were registered by the government. Millions more moved across land borders and small bodies of water, both within the main receiving and sending regions and at the interstices between these main systems. In the Americas, this included millions of people who moved west across North America (including the forced relocation of native Americans); down from the Andes to coastal areas; out from the Caribbean to plantations and construction projects in Central America, Cuba, and the United States, and from Mexico, Canada, and the southern United states into industrial and newly expanding agricultural regions in the northeastern and western United Sates. In Europe, at least a million Irish traveled to England for work, five million Poles moved west, ten million Italians crossed the Alps or moved into France, and millions of other Europeans moved to the industrial northwestern regions of the continent, especially France and Germany. Within Russia, millions more moved into the growing cities and southern agricultural areas.

In India millions of migrants moved to tea plantations in the south and northeast, to the mines and textile producing regions of Bengal, and to newly irrigated lands and urban areas throughout the subcontinent. In China, they migrated to growing coastal cities, to areas of the Yangtze basin left under-populated by the Taiping rebellion, and to borderland areas of the northwest and southwest, including overland migration to Southeast Asia. And in Southeast Asia, at least 500,000 Javanese traveled to plantations in Sumatra and the Southeast Asian mainland, and unknown numbers of Lao speakers settled the sparsely populated regions of northeastern Thailand. In Africa over three million French, Italians, and Spaniards who moved into North Africa, and over a million more

Europeans and Asians migrated to places south of the Sahara. Many millions more also moved within Africa to mines, plantations, and coastal agricultural regions. In western Asia, from 4 to 6 million people also moved back and forth between the Russia and Ottoman empires, while many others moved into Israel and Egypt. And in what may have been some of the densest emigrations anywhere, over 300,000 Pacific Islanders worked as seamen and plantation workers throughout the region.

Emigration was always a geographically uneven process. It became a way of life in some regions and villages, even as another village a few miles down the road barely sent any emigrants—although geographic proximity to emigrant regions always increased the chance that a village or family may turn to migration as a means of making a living. But, where they can be estimated, average emigration and immigration rates were broadly similar in the around the world. At first glance 19 million overseas emigrants from China or 29 million from India seems like a drop in the bucket compared to the several millions from much smaller countries like Italy, Norway, Ireland, and England. But when we look at shifts to regions of comparable size and population, the rates are very similar. Some peak rates of overseas emigration from Europe in the 1910s are 10.8 emigrants per 1,000 population in Italy, 8.3 per 1,000 from Norway, and 7 per 1,000 from Ireland. In comparison, the annual average overseas emigration rate from Guangdong province in south China, which had a slightly larger geographic area and slightly smaller population than Italy, was at least 9.6 per 1,000 in the peak years of the 1920s. Hebei and Shandong provinces (sources of migration to Manchuria) had a rate of 10 per 1,000 during that same decade. In terms of broader regional population, emigration from Europe from 1846 to 1940 amounted to 15.4 percent of the European population in 1900, compared to 11.3 in China and 10.4 in South Asia (world population data from McEvedy and Jones, 1979). This is a significant difference, but one of degree rather than orders of magnitude. From the perspective of the receiving regions, the approximately 35 million migrants who moved into the 4.1 million square kilometers of Southeast Asia from 1870 to 1930 compares quite favorably to the 39 million migrants that moved into the 9.8 million square kilometers of the United States over the same period.

Long distance migration across the three systems also followed similar trajectories over time (Figure 9.1). It expanded until the mid-1870s, after which it stagnated for two decades along with the global economic slowdown. Transatlantic migration and, to a lesser extent, migration from South China experienced a short boom in the early 1880s. But global migration truly exploded in the mid 1890s, nearly doubling to peaks of over 3 million a year around 1910. Transatlantic migration reached a spectacular peak of over 2.1 million in 1913, and migration to Southeast and North Asia also reached unprecedented peaks of nearly 1.1 million a year from 1911 to 1913. World War One caused a global decline in migration, hitting the Atlantic the hardest. But global migration once again reached peaks of nearly 3.5 million a year in the late 1920s, with Asian migration reaching new peaks of 1.25 million migrants to Southeast Asia in 1927 and 1.5 million to North Asia in 1929. Transatlantic migration recovered to 1.2 million migrants in 1924, after which immigration quotas in the United States curtailed migration from southern and eastern Europe. The Great Depression nearly ended transatlantic migration, and slowed migration to Southeast Asia to the levels of the 1880s. In North Asia, however, the command economies of Japan and the Soviet Union used coercion and promotion to generate new peaks of up to 1.8 million migrants a year.

These migrations were part of a significant redistribution of the world's population into burgeoning frontier regions (Figure 9.2). All three main destination regions experienced

165

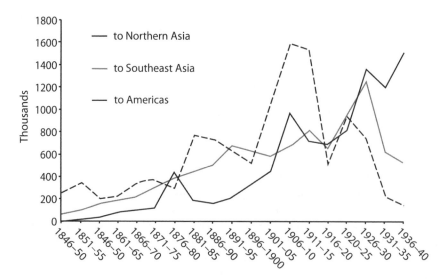

Figure 9.1 Trends in global migration, 1846–1940 (five-year averages).
Source: McKeown 2004: 165.

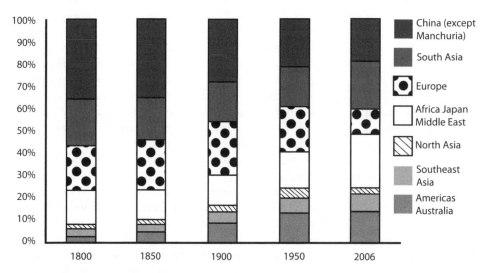

Figure 9.2 World population distribution, 1800–2006.
Source: McEvedy and Jones 1979.

massive population growth, accounting for 10 percent of the world's population in 1850 and 24 percent in 1950. Average annual rates of population increase in northern and south-eastern Asia were over twice the rate of world population growth, while the Americas increased two and a half times as quickly. Population growth in Europe and South Asia, however, was slightly lower than world rates, and in China it was less than 30 percent of world rates. Overall, long distance migration increased more quickly than world population, rising from 0.36 of the planet's population in the 1850s to 0.96 percent in the 1880s, 1.67 percent in the 1900s, and then declining to 1.58 percent in the 1920s.

The most striking evidence of the integration of migration processes around the world is the convergence of return rates in the late nineteenth century (Figure 9.3). Return rates are a good way to measure employments cycles: when employment abroad is high return rates are low, and vice versa The return rates to Europe from the United States, and to India and to China from all destinations grew increasingly similar after the 1890s, not only in terms of the timing of the cycles, but even in absolute proportions. The economic conditions shaping migration flows were increasingly integrated across the globe.

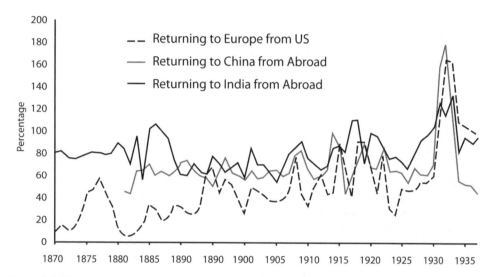

Figure 9.3 Return migrants as proportion of emigrants, 1870–1937.
Source: Carter et al. 2006: 547–8; Davis 1951: 100; McKeown 2004: 186–9.

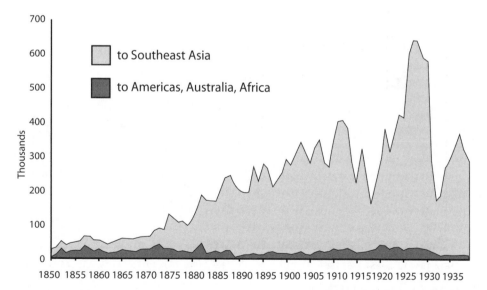

Figure 9.4 Chinese migration, 1850–1940.
Source: McKeown 2004: 188–9.

Even as migration cycles and rates converged around the world, the patterns and directions diverged. For example, from the 1850s to 1870s, up to 40 percent of migrants from south China traveled to the Americas and Australia (Figure 9.4). Nearly 250,000 of them were indentured migrants brought mostly to Peru and Cuba, but over twice that number traveled on their own volition and finances–to the extent of chartering their own ships—to North America and Australia by the mid-1880s. By the 1920s, however, as overall Chinese migration increased twenty-fold, migrations beyond Asia had stagnated. The absolute numbers to places beyond Southeast Asia remained steady, but amounted to less than 5 percent of the total by the late 1920s. This was not a consequence of inadequate resources, earth-bound peasant mentalities or any other distinction that made Chinese migrants categorically different from European emigrants. It was a product of exclusionary laws and hostile attitudes in the non-Asian destinations.

Shifts in the proportions of Indian migration beyond Asia are not so dramatic, but their exclusion from non-Asian destinations was much more complete (Figure 9.5). Nearly 30 percent of Indian overseas migration in the 1840s and 50s was to non-Asian destinations, most of it under indenture contracts. By the 1880s the proportion of migration beyond Asia declined to about 5 percent of total migration, and then down to an insignificant trickle by the 1910s. Unlike Chinese, most Indians moving beyond Asia had traveled to islands with few economic opportunities beyond the plantations, reducing the attraction for new migrants and making it difficult to build migration networks before the imposition of exclusionary measures. South Africa and colonies in eastern Africa were the only non-Asian destinations with established Indian communities and economic opportunities to attract new migrants in the early twentieth century—and South Africa excluded Asians as rigorously as any white settler nation around the Pacific.

Migration to northeastern Asia was probably the most segregated of the three systems, with the fewest migrants leaving to or arriving from places outside of the main receiving

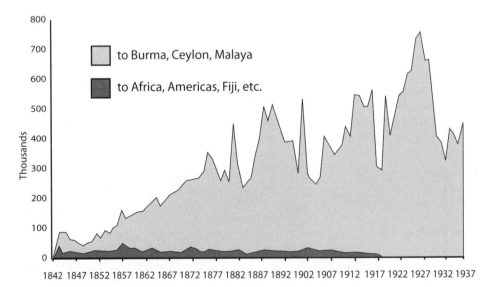

Figure 9.5 Indian migration 1842–1937.
Source: Davis 1951: 100; Heidemann 1992: 99–110.

and sending regions. But rather than the exclusionary policies that constrained migrants to southern Asia, this was more a result of the proactive settlement policies of the three expanding empires of Russia, China, and Japan, all three of which promoted (and, in the case of Russia and Japan, often closely directed and coerced) migration as a way to consolidate their control over territory and reinforce borders against their neighbors (Gottschang and Lary 2000, Treadgold 1957, Weiner 1994). Manchuria remained contested territory until after World War Two. But in the long run the Russian and Chinese migrations rank with the expansion into the American West as the most successful colonizing migrations of this era, successfully integrating new lands into the nation state.

The economic dynamics of these migrations diverged along with the directions. In the Atlantic world migration came with wage convergence, urbanization, and economic development on both sides of the Atlantic. In Southeast Asia, on the other hand, migration generated little wage convergence, substantially less urbanization, and minimal economic development. In the Atlantic migrations, sending destinations shifted in the course of one hundred years from northwest to southeast Europe as American wages converged with those in the main sending regions, and migrant occupations abroad changed rapidly. Asian migration was much less dynamic. Sending regions remained much the same for a century and occupations revolved largely around resource extraction, albeit with a small but significant shift towards retail activities by the early twentieth century.

All of the world was clearly part of the global economy, yet each part was inserted into that economy differently. This segregation and differentiation grew rather than shrunk along with increased flows and economic integration. The segregation of economy and mobility helped make it possible to depict differences as the product of isolation and timeless tradition, rather than as a product of interaction. To phrase it in the rousing cadences of globalization-speak: All fluid, shifting relations, driven by the demands of expanding markets and industry, are fixed anew, and the new-formed differences are ossified under the illusion of history. All that is molten freezes again.

A regulated world

The patterns of integration and segregation in this globalizing world did not merely arise out of elemental forces of economy, communication, and cultural difference. They were also products of intervention and regulation. In particular, the two lines dividing East from West across the Pacific Ocean and across the Mediterranean marked out the basic geographic spaces for the imagination of global difference. These imagined differences helped justify new institutions of border and migration control. Those institutions then made those lines into a concrete reality and enforced the emergence of real differences. In the context of migration, two developments stand out in this production of global difference: the enormous ideological work surrounding attempts to control and understand Asian indenture, and the pioneering institutions of modern migration control forged across the Pacific and Mediterranean.

Indenture—long-term employment contracts entered into by migrants that defrayed their transportation and resettlement costs—was, along with slavery, one of the primary modes of financing long-distance migration around the world before the 1830s. Even with the decline of formal indenture across the Atlantic after the 1830s, many migrants traveled under some kind of formal or informal debt obligation to fellow villagers and labor recruiters (Peck 2000). Most Asians traveled under similar conditions as Europeans, often building migrant networks through the help of labor recruiters and then traveling with the help of family as stronger networks were established. Many of these arrangements took place under government radar, although many colonial and Latin American governments still sponsored a variety of forms of contract labor recruitment. The indenture of Indian and Chinese migrants from the 1830s to 1910s was the most notorious of these processes, because of its massive scale, long term contracts and reputation for coercion and exploitation.

Attempts to understand and regulate Asian indenture created an understanding of Asian migrants as categorically different from European ones. In contrast to free and adventurous European pioneers, Asians came to be characterized as ignorant and impoverished peasants who could never have migrated without direct European intervention, and who even then were inherently unfree and in need of government protection against the abuses of Asian middlemen. In practice, less than 15 percent of Indians and 3 percent of Chinese were ever directly indentured to Europeans (although the great majority of Indians still worked on European-owned plantations). But the amount of publicity, documentation, diplomatic exchange, and historical writing on indenture is inversely proportionate to the actual predominance of indenture as a form of mobility in Asia. Most of the polemics about Asian indenture were incoherent and contradictory, based on recycled second and third hand accounts. Nonetheless, much of this material has since been projected into understandings of Asian migration per se.

From its very beginnings in the 1830s, Indian indenture to the Caribbean and to islands in the Indian Ocean was clouded under debates between those who depicted it as a chance for Indians to free themselves from poverty and ignorance, and those who saw it as a new form of slavery. Both sides appealed to ideals of freedom, progress, and the greater interests of the empire. Pro-indenture activists insisted that contracts and cash advances "freed" impoverished migrants to circulate throughout the empire to places where they could work most effectively for the benefit of themselves and their employers. Indenture alleviated poverty and overpopulation in India while helping British plantations to once again be competitive with those in slave colonies like Cuba and Brazil. To suppress the right of Indians to move and enter into contracts freely was to undermine British ideals. Anti-indenture activists objected that the restrictions on personal liberty entailed in indenture contracts made them akin to slavery. By infringing on freedom, the recruitment of indentured labor also infringed on humanity, family, and Christianity. The empire had a responsibility to protect the well-being of its colonial subjects, especially those who, whether due to ignorance or coercion, were unable to protect themselves against adventurers and self-interested capital (Carter 1995, Kale 1999, Mangru 1987).

Debates over Indian indenture did generate empirical investigations in the form of official commissions. The results were inconclusive. Citations from the many interviews could be used by both factions to support their point, and each side accused the other of manipulating evidence to support its own agenda. But the basic format of these investigations remained much the same until the early twentieth century, as the two positions became ossified into the very structure of the reports and their recommendations. By the 1860s, both sides also found a space of agreement in the idea that, left to themselves, Indians were inherently unfree, mired in ignorance and victimized by the exploitation of Indian middlemen and an irrational caste system. The main disagreement was whether contracts and big capital could liberate them. But, even there, both sides could agree that some level of government regulation was necessary to suppress the abuses perpetuated by Indian middlemen, which undermined both smooth labor markets and the lives and health of the migrants. The oppositional structure of the reports allowed the government to fill a "moderate" position of "benevolent neutrality." This position pretended to balance the two extremes through gentle regulation. In practice, the regulation did little to suppress the middlemen. But it did draw constant attention to the idea that indenture was the best form of migration for people like Indians who could not be trusted with their own mobility, because they would undermine smooth labor markets and collaborate with rapacious capital in exploiting the ignorant (Kale 1999, Mongia 2004).

Debates over Chinese indenture also found common ground in the idea that the corruption and immobility of the Chinese was the root of most problems. They worked out a bit differently, however, because Chinese indenture was an international process and could be placed under the control of a single empire, and was ultimately suppressed in the early 1870s except under highly regulated conditions. In its formative years in the late 1840s, many of the basic assumptions were also quite different than in India. Observers argued that the advantage of Chinese migrants was that they already had well-established migration experience, understood contracts well, and were in many ways more free and competent in the world of commercial labor than were their European counterparts (McKeown 2008: 77–78). It turned out, however, that the British were unable to compete in such an environment, and levels never came close to those of Indian indenture.

Much of the discussion about Chinese indenture over the next three decades was dedicated to randomly distributing out blame for the failure of large scale recruitment. Predictably, much of the blame ended up on the Chinese themselves, with a healthy dose reserved for the coercive practices harbored by the Portuguese in Macao. The Chinese government, once praised for its lack of intervention into coastal migration, was now sometimes criticized for its despotic control of the coast (although critics were hard pressed to find actual examples of intervention and punishment) and other times for its failure to impose regulation that could guarantee smooth emigration. Chinese middlemen, once praised for their organizational skills and market acumen, were now demonized for their exploitation and disruption of free markets. And the migrants themselves, once admired for their diligence and savvy, were now alternately depicted as ignorant, unfree, and unable to act without the help of middlemen, as excessively libertine and uncontrollable once freed from the oppression of the Chinese government, and as motivated by an unbridled commercial greed that made it impossible to enforce a smoothly regulated labor migration that did not reek of slavery (McKeown 2008: 78–88).

The contradictory yet complacent tone of these accusations can be seen in reports on Chinese labor migration produced by the Singapore government. Both Chinese urban elites and white planters, struggling over access to migrant labor, could agree on the suppression of their main competitors, the secret societies, in the 1860s and 1870s. A petition from European planters in 1873 insisted that the free market was the best protection, because once outside the influence of the secret societies, "the competition for labor is so great as to obtain for the newly arrived Immigrant perfect security from extortion or unfair labor bargains. The only danger which assails him is that he may be … hurried and cajoled into engagements to work in countries outside of this Settlement, and in ignorance shipped away beyond the influence and protection of our laws" (Straits Settlements 1874: 146; see also Thio 1960). The Chinese petitioners, on the other hand, wanted immigration depots and stronger government enforcement of contracts as a way to stop runaways. This dovetailed with colonial concerns that, "The government knows little or nothing of the Chinese … and the immense majority of them know little of the Government" (Straits Settlements 1876: 244).

A Chinese protectorate was established to monitor contracts, but less than 10 percent of Chinese migrants ever passed through it and the lodging houses were contracted out to Chinese brokers. European planters were still not getting access to the labor that they wanted. An 1890 investigation made on their behest criticized Chinese brokers for disrupting the labor market by exercising undue persuasion. It asserted that, "It is important that the Coolie should be a free agent, at liberty to choose the employment and country he prefers" (Straits Settlements 1891: 20). To this end it proposed an extensive system of interlinked government operated depots from China to Singapore that channeled migrants directly to their destinations and bypassed the Chinese brokers. As self serving and inconsistent as these ideas of a "free" market may appear on the surface, they succeeded in perpetuating an image of Chinese as unfree, whether due to European colonialism or the nature of Chinese social organization. How Chinese organization was actually organized remains hard to recover from the haze of rhetoric.

Scholars today are much more likely to insist on the agency of Asian migrants. Yet the knowledge produced by indenture still shapes much of the basic understanding about Asian migration in a global context, depicting Asian migrations as categorically different from European. For example, one history of world migrations explains that the causes of Chinese migration were "Imperial Chinese maladministration and revolts, overpopulation, and natural disasters, as well as colonial penetration." reasons that have all been discredited or else are irrelevant in Europe (Hoerder 2002: 12). In this book and others, accounts of indenture far outweigh those of other forms of migration. And discussions of non-indentured migration are frequently mired in attempts to understand their level of "freedom," discussions that rarely bedevil contemporary accounts of European migration regardless of the amount of debt and obligation they undertook on their voyages. These assumptions have shaped the very act of counting migrants. Most English language scholarship counts only 2 to 8 million Chinese emigrants from 1850 to 1940, not the 20 million that can easily be counted and estimated from published reports in China, Singapore, and Hong Kong. The trails of footnotes behind these numbers eventually lead to three secondary works that were very explicitly counting only "coolies" and indentures (T. Chen 1923, Z. Chen 1963, Meagher 2008).

Politicians and anti-Asian activists also drew freely from this trove of indenture knowledge to justify the erection of exclusionary laws to keep Asians out the white-settler nations around the Indian and Pacific Oceans after the 1870s. The borders dividing Asia from the West and its outposts were the most dynamic spaces of innovations in migration control in the nineteenth century. Many of these institutions, originally implemented as somewhat radical attempts to keep Asians out of full participation in the "civilized" Family of Nations, have since become the norm for the regulation of mobility between all nations. In the course of regulating migration, the liberal ideals of free mobility and individual rights were gradually reduced from universal applicability to being contingent on the presence of liberal institutions that are protected behind well-policed walls.

The line dividing the Ottoman Empire from Europe (with Russia sometimes falling on either side) was an important space for the pioneering of medical cordons. The use of passports to regulate the pilgrimage to Mecca served the purposes of both medical and political surveillance against subversion, making the Suez Canal into a window that was permeable in only one direction (Low 2008, Panzac 1986). Although the passport system itself was not a new innovation, its cooperative enforcement across multiple jurisdictions was. Many aspects of modern refugee law were also forged around attempts to regulate the mass movements that accompanied the dismemberment of the Ottoman and Austro-Hungarian

Empires and expansion of Russia. In particular, much of the expansion of refuge and asylum beyond a focus on isolated political offenders to the regulation of mass movements in the context of violence and religious persecution was forged in this context.

On the other side of Asia, the enforcement of Asian exclusion laws around the Pacific in the 1880s created many of the basic institutions, legal categories, standardized paperwork, and diplomatic understandings that shape modern migration control today (McKeown 2008). These include principles that are now taken for granted, such as the idea that migration control happens at international borders, and is a domestic law that can and should be unilaterally enforced by the receiving nation. Before the nineteenth century, there were many possible methods of controlling mobility, including restricted naturalization rights, registration, residential rights, discriminatory taxes and tributes, differential access to civic rights and privileges, and regulation that took place at towns and population centers rather than frontiers. Border control was only one method, and often the most expensive and least effective. All these forms of control were criticized and slowly dismantled by liberal states over the course of the nineteenth century. One of the key points of pride for a liberal state was the fact that it allowed free mobility and equal access to law, as well as the protections to assure those rights. And the powerful states of the world spared little effort in trying to impose these values on the rest of the world. The perceived lack of these values in Asian states was one of the main justifications of extraterritoriality.

Opposition to Asian immigration, however, was a powerful challenge to these liberal ideals. The white-settler nations and colonies around the Pacific, such as Canada, the United States and Australia, were some of the most self-consciously progressive and egalitarian nations in the world. They were also pioneers in anti-Asian agitation, and in the creating and justifying new forms of migration control for a liberal world. Exclusionists argued that the exclusion of Asians was critical to the preservation of a progressive, liberal state. They argued that barbarian Asians who have experienced only despotism could not participate in a self-governing, egalitarian republic, and feared that big capital was using cheap Asian labor to undermine the dignity of the working man. At a more basic level, what could be a more fundamental right of a self-governing people than to control its own membership as it wished?

Extraterritoriality in Asia was the flip side of this logic. Even as these nations were excluding Asians, they demanded that Asian nations open up to world trade and intercourse (McKee 1977). Far from being contradictory, both of these demands revolved around a belief in the necessity of "civilized" institutions that could protect life, liberty, and intercourse in the modern world. As practiced in the late nineteenth century (its origins were quite different) extraterritoriality in Asia was justified by the supposedly uncivilized nature of Asian institutions, which did not provide equal access to law, sufficient property protections, free mobility and guarantees against arbitrary despotism. Just as migration must be controlled if civilized institutions were to prosper in the West, so European institutions were necessary in Asia if successful intercourse and progress was to be achieved.

By the 1890s, the United States—not protected from international diplomacy behind the complicated structures of empire like the British dominions were—had developed extensive political and legal justifications of immigration control in the course of its attempts to impose the exclusion of Chinese laborers. A key issue compelling an explicit formulation of principles was that of protection for foreign residents. In the extraterritorial regime of China, any violence against the person or property of non-Chinese on the interior could not be resolved in Chinese courts, but only through direct indemnity from the Chinese government. But when China tried to demand similar restitution for the massacre of 28 Chinese at Rock Springs, Wyoming in 1885, the United States refused. Secretary of State Thomas Bayard explained to the Chinese Minister that this refusal was based in the nature of US institutions that gave the Chinese residents adequate recourse to civilized courts:

> I should fail in my duty as representing the well-founded principles upon which rests the relation of this government to its citizens. ... and to those who are permitted to come and go freely within its jurisdiction, did I not deny emphatically all liability to indemnify individuals, of whatever race or country, for loss growing out of violations of our public law, and declare with equal emphasis that just and ample opportunity is given to all who suffer wrong and seek reparation through the channels of justice.
>
> (United States Congress 1886: 71)

In an article written for the journal *Forum*, Bayard conceded that the Chinese had not obtained justice from the prejudiced juries of Wyoming. But he further explained that, "The claim now put forward [by China], if allowed, would usurp judicial functions by the executive and legislative branches, and would substitute a government of will for a government of law" (Bayard 1891: 245). To indemnify the Chinese through diplomatic agreement would give them more recourses and rights than those available an American citizen.

This argument quickly segued into a justification of unilateral border control. If the principles of law that are consonant with the Constitution can not be fully enjoyed, argued Bayard,

> because of the presence within our borders of alien subjects ... whose personal wrongs may not be remedied to their satisfaction or to that of their government without the impairment and disorder of our system, then the time has arrived when the unquestionable and sovereign right of the United States to determine by positive law who shall be permitted to enter our gates and who shall be excluded must be exercised.
>
> (Bayard 1891: 249)

In other words, the chaos and injustice of racial animosity was a threat to civilized and liberal institutions. Closing the borders against those threats was better way to protect those institutions of self-rule than domestic surveillance or administrative fiat. But this self-protection came at the cost of no longer being able to assert that the rights and benefits of free mobility were a universal quality that adhered to all humans, but a quality that emanated from the jurisdiction of particular institutions. Such rights began and ended at borders. Claims based on common humanity and those based on the inexorable truth of the benefits of free intercourse were no longer sufficient to demand the right of entry. Such rights and truths were only made possible when enforced by particular institutions. Any rights and due process that a state chose to grant to migrants at borders could only be explained as a result of good will or international pressure. This "good will" has left fertile ground for endless debates over entry policies and treatment of migrants within borders. But it has left little space to question the basic right of exclusion in the first place (McKeown 2008: 149–84).

By the early twentieth century, the United States also developed an extensive machinery to enforce these principles. The Chinese exclusion laws differentiated between laborers who were not allowed to enter, and the "globalizing" classes (merchants, students, teachers, missionaries, US citizens, and their families) who were allowed to move freely. To enforce these distinctions, officials developed painstaking techniques to sift through Chinese migrants one by one, attach an identity to each, determine his or her right to enter, and evaluate the truth of those claims. The establishment of these identities and "truth" entailed ripping the migrants out of the social networks that had once generated identity, and reinserting the pre-fabricated categories of legitimate migrants. These new identities were established and fixed through the production of massive documentary evidence held in cross-referenced files. Whoever a migrant may have thought he really was, he had to constantly perform this new identity in order to be counted among the globalizing classes that were free to partake of the rights of liberal states (McKeown 2008: 215–91).

These were originally conceived as radical measures to protect against the specific and difficult threats of barbarian Chinese. But these principles designed for a specific challenge in segregating the world eventually became, as many US judges and diplomats had feared, universal standards for the regulation of mobility between all nations. By the 1920s, even states that had once mocked US pretensions of unilateral migration control had come to accept the principle, and passports and identity documents had become a nearly universal prerequisite of international travel. The complete story of this diffusion is very complex, but the United States played a key role. With assistance from Immigration Department lawyers, lawmakers wrote the procedural nuts and bolts of exclusion into the general immigration laws. US diplomats pressured other nations to accept those principles, and backed down on their demands to protect the rights of US nationals when other nations asserted the right of sovereign immigration control. Latin American nations borrowed from the American model when creating their own immigration laws. Nations around the world had to produce the paperwork that US and other American nations required. European nations did not always imitate US laws, but admirers often looked on them as more "scientifically advanced" than local regulations (McKeown 2008: 318–47).

Two international conferences on the regulation of migration in 1924 (in Rome) and 1928 (in Havana) largely confirmed that most nations had come to accept the principle of unilateral sovereign control. In large part, this was because the major receiving nations and Japan refused to discuss effective measures of international cooperation. By 1928, however, most nations were willing to constrain their discussion to the "technical" issues of how to streamline and standardize paperwork and immigration categories across nations (*Segunda Conferencia* 1928). By this time, history was already being rewritten in the mode of progressive globalization. The new borders and controls were cast as the vestiges of arbitrary pre-modern "statisms," and discussions to streamline the technical aspects of control were depicted as progressive attempts to overcome these despotisms in the name of liberal mobility.

For example, at the Second Conference of the Institute of Pacific Relations in 1927, the Japanese delegate extensively criticized the validity of the economic and assimilationist arguments used to justify discriminatory immigration laws around the Pacific. Yet he concluded with the assertion that, "We are living in a new day when the notion of unlimited individualism is undergoing a decided change and the spirit of social sharing and co-operation is gradually gaining ground" (Condliffe, 1928: 32). Other delegates held up the British Empire and its internal agreements to restrict Asian migration as a model that pointed to the future of international cooperation in migration matters (Condliffe, 1928: 159). And another delegate summed up the mood with an assertion that, "Questions reserved for 'domestic jurisdiction' are the remnants of what a comparatively short time ago was unlimited state sovereignty." This nineteenth-century emphasis on the rights of nation states was now being overcome and, "There is a clear tendency for questions to pass from the sphere of purely domestic interest and jurisdiction into the sphere of international agreement" (Condliffe, 1928: 158). Conference participants apparently had no difficulty interpreting an era in which national borders were being entrenched around the world as a rising tide of international cooperation and globalization.

Migration and the new globalization

The optimists of the 1920s and their technical negotiations paved the way for the extremes of border control and national purification of the 1930s. Outside the Soviet and Japanese empires, the Great Depression led to a precipitous decline in migration that was reinforced by new migration controls even in the remaining bastions of *laissez faire* such as Singapore. Recovery of previous levels of migration came slowly after World War Two, expanding along with the international economy over the past half century. International immigration in the 1950s and 1960s largely followed the old networks of empire or took the form of guest-worker recruitment into Europe, while other mass movements flowed into the rapidly expanding cities of the Third World. The liberalization of migration laws in many countries of the industrialized world in the 1960s and 70s helped boost global migration, as did demands for labor in the oil rich Persian Gulf states after the 1970s and the fall of the Iron Curtain in 1989. By the 1990s, global migration appeared to have reached the per-capita peaks of the 1910s and 1920s. But the relative stasis of mid-century migration had already become the basis for much knowledge about migration. This was the perspective of those who stayed, settled, and assimilated. Previous experiences of conflict and transnational identities were obscured, making it easier to understand the new waves of migration as an unparalleled challenge to international and domestic stability.

It is hard to be sure if contemporary migration has reached or surpassed the peaks of the past because of the difficulties in counting and comparison. The geometric expansion of short-term tourist and business travel has clearly made mobility more common, and the definition of migrant more arbitrary. Even more significantly, the proliferation of migrant regulation and administrative categories has made it nearly impossible to know who and what is being counted in migration statistics, and created increased incentive to engage in undocumented and illegal migration. The very mechanisms designed to make migration more transparent have ended up making it more obscure. Because of these difficulties, many international organizations prefer to count "migrant stock" rather than migration itself, basing their numbers on foreign born peoples counted in national censuses. By this criterion, the (incomplete) counts made by the International Labour Organization of 2 to 2.1 percent of world population in the 1910s to 1930s remained stable until the 1980s, after which it increased to 2.8 percent by 2003 (ILO 1936: 56, IOM 2003, Zlotnik 1998: 431). But measurement by national stock presents as many problems as attempts to count voyages, because some censuses count foreign birth, while others only count foreign residents who have not become citizens, and others merely note racial or ethnic distinctions. This measurement may also count people who have never moved all their lives while international borders have moved around them, such as the many people who became foreigners without ever having left their homes as new nations were created around them during the break-up of the Soviet Union. The nation has, more than ever, become the unit that defines mobility and integration.

Several new patterns can nonetheless be identified in the past half century of migration. State and private interests have intensified their collaboration in the recruitment and regulation of labor, under new terms such as guest worker and a variety of work visa categories that demonstrate the intensification of state surveillance (Hahamovitch 2003, Herbert 1990). Much of this regulation is designed to guarantee that workers will return when they are finished. Many more migrants also move under the category of refugee, reflecting not only the projects of national purification that came along with the globalization of borders and formation of new states, but also the increasingly aggressive search by migrants to find administrative categories that will support their mobility (Zolberg 1983).

Much of this new migration also crosses the macro-borders that were established in the first wave of mass migration. The Americas, Southeast Asia, the Middle East, and Europe are divided between sending and receiving regions. Inequalities in the accumulation of wealth have overcome population density as the main determinant of the direction of migration. Rather than filling the frontiers, the bulk of recent migration is heading to the cities and factories of wealthy and oil-rich nations as construction, service, and professional workers, with people from poorer countries cleaning the floors, programming the computers, washing the dishes, killing the cattle, picking the vegetables, sewing the clothes, manicuring the nails, mowing the lawns, tending the sick, taking care of old parents and young children, and providing sex for those in the wealthier countries who are too busy manning the bureaucracies and channeling the wealth that make it possible to hire such a huge army of service workers. The effects of this can be seen in the last column of Figure 9.2, where the population trends of the previous century and a half have not continued, especially as concerns the Americas, north Asia and the group of states that includes the Middle East and Japan that were previously not significant net receiving or sending areas.

In terms of the content of the proliferating migration regulations, wealth and education have gone far in replacing race and religion as the main criteria of admission. This is often depicted as a positive and progressive change in the nature of migration laws, selection based on merit and the best interests of the country rather than color of skin (Flynn 2005, Morris 2002). Yet the effects are much the same. Areas and nations that were segregated by migration laws in the first wave continue to be the same ones that have difficulty in producing migrants that fit the criteria of wealth, education, and merit. And visa category, or the lack of a visa, has become a widely accepted justification of domestic discriminations. Those old borders continue to exert their influence not only in access to migration opportunities, but also by encouraging the aura of threat and challenge that pervades many discussions of recent migration. Those old borders lend credence to the claims that this is a new and unprecedented migration, unlikely to go through the same processes of adaptation and assimilation as earlier waves. The main difference, however, is not that these migrants are coming from places that have been outside of the global system and with no experience of mass migration. It is that they are now crossing the segregated systems that had once contained them.

177

Migration and the rhetoric of newness

Following the lead of many recent migration scholars, the International Organization for Migration (IOM) asserts that the world is now experiencing a "migration governability crisis" (IOM 2003: 195). To support this assertion, it explains the difference between "classic" migration to the four "traditional countries of immigration," the United States, Canada, Australia and New Zealand, and modern mobility with its many destinations, new sources, and diasporic formations (IOM 2003: 142). It further explains that,

> Migration movements were long confined to relatively straightforward and linear relations between closely linked poles—a sending country automatically had its receiving country, based on age-old ties that were mostly cultural, emotional, economic or historical in nature; however, these special ties are rapidly giving way to an unprecedented widening of the migration landscape. ... One thing is beyond doubt: migration is gradually eroding the traditional boundaries between languages, cultures, ethnic groups and nation-states. A transnational flow par excellence, it therefore defies cultural traditions, national identities and political institutions, contributing in the long run to curtailing nation-state autonomy and to shaping a global society.
>
> (IOM 2003: 4)

In much the same spirit as Thomas Bayard explained the need for border controls, the IOM explains that the difficulties of regulating migration and appeals to human rights norms to protect them has undermined the institutions of modern nations:

> States feel they have lost the sovereign right to determine who enters and remains in their territories. This feeling of loss of control has real consequences for the health, safety and stability of society and has led to an increase in public anger and frustration both at the government and at the migrant level.
>
> (IOM 2003: 103)

These new challenges demand a new response. "In the long run, only the establishment of an international immigration management framework will make migration—and indeed mobility—safe, fair and constructive" (IOM 2003: 23). The specifics, however, look much like existing regulations developed since the early twentieth century: more government regulation, more biometric data, more collection and sharing of information, more finely defined visa categories, more coordinated management of international labor markets and more policies to promote integration into national societies.

The IOM draws on the same narratives that inspired migration reformers since at least the 1920s and chroniclers of globalization since 1848, but only now are interactions and mobility creating a new world that is overcoming the isolations and traditions of the past. The only consistent fate for all these prophecies of newness is that the next generation will look back on that period as a "classic" era of tradition and separation, when all was still static and isolated. For example, Robert Park, who placed much of his work in the context of the "Great cosmic forces [that] have broken down the barriers which formerly separated the races and nationalities of the world, and forced them into new intimacies and new forms of competition, rivalry, and conflict," is now most widely remembered for being a pioneer of nation-based assimilation theory. Similarly Walt Rostow, of *Non-Communist Manifesto* and modernization theory fame, placed his work in the context of the "great world revolution" of "rapidly accelerating spread of literacy, mass communication, and travel," that is "breaking down traditional institutions and culture patterns, which in the past held societies together," such that "the world community is becoming both more interdependent and more fluid than it has been at any other time in history" (Millikan and Rostow 1957: 4). As with many past prophecies of the new revolution of global integration, modernization theory is now often considered to epitomize the perspective of a fragmented and de-globalized world of isolated nations.

How can we understand this constant reiteration of segregation and newness? Perhaps another look at Marx and Engels can suggest an answer. They deserve a place as godfathers of globalization-speak not only because they set the stylistic benchmark for the rhetoric of newness, but also because they did not sacrifice the nuances and complexities that have so often been lost by the later prophets. This can be seen when we set the citations from the beginning of this paper in a fuller context:

> Constant revolutionizing of production, uninterrupted disturbance of all social conditions, everlasting uncertainty and agitation distinguish the bourgeois epoch from all earlier ones. All fixed, fast-frozen relations, with their train of ancient and venerable prejudices and opinions are swept away, all new-formed ones become antiquated before they can ossify. All that is solid melts into air, all that is holy is profaned, and man is at last compelled to face with sober senses his real conditions of life, and his relations with his kind.
>
> The need of a constantly expanding market for its products chases the bourgeoisie over the entire surface of the globe. It must nestle everywhere, settle everywhere, establish connections everywhere.
>
> The bourgeoisie has through its exploitation of the world market given a cosmopolitan character to production and consumption in every country. ... [Old-established national industries] are dislodged by new industries, whose introduction becomes a life and death question for all civilized nations, by industries that no longer work up Indigenous raw material, but raw material drawn from the remotest zones; industries whose products are consumed, not only at home, but in every quarter of the globe. In place of the old wants, satisfied by the production of the country, we find new wants, requiring for their satisfaction the products of distant lands and climes. In place of the old local and national seclusion and self-sufficiency, we have intercourse in every direction, universal inter-dependence of nations. And as in material, so also in intellectual production. The intellectual creations of individual nations become common property. National one-sidedness and narrow-mindedness become more and more impossible, and from the numerous national and local literatures, there arises a world literature.
>
> The bourgeoisie, by the rapid improvement of all instruments of production, by the immensely facilitated means of communication, draws all, even the most barbarian nations, into civilization. The cheap prices of commodities are the heavy artillery with which it batters down all Chinese walls, with which it forces the barbarians' intensely obstinate hatred of foreigners to capitulate. It compels all nations, on pain of extinction, to adopt the bourgeois mode of production; it compels them to introduce what it calls civilization into their midst, i.e., to become bourgeois themselves. In one word, it creates a world after its own image.
>
> (Marx and Engels 2001: 13–14)

Not only do Marx and Engels claim that they are living through an era of newness, but also that the constant reproduction of newness is a basic constant of this age. This never-ending

179

newness is key to bourgeois power. The agents of that newness are not only the bourgeois centered in Europe, but also the barbarians who capitulate to new wants, cheap prices, and the cosmopolitan processes of production and consumption that have engulfed the world. These barbarians and their descendants constantly slip in and out of globalization, both as its agents and as the conduits to an outmoded world that will soon be engulfed, again. The world created in the image of this global bourgeois is a world of migrant entrepreneurs and labor, a world of integration and difference, whether that difference is defined as class, race, culture, level of civilization, achievement of modernity, or amount of economic development. It is precisely this interplay of integration and difference that makes possible the constant generation of newness, of new markets to conquer, new pieties to profane, new discriminations to overcome, new narrow-minded attitudes to undermine, and new walls to batter. Perhaps the crowning achievement of this process is that it is precisely the analysts of globalization, those that claim to stand outside and evaluate it, that do the most powerful work of perpetuating global power relations through the constant depiction of newness and rewriting of history.

References

Bayard, T. (1891) "State Rights and Foreign Relations," *The Forum*, 11: 235–49.

Carter, M. (1995) *Servants, Sirdars and Settlers: Indians in Mauritius 1834–1874*, Delhi: Oxford University Press.

Carter, S. B., Garter, S. S., Haines, M. R. and Olmstead, A. L. (eds) (2006) *Historical Statistics of the United States: Earliest Times to the Present*, vol. 1, New York: Cambridge University Press.

Castles, S. and Miller, M. (2003) *The Age of Migration: International Population Movements in the Modern World*, New York: Guilford.

Chen, T. (1923) *Chinese Migrations: With Special Reference to Labor Conditions*, Washington, DC: Government Printing Office.

Chen, Z. (1963) "Shijiu shiji cheng xing de tiaoyue huagong zhi" (The nineteenth-century Chinese contract labor system), *Lishi Yanjiu*, 1: 12–17.

Condliffe, J. B. (ed) (1928) *Problems of the Pacific: Proceedings of the Second Conference of the Institute of Pacific Relations*, Chicago: University of Chicago Press.

Davis, K. (1951) *The Population of India and Pakistan*, New York: Russell and Russell.

Emmer, P. (1992) "European expansion and migration: the European colonial past and intercontinental migration; an overview," in Emmer, P. and Mörner, M. (eds.) *European Expansion and Migration: Essays on the Intercontinental Migration from Africa, Asia, and Europe*, New York: Berg.

Flynn, D. (2005) "New borders, new management: the dilemmas of modern immigration policies," *Ethnic and Racial Studies*, 28: 463–90.

Glazier, I. and De Rosa, L. (1986) "Introduction," in Glazier, I. and De Rosa, L. (eds.) *Migrations across Time and Nations: Population Mobility in Historical Context*, New York: Holmes and Meier.

Gottschang, T. and Lary, D. (2000) *Swallows and Settlers: The Great Migration from North China to Manchuria*, Ann Arbor: University of Michigan, Center for Chinese Studies.

Hahamovitch, C. (2003) "Creating perfect immigrants: guest workers of the world in historical perspective," *Labor History*, 44: 70–94.

Hart, M. and Negri, A. (2001) *Empire*, Cambridge, MA: Harvard University Press.

Hatton, T. and Williamson, J. (1998) *The Age of Mass Migration: Causes and Economic Impact*, New York: Oxford University Press.

Heidemann, F. (1992) *Kanganies in Sri Lanka and Malaysia: Tamil Recruiter-cum-foreman as a Sociological Category in the Nineteenth and Twentieth Century*, Munich: Anacon.

Held, D., McGrew, A., Goldblatt, D. and Perraton, J. (1999) *Global Transformations: Politics, Economics, and Culture*, Stanford: Stanford University Press.

Herbert, U. (1990) *A History of Foreign Labor in Germany, 1880–1980: Seasonal Workers/Forced Laborers/ Guest Workers*, trans. William Templer, Ann Arbor: University of Michigan Press.

Hoerder, D. (2002) *Cultures in Contact: World Migrations in the Second Millennium*, Durham: Duke University Press.

International Labour Office (1936) *World Statistics of Aliens: A Comparative Study of Census Returns, 1910–1920–1930*, Geneva: International Labour Office.

International Organization for Migration (2003) *World Migration 2003: Managing Migration – Challenges and Responses for People on the Move*, Geneva: International Organization for Migration.

Kale, M. (1999) *Fragments of Empire: Capital, Slavery and Indian Indentured Labor in the British Caribbean*, Philadelphia: University of Pennsylvania Press.

Low, M. (2008) "The Twin Infection: Pilgrims, Plagues and Pan-Islam under British Surveillance, 1865–1924," *International Journal of Middle East Studies*, 40: 269–90.

McEvedy, C. and Jones, R. (1979) *Atlas of World Population History*, London: Penguin.

McKee, D. (1977) *Chinese Exclusion versus the Open Door Policy 1900–1906: Clashes over China Policy in the Roosevelt Era*, Detroit: Wayne State University Press.

McKeown, A. (2004) "Global Migration, 1846–1940," *Journal of World History*, 15: 155–89.

——(2007) "Periodizing Globalization," *History Workshop Journal*, 63: 218–30.

——(2008) *Melancholy Order: Asian Migration and the Globalization of Borders*, New York: Columbia University Press.

Mangru, B. (1987) *Benevolent Neutrality: Indian Government Policy and Labour Migration to British Guiana 1854–1884*, Hertford: Hansib Publishing.

Marx, K. and Engels, F. (2001 [1848]) *The Communist Manifesto*, London: Electronic Book Co.

Meagher, A. (2008) *The Coolie Trade: The Traffic in Chinese Laborers to Latin America*, Philadelphia, Xlibris.

Millikan, M. F. and Rostow, W. W. (1957) *A Proposal: Key to an Effective Foreign Policy*, New York: Harper, 1957.

Mongia, R. (2004) "Regimes of Truth: Indentured Indian Labour and the Status of the Inquiry," *Cultural Studies*, 18: 749–68.

Morris, L. (2002) *Managing Migration: Civic Stratification and Migrants' Rights*, London, Routledge.

O'Rourke, K. and Williamson, J. (1996) *Globalization and History: The Evolution of a Nineteenth-century Atlantic Economy* Cambridge, MA: MIT Press.

Panzac, D. (1986) *Quarantiens et Lazrets; L'Europe et la Peste D'Orient*, Aix-en-Provence: Édisud.

Peck, G. (2000) *Reinventing Free Labor: Padrones and Immigrant Workers in the North American West, 1880–1930*, Cambridge: Cambridge University Press.

Robertson, R. (1992) *Globalization: Social Theory and Global Culture*, London: Sage Publications.

Sassen, S. (2000) *Guests and Aliens*, New York: New Press.

——(2006) *Territory, Authority, Rights: From Medieval to Global Assemblages*. Princeton: Princeton University Press.

Segunda Conferencia Internacional de Emigracion e Inmigracion, *Diario Oficial* (1928) Havana.

Straits Settlements (1874) *Proceedings of the Legislative Council*, appendix 33, Singapore.

——(1876) *Proceedings of the Legislative Council*, appendix 22, Singapore.

——(1891) *Proceedings of the Legislative Council*, appendix 33, Singapore.

Thio, E. (1960) "The Singapore Chinese Protectorate: events and conditions leading to its establishment, 1823–77," *Journal of the South Seas Society*, 26: 40–80.

Treadgold, D. (1957) *The Great Siberian Migration: Government and Peasant Resettlement from Emancipation to the First World War*, Princeton: Princeton University Press.

United States Congress, House Documents (1886) *Message from the President of the United States Relative to Chinese Treaty Stipulations*, 49th Congress, 1st session, no. 102, Washington DC.

Weiner, M. (1994) *Race and Migration in Imperial Japan*, London: Routledge.

Zlotnik, H. (1998) "International Migration 1965–96: An Overview," *Population and Development Review*, 24: 429–68.

Zolberg, A. (1983) "The Formation of New States as a Refugee-generating Process," *Annals of the American Academy of Political and Social Sciences*, 467: 24–38

10

Climate change, globalization, and carbonization

Ronnie D. Lipschutz and Felicia Allegra Peck

Introduction

In an address delivered on September 30, 1847 to the Agricultural Society of Rutland County (Vermont), then US Congressman George Perkins Marsh warned that "though man cannot at his pleasure command the rain and the sunshine, the wind and frost and snow, yet it is certain that climate itself has in many instances been gradually changed and ameliorated or deteriorated by human action" (Marsh 2001: 10). Some 170 years later, we are witness to the growing impacts of human action on the earth's climate, without any very clear idea of where it might lead. What is clear is that human efforts to address the climate change quandary are, as of yet, more talk than walk. Over the next 50 years or so, what efforts do (or do not) transpire will have significant effects on later twenty-first century societies and ecosystems, in addition to already being felt today. As yet, despite the monumental shift in public opinion regarding the reality of climate change (IPCC 2007a), the world is very far from even beginning to address some very serious matters.

Over its long history, the Earth's climate has never been stable—at best, and in various places, it has been relatively constant for periods of decades and, in a few instances, for centuries. But in those instances, it was variation in exogenous inputs—solar energy—that was largely responsible for climate change—ice ages, interglacial periods, semi-tropical conditions at the poles, etc. Only since the beginning of large-scale industrialization in the late eighteenth century have human beings acquired a major role in affecting *global* biogeophysical systems. One might imagine that, given human adaptability to the wide range of environmental and climatic conditions found across the planet, climate change would pose no great challenge to humanity or its social systems. Yet, it is becoming clear that many people, and even entire societies, could soon find themselves in unviable positions, as a result of climate change and its impacts (IPCC 2007a, 2007b).

What does *globalization* have to do with climate change? The co-occurrence of glo-balization and *global* climate change is hardly coincidental: the two are tightly linked. Indeed, it is the globalization of *carbon burning*, in both physical and social terms, and the vast growth in global economic activity linked to carbon that has led humanity and the Earth to its current precarious position. Consequently, doing something about climate change will require *global* changes in human activities, including massive decreases in carbon burning. To be sure, since Roman times, sea coal has been burned for heat in the British Isles, and probably all over the world. It was not, however, until the beginning of systematic mining of coal in the eighteenth century, for industrial purposes and profit, that anthropogenic emissions of combustion gases into the atmosphere began to change the latter's composition (most famously visible in the graph of rising CO_2 concentration as measured on Manua Loa – see Figure 10.1). Today, the burning of fossil fuels, and generation of other greenhouse gases, emits some 8 billion metric tons of CO_2 per year and some 5 billion metric tons of CO_2-equivalent (in terms of warming). There is little sign of any leveling off in emission rates, not withstanding constant debate over how reductions might be accomplished.

Although the first measurements of atmospheric CO_2 levels at Manua Loa were taken during the International Geophysical Year in 1957–58, it was not until the late 1980s that global climate change became a prominent international concern. The UN Framework Convention on Climate Change (UNFCCC) was introduced at the "Earth Summit" in Rio de Janeiro in 1992; the Kyoto Protocol in 1997. Both mandated emission reductions to 1990 levels by industrialized countries. The Protocol entered into force as international law in 2004 (without accession by the United States) but, overall, has had only minimal impact. Some 20 years after the establishment of the Intergovernmental Panel on Climate Change (IPCC), an international group of climate scientists, policymakers, and national governments continue to squabble over who will reduce greenhouse gas emissions, and when, who is most responsible for rising levels of greenhouse gases, and who will pay for the reductions. At the same time, scientists warn not only that climate change is irreversible—although its severity and extent might be mitigated

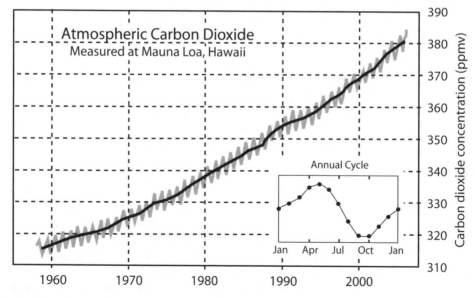

Figure 10.1 Atmospheric carbon dioxide levels measured at Manua Loa, Hawaii
Source: http://www.globalwarmingart.com/wiki/Image:Mauna_Loa_Carbon_Dioxide_png (accessed 26 August 2008).

through near term action—climate change is already here, and much sooner than expected, as seen, for example, in the rapid melting of the Arctic ice cap—a surprise that is somehow not surprising.

What, then, are we to do? The first instinct of many is to propose solutions that align with the scale of the problem. This logic would have it that *global* climate change be addressed *globally*, by institutions whose reach is global, such as the United Nations and its associated institutions and agencies. Individual countries would then follow the dictates of these institutions. The difficulty is that the UN system is only as effective as its members are willing to be; as a result, ever, the roadblock in international negotiations over some kind of binding convention stubbornly holds fast. Given the international impasse among countries, it is worthwhile to examine other approaches, devised and implemented by state and provincial governments, cities, corporations, business associations, individuals, nongovernmental organizations, and social movements. These fall into three broad categories: commodification of pollution, technological modernization of pollution-producing systems and activities, and socialization of individuals and societies into less carbon-intensive "green" behaviors and practices.

The first approach aims to work within or to adjust market logic by putting a cost on greenhouse gas emissions. Such "cap and trade" schemes rely on the sale and purchase of carbon emission permits in markets, by and large viewing governments' role (if any) as making adjustments to the rules under which market transactions take place. Carbon-trading markets are beginning to appear and have even been institutionalized within the European Union. Market logic also applies to attempts to foster "green consumerism," which now dominates the minds of many producers, advertisers, organizations, and individuals. According to the logic of commodification, the market will green itself in response to the demands of ecologically conscious consumers, thus ratcheting down the emissions associated with everyone's goods.

The second approach relies on optimistic promises and the "progress" of technological innovation, relying on decarbonization through "ecological modernization" (EM). The argument is that deployment of new, low-carbon or even carbon-free technologies can reduce producer costs—especially if a price is imposed on emissions—as well as greenhouse gas production. Those advocating EM often call upon statistics and projections to make their case, such as "if everyone replaced an incandescent lightbulb with a compact fluorescent ... " or "if half of all new cars were built with hybrid technology ... ," then so many tons of emissions and so many barrels of imported oil would be avoided. While this discourse of technological admiration extols the glories of efficiency, however, it often fails to mention that improvements in efficiency could well coincide with increases in production of goods, and that the latter could easily cancel out any of the "reductions" brought about by the former (this is called the "rebound effect"; see, e.g., Hilty et al. 2006).

The third approach includes trends that occur at smaller geographic scales or rely on "local action." The logic of such calls and projects is premised on the desire to institutionalize and promulgate greenhouse gas management in ways that are more closely matched to existing institutions, jurisdictions and political economies. In this instance, it would seem that a cost-benefit motive is less prominent or, at least, that a form of ecological civic virtue is the impetus for decarbonization, while climate change itself is the rationale. One drawback of such localized approaches is that most are likely to be implemented in wealthier, "developed" places. Moreover, it is entirely possible that local green initiatives may be undertaken primarily as a form of municipal marketing, with more attention to image than ecological outcomes at a time when "green is in."

Commodification, modernization, and localization each approach the same problem by calling upon different actors—politicians, scientists, and citizens—and pointing to different venues—markets, labs, and communities—for policy and practice. These three approaches are not, of course, mutually exclusive: Municipalities can continue to promote "smart growth" at the same time that automotive technology becomes more fuel efficient and larger-scale cap and trade systems are deployed. In some respects, though, these strategies are theoretically discordant. Market solutions prioritize the power of individual prerogatives, technological approaches place their faith in expertise, and local approaches emphasize the collectivist potential of communities and place. Although these approaches do not comprise the universe of possible responses, as we will later show, they all tend to rely on mechanisms and practices that, by "leaving it to the market," appear to minimize the need for major changes in "lifestyles" or, indeed, in the global capitalist system.

In this chapter, therefore, we investigate what does, and what does not, distinguish these approaches to emission reductions from one another, and link them to globalization. We begin with a "primer" on global climate change: what it is, why it happens, when changes are expected to occur, and who might be affected. We then turn to globalization and carbonization, and discuss how the former—strongly linked to the global expansion of capitalism—has, historically and today, fostered growth in the latter, so much so that climate change is no longer merely a distant theory but an emergent reality. In the third part of the chapter, we describe those international political projects—or "regimes," as they are often called—constructed to encourage national reductions in greenhouse gas emissions. We also discuss the logic behind the regime approach and the shortcomings that have become only too visible after nearly 20 years of efforts. We then turn to an examination of market-based "solutions," all of which are being pursued with considerable enthusiasm but none of which, in our view, can address or ameliorate global climate change very much, if at all. Finally, we ask, if we know what will happen, and we know "what is to be done," why are we doing so little? This section addresses the interacting roles of science, knowledge, politics, and economic interests—and concludes with a discussion of why politics, rather than markets, will be necessary if we are to respond effectively and fairly to climate change

Climate change: coming soon to a location near you

Were it not for the insulating qualities of the Earth's atmosphere, the surface of the planet would be some 15° centigrade (33° Fahrenheit) colder than it is now. This is due to the "greenhouse effect": certain of the gases in the atmosphere are transparent to long-wave solar radiation which, upon hitting the Earth's surface, are re-emitted as shortwave infrared radiation to which these gases are opaque (some of that heat is lost, of course, otherwise the Earth would be much hotter than it is). This phenomenon was first proposed by Jean Baptiste Joseph, Baron de Fourier in 1807, and applied to fossil fuel combustion by Svante Arrhenius in 1896. As noted above, however, scientific recognition of the evidence that has come to be called "global warming" was not available until quite recently.

The most important "greenhouse gases" are water vapor (H_2O), CO_2 and ozone (O_3). Although the first is the most important contributor to the overall greenhouse effect, its concentration in the atmosphere is so large (typically 1–3 percent), and so variable, that human activities have little direct effect; rather, it is through increases in other gases and the consequent temperature effect that global water vapor concentrations might rise—and even then, probably not enough to have a significant effect. By contrast, although the mean atmospheric concentration of CO_2 today is around 370 parts per million (0.037 percent, up from about 260ppm prior to industrialization), molecule for molecule, its contribution to rising temperatures is much more important. That is, all else being equal, water vapor concentrations across the globe have remained more or less the same since 1800, whereas the CO_2 concentration in the atmosphere has increased by about 40 percent.

The result, according to the summary of the synthesis report issued by the IPCC on November 17, 2007, is that

> Warming of the climate system is unequivocal, as is now evident from observations of increases in global average air and ocean temperatures, widespread melting of snow and ice, and rising global average sea level … The temperature increase is widespread over the globe, and is greater at higher northern latitudes. Land regions have warmed faster than the ocean. … Anthropogenic warming over the last three decades has *likely* had a discernible influence at the global scale on observed changes in many physical and biological systems (is our emphasis).
>
> (IPCC 2007b: 1,6)

Although there remain many uncertainties in some of the IPCC's findings, and it is virtually impossible to specify the precise future impacts of climate change on particular locations, groups, and societies, the report provides the following examples, among many:

> *Africa:* By 2020, between 75 and 250 million of people are projected to be exposed to increased water stress due to climate change.
> *Asia:* Coastal areas, especially heavily-populated megadelta regions in South, East and South-East Asia, will be at greatest risk due to increased flooding from the sea and, in some megadeltas, flooding from the rivers.
> *Europe:* Climate change is expected to magnify regional differences in Europe's natural resources and assets. Negative impacts will include increased risk of inland flash floods, and more frequent coastal flooding and increased erosion (due to storminess and sea-level rise).
> *North America:* During the course of this century, cities that currently experience heatwaves are expected to be further challenged by an increased number, intensity and duration of heatwaves during the course of the century, with potential for adverse health impacts.
> *Small Islands:* Sea-level rise is expected to exacerbate inundation, storm surge, erosion and other coastal hazards, thus threatening vital infrastructure, settlements and facilities that support the livelihood of island communities.
>
> (IPCC 2007b: 10–11)

To these must be added other, observed effects, such as the disappearance of glaciers in the Andes (Edwards 2008), changes in mosquito life cycles (Briggs 2001), the death of vast areas of North American pines as a result of beetle infestations (Struck 2006), the widely publicized loss of polar bear habitat, and the submergence of islands such as Tuvalu (Shapiro 2007).

One question that has dogged international negotiations over the years has been the distribution of costs and benefits as a result of both climate change and responding to climate change. Who, for example, should bear responsibility for the increase in atmospheric CO_2 to date? Most of this is due to carbon burning by the wealthy and industry in the global north over the past two centuries. At the same time, as the economies of developing countries grow, especially those of China and India, future emissions will come increasingly from them. Consequently, it is argued, efforts by the billion people in the Global North will be more than canceled out by higher emission levels in the Global South. All of this is further complicated by uncertainties about long-term costs to specific parts of the world. The value of a vacation home on the Atlantic coast of North America is several orders of magnitude greater than a hovel on the delta lands of Bangladesh; which, therefore, is more worthy of attention?

For example, Richard Tol (2002) has estimated that the benefits of a 1°C average global temperature increase could be as high as 2.3 percent of global GDP ($448 billion) and the costs as high as 2.7 percent of global GDP (-$554 billion). In another paper published in 2004, Tol and his colleagues found that the costs are likely to fall most severly on poor countries in the tropics; the annual welfare loss to Africa could be as high as 4 percent of continental GDP (Tol et al. 2004: 261). By contrast, the much-discussed *Stern Review on the Economics of Climate Change*, commissioned by the government of the United Kingdom and published in 2006, suggested that climate change might "reduce [global] welfare by an amount equivalent to a reduction in consumption per head of between 5 and 20 percent" (Stern 2006: x), although this number has been criticized by others for using an unreasonably low discount rate (Varian 2006). The same report proposed that an annual expenditure of 1 percent of global GDP ($400–500 billion) could go a long way toward ameliorating both climate change and its effects (Stern 2006: xii). Of course, the question that remains unanswered is: who will pay for mitigation (though inaction, of course, has its price as well)? The original Framework Convention on Climate Change and the Kyoto Protocol mandated establishment of several different financing mechanisms, although these tended to cover only the additional funds required to build lower as opposed to higher-emission facilities, such as a natural gas-fired power plant instead of a coal-fired one. None of these mechanisms offered a volume of grants and loans necessary to cover anything like the full costs of decarbonization. As we shall see, some hope that a carbon "cap and trade" system might fill this gap.

Globalization: burning carbon for fun and profit

Whether we finger industrialization or capitalism as the culprit behind our carbon-based civilization, the result is the same: an extreme dependence on a finite supply of mineral fuels, laid down over tens of millions of years and, for all intents and purposes, nonrenewable over time frames of interest to humans. But it is not so much the finite supply of fossil fuels that is at issue here; available coal resources could fuel current global rates of consumption for centuries to come.[1] Rather, the problem is the finite capacity of the atmosphere to absorb the greenhouse gases generated as a result of the carbonization of everyday life without resulting in catastrophic changes. How did humans run up against this limit—one largely disregarded by both those who have warned of resource depletion and those who have argued that there are no "limits to growth?" This outcome was not inevitable, inasmuch as the first energy sources harnessed to industrial production were wind and water. Effectively speaking, moreover, solar inputs into agriculture and daylighting date back millennia (Butti and Perlin 1980). As long ago as the early 1950s, the President's Materials Policy Commission, aka the Paley Commission, appointed by

President Truman to investigate potential depletion of US mineral resources, proposed in its report, *Resources for Freedom*, that it was entirely possible to shift to a solar-based energy system (PMPC 1952; Putnam 1952). (In the event, President Eisenhower's "Atoms for Peace" program, as well as new petroleum discoveries in the Middle East, effectively pre-empted any possibility of a non-carbon based energy strategy.)

The replacement of these essentially free energy sources came about as a consequence of two factors: (i) scarcity in terms of the distribution of energy sources; and (ii) the portability and energy content of fossil fuels. As far as the first is concerned, although wood had been used throughout the British Isles for industrial and household purposes, by the eighteenth century, timber was too valuable a resource to burn and it was increasingly reserved for the Royal Navy. Once industrialization began in earnest, factories and mills were built at sites where energy, especially water moving at appropriate speed, was available. But even in the well-watered British Isles, the number of accessible, low-cost sites was not unlimited. Nor was the energy density of usable locations always amenable to expansion beyond a certain level. This is one reason why Britain's main industrial zone was in the Midlands rather than around London, as one might expect, given population distribution and economy. Southeast England lacked the hydraulic resources needed to support expansive industrialization. Thus, when the shift to coal began, industry flowed to the Midlands, where factories were already in operation and coal was nearby.

Although it is exceptionally dangerous when deep mined and dirty when burned, coal was attractive for a number of reasons. First, it was portable—it could come to the factory on the expanding rail system. Second, although the technology for burning coal was expensive and often hazardous—exploding boilers were a common feature of early industrialization—the fuel itself was cheap and plentiful. Third, coal's higher energy density meant it could boil water and raise steam much more efficiently than the wood first used to fuel boilers. Finally, coal gave rise to what came to be a significant British industry in itself, a source of considerable profit to those who owned the mines as well as employment for those who labored in them. Given such advantages, why did oil come to replace coal in industrial applications after World War Two? Not because of greenhouse gas emissions but, rather, Cold War politics. Not only was oil much easier to ship long distances, the labor requirements involved in its extraction were much less than for coal. As a result, there were few, if any, unions involved in the extraction and transportation of oil, especially radical leftist ones that the United States feared might take power and swing British and European politics toward the Soviet Union.

Until the 1970s, any cost advantage of coal over oil was minimized by these factors, as well as the willingness of the transnational oil companies to collude in keeping oil prices low. Today, with oil topping $100/barrel (and who knows how comical this number may sound to a reader only a few years down the line) and global petroleum resources expected to peak sometime over the next 25 to 50 years, coal is once again looking very attractive. Nations that have ample domestic reserves, such as India and China (and even some European countries) are beginning to shift back to coal. Although China still lags far behind the United States in terms of per capita greenhouse gas emissions, in absolute terms it is now the largest emitter of carbon dioxide, in large part as a result of its growing consumption of coal, although another significant contributor, the production of cement (itself responsible for 4 percent of global GHG emissions), indicates that there is still plenty of oil in China's future (Adam 2008).[2]

Across much of the world, the growth of carbonization is being driven (pardon the pun) by "automobility" and "electrification" more than mere industrialization (Freund and Martin 2007; Paterson 2007). Although the latter grew steadily throughout the twentieth century, and today is responsible for some 30 percent of global greenhouse gas emissions, the automobile and expansion in global power generation are likely to have the greatest impacts on climate change during the coming decades. First, the car: By some estimates, there are currently about 800 million fossil-fuelled vehicles in the world, and that number is expected to rise to 2 billion by 2050 (MIT, 2006). Such vehicles currently account for 27 percent of the United States' annual carbon emissions (Greene and Schafer, 2003: 3), and between 15 and 20 percent of the world as a whole. If vehicle growth projections are accurate, however, this fraction could rise as high as one-third or more by the middle of the twenty-first century. Even with relatively high gasoline prices and mileage standards, the sheer proliferation of carbon-burning vehicles—both cars and trucks—will have a significant impact (so-called "plug-in" zero emission cars will still generate greenhouse gases at the power plant, although these may be easier to control). Moreover, given the backward and forward linkages associated with the automobile industry and automobility—not only manufacturers but also highways, repair shops, gas stations, refining, land transformation, expansion of exurban regions, etc.—the actual fraction of global emissions attributable to the car could be significantly higher.

In the absence of a major shift to renewables and nuclear energy, coal burning in the global power generating sector is projected to more than double by 2030, while natural gas consumption will almost triple (EIA 2008). As a result, emissions from power generation will also increase drastically, almost tripling in the developing world, especially Asia, by 2030. Currently, such emissions account for 43 percent of the global total; by 2030, this will rise to 46 percent (Birol 2004). And all of this is exacerbated by rising levels of consumption, which are strongly correlated with electrification, especially in the home. Any large increase in numbers of "zero-emission" plug-in automobiles will also seriously affect this sector, although it is virtually impossible to say with any certainty what such effects might be.

These projections, and more general increases in greenhouse gas emissions, are all imbricated with the shift from Fordist production methods to post-Fordist ones over the past several decades, which has fostered growing rates of consumption and consequent carbonization. Today, global production patterns have become much more complex than they have been in the past. Raw materials, commodities, semi-processed materials, parts and finished goods move among locales in different countries according to both the traditional and intrafirm logics of comparative advantage. The location and sequencing of these processes is determined not only by the absolute cost of factors of production, as we would expect from the classical theory of comparative advantage, but also by cost factors internal to the corporate production chain, the relative costs of capital, both financial and human, the burden of social costs imposed in a specific location and the size of local subsidies, if any (Gereffi and Korzeniewicz 1994; Gereffi et al. 2005). For example, differential national tax rates at various stages of production in different countries might be more important in determining where something is made or assembled than the costs of raw material, labor, technology, and regulation. One result of such globalized commodity chains is that environmental impacts formerly concentrated in one region or country are now spread all over the world (Tol et al. 2004; Peters and Hertwich 2008; Bang et al. 2008). One way of thinking about this problem is to argue, for example, that the United States is "exporting" its emissions to China, as the latter is allocated responsibility for emissions associated with production of goods exported to the former. This presents an accounting problem: who is responsible for emissions, the

189

producer or the consumer? Regardless, the "virtual" emission of carbon associated with the movement of raw materials and goods may actually lead to increased global emissions (Ahmad and Wyckoff 2003).

As this discussion suggests, globalization entails more than just changes in modes and patterns of production and their impacts on the environment; it also affects modes of *consumption* (Firat and Dholakia 1998; Southerton et al. 2004). The global economy has expanded from less than five trillion dollars in 1950 to more than \$55 trillion today (purchasing power parity, in 2005 dollars; UN 2008),[3] while world trade has grown from about \$300 billion in 1950 to more than \$14 trillion in 2006 (in current dollars; Murphy 2007: 5), this even as the population has increased by less than a factor of three (Maddison 2001: 173, 175, 362). In recent years, much of this economic growth has come through expansion of the service, information, and "intellectual capital" sectors, which are generally assumed to have lower environmental impacts than the Fordist industrialism of previous decades (van der Voet et al. 2004; Hilty et al. 2006). Yet, increases in individual incomes around the world, swelling the ranks of potential consumers in the middle class and its upper reaches, especially in North America, Europe, Japan, and parts of Asia have also fostered growing demand for goods and services, such as computers, imported foods and goods, and ecotourism, whose environmental impacts are far from benign (Hawkins 2006; Szasz 2007; see also below). And global consumer demand is further fuelled by the globalization of largely-American cultural norms and practices through media—films, televisions, advertising, magazines—communications networks, international travel, and free trade—all of which may serve to change attitudes and practices (Conca 2001). Even higher levels of education contribute to the globalization of consumerism, in part because of its simple association with higher incomes, and in addition, because Western style education tends to espouse teleological paradigms that equate modernization with "progress."

What is to be done? Technological and social fixes

Technology is simultaneously present and absent in discussions of what is to be done— what *we* must do—about climate change. On the one hand, technological advancement is assumed to be akin to destiny—an extension of human nature. Thus it is seen as largely following a course that may interact with, but is not determined by, politics. On the other hand, when the sense of inevitability associated with technological progress meets market logic, it is assumed that new technologies will naturally spread, via the workings of the "build a better mousetrap" logic of the market. Consequently, technologically-based proposals to alleviate global warming may seem to be politically detached or disinterested—even beyond politics, at the same time they are subsumed by the market. Here we focus, first, on international institutions as agents of action and, second, on the hope that reliance on market-based strategies and solutions, including technology-based approaches, might make it possible to avoid the messiness and complexity of politics.

As a general rule, capitalist societies offer two broad institutional approaches to addressing collective problems centered on politics and markets. The former is based on the notion that, through discussion, bargaining, negotiation, and struggle a polity can agree on a set of notionally-binding practices, legal, customary, and normative, that will, in some way, ameliorate or eliminate the problem of concern (Lipschutz and Rowe 2005). Markets may be a subsidiary element of such a political strategy, but the institutional concomitants come first. The latter arises out of the notion that, in a world of capitalists and consumers, the "proper" signals, transmitted through the prices of goods and bads, can alter preferences and behaviors without direct regulation by the state. Politics are not absent in this instance, but operate only in terms of structuring the rules of the political economy within which markets operate. A simple example of the former can be seen in state-mandated gas mileage standards that must be met by all automobile manufacturers (often called "command and control" regulations); of the latter, a "carbon" tax that doubles the price of gasoline and induces consumers to purchase more fuel-efficient automobiles ("market-based instruments"). In what follows, we discuss one "political" approach, three market-based ones, and a hybrid of the two.

International politics as usual: why can't we all agree?

Over the past several decades, the standard international response to "global environmental problems" has been the creation of an "international regime." A "regime" is an interstate agreement that facilitates collective action among its participants without, it is argued, sacrificing national interests. According to the widely accepted definition, a regime is a set of "principles, norms, rules, and decision-making procedures around which actor expectations converge in a given issue area" (Krasner 1983: 1; the careful reader will note that this is not much different from a sociological description of an institution). Although the sources of greenhouse gas emissions are pervasive and relevant to any number of such regimes—the World Trade Organization, the Food and Agriculture Organization, the UN Development Programme—one has been established specifically to address climate change: the UN Framework Convention on Climate Change (UNFCCC), mentioned earlier. The Convention was not especially ambitious: it divided the world into two categories of countries—in effect, industrialized and developing—and required that the former reduce their greenhouse gas emissions to 1990s levels by 2000. At the time, this did not seem an impossible goal, and members of the old Socialist Bloc, undergoing severe economic recessions as their industrial bases collapsed, were already meeting these terms. But due to disagreements over how the reductions would be measured and paid for, very little happened over the following five years, as government representatives met annually to squabble over terms and actions.

In an effort to launch a more effective process, in 1997 the Conference of the Parties to the UNFCC formulated the Kyoto Protocol, which imposed new reduction requirements, over a longer period, on rich countries while allowing developing countries to increase their emissions until some future, undetermined date. Whereas the United States ratified the Climate Convention, the sailing was not so smooth with the Protocol. The Clinton Administration signed the Protocol but, bowing to warnings from a Republican-dominated Congress, decided not to submit the agreement to the Senate for ratification. Subsequently, President George W. Bush "unsigned" the Protocol. The main complaint, then as now, was that the costs of meeting its terms would be too great for the US economy and, in any case, the United States would not ratify until reduction requirements were also imposed on rapidly industrializing countries, especially India and China. The Protocol was nonetheless ratified without accession by the United States, as well as Turkey, Kazakhstan, and a dozen or so other relatively small states and territories, and went into effect in 2004. It too has had little impact, as global greenhouse gas emissions have continued to rise, substantially propelled by activities in the United States, as well as some developing countries.

Since ratification, annual meetings of both the Conference of the Parties (COP, ratifiers of the UNFCCC) and Members of the Parties (MOP, ratifiers of the Kyotol Protocol) have proceeded on an annual basis without much progress. Because it is not a MOP, the United States has no voting rights in discussions of the Protocol but, as the state responsible for a larger proportion of the world's greenhouse gases than any other,[4] its views and participation receive considerable attention and (dis)respect. The European Union has taken on the role of "champion" of further emission reductions, although its influence over the American position is limited. Finally, there are now discussions underway over a successor to Kyoto, all of this in the face of growing evidence that climate change is no longer something that will happen in the future—it is here, today.

Commodification of the "right" to pollute

The Kyoto Protocol allows for the creation of a transferable permit system in carbon emissions, called "cap and trade." In essence, this would allow parties to buy and sell rights to emit a certain quantity of carbon into the atmosphere, as part of an international effort to limit and reduce such emissions. A standard neo-classical economic argument is that environmental externalities, in the form of wastes, social costs, and other, similar impacts, are a result of market failures in the pricing of factors of production (Coase 1960). That is, a producer is not required to internalize the costs of pollution or labor rights or social costs in the final price of a good; were these to be included, the producer would seek a variety of ways to reduce or eliminate those externalities and, if these proved to be too expensive, would go out of business. In the case of air pollution—and carbon emissions—there was, historically, no financial cost to polluters for dumping wastes into the air, at least not until governments began to impose regulations requiring their reduction and control. But while such "command and control" mechanisms may impose equal requirements on all polluters, they are widely regarded as inefficient—both economically and environmentally—as a consequence of their inflexibility (Fiorino 2006).

The same command and control regulation can affect individual polluters very differently. For example, one polluter might have to spend $10,000 to achieve a mandated emission reduction while the cost for another might be only $1,000. It would be more efficient for the latter to spend $10,000, accomplish a much greater reduction, and sell the "excess" pollution rights to the former for, say $7,500, thereby leading to total lower costs and greater pollution reductions. When institutionalized, this is "cap and trade": a regional, national or global level for pollutants is established, pollution rights are distributed according to some formula, and those who can reduce emissions cheaply can do so and sell their excess rights to those who cannot (Butraw and Palmer 2004). Markets in carbon emissions are already in operation with the European Union and there are numerous private schemes, as well (Hansjürgens 2005). Eventually, if the private and smaller scale markets are any indication, a global market is likely to be established under the terms of the Kyoto Protocol or a successor agreement.

Whether such markets will accomplish their intended goals remains to be seen, but what they do, in effect, is to commodify the right to pollute (Kokaz 2005; Nash 2006).[5] In theory, at least, the price of such an emission right will be determined by supply and demand in a pollution market, and those who can afford to purchase emission permits will do so. Those who cannot will be forced, if necessary, to eliminate those activities that generate excess emissions, although it is envisioned that low-cost emission reduction activities in developing countries, financed perhaps by investors in the Global North, will generate returns through sales to high-cost emission reduction industries and industrialized countries, resulting in a transfer of technology and capital from the rich to the poor. Numerous complications may intervene to make this difficult, however, including measurement and monitoring reductions, agreement on sanctions and penalties for failing to meet targets, different levels and degrees of jurisdiction and management. Furthermore, such schemes are very difficult to get under way, due to the difficulty in determining the initial allocation of pollution permits: who gets them and why (Fiorino 2004).

Cap and trade schemes have worked reasonably well in the United States for pollutants such as sulfur dioxide (Butraw and Palmer 2004), and tend to reduce overall pollution levels. One result of cap and trade, however, is that people living in (or downstream or down-wind of) high-cost emission reduction areas and source points continue to be exposed to high levels of pollutants (Kaswan 2008). In the case of greenhouse gas emissions, of course, the effects are global, and poor people will remain the most ill-equipped to cope with those effects. And carbon dioxide is not the only thing issuing from smokestacks and tailpipes. While this paper concerns itself with climate change, we would be remiss for failing to mention that other environmental problems are often associated with greenhouse gas emissions, including water pollution, heavy metal toxins, smog and unhealthy ozone levels. The focus that comes with establishing clear delineations between "separate" environmental issues is a convenience, but has its limitations, as well.

Ecological modernization

Further differentiations can be made *among* technological proposals. Some technologies are primarily matters of substitution (e.g. electric cars for gas ones) while others would require redistribution (e.g. large-scale wind-power operations would require the erection of transmission lines to windy, frequently remote, areas; see Wald 2008). Additionally, a choice of technology does not occur in a bubble. To illustrate, it is easy to make the case that light rail is more ecological than fossil-fuelled buses. Societies must, however, work with the infrastructure they have, not the infrastructure they wish for. Thus, in places with extensive highway systems, yet relatively few railways, the lower marginal cost and simplicity of adding bus routes may be easier and quicker to implement than a light-rail system. Furthermore, creative uses of old technologies are easy to overlook when the focus is on potential technological panaceas. Short-term auto rentals (e.g., "Zip-Cars") are becoming available in some locations as a quick and affordable substitution for full-time car ownership. This arrangement is a compromise that adjusts to situations in which public transportation is inadequate or not suited to the task at hand. One could also imagine urban, close to real-time ridesharing, arranged through the internet—after all, taxi companies and dispatchers do something close to this all the time.

Cap and trade schemes rely, to a significant degree, on the installation of new, low emission technology and production systems; the deployment of such systems, either as new installations or replacements for old ones, is called "ecological modernization" (EM). Advocates of EM argue that it is technologically-feasible and economically-efficient to reduce waste and emissions through systems and processes that require lower or different inputs and use them more effectively (Mol and Sonnenfeld 2000; Mol 2001, 2002; Carola 2004; Cohen 2006). One example of this is the replacement of chlorine by

193

oxygen in the bleaching of paper (Gunningham et al. 2003); an everyday case involves the automobile. So long as petroleum costs were low and greenhouse gas emissions were not penalized, there was not much reason for manufacturers to build more expensive low- or no-emission vehicles. As the price of gasoline rises, and if a cost is imposed on carbon emissions—most likely as a tax on gasoline or the vehicle—cars will be increasingly designed to go farther on a gallon of fuel and to emit lower levels of greenhouse gases. Although it will be impossible to eliminate totally emissions associated with production and operation of automobiles, their "ecological modernization" could reduce annual global additions to the atmosphere by a considerable amount. At the same time, as noted earlier, the "rebound effect" has been observed to result in *higher* levels of consumption, as the per unit cost of the service associated with a resource declines (Hertwich 2005). In the case of automobiles, in the United States, at least, when more fuel-efficient cars became available in the 1970s, the cost per mile of travel declined. As a result, people tended to travel longer distances, thereby reducing the impact of higher mileage standards.

A similar logic applies to other industries, and other pollutants: as new systems of extraction, transportation, manufacturing, and consumption are developed, processes and products can be designed and deployed that, rather then dealing with "end-of-pipe" pollution, require fewer inputs, use those more efficiently, and generate lower levels of waste. We can assume that any higher costs associated with ecological modernization will be internalized in the costs of goods, services, and waste disposal, thereby making consumers more careful and frugal in their consumption. But there are some serious flaws in the logic of EM (York and Rosa 2003; but see Mol and Spargaaren 2004). First, an absolute increase in the numbers of units—such as automobiles—might cancel out the reductions achieved in each individual unit, or displace the source of emissions from the unit (tailpipe) to the power source (power plant, in the case of electric vehicles). The same kind of logic applies to economic growth more generally: as the global economy expands, EM could well allow stabilization of emissions at a high level, without leading to the anticipated reductions. Second, even with EM and stringent recycling programs, rising rates of consumption around the world will result in growing quantities of wastes and emissions. What Alan Schnaiberg (Gould et al. 2004) has called the "treadmill of production" is the result. Consumers may have to reign in their consumption—but what could motivate such a change in behavior? This leads, in turn, to the third market-based approach: altering consumer preferences and encouraging environmentally virtuous behaviors.

The virtuous consumer

At the end of the day, there is no production without consumption. Globally, people are exposed to the increasing consumption of neighbors as well as media and cultural communications cultivating consumer desire and touting the "freedom" of capitalism. Although no one is certain if advertising "works," there is no gainsaying the globalization of consumer capitalism. Thus, if people can be induced to consume more, through advertising, education, and experience, perhaps they can also be induced to consume in an environmentally-virtuous, "green" fashion (Dobson 2003; Hull 2005). But why be green at all? (It's not easy!) Even though it *appears* to be getting easier to be green, as more "environmentally-friendly" products are being produced and marketed, why do it? And what would motivate businesses and governments in poor countries to go green when so many of their inhabitants live at subsistence levels?[6] There are two aspects to green consumption often lauded by advocates: First, by choosing green products in preference to "brown" ones, consumers can have a real effect on environmental quality and can *feel*, too, that they are doing good for the Earth (whether their impact is ecologically meaningful is another matter). Second, through preferential buying, green consumers can induce corporations to produce more in the way of environmentally-friendly goods (another form of EM), and make the entire market a greener one (Makower, et al. 1993; Peattie 2001).[7] Ultimately, goes the argument, the market for brown goods will disappear, as consumers shift en masse to green ones. In the interim, producers can charge a premium for green goods and realize higher profits.

While there seems to be merit to this approach—after all, if *everyone* changes his or her preferences and behavior together, won't this result in radical reductions of environmental impacts?—the market is a notoriously fickle instrument for altering social choice on a large scale (Lipschutz and Rowe 2005). To be sure, when the costs of a good rise substantially, demand is likely to drop significantly—especially if there is a high elasticity for the product—but this, in turn, should lead to competition that will drive the cost down, thereby leading to resumed growth in consumption. Realistically, only if the good is taxed in order to insulate it from changes in demand as is the case with gasoline in Europe—or a monopoly or concentrated oligopoly dominates the sector—is it likely that changed behavior be maintained over the long term? And if incomes rise, the relative cost of the good will decline, facilitating increases in consumption, too, as happened with gasoline during the 1970s (Hertwich 2005). Finally, consumers may simply decide they don't want to be green, for whatever reason, and refuse to behave in a "virtuous" fashion, or they may feel that buying recycled toilet paper and organic vegetables means they've "done their part," even though they drive a big SUV. Conversely, there may be lots of things keeping someone with green intentions from following through on green actions (e.g. too many responsibilities to take the extra time to walk or bike to work). Consumers may also be tricked into believing that they are making green choices by insidious green-washing marketing ploys. For example, a roll of bathroom tissue by Pronature™, which comes in a muted-color package, has an abstract depiction of a tree at its center and the symbol of recycling (the three arrows forming a triangle on a green background) next to print that reads "100 percent recyc*lable*," not recyc*led* (emphasis added—who recycles toilet paper, anyway?). In other words, absent a firm regulatory policy, the market is a fragile and unreliable instrument on which to rely for long-term change in consumer behavior and public policy (Hardner and Rice 2002). The market can play an important role but it will not do so of its own accord.

Sustainable states and cities[8]

In the face of limited *political* progress at the national and international levels, states, provinces, and cities are, to a growing degree, taking on the task of fostering emission reduction strategies within their borders. Such "sustainability projects" tend to reflect both political and economic objectives, although they are frequently described in terms of the latter. In particular, there is a tendency to adopt urban emission reduction strategies less as a specific response to climate change and more as a calling card for green consumers and businesses. This competitive strategy, as Corina McKendry (2008) has shown, might well be more for show than anything else—and data about actual ecological results of such projects are, so far, lacking.

For example, California has adopted a plethora of climate change laws, regulations, and strategies. In Executive Order S-3-05 (June, 2005), Governor Schwarzenegger set the following targets for the state:

- Reduction of GHG emissions to 2000 levels by 2010 – 59 million tons of emissions less, 11 percent below usual emissions;
- Reduction of GHG emissions to 1990 levels by 2020 – 145 million tons of emissions less, 25 percent below usual emissions;
- By 2050, a reduction of 80 percent emissions below 1990 levels (CCCP 2008a).

The governor has appointed a "Climate Action Team" composed of representatives from a variety of agencies, which has been ordered "to implement global warming emission reduction programs and report on the progress made toward meeting the state-wide greenhouse gas targets that were established in the executive order" (CCCP 2008b). The California Global Warming Solutions Act of 2006 (AB 32) requires the State Air Resources Board (ARB) to "establish a statewide GHG [greenhouse gas] emissions cap for 2020, based on 1990 emissions" and "adopt mandatory reporting rules for significant sources of greenhouse gases," both by January 1, 2008 (CCCP 2008c). The ARB staff has, in turn, issued a 200 page "Expanded List of Early Action Measures to Reduce Greenhouse Gas Emissions in California" (CARB 2007) and the ARB is preparing a

Scoping Plan [that] contains the main strategies California will use to reduce the greenhouse gases (GHG) that cause climate change. The Plan, when it is completed, will have a range of GHG reduction actions which can include direct regulations, alternative compliance mechanisms, monetary and non-monetary incentives, voluntary actions, and market-based mechanisms such as a cap-and-trade system.

(CARB 2008)

As of this writing, the ARB is planning to hold a series of public meetings and to adopt a final "Scoping Plan" by November, 2008. And that will be only the beginning. Among the many uncertainties that will have to be addressed are those involving costs, financing and voter support.

California is often lauded for its environmental legislation, but it should be kept in mind that its regulatory precociousness has an ironic, though perhaps unsurprising relationship with other trends in the state. E.g., the number of miles driven has outpaced population growth in the state by 50 percent for two decades (Barringer 2008). It is also worth keeping in mind that California is larger than many nation-states in terms of geography, population, and economy. The operations and organization of its formal governance institutions—nestled within a federalist system—fit with depictions of local governance. Yet, its sheer scale also indicates that "local" or "decentralized" does not quite describe California's situation. On the one hand, California demonstrates the weaknesses of state-centric approaches to environmental problems, as it has made impressive efforts at environmental protection, even though it is not a nation state. On the other hand, the case of California's environmental governance seems to confirm that larger scales of social organization, which usually come in the form of nation states, are capable of getting things done if there is strong executive and popular interest.

Cities seem to be setting similarly ambitious objectives. According to McKendry (2008: 3–4),

> Over 800 cities around the world have joined the Cities for Climate Protection campaign of the organization Local Governments for Sustainability (commonly referred to as ICLEI because of its former name – the International Council for Local Environmental Initiatives), including four hundred cities and counties in the United States.[9] Over seven hundred mayors have joined the U.S. Mayors Climate Protection Agreement.[10]

Moreover, the US Conference of Mayors (COM) has established a "Mayors Climate Protection Center," whose web site tells of

> an increasingly urgent need to provide mayors with the guidance and assistance they need to lead their cities' efforts to reduce the greenhouse gas emissions that are linked to climate change. Throughout the nation there is clear evidence that mayoral leadership is producing business and community support for policies that reduce emissions. While progress is already being made in many cities, our goal must be to increase the number of cities involved in the effort, and to equip all cities with the knowledge and tools that ultimately will have the greatest impact on undo [sic] the causes of global warming.
>
> (COM 2007a)

Moreover, according to COM, "Under the Agreement, participating cities commit to take following three actions:

> Strive to meet or beat the Kyoto Protocol targets in their own communities, through actions ranging from anti-sprawl land-use policies to urban forest restoration projects to public information campaigns;
>
> Urge their state governments, and the federal government, to enact policies and programs to meet or beat the greenhouse gas emission reduction target suggested for the United States in the Kyoto Protocol – 7 percent reduction from 1990 levels by 2012; and
>
> Urge the U.S. Congress to pass the bipartisan greenhouse gas reduction legislation, which would establish a national emission trading system.
>
> (COM 2007b)

To date, it can probably be said with some assurance that actual reductions resulting from both state and local programs have been difficult, if not impossible to measure. This is not to say that localities are not engaged in measurement, only that the systems of measurement that localities have erected are quite possibly prone to inflating their own results. What their effects might be in the future is, as yet, unclear.

Underlying such plans and programs is the idea that citizens and businesses can be mobilized by urban leaders—and, if necessary, pressured—to actively and enthusiastically participate in efforts to reduce local greenhouse gas emissions. Ignoring, for the moment, the oft-raised question about economic rationality—does it make sense to do something costly if no one else is doing it? (Olsen 1965)—the threat of global warming, combined with the promise of civic virtue, is almost certainly insufficient to "solve" the problem on

197

its own; urban action would only work if it happened just about everywhere. In the face of the seemingly relentless operation of a globalized capitalist system, still hell-bent on carbonization, are any reduction strategies, alone or in combination with others, likely to have the desired impact? To the extent that historical experience offers any insights, it would appear that only war or economic recession have, historically, led to significant decarbonization, and neither is to be devoutly wished. Of course, history is not destiny, and it is possible that decarbonization could happen as a consequence of desirable political changes, rather than war and economic crisis. If we can entertain the notion that economic health, typically measured in terms of sheer growth, as typified by the GDP, is in many ways a poor indicator of societal well-being, then we may get somewhere. During the last 15 years, income inequality has been rising along with the GDP (Uchitelle 2008). We are not necessarily stuck with a choice between different political failures (i.e. economic crisis, environmental devastation, and war). Collective political action *is* possible.

Environmental politics?

Broadly speaking, we know *what* is to be done about climate change: reduce greenhouse gas (GHG) emissions. We also know *how* emissions could be reduced: Use "cleaner" technologies, conserve energy, create more localized production chains *in place* of global ones, make it easier for people to be mobile using collective means of transportation—or even be less mobile, consume less, produce less, conserve more, drive less. But, when an environmentalist or a politician says "we know how to fix the problem," s/he is correct only if the problem is defined as a technical one. Global climate change is, however, as much a political problem as it is a physical one—and its political dimensions are at least as important, probably more so, than its technical ones. Taken together, the elitist terms of environmental discourse, and the institutional advantages of wealthy interests, indicate that the standard approach to the climate change problem—i.e., voluntary, technological, and market-based—continues because it appeases the well-off, not because it is capable of actually addressing climate change.

It is easy to find examples of virtuous, "green" behaviors actually happening—just as we can see global warming actually happening. It would be helpful if the "greening" of human beliefs and practices would occur more rapidly than global climate change but, unfortunately, all indicators point in the opposite direction. The rate at which the climate is changing for the worse is surely outpacing the rate at which humanity is adopting "green" behaviors; indeed, if we are to judge by growing global rates of GHG emissions—which is what matters for the atmosphere and climate—humanity is not getting greener at all. That some people have "green options" and select them in lieu of "brown" ones might slow down the *rate* at which the atmosphere is expected to warm. At best, individuals making "green" choices will delay effects for a relatively short time, especially if global emissions continue to increase (IPCC 2007a: 14) This amounts to a large scale version of the rebound effect: the effort in some places and by some people to conserve resources and increase efficiency occurs even as rates of resource use are dramatically increasing (and for many understandable reasons) elsewhere. In other words, many little "fixes" might be happening in one way or another but, on the whole, nothing is being fixed.

Given the broad and growing political consensus that carbon emissions must be reduced, and so many proposals for halting and reducing them, why is so little being done? There are two basic reasons. The first is that discussions of environmental "politics" typically begin from the assumption that it is best to follow the recommendations of experts (e.g. ecologists and economists). Such faith in expertise leads frequently not to political solutions but, rather, squabbles over technical details. Furthermore, non-experts are encouraged and congratulated for following the advice of experts, especially in their choice of greener, more efficient products (rather than participating in the political conversation). The message conveyed, in other words, is that shopping is a reasonable stand-in for meaningful environmental politics.

The second reason it is difficult to green social practice follows from the first. Detailed, technical proposals will almost always encounter some, often wealthy, actors who have an interest in obstructing them—either as NIMBYists ("Not In My BackYard") or for more mundane economic reasons—and are willing to work against them. To illustrate, consider a law passed by the Seattle City Council requiring stores to charge 20 cents for the choice of plastic (as in "paper or plastic?"). The law is meant to discourage the use of plastic bags and decrease demand for them. The American Chemistry Council, which represents plastic bag manufacturers, objected and financed an aggressive petition drive to put the bag "tax" to a city-wide vote. Proponents had pushed for a fee, instead of an all-out ban such as that in San Francisco, in order to offer shoppers a choice. Opponents, however, framed the issue as a matter of choice, as well: the fee did *not* allow consumers to decide for themselves whether or not use of a plastic bag is justified. The result is considerable resentment toward the "imposition" of the fee (Kaste 2008).

No number of technical solutions and good intentions can surmount the fundamental obstacle to addressing climate change: persuading the necessary numbers of people, especially those in positions of power, to collectively decide what to do, to do it, and to make sure it is done properly. Simply spreading the word about global warming and touting technology, markets, and civic virtue does not amount to "fighting" global warming. To equate "spreading awareness" with a political strategy is akin to running a marathon as an incentive to jog more often and to receive a cool t-shirt. The effort may be fun, and the runner will get some attention, but she is unlikely to finish anywhere close to the winning time.

Conclusion

Some number of pundits, a few politicians, and even fewer scientists maintain a skeptical attitude about the relationship between carbonization and climate change. There is rapidly accumulating evidence—as well as a broad scientific consensus—that climate change is already upon us. At the same time, the politics associated with addressing climate change are such that, despite a burgeoning collective desire to deal with the problem—and to begin sooner rather than later—the enactment of substantive measures is slow in coming. The power distribution between those who are more and less likely to be directly harmed by climate change is not on the side of action and generates considerable resistance to a timely response. In particular, the costs of impacts are likely to fall disproportionately upon the world's poor, while the costs of amelioration will fall heavily on the world's rich. For the most part, many of the latter seem to adopt the view that they can buy their way out of the problem—alternative energy sources, sea walls, air conditioning—and they have no strong interest in helping the former, especially if they (the rich) stand to realize few or no benefits. In other words, the fundamental obstacle to addressing climate change is the present global distribution of power, wealth, and resources, which has only been further exacerbated by globalization. The result, so far, has been international impasse and growing efforts by people and local governments, especially in the Global North,[11] to put in place practices and policies that will reduce urban emissions and give individuals more options for reducing their own. Inasmuch as these strategies are largely voluntary, it is less than evident that they can or will lead to significant and sustained reductions in carbonization and emissions.

What, then, are *we* to do? In our view, a world of nine or ten billion people—the estimated population peak that will be reached sometime around the middle of the 21st century—consuming and carbonizing at current US rates is not only unsustainable, it would mark a monumental political failure. What is required, therefore, is nothing less than a turn away from consumer capitalism and high growth rates to an economic and social system that is fair, just, and equitable and does not privilege excessive consumption and pollution. This could well mean lower levels of consumption for those billion or two of the world's people who are now well off and, ideally, improved lives for the nine or ten billion who will not be. We do know that political and social change take place, that they often result from political movements and activism, and that the resulting changes are often better than what came before. If we are to make this happen, we need to get to work, now.

Notes

1 According to British Petroleum, proved world oil reserves total 1.14 trillion barrels, or about 40 years at current global consumption rates (EIA 2008). World coal reserves total 998 billion short tons (EIA 2007a), or about 150 years at current global consumption rates (EIA 2007b). Lower-grade energy resources are much larger.

2 Cement manufacturing alone is estimated to account for 5 percent of annual global emissions; see Sturrock 2008.

3 By some estimates, Gross World Product might be in excess of $70 trillion in PPP; see Assadourian 2008.

4 Calculations based solely on *where* greenhouse gases are emitted may now place China higher than the US but, considering that the US is the biggest importer of Chinese manufactured products, these numbers are debatable.

5 Many economists and utilitarians would take offense at this idea, arguing that efficiency should take precedence over ethics; see Nash 2006.

6 The flip side of this coin is that people living it at subsistence levels, regardless of whether they have a green consciousness, likely already have small carbon footprints in comparison to most inhabitants of Western countries; see Conca 2001.

7 *Consumer Reports* Greener Choices web site (http://www.greenerchoices.org/home.cfm) illustrates these propositions, as does *The Daily Green* (http://www.thedailygreen.com/).

8 A portion of this section draws on McKendry 2008.

9 "ICLEI Members: Cities for Climate Protection Campaign," ICLEI. Available at http://www.iclei.org/fileadmin/user_upload/documents/USA/members/ICLEI_Local_Governments_Oct07.pdf, accessed on December 28, 2007.

10 "Mayors Climate Protection Center: List of Participating Mayors," *U.S. Conference of Mayors.* Available at http://www.usmayors.org/climateprotection/list.asp, accessed on January 8, 2008.

11 ICLEI lists 852 members, of which 732 are in North America, Europe, Japan, South Korea, Australia, and New Zealand (http://www.iclei.org/index.php?id=772).

References

Adam, D. (2008) "China's Carbon Emissions Soaring Past the US," *Guardian*, June 13, at: http://www.guardian.co.uk/environment/2008/jun/13/climatechange.carbonemissions (accessed September 2, 2008).

Ahmad, N. and Wyckoff, A. (2003) "Carbon Dioxide Emissions Embodied in International Trade of Goods," *OECD Science, Technology and Industry Working Papers*, 2003/15, Paris: OECD Publishing, at: http://titania.sourceoecd.org/vl=4817476/cl=18/nw=1/rpsv/cgi-bin/wppdf?file=5lgsjhvj7ld6.pdf (accessed August 27, 2008).

Assadourian, E. (2008) "Global Economic Growth Continues at Expense of Ecological Systems," Worldwatch Institute, Feb. 14, at http://www.worldwatch.org/node/5456#notes (accessed April 28, 2008).

Bang, J. K., Hoff, E. and Peters, G. (2008) "EU Consumption, Global Pollution," WWF International, Gland/Industrial Ecology Programme, Norwegian University of Science and Technology, Trondheim, at: http://assets.panda.org/downloads/eu_consumption_global_pollution.pdf (accessed March 3, 2008).

Barringer, F. (2008) "California Moves on Bill to Curb Sprawl and Emissions," *New York Times,* August 29, 2008, at: http://www.nytimes.com/2008/08/29/us/29sprawl.html?em (accessed September 2, 2008).

Birol, F. (2004) "World Energy and Environmental Outlook to 2030," Powerpoint presentation, International Energy Agency, at: http://www.oecd.org/dataoecd/37/9/34915156.ppt (accessed September 2, 2008).

Briggs, H. (2001) "Global Warming 'altering genes'," BBC News, November 6, at: http://news.bbc.co.uk/2/hi/science/nature/1639284.stm (accessed September 2, 2008).

Butraw, D. and Palmer, K. (2004) "SO Cap-and-Trade Program in the United States," in Harrington, W., Morgenstern, R. D. and Sterner, T. (eds.), *Choosing Environmental Policy: Comparing Instruments and Outcomes in the United States and Europe,* Washington, DC: Resources for the Future, pp. 41–66.

Butti, K. and Perlin, J. (1980) *A Golden Thread: 2500 Years of Solar Architecture and Technology*, New York: Van Nostrand Reinhold.

CARB (California Air Resources Board) (2007) "Expanded list of Early Action Measures to Reduce Greenhouse Gas Emissions in California recommended for Board Consideration," Sacramento, October, at: http://www.arb.ca.gov/cc/ccea/meetings/ea_final_report.pdf (accessed September 2, 2008).

——(2008) "AB 32 Scoping Plan – Background," Sacramento, n.d., at: http://www.arb.ca.gov/cc/scopingplan/scopingplan.htm (accessed September 2, 2008).

CCCP (California Climate Change Portal) (2008a) "Statistics and Data on Climate Change – California," Sacramento, n.d., at: http://www.climatechange.ca.gov/newsroom/stats/index.html (accessed September 2, 2008).

——(2008b) "Climate Action Team & Climate Action Initiative," Sacramento, n.d., at: http://www.climatechange.ca.gov/climate_action_team/index.html (accessed September 2, 2008).

——(2008c) "Assembly Bill 32 – The Global Warming Solutions Act of 2006," Sacramento, n.d., at: http://www.climatechange.ca.gov/ab32/index.html (accessed September 2, 2008).

Carola, M. S. (2004) "Ecological Modernization Theory: What About Consumption?" *Society & Natural Resources*, 17: 247–60.

Coase, R. H. (1960) "The Problem of Social Cost," *Journal of Law and Economics*, 3: 1–44.

Cohen, M. J. (2006) "Ecological Modernization and its Discontents: The American Environmental Movement's Resistance to an Innovation-Driven Future," *Futures*, 38 (5): 528–47.

Conca, K. (2001) "Consumption and Environment in a Global Economy," *Global Environmental Politics*, 1 (3): 53–71.

Confessore, N. (2008) "Xcel to Disclose Global Warming Risks," *New York Times*, August 28, at: http://www.nytimes.com/2008/08/28/business/28energy.html (accessed September 2, 2008).

Dobson, A. (2003) *Citizenship and the Environment*, Oxford: Oxford University Press.

Edwards, G. (2008) "Andes face Glacial Meltdown," *Guardian*, July 10, at: http://www.guardian.co.uk/commentisfree/2008/jul/13/climatechange.colombia (accessed August 20, 2008).

Energy Information Administration (EIA) (2008) "Figure 6. World Electricity Generation by Fuel, 2005–30," *International Energy Outlook 2008—Highlights*, Washington, DC, June, at: http://www.eia.doe.gov/oiaf/ieo/excel/figure_6data.xls (accessed August 15, 2008).

EIA (2007a) "Table 8.2: World Estimated Recoverable Coal," *International Energy Annual 2005*, Washington, DC, June 21, at: http://www.eia.doe.gov/pub/international/iea2005/table82.xls (accessed September 2, 2008).

——(2007b) "Table 1.4 World Coal Consumption, 1980–2005," *International Energy Annual 2005*, Washington, DC, September 10, at: http://www.eia.doe.gov/pub/international/iealf/table14.xls (accessed September 2, 2008).

Firorino, D. J. (2004) "Flexibility," in R. F. Durant, D. J. Fiorino and R. O'Leary (eds.), *Environmental Governance Reconsidered*, Cambridge, Mass.: MIT Press, pp. 393–427.

——(2006) *The New Environmental Regulation*, Cambridge, MA: MIT Press.

Firat, A. F. and Dholakia, N. (1998) *Consuming People: From Political Economy to Theaters of Consumption*, London: Routledge.

Freeman, A. (2006) "Economics, Incentives, and Environmental Policy," in Vig, N.J. and Kraft, D. (eds.), *Environmental Policy Reconsidered: New Directions for the 21st Century*, Washington, DC: CQ Press, pp. 193–214.

Freund, P. & Martin, G. (2007) "Hyperautomobility, the Social Organization of Space, and Health," *Mobilities*, 2 (1): 37–49.

Gereffi, G. and Korzeniewicz, M. (1994) *Commodity Chains and Global Capitalism*, Westport, CT: Praeger.

Gereffi, G., Humphrey, J. and Sturgeon, T. (2005) "The Governance of Global Value Chains," *Review of International Political Economy*, 12 (1): 78–104.

Hansjürgens, B. (2005) *Emissions Trading for Climate Policy: US and European Perspectives*, Cambridge: Cambridge University Press.

Gould, K. A., Pellow, D. N. and Schnaiberg, A. (2004) "Interrogating the Treadmill of Production – Everything You Wanted to Know about the Treadmill but Were Afraid to Ask," *Organization & Environment*, 17 (3): 296–316.

Greene, D. L. and Schafer, A. (2003) "Reducing Greenhouse Gas emissions From U.S. Transportation." Report prepared for the Pew Center on Global Climate Change, at http://www.pewclimate. org/docUploads/ustransp.pdf (accessed February 25, 2008).

Gunningham, N., Kagan, R. A. and Thornton, D. (2003) *Shades of Green: Business, Regulation and Environment*, Stanford, CA: Stanford Law and Politics.

Hardner, J. and Rice, R. (2002) "Rethinking Green Consumerism," *Scientific American*, 286 (5): 88–95.

Hawkins, G. (2006) *The Ethics of Waste: How We Relate to Rubbish*, Lanham, MD: Rowman & Littlefield Publishers.

Hertwich, E. G. (2005) "Consumption and the Rebound Effect—An Industrial Ecology Perspective," *Journal of Industrial Ecology*, 9 (1–2) (Winter–Spring): 85–98.

Hilty, L. M. et al. (2006) "Rebound Effects of Progress in Information Technology," *Poiesis Prax*, 4: 19–38.

Hull, R. (2005) "All About EVE: A Report on Environmental Virtue Ethics Today," *Ethics & the Environment*, 10 (1): 89–110.

Intergovernmental Panel on Climate Change (IPCC) (2007a) *Climate Change 2007—Synthesis Report*, Geneva: IPCC Secretariat, World Meteorological Organization, at: http://www.ipcc.ch/pdf/assessment-report/ar4/syr/ar4_syr.pdf (accessed 29 April 2008).

——(2007b) *Climate Change 2007—Synthesis Report—Summary for Policymakers*, Geneva: IPCC Secretariat, World Meteorological Organization, at: http://www.ipcc.ch/pdf/assessment-report/ar4/syr/ar4_syr_spm.pdf (accessed 29 April 2008).

Kaste, M. (2008) "Seattle's Bag-User Fee Spurs Backlash," Washington, DC: National Public Radio, at: http://www.npr.org/templates/story/story.php?storyId=93844895 (accessed August 30, 2008).

Kaswan, A. (2008) "Environmental Justice and Domestic Climate Change Policy," *Environmental Law Reporter News & Analysis*, 38: 10287–315 at: http://ssrn.com/abstract=1077675 (accessed July 10, 2008).

Kokaz, N. (2005) "Theorizing International Fairness," *Metaphilosophy*, 36 (1–2): 68–92.

Krasner, S. D. (1983) "Structural Causes and Regime Consequences: Regimes as Intervening Variables," in S. D. Krasner (ed.), *International Regimes*, Ithaca, NY: Cornell University Press, pp. 1–22.

Lipschutz, R.D., with Rowe, J.K. (2005) *Globalization, Governmentality, and Global Politics – Regulation for the Rest of Us?* London: Routledge.

Maddison, A. (2001) *The World Economy—A Millennial Perspective*, Paris: Development Centre of the Organization for Economic Co-operation and Development.

Makower, J, Elkington, J. and Hailes, J. (1993) *The Green Consumer*, New York: Penguin, rev ed.

Marsh, G. P. (2001) "Address Delivered before the Agricultural Society of Rutland County (Vermont)," September 30, 1847, in Trombulak, S.C. (ed.), *So Great a Vision—The Conservation Writings of George Perkins Marsh*, Lebanon, New Hampshire: Middlebury College Press/University Press of New England, pp. 1–23.

McKendry, C. (2008) "Competing for Green: Neoliberalism and the Rise of Sustainable Cities," unpublished MA paper, Department of Politics, University of California, Santa Cruz, May.

Mol, A. P. J. (2001) *Globalization and Environmental Reform: The Ecological Modernization of the Global Economy*, Cambridge, MA: MIT Press.

——(2002) "Ecological Modernization and the Global Economy," *Global Environmental Politics*, 2 (2): 92–115.

Mol, A. P. J. and Sonnenfeld, D. A. (eds.) (2000) *Ecological Modernisation Around the World: Perspectives and Critical Debates*, London: Frank Cass.

Mol, A. P. J. and Spaargaren, G. (2004) "Ecological Modernization and Consumption: A Reply," *Society & Natural Resources*, 17 (3): 261–65.

Murphy, P. (2007) "Recent Developments in World Trade," *Trade Topics – A Quarterly Review of Australia's International Trade* (Spring): 4–9, at: http://www.dfat.gov.au/publications/stats-pubs/downloads/world_trade.pdf (accessed April 28, 2008).

Nash, J. R. (2006) "Framing Effects and Regulatory Choice," *Notre Dame Law Review*, 82 (1): 313–72.

Olson, M. (1965) *The Logic of Collective Action*, Cambridge, MA: Harvard University Press.

Paterson, M. (2007) *Automobile Politics: Ecology and Cultural Political Economy*, Cambridge: Cambridge University Press.

Peattie, K. (2001) "Golden Goose or Wild Goose? The Hunt for the Green Consumer," *Business Strategy and the Environment*, 10 (4): 187–99.

Peters, G. P. and Hertwich, E. G. (2008) "CO_2 Embodied in International Trade with Implications for Global Climate Policy," *Environmental Science and Technology*, 42 (5): 1401–7.

President's Materials Policy Commission (PMPC) (1952) *Resources for Freedom*, Washington, DC: US Government Printing Office.

Putnam, P. (1952) "The Promise of Technology: The Possibilities of Solar Energy," *Resources For Freedom: A Report to the President*, Washington, DC: US Government Printing Office, v. 1: 213–20.

Shapiro, J. (2007). "Tuvalu Envoy takes up Global Warming Fight," Washington, DC: National Public Radio, at: http://www.npr.org/templates/story/story.php?storyId=10950375 (accessed August 30, 2008).

Stern, N. (2006) "Executive Summary," *Stern Review of the Economics of Climate Change*, London: Her Majesty's Treasury Office, at: http://www.hm-treasury.gov.uk/media/4/3/Executive_Summary.pdf (accessed August 26, 2008).

Struck, D. (2006) "'Rapid Warming' Spreads Havoc in Canada's Forests," *Washington Post*, March 1, at: http://www.washingtonpost.com/wp-dyn/content/article/2006/02/28/AR2006022801772.html (accessed August 31, 2008).

Sturrock, C. (2008). "Green Cement May Set CO_2 Fate in Concrete," *San Francisco Chronicle*, September 2, at: http://www.sfgate.com/cgi-bin/article.cgi?file=/c/a/2008/09/02/MNGD129361.DTL (accessed September 2, 2008).

Southerton D., Chappells, H. and van Vliet, B. (2004) *Sustainable Consumption: The Implications Of Changing Infrastructures Of Provision*, Cheltenham: Edward Elgar.

Szasz, A. (2007) *Shopping Our Way to Safety: How We Changed from Protecting the Environment to Protecting Ourselves*, Minneapolis: University of Minnesota Press.

Tol, R. S. J. (2002) "Estimates of the Damage Costs of Climate Change," *Environmental and Resource Economics*, 21: 47–73.

Tol, R. S. J et al. (2004) "Distributional Aspects of Climate Change Impacts," *Global Environmental Change*, 14: 259–72.

Uchitelle, L. (2008) "Hey, Big Number, Make Room for the Rest of Us," *New York Times*, August 31, at: http://www.nytimes.com/2008/08/31/weekinreview/31uchitelle.html? (accessed August 31, 2008).

United Nations (2008) "Tables of Final Results, 2005 International Comparison Program," February, at: http://siteresources.worldbank.org/ICPINT/Resources/ICP_final-results.pdf (accessed 28 April 2008).

US COM (Mayors Climate Protection Center) (2007a) "About the Mayors Climate Protection Center," at: http://www.usmayors.org/climateprotection/about.htm (accessed July 21, 2008).

——(2007b) "U.S. Conference of Mayors Climate Protection Agreement," http://www.usmayors.org/climateprotection/agreement.htm (accessed July 21, 2008).

van der Voet, E., van Oers, L. and Nikolic, I. (2004) "Dematerialization: Not Just a Matter of Weight," *Journal of Industrial Ecology*, 8 (4): 121–37.

Varian, H. R. (2006) "Recalculating the Costs of Global Climate Change," *New York Times*, December 14, at: http://www.nytimes.com/2006/12/14/business/14scene.html (accessed August 30, 2008).

Wald, M. (2008) "Wind Energy Bumps Into Power Grid's Limits," *New York Times*, August 26, 2008, at: http://www.nytimes.com/2008/08/27/business/27grid.html (accessed September 10, 2008).

York, R. and Rosa, E. A. (2003) "Key Challenges to Ecological Modernization Theory Institutional Efficacy, Case Study Evidence, Units of Analysis, and the Pace of Eco-Efficiency," *Organization & Environment*, 16 (3): 273–88.

11

Infectious disease and globalization

Susan Kippax and Niamh Stephenson

[I]n the context of infectious diseases, there is nowhere in the world from which we are remote and no one from whom we are disconnected.

(Institute of Medicine 1992: v)

Introduction: aspirations collapse

The United States' Surgeon General's claim in 1967 that 'it is time to close the book on infectious disease' is held up as a canonical moment because, in retrospect, it actually marked a turning point and upsurge in infectious diseases. Today, despite instances of success (e.g. smallpox eradication coordinated by the World Health Organization (WHO)) the ambition to conquer infectious disease no longer has the same purchase in global public health. It is not simply the re-emergence of infectious disease that has muted such aspirations. Rather, by the mid-1990s a significant transformation in the basic concepts used to understand infectious disease had taken hold in microbiology, virology, immunology, and epidemiology: viruses are increasingly understood as recombinant, unpredictable, and continually in the process of becoming – in short as emergent (Lederberg 1996, Cooper 2006).

The transformation entailed in thinking of viruses as emergent echoes an earlier transformation in biomedical notions of the immune system (and one familiar to medical sociologists) (Martin 1994). The immune system had been characterized as a fixed entity akin to a hierarchical command-control centre that defended the body from invasion through its capacities to recognise 'outsiders'. This notion has been contested by biomedical research which characterizes the immune system as an inherently conflicted network, a non-hierarchal distributed system which no longer operates by discriminating between inside and out, self and other, protector and invader. The immune system is now understood as a distributed system for which '[c]ontext is a fundamental matter, not as surrounding "information", but as co-structure and co-text' (Haraway 1991: 214). Similarly, contemporary characterizations of infectious disease foreground how viruses are not relatively fixed entities that can be studied and known, rather they are unpredictable, unstable modes of existence whose transformations cannot be separated from the contexts in which they arise (Cooper 2006). Viruses are described as situated in the sense that they are 'but one component of a dynamic and complex global ecology, which is shaped and buffeted by technologic, societal, economic, environmental, and demographic changes, not to mention microbial change and adaptation' (Satcher 1995: 4–5). Such accounts of emergence cast viruses as ever changing, recombining and re-assorting in unpredictable ways.

By the mid-90s the notion of emergence had a firm foothold in public health; for instance the Centres for Disease Control (CDC) in the United States of America (US) launched a new journal, *Emerging Infectious Diseases*, or *EID*, in 1996. Here, EID are defined as 'infections that have newly appeared in a population or have existed but are rapidly increasing in incidence or geographic range' (Morse 1995: 1). The pages of *EID* are devoted to familiar emerging and re-emerging diseases (e.g. HIV, TB, malaria, influenza, staph) as well as less familiar zoonoses and diseases transmitted by insects (e.g. rift valley fever virus) and diseases which are becoming increasingly common but attract little in the way of public attention (e.g. norovirus).

The resurgence of infectious disease is commonly explained by those working on EID by invoking 'globalization': 'global factors' are cast as having intensified the risks of bringing people into contact with unfamiliar microbes and of facilitating the dissemination of familiar ones (Lederberg 1998: 464). Thus, in public health discussion, globalization is understood as a set of factors which include: (1) ecological factors, such as dam building or changes in agricultural practices which have been connected to a range of diseases including influenza and Bolivian hemorrhagic fever (Morse 1995); and (2) industrialization and associated demographic changes such as the increased density of populations to be found living in megaslums and the rapidity of travel and contact between people, both of which in turn have been associated with EID (Davis 2006, Lederberg 1998). In addition, EID are explained as a result of (3) technological changes whose uptake across the globe is attributed to some notion of 'globalization' (e.g. the use of air conditioning systems which is connected to Legionnaire's disease, tampons with toxic shock syndrome or faulty water purification with cryptosporidium) (Lederberg 1998). As Lederberg (1998) argues, today there is nothing 'exotic' about diseases that were previously found in far-flung corners of the globe – the amount and rapidity of people's travel around the world together with the extent that goods are being transported means that diseases travel. As the opening quote from an early 1990s report on infectious disease within the US suggests, what has become apparent is the impossibility of successfully deploying familiar public health strategies which rely on national border protection as a means of safeguarding the nation (Institute of Medicine 1992). Epidemiological accounts of EID identify the forms of commerce and travel entailed in the ongoing expansion of global markets as contributing to disease but do not seriously question them. Instead, as we will illustrate, the challenges EID pose to both international health efforts *and* to nation states are increasingly understood to demand 'globalized' solutions.

By connecting EID to 'global factors', EID are cast as situated in particular social contexts. Yet, public health discussions of the 'global factors' contributing to infectious disease neglect, in Farmer's words, how social inequalities 'sculpt not only the distribution of emerging diseases, but also the course of disease in those affected by them' (Farmer 1996: 265). This neglect arises in part, we will argue, because possibilities for public health understanding of and capacity to act on the specificities of different social contexts are under-explored. We develop this argument by examining the failure to grapple with social practices and contexts in the global response to one EID, HIV. The public health response to HIV is rarely informed by analyses of: the power relations at play between high and low/middle income countries; the tensions between different forms of knowledge about disease; or tensions between public health responses that privilege 'exportable', packaged clinical interventions into disease and social interventions that need to be grounded in an engagement with the specificities of local contexts in order to be effective.

Public health accounts of HIV

HIV is a blood borne virus most commonly transmitted by sexual practice, particularly penetrative intercourse (vaginal and anal) with an HIV-infected person. It is also transmitted by the sharing of HIV-contaminated needles and syringes, from an HIV-positive mother to her child during birth and breast feeding, and via the transfusion of HIV-infected blood and blood products. It is now estimated that over 25 million people have died of AIDS and 33 million people are living with HIV, with 95 per cent living in low/middle income countries (UNAIDS 2007, Cohen et al. 2008). In 2007 2.5 million people became infected with HIV, while 2.1 million people died of AIDS (UNAIDS 2007).

Although it is now understood that HIV emerged early in the 20th century (Mokili and Korber 2005), it was not until June, 1981 that a young gay man in the US was 'diagnosed' with the most devastating immune deficiency, referred to by some as the Gay-Related Immune Deficiency (GRID) or the 'gay disease' (McLaughlin 1989). This was the first diagnosis of AIDS although it was not until 1982 that the Acquired Immune Deficiency Syndrome (AIDS) was named. In 1983 the Human Immunodeficiency Virus (HIV) was identified as the cause of AIDS (UNAIDS 2006). With the advent of the HIV test in 1985 rather than having to rely on AIDS cases, epidemiologists began their surveillance work based on HIV testing to provide the needed information about the patterning of the epidemic/s (both internationally and within nations). It soon became evident that HIV was not an exotic disease confined to one population (gay men) or to one country (US) but a disease that had spread around the globe. No country or region has escaped. It was not until 1996 that the first effective treatment – but not cure – of HIV was trialled and later marketed.

In the years that followed the diagnosis of the young gay man in the US, HIV was identified in a number of countries in Europe and the UK, in the Caribbean and Latin America, in Canada, in Australasia – again among gay men but also in injection drug users. In many of these countries transmission was attributed to homosexual transmission (anal intercourse) and to a lesser extent the practice of sharing HIV-contaminated needles, which was more common in southern Europe and, later, in Eastern Europe and the former Soviet Union. A little later, in 1984, heterosexual transmission of HIV was documented in many African countries, particularly in sub-Saharan and southern Africa, where the major mode of transmission was vaginal intercourse (Smallman-Raynor, Cliff and Haggett 1992). In the mid to late 80s, HIV was diagnosed in increasing numbers in the Asia-Pacific region – India, Thailand, Cambodia, Vietnam, and China where transmission is attributed to sex work, injecting, and more recently, to homosexual transmission (Baral et al. 2007).

As the following illustrations show, industrialization and travel of all sorts – for pleasure, for work, for security – was and is clearly implicated in the transmission of HIV (Smallman-Raynor, Cliff and Haggett 1992). The early high prevalence in Switzerland was in large part a function of travel in and out of the international agencies situated in Geneva; in the US many of the early cases in gay men were traced to a French–Canadian airline steward, 'patient zero' (Shilts 1987); and in Australia the first case of HIV was diagnosed in late 1982 in a gay man who had had homosexual contact in the US (Kaldor and Rubin 1994). About 35 per cent of all documented HIV cases in the Philippines are among returning overseas workers, as were 42 per cent of new cases recorded in 2006 (CARAM 2007). Between and within country transmission has also been documented in association with work and mobility. The apartheid system in South Africa established and reinforced patterns of circular migration that persist: men from rural areas and neigh-bouring countries are permitted to work in South African mines and these typically young men live in single-sex hostels with easy access to sex workers. The lifting of the apartheid laws in the early 1990s led to increased mobility throughout southern Africa and probably contributed to the further spread of HIV in the region: the countries of Swaziland, Botswana, Namibia, and South Africa suffer the highest HIV prevalence (around 25 per cent of adults) in the world (UNAIDS 2007). However increased mobility does not necessarily increase HIV risk: mineworkers who return home four or more times per year appear to be at significantly lower risks of HIV (International Organization for Migration and UNAIDS 2003). Truck drivers have been shown to be particularly vulnerable to HIV infection because of a number of structural and environ-mental factors including: movement between regions with different levels of HIV; inadequate access to health care; availability of unregulated sex-work services; and a lack of suitable accommodation at rest stops (International Organization for Migration 2005). Movement between countries in response to conflict by displaced persons and refugees may lead to increased risk of HIV infection. For example, there is evidence that armed conflict and the involvement of soldiers from multiple regions contributed to the trans-mission of HIV from town to town in the early stages of the HIV epidemic in Guinea-Bissau, the Sudan and Uganda (Spiegel et al. 2007). At the same time the isolation and decreased mobility associated with refugee camps can also hinder HIV transmission, as can better access to HIV prevention programmes in some camps (Spiegel et al. 2007).

Globalization was central to the emergence of HIV around the world and there was an international response: early in the 1980s WHO initiated worldwide surveillance for AIDS through a network of collaborating centres, regional offices, and national and international disease surveillance centres. As the epidemiological mapping continued, it became clear that HIV was not evenly distributed around the world: prevalence rates range from less than 1 per cent of the population in most high income countries to more than 25 per cent in some southern African countries. Some countries have 'concentrated' epidemics mainly confined to homosexual men as in northwestern Europe and Australia or to injection drug users as in the states of the former Soviet Union, some such as Botswana, South Africa, and Zimbabwe are experiencing 'generalized' epidemics where the entire sexually active population is affected; while still others such as the US and some countries in South America are experiencing multiple epidemics – among people who inject drugs, among gay men, and increasingly among the poor. In Asia and the Pacific regions the patterning of the epidemic continues to emerge but sex work, injecting drug use, and homosexual transmission are implicated (UNAIDS 2007).

How did public health understand this global patterning of HIV, and what does the public health account of it tell us? In attempting to grasp the patterning of the epidemic in the early 1980s, epidemiologists constructed 'risk categories'. Initially these risk categories were related to behaviours but there was a conflation of behaviour with group identity:

for example, the practice of anal intercourse is conflated with a person's gay identity. Risk categories became 'risk groups' and the earliest 'risk groups' named were gay men, injection drug users, and sex workers, while foreigners and women were added later. The concept 'risk group' became the central analytic category of the epidemiological mapping of HIV and because of the conflation of practice and identity, the deployment of the concept meant that the development of HIV epidemiological knowledge became connected to stigmatizing people thought to belong to particular risk groups (Waldby et al. 1995). These epidemiological categories, which segment the population according to identity (e.g. being gay), occlude the important social and cultural specificities that produce HIV-risk and position HIV-risk as an attribute of individuals or particular sorts of people.

In addition to the deployment of identity categories, the particular ways in which ongoing HIV surveillance is undertaken can (and does) reinforce the positioning of these groups – especially the group 'women' – as vectors of disease (Campbell 1997). As voluntary testing introduces selection and participation bias into any surveillance system, the alternatives are mandatory testing of particular populations judged to be at high risk or unlinked HIV-prevalence studies considered representative of the general population. Although most countries did not pursue the mandatory testing, some do, typically, but not exclusively, among prisoners, STI 'patients', pregnant women, and returning nationals (Mann et al. 1992). Most countries chose to monitor infections nationally via unlinked sero-prevalence surveys in pregnant women, and military recruits (as for example, in Thailand) as these populations, as well as being captive and hence easy to access, are reasonably representative of sexually active populations. Other groups such as blood donors provide some sort of triangulation of the surveillance data. As a result of surveillance a number of other groups were added to the list of 'risk groups': infants/ children of HIV-positive women; military recruits; young people/youth; and prisoners. These 'risk groups' became and continue to be positioned as the vectors of disease – to be avoided and shunned.

This consideration of epidemiological risk categories and surveillance methods illustrates how public health practices support, and even justify, the common perspective of the 'normal' population, in particular adult heterosexual men, that HIV is the disease of 'the other' (Waldby al. 1993). While it is of utmost importance to acknowledge that gay men, injecting drug users, sex workers are in special need, the epidemiological and medical focus on 'risk groups' (now somewhat euphemistically referred to as 'vulnerable groups') feeds into and reinforces already existing understandings and binaries: normal – deviant, strong – vulnerable, clean – dirty. The 'normal' seek to cordon off the 'other' keeping themselves safe – 'cordon sanitaire'. Stigma and discrimination are reinforced by the epidemiological categories developed in order to respond effectively to a virus, a virus that is continuing to spread along societies' fault-lines of gender, sexuality, class, and race. However, as long as risk is associated with identity and not the specificities of social practices, possibilities for understanding and developing public health interventions that engage with these fault lines are occluded and hidden. HIV/AIDS was and, in many countries, continues to be positioned as the disease of 'the other' – the deviant and the undeserving. In the focus on 'the other', social and cultural differences are glossed.

There is a growing awareness that not only is the world facing a global pandemic, but that the HIV pandemic is marked by differences (and inequalities) of class, gender, race and sexual preference, which in turn reinforce the stigma and discrimination that continue to hinder an effective response to HIV and AIDS (Mahajan et al. 2008, Stuber et al. 2008). While it has been difficult for social scientists to make their voice heard, sociologists, economists, and political scientists (for example, Altman 2002; Barnett and Whiteside

2006, Campbell 2003, Friedman et al. 2006, Kippax 2008, Patton 2002, Rao Gupta et al. 2008, Seckinelgin 2008) continue to argue that a more nuanced and socially informed description of HIV-transmission, its causes and its impact is sorely needed. And recently the Head of UNAIDS, Peter Piot, has called on public health researchers to 'know your epidemic' and 'know your response' and has emphasized the central role of social science in achieving these goals (Piot et al. 2008). We are seeing the beginnings of a shift of emphasis to understanding the local and to the particular political, socio-cultural, and economic factors that are associated with (and in many cases drive/produce) the behaviours that produce increases and decreases in HIV rates. It has yet to be determined whether work following this trajectory will continue to be supported and cultivated to the point that we see the development and implementation of more effective interventions into HIV transmission. For this to occur, the apparatuses of national, international, and global public health would need to adopt new tools for understanding HIV epidemics, social scientific tools that enable the understanding of the specificities of social contexts and practices. However currently, it remains the case that public health descriptions and understandings of and responses to HIV remain comparatively unresponsive to difference, and that the social sciences remain peripheral in the search for a sustainable solution. Indeed it might be argued that the public health response – or certain variants of it – is part of the problem.

Responses to HIV: prevention, treatment, and care

There has been a failure on the part of public health to adequately recognize the patterning of HIV infection and how this patterning is shaped by the specificities of social practices and contexts and by relations of power. When we move beyond *descriptions* of the epidemic to examine the global *response* to HIV, what becomes evident is that this failure is magnified, and with disastrous consequences. However, before we develop this argument we want to briefly sketch something of the broader rapidly changing landscape of international/global public health within which HIV responses are being developed.

Before we discuss international health specifically, it is worth noting how the strategies deployed by international development and aid organizations have been affecting the patterning of disease (and the response to it). In the wake of 1970s the oil crises, World Bank loans were given on the basis that recipients would introduce 'structural adjustments'. A 1987 appendix to the structural adjustment policy spelt out how governments were directed to facilitate the privatization of health services, the uptake of private health insurance and the introduction of fees for services. Critics such as the Italian Global Health Watch (2008) argue that these structural adjustment policies required that countries adopt austerity in public spending – including major cuts in health spending. Furthermore they add that such policies helped create the very social and economic conditions and forces that contributed to the spread of HIV infection in developing countries.

Although not so directive, in practice, the conditions tied to IMF loans have meant that recipient governments have had to restrict spending on public services such as health and education. As early as the mid 1980s, UNICEF argued that the poor were being disenfranchised by neo-liberal approaches to development (UNICEF 1987). During the period that these conditions were being introduced, WHO's efficiency was being widely critiqued and its core budget whittled away. The result was that WHO programs were increasingly ad hoc and designed more as vertical interventions and less to strengthen health departments worldwide. The disastrous consequences of neo-liberal economic policies imposed on recipients of IMF and World Bank funds have been widely discussed. For instance, in a hard hitting paper, Whithead et al. (2001) present a list of the consequences produced by World Bank policies in the poorest countries: untreated diseases; reduced access to care; irrational use of drugs; and long-term impoverishment. More specifically, a recent study of former Soviet Union and post-communist Eastern European countries evidences the impact that IMF economic reforms have had on the incidence, prevalence, and mortality rates associated with the re-emerging problem of TB (Stuckler et al. 2008). Their findings suggest that (after correcting for potential confounding factors such as HIV, selection bias, surveillance infrastructure, urbanization, and economic development) there is a strong association between levels of IMF funds and increases in TB incidence, prevalence, and mortality. Moreover, for every year of participation with the IMF TB mortality rates increased by 4.1 per cent and they increased 0.9 per cent for every extra percentage point of funding coming from the IMF.

International health can be effective only when it is able to forge agreements between governments (for example as in the case of smallpox, an initiative suggested by the Soviet Union at the height of the cold war); in the absence of agreement it is virtually impossible to achieve much. As Tarantola (2005a, 2005b) points out, 'international health' agencies work by fostering relations and agreements between nations. The leading international health agency, WHO, has relied on the good will of its member nations: it has little capacity to push governments to decisions or action. In recognition of this weakness, WHO has been trying to strengthen its own capacities to work with member states by developing the new International Health Regulations (IHR) implemented in 2007. These regulations consist of a legal framework to 'ensure international health security without unnecessary interference in international traffic and trade' (WHO 2007). However, the IHR's own articulation of its mechanism to bolster compliance serves as a reminder that although the new IHR are framed as international law they do not carry much weight in and of themselves (this mechanism is vaguely described as the threat of a 'a tarnished international image, increased morbidity/mortality of affected populations' and 'isolation' measures implemented by other states (WHO 2007)). WHO's powers still extend as far as the cooperation and political will of its member states will allow.

The IHR represent one of two very different responses to the weaknesses of international health; they constitute an attempt to strengthen the dimension of international health that hinges on agreements between nations. However WHO, continually faced with the problem of how to fund its activities, has been involved in a proliferation of activities financed by extra-budgetary mechanisms, mainly through public and private donors, which, as we have pointed out above, resulted in vertical programming. In so doing, WHO has been effectively drawing on strategies for addressing global health problems which pertain less directly to the domain of 'international health' than that of, what Tarantola (2005a, 2005b) distinguishes as, 'global health'. In the past decade 'global health' strategies financed by 'global funds' have been widely developed and adopted by those working to address HIV and other EID. Today, philanthropic global funds have channelled an unprecedented level of funding into infectious disease and are now some of the wealthiest actors in the field. For instance, by the end of 2007, the Bill & Melinda Gates Foundation had an asset trust endowment of $US37.6 billion and had spent $US8.5 billion on global health (with another $US5.9 billion on global development and education initiatives in the US). The annual spending of this one fund on global health is on par with WHO's annual budget. Since 2001, another global entity, the Global Fund to Fight AIDS, Tuberculosis and Malaria (the Global Fund) has spent over $US10 billion, money donated by (more than 60) national governments, as well as 'corporate partners' including American Express, Apple, Carphone Warehouse, Converse, GAP, Giorgio Armani, Motorola Inc., O2, Orange UK, Tesco Mobile, and Yahoo!. Since 1999, funding on HIV alone (prevention, treatment, and care) rose dramatically from just under $US1 billion per annum to over $US8 billion in 2005: the key increment was driven by some of the agencies referred to above – the Global Fund and the Gates Foundation – as well as the Clinton Foundation, the World Bank's multi-country HIV/AIDS program (MAP), the WHO '3 by 5' initiative, and the US President's Emergency Plan for AIDS Relief (PEPFAR) (Henderson et al. forthcoming).

We do not want to overdraw this distinction between international and global health – as mentioned WHO is involved in global funds and initiatives, and 93 per cent of the budget of the Global Fund to Fight AIDS, Tuberculosis and Malaria comes from national governments (with the bulk of the remainder coming from the Bill & Melinda Gates Foundation). However, there are some important features of global funds which mark a shift from international health's reliance on diplomacy and international agreements. Firstly, global funds (and national funds that run along the lines of global funds, like PEPFAR, discussed below) are marked, not only by the involvement of private entities as donors (as well as national governments), but also by their willingness to give large grants to bodies such as international non-government organizations (INGOs), which may not include any state actors at all. Secondly, they can weaken state responses by being in a stronger position to decide what health problems to address and how and to attract expertise away from state ministries of health with better employment conditions (Asante and Zwi 2007). Global funds tend to establish 'vertical' programs that typically take the form of public-private partnerships focusing on specific diseases (rather than on working with health ministries to strengthen health services as a whole) (e.g. 70 per cent of PEPFAR funds have gone to – largely faith-based – international NGOs (Cohen 2008)). Whilst real advances in global health can be achieved with this massive influx of funds there are also concerns that the process serves to further distance governments of low and middle income countries from important decisions and processes and to position 'donor' countries as all powerful in such decision-making (Italian Global Health Watch 2008, Tarantola 2005a).

We will argue here through the case of HIV that the vertical, top-down strategies of global health are largely failing to engage with – not only state governments – but with the specificities of how health, illness, and disease transmission are actually lived and understood in particular social contexts, and the implications this has for attempts to intervene – with serious consequences. Notwithstanding the massive increase in HIV funding that global initiatives have managed to introduce, there is growing concern among public health officials and researchers that HIV prevention efforts are failing (Piot 2006; Potts et al. 2008) and that treatments are not reaching those who need them – at least in many low and middle income countries (Italian Global Health Watch 2008). We illustrate by taking two examples: (1) PEPFAR's funding of HIV prevention; and (2) the WHO '3 by 5' initiative aimed at having 3 million people on antiretroviral HIV treatment by 2005.

HIV prevention

Where there has been sufficient funding and support for HIV prevention–from both governments and donors – huge gains have been made (Global HIV Prevention Working

Group 2008). While high income countries, in general, do not face the problems of verticalization often associated with donor funding, Brazil provides an example of a middle-income country which has been successful in HIV-prevention. Brazil has exemplified a remarkable mobilization in the face of HIV, with genuine integration between government officials, particularly from the Ministry of Health, and elements of civil society organizations and activists from gay rights, AIDS service and women's organizations, such as GAPA and Grupo Pela VIDDA (Smith and Siplon 2006). Brazil, in particular, provides an example of the central importance of local initiatives and how they can be mobilized to counter the problems inherent in verticalization.

However, without sufficient funding and in the absence of political and civil support, HIV prevention efforts are unlikely to be successful or sustainable (Henderson et al. in press), and there are danger signs that HIV prevention has slipped off the agenda (Piot 2006). In 2006, the Global HIV Prevention Working Group[1] released an analysis of UNAIDS data, demonstrating not only a prevention funding gap, but also illustrating that access to prevention was low across a range of prevention programmes (Global HIV Prevention Working Group 2006). Fewer than one in five people at high risk for HIV infection have access to prevention programmes. Access to condoms, safe injection equipment, and other preventive initiatives are essential to preventing HIV, yet availability is very low: only 4 per cent of injecting drug users have access to harm reduction programmes; 9 per cent of individuals at risk have access to condoms; 9 per cent of pregnant women at risk have access to treatments that prevent transmission from mother to child; and 11 per cent of homosexually active men, and 16 per cent of sex workers, have access to behaviour change programmes (Global HIV Prevention Working Group 2006). In 2007, the same group warned that effective prevention was not reaching the majority of people who need it (Global HIV Prevention Working Group 2007).

While funding for HIV prevention and treatment has climbed, the percentage of such funds spent on prevention has fallen – because in part of a renewed effort to treat those with HIV. While the number of people on antiretroviral treatment has increased dramatically (UNAIDS 2006), rather less attention has been paid to the number of people accessing prevention (Lancet Editorial 2005, Feachem and Sabot 2006). UNAIDS estimated that in 2006 at least $US4 billion was needed for prevention, and this was not forthcoming.

While PEPFAR pledged $US15 billion dollars towards addressing HIV in a number of badly HIV-affected countries in the world[2] over five years, it restricts how the funds are spent. The distribution of the US PEPFAR funds was authorized by US legislation stipulating that 55 per cent of funds were to be spent on treatment; 20 per cent on prevention; 15 per cent on palliative care and 10 per cent for orphans and vulnerable children (Kates and Lief 2006). Notwithstanding the intention to *prevent* seven million new infections, the end result is that a large proportion of PEPFAR donor funding available for HIV and AIDS activities (80 per cent) has been directed to activities other than prevention. Moreover PEPFAR restricted how prevention funding could be used. These restrictions included and continue to include: (1) that faith-based organizations are permitted to exclude information about contraceptive methods, including condoms, if such information is inconsistent with their religious teachings; and (2) all organizations receiving PEPFAR funding must have an explicit policy opposing prostitution.

In many countries since the late 1990s there has been a move away from proven effective prevention strategies. HIV prevention, with its necessary focus on sex and drugs, is – for some governments – politically difficult (Altman 2006). Governments and

NGOs, particularly those reliant on PEPFAR funding, have ignored the evidence on what have proved to be effective safer sex strategies, and have been reluctant to promote condoms for sexual intercourse – except in the privacy of the clinic – and have, instead, promoted delaying sexual initiation among the young, and monogamy among the sexually active (SIECUS 2005, 2008). The 2005 Sexuality Information and Education Council of the United States (SIECUS) report on PEPFAR country profiles is highly critical of the restrictions placed by PEPFAR on sex and reproductive health education. The Vice President for Public Policy of SIECUS comments in the foreword to the report:

> For two decades our domestic sexuality education and HIV-prevention programs have been under assault – they are battling for their existence under daily attacks from abstinence-only-until-marriage groups who are looking to completely dismantle them and from politicians more concerned with pandering to the agenda of an extreme and zealot constituency than with the well being of people. Money is increasingly being diverted to abstinence and marriage promotion and the use of evidence-based criteria as a standard has been cast into the wind.
>
> (SIECUS 2005: 4)

Similarly many of these same countries have been extremely reluctant to provide clean needles and syringes to injection drug users even though the evidence indicates that this is the most effective means of preventing HIV-transmission among these populations (Wodak and Cooney 2006). The move away from effective HIV prevention strategies has been, in large part, underpinned by a moral conservatism, evident, for example, in requirements in the form of a signed statement imposed on the recipients of PEPFAR funds saying that they the recipient organizations, oppose prostitution and emphasize fidelity and abstinence over condom use. The result is that this emergency fund, PEPFAR, privileges ineffective HIV prevention strategies that fail to acknowledge the realities of people's lives, and, in particular, young people's lives (Crewe 2004).

As well as insufficient funding for prevention, and problematic restrictions on how the funding is to be spent, the most important problem facing HIV-prevention is the proliferation of prevention programs that fail to address the socio-cultural and political contexts in which sexual practice and injecting drug use and the associated risks of HIV-transmission are enacted. This is in part due to the verticalization of much donor funding: prevention policies are informed and even designed by 'outsiders' with little if any knowledge of the specificities of the local cultures and practices, so they are based on public health understandings largely imported from high income countries. This approach reduces the possibilities for input from the recipient countries and their populations in the choice of priorities and the types of interventions adopted (Italian Global Health Watch 2008, Kippax 2008). In particular, the funded agencies, often international non-government organizations (INGOs), fail to engage with the realities of people's sexual lives. Their prevention interventions and health promotion programmes are based on a public health paradigm consistent with the neo-liberal policies and practices of the US and the UK, which positions people as active autonomous agents. As illustrated below, much HIV-prevention takes place within the clinic and people are HIV-tested and advised and counselled to Abstain or delay sexual initiation, or Be monogamous or, if absolutely necessary, use Condoms: the ABC of prevention.

Although HIV prevention is conducted via social marketing and school and peer education, the most dominant mode of promoting HIV prevention is voluntary, counselling and testing (VCT). As VCT takes place in the clinic – people are positioned as patients – as passive. It is simply assumed that these patients, the recipients of VCT, can and will change their sexual practice, that is, it is assumed that people everywhere are neo-liberal subjects. VCT is individualistic (at its best it involves couples) and hence it makes little if any impact on prevailing normative understandings of sex and risk and it has a tendency to reinforce notions of individual responsibility. Consequently, VCT can feed blame and shame, and more generally, reinforce the already existing stigma and discrimination. Even more importantly the use of VCT as a major prevention tool gives governments the excuse to draw back from HIV, the excuse not to have to deal with and face the complexities of talking about sex and drugs, the excuse not to train teachers and those in contact with the young, to raise issues in connection with HIV transmission. Knowledge is privatized and the public and collective voice excised (Kippax 2006). For these reasons, VCT has not proved to be effective in fostering HIV-prevention as some public health researchers (such as Potts et al. 2008) now acknowledge. And as we shall argue below in the next section, VCT is implicated in the disappointing response to the roll-out of HIV treatments.

In general, as Kippax (2008) has argued, prevention programmes and interventions aimed at changing sexual or drug injection 'risk' need to address sexual and drug injec-tion practices as they are locally enacted. They need to address the cultural forms in which sex is enacted: marital sex, sexual concurrency, sex work and so forth, as it is within these forms that safer sexual strategies will be adopted to reduce the risk of HIV transmission. Achieving sustained change requires understanding the structural factors that produce these practices (Friedman, et al. 2006). HIV health promotion that simply addresses the 'behaviour', e.g. condom use, runs the risk of missing the point, because it fails to take into account the varied social and cultural meanings of the practices within which condoms might be used. As a practice, condom use is different in the 'marriage bed' from condom use in a brothel or condom use in a casual sexual encounter, although the behaviour is the same in all three contexts. Furthermore, interventions do not take place in a social vacuum: the people targeted are not individuals isolated from one another but social beings. Social transformation involves working with practices and changing the norms that produce and govern the practices in question (Stephenson and Kippax 2006). Crucially, sustainable change in sexual and drug use practices is a product of community – not individual – action.

This appeal is not new and has been voiced previously (Zwi 1993). It has been repeatedly pointed out that medical and educational interventions aimed at individuals alone are unlikely to work and need to be complemented by interventions or pro-grammes focused on the social and cultural structures that produce the practices in need of change. In places where that appeal has not been heard, the epidemic continues unabated. As Gilbert and Walker (2002) note attempts to intervene in the spread of HIV in South Africa have not been very successful because HIV has been positioned as an 'individual' health issue rather than a 'social' health issue, and often addressed in the context of health-care in the clinic. Such a focus on the individual behaviour, rather than social practice, has meant that it has been impossible to integrate the paradigms of the social and the medical, the biological and the structural.

HIV-prevention programmes have worked when aimed at the community level, the structural level, as well as at the individual level. These successes include programmes such as the early Ugandan success in reducing HIV infection in the general population (UNAIDS 2006), the success in stabilizing HIV infection in gay men in Australia (Kippax and Race 2003), and the success among sex workers in India (Evans and Lambert 2008, Jana et al. 2004) and Thailand (Hanenberg et al. 1994). These successes were, and continue to be due, in large part to an acknowledgement by governments of sexual activity, including marital sex, gay sexual practice, and sex work in all their complexity. Sexual practice is regulated by norms, norms that change in response to gender relations, economic needs, gay liberation, and HIV. HIV-prevention programmes and interventions were not only focused at the individual level, but more importantly at the level of community and network, heterosexual, gay and sex worker, and at the level of structures and institutions: marriage, saunas/baths and sex clubs, brothels … Where prevention has been successful, those at risk of HIV were positioned not as a problem but as part of the solution: they were supported to modify (not abstain from) the practices that placed them at risk.

HIV prevention programs are effective if they are properly resourced and developed with the populations at risk of HIV, developing capacity and supporting local responses that make sense to the people who comprise those populations. They are effective when the health promotion messages address the socio-cultural and political contexts in which sexual practice and drug injection and the associated risks are enacted. It is not that prevention has failed, but that donors and the INGOs funded by these donors have failed HIV prevention – by under-spending on HIV prevention, by failing to engage with and support local initiatives, by failing to build local capacity, and, as a consequence, promoting the 'wrong' sorts of prevention and promoting potentially effective prevention strategies in the 'wrong' ways.

HIV treatment

By the mid-1990s serious concerns were being raised about the massive debt being incurred by middle and low income countries in their fight against HIV and AIDS and there is no doubt that many nations have experienced severe economic downturns because of AIDS. In some African nations, there has already been a decline in agricultural output and a threat to food security. Ill-health means: less time spent on growing crops and more time spent caring for the sick; a concomitant decline in household expenditure on education; a return to rural areas to die thus adding to the problem of scarce village resources; a dramatic increase in health expenditure; and, as a consequence of parental deaths, a rapid increase in the number of children orphaned.

Ill-health can now be delayed, if not for all, for almost all with HIV by the use of the effective HIV treatments, in the form of anti-retrovirals, which became available in the late 1990s. However the cost of anti-retrovirals was and continues to be prohibitive for most low and middle income countries (Seckinelgin 2008). The pharmaceutical companies who had produced the drugs were extremely protective of their patent rights. However growing pressure on the pharmaceutical industry from a number of sources, including UNAIDS, WHO, and activist groups, particularly the Treatment Action Campaign (TAC) in South Africa, led in November 2001 to access-to-treatments issue being taken up and the World Trade Organization meeting in Doha, which issued a ruling allowing for compulsory licensing to produce generic drugs in low and middle income ('developing') countries for emergency health problems such as AIDS, TB, and malaria. However, countries which have the capacity to (and do) produce generic drugs, such as Brazil and India, are not allowed to export these generic drugs to countries who most need them because they have not acquired the technology to manufacture their own generic drugs. So the problem of access to affordable treatments continues to persist in many countries, particularly in Africa (Seckinelgin 2008).

The TAC was founded in South Africa on Human Rights Day 10 December 1998. The TAC among other things asserted that access to antiretroviral therapy is a human right – it was unjust it argued for HIV to have become a chronic disease in high income countries, but to have remained a death sentence in middle and low income countries: it used South Africa's new Constitution with its Bill of Rights to claim the rights of people living with HIV, thus heightening awareness of South African law as an instrument that can be invoked to help people in distress, regardless of whether they are poor or rich. In turn, the TAC took on the South African government, big business, and public prejudice, in order to challenge discrimination, the high price of drugs, and a failure to provide the medication that will keep people alive, not to mention highlighting the government's disastrous failure to provide leadership that acknowledges the reality of HIV and how the epidemic should be handled. Its work continues to be supported by the links that the organization has forged with established global networks of solidarity and political pressure, and the TAC is linked to a wide range of activist groups all over the world which allows for a 'global imaging of protests' (Wasserman 2005: 172). Through extensive internet use, the TAC can on a symbolic representational level simultaneously occupy local, national, and transnational global space.

The TAC had a profound impact on the course of the HIV epidemic – not only in South Africa – but elsewhere. It, like the activist groups in Brazil described above, provides an example of the central importance of local input. However, it is also true that TAC may not have been as successful in escaping the ever-present forces of co-option. In its advocacy of access to treatments, it became part of the WHO, UNAIDS, and Global Fund initiative in 2003 for mass HIV testing campaigns (following the rationale that without testing there is no call for treatments). In particular the TAC supported WHO's '3 by 5' initiative, which aimed to treat 3 million people with HIV in low/middle income countries with antiretrovirals by 2005. Almost all now acknowledge that the results of '3 by 5' were disappointing. At the end on 2005 only 1,300,000 people were on treatment: 43 per cent of the target and 20 per cent of the eligible population, that is, 20 per cent of those in immediate need (Italian Global Health Watch 2008). The lack of adequate population take-up of antiretroviral treatments is directly related to fear of HIV testing and the perceived associated stigma and discrimination associated with an HIV-positive test result. As noted above, treatment cannot take place unless people are tested for HIV. In order to treat 3 million people, around 100 million people would need to be tested (if we assume that on average in low/middle income countries approximately 3 per cent of people are HIV-infected). And people did not come forward to be tested – at least in the numbers required. What research investigating this problem shows is that people fear the disclosure of the HIV-test result – both intentional and unintentional disclosure, and stigma and associated discrimination following an HIV-positive result (Reproductive Health Matters Editorial 2000, Kippax 2006). Among women they surveyed in Dar es Salaam, Tanzania, Maman et al. (2001) found that the most salient barriers to HIV testing and serostatus disclosure were women's fear of: their male partners' reaction; the undermining of decision-making and communication patterns between partners; and their male partners' attitudes towards HIV testing. HIV testing itself positions people 'at risk' – and for women this often means they are positioned as promiscuous. The findings of Burke (2005) in his study of rural men in Tanzania indicate that women have some reason to be fearful of testing and that communication patterns between men and women in rural Tanzania undermined disclosure of test status by the female sexual partner and work against discussion of sexual transmission of HIV. As Grinstead et al. (2001) further illustrate in their study in Trinidad, Tanzania, and Kenya, positive serostatus was associated with the break-up of marriage and being neglected or disowned by their family. Stigma poses considerable barriers to seeking VCT or, more generally, testing, in sub-Saharan Africa – and indeed elsewhere. Not surprisingly given these outcomes, general population readiness for VCT is very low.

The ways in which HIV testing can trigger fear and stigma are well illustrated by Steinberg's (2008) ethnography of a testing centre in a Lusikisiki village in the Eastern Cape of South Africa that he calls 'Ithnanga'. He writes:

> During the course of testing day, some 200 hundred Ithangans drifted to and from the school. Most had come not to test but to watch. Their curiosity was profoundly ungenerous: they had come to see who was HIV-positive. It was, they believed, not hard to tell. As Sizwe (one of his respondents) explains, 'To know who was positive and who was negative, you just had to stand and observe. You looked for how long the people stay. You see, there is counselling before the test, and counselling after the test. The counselling before the test, it's the same for everybody: a few minutes. But the counselling after the test: for some it lasts two minutes, for others, it is a long, long, time. They don't come out for maybe half an hour, even an hour. And then you know. By the time the day ended, the whole village knew who had tested HIV-positive.
>
> (Steinberg 2008: 15)

Steinberg goes on to recount that at the end of the day, nine women had been identified as having tested HIV-positive and had been marked with death. Ithanga went into a state of collective shock.

> Such information is not easily absorbed. In the weeks and months that followed, those who had tested positive were silently separated from the rest of the village. They were watched. Nobody told them that they were being watched. Nobody said to their faces that their status was common knowledge. However, everything about them was observed in meticulous detail: whether they coughed or lost weight or stayed at home ill; whether they boarded a taxi and, if so, whether that taxi was going to the clinic; above all, with whom they slept. These observations were not generous; they issued from a gallery of silent jeerers. In essence, Ithangans were using their knowledge of the nine villagers' HIV status to fuel their sense of denial. By putting an invisible barrier around the nine women and silently jeering at them, the village was in effect putting a barrier around AIDS. To be one of those who jeer is to avoid being one of those jeered at. To jeer is to defend oneself from the knowledge that the virus has no boundaries and might thus be in one's own blood.
>
> (Steinberg 2008: 16)

While we have no argument with the need to treat those with HIV – indeed it is the right of all with HIV to have access to treatment, what was absent from WHO's push to treat was an understanding of people's lived realities in the context of HIV: their fears, their ways of coping; their understandings of HIV. There is a failure on the part of a globalized public health to recognize the relative potency of particular modes of ways of being in relation to the epidemic. This is further evidenced by the most recent push, again from WHO and the major donors, for what is called 'provider-initiated testing' rather than 'recipient-initiated' or 'voluntary' testing (WHO and UNAIDS 2007). While the rights of all those living with HIV to have access to antiretroviral therapy need to be advanced, it is questionable whether the imposition of routine or provider-initiated testing can do this. In regions in the world where testing and associated disclosure mark one as diseased and undeserving – the policy may have dire consequences. It has become increasingly obvious that VCT, which has been adopted as one of the primary tools of both global prevention efforts and treatment initiatives, only works in a supportive environment and one where levels of stigma are not high (Barnett and Whiteside 2006). HIV focuses attention on sex and death, fear and disease in ways that can be and are interpreted to suit the prejudices and the agendas of those controlling particular historical narratives.

Conclusions

Historians have examined how 'tropical health and medicine' played a constitutive role in establishing and sustaining colonial powers (Anderson 1996, Bashford 2006). Early efforts to establish health alliances and agreements between nations arose in the mid-nineteenth century in response to the threats posed by disease to colonial occupiers and economic interests. Western 'rational' and 'progressive' medicine was contrasted with local 'superstitious' practices in ways that justified the expansion of European empires. 'Rational' medical practices were initially targeted towards protecting the health of the settlers and traders, and then extended to the health of native labour forces (King 2002). Irrespective of the actual benefits to local populations or of the hybrid forms in which it was practised (Cunningham and Andrews 1997), western medicine entered the colonies as part of a 'civilizing mission'. While there have been challenges to this approach, Seckinelgin argues that the colonial legacy 'still remains in the politics of global diseases in the form of vertical health policies' (2008:16). That is, something of this colonial mentality lingers on in a more recently developed approach to global public health issues, what King (2002) calls the 'emerging diseases worldview'. In contrast to colonial strategies which explicitly positioned non-Western health beliefs as dangerous and in need of ideological conversion, the primary object of the emerging diseases worldview is to open up new markets for medical goods and expertise and ensure 'free circulation' within them. However, neither approach has moved far beyond adopting top-down, disempowering medical and public health practices, strategies which fail to start from a point of understanding and engagement with the specific social practices through which infectious disease is transmitted and/or contained.

This failure can help us to understand how, to date, the massive influx of funds into global health have largely compounded the problem of decades of eroded health systems. It has been argued that global health funds have extended the demise of existing health services by financing vertical health programs; in fact today this criticism is coming from highly disparate sources and serves very different purposes (Jack 2007). First, it comes in the form of a critique of governance. For instance, in an argument that totally neglects the IMF's own role in undermining health systems, *the IMF* is now pointing the finger at the vertical programs favoured by global donors and deeming them unnecessarily wasteful because they reproduce bureaucracies (Hsiao and Heller 2007). Second, verticalization is being criticized as part of a broader attempt to privilege medical knowledge and practices over other forms. For instance Roger England's (2007) critique of verticalization contains a thinly veiled attack on the way 'new public health' positions the social sciences as having useful tools and approaches to offer the struggle to prevent and treat HIV. England contests the ways that most HIV funding goes on '"multisectoral" activities and "mainstreaming" HIV into just about every social activity. These have become the emperor's new clothes of public health' (2007: 344). England's argument hinges on an opposition between 'new public health' attempts to understand how HIV affects multiple domains of life and is best tackled in those multiple domains with what he calls 'rational resource allocation'.

Although England fears the potential of the new public health, the third critique of verticalization, and the one we have been advancing here, is that the imperative to approach HIV as socially situated has largely been smothered by the top-down imposition of funders' pre-existing notions of what HIV is and how it is best addressed. Certainly, arguments in favour of strengthening medical systems are important, but it is also vital to recognize that the problem of 'verticalization' *extends beyond* the by-passing of low and middle income countries' health systems through the imposition of top-down agendas. The neglect of state ministries of health extends to the neglect of a wide range of actors, including members of governments, health care professionals, members of community based organizations, and ordinary people whose everyday social practices function to contain or augment HIV transmission, the problems of stigma and discrimination and the development of modes of care for those infected with the virus. Without these local voices, without the means to situate medical or biological understandings of HIV within the social and the cultural contexts in which they are developed and adopted, any response to infectious disease is likely to be unsustainable.

We want to suggest that global policies have failed not because they are explicitly colonialist in their aims of ideological conversion, but because, as with the emerging diseases worldview identified by King, their primary goal is to expand the market for the medical and public health expertise and knowledge being produced in donor countries. They pay little if any attention to the local social and cultural specificities of the populations and communities affected by HIV. Our consideration of HIV demonstrates that the challenges posed by infectious disease cannot be met from the starting point that EID are affected by a number of 'global factors' which, once named (e.g. patterns of mobility, patterns of sex, etc.), can then be apprehended by health promotion strategies (abstain, be faithful, use condoms, be circumcised, be tested, etc.) that target individuals through top-down interventions (e.g. counselling and testing, school education or mass campaigns). Rather what is needed is a detailed and nuanced understanding of the practices that give rise to HIV transmission risk, with reference to the social, economic and political structures, such as gender, race and class, that produce these practices, and an understanding of the ways in which communities and people have already begun to respond to HIV, their fears and hopes, as well as the strategies they have put in place to protect themselves. Armed with this information, public health professionals need to work in partnership with governments and communities to build the required health infra-structure and services, provide support and care, and promote the HIV-prevention and treatment strategies that are efficacious but also acceptable to communities and people, and implement them in a manner that is likely to engage those in need. Without socially informed understandings and without genuine partnerships, prevention and treatment strategies are unlikely to be adopted or sustained.

Coda

If public health organizations and professionals are to 'know their epidemics' and 'know their responses' they need to better understand the social contexts and practices through which EID come into being, are transmitted and contained. Whilst both understandings of disease and the development and implementation of public health responses are situated in political as well as social contexts, here we have focused on social contexts. We want to conclude by suggesting the importance of developing adequate tools for grasping how changing political contexts impact infectious disease, and we do this by sketching one emerging trajectory in the planning and delivery of public health strategies designed to tackle epidemics: 'preparedness'. Although neither the rationale nor many of the practices of preparedness are entirely new (Fearnley 2005), they have been rapidly proliferating through international and national public health efforts in the past decade.

What is distinct about preparedness? Identifying and managing risk has been integral to public health responses to infectious diseases. But this broad approach to risk only works if risk can be thought of as something that is basically calculable and manageable. However, as we noted at the outset of this chapter, as infectious disease is recast as 'emergent' and ever-changing it comes to be seen as fundamentally unpredictable, incalculable, and potentially catastrophic (Cooper 2006). One response to the problem posed by EID is to try to extend disease surveillance efforts, to develop new modes and tools and to incorporate new actors in the work of calculating, predicting, and preventing. Such attempts have brought the US military to the fore in the field of international health; for instance the Department of Defence-Global Emerging Infections Surveillance and Response System (DoD-GEIS) is leading the global response to EID surveillance as it collaborates with military epidemiology units around the globe and at home with NASA, the Centres for Disease Control and university based researchers as well as with WHO (Chretien 2007). More recently, in October 2008, Google.org announced its new 'predict and prevent' initiative to bolster the global surveillance of EID. An alternate response, that of preparedness, involves breaking with the risk management rationale of 'predict and prevent' efforts which rely on an epidemic's calculability, and – in the words used by the head of WHO's Global Influenza program to describe the aim of global pandemic influenza preparedness – switching to planning and designing strategies for 'damage control'.

Preparedness efforts centre around the coordination of 'vital systems security' with the involvement of all relevant state and non-state agencies (Collier and Lakoff 2006, Lakoff 2007). Taking such an approach to the challenges of infectious disease means situating them as one of multiple possible emergencies faced at the national and transnational levels; exceptional and potential catastrophic events which – by threatening critical infrastructure and communications – jeopardize states' as well as non-state actors' capacities to connect and function. Hence, a distinct set of concerns take centre stage in public health displacing traditional concerns with the population: intra- and inter-governmental vulnerabilities, weaknesses in organizations and systems (Winner 2006). The security offered by a rationality of preparedness invokes neither the promises of prevention nor insurance, but a continuous readiness for operating in an unpredictable, porous transnational network.

Public health's recent turn to preparedness can be understood as part of a broader, contemporary political shift, a political shift in which the problematization of security agendas has been taken up in diverse realms of governance (Bigo 2006). Of course, the connections between public health and security agendas are longstanding and have occurred on many levels, ranging from the use of militaristic language and metaphors to describe infectious disease (Martin 1994) to the involvement of (and even reliance on) military personnel and expertise for the surveillance of and response to outbreaks of infectious disease. However now and (we anticipate) increasingly in the near future, EID are acting as the trigger for the formation of new and increasingly dense connections between these two domains such that political concerns about security are shaping and strengthening a distinct approach to the management of infectious disease. One of the questions raised by this evolving trajectory is what openings people will find and carve out for contesting, supporting, participating in or subverting public health responses to EID which no longer directly focus on the health of population. Without adequate tools for engaging with the politics of disease and the social practices and structures which contribute to disease transmission and/or containment, public health cannot begin to address such questions. As Barnett and Whiteside argue in their analysis of the global problem of HIV, an epidemic such as HIV 'is more deeply seated' than in the bodies of people it infects, as it

> reveals many of the fractures, stresses and strains in a society … it is but a symptom of the way in which we organise our social, [political] and economic relations. Concern with clinical-medical issues and with individual behaviour change, to the almost total exclusion of the structural and distributional factors which result in those behaviours, has had serious implications.
>
> (2006: 78)

Acknowledgement

We acknowledge Mary Crewe, Director of the Centre for the Study of AIDS, University of Pretoria, South Africa for her valuable contribution to this chapter.

Notes

1 In 2002 the Global HIV Prevention Working Group was established with the backing of the Bill & Melinda Gates Foundation and the Henry J. Kaiser Family Foundation. The aim of the group is to inform decisions on prevention and advocate for a comprehensive response to HIV/AIDS that integrates care and prevention.
2 The main countries funded by PEPFAR are: Botswana, Côte d'Ivoire, Ethiopia, Guyana, Haiti, Kenya, Mozambique, Namibia, Nigeria, Rwanda, South Africa, Tanzania, Uganda, Vietnam, and Zambia.

References

Altman, D. (2002) *Global Sex*. Chicago: Chicago University Press.
——(2006) 'Taboos and denial in government responses', *International Affairs*, 82: 257–68.
Anderson, W. (1996) 'Race and acclimatization in colonial medicine disease, race, and empire', *Bulletin of the History of Medicine*, 70(1): 62–67.
Asante, A. D. and Zwi, A. B. (2007) 'Public-private partnerships and global health equity: Prospects and challenges', *Indian Journal of Medical Ethics*, 4(4): 176–80.

Baral, S., Sifakis, F., Cleghorn, F. and Beyrer, C. (2007) 'Elevated risk for HIV infection among men who have sex with men in low- and middle-income countries 2000–2006: a systematic review', *PLoS Medicine*, 4, 12, e339. www.plosmedicine.org.

Barnett, T. and Whiteside, A. (2006) *AIDS in the Twenty-First Century: Disease and Globalization*, 2nd edn. New York: Palgrave.

Bashford, A. (2006) 'Global biopolitics and the history of world health', *History of the Human Sciences*, 19(1): 67–88.

Bigo, D. (2006) 'Gobalized (in)security: The field and the ban-opticon', in D. Bigo and A. Tsoukala (eds) *Illiberal Practices of Liberal Regimes: The (in)Security Games*. Paris: l'Harmattan

Burke, M. (2005) 'Medicalisation of prevention in Tanzania, East Africa', paper presented at the 7th AIDS Impact Conference, Cape Town, South Africa, April.

Campbell, C. (1997) 'Migrancy, masculine identities and AIDS: the psychological context of HIV transmission in South African gold mines', *Social Science & Medicine*, 45(2): 273–81.

——(2003) *Letting Them Die: Why HIV/AIDS Prevention Programmes Fail*. Oxford: James Curry.

CARAM. (2007) *State of Health of Migrants*. Kuala Lumpur: CARAM Asia.

Chretien, J.-P. (2007) 'Evaluating pandemic influenza surveillance and response systems in developing countries: Framework and pilot application', *Advances in Disease Surveillance*, 2: 146.

Cohen, J. (2008) 'The great funding surge', *Science*, 321: 512–19.

Cohen, M. S., Hellmann, N., Levy, J. A., DeCock, K. and Lange, J. (2008) 'The spread, treatment, and prevention of HIV-1: Evolution of a global pandemic', *Journal of Clinical Investigation*, 118: 1244–54.

Collier, S. J. and Lakoff, A. (2006) *Vital Systems Security, ARC Working Paper No. 2, February 2, 2006*, Laboratory for the Anthropology of the Contemporary. Online. Available HTTP: http://anthropos-lab.net/wp/publications/2007/01/collier_vital-systems.pdf (accessed 4 June 2008).

Cooper, M. (2006) 'Pre-empting emergence: The biological turn in the war on terror', *Theory, Culture & Society*, 23: 113–36.

Crewe, M. (2004) 'A PEP talk too far? The power of AIDS education', plenary paper presented at the XVth International AIDS Conference, Bangkok, July.

Cunningham, A. and Andrews, B. (1997) *Western Medicine as Contested Knowledge: Studies in Imperialism*, Manchester: Manchester University Press.

Davis, M. (2006) *Planet of Slum*. London: Verso.

Epstein, H. (2007) *The Invisible Cure: Africa, the West, and the Fight against AIDS*. New York: Farrar, Straus & Giroux.

England, R. (2007) 'Are we spending too much on HIV?', *British Medical Journal*, 334: 344.

Evans, C. and Lambert, H. (2008) 'The limits of behaviour change theory: Condom use and contexts of HIV risk in the Kolkata sex industry', *Culture Health & Sexuality*, 10:27–42.

Farmer, P. (1996) 'Social inequalities and emerging infectious diseases', *Emerging Infectious Diseases*, 2(4); 259–69.

Feachem, R.G.A. and Sabot, O. (2006) 'An examination of the Global Fund at 5 years', *The Lancet*, 368 (9534): 537–40.

Fearnley, L. (2005) *Pathogens And The Strategy Of Preparedness: Disease Surveillance In Civil Defense Planning, Report II*, Laboratory for the Anthropology of the Contemporary. Available HTTP: http://anthropos-lab.net/wp/publications/2007/01/fearn_pathogens.pdf (accessed 4 April 2006).

Friedman, S. R., Kippax, S., Phaswana-Mafuya, N., Rossi, D. and Newman, C. (2006) 'Emerging future issues in HIV/AIDS social research', *AIDS*, 20:959–65.

Gilbert L. and Walker, L. (2002) 'Treading the path of least resistance: HIV/AIDS and social inequalities: a South African case study', *Social Science & Medicine*, 54:1093–1110.

Global HIV Prevention Working Group (2006) *Global HIV Prevention: The Access and Funding Gap*. Online. Available HTTP: http://www.globalhivprevention.org/pdfs/pwg_access_factsheet_6_07.pdf (accessed 14 June 2008).

——(2007) *Bringing HIV Prevention to Scale: An Urgent Global Priority*. Online. Available HTTP: www.globalhivprevention.org/pdfs/PWG-HIV_prevention_report_FINAL.pdf (accessed 14 June 2008).

——(2008) *Behavior Change and HIV Prevention: (Re)Considerations for the 21st Century.* Online. Available HTTP: http://www.globalhivprevention.org/pdfs/PWG_behavior per cent20report_FINAL.pdf (accessed 16 August 2008).

Grinstead, O. A., Gregorich, S. E., Choi, K.-H., Coates, T. and the Voluntary HIV-1 Counselling and Testing Efficacy Study Group (2001) 'Positive and negative life events after counseling and testing: The Voluntary HIV-1 Counselling and Testing Efficacy Study', *AIDS*, 15(8): 1045–52.

Hanenberg, R. S., Rojanapithayakorn, W., Kunasol. P. and Sokal, D. C. (1994) 'Impact of Thailand's HIV control programmes as indicated by the decline in sexually transmitted diseases', *The Lancet*, 344: 243–45.

Haraway, D. J. (1991) *Simians, Cyborgs, and Women: The Reinvention of Nature.* New York: Routledge.

Henderson, K., Worth, H., Aggleton, P. and Kippax, S. (forthcoming) 'Enhancing HIV prevention requires addressing the complex relationship between prevention and treatment', *Global Health*.

Hsiao, W. and Heller, P. (2007) *What Should Macroeconomists Know about Health Care Policy? IMF Working Paper No. 07/13*, IMF. Online. Available HTTP: http://imf.org/external/pubs/ft/wp/2007/wp0713.pdf (accessed 16 November 2007).

International Organization for Migration and UNAIDS (2003) *Mobile Populations And HIV/AIDS In The Southern African Region.* Geneva: IOM and UNAIDS. Online. Available HTTP: http://www.queensu.ca/samp/sampresources/migrationdocuments/documents/2003/unaids.pdf (accessed 4 February 2007).

International Organization for Migration (2005) *Population Mobility and Migration in Southern Africa: Defining a Research and Policy Agenda.* Pretoria: IOM. Online. Available HTTP: http://www.queensu.ca/samp/migrationresources/reports/PopulationMobilityReport.pdf (accessed 4 February 2007).

Institute of Medicine (1992) *Emerging Infections: Microbial Threats to Health in the United States,* Washington, DC: National Academy Press.

Italian Global Health Watch (2008) 'From Alma Ata to the Global Fund: The history of international health policy', *Social Medicine*, 3(1): 36–48.

Jack, A. (2007, September 28) 'From symptom to system', *Financial Times*. London. Online. Available HTTP: www.ft.com/cms/s/0/2318ea9c-6d60–11dc-ab19–0000779fd2ac.html (accessed 4 November 2007).

Jana, S., Basu, I., Rotheram-Borus, M. J. and Newman, P. A. (2004) 'The Sonagachi Project: A sustainable community intervention program', *AIDS Education & Prevention*, 16(5): 405–14.

Kaldor, J. and Rubin, G. (1994) 'Epidemiology of HIV infection' in J. Gold and D. Rubin (eds) *The AIDS Manual: A Comprehensive Reference on the Human Immunodeficiency Virus*, 3rd edn. Albion Street (AIDS) Centre. Sydney: MacLennan and Petty.

Kates, J. and Lief, E. (2006) *International assistance for HIV/AIDS in the developing world: Taking stock of the G8, other donor governments, and the European Commission.* Kaiser Family Foundation. Online. Available HTTP: http://www.kff.org/hivaids/upload/7344–02.pdf (accessed 5 May 2007).

King, N. (2002) 'Security, disease, commerce: Ideologies of postcolonial global health', *Social Studies of Science*, 32(5–6): 763–89.

Kippax, S. and Race, K. (2003) 'Sustaining safe practice: Twenty years on', *Social Science and Medicine*, 57: 1–12.

Kippax, S. (2006) 'A public health dilemma: A testing question', *AIDS Care*, 18: 230–35.

——(2008) 'Understanding and integrating the structural and biomedical determinants of HIV-infection: A way forward for prevention', *Current Opinion in HIV & AIDS*, 3: 489–94.

Lakoff, A. (2007) 'Preparing for the next emergency', *Public Culture*, 19(1): 247–71.

Lancet Editorial (2005) 'The Global Fund plans an image makeover', *The Lancet*, 366(9485): 522.

Lederberg, J. (1996) 'Infection emergent', *Journal of the American Medical Association*, 275: 243–45.

——(1998) 'The future of infectious diseases', *Journal of Urban Health*, 75(3):4 63–70.

Mahajan, A. P., Sayles, J. N., Patel, V. A., Remien, R. H., Sawires, S. R., Ortiz, D. J., Szekeres, G. and Coates, T. J. (2008) 'Stigma in the HIV/AIDS epidemic: a review of the literature and recommendations for the way forward', *AIDS*, 22 (suppl. 2): S67–79.

Maman, S., Mbwambo, J., Hogan, N. M., Kilonzo, G. P. and Sweat, M. (2001) 'Women's barriers to HIV-1 testing and disclosure: Challenges for HIV-1 voluntary counselling and testing', *AIDS Care*, 13(5): 595–603.

224

Mann, J., Tarantola, D. and Netter, T.W. (1992) *AIDS in the World: A Global Report*. Cambridge, MA: Harvard University Press.

Martin, E. (1994) *Flexible Bodies*. Boston: Beacon Press.

McLaughlin,L. (1989) 'AIDS: An overview' in P. O'Malley (ed.) *The AIDS Epidemic: Private Rights and the Public Interest*. Boston: Beacon Press.

Mokili, J. and Korber, B. (2005) 'The spread of HIV in Africa', *Journal of Neurovirology*, 11, Suppl. 1, 66–75.

Morse, S. S. (1995) 'Factors in the emergence of infectious diseases', *Emerging Infectious Diseases*, 1(1):8–15.

Patton, C. (2002) *Globalizing AIDS*. Minneapolis: University of Minnesota Press.

Piot, P. (2006) 'AIDS: From crisis management to sustained strategic response', *The Lancet*, 368 (9534): 526–30.

Piot, P., Bartos, M., Larson, H., Zewdie, D. and Mane, P. (2008) 'Coming to terms with complexity: A call to action for HIV prevention', *The Lancet*, 372(9641): 845–59.

Potts, M., Halperin, D., Kirby, D., Swidler, A., Marseille, E., Klausner, J.D., Hearst, N., Wamai, R. G., Kahn, J. G. and Walsh, J. (2008) 'Reassessing HIV prevention', *Science*, 320: 749–50.

Rao Gupta, G. Parkhurst, J. O., Ogden, J. A., Aggleton, P. and Mahal, A. (2008) 'Structural approaches to HIV prevention', *The Lancet*, 372(9640): 764–75.

Reproductive Health Matters Editorial (2000) 'Efficacy of voluntary counselling and testing for HIV in reducing risk', *Reproductive Health Matters*, 8 (16): 176–77.

Satcher, D. (1995) 'Emerging infections: Getting ahead of the curve', *Emerging Infectious Diseases*, 1(1): 1–7.

Shilts, R. (1987) *And The Band Played On: Politic, People and the AIDS Epidemic*. New York: Penguin Books.

Seckinelgin H. (2008) *International Politics of HIV/AIDS: Global Disease – Local Pain*. London and New York: Routledge.

SIECUS (2005) *PEPFAR Country Profiles*: Online. Available HTTP: www.siecus.org/countryprofiles (accessed 14 October 2008).

——(2008) *PEPFAR Country Profile Updates*. Online. Available HTTP: www.siecus.org/countryprofiles (accessed 14 October 2008).

Smallman-Raynor, M., Cliff, A. and Haggett, P. (1992) *The London International Atlas of AIDS*. Oxford: Blackwell.

Smith, R. A. and Siplon, P. D. (2006) *Drugs into Bodies: Global AIDS Treatment Activism*. USA: Praeger.

Spiegel, P., Rygaard Bennedsen, A., Claass, J., Bruns, L., Patterson, N.,Yiwesa, D. and Schilperoord, M. (2007) 'Prevalence of HIV infection in conflict-affected and displaced people in seven sub-Saharan African countries: A systematic review', *The Lancet*, 369: 2187–95.

Steinberg, J. (2008) *Aids and Aids Treatment in a Rural South African Setting*. Monograph 149, Institute for Security Studies: Pretoria, South Africa. August. Also published as *Three-Letter Plague: A Young Man's Journey through a Great Epidemic*, Johannesburg: Jonathan Ball.

Stephenson, N. and Kippax, S. (2006) 'Transfiguring relations: Theorising political change in the everyday', *Theory & Psychology*, 16: 391–415.

Stuber, J., Meyer H. and Link, B. (eds) (2008) 'Stigma, prejudice and discrimination and health', Special Issue of *Social Science and Medicine*, 67: 351–486.

Stuckler, D., King, L. and Basu, S. (2008) 'International monetary fund programs and TB outcomes in post-communist countries', *PLoS Med*, 5(7): 1079–89.

Tarantola, D. (2005a) 'Global health and national governance', *American Journal of Public Health*, 95(1): 8.

——(2005b) 'The tensions and interface between international health, global health and human rights', Inaugural John Hirshman Lecture, University of New South Wales, October.

UNICEF (1987) *Adjustment with a Human Face. Volume 1: Protecting The Vulnerable And Promotion Growth*. Oxford: Clarendon Press.

UNAIDS (2006) 'Report on the Global AIDS Epidemic, Introduction', Geneva: UNAIDS. Online. Available HTTP: http://data.unaids.org/pub/GlobalReport/2006/2006_GR_CH01_en.pdf (accessed 28 August 2007).

225

——(2007) *AIDS Epidemic Update: December 2007*. Online. Available HTTP: http://www.unaids.org/en/KnowledgeCentre/HIVData/EpiUpdateArchive/2007 (accessed May 5 2008).

Waldby, C., Kippax, S. and Crawford, J. (1993) 'Cordon Sanitaire: "Clean" and "unclean" women in the AIDS discourse of young men', in P. Aggleton, P. Davies and G. Hart (eds) *AIDS: Facing the Second Decade*. London: Falmer Press.

——(1995) 'Epidemiological knowledge and discriminatory practice: AIDS and the social relations of biomedicine', *Australian and NZ Journal of Sociology*, 31(1): 1–14.

Wasserman, H. (2005) 'Connecting African Activism with Global Networks: ICTs and South African Social Movements', *Africa Development*, XXX, Nos 1 & 2: 163–82.

WHO (2007) *International Health Regulations (2005)*. Online. Available HTTP: http://www.who.int/csr/ihr/en/ (accessed December 2007).

WHO and UNAIDS (2007) *Guidance on Provider-Initiated HIV Testing and Counselling in Health Facilities*. May. WHO, Geneva. Online. Available HTTP: http://www.who.int/entity/hiv/who_pitc_guidelines.pdf (accessed May 31 2007).

Whithead, M., Dahlgren, G. and Evans, T. (2001) 'Equity and health sector reforms: Can low-income countries escape the medical poverty trap?' *The Lancet*, 358: 833–36.

Winner, L. (2006) 'Technology studies for terrorists: A short course', in T. Monahan. (ed.) *Surveillance and Security*. New York: Routledge.

Wodak, A. and Cooney, A. (2006) 'Do needle syringe programmes reduce HIV infection among injecting drug users: A comprehensive review of the international evidence', *Substance Use and Misuse*, 41(6–7): 777–813.

Zwi, A. (1993) 'Reassessing priorities: Identifying the determinants of HIV transmission', *Social Science & Medicine*, 36: iii–viii.

12

Globalization, disasters, and disaster response

Habibul Khondker

Introduction

The sociology of disasters is concerned commonsensically with disasters, which may be defined as unscheduled events caused by nature or by human interventions. It deals with their consequences for human societies, responses to post-disaster adjustments, and long-term recovery. These disasters include a wide variety of calamities from natural to nuclear disaster. Over the years, as the field has grown, it has included within its range of investigation diverse types of disasters and hazards, their causes, both short- and long-term consequences and the processes of rehabilitation. In recent years some authors have included subjects such as wars, civil wars, large-scale human rights violations, and even terrorist attacks within the purview of disaster sociology. The growth of the field has been slow, partly owing to the penchant for sociology as a discipline to study social order and continuity in society. As sociology evolved into more inter-disciplinary fields and began to expand its horizons, social discontinuity and more atypical aspects of society came under its purview. This development opened the door to the study of disasters and other disorderly and disruptive events and processes in society. Over time policy makers too recognized the importance of disaster research in public-policy making that would minimize disaster losses and became supportive of this field of study.

Unlike other fields of sociology, disaster sociology lacks the benefit of contributions from classical sociologists. The first systematic social and behavioural study of a disaster was Samuel Prince's study of the Halifax explosion in 1920 based on the disastrous collision of a Belgian and a French ship carrying TNT. Although it was the study of a single case, important propositions and hypotheses were contained in that study (Drabek, 1986: 1). After a hiatus in the 1960s, disaster as a topic and a research area once more attracted the attention of social scientists and policy makers. In social sciences, disaster as a topic was initially viewed as an example in the field of social problems and thus a chapter on disaster written by C. E. Fritz was included in *Social Problems*, which was edited by Robert Merton and Richard Nisbet (1961). Nearly a decade later, Allan Barton (1970) presented a sociological contribution highlighting individual behaviours in times of disasters with a focus on role definition, competence, and conflict under disaster conditions

(Quarantelli and Dynes, 1977: 26). After a lull of over two decades came Pitirim Sorokin's *Man and Society in Calamity* (1942). Owing to the influence of behaviourism, earlier works on disaster focused more on the psychological consequences of disasters viewing them as generating high stress in individuals (Baker and Chapman, 1962). In 1963 the Disaster Research Center was established at Ohio State University by two of the pioneering figures in disaster sociology, E. L. Quarantelli and Russell Dynes. The Disaster Research Center, according to the Center's website, is the first social science research centre in the world devoted to the study of disasters. The Center was moved to the University of Delaware in 1985. Accordingly,

> [t]he Center conducts field and survey research on group, organizational and community preparation for, response to, and recovery from natural and technological disasters and other community-wide crises. DRC researchers have carried out systematic studies on a broad range of disaster types, including hurricanes, floods, earthquakes, tornadoes, hazardous chemical incidents, and plane crashes.
>
> (DRC Website, accessed on 30 August 2008)

Since Barton's (1970) analysis, and with conscious efforts of the Disaster Research Center, disaster research began to focus more on organizational and structural issues rather than the psychological consequences. Studies conducted by the researchers at the Disaster Research Center, such as Russell Dynes (1974) and disaster researchers elsewhere (Stallings, 1978; Turner, 1978) began to focus more on the institutional and organizational aspects of disaster response. Although the sociology of disasters in North America originated in the wake of the rise of risks from industrial disasters, it gradually came to include natural calamities within its research agenda. Following the Buffalo Creek floods, Kai Erikson wrote a report, which was later converted into a book entitled *Everything in its Path* (1976) which became a landmark study of disasters and their consequences. The study examined the destruction and reconstruction of the community in the aftermath of the disaster. Erikson argued that the trauma was caused not by the disaster itself but by the sense of loss or destruction of the community or, in his words, *communality*, since the people of Buffalo Creek in the Appalachian Range lived in *gemeinschaft*-like relationships.

This chapter will outline the nature of disasters, their consequences and responses to disaster in the contemporary world. All these processes reveal, not only the interconnected nature of the global world, but also some underlying social structural features and the issues of governance in dealing with disasters.

Definitions

Disasters may be defined as unscheduled events that destroy human lives and property, and which eventually impact on social stability. While a cyclone or earthquake is a visible 'natural' disaster with dramatic television footage of ruination in its path, there are also creeping disasters – disasters that build slowly and steadily over a period of time. The consequences of these creeping disasters are no less lethal, and the damage and disruption no less catastrophic. Food shortage and famine are disasters which have also been labelled as 'creeping disasters' (Khondker, 1989), because the build-up to such events is typically long term. The rapid inflation in food prices in 2008 led to a 'silent famine' in many parts of the world. Since politicians are loath to use the term 'famine', various euphemisms have surfaced to describe the crisis, which in itself is suggestive of the link between politics, the media, and disasters.

Disasters as unscheduled events have led to emergent communities in post-disaster situations. The phenomenon of the emergent community was an interesting conceptual development permitting sociologists to examine the non-permanence and malleability of human communities. Disasters had both long-term and short-term consequences. In the context of industrialized, advanced economies, the focus has been confined to the community level since this was also the time when community studies occupied a central place in sociology and related social sciences. Sociology in the 1950s and 1960s was also viewed as a discipline with a limited brief. Related fields like social geography and public administration also played a key role in disaster research. Social geographers studied human responses to various types of natural disasters or in their language to hazards. The Natural Hazards Research Center was set up in University of Colorado in 1984 (Drabek, 1986: 4).

As attention expanded to consider disasters in other parts of the world and as more varieties of disasters came to attract the attention of the social scientists, sociology became somewhat more open to non-traditional community studies and included research on nation-states, regions and even the global society as its field of investigation. Thus the scope of disaster sociology widened beyond community studies. Sociology as a field also underwent changes in the late 1970s and 1980s as a result of an infusion of political economy, macro sociology, and historical sociology. With growing attention to social discontinuity, some sociologists became increasingly interested in the political economy of disasters, famines, and other large-scale crises and with their historical roots. More interdisciplinary research became the norm with the cooperation of researchers from various fields.

The International Sociological Association organized special sessions on disaster sociology and in 1986 established a Research Committee (RC39) on the Sociology of Disasters. By 1986, special disaster sociology sessions were organized under the rubric of Third World disasters. Many Third World societies were of course extremely vulnerable to disasters which were produced by a complex set of causes. For example, famines in Africa and Bangladesh were rooted in multiple causes spanning both local and the international political economy. In the advanced societies, the concerns of social scientists were slightly different; for example insurance was a key issue in the discussion of floods in North America. In developing societies, people often turned to their extended families and to larger kinship groups for help in post-disaster situations and hence the issue of insurance coverage was less relevant. Sessions on famines were also organized under the rubric of Disaster Sociology. In 1988 a Thematic Group was organized on 'Famine and Society' and in 1998 it graduated into a Working Group (WG05) of the International Sociological Association.

Journals related to disasters began to appear in Japan in early 1950s and in Europe in the late 1970s. Kyoto University's Disaster Prevention Research Institute's Bulletin was launched in 1951. *Disasters: The Journal of Disaster Studies, Policy and Management*, a publication of the Overseas Development Institute in the United Kingdom, was launched in 1977. *International Journal of Mass Emergencies and Disasters* in the United States began to appear in 1983. *Disaster Management* was published in India in 1981 and in 1993 *Journal of Contingencies and Crisis Management* appeared.

Industrial accidents such as the near-meltdown at the nuclear plant at the Three Mile Island at Harrisburg, Pennsylvania in 1977, the deadly Methyl Isocyanate (MIC) gas

229

leakage at Union Carbide plant in Bhopal, India in 1984 and the nuclear accident at Chernobyl Nuclear Plant in 1986 generated interest in industrial disasters. A whole range of disasters or 'crises' as they were called in the language of policy makers were investigated (Comfort, 1988; Rosenthal et al., 1989). Policy-oriented social scientists were interested in public-policy making, mitigation and prevention of these crises. In response to growing technological threats, a number of writers in the 1980s developed the notion of risk and the normalcy of crises (Perrow, 1984; Short, 1984).

In December 1987 at its 42nd session, the General Assembly of the United Nations designated the 1990s as the International Decade for Natural Disaster Reduction (IDNDR). The basic idea behind this proclamation of the Decade was, and still remains, the unacceptable and rising level of losses which disasters continue to incur on the one hand, and the existence, on the other hand, of a wealth of scientific and engineering know-how which could be effectively used to reduce losses resulting from such disasters. As its name implied, the IDNDR officially came to an end in 1999. However, during its ten-year span of activities, it achieved such important successes – especially in terms of forging vital links among the political, scientific, and technological communities – that the United Nations created a successor body to carry on its work. This new body of coordinated action programs, with a secretariat in Geneva, is ISDR. Some of the major conferences under IDNDR on natural disaster reduction took place in Japan, which stoked interest in international disasters. Disasters such as earthquakes were a preoccupation of Japanese sociologists and many of them were very interdisciplinary in their orientation. There were also historians and engineers who took an interest in a variety of disasters, their consequences and mitigations. Their contributions enriched the field which was otherwise quite parochial.

How natural is a natural disaster?

There is some debate over the idea of 'risk society' as outlined by the German sociologist Ulrich Beck. He views modern society as a risk society which tends to deal with the hazards and insecurities induced and introduced by the very conditions of modernity in a systematic way. In other words, risk society is an aspect of the present level of modernization itself (Beck, 1992: 21). History of disasters and calamities provide ample evidence that human beings have always been at risk of disasters. The risk theorists (Beck, 1992; Giddens, 1999), however, suggest that modern risks are different because they are the products of human agency, and in this sense they are manufactured risks. To illustrate the idea of the modernization of risk, examples are often drawn from environmental crises. A closer examination of historical disasters would reveal that the difference between 'external' or natural disasters and the so-called man-made disasters is not always clear. There are significant overlaps between the two types of risk. The advantage of modern society over its pre-modern counterpart lies in the mitigation of hazards. Modern society with the advantage of systematic storage and sharing of information capabilities has become not only more future oriented which heightens the awareness of risk perceptions, its preparedness for dealing with disasters has improved considerably as seen in the reduction of the losses. Beck (1992) has argued that in the advanced modern world, the risks have also been complicated and preparedness against risk has become a major feature of all modern nation-states. In this modern risk environment, international organizations are also geared to dealing with disasters and crises of all kinds.

Disasters come in many forms and shapes, causing varying levels of destruction to life and property, thereby disrupting society as a whole. Some disasters are caused by nature, others by human beings, and even those caused by natural phenomena are often either aggravated or mitigated by human interventions. Sometimes it is difficult to untangle human involvement from such 'natural' disasters. In the globalized world, local disasters have global consequences and global crises have serious local impacts. Global and local are often enmeshed with each other.

For a long time social scientists and philosophers have questioned the nature-centric view of disasters. The mediating influence of social arrangements on disaster was noted even by J.-J. Rousseau (1712–78) in the eighteenth century. The Lisbon earthquake of 1755 became a subject of some philosophical musings by the Enlightenment philosophers who pondered over the meaning of the earthquake in the context of human reason, divine purpose, and human evil. Voltaire – the pen name of Francois-Marie Arouet (1694–1778) and one of the key Enlightenment figures – saw the earthquake which took a toll of 90,000 lives as a metaphysical event. In a poem, he raised the problem of evil, doubting the Enlightenment view of progress and optimism:

> Rousseau's reply to Voltaire outlined a surprisingly modern social science view. Rousseau pointed out that it was not the seismic event itself which was important but the nature of the human community. 'Without departing from your subject of Lisbon, admit, for example, that nature did not construct twenty thousand houses of six to seven stories there, and that, if the inhabitants of this great city had been more equally spread out and more lightly lodged, the damage would have been much less and perhaps of no account.'
>
> (Rousseau quoted in Dynes, 2000)

Similar discussions took place following the devastating earthquake losses in Pakistan in 2005 with fatalities estimated at 86,000 or 31,000 deaths in Bam, Iran in 2003 or the Turkish earthquake of Izmit in 1999 with a death toll of over 1,700 or the Tokyo earthquake – one of the most devastating earthquakes in the history of Japan – in which the resulting fire took a toll of 143,000 lives in 1923. A number of historical studies on the consequences of the Tokyo earthquakes followed. Some argued that the earthquake had a lasting influence in changing the architectural designs of houses in Japan. These illustrations reveal that disasters are events that not only affect the assets of society and organized social life, but also lead to changes in social organizations and the consciousness of the people.

Human history with its litany of experiences with a great variety of disasters has been a history of the constant struggle of society against disasters. One of the measures of social progress is the human ability to tackle disasters by foretelling, preventing whenever possible, and mitigating the losses. Human agency and organized social response have reduced our collective vulnerability. However, calamities such as the Asian Tsunami of December 2004 or the Sichuan Earthquake of 2008 in China are reminders of the helplessness of people in the face of the fury of nature. A true measure of social progress is the reduction of vulnerability caused both by the forces of nature as well as by society.

Some countries such as the Philippines and Bangladesh are regularly visited by a whole range of 'natural' calamities ranging from cyclones to earthquakes. It would be impossible to deny the role of nature in the causation of disasters, but natural causes are mediated by social and political processes and hence we put quotation marks around the word 'natural'.

The Asian Tsunami is a case in point which affected countries as far afield as Somalia and India. The worst affected countries were Sri Lanka, Thailand, and Indonesia. Of the estimated death toll of 220,000, the majority were from the Indonesian province of Ache. The beaches that faced the brunt were the ones developed for tourists and were thus denuded of mangroves. Seashores lined with mangroves would have offered some protection against the ferocity of the tidal waves. As human intervention was visible in the clearing of the mangroves, the other facet was in the subsequence administration of disaster relief. Some societies are obviously better able to cope with disasters than others depending on their level of efficient and reliable state administration and the presence of effective civil society institutions, especially active voluntary associations.

China suffered a 7.9 magnitude earthquake in May 2008. It is estimated that 70,000 people perished in the earthquake with another 18,000 people went missing. Many of the victims were school children. It appeared that the school buildings were not built to the appropriate safety specifications despite the fact that, following the Tangshan earthquake in China in 1976 with a death toll of 240,000 administrative orders were in place for earthquake proofing of the constructions (Fong, 2008). However, the government of China mounted a massive relief operation following the calamity. About 130,000 army and paramilitary troops assisted the search and rescue effort in Sichuan (*Gulf News*, 16 May 2008: 19).

Globalization and disasters

Disasters in times of globalization have consequences far beyond the location where they strike. The globalization of the consequences of disasters is revealed clearly in epidemiological crises such as avian flu (popularly known as bird flu), SARS, TB, or swine flu. These have become transnational diseases as a result of the migration of people across national borders. There are several examples of epidemics in history which were also the result of the movement of people. Bubonic plagues in medieval Europe were a consequence of the crusades because the crusaders unintentionally brought rats in their ships back to Europe. The rats were hosts to fleas that transmitted disease to humans. Similarly, the European colonialists infected the Indigenous people in what is now known as Central America and North America with conditions such as measles and whooping cough against which these aboriginal communities had little or no resistance. In the early part of the twentieth century, an influenza virus wiped out millions of people in Asia and Europe – an infection that was eventually taken from Europe to America and Asia. The influenza was incubated in Italy with the detachment of American troops who brought it back to the USA and was later moved to parts of Asia where the troops went. The connection between war and the spread of diseases provides us with many such examples. However, the silent disaster of the twenty-first century is hunger which is caused by poverty that keeps nearly a quarter of world population at a level of vulnerability where simple shocks can put their lives at stake.

The 2008 crisis in food prices and the threat of global hunger were a surprise to many observers, because for a decade food prices had been stable or falling. In 1987, writing about futurology in an article called 'The World and the United States in 2013', Daniel Bell (1987: 18) made a number of valuable and precise predictions, for example about the growing economic influence of China and India, but he also made a surprising statement about the supply of food. He claimed that 'almost every country in the world is just about self-sufficient in food, and seeking export markets. ... Until the twentieth century, a famine was recorded almost every year somewhere in the world. Today famines are rare ... the problems of food production are *political*. Bell was obviously too optimistic about the disappearance of famine, but he was surely correct in claiming that the principal causes of famine arise from political conflict, mismanagement, and violence. Many of the causes of malnutrition and famine in contemporary Africa – Darfur, Ethiopia, and Zimbabwe – are political.

In March 2008, a sudden rise of cereal prices caused a great deal of uncertainty in various parts of the world. In Egypt women were out on the streets protesting and fighting the police over the disappearance of bread. There is a certain irony to this situation for Egypt was not only the cradle of human civilization but also the birthplace of systematic agricultural production based on irrigation. The Cairo-based regional office of the World Food Program (WFP) identified greater demand of food with a dwindling supply in the emerging big economies of China and India, the increased use of land for bio-fuels, climate change and failed harvests, high oil prices and increasing transport costs as causes for the surge in food prices. Added to those factors were the lack of liquidity in the financial market and the problems of governance in various developing countries where hoarding of food grains distorted the market. Flooding in the American Mid-West also damaged the harvesting of crops such as soya bean and maize in 2008 further driving up the price of grain. A concern for improved ecology was one of the factors in the demand for ethanol which is less polluting. But the diversion of crops from human consumption to fuel production compounded by drought in Australia exacerbated the food situation leading to hunger in many countries. Global warming contributed to the increased frequency of floods and other natural calamities. It is difficult to gauge exactly how much the increase in commodity process was a result of speculation, but these price fluctuations will obviously continue. In response to demand, farmers planted more wheat and by late 2008 it looked as if wheat prices would stabilize following an increase in supply, but the overall trend appears to be inflationary with unsatisfied demand continuing to drive up prices.

Suddenly countries until recently touted as breadbaskets of the region covering parts of the Middle East and Africa such as Iraq and Sudan were short of food. Bangladesh which attained self sufficiency in food in 1999–2000 faced a serious food crisis in late March and early April 2008 while government and the opposition parties squabbled over terminology as to whether that was a silent famine, or a food shortage, or a crisis of subsistence. While politicians debated over semantics, many poor starving members of the underclass and working class stood in food lines at government-run shops that sold food grains (such as rice) at fixed prices.

In early 2008 William Paddock, an American agronomist, died in Uruguay. He had co-authored a book entitled *Famine 1975!* in 1967 predicting starvation and famine in large parts of the world which would be dependent on American food aid. In this crisis, the Paddock brothers recommended 'triage' arguing that some countries cannot be saved and scarce food aid should be channelled to those that could be saved and that would be in the US interest. India was included along with Egypt and Haiti in their list of countries that cannot be saved (Paddock and Paddock, 1967: 222). By the mid-1970s, India was close to solving the problem of mass hunger. With the exception of the 'panic famine' of 1967–68 which was averted as a result of US food aid under the scheme of P.L. 480, India avoided famine in the post-independence period. The last widespread famine was in 1942–43 during World War II when war conditions directly contributed to food scarcity and famine. That famine was depicted with brutal clarity in the famous Satyajit Ray film *Distant Thunder*. Indian democracy had become a bulwark against famine.

Research on famines

Sociologists did not traditionally take research on famines seriously. In sociology, natural calamities and disasters which are familiar to the underdeveloped world received much of the attention. But in general the experience of famine has been too remote from the experience of the developed countries to be included in their research agenda. The only leading sociologist who paid attention to unusual and out of the ordinary events was Pitirim Sorokin, a Russian émigré who wrote on food crisis and famine in Russia in the 1920s. Sorokin's study on the Russian Famine of 1921–22 was published posthumously (Sorokin, 1975) and the importance of his works was not recognized until much later. While his experience in Russia was invaluable, sociology as an academic field developed mostly in North America where there was little demand for research on disasters. Apart from the work of Sorokin in the 1940s, systematic sociological research on famine is still a rarity.

This is ironic because famine as a catastrophe has been known throughout human history. The earliest reference to famine is biblical, namely the famine that affected Egypt and was handled with the prudent food reserve policy of Joseph. The bulk of the existing literature on famine is historical. These historical studies offered plausible explanations of the causes and consequences of famines in various parts of the world. These works span a variety of regions as well as periods in history. W.H. Mallory (1928) on China, Pierre Goubert (1970) and Le Roy Ladurie (1973) on France, A. Loveday (1908) and B. M. Bhatia (1967) on India, Andrew Appleby (1978) on England, R. D. Edwards and T. D. Williams (1976) on Ireland, H. H. Fisher (1935) and R. G. Robbins (1975) on Russia are works which have enhanced our understanding of the major famines in history. Jack Shepherd (1975) on Ethiopia, R.W. Franke and B. Chasin on Shahel (1980), Rehman Sobhan (1979), Mohiuddin Alamgir (1980), Amartya Sen (1981), Paul Greenough (1982), and Habibul Khondker (1984) on Bengal (including Bangladesh) add to the rich literature on famine in the twentieth century. A growing concern for the need for public action and international cooperation has led to important contributions by Jean Dreze and Amartya Sen (1989).

Famines which were matters of the past, a subject fit for history books, lingered into the last decades of the twentieth century only in Africa and North Korea. The fear of famine was back on newspapers and television talk shows as much as in the hungry neighbourhoods of Bangladesh and Sudan and Somalia in 2008. Ethiopia, according to one media report, faced a 'toxic cocktail' of global inflation, armed conflict, and associated plagues that threaten fourteen million people who are in need of food aid. North Korea, largely for political reasons, remains globally isolated and is faced with famine on a more or less constant basis, despite the efforts of South Korea to normalize relationships (www.usatoday.com/news/world/2008-08-17-ethiopia_N.htm [accessed on August 23, 2008]).

Bangladesh suffered a famine in the mid-1970s as the country was trying to recover from a trail of devastations left behind by a bloody war of liberation in late 1971. Wars and famine are natural allies. Poverty lies at the heart of famine. Amartya Sen reminded us that the entitlement failure, often translated into lack of purchasing power, and not the shortages of food, is the real cause of famine. This idea was, by no means, a new discovery, though the formulation was. But in some famines, failure of entitlement and shortage of food occur simultaneously. More than half a century before Amartya Sen's *Poverty and Famines*, which was published in the early 1980s, W. H. Moreland (1923) made a distinction between 'food famines' and 'work famines'. In a straightforward manner, he said that some localized famines were caused simply by the shortage of food. Other famines which characterized the colonial period in India were caused by the lack of employment. No work, no income, therefore, no food. And in 1900, such explanations were presaged by J. T. Sunderland (1900) who in an article entitled 'The Cause of Indian famines' attributed famines to 'the extreme poverty of the Indian people – a poverty so severe that it keeps a majority of all on the verge of suffering, even in the years of plenty … ' (Sunderland, 1900: 58).

Those realities have not changed significantly two centuries later. Unemployment in Zimbabwe is running at 80 per cent. Unsurprisingly Zimbabwe is in the grip of a famine. A bad economic situation caused by the compulsion of history and a spate of bad policies by a national hero turned dictator President Mugabe brutalized the population, mismanaged the economy and famine was a natural consequence. Price inflation at an unimaginable level ensures that the mass of people cannot afford to feed themselves.

Famines and starvation often culminate in social collapse. Famines are rarely equal opportunity disasters unlike a tidal wave that sweeps everybody and everything in its path. Famine and starvation affect a society unevenly. It is the poor who become the first line of casualties. This historical knowledge has driven such programmes as feeding the poorest of the poor, the unemployed or in Sen's terms those whose entitlements to food cannot be assured by the play of the market forces alone. Hence public action, involving the state in mitigating hunger, becomes essential. In a globalized world, states are able to mobilize resources not only from the international food market but also from food-surplus nations as well as from multilateral agencies.

Unlike in previous centuries, by the middle of the twentieth century international cooperation and global institutions evolved to tackle precisely these sorts of problems. By the late twentieth century, the World Food Program was feeding the hungry around the world. Although most writers avoid any discussion of the Malthusian apocalyptic vision of population growth outstripping the food supply in view of a dramatic increase in the production of food, population growth as one of the factors in the modern food crisis cannot be completely ignored. 78.5 million babies are born into the world every year. It is like adding more than the entire population of Turkey (74 million) or Egypt (73 million) each year to the world population of 6.7 billion in 2008. The world population is projected to increase from 6.7 to 9.3 billion by 2050 (Population Reference Bureau, *Data Sheet*, 2008) which is likely to stretch the capacity of global food production.

It was believed that human progress would confine famine to history. We have already referred to Professor Bell's predictions from the 1980s. To some extent the recurring famines of the Middle Ages became a subject of history. Of the famous nineteenth-century famines, we remember famines in the colonies and the one in Ireland. Famines often triggered mass migration. Irish people went to America for a better life, a life without starvation. Chinese from the Southern and Central regions, Canton or what is now called Guangzo and Hainan migrated to Hong Kong and Singapore to work as coolies. The labour migration of the nineteenth century bears witness to famines and starvation. An exodus of Irish migrants to the United States followed the Irish famine of the 1840s which is also known as the 'potato famine'.

In the first decade of the twenty-first century, China and India, which vied for world attention for their rapid economic developments, have moved up the ranks of developing nations from poor to industrializing countries. In the historical discussion of famines and disasters, ironically these two countries would often be mentioned for disasters and in fact they competed with each other for the title 'land of famines'. As we have seen books were written even in the 1960s with titles such as *Famine 1975!* predicting impending famine in India which was teeming with poor people. The predictions were falsified by India's ability to feed its population. Poverty remained but hunger was no longer an endemic problem. Famines did not strike nor did it stalk the poor people.

In one view, as societies have developed they have achieved more capacity to control natural and man-made disasters. Famines which were common in Europe in the Middle Ages and the early modern period became relics of history with the advancement of social development and industrialization. The only famine in Europe in the twentieth century was the Dutch famine caused by a deliberate strategy by the Nazis during World War II.

Although famines have been contained in parts of Africa and Asia, countries well known for famines have overcome this scourge in the late twentieth century. India experienced the last famine during World War II which was linked to the war efforts of the British. Post-independent India suffered one panic famine in Punjab in the late 1960s, but India averted this crisis following US President Johnson's timely intervention. China suffered a major famine during the so-called Great Leap Forward movement in the heyday of Maoist communism when local officials inflated production figures and hid the real picture from the central authorities. In other words, political and bureaucratic mismanagement was the root cause. This led Amartya Sen to develop his theory that democracy is a viable antidote against famine and other similar crises.

Famines were always complex crises. A host of social, economic and political factors often conspired in the past to create famine situations. The march of progress minimized the threats of famine or contained it in the high-poverty regions of the world. Although in the advanced age of information and communication revolutions, news of the shortages spreads very rapidly and interventions and assistance can be mobilized on a short notice. Yet the world is not free from the threats of food crises. As we have seen in 2008 there was a shortfall of wheat production causing sharp price increases in various countries pushing tens of thousands of people to the brink of starvation.

Tyranny and famines

In the twentieth century many large famines were caused by oppressive political regimes. These include British rule in India, the Dutch famine caused by the Nazis and the communist famines in the Soviet Union and China in 1930s and 1950s respectively. With the decline of the bureaucratic and centralized socialist systems and the rise of democracy in the 1990s, it was hoped that famines would disappear. They did not. Globalization introduced a new dimension to famine. As economies became more and more connected and linked, an economic crisis in one place spilled over not only into neighbouring regions but also into distant places. Food shortages in the first decade of the twenty-first century revealed some of the deep-seated problems of globalization. Financial instability in the credit crunch of 2008 is one rather obvious example of this interconnectivity.

The world-wide shortage of food grains was caused by a complicated set of factors. With rising petroleum fuel prices, the demand for bio-fuel grew, with more ethanol coming from corn and other edible food grains, the price of marketed food grains for human consumption sky-rocketed. As China and India became prosperous, the demand for meat and a more sophisticated cuisine grew putting further strain on food prices. While the rich ate more meat and drove ethanol powered cars, the poor starved and walked miles in search of food. The international political and economic arrangements of inequality between nations sustain the conditions for global hunger.

Yet, the crisis of subsistence is often exacerbated by the local or national political economy. The case of Burma illustrates the problem only too well. The military regime in Burma had usurped political power by denying the results of a democratic process that had elected Aung San Suu Kyi in 1990. The resultant political crisis in Burma has not only resulted in a stagnant economy, but Burma is perceived as a pariah state and a large number of Burmese have crossed into neighbouring Thailand as refugees and migrants creating a humanitarian crisis. In the wake of devastation left by Cyclone Nargis, the military rulers in Burma, rather than mounting all-out relief operations, carried out a national referendum to legitimize the military regime-sponsored constitution in May 2008. The Burmese military regime did not want the presence of foreign aid workers except to give a token amount of foreign aid. The distribution of aid is often a political act – the aid goes to the supporters of the regime as exemplified in a number of similar cases, while the opponents of the regime are excluded. Rangoon was cleaned up relatively quickly partly for strategic and partly for cosmetic reasons, while the hinterland which was out of site languished. It was reported that in the middle of these devastations and acute shortages of food, Burma was exporting rice to Malaysia and Singapore (*International Herald Tribune*, 11 May 2008).

The world is beset with problems – some routine, some structural; some anticipated, some unanticipated, and some in-between. Consider for example natural calamities. They occur almost at regular intervals and have become almost routine annual features in certain countries, yet one cannot predict exactly when they will occur. The US has been visited by tornadoes and flash floods regularly, yet even with advanced science and technology it was not possible fully to anticipate the consequence of such disasters. In March 2008, a sudden flash flood in the Midwestern states of the USA killed eighteen people and washed away properties worth millions of dollars. Hurricane Katrina in 2005 which affected Louisiana and three other southern states caused hardships and social dislocation of such magnitude that we cannot escape the conclusion that we are all vulnerable. It is the common denominator of the human condition, no matter where human beings live. A major tidal wave, named *Sidr* lashed Bangladesh in November 2007 washing away tens of thousands of human lives, livestock, and houses, and ruined agricultural land pushing people to starvation. The death toll of the 2007 tidal wave when huge walls of water swept away everything in its path was estimated at 138,000. Fortunately massive international assistance helped to mitigate the full horror of this crisis. An earlier cyclone-driven tidal wave in November 1970 had an even higher death toll – estimated between 200,000 and half a million which was did not receive the same level of attention by the Pakistan government of the day triggering resentment and fomenting a nationalist movement in Bangladesh. These national leaders could then use the lack of response as an instance of the neglect of East Pakistan (now Bangladesh) by the military rulers of Pakistan.

Hurricane Katrina – a case study

It may be useful to examine the disaster of Hurricane Katrina and its consequences in the states of Mississippi, Alabama, and Louisiana, especially of New Orleans and compare this

American disaster with that of the Asian tsunami. The comparison in so far as the death toll is concerned may be preposterous – the Asian tsunami killed about 300,000 human beings, whereas the death toll from hurricane Katrina may be less than a thousand, despite the initial estimates on the higher side. The Asian tsunami was perhaps the costliest calamity in terms of the loss of human lives. Hurricane Katrina was the costliest in terms of dollar value. This reveals an intriguing aspect of globalization. The US government in both events responded first in a sluggish manner and then after much media criticism, as in the New Orleans case, with a huge outpouring of generosity. President George Bush committed $60 billion in recovery and rehabilitation promising to rebuild New Orleans even better than it had been before disaster struck in a speech delivered from the flood soaked city on 15 September 2005. In that speech President Bush not only admitted the failures of the Federal government but also admitted the social historical causes that exacerbated the sufferings of the victims, a disproportionate number of whom were African Americans. 'As we clear away the debris of a hurricane, let us also clear away the legacy of inequality', declared President Bush (*International Herald Tribune*, 16 September 2005).

Apart from the failures of the government, the sudden nature of the disaster and the magnitude of the losses produced comparisons of a cosmological nature. In a Reuters report entitled 'Some evacuees see religious message in Katrina' it was said that 'Natural disaster is caused by the sin in the world' according to Major John Jones, area commander for the Salvation Army, who led the service. 'The acts of God are what happen afterwards … all the good that happens.'

> 'God made all this happen for a reason. This city has been going to hell in a handbasket spiritually,' Tim Washington, 42, said at New Orleans' Superdome Saturday as he waited to be evacuated.
>
> 'If we can spend billions of dollars chasing after [Osama] bin Laden, can't we get guns and drugs off the street?', he asked. Washington said he stole a boat last Monday and he and a friend, using wooden fence posts as oars, delivered about 200 people to the shelter. 'The sheriff's department stood across the street and did nothing,' he added.
>
> (Source: www.msnbc.msn.com/id/9206991/ [accessed on 12 September 2005])

Soon after the Asian tsunami that lashed the coasts in Ache, Indonesia, Southern Thailand, and parts of India, Sri Lanka, and the Maldives ten months earlier, the disaster evoked similar connections between sin furthermore God's wrath. In the Asian case, of course, the discussion was much more pronounced and broadened to include some Gulf nations as well. Following the tsunami, some Muslim commentators in Saudi Arabia and elsewhere suggested that the disaster was a response to wanton behaviour. On an Islamist website, one commentator wrote: 'Asia's earthquake, which hit the beaches of prostitution, tourism, immortality and nudity, is a sign that God is warning mankind from persisting in injustice and immorality before he destroys the ground beneath them' (www.dailytimes. com.pk/default.asp?page=story_6-1-2005_pg7_51 (*Daily Times*) [accessed on 15 September 2005]).

As regards Hurricane Katrina, apart from right-wing Islamic websites, no one took such alleged connections seriously. But the similarity between the cases of the New Orleans tragedy caused by Hurricane Katrina and the Asian tsunami of December 26, 2004 does not end here.

In both instances the disasters were man-made though the events – tsunami and hurricane – that caused them may have been the hazards of nature. Even the 'natural hazard' was in part brought about by global warming and other human interventions.

The two disasters also reveal certain processes of globalization at work. Disasters often bring to the surface deeper aspects of society that otherwise remain hidden under normal circumstances. As commentators put it:

> The violence of the storm and his faltering response to it have left to Bush the task not just of physically rebuilding a swath of the United States, but also of addressing issues like poverty and racial inequality that were exposed in such raw form by the storm.
>
> (*International Herald Tribune*, 18 September 2005)

The incidence of looting, criminal activities, rape, and breakdown of law and order reflected a social collapse in New Orleans that remained hidden from the public view. The real crisis in New Orleans was a social collapse manifested in the weakness of governance. New Orleans, for some time in the 1980s, had the dubious distinction of being the murder capital of the United States (a position that it yielded to Washington, DC in the 1990s).

New Orleans, despite its reputation as the jazz capital of the world and a tourism hub, was a city in which 27.4 per cent of the people were living below the poverty line and of these over two-thirds were African Americans (DeParle, 2005). According to NBC news programme, most of the poor did not have insurance. Some 134,000 people could not leave because they could not afford transportation (www.msnbc.msn.com/id/9163091/ [accessed on 12 November 2008]). According to the *New York Times*, 35 per cent of the black households did not have access to a car compared with just 15 per cent for whites (Deparle, 2005).The ills of New Orleans were a microcosm of the social ills of the United States, a nation adrift. The hurricane was only the fuse of a time bomb created by years of neglect by the Republican agenda such as 'freedom' of hand gun ownership, compounded by the neo-liberal strategies of privatization and deregulation of services resulting in a further erosion of social services. The fact that the sale of guns rose following the hurricane reflects some of the deeper problems of American society. Former President Clinton in an ABC interview said, 'You can't have an emergency plan that works if it only affects middle-class people up' (*International Herald Tribune*, 19 September 2005). Clinton pointed out that the tax cuts for the rich and the welfare cut for the poor in the preceding decade made the poor people poorer who did not have the means to evacuate to safety.

Yet the link between poverty and social collapse may not be automatic. The case of impoverished Bangladesh is illustrative. Bangladesh is no stranger to floods and assorted calamities, yet in 1988 when a massive flood engulfed the elite part of the capital city Dhaka there was an unprecedented response. The government woke up to the realities of flood management that would protect the capital city, whereas the coastal regions of Bangladesh experience flood almost on an annual basis with little consequence and alarm on the part of the government (Khondker, 1992). The aftermath of floods in Bangladesh often show a high degree of fellow-feeling – an aspect of social capital that remains unnoticeable in everyday life. Civil society organizations spring to action spontaneously cross-cutting socio-economic classes. Only on rare occasions do the authorities have to worry about social collapse. A number of commentators in Bangladesh press suggested how the lessons of Bangladesh could be used in handling flood disasters in the USA.

The Asian tsunami of 2004 also revealed a number of interesting social, cultural, and political processes. Both Indonesia and Thailand were recently restored democracies that had to encounter this challenge. In Sri Lanka, as in Indonesia, the disaster hit regions that were experiencing civil unrest emanating from years of separatist movements. One of the positive outcomes in Aceh which was the hardest hit disaster area was the arrival of a peaceful settlement in August 2005.

However, crimes were not unknown – though not rampant – to the victims of the Asian tsunami. The BBC reported that given the scale of the disaster, it was remarkable that only isolated examples of crime had emerged. But for the already traumatized victims, the impact can be devastating. There are already reports of looting in many of the affected countries – with homes, shops, and even dead bodies being targeted. In Sri Lanka, some of the disaster victims have allegedly been raped in refugee camps.

One of the most disturbing allegations is that criminal gangs were befriending children orphaned by the tsunami, and selling them to sex traffickers. The Indonesian government has banned children under the age of 16 from being transferred from the devastated province of Aceh amid fears that trafficking syndicates were moving into the area. UNICEF (the children's agency) said it had received several reports of criminals offering kidnapped children from Aceh for sale or adoption.

A spokesman for UNICEF in Indonesia, John Budd, said there had been one confirmed case of a child being smuggled from the devastated Indonesian province of Aceh to the nearby city of Medan for trafficking purposes (http: //news.bbc.co.uk/2/hi/asia-pacific/4145591.stm [accessed on 15 September 2005]).A women's group in Sri Lanka said rapists were preying on homeless survivors. 'We have received reports of incidents of rape, gang rape, molestation and physical abuse of women and girls in the course of unsupervised rescue operations and while resident in temporary shelters', the Women and Media Collective group said. Save the Children warned that youngsters orphaned by the tsunami were vulnerable to sexual exploitation. 'The experience of earlier catastrophes is that children are especially exposed', said its Swedish chief, Charlotte Petri Gornitzka.

> In Thailand thieves disguised as police and rescue workers have looted luggage and hotel safes around Khao Lak beach, where the tsunami killed up to 3,000 people. Sweden sent seven police officers there to investigate the reported kidnapping of a Swedish boy of age 12 years whose parents were carried off by the wave.
> (http: //uk.news.yahoo.com/050103/325/f9k58.html
> [accessed on 15 September 2005])

The incidents of crime and preying on the victims are not limited to the American disasters anymore. The crimes reflect social blights and failures of governance which have taken on global proportions. Apart from the failures of everyday governance, it also touches on the issues of the relationship between state and its citizens. Rev. Jesse Jackson, amongst others, was peeved by the media reference of the evacuees as 'refugees'. He reminded the press that they are citizens of the United States and not refugees.

'It is racist to call American citizens refugees', the Rev. Jesse Jackson said, visiting the Houston Astrodome on Monday. Members of the Congressional Black Caucus have expressed similar sentiments. Others have countered that the terms 'evacuees' or even 'displaced' are too clinical and not sufficiently dramatic to convey the dire situation that confronts many of Katrina's survivors.

President Bush, who spent days trying to deflect criticism that he responded sluggishly to the disaster, came to address the problem. 'The people we're talking about are not refugees', he said. 'They are Americans, and they need the help and love and compassion of our fellow citizens' (www.msnbc.msn.com/id/9232071/#storyContinued [accessed 15 September 2005]).

In the aftermath of the Turkish earthquake of 17 August 1999, known as the Izmit earthquake, it was found out that the citizens received assistance only after a prolonged period of negotiations with the authority. This problem shows that citizenship is more than a juridical matter; it also entails traditional rights. In many situations, the entitlements of the victims of a disaster cannot be taken for granted. In the American case, the Hurricane also exposed the issue of the rights of citizenship and the links between social class and the enjoyment of citizenship entitlements. The poor in New Orleans were denizens without access to their complete citizenship rights which were undercut by economic deprivations.

The slowness of the response from the federal government and the practice of finger pointing where the Mayor of New Orleans blamed the State Governor and both pointed fingers to Washington, DC created a political crisis in the middle of a humanitarian calamity. The fact that President Bush was vacationing did not help either. However, once the barrage of media criticism, international attention and public outrage pushed the US government into action, it acted decisively. The chief of Federal Emergency Management Agency (FEMA) was fired for his lethargic response and massive search and recovery plans were implemented. President Bush, having had only an aerial view of the initial disaster, returned to onsite inspection thus regaining part of his lost public ratings.

Globalization of disaster response

The international response was both generous and widespread reflecting another aspect of globalization. Singapore committed its military helicopters usually based in the US for training purposes which with Asian alacrity went into immediate action. Air Canada mounted a massive help line. India, Cuba, Venezuela, Kuwait, Bangladesh, and even Afghanistan came up with financial assistance not so much to provide material aid but to express solidarity with the suffering people in the most powerful nation of the world. Symbolic though it was, it was unprecedented.

Such disasters remind us that vulnerability is the basis of our common humanity. The collective, global response to such crises also points to the emergence of an incipient global moral system. Although the disasters befell New Orleans or coastal regions of Bangladesh, they are by no means local disasters. Scientists have argued that global warming has contributed to the frequency of tornados and cyclones in recent years.

In one sense 9/11 can be seen as a major 'man-made' disaster. In the USA Hurricane Katrina also alerted us to the importance of disasters caused by nature and complicated by society. In 2004 the Asian tsunami affected not only several Asian countries but involved hordes of European tourists who were on vacation in Thailand and elsewhere in Sri Lanka and Bali. People who are not necessarily familiar with natural disasters such as surges of the ocean had a first-hand experience of natural calamities. The response to the disaster was global as the tragedy itself was global affecting a large number of countries and affecting people of any nations.

The globalization of disaster response has been linked in part to the role of the media in bringing the news of disaster to the living rooms of those who were lucky to avoid

241

such disaster spots. In the 1980s when Ethiopia and several other African countries were in the throes of famine, a massive humanitarian appeal was made by a number of musicians and aid-workers who organized 'Band Aid'. This was a milestone event, linking people in the West who were ready to help and the plight of the victims of famine.

At one level, it is ironic that people starve in times of global affluence. Yet, the response was a sure sign of a global sentiment – a vindication of what we will call a global morality. The world is not completely devoid of generosity. The idea of a global moral economy (Khondker, 1984) was an elaboration of the approach of E. P. Thompson and James Scott who found norms of reciprocity in early England and in Southeast Asia. The norms of reciprocity and their discovery by historians and anthropologists questioned the economic rationality and the transactional or exchange model of society. Historians have shown how economies are embedded in societies. At the heart of social organization, there lies a moral nexus. With modernization and growing individualization, the moral system transforms society – to use the terminology of Émile Durkheim – from a system of social solidarity that is mechanical to an organic phase. Society is hardly able to survive without a moral framework. It is likely that a global moral economy is a viable response to the problems besetting the world.

Environmental crises have been at the forefront of international headlines for quite some time, at least since the 1970s. Books such as *The Silent Spring* (Carson, 1962) or *The Poverty of Power* (Commoner, 1976) played an important role in creating awareness about the plight of the earth's ecological condition. In this regard, the movie made by Al Gore *An Inconvenient Truth* (2006) played a significant role in shocking people to accept the reality of the crisis. Yet, this has been a highly politicized issue. When George W. Bush became the president of the United States with some help from the US Supreme Court in 2000, one of the first acts of the newly elected president was to withdraw from commitment to the Kyoto Protocol which had been achieved through hard negotiations. The Protocol had been based on a collective responsibility to stem the deterioration of the ecological system by reducing emission of greenhouse gases to the atmosphere.

Scientists have predicted long-term climatic change for a number of years. Public-minded scientists have always predicted a scenario where economic and political matters are implicated in causing environmental degradation. The ecosystem in their view was part of a more complex and larger historical system. Even before the term 'ecology' – a term borrowed from botany – was coined, historians paid a great deal of attention to geographical factors. In that view the geographical system was a limiting and in some cases, an enabling factor; it was not acted upon. The idea that human action can change nature had novel implications.

While it is well known that reckless economic development in China has put China's ecosystem at risk, it is not well known that China is also taking important step towards containing ecological damage. In other societies such counter measures are often the result of democratic mobilization and the action of the civil societies. In that respect democracies have a natural advantage. The case of Indian civil society organizations in resisting a mega-project that threatened the ecosystem as well as the economic livelihood of many illustrates this difference. In China, the resistance against the Three Gorges Dam project was feeble at best and the state could go ahead with the project as scheduled. In India, such mega projects as the Narmada project was shelved or adjusted in part owing to the mobilization of NGOs and public intellectuals. Such prominent cultural figures as Arundhati Roy and Shabana Azmi as well as NGO activists all help play a part in social mobilization and activism.

Conclusion

Over the years, an increasing number of musicians and popular figures have joined in the fight against hunger and related disasters. In the 1980s Live Aid, where the leading pop artists from Europe and North America took part in concerts, raised funds to help famine victims in Africa. Bob Geldof in the UK launched a crusade against hunger in Africa and his efforts have resulted in an enhanced global awareness of the poverty and famine crisis in Africa. Globalized mass media and popular culture joined hands in aiding disaster management and raising global awareness of the problems of development in the poorer regions of the world. The rise of world-wide disasters coincided with global responses to disasters often bolstered by the global civil society point to the possibility of the emergence of a global moral economy.

References

Alamgir, M. 1980. *Famine in South Asia*. Cambridge: Oelgeschlager.

Appleby, A. B. 1978. *Famine in Tudor and Stuart England*. Stanford: Stanford University Press.

Baker, G. W. and Chapman, W. D. (eds) 1962. *Man and Society in Disaster*. New York: Basic Books.

Barton, A. H. 1970. *Communities in Disaster*. Garden City, NY: Anchor, Doubleday.

Beck, U. 1992. *Risk Society*. London: Sage.

Bell, D. 1987. 'The World and the United States in 2017', *Daedalus*, 116(3): 1–31.

Bhatia, B. M. 1967. *Famines in India*. Bombay: Asia Publishing House.

Carson, R. 1962. *The Silent Spring*. New York: Houghton Mifflin.

Comfort, L. K. 1988. *Managing Disaster: Strategies and Policy Perspectives*. Durham: Duke University Press.

Commoner, B. 1976. *The Poverty of Power*. New York: Alfred Knopf.

DeParle, J., 2005. 'What Happens to a Race Deferred', *New York Times*, 4 September.

Drabek, T. E. 1986. *Human System Responses to Disaster*. New York: Springer-Verlag.

Dreze, J and Sen, A. K. 1989. *Hunger and Public Action*. Oxford: Clarendon Press.

Dynes, R. R. 1974. *Organized Behavior in Disaster*. Lexington, MA: Heath.

——2000. 'The Dialogue between Voltaire and Rousseau on the Lisbon Earthquake: The Emergence of a Social Science View', *International Journal of Mass Emergencies and Disasters*, 18(1): 97–115.

Edwards, R. D. and Williams, T. D. 1976. *The Great Famine*. New York: Russell and Russell.

Erikson, K. 1976. *Everything in Its Path*. New York: Simon and Schuster.

Fisher, H. H. 1935. *The Famine in Soviet Russia*. Stanford, CA: Stanford University Press.

Franke, R.W. and Chasin, B. 1980. *Seeds of Famine*. Montclair, NJ: Allanheld and Osmun.

Fritz, C. E. 1961. 'Disasters', in *Social Problems,* ed. R. Merton and R. Nisbet, pp. 651–94. New York: Harcourt, Brace and World.

Giddens, Anthony 1999. 'Risk and Responsibility', *Modern Law Review*, 62(1): 1–10.

Gore, A. 2006. *An Inconvenient Truth: The Plaentary Emergency of Global Warming and What We Can Do about It*. Emmaus, PA: Roddale Press.

Goubert, P. 1970. *Louis XIV and Twenty Million Frenchmen*, translated by Anne Carter. New York: Random, Pantheon Books.

Greenough, P. 1982. *Prosperity and Misery in Modern Bengal*. New York: Oxford University Press.

Khondker, H. H. 1984. 'Governmental Response to Famine: A Case Study of the 1974 Famine in Bangladesh', PhD Thesis at the University of Pittsburgh, USA.

——1989. 'The 1984–85 Ethiopian Famine' in Rosenthal, U., Charles, M. and Hart, P. (eds) *Coping With Crisis: The Management of Disasters, Riots and Terrorism*. Springfield, IL: Charles C. Thomas, pp. 278 – 299.

——1992. 'Floods and Politics in Bangladesh', in *Natural Hazards Observer*, 16(4), March: 4–6.

Kreps, G. A. 1984. 'Sociological Inquiry and Disaster Research', *Annual Review of Sociology*, 10: 309–30.

Ladurie, E. Le Roy. 1973. *Times of Feast, Times of Famine*. New York: Doubleday.

Loveday, A. 1908. *The History and Economics of Indian Famines*. London: G. Bell.

Mallory, W. H. 1928. *China: Land of Famine*. New York: American Geographical Society.

Moreland, W. H. 1923. *From Akbar to Aurangzeb*. London: Macmillan.

Paddock, W. and Paddock, P. 1967. *Famine 1975!* Boston, MA: Little, Brown and Company.

Perrow, C. 1984. *Normal Accidents: Living with High-Risk Technologies*. New York: Basic Books.

Population Reference Bureau. 2008. *Data Sheet*.

Quarantelli, E. L. and Dynes, R. R. 1977. 'Response to Social Crisis and Disaster', *Annual Review of Sociology*, 3: 23–49.

Robbins, R. G. 1975. *Famine in Russia, 1891–92*. New York: Columbia University Press.

Rosenthal, U., Charles, M. and Hart, P. 1989. *Coping With Crisis: The Management of Disasters, Riots and Terrorism*. Springfield, IL: Charles C. Thomas.

Sen, A. K. 1981. *Poverty and Famine*. Oxford: Clarendon Press.

Sheperd, J. 1975. *The Politics of Starvation*. New York: Carnegie Endowment for International Peace.

Short, J. F. 1984. 'The Social Fabric of Risk: Toward the Social Transformation of Risk Analysis', *American Social Review*, 49: 711–25.

Sobhan, R. 1979. 'Politics of Food and Famine in Bangladesh', in *Economic and Political Weekly*, XIV, No. 48, Bombay,

Sorokin, P. A. 1942. *Man and Society in Calamity*. New York: E. P. Dutton & Co., Inc.

——1975. *Hunger as a Factor in Human Affairs*. Gainesville, FL: University Press of Florida.

Stallings, R. A. 1978. 'The Structural Patterns of Four Types of Organizations in Disaster', pp. 87–103 in E. L. Quarantelli (ed,) *Disasters: Theory and Research*. Beverly Hills, CA: Sage.

Sunderland, J. T. 1900. 'The Cause of Indian Famines', *New England Magazine*, September, 23(1): 50–60.

Turner, B. A. 1978. *Man-Made Disasters*. London: Wykeham www.msnbc.msn.com/id/9163091/USGS (United States Geological Survey).

13

The globalization of crime

Robert Winslow and Virginia Winslow

Introduction

In the text *Criminology: A Global Perspective* we maintain that "crime comes from everywhere and goes everywhere" (Winslow and Zhang 2008: 25). By implication, one cannot understand crime in one country without studying crime globally or internationally. The global or international study of crime is called *comparative criminology*. *Criminology: A Global Perspective* is a global study of crime from the United States point of view. Similarly, in this chapter on the globalization of crime, we will be studying the globalization of crime from the US point of view, based, in part, upon the fact that the US is a major player in economic globalization (Central Intelligence Agency 2008). In saying that one cannot understand crime in one country without studying it globally, we are saying that US criminology should become comparative criminology. Adler, Mueller, and Laufer indicate the need for global criminology in the following quote:

> Crime, like life itself, has become globalized, and responses to law-breaking have inevitably extended beyond local and national boarders ... the countries of the world gradually became more interdependent. Commercial relations among countries increased. The jet age brought a huge increase in international travel and transport. Satellite communications facilitated intense and continuous public and private relationships. The internet added the final touch to globalization ... These developments, which turned the world into what has been called a "global village," have also had considerable negative consequences. As everything else in life became globalized, so did crime. Transnational crimes ... suddenly boomed. ... many apparently purely local crimes, whether local drug crime or handgun violence, now have international dimensions ... Consequently, national criminology had to become international criminology. *Criminology has in fact been globalized* ... Economic globalization, as much as it promotes useful commerce, also aids organized crime and fosters the global spread of frauds ... Consider that drugs produced abroad and distributed locally create a vast problem of crime: Not

only is drug dealing illegal, but a considerable portion of street crime is associated with narcotics.

(Adler et al. 2004: 18–19, 386)

Just as US criminology is provincial in nature, so is US criminal justice in the sense that the US criminal justice system departs from the civil law justice model used by most other developed nations (Winslow and Zhang 2008: 21). The US system of justice is based partly upon British common law and partly upon Puritan evangelical beliefs, a system lagging behind the fast-changing largely secular civil law legal systems of the majority of the countries of the world.

There are essentially five legal systems in the world. These include (a) civil law, (b) common law, (c) Islamic law, (d) socialist law, and (e) customary law systems. These are discussed in descriptions of the countries of the world on a global criminology website linked to this article. The website, which we term the Comparative Criminology Website, can be located at http://www.rohan.sdsu.edu/faculty/rwinslow/index.html. The two dominant legal systems are the civil law and common law systems, while the remaining three systems generally exist in combination with the first two (see Table 1.1 entitled "Legal Systems of the World's Countries," in Winslow and Zhang 2008: 21). Due to their dominance in the world, the focus in this chapter will be upon the civil law and common law legal systems.

Civil law systems (not to be confused with American civil vs. criminal courts) resulted from the Roman legal tradition of codifying law done originally by the 6th century Roman emperor Justinian. Subsequently, Napoleon developed a similar written law known as *Code Civil* or Code Napoleon, proclaimed in 1804. What characterizes a civil law system is that it is written law and is revolutionary in nature, because when a new code is developed in civil law countries, all prior law is repealed. Civil law systems characterize most European countries and are generally associated with parliamentary forms of government in which the legislative branch of the government is the most powerful branch. Civil law systems have an obvious advantage of being able to quickly adapt to newly emerging crimes, such as terrorism or computer crimes, because laws to control such crimes can be quickly passed and enforced with less possibility of judicial nullification. Courts in civil law countries typically do not use juries to decide innocence or guilt, and focus upon determining the facts of the case rather than whether or not due process has been followed (Reichel 2005: 109–23).

Common law systems are sometimes referred to as being based, historically, upon a tradition of unwritten law. *Common law* developed in Britain to resolve conflicts between landlords and vassals (tenants) during feudalism. Essentially, common law courts, with the aid of a jury of peers, settled disputes on the basis of what was customary. What evolved was the principle of *stare decisis*, which meant that the court was expected to abide by previously decided cases. Based upon the principle of *stare decisis*, it is difficult to overturn existing laws and prior court decisions. Thus, in common law countries, laws supporting traditional morality are more likely to continue, while new laws pertaining to new social problems are less likely to be developed than in civil law countries. While legislated law is given priority in civil law countries, the judiciary is given much more power in common law countries.

Being a common law country, America is to some extent bound by tradition, based upon the principle of *stare decisis*. Thus, much of what was defined as crime during colonial days became a basis for case law precedent in modern America. An important point to highlight is that America was founded initially by Puritans, a fundamentalist Protestant sect who escaped to the colonies to avoid religious persecution. The Puritans were advocates of the Protestant Reformation in England. They were persecuted by English royals, such as Queen Mary I, because the royals wanted to retain much of Catholic liturgy and ritual forms, whereas the Puritans wanted to suppress remaining Catholic forms. The Puritans developed an extreme form of Protestantism when they formed their independent colony at Massachusetts Bay in 1630. The Puritans criminalized moral offenses such as fornication, adultery, misbehavior on the Sabbath, consumption of alcohol, and idleness, and sanctioned violation of the moral code with extreme penalties.

The Puritan experiment in Massachusetts ended in 1700 after England took actions to regularize the legal systems of the colonies, which were found to be divergent from those of English common law (McClendon 1990). Nevertheless, the early Puritan experiment left an indelible stamp upon American culture. From time to time, the return to fundamentalist harsh punishments for moral offenses has occurred in the US in the form of evangelical moral enterprise culminating in today's "War on Drugs."

The scope of this analysis

Due to space limitations, the focus of our analysis here will be upon selected crimes. We will spend less time in this chapter studying crimes that are only crimes in a minority of countries, and will, instead, restrict our analysis to acts that are recognized as crimes by international organizations such as the United Nations, Interpol, and the World Health Organization. We will also focus on crimes that are considered to be serious crimes in the US. These include the seven major crimes in the FBI's index of crime: (1) murder and nonnegligent manslaughter, (2) forcible rape, (3) robbery, (4) aggravated assault, (5) burglary, (6) larceny-theft, and (7) motor vehicle theft. These crimes have the virtue of including two of the three criteria of seriousness, bodily harm and theft, determined by Sellin and Wolfgang, that were agreed upon through measurement of public opinion on the topic of what is a serious crime. The three criteria of a serious crime they found to be *bodily harm, property damage, and theft* (Sellin and Wolfgang 1964: 62–70). Another advantage of accepting this typology of offenses is that they are represented in the international databases assembled by both the United Nations and Interpol. Because the FBI's Index Crimes are considered to be serious both in domestic public opinion research and internationally by the United Nations and Interpol surveys, they will serve as a framework for the organization of this article.

Does the U.S. have the highest rate of crime in the world? Where does the US stand in terms of violent crime? What about property crime—theft? The answer is *no* to all three questions. In a database developed from Interpol and UN data posted on the Comparative Criminology Website, the US ranks 12th out of 165 countries in the world in its overall Crime Index. In terms of violent crime, the US ranked 19th out of 164 countries of the world, which is not even in the top 10 percent. The US ranks 13th out of 160 countries in terms of theft (burglary, motor vehicle theft, and larceny-theft), which is near the bottom of the top 10 percent of nations (Winslow and Zhang 2008: 31–32).

The globalization of street crimes

Today, even ordinary street crimes normally thought of as localized can be influenced by globalization. We will focus in this discussion upon the serious crimes of murder, forcible rape, robbery, aggravated assault, and theft.

Murder

Historically, countries that have the highest murder rates are those who have high rates of socioeconomic inequality traced to the colonialism of European powers, while today, the domination of the US in the world is making an additional impact upon murder rates.

Historically, the domination of colonial powers led to enhanced socioeconomic inequality in countries dominated by colonial powers which, in turn, led to higher rates of murder in those countries. Today, one can point to South Africa as a country with nearly the highest rate of both inequality and murder in the world. The high degree of social inequality that exists in South Africa today is a historical product of colonialism. Starting in 1488, Portuguese, Dutch, French Huguenot refugees, and Germans settled in the Cape of Good Hope, collectively forming the Afrikaner segment of today's population. Subsequent British settlement, stimulated by the discovery of diamond and gold deposits, led to conflict between the Afrikaners and the English, culminating in the Anglo–Boer Wars in 1880 and 1899, won by the British who subsequently formed the Union of South Africa, a dominion of the British Empire (Winslow and Zhang 2008: 206). In 1948, the National Party won the all-white elections and began passing, codifying, and enforcing a strict policy of white domination and racial separation known as *apartheid* (separateness), thus enhancing socioeconomic inequality based upon race. Subsequently, guerrilla warfare and popular uprisings characterized South Africa, even after the election of Nelson Mandela in the first nonracial elections held in 1994. After Mandela's election, right-wing terrorists, including groups such as the White Liberation Army, the White Republican Army, the Boer Republican Army, the White Wolves, and the Order of the Boer Nation, have claimed responsibility for some thirty-five bombings. Currently, the high rate of violence in South Africa is related to taxi drivers' street rivalries, vigilante action and mob justice, murders of farm families and of black farm laborers, and witchcraft-related incidents. Human rights organizations have claimed that rural police and courts refuse to arrest or prosecute white perpetrators of crimes against the black workers and farm families. Evidence exists that, of all racial groups, the blacks are the most victimized by violent crime in South Africa. A 1981 survey revealed that 20 percent of the black respondents, 10 percent of colored, 5 percent of Indian, and 2 percent of white respondents reported being victims of assault (Winslow and Zhang 2008: 207–8). The administration of Nelson Mandela helped to heal the wounds created by apartheid through creating a Truth and Reconciliation Committee and began to reintroduce South Africa into the global economy through implementing a market-driven economic plan known as Growth, Employment and Redistribution (GEAR). However, this plan ironically opened South Africa to the drug trade, with the trappings of violent and property crime that go with it.

Today, the domination of the US in world markets has affected an expansion of the domain of US policies, impacting murder in countries around the world. Just as the drug trade is beginning to affect violence in South Africa, it has, for some time, contributed to the high rate of murder in Colombia. Just as in South Africa, whites constitute a minority of the population who, nevertheless, control the government as they do throughout South America. White minority rule and inequality constitutes a backdrop for much of the violence that has occurred in Colombia through the years. In terms of inequality, as measured by the Gini Index (a measure of socioeconomic inequality in which high scores indicate higher inequality), Colombia ranks 9th of 118 countries for which data are available, while South Africa ranks 7th, with Gini Indices of 57.1 for Colombia and 59.3 for South Africa (Winslow 2003). South Africa's white minority rule probably led to greater inequality in that country compared to Colombia, because it was backed by *apartheid*, which imposed strict legal barriers enforcing segregation not found in South America, which also permits greater intermarriage than found in South Africa (Wikipedia 2008). By way of comparison, the US has a Gini rate of 40.8. One of the strongest demographic correlates of murder internationally has been the Gini Index with a correlation coefficient of .41 using Interpol data and .57 using World Health Organization (WHO) data (Winslow and Zhang 2008: 203).

Colombia is second in the world to South Africa in its murder rate (Winslow and Zhang 2008: 208). Colombia is, perhaps, an example of a country's attempt to curtail the drug trade contributing to high homicide rates, since that government has been battling drug cartels, as well as narcoterrorist organizations, for some time and has received US support in its effort. Class conflict has been even more problematic in Colombia, and Colombia's government has been less successful than other South American governments in suppressing guerrilla organizations, historically, as well as in dealing with narcoterrorist organizations, since the 1960s. In Colombia the police have supported paramilitary organizations that have attempted to battle left wing insurgencies. Colombia leads the world not only in its murder rate, but also in kidnappings, cocaine production, previously in marijuana production, and increasingly in heroin production. The chief market for Colombian drugs is the US, with Colombia benefiting both from its proximity to the US and easy accessibility to the US via Central America, as well as by sea and air.

Colombia has a long history of violence. Resulting from the bitter rivalry between the Conservative and Liberal parties, the War of a Thousand Days (1899–1902) cost an estimated 100,000 lives, and up to 300,000 people died during La Violencia of the late 1940s and 1950s. Starting in the 1960s, a link between the drug trade, terrorism, and murder developed in Colombia. An escalation of Colombian marijuana production began in the mid- and late 1960s as a result of the growing demand generated by the US market. When, in the early 1970s, the US tightened up drug enforcement along the US–Mexican boarder, and Mexico launched a major drive against its domestic producers, the epicenter of marijuana production in the hemisphere rapidly shifted to Colombia, which developed a similar percentage of the cocaine trade in the 1980s. By the end of the decade, Colombia accounted for about 70 percent of the marijuana reaching the US from abroad. The drug trade facilitated the development of numerous terrorist organizations in Colombia, including drug cartels, leftist guerrilla organizations, and paramilitary right-wing anti-guerrilla forces. Drug cartels that engaged in terrorist acts in Colombia included the Medellin Cartel and the Cali Cartel. The Cali Cartel had its own military wing.

Colombia's first generation of traffickers, the "cocaine cowboys" typified by Pablo Escobar's Medellin Cartel, trained legions of young assassins, kept mounds of cash in wicker baskets and concentrated operations in specific regions. Flaunting their wealth and defying authorities, they went down in flames in the early 1990s with the death of Medellin cartel leader Pablo Escobar in a police shootout in 1993.

Both leftist anti-government guerrilla organizations and right wing paramilitary organizations arising to combat the leftist groups have engaged in acts of terrorism and have been financed through drugs. The leftist groups included the Revolutionary Armed Forces of Colombia (FARC), the 19th of April Movement (M019), the National Liberation Army (ELN), and the Popular Liberation Army (EPL). The ELN was formed in 1965 by Cuban inspired urban intellectuals and is financed through drugs and the Iranian-backed "Hezbollah of Colombia and Venezuela" (Cromwell 2003). FARC was established in 1964 as a military wing of the Colombian Communist Party, with 9,000–12,000 armed members, operating with impunity throughout much of the country. The FARC has become increasingly involved in the illegal drug trade, including both the processing and the exporting of cocaine.

The FARC was said to demand as much as $15,000 per flight of every drug-carrying plane that takes off from an airstrip that they guard. The drug cartels were willing to pay the guerrillas $20,000 for every plane or helicopter involved in anti-narcotics operations that is shot down (Macko 1996). Right-wing terrorist groups became increasingly active during the Barco administration and repeatedly targeted for assassination many public officials and guerrilla organizations. Several groups have distinguished themselves for their national-level operations. The most prominent of these were Death to Kidnappers (MAS) and the Extraditables (Los Extraditables), both of which had ties to the narcotics traffickers. Non-governmental organizations have attributed a large majority of political killings, social cleansing killings, and forced disappearances to paramilitary groups. According to military estimates, the United Self-Defense Forces of Colombia (AUC), a paramilitary umbrella organization, has a membership of 8,000 and 11,000 combatants. The AUC exercised increasing influence during the year 2001 and fought to extend its presence through violence and intimidation into areas previously under guerrilla control while conducting selective killings of civilians whom it alleged collaborated with guerrillas. Throughout the country, paramilitary groups killed, tortured, and threatened civilians suspected of sympathizing with guerrillas in an orchestrated campaign to terrorize them into fleeing their homes, to deprive guerrillas of civilian support and allow paramilitary forces to challenge FARC and ELN for control of narcotics cultivations and strategically important territories. They also fought guerrillas for control of some lucrative coca-growing regions and engaged directly in narcotics production and trafficking. On the other hand, the FARC and ELN regularly attacked civilian populations, committed massacres and summary executions, and killed medical and religious personnel. In many places, guerrillas collected "war taxes," forced members of the citizenry into their ranks, forced small farmers to grow illicit crops, and regulated travel, commerce, and other activities.

Both South Africa and Colombia demonstrate the conditions leading to extremely high rates of murder. These conditions include very high rates of inequality and a history of colonial domination by one race (whites) over another (blacks in the case of South Africa, Indians or Mestizos in the case of Colombia). While these conditions lead to anger and hatred between the underclass and elites, they are not solely responsible for high rates of murder. What led to violence in these two countries was the development of opposition groups (pro and antigovernment) with the means to engage in widespread combat. While the Zulus of South Africa may have carried out some murders using knives and spears, semi-automatic guns are much more effective in waging guerrilla warfare, and these are expensive. It takes money to wage civil warfare on the level of South Africa and Colombia. In the case of Colombia, that money was supplied by the trade in drugs, and in South Africa, drugs are augmenting "conflict diamonds" as a source of funding violence.

One point referred to in both country profiles above is the role of the police in "extra-judicial killings," as well as the support by the police for pro-government paramilitary and/or vigilante groups.

How does this observation apply to the US? The objection may be raised that police violence and vigilante activity cannot account for America's relatively high rate of murder. It is true that it is difficult to investigate extralegal killings by police in America due to the geographical dispersion of the police, as well as the lack of civilian oversight in regard to police activities in the US. However, vigilante activities in the US date back to the legendary "lynch laws" of the nineteenth century. There can be no doubt that vigilante groups, such as the Ku Klux Klan, skinheads, and militias, are quite active in America. Furthermore, retaliatory violence on the part of urban youth gangs is often construed by the gangs as vigilante activity. Thus, it seems logical that investigation of police and/or vigilante violence may yield fresh incites into the relatively higher rate of murder in the US when the US is compared with other developed nations.

Forcible rape

Forcible rape is an international crime when it occurs during wartime and when it is associated with international trafficking in persons. Throughout history, soldiers of conquering armies have assumed that sexual intercourse with their enemies' women was one of the spoils of war. During warfare, rapes of women were socially acceptable as part of the rules of warfare among the ancient Greeks and even by knights and pilgrims during the Crusades (Siegel 2004: 329). Some 200,000 Korean women were raped by the Japanese army during World War II, as were some 20,000 Chinese women during the "Rape of Nanking" in 1937. In 1971, Pakistani soldiers raped an estimated 200,000 to 400,000 Bengali women during East Bengal's war of independence, after which it became Bangladesh (Neill 2000). Rape has been used as a tool of war in a variety of armed conflicts such as those in Algeria, India, Indonesia, Liberia, Rwanda, and Uganda (Krug et al. 2002: 156). Data from the Office of the United Nations High Commissioner for Refugees indicate that among the "boat people" who fled Vietnam in the late 1970s and early 1980s, 39 percent of the women were abducted or raped by pirates while at sea (Swiss and Giller 1993). The Serbian army engaged in "genocidal rape" of Bosnian and Kosovar women during the civil war in the former Yugoslavia. Rape in this case was sometimes intentionally used to impregnate Bosnian women with Serbian children (Allen 1996). While some assume that the US military would never become involved in wartime rape, it has been charged that US servicemen in Vietnam did, in fact, engage in rape. From the individual rape of barroom girls in Saigon to the mass rape and murder of dozens of civilian women in the village of My Lai, the Criminal Investigative Division of the US Army is rife with documentation concerning abuses by Americans. Beyond the brutality of rape, however, was the American military's involvement in the commercial sex business. In order to maintain soldiers' morale in fighting an unpopular war, the Pentagon knowingly allowed the formation of brothels on base camps throughout Vietnam. Military authorities also organized thinly veiled "sex tours" for Army troops, sailors, airmen, and Marines on leave in Thailand, the Philippines, Taiwan, and other locales (Neill 2000: 4).

251

There is some evidence of a link between wartime involvements in rape and rape in the homeland of combatant countries as a byproduct of war. A study of questionnaires filled out from calls to the SOS Hotline for Women and Children in Serbia revealed that the frequency and duration of violence toward women was increased as result of men's participation in the wars in Croatia and Bosnia. The majority of incidents involved physical and verbal/emotional violence, while a minority involved sexual and economic violence. A large amount of violence against women was that of sons against their mothers (Mrsevic and Hughes 1997).

While it is not suggested here that all rape is a product of wartime military involvement, a rising trend in rape during or immediately after a war is a hypothesis that should be investigated. In addition to actual war experience of rape of military personnel based on opportunity and role modeling, military personnel may become involved in trafficking in women as a product of their military experience. Between the early 1950s and early 1990s, over 100,000 Korean women immigrated to the US as wives of US servicemen. An estimated 80 percent of Korean–G.I. marriages resulted in divorce, and a large number of the women entered the sex trafficking circuits in the US. US servicemen have been paid by traffickers to marry women in Korea and bring them to the US for use in massage parlors and brothels here. In addition, some servicemen are reported to be involved in direct trafficking of women, not only from Korea, but also from Vietnam and Okinawa, Japan. The rise in numbers of sex establishments around military bases has been linked to the Vietnam War period. At that time, Fayetteville, North Carolina, with the largest military base in the US, became known as "Fayettenam." The red light district of the town came to resemble the prostitution areas for the US military on R and R (rest and recreation) leave in Saigon. Street prostitution is also common in military towns. Prostitution around military bases is facilitated by military personnel when military men marry prostitutes around military bases abroad, bring them back the US, and coerce them to engage in prostitution (Raymond and Hughes 2001: 38, 48, 52; Winslow and Zhang 2008: 528). The relationship between trafficking and rape is that trafficking in women by military personnel is invariably for purposes of prostitution, and such women are typically abused, sexually exploited, and coerced into prostitution. In other words, the women were often forcibly raped as a means of initiating them into prostitution.

Robbery

Robbery is another crime that is considered to be domestic in origin, but which can also have a strong international component. Among international components may be migration of potential robbers from a foreign country, the use of a foreign country as a hideout for robbers wanted in another country, and the enforcement of drug laws "imported" from a foreign country, i.e. drug laws of the US and related displacement of crime (from a less serious to more serious crime).

In the US, children of immigrants from war-torn countries have been involved in robbery. Examples of this include Southeast Asian gang members in the US from Vietnam, Cambodia, and Laos who are known to commit home invasion robberies (HIR). Also included would be the *chapulines* (grasshoppers) of Costa Rica and Haitian immigrants in the Bahamas.

While Asians in the US often have been portrayed as largely exempt, from crime living in "Oriental enclaves" insulated from criminalizing outside influences (Winslow 1968:

156–57), during the past 25 years, youth from refugee families, from such war-torn countries as Laos, Cambodia, and Vietnam, have formed the basis for Asian gangs that have specialized in home invasion robberies. One study based upon law enforcement sources portrayed the Asian gangs as "home invaders," who travel across the US robbing, terrorizing, and intimidating Asian families (Burke and O'Rear 1990). Another study found that Asian gang membership was traced to a breakdown in the traditional family structure. The gang members had experienced victimization and abuse in their families, which prompted the youth to seek gang membership as a source of support (Toy 1993).

The *chapulines* (grasshoppers) of Costa Rica, which has a high rate of recorded robbery, constitute another instance of immigrant robbers from other countries torn by civil disorder or war. The youngsters are mostly homeless children who use their numbers to steal from unwary passersby through rolling them or stripping them of valuables. While Costa Rica is 94 percent white in race, it is estimated that from 10 percent to 15 percent of the population is Nicaraguan and primarily Mestizos in origin (Winslow and Zhang 2008: 282). Perhaps the offenses of these children are influenced by Costa Rican's penal system because in Costa Rica the *chapulines* are considered too young to prosecute. However, it also seems likely that these children are refugees from countries such as Nicaragua, Guatemala, and Honduras where hundreds of children and youth have been murdered over the past several years by police, who target unidentified individuals and groups in a so-called effort of "social cleansing" (Costa Rica Staff 2002).

The high rate of robbery in the Bahamas may be traced to the existence of "stateless children" (not recognized as citizens by either Haiti or the Bahamas), migrants from Haiti, who have emigrated illegally from Haiti, seeking a better life in the Bahamas (Treco 2002). The stateless children are not recorded in the census of the Bahamas, but they and other recent immigrants, totaling as high as 60,000, are blamed for the high rate of crime because their numbers contribute to a high rate of unemployment in the Bahamas (Jelsoft Enterprises Ltd. 2008).

Migration *from* a foreign country is not the only international link to robbery. Foreign countries are often used as hideouts for robbers who are being pursued by the police, who lack jurisdiction in the foreign country. Once their crime becomes a "cold case," the robbers then return to their country of origin. For the US, Mexico has often been used as a hideout for robbers, since the early days of bank and train robbery in the old West. In England, one of the leaders of the gang that pulled off the Great Train Robbery of 1963, Ronnie Biggs, after being imprisoned for the crime, escaped from prison and was smuggled across the English Channel to Belgium, where he underwent plastic surgery to hide his identity, and was given money, new passports, and clothes. He then spent until 1968 with his family in Australia, after which he migrated to Panama and then to Rio de Janeiro (Bevan 2008). In Namibia, a gang known as the Red Eye Gang combines both elements of immigration and escape after a robbery. Famous cases of cash-in-transit armed robbery in Namibia include the Karibib Heist, involving one million Namibian dollars, and the Brakwater Heist of over six million Namibian dollars. Frequently, the criminals are from South Africa, and abscond to Angola, a country with which Namibia does not have formal extradition arrangements, as well as South Africa, where many Namibians still hold citizenship, which makes extradition nearly impossible (Winslow and Zhang 2008: 345).

Migration of crime-prone groups into a country and the use of foreign countries as hideouts are two important factors in the globalization of robbery; however, the export of US drug policy can impact countries outside of the US. This is because every country must make a choice in its criminal justice policy in enforcement of laws—essentially between enforcement of drug laws or laws pertaining to robbery—a *quid pro quo* decision-making process. A country's orientation in regard to drug laws can have an impact upon robbery and other crimes against property. If drugs are illegal, there will be a black market for prohibited drugs in which illicit drugs are sold at a highly inflated price compared with the cost of the manufacture of these drugs. Thus, potential thieves can make money through trafficking in drugs, or simply selling the drugs to friends and acquaintances. If a thief uses addictive illegal substances, his need for those drugs may increase to the point that selling drugs does not generate enough revenue to pay for the drugs he needs. He may then engage in petty theft and other crimes to raise the extra money. If the addict/thief becomes even more desperate, he may engage in robbery as a more certain and quick way of obtaining funds. He may go directly to the source of drugs by robbing a drug dealer, who possesses large sums of money and the drugs craved by the addict/thief. This vicious circle of drug addiction and robbery is what a country has to face when developing laws regarding drugs. If a large proportion of people in prison are there for possession or sale of drugs compared to robbery and a large proportion of persons convicted of robbery are released on probation to make room in prison for drug users, then the country has chosen drug prosecutions over robbery prosecutions. As a consequence of this, criminals will rationally engage in robbery as a crime of choice since it is relatively unsanctioned, compared to drug use. This process of punishing (in public opinion) a relatively less serious crime (possession or sale of drugs) more so than (in public opinion) a more serious crime (robbery) is a *quid pro quo* (something for something) choice taken by many countries that can exacerbate the countries' overall crime problem. If robbers go free while drug peddlers are confined in prison, then more crimes are committed by the robbers (robberies as well as other thefts), while drug peddlers receive a liberal education on crime in prison. Indeed, many criminologists consider prisons to be "schools for crime." Drug peddlers in prison will learn techniques for committing crimes, such as robbery, and can learn that robbery is relatively unsanctioned, and, when released, may graduate to the more serious crime of robbery. This process seems to have taken place, not only in the US, where the War on Drugs has led to unprecedented rates of imprisonment, but in countries outside of the US that have recently adopted US drug policies.

What we have suggested in the last paragraph is that in the US and many countries that have adopted the US drug policy, drug prosecution flourished while the prosecution of a serious crime, robbery, has been left by the wayside. William Chambliss has made a point about "instrumental" versus "expressive" offenses that actually shows that prioritization of drug offenses aggravates the situation still further because robbery is more amenable to penal sanction than drug offenses. He found that research findings show a low deterrent effect of legal punishment for offenses that involve a high commitment to crime as a way of life combined with involvement in an act that is "expressive" in the sense of being an end in itself (e.g., murder and illicit drug use). On the other hand are acts in which the commitment of the agent to crime is low and the act is "instrumental," i.e. a means to some other end. These crimes have a high capability of being deterred by the legal system. Robbery is said to be a good example of an "instrumental crime" in the sense that it is typically not done "for the fun of it" but as a means to another end (money, drugs, etc.) (Chambliss 1967). Application of deterrence theory in the case of robbery is not shown by America's criminal justice system. Clearance rates have remained steady at round 25 percent for the past decade. There is evidence of a 50 percent to 60 percent attrition rate (failure to convict) after arrest (Feeney, Dill, and Weir 1983). Furthermore, cases that do result in felony conviction may be "pled out." The result is often more lenient misdemeanor convictions and sentences of "local time" or probation rather than state prison. In California, a study done in 1980 indicated that jury trials for robbery had become rare, and that most sentences were the product of a plea bargain with the prosecution. This resulted in a lighter sentence, which was not likely to be state imprisonment (California Legislature Joint Committee for Revision of the Penal Code 1980). There are fairly clear examples of these increasing rates of "real crime" as a consequence of application of the US drug policy, not only in the US, but in countries outside the US. Several countries where this has happened include Portugal, Spain, Australia, and Great Britain.

One basis for the US War on Drugs is the assumption that the consumption of illicit drugs causes other forms of crime, both violent and property crime. If that assumption is true, then prosecution of use and sale of drugs should lead to a reduction in violent and property crime. However, a study of various countries leads to another conclusion, the *quid pro quo* finding referenced above. That is, the criminal justice system has only so many resources, so if drug offenses are vigorously prosecuted, then it is necessary to forgo the prosecution of other and often more serious offenses, such as robbery. What has happened to robbery and related crimes since various countries have joined the War on Drugs? From 1995 to 2001, Portugal increased its drug enforcement efforts, doubling its drug offenses from 27.72 per 100,000 inhabitants in 1995 to 54.54 in 2001. During this same time period, robbery increased by 137 percent, burglary by 167 percent, larceny by 287 percent, and motor vehicle theft by 371 percent. Rather than being a mere exchange of one crime for another, overall crime increased in Portugal from 529.3 to a much higher rate of 1,776.35 per 100,000 inhabitants during the same time period. A similar process has happened in Spain (Winslow 2003: Portugal) and Australia (Maher, Dixon, and Hall 2002). There is evidence that the experience of being in prison encourages drug use (Swann and James 1998), and one study even found that 22 percent of inmates in the study had begun using drugs in prison (Korte et al. 1998). Thus, the growth of imprisonment that has resulted from the War on Drugs may contribute to the link between robbery and drug addiction through actually adding to the amount of addiction among the criminal population. This contributes to rates of robbery outside of prison when the released and often unemployable inmates must support their drug habits through criminal means. In addition, knowledge of the techniques of committing the crime of robbery may have been acquired through time spent in incarceration. Thus, it seems that drug use causes crime primarily when drug users are incarcerated for that offense, increasing their association with other criminals. A similar process has occurred in Great Britain, a country that fought two Opium Wars with China, asserting its right to sell opium to that country. Just as China tried to do in the past, Britain has attempted to prohibit the trade in heroin, among other opiate derivatives. While Britain had a practice of prescribing heroin to addicts from the 1920s to the 1960s, in response to political pressure from the US, heroin maintenance was severely curtailed in 1971 with the passage in Britain of the Misuse of Drugs Act. The result was an unregulated illicit market and a jump in the number of heroin users from fewer than 2,000 in 1970 to upwards of 300,000 today (Drug Policy Alliance 2003). Along with that increase in addicts was a significant jump in crime, particularly property crime, in Britain. From 1981 to 1995 according to victim surveys done in Britain, robbery rose 81 percent (4.2 per 1,000 inhabitants, rising to 7.6) (Bureau of Justice Statistics 1998).

While Britain experienced an increase in robbery coinciding with its participation in the War on Drugs, Switzerland experienced the opposite effect when it experimented with a prescription heroin program that deviates from the US promulgated drug laws. Switzerland's rate of robbery in 2002 was 33.4 per 100,000 inhabitants—perhaps the lowest rate for developed countries. A possible explanation for this low rate is Switzerland's prescription program for heroin users, as well as a needle exchange program. A significant percentage of Switzerland's some 30,000 addicts are allowed to obtain heroin legally, in some cases, provided free of charge by the government. The heroin prescription program for addicts may very well have targeted the drug of choice for robbers (heroin), thus keeping the robbery crime rate low (Winslow, 2003: Switzerland). A study done in Switzerland, published in 1998, found that the number of heroin patients involved in muggings has decreased by more than 80 percent since the program of prescription heroin began in 1992. In addition to robbery, it was found that users had previously raised cash through selling hard drugs to consumers from their own social network. Thus, the Swiss heroin prescription program may be vital to breaking the link between dependence and resale to new consumer recruits (Killias and Rabasa 1998).

Critics of the War on Drugs have argued that the crack down on drugs has led to an increase in robbery in two ways. One is a reduction in prison sentences for robbers to make room for the increased population of drug offenders (Kykeon@lycaeum.org 1991). Critics have also argued that harsher enforcement of drug laws has resulted in robberies motivated by the drug addict's need to obtain money to pay for artificially higher-priced drugs (Hornberger 2000).

Assault

Assault seems like the epitome of a localized crime, typically resulting from family violence or a feud between members of rival gangs, occurring within local neighborhoods within a country. However, assault can also occur in one nation as a result of immigration policy or covert activities of another nation regarding the first nation's political activities.

Transnational assault occurs when a gang member or members from one nation go to another country to assault individuals or gang members in that nation. A current-day example of this is Mara Salvatrucha, or MS-13, which the FBI has declared to be the most dangerous gang in the US The MS-13 gang has cliques, or factions, located throughout the US and in other countries, but it is composed mostly of El Salvadorans and retains its ties to its El Salvadoran counterparts. This gang originated in El Salvador and was organized by convicted criminals deported by the US back to their country of origin, El Salvador (Wikipedia 2007).

The *deportation* of El Salvadoran gang members resulted, upon their return to the US, in assaulting US gangs in the case of MS-13. However, the *importation* of gang members from Jamaica into the US may have profoundly influenced gang violence in the form of the "drive-by shooting" during the 1980's. There is some evidence that the emergence of drive-by shootings and, in fact, the US cocaine epidemic may have been influenced by the immigration of Jamaican "posse" members (also called "Yardies") during the late 1970s and early 1980s. These events were said to be the unintended consequences of a US government covert operation in Jamaica gone awry, an example of what has come to be termed *blowback* by the intelligence community.[1] The "Yardies" were an outgrowth of Jamaican violent elections, starting out as gangs who would be given guns and money by political parties to ensure that certain communities would stay loyal or vote in a particular way. When the party supporting a particular gang lost power, the gang members moved abroad (typically to America or the UK) where they sold drugs, and then sent money to Jamaica to continue the fight (Thompson 2002: 2). Jamaican posses in the US sold Jamaican *ganja* (marijuana and hashish) during the 1970s, but subsequently trafficked in cocaine in cooperation with Colombian narcotics cartels. Yardies were said to be almost single-handedly responsible for the explosion in crack cocaine use in the US during the 1980s (Small 1995). The posses established working relationships with West Coast street gangs, as well as traditional organized crime groups (Gay and Marquart 1993).

Since Jamaica became a sovereign nation in 1962, two political parties have rivaled each other in closely contested elections—the Jamaica Labour Party (JLP), and the Democratic Socialist Party (PNP). The JLP favored a free market economy compatible with conservative corporate America and held power during the first two governments. The PNP attempted to retain some profits from industry for Jamaica, to obtain worker benefits, and to move toward socialism through working collaboratively with noncapitalist countries, such as Cuba. The PNP held power from 1972 to 1980. Allegedly, this resulted in the development of a plan by the US CIA to topple the regime. A violent election in which almost 700 people lost their lives resulted in the return to power by the JLP in 1980. After nearly a decade of economic problems, the PNP returned to power in 1989 with a more conservative open market approach (Mustard Seed Communities, 2003). The aforementioned plan by the CIA to topple the PNP regime and its leader, Michael Manley generated considerable comment on the internet, particularly because former President George Bush was director of the CIA from January 1976 to January 1977. Furthermore, there were accusations that it was CIA backing for Jamaican posses in the fight against Manley that may have accelerated the posses' involvement in the distribution of crack cocaine in the US, as well as posse involvement in violent crime in the US (Gunst 1989; Shalif 1997; Conscious Rasta Press 1998; Blake 1999).

Theft

Theft becomes global crime when it is committed in one country against citizens of another country, or when things stolen are taken across international borders, possibly for resale in a foreign country or (in the case of vehicle theft) as a means of getting items or persons trafficked to or from a foreign country. For instance, Great Britain has become a major center for international motor vehicle thefts, particularly since completion of a land bridge (the "Chunnel") under the English Channel.

Great Britain is by several measures number one in the world for motor vehicle theft (Winslow and Zhang 2008: 406–7). However, the advent of the Chunnel is not the only factor accounting for the high rate of vehicle theft in Britain. Other factors include a lenient treatment of vehicle theft as a crime, high rates of unemployment, immigration, and high rates of various forms of drug and human trafficking. Similar factors converge for two other countries that top the world for burglary and larceny-theft, Australia and Sweden, respectively. All three countries share an anomaly: they have high rates of theft despite being affluent countries. Though there may be great wealth in these countries, it is not shared equally. In particular, young working-class people and immigrants just entering the job market must share relative poverty compared to older citizens of the country and those with accumulated wealth. So both groups experience relative deprivation possibly motivating them to commit theft, with Australia extremely high among the countries of the world in burglary, Sweden in larceny-theft, and Great Britain in motor vehicle theft. While this process occurs in all three countries, we shall focus here upon Great Britain and vehicle theft, because the country illustrates not only the marginalization of youth and immigrant minorities, but it also displays the internationalization of vehicle theft because of that country's unique history.

The Chunnel provides a portal through which stolen vehicles can be transported from Britain to other countries. Freedom of trade with other European nations is another recent phenomenon that has led to increased vehicle theft. Britain was one of the original signators of the Treaty on European Union (commonly called the Maastricht Treaty) in 1991, along with Belgium, Denmark, France, Germany, Greece, Ireland, Italy, Luxembourg, The Netherlands, Portugal, and Spain. The Maastricht Treaty permitted relaxed border controls. Also, customs and immigration agreements were modified to allow European citizens greater freedom to live, work, and study in any of the member states (Urwin 2004: 1). Vehicle theft became an extensive problem in the European Union, where the number of stolen cars almost tripled between 1989 and 1993 (World's Vehicle Documents 2001: 2; Neilson 2000).

The Chunnel and EU are enabling factors providing an opportunity for vehicle theft in Britain; however, the lenient legal treatment of vehicle theft is another facilitating factor. Government statistics in Britain indicate that over 50 percent of vehicle thefts are committed by juveniles age 10 through 17 in England and Wales (Richardb 2003). A possible reason for the juvenile involvement in vehicle theft is a lack of deterrence on the part of the juvenile justice system in Britain. If a juvenile admits to his crime and there is supporting evidence, he may typically receive a "caution" (Richardb 2003). A caution is merely a warning in Britain, a summary judgment which requires the offender to serve neither jail nor prison time as a penalty. Another explanation for youth involvement (as well as adult involvement in theft) in the United Kingdom is unemployment (Carmichael and Ward 2001). Unemployment is aggravated by the fact that in Britain, youth complete their secondary education at age 16, and nearly 30 percent of the age cohort leaves school at age 16, entering into the job market or facing unemployment (Hammer 2004). When young people are unemployed, attempting to enter the job market in a country of great affluence, they can experience a sense of relative deprivation, feeling they have been unjustly excluded from the opportunity to obtain their "piece of the pie." This sense of relative deprivation could motivate a youthful offender to take a quick trip through the Chunnel with an expensive stolen automobile, one of the major status symbols of wealth.

Like young people in Britain, immigrants to the country may experience relative deprivation and resort to vehicle theft as a means of wealth acquisition. We use the term "may" because approximately 98 percent of all incarcerated immigrants had been convicted of drug offenses (Simon 24 June 2004).

The prosecution of immigrants for drug offenses very likely obscures the actual number of vehicle thefts done by immigrants. This is because, while drug offenses are typically prosecuted as "indictable" (more serious) offenses (Jason-Lloyd 1998), unauthorized taking of a motor vehicle was downgraded from an indictable to a summary offense in the Criminal Justice Act of 1988 (Farrington and Jolliffe 2004: 17). Immigrants include not only those from EU countries, but also immigrants from Commonwealth nations, colonial possessions of Britain who are now independent and sovereign nations who voluntarily associated with each other and with Britain after sovereignty (Wikipedia 2004). Members enjoy privileged access to each other's markets, as well as free or preferred right of migration from one Commonwealth country to another. In a sense, Britain's history of colonial domination has come to haunt this country. Former British "subjects," many of whom are descendants of slaves under colonial domination, may freely migrate to Britain. Many of these migrants may come from a background of poverty and unemployment in home countries such as Jamaica and the Bahamas. When they arrive in Britain, they may observe the relative affluence of that country and compare it with their own abject poverty. They also may become aware of the leniency of a court system that typically dismisses vehicle theft as a "summary offense." As a consequence, the "underclass" of these Commonwealth countries visiting or living in Britain may seek redress through crime. They may acquire "seed money" through trafficking in cocaine and heroin from Colombia, or if they are from Asian countries, heroin and opium from South Asia. In this regard, there is a growing volume of literature that suggests that vehicle theft in Britain is a key element in a cluster of crimes that includes motor vehicle theft, trafficking in stolen automobiles, drug trafficking, and even human trafficking. As a result of the open borders policy made possible by the European Union, vehicles may be stolen in Britain (and other European countries) and driven across many international borders, even before the owners discover or report the theft. The vehicles are driven to countries such as Poland, the Baltic Republics and on rarer occasions to Slovakia and Hungary, where they are renovated or "laundered," given new vehicle identification and documentation. Many are then shipped to Eastern European countries, such as Russia, that have a high demand for these vehicles. To make the theft even more productive, the proceeds from the sale of these automobiles may be used as a source of "seed money" to purchase illicit drugs, which, in turn, are smuggled back to Britain, either by themselves or in conjunction with the smuggling of illegal aliens (World Vehicle Documents 2001). Thus, the crime of auto theft may be a key crime, at least for the small-time operator, in funding a whole circuit of profitable crimes. It may also be an enhancement when used by larger organized crime syndicates. Named as involved in the trade in stolen cars have been Russian groups, Turkish groups that traffic in 75–85 percent of the heroin and other opiates in Europe, Jamaican posses, Hell's Angels biker gangs, and Iranian groups (Sands 2002: 8–10).

The globalization of high-level crimes

The term "high-level crimes" refers to organized crime, white-collar crime, and terrorism. These crimes differ from street crime insofar as they refer not to just single crimes, but sets of crimes carried out not by individuals but by organized groups. These groups often include government officials or agencies and sometimes involve members of the highest social status of society.

Organized crime

Like many street crimes discussed above, organized crime in the US has evolved from being a local phenomenon, with a similar hierarchal social structure involving one or two ethnic groups to a multi-national phenomenon involving many organizational structures and many ethnic groups and nationalities. Thus, organized crime has developed from a local to global phenomenon.

Organized crime (OC) refers to "a conspiratorial enterprise pursuing profit or power through provision of illegal goods and/or services, involving a systematic use of force or threat of force" (Winslow and Zhang, 2008: 430). Based upon this definition it is apparent that OC in the US includes not just the Mafia, rooted in Sicily, with its hierarchical organization structure, but a large number of organization structures, ethnicities, and nationalities. Besides Italians, OC includes a wide variety of racial, national, and ethnic groups. These included blacks, Canadians, Chinese, Colombians, Cubans, Irish, Japanese, Mexicans, Russians, and Vietnamese (President's Commission on Organized Crime 1986: 75–128). More and more it is being recognized that OC, rather than being a national crime syndicate of a single ethnic group (Italian Americans) is actually a "transnational" endeavor of a multitude of national, ethnic, and racial groups. The term "transnational" is used here to refer to crime committed in more than one country, or more specifically according to the Convention against Transnational OC developed by the United Nations in 1998:

> ... an offence is transnational if "(a) It is committed in more than one state; (b) It is committed in one state but a substantial part of its preparation, planning, direction or control takes place in another state; (c) It is committed in one state but involves an organized criminal group that engages in criminal activities in more than one state; or (d) It is committed in one state but has substantial effects in another state."
>
> (Transnational Organized Crime Convention, Article 3 (2) as cited in United Nations Office on Drugs and Crime 2002)

Transnational OC groups include Chinese Tongs and Triads, the Medellin and Cali drug cartels of Colombia, Jamaican Posses, Japanese Yakuza, outlaw motorcycle gangs, Russian Mafiya, and Vietnamese Triad groups and gangs of Vietnamese origin (Faculty.ncwc.edu 2004). In 1995, the United Nations identified eighteen categories of transnational offenses, whose inception, perpetration and/or direct or indirect effects involve more than one country. These offenses include:

> ... money laundering, terrorist activities, theft of art and cultural objects, theft of intellectual property, illicit arms trafficking, aircraft hijacking, sea piracy, insurance fraud, computer crime, environmental crime, trafficking in persons, trade in human body parts, illicit drug trafficking, fraudulent bankruptcy, infiltration of legal business, corruption and bribery of public or party officials.
>
> (United Nations Office on Drugs and Crime 2002: 4)

Little analysis exists in the literature on OC regarding the causes of OC. The lack of causal analysis of OC may be, in part, because it has not been studied globally. Cross-national analysis helps to expand the classification of types of OC, and clarifies when, where, and why OC develops in a society. In *Criminology: A Global Perspective*, we itemize the variety of OC types as including the standard hierarchy, clustered hierarchy, core groups, and criminal networks (a more detailed discussion is contained in the text, pp. 436–38). We also extend the discussion to causal analysis of OC through studying it from the comparative, historical point of view. Briefly, we hypothesize that OC develops in countries that have, over a fairly long period of time, been subject to military rule. This is in part because military rule imposes restrictions upon the distribution of various needed or desired commodities or services through rationing or outright prohibition, resulting in a black market for those goods or services. In our text, we discussed the hypothesis of military rule and OC through a qualitative analysis of countries that illustrate the hypothesis—China, Japan, Mexico, Italy, Russia, Nigeria, Pakistan, Germany, and the US. While it is debatable that the term "military rule" has ever applied to the US on the scale found in other countries, it cannot be doubted that the US has been involved with military activities and war since its inception, roughly every 20 years up until recently. Since WWII, the pace of military involvement has increased precipitously, with the Korean and Vietnamese incursion and various "secret wars" carried out by US intelligence organizations, and, more recently, the US "War on Drugs" and "War on Terrorism."

Criminology: A Global Perspective traces how US military activity has had a causative influence upon the drug trade. The globalization of trade in illicit drugs is influenced, in part, because these drugs may grow best in countries outside the US and also because of the military involvement of the US in or near opium producing countries including the *golden triangle* countries of Myanmar, Laos, and Thailand, as well as the *golden crescent* countries of Afghanistan, Iran, and Pakistan. However, wars outside of the US have also led to the development of familiarity of American military personnel with these source markets for illicit drugs. Military personnel, when faced with poor employment prospects after war, may turn to international trade in drugs as a profitable career. Knowledge of global source markets may fund not only the drug trade as an OC enterprise, but also international terrorism, a surprising finding of our global study of OC to be discussed in more depth below.

White-collar crime/internet crime

In *Criminology: A Global Perspective* we discuss a variety of forms of white-collar crime, including a broad spectrum of frauds to which the public is frequently subjected. These include securities fraud, employee petty larceny, food and drug violations, check-kiting, deceptive advertising, bankruptcy fraud, home improvement schemes, debt consolidation schemes, personal improvement schemes, Ponzi schemes, and various forms of identity theft.

Damage from these crimes often goes unabated, and white-collar criminals often operate with impunity in the US because criminal sanctions for these crimes are not provided (or enforced) by the US criminal justice system.

Due to space limitations in this chapter, we shall focus in this section upon identity theft, because this is a crime that emerged recently as a white-collar crime that is global in its scope and one with which a large number of individuals have direct personal experience, particularly individuals who own personal computers and access the internet. Identity theft crimes include ATM fraud, credit card fraud, and advance fee swindles.

Most computer owners who browse the internet have been subjected to *malware*—computer viruses, worms, trojan horses, spyware, dishonest adware, and other malicious and unsolicited software. Malware slows down or even disables computers and is the product of contact through browsing websites which plant malware upon the user's personal computer.

While malware causes inconvenience to computer users, quite possibly the most malicious, frightening, and aggressive of internet computer contacts result from unsolicited email or spam which can cause severe financial loss to computer user victims. Probably the most frequent of these emails are termed *Nigerian advance fee scams* (often known internationally as "419" fraud, after the section of the Nigerian penal code which addresses fraud schemes). Similar email frauds include the *lottery scams* which emanate from UK, Spain, and the Netherlands.

Quite possibly because *Criminology: A Global Perspective* is linked to a website that includes a contact email address, we receive numerous examples of these fraud letters. We conducted a content analysis of approximately 300 letters that appeared in our email inbox from March 1, 2008 through May 12, 2008. As suggested by the term Nigerian advance fee scam, the vast majority of such emails appeared to originate in Nigeria, although others originated in other African countries (Benin, Ghana, Ivory Coast, Sierra Leon, South Africa, Togo, and Zimbabwe). The lottery scam letters typically appeared to originate in Britain, the Netherlands, Spain, and Switzerland.

The pitch varied with the type of email scam. Lottery scam letters stated that your email address has been entered in a lottery and that your address has been randomly selected as a winner. You are then asked to provide personal information (e.g., Social Security number, bank account numbers, home address, etc.) so that funds can be sent to you or transferred to your bank account.

With Nigerian 419 emails, the pitch is more complicated, perhaps because more explanation is required to enhance credibility. Often they begin with an affectionate greeting ("Dearest One," "Dear Beloved," or "Dear Honest One") or a religious greet- ing ("Greetings in the Name of our Lord Jesus Christ"). Next a description is given of the funds that will be offered to you. These include funds left abandoned in a national bank derived from an inheritance from a distant relative, or funds left in a bank from a person who died without a will, or funds left in a bank from a tragedy in which all surviving relatives died in an airplane crash or natural disaster, such as a tsunami. Funds may also be described as derived from an unclaimed insurance policy (about to expire), a bank client who wants to invest in the US, excess funds from a government contract, or a benefactor whose identity cannot be disclosed. In some cases, the email is stated to be from a wife or daughter of a deceased person. The wife is often described as a victim of terminal cancer, while the daughter indicates her desire to continue her education in the US. In some cases the funds were said to be left dormant, known only to a bank insider. In three cases, funds were claimed to have been accessed by US military personnel from Saddam Hussein's storage vault.

Next is a description of why the email writer wants to transfer funds to your bank account, usually via a bank-to-bank transfer and in exchange for a fee of, typically, 15 percent in the form of cash, use of an international ATM card, a bank draft, or a wire transfer. Often the purpose of the intended transfer is to "repatriate" abandoned funds to prevent government takeover of the funds, and you are described as serving as a stand-in for the next of kin. The said purpose for the transfer is to facilitate investment of money in the US, contribution of money to a worthy cause, or to further your education or the email author's education in the US.

By reply email or through a link, you are then asked to provide personal information that may include your full name, age, sex, marital status, occupation, company name, position, home address, telephone/fax/mobile phone number, nationality, state, country, zip code, nearest international airport, bank name, bank address, password, account number, routing number, swift code number, date of birth, and next of kin. The usual method of extracting money from the victims of such letters is to require an advance fee, or payment up front to extend credit, grant COD privileges, pay for processing of the money from the bank, and the like. However, armed with this information, the recipient can easily assume your identity, doing business in the form of transferring your bank funds from your bank to his, making credit card purchases, and/or conducting ATM withdrawals.

Some email scam letters, often displaying a bank's logo, more directly solicit your identification information saying that someone has tried to access your bank account, that your credit or debit card has been suspended because of fraudulent use, or that your online banking privileges have been suspended. Other direct internet fraud email letters indicate that you need to provide identification information because you have a tax refund owed you by the IRS, to prevent your web mail account from closing, so that they can compensate your for helping with the bank transfer pertaining to someone else's account, or even to qualify for UN compensation for being a past victim of a Nigerian scam.

While for most email recipients, the major cost of unsolicited scam letters consists of the time lost deleting such spam, there is evidence that a sizable percentage of recipients of the email scam letters become victims. It has been estimated that the Nigerian scam alone constitutes a $5 billion loss worldwide (419 Coalition 2008). It should be noted that in *Criminology: A Global Perspective*, Nigeria is cited as a major home base country for organized crime (OC), indicating that when high level crimes are viewed on a global or comparative basis, there is a close link between organized crime and white-collar crime. The close connection between OC and white-collar crime in the case of the advance fee scam is probably related to its historical connection to *money laundering*, the means by which the proceeds of OC are made to appear legitimate through illicit bank transfers, wire transfers, parcel delivery, illicit international traffic in currency, and other similar means of money transfer.

Terrorism

A great deal of interest has been focused, in particular, upon the role that the US Central Intelligence Agency (CIA) has played in the affairs of foreign countries. An excellent chronicle of the CIA's involvement in clandestine activities at home and abroad was provided by whistleblower Steve Kangas. His essay, *Timeline of CIA Atrocities*, was published online prior to his 1999 unsolved murder outside the office of billionaire Richard Mellon Scaife, who was said to be Kangas' nemesis. Steve Kangas (1961–99) was found dead, shot twice in the head, on the 39th floor in the bathroom of the offices of Richard Mellon Scaife (Bashford 1999). Kangas, known as an "internet warrior," had served in US Army intelligence. After serving in the army he became a Doctoral Candidate at the University of California at Santa Cruz (UCSC) in economics and political science (Kangas 1999). Kangas' "tell all" analysis of the role of the CIA in foreign policy begins his Timeline article:

> CIA operations follow the same recurring script. First, American business interests abroad are threatened by a popular or democratically elected leader. The people support their leader because he intends to conduct land reform, strengthen unions, redistribute wealth, nationalize foreign-owned industry, and regulate business to protect workers, consumers and the environment.
>
> So, on behalf of American business, and often with their help, the CIA mobilizes the opposition. First, it identifies right-wing groups within the country (usually the military), and offers them a deal: "We'll put you in power if you maintain a favorable business climate for us." The Agency then hires, trains and works with them to overthrow the existing government (usually a democracy). It uses every trick in the book: propaganda, stuffed ballot boxes, purchased elections, extortion, blackmail, sexual intrigue, false stories about opponents in the local media,

infiltration and disruption of opposing political parties, kidnapping, beating, torture, intimidation, economic sabotage, death squads and even assassination.

These efforts culminate in a military coup, which installs a right-wing dictator. The CIA trains the dictator's security apparatus to crack down on the traditional enemies of big business, using interrogation, torture and murder. The victims are said to be "communists," but almost always they are just peasants, liberals, moderates, labor union leaders, political opponents and advocates of free speech and democracy. Widespread human rights abuses follow.

(Kangas 2002)

Kangas gave numerous examples of covert actions by the CIA in favor of US corporate interests including a "black bag job" providing money to candidates for the Christian Democratic Party in Italy who in 1948 won the national election defeating the communist party, the 1953 Iran overthrow of the democratically elected Prime Minister of Iran, Mohammed Mossadegh and installation of the monarchy of Shah Reza Pahlavi, the 1954 Guatemala replacement of democratically elected leader Jacobo Arbenz with a dictator Castillo Armas, and subsequent CIA backed military coups/or assassinations in countries with democratically elected leaders, including the Dominican Republic (1963), Ecuador (1963), Brazil (1964), Indonesia (1965), Greece (1967), Cambodia (1970), Bolivia (1971), Chile (1973), Panama (1989), and Haiti (1990). The CIA has also participated in the form of black bag jobs (black bags filled with money for candidates) in elections in various countries, including Jamaica (1980) and even Australia (1970).

The above-mentioned covert operations of the CIA may be construed as in the national interest of the US From the vantage point of criminology, however, these activities by the CIA make for a continuing crime problem, both in the US and in other countries, in a variety of ways:

1 Forcing countries to accept terms of the US under a brutal dictatorship often results in political instability and civil disorder in those countries, and rebel groups may fund their insurgency through illicit traffic in drugs and other illicit commodities, with the US as a major market place for the illicit traffic.
2 Brutal dictatorships create a refugee problem of people escaping from such oppression, and the US is often a target destination for human traffic.
3 Often in order to fund a clandestine war, the CIA has found it necessary to fund its activities through illicit means—most particularly, through the drug trade and money laundering. CIA involvement in drug trafficking has been discussed in relation to military intelligence operations during WWII, the French Connection, Air America, Operation Cyclone, and the Iran-Contra Affair.

(For further discussion of these topics, see Winslow and Zhang 2008: 624–25.)

While global crime may have been exacerbated by the activities of the CIA, activities of the Agency may also have been conducive to terrorism. Terrorist organizations, no doubt, have found it easier to recruit followers in countries were CIA activities have generated an unfavorable view of the US CIA activities may have more directly led to terrorism in situations when the Agency ignored or even participated in drug trafficking and terrorism, such as the case listed above as Operation Cyclone. This was a CIA operation secretly authorized by the Carter Administration. In 2002, Zbigniew Brzezinsky, National Security Adviser to President Jimmy Carter, revealed that President Carter secretly authorized $500 million to create an international terrorist movement that would spread Islamic fundamentalism in Central Asia and "destabilize" the Soviet Union. They called this plan Operation Cyclone and poured $4 billion into setting up Islamic training schools in Pakistan. Young zealots were also sent to the CIA's spy training camp in Virginia, where future members of Al Qaeda were taught "sabotage skills" (Friends of Liberty 2002). The Mujahidin in Afghanistan, as they became known, financed their war against the Soviet Union through drug trafficking, in this case heroin. The CIA reopened trade routes to supply the Mujahidin with weapons. The Afghani rebels smuggled the drug into the world market, making the areas they controlled the world's leading source of heroin exports to the US and Europe (Potter 2005).

We have tested a number of theories regarding the causes of international terrorism using international indices. Using the number of terrorist organizations in a country as a measure of terrorism, we found that the strongest correlation among the variables tested and terrorism was the number of kilograms of heroin seized by country, supporting the theory that the illicit traffic in heroin, though not a "cause" of terrorism, may provide a funding source for terrorist organizations (r = .39) (Winslow and Zhang 2008: 638–39). As recently as 2003, Pakistan was number one in the world in seizures of heroin (United Nations Office on Drugs and Crime 2005: 54). It is interesting to note that, just as Pakistan was number one in the world for heroin seized, it was also number one in the world in the number of terrorist organizations that exist in a single country. According to data published by the Terrorism Research Center, in 2006, Pakistan had 67 terrorist organizations within its borders. That is 11 more organizations than the next highest country, India, which has 56 terrorist organizations (The Terrorism Research Center 2006).

Conclusion

From the vantage point of the US, much of life has been globalized, including commerce, transportation, labor, and communication. It seems logical that crime also has become globalized. As such it cannot be fully understood in the US without taking a global or comparative perspective, rather than a provincial or isolationist one. We have seen that with many crimes, whether they be common crimes such as murder, rape, or theft, or higher level crimes such as OC, white-collar crime, or terrorism, full understanding of these crimes cannot be reached without viewing them globally. Thus, comparative criminology studies should not simply be confined to obscure journals or occasional association meetings; they should be a central concern of mainstream sociology and criminology. To understand crime in the twenty-first century, it is imperative that it be viewed from a global perspective.

Acknowledgment

Portions of this chapter were drawn from Winslow, Robert W. and Zhang, Sheldon X., *Criminology: a global perspective*, 1st Edition © 2008. Reprinted by permission of Pearson Education, Inc., Upper Saddle River, NJ.

Note

1 In *Blowback: The Costs and Consequences of American Empire,* Chalmers Johnson refers to blowback as "unintended consequences of policies that were kept secret from the American people." He adds, "What the daily press reports as the malign acts of 'terrorists' or 'drug lords' or 'rogue states' or 'illegal arms merchants' often turn out to be blowback from earlier American operations" (Johnson 2000: 8).

References

419 Coalition, The (2008) *Nigeria—the 419 Coalition Website,* Online. Available HTTP: http://home. rica.net/alphae/419coal/ (accessed 14 August 2008).

Adler, F., Mueller, G. O. W. and Laufer. W. S. (2004) *Criminology and the Criminal Justice System* (5th ed.), New York: McGraw-Hill.

Allen, B. (1996) *Rape warfare: the hidden genocide in Bosnia-Herzegovina and Croatia,* Minneapolis, MN: University of Minnesota Press.

Bashford, D. (1999) *Who killed Steve Kangas?* Online. Available HTTP: www.psnw.com/~bashford/ kang-ev0.html (accessed 30 April 2005).

Bevan, R. (2008) *Great crimes and trials: the great train robbery,* Online. Available HTTP: www.crimeandinvestiga tion.co.uk/famous_crime/36/the_crime/1/The_Great_Train_Robbery.htm (accessed 4 June 2008).

Blake, D. (1999) "Shower posse: the most notorious Jamaican criminal organization", [Book Review], Online. Available HTTP: www.headstartbooks.com/cstudies/ carribbean.htm (accessed 17 October 2003).

Bureau of Justice Statistics. (1998) *Crime and Justice in the United States and in England and Wales, 1981– 96: crime rates from victim surveys,* Online. Available HTTP: www.ojp.usdoj.gov/bjs/pub/html/ cjusew96/crvs.htm (accessed 13 June 2004).

Burke, T. W. and O'Rear, C. E. (1990) "Home invaders: Asian gangs in America," *Police Studies,* 13(4), 154–56.

California Legislature Joint Committee for Revision of the Penal Code. (1980) *Plea bargaining,* Sacramento, CA.

Carmichael, F. and Ward, R. (2001) "Male unemployment and crime in England and Wales," *Economics Letters,* 73, 111–15.

Central Intelligence Agency. (2008) *The 2008 world factbook: field listing – rank order-GDP (purchasing power parity),* Online. Available HTTP: https://www.cia.gov/library/publications/the-world-factbook/ rankorder/2001rank.html (accessed 15 May 2008).

Chambliss, W. J. (1967) "Types of deviance and the effectiveness of legal sanctions," *Wisconsin Law Review,* 3, 703–19.

Costa Rica Staff. (May 7, 2002) *Bands of children back on streets in San Jose,* Online. Available HTTP: http:// streetkidnews.blogsome.com/category/1/north-south-america/costa-rica-streetkid-news (accessed 5 June 2008).

Conscious Rasta Press. (1998) *CIA and Reggae: Part 3 of a series excerpted from high crimes of murder,* Online. Available HTTP: www.7mac.com/7MAC/academy/CIA_reggae5.htm (accessed 11 November 2003).

Cromwell, B. (2003). *Colombia,* Online. Available HTTP: www.cromwell-intl.com/security/nu/co. html (accessed 31 July 2003).

Drug Policy Alliance. (2003) *Drug policy around the world: England,* Online. Available HTTP: www. lindesmith.org/global/drugpolicyby/westerneurop/england/ (accessed 13 June 13 2004).

Faculty.ncwc.edu. (2004) *Organized crime: characteristics, history, enforcement, genre, activities,* Online. Available HTTP: http://faculty.ncwc.edu/toconnor/427/427lect11.htm (accessed 4 November 2004).

Farrington, D. P. and Jolliffe, D. (2004) "England and Wales," in D.P. Farrington, P.A. Langan and M. Tonry (eds.). *Cross-National Studies in Crime and Justice,* Washington, DC: US Department of Justice Office of Justice Programs. Online. Available HTTP: www.ojp.usdoj.gov/bjs/pub/ascii/cnscj. txt (accessed 15 October 2004).

Feeney, F., Dill, F. and Weir, A. (1983) *Arrests without conviction: how often they occur and why,* Washington, DC: US Government Printing Office.

Friends of Liberty (2002) "The CIA's 'operation cyclone' and Osama bin Laden," Online. Available HTTP: http://members.iimetro.com.au/~hubbca/cyclone.htm (accessed 9 May 2006).

Gay, B. W. and Marquart, J. W. (1993) "Jamaican posses: a new form of organized crime," *Journal of Crime and Justice*, 16 (2), 139–70.

Gunst, L. (1989 November) "Johnny-too-bad and the sufferers," *The Nation*, 13, 549–53, Online. Available HTTP: http://debate.uvm.edu/dreadlibrary/thielen.html (accessed 21 October 2003).

Hammer, T. (2004) *Youth unemployment and social exclusion in Europe*, Online. Available HTTP: www.celpe.unisa.it/DP/Torild_Hammer.pdf (accessed 8 October 2004).

Hornberger, J. G. (2000) *Crack down in the war on drugs ... or end it? Commentaries*, Online. Available HTTP: www.fff.org/comment/ed0200b.asp (accessed 18 November 2003).

International Centre for Prison Studies. (2004) *Prison brief for United Kingdom: England and Wales*, Online. Available HTTP: www.kcl.ac.uk/depsta/rel/icps/worldbrief/europe_records.php?code=168 (accessed 14 October 2004).

Jason-Lloyd, L. (1998) *UK drug and alcohol misuse white papers—UK drugs legislation*, Online. Available HTTP: www.nadt.org.uk/suba/legislation.html (accessed 15 October 2004).

Jelsoft Enterprises Ltd. (2008) *Illegal immigration and crime*, Online. Available HTTP: www.bahamasissues.com/showthread.php?t=13635 (accessed 5 June 2008).

Johnson, C. (2000) *Blowback: the costs and consequences of American empire*. New York: Henry Holt.

Kangas, S. (1999) *About me*, Online. Available HTTP: www.psnw.com/~bashford/aboutme.html (accessed 1 May 2005).

——(2002) *Timeline of CIA atrocities*, Online. Available HTTP: www.serendipity.li/cia/cia_time.htm (accessed 30 April 2005).

Killias, M. and Rabasa, J. (1998) "Does heroin prescription reduce crime? Results from the evaluation of the Swiss heroin prescription projects," *Studies on Crime and Prevention*, 7 (1), 127–33.

Korte, T., Pykalainen, J. and Seppala, T. (1998) "Drug abuse of Finish male prisoners in 1995," *Forensic Science International*, 97(2–3), 171–83.

Krug, E. G., Dahlberg, L. L., Mercy, J. A., Zwi, Anthony, B. and Lozano, R. (eds.). (2002) *World report on violence and health*, Geneva: World Health Organization.

Kykeon@lycaeum.org. (1991) "The duplicity of the war on drugs," Online. Available HTTP: www.lycaeum.org/drugwar/dupe.html (accessed 16 November 2003).

Macko, S. (1996) "Security problems in Latin America," *ENN Daily Report, 2* (237) Online. Available HTTP: www.emergency.com/ltn-scty.htm (accessed 3 August 2003).

Maher, L., Dixon, D. and Hall, W. (2002) "Property crime and income generation," *Australian and New Zealand Journal of Criminology*, 35(2), 187–202.

McClendon, J. G. (1990) *Puritan jurisprudence: progress and inconsistency*, Online. Available HTTP: www.reformed.org/webfiles/antithesis/v1n1/ant_v1n1_juris.html (accessed 3 March 2005).

Mrsevik, Z. and Hughes, Donna M. (1997) "Violence against women in Belgrade, Servia: SOS Hotline 1990–93," *Violence Against Women*, 3(2), 101–28.

Mustard Seed Communities. (2003) *Jamaica. Mustard Seed Communities*, Online. Available HTTP: www.mustardseed.com/locations/jamaica.html (accessed 17 November 2003).

Neill, K. G. (2000, November) "Duty, honor, rape: sexual assault against women during war," *Journal of International Women's Studies*. Online. Available HTTP: www.bridgew.edu/depts/artscnce/jiws/nov00/duty.htm (accessed 17 October 2003).

Neilson, A. (2000) *Organized crime in Europe*, Online. Available HTTP: www.ex.ac.uk/politics/pol_data/undergrad/Neilson/index.html (accessed 14 October 2004).

Potter, G. (2005) *State-sponsored terrorism in US foreign policy*, Online. Available HTTP: www.policestudies.eku.edu/POTTER/Module9.htm (accessed 12 February 2005).

President's Commission on Organized Crime. (1986) *The Impact: Organized crime today*, Washington, DC: US Government Printing Office.

Raymond, J. G. and Hughes, D. M. (2001) *Sex trafficking of women in the United States*, New York: NY Coalition Against Trafficking in Women. Online. Available HTTP: http://action.web.ca/home/catw/attach/sex_traff_us.pdf (accessed 14 December 2004).

Reichel, P. L. (2005) *Comparative criminal justice systems*, Upper Saddle River, NJ: Pearson/Prentice Hall.

Richard, B. (2003) *Angliacampus: car crime*, Online. Available HTTP: www.angliacampus.com/grwn/prnt/beyond/CarCrime/ (accessed 14 October 2004).

Sands, J. (2002) *Europe in the age of globalization: a hotbed of transnational organized crime?* Online. Available HTTP: http://members.lycos.co.uk/ocnewsletter/SGOC0902/sands.html (accessed 10 October 2004).

Sellin, T. and Wolfgang, M. E. (1964) *The measurement of delinquency*, New York: John Wiley and Sons.

Shalif, I. (1997) *Scotland Yardies Part 2*, Online. Available HTTP: www.ainfos.ca/A-Infos97/4/0610.html (accessed 21 November 2003).

Siegel, L. J. (2004) *Criminology: theories, patterns, and typologies* (8th ed.), Belmont, CA: Wadsworth/Thompson Learning.

Simon, Rita J. (2004) "Immigration and crime across seven nations," Talk given at Forschungsinstitut zur Zukunft der Arbeit GmbH (IZA) Annual Migration Meeting Online. Available HTTP: http://216.239.41.104/search?q=cache:XnW-1U5rcIQJ:www.iza.org/conference_files/amm_2004/simon_r1669.pdf+immigration+and+crime+across+seven+nationsandhl=en (accessed 15 October 2004).

Small, G. (1995) *Ruthless: the global rise of the yardies*, London: Warner.

Swann, R. and James, P. (1998) "The effect of the prison environment upon inmate drug taking behavior," *Howard Journal of Criminal Justice*, 37(3), 252–65.

Swiss, S. and Giller, Joan E. (1993) "Rape as a crime of war: a medical perspective," *Journal of American Medical Association*, 270(5), 612–15.

The Terrorism Research Center. (2006) *Country profiles: May 9, 2006*, Online. Available HTTP: www.terrorism.com/modules.php?op=modloadandname=Countriesandfile=index (accessed 9 May 2006).

Thompson, T. (2002 October) Look at Jamaica: Jamaica's poll bloodbath, *Observer*. Online. Available HTTP: www.trinidadandtobagonews.com/forum/webbbs_config.pl/noframes/read/845 (accessed 20 November 2003).

Toy, C. (1993) "A short history of Asian gangs in San Francisco," *Justice Quarterly*, 9(4), 647–665.

Treco, R. N. M. (2002) *The Haitian Diaspora in the Bahamas*, Online. Available HTTP: http:/lacc.fiu.edu/research_publications/working_papers/WPS_004.pdf (accessed 5 June 2008).

United Nations Office on Drugs and Crime. (2002) *Global program against transnational organized crime: results of pilot survey of forty selected organized criminal groups in sixteen countries*, Online. Available HTTP: www.unodc.org/unodc/en/organized_crime.html (accessed 2 November 2004).

——(2003) *Pakistan: country profile*, Online. Available HTTP: www.unodc.org/pakistan/country_profile.html (accessed 7 May 2006).

Urwin, D. W. (2004) European Union. *Microsoft Encarta Online Encyclopedia 2004*, Online. Available HTTP: http://encarta.msn.com/text_761579567 – 0/European_Union.html (accessed 12 October 2004).

Wikipedia. (2004) *Commonwealth of Nations*, Online. Available HTTP: http://en.wikipedia.org/wiki/Commonwealth_of_Nations#Benefits_of_membership_and_Contemporary_Concerns (accessed 16 October 2004).

——(2007) *Mara Salvatrucha*, Online. Available HTTP: http://en.wikipedia.org/wiki/Mara_Salvatrucha (accessed 7 January 2007).

——(2008) *Dominant minority*, Online. Available HTTP: http://en.wikipedia.org/wiki/Dominant_minority (accessed 26 May 2008).

Winslow, R. W. (1968) *Crime in a free society: selections from the President's Commission on Law Enforcement and Administration of Justice*, Belmont, CA: Dickenson Publishing Co.

——(2003) *Crime and society: a comparative criminology tour of the world*, Online. Available HTTP: http://www-rohan.sdsu.edu/faculty/rwinslow/index.html (accessed 13 December 2003).

Winslow, R. W. and Zhang, S. X., (2008) *Criminology: a global perspective*, Upper Saddle River, NJ: Pearson/Prentice-Hall.

World's Vehicle Documents. (2001) *Vehicle crime in Europe*, Online. Available HTTP: www.vehicle-documents.it/articoli_veicoli/art_47.htm (accessed 7 October 2004).

14

Religion out of place?

The globalization of fundamentalism

Peter Beyer

The dependent co-arising of globalization and fundamentalism

As a word and a concept, "globalization" is a relative neologism, appearing in English dictionaries no earlier than the late 1950s and only attaining its current popularity as of the 1990s. "Fundamentalism" has a somewhat older history, dating back at least to the early twentieth century. Yet the meaning of the term that is currently dominant, referring to a particular kind of religious and usually also political movement, only gained widespread use after the end of the 1970s. This rough simultaneity is not a mere coincidence. Religious movements that have been labelled fundamentalisms over the past few decades are the sort of critical events that, for many, signalled the need to speak about our broader social world in new terms; "globalization" has become the term of choice in this regard (although the idea of "postmodern" arose at the same time and speaks to the same shift in perception; see (Lyotard 1984, French original published 1979)). They are not the only such events, to be sure. Indeed, the currently still prevailing understanding of globalization sees it in primarily economic terms, pertaining to the supposed late twentieth-century worldwide integration of capitalist markets and investment along what is sometimes called a "neo-liberal" model, which stresses minimal restriction on the global flow of trade and capital (for a balanced introduction, see Scholte 2005). Yet even here, to the degree that religion appears at all under this rubric, it does so as "fundamentalisms", which are generally understood as reactions against the homogenizing and generally "secularizing" forces of (economic) globalization, different but analogous to other anti-(or alternative) globalization movements.

A different understanding of globalization has been somewhat overshadowed by this economic conception, although the balance may be shifting. It stresses not just its integrative or homogenizing character, but also the way that the contemporary world simultaneously generates renewed and powerful assertions of difference or heterogeneity (Robertson 1992). In this conception, what are called fundamentalisms can appear rather more central given that one of their characteristics is an insistence on difference. In the more popular literature on this subject, this stress on and even anxiety about difference is perhaps best expressed in Samuel Huntington's "clash of civilizations" thesis or in

Benjamin Barber's notion of "Jihad vs. McWorld" (Barber 1996, Huntington 1996). The "civilizations" that are in conflict mostly have a presumed "religious" basis (Confucian, Western Christian, Eastern Christian, Islamic, Hindu, Buddhist, and so on); what opposes economic neo-liberalism (McWorld) is based in religion (Jihad).

One can go further with this parallel. Within globalization discussions, one of the more persistent questions concerns when this process supposedly began and, in relation to this, through what historical phases it may have gone since its beginning (Campbell 2007, Held et al. 1999: 414–44, Robertson 1992: 57–60, Scholte 2005: ch. 3, Wallerstein 1974–80). While there is little agreement on the answers to this question, a prevailing understanding distinguishes between "modern" globalization, beginning somewhere in the late 15th to 16th centuries, and antecedent developments around the world before that time and stretching back as far as the beginning of recorded human history. The modern period is associated with the beginnings of European expansion and the gradual development of what Wallerstein first called the capitalist world-economy (Wallerstein 1979). Within such an economy-centred approach, phases correspond to periods of expansion and contraction or consolidation of this global economy between the sixteenth and twenty-first centuries, as more and more of the world becomes incorporated within the world-system. Not nearly as often noted, however, are the significant, and increasingly global, religious developments that have also characterized these same centuries. Critical among these would be the Protestant and Catholic Reformations in sixteenth century Europe, religious transformations that were also central to the development of the European state system that eventually expanded to the entire globe. To this corresponded the expansion of Christianity in the form of European colonizers, but especially through missionaries that accompanied, followed, or even preceded the economic and political bearers of European power. From the sixteenth century onward, Catholic missionaries were active in virtually every corner of the globe, in the Americas, in Africa, in the Indian subcontinent, and in China and Japan (see Neill 1986). Moreover, much as in the case of the global capitalist economy, the real "take-off phase" (Robertson 1992) came in the nineteenth century, and most especially toward the end of that century and into the twentieth. Protestant and Orthodox Christian missions joined Catholic ones to consolidate and further the spread of their religion to other regions.

Perhaps even more important, the period from the late eighteenth to the early twentieth century witnessed significant changes in the non-European world as well. These were in part responses to incorporation and they very much included religious transformations. Reformation movements of diverse sorts in East and South Asia, in the Middle East, Africa and in Latin America, not to mention Europe, refashioned for this increasingly globalized context the religious traditions and cultures of these regions to face up to, compete with, and in certain cases to emulate or expressly reject the Christian model presented and developed during these centuries by the Europeans (Beyer 2006, 2007b). These developments, which are still very much ongoing, resulted in the gradual formation and mutual identification of the set of so-called "world religions" that are today recognized and present virtually around the world. It is in terms of these religions that twentieth century "fundamentalisms" have come to be understood. The "world religions", in other words, both in conception and to a large degree in form, have been as much an aspect and a symptom of the historical process of globalization as has the globalized capitalist economy and the global system of formally sovereign and territorially defined nation-states. Moreover, analogous to the situation in this world economy and global state system, the relations among these (re)constructed religions range along a continuum from one of mutual recognition, toleration, and collaboration in a perceived common enterprise called religion, to outright hostility and conflict as they compete for influence, presence, and adherents. Issues such as religious "conversion", the changing of religious loyalty and participation, and the "accommodation" of different religions have become persistent and controversial issues in virtually every part of the world, making the question of religious pluralism one of the most central concerns of religious insiders and outsiders alike (Beyer 2007a).

Much as in the domain of the global economy and the global system of states, the religious dimension of globalization has therefore also been, to say the least, conflicted and contested. Contestation among religious actors, in religious terms, and implicating religion have been and continue to be a characteristic feature as the idea of the religions has formed and taken hold; and as religious cultures themselves have taken shape and reformed for the globalizing context. Such contestation has concerned chiefly three sorts of boundary questions. First, which religions are to legitimately count among the religions? Second, what, internally, is the proper content of those religions and, relatedly, which subdivisions of these religions are to be recognized? Third, what should be the range of religious influence or operation? Moreover, certain periods in modern global history have witnessed a far greater presence and frequency of such religious contestation than others, and these periods correspond more or less to certain phases of globalization. Among these, two stand out for our purposes here, the late nineteenth and early twentieth-century period that, as noted, Robertson identifies as the "take-off" phase of globalization; and the later twentieth- and early twenty-first-century period in which we find ourselves now. Not at all coincidentally, the first witnessed the advent of the word "fundamentalism" and the second its global application beyond the realm of American Protestant Christianity.

The arrival of fundamentalism as a descriptive term occurred in the context of early twentieth-century American Protestant Christianity. The Fundamentalists represented a movement which opposed a different and "liberal" form of Christianity (Marsden 1980); it was an example of inner-religious contestation over, roughly speaking, "orthodoxy" or "correct religion". Just as important, however, was why the Fundamentalists thought that liberal Christianity was problematic, namely that liberals supposedly were allowing a "de-Christianization" and thus, for the Fundamentalists, a critical weakening of the influence of religion and thereby an undermining of the health of American society. Fundamentalism was in that sense a dispute about the content of a religion and how determinative religious understandings should be in society. It was an attempt at religious re-formation or re-assertion at a critical juncture in not only the history of the United States but, as already outlined, in the development of today's global system.

While the American case marks the advent of the word "fundamentalism" and refers to such re-formation and re-assertion processes, it was by far not the only significant religious occurrence worldwide during the "take-off" phase. In China, the New Text movement was leading to an eventually completely unsuccessful attempt to re-imagine the Confucian tradition as the religion of Confucius (*kongjiao*), or, to use Lionel Jensen's term, "Confucianity" (Jensen 1997). In Japan, the post-Meiji Restoration elite was busily refashioning Shinto into what one could call a "state orthodoxy", thereby relegating all other religions (*shukyo*) to a privatized domain and expanding State Shinto beyond the category of religion to make it a foundational ideology of the society (Hardacre 1989). In India, movements like the Arya Samaj and the Ramakrishna Math and Mission sought to imagine a reformed and united Hinduism for the first time in history, bringing to one of

271

its high points a process of religion formation that had begun earlier in the century and that featured a corresponding assertion of a counter-orthodoxy in the form of what was becoming known as Sanatana Dharma, the eternal teaching (Dalmia and von Stietencron 1995). Here reform movements, much as in the case of American Protestant Christianity, engendered counter-orthodoxy responses. In the Punjab region of India, the Singh Sabha movement in the late nineteenth century and its successor Akali movement of the early twentieth century not only succeeded in asserting a renewed Khalsa Sikh orthodoxy and thereby progressively marginalizing other forms; they also for the first time in Sikh history brought about a clear distinction between Sikhism and Hinduism as religions (Kapur 1986). A bit farther south, the early twentieth century saw the rise in Sri Lanka/Ceylon of Angarika Dharmapala's attempt to reform Buddhism in a way that attenuated the distinction between monastic and lay Buddhism (Dumoulin and Maraldo 1976). In sub-Saharan Africa, Indigenous Christians gradually became the dominant missionizing force among their fellow Africans, leading both to the explosive growth of this religion in that region and to the rise of a number of Indigenous Christian movements, above all the African Instituted Churches that today are such a significant part of the African Christian landscape (Isichei 1995). Across the Muslim world from Northern Africa to Southern Asia, various reform movements associated first with names like Jamal al-din al-Afghani and Muhammad Abduh in the nineteenth century, and then Rashid Rida, Hasan al-Banna and Mawlana Mawdudi in the twentieth century initiated a revisioning of Islam that formed the basis of many and even most subsequent Islamic and Islamist movements of the later twentieth century (Voll 1982). The late nineteenth and early twentieth century also witnessed the rise of the Zionist movement among Jews in Europe, a development that eventually led to the foundation of the State of Israel in the mid-twentieth century, but just as importantly to assertions of Jewish orthodoxy, such as Agudat Israel, to counter the secularist Zionists; and the beginnings of specifically religious Zionism under Rabbi Kook (Lustick 1988).

This is only an incomplete list of important examples, but what is particularly noticeable among so many of them is their close association with corresponding nationalist movements in the respective regions. In other words, just like in so-called fundamentalist movements of the late twentieth century, religion (re)formation and state (re)formation have usually been closely associated and often even intimately related. Most of the movements just mentioned were an important moment in how particular parts of the world responded to their increasing integration into a single social system that today so many people analyze under the rubric of globalization. These religious developments were often aspects of a "reaction against", usually against the domination of Western powers; but they were for the most part not specifically "reactionary", meaning that they did not seek to re-establish some prior situation, some "ancien régime", as it were. In point of fact, to the extent that many of them could be styled as defensive, they were also innovative and historically unprecedented even as concerns their religious content.

The expansion in meaning of the word "fundamentalism" from one that refers for the most part to a certain direction in American Protestant Christianity to a globally applicable term corresponds roughly with the advent of late twentieth century religio-political events in different parts of the world, especially two of them virtually simultaneously in two different religions: 1979 saw the rise of the *New* Christian Right in the United States, signalled especially through the foundation of the Fundamentalist Rev. Jerry Falwell's Moral Majority; and the Iranian revolution with its theocratic face in the person of the Ayatollah Khomeini. It was in the aftermath of these occurrences that one sees the rather sudden and much more widespread use of the term, "fundamentalism". Where before, the word was occasionally used to refer in general to rigid ideological orientations and in some cases to certain Islamic directions (such as those of Mawdudi in Pakistan; see Binder 1957), from this time forward one witnesses, first widespread reference to "Islamic fundamentalism", and then more generally to fundamentalism in the form of various other religio-political movements that sought to move religious orientations and determinations (back) into the state-political arena (for earlier collections, see Hadden and Shupe 1986, 1989, Robertson and Garrett 1991, Shupe and Hadden 1988). In subsequent years, "fundamentalisms" appeared to arise from virtually every one of the recognized "world religions": Jewish fundamentalism in Israel with the radicalization of religious Zionism in Israel after 1977 (but see the earlier use by Charles Liebman [Liebman 1966]); Sikh fundamentalism in the context of the Punjab crisis of the early 1980s; and then a few years later, Hindu fundamentalism in the form of the Hindu nationalist movement embodied in the Rashtriya Swayamsevak Sangh (RSS) and its associated "family of organizations" (Sangh Parivar). The term was even applied to Buddhist movements such as the Soka Gakkai and its associated Komeito party in Japan, and the Sinhalese nationalism embroiled in the ongoing civil war in Sri Lanka (for a wide range of examples from around the world, see Marty and Appleby 1991–95). To a large degree, the movements in question did indeed arise at this time, and therefore it may not be surprising that observers paid so much attention to them. Yet equally as significant is what all these otherwise very diverse movements supposedly had in common that would warrant using a single and such a singular descriptor for them.

Much like the co-arising idea of globalization, applying the term fundamentalism to such a wide variety of religious, and generally religio-political, movements pointed to what was perceived to be unprecedented or special about them all. Globalization, appearing as a concept at the same time, seemed a necessary neologism because of a realization that, somehow, all of us on the globe were living in a single social world in a way and with an intensity that had not existed before or that we had not noticed as clearly before. Fundamentalism signalled an analogous realization: religion and the religions seemed to be taking forms that, for most of the observers who used the term, were not just unexpected, but perhaps even out of place and out of time. For most, but not all, of those using the term, the kind of religion that claims to be at the centre of human affairs, that *successfully* seeks to have its *religious* precepts exert determinative influence in the "public" realm of "modern" and supposedly secular societies should not have been happening, but it was and it was happening all around the very same world which now appeared to be increasingly integrated. It was not a great leap from here to see the two as related, and specifically to see fundamentalisms as a reaction against globalization or, what amounts to the same, against the "secularity" of the dominant forces in this world-wide social world: the modern state, the capitalist economy, and scientific rationality (Almond et al. 2000, Juergensmeyer 1993, Keddie 1998, Marty and Appleby 1991–95). Initially, especially before the fall of the Soviet empire and the collapse of state-centred socialism as a believable alternative to global (neo-liberal) capitalism, the idea of fundamentalism could help sustain the (still) widespread notion that, somehow, the "religious" and the "modern" were at odds, that a "modern" society is *ipso facto* a secularized or secularizing society, where religion at best maintains itself as a privatized concern. To the extent that "globalized" society was also modern – and its understanding as globalized capitalism pointed in this direction – the "resurgence" of something that was decidedly "unmodern", perhaps even "medieval", could be understood as "reaction against". Since then, however, as globalization has taken on the status of a buzzword as much as an understandable concept, that mode of understanding may be becoming less convincing. In the age of the "clash of civilizations" and the "war on terror", fundamentalisms now appear, not simply or even primarily as "reaction against", but more as – still often problematic – "symptom of" globalization. In a post-Cold War context where popularized terms like "New World Order", "clash of civilizations", and "the war on terror" seek to capture what are now the key characteristics of the current global order, religion more generally, but religio-political fundamentalisms in particular, appear increasingly as a regular feature of that order, something expressive of it rather than a rearguard action on the part of those who hanker for the communal and isolated security of a bygone world.

Fundamentalist religio-political movements of the late twentieth century

A brief look at several late twentieth-century religious movements that have often been labelled fundamentalisms, and that have received the most sustained attention in the literature, can serve to put flesh on this general argument. In each case, what becomes evident is that what are called "fundamentalist" movements are symptomatic of the repositioning and restructuring of various world regions, certain states in particular, within the context of globalization. They are better seen as "appropriations of" globalization than "reactions against": they are not expressive so much of a wish to "turn back the clock" as they are of "doing it our way" and in a way that is deliberately and noticeably different from "your way".

The case of the fundamentalist Islamic revolution in Iran

Like most religio-political movements understood as fundamentalist, the Iranian revolution was in important ways but a late twentieth century manifestation of a religious direction and movement that had its antecedents already in the nineteenth century. It was in that earlier period, when the Qajar Shahs ruled Iran during a century of ever increasing influence of European colonial powers, that the Shi'a clerical hierarchy which gave us the title, Ayatollah, solidified and gradually institutionalized its relative independence from the political structures of the day (Arjomand 1984). The Shi'a clerics played key leadership roles in late nineteenth- and early twentieth-century Iranian movements of national and nationalist assertion against Western colonialist control of their country, and against the reigning monarchy which many in Iran came to regard as an agent of that control. The Tobacco Revolt of 1890 successfully forced the Shah to rescind concessions he had made to British concerns in an effort to finance of his own modernization efforts. Shi'a clerical support and leadership were instrumental in this success. Then, during the Constitutional Revolution of 1906, the leading clerics were divided, but enough of them supported the revolutionaries to make the promulgation of Iran's first modern constitution possible. Two decades later, they again appeared as necessary allies in Reza Khan's successful attempt to replace the Qajars with his own Pahlavi dynasty, even though Reza Shah subsequently cast them aside as agents of backwardness who blocked his project of rapid modernization of the country. Reza Shah accepted the idea – as did his contemporary slightly to the west, Mustapha Kemal (later, Atatürk) of the new Republic of Turkey – that Islam was antithetical to this modernization. The clerical hierarchy again were critically involved in the post-Second World War accession of Mohammed Mossadegh and his National Front to power in Iran; and in the subsequent British and American led coup that overthrew him. Although the clerics were, as before, divided on whom they supported, their dominant impulse was what later discourse would call fundamentalist: they sought to free Iran from the control of colonialist powers, but this in order to (re)establish a society in which Islam informed all sectors and domains of society, including the political and the legal (Keddie 2003). What is additionally important, however, is that the aim was not thereby to "go back" to some imagined traditional past, for instance the early community of the Prophet Muhammad himself or the sixteenth- and seventeenth-century glory days of the Shi'a dominated Safavid empire in Iran. Rather it was to establish a newly Islamic society along Shi'a lines.

The 1979 revolution was in direct continuity with these earlier developments. It was in certain senses their further development (cf. Arjomand 1988). The Pahlavi Shah then in power, Reza Mohammed, embodied to most of those who opposed him not only local oppression, but also foreign and Western domination of Iran. To the degree that "Islam" was their unifying rallying cry, it represented what the Shah and the ideology of his regime were not, more than it pointed to some sort of unified, reactionary religious opposition. What the revolutionaries meant by Islam was in fact quite diverse. It ranged from the frankly socialist vision of Ali Shariati – at the time as iconic a figure of the opposition as the Ayatollah Khomeini – through the "Islamic democrats" represented by Mehdi Bazargan (the head of the provisional government immediately after the overthrow of the Shah), all the way to the radical Khomeinists who envisioned a post-revolutionary theocratic state in Iran. Only the latter would qualify as clearly fundamentalist in their emphasis on religious authority and socio-moral conservatism. The former bore a much stronger resemblance to the socialist orientation of then contemporary Latin American liberation theological movement or the post-World War II Christian democrats of Western Europe (Abdel-Malek 1988, Chebabi 1990, Sachedina 1983). The outlook of virtually all opposition currents was implicitly or explicitly nationalist, concerned in the first instance with freeing Iran from the dictatorial clutches of the "anti-religious" monarchy and from Western colonialist domination. The Iranian Revolution of 1979 was in that sense a national revolution analogous to other "modern" revolutions like the French, the Russian, the Chinese, and notably the Nicaraguan revolution that occurred in the same year (see Farhi 1990, Skocpol 1979). The difference with respect to these was in the way that a traditional religion provided the symbolic resources to express the revolutionary impulse, and in the outcome of the post-revolutionary power struggle.

The Khomeinists were better organized and astute in their strategy, including in the use of modern communication technologies. They had greater institutional resources and, critically, the mass power base in the form of large numbers of recently urbanized and relatively marginalized people who regarded the Shi'a clerics as their natural leaders (see Bakhash 1990). The vision that Khomeini and his devotees tried to implement was certainly fundamentalist in the sense that it expressly sought to make traditional Shi'a Islam, as they understood it, the central orienting force in the new Islamic Republic of Iran (IRI). Yet already the middle term in that title for the new state regime indicates that this was not simply a "reactionary" impulse. Like other modern states, the Islamic republic was supplied with a new constitution which, to be sure, gave Islam and religious leaders a central role, but also provided for a democratically elected parliament and president alongside the newly minted and innovative Islamic political structures of the Supreme Leader (*Faqih*) and the Guardianship Council. The autocratic restrictions that have since been applied to this system, although justified in the name of Islam and rendering the state structures far from democratic in the Western liberal sense of that term, are in their own way no more "anti-modern" than what prevails in any number of other states around the world. Moreover, and perhaps more important, the policies that successive IRI governments have implemented since 1979 have, as in most other countries, pursued the further economic, educational, scientific/technological, and cultural development of the country, as well as its political aggrandizement and the extension of its international influence (also Khosrokhavar and Roy 1999; see, for the first decade after the revolution, Rahnema and Nomani 1990). All this, however, in the key of Shi'a Islam, interpreted by the reigning clerics in a way at least as much in discontinuity as in continuity with the Iranian Islam of past centuries.

This combination of using "tradition" for "modern" purposes is further illustrated through the vexed question of the role and position of women in the revolution and in the IRI thereafter. During the period leading up to the revolution, for instance, many Iranian women regarded the wearing of the Islamic *chador* (black garment covering the body and head) as a symbol of protest, whether or not they were devout Muslims. It demonstrated their opposition to the Shah and all he stood for (Keddie 2003: 229f). In the wake of the Khomeinist post-revolutionary take-over, however, what had been for some a voluntary gesture of protest became mandatory when the new regime forced all women to "cover" in public. As with most other movements labelled fundamentalist, the Khomeinists expressed their vision in part through the religiously justified and patriarchal control of women (cf. Riesebrodt 1993). Requiring women to cover was an important symbol in this regard. From one perspective, this was "reactionary", part of stating one's anti-Western identity. Yet, especially for women in the lower and often recently urbanized classes, the regime's policies made possible their participation in public life, including many professions and the political arena, in ways that had been closed to them before; and they could do this on a traditionally Islamic basis (see Khosrokhavar 1993: ch. 2).

Summarizing, what made the 1979 revolution different was not the sudden rise of "fundamentalism" in reaction against the encroachments of the modern globalizing world, but rather the better strategy adopted by those forces that had been carrying the fundamentalist or religious option throughout the entire historical process that has been modern globalization, in the Iranian case, at least since the early nineteenth century. The difference was not the presence of fundamentalism, but rather the context which, for the first time, allowed its representatives to gain ascendancy. Fundamentalism has here been part of a particular path to modernization, and only an attitude which insists that the presence of religion is *ipso facto* anti-modern, would see in this an inherent contradiction.

The case of American Christian fundamentalism

In spite of the fact that the United States has been one of the most powerful countries in the twentieth-century world system – and since the Second World War, the most powerful – and therefore a projector of global hegemonic power rather than a victim of it, the situation of American fundamentalism is in many ways analogous to the Iranian case. As already noted, American Protestant fundamentalism of the early twentieth century was the movement that gave us this term in its current meaning, referring to an intra-religious but also religio-political movement of that period which played a key role on the American political scene during and after the First World War (see Liebman and Wuthnow 1983). Much as in Iran, religious actors and religious interpretations were at the centre of the most important developments, not part of a peripheral backwater. Fundamentalist leader William Jennings Bryan was a three-time presidential candidate for the Democratic Party. Fundamentalist ideas seriously informed American attitudes toward the war and toward the German enemy in that the war. They were also at the forefront of the successful drive toward Prohibition (see Marsden 1980). The fundamentalist orientation did experience a nadir of public presence and influence in the aftermath of the Scopes trial in 1925, where one of its central issues, the teaching of evolution in public schools, was the focus of attention. This, however, is roughly parallel to what happened to the clerical caste in Iran during Reza Shah's regime. Similarly, one detects a kind of resurgence of religiously inspired orientations in the immediate post–World War II period, where the McCarthy era was much more in tune with them; and this is exactly parallel to the Mossadegh era in Iran. In that light, it is hardly surprising that the current ascendancy of what was originally called the New Christian Right in the United States runs parallel with the establishment of the Islamic Republic of Iran.

The reappearance of American fundamentalism on the political scene toward the end of the 1970s did seem to catch many observers by surprise, evidently still convinced that religion was and should be on the decline in the United States as elsewhere. The period of apparent decline during the 1960s and early 1970s along with the dominance of very non-fundamentalist religious and cultural trends as exhibited in the counter-cultural, civil rights, feminist, and new religious movements of that era, gave some credence to that impression, parallel again to the secularist orientations of the Shah's regime in Iran at the same time. Yet during all that time, the conservative religious sector continued to grow (cf. Kelley 1972) and the fundamentalist opposition to the just-mentioned directions had been mounting since the early 1970s (see Brown 2002). With the foundation of Jerry Falwell's Moral Majority, Inc. in 1979 and its claim to have been instrumental in the election of Ronald Reagan as president in 1980, what was going relatively unnoticed could no longer be ignored. Since that time, the Religious Right in the United States has had at best moderate success in American politics (cf. Beyer 1994: ch. 5, Bruce 1988); nothing like the Iranian situation has been repeating itself. There can be no doubt, however, that it has become a solidly institutionalized fixture both in the political system – especially through its influence in the Republican Party – and more broadly in the cultural ecology of the United States (Durham 2000, Wilcox 2000).

Given this established influence, it is important to note that, much as the Islamic revolution in Iran, the Christian Right in the United States can also not be understood simply as "reaction". To be sure, there is a kind of defensiveness about this movement, as it is centrally concerned with the decline of American power in global context and the supposed moral and religious decadence of American "secular humanism" that it holds responsible for bringing about this decline. Strong currents within it are deeply suspicious of the "other", not just the old enemy of "Godless communism" or even militant Islam, but a somewhat amorphous global homogenizing force represented in, for instance, the fear of "one world government", this latter again paralleling what in the Iranian case is given voice in phrases like "global arrogance" and the "Great American Satan". None-theless, the American Christian Right is really no more isolationist, wishing to keep the rest of the world out, than other trends in contemporary American society; and it has no difficulty supporting the continued and aggressive projection of American economic, political, and military power around the world. As such, American fundamentalism in its early twenty-first-century incarnation is also about making globalization work in a cer-tain way, and in the process furthering globalization not just through the greater

277

integration of the different regions of the world into global economic and political structures, but also through the renewed assertion of difference, in this case American difference. In this light, it cannot be insignificant that the same forces that generate the American fundamentalist right are also solidly behind efforts at the further missionary expansion of conservative forms of American Christianity all around the world. This is globalism of a particular sort, not anti-globalism.

The case of Jewish fundamentalism in Israel

It was after the victory of the nationalist Likud party in the 1977 Israeli elections that what has since been labelled Jewish fundamentalism took on a new importance in that country. The periodization therefore corresponds to the previous two examples. What is more, the antecedents of this movement also date rather precisely to the late nineteenth- and early twentieth-century period. During that time, in the context of the development of the largely secularist Zionist movement there arose, first a religiously traditionalist anti-Zionist movement, especially in the form of the Agudat Israel organization (Schiff 1977); and then, in the 1920s, a positive religious Zionist direction inspired by Rav Kook. The difference between the two was not that one was fundamentalist and the other was not; it was rather in the differing attitudes they took to the religious legitimacy of the Zionist project of establishing a Jewish homeland in Palestine: Agudat Israel opposed it for religious reasons and Kook supported it for religious reasons. But both objected to the non-religious character of secular, and in particular socialist, Zionism. They could both be styled as "conservative" religious directions, but Rav Kook's nascent movement more clearly representing the will to appropriate the new developments rather than just reject and react against them. From that perspective, Agudat Israel might be considered the more fundamentalist if one identifies this term with "reaction". Yet, in the post World War II period, in the aftermath of the Holocaust and of the foundation of the State of Israel in 1948, the religious anti-Zionists (with minor exceptions such as the Neturei Karta) joined the religious Zionists in this appropriation effort, a move exemplified in the founding of religious political parties, which have been important partners in almost every Israeli government since then (Cohen and Susser 2000). That noted, as in the Iranian and American cases, the post-1920s period marked something of a nadir in the presence and influence of this direction, as did the post-war years when the socialist Zionism of Ben Gurion and the Labour party largely characterized the identity of Israel, and the religious parties played rather minor roles (Liebman and Don-Yehiya 1983).

In this light, what was different about the post-1977 rise of Jewish fundamentalism in Israel, again as in the previous two cases, was not the birth of a movement that had not been there before, but rather the visibility and success of the political activism of this renewed religious Zionism and Jewish fundamentalism. Although the Likud government of the day was itself more nationalist than religious, it proved a valuable ally and even catalyst for this development, perhaps somewhat parallel to the role of the Republican Party in the United States for the Christian Right. The Likud nationalists, from Menachem Begin to Ariel Sharon, held an expansionist view of Israel's legitimate boundaries. In that light, they were also more positively disposed toward basing that legitimacy in biblical warrant. The combination dovetailed nicely with the revisioning of the new religious Zionists, especially through the concrete mobilization strategy of planting (religious) Jewish settlements in the territories occupied by Israeli forces during the six-day war of 1967 (see Lustick 1988). Although Jewish fundamentalism more broadly seeks also to create a more religious Israeli state and society, one where, for instance, Jewish religious law strongly informs the country's legal system, the settlements have in practical effect and symbolic importance been the keystone of religious Zionist mobilization and political success. They have translated the religious impulse into the most concrete expression of modern political reality: sovereign state control of territory and all that takes place on it.

That said, it is important to point out that this political fundamentalism, and in particular the religious Zionist dimension of it, is part of a very diverse religious picture in Israel. The same is, of course, the case for all the other countries examined here, but in the Israeli case it is especially important because most religion in that state could be styled as "fundamentalist" if by that we mean tending toward conservatism and traditionalist orthodoxy. Orthodox Jewish religion, including religious Zionism, is internally a very diverse force in Israel, incarnating a wide variety of visions of state and society (Efron 2003). Thus the most religiously traditional and orthodox, and from that perspective fundamentalist, are not necessarily the most aggressively nationalist. There exist not only anti-Zionist ultra-orthodox groups, but also "peace" oriented (i.e. making no claim to the "biblical Land of Israel" as legitimate state boundaries, and promoting the peaceful coexistence of all religious groups in broader Palestine) orthodox groups, as well as tendencies all along the political spectrum from moderately or ambiguously nationalist/expansionist to aggressively so. The fundamentalist religious Zionists do, nonetheless, have the effect of making this spectrum that much more visible. The fate of religion in Israel as elsewhere in the context of a global world, cannot thus be reduced to fundamentalism/traditionalist orthodoxy on the one hand and privatized, publically irrelevant religion on the other. If anything, the fundamentalist movements make the complexity of religion in modern societies – and hence in global society – more visible and evident.

As in those cases already examined and in those analyzed below, Jewish fundamentalism in the form of the religious Zionist movement has been anything but a simple "reaction" to modernizing and globalizing forces. One could say that the State of Israel always did have implicitly religious roots, at least to the extent that Jewishness is and always has been simultaneously a national/cultural and a religious identification. The religious Zionists merely rendered that relation in a certain form, activating and appropriating the religious dimension in a concrete historical situation and one intimately expressive of how the modern and global system of political states functions. Religion is not an anomaly here, not a rejection of modern society, let alone the insistence on creating some kind of religious enclave in an otherwise secular society. Rather it is a critical resource and social form through which that society can and does reproduce and transform itself, here in the modern, contemporary, and global context.

The case of Sikh fundamentalism in Punjab

These instances of the continuity and role of so-called fundamentalist movements is not limited to cases where the Abrahamic religions of Islam, Christianity, and Islam are involved. The Sikh example bears many of the same main features, although, like them, in partial emulation of them rather than only out of its own historical tendencies and resources.

The already mentioned Singh Sabha movement of the late nineteenth century had the goal and effect of solidly distinguishing Sikhism as a religion apart from Islam and Hinduism, but it was also part of a broader Indian nationalist movement of which Congress and the Muslim League became the prime expressions in the twentieth century on the Hindu/Secular and Muslim sides. Singh Sabha wished to solidify the religious difference, to generate a clearly different Sikh form or orthodoxy that would be distinct from Islam and Hinduism. In so doing, however, the movement took on or at least led to a much more explicitly political expression in the form of the early twentieth-century Akali movement. The successful creation in 1925 of the Shiromani Gurdwara Prabhandak Committee, usually referred to simple as the SGPC, a quasi-parliamentary body in charge of the Punjab's Sikh gurudwaras, marked both an important achievement of Sikh "orthodox" religious power and control and the creation of specifically Sikh and very modern political governing structures that, as such, were unprecedented in Sikh history (Oberoi 1994). This development could have led to the formation of an independent Sikh state alongside the creation of the states of independent India and Pakistan in 1947, but the fact that Sikhs are, demographically speaking, a tiny minority in South Asia precluded this as a practical possibility. Following on the high points of this Sikh movement in the late nineteenth and earlier twentieth century, this failure marked a period of relative decline in at least the political visibility of this historical movement, parallel to the nadir suffered by the previous examples. During the post-Second World War period, then, one witnesses another gradual resurgence, one that had as its first significant success the 1966 creation of a new and smaller federal Punjab state. The boundaries of this state were drawn along linguistic and not religious lines – the latter unthinkable in an India traumatized by Partition only two decades earlier – but the effect, very much intended on the part of the Sikhs that mobilized over decades to create it, was to bring about the first demographically Sikh majority political unit in history (Deol 2000). Punjab was nonetheless thereby not (yet) a Sikh state, and therefore the religio-national impulse did not lose its elan (Gupta 1996).

The historical push for what Rajiv Kapur titled Sikh separatism (Kapur 1986) in fact continued virtually without interruption after the creation of the new Punjab state. It was the combination of this continuity and other contextual factors, however, that brought matters to a head at more or less precisely the same time as happened in Iran, the United States, and Israel. Economic transformations in Punjab after 1966, state/federal disputes over economic, administrative, and political control, and the ongoing policies of Indira Gandhi to maintain and enhance the Congress Party dominance over the Indian government bequeathed by her father, Jawaharlal Nehru; these all contributed to an atmosphere in which rival Sikh factions sought to outdo one another in their efforts to represent the best interests of Sikhs. Among these factions were those that adopted more militant tactics beyond civil disobedience and mass protests, leading the escalating violence of the early 1980s that culminated in, Operation Bluestar, the 1984 invasion by the Indian army of the Sikh's most holy shrine, the Golden Temple in Amritsar. It was in this context that observers began to speak of Sikh fundamentalism, an unsurprising development given the emphasis that some militant leaders, especially Sant Jarnail Singh Bhindranwale, put on various symbolic elements of the Sikh orthodoxy that had been solidifying since the Singh Sabha movement of a century earlier (Madan 1991).

In this context of polarization and violence, the Sikh movement took on its most politically separatist face to date. In the several years before and after Bluestar, the movement toward an independent Khalistan, a hoped-for orthodox Sikh state, attained its greatest strength, to the consternation of more than a few observers (Embree 1990, Jeffrey 1985, Larson 1995). The Khalsa orthodoxy gained significantly among Sikhs in India as elsewhere (Tatla 1999). Yet, unlike as in the already treated examples, this result was not to last. The militant Sikh movement experienced no corresponding lasting success, but was quite brutally suppressed, in part through the agency of other Sikhs who did not share the "fundamentalist" vision of a religiously inspired independent Sikh state (Singh 1996). By the mid-1990s, the movement had effectively lost its force, while world attention shifted more to the Hindu nationalist movement that was reaching its apogee at about the same time. This is the subject of the next section.

The Sikh fundamentalist or revolutionary religio-national movement of the last decades of the twentieth century did not experience the success of its contemporary Islamic version in Iran, but the two were similar in that they sought to take political control of or to create a modern sovereign state. They were in this and other ways similar to their other contemporary revolutionary movement, that of Nicaragua. The reason that most observers would not call the latter fundamentalist – in spite of the significant implication of religiously motivated actors such as liberation theological Roman Catholic priests, three of whom subsequently held cabinet posts in the post-revolutionary Sandinista government – whereas the former are generally seen as prime examples of this phenomenon, is that the dominant revolutionary ideologies in Punjab and Iran were based in religion, a recognized world religion at that. The Nicaraguan priests did not aim to create a state in which, in their case, a revitalized and avowedly traditionalist Roman Catholic Christianity would inform the very identity of state and society; the Khomeinists and Khalistani Sikhs had precisely this in mind using Shi'a Islam and Sikhism. It is because the corresponding ideology in the Nicaraguan case was socialist – albeit for many a Christian-inspired socialism – and because most observers deem socialism modern and non-religious, that this revolution is not deemed fundamentalist. Fundamentalism again appears as the use of "tradition" for "modern" purposes, and only a perspective that sees tradition and modernity as mutually exclusive would find this in any way odd.

The case of Hindu fundamentalism in India

The final example, that of Hindu fundamentalism, essentially repeats the pattern evident in the others. In this case, the movement is even more commonly referred to as Hindu nationalism rather than fundamentalism, underscoring the semantic link between this term and religio-nationalisms. One can go further. In a way analogous to the role that Agudat Israel and then the religious Zionism of Rav Kook played with respect to secular Zionism in the Jewish case, a specifically Hindu nationalism attached itself to the larger "secularist" (read: not identified with a particular religion) Congress-led Indian nationalist movement at the beginning of the twentieth century, notably in the form of the Hindu Mahasabha (Jones 2001). And, parallel to the Sikh case, this occurred during an era that saw the parallel formation and imagining of Hinduism as a distinct and united mass religion for the first time in its history (Chatterjee 1995). If one considers that a third religio-national option, in the form of the Muslim League, arose at the same time as the Hindu Mahasabha and the Singh Sabha/Akali movement, then the overall Indian developments of the late nineteenth and early twentieth centuries show with great clarity how religious (re)formation of that period – in India as elsewhere around the entire globe – was so often intimately tied to the development of the particular identities that most observers today recognize as among prime "actors" in the global social system to which the idea of globalization primarily refers: nations, but also religions. Moreover, and underscoring the common logic of the religio-national events of this time, just as in the American case the term "fundamentalism" was coined at this time to refer to this type of (re)formation movement, so did the strictly parallel Indian term "communalism" arise at more or less exactly the same time (see Pandey 1992) and with reference to the same sort of movement. The two terms are parallel if not entirely synonymous; they are both defined in opposition to "secularism"; they could in fact be used interchangeably.

Although the Hindu Mahasabha represented the organized beginning of specifically Hindu nationalism at the beginning of the twentieth century, developments during the 1920s put this religio-national movement on a solid and uniquely Indian footing. In 1923, V. D. Sarvakar published what has become a kind of manifesto or sacred text of this movement, entitled *Hindutva*, or "Hinduness". A few years later saw the foundation of the Rashtriya Swayamsevak Sangh (RSS), an organization that has, ever since, been the core organization eventually of a whole family of Hindu nationalist organizations often referred to as the "family of organizations", the *Sangh Parivar* (Andersen and Damle 1987, Jaffrelot 2005b). As in the other cases examined above, in the years after the 1920s, including the first two to three decades after Indian independence in 1947, the movement did gradually grow but was eclipsed in terms of power and influence – if not exactly in visibility, even notoriety – by the secular nationalists in the form of Congress and its primary leaders, Gandhi and Nehru. Yet from 1947, the Hindu nationalist family, as in the Israeli case, included political parties, first the Jana Sangh founded in 1951, and then, at the beginning of the 1980s, the Bharatiya Janata Party (BJP), which became the governing party in several Indian states and at the federal level during the 1990s and early 2000s (Bhatt 2001). Most observers only started to look seriously at this party and what it represented in the very late 1980s when it began to achieve electoral success, and especially after the violence surrounding the destruction of the Babri Masjid in Ayodhya in 1992. Yet its founders and main leaders, Advani and Vajpayee, had already held substantial power in the 1977–80 government of the Janata Dal, an anti-Congress coalition formed to oust Indira Gandhi from power after the two-year Emergency she had perpetrated in the two years previous.

What one witnesses in the Hindu nationalist case as in the others is, again, not the sudden rise of an unprecedented fundamentalist "reaction" in the late twentieth century, but rather the greater and partially unprecedented prominence of a movement that had for almost a century been a significant actor in the development century India both as a state and as a particular society within the global system. The late decades of that century provided the contextual opportunity for the movement's greater success. Moreover, in this Hindu nationalist case, there is also little question that it represents much more a different kind of appropriation than of reaction given the decidedly neo-liberal directions that BJP governments ended up taking (in spite of an RSS ideology to the contrary) and the degree to which this Hindu nationalism has now become part of the Indian electoral mainstream (Jaffrelot 2005a). In fact in four of the cases examined here (assuming the Sikh political party, the Akali Dal, as the religio-nationalist survivor in the Punjabi case) the fundamentalisms have become a regular part of the liberal democratic mainstream, rather than the leaders of a theocratic and isolationist authoritarianism or an ultimately futile cry of anguish destined for the garbage heap of history.

Globalization, particularization, and fundamental difference

The strong connection, sometimes to the point of identification, between the religion and the nationalism of these fundamentalist movements is one of the strongest indicators of the degree to which they are more expressive of the current situation of globalization than they are reactions against it. Globalization, as indicated at the outset, is only incompletely understood if one focuses simply on its "homogenization" aspects, on the ways that greater connectivity among all social parts of the world is leading to the sameness of those parts. From that truncated perspective, all insistence on difference and heterogeneity can only appear as resistance and reaction. In that case, the global and the local must always be opposed. The wider view of globalization, however, recognizes that the world's people becoming more tightly integrated has indeed generated a great amount of imitation, and not just of the so-called West by the non-West. Global flows, as communications of all sorts across the world are sometimes called, go in all directions, from West to East, from North to South to be sure; but also from East to West, from South to North, and from South to East, East to South. Yet, what flows through those networks are not just goods, people, and ideas. These also implicate various sorts of, often very unequal, power relations. Global relations thereby generate more than imitation, fusion, and hybridity as old identities become transformed. They also bring about coercion and competition; and it is this combination of flows of meaning and power that raises serious questions for all the world's people not just of "who am I?", "who are we?", but just as importantly "who controls who I am or what we are and will become?" In this context, questions of identity, and how "our" or "my" identity is different from "others'" become more than existential speculation; they become matters of life-chances, integrity, dignity, and worth. As a result, the processes of globalization have always carried with them and generated, not just sameness, but difference, not just homogeneity but at the same time heterogeneity, both in a comparative and competitive way. Not only do we all thereby end up doing the "same thing" differently, but these differences typically come to express themselves in analogous ways. It is in this context that globally spread concepts like culture, religion, nation, people, race, ethnicity, class, and gender take on a peculiar importance. They have become the "re-formed" or "invented" vehicles of different identities in global context. Fundamentalist religious movements, such as the ones just examined, are examples of this assertion of difference in global context, the use of religious meaning and power to assert and manufacture meaningful and powerful differences. They are not the only such example, by any means; but they belong to the current context quite as much as movements that are more "liberal" (not conservative or traditional) and more "secular" (not religious).

The context of globalization thus shows that fundamentalisms are not, for the most part, "reactionary" expressions of the yearning for a traditional and bygone world. They are rather modern developments in a globalized world. If that conclusion can be taken as given, then it also has implications for religion more generally. As the title of one book on the subject indicates (Almond et al. 2000), the meaning of fundamentalism is frequently not limited to the sort of national, state-centred religio-political movements that have been the primary empirical focus of this chapter, but includes any "strong" religion, any religious movement that seeks to create strong "communal" boundaries against the perceived "other", the "secular" world (cf. Kepel 1994). What should be evident from the foregoing analysis is that, even if one extends the meaning of the word in this way, "strong" religion is not necessarily a way of being "un-modern", of rejecting the modern globalized world and its strong secularity. Instead, as is the case with the vast majority of "communal" or even sectarian religious movements that would in this view fall under the title of fundamentalism, they are ways of participating in this world quite on a par with any other, more clearly non-religious ones. Whether one is looking at Pentecostalists in Brazil, Lubavitchers in the United States (and Israel), Communione et Liberazione in Italy, Pushti Marga in India, just to name a few examples, these forms of religion, like the religio-political fundamentalisms, are ways of engaging in the contemporary world, but with an identity that is different. The context of globalization, which switches the primary unit of analysis so that the entire world rather than just one piece of it is included, just makes this conclusion that much easier to observe.

References

Abdel-Malek, K. (1988) *Towards and Islamic Liberation Theology: Ali Shari'ati and His Thought*, Montreal: McGill University Press.

Almond, G. A., Appleby, R. S. and Sivan, E. (eds.) (2000) *Strong Religion: The Rise of Fundamentalisms around the World*, Chicago, IL: University of Chicago Press.

Andersen, W. K. and Damle, S. D. (1987) *The Brotherhood in Saffron: The Rashtriya Swayamsevak Sangh and Hindu Revivalism*, Boulder, CO: Westview.

Arjomand, S. A. (1984) *The Shadow of God and the Hidden Imam: Religion, Political Order, and Societal Change in Shi'ite Iran from the Beginning to 1890*, Chicago, IL: University of Chicago Press.

——(1988) *The Turban for the Crown: The Islamic Revolution in Iran*, New York: Oxford University Press.

Bakhash, S. (1990) *The Reign of the Ayatollahs: Iran and the Islamic Revolution*, New York: Basic Books.

Barber, B. R. (1996) *Jihad vs. McWorld*, New York: Balantine Books.

Beyer, P. (1994) *Religion and Globalization*, London: Sage.

——(2006) *Religions in Global Society*, London: Routledge.

——(2007a) "Globalization and Glocalization", in J. A. Beckford and N. J. Demerath III (eds) *The Sage Handbook of the Sociology of Religion*, London: Sage, pp. 98–117.

——(2007b) "Globalization and the Institutional Modeling of Religion", in P. Beyer and L. Beaman (eds) *Religion, Globalization, and Culture*, Leiden: Brill Academic Publishers, pp. 167–86.

Bhatt, C. (2001) *Hindu Nationalism: Origin, Ideology and Modern Myths*, Oxford and New York: Berg.

Binder, L. (1957) "Pakistan and Modern Islamic-Nationalist Theory, Part 1", *Middle Eastern Journal*, 11, 382–96.

Brown, R. M. (2002) *For a "Christian America": A History of the Religious Right*, Amherst, MA: Prometheus Books.

Bruce, S. (1988) *The Rise and Fall of the New Christian Right: Conservative Protestant Politics in America 1978–1988*, Oxford: Clarendon.

Campbell, G. V. P. (2007) "Religion and Phases of Globalization", in P. Beyer and L. Beaman (eds) *Religion, Globalization, and Culture*, Leiden: Brill Academic Publishers, pp. 281–302.

Chatterjee, P. (1995) "History and the Nationalization of Hinduism", in V. Dalmia and H. von Stietencron (eds) *Representing Hinduism*, New Delhi: Sage, pp. 103–28.

Chebabi, H. E. (1990) *Iranian Politics and Religious Modernism: The Liberation Movement in Iran under the Shah and Khomeini*, Ithaca, NY: Cornell University Press.

Cohen, A. and Susser, B. (2000) *Israel and the Politics of Jewish Identity*, Baltimore, MD: Johns Hopkins University Press.

Dalmia, V. and von Stietencron, H. (eds) (1995) *Representing Hinduism: The Construction of Religious Traditions and National Identity*, New Delhi: Sage.

Deol, H. (2000) *Religion and Nationalism in India: The Case of the Punjab*, London: Routledge.

Dumoulin, H. and Maraldo, J. C. (eds) (1976) *Buddhism in the Modern World*, London and New York: Macmillan.

Durham, M. (2000) *The Christian Right, the Far Right, and the Boundaries of American Conservatism*, Manchester: Manchester University Press.

Efron, N. J. (2003) *Real Jews: Secular Versus Ultra-Orthodox and the Stuggle for Jewish Identity in Israel*, New York: Basic Books.

Embree, A. (1990) *Utopias in Conflict: Religion and Nationalism in Modern India*, Berkeley, CA: University of California Press.

Farhi, F. (1990) *States and Urban-Based Revolutions: Iran and Nicaragua*, Urbana, IL: University of Illinois Press.

Gupta, D. (1996) *The Context of Ethnicity: Sikh Identity in Comparative Perspective*, New Delhi: Oxford University Press.

Hadden, J. K. and Shupe, A. (eds) (1986) *Prophetic Religion and Politics*, New York: Paragon House.

——(eds) (1989) *Secularization and Fundamentalism Reconsidered*, New York: Paragon House.

Hardacre, H. (1989) *Shinto and the State, 1868–1988*, Princeton, NJ: Princeton University Press.

Held, D., McGrew, A., Goldblatt, D. and Perraton, J. (1999) *Global Transformations: Politics, Economics and Culture*, Stanford, CA: Stanford University Press.

Huntington, S. P. (1996) *The Clash of Civilizations and the Remaking of World Order*, New Delhi: Viking Penguin.

Isichei, E. A. (1995) *A History of Christianity in Africa: From Antiquity to the Present*, Grand Rapids, MI and Lawrenceville, NJ: W.B. Eerdmans and Africa World Press.

Jaffrelot, C. (2005a) "The BJP and the 2004 General Election: Dimensions, Causes and Implications of an Unexpected Defeat", In K. Adeney and L. Sáez (eds) *Coalition Politics and Hindu Nationalism*, London: Routledge, pp. 237–53.

——(ed.) (2005b) *The Sangh Parivar: A Reader*, New Delhi: Oxford University Press.

Jeffrey, R. (1985) *What's Happening to India: Punjab, Ethnic Conflict, Mrs. Gandhi's Death and the Test for Federalism*, New York: Macmillan.

Jensen, L. M. (1997) *Manufacturing Confucianism: Chinese Traditions and Universal Civilization*, Durham, NC: Duke University Press.

Jones, K. W. (2001) "Politicized Hinduism: The Ideology and Program of the Hindu Mahasabha", In R. D. Baird (ed.) *Religion in Modern India*, Delhi: Manohar, pp. 241–73.

Juergensmeyer, M. (1993) *The New Cold War? Religious Nationalism Confronts the Secular State*, Berkeley, CA: University of California Press.

Kapur, R. (1986) *Sikh Separatism: The Politics of Faith*, London: Allen & Unwin.

Keddie, N. R. (1998) "The New Religious Politics: Where, When, and Why Do 'Fundamentalisms' Appear?" *Comparative Studies in Society and History*, 40, 696–723.

——(2003) *Modern Iran: Roots and Results of Revolution*, New Haven, CT: Yale University Press.

Kelley, D. M. (1972) *Why Conservative Churches Are Growing: A Study in Sociology of Religion*, New York: Harper & Row.

Kepel, G. (1994) *The Revenge of God*, Oxford: Blackwell.

Khosrokhavar, F. (1993) *L'Utopie sacrifiée: Sociologie de la révolution iranienne*, Paris: Presses de la Fondation nationale des sciences politiques.

Khosrokhavar, F. and Roy, O. (1999) *Iran: Comment sortir d'révolution religieuse*, Paris: Seuil.

Larson, G. J. (1995) *India's Agony over Religion*, Albany, NY: SUNY Press.

Liebman, C. S. (1966) "Changing Social Characteristics of Orthodox, Conservative and Reform Jews", *Sociological Analysis*, 27, 210–22.

Liebman, C. S. and Don-Yehiya, E. (1983) *Civil Religion in Israel: Traditional Judaism and Political Culture in the Jewish State*, Berkeley, CA: University of California Press.

Liebman, R. C. and Wuthnow, R. (eds) (1983) *The New Christian Right: Mobilization and Legitimation*, New York: Aldine.

Lustick, I. S. (1988) *For the Land and the Lord: Jewish Fundamentalism in Israel*, New York: Council on Foreign Relations.

Lyotard, J.-F. (1984) *The Condition of Postmodernity*, Manchester: Manchester University Press.

Madan, T. N. (1991) "The Double-edged Sword: Fundamentalism and the Sikh Religious Tradition", in M. E. Marty and R. S. Appleby (eds) *Fundamentalisms Observed*, Chicago, IL: University of Chicago Press, pp. 594–627.

Marsden, G. (1980) *Fundamentalism and American Culture: The Shaping of Twentieth Century Evangelicalism, 1870–1925*, New York: Oxford University Press.

Marty, M. E. and Appleby, R. S. (eds) (1991–95) *The Fundamentalism Project*, 5 vols, Chicago, IL: University of Chicago Press.

Neill, S. (1986) *A History of Christian Missions*, Harmondsworth: Penguin.

Oberoi, H. (1994) *The Construction of Religious Boundaries: Culture, Identity, and Diversity in the Sikh Tradition*, Chicago, IL: University of Chicago Press.

Pandey, G. (1992) *The Construction of Communalism in Colonial North India*, Delhi: Oxford University Press.

Rahnema, A. and Nomani, F. (1990) *The Secular Miracle: Religion, Politics, and Economic Policy in Iran*, London: Zed Books.

Riesebrodt, M. (1993) *Pious Passion: The Emergence of Modern Fundamentalism in the United States and Iran*, Berkeley, CA: University of California Press.

Robertson, R. (1992) *Globalization: Social Theory and Global Culture*, London: Sage.

Robertson, R. and Garrett, W. R. (eds) (1991) *Religion and Global Order*, New York: Paragon House.

Sachedina, A. (1983) "Ali Shariati: Ideologue of the Iranian Revolution", in J. L. Esposito (ed.) *Voices of Resurgent Islam*, New York: Oxford University Press, pp. 191–214.

Schiff, G. (1977) *Tradition and Politics: The Religious Parties of Israel*, Detroit, MI: Wayne State University Press.

Scholte, J. A. (2005) *Globalization: A Critical Introduction*, London: Palgrave Macmillan.

Shupe, A. and Hadden, J. K. (eds) (1988) *The Politics of Religion and Social Change*, New York: Paragon House.

Singh, G. (1996) "Punjab since 1984: Disorder, Order and Legitimacy", *Asian Survey*, 36, 410–21.

Skocpol, T. (1979) *States and Social Revolutions: A Comparative Analysis of France, Russia, and China*, Cambridge: Cambridge University Press.

Tatla, D. S. (1999) *The Sikh Diaspora: The Search for Statehood*, Seattle, WA: University of Washington Press.

Voll, J. O. (1982) *Islam: Continuity and Change in the Modern World*, Boulder, CO: Westview Press.

Wallerstein, I. (1974–80) *The Modern World System*, 3 vols, New York: Academic Press.

——(1979) *The Capitalist World-Economy*, Cambridge: Cambridge University Press.

Wilcox, C. (2000) *Onward Christian Soldiers: The Religious Right in American Politics*, Boulder, CO: Westview.

15

Globalization and Indigenous peoples

New old patterns

Carlos Gigoux and Colin Samson

Norwegian energy company SN Power recently agreed to temporarily suspend activities on its hydroelectric project due to the vocal opposition from local Indigenous groups (...) During a seminar in Oslo, Norway, last month Mr. Antimilla suggested that the project would constitute an intervention in Mapuche territories, interfere with Mapuche-operated tourism, and threaten the surrounding environment.

(*Santiago Times*, 3 January 2008)

Denouncing it as a threat to Indigenous ways of lives and the environment, local Mapuche communities and the nearby non-Indigenous towns of the Región de Los Ríos, southern Chile, have raised stiff opposition to the building of hydroelectric power plants. Different national and international strategies have been devised to stop the Norwegian energy company SN Power diverting the rivers of the Mapuche territories for hydro-electric power generation. The project has been challenged on many grounds, but two issues have predominated: first, the acquisition of water rights infringed Mapuches' rights over their territories and, second, the government's provisional concession for the development of the hydroelectric projects did not consult the local communities affected by it (Nordbø and Utreras 2007). In this context, the conference held in Oslo – and sponsored by the Norwegian NGO FIVAS – had a positive effect insofar as the company agreed to halt their initial surveys in the region and engage in open discussions with local communities. However, despite this agreement and subsequent meetings, the project – and the conflict – continues. Even though there are massive power disparities between the Mapuche and SN Power, this case exemplifies the increasing emphasis of Indigenous groups to make local violations of their rights a global issue in the fight for the protection of their territories, resources, and ways of life. Furthermore, it highlights a new strategy that requires alliances with national and international NGOs who contribute funding, research data, publicity, and contacts with national governments and international organizations, but also reflects a tendency to bypass the nation state in order to counter such projects. The multinational threat to Indigenous territories has created a global strategy.

The Mapuche challenge to the plunder of their lands and waters is just one among many that highlight the ongoing conflicts to which Indigenous peoples are exposed as a consequence of private and state sponsored projects that seek to physically transform the territories in which they live, and which are at the centre of their ways of life. Although not new, such threats have acquired an increasing global dimension that involves trans-national actors whose objective of profit maximization cannot be reconciled with the social and cultural stability of local populations. Many of the laws and policies of states are designed to facilitate the operations of these enterprises, and in many parts of the world this inevitably involves, first, the appropriation of Indigenous lands and, second, in almost all cases, negative social and psychological transformation of the peoples themselves.

This chapter focuses on the consequences of contemporary global events on Indigenous peoples. The first part will deal with the connections between globalization and Indigen-ous peoples. This serves both as a starting point and as an analytical frame. We will then examine sites of contestation such as Indigenous mobilizations, the international recog-nition of Indigenous rights, the court cases, the role of advocacy groups and the quest for Indigenous identity revitalization.

'New old patterns': globalization and Indigenous peoples

There is much debate about what globalization actually is. Described as the 'Global Vil-lage' or the 'Network Society', globalization as a term remains elusive (See Castells 1996, McLuhan 1962. Van Dijk 1991). Is it a theory, a process or a historical period? Is it the extension of modernity or a shift to a new phase in history? Is it just a euphemism for neoliberal economic universalism? Is it a process that leads to open markets and demo-cratization or does it simply deepen longstanding injustices and divisions? The discussion goes on and on, but undoubtedly it is possible to recognize some of its salient features. Robinson (2007: 125) provides a good summary of some of its key points:

- A globalized economy involving new systems of production, finance, and consumption and world economic integration.
- New transnational or global cultural patterns, practices, and flows, and the idea of 'global culture(s)'.
- Global political processes, the rise of new transnational institutions and, concomitantly, the spread of global governance, and authority structures of diverse sorts.
- Unprecedented multidirectional movement of peoples around the world involving new patterns of transnational migration, identities, and communities.
- New social hierarchies, forms of inequality and relations of domination around the world.

However, examining Robinson's definition it is possible to recognize that, although globalization exhibits unprecedented characteristics, especially in regard to the develop-ment of information technology and massive migration movements, it remains very much a new version of an old story. It is impossible to separate globalization from its Western historical roots anchored in liberalism, capitalism, and colonialism. The forms may have changed, but globalization is mainly an economic process steered by those in positions of political and commercial power. It continues to structure worldwide social hierarchies of domination that consign large segments of the population to inadequate levels of food and shelter and few realistic possibilities for social justice. Moreover, if globa-lization has compressed time and space, making the world smaller and more interconnected, the most beneficial effects accrue to the affluent and political elites. From the perspective of many Indigenous peoples, globalization is just a new variation of an old pattern of intrusion and dispossession.

The term 'Indigenous peoples' also poses various difficulties. Who are considered Indigenous peoples and what defines them as such? What ways of life defines Indigenous peoples: farmers, hunter-gatherers, pastoralists, all of them? Are Indigenous peoples who migrate to urban areas still Indigenous? Does this generic term respect the cultural and historical specificities of thousands of peoples worldwide or just artificially homogenize them? Is it possible to speak of Indigenous peoples in the decolonized nation states of Asia and Africa where all populations are regarded by the states as Indigenous?[1] Its official international use is strictly connected with the need for a standardized legal terminology that can assist the advancement and protection of specific human rights. In this context, the definition of José Martínez Cobo in his study *On the Problem of Discrimination against Indigenous Populations* (1986) has been highly influential within the United Nations:[2]

> Indigenous communities, peoples and nations are those which, having a historical continuity with pre-invasion and pre-colonial societies that developed on their territories, consider themselves distinct from other sectors of the societies now prevailing on those territories, or parts of them. They form at present non-dominant sectors of society and are determined to preserve, develop and transmit to future generations their ancestral territories, and their ethnic identity, as the basis of their continued existence as peoples, in accordance with their own cultural patterns, social institutions and legal system (...) On an individual basis, an Indigenous person is one who belongs to these Indigenous populations through self-identification as Indigenous (group consciousness) and is recognized and accepted by these populations as one of its members (acceptance by the group). This preserves for these communities the sovereign right and power to decide who belongs to them, without external interference.[3]

Martínez Cobo's definition emphasizes the personal and the historical dimensions of indigeneity, the essential colonial context, the self-consciousness of cultural identity and the longstanding connections to territory.[4] Furthermore, the International Labour Organization (ILO) definition of 1989, recognized as an international Indigenous rights instrument, draws from this definition by further affirming Indigenous peoples right to self-determination.[5] This definition has been a cornerstone for Indigenous peoples advancing their rights through the United Nations and is incarnated in the 2007 UN Declaration on the Rights of Indigenous Peoples. However, the definition has also been opposed by states, many of which do not accept the designation 'peoples' or the notion that specific rights attach to longstanding connections to land.

So what is the relation between globalization and Indigenous peoples? From the perspective of many Indigenous peoples, globalization is just an extension of previous socio-political processes that have dispossessed them of their lands and, following numerous extinctions in the nineteenth century and continuous erosion of their land bases and political autonomy, threaten their survival as distinct ethnic groups.[6] Although globalization has some new features, distinctive from previous historical periods, there are three major features that remain largely unchanged: first, the economic imperative driving the exploitation of Indigenous territories for natural resources, industrial activities and/or space for urbanization; second, the lack of recognition of Indigenous societies and cultures by the nation state;[7] and third, the relative indifference on the part of states towards Indigenous peoples' lives. 'Wherever there is evidence in the contemporary world,' as Kunitz (2000: 1531) argues, 'Indigenous peoples who have been incorporated into the state have lower life expectancy, lower income, and worse health than non-Indigenous inhabitants of the same state.' Part of the indifference to this, of which its persistence is a measure, is grounded in social Darwinist notions of competition between superior and inferior races and Indigenous impoverishment, ill health and social pathology as a stage in the adjustment to civilization or modernity.[8] Globalization has only increased such historical patterns, and while creating new opportunities for Indigenous peoples' resistance, the fact remains that nowadays, Indigenous peoples continue to be exposed to the powerful forces of the worldwide capitalist economy and consumer culture. Therefore, any reflection on the relationship between globalization and Indigenous peoples has to start acknowledging the impact of these forces on the ways of life and distinctive identities of Indigenous peoples.

Patterns of violence: dispossession, destruction of the land, and racial stereotypes

Tropic of Capricorn, a 2008 BBC documentary, provided a glimpse of the local consequences of globalization for Indigenous peoples.[9] The increasing demand for soybean – mostly in Europe and China – for livestock feed and the production of biofuels has led to deforestation in many regions of South America, especially in the regions of Amazonas and El Chaco. Lands with abundant biodiversity have been turned over to mono-crop agriculture. The documentary showed how the hunting, gathering, and honey procuring activities of the Wichi peoples in the northern Argentinean region of Salta were made impossible. Gigantic bulldozers were shown standing besides upturned trees in the depleted forests. This was a powerful image of a violence unleashed on both the forests that are cleared, the animals that live in them and the biodiversity needed to live as Indigenous peoples who are dependent upon animals, plants, and honeybees.

Another recent film, *Invisible*, by British artist Roz Mortimer, exposes the paradox – and drama – of Inuit mothers whose breast feeding transmits high levels of persistent organic pollutants into their children's bodies. Mortimer's camera pans slowly over the beauty of the deep white of the landscape, and the red stained snow as Inuit hunters bring back seal and whale meat to Igloolik on Baffin Island in the Canadian territory of Nunavut. The vivid and sometimes enigmatic imagery becomes a backcloth to the words of Inuit mothers and scientists commenting on the contamination of the seas and the marine life that is at the heart of Inuit culture.[10] Dioxins and other pollutants known as polychlorinated biphenyls (PCBs) from iron plants, copper smelters, cement kilns, pesticides, and municipal waste plants emanating from Southern Canada and the United States have already been found in abundance in the Indigenous territories of the Far North. These are absorbed by plankton, small fish, and even seals, and are now in the Inuit food chain in Alaska and Canada. As early as 1994, studies discovered the Inuit to have extremely high levels of organochlorine compounds such as the pesticide DDT and PCBs in their bodies, even though the sources of these toxins are thousands of miles away (Dewailly et al. 1994). Some of it is passed from mother to baby in breast milk. This means that mothers have to choose between eating the otherwise highly nutritious fish and meat that is the mainstay of the Arctic diet and thereby risking their babies'

health or abandoning this diet in favour of the unhealthy flown-in store bought processed food products that are ubiquitous in the Far North and are causes of the Western
diseases that are proliferating across the Indigenous world.[11]

The global effects of fossil fuel consumption, manufacturing, and industrialized agriculture now means that no matter how far a group is from the centres of production,
they are never immune from the environmental effects. With their own food sources in
jeopardy from resource extraction and industrialization, the exchange of healthy wild
foods for unhealthy junk foods is a key element of the 'new' globalization. This is the
story for Indigenous peoples in huge swathes of the circumpolar North, the deserts, and
rainforests. Such areas were initially perceived as having little economic productivity.
However, this has all changed. Indigenous peoples' territories no matter how 'remote,'
are prime targets for the situation of dams, logging, industrial farming, roads, housing,
fishing, national parks, tourism, and conservation projects. Such projects are often pushed
through by national legislation following from the cooperation of politicians with lobbyists of powerful corporations. They are often subject to direct government endorsement, with only the most perfunctory environmental impact review and virtually no
consultation with the peoples whose lands are being usurped.[12] Significantly, it is the case
in many countries that the cooperation of government-appointed, paid or endorsed
Indigenous political elites is also required. Whether hunter-gatherers, farmers or pastoralists, Indigenous peoples require a territory in order to live and maintain distinct Indigenous identities. Major resource extraction and other projects such as the establishment
of semi-urban settlements represent major threats to this aim. The consequences of
development activity in this context are well documented: (a) deterioration of living
conditions; (b) negative impact on their distinct cultures; (c) migration to urban areas; (d)
diseases; (e) alteration of food supplies; (f) pollution of the environment; (g) deforestation;
(h) destruction of wildlife; (i) violent deaths; and (j) forced resettlement.

In many cases, industrial development directly causes the devastation of well-functioning
societies. Many of these stories unfold only in the periphery of mainstream media and
political and academic commentary. Academic research provides useful snapshots of
specific zones of misery but sustained long-term research on the politics of Indigenous
survival, however, is not common. By contrast, the dynamic and ongoing process of
threats and resistance can be followed in the Indigenous and NGOs websites. On a daily
basis, information springs up on the computer screen but seldom makes it to the headlines
of mainstream media.

To take a few examples from South America; a recent Report of the Conselho Indigenista Missionário (CIMI) documented that in 2007, 48 Guarani-Kaiowá Indians were
killed in Matto Grosso do Sul as a consequence of illegal deforestation.[13] In 2007, CIMI
estimated that about a third of the remaining uncontacted Indigenous groups in the
Amazon are threatened with extinction as ranchers, loggers, and miners have expanded
into the rain forest. This has been enabled by the Brazilian government's slow demarcation of defined boundaries that would prevent the theft of Indigenous lands. At the same
time, the Brazilian Amazon is endangered by oil and gas projects. In Rio Juruá, in the
Acre region, such projects are opposed by local Indigenous communities for fear of
pollution and deforestation. In the Putumayo border region between Colombia and
Ecuador, the Cofán peoples are exposed to the intertwined threat of oil, narcotic production,
and military conflict. The Putumayo case exemplifies very well the continuous nature of
such threats. These reports recall the dramatic overtones of the Roger Casement's Putumayo
Report of 1912 (Taussig 1987: 37–47).

The mass media now reaches a global audience in publicizing Indigenous peoples' sufferings from political violence or war between antagonists within the state on their territories. For instance, the Indigenous peoples in Colombia have been exposed to violence involving the conflict between the guerrillas, the army, and the paramilitaries that has resulted in massive displacements, murders, and poverty (Villa and Houghton 2005). Underneath the conflict is the appropriation of territories for the industrial production of drugs for the United States and European markets, which in turn sustains the ongoing armed conflict and maintains profits. Therefore, drug consumption in New York, Amsterdam or London becomes entangled with the violent dispossession of Indigenous peoples' territories and the imperilling of their lives.

Yet, this new — and old — globalized world has produced new kinds of threats to Indigenous peoples. Although generally not violent in character, some tourist and environmental projects are perceived by many Indigenous peoples as new forms of colonialism. Minority Rights Group International (MRG) has recently launched a campaign in order to create awareness of the damaging effects of some tourist projects sponsored by national governments that force Indigenous peoples off their lands. For instance, in Kenya the Maasai Mara Game Reserve and the Amboseli National Park have a long history of conflicts with the pastoralist Maasai (Rutten 2002). In Botswana, the San were denied access to their hunting lands in order to build the Central Kalahari Game Reserve.[14] Neumann (1998) shows how the Tanzanian state built upon the colonial model of land appropriation, commandeered natural resources and then established limited zones of conservation at places like Mount Meru. This has led to the displacement and impoverishment of peoples who historically used the areas for a wide variety of subsistence activities and whose own histories and beliefs are bound up with the mountain region.

A recurrent theme in the state response to the displacement of Indigenous peoples is the argument that only solutions that bind populations into the social and cultural order of the state by using its own scientific, medical, educational, and political institutions will address the poverty, ill health, and dysfunction of Indigenous groups. In the eyes of many national politicians, these forms of intervention will help stabilize the Indigenous populations, but in order to reduce poverty and marginalization, Indigenous peoples must be taught how to take advantage of opportunities for economic gain.[15] Under the guise of citizenship policies, many states have and continue to require assimilation through permanent settlements, schooling, missionary activities, supervised wage labour, and entrepreneurial tutelage. Thus, instead of tackling the problems by examining the sources, such as *externally* induced displacement, states often displace the problem itself and depict it as *internal* to the Indigenous group itself.

The paradox is that most Indigenous peoples were largely self-sufficient until brought under the authority of nation states when their dispossession created dependency and thus the demand for ameliorative assistance from state welfare institutions arose. The Indian reservations in the United States, the Aboriginal reserves in Canada, and the Aborigine compounds in Australia are vivid examples of such realities, and rather than being a thing of the past remain a very lively reminder of the negative consequences of dispossession.[16] Rather than contributing to the improved welfare of the Indigenous populations, these enclaves act as physical contexts for serious deterioration of their physical and mental health. Several studies document the specific patterns of collective self-destruction that no amount of welfare, medical services or education has been able to combat. In all these cases, the rates of alcohol and drug abuse, imported Western illnesses, death and suicide rates are much higher than those for the average state population.[17]

Finally, and deeply intertwined with these economic patterns of dispossession, is the role that discourses on ethnicity play in the justification of such actions and/or in shaping the social indifference towards them. Despite decades of deconstructing narratives and postcolonial theory, social Darwinist assumptions still linger underneath social representations that not only proclaim the inevitability of the assimilation of Indigenous peoples into the 'modern world', but also reinforce the stereotype that they are living relics of the past. Such discourses function to naturalize dispossession and at the same time nourish the apathy towards Indigenous tragedies. They also foster a conception in Western development circles that policy ought to emphasize change not continuity because Indigenous peoples are mired in the 'stone age' or the 'Mesolithic era.' This was the contention of British peer Baroness Lady Jenny Tonge in entering into a highly public debate with the NGO Survival International in Britain over their support for the San Bushmen to return to their hunting territories from the relocation camps set-up by the government of Botswana.[18] What is staggering is the persistence of the assumption that Indigenous peoples have almost nothing to offer dominant societies.

While the overwhelming forces that threaten Indigenous peoples cannot be simplified, overlooked or ignored, it is also worth analyzing the extent to which globalization has provided a space for resistance and contestation. First, the international scene has provided Indigenous peoples with an opportunity to acquire a broader visibility and a platform from which to create networks to support their claims for recognition. In particular these aims have been achieved through a series of linked factors: social mobilizations; UN recognition of Indigenous rights as human rights; the emergence of international advocacy groups; the creation of international Indigenous networks; the increasing jurisprudence on Indigenous peoples' rights; revitalization movements; and historical recognition and reconciliation.

Indigenous rebellions: uprisings, networks, and the artist

The Zapatista uprising in 1991 is a milestone for contemporary Indigenous mobilizations. The contexts and rationales for the uprising did not differ significantly from any other Indigenous mobilizations around the world – marginalization, discrimination, poverty – but three elements made it a global event: first, the timing of the uprising at the beginning of the North American Free Trade Agreement (NAFTA) agreement between the United States and Mexico; second, the global mass media coverage; third, the discussions surrounding the anniversary of the conquest of the Americas in 1492. Suddenly, the marginalized Indigenous communities of southern Mexico were a worldwide event and the masked faces of their leaders become part of the iconography of the late twentieth century. As Lee (2006: 455) argues, 'the current prominence of Indigenous social movements indicates not only the coming to political consciousness of marginalized peoples, but also a new global acceptance of these peoples and the legitimacy of their claims'. The local Indigenous communities' mass media attention strengthened their use of the global space to invert hierarchical structures of power by developing highly visible symbolic actions, such as the presence of Comandante Esther at the Mexican Congress in 2001. The fact that an Indigenous woman, holding a leadership position in the structure of the Ejército Zapatista de Liberación Nacional (EZLN), was able to take centre stage at the heart of Mexico's political system highlights this inversion. The Zapatista's have developed, alongside their military capacity, a strong use of information technology in

293

order to maintain worldwide attention of their mobilization. In this context, the use of internet has contributed in great extent to their aims (Kahn and Kellner 2007: 663–664).

The Zapatista rebellion only highlights the connections between mobilization and visibility. Many Indigenous peoples live very much marginalized from the main populations of states, whose members take little notice of their existence. Therefore, countering state policies and widespread social stereotypes requires the appropriation of geographical space in order to gain visibility and to counter social indifference. As Clifford (2007: 198) comments, 'the increase of Indigenous movements at different scales – local, national, regional and international – has been one of the surprises of the late twentieth century. 'Tribal', 'archaic', 'primitive', or 'stone age' peoples, in Baroness Tonge's parlance, were, after all, destined to wither in the relentless winds of modernization. It now takes just a few minutes to scroll around the internet to find endless Indigenous mobilizations across the world and to realize the implications that such mobilizations have on Indigenous peoples. Nicholas (2000: 233) explains how the increasing threat over Orang Asli's territories and resources in Malaysia pave the way to 'a new and broader pan-Orang Asli consciousness'.

In effect, Indigenous peoples which have been independent and sometimes in conflict with each other have realized the need for creating common alliances in opposition to the political, economic, and social threats. From small local alliances to national and international networks, Indigenous peoples have created their own institutional networks in order to support their struggles. Just a few examples would include, The Confederación Nacional Indígena de Ecuador (CONAIE); the Amerindian Peoples Association in Guyana; the Assembly of First Nations in Canada; the Cordillera Peoples Alliance in the Philippines CPA; the Organización Nacional Indígena de Colombia (ONIC), the National Congress of American Indians in the United States, the Asociación Interétnica de Desarrollo de la Selva Peruana (AIDESEP), the International Alliance of Indigenous and Tribal Peoples of the Tropical Forests and the Asian Indigenous & Tribal Peoples Network. These all have developed a range of activities from political lobbying to educational, artistic, and tourist projects. Again, their websites are a good example of the interconnection with information technology, creating a discordant note with the persistent images of Indigenous primitivity. While these organizations have been established to fight for Indigenous peoples' rights and cultural distinctiveness, being dependent on state funding can compromise some pan-Indigenous organizations. In these cases, their goals can easily become depoliticized, as for example in Canada, when the state slashed funding for the organization in response to Assembly of First Nations (AFN) National Chief Matthew Coon-Come's frank criticisms of the racism embodied in Canadian Indian policies in the international arena which had embarrassed the government. This act ultimately enabled the victory of his moderate and more domestically focused opponent Phil Fontaine in the AFN election of 2000 (Ross 2003).

In Latin America, Indigenous peoples have gone further by creating their own political parties in which Indigenous rights are at the forefront of their quest for power. So diverse is the ethnically structured political landscape in Latin America that it has attracted the attention of scholars intrigued by the communal nature of such parties and their distinctiveness from traditional Western political parties (Rice and Van Cott 2006). The success of Evo Morales and the Movimiento al Socialismo (MAS) party in Bolivia highlights the entry of Indigenous interests into state politics, as does the candidacy of Rigoberta Menchú in Guatemala, although by contrast her political bid was unsuccessful. In countries like Ecuador, Colombia, Guyana, and Panamá there are also Indigenous representatives in the national Parliaments – either elected or appointed – while the EZLN in México exercise their self-determination by maintaining control over territories claimed by the Mexican state.

Another important aspect of Indigenous contestation in the global stage is the increasing role taken by Indigenous artists, musicians, and writers in the representation, not only of their own communities, but of themselves as legitimate contemporary artists who defy, enlarge and extend the meaning of art itself by challenging some of the canonical assumptions of Western arts and letters. By refusing to collaborate with either craft or artefact genres, much Indigenous art defies the colonial – and passive – settings of the many displays of Indigenous cultures in Western museums and galleries. In this context, Indigenous artists have become a common place within the cultural landscape of galleries, museums, and art spaces around the world. Moreover, the global stage has also provided the opportunity for Indigenous performers to directly challenge pervasive stereotypes and to denounce the social and political marginalization. For instance in 1987 the Luiseño American Indian James Luna staged an installation, *The Artifact Piece*, in the Museum of Man in San Diego. Luna, barely covered by a loincloth, laid down still inside a glass box surrounded by objects such as his personal documentation while visitors walked by.[19] The performance subverted the notion that Indigenous cultures were part of the past and the fact that it was staged inside a museum challenged the very institution where such assumption has been produced and reproduced. But also Luna has staged performances in which he raises issues concerning white-Native American relations that are often uncomfortable for white audiences. Recently, at the George Gustav Heye Center, New York, he staged *Emendatio* in which he highlights the serious health problems that affects Indigenous peoples.[20] Other North American native artists include Jimmie Durham, Shelley Niro, Edgar Heap of Birds, Jolene Rickard and Juane Quick-to-see-Smith.[21]

'The minimum standards for their survival, dignity, and well-being':[22] the United Nations, recognition of Indigenous rights

If political and cultural mobilizations have been at the forefront of Indigenous actions to defend their territories and counter racism, discrimination, and marginalization, the twentieth century has also witnessed the increasing recognition of Indigenous rights in international forums transforming Indigenous peoples into distinct subjects of international law (Morgan 2004). The International Labour Organization (ILO) Convention No. 107 (1957) 'On Living and Working Conditions of Indigenous Populations' was the first explicit text of the United Nations that dealt extensively with Indigenous peoples within the framework of labour rights. In 1982 the United Nations Economic and Social Council established the Working Group on Indigenous Populations (WGIP) and integrated into its structure five experts of the Sub-Commission on the Promotion and Protection of Human Rights. The Working Group has provided a space for Indigenous peoples to participate within the UN system and as a consequence to be able to put forward initiatives on issues of concern to Indigenous groups around the world. But the most important document concerning Indigenous peoples sprang from the ILO, when in 1989, it published its Convention (N°169) concerning Indigenous and Tribal Peoples in independent countries.[23] Consequently, a series of initiatives took place that helped to establish a new UN consciousness about Indigenous peoples. 1993 was declared the International Year for the World's Indigenous Peoples. In 1994 the United Nations

General Assembly launched the first International Decade of the World's Indigenous Peoples (1995–2004) and subsequently the second one (2005–2014) which aims to promote a whole range of social, cultural, and economical initiatives concerning Indigenous peoples. In 2000 the UN established a Permanent Forum on Indigenous Issues (UNPFII) that has created a space for Indigenous peoples, advocacy groups and independent researchers and experts to meet and discuss on a whole range of issues.[24] However, the most important development was the UN adoption of the Declaration on the Rights of Indigenous Peoples on 12 September 2007. Despite opposition from the United States, Australia, New Zealand, and Canada, and containing limitations which enable state vetoes of exercises of Indigenous rights, the Declaration is a significant step in creating an international legal framework for the recognition of the rights of Indigenous populations.

Altogether, these UN developments have generated an increasing legal corpus on Indigenous peoples' rights. International institutions such as the World Bank, the European Union and the Inter American Bank have adopted guidelines, especially in regard to free, fair and informed consent for development projects.[25] In a global world, where the UN system *should* play a central role, the recognition of Indigenous peoples as distinctive peoples is a major step forward in creating international awareness of their rights, and at the same time establishing specifically Indigenous social and cultural rights in international law. The main result of all this is the recognition of their cultural and social identity, territorial rights and of the principle of self-determination. However, as history has shown such legal advancement does not guarantee the well-being of Indigenous peoples, as it requires the effective implementation and enforcement of such policies by the nation states where Indigenous peoples live. This tension is well reflected in the increasing use of national and international courts by Indigenous peoples in order to enforce their rights.

The court and the politics of Indigenous ethnic identity

Not only have international organizations taken into consideration the body of Indigenous peoples rights, states have also needed to adapt their internal legislations to such international agreements, or failing that to react to them in some fashion. As a consequence, Indigenous peoples are increasingly using this new framework in order to challenge governmental decisions affecting their territories in the national and international courts.

Such actions have created new dynamics concerning the scholarly understanding of cultural identity. It was a common feature of nineteenth-century ethnology to elaborate complex biological traits as codes for the conceptualization of race. The twentieth century witnessed a shift from race to culture with the consolidation of anthropology as a discipline. Under the rubric of culture, the activities, manners, and habits of Indigenous peoples became distinctive objects of study for Western social scientists who, through ethnographic fieldwork, elaborated the forms and functions of Indigenous societies. Much, if not most, of this research was undertaken under the authority of the colonial powers that occupied the lands of the research subjects. Anthropological knowledge often served these same colonial interests by providing useful cultural knowledge to colonial administrators while largely ignoring the coerced transformations that occurred through colonialism.[26]

However, after formal decolonization, the politics of cultural identity has shifted from the lecture hall and the journal to the courtroom.[27] The growing corpus of International law on Indigenous rights has provided Indigenous peoples' organizations with a new frame for the protection of their rights (Pasqualucci 2006: 282). In the last ten years or so, an increasing number of Indigenous plaintiffs have filed suits in national and international courts, and the cases that resulted have added a whole range of legal resolutions to the corpus of Indigenous laws. Table 15.1 provides a glimpse of these new realities.

These court cases demonstrate an ever-increasing judicialization of Indigenous rights. A closer examination of each one of them reveals some common patterns. First, the central issue of contention is land. Second, the parties involved in the conflict are Indigenous peoples and nation states. Third, they all ended with favourable resolutions in favour of the plaintiffs. Fourth, the trial became a site of anthropological debate within a context of legal control. In 1997, the Supreme Court of Canada recognized the underlying ownership and jurisdiction of Indigenous groups to lands in North Western British Columbia, challenging in the process the assumption that underlying native title could simply be extinguished by conquest or through some criteria of *terra nullius*. It also paved the way for the introduction of oral evidence alongside physical evidence of historical occupation of lands.[28] In 2001, the Inter American Court of Human Rights ruled in favour of the collective rights of the Mayagna Community to their traditional lands, natural resources and environment and therefore ruling against the concessions given by the Nicaraguan government to international companies for timber exploitation in these territories.[29] As a consequence it ordered the Nicaraguan government to reverse the authorization given to a timber company in order to operate in the communal lands. In 2002, the Federal Court of the Selangor State in Malaysia established that the Orang Asli were not tenants on their lands but have full native titles based on the right to their customary and ancestral lands. Therefore, it ruled that the eviction from their lands in order to accommodate a highway to the International Airport contravened these rights and that they were entitled to a full compensation for such unlawful actions.[30] The final

Table 15.1 Selected Indigenous rights court cases.

Year	Country	Indigenous peoples	Case	Court
1997	Canada	Gitxsan and Wet'suwet'en Nations	Delgamuukw vs. British Columbia	Supreme Court of Canada
2001	Nicaragua	Awas Tingni	Mayagna (Sumo) Community Awas Tingni vs. Nicaragua	Inter American Court of Human Rights
2002	Malaysia	Orang Asli	Sagong Tasi vs. Selangor State Government	Federal Court
2002	United States	Shoshone	Mary and Carrie Dann vs. United States	Inter American Commission of Human Rights
2005	Paraguay	Yakye Axa	Yakye Axa vs. Paraguay	Inter American Court of Human Rights
2006	Botswana	San	Roy Sesana & 242 others vs. The Botswana Government	Botswana High Court
2007	Belize	Maya	Aurelio Cal et al. vs. Attorney General of Belize	Supreme Court of Belize

resolution in the *Dann* case issued two recommendations to the US; (1) To hold a leg-islative or judicial hearing on the issue of land title, since the confiscation of lands for military testing and other purposes amounted to a reneging on the guarantees the US had already granted the Western Shoshone in the 1863 Treaty of Ruby Valley, and (2) Review all US law and policy on Native American rights to property (Gómez 2003).

In 2005, once again the Inter American Court of Human Rights was called upon to address the rights of the Yakye Axa to their lands, rights persistently denied by the Para-guayan state. According to the Inter American Commission on Human Rights, this situation 'has implied the impossibility, for its members, to access the property and possession of their territory and has kept them in a vulnerable alimentary, medical and sanitary condition that continuously threatens the survival of its members and the integrity of the commu-nity'.[31] The Court ordered Paraguay to comply with the resolution. In 2006, the Botswana High Court ruled in favour of the right of the Kalahari San to return to their hunting lands in the Central Kalahari Game Reserve where they were forcibly evicted.[32] More recently, the Supreme Court in Belize ruled that the Maya Villages of Santa Cruz and Conejo 'hold collective and individual rights in the lands and resources that they have used and occupied according to Maya customary practices and that these rights constitute "property ... "'. It instructed the Belize government to demarcate the Indigenous terri-tories and refrain from any act that may contravene this right.[33] This ruling sets a new benchmark as far as it is the first court case to invoke the UN Declaration on the Rights of Indigenous Peoples as a legal precedent in the protection of Indigenous native titles.[34]

In addition to having implications for the state monopoly of power within a territory, the judicialization of Indigenous struggles brings into question the activities of transna-tional corporations in various host countries. In 1993, the Achuar from the Ecuadorian Amazon filed a lawsuit against the oil company Chevron in a Federal Court in the United States for environmental and health damages as a consequence of their industrial activity. After many years of litigation, the jurisdiction of the case was transferred to a court in Ecuador where a resolution is still pending.[35] More recently, the Achuar from the Per-uvian Amazon have also filed a lawsuit against the US Oil Company Oxy (Richardson 2008). In both cases the operation of the Oil Companies left pollution that affected the environment and the health of Indigenous populations. Similar charges have been levelled against multinational resource extraction companies in North America. Following wide-spread environmental damage across the entire Far North and Arctic regions and a suit filed by the Inuit of Alaska and Canada in the Inter-American Court against the US government, in 2008, the village of Kivalina, Alaska sued Exxon Mobil Corporation and six other corporations in a lawsuit in a Federal Court. They claim that global warming threatens the existence of the village through soil erosion, pollution, and the loss of animal habitats.[36] By suing the companies, Indigenous peoples have bypassed the national gov-ernments and displacing the site of struggle from the apparently invisible rain forests to the highly visible corporate skyscrapers in New York or Los Angeles. In the process, they have managed to create a wider public impact, whilst highlighting the interconnections between decisions taken in the economic centres of the world and the peoples of the peripheries. Mobilizations, political representation, and legal actions are part of these new strategies that take into account the global nature of the challenges that threatened their ways of life.

Overall, how are we to interpret this judicialization of Indigenous rights? In the broader context of colonial relations between nation states and Indigenous peoples the law, far from being a neutral and impartial set of norms, has been an instrument legitimating the dis-possession of Indigenous peoples through its use of concepts such as the doctrine of discovery and *terra nullius* and its insistence on the sanctity of the private property rights of colonists and their descendents against original inhabitants of colonized territories around the world (Weaver 2003, Robertson 2005). Indeed, filing suits and claims in state courts has been often been unsuccessful even when the violation to Indigenous peoples pre-existing rights or damage to their lands is blatant.[37] The positivist and enlightened nature of the law has been a permanent weapon of dispossession and deception for continuing colonial practices.

If yesterday's treaties between colonial powers and Indigenous communities facilitated dispossession, nowadays land claims agreements, business contracts, and environmental impact studies pave the way for a second or third wave of dispossessions. Therefore, it is a novelty to see Indigenous peoples battling through national and international courts in order to interrogate these state procedures. Indeed, the development of a body of international law and jurisprudence has provided strong support in Indigenous rights and cultural continuity cases. A good case in point is the efforts of Aboriginal lawyers and activists in exposing Canada's notorious extinguishment policies at the UN. Interventions at the UN in New York and Geneva from lawyers such as the Armand McKenzie (Innu) and Sharon Venne (Cree), along with activists such as Kenneth Deer (Mohawk) and Romeo Saganash (Cree) has led to persistent interrogation of these policies, which in effect mandate that in order to 'claim' their own lands and achieve limited self-government rights, the property rights to ancestral lands must first be signed over to Canada.[38]

Nevertheless, the shuttling back and forth to the UN and the fighting of court cases is a great burden on Indigenous peoples' resources and requires a whole range of parallel initiatives like lobbying, fundraising and research in order to support their claims. They also need to find funds to hire lawyers, environmental scientists, and anthropologists, many of whom are necessarily non-Indigenous and have joint loyalties to the state of which they are citizens and which often actually pay their substantial salaries.[39] Because of these limitations, the role of national and international NGOs becomes more important. Indigenous peoples' organizations are at the forefront of their struggles, but in the process they have needed to create partnerships and alliances with non-Indigenous organizations.

Global alliances: the role of the INGOs

If the new global economy is characterized by global business networks, Indigenous peoples have mirrored this by creating national and supranational collaborative institutions. In this regard, they have adopted the institutional frame of modern institutions and with it created parallel bureaucratic apparatuses. In this context, the use of IT skills has led to the creation of hundreds of websites that help to create a virtual platform for Indigenous issues and networks. Since the 1960s a growing number of International NGOs (INGOs) have been created in order to support Indigenous peoples' rights in their struggles with national governments and corporations. They also provide economic and technical support, wage media campaigns, engage academic expert research, and generally facilitate linkages between Indigenous groups and sources of potential assistance for fund raising, human rights recognition, lobbying of national governments and litigation. INGOs such as the Minority Rights Group, MRG (founded in 1965); IWGIA (1968); Survival International (1969); Cultural Survival (1972); Conselho Indigenista Missionário, CIMI (1972); The Kalahari Peoples Fund, KPF (1973); Centre for World Indigenous Studies, CWIS (1984); Working Group of Indigenous Minorities in Southern Africa,

WIMSA (1996); and the European Network for Indigenous Australian Rights, ENIAR (1998) are just some of the most prominent examples of a whole list of Indigenous peoples' advocacy groups. They all share a concern for Indigenous peoples' rights and generally act as brokers in the way that anthropologists once saw themselves as acting (Henriksen 1985). Advocacy group strategies and methods vary a great deal from one to another, and some have been bitterly opposed to others, some have preferred media campaigning, others litigation and yet others have focused more on academic research.

The information collected through the Commission Internationale pour les Droits des Peuples Indigènes (ICRA) provides a wealth of sources and information on the threats to Indigenous peoples interests. Many academics involved in providing the kind of research that feeds into this data bank do not operate in the positivistic paradigm of much of social science. Instead they maintain that research about Indigenous peoples must also by *with* those peoples. Many have become advocates of Indigenous rights in the international arena, but this has not been without controversy. Within professional anthropology debates collaboration with such organizations and/or support for Indigenous rights campaigns has been heavily contested.[40] Critics like anthropologist Adam Kuper (2003) allege that the Indigenous peoples movement and those who support collective rights as incarnated in the UN Declaration of 2007 and other international human rights instruments are 'essentializing' Indigenous peoples. Kuper argues that the INGO Survival International reflects a move back to regarding Indigenous peoples as primitive peoples or 'noble savages', whose fragile, primordial, and ancient way of life must be protected. Anthropologists who Kuper believes to promote such views are depicted as subscribing to a 'natural harmony' thesis of Indigenous societies. Using the example of the San Bushmen of the Central Kalahari Game Reserve, Kuper additionally argues that the campaigns to safeguard Indigenous land rights locks them into a static way of life and prevents them from participating in development. Kuper, in tandem with several other anthropologists, ignores the extensive evidence that 'development' has often been catastrophic for Indigenous peoples, leading in some cases to the complete disintegration of groups. Kuper presupposes that progress as defined by Western states and the corporations they largely represent *is* universal progress and that the various kinds of development projects before which distinct Indigenous identities must yield *are* inevitable. This further assumes that there is some sort of foreseeable trajectory of human history that makes the continued practice of Indigenous ways of life impossible, and that it is some unseen force akin to the 'invisible hand', and not human actions such as the exercise of power and violence that create the world we live in.[41] In effect, by assuming some sort of inevitable future, Kuper and others 'essentialize' the human condition!

The position that development is inevitable and largely benign fits a parallel vision of globalization as having effectively erased cultural distinctiveness in the world. Ronald Niezen (2005: 34, 55) argues that resistance to globalization, as is apparent in the Indigenous rights movements, leads more completely to integration, often through human rights processes, which bind people into a European legal, normative, and cultural order. As he argues, 'efforts to resist the forces of social transformation are paradoxically contributing to them', and there is 'no escape from the forces of social convergence'. That is, in the process of configuring themselves into organizations and institutions to protect their rights, Indigenous peoples inevitably lose their distinctiveness ending up only in celebrating symbolic differences and 'invented traditions.' Familiarity with the law marks a move away from the sensibilities and traditions of oral cultures. This proceeds further with digital and internet cultures of abstraction. However, if this is the case, it presupposes that the many Indigenous groups that are actively attempting to reclaim threatened ways of life, diets, subsistence activities, languages, and religious observances cannot 'play the game' while also being loyal to their Indigenous beliefs and ways of life.[42]

Revitalization: Indigenous challenges to cultural homogenization

Article 17 of the UN Declaration on the Rights of Indigenous Peoples establishes that 'Indigenous peoples have the right to practice and revitalize their cultural traditions and customs.' This article reflects an ongoing process in many parts of the world where small Indigenous communities have started an active process of cultural revival. According to the Oxford Dictionary, to revitalize is 'to make something stronger, more active or more healthy'. The purpose of revitalizing cultural identity has to be understood as a dynamic and creative process that varies according to different contexts. This is a side effect of the increasing internationalization of Indigenous peoples' organizations and the recognition of their rights. It presupposes the existence of a group of people – normally attached to a territory – that share a cultural identity regardless of the fact that the exercise of such identity as a distinct way of life might have been weakened by assimilation policies and dispossession. In some cases, the Indigenous language and cultural symbols might have substantially diminished.

Across the globe, there are signs that Indigenous groups are attempting to reinvigorate practices that were abandoned under the pressures of colonial domination and adapt these to contemporary economic and social conditions. In some instances, elements of this revitalization are undoubtedly symbolic, amounting to simulations of past practices that can only partially be resuscitated because land, languages, and knowledge have all died or been eroded. But in certain locations, particularly regions of the Far North such as Nunavut and Labrador-Quebec in Canada, Greenland, Alaska, and the Saami territories in Scandinavia, lands are more abundant, Indigenous languages are still widely spoken, and the encroachments of non-Indigenous populations have not been so concentrated. Despite all the adversities to hunter-gatherers in the Amazon and parts of Africa, links with the land are also multifarious in those locations.

As evidence is rapidly accumulating of the toxic consequences of the contemporary Western diet based on industrialized agriculture with its concentrations of saturated fats and carbohydrates, Indigenous peoples fortunate enough to have wild foods available to them may enhance their chances of physical and cultural survival (Samson and Pretty 2006; Damman et al. 2008; Pollan 2008). Often efforts to reclaim Indigenous diets are also twinned with recovery of medical systems, natural pharmacies, and educational systems.[43] Indigenous groups also need to find an economy to support revitalization. Some have been able to tap into state and international donor funds. Others have taken an entrepreneurial approach, opening up ecotourism ventures, educational projects, trekking, fishing camps, and wildlife viewing.[44] The United Confederation of Taíno People recently requested from the Expert Group Meeting on Indigenous Languages that the Caribbean Indigenous Peoples be included in the process of fighting discrimination against Indigenous languages and in promoting actions concerning 'the revitalization and rescue of threatened Indigenous languages'.[45] Contrary to the longstanding perception that the Indigenous peoples from the Caribbean have vanished, these events show active efforts of revitalization. As Forte (2006: 3) explains 'contemporary Indigenous peoples of the Caribbean refuse to be measured by the relics of their past or to be treated

301

condescendingly as mute testimonials to a disappearing history, or a history of disappearance'. By the same token, the seldom acknowledged Ainu peoples of Hokkaidō, Japan provide another interesting example of such process. Groups such as Yay Yukar no Mori based in Sapporo, and the Foundation for Research and Promotion of Ainu Culture have embarked on several projects to promote the Ainu language, religious observances and hunting and fishing practices in the midst of one of the most assertively technological societies on the planet.[46]

Most Indigenous cultural revitalization has been led by the communities themselves, sometimes in partnership with national governments, international agencies or even private companies.[47] This revitalization process must be understood in the context of the resilience of Indigenous peoples but also as the shifting and dynamic nature of cultural identity. As Clifford (2007: 198) argues, 'this "survival" has been an interactive, dynamic process of shifting scales and affiliations, uprooting and re-rooting, the waxing and waning of identities'. Moving away from fixed notions of cultural identity, mostly imposed by non-Indigenous peoples, cultural revitalization reflects how Indigenous peoples represent themselves and how these identities are produced and negotiated in a global stage.

The limitations on revitalization

Of course, not all Indigenous peoples are in a position to be as inventive as Clifford suggests. Much depends on how Indigenous peoples are situated in relation to states and corporations, what kinds of states they find themselves in, and the extent to which their land is coveted for exploitation. If a group finds themselves in a state not particularly concerned about either Indigenous cultural identity or human rights, and at the same time eager to take advantage of global economic opportunities, then Indigenous groups are in a precarious position to do anything other than *react* to growing encroachments. Much will also depend on what they wish to be inventive about. If land, languages, religions, and social organization have been lost or already substantially altered, then there is less to use as a basis for invention other than the tools handed them by the institutions of the dominant society. Their 're-rooting' is therefore not in conditions of their own choosing, to paraphrase Marx.

States and corporations often work in tandem. While states are responsible for the drafting and enforcement of domestic laws and policies, the operations of multinational corporations are vital to the economic conditions that serve as legitimation of the state itself. Thus, in numerous realms of activity, corporations are allowed liberties, both legal and extra-legal, not permitted of citizens. States are notorious for turning a blind eye to activities of corporations, and in turn the neo-classical and neo-liberal economic theories that underpin most economic activity view government intrusion into the workings of business as a perversion of market mechanisms. This is why either protection of such market mechanisms has been written into law or excesses that violate laws have been ignored (see Mattei and Nader, 2008). Indeed, all colonial and post-colonial plunder have had either a legal or extra-legal sanction. Even the property rights that were supposedly sacrosanct to Enlightenment notions of democratic order were quietly ignored or even sanctioned by the British state and its postcolonial offspring in North America, Australia, New Zealand, and South Africa when settlers claimed Indigenous lands (Weaver 2003).

All this means that Indigenous peoples protests directly to states may have little effect. Direct confrontation with corporations, as shown by the Mapuche strategy described at the beginning of this chapter, may achieve better results since unfavourable publicity may be seen by corporate executives to reflect badly on the reputation – and potentially the future profitability – of the business. However, from the corporate point of view, this can be avoided to some degree by a further deflection of responsibility when there is international financing of operations. Many resource extraction projects on Indigenous lands are enabled via organizations such as the World Bank that make loans to corporations which are bound only by the voluntary codes of corporate social responsibility. There are numerous examples whereby World Bank financing of resource extraction activities on Indigenous lands have led to land confiscation, toxic contamination, damage to property, and even the murder or criminalization of protesters. In these cases, Indigenous peoples have little recourse to justice from the state, since the World Bank takes responsibility through its funding and then points to the 'corporate social responsibility' as a guarantor of just treatment – even though this voluntary code guarantees very little.

Such is the Kafkaesque case with the giant Canadian mining company Goldcorp's operations at the Marlin mine in Guatemala and elsewhere in Central America, where there have been persistent complaints from Indigenous and other communities about lead and arsenic levels in Honduran villages adjacent to a Goldcorp gold mine.[48] In Guatemala the Indigenous peoples on whose land the Marlin mine is situated were not consulted about the mine, the perimeter fence of which extends to just outside the houses of villagers. Consultation is of course a basic right guaranteed by ILO No. 169, which Guatemala is bound to, having ratified it in 1996, and the 2007 UN Declaration on the Rights of Indigenous Peoples, which it also supported. There have been outbreaks of what appear to be environmentally induced illnesses in the village, but complaints about contamination of the nearby river and a request for independent testing has been refused by the company, who will only test samples in their own laboratories in Vancouver. However, an independent hydrological study (Bianchini 2006) 'indicates that downriver from the mine, heavy metals are beginning to accumulate, and levels of copper, aluminium and manganese are already over the limits prescribed by the World Bank' (Paley 2007). Protests at the mine have also been criminalized by company security forces arresting and imprisoning protesters, seemingly on their own asserted authority independent of the state (Deonandan 2008). The controversy over the Marlin mine is simply one example of the limitations on Indigenous peoples' abilities to assert and practice autonomy. In this case the Indigenous peoples are coping with potentially toxic effects of arsenic and cyanide (used to leech gold from the earth) into their bodies, facing violence from mining company security officials and miners, and have little appeal bar the almost completely inaccessible World Bank. This means that the global interlinking of the state, corporations, and the World Bank with instruments of violent suppression place severe limitations on Indigenous autonomy, and dictate that much of their energies are sapped by simply reacting to new and often unjust situations that are foisted upon them.

Conclusion: symbolism and beyond

On 13 February 2008, Kevin Rudd, the Australian Prime Minister made an official apology to Australia's Indigenous peoples for the state sponsored policies that forcibly removed children from their families since the late 1860s up to the 1970s. The apology was delivered at the Australian Parliament in front of aboriginal leaders and members of the Stolen Generation and broadcasted live on national TV.

We apologise for the laws and policies of successive Parliaments and governments that have inflicted profound grief, suffering and loss on these our fellow Australians.

We apologise especially for the removal of Aboriginal and Torres Strait Islander children from their families, their communities and their country.

For the pain, suffering and hurt of these Stolen Generations, their descendants and for their families left behind, we say sorry.

To the mothers and the fathers, the brothers and the sisters, for the breaking up of families and communities, we say sorry.

And for the indignity and degradation thus inflicted on a proud people and a proud culture, we say sorry.

We the Parliament of Australia respectfully request that this apology be received in the spirit in which it is offered as part of the healing of the nation.

(Rudd 2008)

The official apology represents an important statement of the Australian government concerning its historical – and genocidal – relationship with Indigenous peoples. Like other apologies, it plays a symbolic political role in redeeming the settler society and the British colonial powers that oversaw the atrocities, but at the same time it highlights the important partnership between Indigenous peoples, intellectuals, and advocacy groups in pushing forward a small measure of recognition that the apology also symbolizes. The *Report of the National Inquiry into the Separation of Aboriginal and Torres Strait Islander Children from Their Families* issued in 1997 was largely due to their persistent and intensive social pressure and lobbying. Indeed, the official apology responds to the long struggle of Indigenous peoples in Australia for cultural recognition after decades of denial by the Australian state and much of the settler population. The apology, however, does nothing to address the serious economic and social issues that affect Indigenous communities, reclaim the enormous amounts of stolen land, or recover the self-confidence robbed of peoples forcibly inducted into assimilation regimes.[49]

Clearly, Indigenous peoples' struggles for physical survival and cultural continuity will require more than apologies from magnanimous colonial states. It will depend upon the efforts of Indigenous peoples themselves on global stages. As we have discussed in this chapter, social mobilizations, the international recognition of Indigenous rights, court cases, the role of advocacy groups, and the quest for Indigenous identity through revitalization projects are major features in the process of active resistance and re-creation led by Indigenous peoples themselves. However, the apologies, the UN Declaration on the Rights of Indigenous Peoples and 'corporate social responsibility', will not be sufficient to meet the aspirations of many Indigenous peoples to retain their ways of life and autonomy and reverse the worst effects of colonialism such as the adoption of the Western diet and the import of Western diseases. Persistent efforts both to find practical ways of living the lives they wish to and negotiating the often-Kafkaesque global order will be needed to ensure that what are ostensibly gains in terms of rights and opportunities are more than symbolic.

Notes

1 For a discussion on the term 'Indigenous', see Lee (2006). Also see UN Permanent Forum on Indigenous Issues, Fifth Session, 6th & 7th Meetings, 2006. It is important to note, however, that while states argue that all populations within its borders are Indigenous citizens, the states themselves

often comprise an urbanized elite ethnic group configured by the departing colonial power. This is especially true of African states; see Davidson (1992).

2 United Nations, Department of Economic and Social Affairs. Workshop on Data Collection and Dissagregation for Indigenous Peoples. *The Concept of Indigenous Peoples*. PFII/2004/WS. 1/3.

3 UN Doc. E/CN.4/Sub.2/1986/7 and Add. 1–4.

4 The definition by its very nature glosses over vast differences between groups designated as 'Indigenous peoples'. Some groups remain rooted to lands, languages, religions, and cultural practices, while others have intermarried with other populations and have moved away geographically and culturally. Yet others have reinvented themselves with an Indigenous identity that distinguishes them from the dominant populations. Many groups are, as a consequence unrecognized by this definition; see Miller (2003).

5 Seventy-Sixth Session, General Conference of the International Labour Organization (ILO). Convention N°169 concerning Indigenous and Tribal Peoples in Independent Countries, June, 1989.

6 A number of Indigenous genocides occurred in the nineteenth century, especially within the British Empire. On Canada, see Marshall (1996). On Tasmania, see Lemkin (2007); Brantlinger (2004). On Tierra del Fuego, see *Comisión Verdad Histórica y Nuevo Trato* (2003: 115–146). Known as the 'Black Legend', earlier genocides were committed by the Spanish in the Caribbean and immortalized in the contemporary writings of Bartolomé de Las Casas (1992).

7 This lack of recognition is closely linked to the challenge that such recognition would represent to the assumption of the 'state-centered, historical sovereignty' of the modern imagined nation state; see Anaya (2004: 7).

8 See, for example, Horsman (1981); Lindqvist (2007).

9 *Tropic of Capricorn*, BBC, Sunday, 2 March, 2008.

10 See Mortimer (2007) [DVD] *Invisible*.

11 On the connections between changes in diet and mental health in the Arctic, see McGrath-Hanna et al. (2003). On the relationship between the abandonment of traditional diets and Western diseases, see Pollan (2008: 85–98).

12 On the attempts by the Bush administration to promote oil drilling along the North Alaska coast occupied predominantly by Inuit and Gwich'in Indians, see the comments of Matthiessen (2007: 57–64).

13 On the violent patterns to which Indigenous peoples are exposed, see for example Bonin (2008); Olmos (2006). On the Putumayo, see Misión Internacional de Verificación de la Verdad en Pueblos Indígenas (2006).

14 Minority Rights Group International, *Press Release*, 9 August 2007.

15 Indeed one of the primary justifications for assimilation measures in North America was the inculcation of the profit motive. While preparing the Allotment Act of 1883, which allocated reservations in individual parcels of land under private property ownership, the architect of the policy, Senator Henry Dawes complained that Indian tribes had, ' … no selfishness, which is at the bottom of civilization' (see Debo 1940: 22). On the connection of these policies with citizenship, see Hoxie (1984: 34).

16 In Canada, Aboriginal infant mortality, suicide, alcoholism, and chronic diseases are all substantially higher than for the general population; see Health Canada (2003). According to a report by the United States Commission on Civil Rights (2004), Native Americans in the US are 770 per cent more likely to die from alcoholism, 650 per cent more likely to die from tuberculosis, and 420 per cent more likely to die from diabetes than the general population. See also the Report (2005) of the American Psychiatric Association to the United States Congress on the status of the mental health of American Indians and the results from the 2005 National Survey on Drug Use and Health (2006). The same pattern of extremely high rates of suicide, alcoholism and very low life expectancies are also to be found among Aborigines in Australia, see information compiled by Short (2008: 2–3) and Australian Indigenous HealthInfoNet (2008).

17 For the Innu of Northern Labrador, Canada, see Samson (2003, 2004). On the Orang Asli of Malaysia, see Nicholas (2000). On the San, see Saugestad (2001). On the Ik of East Africa, see Turnbull (1973). On Australian Aborigines, see McKnight (2002).

18 On the debate, see Tonge (2006) *The Guardian*, 24 March, and Monbiot (2006) *The Guardian*, 21 March.

19 For a description of the installation of the *Artifact Piece*, see Thompson (1998).

20 For a viewing of the exhibition/installation *Emendatio* see www.nmai.si.edu/exhibitions/emendatio [accessed 14 August 2008].

21 Similar points could be made about literary figures such as Gerald Vizenor, Leslie Marmon Silko, and N. Scott Momaday, who won the Pullitzer Prize for Literature for his *House Made of Dawn* in

1969. On Native American visual artists see, for example, Alison (1998); Durham (1991); Rushing (1999); Ryan (1999).

22 Press conference made by Roberto Mucaro Borrero, of the Indigenous Peoples' Caucus and Chair of the NGO Committee on the Decade of the World's Indigenous People, United Nations Press Conference, 12 December 2006.

23 International Labour Organization (1989) *Convention 169 concerning Indigenous and Tribal Peoples in independent countries.*

24 This year, the special theme of the Seventh Session of the UNPFII is on 'Climate change, bio-cultural diversity and livelihoods: the stewardship role of Indigenous peoples and new challenges', New York, 21 April–2 May, 2008.

25 See European Union Council Resolution (1998) *Indigenous peoples within the framework of the development cooperation of the Community and the Member States*; World Bank (2005) *Revised Operational Policy and Bank Procedure on Indigenous Peoples* (OP/BP 4.10); Inter American Development Bank (2006) *Operating Guidelines Indigenous Peoples Policy* (OP-765). As we shall see later, however, it is a different question as to whether these guidelines are respected by corporations and enforced by the international institutions.

26 This was true of prominent British anthropologists such as Radcliffe-Brown in Australia and Malinowski in Africa as they contributed numerous insights into the British technique of 'indirect rule', see Lindqvist (2007: 112–116) and Malinowski, (1945: 138–150).

27 For a discussion on the politics of identity developed within a court case, see for example Sapignoli (2007: 23–66).

28 Delgamuukw vs British Columbia. [1997] 3 S.C.R. 1010.

29 Corte IDH. Caso de la Comunidad Mayagna (Sumo) Awas Tingni vs Nicaragua. Sentencia de 31 de Agosto de 2001. Serie C, N° 79.

30 Sagong Tasi vs Selangor State Government [2002] Part 3 Case 5 H.C.M.

31 Corte IDH. Caso Comunidad Indígena Yakye Axa vs Paraguay. Sentencia 17 de Junio de 2005. Serie C N°125. I.2.

32 The Indigenous rights NGO Survival International have closely monitored the situation of the San relocates and extensive information about their contemporary circumstances is available at their website: www.survival-international.org/tribes/bushmen [accessed 14 August 2008]. Information is also available through the First People of the Kalahari organisation website: www.iwant2gohome.org/index.htm [accessed 14 August]. See also Olmsted (2004).

33 Supreme Court of Belize. Claim 121/2007. 18 October 2007. Art. 136. (a)

34 Ibid. Art. 131–134.

35 Information available through the Amnesty International USA website: www.amnesty.usa.org/print.php [accessed 14 August].

36 Native Village of Kivalina and City of Kivalina vs. Exxon Mobil and other Corporations, [2008], United States District Court, Northern District Of California, San Francisco Division.

37 The Western Shoshone filed a Federal lawsuit to stop the entombment of 77,000 tons of nuclear waste at Yucca Mountain, guaranteed to them by the 1863 Treaty of Ruby Valley in March 2005, but a Federal judge rejected the injunction of the Shoshone's to stop the operation in May 2005. The rejection was based on the premises that the tribe could not demonstrate 'immediate and irreparable harm'. See http://a4nr.org/library/waste/waste.pfsgoshute/2005.05.18-lasvegassun [accessed 11 August 2008]. Similarly in August 2008, The Indian Supreme Court ruled against the objections of the Dongria Kondh hill tribe to give approval to Vedanta Resources to mine a mountain revered and used by the tribe since times well predating the establishment of the Indian state (Leahy and Bream, 2008).

38 UN Human Rights Committee, (2005), Concluding observations of the Human Rights Committee: Canada. 02/11/2005, Eighty-Fifth Session, Geneva: UN.

39 On the compromised positions of non-Innu advisors in Innu land claims in Canada, see Samson (2003: 64–86).

40 Interestingly, no such debate was conducted by anthropologists in the past about their collaborations with colonial governments.

41 Among the responses to Kuper, see Asch and Samson (2004: 261–265) and Kenrick and Lewis (2004: 4–9).

42 For example, the Innu lawyer Armand McKenzie, who has been in the forefront of Indigenous rights discussions at the UN, speaks his own language as a first language, French as a second language, English as a third language, and he is also proficient in Italian. He is trained in law, knowledgeable

about international legal instruments, but also spends time hunting and fishing with his family and friends in what the Innu call 'Nitassinan', the interior of the Labrador-Quebec peninsula.

43 One such example in East Africa is the Aang Serian organization based in Arusha, Tanzania, see their website at: www.aangserian.org.uk/ [accessed 14 August 2008]. In Northern Canada the alliance of Innu hunting families called the Tshikapisk Foundation is also an excellent example www.tshikapisk.ca/home/ [accessed 11 August 2008].

44 As well as Aang Serian and Tshikapisk mentioned above, a few diverse examples include the Kiana Lodge in British Columbia, the Maniilaq Association in Kotzebue, Alaska, and the Ka'ala Cultural Learning Center in Hawaii. See their websites available at: http://kianalodge.com/about.html; www.maniilaq.org/flash.html and www.k12.hi.us/~waianaeh/HawaiianStudies/kaala.html [accessed 14 August 2008].

45 United Nations (2008). International Expert Group Meeting on Indigenous Languages. PFII/2008/EGM1/18.

46 Comments based on visit of Colin Samson to Sapporo and Nibutani, January 2008, Interviews with Mitsunori Keira and Shiro Kayano. See Foundation for Research and Promotion of Ainu Culture (2007). Also see their website available at: www.frpac.or.jp/eng/e_prf/index.html [accessed 14 August 2008].

47 See National Geographic Mission Programs in partnership with the Living Tongues Institute for Endangered Languages (2007).

48 For a general description of the mining conflict in the region, see Leahy (2007).

49 On the inadequacies of Australian reconciliation policies and the failure to return stolen lands; see Short (2008). The apology also ignored numerous other British and Australian policies such as settler murders, land theft, and the Lock Hospitals where Aboriginal peoples were forcibly quarantined and separated from their people for no apparent reason other than that they were considered by settlers to be 'unhygienic'; see Barta (2008) and Stingemore (2008).

References

Alison, J. (1998) *Native Nations: Journeys in American photography*, London: Barbican Art Gallery.

Amnesty International USA (2008) *Chevron (CVX) in the Amazon – Oil Rights or Human Rights? Texaco's legacy, Chevron's responsibility*. Available at: www.amnestyusa.org/chevron-corp/chevron-in-ecuador/page.do?id=1101670&n1=3&n2=26&n3=1242 [accessed 14 August 2008].

Anaya, J. (2004) *Indigenous Peoples in International Law*, New York: University Press.

Andersen, L. (ed.) (2008) 'Norwegian Company Suspends Hydroelectric Project in Chile', *Santiago Times Online*, 3 January. Available at: www.santiagotimes.cl/santiagotimes/2008010212607/news/business-news/norwegian-company-suspends-hydroelectric-project-in-chile.html [accessed 14 August 2008].

Asch, M. and Samson, C. (2004) 'On the Return of the Native', *Current Anthropology*, 45(2): 261–265.

Barta, T. (2008) 'Sorry and Not Sorry, in Australia: How the Apology to the Stolen Generations Buried a History of Genocide', *Journal of Genocide Research*, 10(2): 201–214.

BBC (2008) *Tropic of Capricorn*, Sunday 2 March.

Benton, B. (2005) *APA Urges Congress to help Improve Mental Health of American Indians*. Available at: www.psych.org/MainMenu/Newsroom/NewsReleases/2005NewsReleases/05–22apatocongressimprovveai_an_mh.aspx [accessed 14 August 2008].

Bianchini, F. (2006) *Calidad de agua del Río Tzalá (municipio de Sipakapa; departamento de San Marcos)* Available at: http://blog.reportero.org/wp–content/estudio_de_agua_del_rio_tzal.pdf [accessed 14 August 2008].

Bonin, I. T. (2008) *48 índios Guarani assassinados em Mato Grosso do Sul no ano de 2007 ... O que temos a ver com isso?* Available at: www.cimi.org.br/?action=read&eid=259&id=2872&system=news [accessed 14 August 2008].

Brantlinger, P. (2004) '"Black Armband" versus "White Blindfold" History in Australia', *Victorian Studies*, 46(4): 655–674.

Castells, M. (1996) *The Rise of the Network Society, The Information Age: Economy, Society and Culture*, Vol. I. Oxford: Blackwell.

Clifford, J. (2007) 'Varieties of Indigenous Experience: Diasporas, Homelands, Sovereignties', in M. Cadena and O. Stern (eds) *Indigenous Experience Today*, Oxford: Berg.

Corte Interamericana de Derechos Humanos (2000) *Caso de la Comunidad Mayagna (Sumo) Awas Tingni vs Nicaragua*. Available at: www.corteidh.or.cr/docs/casos/articulos/Seriec_66_esp.pdf [accessed 14 August 2008].

——(2005) *Caso Comunidad Indígena Yakye Axa vs Paraguay*. Available at: www.corteidh.or.cr/docs/casos/articulos/seriec_125_esp.pdf [accessed 14 August 2008].

Damman, S., Eide, W. B. and Kuhnlein, H. (2008) 'Indigenous Peoples' Nutrition Transition in a Right to Food Perspective', *Food Policy*, 33(2): 135–155.

Davidson, B. (1992) *The Black Man's Burden: Africa and the Curse of the Nation State*, New York: Times Books.

Debo, A. (1940) *And Still the Waters Run: The Betrayal of the Five Civilized Tribes*, Princeton, NJ: Princeton University Press.

Deonandan, K. (2008) 'The Mining Industry, Indigenous Peoples and Corporate Social Responsibility in Latin America: The case of Guatemala', paper presented at the Third International Conference on Interdisciplinary Social Sciences, Prato, 23 July.

Dewailly, E., Ryan, J. J., Laliberté, C, Bruneau, S., Weber, J. P., Gingras, S. and Carrier, G. (1994) 'Exposure of Remote Maritime Populations to Coplanar PCBs', *Environmental Health Perspectives Supplements*, 102 (supp 1): 205–209.

Durham, J. (1993) *A Certain Lack of Coherence: Writings on Art and Cultural Politics*, London: Kala Press.

European Union (1998) *Council Resolution on support for Indigenous peoples in the development co–operation of the Community and the Member States*. Available at: http://ec.europa.eu/external_relations/human_rights/ip/work_doc98.pdf [accessed 14 August 2008].

First People of the Kalahari (2008) *I want 2 go home*. Available at: www.iwant2gohome.org/index.htm [accessed 14 August 2008].

Forte, M. C. (2006) *Indigenous Resurgence in the Contemporary Caribbean: Amerindian Survival and Revival*, New York: Peter Lang Publishing Group.

Foundation for Research and Promotion of Ainu Culture (2007) *History and Culture*, Sapporo: FRPAC.

Comisión Verdad y Nuevo Trato (2003) *Informe de la Comisión Verdad Histórica y Nuevo Trato de los Pueblos Indígenas*. Santiago: La Nación.

Gómez, V. (2003) 'The Inter-American System', *Human Rights Law Review*, 3(1): 127–133.

Hall, G. and Patrinos, H. A. (2005) *Indigenous Peoples, Poverty and Human Development in Latin America, 1994–2004*, Houndmills: Palgrave Macmillan.

Health Canada (2005) *First Nations Comparable Health Indicators*. Available at: www.hc–sc.gc.ca/fniah–spnia/diseases–maladies/2005–01_health–sante_indicat–eng.php [accessed 14 August 2008].

HealthInfoNet (2008) *Summary of Australian Indigenous Health*. Available at: www.healthinfonet.ecu.edu.au [accessed 14 August 2008].

Henriksen, G. (1985) 'Anthropologists as Advocates: Promoters of Pluralism or Makers of Clients?' in R. Paine (ed.) *Advocacy and Anthropology, First Encounters*, St. John's: Institute of Social and Economic Research Press.

High Court of Malaya (2002) *Sagong Tasi vs Selangor State Government*. Available at: www.ipsofactoj.com/highcourt/2002/Part3/hct2002(3)–005.htm [accessed 14 August 2008].

Horsman, R. (1981) *Race and Manifest Destiny: The Origins of American Racial Anglo Saxonism*, Cambridge, MA: Harvard University Press.

Hoxie, F. (1984) *A Final Promise: The Campaign to Assimilate the Indians, 1820–1920*, Lincoln: University of Nebraska Press.

Inter American Development Bank (2006) *Operating Guidelines Indigenous Peoples*. Available at: www.iadb.org/sds/doc/ind–111PolicyE.pdf [accessed 14 August 2008].

Johnston, A. M. (2006) *Is the Sacred for Sale? Tourism and Indigenous Peoples*, London: Earthscan.

Kahn, R. and Kellner, D. (2007) 'Resisting Globalization', in G. Ritzer (ed.) *The Blackwell Companion to Globalization*. Oxford: Blackwell.

Kenrick, J. and Lewis, J. (2004) 'Indigenous Peoples' Rights and the Politics of the term "Indigenous"', *Anthropology Today*, 20(2): 4–9.

Kunitz, S. (2000), 'Globalization, States and the Health of Indigenous Peoples,' *American Journal of Public Health*, 90(10): 1531–1539.

Kuper, A. (2003) 'The Return of the Native', *Current Anthropology*, 44(3): 389–402.

Las Casas, B. de. (1992), *A Short Account of the Destruction of the Indies*, edited and translated by Nigel Griffin, London: Penguin.

Leahy, J. and R. Bream, (2008), 'Hill Tribe Protests to Go On at Indian Mine Site', *Financial Times*, 9–10 August, 7.

Leahy, S. (2007) 'Enviromental Protests at Canada's Goldcorp Mines in Honduras and Guatemala'. Available at: http://stephenleahy.wordpress.com/2007/02/22/environmental–protests–at–canadas–goldcorp–mines–in–honduras–and–guatemala/ [accessed 14 August 2008].

Lee, R. B. (2006) 'Twenty–first Century Indigenism', *Anthropological Theory*, 6(4): 455–479.

Lemkin, R. (2007) 'Tasmania', edited by Ann Cuthoys, in D. A. Moses and D. Stone (eds) *Colonialism and Genocide,* London: Routledge.

Lindqvist, S. (2007) *Terra Nullius: A Journey Through No One's Land*, London: Granta Books.

McGrath-Hanna, N., Greene, D., Tavernier, R. and Bult-Ito, A. (2003) 'Diet and Mental health in the Arctic: Is diet an important risk factor for mental health in circumpolar peoples? A review', *International Journal of Circumpolar Health*, 62 (3): 228–241.

McKnight, D. (2002) *From Hunting to Drinking: The Devastating Effects of Alcohol on an Australian Aboriginal Community*, London: Routledge.

McLuhan, H. M. (1962) *The Gutenberg Galaxy: The making of Typographic Man*, Toronto: Toronto University Press.

Malinowski, B. (1945) *The Dynamics of Culture Change: An Inquiry into Race Relations in Africa*, New Haven, CT: Yale University Press.

Marshall, I. (1996) *A History and Ethnography of the Beothuk*, Montreal: McGill-Queen's University Press.

Martínez Cobo, J. (1986) *Study on the Problem of Discrimination against Indigenous Populations.* Available at: www.un.org/esa/socdev/unpfii/en/spdaip.html [accessed 14 August 2008].

Mattei, U. and Nader, L. (2008) *Plunder: When the Rule of Law is Illegal*, Oxford: Blackwell.

Matthiessen, P. (2007) 'Alaska, Big Oil and the Whales', *New York Review of Books*, 22 November.

Miller, B. (2003) *Invisible Indigenes: The Politics of Nonrecognition*, Lincoln, NE: University of Nebraska Press.

Minority Rights Group (2007) *As UN marks World Indigenous Day, Minority Rights Group International warns of Trouble in Paradise.* 9 August. Available at: www.minorityrights.org/?lid=1682 [accessed 14 August 2008].

Monbiot, G. (2006) 'Who really belongs to another age – bushmen or the House of Lords?', *Guardian*, 21 March.

Misión Internacional de Verificación de la Verdad en Pueblos Indígenas (2006) *Informe Actual sobre la Situación de Violencia en los Pueblos Indígenas del Departamento dePutumayo/Colombia y en particular, de la Población Indígena Desplazada en Mocoa.* Available at: www.onic.org.co/mision/informe_putumayo.pdf [accessed 14 August 2008].

Morgan, R. (2004) 'Advancing Indigenous Rights at the United Nations: Strategic Framing and its Impact on the Normative Development of International Law', *Social & Legal Studies*, 13(4): 481–500.

Mortimer, R. (2007) *Invisible*, [DVD], London: Wonderdog Productions.

National Geographic Mission Programmes and the Living Tongues Institute for Endangered Languages (2007) *The Enduring Voices Project.* Available at: www.nationalgeographic.com/mission/enduringvoices [accessed 14 August 2008].

National Museum of the American Indian (2008) *Emendatio.* Available at: www.nmai.si.edu/exhibitions/emendatio [accessed 14 August 2008].

Neumann, R. (1998) *Imposing Wilderness: Struggles over Livelihood and Nature Preservation in Africa*, Berkeley: University of California Press.

Nicholas, C. (2000) *The Orang Asli and the Contest for Resources: Indigenous Politics, Development and Identity in Peninsular Malaysia*, Copenhagen: IWGIA.

Niezen, R. (2005) *A World Beyond Difference: Cultural Identity in the Age of Globalization*, Oxford: Blackwell.

Nordbø, I. and Utreras, M. (2007) *¿Los Nuevos Conquistadores? SN Power: hidroeléctricas en territorio Mapuche*, FIVAS: Oslo.

Olmos, H. (2006) 'Violence Threatens Extinction of Brazil's Isolated Indians Report Says', *Associated Press State and Local Wire*, 31 May.

Olmsted, N. (2004) 'Indigenous Rights in Botswana: Development, Democracy and Dispossession', *Washington University Global Studies Law Review*, 3(3): 799–866.

Paley, D. (2007) *In Guatemala, angry locals vote no, but BC firm presses on.* Available at: http://thetyee.ca/News/2007/02/07/MarlinProject/ [accessed 14 August 2008].

Pasqualucci, J. M. (2006) 'The Evolution of International Indigenous Rights in the Inter–American Human Rights System', *Human Rights Law Review*, 6:2: 281–322.

Pollan, M. (2008) *In Defense of Food: The Myth of Nutrition and the Pleasures of Eating*, London: Allen Lane.

Rice, R. and Van Cott, D. L. (2006) 'The Emergence and Performance of Indigenous Peoples' Parties in South America: A Subnational Statistical Analysis', *Comparative Political Studies*, 39(6): 706–732.

Richardson, L. (2008) 'Rumble in the jungle: Amazon pollution lawsuit leaves L.A. for Peru'. *Los Angeles Times Online*, 18 April 2008. Available at: http://opinion.latimes.com/opinionla/2008/04/rumble–in–the–j.html [accessed 14 August 2008].

Robertson, L. (2005) *Conquest by Law: How the Discovery of America Dispossessed Indigenous Peoples of their Lands*, New York: Oxford University Press.

Robinson, W. I. (2007) 'Theories of Globalization', in G. Ritzer (ed.) *The Blackwell Companion to Globalization*, Oxford: Blackwell.

Rojas, R. (2005) *Programa Salud de los Pueblos Indígenas de las Américas: Plan de Acción 2005–2007*. Washington, DC: THS/OS, Organización Panamericana de la Salud.

Ross, M. (2003) 'Fontaine Returns as AFN Grand Chief', *Indian Country Today*, 29 July. Available at www.indiancountry.com/content.cfm?id=1059508081 [accessed 14 August 2008].

Rushing, W. J. (1999) *Native American art in the Twentieth Century: makers, meanings, histories*, London: Routledge.

Rudd, K. (2008) *Apology to Australia's Indigenous Peoples.* Available at: www.aph.gov.au/house/rudd_speech.pdf [accessed 14 August 2008].

Rutten, M. (2002) 'Parks Beyond Parks: Genuine Community Based Wildlife Eco-tourism or Just Another Loss of Land for Maasai Pastoralists in Kenya?' London: International Institute for Environment and Development (IIED), Issue Paper (no. 111).

Ryan, A. (1999) *The Trickster Shift: Humour and Irony in Contemporary Native Art*, Vancouver: University of British Columbia Press.

Samson, C. (2003) *A Way of Life that Does Not Exist: Canada and the extinguishment of the Innu*, London: Verso Books.

——(2004) 'The Dis-ease over Native North American Drinking: Experiences of the Innu of Northern Labrador', in R. Coomber and N. South (eds) *Drug Use and Cultural Contexts: Beyond the West*, London: Free Association Books

Samson, C. and Pretty, J. (2006) 'Environmental and Health Benefits of Hunting Lifestyles and Diets for the Innu of Labrador', *Food Policy*, 31(6): 528–553.

Sapignoli, M. (2007) *Indigenato e strategie politiche in Botswana: il caso dei Boscimani del Central Kalahari Game Reserve*, unpublished thesis, Università di Bologna.

Saugestad, S. (2001) *The Inconvenient Indigenous: Remote Area Development in Botswana, Donor Assistance and the First People of the Kalahari*, Uppsala: Nordic Africa Institute.

Short, D. (2008) *Reconciliation and Colonial Power: Indigenous Rights in Australia*, Aldershot: Ashgate.

Stingemore, J. (2008) 'Surviving the Cure: Life on Bernier and Dorre Islands under the Lock Hospital Regime', paper presented at the Third International Conference on Interdisciplinary Social Sciences, Prato, 23 July.

Supreme Court of Belize (2007) *Aurelio cal, et al. v. attorney general of Belize.* Available at: www.elaw.org/node/1620 [accessed 14 August 2008].

Supreme Court of Canada (1997) *Delgamuukw vs British Columbia.* Available at: http://scc.lexum.umontreal.ca/en/1997/1997rcs3–1010/1997rcs3–1010.html [accessed 14 August 2008].

Survival International (2008) *Botswana government targets Bushman hunters.* Available at: www.survival–international.org/tribes/bushmen [accessed 14 August 2008].

Taussig, M. (1987) *Shamanism, Colonialism, and the Wild Man: A Study in Terror and Healing*. Chicago: University of Chicago Press.

——(1991) *Shamanism, Colonialism, and the Wild Man: A Study in Terror and Healing*, Chicago: University of Chicago Press.

Thompson, K.A. (1998) *Post–Colonial Performance and Installation Art*. Available at: www.english.emory. edu/Bahri/ArtifactPiece.html [accessed 14 August 2008].

Tonge, J. (2006) 'Don't romanticise the Kalahari Bushmen. They're part of the modern world too', letter to *Guardian*, 24 March.

Turnbull, C. (1973) *The Mountain People*, London: Picador.

United Nations (1989) *Convention 169 concerning Indigenous and Tribal Peoples in independent countries*. Available at: www.unhchr.ch/html/menu3/b/62.htm [accessed 14 August 2008].

United Nations, Department of Economic and Social Affairs, (2004) *The Concept of Indigenous Peoples*. Available at: www.un.org/esa/socdev/unpfii/documents/PFII%202004%20WS.1%203%20Definition. doc [accessed 14 August 2008].

United Nations, Human Rights Committee (2005) *Concluding observations of the Human Rights Committee: Canada. 02/11/2005*. Available at: www.treatycouncil.org/PDFs/Concluding_observations_Canada_ HRC.pdf [accessed 14 August 2008].

United Nations, Permanent Forum on Indigenous Issues (2006) *Fifth Session, 6th & 7th Meetings*. Available at: www.un.org/esa/socdev/unpfii/en/session_fifth.html [accessed 14 August 2008].

United Nations (2006) *Conference On Declaration Of Indigenous Peoples' Rights*. Available at: www.un. org/News/briefings/docs/2006/061212_Indigenous.doc.htm [accessed 14 August 2008].

United Nations, Economic and Social Council (2008) *Report of the international expert group meeting on Indigenous languages*. Available at: www.un.org/esa/socdev/unpfii/documents/E_C19_2008_3_revised_24% 20Jan.pdf [accessed 14 August 2008].

United States Department of Health and Human Services, Office of Applied Studies (2006). *Results from the 2005 National Survey on Drug Use and Health: National findings*. Available at: www.oas.samhsa.gov/ NSDUH/2k5NSDUH/2k5Results.htm [accessed 14 August 2008].

United States Commission on Civil Rights (2004) *Broken Promises: Evaluating the Native American health care system. Draft report for commissioners' view*, Washington DC: Office of the General Counsel.

United States District Court Northern District of California San Francisco Division (2008) *Native Village of Kivalina and City of Kivalina vs. Exxon Mobil and other Corporations*. Available at: www.adn.com/ static/adn/pdfs/Kivalina%20Complaint%20–%20Final.pdf [accessed 14 August 2008].

Van Dijk, J. (1991) *The Network Society: Social Aspects of New Media*, London: Sage.

Villa, W. and Houghton, J. (2005) *Violencia Política contra los pueblos Indígenas en Colombia 1974–2004*. Copenhagen: IWGIA.

Weaver, J.C. (2003) *The Great Land Rush and the Making of the Modern World, 1650–1900*, Montreal & Kingston: McGill-Queen's University Press.

World Bank (2005) *Revised Operational Policy and Bank Procedure on Indigenous Peoples (OP/BP 4.10)*. Available at: http://wbln0018.worldbank.org/Institutional/Manuals/OpManual.nsf/toc2/9367A2A9D 9DAEED38525672C007D0972?OpenDocument [accessed 14 August 2008].

Websites

Aang Serian (2008) Available at: www.aangserian.org.uk/ [accessed 14 August 2008].

Foundation for Research and Promotion on Ainu Culture (2007) www.frpac.or.jp/eng/e_prf/index. html [accessed 14 August 2008].

Ka'ala Cultural Learning Center (2008) Available at: www.k12.hi.us/~waianaeh/HawaiianStudies/ kaala.html [accessed 14 August 2008].

Kiana Lodge (2006) Available at: http://kianalodge.com/about.html [accessed 14 August 2008].

Maniilaq Association (2003) Available at: www.maniilaq.org/flash.html [accessed 14 August 2008].

Tshikapisk Foundation (2008) Available at: www.tshikapisk.ca/home/ [accessed 11 August 2008].

16

Genocide in the global age

Martin Shaw

The word 'genocide' was invented by Raphael Lemkin (1944), and its legal status was defined by the United Nations (1948) in the Convention on the Prevention and Punishment of the Crime of Genocide, in the light of the Nazi German suppression of Europe's peoples and attempted extermination of its Jews. Genocide has ever since been identified with this period in the Western political imagination, so that it seems to be primarily a phenomenon of what Eric Hobsbawm (1994) called the 'age of extremes', the 'short twentieth century' from 1914 to 1989. The Nazi genocide was preceded by the Ottoman genocide of the Armenians and the Stalinist 'liquidation of the kulaks', and followed by the murderous famine of Mao's Great Leap Forward and the Cambodian genocide. In short, genocide and related policy-driven mass death seem closely linked to the era of totalitarianism and world war.

Thus for many the twentieth century was 'the century of genocide' and few expected the twenty-first to be scarred by the phenomenon to anything like the same extent. The 'global age' ushered in by the end of the Cold War was often envisaged as an era of peace and global order, in which totalitarianism and major wars belonged to the past and any residual tendency for regimes to commit mass atrocities would be countered by international authority, law, and intervention. However the murderous 'ethnic cleansing' in former Yugoslavia between 1991 and 1999 and, above all, the Rwandan genocide of 1994 – in which the rate of killing outstripped even the Holocaust – quickly shattered any idea that globalization meant the decline of genocide. These and other events have even led some to suggest that the new century might equal, if not exceed, the destructive record of the old. As investigations have revealed the extent of genocidal phenomena before the twentieth century, as well as the implication of fundamental relations of modernity in genocidal events, the new field of 'genocide studies' is providing support for these fears.

This chapter will address the following main dimensions of this problem. First, I shall deal with the question of definition: genocide is a contested concept and the changing manifestations of political violence in the global era have stimulated new differences over its meaning and scope, in both political and academic debate. Second, I shall address the record of genocidal violence in the post-Cold War period and suggest some of the questions this raises for analysis. Third, I shall look at how the changed political, economic, social, and cultural relations of the global era have affected the conditions for genocide – whether they make it more or less likely, and how changed social relations are affecting the forms of genocide in the twenty-first century. Finally, I shall ask how adequate our resources for preventing genocide are in the era of globalization.

The debate about the meaning of genocide

The over-identification of genocide with the archetypical Nazi case has predisposed some genocide scholars, as well as many participants in political debates, to assume that genocide is simply a matter of large-scale mass murder and that genocide pertains primarily to those few cases (like the mass killings of Armenians, Rwandans, and Cambodians) which most closely approximate the Final Solution (the last, simply murderous, stage of Nazi violence against the Jews during the Second World War). The idea of genocide proposed by Lemkin was, however, a *general* concept of *social* destruction – he believed that his concept applied to the destructive Nazi rule in occupied Europe as a whole, with its political, economic, and cultural attacks on societies, not just to the Nazis' 'physical destruction' of the Jews. The Genocide Convention, while narrowing the concept in the direction of emphasizing killing and physical harm, also allowed that mental harm as well as measures of biological control, when perpetrated with the intention of destroying an ethnic, national, racial or religious group, could constitute genocide. The simple equation of genocide with deliberate mass murder has thus been a further narrowing of the concept. This has been partly a consequence of the increased importance of the Final Solution, now named 'The Holocaust' or 'The Shoah', in Western perceptions of twentieth-century history, but also because new episodes in Cambodia and Rwanda have shown similarly extensive killing. This narrowing has been reflected in academic definitions of genocide which have also frequently moved closer to limiting it to mass murder (e.g. Chalk and Jonassohn 1990, Charny 1994).

This chapter reverts, however, to Lemkin's broader concept of genocide as social destruction, following an argument I have made elsewhere (Shaw 2007). To summarize, the broader definition is more appropriate for several reasons:

1   Even when regimes commit mass murder this is not an end in itself: murder is a *means* of destroying a population, and is usually combined with other means like terror, rape, concentration, expulsion, forced migration, and conversion of children. It makes better sense to define a social phenomenon like genocide by the *ends* for which actions are undertaken, rather than by particular means. I shall therefore assume that in genocidal action, *armed power organizations treat civilian social groups as enemies and aim to destroy their real or putative social power, by means of killing, violence, and coercion against individuals whom they regard as members of the groups.* Genocide, however, is more than one-sided action: it is *a form of violent social conflict or war, between armed power organizations that aim to destroy civilian social groups and those groups and other actors who resist this destruction* (Shaw 2007: Chapter 10).

2   We should not artificially separate episodes of anti-civilian violence and coercion as different *kinds* of phenomena according to the *extent* of killing that is intended, or occurs, within them. The narrow approach leads to regarding only cases where the aim is to kill a majority of a group as genocide, so that others where the aim is

only to kill a minority (political leaders as potential leaders, adult men as potential resisters, and others in order to terrorize the majority into fleeing) are regarded not as genocide but as some lesser crime (e.g. 'politicide' or 'ethnic cleansing'). I shall assume that all attempts to destroy population groups, whether through forced migration achieved by killing a minority, or through extensive killing that potentially targets all the members of the group, constitute genocide. (Of course the movement from one type of destructive means to another remains an important element in any analysis of genocide.)

3   The kind of categorical separation assumed by a narrow definition of genocide leads to artificial distinctions not only between cases, but also within cases. In the case of the Nazis' actions against the Jews, for example, it would lead to us to say that policies of terrorised flight (in Germany, before 1939), and expulsion and brutal ghettoization (in Poland, 1939–41), were not genocide, while the extensive murder in villages and towns (during the conquest of the Soviet Union, 1941–42) and especially the industrial mass murder (in extermination camps, 1942–45) were. With a broad definition, all can be recognized as manifestations of the same genocidal thrust, which became more extreme in the course of the war, but which had throughout the aim of destroying the Jewish population and culture in Europe. A broad definition therefore helps to understand genocide as a developing process.

4   We should not neglect the importance of small-scale, even localized, episodes of social destruction, both as dangerous violent events in their own right, and as possible harbingers of large-scale destruction. The narrow approach concentrates attention on the relatively few cases of achieved, large-scale mass murders (thus taking attention away from colonial genocides, which typically involved smaller-scale violence: see Kiernan 2007), and leads to the conclusion that, as Scott Straus (2007: 479) has put it, genocide is a 'rare' phenomenon. If we recognize that the much larger number of small-scale episodes of violence against particular groups are driven by similar aims of destroying the groups concerned, at least locally, then we can see that genocide is not extremely unusual or exceptional but a much more widespread danger in modern society. The idea of 'genocidal massacres' was developed by Leo Kuper (1981: 32) to describe small-scale murderous events, but we should note that such events, like larger-scale episodes of destruction, may involve forced migration, rape, etc., as well as killing. This chapter will therefore use the broad approach to examine contemporary genocide, focusing on the relations between smaller and larger episodes.

5   The focus on a few large, discrete 'genocides' decontextualizes these episodes themselves. The Nazi campaign against the Jews was not an isolated policy, but part and parcel of the murderous Nazi programme to 'racially' restructure European society, and involved simultaneous genocide against a range of groups, including the disabled, homosexuals, Gypsies, and Slavs, and wider destructive policies against occupied peoples across Europe. Moreover Nazi genocide was part of a wider genocidal context in the Second World War, during or at the conclusion of which other protagonists also developed genocidal policies, such as the Japanese against the Chinese population (for example, in the Rape of Nanking), Germany's Croatian puppet state against Serbs, Stalin's USSR against Soviet population groups like the Volga Germans and Chechens, seen as potentially pro-German. This larger pattern of total war and genocide is important to understanding

the individual episodes. A similar pattern can be observed with the Armenian Genocide, which Bloxham (2007) has shown was the murderous peak of a 'great game
of genocide' involving destructive policies against various national groups both by
the Ottoman Empire and by the new nation-states emerging from the Empire's
collapse, often supported by rival empires.

Genocide studies, at the beginning of the twenty-first century, are divided between
these narrow and broad approaches. The former have led to a series of studies comparing
a few major cases (e.g. Midlarsky 2005), although sometimes showing how smaller
massacres escalate to large-scale genocide (Sémelin 2007). The latter, in contrast, have
shown how patterns of genocide characterize sets of relationships in whole historical
periods, for example during European colonisation of the Americas and Australia (Moses
2008, Kiernan 2007). This chapter will sketch how this approach can help us understand
the problem of genocide in our own times.

Genocidal violence in the global age

The problem with historical periodization is, of course, that even if events can be dated
precisely within them, the relations and processes that link these events never fit neatly
within whatever historical boundaries we try to draw. So while this chapter uses the terms
'global age' and 'twenty-first century' interchangeably, and regards these as marked off by
the end of the Cold War, itself conventionally delimited by the fall of the Berlin Wall in
1989, we need to remember that there is a certain arbitrariness in all these usages. I shall
argue, certainly, that the end of the Cold War was the most profound historical turning-
point of recent times (more so, for example, than 9/11), and that the changes it signalled
have been important for genocide. But we need to be aware that in every case of 'global
era' genocide there are important antecedents in the twentieth century, and often earlier.

Genocide had been important to the origins of the post-Second World War world
order. The Nazis' policies were not only the archetype of genocide for Lemkin and for
the drafters of the 1948 Convention. Knowledge of the Nazi genocide helped to define
the struggle just ended as one of good over evil, and inspired the foundation of the
United Nations and the loftier goals it proclaimed in its Charter and the Universal
Declaration of Human Rights. Indeed the post-war order was supposed to be one of
'universal' values and institutions: a global order in which neither war nor genocide had a
place. Although the language of 'globalization' and 'globality' did not develop until the last
quarter of the twentieth century, the 'global' idea already carried these strongly anti-genocidal
connotations.

However by the time the Genocide Convention and the Universal Declaration were
adopted at the end of 1948, the United Nations and its founders had themselves been
complicit in genocidal policies. During the drafting of these foundational documents, the
Soviet Union, Poland, and Czechoslovakia brutally, often murderously, destroyed German
minorities in Eastern Europe; India and Pakistan were founded amidst large-scale mutual
destruction of their minority populations by local militia often encouraged and protected
by regional political leaders; and Israel was founded through the destruction of the Arab
population in the larger part of Palestine. None of these situations, of course, was as
totally murderous as the Final Solution; but Britain, the USA, and/or the UN itself bore
a high degree of responsibility for all these socially destructive developments.

315

By late 1948, too, the 'Cold War' was developing between the emerging Western and Soviet blocs, and rapidly developed into a worldwide system of conflict. For both sides, *Realpolitik* overshadowed the universal values so recently proclaimed, and the UN itself became a weak institution. The Convention, although it continued to collect signatories from the growing number of UN member-states, was honoured more in the breach than in observance. In Communist China, Mao's policies caused tens of millions of deaths in the Great Leap Forward of 1958–61, in Cambodia the Khmer Rouge murdered millions in the genocide of 1975–79, and in Ethiopia hundreds of thousands died under the pro-Soviet Menghistu regime. The pro-US dictatorship in Indonesia killed half a million suspected Communists in 1965 and caused the deaths of hundreds of thousands of civilians in East Timor which it invaded in 1975; similar dictatorships in Latin America carried out mass destruction in Guatemala and elsewhere. Yet no one was prosecuted internationally under the Genocide Convention until after 1989. Indeed the international criminal court foreseen after 1945 did not materialize until 2002.

Yet if the Cold War era saw genocidal episodes in Asia, Africa, and Latin America, it was also a framework of international discipline in which states and populations were held in place by the blocs and their rivalries. In Europe especially, the Cold War largely froze political systems until the 1980s. In a continent bristling with nuclear weapons, war was too dangerous and radical political change seemed near-impossible, as the Soviet suppression (unchallenged by the West) of successive revolts in East Germany, Hungary, Poland, and Czechoslovakia showed. In Europe at least the twentieth century's history of genocide had halted by 1949.

Europe: the Caucasus and Yugoslavia

This was all to change with the end of the Cold War and of Communism. Although the question of recent genocide in Europe is linked in most minds with Bosnia, it should really be considered as a general problem of two major post-Communist regions, the areas of the former Soviet Union and Yugoslavia. Although the most publicized and internationally important incidence has been in former Yugoslavia, the democratization and break-up of the Soviet bloc, and especially the Union itself, also led to genocidal conflict. The loosening of Moscow's control over political life under Mikhail Gorbachev between 1985 and 1991 led to nationalist self-assertion by the Communist party leaderships, intellectuals and populations in Eastern Europe and also in the many non-Russian republics of the Union. In Eastern Europe, national autonomy, and democratization, and even the break-up of Czechoslovakia into two states, were achieved almost largely without violence. Likewise in the Baltic states (Lithuania, Latvia, and Estonia), nationalist politics focused on secession from the Soviet Union, and although there was repression of Russian speakers, seen by many nationalists as non-nationals, this did not become genocidal.

In the Caucasus and central Asia, however, some conflicts between and within republics did lead to episodes and policies of social destruction. Reviving conflicts between Armenians and Turks and other Muslims that went back to the period of the Armenian Genocide, and following a massacre of Armenians in Sumgait, Azerbaijan, in 1988, *Armenia* and *Azerbaijan* went to war over the largely Armenian enclave of Nagorno-Karabakh, from 1988 to 1994: both sides expelled and at times murdered members of the 'enemy' population. In the Abkhazian region of *Georgia*, thousands were killed as local secessionists expelled hundreds of thousands of Georgians; Abkhaz civilians also died at Georgian hands. Similar genocidal violence occurred in *Tadjikistan*, in Central Asia, in 1992–93.

In *Yugoslavia*, reconstructed after 1945 as a Communist federation of national republics and provinces, the break-up of the multinational state led to a complicated set of conflicts in which several sides developed genocidal policies. Especially after the death of President Josep Broz Tito in 1980, the Communist leaderships of the different republics all pursued increased national autonomy. Yugoslavia was not part of the Soviet bloc – indeed it had long become closer to the West in order to increase its autonomy from Moscow – but it was radically affected by the late 1980s climate of democratization and de-Communisation in Eastern Europe. By the end of the decade, Yugoslav republics were organizing democratic elections and national Communist parties were re-inventing themselves as nationalist parties.

The resulting dynamics of genocidal conflict were largely driven by political developments in *Serbia*, the largest republic, where Slobodan Milošević came to power in 1989. Milošević mobilised Serbian nationalism by exploiting the grievances of Serbs in *Kosovo*, a province of Serbia in which 90 per cent of the population were Albanians, against its Albanian-dominated provincial government. Suspending Kosovo's autonomy and driving Albanians from public institutions, Milošević also gained the votes of Kosovo and another province, Vojvodina, on the federal Yugoslav presidency, where with those of Serbia itself and its ally Montenegro he was now able to wield a majority to assert Serbian over other interests. But Milošević's drive to increased Serbian hegemony in Yugoslavia pushed other Yugoslav republics, especially wealthier Croatia and Slovenia which were closer to Western Europe both geographically and culturally, towards secession from the federation. In 1991, Slovenia broke away successfully after an 11-day war with few casualties, when the Serbian-led Yugoslav National Army (JNA) withdrew.

In *Croatia*, however, there was a large minority Serb population, and Milošević was determined that if Croatia seceded, Serbian-controlled areas would be annexed to a greater Serbia. The Croatian declaration of independence, also in 1991, was therefore the trigger for genocidal campaigns by the JNA and Serbian nationalist paramilitaries, supported by Milošević, against the Croat populations in eastern Slavonia and the region renamed the Krajina by Serbian nationalists. The Serbian forces carried out the 'ethnic cleansing' of these regions through brutal assaults on civilian populations in towns and villages, yet the secession of Croatia, whose government controlled the majority of the republic, was achieved, and this put the government of *Bosnia and Herzegovina*, a republic with no ethnic majority – Muslims constituted about 40 per cent of the population, Serbs 30 per cent, and Croats 20 per cent – in an untenable position.

In 1992, the Bosnian government proclaimed independence with the support of Muslim and Croat voters in a referendum, but the Serbian nationalist party, with the backing of the JNA in Bosnia which was now converted into a Bosnian-Serbian army, as well as paramilitary groups from Serbia, began a campaign of 'cleansing' across northern and eastern Bosnia and set up its own statelet, Republika Srpska, in this area. In the course of a year the Serbian campaign destroyed almost all Muslim and Croat society across Serbian-controlled regions, leaving barely 10 per cent of the original non-Serb population, which had constituted about half of the total. Tens of thousands were killed, many of them civilians, many Muslim men were incarcerated, tortured or killed in concentration camps, and many women were raped, to create this Serbian state and wipe out resistance.

The Bosnian 'ethnic cleansing' introduced this Serbian phrase into global discourse – translated into English it found its way into international documents and mass media, soon losing its inverted commas. This euphemistic term – 'there is nothing clean about "ethnic cleansing'" as Norman Naimark (2001) pointed out – was soon used to describe expulsion and forced migration not only in Yugoslavia but worldwide. As 'genocide' was narrowed to annihilationist mass murder, destructive policies that fell short of total extermination were increasingly categorized as 'cleansing'. Historians like Andrew Bell-Fialkoff (1996) and Naimark adopted the new term and read it back into earlier periods, including, ironically, the Nazi genocide. For these scholars, 'ethnic cleansing' was a broad category and genocide a narrow one; sociologist Michael Mann (2005) completed this tendency in an ambitious work which used 'ethnic cleansing' as the master-concept of the sociology of political violence, of which genocide was a (relatively rare) variant. For all these writers, as for 'narrow' genocide scholars like Jacques Sémelin, Bosnia-Herzegovina was a case that generally fell short of genocide.

Events in Bosnia-Herzegovina posed important challenges too for the legal inter-pretation of genocide. In 1993 the government of Bosnia-Herzegovina sued rump (Serbian-controlled) Yugoslavia, for genocide committed over the previous year, in the International Court of Justice – the case was to last 14 years. Meanwhile, in 1993, the United Nations took the important decision to establish an International Criminal Tribunal for former Yugoslavia (ICTY), charged with bringing to justice the individual perpetrators of inter-national crimes in the conflicts. The Tribunal, like that established for Rwanda in 1994 has had to make the first international decisions over prosecution for genocide since the crime was instituted in 1948. In general the ICTY has preferred to use the charges of 'war crimes' and 'crimes against humanity', and although some judges have given opinions that 'ethnic cleansing' constitutes genocide, and in the Blagojevic case the court ruled that it constituted serious 'mental harm' within the terms of the Genocide Convention, the Tribunal has not generally seen 'cleansing' as a form of genocide.

However there is one incident which the Tribunal has consistently ruled as genocide, the massacre of around 7,000 Bosnian Muslim men and boys at *Srebrenica* in 1995, and the International Court of Justice, when it finally ruled on Bosnia-Herzegovina's case in 2007 (by this time Yugoslavia had ceased to exist, so Serbia was the defendant) con-tinued this line of argument, maintaining that only in this incident had there been the 'specific intent' to commit genocide. This was a curious, even perverse, ruling, in that the Serbian regime and the Serbian nationalist regime in Bosnia had consistently pursued a policy of destroying the non-Serb population within the territory they controlled since 1992: the difference at Srebrenica was not the intention but the means – the policy of physically exterminating the (male) Muslim population. It seems that, despite the legal phrasing, the Court was adopting the narrow understanding of genocide which we have seen has been a tendency of recent years, especially over Bosnia.

At the beginning of the Bosnian war, Milošević had met Franjo Tudjman, president of Croatia, to discuss a carve-up of Bosnia-Herzegovina between Serbia and Croatia, as the Croatian regime also regarded (western) parts of the republic, where many Croats lived, as belonging to their new state. In 1992 Croatia and Croatian nationalists in Bosnia sided with the Bosnian government, but in 1993 they began their own 'cleansing' campaign against Muslims, notoriously in the murderous siege of the eastern part of the city of Mostar. By late 1994 the Croatians were aligned once more with the Bosnians against the Serbian forces, and in 1994–95 they drove the Serbians out of significant areas that they had conquered. However the Croatians expelled not just Serbian nationalists but the Serb population, in a genocidal campaign that included significant local massacres.

This Croatian-Bosnian offensive shifted the balance of forces in Bosnia-Herzegovina sufficiently for the USA to force the parties to the Dayton settlement of 1995. This compromise maintained Bosnia-Herzegovina as a unitary state but allowed the Serbians to preserve their statelet, achieved through genocide, within this state. Although refugees were supposed to be allowed to return, the subsequent decade and a half of international administration and occupation failed to achieve significant progress on this aim: genocide, once achieved, is difficult to reverse even where there are large numbers of survivors. And Dayton left at least one major problem in Yugoslavia unaddressed: the precarious situation of the Kosovo Albanians, who by engaging in civil rather than armed resistance had avoided war, but also failed to gain sufficient international attention to address their grievances. Around this time, therefore, some Albanian activists formed the Kosovo Liberation Army (UCK) and began a campaign of armed resistance against the Serbian regime.

By 1998 the UCK were strong enough to be a serious problem for the Serbian administration and forces in Kosovo. Milošević responded with a military crackdown directed at the Albanian population, suspected of hiding and supporting the armed resistance, which included burning of villages and small massacres and caused many to flee their homes. This in turn led US and European leaders, who had been forced to bring the violence in Bosnia to an end, to try to achieve a settlement in Kosovo. When talks failed to achieve Serbian concessions, and Serbian atrocities on the ground escalated, the North Atlantic Treaty Organization (NATO) began a limited aerial bombardment of Serbia and Serbian forces in Kosovo, in order to force Milošević to back down. Milošević, believing that the 19 NATO governments lacked the unity and determination to fight to the end, responded to the bombing with a very radical escalation of his campaign against the Albanian population.

There is controversy over how far Milošević pre-planned this escalation, but little doubt that after the NATO bombing began Serbia pursued a systematic policy to violently destroy the larger part of the Albanian society in the province and remove the majority of the population – an attempted genocide. The Kosovo capital, Pristina, was emptied, the Albanian population shipped by train to the borders, while armed police and troops attacked villages, killing men and terrorizing the population into flight. Around 10,000 were killed, a million fled to camps in Albania and Macedonia, and many tens of thousands hid in mountainous regions of Kosovo itself. As a result, in order to reverse the mass expulsion and return the refugees to their homes, NATO became locked into a more serious war than it had envisaged, and escalated its bombing to the point where Serbia agreed to negotiate its withdrawal. Kosovo became an international protectorate in which parties of the Albanian majority held power, and now the boot of 'ethnic cleansing' was largely on the other foot, as some former UCK fighters and others forced many of the remaining Serbs in the province to flee. The tensions produced by this episode spilled over into further attempts at violent expulsions in Macedonia and in the Preševo Valley of Serbia itself, but these were contained.

This account of genocide in the former Yugoslavia has shown that, as in the former Soviet Union, there was a complex pattern of genocidal violence, entwined with war between the former republics and armed factions, which spread over several regions in succession. The genocidal project of Milošević's Serbia and local Serbian nationalists expanded over Croatia, Bosnia-Herzegovina and Kosovo, but Tudjman's Croatia and Croatian nationalists pursued similar policies in Bosnia-Herzegovina and so, in a more covert manner and on a smaller scale, did some Kosovan nationalists. The post-Yugoslav genocidal wars also raised important issues about international response, intervention, and law, as well as, of course, the concept of genocide and its relation to 'ethnic cleansing'. All of these issues reverberate in other global-era episodes of genocide.

Africa: Central and North-east Africa

The best-known, most studied and only universally recognised recent case is the Rwandan Genocide of 1994, in which an estimated 800,000 or more Tutsis and political opponents of the Hutu Power regime were slaughtered. Because this is the only genocide not just of the global era but of modern times as a whole to fully match the single-minded murderousness of the Nazi Final Solution, Rwanda fits the 'narrow' as well as the 'broad' definition of genocide. However this retrospective validation of genocide, echoed in international politics by widespread official acknowledgement, does not mean that defining this genocide is, let alone was at the time, entirely straightforward.

The 1994 genocide was an outcome of international-regional, as well as national, dynamics, which also affected how it was understood as it occurred. All postcolonial states in Africa are characterized by complex inter-group relations, often perceived as 'tribal' and 'ethnic' by Western observers, which help mould but are also moulded by the modern politics of these states. Colonial regimes had shaped these inter-group relations as they attempted to manage their subject populations, and their policies have had lasting effects. Since the distribution of population groups crosses borders, the internal politics of states, as well as their international policies, affect each other.

Although Rwanda was unusual in the relatively simple polarization of its inter-group politics – the majority Hutu had been dominated by the minority Tutsi before and during the colonial era, but then Hutu politicians gained control of the state after independence – it did not escape from these general rules. 1963–64 massacres of Tutsis by the Rwandan Hutu nationalist regime had forced many to flee to Uganda. Meanwhile in neighbouring Burundi in 1972 a Tutsi-dominated regime committed genocide against Hutus, which had repercussions in Rwanda. In Uganda some Rwandan Tutsis later formed part of the resistance to the violent, even genocidal regimes of Idi Amin and Milton Obote, helping to bring Yoweri Museveni to power in 1986. Under him exiles were able to form the Rwandan Patriotic Front (RPF), which invaded Rwanda in 1990, in turn committing some massacres of Hutus. The RPF's invasion destabilized the dictatorial regime of President Juvénal Habyarimana and prompted a United Nations intervention which led to the 1993 Arusha accord, obliging the regime to share power with the RPF and the internal opposition and open the way to democracy.

The powerful elements of the Habyarimana regime who organized the 1994 genocide feared that the president was being forced to implement power-sharing, but above all they mistrusted the RPF, which in early 1994 invaded Rwanda again, bringing atrocities against Hutus. Habyarimana was assassinated when his plane was blown up, possibly by the RPF, on 6 April, and at this point the *génocidaires* moved to attack the political opposition and the small number of UN soldiers, followed by a total onslaught on Tutsi members of the population, whom they identified with the RPF. Wholesale killing, accompanied by widespread rape, led by the army and Hutu Power party militia, mobilised ordinary Hutu through the communal labour system: it is estimated that 14–17 per cent of the Hutu population took part, the highest civilian participation ratio of any major genocide (Straus 2006)

The speed of mass murder was unmatched in recent times, but a quick reinforcement of the UN force might have deterred or helped to halt the slaughter. In New York, however, the UN secretariat and the major powers in the Security Council muffled the warnings of the local UN commander, Canadian General Roméo Dallaire, that genocide was taking place, preferring to talk of the 'excesses' of 'civil war'; they withdrew most of the already inadequate number of peacekeepers. Neither US President Bill Clinton nor Secretary-General Boutros Boutros-Ghali was prepared to use the 'genocide' word during the crisis, although Clinton and Boutros-Ghali's successor Kofi Annan (as a UN official complicit in the evasion of responsibility at the time) subsequently apologized in Kigali, the Rwandan capital. The only power willing to intervene was France, which had sponsored the Habyarimana regime and whose operation in south-western Rwanda saved *génocidaires* as well as victims. The genocide was only ended nationally by the victory of the RPF, although its campaign also continued to be marred by (very much smaller-scale) atrocities.

Just as the 1994 genocide was preceded by linked smaller genocidal episodes in Burundi as well as Rwanda itself, so its conclusion was hardly the end of genocidal violence in the region. Many Rwandan *génocidaires* fled to refugee camps in neighbouring Zaïre (formerly Congo), where they joined elements of the crumbling dictatorial regime of Mobuto Sese Seku in attacking Congolese Banyumalenge (a section of the population linked to the Tutsi) as well as making incursions back into Rwanda. The new Rwandan government with its ally Uganda then invaded Zaïre and allied with Congolese rebels led by Laurent Kabila to overthrow Mobuto. Kabila (who renamed the country the Democratic Republic of Congo, or DRC) was installed as President, but was quickly assassinated, to be replaced by his son Joseph. However, Rwanda and Uganda fell out with the Kabila regime, supported new rebel movements, and the DRC lapsed into a new war, further internationalized (this was called 'Africa's Great War') by the participation of Zimbabwe, Namibia, and Angola on Kabila's side.

Despite the official withdrawal of all foreign powers and the introduction of a UN peacekeeping force (large in relation to other such forces but small in relation to the huge size and complex problems of the DRC, where a national economy and infrastructure hardly exist), the country saw new phases of civil war throughout the 2000s. Most armed organizations in the many-sided conflicts saw 'other' ethnic groups as enemies and committed genocidal atrocities against civilians: as well as killing, rape was practised on an extraordinarily wide scale and by many different factions. Altogether death tolls in the DRC in the late 1990s and 2000s have been estimated at up to 4–5 million, many of which have been directly caused by violence, but the vast majority from hunger and disease caused by the disruption that the conflicts have caused.

Nor are the Great Lakes the only region of Africa in which genocidal violence has taken place. As Alex de Waal (2007: 28) has noted, 'If we applied the letter of the convention, … at least half a dozen episodes in the Sudanese civil war would be genocide, as well as episodes in Ethiopia in the 1980s, Uganda in 1983, Somalia in 1988 and 1992–3 and again in [2007], numerous episodes in the DRC and various others would all be genocide.' To the northeast as well as directly around the Great Lakes, therefore, genocidal violence has occurred sporadically in the context of ethnicized armed conflict, yet the only case around which a 'genocide' debate has developed is that in Darfur, western Sudan, ongoing since 2003. De Waal went on to add, 'Many scholars prefer to use a narrower interpretation of the genocide convention to apply to projects of racial or ethnic annihilation – which Darfur is not.' It is certainly true that what has happened in Darfur does not meet the narrow, Holocaust or Rwanda definition of genocide. Yet the extensive, coordinated attacks by the Janjaweed militia, backed by the Sudanese government and often reinforced through bombing by its airforce, were certainly conducted with the intention to substantially destroy the social existence of the non-Arab peoples of Darfur, through massacres, rape, pillage, and burning of villages. Hundreds of thousands were dead, many of them killed by the Janjaweed but even more from disease, and millions displaced.

The peak of violence in Darfur coincided with the tenth anniversary of the Rwandan Genocide, which world leaders marked with 'never again' proclamations. Yet the international response to the largest-scale genocidal violence anywhere in the world since 1994 was, once again, too little and too late. For two years world leaders and the UN, while acknowledging a 'humanitarian crisis', were very reluctant to recognise 'ethnic cleansing', let alone genocide. Even when, in late 2004, the US administration took the unusual step of pronouncing that 'genocide' was indeed occurring in Darfur, it coupled this with a weakening of the corresponding duty to act to halt genocide, to which it was bound by the Convention. The United Nations, on the other hand, continued to avoid the genocide determination, although it did eventually support the sending of an African Union force. Although this provided some protection for some of the displaced people in Darfur's camps, it was unable to prevent further waves of genocidal attacks or secure humanitarian aid in the face of the Khartoum regime's attempts to block it. In 2006 the Security Council recognised this failure and authorized an enhanced UN force, but Khartoum blocked its deployment, and at the time of writing in 2008 the situation in Darfur was still dire.

An indication of the underlying genocidal dangers in sub-Saharan Africa was given by developments in Kenya in 2008. This country was widely considered a bastion of stability – indeed it had been a base from which international operations in Rwanda, Congo and Sudan had been carried out. Yet a rigged presidential election on 30 December 2007 triggered violent protests which were quickly turned into genocidal campaigns, aimed at destroying the presence of ethnic groups identified with the regime across substantial areas of the country. These campaigns quickly claimed hundreds of lives, forced hundreds of thousands from their homes, and led to counter-violence by armed groups based among those originally attacked. A genocidal massacre at Eldoret, where up to 30 people were burnt alive in a church, reminded some commentators of Rwanda. Although others dismissed this comparison – the violence was locally organized and perpetrated and the number of victims vastly fewer – the crisis spread quickly across wide areas, highlighting underlying conflicts over land ownership and the extent to which politicians, engaged in electoral competition, were complicit with ethnically based militia who led the attacks. The crisis drew attention to ongoing campaigns by armed gangs against some groups in western Kenya – as well as earlier violence, sponsored by the former regime, in the 1990s. At the time of writing it is uncertain whether Kenya's rival politicians will be able to contain this violence by managing their own conflict, or whether the difficulties of achieving a political settlement, together with the polarization caused by the 2008 crisis, will result in even more destructive conflict.

The worldwide prevalence of genocidal conflict

These two regional surveys have shown that the recent 'genocidal episodes' of which Western public opinion is aware – in Bosnia, Rwanda, and Darfur – are the peaks of larger regional patterns of genocidal violence, which are in turn closely linked to the forms of political and especially armed conflict in these regions which have developed over several decades. There is not space in this chapter to develop a comprehensive global survey, and indeed no one has yet carried out the necessary research to achieve this. Yet it is important to understand that Europe – where genocidal conflicts developed in the late 1980s but were largely contained by 2000 – is less typical of the worldwide picture than central and north-east Africa, where the genocidal episodes of the 1990s and 2000s were often continuations of earlier conflicts, and where genocidal dangers have not been overcome to the same extent.

A brief survey can indicate some of the other main regions of genocidal violence. In Indonesia, where the US-sponsored regime of General Suharto originated in the genocidal massacre of Communists in 1965 and then perpetrated the genocidal conquest of East Timor in 1975, the collapse of authoritarianism led to new genocidal threats at the beginning of the 1990s. In East Timor, the Indonesian military sponsored paramilitary gangs which massacred pro-independence Timorese during the build-up to a UN-sponsored referendum; in Aceh and Borneo, the military and local armed groups were also involved in massacres of presumed pro-secessionist populations. In *India*, there were echoes of the Partition violence in the massacres of Muslims by Hindu nationalists in Gujarat in 2002. In Iraq, where the Saddam Hussein regime had carried out the notorious Anfal campaign against Kurds in the late 1980s, the USA's invasion to overthrow him in 2003 precipitated a nationalist armed 'resistance', based in the same Sunni section of the population from which Saddam had drawn support. This turned its violence into genocidal attacks on Shia Muslims in parts of the country they considered their own, and eventually provoked similar attacks on Sunnis by Shi'ite militia. In Latin America, where episodes of settler violence against Indigenous peoples and anti-Communist political genocide had both taken place in several countries during the Cold War period, post-Cold War democratisation brought no simple end to violence. This survey is by no means exhaustive – as de Waal put it, the UN definition of genocide 'would include most ethnic wars and counterinsurgencies' and so the genocidal danger remains worldwide.

Globality and the conditions for genocide

The question to which genocide scholars have devoted most attention is that of the conditions under which political violence escalates to large-scale mass murder, as in the Holocaust and the Rwandan Genocide (This has led to *comparative* studies of cases that are historically separated, as these two cases are.) This is an obviously important question, but this survey raises another another question which is in a sense prior – under what conditions does low-level genocidal violence develop? This question has been addressed more in *historical* studies that examine linkages between cases over time – for example, in studies of the development of settler colonialism, and of the connections between different episodes in the decline of the Ottoman Empire. This question is difficult to answer except in the most general terms, because of the sheer variety of circumstances in which broadly genocidal practices have developed. At a general level, a number of different answers have been given for the genocidal developments of recent centuries – for example, some see modernity as harbouring genocide, others see cultural and economic factors as instrumental, while most emphasize specific political conditions and the close connections between genocide and war.

In trying to establish the conditions that are affecting the prevalence of genocidal violence in the global age, it seems helpful to distinguish the roles of 'old' factors, familiar in the literature from earlier historical periods, and a number of 'new' factors which are specific to the post-Cold War, 'global', context, in stimulating genocidal developments.

The connection of genocide with *empire*, which some might consider a pre-global phenomenon, remains strong in the global age. Many of the genocidal episodes I have

323

discussed occurred in the contexts of the break-up of states that, while not formally empires, had a strongly quasi-imperial character. The Soviet, Yugoslav, Indonesian, and Iraqi states, although formally modern nation-states, all possessed strongly multinational or multiethnic characters, and the political violence accompanying centrifugal tendencies within them – leading in the first two cases to complete break-up – is reminiscent of the problems attending break-up of the Ottoman Empire a century ago. This prime context for possible genocidal violence has not been ignored in the literature: according to Mann (2005: 517), the most dangerous ethnopolitical conflicts today 'mostly exist around the fringes of the bigger imperial countries', India, Indonesia, Russia, and China, as well as the peripheral territories of states like Turkey, Iran, Iraq, Burma, and the Philippines.

In this context, some familiar processes are at work. On the one hand, 'subaltern' resistance can often be seen as a trigger: independence moves in Croatia, Bosnia, and East Timor, and armed resistance in Rwanda and Kosovo, as well as the attempt by Armenians by Nagorno-Karabakh to break away from Azerbaijan, have often provoked 'quasi-imperial' regimes. In some cases, moreover, a sort of 'sub-imperial' expansionism has been important, for example in the Indonesian annexation of East Timor and the Serbian attempts to annex parts of Croatia and Bosnia. In all cases, too, war has been an important context of genocidal violence, and the general decline of major interstate war in the global era has not radically altered the general connection of war and genocide. On the contrary, 'civil' wars, or indeed 'new' (globalized interstate-civil) wars, as Mary Kaldor (1999) has called them, are often pivoted around ethnopolitical conflicts, and so many conflicts could be called 'genocidal wars' in the sense that genocide is often a distinct aim of organized violence alongside more conventional military aims.

On the other hand, we can see some distinctive 'new' factors leading to genocide violence, which are closely linked to the new political conditions of the global age. Democratization, far from leading automatically to a peaceful resolution of the ethnopolitical conflicts arising from the ending of quasi-imperial and authoritarian regimes, is often a context for genocidal violence, as has happened in Yugoslavia, Rwanda, and Indonesia. Within democratization processes, referendums and elections – precisely because they are pivotal moments when political power is brought into question – are often catalysts for genocidal violence, as happened over independence referendums in Bosnia and East Timor and over the presidential election in Kenya in 2007. Electoral logic can be part of the logic of genocide in a broader sense – since nationalists know that in global-era terms they must legitimate their rule electorally, there is an obvious incentive to rig the electorate, by expelling or minimizing other ethnic and national groups, so that there will be less necessity to rig the elections. Genocidal violence also has the by-product of intimidating the nationalists' 'own' group into supporting them.

If democratization can destabilize social and political relations and create the conditions for genocidal violence, so can international surveillance and intervention. It is global surveillance, by Western states, the UN, NGOs and mass media, as well as internal pressure, which creates the 'democratic imperative' for proto-genocidal regimes to internalise electoral logic. Global surveillance, backed up by the threat of international legal action through the International Criminal Court and the *ad hoc* international tribunals, gives genocidal actors additional reasons to permanently silence witnesses to their crimes. And international intervention, often thought of as a means by which genocide is prevented or halted, can also enter into the conditions *for* genocide. Intervention can make local authoritarian regimes feel threatened and thus increase the incentive for a more drastic solution, leading to an *escalation* of violent action.

Thus the implementation of the UN-brokered Arusha agreement was seen as a threat to Hutu Power in Rwanda, and the aim of blocking it was one of the key reasons for the genocidal plan which was put into action in April 1994. NATO's intervention over Kosovo in 1999, with its bombing of Serbia, was the provocation that led Milošević to escalate his war against the Albanian population to a campaign of murderous expulsion on a province-wide basis. Similarly, the US invasion of Iraq in 2003 was the stimulus for a 'resistance' which became as much anti-Shia as anti-American, so leading to genocidal massacres of Shia and provoking a counter-genocidal conflict between Sunnite and Shi'ite militia. Moreover even where intervention has halted genocide, as in Kosovo, this has been at the cost of unnecessary civilian casualties (because Western governments rely heavily on airpower which does not discriminate enough between civilians and enemy combatants). And in most cases, as even in Rwanda, intervention has either not come at all or has been insufficient to quickly halt extensive mass violence.

In sum, while many of the old causes of genocidal violence have re-appeared in new forms, troubling new ones connected with character of 'global era' political relations have also emerged. Mann has of course argued that genocidal violence is the 'dark side of democracy', but he acknowledged that historically, in many cases, the connections of genocide with democracy were quite indirect. But if his thesis was not entirely convincing for much twentieth-century genocide, it seems to work all too well in twenty-first-century cases. The connection of democracy with genocidal 'cleansing' and killing is now often much more direct than in the past. Genocide is a 'dark side' not just of democracy, but of international intervention and indeed of globalization, in so far as global surveillance and mass mediation play crucial roles in its current manifestations.

How genocidal, then, will the global era be? On the whole genocide scholars study past events and are reluctant not only to predict – a normal tendency for social scientists because of the complexity and indeterminacy of social life – but also to define the parameters of twenty-first century genocide. Mann (2005: 506–18) is a rare recent author who has considered current historical trends in 'ethnic cleansing' and genocide. He argues that there had been a decline in the global North, largely as a result of the success of earlier waves in creating mono-ethnic states. In the remaining multi-ethnic states, politics is largely defined by class, region, and gender, while continuing ethnic politics, both historic and new, is largely non-violent. We might add that, where genocidal violence has emerged in the North, as in the former Soviet and Yugoslav regions, it has been internationally managed – if not well – then *relatively* well compared to most other world regions where it has often been hardly contained at all. The genocidal violence of the 1990s appears to have subsided in Europe a decade later. Mann argues that in the South, in contrast, the diffusion of the 'ideal of the nation-state' and the confusion of *demos* and *ethnos* are creating new threats of 'cleansing', reinforced by the decline of class politics, the weakening of liberalism and socialism and the rise of fundamentalism (including 'theo-democracy', which Mann suggested could represent a third variant of his perversion of democracy thesis, alongside ethnic and class versions). Settler 'cleansing' continues against Indigenous peoples, especially in Latin America; 'middlemen ethnicities' like the Chinese in Southeast Asia remain vulnerable.

There remains the question of whether extensive, low-grade, localized genocidal violence is likely to lead to intensive, large-scale, national genocides, especially exterminatory genocide, as in Rwanda. Mann (2005: 517) argues that there are few cases in which rival bi-ethnic claims are capable of fuelling the most murderous genocidal developments that occurred in Yugoslavia and in Rwanda and Burundi: 'I can think of no other closely

325

analogous case to Rwanda/Burundi elsewhere in the world. Perhaps this was the last of the world's [large-scale] genocides.' In line with his belief in the possibility of more or less peaceful cleansing, Mann even recommended that '[i]n some cases it may be better to deflect hatreds onto milder stages of cleansing achieved by mutual negotiation through agreed-upon population and property exchanges, border alterations and so on than to risk further cleansing by force' (Mann 2005: 525). Perhaps, he implied, we are entering an era in which 'cleansing' can be managed so as to avoid genocide. Morever, genocidal violence might be less globally important: 'Most [ethnopolitical] conflicts occur in some of the poorest, most isolated parts of the world, and so they become only local black holes' (Mann 2005: 518).

It is difficult to feel convinced by Mann's optimism, even though it is cautiously expressed. Large-scale, and totally murderous, genocides are always relatively rare, and escalation is difficult to predict, as Rwanda showed: no one foresaw the scale or intensity of that genocide. However, the Darfur crisis – although the main direct perpetrators, the Janjaweed, did not control the Sudanese state, but were manipulated by it, and the violence was less totally exterminatory than in Rwanda – was on a large scale. Although it occurred precisely in a poor, isolated part of the world, it *did* slowly become a global crisis through political campaigning and media coverage in the USA and elsewhere. The Congolese crisis, although including fragmented, decentralized, episodic genocidal violence by multiple perpetrators, has also been on a large scale. These cases underline the theoretical and political danger in looking for genocide only in Holocaust-type centralized campaigns. Moreover many attempts to 'manage' ethnopolitical crises, for example through 'transfers' and partitions, have often made them worse as well as causing much additional suffering.

The sociology of global-era genocide, even more than the historical sociology of twentieth-century and earlier genocide, is in its infancy. Yet questions like whether the targets and perpetrators of genocide are changing are beginning to arise. The decline of totalitarianism and especially its Stalinist variant have made totalizing genocides of the Cambodian type, and especially 'class' targeting, less likely. The ethnicization of electoral politics in emerging democracies, on the other hand, raises the spectre of spreading genocidal violence, led often by local and regional movements within states rather than by national regimes, and so of elusive networks of perpetration. The partial Islamization of politics within Muslim communities, and especially the emergence of violent Islamist 'terrorist' movements, gives a new salience to religious definitions of targets and raises the danger of shadowy underground networks of perpetrators.

Does the global age experience of genocide give new grounds for hope that genocide will be prevented, or at least halted once it is underway? The new international determination to address gross human rights abuses since the end of the Cold War and first legal uses of the Genocide Convention give the politics of anti-genocide starting points that it largely lacked in the Cold War period. Global media coverage of distant atrocities and the possibility to create mass protest movements speedily through the internet should help to influence governments to protect civilians. Yet so far, even prominent cases like Bosnia, Rwanda, and Darfur have been under-covered and misrepresented by mainstream media, especially in their key, early stages; media have often taken their cue from Western governments on these crises; and they have often seemed more complex to publics than they really are, so that movements of solidarity have been slow to arise. Most of the other cases discussed in this chapter have hardly made the headlines at all, certainly not for sustained periods. It is difficult to argue that the anti-genocidal impacts of global change are greater than the genocidal impacts. Yet the knowledge and understanding that genocide scholars are beginning to develop can help to change this.

References

Albrow, M. (1996) *The Global Age*. Cambridge: Polity.

Bell-Fialkoff, A. (1996) *Ethnic Cleansing*. Basingstoke: Macmillan.

Bloxham, D. (2007) *The Great Game of Genocide*. New York: Oxford University Press.

Chalk, F. and K. Jonassohn (1990) *The History and Sociology of Genocide: Analyses and Case Studies*, New Haven, CT: Yale University Press.

Charny, I. W. (1994) 'Toward a Generic Definition of Genocide', in G. A. Andreopoulous, ed., *Genocide: Conceptual and Historical Dimensions*, Philadelphia, PA: University of Pennsylvania Press, 64–94.

De Waal, A. (2007) 'Reflections on the Difficulties of Defining Darfur's Crisis as Genocide', *Harvard Human Rights Journal*, 20, Spring, www.law.harvard.edu/students/orgs/hrj/iss20/dewaal.pdf.

Hobsbawm, E. (1994) *Age of Extremes: The Short Twentieth Century 1914–89*. London: Michael Joseph.

Kaldor, M. (1999) *New and Old Wars*. Cambridge: Polity.

Kiernan, B. (2007) *Blood and Soil*, New Haven, CT: Yale University Press.

Kuper (1981) *Genocide*, Harmondsworth: Penguin.

Lemkin, R. (1944) *Axis Rule in Occupied Europe: Laws of Occupation, Analysis of Government, Proposals for Redress*. New York: Carnegie Endowment for International Peace.

Mann, M. (2005) *The Dark Side of Democracy: Explaining Ethnic Cleansing*, Cambridge: Cambridge University Press.

Midlarsky, M. (2005) *The Killing Trap: Genocide in the Twentieth Century*, Cambridge: Cambridge University Press.

Moses, A. D., ed. (2004) *Genocide and Settler Society: Frontier Violence and Stolen Indigenous Children*, Oxford: Berghahn Books.

——(2008) 'Empire, Colony, Genocide', in A. D. Moses, ed., *Empire, Colony, Genocide*, Oxford: Berghahn, 3–54.

Naimark, N. M. (2001) *Fires of Hatred: Ethnic Cleansing in Twentieth-Century Europe*. Cambridge, MA: Harvard University Press.

Prunier, Gérard, *From Genocide to Continental War: The 'Congolese' Conflict and the Crisis of Contemporary Africa*, London: Hurst, 2008.

Sémelin, J. (2007) *Purify and Destroy*, London: Hurst.

Shaw, M. (2007) *What is Genocide?* Cambridge: Polity.

Straus, S. (2006) *The Order of Genocide*, Ithaca, NY: Cornell University Press.

——(2007) 'Second-Generation Comparative Research on Genocide', *World Politics*, 59, April, pp. 476–501.

United Nations (1948) *Convention on the Prevention and Punishment of the Crime of Genocide*. New York: United Nations.

17

Global elites

Jan Pakulski

The concept of 'global elite' is anchored in both the elite theoretical tradition and a rather nebulous contemporary body of thought about globalization and its effects. It has three main referents:

1   The first, and perhaps most popular, is a new concept of 'global elite', also called 'superclass', referring to an allegedly new grouping consisting primarily of the 'super-rich' and other powerful and supra-national figures, such as CEOs of the largest transnational corporations, the most influential national political leaders, heads of the most powerful military establishments, leaders of the largest religious movements and organizations, as well as, somewhat surprisingly, heads of the most notorious transnational terrorist and criminal groups. According to Rothkopf (2008), the emergence and integration of all these powerful figures into a 'global elite' ('without a country') is the result of economic and political globalization, including a rapid concentration of wealth, mergers, and expansion of transnational corporations, widening information and communication networks, and mobilization of global movements.

2   The second referent derives from (neo-)Marxist analyses of 'transnational capitalist class' (or, in some versions, class*es*). The professional and executive 'apex' of this class (or classes) forms a 'transnational elite' of professional experts, corporate leaders and their political sponsors, all supporting deregulation and expansion of markets. This 'transnational' or 'global elite' also includes the top political executives and bureaucrats in the international associations and alliances (for example EU, NAFTA, ASIAN) as well as heads of regulative and coordinating bodies promoting 'global economic governance' (such as WTO, World Bank, IMF). According to Sassen (2007) and Robinson (2004), the members of this new 'transnational elite' operate in a coordinated fashion, support and promote the neo-liberal program of deregulation and global expansion of capital, and thus become the key management committee of transnational capitalism (see also, Chase-Dunn 1998, Sklair 1995).

3   The third referent is more in line with the 'classic' elite theory and contemporary research. In some political and historical analyses 'global elite' means 'power elite'

of the dominant superpower that acquires a 'global reach', typically the USA. Thus, according to Fukuyama (1992) and Kagan (2006), America has emerged from the Cold War as a 'sole superpower' capable of exercising influence on the global scale. This is due to the American political, military and economic might, as well as a world-wide impact of American ideology and popular culture. Consequently, the American elite became *de facto* 'global elite'.

These three referents are embedded in three arguments, respectively: (1) about the supra-national power concentration and the emergence of the new dominant 'international class of powerful elites' (the global 'superclass'); (2) about the economic and political ascendancy of the 'transnational capitalist class' with its top executives (transnational elites) promoting and aiding deregulation and global capitalist expansion; and (3) about the emergence of hege-monic 'sole superpower', the USA, whose elite operates internationally, on the global plane.

All three arguments are problematic. More specifically, arguments (1) and (2) are based on some controversial premises about 'de-nationalization' and group integration of the top wealth- and power-holders. There are also some analytic and theoretical problems. For a start, the deployment by the advocates of 'global elite(s)' of the key concepts, especially 'power', 'elites' and 'globalization', is bound to raise the eyebrows of con-temporary elite researchers respectful of the elite theoretical tradition (as represented by Pareto, Mosca, Michels, and Weber). In this tradition, power is treated as a largely positional-organizational capacity, elites are national in scope, and their small size, com-bined with strong integration, are seen as foundations of elite power. By contrast, most neo-Marxist advocates of 'transnational class-elite' tend to see political influence as a reflection of economic power, identify the latter with capital ownership, and anchor power in the entire ownership classes. Because of this anchoring, classes and elites tend to be conflated; it is not clear where one ends and another starts. Yet, as insisted by elite theorists, 'classes' and 'elites' are quite distinct entities, and they belong to quite distinct analytic vocabularies and theoretical traditions, in spite of the fact that many scholars use the terms 'elite' and 'class' interchangeably. Starting with the most obvious, classes are far more numerous and diffuse than elites. Moreover, classes are typically seen as the key ele-ments of the socio-economic structure and as large socio-economic categories-collectivities, distinguished by their employment and/or occupational status (and the derived 'class interests'), rather than political criteria of power and influence. Classes differ in the degree of their social formation (awareness, consciousness, solidarity, and organization), while elites are, almost by definition, integrated and organized *groups*. Therefore frequent conflation of the two concepts by the advocates of 'global elites' poses serious problems.

The above criticisms do not apply to the (third) argument about the newly acquired global status and 'global reach' of the American elite. This argument is theoretically consistent and factually plausible. However, its popularity (at the peak in the 1990s), has recently waned, and it has been challenged on empirical grounds. Therefore it has to be taken with a degree of scepticism, especially in the light of the most recent analyses by the advocates of the 'post-American world order' (for example Zakaria 2008).

This chapter reflects these critical considerations. It starts with a brief theoretical over-view that highlights the differences between the elite and class concepts and perspectives. This overview helps in identifying the main shortcomings of arguments (1) and (2), both of which are summarized in more detail. This is followed by a brief exposition of argu-ment (3), about the global American hegemony, also followed by critical comments, and ends with a short summary of arguments and debates about 'global elite'.

Power, elites, and classes

The concept of elite was elaborated and popularized at the turn of the twentieth century by Vilfredo Pareto (1848–1923), Gaetano Mosca (1858–1941), and Robert Michels (1876–1936) under a strong influence of Max Weber's (1864–1920) analyses of rationalization, bureaucracy, and charisma. Both the concept of elites and the 'classic' elite theory in which it was embedded carry a strong imprint of political and ideological controversies of the time: intellectual confrontations with Marxism, widening popularity of the normative 'democratic theory' (promoting democracy as 'rule of the people, for the people and by the people'), and concerns with separating science from ideology. Elite theorists took a strong stand on all these turn-of-the-century controversies. They rejected the key tenets of both Marxism and the radical democratic political theory alike by arguing that both confuse ideology with reality. In their place, elite theorists proposed an alternative account of power and politics, based on what they believed to be solid empirical grounds and sober scientific-historical analysis. In contrast with Marxist scholars, who saw political power as derived principally from economic domination, elite theorists perceived political power as autonomous, derived mainly from organization, and attached to a broad range of 'power resources'. In Michels' (1958) famous formulation of the 'iron law of oligarchy', large-scale organizations, even those professing egalitarian principles, inevitably spawn powerful minorities that dominate 'the masses'. These minorities, variously called 'elites', 'ruling classes', 'political classes', 'oligarchies', 'aristocracies' and so forth, become the key social and political actors, and they use their political-organizational resources, as well as their small size, to secure effective domination over the unorganized majorities. According to Pareto (1935), elite power derives not only from its small size and superior organizational capacities, but also from talent, certain psycho-social features and from the capacity to use force and/or cunning. While history abounds with examples of diverse elite groups, the most powerful elites are the products of complex organization and power concentration, particularly within the modern state. The formation of massive governmental and party bureaucracies, the control extended by these bureaucracies over national economies, the monopoly for coercion and military command, the widening financial influence, and the capacity to manipulate public opinion via the budding mass media, all created the foundations for irresistible domination of elites, especially those commanding modern state apparata. This is why all elite theorists have emphasized the central role of *political* elites – the incumbents of executive positions at the apex of the state – as 'core' elements of modern 'oligarchies'. Political elites merge and overlap with non-political segments of the ruling oligarchies; their ranks encompass the top executives of the largest (and state-supported) business organizations, military forces, and media organizations. Their members interact frequently, and they posses social cohesion and solidarity that facilitate coordinated action (for instance Mills 1956, Bottomore 1964/1993).

Elite accounts attribute to elites a status of key social actors. This contrast with Marxist visions of power concentrated in capital and social classes – large socio-economic categories anchored in property relations – and with Marxist insistence on the centrality of classes as key structural entities and social actors. Unlike elites, classes are numerous; their power derives partly from their large size. Elite theorists, by contrast, see the power of elites as enhanced by their *small* size and the accompanied group cohesion and solidarity. Such strong elite cohesion does not preclude internal divisions, but it facilitates communication, collaboration, and collusion, especially the formation of extensive networks.

Charting and studying these networks became a key preoccupation of elite researchers at the end of the twentieth century (e.g. Scott 1990). The network studies show strong interconnections – interlocking positions and overlapping membership – within elite sectors (especially business and political), between elite sectors and, above all, within the 'cores', 'inner circles' or 'central circles' of national elites. These interconnections allow elite members to interact regularly, coordinate their policies, and act as a group, in a solidary manner, thus increasing the effectiveness of their action (Useem 1984).

Elites not only coordinate their policy decisions but also manage their succession. Save for some dramatic elite failures (resulting in sudden and violent revolutionary replacements), access to elite ranks is controlled by elite 'selectorates', typically involving exclusive schools, party machines, parliamentary factions, and corporate hierarchies. Elite selectors favour certain elite types selected in terms of outlooks, social orientations, and social backgrounds, and that facilitates smooth power succession. While contemporary elites tend to be increasingly socially open – or predominantly 'middle class' – they remain biased in their ethno-racial and gender composition, and restricted to those with tertiary education (Parry 1969/2005, Putnam 1976).

Another issue of contention concerns the role of elites and classes in social change. Marxist scholars see change as propelled by class conflicts, and they diagnose the widening class polarization and escalating conflicts, both accompanied by successful mobilizations of the dominated masses into nationally organized working classes. Such 'mass classes', acting in a solidary manner under the revolutionary leadership, are likely to engineer, according to Marxist observers, revolutionary take-overs, followed by the evolution in the direction of classless egalitarianism. Elite theorists present quite different – in their view, more realistic – diagnoses and prognoses. They agree with the social polarization thesis, but see this polarization as a widening elite-mass gap. Moreover, they insist that the gap between powerful elites and the masses is inevitable, and that it cannot be bridged by revolutions. Elite rule *is* vulnerable to challenges, but only from other competing elite groups. Those elites who fail to effectively use persuasion and coercion are replaced by more politically skilful competitors. In most cases, such elite replacements occur gradually and peacefully through what Pareto termed 'elite circulation', that is gradual change in elite composition. Occasionally, however, elite succession may take a more sudden and violent form of coups and revolutions. Such revolutions, however, should not be confused with elimination of elites or assertion of power by the masses. As the French and Russian Revolutions have demonstrated, revolutions simply replace one elite with another: history is a graveyard of successive oligarchies, notes wryly Pareto. Post-revolutionary elites typically exercise power in a less restrained and more coercive manner than their predecessors, though their ideologies may evoke democracy, equality and human rights.

While elites enjoy political autonomy, in order to cement their rule under growing democratic pressures, they have to use demagogy and enter alliances with diverse 'social forces'. Again, elite theorists strongly disagree with Marxists on the nature of these political alliances. Marxist scholars see elites as firmly embedded (socially and functionally, in terms of their power interests) in dominant classes, and they focus on class-elite alliances. Elite analysts study elites as largely autonomous power-wielders who may ally themselves with a wide variety of 'forces', including social movements, ethno-racial minorities, religious segments, occupational categories, or regional groupings – depending on the opportunities for enhancing power and maximizing support. The European fascist elites, for example, enjoyed the support of radical nationalist movements, paramilitary groups and small businessmen. Similarly, the contemporary liberal democratic regimes are the products of consensual elites that represent wide alliances of organized political groups, business organizations, and voluntary associations (for example Higley and Burton 2006).

This brings us to another controversy in 'global elite' literature: about anti-democratic nature of elites and authoritarian bias allegedly inherent in 'classic' elite accounts. Mosca's critique of 'democratic illusions', Pareto's rants about 'demagogic plutocracy', and Michels' final endorsement of fascism, have contributed to this misperception, and gave elite theory a bad name among many liberal political analysts. This was in spite of the fact that the 'classic' theorists (save for Michels in his final days) were 'critical liberals' who normatively endorsed liberal democracy, while criticizing 'democratic illusions' of the day (Femia 2006). However, the anti-democratic label stuck, and the image of elite theory as ideologically biased lingered well until 1960s. It was accompanied by an image of 'power elites' as inimical to democracy (Mills 1956) and as tools of the dominant/ ruling classes (Domhoff 1967). The change of the image, and the theoretical reconciliation between elites and democracy, has occurred gradually over the last half a century. First, throughout the 1950s and 60s the elite concept was endorsed by growing number of 'pluralists', who identified modern democracy with a 'polyarchy' of competing elites (Dahl 1971). This was reinforced by the Schumpeterian interpretation of the 'democratic method' as elite competition for leadership embraced by 'plural/strategic' elitists, as well as 'demo-' and 'neo-' elitists, especially popular in the USA (Keller 1963). In their accounts, competing elites were accepted as an integral part of liberal-democratic politics. The second step took a form of studies of liberal elites and their alliances ('coupling') with broadly based and egalitarian social forces, including working class organizations and movements (Etzioni-Halevi 1993). This coincided with studies of elites successfully managing stable liberal-democratic regimes. Finally, a powerful wave of democratization (1974–1991), brought mainly 'from above' by determined leaders supported by prodemocratic reformist elites (for example organized around King Juan Carlos in Spain, Michail Gorbachev in the Soviet Union, Lech Walesa in Poland, and Nelson Mandela in South Africa) triggered more elaborate theoretical analyses of the role of liberal elites in the process of democratization and democratic consolidation of regimes (Higley and Pakulski 1995, Higley and Burton 2006).

As a result of these changes, the concept of elites has emerged at the beginning of the twenty-first century as an ideologically neutral and popular analytic tool. It has been absorbed in the mainstream and Marxist analyses alike (in the latter as an appendage to class), and given a more precise meaning. While the empirical delineations of elites continue to be arbitrary in recognition of the fact that power and influence are a matter of degree, elite researchers agree that power is concentrated at the apex of the largest and resource-rich organizations, and that the top power-holders, national elites, are small groups or networks. They typically restrict their size to 300–1,000 persons, with political 'inner circles' consisting of few dozen key decision-makers. Elite members are identified 'positionally', as holders of the top executive positions in the largest organizations, primarily the state, or by involvement in making key decisions, or by reputation among their powerful peers, or by all three methods combined. At the other end of the power spectrum are 'non-elites', typically treated as 'pressure groups' and 'support constituencies' of elites. Between these two extremes, social scientists also distinguish various political strata of 'influentials' from which elites are drawn and on which they rely in wielding power.

Elites and globalization

Contemporary elite analyses have managed to liberate themselves from ideological visions associated with the twentieth-century debates. However, they are in danger of succumbing to a new ideological perspective, a new form of skewed vision, this time associated with the concept of globalization, understood as the increasing worldwide economic, informational, and cultural *interdependence*. Interest in globalization started to grow in the 1960s stimulated by the analyses of global media by Marshall McLuhan (who coined the term 'global village'), then by the 'world-system' analyses by the so called dependency theorists, primarily Immanuel Wallerstein and his followers, and finally by liberal analysts of trade and financial liberalization accompanied by a rapid expansion of international regulatory bodies, and by the students of informational revolution, especially the phenomenal expansion of the information and communication technologies (ICT). The collapse of the Soviet Union, the expansion and further integration of the EU, the market liberalization, especially in China and the US-led trading blocs, and the expansion of the internet, formed the key focus of the more recent studies of globalization. The concept turned into a 'buzz word' in the 1990s following the publication of popular accounts of globalization by Roland Robertson (1992) and Anthony Giddens (1990).

Globalization means increasing interdependence on a world scale caused by intensified cross-border circulation of capital, goods, information, and people, and facilitated by the ICT. Although most observers see market liberalization as the key aspect of globalization, there is also an agreement that the distinctive feature of the current 'globalization wave' is the coincidence of the information/communication revolution with the market liberalization and political integration (especially in Europe). National elites of the most developed countries, especially their business-corporate sections, emerge as key agents of globalization. They embrace liberal policies, form regional alliances, and position themselves favourably in the increasingly global competition. The advantageous position in this competition offers immense rewards: broadened scope and scale of operations, increased profits, access to scarce labour, and widening spheres of influence. Hence globalization also triggers fierce competition in this international positioning, and it accompanies concentration of power through corporate mergers, 'executive shift' of power within political elites, and political alliances between national elites. National elites compete with a help of regional associations, such as the EU, NAFTA, and ASEAN, and they use transnational regulatory agencies, such as the World Bank, the International Monetary Fund, and various UN instrumentalities. Pro-globalization elites extend the networks of communication, investment, production, trade, and consumption; encourage international circulation of capital, goods, and services; aid the progressive integration of the financial markets; and support the free circulation of labour (Bauman 1998; Beck 2000). Political globalization accompanies the widening economic links, and it takes the form of a shift of power to political executives (especially the leaders), widening political alliances, closer engagement of formerly insulated countries, and increasing involvement of non-state political actors. A new global world politic is in many respects similar to the globalizing world economy: increasingly complex, cross-national, and less predictable than the old state-controlled politic. The power of the 'core' states, especially the USA and the rising competitors, China and India, increases proportionately to their success in positioning themselves as 'global players'. This results in the emergence of transnational political alliances that mirror financial and corporate networks.

With the global expansion, competition, and concentration of power come also increasing complexity, uncertainty, and risk. This is the point seldom appreciated by students of globalization. Increasing communication, interaction, and interdependence do not change the nature of political power. Nor do they alter the locus of power; power continues to rest at the apex the largest and resource-rich organizations. What globalization does is to alter the way power is *exercised*. The increasing interdependence, as the most apt observers note, widens the domains of decisional power, increases the complexity of problems faced by decision-makers, and amplifies the risks of unintended and adverse consequences. In the globalizing world, elites enjoy more influence, but suffer more uncertainty and risk. Their control over the outcomes of decisions is reduced by increasing 'systemic complexity' of the interconnected world, by the growing number of 'power stakeholders' – those who can influence the outcomes, often through disruption – and by a sheer novelty of complex and dynamic power arrangements that make past experiences irrelevant.

This is another way of saying that while elite power becomes more concentrated, it also becomes more difficult to wield. Consequently, elite positions become more precarious. This propels increasing elite interaction. In order to reduce the risks, elite groups contact and consult each other more widely and more regularly, coordinate their steps, form alliances, build protective political cartels and cooperate in executing policies. However this intensified interaction does not necessarily imply – and it should not be confused with – global *integration*. Deep divisions and conflicts persist, even though along different and rapidly changing fault lines. The fact that these divisions are often new and complex (cross-cutting, rather than overlapping) makes them more challenging, more difficult to control and contain. The proliferating elite summits, forums, and ad hoc meetings reflect these risk concerns and exemplify risk-reducing strategies. But even these intense and regular contacts do not defuse conflicts, and inter-elite competition remains fierce, culminating in occasional violent confrontations.

This intensifying inter-elite interaction (but not necessarily integration) is both facilitated and undermined by the third aspect of globalization involving communication and culture. Cultural globalization involves a world-wide circulation of ideas, images, values, and norms. The improving infrastructure of global communication, the widening networks of the mass media, and the declining effectiveness of distance and national boundaries in insulating nations, regions and communities amplifies what McLuhan called a 'global village' effect: a widening awareness of publicized ideas and events. While the cultural-informational globalization may aid the ultimate world-wide cultural integration, its short-term effects tend to be as disruptive as they are integrative. The intercultural contacts facilitated by ubiquitous mass media, amplify and aggravate the tensions between incompatible values and norms, especially between modernized and traditional cultures. Under their combined impact, incompatible cultures clash, the established (and often sacred) traditions crumble, and the formerly insulated communities confront each other, thus triggering cultural-communal backlash. One of the symptoms of this backlash are eruptions of intensified nationalism and communitarian-religious fundamentalism, both posing a serious challenge to political elites.

This leads us to one of the central controversies among the students of globalization and elites. The advocates of 'global elite' take an exaggerated position in this controversy by embracing the concept of 'de-nationalization', especially at the higher rungs of power. Upper classes and elites are seen by them as increasingly de-statized, 'transnational', 'without the country', politically and ethnically deracinated, and progressively integrated on the global level. Such a vision, and the accompanying argument about 'denationalization' of elites, seems to conflate three quite different global processes. One, widely recognized and quite well supported by evidence, is the declining capacity and willingness of nation-states to regulate national economies and societies. Globalization coincides with liberalization, with 'freeing' economic activities from restrictive regulations, recognition of 'rights', and reduction of taxes – all accompanied by the shift from ruling to governance, from using thumbs to using fingers. In a sense, this liberalization can be seen as a 'horizontal' redistribution of state power. The second process is 'internationalization' of perspective, increasing recognition of links and connections between domestic and international issues and problems, ranging from pollution to crime. Internationalization prompts elites to think globally, even when they deal with the local issues. Finally, there is a much less widespread cultural trend of 'cosmopolitanism', that is detachment from national cultures and identities. It seems to be limited in scope, affecting only some sections of metropolitan cultural upper strata.

These processes do not add up to 'de-nationalization', especially on the elite level. This is because the key organizational bases of elites, nation states, remain the major containers and the principal *loci* of power. Nation states continue to (i) hold monopoly for coercion, and therefore the concentrated control over the military and police forces; (ii) hold the supreme capacity for mobilizing various 'power resources' (economic, political, and ideological) and coordinating their deployment; and (iii) maintain the supreme legitimacy based on their claim to represent nations, defend national interests, and sustain national cultures and identities. States also claim a unique representation of the *democratic principles* and the key defenders of rights (civil, political, social, and cultural) that lie at the heart of dominant liberal-democratic ideologies. Finally, state arenas provide privileged forums for elite interaction and integration. Networks that are national in scope prevail among elites, in spite of the increasing international contacts and consultations. For all these reasons power remains concentrated on the national level, in the hands of national elites. Members of these elites also tend to be more nationalistic than the masses, mindful of the centrality of national commitments and the importance of nation-states in securing and defending their power interests. This is why powerful interests, especially transnational interests, use national idioms of legitimation, cultivate national networks, maintain national lobbies, and seek national alliances. The success of the European integration is due mainly to the strong championing of the union by the French and German elites who see a strong EU as a 'Franco-German project' promoting their national interests. Similarly, the current slow-down of the European integration reflects the growing influence of more Euro-sceptical and nationalistic elites in Britain, Northern and Eastern Europe. The importance of national elites is also highlighted by the fact that all elite members (like Rupert Murdoch, the powerful media magnate who changed his nationality from Australian to American), carefully choose what passports they carry.

To reiterate, globalization does not 'de-nationalize' power, and it does not promote elite integration on a global scale. Instead, it facilitates and stimulates inter-elite contacts aiming at enhancing elite security and reducing risks. Wide international consultation, coordination of action, power alliances, political coalitions, and protective cartels became routine risk-managing measures adopted by elites. Such measures do not reduce power competitions, and they do not eliminate inter-elite conflicts, but allow for their management with reduced risk of political fall-outs, especially violent confrontations. There is evidence of closer links and personal contacts between elite groups not only sharing sectional or regional interests, but also competing for influence. There are also signs of closer and more systematic collaboration and *reproachement* between the most powerful national leaders and elites – the trend correlated with a post-Cold War reduction in violent confrontations. But there are also persisting conflicts in the Middle East and Southern Asia, as well as growing competitive tensions, especially between the allied US and EU elites on the one hand, and the increasingly assertive and expansionist Russian elite (Putin's *siloviki*) on the other. Indeed, among the most alarming scenarios are those that depict new and widening regional and cultural-religious conflicts (the 'New Cold War', the 'clash of civilizations'), the management of which may exceed the capacity of elites. Elites, in other words, do communicate and interact more widely and regularly across the national borders without necessarily abandoning national commitments and without integrating on a global scale.

With these critical comments in mind, we can look at the most popular versions of arguments about the emergence of 'global elites' and the accompanying claims about the impact of globalization on the power structure.

'Global elite' or 'superclass'

Rothkopf's (2008: 10–11) argument about the formation of powerful 'global elite' a 'new class without a country' sounds plausible, because three (out of four) central premises are plausible and well supported. For a start, there is convincing evidence of centripetal trends in power distribution: concentration of wealth in the hands of the new billionaires, concentration of executive power in the boards of largest transnational corporations, especially the corporate giants spawned by the 'merger-mania' at the end of the twentieth century, concentration of political power in the hands of leaders and their 'court governments', and concentration of influence in the large religious churches and movements. There is also little doubt that '[e]ach member of this superclass [allegedly the emergent "global elite"] has the ability to regularly influence the lives of millions people in multiple countries worldwide' (2008: xiv). The 'superclass', as Rothkopf claims, includes not only political leaders and CEOs of largest international corporations, but also 'media barons, billionaires who are actively involved in their investments, technology entrepreneurs, oil potentates, hedge fund managers, private equity investors, top military commanders, a select few religious leaders' and, more controversially, 'a handful of renowned writers, scientists and artists, even terrorist leaders and master criminals'. Altogether, over 6,000 people qualify as members of the 'superclass'.

The second premise is equally plausible. Rothkopf shows that the 'global elite' consists of predominantly *new* power-wielders, whose power – linked to recently accumulated wealth, newly acquired political authority, centralized executive control, widening communication, and broadening networks of influence – has been either created or enhanced in/by the processes of globalization. These are, in other words, the winners in the globalization stakes: the offspring of the economic boom triggered by the powerful wave of market expansion and deregulation that started in the late 1970s and accelerated at the turn of the century, the beneficiaries of power reshuffle that followed the 'fall of the Wall', those who emerged out of the energy crisis, who gained international influence in economic exchange, earned billions in war-boosted arms trade, and caught the limelight in the widening market for attractive ideas. Finally, there are those who control large populations and enjoy the loyalty of millions of followers, again, thanks to the enhanced means of mass communication, intensified circulation of ideas, and widening markets for those ideas. This is an uncontroversial claim, typically made by supporters of globalization.

Slightly less plausible and less supported is the third claim about 'de-nationalization' of the 'superclass'. The argument that members of the 'superclass' enjoy international influence is indisputable. But this is not new, and it does not prove international integration. Significant power has always radiated internationally. But the international scope of communication, consultation, and power-wielding does not necessarily indicate the weakening national interests, loyalties, and identities. The most powerful organizations, nation-states, still command primary loyalties, and identities of citizens and elites. Elites champion predominantly national interests, even if these interests overlap with the interests of other allied national elites, and even if they champion these interests internationally. At the core of national interests lie the support for national economies, promotion of domestic businesses (especially against international competitors), widening of national political influence, and aiding national cultures, including their mass/popular products. To argue otherwise would risk ignoring overwhelming evidence of strong national commitments, especially among the leaders of superpower nations: the USA, Russia, and China. It would also ignore overwhelming support given by national political elites to 'their' (that is nationally embedded) businesses. Corporations like Wal-Mart, with high economic profiles (in employment, technology, innovation, import-exports, and so forth) are as protected and supported as the 'government sponsored' enterprises, even if they are privately owned and their ownership and operations are international in scope. If they find themselves in trouble, like Microsoft in the 1990s, national political leaders let them off the hook. If they go broke, like the loan mortgage giants Freddie Mac and Fannie Mae in recent years, the US government bails them out. Their interests are protected by national elites.

However, some provisos are necessary: as argued above, the process of globalization has undoubtedly weakened *some aspects* of national loyalties and identities by giving more influence to both regional (sub-national) organizations, and supra-national ones, including transnational religious and secular movements. However, the power and influence of such organizations and movements is typically proportionate to the support they receive from national elites. The anti-Western Islamist movements, such as the Hezbollah and the Taliban, for example, rely on support of national elites in Iran and Pakistan. Their actions enhance the influence of Iranian and Pakistani political elites, both competing for a status of international champions and defenders of Islam and the Palestinians.

This leads to the fourth, and as we have already noted, highly problematic part of Rothkopf's argument: namely that the members of the 'superclass' form a single and relatively integrated 'global elite', show some social cohesion, as well as commonality of interests and orientations. While stressing that the 'global elite' is *in statu nascendi*, Rothkopf (2008: xiv) nevertheless refers to it as a 'group'. Moreover, he compares the members of the 'superclass' to the American 'power elite' as depicted by C. Wright Mills (1956), overlooking the fact that, according to Mills, the three segments of the American power elite were united by shared commitment to national interests and 'American values'. Rothkopf seems to be aware of the problem, and he occasionally alludes to differences and divisions within the ranks of the 'superclass'. He also distances himself from conspiracy theorists who see the 'world rulers' as a well integrated clique. But he also assumes a commonality of interests, orientations, and actions that are typical of a group:

> The influence of this transnational superclass is often amplified as the members act
> in clusters knit together by business deals, corporate boards, investment flows, old

337

school ties, club memberships, and countless other strands that transform them if not into the conspiring committees of legend then at least into groups that are proven masters at advancing their aligned self-interests.

(2008: xvii)

While this passage would sound plausible as a description of a national elite, it is bound to raise the eyebrows as a portrayal of the 'global superclass'. The key members of this 'superclass': Bill Gates, Hu Jintao, Vladimir Putin, and Osama bin Laden, have remarkably little in common as far as their backgrounds, orientations, core commitments and identities, and self-interests are concerned. While powerful, they are members of quite disparate elite clusters, and they compete with each other. Such persons are not likely to meet at the Davos promenade.

Paradoxically, one may say, the label 'superclass', while analytically exotic, seems more suitable as a descriptor of these disparate category of winners in the globalization stakes than the label 'global elite'. For a start, the core members of the superclass are the super-rich and 'leaders in business and finance' (Rothkopf 2008: 33, 39, 81, 116, 155). This makes the 'superclass' somewhat similar to the 'transnational capitalist class' analyzed by Marxist scholars – in spite of Rothcopf's frequent and approving references to Pareto and Mills, rather than Marx. The large size (6,000) and internationalism of the 'superclass' also fit better the image of a class rather than an elite. Finally, Rothkopf's reluctance to depict the 'superclass' as an actor also seems to fit better a class image than an elite image. Classes are seldom considered political actors. Elites, by contrast, show what Meisel (1965) labelled as '3Cs': consciousness, cohesion, and conspiracy, the latter understood as the capacity for solidary action.

Does this 'class interpretation' make Rothkopf's arguments more plausible? In order to answer this question, we have to look first at the neo-Marxist arguments that explicitly anchor 'transnational elites' in a broader 'transnational capitalist class'.

'Transnational elites' and 'transnational capitalist class'

The family of arguments that depict 'global elites' (typically in plural) as incumbents of the top rungs in the emergent 'global classes', especially the 'transnational capitalist class', is quite sizable. This reflects the popularity of class-elite interpretations of globalization (for example Sklair 1995, 2001, Robinson 2004, Boswell and Chase-Dunn 2006, Sassen 2007). We focus here on two relatively new but quite typical members of this family: the versions outlined by Saskia Sassen (2007) and William Robinson (2004).

According to all neo-Marxist scholars, the globalization of classes, especially the ruling class, follows the logic of capitalist development, as charted by Marx and updated by the 'dependency' or 'world system' theorists. The global expansion of capital, according to them, results in a gradual detachment of class interests and identities from nation-specific interests and identities. The dependency theorists tend to see this supra-national class formation and integration as different in the 'core', 'periphery', and the 'semi-periphery' of the capitalist world system (Chirot 1977). More orthodox neo-Marxists ignore these structural-regional differences in class formation and analyze the world-wide integration and 'denationalization' of classes and class-embedded elites (Robinson 2004: 49–57). There are some differences even between the closely allied visions. Thus Robinson sees globalization and transnational class integration as asymmetric, whereby in the last half-a-century 'capitalist globalization has increased the relative power of global capital over global labour by acting as a centripetal force for the capitalist class and a centrifugal force for the working class.' Sassen (2007: 168–9), by contrast, sees the transnational integration as occurring on both ends of the polar class divide. She distinguishes three emergent global (at least partly 'de-nationalized') classes: transnational corporate professionals and executives, top state executives embedded in 'transnational networks of government officials' (experts, judges, law enforcement, and so forth), and 'an emergent class of disadvantaged or resource-poor workers and activists'. Thus the process of 'denationalization' and integration of classes occurs at the both extremes of the class structure; the 'middle' classes remain less globalized and more 'nationalized'.

Sassen (2007: 173–5) also distinguishes within the top two globalizing classes another entity: 'an international class of powerful elites' or 'transnational elites', thus suggesting that elites form at least partly independently of transnational classes, though within them, that is within class-embedded international corporations, financial organizations, government networks, regulative and facilitative bodies, especially in the organizational hubs of global metropolies. These organizations form 'a kind of operational infrastructure for corporate economic globalization', and are run by groups of 'professionals, managers, executives, and technical staff members' – a 'new transnational professional class' of controllers, rather than owners, of the main class organizations. The key assets of members include expertise, information and networks (social capital). They are well-trained, well-connected, well-informed and highly mobile functionaries of capital. They inter-twine with the second constitutive part of 'global elites' – a transnational network of top government officials whose function is facilitative and (de-)regulatory: they are 'in charge of critical work in the development of a global corporate economy' (2007: 179). Finally, there are also informal networks of economic and financial experts and advisors operating outside transnational corporations and intergovernmental regulatory bodies. Their function is important but largely facilitative. They, nevertheless, are also included in the ranks of 'transnational elites' that are increasingly independent of national bodies and committed to promoting the international 'deregulatory project'.

According to Robinson (2004: 75–82) the 'global elites' are a part of the 'globalist bloc' (a Gramscian concept denoting a hegemonic coalition of social forces supporting the global expansion of capital) that includes the 'core' member of the transnational capitalist class (TCC): owners and managers of the transnational corporations (TNC), as well as the key functionaries of regulatory and facilitative agencies, such as the International Monetary Fund, the World Bank and the World Trade Organization. The 'bloc' includes also top officials of 'dominant political parties, media conglomerates, and technocratic elites and state managers in both North and South along with select organic intellectuals and charismatic figures who provide ideological legitimacy and technical solutions'. The distinctive feature of this broad 'bloc-elite' is not so much high power and influence, as a shared neo-liberal agenda of de-regulation, liberalization of trade, privatization, and unconstrained capital circulation – all promoting the 'unfettered operation of the new global capitalist production system'. Democratic 'polyarchy' – a system of competing (plural) political elites – 'has been promoted by the transnational elite as the political counterpart to neoliberalism'.

As these short summaries suggest, the neo-Marxist arguments about 'global elites' share certain characteristics. All of them are vague in distinguishing and delineating classes, blocs and elites, and they tend to conflate them. All depict the elite as embedded in the capitalist class, and as functionally allied with international capital. The nature of this alliance, however, is seldom spelled out in a clear way. On the one hand, the global elite is supposed to be embedded in and subservient to the TCC, as an 'executive committee' of the dominant class, on the other hand, it is also credited with a fair degree of political agency and autonomy – a clear symptom of unresolved theoretical tensions between the elite and class perspectives. This poses a dilemma: if power is concentrated in economically dominant classes or blocs, then the concept of elite becomes superfluous. It becomes a mere rhetorical concession to the current terminological fashion. On the other hand, if elite is really important, if it enjoys political autonomy and authentic power-agency in promoting the international expansion of capital, this undermines the very foundations of the Marxist class theory and questions the utility of class analysis.

There is also a perennial problem of elite (and class) unity. If the class and elite members share basic interests (sometimes identified with the maintenance of the capitalist status quo, sometimes seen as promoting global restructuring), how can we account for divisions and conflicts within the 'capitalist class' and among national political executives? Are these conflicts (for example about territories or control of energy resources) to be dismissed as insignificant 'fractionation' (Robinson 2004)? Are they, as many advocates of 'global elite' suggest, just residues of 'old' conflicts between the 'national' ruling classes and elites? The answers to these questions suggested by the advocates of 'transnational class-elite' are less than satisfactory.

This leads us to the third usage of the term 'global elite' and the accompanying argument about the emergence of the hegemonic super-power, typically the United States, whose elite becomes de facto 'global' due to the unchallenged 'sole superpower' status of its nation-state and the unchallenged 'global reach'.

Global elite of the sole superpower

These arguments were popularized in the 1990s following the collapse of European communism and the period of assertive political leadership of Ronald Reagan, George Bush (Snr) and Bill Clinton. Among the most popular was the 'global American hegemony' argument, according to which the USA exercised largely consensual and benign domination, and became the unchallenged economic, military, ideological and cultural super-power on the world scale. This global ascendancy had followed the military victory of the (US-led) Allies in World War II, was reinforced by the post-war military-nuclear hegemony, and was confirmed by the political-ideological victory in the Cold War that culminated in the sudden collapse of the Soviet bloc. The unprecedented economic expansion of the USA in last decades of the twentieth century reinforced this vision of global American hegemony. One of the offshoots of this vision was a claim that American power elite turns into a global power elite, whose world-hegemonic status gives it a global responsibility and power-reach (for example Nye 1990, Fukuyama 1992, Kagan 2006).

Hegemony is an apt term to describe the largely consensual, multifaceted, and diffuse form of domination. Its scope is quite stunning. With its young and expanding population amounting to less than 5 per cent of the world population, the USA in 2001 accounted for 31 per cent of global GDP, 36 per cent of global defence spending; 45 per cent of the global conventional weapons export; 41 per cent of global spending on research and development; 60 per cent of global export and capital investment; and a staggering 83 per cent of global cinema and box-office revenues. The American leaders combine the 'hard' and 'soft' forms of power. US military power is projected worldwide through over 700 military installations outside the American territory and with the help of a 1.4 million-strong army, approximately a quarter of which is permanently stationed abroad. The hegemony is also exercised through the US-dominated international bodies, such as the World Bank (which traditionally appoints an American head), the IMF and the WTO, as well as increasing foreign aid, estimated at c. $US 15 billion a year in 2006. On the 'soft' end of the power spectrum, American English has become a new *lingua franca*, American popular culture has dominated the (mostly American) mass media, and – perhaps most importantly – the American version of liberal-democratic ideology has become the dominant creed among Western political elites and masses. Increasingly, it has also been embraced by the elites of modernizing nations (*The Economist*, 2002). Even after the military debacle in Iraq, and following the 'relative decline' (mainly in economic growth, indebtedness/deficit, and political reputation) during the post-2001 years, the US continues to be depicted as the superpower that dominates in the key areas of science, technological innovation, economic efficiency, and military might. In spite of economic and political woes, the US continues to have the best universities, lead in technological innovation, have the most competitive industries and produce (consistently over the last 120 years) about 25 per cent of the world economic output (Zakaria 2008).

The United States, as stressed by the advocates of the 'global American elite', is also home of the largest and most competitive transnational corporations. Perhaps the best known, Wal-Mart, has revenue that exceeds the GDP of most countries and is eight times the size of Microsoft's revenue, and accounts for about 2 per cent of the American GDP. Because it employs 1.4 million workers, leads in innovation and (ruthless) efficiency, is regarded as technological standard-setter in retail and the key inflation-checker (due to massive price reductions and $18 billion import from China), Wal-Mart is also regarded as a 'national asset' strongly supported by American political elite.

This argument and the underlying theoretical equation (global elite = elite of the hegemonic superpower) is by far the most clear, theoretically most consistent and best supported of the three arguments about the emergence of the 'global elite'. It is consistent with the classic elite theory, it clearly delineates elite members (especially the core 'political leadership'), and it is plausible, that is fits the popular interpretations. But it has also been exaggerated. The scope and strength of the American hegemony, in particular, has been questioned, especially in the light of the most recent 'rise of the other powers' (Zakaria 2008). According to critics (such as Kennedy 1987, Schlosstein 1989, Brzezinski 2007), American hegemony has been waning, not so much due to the decline of American power, as to the rise of the other powers, especially China and India, and to the failure of American political elites, especially the leonine 'G.W. Bush elite', to provide effective 'global leadership'. The rise of potential challengers makes American elites *relatively* weaker on the global scene, less capable of influencing events on the world scene. The USA may have been a sole superpower immediately after the WWII and then, again, after the collapse of the Soviet Union in the 1990s. However, this period of unchallenged supremacy has passed. The inability to capitalize from the collapse of the Soviet Union, the prolonged, unilateral, unpopular, and prohibitively expensive invasion of Iraq, the ineffective tackling of insurgencies in Iraq and Afghanistan, the accompanying economic slow-down (partly due to military over-stretch), and the massive trade deficit with China, have weakened American hegemony in all dimensions and limited the 'soft power' of the American elite, that is 'the ability to get what you want through attraction rather than coercion or payments ... [that] arises from the attractiveness of a country's culture, political ideals, and policies' (Nye 2004: 4). This weakening, according to sceptics, marks a decline in American 'global reach'. Brzezinski (2007) sees this as the result of poor leadership and the errors of the last three administrations. According to Stiglitz and Bilmes (2008), this is the case of imperial 'over-stretch' and the ballooning costs of the war in Iraq war (estimated at $3 trillion). In Zakaria's (2008) view, this is a case of 'relative decline' reflecting the rise by China and 'the rest'. Whatever the reason, critics argue, the American elite has been losing its hegemonic power and global reach.

Conclusion: problems with 'global elite'

The supporters of 'global elite' arguments (especially (1) and (2)) question the core theoretical premises of classical elite theorists concerning the sources and locus of power. They claim that the old power concentrations within nation states/governments and economies have been – or are being – replaced by new concentrations in the hands of new 'global' and 'denationalized' elite 'without a country', with few national attachments and nation-specific interests, but with strengthening international links and increasing internal integration *cum* cohesion. This claim not only stretches the meaning of 'power' and 'elites', but also misrepresents the changes associated with globalization. As noted by critics (such as Stiglitz 2002, Zakaria 2008), globalization does not weaken national attachments and identities, but enhances some alternative – local, regional, gender, racial, and religious – identities and commitments. In fact, globalization seems to accompany a rise in nationalism, a 'global political awakening' (Brzezinski's term) that affects both the elites and the masses. These national 'awakenings' have been most apparent in the Balkans and Central Asia following the collapse of the Soviet Union and Yugoslavia. In extreme cases, the 'awakening' combines xenophobic demagogy with militancy and populist mobilizations – all facilitated by the information and communication revolution. But the less extreme awakenings are also noticeable in America, China, and India, all of which seem to experience resurgences of patriotic zeal and rhetoric. These outbursts of nationalism have been both articulated and seized by political elites. The resurgent American nationalism has been harnessed by the neoconservative 'Vulcans' at the inner core of George W. Bush's elite. The nostalgic and imperial Russian nationalism has been embraced by Vladimir Putin's violent and prickly elite; the assertive Chinese nationalism found its expression in the tough rhetoric of Hu Jintao's elite, especially in response to the demands for human rights and autonomy in Tibet.

Similarly, the suggestion that the majority of capitalist classes, including the largest corporations and national political elites, support globalization, appears to be exaggerated, to say the least. There are significant differences of views on the merits of globalization, especially the 'free' population movements, among elite groups. There are also emerging anti-globalization elite groups and coalitions both within the USA and internationally (for example in South America led by Venezuela's Hugo Chavez). Significant business interests in the Unites States and Great Britain define themselves as threatened by globalization, and they demand national trade and workforce protection. This ambivalence towards globalization has been well articulated by Stiglitz (2002) and Soros (2002). Like debates about national interests, the controversies about the impact of global expansion of trade, investment, global production, information, and circulation of people, continue to divide the top power-holders. Some even predict that the political elite of the Republican Party in the US may split on the issue, with a fraction taking an anti-global, protectionist, and unilateral stance.

To put it differently, the advocates of 'global elite' arguments seem to exaggerate the popularity of global 'opening up', and overestimate the 'de-nationalization' cosmopolitanism and open mobility. In the globalizing world, especially in elite circles, nationalism seems to thrive, cosmopolitanism is restricted to metropolitan enclaves, and open mobility encounters serious restriction and opposition (Turner 2007). The 'global elite' arguments also confuse some of the aspects of globalization: the change in the *location/distribution of power* (not backed by evidence) and the change in *the way power is deployed/exercised* (well documented). The latter, that is the change in the deployment and exercise of power, is as significant as it is uncontroversial. It involves broadening (inter-)action, as reflected in intensifying contacts, coordination, and collaboration among elite groups – all in response to growing interdependence, growing complexity, declining certainty, increasing risks, improved communication, and the multiplication of 'transnational' problems, such as uncontrolled migrations, energy shortages, environmental degradation, pollution, climate change, trade in illegal drugs, terrorism, cyber-crime, and threat of pandemics (such as AIDS). As far as the deployment of power by elites is concerned, globalization breeds five Cs: contacts, coordination, collaboration, collusion, and competition. National elites rely on widening contacts in improving the effectiveness of their policies and reducing risks of failures. For the same reasons they create and support transnational coordinative, regulative, collaborative bodies, such as the IMF, the World Bank and the agencies of the UN. The proliferation of such bodies, however, does not mean that power, especially the ability to enforce compliance, shifts away from the states. The transnational bodies rely on political support as well as funding by national elites.

This picture, if accurate, would vindicate the classic elite theorists who have always claimed that in modern societies power derives from organizational sources and follows the highly skewed but principally national pattern of distribution. It remains heavily concentrated in national states and in the hands of national elites. Such elites should not be confused with the ownership/property classes (as identified by Marxist scholars) or with the groups of publicity-seekers. The super-rich do command power and influence, and they also acquire high status, but their power is dwarfed by the commanders of the state apparata and corporate giants. Similarly, the international celebrities may acquire significant influence and even succeed as candidates for political offices. But they seldom secure systematic and authoritative decisional power and remain mere 'influentials'. As noted by Pareto, Mosca, and Mills, elites cultivate friendly 'gliteraties' and surround themselves with celebrities. They also rub shoulders with the 'super-rich'. However, their power is principally dependent on their positions, on the organizational resources these positions command, and they often use this organizational power to assert their will and interests over the super-rich. President Putin's brutal and swift political 'decapitation' of the recalcitrant super-rich 'oligarchs' in Russia demonstrates it clearly.

This leads us to the second general criticism of the 'global elite' concepts and arguments. Globalization – increasing interdependence – is confused by many proponents of 'global elite' with global integration, that is, bringing together and unifying disparate groups, positions, and organizations. In fact, the two – global interdependence and integration – seem to vary independently. In some cases globalization accompanies integration (for example the strengthening of the European Union), in other instances it accompanies disintegration (such as the fragmentation of the Soviet Union, disintegration of Yugoslavia, and the Balkan conflicts). Globalization, in other words, does not necessarily promote unity and harmony. It does not weaken inter-elite competition as demonstrated by recent political flare-ups in the Middle East, Central and South Asia, and throughout Africa. If anything, globalization seems to aggravate tensions and animosities.

Again, this seems to vindicate the classic elite theory that stresses the importance of *intra*-elite integration and *inter*-elite competition. Only the cohesive and solidary groupings of power-holders, capable of articulating and defending their interests – typically against power competitors and other elites – can be considered 'elites'. The proponents of 'global elite' (both understood as a 'superclass' of new rich, and defined as the executive of the 'transnational capitalist class') ignore these classic theoretical tenets. They suggest that globalization can spawn a 'global elite' of the size that precludes a possibility of regular interaction and therefore social integration and cohesion.

In spite of the increasing interconnectedness and interdependence, in spite of progressive concentration of economic and political power in executive bodies of states and TNCs, and finally, in spite of increasing international consultation, collaboration, coordination, and cooperation, there is little evidence of the emergence of a *single and integrated* 'global elite' or dominant 'superclass'. Instead, most political analysts see multiple power centres and competing national elites, the latter forming a steep hierarchy with the superpower and 'global powers' at the apex. The American elite remains at the top of the international power hierarchy, although its hegemony and power reach have been weakened by the rising 'others'.

References

Bauman, Zygmunt (1998) *Globalization: The Human Consequences*, New York: Columbia University Press.
Bottomore, Tom (1993/1964) *Elites and Society*, 2nd edition, London: Routledge.
Brzezinski, Zbigniew (2007) *Second Chance*, New York: Basic Books.
Boswell, Terry and Chase-Dunn, Christopher (2006) 'Transnational Social Movements and Democratic Socialist Parties', in C. Chase-Dunn and S.J. Babones (eds), *Global Social Change*, Baltimore: Johns Hopkins University Press, pp. 317–36.
Chase-Dunn, Christopher (1998) *Global Formations*, updated edition, Lanham, MD: Rowman & Littlefield.
Chirot, Daniel (1977) *Social Change in the Twentieth Century*, New York: Harcourt Brace Jovanovich.
Dahl, Robert A. (1971) *Polyarchy: Participation and Opposition*, New Haven, NJ: Yale University Press.
Domhoff, William (1967) *Who Rules America?* Englewood Cliffs: Prentice-Hall.
Economist, The (2002) 'Present at the Creation. A survey of America's world role', 29 June.
Etzioni-Halevi, Eva (1993) *The Elite Connection*, Cambridge: Polity.
Femia, Joseph (2006) *Pareto and Political Theory*, London and NY: Routledge.
Fukuyama, Francis (1992) *The End of History and the Last Man*, London: Penguin.
——(2006) *America at the Crossroads*, New Haven: Yale University Press.
Giddens, Anthony (1990) *The Consequences of Modernity*. Cambridge: Polity.
Higley, John and Burton, Michael (1989) 'The Elite Variable in Democratic Transitions and Breakdowns', *American Sociological Review*, 54: 17–32.
——(2006) *Elite Foundations of Liberal Democracy*, New York and Oxford: Rowman & Littlefield.
Higley, John and Pakulski, Jan (1995) 'Elites and democratic transitions in Eastern Europe', *Australian Journal of Political Science*, 30(2): 32–54.
Higley, John, Pakulski, Jan and Wesolowski Wlodzimierz (eds) (1998) *Postcommunist Elites and Democracy in Eastern Europe*, Houndmills: Macmillan.
Kagan, Robert (2006) *Dangerous Nation: America's Place in the World from its Earliest Days to the Dawn of the Twentieth Century*, New York: Alfred Knopf.
Keller, Suzanne (1963) *Beyond the Rulling Class: Strategic Elites in Modern Society.* New York: Random House.

Kennedy, Paul (1987) *The Rise and Fall of the Great Powers*, New York: Vintage.

Linz, Juan (2006) *Robert Michels, Political Sociology, and the Future of Democracy*, New Brunswick, NJ: Transaction Publishers.

Meisel, James H. (1958) *The Myth of the Ruling Class*, Ann Arbor, MI: University of Michigan Press.

Michels, Robert (1958) *Political Parties*, Glencoe, IL: Free Press.

Mills, C. Wright (1956) *The Power Elite*, Oxford: Oxford University Press.

Mosca, Gaetano (1939) *The Ruling Class*, New York: McGraw-Hill.

Nye, Joseph S. (1990) *Bound to Lead: The Challenging Nature of American Power*, New York: Basic Books.

——(2004) 'The Decline of America's Soft Power', *Foreign Affairs*, 83(3), May/June, 7–29.

Pareto, Vilfredo (1935) *The Mind and Society*, New York: Dover.

Parry, Geraint (1969/2005) *Political Elites*, London: Allen & Unwin.

Putnam, Robert (1976) *Comparative Study of Political Elites*, Englewood Cliffs, NJ: Prentice-Hall.

Robertson, Ronald (1992) *Globalization. Social Theory and Global Culture*, London: Sage.

Robinson, William I. (2004) *A Theory of Global Capitalism*, Baltimore, MD: Johns Hopkins University Press.

Rothkopf, David (2008) *Superclass: The Global Power Elite and the World They are Making*, New York: Farrar, Straus & Giroux.

Sassen, Saskia (2007) *A Sociology of Globalisation*, New York & London: W.W. Norton.

Sartori, Giovanni (1987) *The Theory of Democracy Revisited*, Chatham, NJ: Chatham House.

Schlosstein, Steven (1989) *The End of the American Century*, New York: Congdon & Weed.

Schumpeter, Joseph (1954/1942) *Capitalism, Socialism and Democracy*, London: Allen & Unwin.

Scott, John (ed.) (1990) *The Sociology of Elites*, London: Edward Elgar.

Sklair, Leslie (1995) *Sociology of the Global System*, 2nd edition revised and updated, London: Prentice Hall, Harvester Wheatsheaf.

——(2001) *The Transnational Capitalist Class*. Oxford: Blackwell.

Soros, George (2002) *George Soros on Globalisation*, London: Public Affairs.

Stiglitz, Joseph (2002) *Globalisation and Its Discontents*, New York: W.W. Norton.

Stiglitz, Joseph and Linda Bilmes (2008) *The Three Trillion Dollar War*, New York and London: W.W. Norton.

Turner, Bryan S. (2007) 'The Enclave Society: Towards a Sociology of Immobility', *European Journal of Social Theory*, 10(2): 287–304.

Useem, Michael (1984) *The Inner Circle*, Oxford and New York: Oxford University Press.

Zakaria, Fareed (2008) *The Post-American World*, New York and London: W.W. Norton.

18

Globalization, ethnic conflict, and nationalism

Daniele Conversi

This chapter begins by tracing a parallel: the advent of modernity lies at the very heart of nationalism, while both modernity and nationalism are related to the expansion of warfare. A similar relationship can be said to apply to globalization and its close links with ethnic conflict, civil strife, and militarism. The case studies which follow illustrate the direct and indirect consequences of both modernization and globalization in instigating the explosion of nationalism. More substantially, the overlap between globalization and Americanization is addressed as a recurrent phenomenon in the explosion of ethnic conflict.

Modernity, globalization, and nationalism

The idea that nationalist conflicts erupted as a consequence of social changes brought about by modernity has remained an incontrovertible paradigm in the study of ethnic conflict and nationalism. However, many also argue that nations as such could not exist before the modern age. This approach is often referred to as 'modernism' (Smith 1996, 1998, 2004). Some authors go as far as saying that nations are entirely 'invented' (Hobsbawm 1983, Gellner 2006) or 'imagined' (Anderson 1993) by modern elites and reading publics.

The force of nationalism has spread well over the nineteenth century into the age of globalization. There are thus parallels between modernization and globalization as stimulating factors for nationalism and ethnic conflict. Although the reach of globalization is historically unprecedented, some of its features accompanied the rise of modernity and the advent of the modern nation state. In particular, both resulted in the demise of older boundaries and the construction of new ones. Whereas industrialization destroyed local and regional boundaries by superimposing national boundaries on them, globalization destroyed national boundaries by superimposing a plethora of supra-national and corporate networks on them, including mafias, organized crime, and multi-national corporations (MNCs), none of which are as easily identifiable on a political map as 'sovereign' countries still are. The adoption of planetary rules to comply with the standards set by the International Monetary Fund (IMF) and the World Bank has unsurprisingly resulted in global disempowerment, at least according to the perception of influential NGOs activists (Korten 2001).

Has all this also led to a decline in national identities? Not at all. Partly because national cultures have been seriously damaged or reshaped by globalization, we have seen a global intensification of ethnic belligerence. Moreover, the formation of new elites and the spread of capitalist wealth have led to nationalist self-assertion, while cultural impoverishment spurred a generalized need for compensatory ethnic assertiveness.

Despite some divergence over the nature and time-span of modernity, modernism has continued to inform scholarly accounts of nationalism and ethnic conflict. On the other hand, longstanding assumptions of modernity as founded on a historical rupture have been challenged by the exploration of continuities with the past: Anthony D. Smith's ethno-symbolic approach argues that, although nationalism is a modern phenomenon, nations are not necessarily modern creations and are indeed based on ancient, pre-modern ethnic roots which became re-activated by adapting to the new political climate (Smith 2004, Leoussi and Grosby 2006). The challenge of modernity constrained ancient *ethnies* or ethnic groups to find ways out to ensure their survival and protect their mil-lennial identity. Only through nationalism could they find a new 'security', and via national mobilization could they hope to ensure their survival by attaining either power-sharing or separate statehood. It should be noted that Smith's ethno-symbolism emerged primarily as a critique of extreme forms of modernism postulating that nations are wholly fabricated (Gellner 2006) or that many institutions we often call 'traditions' are simply modern inventions (Hobsbawm 1983).

In general, both modernists and anti-modernists (of which, more later on) could not fail to recognize that modernity, however one defines it, provided the main incentive and stimulus for nationalist conflict. Therefore, both 'modernists' and 'anti-modernists' share the view that modernity was *the* catalyst, although the latter would not describe modernity as leading to ethno-genesis. In fact, given that their focus was on persistence and *longue-duree*, anti-modernists also anticipated the fact that globalization could not lead to the demise of nations and the erosion of nationalism (Leoussi and Grosby 2006). On the contrary, it would provide a further boost to ethno-national mobilizations (Smith 1996).

Globalization has been described as either a deepening of modernity or as a wholly new departure, often celebrated as 'postmodernity'. Whether one stresses continuity or rupture, the shared view is that both industrialization and globalization were characterized by massive change and the breakdown of ancient boundaries. In this way, the advent of industrialization contained and anticipated most of the problems faced in the era of glo-balization. Later on, the history of Basque nationalism provides a telling example to illustrate this relationship.

If nationalism cannot be explained independently from the onset of modernity and modern state-making, both are enmeshed in the expansion of warfare. Nationalism manifested itself in an era of inter-state competition, the collapse of boundaries, eco-nomic expansion, mass migration, general insecurity, political centralization, obsessive law-making, societal policing, and drastic militarization, finally leading to war. In the meanwhile, the *Pax Britannica* ensuing Waterloo provided the impetus for colonial expansion while fomenting inter-imperial rivalries and competition (Conversi 2007). Thus, just as Europe was accumulating wealth, power, and armaments in anticipation of the unprecedented conflagration, its global economic reach affected broader and broader areas of the world. Economic competition and destructive warfare were just being exported beyond European borders. Linda Colley notes: 'the profit and the price of this hundred-year partial European peace was unprecedented Western, and especially British, freedom to concentrate on global empire. In 1800, the European powers, together with

Russia and the United States, laid claim to some 35 percent of the globe's total land area. By 1914 ... [their] proportion of the globe ... had risen to 84 percent' (Colley 2002: 311). By 1914, the West had also accumulated enough economic wealth and weapons of mass destruction to unleash the greatest manslaughter in human history. The totalitarian era following the First World War has been described as the culmination of a pattern of mass dislocation founded on modernity (Arendt 1958; Bauman 1989). As we shall see later, the emergence of totalitarianism in Europe coincided with the first wave of 'deep Americanization', including the triumph of Hollywood, cigarette consumption, the car culture, and other US products meant for mass distribution.

Nationalism as Westernization

Most modernists argue that nationalism is historically specific and set its origins with surgical precision in the year 1789. For instance, the political scientist Walker Connor (2004) clearly situates its sources in the advent of the French revolution. The overwhelming majority of historians and social scientists agree with this periodization. Although the final partition of Poland in 1795 is occasionally indicated as an alternative date, its bearing upon European developments was negligible in comparison to the French Revolution. Arguably, not even the American Revolution (1776–83) had such an immediate impact on European cultural, political, and military affairs. Finally, a few scholars see nationalism as manifesting itself first in England (Greenfield 1992, Hastings 1997) or the Netherlands (Gorski 2006).

The expansion of nationalism throughout the globe is hence the spreading out of a Western idea. In other words, nationalism is an essential component of Westernization. As I have argued, nationalism cannot be understood outside the devastating impact of modernity, particularly industrialization, with its demise of traditional lifestyles, skills, cultures, and communities (Gellner 2006). Such a devastation was sufficiently all-pervasive to argue that the victory of nationalism represented the victory of a surrogate sense of community, which for some was a colossal 'fraud' (Gellner 2006) or an 'invented tradition' (Hobsbawm 1983). Thus, for Gellner the nationalists spoke in defence of a hypothetical *Gemeinschaft*, but actually practiced the construction of a novel *Gesellschaft*, the two being largely incompatible. For both Gellner and Hobsbawm nationalism was not much less than a form of cultural 'brainwashing'. For others, the whole process was not only counterfeit, it was based on the conspiracy of emerging rapacious economic and political elites, which used selected elements of popular tradition while invoking nationhood, just as populists often invoke the defence of the people. For instance, the role of secret societies like the Italian *carbonari* is a widely known and omni-present feature of nineteenth-century century mobilization. Secret paramilitary groups of patriots played a pivotal role in the spread of most nationalist movements. Karl Marx's characterization of nationalism as a form of 'false consciousness' manipulated by the bourgeoisie is a well-known example of this conspiracy approach. Traditionalist, anarchical, conservative, and even liberal approaches often share similar views of nationalism as a strategy of elites. The broader trend is often known as 'instrumentalism' (Smith 1998), because it emphasizes the mere instrumentality of nationhood. Nations do no exist as such; they are simply cultural tools in the hands of elites or proto-elites who seek to mobilize the masses on the basis of an emotional appeal to a common but fictitious nationality.

The staunchest critic of instrumentalism has again been Anthony D. Smith, who identified its opposite view as 'primordialism' (Smith 1996, 1998). For Donald Horowitz (2004), the 'primordialists' have become 'the straw men of ethnic studies', indeed 'the most maligned for their naiveté in supposing that ethnic affiliations are given rather than chosen, immutable rather than malleable' (Horowitz 2004: 72–73).

By accentuating the explosive, unpredictable nature of ethnic bonds, primordialists seem to discourage further scholarly enquiry, particularly into the causes of, and possible solutions to, ethnic conflict. However, it is necessary to point out that this bad reputation is relatively recent. Before the Second World War, primordialism was *à la mode* and provided the dominant way of presenting one's own nation, while history books were crammed with reminiscences of the nation's primordial bonds, glories, and grandeur. In fact, the heyday of nationalism also saw the zenith of primordialism. Once nationalism fell into disrepute, so primordialism fell into disrepute.

Although *nationalism* as an ideology is quintessentially modern, it remains very difficult to identify a precise date and location when and where one can begin to speak of *nations*. A necessary tautology would say that nations in the modern sense could not exist before modernity. The central point here is that, whenever one dates it, nationalism was a Western phenomenon fully originated and developed in the West. As such, it is possible to extrapolate parallels with globalization, which also fanned out from the West to the wider world.

Most nationalist movements appropriated the West's hierarchy of values and adapted effortlessly to it. Hence, Westernization went hand in hand with the spread of nationalism. The view that the national idea spread out from a Western core to the rest of the globe is called *ideological diffusionism*. For Ellie Kedourie (1993), nationalism consisted in a series of imitations and mimicking acts carried eastward from its European core by the spread of ideas. Accordingly, nationalism is a form of Westernization in itself, because it incorporates a model of governance and state legitimacy originally envisioned in Western Europe – although Kedourie incorrectly argued that Kant's idea of *individual* self-determination was at the core of nationalism's political career. In international relations, this world-shattering process has been associated with 'the Westernization of the political order through the imported state system' (Badie 2000).

On the other hand, nationalism is perfectly compatible with broader processes of past and present homogenization, occurring either under industrialization or globalization. The competition in emulating the 'superior' West became an intrinsic part of the eastward expansion of nationalism. Thus, ethnic nationalists and patriots participated in a perverse game centred on mutual humiliation. In a downward spiral of resentment, they often inflicted humiliation on their own victims, usually neighbours and minorities, which in turn acted similarly against their victims.

As we shall see, in its current shape cultural globalization is often understood as a one-way importation of standardized cultural items and icons from a single country, the United States of America, to the rest of the world – regardless of the fact that most of the items are actually 'made in China'. For many, globalization is synonymous with Westernization (la Branche 2003, 2005, Latouche 1996) or, more accurately, Americanization. The international consequence of Americanization is a widespread sense of 'cultural insecurity' *vis-à-vis* an unfathomable force that nobody seems capable of containing (Amin 2004). Because this perception has been so far unable to produce organized, rational and universal responses, it tends to express itself through visceral, rudimentary, and unpredictable forms of anti-Americanism (Barber 1995).

In the two cases studies, I will explore the role of modernization and globalization in engendering ethno-national conflicts through the example of two nationalist movements, one leading to the rise of Basque nationalism, the other to the breakup of Yugoslavia.

Industrialization and the rise of Basque nationalism

As I have argued elsewhere (Conversi 1997), the inception of Basque nationalism can be dated back with some precision as a consequence of Spanish industrialization, following the end of the Carlist wars (1876). Unlike other types of nationalism, Basque nationalism was specifically born in those areas most affected by industrialization, which first saw the collapse of traditional community bonds and vernacular culture. Indeed the founder of Basque nationalism, Sabino Arana Goiri (1865–1903), was the son of a small semi-rural industrialist whose fortunes were dramatically reversed by industrialization. Arana's birthplace, Abando, was soon absorbed into greater Bilbao, its popular neighborhoods demolished and swamped by immigrants. Throughout the industrial areas of Euskadi (the Basque Country), traditional culture was mostly erased by modernity in the form of urbanization, industrialization, and occupational de-skilling. The rise of a rich bourgeois class was accompanied by the destitution of previously rural labourers, small holders and lesser industrialists, and by the growth of a newly dispossessed urban proletariat. Basque nationalism was born as an attempt to restore order and tradition out of this chaotic scenario. Therefore, one can hardly speak of Basque nationalism before the advent of industrialization and no serious scholar of Basque nationalism would deny that industrialization, as a consequence of the globalization of capitalism, was the main catalyst in the conflict.

The movement rapidly expanded from its inner core of radical activists to larger portions of the middle classes and the impoverished urbanized labourers. For a long while, it remained peaceful and unwilling to use violence, despite its uncompromising separatism and virulent anti-immigrant ideology – although one can doubt whether Arana was a fully-fledged racist (see Douglass 2004). This nonviolent attitude continued throughout the early evolution of Basque nationalism.

However, several years later the peaceful radicalism of the early pioneers was slowly transformed into a virulent form of terrorism. In practice, two main changes had occurred: the advent of a centralist Spanish dictatorship (1939–1975), which took away the remaining Basque liberties and banned most of its cultural expression; and a second phase of massive industrialization pushing into the area new waves of immigrants (1960–1973). Owing to the resulting profound crisis of regional identity, nationalism was no longer a response to industrialization. Now it was a matter of the very survival of the Basque nation. While most Basques had to deal with a ferocious dictatorship which did not hesitate to use torture in order to extort confessions from militants, Basque culture appeared to be under a final threat. The crisis could be seen above all in the rapid decline of the Basque language (Euskara), now spoken by a small minority and virtually unknown among city-dwellers. This predicament prompted the foundation of ETA (*Euskadi 'ta Askatasuna*) in 1959. Although the organization was initially non-violent, its radicalization increased with the intensification of the two factors, namely the escalation of state repression and the spiraling destruction of Basque traditional culture. Moreover, the immigrants happened to be Spanish-speakers, hence using the oppressor's tongue. The first political murder committed by ETA dates back to 1968. It immediately gained the popularity and attention of the Basque youth from most social classes and backgrounds, including many immigrants. ETA rejected Arana's obsolete ethnicism and fully committed itself to build a 'civic' form of nationalism which would encompass militants from all social milieux, beyond their ethnicity. Recurrent internal splits characterized ETA's pre-violent phase. In fact, ETA began to compensate for potential fragmentation and internal conflict by strategically using violence as a community-building device (Conversi 1997). This functioned to mobilize a significant spectrum of public opinion, mostly because violence was the only means of breaking through the curtain of censorship at a moment when no distinctive markers of Basque identity, such as language or religion, could be shared any longer.

The national homogenization plans established by the Francoist dictatorship made it impossible to establish sustained inter-cultural dialogue. As I have demonstrated (Conversi 1997), this was a key factor in the rise and expansion of conflict. All forms of inter-communications being squashed by a conspiracy of silence, only violence was able to lift the veil of secrecy. Violence became a tool of communication and a language *per se*, while a popular counter-culture slowly coalesced around it. As inter-cultural dialogue had practically closed down, terrorism provided *the* voice that nobody could fail to hear. As most Basques could only judge ETA by the violent actions it committed, violent attacks increased in tandem with ETA's popularity. It seemed that the more terrorism was used, the more popular ETA became.

This trend continued until 1980, when the Basque Country was finally granted autonomy. By then, the dictator Francisco Franco had long been dead (1975) and a new Constitution had been passed in 1978. Therefore, the concession of autonomy was the first effective measure to end violence and the Statute of Autonomy (1980) was particularly important since it addressed the core concern of many Basques, that is, their survival as a distinctive people and culture.

Like in other areas of Europe during the late 1970s, de-industrialization saw the simultaneous 'diversification' and 'homogenization' of the socio-economic structure. In the meantime, 'McDonaldization' and other forms of Americanization affected Basque culture not differently from other regions around the globe. Moreover, nationalist rock music (*rock nacionalista vasco*) became popular among the youth. It remained Anglo-Saxon in form, but was easily adapted to the conflictual logic of the area as a 'localized' variety of 'global' culture.

Of course, one of the key factors in the de-escalation of violent activity was that Basque culture was finally able to recover some of the ground lost in the preceding century. In a variety of areas, there was a revival of selected aspects of regional culture, both at the elite and the popular levels. Although this revival affected only a minority, there was a broader consensus that Basque culture was now being revitalized.

What did really change with globalization? In general, the bipolar conflict had become triangular: a broader conflict was superimposed on the ancient Basque-Spanish one, with 'cultural globalization' (or, to many, 'Americanization') providing a new source of discord. Paradoxically, the same antagonism towards the emulation of American consumerist models was diffused among both Spaniards and Basques, and was shared by both nationalists and non-nationalists. However, neither Basque nor Spanish nationalisms have been able to halt Americanization, while both seem to have found ways of accommodating to it. Within the Basque cultural scene, the term 'McGuggenization' has been used to explore the popular resistance to US-inspired forms of retail and cultural franchises (McNeill 2000). Local analysts, opinion-makers, and social scientists used this and

351

similar terms to describe a phenomenon which was not only exemplified by the Guggenheim's Bilbao venture, but also affected numerous other areas from the all-pervasive shopping mall to the destruction of small-scale businesses in the local economy.

Globalizing and fragmenting Yugoslavia

The creation of Yugoslavia in 1918 was at heart US President Woodrow Wilson's gift to Serbian elites, although in the long-term it proved to be quite a poisoned one. After lengthy negotiations, the 'Kingdom of Slovenes, Croats and Serbs' with its capital in Belgrade (1918) was set up as a loose alliance between several nationalities in common defence against Italian irredentism. By 1929 this Kingdom was rechristened 'Yugoslavia', the land of the South Slavs. In a very short time, it was transformed into a centralized state under rigid dictatorial Serbian control. In the 1920s, Belgrade's drift towards the centralization of power reflected a general European movement towards authoritarianism, elsewhere accompanied by mega-projects of cultural and social engineering culminating with National Socialism. During the Second World War, the great powers chose to support the socialist Partisans, abandoning the monarchic nationalists, who in Yugoslavia were mostly Chetniks, that is hard-line Serbian ultranationalists.

The post-war socialist state took on a progressively more federal structure. The power of the constituent units, the Republics of Slovenia, Croatia, Bosnia-Herzegovina, Serbia, Montenegro, and Macedonia, increased with every new constitutional re-arrangement (Ramet 2006). Only the Socialist Party and the army remained highly centralized, at least under the charismatic leadership of Marshall Tito (1945–1980).

The strengthening of internal pluralism corresponded to an opening to foreign markets in the form of economic liberalization. Departing sharply from the strong centralizing patterns common to most socialist 'federations', Tito's Yugoslavia reached a unique level of self-determination for its constituent Republics. Since 1974, Serbia's two autonomous provinces, Kosovo and Vojvodina, also gained a high degree of self-government.

When Tito died in 1980, he left a precarious legacy, a union of semi-sovereign republics and provinces whose continuity as a single entity heavily depended on checking incompatible forces of nationalism, particularly Serbian irredentism. Given its autonomy from the Soviet bloc, Yugoslavia was the first socialist country to yield to the pressures of globalization, well before these developments became truly global phenomena. However, liberalization did not result in the long-term increase of general domestic product, or in enduring welfare among ordinary citizens. An economic recession was particularly dramatic in the 1980s. Economic globalization came to Yugoslavia in the form of significant loans from the IMF, which were characteristically attached to stringent political and social conditions (Blitz 2006: 1–2). These included an unprecedented request by the IMF to re-centralize the country, particularly in financial matters. Such a historical turn-around was promptly seized on by Serbian elites who embarked on a plan to recentralize Yugoslavia apparently assisted by the 'international community'. Since the beginning, Slovenia (and subsequently Croatia) had opposed any international plan to dilute or re-open any discussion of Yugoslavia's federal structure, which had been achieved through decades of lengthy and strenuous negotiations (Ramet 2006). Given its resistance, Slovenia was henceforth described by both the state-run media and many international observers as an outcast. As scholars of nationalism could have easily anticipated, re-centralization backfired and the Slovenian government, tacitly supported by other Republics, presented a counter-plan to co-federalize the country. In practice, this meant that most non-Serbs had begun to feel insecure within the current federal arrangements and no longer accepted a plain federation: Confederation was now a prerequisite, which to all intents and purposes meant a kind of 'sovereignty-association' agreement for all Republics. In other words, nobody was any longer in favour of the *status quo*, but each side was tearing the country apart in opposite directions. In the era of globalization, no key player except the army was any longer interested in keeping Tito's federation intact.

Once it was recognized that Slovene and Croat elites were not willing accomplices to any plan for re-centralization, Serbian nationalists embarked onto a unique path of ethnic secession. This strategy was destined to become ruthless because the Serbs, a minority within Yugoslavia representing only around thirty-seven per cent, were both territorially dispersed and inter-mixed with many other groups. Any attempt to separate Serbs from non-Serbs would inevitably require violence. With increasingly hesitant support from the US and a few European countries, the new Serbian leadership under Milošević posed as saviour of the country's unity, while moving fast ahead with its undeclared, violent politics of dissolution. Such a conjuncture between national and international interests was so peculiar as to deserve a new concept: 'secession by the centre' or 'central secession' (Conversi 2003). Of course, this development cannot be the only explanation for the country's violent disintegration. For many scholars, the way in which Western-style democracy and liberalization were 'imposed' on Yugoslavia was more important. Other scholars argue that when democratization is not preceded by institution-building and the protection of minorities through the creation of liberal-civic institutions, then free elections are likely to result in the explosion of violent conflicts. Political leaders are thus 'elected to fight' (Mansfield and Snyder 2006).

In contrast with the previous section, this brief excursus into the background of the Yugoslav tragedy has served to highlight how globalization directly impacted upon the precarious balance of a country which had achieved a high level of decentralization within a socialist framework through decades of arduous political negotiations. Yugoslavia's modernization was largely carried out at the time of socialism and included industrialization, urbanization and the expansion of the welfare state. However, differently from Franco's Spain, socialist rule was able to create a supranational, quasi-cosmopolitan, framework, which in all good faith attempted to promote harmony, inter-connectedness and mutual respect among its constituent peoples, while cultivating the existing culture(s) of each republic. In contrast, economic liberalization implied a considerable degree of one-way, unilateral measures under the catchall banner of Westernization. Initially, this was a slow incursion and most official media were allowed to continue broadcasting national, regional, and local productions, while taking great care to avoid any form of discrimination against specific groups. For instance, radio broadcasts were articulated at both the republican and regional levels, their programmes championing the diffusion of popular art forms from each recognized nationality. In theory, all groups had equal access to their own cultural traditions and the same chance to know the traditions of all other groups. This situation was possible insofar as cultural Westernization remained less significant. Tito considered intercultural dialogue as a prerequisite for good citizenship and a prelude to the consolidation of a multinational state independent from both East and West. Despite authoritarian rule, for many decades the prevailing feeling was one of security and self-preservation, while citizens could share equal access to a common pool of information and cultural traditions.

However, such a solidaristic framework began to unravel once globalization set off to erode Yugoslavia's federal structure. The crisis deepened in the 1980s following Tito's death. While the rising nationalist tide made inter-ethnic dialogue increasingly difficult,

353

Americanization and westernization made major inroads through neighbouring European-based radio and TVs stations (Italian, Austrian, and, most important, various US Cold War propaganda stations directed towards the Eastern Bloc and interspersing news with rock music). These gained large audiences and Americana soon began to permeate all aspects of youth 'culture' (Ramet and Crnkovic 2003). The 'invasion' was initially welcomed by the local youth and identified as a new 'wave of freedom'. Such a common terrain offered an apparent patina of formal uniformity, mistakenly embraced by many as an alternative kind of openness and prelude to cosmopolitanism. In fact, it better concealed the germs of reactive nationalism, while voices of dissent against the unstoppable invasiveness of US cultural domination were soon to be heard among intellectuals, artists, and members of the public in all republics – although some felt more victimized than others. For instance, Belgrade's studios and media productions, until then market leaders in the Balkans, began a slow drift towards decline. In order to survive, they had to depend increasingly upon the regime. Thus, while Milošević's regime was not particularly interested in the preservation of Serbian culture, it was happy to finance movies, which subtly presented the ultra-nationalist viewpoints portraying non-Serbs as aggressors, therefore diametrically inverting years of positive discrimination efforts. The personal trajectory of the Bosnian director Emir Kusturica will be compared later on with Russian's patriotic build-up as extreme defence against Americanization. Finally, once reciprocally hostile nationalisms had seized the state, inter-ethnic dialogue became virtually impossible, as mutual recriminations made it unworkable to reconstruct the texture of inter-connectedness that had finely preserved the country's unity.

Global Islam, Americanization, and ethnic conflict

The previous two sections have addressed the impact of modernization, particularly industrialization and globalization, in the explosion of ethnic conflict. We now briefly explore how this impact has affected a much broader area which, trespassing state boundaries, is also a contributing factor to globalization.

Oliver Roy's (2005) path-breaking work on global Islam joins a large body of literature exploring the links between ethno-religious conflict, fundamentalism, and globalization. For Roy, neo-fundamentalism is simultaneously a product and a vehicle of globalization: 'Religion, conceived as a de-contextualized set of norms, can be adapted to any society, precisely because it has severed its link with a given culture and allows people to live in a sort of virtual, de-territorialized community that includes any believer' (Roy 2005: 287). He then advances some intriguing thoughts about the substantial Americanization of radical fundamentalism. Roy begins by stressing the decline of traditional cuisine under the encroachment of the fast-food industry, which has been fully assumed by neo-fundamentalists:

> 'Food versus cuisine is a good example of the opposition between code and culture. Neofundamentalists care nothing for cuisine. Anything that is *halal* is good, whatever the basics ingredients and the recipe. When they open a restaurant it never promotes Ottoman or Moroccan cuisine, but *halal* food, and more often than not will simply offer the usual Western fast-food products. Similarly, *halal* dress can be based on Western raincoats, gloves, fashionable scarves (*cha-Dior*, as the Iranians joke), and so on. *Halal* is thus a code that is adaptable to any culture. Objects cease to have a history and to be culturally meaningful; once chosen they meet a normative requirement and do not refer to a specific culture. ... For the

neo-fundamentalist the hamburger is seen as culturally neutral a long as it is made along the lines of their religious norm (*halal*) (Roy 2005: 271).

In fact, global Islam appears to be more culturally neutral than Americanization. Whereas the latter is based upon the imposition of a global cultural matrix (and hence on a process of de-culturation), global Islam is more interested in establishing new codes, norms and values, irrespective of their cultural forms. The launching of *Mecca-Cola* in France during the apex of global anti-Americanism (2002–2003), with exactly the same ingredients as Coca-Cola bar a different name, confirms that symbolic opposition to Americanism is compatible with deeper, and perhaps more substantial, forms of 'Americanization' (Roy 2005: 271–2). This seems to go partly against Benjamin Barber's (1995, 2008) view that 'global jihad' is a reaction against McWorld and Americanizing globalization. It also differs from George Ritzer's argument about the symbolic anti-consumerist nature of the pro-jihadist world-view (Ritzer 2002; Ritzer and Ryan 2004; Seidler 2004).

However, certain aspects of neo-fundamentalism are also a war waged against US domination. In order to win this war, it has to appropriate the globalizing tools of McDonaldization, including its rigid, de-territorialized and global bureaucratic functioning. This includes the 'replacement of culture by code' and of traditional community by para-military groups. With some notable differences, such a *déjà vu* experience reminds us of the early twentieth-century drift towards totalitarianism as a result of industrialization and the end of traditional communitarian relations. As we have seen, most scholars link modernization with the rise of nationalism. In this sense, Islamic fundamentalism or non-traditional Islam can be described as a form of 'supra-national' nationalism (see Gellner 1981). Mary Kaldor also points out how the ideology of global Islam should be seen as a new variant of nationalism, insofar as the 'ideologists of the movement talk about the "Islamic nation" and the basic idea of uniting around a common culture, Islam and a religious language, Arabic, is a nationalist idea' (2004: 171). Whether nationalist or not, the most violent fringes of radical Islam have been identified as an aspect of Westernizing modernity (Gray 2003).

Global Islam has found an ideal terrain amongst the conflicts erupting along Islam's civilizational fringes. In fact, many contemporary conflicts emerge when political Islam meets other religious traditions associated with dominant ethnicities in control of specific states. In these cases, Muslims are contextualized as oppressed minorities in Chechnya, Bosnia, Kashmir, southern Thailand, Ambon/Moluccas, Azerbaijan, Palestine, Mindanao, and Xingjian. These regions have witnessed the reactive politicization of Islamic communities as a response to the resurgence of dominant nationalism/state patriotism. They have found in global Islam a handy package offering unique organizational support and new networks of international solidarity.

The failed communication approach

So far, we have implicitly recognized throughout our case studies that inter-cultural dialogue remains an essential component for safeguarding peace and stability. In both the Basque and Yugoslav cases, the breakdown of inter-cultural dialogue was a contributing factor in the resulting conflicts. The key argument to be developed here is that, despite the internet and other multi-directional flows of communication, the current 'cultural world order' retains a vertical communicational structure, where groups have few opportunities to inter-communicate or interact in meaningful ways and know each other's traditions. This may appear to be counter-intuitive, if one considers the information revolution bringing previously disconnected individuals 'together' and enabling unprecedented flows of multi-directional information (see Castells 2000). However, such a technologically-oriented view is limited. With the exception of specifically designed EU policies aimed at cultural exchange, there are few incentives for neighbouring regions, groups and nationalities to establish sustained and systematic inter-cultural exchanges. Outside the EU framework, inter-cultural dialogue remains extremely difficult, its place being often taken over by Americanization. As we know, most ethnic conflicts occur precisely among neighbouring groups and are not 'long-distance conflicts'.

This contrasts with policies adopted under Communism, at least at a discursive level. In the early post-Soviet years, cultural Americanization has hampered any such attempt at inter-ethnic, inter-state, and inter-cultural exchange. Once the Soviet imperial communication network was dismantled, its place was immediately filled by its victorious rival, which had already made significant inroads into Soviet cultural audiences by the distribution of US pop icons (Lucas 1999). The message systematically proposed 'America' as the only reference model and Americans as the only 'reference group', to use a sociological concept from the 1950s (see Williams, 1970).

The pervasiveness of US consumerist iconographies may be considered normal today, just as nationalist homogenization was considered normal in the heydays of nationalism. McDonaldization has been broadly driven by a thrust towards profit at the expenses of culture. The result has been more profit and less culture, notably less inter-cultural communication, hence a greater potential for conflict.

On the other hand, if cultural globalization can be simply identified as naked Americanization, then it may well be associated with a new type of colonial or imperial domination (Barkawi 2005). Has this awareness stimulated some genuine forms of global resistance?

In fact, nationalism and ethnicity have sometime been spurred by attempts to mobilize noncompliance to globalization. Sentiments of hostility towards global Americanism can be appropriated by both popular movements of local resistance and more aggressive forms of state-led patriotism. In those rare instances where Americanization has been accompanied by territorial intervention, such as Afghanistan or Iraq, the unintended consequence is to create broader nationalist discourses and frameworks. These may transcend the boundaries of ethnicity, although in Iraq the opposite effect was initially visible. In addition, powerful authoritarian states, like China and Russia, have already capitalized on state patriotism by mobilizing widely shared anti-American attitudes.

On the other hand, an apparent acceptance of US iconography, such has the kilometric queues at the opening of McDonalds's in Moscow (1990) and Beijing (1992), is no proof that either the surface or the substance of Americanism will be passively accepted in the long term. In fact, anti-Americanism is particularly widespread in the above countries, both at the elite and popular levels. The implication of this for global Islam (and its intersection with ethnic conflict) has been addressed earlier on. Concomitantly, the McDonaldization of Russia, China, and Saudi Arabia was followed by a reassertion of anti-American 'revanchism' at all levels of society. These anti-American sentiments were being expressed oddly enough just while McDonald's were opening new outlets.

Americanization and globalization

Despite a considerable body of literature describing globalization as different from Americanization (see Turner and Khondker 2010), this section sets out from the opposite premise. It shows that, insofar as globalization is grounded upon American fashions and norms, it directly instigates national and ethnic conflicts at both the state and sub-state level. The linkage between Americanization and globalization is moreover assumed by many ethnic and patriotic groups, as well as by alternative universalistic movements. Therefore, it should be treated more rigorously and systematically in the globalization literature, rather than being dismissed as over-simplification or trivialization.

To many, the very patterns through which globalization spreads appear to be moulded by American cultural domination. Thus, George Ritzer's (1996) neo-Weberian description of McDonaldization as the bureaucratic regulation of society at a global level begins by analyzing the functions of a brand name that stands as the symbol of American consumerism in its most contested and aggressive forms.

How should 'Americanization' be defined for the purpose of analyzing its effect on ethnic conflict? Ritzer and Stillman (2003) identify it as a 'powerful one-directional process that tends to overwhelm competing processes'. In contrast, Ulrich Beck's (2003) argument is that the concept of 'Americanization' implies a narrower 'national under-standing' of globalization that substantially limits its utility. However, this makes it even more relevant to the study of ethno-national conflicts. Moreover, Americanization has been a driving force throughout the previous century and can only be ignored at the risk of adopting an a-historical perspective.

According to Schörter (2008a), Europe experienced three main waves of American-ization. These were firstly in the 1920s, coinciding both with the rise of fascism and the adoption of economic rationalization aimed at increasing competitiveness and efficiency (Taylorism, Fordism, the mass media, and so on); the second wave took place in the period of economic expansion of 1949–1973; and the final wave lasted from about 1985 until the present, when the idea of globalization became dominant and all-pervasive. In each phase, Americanization deepened, encountering less and less resistance, until it became a normal feature of the European scene. The above tripartite division applies to both the cultural and the economic spheres, including an account of why Hollywood and the US film industry became dominant in the 1920s and 1930s (Schörter 2008a).

The process of Americanization should not be understood as the substantial incorporation or espousal of American values. The term should more often serve to describe a super-ficial, incoherent, fractional, and flawed appropriation of external items and ephemera. In particular, Americanization does not automatically mean exporting American ideals, but rather more trivial US mass-consumer products, often through superficial imitation.

Former Secretary of State Madeleine Albright showed insights about the US' 'full-spectrum dominance' cultural policy when she said that 'Cultural factors play a pivotal role in many of the international challenges we face … our cultural programs are cen-tral—and I underline that—central—to the success of American foreign policy' (Albright 2000). Once out of office, she adopted a more cautious position, considering the risks and damages inflicted by extreme forms of Americanization. For Bacevich (2002), the economic 'openness' implicit in neo-liberalism produces a form of globalization that is inevitably synonymous with Americanization, since it is predicated on a national security approach founded on global dominance.

How far has Americanization contributed to the disintegrative trends described in this chapter? If so, how did it? In recent years several studies have been devoted to the critical analysis of 'Americanization' in various areas (see Barber 2008, de Grazia 2006, Stonor Saunders 1999, Wagnleitner 1994). Some of these have explored the response to Americanization either as the enthusiastic embrace of, or as the embittered rejection of,

357

Americanism. But the consequences of cultural Americanization remain among the least studied, yet most critical, aspects of globalization. In many countries, unrestrained Americanization has led to an all- devouring introduction of consumerist homogenization in which thousand-year old cultures have been replaced by serially crafted ephemera destined for rapid consumption.

For some authors, Americanization seems to be increasingly challenged by Indigenous practices and products through processes of vernacularization, domestication, and hybridization (Appadurai 1997: 81). However, the latter have customarily had to Americanize their products in order to survive in the market. The neo-liberals' populist rhetoric of 'let's give to the people what they *really* want' articulates an ideology specifically wrought to tear down the traditional barriers of both local cultures and national communities. Yet, indigenized forms of 'Americana' have been even more 'effective' in destroying local cultures as they could be more easily camouflaged behind a mask of national Indigenousness.

For instance, despite claims that it heralds a national assertion of Indian identity, the very designation 'Bollywood' visibly echoes, and originates from, its American namesake. Its cultural content increasingly impersonates American tastes, rules, behaviour, norms, customs, and fashions (Rao 2007). As for the globalization-nationalism nexus, Hindu ultra-nationalist and globalist ideologues fully converge in granting 'Bollywood' a patent of 'Indianness' (Rajadhyaksha 2003, Ranganathan and Lobo 2008). Militant *Hindutva* groups use it to promote an image of India 'among the most powerful nations in global modernity' in an effort to subvert, essentialize, and homogenize contemporary Indian culture (McDonald 2003: 1563). At the same time, recent ethnographic works have shown that the artificiality and elitism of the highly Westernized, consumerist, urban middle class portrayed in these films is entirely grasped by non-elite audiences, who discern in them 'the brand logic of transnational capital which is redefining the meaning of the masses' (Rao 2007: 57). Similarly, Egyptian marketers promoted the *infitahs* as an attempt to 'glocalize' international business in order to twist local economic conditions by 'Egyptianizing' (or 'mediating') imported goods, brands, and logos as promoted by global MNCs (Shechter 2008).

Corporate populism upholds the need to 'indigenize' profit-making transnational flows. This approach has long been flagged by multinational business while adopting a rhetoric of 'respecting' local values in the very act of dispensing with them. Rather like the 'green' credentials assumed by environmentally destructive mega-corporations, a populist rhetoric defending the people's 'spontaneous' attractions to global logos and brands is often accompanied by a discourse claiming that the company is striving to incorporate 'Indigenous values'. Can this be simply discounted as 'glocalization'? The philosophy of contemporary marketing is anthropologically rooted, sociologically informed, and conveyed by a pseudo-pluralistic parlance which promotes an 'understanding' of local and national cultures so that the corporation can better penetrate new foreign markets. Similar processes have been reassuringly referred to as 'creolization' or as forms of contamination of non-dominant cultures by Western consumption models spread by mass media.

Critics of globalization agree that large portions of 'national sovereignty' have to a great extent been seized by multinational corporations (see Barnet and Cavanagh 1994). As mentioned earlier, this demise of national sovereignty has directly or indirectly contributed to boost nationalism and other boundary-building practices (Conversi 1999). However, some institutions seem to have remained immune from it. For instance, despite rapidly increasing legal uniformity throughout the world, the leniency or severity in which global laws are applied across countries varies widely (Lacey 2008). Thus, the

US-led global securitization framework has steered various state laws to incorporate a rash of illiberal legislations (see Bowring 2008). While countries like Uzbekistan have arbitrarily used the original US template to eliminate political opponents (Kendzior 2007, Murray 2007, Scheuer 2004: 12 and 263), countries such as Italy use a similar securitization discourse against various internal 'others' with more leniency (Sigona 2005), and China exploits the global 'war on terror' more systematically against a host of religious and ethnic groups, notably the Tibetans and the Uygurs of Xinjiang (Steele and Kuo 2007).

New cultural hierarchies and ethnonationalism

Contrary to the globalists or ideologues of globalization (Steger 2005), both Marxists and liberals have highlighted the 'pyramidal' structure underlying globalization. This metaphor applies well to cultural dissemination. An elite of corporate, media, and governmental agencies sits at the pyramid's top level, small regional intermediary elites sit immediately below, while the overwhelming majority of humans are pushed well down towards the pyramid's bottom. In the realm of 'global culture', this looks like a master-servant relationship with much of the world at the boot-licking end. Whether such a relationship really exists, or is even practical, this metaphorical dramatization can nevertheless help to understand collective self-perceptions.

The consequences in the area of ethnic conflict are significant. Such a hierarchical structure makes it impossible for global exchanges to turn into egalitarian relationships based on evenly balanced inter-cultural communication and dialogue. On the contrary, cultural globalization is not reflected in a genuine increase of inter-personal, inter-ethnic and inter-cultural contacts. As I shall argue, in most public areas 'cultural globalization' really means the unreciprocated, one-way flow of consumerist items from the US media and leisure machine to the rest of the world. This top-down distribution ensures that a few individuals and groups, nearly all in the USA, firmly establish the patterns of behaviour and taste to be followed by the rest of mankind.

Is this congruent with the view that there is a form of 'global centralization' in cultural-legal matters leaning towards Washington, DC? As for a supposed 'global culture', the symbolic capital would ideally be located in Hollywood, rather than Washington. In fact, the term 'Hollywoodization' insinuates a media-enforced hierarchical structure with immediate symbolic resonance. It also offers a more cultural, perhaps less sociological, focus than the Weberian concept of bureaucratic 'McDonaldization' (Ritzer 1996). Competing terminologies include 'Disneyfication'/'Disneyization', with its stress on extreme predictability and the infantilization of leisure (Bryman 2004), 'Walmarting' as the streamlining of the retail sector (Fishman 2005, Morrow 2004), or earlier Cold War terms like 'Coca-Colonization' (Wagnleitner 1994). We previously saw how the term 'McGuggenization' has been used to indicate art-related cultural franchising and other forms of Americanization in the Basque Country (McNeill 2000). All these equally refer to socio-economic trends originated in the USA and are hence forms of Americanization.

However, 'Hollywoodization' has broader implications for ethnic relations and nationalist conflicts. In practice, Hollywood-inspired simplifications have become the daily staple for millions of peoples around the world in their leisure time. In the area of ethnicity, 'Hollywoodization' has been elevated to the only known reality and the unique source of information about the outside world for increasing numbers of people, not only in the USA. Thus, the world is more likely to get its stereotypes of the Brits from US movies like *The Patriot* or *Saving Private Ryan* than via British productions. Similarly, most of the world is likely to see Scotland through the lenses of US-made *Braveheart*, as the larger public can barely afford any access to Scottish cultural productions. This monopoly of global stereotyping and ethnic imagery has serious implications for the spread and continuation of ethnic conflict.

The tools of primary socialization were once under firm control of the family, either nuclear or extended. They were subsequently assumed by the state in the industrialization 'phase', notably with post-1789 mass militarization and compulsory schooling (Conversi 2007, 2008). Under neo-liberal globalization, primary socialization has been seized by unaccountable cash-driven corporations and media tycoons. This has further reduced the space of inter-generational transmission and family interaction. If a community can no longer socialize its children according to its culture and traditions, then the very bases of local, regional, and national continuity are all visibly at stake. This threat to a group's survival is often seized upon by patriots and ethno-nationalists, whose political programs are founded on providing a new sense of social cohesion and security – even if the targets are often hapless and unprotected minorities. That is partly how nationalism and xenophobia have expanded in tandem with globalization. Ethno-nationalism not only persisted through change, but is perceived by many as a response to the growth of globalization, providing a *prêt-à-porter* hope for national resistance and resilience.

By depending on Hollywood as unique conveyor of 'globalization', inter-ethnic interaction is inevitably undermined. In some instances, international communication has practically evaporated. Following the fall of the Soviet Union, the explosion of chauvinism, racism, neo-fascism, and xenophobia seems to go hand in hand with a blind faith in mass consumerism (Hockenos 1993).

Under socialism, it was relatively common to see on cinemas and television film masterpieces from France, Yugoslavia, Russia, Italy, or Britain until about 1989. Ensuing the Comecon's dismantling and its absorption into the free market area, this was no longer possible. Only the full panoply of Hollywood and MTV-inspired products could then be seen every day on every post-socialist TV channel and in every movie theatre. The same phenomenon recurs in Poland, Hungary, Russia, Uzbekistan, Georgia, Mongolia, and nearly all other post-communist societies. Here, by the early 1990s the local film industry had collapsed with little hope of recovery. In Russia, thousands of actors, directors, screenwriters, players, producers, writers, editors, musicians, consultants, sceno-graphers and other artists became jobless virtually overnight.

The political trajectory of one of the greatest living film directors, the multi-award winner Nikita Mikhalkov, conveys an important lesson about the impact of Americanization on the rise of Russian nationalism. Born into a family of distinguished but moderate patriots, Mikhalkov moved from global masterpieces like *Oblomov* (1980), Chekhov's transposition of *Dark Eyes* (1987), *Burnt by the Sun* (1994) and his world-acclaimed epic on the Mongols, *Urga* (1992) (Tavis 1994), to increasingly patriotic movies destined for domestic audiences. These were accompanied by growing involvement into nationalist politics. Mikhalkov became more and more vocal in his claims that the West had launched a 'war against Orthodoxy', endorsing the latter as 'the main force which opposes cultural and intellectual McDonald's' (Foglesong 2007: 204 and 215–216, Hashamova 2007, Larsen 2003). A militaristic extravaganza like *The Barber of Siberia* (*Sibirskij tsiryulnik*, 1999) (Siefert 2006: 208–9) reads like an act of defiance against the neo-liberal obliteration of Russian culture. Moreover, under invitation from his Serbian colleagues, Mikhalkov travelled to Belgrade in support of Serbia's claims over Kosovo, becoming furthermore involved in genocide denial. Before neo-liberal globalization, Russian and Serbian studios were home to some of the world's most prolific and rich cinematic productions. Now both cultures shared a common fate, the global neo-liberal devastation of the domestic and independent film industry. Finally, Mikhalkov championed Serbian nationalism as a form of resistance against American aggression. Americanization was no doubt the prime crime – and he went as far as comparing the effects of McDonaldization to Stalinism.[1] The theme of humiliating McDonaldization resurfaces in the movies and interviews of another Russian director who converted to patriotism, Aleksei Balabanov (Larsen 2003).

A similar trajectory from cosmopolitanism to ultra-nationalism was experienced in Yugoslavia by another world-famous cinema director, Emir Kusturica (b. 1954). While shooting his *Underground* (1995), partly financed by the state-owned Belgrade Radio Television, official Yugoslav army equipment was employed in the set. Mixing grotesque irony with surrealistic war drama, the film was accused of propagating the Serbian nationalist tale just as genocide was taking place. Kusturica allegedly defended Slobodan Milošević, rebuking Western media as the real cause of the war.

A recurrent slogan appearing in the Russian daily *Pravda* (Truth) reads verbatim: 'McDonald's had killed more Americans in 2001 than Osama bin Laden & al Qaeda'; another reads 'McDonald's food demoralizes the globe'. *Pravda* has become the talking head for Russia's anti-American audiences and its global popularity has correspondingly amplified in tandem with the spread of anti-Americanism ensuing Guantánamo and the 'war on terror'.

The case of Russia seems to confirm Barber's thesis: the slow build-up of an 'Eastern Jihad' first revealed itself in a chaotic, implicit, nearly secretive way. Then, it gradually began to be channelled and harnessed under the authoritarian banner of Russian patriotism, as this gained inroads into most institutions. In post-communist countries, the collapse of national cultures was assisted by the legacy of totalitarianism which had already turned whole societies into a cultural *tabula rasa*, preparing the ground for the onslaught of cultural globalization. In all these cases, economic, political and cultural Americanization has substantially replaced Sovietization. While McDonalds, MTV, and Hollywood triumphed eradicating potential Indigenous rivals, the ancient régime's political structures were inherited almost intact by Western-led corporate power and simply 'accommodated' to the new rules of the game.

Conclusion

This chapter has focused on the political and cultural dimensions of globalization, relating it to ethnic conflict, patriotism, and nationalism. In short, one of the long-term legacies of the era of globalization is the global spread of oppositional ethnic and religious conflict. I have described, and subsequently dismissed, the profit-oriented ideology that globalization, intended as Mcdonaldization and Hollywoodization, can contribute to better international understanding. On the contrary, it has ushered in a process of planetary cultural and environmental destruction, while hampering inter-ethnic communication and fostering human conflict. The notion of cultural security, so central to international relations and peaceful coexistence, has undergone unprecedented challenges.

We began by addressing parallels between modernity, particularly industrialization, and globalization as harbingers of ethno-national conflict. We then explored three main cases (the Basque Country, Yugoslavia, and global Islam) and two minor ones (India and Russia) through the lens of the movie industry. Insofar as cultural globalization is understood as uni-dimensional import of standardized cultural icons, symbols, practices, values, and legal systems from the United States, it can simply be re-described as Americanization (rather than Westernization in the broad sense), or 'globalization by Americanization' (Hilger 2008). This is of central importance for the study of ethnic conflict.

In fact, the outcome is scarce hybridization, amalgamation, and *metissage*. Rather than providing an inter-cultural bridge, this unilateral drive has often eroded the basis for mutual understanding, impeding inter-ethnic, inter-cultural, and international interaction. Given the current vertical, pyramidal structure of the 'cultural world order', the opportunity of distinctive groups to communicate directly and appreciate each other's traditions has decreased, except in the virtual area of long-distance communication. For an increasing number of individuals, an American mass consumer culture remains the only window on the world. Hence, to know and appreciate one's neighbours has become an ever-arduous task.

To recapitulate my point, wherever cultural globalization appears as synonymous with Americanization, it engenders conflicts on a variety of levels. Because the process is one-way and unidirectional, the result is unlikely to be a fusion between cultures or, even less, the blending of ethnic groups. Contrary to the globalist utopia, the imposition of more and more American icons means less and less possibility for direct inter-ethnic encounter and communication among nations. Together with the collapse of state legitimacy, this substantially contributes to the spread of ethnic conflict and nationalism.

Despite the internet, the crucial factor remains the reduction of real, effective, inter-ethnic, and international communication outside American direction and control. After years of mimicking the successful US model, many local entrepreneurs have been spurred into beginning their US-inspired ventures, in a sort of 'self-Americanization'. However, globalization *qua* Americanization is not simply a matter of 'free choice'. The reach of US cultural propaganda has been driven by the need to manage a host of regional conflicts (Hixson 1997, Snow 2003, Snyder 1995, Sorenson 1968), such as the Korean war (Casey 2008), or the building of post-Cold War European order (Wagnleitner 1994).

The resulting sense of cultural insecurity has hence spread onto a planetary scale, increasingly accompanied by the reassertion of hurt pride and a rise of patriotism which can easily seize anti-American themes, whenever elites chose to use these in order to gain popular consensus. As convincingly argued by Dennis Smith, the 'stirring up a tide of global resentment' has so far been 'held back by fear of American military power. When that power falters, the revenge of the humiliated world will strike the West' (2006: 1).

Moreover, owing to globalization, the legitimacy of the state and even the rule of law have declined in many affected countries. In several areas, organized crime is more powerful than central governments. This is particularly true for countries ravaged by ethnic conflict: In fact, when ethnic conflict and globalization merge, the result is often the empowerment of 'McMafias' (Glenny 2008). Central governments in various countries, including Serbia under Milošević, Italy under Berlusconi, and Russia under Putin, have sought to consolidate their powers by simultaneously reaching deals with both organized crime and ethno-nationalist forces. In other areas, given the lack of state authority, rulers have attempted to claim back legitimacy by using the easiest mobilizing tool which they can still muster up: patriotism imbued by fear, that is, the double-faced politics of terror and 'national security'.

Dialogue remains essential as peace itself is made up of a plurality of co-existing visions. Yet, 'globalization produces conflict because the different conceptions of peace prevalent in each society are unable to enter into dialogue with each other' (Gasparini 2008: 27). Whether the idea of a 'global civil society' has anything to do with globalization as described in these pages will remain an issue of contention. In all, the impact of globalization is clearly linked to the spread of ethnic conflict, patriotism, and nationalism. This chapter has contested optimistic visions of globalization, insofar as the latter remains hetero-directed, deeply in-equalitarian, environmentally unsustainable, and culturally self-destructive.

Note

1 See www.runewsweek.ru/theme/?tid=150&rid=2326; www.sentieriselvaggi.it/articolo.asp?sez0=3& sez1=33&art=26452.

References

Albright, Madeleine 2000 conference chair, remarks at the White House Conference on '*Culture and Diplomacy*', Washington, DC, November 28, 2000. Washington, DC: Bureau of Educational and Cultural Affairs/ Organized by the Department of State in cooperation with the Office of the First Lady, the White House Millennium Council and the National Security Council [www.state.gov/r/whconf/final_rpt.html].

Amin, Samir 2004 *The Liberal Virus: Permanent War and the Americanization of the World*. London: Pluto Press.

Anderson, Benedict 1993 *Imagined Communities*. London: Verso [1st edn, 1982].

Appadurai, Arjun 1997 *Modernity at Large: Cultural Dimensions of Globalization*. Minneapolis: University of Minnesota Press.

Arendt, Hannah 1958 *The Origins of Totalitarianism*. Cleveland/New York: Meridian Books.

Bacevich, Andrew J. 2002 *American Empire*. Cambridge, MA: Harvard University Press.

Badie, Bertrand 2000 *The Imported State: The Westernization of the Political Order*. Standford, CA. Stanford University Press.

Barber, Benjamin R. 1995 *Jihad vs. McWorld*. New York: Ballantine Books.

——2008 *Consumed: How Markets Corrupt Children, Infantilize Adults, and Swallow Citizens Whole*. New York: W. W. Norton.

Barkawi, Tarak 2005 *Globalization and War*. Lanham/ Oxford: Rowman & Littlefield.

Barnet, R. J. and J. Cavanagh 1994 *Global Dreams: Imperial Corporations and the New World Order*. Simon & Schuster.

Bauman, Zygmunt 1989 *Modernity and the Holocaust*. Ithaca, NY: Cornell University Press/Polity Press.

Beck, Ulrich 2003 'Rooted Cosmopolitanism: Emerging from a Rivalry of Distinctions', in Ulrich Beck, Natan Sznaider and Rainer Winter (eds) *Global America? The Cultural Consequences of Globalization*. Liverpool: Liverpool University Press, pp. 15–29.

Blitz, Brad 2006 'War and Change', in Brad K. Blitz (ed.) *War and Change in the Balkans: Nationalism, Conflict and Cooperation*. Cambridge: Cambridge University Press.

Bowring, Bill 2008 *The Degradation of the International Legal Order? The Rehabilitation of Law and the Possibility of Politics*. Abingdon, Oxon/New York: Routledge–Cavendish.

la Branche, Stéphane 2003 *Mondialisation et terrorisme identitaire, ou, Comment l'Occident tente de transformer le monde*. Paris: Harmattan.

——2005 'Abuse and Westernization: Reflections on Strategies of Power', *Journal of Peace Research*, vol. 42, no. 2, pp. 219–235.

Bryman, Alan E. 2004 *The Disneyization of Society*. London: Sage.

Casey, Steven 2008 *Selling the Korean War: Propaganda, Politics, and Public Opinion in the United States, 1950–1953*. Oxford: Oxford University Press.

Castells, Manuel 2000 *End of Millennium: The Information Age – Economy, Society and Culture: Vol. 3.* Oxford: Wiley Blackwell.

Colley, Linda 2002 *Captives.* London: Pimlico/ New York: Pantheon Books.

Connor, Walker 2004 'Nationalism and Political Illegitimacy', in Daniele Conversi (ed.) *Ethnonationalism in the Contemporary World.* London/New York: Routledge.

Conversi, Daniele 1997 *The Basques, the Catalans, and Spain: Alternative Routes to Nationalist Mobilization.* London: Hurst/Reno: University of Nevada Press.

——1999 'Nationalism, Boundaries and Violence', *Millennium. Journal of International Studies,* vol. 28, no. 3, pp. 553–584.

——2003 'The Dissolution of Yugoslavia: Secession by the Centre?', in John Coakley (ed.) *The Territorial Management of Ethnic Conflicts.* London: Frank Cass, pp. 264–292.

——2007 'Homogenisation, nationalism and war: Should we still read Ernest Gellner?' *Nations and Nationalism,* vol. 13, no. 3, pp. 371–394.

——2008 '"We are all equals!" Militarism, Homogenization and "Egalitarianism" in Nationalist State-building (1789–1945)', *Ethnic and Racial Studies,* vol. 31, no. 7, pp. 1286–1314.

de Grazia, Victoria 2006 *Irresistible Empire: America's Advance through Twentieth-Century Europe.* Cambridge, MA: Harvard University Press.

Douglass, William 2004 'Sabino's Sin: Racism and the Founding of Basque Nationalism' in Daniele Conversi (ed.) *Ethnonationalism in the Contemporary World.* London/New York: Routledge.

Fishman, Charles (2005) *The Wal-Mart Effect: How the World's Most Powerful Company Really Works – and How It's Transforming the American Economy.* London: Penguin Press.

Foglesong, David S. 2007 *The American Mission and the 'Evil Empire' – The Crusade for a 'Free Russia' since 1881.* Cambridge: Cambridge University Press.

Gasparini, Alberto 2008 'Globalisation, Reconciliation and the Conditions for Conserving Peace', *Global Society,* vol. 22, no.1, pp. 27–55.

Gellner, Ernest. 1981 *Muslim Society.* Cambridge: Cambridge University Press.

——2006 *Nations and Nationalism.* Oxford: Basil Blackwell/Ithaca: Cornell University Press [1st edn 1983].

Glenny, Misha 2008 *McMafia: A Journey Through the Global Criminal Underworld.* Bodley Head/New York: Alfred A. Knopf.

Gorski, Philip S. 2006 'Premodern Nationalism', in Gerard Delanty and Krishan Kumar (eds), *Handbook of Nations and Nationalism.* London: Sage.

Gray, John 2003 *Al Qaeda and What It Means to Be Modern.* New York: Faber and Faber.

Greenfeld, 1992 Liah. *Nationalism: Five Roads to Modernity.* Cambridge, MA: Harvard University Press

Hashamova, Yana 2007 *Pride and Panic: Russian Imagination of the West in Post–Soviet Film.* Bristol/Chicago: Intellect.

Hastings, Adrian 1997 *The Construction of Nationhood.* Cambridge University Press.

Hilger, Susanne 2008 'Globalisation by Americanisation: American Companies and the Internationalisation of German Industry after the Second World War', *European Review of History/Revue Europeenne d'Histoire,* vol. 15, no. 4, pp. 375–401.

Hixson, Walter L. 1997 *Parting the Curtain: Propaganda, Culture, and the Cold War, 1945–1961.* New York: St. Martin's Press.

Hobsbawm, Eric 1983 'Introduction: Inventing Traditions' and 'Mass Producing Traditions: Europe, 1870–1914', in Hobsbawm, Eric J. and Terence Ranger (eds) *The Invention of Tradition.* Cambridge: Cambridge University Press.

Hockenos, Paul 1993 *Free to Hate: The Rise of the Right in Post–Communist Eastern Europe.* London: Routledge.

Horowitz, Donald 2004 'The Primordialists', in Daniele Conversi (ed.) *Ethnonationalism in the Contemporary World.* London/New York: Routledge.

Kaldor, Mary 2004 'Nationalism and Globalisation', *Nations and Nationalism,* vol. 10 no. 1/2, pp. 161–177.

Kedourie 1993 *Nationalism.* Oxford, UK/Cambridge, MA: Blackwell [4th expanded edn].

Kendzior, Sarah 2007 'Poetry of Witness: Uzbek Identity and the Response to Andijon', *Central Asian Survey,* vol. 26, no. 3, pp. 317–334.

Korten, David C. 2001 *When Corporations Rule the World.* Bloomfield, CT: Kumarian Press.

Lacey, Nicola 2008 *The Prisoners' Dilemma Political Economy and Punishment in Contemporary Democracies*. Cambridge: Cambridge University Press.

Larsen, Susan 2003 'National Identity, Cultural Authority, and the Post–Soviet Blockbuster: Nikita Mikhalkov and Aleksei Balabanov', *Slavic Review*, vol. 62, no. 3, pp. 491–511

Latouche, Serge 1996 *The Westernization of the World: The Significance, Scope and Limits of the Drive Towards Global Uniformity*. Cambridge: Polity.

Leoussi, Athena S. and Steven Grosby (eds) 2006 *Nationalism and Ethnosymbolism: History, Culture and Ethnicity in the Formation of Nations*. Edinburgh: Edinburgh University Press.

Lucas, Scott 1999 *Freedom's War: The American Crusade against the Soviet Union*. New York: New York University Press.

Mansfield, Edward D. and Jack Snyder 2006 *Electing to Fight: Why Emerging Democracies Go to War*. Cambridge, MA: MIT Press.

McDonald, Ian 2003 'Hindu Nationalism, Cultural Spaces, and Bodily Practices in India', *American Behavioral Scientist*, vol. 46, no. 11, pp. 1563–1576.

McNeill, Donald 2000 '*McGuggenisation*? National Identity and Globalisation in the Basque Country', *Political Geography*, vol. 19, no. 4, pp. 473–494.

Morrow, Karen 2004 'Megamall on the Hudson: Planning, Wal–Mart, and Grassroots Resistance', *Journal of Environmental Law*, vol. 16, no. 1, pp. 147–149.

Murray, Craig 2007 *Murder in Samarkand: A British Ambassador's Controversial Defiance of Tyranny in the War on Terror*. Edinburgh: Mainstream Publishing.

Ramet, Sabrina P. 2006 *Thinking About Yugoslavia: Scholarly Debates About the Yugoslav Breakup and the Wars in Bosnia and Kosovo*. Cambridge: Cambridge University Press.

Ramet, Sabrina P. and Gordana Crnkovic (eds) 2003 *Kazaaam! Splat! Ploof! The American Impact on European Popular Culture, since 1945*. Rowman & Littlefield.

Rao, Shakuntala 2007 'The Globalization of Bollywood: An Ethnography of Non–Elite Audiences in India', *The Communication Review*, vol. 10, no.1 January, pp. 57–76.

Rajadhyaksha A. 2003 'The "Bollywoodization" of the Indian Cinema: Cultural Nationalism in a Global Arena', *Inter-Asia Cultural Studies*, vol. 4, no.1, April, pp. 25–39.

Ranganathan, Maya and Bernadette Lobo 2008 'Localizing the Global: Analysis of Nationalist Ideologies in MNC Advertisements in Indian TV', *Nationalism and Ethnic Politics*, vol. 14, no. 1, January, pp. 117–142.

Ritzer, George 1996 *The McDonaldization of Society*. Thousand Oaks: Pine Forge.

——2002 'September 11, 2001: Mass Murder and its Roots in the Symbolism of American Consumer Culture', in *McDonaldization: The Reader*. Thousand Oaks, CA: Pine Forge Press/London: Sage.

Ritzer, George and Michael Ryan 2004 'Americanisation, McDonaldisation, and Globalisation,' in Neil Campbell, Jude Davies and George McKay (eds) *Issues in Americanisation and Culture*. Edinburgh: Edinburgh University Press, pp. 41–60.

Ritzer, George and Todd Stillman 2003 'Assessing McDonaldization, Americanization and Globalization', in Ulrich Beck, Natan Sznaider and Rainer Winter (eds) *Global America? The Cultural Consequences of Globalization*. Liverpool: Liverpool University Press, 30–48.

Roy, Oliver 2005 *Globalized Islam: The Search for a New Ummah*. London: Hurst/New York: Columbia University Press.

Scheuer, Michael 2004 *Imperial Hubris: Why the West is Losing the War on Terror*. Washington, DC: Brassey's.

Shechter, Relli 2008 'Glocal Mediators: Marketing in Egypt during the Open–Door Era (*infitah*)', *Enterprise and Society*, vol. 9, no. 4, pp. 762–787.

Schörter, Harm G. 2008a 'Economic Culture and its Transfer: An Overview of the Americanisation of the European Economy, 1900–2005', *European Review of History: Revue Europeenne d'Histoire*, vol. 15, no. 4, pp. 331–344.

——2008b 'The Americanisation of Distribution and its Limits: The Case of the German Retail System, 1950–1975', *European Review of History: Revue Europeenne d'Histoire*, vol. 15, no. 4, pp. 445–458.

Seidler, Victor 2004 'Freedom, Anger and Global Power: Accusing Others' in Neil Campbell, Jude Davies and George McKay (eds) *Issues in Americanisation and Culture*. Edinburgh: Edinburgh University Press, pp. 61–76.

365

Sigona, Nando 2005 'Locating "The Gypsy Problem". The Roma in Italy: Stereotyping, Labelling and "Nomad Camps"', *Journal of Ethnic and Migration Studies*, vol. 31, no. 4, July, pp. 741–756.

Siefert, Marsha 2006 'From Cold War to Wary Peace: American Culture in the Soviet Union and Russia', in Alexander Stephan (ed.), *The Americanization of Europe: Culture, Diplomacy, and Anti-Americanism after 1945*. Oxford: Berghahn Books.

Smith, Anthony D. 1996 *Nations and Nationalism in a Global Era*. Cambridge: Polity.

——1998 *Nationalism and Modernism: A Critical Survey of Recent Theories of Nations and Nationalism*. London: Routledge.

——2004 'Dating the nation', in Daniele Conversi (ed.) *Ethnonationalism in the Contemporary World*. London/New York: Routledge.

——1991 *National Identity*. Harmondsworth: Penguin/Reno: University of Nevada.

Smith, Dennis 2006 *Globalization: The Hidden Agenda*. Cambridge: Polity.

Snow, Nancy 2003 *Information War: American Propaganda, Free Speech and Opinion Control Since 9/11*. Seven Stories Press.

Snyder, Alvin A. 1995 *Warriors of Disinformation: American Propaganda, Soviet Lies and the Winning of the Cold War*. New York: Arcade.

Sorenson, Thomas 1968 *The Word War: The Story of American Propaganda*. New York: Harper & Row.

Soros, George 1998 *The Crisis of Global Capitalism: Open Society Endangered*. New York: Public Affairs.

Steger, Manfred B. 2005 'Ideologies of Globalization', *Journal of Political Ideologies*, vol. 10, no. 1, pp. 11–30.

Steele, Liza and Raymond Kuo 2007 'Terrorism in Xinjiang?', *Ethnopolitics*, vol. 6, no. 1, pp. 1–19.

Stonor Saunders, Frances (1999) *Who Paid the Piper? The CIA and the Cultural Cold War*. London: Granta.

Tavis, Anna A. 1994 'Review of *Close to Eden* by Nikita Mikhalkov', *Slavic Review*, vol. 53, no. 2, pp. 549–550.

Turner Bryan S. and Habibul Khondker 2010 *Globalization East and West*. London: Sage.

Wagnleitner, Reinhold 1994 *Coca-Colonization and the Cold War: The Cultural Mission of the United States in Austria after the Second World War*. Chapel Hill, NC: University of North Carolina Press.

Williams, Margaret A. 1970 'Reference Groups: A Review and Commentary', *Sociological Quarterly*, vol. 11, no. 4, pp. 545–554.

19

The global drive to commodify pensions

Robin Blackburn

We live in an ageing world – by which I mean that the proportion of those over 60 or 65 has risen and is projected to continue to rise. Public and private pension arrangements involve huge financial flows because they are required to cover increasing sections of the population. The course of globalization itself has been shaped by institutional investors, many of them pension funds. At the present time systematic pension provision is largely confined to the richer countries but it is gradually dawning that pension arrangements are needed everywhere.

The ageing of the population is rooted in a global, if uneven, decline in the birth rate as well as an uneven, but also global, rise in life expectancy. In most developed countries the birth rate has fallen below the level at which it reproduces the existing population. Life expectancy in these countries is growing by about two years in every decade. China has gone through a similar demographic transition and it is spreading in most parts of the developing world. Trends like this cannot be extrapolated endlessly into the future but they have been established long enough to make very likely the overall growth of the proportion of the elderly in the total population.

An ageing world

By 2050 the UN Population Division expects there to be 2 billion persons aged 60 or over worldwide, with 1.6 billion of these in the less developed countries. Ageing is most marked in Europe and Asia but it is advancing elsewhere too. By 2050 the size of this older group in Africa is set to quadruple to reach 207 million, comprising 10.3 per cent of total population. Africa will have more older persons than Latin America and the Caribbean (with 187 million aged 60 and over), and nearly as many as Europe (with 229 million of that age). By 2050 Asia, a category that includes India and China, is expected to have no less than 1,249 million older persons, comprising a fifth of the total population in India and as much as 28 per cent in China (UN Population Division 2006).

Today women comprise 55 per cent of those aged 60 and above worldwide, 65 per cent of those aged 60 plus in North America and 70 per cent of those aged 60 plus in

Europe. World-wide women comprised 63.5 per cent of those aged 80 and above in 2005, a figure that is expected to drop slightly to 61.4 per cent by 2050. The frail and vulnerable 'old old' are the most rapidly growing age cohort in all parts of the world. There were 88 million persons aged 80 and above worldwide in 2005, a figure that is projected to rise to 402 million by 2050 according to the UN Population Division mid-range projections.

The ageing trend will already be evident long before 2050. Ageing will double the number of US citizens who are 65 or older from 35 million in 2004 to 70 million by 2035. Because of both projected immigration and a somewhat higher birth rate than Europe the share of the old in the US proportion will not quite double but rise from 12 to 20 per cent. India's over-60 cohort will number 175 million by 2024. By 2040 there are expected to be 98 million persons aged 80 plus in China, 47 million in India and 13 million in Brazil. These people are all already born, a circumstance that gives the projection a high degree of probability.

There are few countries which have arrangements fully adequate to the rising future need for the care and support of the elderly. In the developing world and poor countries many of the aged are sunk in absolute or extreme poverty. A UN report, *Development in an Aging World* (United Nations 2007) observes:

> The demographic transition poses an enormous challenge ... For the unprotected the notion of retirement does not exist; they must continue to rely on their work, which is a greater challenge for those in advanced age (80 years or over). To survive, older persons also count on the support of the family and the community, which, if also resource-constrained, may not be able to offer solid social insurance. In this regard, older persons who are single, widowed or childless (particularly women) face an even higher risk of destitution.

The ageing process is more advanced in the richer countries of Western Europe, Japan, and North America and this is matched by much stronger pension provision. Nevertheless, as we will see below, an increasing number of the aged in these countries are likely to suffer relative poverty if current arrangements are not improved. As aged populations double or treble both these problems will grow. As the baby-boomers retire the number of the aged will double in two or three decades. Rising health costs are a special problem. The over-60s are today fit for longer than used to be the case but their health expenditures tend to be four times as great each year as those under 60 (Reinhardt 2001).

Less than a quarter of the world's population have arrangements in place to pay them pensions when they are old. While the old in the OECD group of rich countries enjoy the best coverage, some are much better covered than others. Nearly every advanced country has a public old age pension system, usually financed by a pay-as-you-go system of pay-roll taxes or insurance contributions. During the working life of the famous postwar 'baby boom' some of these schemes built up a trust fund. Japan and Singapore used such contributions to finance large-scale investments in public infrastructure in the 1950s and after. More recently a number of other states – notably Norway, Australia, and China – have established state pension funds in order to be able to supplement pay-roll contributions in the future. Such funds can also be used to promote macro-economic stability.

The rise of public pensions

The public and the private have long had a stake in pension provision, sometimes a clear division of labour, sometimes, as recently, in stark competition with one another. Since at least the mid-eighteenth century the rich could purchase pension annuities from banks and insurance houses and in 1853 William Gladstone, the British Chancellor of the Exchequer, made contributions tax deductible. The first state-supplied social insurance schemes were introduced to fill the yawning gaps left by commercial suppliers and to furnish at least a measure of social security to all at times of general economic distress. Commercial suppliers of pensions and company retirement schemes did not aim to cover the whole population, and often failed their beneficiaries in economically troubled times. Between 1914 and 1950 political and economic shocks – war, Depression, hyper-inflation, and bank collapse - destroyed many pre-Second-World-War pension schemes and revealed others to be vulnerable or incomplete. The Second World War was a watershed after which universal public pensions schemes spread within most of the industrial nations. Universal coverage was expensive but the war had shown that huge sums could be raised from taxation.

In the US social security was widened in 1949 to embrace the whole population while in Western Europe and Japan around this time universal provision of old age pensions was put on a new and, as it turned out, viable basis by resort to pay-as-you-go financing principles. As contributions flowed into the new schemes from a pay-roll (national insurance) tax, these revenues were paid out to cover the first pension entitlements. It helped a lot that the size of the workforce was growing while the ageing effect was checked for about three decades by the postwar baby boom. Pay-as-you-go was also sustained by strong economic growth, so that revenue streams from the pay-roll tax easily kept pace with, or outstripped, retiree entitlements. And so far as the future was concerned the government was able to pledge its taxing power to promise that the entitlements created by current contributions would be redeemed by future streams of revenue. Private pension providers could not match this pledge. They needed to build up a fund before they could make any pay-outs. And while citizens were confident that there would be a government in fifty years time, financial concerns were vulnerable to market upsets. The Harvard economist Paul Samuelson, later to be awarded the Nobel Prize, published an article confirming the soundness of pay-as-you-go financing (Samuelson 1958).

When Gosta Esping-Andersen published *The Three Worlds of Welfare Capitalism* in 1990 he was able to chart the advance of public pension provision in most European states, earning them a correspondingly high rating for the 'de-commodification' of protection in old age. By this he meant that the aged had rights in a public pension scheme so that they did not need to buy it as if it were a commodity. Typically every employee paid into such a scheme and every retired person had a pension. While those who contributed more usually received a somewhat higher pension the differentials were low and there was significant redistribution from the higher paid to the lower paid.

The United States, Britain, and a few other states (Netherlands, Switzerland) still had commercial pensions. These states, with their 'mixed' or 'divided' pension regime, had long-established stock markets and politically influential financial corporations. Their pension systems were not purely private since they benefited from tax relief on contributions made to the plans. They also had pre-funded and tax-favoured occupational schemes sponsored by employers, both public and private. In most other countries commercial provision made a negligible contribution to pension provision, though it is common for

369

public sector employees to have pension entitlements, often paid from a fund to which their employer contributes.

The high tide of public pensions was reached in about 1980 – the date of the main data in Esping-Andersen's research – after which determined efforts were to be made to weaken public provision in a pattern that has been called 'implicit privatization', since the mass of citizens were urged to look to commercial pensions to make up for the public shortfall. While Esping-Andersen showed that public systems, whether social democratic (Sweden) or social conservative (Germany), could generate impressive levels of public pension provision, the more surprising finding was that private pension delivery still had an elite rather than popular character in the United States and Britain, generating pensions amounting to only about 1 per cent of GDP in 1980 (Esping-Andersen 1990). While pay-as-you-go had immediately generated large streams of pension payments, the commercially funded approach would take decades to mature and until it did its efficiency and reliability remained unclear. However the very success of public provision seemed alarming to some observers, especially free market economists like Milton and Rose Friedman who attacked US social security as a socialist cuckoo introducing an alien collectivism to the cosy nest of US capitalism (Friedman and Friedman 1980). The woes of capitalism in the 1970s and 1980s were laid at the door of a collectivism that was crowding out capital accumulation.

From implicit to explicit privatization

Margaret Thatcher was the first to take a small but significant step towards what came to be known as 'implicit privatization'. In 1980 the indexation of Britain's already modest Basic State Pension was switched from earnings to prices. In 1987 the returns to the State Earnings Related Pensions (SERPS) were slashed. While public pensions shrivelled, new opportunities and tax breaks were opened to commercial suppliers. Members of occupational schemes, whether public or private, were encouraged to leave them and to establish individual pension pots instead. This laid the basis for a gigantic 'mis-selling' scandal in which one and a half million savers were able to sue the commercial pension suppliers for having promised, but not delivered, better returns than the occupational schemes they had been persuaded to leave.

The relative value of the British state pension declined remorselessly – worth 20 per cent of median earnings in 1980 it dropped to 14 per cent by 1997. The incoming New Labour government made no move to restore its value. This steady decline in public provision meant that employees needed to take out a private plan if they wished to avoid the breadline in old age – the logic dubbed 'implicit privatization' by Paul Pierson (Pierson 1995). In the 1990s and 2000s fund managers found a ready market for their tax-favoured pension plans. London's facilities as an international financial centre helped them to distribute the money entrusted to them amongst a wide range of investments throughout the globe.

While the UK showed what 'implicit privatization' could achieve, a small South American state was to be hailed as the model for 'explicit' privatization. Chile suffered hyperinflation and a military coup in the 1970s and then a deep depression in the early 1980s. The public pension scheme was drastically weakened. José Pinera, the finance minister appointed by the military dictatorship, spotted an opportunity to apply the market-oriented approach he had imbibed while studying at the University of Chicago. He proposed that the state pension be phased out and replaced by 'mandatory' privately managed accounts. Pinera believed that a private, funded scheme that was also compulsory and universal would solve two problems at one stroke. It would relieve the government of the headache of pension provision while also deepening local capital markets. The obligatory contributions were to be invested in property, shares, and other marketable assets. In contrast to many developing states Chile had long-established financial institutions. Following the introduction of the mandatory contributions, these could rely on a steady stream of business. The AFPs offered 'defined contribution' benefits so their members were directly at risk from high charges and rocky markets.

The banks and insurance houses set up pension associations (AFPs) which received the pension contributions, managed the resulting funds – and would be responsible for paying pensions when they became due. There were many competing AFPs, based on financial and professional networks, but also eager to attract contributions from as many as possible. While the scheme of pension privatization was market-oriented in conception it was also state-sponsored, with the AFPs able to claim generous tax relief on contributions. However one feature of the AFP arrangements was inspired not by neo-liberalism but by the heritage of Latin American developmental economics, namely a requirement that the AFPs had to invest in the local economy. The hope was that the new pension regime would channel resources to the Chilean banks and stock market helping to promote domestic growth (Riesco 2007). Chilean employees opted out of a state scheme in which the government itself had no confidence. By 1990, 70 per cent of the country's regular workforce had enrolled in an AFP and the savings rate was rising (Ferguson 2008: 216).

While the Chilean scheme was to become famous, a less-heralded pension reform, in Switzerland in the 1980s, was based on mandatory membership of an occupational scheme operated by one of the country's insurance houses (Leimgruber 2008). The Swiss version of compulsory contributions was not so appealing to privatizers for two reasons – because it did not replace the state pension and because it offered savers a guaranteed minimum annual rate of return of 4 per cent. Given the strength of the Swiss franc contributor risk was very limited, a fact which rendered the scheme unattractive to commercially-minded 'pension reformers'. (In 2003 the guaranteed return dropped to 2 per cent but was still a feature that savers in US or UK pension plans might envy.)

The 1980s and 1990s were marked by a gathering process of financialization as the financial services industry offered sophisticated new products which, so it was claimed, would help customers to negotiate the longer life course and would also furnish new revenue streams to the finance houses. Such instruments included student loans, 'baby bonds' and credit card debt but the real money related to housing mortgages and pension funds, especially personal pension plans (Blackburn 2006a and 2006b: 20–9, 172–77).

By 2006 the US mortgage market, inflated by a housing bubble, was worth $11 trillion. The global value of all assets in pension funds in December 2007 was $26 trillion, compared with global GDP of $55 trillion. In 1998 the value of equities held by pension funds was around $5 trillion (Monks 2001). By the end of 2007 this had grown to around $15 trillion of equities and $11 trillion of other assets. The tripling of pension fund equity holdings in a decade reflected both continuing net contributions to these systems and a stock market peak. While US pension funds might place around 10 to 20 per cent of their investments overseas, the European states often placed a half or more of their investments in foreign, often US, capital markets. By 2007 the US and British funds still managed about a third of all pension assets, but public funds in Japan, China, Singapore, and Norway, as well as the US and UK, accounted for 67 per cent of the pension assets held by the world's 300 largest funds (Watson Wyatt 2008).

The resilience of US social security

French insurance houses and German banks wanted legislation that would prune back public pensions and encourage savers to go for individual accounts by giving tax relief. The campaign for pension privatization certainly reflected the banks' hunger for new business but there was also a strong ideological component as free market think tanks identified public pension systems as a drag on capital accumulation. Privatization would widen capital markets and would diminish the role of the state in redistribution. However those who wished to cut state provision right back still demanded tax concessions and a degree of compulsion. Around the year 2000 tax concessions on pension saving cost the US Treasury about $100 billion a year while the UK Treasury lost about £14 billion annually.

Most US neoliberal or conservative think tanks supported social security 'reform'. The Cato Institute, with an endowment worth $300 million in the early 2000s, was the most energetic and persistent. However, the privatizing lobby in the United States found that there was fierce resistance to even partial privatization of social security. When George W. Bush proposed in 2004–5 to divert a portion of the pay-roll tax to 'individual accounts' to be invested in the stock market they encountered stiff resistance from the American Association of Retired Persons (AARP). Raising a public loan of $2 trillion to fix the transition problem – maintaining payments to today's retirees while building the personal accounts of today's workers – seemed a risky procedure. What would be the terms of the loan? And what if the stock market tanked? Republican Congressmen quickly learned that social security reform alarmed their voters. The programme transfers income from rich to poor both within states and between them. Large, rich states, like New York, are net contributors while poor ones, like Kansas, are net recipients. Republican representatives from poor and small states saw no reason to jeopardize these arrangements.

Current retirees worried that there would be less income flowing in to pay their pensions while their children did not want to put at risk either their parents or their own pension entitlement. The White House pet project was dropped like a hot brick. The rebuff to George W. echoed the defeat of earlier schemes to part-privatize social security. Reagan abandoned an attempt to downsize social security in 1983 while in 1999 President Clinton junked an elaborate plan to establish private accounts drawn up by his Treasury Secretary, Lawrence Summers, the former World Bank Chief Economist, who, as we will see, was a strong partisan of pension privatization. In this case the improbable saviour of the programme was Monica Lewinsky – Clinton had the political instinct to see that he could not escape impeachment if he tried to tamper with social security (Blackburn 2002: 396–9, 2006b). It will be interesting to see whether, following these debacles, any new attempt is made to 'save' – that is downsize or part-privatize – social security.

The World Bank focuses on privatization in richer markets

Though checked at home the US privatizing lobby, together with local allies, vigorously pursued their cause overseas. While US administrations could not persuade their own electorate to swallow the medicine of pension privatization they had much more success in foreign lands. The collapse of Communism in Eastern Europe and the Soviet Union in 1989–91 supplied a shock which was registered far and wide. The cause of pension privatization was given priority by the World Bank, with strategic support from the IMF and USAID, Washington's own development agency. While these institutions took the lead in promoting the replacement of public by commercial pension provision the neo-liberal think tanks and the big banks played a supporting role, helping to cover the cost of seminars, surveys, and position papers, and undertaking a major promotional effort once legislation was imminent (Orenstein 2008).

The rationale for the campaign of pension privatization was given by a landmark report issued by the Bank in 1994, *Averting the Old Age Crisis: Policies to Protect the Old and Promote Growth* (World Bank 1994). The Bank claimed to address the global ageing problem but in practice it had little to say about preventing destitution among the elderly in the poorer and less developed countries. If one considers the plight of the world's two billion poorest inhabitants, living on $2 a day or less, it is clear that they are not a realistic target for financial products and that expecting highly-paid fund-managers in the world's financial centres to handle their money would be a grotesque mismatch. In fact it would be much more appropriate to levy a world-wide Tobin-style tax on financial transactions – or a share levy on corporate profits – in order to fund a global old age pension of, say, one dollar a day (Blackburn 2007). But this was the very last thing on the minds of the World Bank.

The World Bank's real focus was instead on middle income states in Eastern Europe and Latin America – and on developed states with a 'dominant' public pension system. The former Communist states were already shaken by free market 'shock therapy' and were consequently less resistant to drastic neo-liberal reform than, say, the Asian 'tigers'. In Latin America the recent experience of hyper-inflation, military dictatorship, and 'structural adjustment' traumatized public opinion and prepared the way for privatization: public pensions had already become practically worthless and few rallied to their defence.

The Bank's idea was to replace exhausted public pension systems with 'mandatory' (i.e. compulsory) individual pension plans offered by commercial suppliers. Finance ministers in middle income states in Latin America and elsewhere that had recently experienced hyper-inflation and 'structural adjustment' programmes proved quite receptive to the sales pitch of the privatizers. With drastically reduced social budgets they were interested in a strategy that lifted from them the responsibility to finance better pensions. Instead they continued to pay debased pensions as a species of poor relief.

One of the thorniest problems faced by the advocates of pension privatization was that of explaining how the transition from pay-as-you-go to funded personal accounts could be negotiated. The case for privatization stressed that it was far better for pension contributions to be invested in the stock market than used to pay current pensions. The returns would be better and the arrangement would not be vulnerable to big differences in cohort size, with a small working age cohort obliged to fork out ever higher contributions to pay pensions to a large retired cohort (such as the baby-boomers). But if pay-roll taxes were paid into personal accounts they would not be available to pay the pensions of current retirees in the public system. This was a political as well as economic problem since voters would worry about the fate of their own entitlements. Peter Ferrara of the Cato Institute urged that governments could take out a huge loan to enable US social security to continue to pay pensions while much of its former income stream was diverted to individual share accounts managed by a commercial supplier (Ferrara 1985). As we have seen this idea failed to gain acceptance in the United States but was even less viable in states that were not in a position to float huge loans. However in Eastern Europe and Latin America the transition problem was much less daunting, as we have seen, because of the devaluation of pubic pension promises. With diminished expectations, the incomes of the elderly were allowed to dwindle and attention was focused on the new private funds.

The European prize

The campaign for pension privatization was to win its first victories in Eastern Europe and Latin America but the real prize was a change of regime in the world's richer countries, with their potentially valuable contributor base. Japan was an unrealistic target. It already possessed a mixed regime of public and private pensions and the nineties – the aftermath of the collapse of the 'bubble economy' of the late eighties – was scarcely the right moment to compel citizens to put their life savings in the stock exchange. But Europe was another matter. There was unhappiness at the performance of the European economy. Strong public pension systems were blamed for labour market 'rigidity' and high unemployment. Pension systems in Germany, Italy, and France offered pensions to which all employees contributed and paid out pensions which all could claim. Though quite complex, with special schemes for different types of employee and some reliance on employer support, these arrangements were all overseen by, and backed by, the state.

The advice offered by the World Bank proposed a variant of the Chilean 'model', whereby all employees would be required to save in commercially-managed individual pension accounts (and with no Swiss-style guarantee). The public pension would be cut right back until it offered only a safety net. The citizens of the European Union were suspicious of the World Bank's market-friendly message but the centre left and left parties seemed to have reached an impasse and could not see an alternative. It made a demoralizing accommodation to market economics. The failure of Gorbachev's reforms weakened the Left everywhere.

Most countries belonging to the European Union still had little commercial pension provision. The publicly-mandated schemes in France, Germany, and Italy had close to universal coverage and delivered a pension, together with occupational supplements, of 60–70 per cent of pre-retirement earnings. These deeply entrenched public pension systems, and the collectivist welfare arrangements of which they were a part, represented a hold-out against the now triumphant formulas of free market economics. At the same time they acted as a barrier against the ambitions of the global financial services industry – unless it was breached the impetus to financialization would be kept at bay in the world's second largest – soon largest – economic zone.

Since the Christian Democrats and the Gaullists had helped to build Europe's collectivist welfare capitalism, weaning them away from these arrangements would not be easy. The only reason that there was any hope of this happening was that the European economy had been underperforming for some time, with lower profits and rising unemployment. Germany was struggling to finance the heavy costs of reunification. And at Maastricht in 1992 the member states had adopted a sternly deflationary programme in preparation for the launch of a common currency. This made a major contribution to subsequent stagnation (Boltho 2003). The custodians of financial orthodoxy argued that the priority was to promote labour flexibility, restore profit levels, and keep down social costs. Some sections of the European financial services industry, notably the French insurance houses and some of the German and Swiss banks, became strongly committed to pension reform since it would open up impressive new business opportunities. Some French Socialists and German Social Democrats urged the need for a grand scheme of Keynesian expansion but the Bundesbank vetoed this. However, politicians still hesitated to question popular and well-entrenched welfare programmes. Powerful arguments and moral support would be needed to stiffen the confidence of politicians before they would be brave enough to take the cause of pension reform to the people – and risk being mowed down by their opponents in the process. The World Bank report on pensions and ageing helped to supply the needed arguments and legitimacy.

Averting the Old Age Crisis had been commissioned by Lawrence Summers, the Bank's Chief Economist. Pensions absorb so much public money that their financing is bound to have large implications for the overall economic pattern. While simulating balance and judiciousness the report was, in fact, quite prescriptive, with implications for the core developed OECD states, with their ageing populations, as well as for 'young countries', 'emerging markets', and those 'in transition'.

The starting point of the report was a species of demographic determinism. The advance of ageing meant that public pay-as-you-go (PAYGO) systems were 'financially unsustainable' and had to be cut to the bone or even phased out. The report quoted some unguarded comments by Paul Samuelson, the economist who had explained the success of PAYGO pensions and given them credibility amongst his colleagues. In a 1967 *Newsweek* article Samuelson wrote:

> The beauty of social insurance is that it is actuarially unsound. Everyone who reaches retirement age is given benefit privileges that far exceed anything he has paid in … How is this possible? It stems from the fact that the national product is growing at compound interest and can be expected to do so for as far ahead as the eye cannot see. Always there are more youths than old folks in a growing population. More important, with real incomes growing at some three percent a year, the taxable base upon which benefits rest in any period are much greater than the taxes paid historically by the generation now retired.

These breezy remarks now looked to be based on false assumptions. The numbers of the old folks were set to rise everywhere and the advanced countries were dogged by lower growth and stagnant earnings. The report was able to cite a contrite Samuelson himself warning about the 'primrose path' of unfunded, or inadequately funded, pension programmes, when population and income growth had stalled (World Bank 1994).

The World Bank model

As the analysis of the report unfolded public pension provision, and the payroll taxes used to finance it, were indicted for being major culprits generating stagnation, firstly because of the economic distortions they generated and secondly because they stood in the way of private pensions which would expand the capital market: 'behind the government's fiscal crisis lies the deeper crisis of labour and capital markets that are malfunctioning, preventing the growth that is ultimately the only way out of these difficulties' (World Bank 1994: 138). Payroll taxes deterred employers from taking on workers, leading to unemployment and a growth of the 'informal sector'. Combined with generous public pensions they promoted early retirement and, especially in Europe, a consequent decline in labour participation rates for those over 50. Moreover the early retirement of skilled workers was a dead loss to the economy; younger, unskilled workers did not take their place. And the impact on capital markets of overweening public systems was as nefarious as the impact on labour markets, squandering savings, deterring private entrepreneurs, and blocking the inventiveness of the financial services industry.

The report advocated a change in the weight and importance of the three pillars of pension provision: (1) The first pillar was the tax-financed public pension, which was to be reduced to a safety net; (2) the second was occupational pension schemes, which were to move from 'defined benefit' to 'defined contribution' (on which more below) and to be managed by the financial services industry; and (3) the third pillar was personal savings, which were to become mandatory, with contributions channelled to and managed by commercial suppliers.

The prescriptive bias of the report was thus directed against the 'dominant public pillar', which was the problem, and towards mandatory personal savings plans, which were the solution (World Bank 1994: 107). State pension entitlements needed to be cut right back. They were cursed by increasing dependency ratios, overgenerous and ill-thought-out benefits, overmaturity and negative side effects. Existing schemes were 'financially unsustainable' because they could only be paid for by doubling or trebling payroll taxes that were already too high. The 'tough choices' imposed by the 'unsustainability' of the PAYGO systems included cutting back benefit levels, raising the retirement age, raising taxes – and moving to a new regime where state pensions no longer bore the brunt of retirement provision but instead acted as a safety net. The occupational pillar was treated with a little more respect but with an emphasis on moving to a fully commercial basis. Overall the retention of the re-assuring and time-hallowed image of three 'pillars' – each of which was meant to be strong – accommodated a shift to an ungainly structure with a weak first pillar, a shifting second pillar, and a dominant third pillar.

The bias in favour of personal accounts

While the report emphatically supported private over public provision it also favoured personal accounts, organized on the 'defined contribution' (DC) model, over occupational schemes, organised on the 'defined benefit' (DB) model. (In the former the pension is whatever annuity can be purchased with what is in the pension pot at retirement; in the latter the level of the pension relates to salary and is guaranteed by the employer that sponsors the plan). The second pillar was preferably to be organized on a Defined Contribution basis. Already some employers were phasing out their DB schemes and replacing them with DC plans. In doing so they were transferring market risk from the company to the employee. If a DB fund was unable to honour its pension promise then the sponsoring company and its assets were liable. The report obviously did not like this aspect of traditional DB arrangements. Requiring employers to guarantee the level of future pensions made the beneficiaries of these schemes into residual owners of the corporation. DC schemes usually had (and have) a lower employers' contribution, but they were more likely to be portable. An advantage of the traditional occupational schemes was that contributions could be easily implemented through payroll deductions. If employees were to have a choice of personal pensions, as in the US 401(k) DC-style schemes, then this would lead to extra marketing and administrative expenses. However by making deductions mandatory at least some of these costs could be reduced, allowing the report blandly to conclude: 'Overall, personal savings schemes would seem to have the edge for the privately managed mandatory pillar' (World Bank 1994: 246).

The case against ever-higher payroll tax rates was, by itself, not without merit. Unlike income tax, payroll taxes are not 'progressive', that is they do not take more from the rich than the poor. Analysis showed that the workers actually bore the cost of so-called 'employers contributions' to the payroll tax. But the decisive argument against high payroll taxes – say above about 15 per cent of salary – is that this would sap demand and raise labour costs, leading to unemployment. The deflationary policy pursued by the monetary authorities was a factor here but there is evidence that a total 'tax wedge' of about 40 per cent on European incomes – half of it connected to pension finance – did explain about a half of the rise in unemployment as the European average rose above 10 per cent of the registered labour force (Directorate General 2003: 12).

Public funds can supplement PAYGO

However, the criticisms made by the report strained logic and credulity when they claimed that the answer was pension privatization and mandatory membership in commercially-managed schemes. The demographic challenge, in itself, yielded absolutely no conclusions about the best way of delivering pensions. If the proportion of over 65s is set to double over three decades, then either the money going to pensioners as a whole rises, say from 8 per cent of GDP in 2004 to 16 per cent of GDP by 2034, or individual pensioners will drop behind the growth in prosperity. If the proportion of GDP available to the over-65s stays roughly the same (we will see below that this is forecast for the post-reform EU) then relative poverty will grow sharply. While public pension systems have met the challenge of raising great chunks of GDP, private pension funds have yet to equal this ability. The greying of the population does indeed demand supplementary sources of finance – perhaps the taxing of capital not labour – but this does nor require commercial fund management. Already in 1994 there were many successful public sector pension funds.

Notwithstanding the historic success of payroll taxes in raising pension revenue, the argument that they were counter-productive or inefficient above a certain level was a serious one. It would imply both finding the best level for efficient pay-roll taxes, and a search for other taxes – on high incomes, financial transactions, property or capital – to take up the shortfall. As globalization advanced inequalities in income and wealth within states was growing. There was a strong argument from social justice to close tax havens and increases taxes on the wealthy (Blackburn 2006b). The report did not address the problem that compulsory contributions would themselves function very much like a payroll tax, for example by reducing demand and raising labour costs.

In fact the case for allowing pay-as-you-go (PAYGO) to remain a major source of pension finance was never squarely addressed. It was claimed that PAYGO was 'unsustainable' when it really meant that pay-roll taxes were likely to raise something less than 100 per cent of the target level, instead of being grateful that PAYGO could raise 80 or 90 per cent of needed revenues and looking for a supplement. It also neglected the efficiency of pay-roll taxes. The deduction of such taxes at source – and without any need for the expense of choice between different commercial suppliers – made such public schemes very cost-effective. In the US the social security administration – with a staff of just 65,000 – collects contributions from 120 million employees and then pays out pensions to 44 million beneficiaries. By comparison, even post-credit-crunch, a single large US bank or fund manager would employ more people – and on higher salaries.

While the authors of the report rule out tax increases as politically unfeasible, they instead assume that citizens will accept compulsory deductions from their earnings so long as they are put into approved, tax-favoured personal or occupational funds. At this point their argument could have concluded that social insurance contributions should go

377

into a publicly managed fund or network of funds and not be treated as another tax and that the social funds should be visibly more accountable to those they were supposed to benefit. Likewise the report could have suggested that taxes on corporations or the rich could have been called on to make up for shortfall in pension receipts. But the report is, in fact, hostile to such approaches. Instead it insisted that pension funds had to be commercially managed and subject to lighter public regulation. It claimed that those forced to pay contributions will see them as the price they are paying for a purchase and that this perception will banish all the negative aspects of payroll taxes.

The cost disease of private pensions

While singing the praises of privately furnished pension schemes the report seemingly balanced this by conceding some of their limitations. It was admitted that the coverage of private pension funds is usually too narrow and that is why a mandatory approach is needed. The report urged that pension funds should be freed from political interference and that they should be 'liberated' – an 'idea whose time has come' – from such irksome restraints as minimum holdings of public bonds or controls on the export of capital. It helpfully explained: 'Easy capital outflow helps to stimulate capital inflows, because a prime concern of international investors is to be able to get out of a market quickly when the need arises' (World Bank 1994: 219).

Employees would accept the obligation to pay a proportion of their earnings to the financial services industry because of the promise of good returns from the stock market. The capital markets would receive a much-needed boost and the employment-harming effects of high taxes would be avoided. Tax breaks were to continue. The pension fund industry, having been created in its present form by lavish tax concessions, was thus now to be further boosted by compulsory, government-subsidised contributions from the entire workforce. The report's recommendations supposedly applied to a swathe of developing countries too. It was urged that lack of trained administrators need be no obstacle:

> The shortage of local expertise in many developing countries may be overcome by using foreign fund managers in joint ventures with local firms. Developing countries reluctant to use joint ventures may have a hard time assembling the expertise needed to run pension funds well, especially in the early years.
>
> (World Bank 1994: 139–40)

The report, as we have seen, mildly favoured personal savings plans over occupational funds, but strongly favoured private funds of any description over state sponsored provident funds – despite what was admitted to be the higher administrative and marketing charges involved in the former. Administrative charges in the Chilean system had been heavy to begin with and remained rather high in 1990 at 2.3 per cent of assets. Over forty years a 1 per cent cost ratio brings a 20 per cent reduction in yield so the 1990 rate would imply substantial erosion. Although employees had to join a scheme they could choose from more than a score of AFPs and, if they became unhappy, could switch. This lead to intense competition between rival sales teams and consequent expense. Costly promotion led employees who already contributed to switch from one supplier to another but did not widen overall coverage. Enrolment was meant to be universal but actual contributions remained stubbornly stuck at around half of the total labour force, with scant participation in the rural sector or in the poorest urban districts. There was also great inequality of coverage within the ranks of those enlisted, so that many have only a nominal pension to look forward to. In 2006 the state pension system which had been 'frozen' in 1981 was still paying out more in pensions than the AFP and the Chilean government was obliged to introduce a basic state pension (Riesco 2007).

By contrast the Central Provident Fund of Singapore had near-universal enrolment and annual administrative costs of only 0.16 per cent of assets a year in 1990. And the Malaysian Provident Fund had expenses of only 0.18 per cent. However the investment returns of the Chilean AFPs had been 7.5 to 10.5 per cent in 1990 while the Malaysian return was 4.82 per cent and that in Singapore 2.86 per cent. (World Bank 1994: 224) The AFPs had yet to pay out any pensions, which should have reduced costs. And the Singapore CPF, as the report noted, had a remit to help participants buy their dwellings or meet other permitted expenditures (e.g. training fees), lowering the current rate of return but with some returns to come in the future. These contrasts, already observable in 1990, were to become even more marketed in the subsequent decade and a half.

Averting the Old Age Crisis did not explore the successes of provident funds in Singapore and Malaysia, nor that of the huge contribution of similar state-sponsored saving in Japan. Japan's remarkable postwar growth had been greatly facilitated by public retirement funds which had paid for huge infrastructure investments in roads, harbours, railways, and airports. By the early 1990s this phase of Japanese growth had come to an end but this was no good reason to ignore its huge role in the preceding four decades (Ecclestone 1989: 97). Instead of scrutinizing the East Asian model *Averting the Old Age Crisis*, dwelt on the failures of state-sponsored pension systems in Africa and parts of Latin America. The report failed to register that stock markets and private savings in these same countries had also delivered miserable results.

The report offered a strategically located table on investment rates of return which signalled the superiority of private over public fund management – though in fact no information was given on administrative charges. It was not noted that the public funds in question were obliged to invest almost exclusively in specially denominated public bonds. Covering periods of between five and ten years in the eighties the table showed that the rate of return in Peru, Zambia, Venezuela, Egypt, and Kenya had been negative, sometimes strongly so; but no information was supplied on conditions in these countries, including rates of return on equity capital. The public bonds given to the funds in exchange for contribution income had steadily lost value, usually because of inflation. This funding device was, in effect, a way whereby the governments concerned treated pension contributions as tax income. The table, not surprisingly, showed better rates of return for the advanced countries, though once again public funds have often been required to invest in special government bonds. The surplus in the US social security account was allotted interest of 4.8 per cent annually. Again this was a reflection of a government-sanctioned Treasury dictat. The investment income reaped by privately managed funds was higher, according to the table. During the eighties Dutch occupational schemes returned 6.7 per cent annually, compared with 8.0 per cent for US occupational funds and 8.6 per cent for those in the UK. The Singapore CPF return averaged 3.0 per cent in the eighties and the Malaysian CPF 4.6 per cent while the Chilean AFPs came top of the class with 9.2 per cent. The conclusion: 'Privately managed funds beat publicly managed funds hands down' (World Bank 1993).

In fact this conclusion was produced by fixing the contest in advance, with no account taken of charges, no information on the returns of personal pensions in the UK or US, and the exclusion or misattribution of evidence concerning public or social funds that were not commercially managed. If information had been given concerning individual pension plan holders in the UK and US some would have shown negative or very low returns where participants had been penalized for not maintaining payments. And the figures given in the table lumped the rather successful public sector pension funds in Britain, the United States, and the Netherlands into the 'privately managed' category. The exclusion of costs also tilted the comparison against the public funds.

The report did not completely ignore over-charging and competitive waste in privately run schemes. It also noted that commercial fund managers could be guilty of 'short-termism', herd-like behaviour, and elitism vis-à-vis the local or small-scale. But whereas the failures of private pension schemes posed 'regulatory issues' which could be addressed, those of funded public schemes were irredeemable, so they should be abandoned. In fact the 'public funds' to which the report paid most attention scarcely deserved the name but were simply accounting devices used by public treasuries. If the record of public sector funds had been scrutinised no doubt some problems would have been encountered but financial performance would not generally have been among them. However the report was not interested in exploring ways of improving non-commercial pension funds. Indeed the very possibility that pensions funds could be pre-funded and run by public trustees, or by autonomous non-commercial social institutions, was scouted. This would, it warned, pose a threat to free enterprise capitalism. The report worried that if 'centralized provident funds' were to 'invest in corporate equities, public officials could gain control of corporate affairs, a back door to nationalization' (World Bank 1994: 93–4).

The message of the report offered a one-size-fits-all recipe. But the main pre-occupation was not reaching out to the majority of the world's population who have no pension coverage, but rather to concentrate on dismantling public provision in richer countries where this might deliver new business to the fund managers. Notwithstanding the references to the 'multi-pillar' approach, few readers could miss the emphasis on, and the novelty of, the proposal for mandatory personal savings plans. Indeed the strong standpoint emanating from the report and the wide range of evidence it marshalled helped, together with the Bank's authority, to make this a bench-mark study (Ney 2000). Joseph Stiglitz, a later Chief Economist at the World Bank, became alarmed at the the the new dogma of pension privatization and co-authored (with Peter Orszag) a trenchant critique of *Averting the Old Age Crisis* in 1999. Some of the Bank's operational staff admitted that there were risks in scrapping public provision and placing all resources in vulnerable commercial funds. But the momentum of the privatization campaign was only momentarily disturbed. Shortly thereafter Stiglitz was removed from his post (Stiglitz and Orzsag 2001, Stiglitz 2002).

The report had strong bureaucratic backing in the Bank and IMF and from the Clinton administration, where Summers, who had commissioned the report, was successively Assistant Treasury Secretary and then Treasury Secretary in the years 1995 to 2000. Summers remained widely influential and the critiques did not prevent ever more ambitious attempts to ram through 'pension reform' in a widening circle of countries. Governments coping with the aftermath of free market 'shock therapy' and wrestling with the aftermath of IMF-sponsored 'structural adjustment' were persuaded to commit to pension reform, especially if they were middle income (Mexico, Poland) and/or resource rich (Kazakhstan, Nigeria). In many cases hyper-inflation had destroyed pension reserves and left employees with miserable benefits. Privatization often meant that public pensions could be cut to the bone and pay-roll taxes converted into contributions to a local branch of the international financial services industry. Whether stock market investments would really lead to better pensions in the future was something that only time would tell – for the moment it meant one less headache for the authorities. Meanwhile the World Bank and IMF offered expert assistance and conveyed the message that governments that followed their advice would get better credit scores and favoured treatment from international lenders.

Classic accounts of public pension provision in the first industrializing countries stressed that public provision had been forthcoming in response to pressure from labour movements and from employers who did not want to be encumbered by running their own schemes. Different national traditions and labour markets have also set up a degree of path dependence. Esping-Andersen had identified three types of social security regime – conservative, social democratic, and liberal – with the evolution of each country's welfare regime reflecting dominant values and structures.

In the debate on the origins of the welfare state a central idea became the importance of 'path-dependence' in pension systems. Those who had accrued entitlement in public pay-as-you-go pension systems had a strong interest in their continuance and in the indexing of benefits to national prosperity. On the other hand 'liberal' regimes, which had granted tax relief to private savings, also create a vested interest in continued public subsidy of commercial saving (Hacker 2002). The rapid spread of something quite close to the 'liberal model' in the 1990s and early 2000s challenged the path dependent model. Former Communist countries switched from a completely public (though semi-'conservative') regime to almost complete reliance on commercial provision and the market. In Latin America and Eastern Europe the World Bank model was widely adopted contrary to the 'path dependent' model. Just as the consolidation of modern public systems in mid-century reflected the collectivist response to depression and war so the privatization of social protection was made to seem a plausible solution by political ruptures which seemed to discredit the welfare state and socialism. Neo-liberal discourse insisted that there was only one effective response to globalization, that which sought to replace social guarantees with the canny commercial bets of 'responsible risk takers' (Giddens 1997, 119–20). Pension reform was made to seem attractive and responsible to political leaders in many countries – especially after they had been instructed in how advantageous this would be by emissaries from the World Bank.

In July 2001 the director of the Bank's Social Protection unit claimed that '(t)he World Bank has been and remains one of the main drivers behind the pension revolution' and noted that mandatory private schemes now operated in eleven Latin American countries and three former Communist states (Holzmann 2001). In a study of pension privatization published in 2008 Mitchell Orenstein found there to have been 30 instances where World Bank help had been influential (Orenstein 2008).

Notwithstanding popular opposition, the decade 1995 to 2005 witnessed major gains for the cause of pension reform in the core countries of continental Europe. One of the most surprising gains was in Sweden where 1995 saw the enactment of a pension reform that removed the previous 'defined benefit' offered by the public pension and substituted a so-called 'notional defined contribution' model which offered a proportionate share of the income that would be raised by a static payroll tax. On top of this, two and a half per cent of income was to go to a personal accounts system which would invest in funds offered by the main commercial suppliers. Sweden had been badly shaken by an economic and financial crisis in 1992 and this undoubtedly helps to explain the decision of its political elite to make a sudden – and secretive – lurch in the direction of implicit privatization. The public pension authority retained oversight of the pension system and insisted on cost ratios – around 0.3 per cent of assets – that contrasted with the two per cent or more which the finance houses were able to charge in Hungary and Poland. Nevertheless, for Europe's most famous welfare state to adopt such a measure was a symbolic gain for the privatization cause. Around the same time Norway was also hit by a financial crisis but the government responded by taking over the banks and setting up what became the State Pension Fund, an entity that was to build up assets of $240 billion by 2008.

The 'privatizing' of pensions matched the privatization of public assets that was already underway. Shares in privatized railways and telecoms could be purchased by the fund managers with money supplied by scheme participants. This offered lush new grazing grounds to banks, insurance houses, fund managers, and stock exchanges. The fund managers would also be able to purchase US securities, adding zest to the US exchanges. To call this a recipe for wild capitalism would not be fair since, as we have seen, it required a new regime of publicly mandated, publicly organized and publicly subsidized contributions from the mass of employees. Governments were not only to offer handsome tax incentives but were often expected to turn public bodies into collection agencies for commercial concerns. However, even the magic of financial engineering finds more difficulty in conjuring a profit out of public obligations than out of public assets. While undervaluing the latter led to the brisk take-up of shares, the devaluing of public pension obligations by no means ensured that commercial funds would be able to take their place.

Private pensions

Supposedly Western Europeans could replace lost public pensions by taking out private pension coverage. Fearful of popular reaction, and aware that it would aggravate the deflationary climate, their governments had declined to make commercial provision compulsory. Those who reach retirement age around 2030 are headed for a double short-fall. Their public pension has shrunk and accumulation in commercial funds will not be able to take their place. The advocates of pension privatization claimed that savers could look forward to an annual rate of return of 7 per cent or more in real terms. But this is a delusion. The roller coaster of the stock markets in 1997–2008 – ending close to where they began – have confounded such expectations. The loss of a decade of growth will be very difficult – perhaps impossible – to make up prior to the retirement of the baby-boomers. Financial crises have not been external to the regimes of financialization and globalization but integral to it (Brenner 2006, Glyn 2006, Turner 2008). The credit crunch of 2007–8 was the forty-second major financial crisis since 1971, when the Bretton Woods system was abandoned. If the difficult but necessary work of negotiating a new global financial regime is carried through – which will have to fully involve such states of Brazil, India, and China – and if such challenges as climate change and world poverty are properly addressed, then pension funds should be happy with less than half of the rate of return postulated by the privatizers.

Despite tax concessions fund managers have failed to demonstrate that they can generate the huge sums needed to avoid pensioners falling further and further behind the rest of the population. In the United States or Britain, with their long history of private provision, commercial pensions are on course to make only a very modest contribution to future pension income. While the UK state pension and the US social security pension will furnish 5–7 per cent of GDP in the 2030s, their financial services sector is on course to supply about a third of this. The first report of the UK Pensions Commission estimated that private pensions were on course to supply pensions worth only 2 per cent of GDP and the figure for the US seems very similar. There is little sign that the authors of *Averting the Old Age Crisis* were thinking in comprehensive or realistic terms since at no point did they estimate the size of pension fund needed to supply a target level of GDP as pension income. The UK Pension Commission never managed to fill the hole it identified but had the candour to acknowledge that the pension system would need to raise 14 per cent of GDP by mid-century, if it was to maintain the relative income of those of pension age, but was only likely to raise about 10 per cent of GDP. Projections made for the US in the period 2040 to 2050 show a shortfall that is also around 4 per cent of GDP (Pensions Commission 2004: 17; Blackburn 2006b: 61–74). These shortfalls suggest that the incomes of the old will lag behind the growth of average income by about a third.

The cause of social security or pension 'reform' might be attractive to financial lobby groups but usually inspired great reserve amongst those who had already built up entitlement in an existing public regime. However, as we have seen, Eastern Europe and Latin America were softened up for pension reform, by some combination of military dictatorship, hyper-inflation, 'shock therapy', and structural adjustment, as noted above. Pensions had become almost worthless and in some cases were only paid months late. Fragile new governments found themselves the targets of a high-powered campaign of persuasion.

In *Pension Privatization*, Mitchell Orenstein notes that the World Bank identified key political leaders, state officials, and opinion-formers and invited them to conferences on pension privatization in 'attractive locations'. The World Bank paid for public relations campaigns – $1.4 million in the case of Poland. He adds: 'The World Bank not only seconded or released its own employees to participate in the reform teams for pension privatization. ... it has also hired prominent [local] pension reform officials onto its staff' (Orenstein 2005: 91). The IMF played a different but complementary role. In another dimension of what Orenstein terms 'resource leverage' it indicated that loans would not be forthcoming unless and until pension reform was tackled. Loans to assist transition costs, on the other hand, were made available by the Bank not the IMF. The free market think tanks and USAID also furnished help focussed on 'norms teaching'. Only in a few cases – Poland being one – did the campaign meet open resistance. In the Polish case Solidarity and the Ministry of Labour both had marked objections to features of the reform but did not come together with an alternative. (Solidarity wanted the concurrent privatization of state industry to be effected by distributing shares to the work force.) In a number of former Soviet republics authoritarian structures smoothed the path: 'The solution Kazakhstan adopted was heavily influenced by transnational actors [ie World Bank, IMF] but was facilitated by the small number of veto actors in its strong presidential political system' (Orenstein 2008: 130).

'Resource leverage' had more limited application in Western Europe where there was anyway still much support for generous public pensions. Rather than the grand slam approach which prevailed in Eastern Europe and Latin America Europe's pension reformers adopted 'salami tactics', with successive moves to cut back on public provision. The first attempts to weaken the public programmes led not simply to massive demonstrations and strikes but to the downfall of three centre-right governments in the mid-1990s – the governments of Silvio Berlusconi in Italy, Alain Juppé in France, and Helmut Kohl in Germany. Even in Britain pension scandals and disappointments contributed to the downfall of John Major's government in 1997 and disenchantment with Margaret Thatcher's legacy.

The centre-left coalitions which replaced these governments acted with great circumspection. They sought to avoid a head-on clash over most existing pension commitments and entitlements but nevertheless harped on the need for 'reform'. They singled out a few instances of apparently excessive pension generosity and then proceeded to a general – but strategically delayed – downsizing. Europe's stagnation and unemployment was blamed not on the policies of central banks obsessed by monetary union, or on the regressive features of payroll taxes, but on the burden of pension and welfare provision. The Dini centre-left administration in Italy negotiated a major instalment of reform in 1995 when it severely cut future entitlements while respecting those of workers aged forty and above. This formula of longitudinal 'reform' was eventually adopted, notwithstanding much resistance, by the Shroeder government in Germany and the Raffarin centre-right administration in France. The failure of the centre-left governments to come up with an effective response to mass joblessness undercut and demoralized opposition to successive doses of 'implicit' privatization, often accompanied with legislation offering tax relief to those who signed up with a private supplier.

Already in 2001, prior to a new wave of cuts in the next few years, projected public expenditure per person aged 65 plus by EU states was planned to shrink dramatically from its former level. In terms of expenditure per head as a percentage of GDP per head the drop was to be from 72.0 per cent in France in 2000 to 57.5 per cent in 2040; in Italy from 72.3 per cent of GDP per head in 2000 to 45.9 per cent in 2040, in Germany from 67.4 per cent of GDP per head in 2000 to 54.8 per cent in 2040 (Math 2004: 122).

This was simply a first instalment of downsizing with more to come from Raffarin, Berlusconi, Shröder, and Merkel in the mid-2000s. A February 2006 report by the European Commission and its Economic Policy Committee predicted declining 'benefit ratios', that is a decline in the ratio of per capita pension benefits to per capita output, for 2030 and 2050. It showed that in terms of per capita GDP, public pension income per aged citizen is expected to drop year by year until by 2050 it will be only a little over half its level in 2004. In absolute terms public spending on old age pensions, elder care and health creeps up but numbers of the aged roughly double. The EU-wide projections, covering 25 countries and some 450 million people, show overall public pension spending growing even more slowly despite a rapidly increasing aged population (European Commission 2006). Most of the new member states switched from public to private provision with haste and their funds were nearly wiped out in 2008.

The cuts made to pension provision in 'old Europe' left a gaping hole that the private suppliers sought to fill. But the perennially hopeful financial services found it tough going. Reforming governments boasted that public pensions were affordable but failed to make it brutally clear to their citizens that they were on their own now. Not only did they need to save a tenth or more of their earnings but they also needed to find a reliable and efficient savings vehicle. Failing these two tests they would have a pinched old age at best. Legislation was introduced to give tax favours to DC-type pension accounts but the choice amongst them could be bewildering. In boom times the suppliers implied that their skill explained the growth in their funds and gave scant information on charges, yet studies show that charge ratios are the best predictor of yield (Blackburn 2002). Only a few had access to the most efficient schemes, applying to a whole occupation group but with transferable benefits. The US money managers had greater marketing expertise and, for a while, their individualized products seemed attractive. Local banks and insurance houses resented the competition.

An article in the *Institutional Investor* magazine explained: 'Money managers have stormed the continent. But so far they are fighting over scraps.' Italy had introduced a new law in late 1998 allowing personal pension plans, but 'without the tax incentives that make them exciting' and with a high hurdle for foreign money managers. It worried that 'The fledgling equity revolution in Europe is at risk, along with the future of economic and monetary union.' The timid response of European governments was a poor recompense to all the interest that had been shown: 'Take a seat on an airplane going to one of the capitals of Europe and the chances that a fellow passenger is a salesman or investment manager is high.' Among those who had set up 'base camps' were Goldman Sachs, Morgan Stanley, J. P. Morgan, Invesco, Vanguard, and Merrill Lynch. They encountered stiff competition for the modest business available from BNP-Paribas, Caisse de Depots et Consignations, Westdeutsche Landesbank, and Dresdner RCM Global Investors. The regulations imposed by European governments were generally too tough on the managers and too timid with the employees. The Swedish public pension fund offered only a 'paltry' 0.2 per cent management fee for funds of $3.5 billion or more. 'The bad news for investment managers is that Sweden could become the template of Europe.' This treatment could not be in harsher contrast to Eastern Europe: 'In Poland, at least, the fund managers have been helped in recouping their costs by management fees as high as 10 per cent.' There was also the problem that the European governments had left too much discretion to employees. An Italian occupational scheme was found wanting on these grounds: '"The sign-up for the funds was less than people had hoped for," says Alan Rubenstein, managing director of the pensions group at Morgan Stanley Dean Witter. "The new system needs to be made obligatory"' (*Institutional Investor* 2000). Here was a business arrogant enough to believe that purchase of its products should be compulsory!

In subsequent years more progress was made but the money management industry in Europe failed to take off. One problem was that it was essentially a vehicle for making high-cost, individually packaged investments in the United States when, firstly, this was a disadvantageous way of investing there, and secondly, European investors might have better prospects elsewhere. Investing in the US via Fidelity or Pimco meant incurring heavy marketing and admin charges. It also locked the investor into US asset bubbles like the dotcom and housing booms. Investing at home or in the Far East might have made better sense.

Nevertheless, the pension fund managers did help to attract a flow of European capital to the US and thus to cover current account deficits that were placing great pressure on the financial systems. The Harvard economist Martin Feldstein was a prominent champion of pension privatization. He also worried about the huge inflow of capital into the US (Blackburn 2002: 392–99). This was less inconsistent than it might appear. If the US needed an inflow of funds to offset its deficits then better that it should be in the form of penny-parcels managed by US finance houses than that it take the form of the purchase of entire corporations, as happened with Japanese investments. However, from the standpoint of the European savers, prospects were bleak. When the crash came in 2007–8 many European banks and insurance houses were left holding toxic assets. Those who had invested in the new pension schemes found that the value of their funds had fallen by a half or more.

It is a testament to the persuasive powers and 'resource leverage' of the financial services industry and the free market think tanks that they persuaded so many governments to jettison public systems that simply needed supplementary finance (on which more below) and instead plumped for private systems which were a recurrent source of scandal in the US and UK, and whose returns had always been poor. The global growth in pension funds was part of a wave of financialization which helped to generate a succession of asset bubbles and their eventual collapse.

The private pension bonanza 1990 to 2007

In the US and Britain de-regulation of financial institutions and privatization of non-commercial entities allowed for a dramatic expansion of commercial money management. DB schemes were withdrawn by many employers and DC pension plans took their place. Britain's mutually-owned building societies became banks like Northern Rock and TSB. Repeal of the Glass-Steagal Act in 1999 allowed Wall Street's investment banks to get into the field of retail finance.

Already by the 1990s pension funds of various sorts had become major investors and potential customers for the new structured finance products and Special Purpose Vehicles offered by the banks and brokers. Around this time US pension funds held assets worth about $7 trillion. The types of funds included public and private sector employer-sponsored occupational funds (worth about $3.4 trillion), usually organised on a DB basis, and individual savings plans, operated by money managers like Fidelity, Pimco, and Vanguard, offering DC pensions. So far as private sector employees were concerned the DC schemes grew steadily from the early 1980s using the tax advantages offered by the 401 (k) clause of the Internal Revenue Service schedule. Employers needed to sponsor these schemes but had no responsibility whatsoever for supplying any given level of pension. By 2007 some 45 million US workers had 401(k)s, though the average holding of about $59,000 was not going to buy more than a modest supplement to the social security pension. Employees were also encouraged to hold large proportions of their employers' shares. The highly paid made disproportionate gains from the 401(k)s. The top ten per cent of savers received 50 per cent of all tax relief (Hughes and Sinfield 2004: 171) and their larger holdings attracted lower charge ratios.

Meanwhile there was the slow agony of the well-established DB funds at the large steel plants, airlines, and auto-makers. These had mostly sponsored their own DB plans since the 1950s but now ran into trouble as the number of retirees massively outnumbered the numbers of workers paying into the schemes. The plans each had a fund but sponsoring employers often allotted themselves a contribution holiday when the stock market went up. In the UK, companies with DB schemes skipped contributions worth £28 billion between 1988 and 2001. The plan trustees were mainly appointed by the employers and the company's chief financial officer would work closely with the executive manager of the pension fund (they might even be the same person). In working out the scheme's liabilities much depended on the choice of the discount rate used to make the estimate.

The US authorities left the corporations great latitude in estimating future liabilities since to have done otherwise would have risked pushing them into bankruptcy. Nevertheless several giant steel, airline, and auto companies were driven close to bankruptcy. This created a new type of entrepreneur, the 'vulture capitalist' who bought up troubled companies, and took them into Chapter 11 bankruptcy protection. They then applied to the bankruptcy court to allow them legally to transfer the company's pension and health care promises to the Pension Benefits Guarantee Corporation (PBGC), a Federally-mandated insurance scheme set up in 1974. On average the PBGC pays out about 70 per cent of the benefits promised by the schemes it has taken over. If the courts agree to this transfer of liability, as they usually do, then the value of the company rises and it can be sold for a healthy profit. This operation is colloquially known as 'scouring the barnacles'. Hundreds of thousands of workers find that their pensions have shrunk – and some may lose their jobs too. While this spectacle is a wretched one the brutality of the vulture capitalists is only part of the problem. The root flaw is that the pension fund is sponsored by a single employer which, over a few decades, may go from blue chip to a basket case (Blackburn 2006a and 2006b).

Public sector workers have been in a somewhat stronger position since their employers find it more difficult to escape the promises they have made. They have also had the advantage of cost-effective and sometimes enlightened fund management. Given their huge size – Calpers, the California Public Employee Retirement System has a fund of about $250 billion in 2007 – they tend to invest in everything in order to achieve diversification. US pension funds began investing overseas on a large scale in the 1990s and foreign pension funds have increased their US holdings. However portfolio theory urges funds to avoid currency risk and place their main investments in the currency area in which their liabilities are denominated, so domestic securities dominate the holdings of most types of pension fund. However the speculative fevers of financialization communicated themselves to even staid pension funds and they began to take stakes in hedge funds and private equity partnerships. While some of these might do well others went bust. Even the successful bets came with heavy charges under the 'two and twenty' formula (an annual 2 per cent of fund value and 20 per cent of any capital gain).

The individual plans beloved of pension reformers have been the most vulnerable to poor returns and the gaming of the small saver. The years 2001 to 2008 were marked not only by market fluctuations but also by an extraordinary succession of scandals associated with insider dealing, phony accounting, off balance-sheet entities (SPEs), backdated executive options, exorbitant bonuses, bid-rigging by insurers, and fund managers permitting after-hours arbitrage at the expense of their own customers. The term 'grey capitalism' evokes important features of a financial regime riddled by insider abuse and in which pension beneficiaries do not know what is happening to their savings. Fund managers were not responsible to policy holders and CEOs were not accountable to share-holders (Useem 1996, Bogle 2005). The term also sought to draw attention to the murky practices of financialization, including the growth of an unregulated secondary banking system (Blackburn 2006b and 2008).

The credit crunch

So we arrive at the credit crunch and the swooning stock markets of 2007–8. At its core the crisis was caused by politicians who believed in the magic of markets and in the exemplary qualities of business. They did what the consultants and special interest lobbies told them made business sense. Tame regulators were found who contemplated great mountains of debt with equanimity, and who found nothing amiss in 'self-cert' mortgages, buy-to-let bubbles, CDO pyramids, and an entire, off-balance-sheet, shadow banking system.

Huge global imbalances – China's mountainous surpluses and the chasm of the US deficit – prompted the US Federal Reserve Bank to adopt absurdly low interest rates in 2001–6, which in turn led to 120 per cent mortgages, a shower of gold cards and a proliferation of structured finance products, better thought of as instruments of mass self-deception.

US households were cast as the world's 'customers of last resort' but had to go deep into debt to carry this off. But this applied not only households. The banks and hedge funds took on huge amounts of 'leverage' and companies taken over by private equity groups were burdened with massive debt. Politicians helped the party along by de-regulating and privatizing. Investment banks were no longer barred from retail finance and the pressure to financialize became ubiquitous. People were encouraged to see themselves as two-legged profit and loss centres. Households were meant to behave like businesses, businesses to behave like banks, and banks to behave like hedge funds. By taking on leverage one supposedly did away with 'unrewarded risk'. Giant companies like GM and GE now made their profits not from selling their products but from arranging the accompanying consumer finance.

The derivatives revolution made poor people's debt the caviar of the finance houses. Subprime mortgages could be bundled and tranched as Collaterized Debt Obligations (CDOs), and then sold on to institutional investors which were themselves the reposi-tories of the savings of those on middle or even low incomes. But already in 2006 many institutions – especially public sector pension funds and college endowments – became stand-offish and the banks found that they had large unsold stocks of their complex credit derivatives. But the bankers and rating agencies had long ago learnt that the mere absence of paying customers was no bar to obscene fees and bonuses. They booked fees in advance and used 'over the counter' transactions to sell off the credit derivatives to the unwary – or simply to their own off-balance sheet entities – at 'model' prices. They bor-rowed money from wholesale markets to finance the acquisition of CDOs and other collateralized receivables (Blackburn 2008, Turner 2008). Yawning inequality made for shaky structures. If China's workers and farmers had been better paid the international imbal-ances would have been more manageable and if there was less poverty in the US there would not have been such a large pool of subprime and Alt A mortgages to turn sour.

Free market economists had always warned that planned economies could not work for long because they used administered prices. Clinton, Blair, and Brown completed the work of Thatcher and Reagan, 'liberating finance' and cultivating a market in everything from public services to student debt, baby bonds to air traffic control, water to pension products. Yet in the end they created a world whose 'light touch' regulation allowed the heart of the financial system to be clogged up with non-performing – and unpriceable – assets. … a predictable recipe for a heart attack. By 2007 the value of credit derivatives valued at model prices held off-balance sheet by the major banks exceeded their equity capital.

No one knew the problem better than the banks themselves. A spate of defaults in summer 2007, led them to refuse to lend to one another. The central banks sought to revive them by offering great dollops of liquidity. But offering easy loans to institutions suffering from insolvency simply delays the day of reckoning.

The Scandinavian experience of 1988–92 showed that governments needed to use their bail out powers and cash to enforce recognition of losses, to take over the large banks and then to use public credit to revive the real economy, with an emphasis on investing in infrastructure and the knowledge economy. The US and British authorities adopted a more partial and less effective response.

Anglo-Saxon economics was based on the centrality of a national debt. The folly of financialization compounded this with massive levels of personal and finance-sector debt. The states that thrive today are those which balance a public debt with a sizeable – often larger – publicly managed pool of assets, like Norway's State Pension Fund, Australia's Future Fund, Singapore's Provident fund, or Sweden's national research foundations, established in 1992 with the assets of social funds set up a decade earlier with the proceeds of a levy on corporations.

While the term 'grey capitalism' draws attention to the lack of accountability and transparency in the financial and corporate worlds it remains to explain how collective social funds could be organized in a way that would help to cover future social expenditure on pensions and health. Firstly they would have to be universal in character. Serious resources could be raised by exacting a share levy on all corporations equivalent to 10 per cent of the profits each year. Companies could discharge this obligation simply by issuing new shares, without any need to subtract from their cash-flow. The shares would not be sold but held to generate future dividend income (which is less volatile than share price). Rudolf Meidner, architect of the Swedish welfare state, urged arrangements of this sort to foster agencies of economic self-government as well as supplementary pensions (Blackburn 2006b: 245–9, 272–99).

The purposes and nature of the fund would be laid down in legislation and monitors established to see that they were strictly adhered to. For example the funds should only be used for the paying of pensions and that these should reflect common criteria across the system. I have elsewhere suggested that the funds should constitute a regional network within and between states. The management boards of these funds would be elected at regular intervals. They would have some scope in the use of the investment income accruing to the fund and would have to explain this to the citizens of their region. They would be allowed to – even encouraged to – vote the shares they held at AGMs. This would allow them to pursue policies on carefully chosen topics, such as executive remuneration, energy use or labour contract norms.

The privatized model of pensions provision has been engulfed by the onset of the credit crunch. Tens of millions have been persuaded to invest in commercially-managed schemes that have lost much of their value. Recession and/or unemployment has forced many to raid their savings to meet current living expenses. Those who run the financial services industry have been suffered a setback but show every sign of attempting to get back to 'business as usual' as soon as possible. Nevertheless the crisis has witnessed a resort to collective solutions that could point in a quite different direction. States which still have a pay-as-you-go system of pension finance will want to protect it. Even before the ravages of the credit crunch were clear the government of Chile, responding to a public campaign, moved to restore a modest, non-contributory public 'solidarity' pension to those with no pension entitlement, financed by taxation. In many countries, including the US, it no longer seems wise to denounce PAYGO as 'unsustainable' when all that is meant is that it can supply 80 or 90 per cent of pension needs, not one hundred per cent. The restoration or continuation of PAYGO will make a huge contribution to meeting ageing costs but social funds financed by taxes on capital could furnish a useful supplement.

The recession, aggravated by the credit crunch, will deliver a heavy hit to the pension funds; the yield of PAYGO schemes will also drop, but less drastically. *Global Pensions* cited a study estimating that US pension fund of all types had lost $3.4 trillion – $2 trillion for the DC schemes and £1.8 trillion for the DB schemes – between January and October 2008 (Legorano 2008). The shock to non-US funds could be larger or smaller depending on their portfolio and currency. As the recession shrinks the labour force and earnings, the yield of PAYGO pension systems will also be reduced. The answer is to find measures that restore the health of the economy and to introduce efficient and benign taxes that pump extra resources into the pension systems. Poverty helped to create the credit crunch, both the domestic poverty of subprime borrowers and the low earnings of China's workers and farmers, since the latter led to huge global imbalances (Blackburn 2008, Turner 2008, Glyn 2006). A well-balanced pension regime could contribute to re-distribution and better governance, helping to mobilise investment resources in needed directions.

Following the credit crunch the siren song of privatization is now likely to be muted. However it would be foolish to suppose that schemes of implicit or explicit privatization will not again be pressed as solutions to the pensions crisis. Such proposals are backed by powerful lobbies and will not disappear until the underlying pension challenge has been met.

Acknowledgements

I would like to thank Matthieu Leimgruber and Manuel Riesco for comments on an earlier draft. They are not, of course, responsible for my errors or interpretations.

References

Blackburn, Robin 2002 *Banking on Death or Investing in Life: The History and Future of Pensions*, London: Verso.

——2005 ' Capital and Social Europe', *New Left Review*, no. 34, July–August.

——2006a 'Finance and the Fourth Dimension', *New Left Review*, no. 39, May–June.

——2006b *Age Shock: How Finance Is Failing Us*, London: Verso.

——2007 'The Case for a Global Pension', *New Left Review*, no. 47, November–December.

——2008 'The Credit Crunch', *New Left Review*, no. 50, March–April.

Bogle, John 2005 *The Battle for the Soul of Capitalism*, New Haven, CT: Yale University Press.

Boltho, Andrea 2003 'What's Wrong With Europe?', *New Left Review*, no. 23, July–August.

Brenner, Robert 2006 *The Economics of Global Turbulence*, London: Verso.

Castles, Francis 2004 *The Future of the Welfare State: Crisis Myths and Crisis Realities*, Oxford: Oxford University Press.

Directorate-General for Economic and Social Affairs 2002 'Germany's Growth Performance in the 1990s', Economic Paper no. 170, May.

Directorate-General for Economic and Financial Affairs, 2003 'European Commission', Economic Paper no. 183, May.

Ecclestone, Bernard 1989 *State and Society in Postwar Japan*, Oxford: Wiley.

Economic Policy Committee and the European Commission, Directorate General for Economic and Financial Affairs, 2006 *The Impact of Ageing on Government Expenditure: Projections for the EU25 Member States on Pensions, Health Care, Long term Care, Education and Unemployment Transfers*, Brussels.

Ferguson, Niall 2008 *The Ascent of Money: A Financial History of the World*, London: Allen Lane.

Ferrara, Peter 1985 *Social Security: Prospects for Real Reform*, Washington, DC: Cato Institute.

Friedman, Milton and Rose 1980 *Free to Choose*, New York: Harvest Books.

Giddens, Anthony 1997 *The Third Way*, Cambridge: Polity.

Glyn, Andrew 2006 *Capitalism Unleashed*, Oxford: Oxford University Press.

Hacker, Jacob 2002 *The Divided Welfare State: The Battle over Public and Private Benefits in the United States*, Cambridge.

Hill, Michael and Lian Kwen 1995 *The Politics of Nation-Building in Singapore*, London: Routledge.

Holzmann, Robert 2001, 'World Bank Supports Pension Reforms', *Financial Times*, 11 July.

Institutional Investor, 2000 'The Stalled Promise of European Pension Reform', February.

Legorano, Giovanni 2008 'US Schemes Hit by 3.9 trillion Losses Equity Fall', *Global Pensions*, 23 October.

Leimgruber, Matthieu 2008 *Solidarity Without the State? Business and the Shaping of the Swiss Welfare State, 1890–2000*, Cambridge: Cambridge University Press.

Math, Antoine 2004 'The Impact of Pension Reforms on Older People's Income', in Gerard Hughes and Jim Stewart (eds), *Reforming Pensions in Europe: Evolution of Pension Financing and Sources of Retirement Income*, Cheltenham: Edward Elgar, pp. 105–38.

Monks, Robert 2001 *New Global Investors*, Oxford: Capstone.

Ney, Stephen 2000 'Are You Sitting Comfortably. … Then We'll Begin: Three Gripping Stories About Pension Reform', *Innovation*, vol. 13, no. 4, December, pp. 341–71.

Orenstein, Mitchell 2008 *Privatizing Pensions: The Transnational Campaign for Social Security Reform*, Princeton: Princeton University Press.

Pensions Commission 2004 *Pensions: Challenges and Choices: the First Report*, London.

Pierson, Paul 1995 *Dismantling the Welfare State?* Cambridge: Cambridge University Press.

Reinhardt, Uwe 2001 'On the Apocalypse of the Retiring Baby Boom', *Aging/Vieillissement*, Summer Toronto, Canada.

Riesco, Manuel 2007 *Se Derrumba Un Mito*, CENDA Santiago (Chile).

Stiglitz, Joseph and Orzsag, Peter 2001 'Ten Myths About Social Security 2001', in Robert Holzmann and Joseph Stiglitz (eds), *New Ideas About Old Age Security*, World Bank, Washington, DC.

Stiglitz, Joseph 2002 *Globalization and its Discontents*, New York: Penguin.

Samuelson, Paul 1958 'An Exact Consumption-Loan Model of Interest, With or Without the Social Contrivance of Money', *Journal of Political Economy*, December.

Turner, Graham 2008 *The Credit Crunch*, London: Pluto.

UN Population Division 2006, *World Population Prospects*, New York.

United Nations 2007 *Development in an Aging World*, New York.

Useem, Michael 1996 *Investor Capitalism: How Money Managers Are Changing the Face of Corporate America*, New York: Basic Books.

Watson Wyatt, 2008 *The World's 300 largest Pension Funds*, October.

World Bank 1994 *Averting the Old Age Crisis: Policies to Protect the Old and Promote Growth*, Washington, DC.

Part III

New institutions and cultures

20

Popular culture, fans, and globalization

Cornel Sandvoss

Introduction

Few aspects of contemporary everyday life capture the imagination of scholars of globalization as much as global media events. The Football World Cup, Olympic Games, the Wimbledon Lawn Tennis Championships, the Super Bowl or the Eurovision Song Contest in their seemingly exceptional and spectacular, yet in their sum almost quotidian nature, evoke passion, enthusiasm, and committed consumption among audiences across the globe. Box office hits such as the *Lord of the Rings* and *Star Wars*, internationally distributed and franchised television shows from *24* to various casting and reality shows have led to a convergence of audiences' viewing practices and experiences across different global regions. The images of stars and celebrities—from John Lennon, who notoriously proclaimed to be more famous than Jesus, to Mohammed Ali and David Beckham—are among the cultural resources that enjoy widespread transnational recognition and adoration.

Global communication, then, more often than not is *popular* communication. While 24-hours news channels such as CNN or more recently Al Jazeera are frequently identified as iconic examples of the globalization of communication, media genres such as sports, music and film have attracted much larger global audiences. This chapter explores the premises and consequences of these audiences' individual and collective participation in popular culture and popular media in their transnational and global distribution.

Modernity and popular culture

Most research on popular culture and its consumption is of a contemporary nature, focusing on the study of popular culture as media culture, tied to the rise of audiovisual and broadcast media. However, the interplay between popular culture and globalization is rooted in the shared social, cultural, and economic premises that inherently tie leisure and popular culture to the macro transformations of everyday life in global modernity.

In this context it is important to distinguish between free time and our modern understanding of leisure. While agricultural life of the middle ages was marked by an acute lack of geographical and social mobility and occasional hardships resulting out of crop failures, epidemics or war, the population in pre-industrial societies had considerable amounts of free-time at their disposal, as rhythms of work were determined by the cycles of agricultural production and dependent on weather conditions and daylight hours. The home was generally a centre of production rather than recreation. Work and leisure thus lacked a sharp differentiation in a spatial and a temporal sense. Popular recreational practices during this time such as rambling or what in retrospect became known as "folk football" remained largely unstructured in terms of time, place, and participation. Folk football, for instance, was played between whole villages in which the aim was generally to carry a filled pig's bladder into the opposing village. The game was played on the open land between villages, the time of play was limited only by daylight hours and participation was left open to all villagers not deterred by the general absence of rules which made homicides a not uncommon occurrence at such events.

Such practices stand in sharp contrast to modern sports that first developed in early modern institutions such as private schools and universities and that accelerated in their diffusion in the second half of the nineteenth century, corresponding with the demands of modern industrial life: the proliferation of clock-regulated industrial labor introduced a sharp division between work and free time; the rise of capitalism fuelled the growing commodification of place in many European countries, putting formerly public recreational spaces into private ownership. The rapidly progressing urbanization through the nineteenth century in turn resulted in new levels of population density in industrial centers. In these overcrowded living conditions and with the gradual reduction of working hours in industrial employment (a consequence of the growing leverage of increasing demand for skilled labor as industrial production increased in complexity) distinct times and spaces of leisure consumption emerged: alongside parks, museums, and public houses, theatres, stadia, and later cinemas became popular recreational venues.

These transformation in the experience of time and place as part of the process that Giddens (1990) has summarized as time–space distanciation, have themselves been identified as important aspects in the nexus of modernity and globalization. Patterns of daily life becoming regulated by clock time thus allowed for the rise of standardized and centralized forms of leisure. Alongside the transformations of time and space—with the modern differentiation between work/leisure time and public/private space—new forms of entertainment such as sports, theatre or film introduced a third divide that mirrored the new regimes of industrial production: the Taylorist divide between participant and spectator. In the commercial logic of capitalism this separation between actor and spectator thus inevitably translated into a distinction between producer and consumer, and defined leisure as a sphere of consumption and a field of tension between the increasingly industrial production of popular entertainment by the cultural industries and their consumption. In sports the logic of this distinction, formalized in the rules implemented by the emerging, national sports governing bodies, allowed for the professionalization of sport in Europe and North America from the 1860s onwards. Similarly, Dan Cavicchi (2007: 237) observes in his study of nineteenth-century music lovers in North America that while "before 1800, music had primarily existed either as a private amateur pastime, made among friends and family, or as an elaborate public ritual, either in street performances in street parades or church services," soon "concerts and public performances, especially, segmented musical experiences into distinct phases of production (composition), distribution (performance), and consumption (listening)."

While popular culture was thus initially situated in local, physically manifest contexts, the divide between spectators and participants from its beginning facilitated the link between the local and the distant: museums such as the British Museum, opened in 1753, put on show artefacts from overseas locations; professional theatre companies and orchestras toured from town to town; and professional sport clubs moved from the recruitment of players from the vicinity of the club to attracting talent from ever further afield as the introduction of gate money and players' salaries created incentives for professional athletes to migrate in the pursuit of their sporting careers.

The centralization of leisure in urban markets giving rise to mass audiences and (communal) mass consumption was thus not only embedded in but also contributed to the advancement of complex administrative, economic, and social dependencies across space. On the one hand, the diffusion of modern sports such as football throughout the home nations, Europe and subsequently America, Asia, and Australia thus followed the routes of emerging international trade and of emigration from Europe. One the other, football's international diffusion became itself an agent of globalization and its sub-processes such as hybridization as these migrant populations became founding members of clubs that were soon transformed into focal points of local and regional identities. This role of modern sports as both consequence and driving force of globalization is in turn reflective of principles of modernization and rationalization, in particular through the agency of Protestant entrepreneurs and of those in technical professions of the middle classes. As Stephen Wagg (1995: 104) argues: "in general it can be assumed that, in each country, the growing power of urban, industrial middle-class was a factor in the spread of the game; indeed, the zeal of bourgeois figures to promote a rationalized, codified competitive game and their related concern to displace political energies have become the conventions of sports history."

Despite its territorial focus centralized forms of urban popular entertainment thus deepened the connectivity of local cultural practices to wider, international and transnational transformations and frames of reference. Not only were popular high-modern recreational practices shaped by the multiple influences and traditions of migrant populations—such as America's national pastime baseball, based on the English public school game of rounders—but such practices also offered experiences of and encounters with the distant Other through play, music, sound, and vision. World Exhibitions offered urban masses first glimpses at distant urban centers and countries, as well as often leaving a legacy of local landmarks positioning cities within an emerging network of global centers such as London's Crystal Palace (1851), the Eiffel Tower in Paris (1890) or the Atomium in Brussels (1958). American music lovers following the works of great European composers—themselves often mythological representations of European regions and histories such as Wagner's *Ring der Nibelungen* (completed in 1874) (loosely based on folk songs and Nordic mythologies), Rossini's *Guillaume Tell* (1829) (drawing on Friedrich Schiller's *Wilhelm Tell*) or Verdi's *La Traviata* (1853) (based on Alexandre Dumas' *La dame aux Camélias*)—sought to complement these textual encounters with journeys to the Old Continent (Cavicchi 2007).

While leisurely travel to distant places encountered in and through popular culture remained the privilege of the wealthy upper middle classes until the late twentieth century, centralized urban leisure established a mode of engagement with those geographically distant through sporting competitions, music, and theatre, that laid the fundament for the subsequent rise of mass media such as the press and broadcast media. As Cavicchi (2007: 236) concludes: "music lovers not only transformed America's musical life, setting the ground for late-nineteenth-century music business based on listening technologies like the phonograph, but also produced models for cultural consumption that would be adopted and extended in twentieth-century mass culture, particularly by those we today call fans." Nineteenth-century urban leisure markets thus reflected and advanced forces of the rational reorganization of everyday life and of the increasing interconnectivity of cultural practices and experiences that were to excel in the subsequent phase of decentralization, suburbanization, and mediation.

The modern home, national broadcasting, and community

Modern popular culture and entertainment thus laid the social and cultural grounds for the rise of what Raymond Williams (Williams, 1974: 26) aptly described as "mobile privatization," reflecting "the two apparently paradoxical yet deeply connected tendencies of modern urban industrial living: on the one hand mobility, on the other hand the more apparently self-sufficient family home." With the migration of urban populations to the suburbs, driven by both the intolerably cramped conditions of urban housing and the rise of affordable mass transportation technologies, the focus of leisure and recreation shifted from public, urban spaces to the private home. However, the privatization and individualization of popular culture did not lead to the disappearance of communities, but their profound transformation. Centralized urban leisure had set in motion the formation of mass audiences and thus provided a frame for the emergence of modern communities that were no longer primarily based on kinship, face-to-face interaction and economic dependency. With the proliferation of regional and national, rather than local, newspapers and of broadcasting technologies, the frame against which these communities in the consumption of popular culture were constructed shifted from the local to the national, mirroring the shift from urban leisure to national broadcast markets.

The decentralization of audiences in mass communication was mirrored by the centralization of institutional power and control as popular entertainment shifted from physical venues to electronic media. In most European countries the broadcasting monopoly of public service broadcasters tied broadcasting to the institutional power of the nation state. In the United States, networks, while commercial and marked by greater local differentiation, also led to the establishment of a national broadcasting market.

Various writers and broadcast historians have explored the power of popular entertainment in creating national communities and a sense of national belonging (see, for example, Scannell 1996). In Britain annual events such as the Cambridge–Oxford Boat Race or the FA Cup Final were turned into national events and spectacles around which a sense of national cohesion and belonging was built. Live broadcasts were commonly complemented with a national diet of magazine formats such as *Grandstand* and *Sportsview* that corresponded with the gendered, domestic leisure pattern of the Fordist, suburban weekend. In addition to relaying forms of *in situ* entertainment such as sport, theatre or opera into the homes of audiences, radio and television also developed genres and textual formats distinctly tied to the centralized and quotidian nature of broadcasting: serial drama, often known as soap operas, quiz shows, talk shows, cooking and lifestyle programs. Such broadcast entertainment promoted popular texts shared within a distinctly national frame and often unknown beyond the frontiers of national broadcasting. Broadcast entertainment thus offered both unity and synchronicity of experience on a national level (cf. Morley 2000).

While national broadcast entertainment has been a crucial agent in building a shared national cultural horizon, mediated popular culture has nevertheless been tied to forces and process of globalization throughout the era of national broadcasting in three important respects.

First, while broadcast channels and networks operated largely on a national level until the 1980s, television programming outside the United States has generally drawn on a mixture of domestic, imported, and coproduced programming. Australian game shows, English crime drama, Czech children's television or Japanese animation all frequently featured in the schedules of different national broadcasters around the world. Similarly, in less regulated media sectors, distinctly international industries and markets developed from their outset, with Hollywood studios playing a central role in international film production and distribution since the 1920s (see Chapter 21).

Second, the elevation of popular entertainment to the national level through broadcasting accelerated the process of deterritoialization of (popular) culture and constituted a further manifestation of cultural globalization rather than its antithesis. Broadcasting elevated musicians, entertainers, athletes, and actors to levels of national recognition. The popularity of these cultural texts and icons was thus tied to their mediation and its frontiers—frontiers that only temporarily coincided with the nation state as a manifestation of the mercantile forces of high modernity. With the decline of the economic-regulatory power of the nation state in the late twentieth century, these frontiers of broadcasting have both broadened and fragmented.

Third, the work of broadcast historians emphasizing the merits of particularly European public–service broadcasting in building national cohesion, communities, and sociability have attracted substantive criticism. As Morley (2000) notes in his critique of Scannell's work emphasizing the seemingly unpolitical patterns of daily broadcast entertainment, mediated popular culture carried a mode of address that was far from equal in its invitation to members of different social, ethnic, and class groups to be part of the audience and by extension the national community. Migrant populations in particular often expressed a distinct feeling of exclusion from the programming diet of national broadcasters.

Communities below and beyond the nation

This third point raises a further concern in the academic analysis of popular culture within and beyond the nation state. Hitherto I have treated the notion of popular culture synonymously to the realms of mass entertainment, recreation, and leisure. In Cultural Studies, however, the term has been used in a narrower, on occasion normative sense that describes the realm of the popular as a space of resistance and emancipation for disempowered sections of society. According to John Fiske (1992) in the realm of popular culture strategies of the "power bloc" these are countered by the tactics of the weak through acts of negotiation and appropriation in which mass culture is transformed and derives significance to its consumers in the act of consumption itself ("audience activity").

While recent work in audience studies has sought to move beyond Fiske's bipolar model of power in popular culture as accounting insufficiently for the complexity of power in contemporary culture, it does raise the important question of the relationship and discontinuities between media production and consumption that inform processes of cultural globalization. As Lynn Clark (2005: 154) notes, while the tension between conceptualizations of the audience as active, empowered agents on the one hand and as ideologically shaped on the other remains at the heart of popular communication research (reflecting the fundamental question of the interplay between structure and agency), "globalization has made necessary a reconceptualization of the relation among media, audiences, and power" as their interplay has shifted from the national to transnational levels.

This interplay between media industries and audiences of popular media texts has impacted on the formation of communities underneath and beyond the nation state. Beyond the nation state, the deregulation of broadcast markets across Europe and much of the developed world since the early 1980s has aided the further concentration of media industries reflected in the rise of a small group of transnational media corporations (TNCs) such as Time Warner, Disney, Viacom, Bertelsmann, and News Corporation. Reflecting the political forces of neo-liberalism, international free trade agreements have offered these TNCs increased access to local and national markets beyond the core of Anglo-American media production. The growing presence of primarily American programming in different national markets has fuelled the rise of the Cultural Imperialism thesis in mass communication scholarship (for a detailed discussion see Tomlinson 1999). While highlighting significant inequalities in the distribution of means of cultural production and in access to international markets, such work has tended to give insufficient attention to audiences and their ability to appropriate, or what in the context of global communication Morley (1991) labels as "indigenize," cultural texts. A range of studies of the local appropriation of American media texts in regions and nations on the semi-periphery or periphery of global economic relations has thus highlighted the role of local audiences in processes of cultural globalization. The simultaneous forces of globalization and localization are, for instance, usefully documented in Daniel Miller's (1992) study of the appropriation of the CBS produced daily soap *The Young and the Restless* in Trinidad. Miller (1992), an anthropologist, was confronted with the enormous popularity of the show amongst local residents while conducting fieldwork on the island. On the surface, the success of an American daytime soap in the Caribbean state would appear to confirm charges of Americanization and Cultural Imperialism. Yet, Miller carefully documents how the reading and appropriation of the show was embedded in local cultural practices and social norms, echoing in particular motives of transgression and subversion equally evident in the local popularity of bacchanal. Viewers' talk accordingly centered on different themes of scandal and transgression in the show and served as a vehicle to evaluate social and interpersonal relations among its Trinidadian audience. In turn, these themes were reworked into local cultural forms such as a Calypso dedicated to the show. In documenting the hybridity of cultural forms—both bacchanal and Calypso being reflections of the multiple cultural and migratory influences on the island—Miller not only implicitly marks Trinidad out as a suitable space to study and anticipate the consequences of cultural globalization but also puts into question notions of local and national authenticity. Miller's study thus informs Morley's (1991: 9–10) claim "that the 'local' is not to be considered as an Indigenous source of cultural identity, which remains 'authentic' only in so far as it is unsullied by contact with the global. Rather, the 'local' is itself often produced by means of the 'indigenization' of global resources and inputs," an assessment equally applicable to the international diffusion of other popular cultural practices.

However, while *The Young and The Restless* attracted large audiences in Trinidad (Miller estimates ratings in excess of 70 percent), the show was more popular among the island's lower income population. The varying popularity of an internationally distributed programme within a local or national market, again reveals the limits of inclusivity in national popular, mediated cultures. Transnational networks and imported television have thus enjoyed particular popularity among the many communities underrepresented in the visions of nationhood by national broadcasters such as ethnic minorities (for a useful summary of such studies see, Morley 2000) or those disempowered on counts of class, age or gender. If the national community was thus imagined through shared practices of (popular) media consumption, the increased availability of mediated, symbolic resources within national media markets allowed for the formation of new communities. Yet such communities emerged not only through the international distribution of television programming, but also below the level of the nation state. Since the late 1980s one of the fastest growing fields within popular communication research has been the study of fan audiences. Scholars such as Henry Jenkins, Camille Bacon Smith, and Janice Radway in their study of popular North American media texts such as *Star Trek*, *The Beauty and the Beast* or romance novels have all documented the formation of fan audiences as fan communities in which viewers who tend to feel marginalized within "official" (national) culture find a rallying point in their affection for particular media texts.

Yet, whether such cultural practices are shared subculturally, nationally or transnationally does not render them more or less "authentic" as they, first, are all based on (deterritorializing) media consumption and, second, authenticity inadequately accounts for the inherent hybridity in the formulation of local and national cultures. Neither, to return to Fiske's bipolar model of power in popular communication, can national nor transnational fan communities be identified as emancipatory *per se*. While many studies of fan communities have emphasized their formation vis-à-vis existing power blocks, local appropriation of transnational media texts can equally support the interests of local elites. While, for instance, fandom of European soccer in the United States has thrived in particular among Hispanic migrant communities and internationally minded urban liberals, in South Africa support of European and in particular English clubs serves a marker of cultural distinction for white South Africans distancing themselves from the local game cherished by the country's black majority (Sandvoss 2003). To explore the complex fields of power in global popular culture, we therefore need to shift our attention from the macro (media industries and audience communities), to the micro in the interrelation between popular media, identity, and the self (consumers and fans).

Fans, self, and transnational media

Globalization theory is centrally concerned with the growing distanciation of economic, social, political, and cultural relations and thus processes of deterritoialization; it traces the widening gap between physical space on the one hand and social and cultural space on the other. The same process of distanciation is central to the proliferation of popular culture in modernity documented in this chapter. Both processes are driven by the international diffusion of industrialism and (consumer) capitalism. Moreover, as a non-reductive theory (see introduction), globalization theory has acknowledged the importance of social and cultural practices not unrelated to—and in many ways closely framed by—but not solely predetermined by economic causes. The study of popular culture has focused on precisely these processes and on the "soft" experiences and emotions in and through which media audiences relate to others in a globalizing world: affection, belonging, identification, and identity. The remainder of this chapter therefore explores how the participants in popular culture, those we commonly call "fans," engage with and relate to distant Others.

In a contribution that broke with the established conceptual canon of fans studies but usefully situates media fandom within the wider analysis of modernity, John Thompson (1995) has described the relationship between media consumers, fans, and their favorite stars as a form of "mediated quasi interaction." According to Thompson the intimate bond between fans and stars rests on media fans' ability to meaningfully appropriate the star text to the individuals' experiences and demands of everyday life in industrial modernity. Mediated personae, in Thompson's words (1995: 219) "can be slotted into the time-space niches of one's life more or less at will. They are regular and dependable companions." The affective engagement in popular culture is thus not only aided but premised on mediated distance. It is non-reciprocal intimacy at a distance that enables fandom: "the non-reciprocal character of mediated relationships does not imply that recipients are at the mercy of distant others […] on the very contrary that others are not situated in the same spatial-temporal locales as recipients, and are not normally in face-to-face interaction with recipients, means that recipients have a great deal of leeway in shaping the kind of relationship they wish to establish and sustain with distant others" (Thompson: 1995: 220). Thompson illustrates this point with extracts from Vermorel and Vermorel's (1985) extensive collection of fan letters and testimonies, in which a 42-year-old female fan of Barry Manilow, Joanne, describes how the singer offers a counterpoint to the uncertainties and frustrations of her own everyday life and in Joanne's fantasies serves as a parallel romantic relationship that helps her to overcome the shortcomings of her own marriage. Thompson thus links fandom back to an understanding of mass communication in modernity that evokes Giddens' (1990) analysis of modern life. "Being a fan," in this sense, "is one way of reflexively organizing the self and its day-to-day conduct" (Thompson 1995: 222). More specifically it is linked to mediated distance as Thompson (1995:221) concludes that Manilow is "a malleable object of affection who can be summoned upon more or less at will", precisely because he is "a distant other encountered primarily through the media."

The process of distanciation through mediation at the heart of cultural globalization—which conversely is based on establishing textual proximity to the socially, culturally or geographically distant Other—is thus integral to building attachments and affection in popular culture. Notably, those media that are most closely associated with globalization—electronic and broadcast media—are also those through which affective bonds with distant Others in fandom are facilitated. Yet, the distancing between actor/performer and consumer/fans is a premise, but not a sufficient explanation for the emergence of fan cultures within and across local and national media cultures. Thompson's (1995) *en passe* treatment of fandom in his wider analysis of mass communication thus reveals important structural conditions of fandom, yet does not progress substantially beyond a uses and gratifications approach in explaining how and why fandom has grown into a prevalent mode of media consumption.

In drawing on examples of fans adoring a star of their choice to the extent that they profess to the star entering their romantic imagination, Thompson inadvertently also invites the pathologizing of fans, his analysis seeks to dismiss (for a detailed representation of fans in academic discourses see Hills 2002). Desires for sexual intimacy certainly play a role in popular media consumption as even the most unsystematic survey of contemporary celebrity coverage or music videos will confirm. Moreover, all regional variation in morality and sexual norms alike, such desires appear among the most universal and consistent motivations in the consumption of popular culture on a global scale. However, they easily obstruct other profound articulations of attachment and belonging in transnational media fandom. Take the following two accounts from fans of different popular texts and icons: a US soldier and *Star Wars* fan stationed in South Korea and a Bruce Springsteen as well as sports fan from Massachusetts:

> Here in South Korea, the US army has a programme that lets Korean soldiers join the ranks of the US Army [. …] I was walking down with one the other day and

passed a *Phantom Menace* poster. [He] told me I should go and see the movie because it was great. As his English was not too good, I started to explain to him that I was a huge *Star Was* fan […] we ended up trading several different collectibles and have been good friends ever since.

(Jacob Neher, quoted in Brooker 2002: 26)

I am attached to [Bruce Springsteen's music]. Like the sports teams, here [in New England]. Like Fenway Park, like the Celtics. I mean, I feel the same way about them as I do about Bruce Springsteen. It's something that I'll never change; it will always be apart of my makeup, a part of what I am about a little bit.

(Andy Sirk, quoted in Cavicchi: 1998: 134)

These extracts both reflect the dual sense of ownership and sharing in fandom as an act that positions the media consumers' self in the modern world by creating a sense of belonging, attachment, and community in ways that reflect the challenges on the modern self. They indicate how, as media audiences' lifeworlds are increasingly phantasmagoric, the affective consumption of popular media has taken on three interrelated functions that have allowed media consumers to manage and sometimes utilize disembedding and distanciating forces: the facilitation of (a) deterritorialized communities, (b) social distinction and (c) belonging and affective attachment in a globalized world. The prevalence of these processes in turn invites a framework that shifts from a definition of globalization and modernity broadly based on Giddens' work (1990) to the recent work of Zygmunt Bauman, which has emphasized processes of individualization, marketization, and the fluidity of contemporary social and cultural relations. In a series of recent works Bauman portrays modern life as one of uncertainty at an ever accelerating pace. In Bauman's (2005: 1) words "'Liquid modern' is a society in which the conditions under which its members act change faster than it takes the ways of acting to consolidate into habits and routines." In contemporary life this liquidity is experienced both as an opportunity by the winners of the global competition driving such instability, who gain not only freedom of movement but have an ever increasing range of identity resources at their disposal, and a threat to those at the bottom of the pyramid who "cling fast to the sole identity available and to hold its bits and parts together while fighting back the abrasive forces and disruptive pressures" (Bauman 2005: 6); most of us find ourselves between these poles confronted with a mixture of these risks and opportunities.

Consumption, in turn, is the modus operandi by which these identities are articulated and transformed, whereas the varying ability to engage in acts of consumption reflects the relative multitude or lack of identity resources described by Bauman. For all the methodological and empirical limitations of Bauman's brushstroke analysis, it usefully highlights a state of flux, uncertainty and focus on the project of self, that resonate in fan consumption and its interplay with globalization.

Fan communities and deterritorialization

The forces of deterritoialization, which sees social, cultural, and economic life detached from singular, territorial space, are central to the proliferation of the liquid life Bauman describes. Yet, deterritorialization reworks, not erodes social and cultural connections. Fan communities mirror these profound changes in facilitating a spectrum of different

403

communities from tight-knit social groups based on face-to-face interaction to "imagined communities" in the mould of Anderson's (1991) analysis.

On one end of the spectrum, fans not only create meaning in the consumption of media texts ("semiotic activity"), but also engage in a range of further activities as part of their fandom. Fiske (1992) describes these as "enunciative" and "textual productivity." Enunciative productivity describes the interactions between different fans—the so called water-cooler moment of discussing one's favorite TV show in the office, the chat and banter between season ticket holders at sports events, the mingling at music festivals or the avid discussions in fan fora online. While these communities form around a shared object of fandom, they over time function as actual social networks. These networks also serve as spaces in which fans' can circulate their own "textual productivity": fan fiction such as so-called slash writing, fanzines, mash-ups, re-edits of favorite films or blogs.

The role of fan consumption in establishing such networks is maybe best captured by the rapidly expanding social networking site Facebook. Facebook allows for two types of social relations: either to be "a friend" of another Facebook user or to be "a fan" of a given popular texts or icon. Echoing Thompson's notion of non-reciprocal intimacy, the first requires confirmation by those considered to be a friend, while becoming a fan is a one-way process open to all users. Yet, the latter still results in group memberships in which we are likely to interact with other users who eventually may also become "friends." The rise of the world wide web as a virtual space for the formation of such communities in turn reflects the deterritoialization of social networks, although the technological advancement of communication technologies and formats such as the internet and social networking sites is driven by the increasing need for such spaces that arise out of the international distribution of popular music, sports, film, and TV programs.

Of course not all fans engage in textual and enunciative productivity in equal measure. Many follow their object of fandom without ever joining formal or informal networks. Abercrombie and Longhurst (1998) offer a useful typology of fans that correlates such levels of activity with levels of engagement with social networks and the specificity of media use. At the one end of this spectrum we find the fan who engages with the fan text largely through mainstream mass media yet spends little time interacting with other fans. On the other end, fans are embedded in close social networks and their object of fandom often shifts from the mainstream media texts to their own activity and productivity.

Yet whether fans are part of close social networks forming "interpretive communities" or whether their engagement with their object of fandom remains largely solitary, all fans are part of a wider, imagined community centering around a given fan object. When sport fans resort to the categorized "we" in talking about their favorite team, most include themselves, the team and their fellow supporters (those that are part of their social network as much as those they have never and will never meet) within this imagined community. Such imagined communities in sports fandom have historically evolved along the territorial and institutional lines of the nation state, in particular in nominally amateur sporting events based on the participation of national federations. Thus even global events such as Olympic games—take for example the 2002 Winter Olympics in Salt Lake City in which a torn flag alleged to have been rescued from the World Trade Center after the September 11 attacks was presented at the opening ceremony or the Beijing Olympics with its extravagant displays of Chinese economic and developmental success, offer spaces of national identification to national and diasporic communities (Sandvoss 2003). Yet, sports consumption has increasingly moved beyond national frames in building transnational fan communities: in major professional sports such as football the increasing migration of athletes in a global market place has reworked and shifted allegiances as leading clubs field international teams attracting a transnational following. The English Premier League teams, for instance, attract lively fan communities from Scandinavia to South East and East Asia—the later having become a regular stop in preseason preparations of many big European teams seeking to cater to (and profit from) these emerging transnational fan communities. At the same time, fans in economic centers of the global sports market have responded to the international makeup of the teams they support by frequently putting "club before country," in other words privileging the simultaneously local and transnational fan community of their favorite team over allegiances to the nation state and its sporting representatives. Similarly, Cavicchi (1998: 161) describes a distinct feeling of a community—"a sense of belonging together" among Bruce Springsteen fans both in the US as well as among those from around the world. From Elvis to Michael Jordan, from horror films to Japanese Anime, a range of cultural texts and icons have served as the focal point for these imagined communities beyond the nation state.

The communities of fans that emerge around a variety of popular texts, whether produced locally or imported from other countries (and more often than not the United States), thus take on important roles in fans' self-understanding and identity. Notably, these communities are not more or less "real" or authentic than earlier modern communities centering on the nation state. Both, for their sheer size, are necessarily imagined, yet both are real in their consequences. Neither does the question of how deterritorialized they are determine their authenticity. As Tomlinson (1999: 149) notes, rather than ever further separating lifeworlds from physical spaces, deterritoialization is limited by "the simple but important fact that we are all, as human beings, *embodied and physically located*. In this fundamental material sense the ties of culture to location can never be completely severed [...] So deterritorialization cannot ultimately mean the end of locality, but its transformation into a more complex cultural space." Thus, even deterritorialized fan communities are manifested locally. The globalization of the distribution of popular media has equally driven non-mediated events: the rise of file-sharing has led to a rise in attendance at concerts and music festivals. Many sports such as football or baseball have seen their growing exposure on television matched by increasing numbers of *in situ* spectators. Similarly, recent fan studies have documented the rise of fan pilgrimages in which fans, often from far afield, visit the sites in which their favorite film or show is produced or celebrities live. Graceland for Elvis fans, the streets of Vancouver for X-Files fans, and the guided Sopranos Tour of New Jersey all are evidence of fans' wish to experience their fan text and their fellow fans not only in textual, potentially global but also physical, local place (cf. Sandvoss 2005).

The difference between these fan communities and early modern, national communities is thus not one of authenticity, but that fan communities are *elective*. As opposed to national or pre-modern communities, they reflect individual preferences allowing fans to articulate different aspects of their identity through their participation in popular culture. Equally, in elective communities membership can cease or change over time; though many fans display loyalty to their object of fandom. Here fan's engagement with popular culture diverges from the ephemeral of nature of consumption upon which Bauman's account of liquid modernity rests in two important respects: first, fan consumption not only articulates increasingly liquid identities and community memberships, but also the ways in which consumers through acts of agency seek to re-create stable points of references and group membership in a liquid world; second, while fan communities are elective, our initial choice of object of fandom, for all its seeming idiosyncrasies, is not coincidental.

Social distinction and transnational popular culture

Fan communities, as with all social groups, are based on inclusion and exclusion. In the increasing cultural interconnectivity of globalization, fans' participation in selected aspects of popular culture thus not only enable fans' membership of networks and communities but also becomes a tool of both deliberate and inadvertent distinction. A number of studies of fan communities and subcultures since the early 1990s have therefore turned to Pierre Bourdieu's (1984) influential sociology of consumption in which he identifies taste as structured by the habitus—itself a structuring and structured structure. Bourdieu identifies the habitus as an articulation of individuals' position in his multidimensional model of class based on economic, social, and cultural capital. Subsequent work has sought to extend this focus by arguing for the inclusion of age, gender, and ethnicity alongside class as lines of distinction articulated through (media) consumption. In these studies Bourdieu's model serves to explain fans' choices of their fan object as an articulation and reinforcement of their relative socio-demographic position, as Lynn Thomas's (2002) study of listeners to the daily British radio soap *The Archers* and the TV crime drama *Inspector Morse* suggests.

While most of this work has followed Bourdieu in drawing on an implicitly national frame within which such distinctions of class are drawn, social and cultural globalization in the form of migration and symbolic exchange have increasingly broadened the points of reference against which our fan consumption serves as an articulation of difference. As class itself moves beyond the nation state in the emergence of a transnational capitalist class (Sklair 2001) so does the habitus. Sports such as golf or yachting, for instance, attract fan audiences which are distinctly international, but rather more coherent with regard to other socio-demographic factors such as economic capital. Their stars, and none more than Tiger Woods, are in turn employed in marketing efforts aimed at this transnational following—note the particular prominence of advertising featuring the American golfing prodigy of distinctly mixed African, Asian, European, and native American origin, in the hubs of international business travel such as Heathrow or JFK.

Similarly, the hybrid influences of ethnicity and cultural capital across and beyond nation states are highlighted in the objects of fandom among diasporic audiences that have emerged as distinct entities in transnational media markets. The texts favored by diasporic fan cultures function as important identity resources reflecting their transnational biographies. As Punathambekar (2007: 208–9) suggests in his analysis of Bollywood and its fans, we need to "think beyond the "national" as the most important scale of identity construction" as "it has become clear that the creation of Bollywood properties— films, musical, apparel, web portals, mobile games, etc.—is an enterprise that takes place in many locations around the world, and involves people with affiliations and stakes that criss-cross varied regional, national, and diasporic boundaries."

In this sense, studies of transnational popular culture drawing on Bourdieu provide us with an important conceptual tool in understanding a seeming paradox of Bauman's account of global liquid life: the fact that despite the seeming fluidity of social and cultural relations, social and economic inequalities and hierarchies not only persist but deepen. Yet, at the same time, the intersubjective reinforcement of individual fans' position through their choice of fan object is weakening within transnational frames of popular culture, as the meaning attached to particular popular icons is subject to the local variations documented above. In light of the emergence of transnational popular culture and growing global symbolic and material exchange, the criticism of Bourdieu's work as overstating the degree to which objects of consumption assume fixed meanings appears

406

particularly apt. To fully understand how fandom in global media markets serves as a powerful form of attachment through which fans derive a sense of enjoyment as much as of belonging, we thus turn to the realm beyond the intersubjective meanings of consumption: the psychological bond between fan and fan object.

Self, identity, and belonging in fan consumption

While the focus on fan communities and on fandom as social distinction broadly mirrors the first and the second wave of empirical and conceptual approaches to the study of fans, a third wave has sought to explore the intrapersonal processes on which the engagement between fan and fan object rests: the motivations, emotions, and fantasies through which fandom is enjoyed and maintained, rather than its social function (which might be of little significance to the fan him- or herself). A first body of work has drawn on the work of object relations theory in this endeavor. Alongside the work of Melanie Klein, the notions of transitional spaces and transitional objects in the work of D.W. Winnicott (1971) have attracted particular attention in studies of fan audiences (see Harrington and Bielby 1994, and Hills 2002). Winnicott describes the developmental coping mechanisms with which the infant seeks to respond to the growing realization of its separation from the primary caregiver through an affective investment in external objects. The child discovers these objects such as teddy bears, blankets, or pillows and while experiencing them as external objects also develops a claim of ownership over them in which the object is not only found but its affective significance is created by the child (and illustrated by the distress the child suffers when the object is changed by others). The child often holds or hugs the transitional object when engaging in activities seeking to re-enact its lost state of complete nurture such as thumb sucking. The external object is thus claimed to be both part of the self and the object world. At the same time, it is also an object of play and reality testing. It thus provides a link between the self and the object world, a transitional space. It is our first affective investment into the material world beyond, if in the mould of, the primary caregiver. Given this emphasis on developmental processes that allow the forming self to engage with a complex world, it is unsurprising that Winnicott's analysis has been frequently drawn upon in recent work by social and media theorists alike. Yet, fans' engagement with popular texts possibly best replicates the function of the transitional object in the symbolic realm as the object of fandom is not only experienced as a source of (ontological) security but also of enjoyment, play, and attachment. Indeed, many fan objects such as one's favorite band or TV show are rooted in childhood media consumption and retained in adulthood.

These textual possessions thus offer a meaningful link between the self and the world as a space that is both familiar, yet reaches beyond the self, a space that is maintained through fantasy and affective investment, but that also has an external reality. The object of fandom as a transitional object thus offers a nonthreatening mode of engagement with the world as a wider cultural field. As a "textual home" fan objects thus serve as symbolic space of belonging that fills the void resulting out of the decline of the cultural predominance of the nation state and other modern institutions in liquid life. In this sense, the centrality of popular communication in building and maintaining identities beyond the nation state can hardly be overestimated. International competitions such as the Eurovision Song Contest (Sandvoss 2008) or Olympic games—all their overt performances of nationalism aside—create distinctly international transitional spaces; globally popular stars such as Elvis or Mohammed Ali or texts such as *Harry Potter* or *Lord of the Rings*, function as transitional objects which to many fans are based on transnational and transcultural readings. These fan objects thus provide a symbolic *Heimat* which is not based on territoriality and that, like fan communities, is elective.

A second conceptualization of the bond between fan and fan text in recent work on fan audiences similarly suggests that popular media texts provide an interface between audiences' selves and a (globalizing) world. If the transitional object reflects a relationship between fan and fan object marked by a claim of ownership and control ("mine"), the levels of identification and attachment displayed by many fans suggest a yet deeper engagement in which the external fan object is appropriated and misrecognized as part of self ("me")—when for instance fans of team sports speak about their favorite team, they more commonly use personal pronouns such as "us" and "we" than possessive pronouns "my" or "our" team (Sandvoss 2003). Beyond this semantic level that is more common in sports fandom than elsewhere, the degree to which appropriations of fan objects serve as a self-reflective extension of the fan's self is illustrated by the diverging, sometimes diametrically opposed readings by individual fans of the very same fan text. To use two of the examples introduced in this chapter, when football fans or fans of a musician such as Bruce Springsteen describe their fan object, they project their beliefs and experiences, expectations and hopes onto the fan object. Understanding fan consumption as an act of self-reflection thus returns us to one of the early contributions to the analysis of the role of communication in globalization, the work of Marshall McLuhan (1964). According to McLuhan (1964) electronic media function as extensions of our bodies into space (television, for example, enables us to see what is geographically distant). This extension in mediation to McLuhan constitutes a form of narcissism, in which we, just as Narcissus falling under the spell of his reflection in the water, are fascinated with our extension into the external world without, however, recognizing the source of our fascination in this unwitting (mis-)recognition of the self in the external object. In this sense, the fan's fascination with the fan object is based on a narcissistic, self-reflective bond in which the fan's attachment is rooted in projecting aspects of the self onto the fan object.

The fan object is hence experienced as a part of the fan's self (if not recognized as self-reflection). It is before this background that some fans' willingness to prioritize their fandom even over their closest interpersonal relationships can be explained. When Chelsea FC Benny proclaims that "if it comes to choosing between my wife and football, Chelsea, there would only be one winner" (quoted in Sandvoss 2003: 32) his preference for the fan object over his partner is reflective of the degree to which the former is constitutive of Benny's self and identity. In the everyday life of media consumers objects of fandom—whether they function as transitional objects or as self-reflections—thus become sources of enjoyment and stability, providing a "solid" core to fans' identity counteracting the erosion of other stable sources of identity in liquid life, including kinship and families. While marriages, for instance, are increasingly at the risk of break down, the non-reciprocal bond with the fan object provides a more stable, if never entirely secure point of reference in identity construction.

On the surface, the proliferation of media fandom therefore appears to be another articulation of individualization. The historical trajectory portrayed in this chapter indeed suggest centrifugal forces from the centralization in urban leisure markets, via decentralized suburban media consumption to mobile, individual fans who form self-reflective readings of the fan object. However, this self-reflective bond between fan and fan object should not be misinterpreted as disengagement with the object world. As McLuhan (1964) implies, the extension of self through media and in mediated texts leads to an investment of the self in the object world that makes the individual more receptive and vulnerable to the outside world. Rather, the narcissistic bond between fan and object of fandom thus evokes Marcuse's (1956) account of narcissism as the fundamental process through which the ego is integrated into the object world: the misrecognition of the self in the external object is thus the premise to affective engagement with the object world. In the music they listen to, TV shows and films they watch, sport teams they follow, actors they adore, consumers of popular culture thus find cornerstones through which their engagement with their social, cultural, and economic environment are built. And as the distribution of the mediated texts upon which most fandom rests has become increasingly transnational, bypassing the nation state on a local and global level, these attachments are themselves becoming increasingly independent of early and high-modern institutions. For contemporary fans their geographical location and their nationality are therefore only two of many identity discourses that can be drawn upon in articulating and reinforcing their identity in the consumption of popular culture.

Globalization, intertextuality, and the proliferation of fandom

The close emotional bond that fans maintain with their object of fandom—whether as a transitional object or in its self-reflective reading—establishes an interface between the micro forces of individual agency and economic, social, cultural, and technological macro transformations manifested in the globalization of cultural industries. As such the participation in popular culture through media consumption and fandom is one of the central realms of contemporary everyday life in which globalization is experienced and negotiated and impacts on individuals' conceptualization of their lifeworlds and formation of their identity. Watching television shows and formats originating in different markets, following professional sport teams that increasingly recruit players in a global labor market, listening to popular music distributed via the world wide web, media consumption offers an increasingly transnational horizon of experience.

Yet, assessing the complex power relations in this interplay between consumers and industries, between the local and the global remains a central challenge to globalization theory and popular communication research alike. In emphasizing the ephemeralness of consumption patterns and the commodification of contemporary lifeworlds through consumerism, Bauman's (2005) notion of liquid life, while capturing key transformations of identity construction in a globalizing world, fails to account for the profound affective investments made in the consumption of popular culture, in which fan consumption aims to overcome the instability of social and cultural relations. Similarly, theses of media imperialism fail to engage with the complexities of the readings of mediated texts in their local contexts, proposing a too singular model of the relationship between state power, economy, and culture. However, the emphasis on fans' agency and the role of popular culture as a realm of resistance and empowerment in Cultural Studies has frequently failed to acknowledge the degree to which practices of contemporary consumption are embedded in industrial everyday life and consumerism. The growing fandom for European football clubs in sub-Saharan Africa is not a case of cultural imperialism, but an important aspect of local culture, play, enjoyment, and dreams. Yet at the same time, the interest in the game its leading European clubs is undoubtedly part of the modernization of economic and cultural life in Africa and thus its integration into a global capitalist

409

system. In the developing world as much as in the heartlands of consumerism and transnational media production, the ability to negotiate texts, to appropriate them to local audiences groups, to participate in fan communities in which fans' own enunciative and textual productivity offers alternative discourses beyond the control of media industries, are all premised upon the separation of actor and spectator in modern leisure and the growing distanciation between text and reader through mediation.

This non-reciprocality of mediated communication at the heart of fans' ability to appropriate fan objects is advanced through the transnational distribution of media texts, often adding to the social and cultural distance across which such fan texts are read. Similarly, related processes of deregulation and convergence have further tipped the balance of power in meaning construction towards media consumers, as cultural, technological, and regulatory changes driving cultural globalization have not only transformed the distribution of media texts, but also impacted on the nature of mediated textuality itself. Recent work on the affective and emotive significance of the bond between fans and fan objects, in which the latter is conceptualized as transitional object or a form of self-reflection, suggests that fans have gained far-reaching autonomy in their reading of mediated texts, to the extent that such texts are no longer polysemic (accommodating a multiplicity of different readings) but neutrosemic, devoid of intersubjective meaning (Sandvoss 2005). The ability of fans to construct such readings is not only a result of distanciation and non-reciprocality in the consumption of transnational popular culture, but of the proliferation of intertextuality within and across popular media. Objects of fandom are not singular texts but rather textual fields that span across different media, advanced by processes such as convergence and deregulation: fans can follow their favorite star through a range of newspapers, magazines, radio and television shows, many of which are accessible globally via the internet, which also hosts non-commercial websites and blogs run by fellow fans. Out of this plethora of global intertextuality fans privilege choose certain texts over others—and thus create textual boundaries, thereby ever further shifting the balance of meaning construction on the spectrum between author/producer and reader/audience towards the latter.

Globalization in this sense is not only a process of deterritoialization and disembedding of cultural and social relations, but also of advancing cultural interconnectivity and intertextuality that drives two seemingly opposing developments: on the one hand standardization and homogenization as fan objects attract a global fan following, and of fragmentation and individualization on the other, as the meanings and identities derived from these fan objects vary widely from fan community to fan community and from fan to fan. Similarly, global popular culture and fandom evade easy evaluations as practices of hegemony or resistance as they mirror the complex and sometimes contradictory forces of localization, elective community membership, commodification, and deterritoialization. Fans often seem most embedded in the commercial logic of cultural industries, but it is precisely for their affective attachment to aspects of popular culture that they are most aware of its commercial logic and most creative in circumventing it, while nevertheless remaining firmly entrenched in the parameters of modern, globalized life. What is certain, however, is that as social and cultural relations continue to be stretched across space, as our lifeworlds become increasingly phantasmagoric, as convergence further advances the presence and availability of communication media in our everyday life, and as entertainment continues to proliferate in transnational media markets, fandom will become an increasingly important mode of engagement with the world around us—and its study an import tool in understanding of how attachment, belonging and identities are transformed in a mediated, globalizing world.

References

Abercrombie, N. and Longhurst, B. (1998) *Audiences: A Sociological Theory of Performance and Imagination*, London: Sage.

Anderson, B. (1991) *Imagined Communities*, revised edition, London: Verso.

Bauman, Z. (2005) *Liquid Life*, Cambridge: Polity Press.

Bourdieu, P. (1984) *Distinction: A Social Critique of the Judgement of Taste*, London: Routledge & Kegan Paul.

Brooker, W. (2002) *Using the Force: Creativity, Community and Star Wars Fans*, London: Continuum.

Cavicchi, C. (2007) "Between Rowdies and *Rasikas*: Rethinking Fan Activity in Indian Film Culture," in J. Gray *et al.* (eds.) *Fandom: Identities and Communities in a Mediated World*, New York: New York University Press.

Cavicchi, D. (1998) *Tramps Like Us: Music and Meaning among Springsteen Fans*, New York and Oxford: Oxford University Press.

Clark, L. (2005) "Globalizing Popular Communication Audience Research: Looking to our Sister Fields for New Directions," *Popular Communication*, 3(3): 153–66.

Fiske, J. (1992) "The Cultural Economy of Fandom," in L.A. Lewis (ed.) *The Adoring Audience*, London: Routledge.

Giddens, A. (1990) *The Consequences of Modernity*, Cambridge: Polity Press.

Harrington, C. L. and Bielby, D. (1995) *Soap Fans: Pursuing Pleasure and Making Meaning in Everyday Life*, Philadelphia: Temple University Press.

Hills, M. (2002) *Fan Cultures*, London: Routledge.

Marcuse, H. (1956/1987) *Eros and Civilization: A Philosophical Inquiry into Freud*, London: Routledge.

McLuhan, M. (1964) *Understanding Media: The Extension of Man*, London: Routledge.

Miller, D. (1992) "The Young and The Restless in Trinidad: A Case of the Local and the Global in Mass Communication," in R. Silverstone and E. Hirsch (eds) *Consuming Technologies: Media and Information in Domestic Spaces*, London: Routledge.

Morley, D. (1991) "Where the Global Meets the Local: Notes from the Sitting Room," *Screen*, 32 (1): 1–15.

——(2000) *Home Territories: Media, Mobility and Modernity*, London: Comedia, Routledge.

Punathambekar, A. (2007) "Loving Music: Listeners, Entertainments, and the Origins of Music Fandom in Nineteenth-Century America," in J. Gray *et al.* (eds.) *Fandom: Identities and Communities in a Mediated World*, New York: New York University Press.

Sandvoss, C. (2003) *A Game of Two Halves: Football, Television and Globalization*, London: Comedia, Routledge.

——(2005) *Fans: The Mirror of Consumption*, Cambridge: Polity Press.

——(2008) "One the Couch with Europe: The Eurovision Song Contest, the European Broadcast Union and Belonging in Europe," *Popular Communication: The International Journal of Media and Communication*, 6(3): 190–207.

Scannell, P. (1996) *Radio, Television and Modern Life: A Phenomenological Approach*, Oxford: Blackwell.

Sklair, L. (2001) *The Transnational Capitalist Class*, Oxford: Blackwell Publishing.

Thomas, L. (2002) *Fans, Feminism and Quality Media*, London: Routledge.

Thompson, J. B. (1995) *The Media and Modernity: A Social Theory of the Media*, Cambridge: Polity Press.

Tomlinson, J. (1999) *Globalization and Culture*, Cambridge: Polity Press.

Vermorel, F. and Vermorel, J. (1985) *Starlust: The Secret Fantasies of Fans*, London: Comet.

Wagg, S. (1995) "On the Continent: Football in the Docieties of North West Europe" in S. Wagg (ed.) *Giving the Game Away: Football, Politics and Culture on Five Continents*, Leicester: Leicester University Press.

Williams, R. (1974) *Television: Technology and Cultural Form*, London: Fontana.

Winnicott, D. W. (1971) *Playing and Reality*, London: Pelican Books.

21

Film and globalization

From Hollywood to Bollywood

Stephen Teo

Introduction

Ever since cinema was invented in the West, it has seeped into different parts of the world, exerting a globalizing influence. The earliest films, produced by the Lumière Brothers, were shown in France to paying audiences in 1895 (Monaco, 1977: 199), and by 1896 were circulating in India and China. From there on, filmmakers in Asia and elsewhere have attempted to integrate the new technology of cinema with their local culture and thereby establish national film industries.

This chapter examines the progression of film in its globalizing path from Hollywood to Bollywood. These two terms are used as metaphors to suggest two different and distinctive processes of the globalization of film. Hollywood embodies the spirit of Western cinema, but more than that, it has come to be regarded as *the* cinema of all humanity. Its successful adoption of an industrial mode of production as far back as the early days of the silent cinema enabled it to outperform other cinemas based on more craft-based, less specialized type of production methods. The industrial mode of the Hollywood system comprising the setting up of studios, the promotion of famous stars, and the production of big budget blockbusters as efficiently and profitably as possible have come to be the yardstick by which other media production systems are measured.

Bollywood, on the other hand, embodies the spirit of Asian cinema and is treated as *the* alternative cinema of humanity – a poor man's Hollywood perhaps but one which is constantly climbing the ladder and aspires to the same universal dream. Bollywood infuses elements of Indigenous cultures with the Hollywood system of production adopted by Asian film industries. Though the Hollywood paradigm is held to be the universal standard, it is modified by the diversity of cultures and economic regimes around the world creating a phenomena epitomized most obviously by the term "Bollywood". My aim in this chapter is to demonstrate that the process by which Hollywood becomes Bollywood is quite complex, and that the globalization of film is far from a one-track process.

The Hollywood mode of representation and the universal paradigm

"Hollywood" is both an idea as well as the name of a place. Originally a "sleepy village (in Los Angeles) surrounded by farms and citrus groves" (French and Rosencrantz, 1979: 1), it was transformed by filmmakers early in the first decade of the twentieth century into the headquarters of a film industry producing motion pictures in the United States. As its influence spread worldwide, Hollywood has become a cliché and its meaning expanded to refer simply to a film industry or the social phenomenon of the cinema. In Asia, India's film industry is popularly known as "Bollywood" (the "B" refers to the city of Bombay, now known as Mumbai, which is where India's mainstream Hindi-speaking commercial film industry is concentrated); Hong Kong's film industry is known as "the Hollywood of the East", and South Korea's is known as "Hallyuwood" (the term "hallyu" meaning "Korean wave", indicates the surge of South Korean cultural influences sweeping over Asia since the beginning of the new millennium, and "Hallyuwood" refers to South Korean movies). The film industries of India, Hong Kong, and South Korea are regarded as exemplary models that follow the institutional and aesthetic patterns of production, distribution, and viewership set by Hollywood. One could justifiably claim that Hollywood is the mother of all film industries.

The power of Hollywood is effectively the power of the movies. As Jean Benoit-Levy in *The Art of the Motion Picture* has put it, "The motion picture is certainly the most powerful medium for the diffusion of human thought that man has discovered since the invention of printing in the fifteenth century" (Benoit-Levy, 1946: xi). Hollywood institutionalized the new medium by devising a systematic industrial mode of production and distribution, which the critic Noël Burch called "the institutional mode of representation" (Burch, 1979). It did this by setting up studios, implementing the star system, and making films that employ conventional formulas. The studios were the companies that produced the movies; they concentrated large amounts of money, manpower, and other resources to make movies utilizing factory type production methods, such as division of labour between various specialists and departments, top down decision making by bankers and managers, and the simultaneous production of numerous films at one time.

However, studios by themselves could not ensure a stable system of production. Instead, it was the star who "became a prime means of stabilizing production", and films in which a reigning favourite appeared could be counted on to attract movie goers fairly regularly, hence "they could be manufactured faster and ... more profitably" (Jacobs, 1939: 162). The star system, as Charles Higham tells us, "was based on contractual employment of figures which gave a studio the image it wanted" (Higham, 1972: 6). Finally, the studios had to tell stories in a way that audiences could easily recognize in terms of characters, plots, themes, and techniques. Films produced according to conventions or genres, such as the melodrama, romances, comedies, thrillers, Westerns, horror, and so on were popular with audiences and thus profitable for the studios to make in large numbers. Film genres therefore became an entrenched part of the system very early on.

The use of stars and generic film conventions are still the fundamental means of producing movies on a regular, commercial basis, and it is the principle followed by the film industries of Asia's most popular cinemas in India, Hong Kong, China, Japan, and South Korea. Without stars and genres, it is doubtful whether these national cinemas could have flourished in the way they did, or continue to do so today.

Other contributing factors to Hollywood's rise to global influence were America's geography and financial power: America had the advantage of being cut off from both

Europe and Asia during the disastrous conflicts that afflicted both continents; migrants and refugees fleeing wars and deprivation augmented its population, thus enhancing the dynamism and vibrancy of its cultural milieu as well as boosting its economic power. With a stable market at home, Hollywood could produce movies efficiently and regularly and on a grand scale. It also universalized its products in order to make them more accessible and appealing to the different ethnic and migrant groups that made up its population. It was thus well prepared to conquer the world. Today, the global market makes up its most important market: in 2007 and 2006, the international market constituted 64% of worldwide box-office gross of Hollywood films (Motion Picture Association of America, 2007).

Yet, there is more to this story of Hollywood's pervasive influence on the film industries of the world. Hollywood movies in themselves have such universal appeal that one is prompted to probe further the tenacity of Hollywood's influence. What is the secret of Hollywood's power? According to Lewis Jacobs, there were three things from the outset: "a commodity, a craft, and a social force" (Jacobs, 1939: 21). Hollywood's influence since its rise in the 1910s and 1920s is clearly due to its ability to make movies that are all three things. They remain unsurpassed in terms of their glossy packaging; superiority of craftsmanship backed up by technological finesse and talented stars, directors, and producers; and a facility at keeping the masses engaged.

Lewis Jacobs has therefore pinpointed the capacity of Hollywood to influence others through an industrial mode of producing commodities that are more than mere products. The movies are unlike cars or shoes because they have something akin to a soul. The German scenarist Walter S. Bloem published a book in the 1920s entitled *The Soul of the Moving Picture*, in which he wrote that the moving picture is an art "based on feeling, and not on thought" (Bloem, 1924: xi). "The inexpressible, the unspeakable, that regarding which even poetry itself can do no more than merely touch or indicate, has been taken up by the film and made a reality in the sphere of art" (ibid.: 8). Bloem had articulated an abstract vision of the movies as a universal force. "Art based on emotions is art for the masses" and the motion picture is an "art for the masses" (Bloem, 1924: xvii). The question then is whether Hollywood, the "factory" that produces films as commodity could also, at the same time, produce a universalizing quintessence of the human heart. As Stanley Aronowitz has phrased it, "The real question … is the question about the status of film as an object-form of which the entire repertoire of human emotions is the subject-form" (Aronowitz, 1979: 110).

Is Hollywood, more than any other national film industry, the embodiment of both the "object-form" and the "subject-form"? There seems little doubt that Hollywood enculates the universal idea of the movies because of its sheer power as a social force in having captured the markets of the world from its very beginning. In copying Hollywood, other film industries of the world have replicated its identity as both industrial machine and expression of soul. They seek to produce movies efficiently, and be an art for the masses.

There is something ironic about the fact that the movies, while being a mass art whose system of representation derives little "from the characteristically bourgeois art forms of the eighteenth and nineteenth centuries" (Burch, 1979: 77), made itself felt by relying on the capitalist-industrial mode of production that came into being during that period. Such an irony is detectable in a study of Hollywood in the post-war 1940s by the anthropologist Hortense Powdermaker, who questioned whether the Hollywood system is "the most appropriate one for the making of movies", given that such a new technology of storytelling "makes it dependent on mass rather than individual production" (Powdermaker, 1951: 39).

The characteristics of mass production are the uniformity of a product and its systematic distribution throughout a wide network of outlets. Powdermaker's comments throw into relief the opposing idea: that movies are an art form of individual expression and not "prefabricated daydreams" produced in a factory (Powdermaker, 1951: 39). On such a note, Hollywood remains suspect as an idea in that the quest of art and individual expression remains moot, even when we accept Hollywood as a superior model in terms of its industrial machine.

Given Hollywood's penchant for making blockbuster entertainments achieved through technological wizardry, from camera trickery in the old days to computer-generated imagery in the present – there will always be sceptics questioning its legitimacy as art. "For many of us," David Bordwell writes, "today's popular American cinema is always, fast, seldom cheap, and usually out of control" (Bordwell, 2002: 16). Hollywood movies will always be for some an "art without soul", to quote Bloem, who decries "the trick film" of the silent cinema, the early equivalent to what is now the blockbuster leaden with special effects (Bloem, 1924: 34).

But even sceptics cannot deny Hollywood's achievement in pioneering and cultivating innovative techniques and styles through filmmakers such as D. W. Griffith, Orson Welles, William Wyler, and many others, which were admired and copied by filmmakers throughout the world. The French critic Alexandre Astruc, writing in 1946, lauded Hollywood's technicians for bringing to perfection "the most economical and transparent technique possible" in the making of sound films:

A film was made of a series of sequences in *plan américain* (knees-up framing), with some camera movements and a constant play of shot and reverse-shot. Montage which had been of the essence in the silent era, was abandoned and replaced by découpage. The movements of the camera were utilized in very precise framings: the tracking shot to give the impression of depth, the pan shot to give a sense of breadth.

(Astruc, quoted in Bordwell, 1997: 55)

The *plan américain*, literally "American shot", referred to the classical medium shot that American cameramen devised to shoot actors from the knee up, while *découpage* was a French term to refer to the American system of cutting together scenes in an unobtrusive manner that respected spatial and temporal integrity – as opposed to the montage system piecing together unconnected, fragmentary shots used by the Soviet directors (Bordwell, 1997: 53).

Even if Hollywood had not actually invented the techniques, it had perfected the style such that it became a tradition shared or imitated around the world (Bordwell, 1997: 55). In many fields, such as animation, the introduction of sound, the introduction of Technicolor, and the use of widescreen and stereophonic sound, Hollywood was the pioneer. It also developed certain genres, such as the musical, the gangster movie, and the Western, that came to be known as quintessentially American genres. It pioneered a unique style such as film noir (or "black film") which exploits shadow and darkness in pictorial representation to create poetic atmosphere and suspense. But perhaps the most important achievement of Hollywood films was that they transmitted "a sense of film-ness", as the Soviet director Lev Kuleshov described it.

Film-ness is defined as that quality that "differs from photography in that it moves and introduces the temporal dimension". It is therefore not static and not related to the photographic sense of realism. Hollywood had mastered "film-ness" with its techniques

415

of découpage, "shortening the length of each component part of the film ... by shooting only the element of movement without which at any given moment a necessary vital action could not occur" (Kuleshov, quoted in Aronowitz, 1979: 111). Film-ness in this way can be defined more succinctly as a plastic form specific to cinema, emphasizing action, speed, rhythm, and narrative brevity, which might be summed up in a phrase coined by the poet and early film theorist Vachel Lindsay, "Sculpture-in-Motion" (Lindsay, 1922). To emphasize the plasticity of the moving picture, Lindsay also came up with such terms as "Painting-in-Motion" and "Architecture-in-Motion". The plastic materiality of the moving picture cannot be replicated on the live stage, for example, and certainly not by a still photograph. In Hollywood films, it is a vital part of its success, and it is imitated in certain Asian cinemas that follow the Hollywood model, particularly Hong Kong and Bollywood.

Despite the achievements of Hollywood, the essence of its soul is very often attacked. Authors like F. Scott Fitzgerald and Nathanael West wrote novels addressing the depravity and the spiritual corruption of its denizens. Sex, money, drugs, and the craving for fame and success are the corrupting elements that gnaw away at its soul. Hollywood was also never as progressive or as liberal as one might think. Racial stereotyping, sexism, censorship and self-censorship, the political witch hunts of the late 1940s and early 1950s and the subsequent blacklist, make up some of the inglorious episodes in the history of the dream factory. It was not above jingoistic propaganda, and it could be argued that the dream factory was always too keen on purveying the American dream when the dream was supposed to be universal. Hollywood movies were at the frontline of the cultural cold war, dispensing a vision of the capitalistic lifestyle to the Third World, and we are still living through the legacy of this war. Hollywood was also guilty of Orientalism, of falsifying history, and of perpetuating misconceptions through myths.

Hollywood is therefore a paradox. On the one hand, it is looked up to as a model and on the other hand, it is put down as a corrupting influence. Whatever the case, Hollywood is indisputably the hegemonic power in the global arena of cinematic culture. Like a magnet, it attracts talent from all over the world, which it mobilizes with its money to foster an aura of interdependence between itself and the other cinemas of the world and also to compete with them (Miller, et al., 2005: 131). Should such interdependence be accepted wholeheartedly? It is pertinent to ask how one should respond to Hollywood as a mode of representation and as a universal paradigm. It is worthwhile noting that within America itself, the Hollywood mode of filmmaking did not go unchallenged and there were other systems and modes of representation that came into operation – such as the concept of independent production, short films, animated films, experimental films, and documentary films. Sometimes such forms were incorporated by Hollywood, but on the whole, they remained on the margins. Within the United States, the Hollywood mode of representation was predominant.

The dominance of Hollywood has led other countries to push for "local content", a phrase more often applied to the television industry but also sometimes heard in the film industry – the idea being to protect local jobs and ensure the cultural subsistence of Indigenous artists. "Local content" is a nationalistic response to globalization. Ironically, however, national cinemas themselves seek to show their culture to the world. The interesting question is whether Hollywood can be supplanted by the local, national cinema as a universal paradigm. Thus far, it is Hollywood that has supplanted other national cinemas but the question of an alternative paradigm to Hollywood is not a new one, and has been raised for as long as Hollywood has existed. In the early years of cinema, filmmakers in the Soviet Union did attempt to devise an alternative cinematic system and mode of representation by "*appropriating* the codes governing the major genres of the capitalist film industries" (Burch, 1979: 85). There is an acute sense of paradox here in that alternative models, even as envisaged in the Soviet Union, are themselves closely sourced from and connected with Hollywood. The truth of the matter was that the efficiency of Hollywood's production methods so impressed Soviet filmmakers that the state itself tried to build a "Soviet Hollywood" in the 1930s (Taylor, 1986: 58–59).

In the context of the contemporary rise of Asia as an economic and political power-house, its cinemas have also made an impact in international film festivals and in the cinema circuits of the West. With the rise of Asian cinemas in disparate countries ranging from Iran to Thailand, from Singapore to South Korea, and with the solidifying of tra-ditional major cinematic powers such as India, China, and Japan, theorists have raised the possibility of seeing Asian cinema as a single unitary force forming an alternative para-digm to Hollywood. This is the crux of an emerging discourse on Asian cinema that has come out of the growing literature and the pedagogical modules taught in universities and institutions that seek to assess and explain the films, genres, stars, and directors of the Asian film industries. But since these industries are closely modelled on Hollywood, is an alternative paradigm a viable idea? Should it be comparative? Mitsuhiro Yoshimoto has raised the problem of what he perceives to be "a pervasive dichotomy of Hollywood and the rest" (Yoshimoto, 2003: 455). For Yoshimoto, the problem lies in looking at Hol-lywood as the universal standard-bearer of classical cinema, with every other cinema rebounding off Hollywood, adopting its standards. "To be critically viable, the idea of Asian cinema should *not be a derivative* of the Hollywood-centered paradigm" (my italics).

However, Yoshimoto concedes that it is not easy to re-conceptualize Asian cinema completely outside of this paradigm. The reason for this is not only that Hollywood's industrial and economic model is hard to refute, it also embodies the essence of the moving picture. Imitation of Hollywood is not simply a matter of adopting the capitalistic-industrial mode of production which Hollywood represents and seemingly imposes on the film industries of the world as a sort of universal practice. Its spiritual impact is even greater. As a cultural and social force, Hollywood is intrinsic to the films of the various Asian film industries. In this respect, Hollywood has shown the greatest capacity to capture the emotions. The Hollywood spirit is inherent in the films of other national cinemas inasmuch as they replicate the same desire to emit the passion of the soul and capture the emotion of viewers around the world. Hollywood is therefore not just an economic hegemon but "an integral and naturalised part of the national culture, or the popular imagination, of most countries in which cinema is an established entertainment form", to quote Andrew Higson (1989: 39).

In the final analysis, because Hollywood has set the classical standards of filmmaking and because many of the film industries in the rest of the world are effectively modelled after Hollywood, it is necessary that we engage with Hollywood on various levels. If Asian cinema is to develop as an alternative paradigm, its viability is increased, not les-sened, through engagement with Hollywood and its norms. The great Japanese director Yasujiro Ozu, for instance, was able to develop his own inimitable method and style of cinema by drawing on references to Hollywood cinema, as David Bordwell has demonstrated in a book-length study on the master published in 1988. The case of the Soviet director Lev Kuleshov is also instructive. As David Bordwell tells us, Kuleshov "turned toward violent stunts, chases, and fistfights, all rendered in a rapid editing derived from American films" and he "repudiated stylistic schemas cultivated in his milieu for the sake of creating a modern popular cinema for the new Soviet state"

417

(Bordwell, 1997: 154). From this approach, the Soviet filmmakers developed their own distinctive form of montage.

Most of us grew up with Hollywood and are probably not as prone to see it as the "Other" as we might other national cinemas. It is not alien to us. The Hollywood mode of representation is seemingly natural and conducive to our senses and emotions but it also mirrors a contingent space where we question ourselves and experiment with identity and shapes. Such a space is not always manifested, but it is immanent and can be shaped by creative forces both hostile and friendly to the Hollywood mode. It is exactly in this kind of space that a filmmaker like Ozu experimented. The space is contingent because of the intractable factor of culture. Differences in culture means that Hollywood influences are necessarily transformed – the expression "Bollywood" is a transformation of "Holly-wood". As an idea, Hollywood gives us the possibility of the union and celebration of common humanity but at the same time, it offers us the open space for change and transformation.

Bollywood and other Asian cinemas as the alternative mode of cinematic representation

Bollywood, like Hollywood, is an idea, which, for the purposes of this chapter, refers to a different kind of Hollywood, one that could serve as a metaphor for an Alternative Mode of Cinematic Representation (AMCR). "Bollywood" is here used to signify a system of production and cinematic representation that is based on the idea of national cinema but which replicates the Hollywood model to produce films. Whereas Holly-wood is a global mode of cinematic representation, "Bollywood" is a national mode of cinematic representation, and the films that are produced from this latter mode are significantly marked by national characteristics. However, national cinemas also employ the transcultural techniques of filmmaking which conjoin them to Hollywood and other national cinemas. We shall therefore be examining more specifically how transcultural techniques of cinema can transform Hollywood styles into "Bollywood" (meaning national) styles, and how national cinemas in Asia might function as alternative modes.

While Bollywood refers to the popular Indian cinema based in Mumbai, the metaphorical "Bollywood" includes other Asian national cinemas (such as Japan, South Korea, and the "three Chinas") which are simply different from Hollywood by virtue of their incorporation and expressions of national styles. In the first instance, one could see "Bollywood" as a substitute Hollywood, as developing countries in Asia seek to initiate film production and integrate the marvel of cinema into its own national-cultural environment in the early twentieth century. This "substitute Hollywood" then transforms itself into a distinctive cinema in its own right and we could begin to see this film industry as an alternative to Hollywood even though it retains many of the features and characteristics of Hollywood.

The Indian Bollywood is the largest of the film industries in Asia that followed the Hollywood model while transforming themselves into "national cinemas". Indeed, the Indian national cinema, which comprises of Bollywood and several other regional film industries (including Tamil, Telugu, Bengali, Malayalam, and Kannada), is the largest in the world. Bollywood itself already produces over 1,000 movies a year and this industry is expected to expand to US$4.4 billion a year in 2011 (Giridharadas, 2007). What the numbers demonstrate above all is that Bollywood films dominate India's domestic market. "India is the one major market Hollywood has never figured how to crack", Chidananda Das Gupta tells us (1980: 34). From the moment that India produced its very first film in 1913, *Raja Harishchandra*, directed by Dadasaheb Phalke, it was engaged with "the struggle to establish a film industry, and nurture it into self-sufficiency" (Rajadhyaksha, 1987: 65). Bollywood is the living testament of the self-sufficient Indian film industry. It challenges the view of Hollywood as global hegemon, causing us to reconsider just what kind of role Hollywood is really playing in the global stage relative to the national cinemas of the world. Toby Miller makes the point that Hollywood's output is actually mediated by Indigenous cultures such that the thesis of Hollywood cultural imperialism has to be strongly qualified (Miller et al., 2005: 78). In this process, Indian filmmakers saw in Hollywood a model to emulate, and "Bollywood" was the result, an Indian film industry which is clearly "mediated" by Hollywood, and a case of a "strategic making-do, not of being overwhelmed" by Hollywood (Miller et al., 2005: 79).

The appeal of Bollywood films has been attributed to filmmakers adopting the norms of the oral epic narrative and its melodramatic conventions, which are easily communicable to uneducated, non-literate audiences (Nayar, 2004, 2005; Booth, 1995; Rajadhyaksha, 1993). Gregory Booth tells us that one feature of traditional epics "is their great emotionality, and their tendency to portray a wide variety of emotions in sometimes rapid (and, for Western audiences, bewildering or inconsequent) succession" (Booth, 1995: 175). Ashish Rajadhyaksha identifies more specifically the epic melodrama as the form with which the Hindi-speaking Bollywood cinema and other regional cinemas could adopt as a national cinematic form – as being something more than just a genre, "as, indeed, something like a mode of cultural production/assimilation" (Rajadhyaksha, 1993: 59). The epic melodrama also "crucially revitalized the star system" (ibid., p. 57), which is of course an important plank in the Hollywood institutional mode that Bollywood wholeheartedly took onboard. In adopting the traditional epic form, Bollywood has actually followed the principle that an art based on emotions is an art for the masses, but it is worth our while to consider more concretely how Bollywood was able to absorb Hollywood into itself, making something uniquely its own rather than be immersed by Hollywood.

While making *Raja Harischandra* in 1913, the director Phalke was preoccupied "with the depiction of Indian images" (Rajadhyaksha, 1987: 65). One problem was how to create images from the Indian *point of view* while incorporating the foreign technology of the movies into the local culture and environment. Phalke resolved this problem, according to Ashish Rajadhyaksha, by letting the audience become a part of the cosmos of the characters' frontal gaze on screen (frontality was the common method at the time of performing for the camera: actors quite literally stood in front of the camera and gazed at it). "The story ... is a continuous back-and-forth interaction between the viewers and the object viewed; we are shown the imaginary universe condensed into the object, our seeing is reciprocated" (Rajadhyaksha, 1987: 71). Obviously, Bollywood and Hollywood would differ in terms of their points of view, a difference that inevitably marks the aesthetics of their images.

Much of the aesthetics of Bollywood movies relate to the cultural influences of Indigenous music and oral performances – since song and dance play a dominant role in Bollywood films. Anna Morcom has looked at how music, for example, is a sign of the transformation of Hollywood influence into something culturally specific in Bollywood films (2001), and I will follow her analysis to explore how this is done. Although music is perhaps the single most important Hollywood influence, the manner in which it is used is uniquely Bollywood. Motifs and conventions in Hollywood based on Western tonal music convey different meanings in the Bollywood context. In Bollywood music, feelings, and emotions are largely expressed through the melodic musical tradition known as *rāga*, and only heroes and heroines sing, villains do not (Morcom, 2001: 80). Hollywood techniques in music are incorporated in Bollywood films only to the extent of constituting "an antithesis of *rāga* and classical melody and also film and folk song melody", and "can therefore be used as a powerful means to express distortion, destruction and disturbance of these qualities (of the sacred, love, romance and celebration) in a range of dramatic situations" (Morcom, 2001: 81).

The moral universe of Bollywood films is in this manner shaken by the introduction and incorporation of Western music. Morcom points out that it is "not the fact that this music is mostly Western in origin and probably came from Hollywood that makes it negative in this way, but rather that it is profoundly at odds with the strongly positively coded phenomenon of *rāga* or melody" (2001: 81). Here, we have a sense of how cultural forms from the East and the West are "profoundly at odds" with each other but yet can co-exist in a unified film narrative set to music, incorporating techniques that are often considered to be transcultural. When Western musical techniques as employed in Hollywood films are applied in Bollywood films, they convey different meanings, and it is this difference in values that demands our attention. Somewhere in that exchange of values lies the difference between Hollywood and Bollywood. While the exchange is made possible through the transcultural techniques of film and music, a transmutation occurs half way through. Transculturalism is far from a smooth and linear process, which is a point that I will return to.

The cinema is one huge transcultural medium, and David Bordwell is the most prominent exponent of this principle, tirelessly demonstrating that film techniques cross borders and transcend cultures. In the use of techniques and styles, different national cinemas and Hollywood engage on common ground. Bordwell, who has assiduously studied film styles and techniques as practised by filmmakers from most of the major film industries in the world, has recently turned his attention to the Chinese-language cinemas and their achievements of film style that owe debts to Hollywood practices but also transcend them. He asserts that "Chinese films, to put it bluntly, are Chinese," but they are also films, "and films are a powerful transcultural medium, drawing not only on local knowledge but also on a range of human skills that are shared across many cultures." "By mastering several transcultural possibilities of cinema, Chinese films have gained the power to cross national boundaries and be grasped by audiences around the world" (Bordwell, 2005: 144).

Bordwell's thesis of transculturalism allows us to understand that the globalization process in cinema is not a one-way track and that there are multiple players involved. However, his focus on form and technique raises the question whether Chinese films cross national boundaries through its use of the medium alone. In other words, is transculturalism primarily a matter of conversing through film technique? How is an abstract notion such as culture actually transmitted through the use of film? These questions do not have easy answers but from the discussions above regarding Bollywood and the issues I will address below, we will attempt to gain a better understanding of the complex process of film and globalization.

At this point, let us briefly consider how Chinese cinema can be taken as another possible AMCR. The creation of a Chinese national cinema in Shanghai during the 1920s was marked by the appropriation of Indigenous genres. One such genre is the martial arts tales of chivalry and romance known as *wuxia* (literally, "martial chivalry"). It is passed on through history, literature, and folklore, as well as performing traditions such as *tanci*, an oral storytelling form accompanied by music, and opera traditions (Beijing Opera, and other regional forms of opera). Chinese intellectuals and writers, principally intellectuals of the May Fourth Movement in the 1910s and 1920s, often talked about a "national form" in the arts and literature. The genre of the martial arts in Chinese cinema and other closely related genres – such as the opera film, the historical costume film, and the fantastic *shenguai* (gods and demons) film – exuded just such a "national form" that was recognizable to a Chinese audience even though the form was also influenced by Hollywood genres such as the Western and the swashbuckler (popular among Chinese audiences in Shanghai in the 1920s).

So the presence of Hollywood and other foreign cinemas, mostly European, provided an impetus towards the creation of a national Chinese cinema. That Hollywood is seen as a model of the "national" is not a surprise. It is in reality a nationalistic cinema itself, having been endorsed by the state and used by the United States government to propagate American values (Wan and Kraus, 2002: 428). It is precisely this kind of model that the government of the People's Republic of China sought to emulate when it decided to open up the China market to Hollywood in the 1990s. It believed that through interactions with Hollywood, Chinese cinema would evolve as a film industry swerving nationalistic interests. A cinema could be developed that allowed the state "to create a more attractive form of propaganda through a peculiar hybrid of political authority and market forces" (Wan and Kraus, 2002: 429).

Chinese cinema, like Bollywood, exists as an appropriation of many forms and styles which can be both Indigenous and foreign. It is imperative on the intelligent viewer to consider how Indigenous, national styles are corrupted by or informed by foreign styles and all that that implies. For example, a film like Ang Lee's *Crouching Tiger, Hidden Dragon* (2000) subscribes to the conventions of the traditional *wuxia* genre, including the staging of fantastic martial arts action scenes. It became the most successful Chinese film to break into the American market, and critical commentaries have since scrutinized the film and concluded that it was essentially made for Westerners rather than for the Chinese audience. *Crouching Tiger* actually demonstrates how the genre was already infused with foreign influences in that it absorbed the styles of Hollywood genres that were popular with Chinese audiences. The foreign influences in Chinese cinema often vie for attention with apparently Indigenous cultural norms such that one can see currents of modernism and postmodernism interacting with traditional forms, and nationalism and transnationalism crossing paths. There is no doubt that the director Ang Lee and his artistic collaborators intended to make *Crouching Tiger* as a Chinese film that could also at the same time be seen and appreciated by large global audiences. Having succeeded in this aim, *Crouching Tiger* is the classic transcultural film, one which crossed over into the global market dominated by Hollywood thus far.

The concept of national cinema, as I have tried to show above, contains contradictory impulses, but fundamentally, it might be summed up as a quest based "on recovering or reinventing (the) 'national' aesthetic and narrative traditions against the homogenizing impulses of Hollywood in its domination over markets and normative standards" (Vasudevan, 2006: 295). The Indian and Chinese experience shows that the first aim of any national cinema is to build up a stable industry and market, ultimately perhaps to achieve a certain parity of status with Hollywood, or as in the case of *Crouching Tiger, Hidden Dragon* to make films that can successfully compete with Hollywood films in the global market. However, creating national cinemas in the contexts and structures of colonialism (in the case of India) and semi-colonialism (in the case of China) and maintaining them as viable industries in the postcolonial era amidst pressures of globalization (entailing a parallel development and competition with Hollywood) would not have been and still is not easy. The task of creating an alternative paradigm to Hollywood is enormous, but it is in the realm of the transcultural medium of film practices that we can discover the potential of the Asian AMCR.

The essence of an alternative mode is that it is not only transcultural but unique. Bordwell speaks of the convergence of cultures, "the development in different cultures of a remarkably similar way of constructing space for the viewer" (Bordwell, 2005: 156), but he actually tenders the idea of uniqueness to consider the question of difference or the possibility of an alternative to the norms of Hollywood. The construction of space is where uniqueness lies. The concept of uniqueness is therefore not tied to any abstract notion of culture but rather to a methodology of form – and it is the methodology of directors which appears to illuminate the idea of uniqueness.

Bordwell holds up Yasujiro Ozu as the exemplar of transculturalism and uniqueness. Once regarded as the "most Japanese of Japanese directors", Ozu, who was the master of the home drama (his classics include *Tokyo Story*, from 1954, and *An Autumn Afternoon*, his last film, released in 1962) is recognized today as one of the greatest filmmakers in the world, admired in both the East and in the West. To Bordwell, Ozu is quite likely the greatest "experimental filmmaker" for his unique style of *mise-en-scène* and cutting (Bordwell, 1988: 6–7). Here Bordwell shows his tendency to disregard culture in considering a director's employment of stage blocking techniques and use of space (what the French call *mise-en-scène*, a term now generally used in the English language to refer to direction which includes all aspects of paying attention to the actors' performances, camera movements, décor, etc.). He does not see Ozu's "Japaneseness" as the decisive factor in his art and proceeds to analyze the director's work from a transcultural perspective of cinematic practice.

Bordwell situates Ozu against the historical background of the artistic and cultural developments of post-Meiji Japan, during which time notions of "Japaneseness" are constantly shifting based on the interchanges of Indigenous cultural norms and external, extrinsic norms. While influenced by Hollywood, Ozu draws on Indigenous Japanese norms of poetry, literature, and religion for a kind of "decorative classicism". But ultimately, Ozu works against both norms, constructing his own rules by adopting a "ludic quality" which "consistently challenges the stability of coherent representation" (Bordwell, 1988: 108). As Bordwell has dissected it, Ozu's style is very piecemeal: based on the method of *découpage*, it is at the same time highly rigorous and conforms to a strict pattern of staging.

Ozu's uniqueness means that he is quite unlike both Western directors and his Japanese contemporaries. This uniqueness explains how Ozu is both modern and experimental, and both Japanese and Western. Ozu's quality of uniqueness is that quality which we might see as an alternative mode of cinematic representation. Significantly, though Ozu's style is said to be uniquely Japanese, he has influenced many directors in Asia, which shows that this uniqueness is transcultural. Other examples of contemporary Asian directors who could be considered heirs of Ozu in the sense of having unique styles yielding alternative modes of cinematic representation: the Taiwanese directors Hou Hsiao-hsien, Edward Yang, and Tsai Ming-liang, the Mainland Chinese director Jia Zhangke, the Hong Kong directors Wong Kar-wai and Johnnie To, the Thai director Apichatpong Weerasethakul, the Malaysian director Amir Muhammad, the Iranian director Abbas Kiarostami. The late Indian director Satyajit Ray also possessed the same kind of unique quality, and fittingly, he too, like Ozu, was different from his own contemporaries and from his Western counterparts (Ray was definitely different from the Bollywood directors but he also remains an unparalleled *auteur* director in the so-called "parallel" cinema that produces more socially committed art films usually in the regional industries away from Bollywood).

It is within this group of directors that we might seek to define an Asian cinematic practice that can be taken as an alternative mode to that of Hollywood. Here we might speak of a transculturalism inscribed within Asianness and the state of being Asian and inter-Asian (directors like Hou Hsiao-hsien and Tsai Ming-liang are heavily influenced by Ozu, for example, and they in turn influence others) as well as being transnational. The fact that the films of such demanding directors as Hou Hsiao-hsien, Tsai Ming-liang, Wong Kar-wai, Edward Yang and others are seen and appreciated in the West illustrates a certain paradox in highlighting the concept of an Asian cinema as an AMCR. These directors are problematic directors in their home countries; their films usually do not perform well at the box-office because they are shunned by the mass audience who see them as too arty and pretentious, while in the West, their films are highly praised by critics and academics. The Western appreciation of difficult Asian directors heightens the sense of contestation, whether it is seen as the West applying Orientalist knowledge on a crop of Asian films or Asian directors themselves exploiting and mobilizing Orientalism to benefit their works in the West (*Crouching Tiger, Hidden Dragon*, for example, has been attacked as a model of "self-Orientalism").

This sense of contestation keeps the concept of Asian cinema and its possibilities as an AMCR very much alive. The theoretical point I am making is that Asian cinematic space is a discursive space where culture itself is problematized and transculturalism is not a perfectly symmetrical process. Orientalism, nationalism, and transnationalism are bound together as Asia is bound together with Hollywood because its institutional mode of representation is embedded into Asian cinematic practice. The transculturalism that takes place will always produce counterintuitive effects, and the idea of an alternative mode is ever present in the exchange.

Transculturalism through Asian cinematic space

While Bordwell emphasizes transculturalism to show how cinemas of different nations and cultures share and partake in a filmmaking culture, there is obviously more to the concept of transculturalism inasmuch as the intangible and abstract aspect of culture makes it an unpredictable process. While we may all accept that film is a transcultural medium (i.e. that there is some intrinsic value in film that can cross cultures), the question of cultural difference and how different cultures value film must be considered thoroughly.

In emphasizing culture as difference and suggesting an idea of an Asian cinema as an alternative paradigm to Hollywood (or more broadly, the cinemas of the West), there is always the possibility of "reverse ethnocentrism", as Yoshimoto cautions us (2003: 455). There is always a risk of falling into a trap of cultural essentialism – of trying to define essentialist qualities of "Asianness" where none exist. Asia is in reality made up of diverse nations, many of which emerged out of the cocoon of colonialism around the middle of the twentieth century. As independent nation states, their cinemas contain nationalistic discourses which point to the subject of identity and distinctiveness, often in the process

423

accentuating ethnicity. However, I would argue that rather than suggesting ethnocentrism, the use of the term "Asian" is actually transcendent of nationalisms and ethnocentrism. Thus there is no question of reverse ethnocentrism since the problem of ethnocentrism is actually avoided by the adoption of the term "Asian cinema". As with the idea of Europe, the idea of Asia transcends nationalism and ethnicity. But perhaps Asia and an Asian cinema has not yet come of age, and it is not as yet politically acceptable to speak of Asia as a transcendent political entity, much less Asian cinema as an entity that transcends nationalism and ethnocentrism.

Historically, the notion of Asia as a politically transcendent entity has acquired negative connotations. In Japan, "Asian" conjures up memories of the Second World War and the attempt by Japan to impose a "Greater East Asia Co-prosperity Sphere", such that the word is too politically incorrect to be in general usage. Similarly, in South Korea, where memories of Japan's colonial rule remain fresh or are constantly invoked, the word "Asian" smacks of power and conquest. China too has its bitter memories of war with Japan and it has its own imperialist baggage to shed where Asia is concerned. Thus as the idea of an Asian cinema is put forward, its insufficiency as a historical concept makes it too elusive. However, the idea of an Asian cinematic space that is transcultural points to an arena in which several national cinemas interact, perhaps even compete. The films function as the textual references for an alternative mode of cinematic practice vis-à-vis each other and vis-à-vis Hollywood.

Asian cinema exists within a transnational, transcultural, heterogeneous, and hybrid realm of world cinematic spaces and cultures – and any theoretical formulation of Asianness, or Asian uniqueness, in the cinema is not meant to be exclusive and cannot possibly be so. The concept of Asian cinema needs to be theorized more than it has been, to which end, I believe, there will be more claims and counterclaims of Asian uniqueness and distinctiveness which can be both positive and negative. Asian cinema *is* a transcultural medium. It is transcultural *within itself*, which is to say that there are many Asian cinemas which all mutually submit to the universal language of cinema (to return to the metaphor of "Bollywood", there is not one but many Bollywoods).

Within Asia, transculturalism is manifested through the practice of so-called "Pan-Asian" co-production, where several film industries get together to produce a film utilizing talent from all these industries. A Pan-Asian film recognizes that Asia possesses common cultural traits that can easily cross borders such that one part is seen as no different from the others. A film like *The Myth* (2005), a Hong Kong production starring Jackie Chan teams the star with co-stars from Bollywood, South Korea, and China. *The Promise* (2005), a Mainland China production directed by Chen Kaige, features stars from Japan, South Korea, Hong Kong, and China. These films, and many others like them, are Pan-Asian but they also seek to be global. The idea of transculturalism is intrinsic to all of them.

However, transculturalism may not necessarily be unproblematic, not least because the term "Asia" itself is problematical but also that common properties of culture are insufficient indicators of transculturalism. There are transmutations involved in the passage of transculturalism which need to be assessed more rigorously – an exercise which falls beyond the scope of this chapter. Suffice to say that while transculturalism is a fairly established practice in Asia inasmuch as most urban Asians have the facility for switching back and forth from Western to Eastern references, from local to foreign traditions, there is a lot of tweaking and readjusting. In the cinema, a good example is Wisit Sasanatieng's *Tears of the Black Tiger* (2001). The film is an amalgam of two quite separate and distinctive genres. It incorporates the Western, which is considered a distinctively American genre, and shows Thai cowboys and gunslingers shooting it out in carefully choreographed gunfight sequences. It is consciously aware of popular conventions used in the Hollywood Western (and also the Italian so-called "spaghetti" Western). This foreign genre is integrated into the fabric of the picture that is patterned along the lines of the local Thai melodrama, describing a romantic tale between the working-class hero and the young rich girl he loves.

In its evocation of the local conventions of melodrama and the incorporation of a foreign genre, the film demonstrates that transculturalism is a two-way process. Any incongruities are either tided over or completely ignored. Furthermore, considering the film from the audience's perspective, it is probably easier for non-Thais to grasp the conventions of the Western than those of the Thai melodrama. This is because most of us are less familiar with the Thai cinema and its genres than with Hollywood cinema and its genres. *Tears of the Black Tiger* is an entertaining film that introduces the conventions of Thai melodrama to a global audience while integrating a Hollywood genre into its overall narrative. In the process, it prompts the audience to re-examine what it knows about Thai cinema and the way the filmmakers have used the practice of transcultural exchange. Is *Tears of the Black Tiger* a parody or satire of transculturalism, or is it really transcultural to the extent that it conveys the same meanings to everybody, East and West, North and South?

Though transculturalism, as used by Bordwell, has a specific application to cinema techniques and styles, we need also to examine how it is related to other terminologies such as globalism, transnationalism, and Pan-Asianism. All these terms have parallel meanings which may or may not converge, but I would suggest that they have one thing in common: Hollywood, as an idea and as a paradigm of universality. In fact, as transculturalism is a two-way process, Hollywood itself has absorbed the talent of Asian cinemas and has made its own Pan-Asian films. A famous example is *Memoirs of a Geisha* (2005) featuring Mainland Chinese stars Zhang Ziyi and Gong Li, the Chinese-Malaysian star Michelle Yeoh, and Japanese actors. Hollywood has also made Asian films – an example being Clint Eastwood's *Letters from Iwo Jima* (2007), spoken entirely in Japanese and featuring all-Japanese actors. It is also making its own Bollywood films, with Indian directors and stars speaking Hindi, as a ploy to join Bollywood rather than conquer it (Giridharadas, 2007). As Quentin Tarantino's *Kill Bill* (2003/04) shows, Hollywood is as capable of adopting Asian influences and styles as Asian cinemas are in adopting from Hollywood.

Hollywood has shown its awareness of the fact that there are many other national cinemas with their own distinctive styles. The propensity of Hollywood to absorb and to copy from others is perhaps not as obvious as others copying from Hollywood. Nevertheless, it is strong and likely to continue. Hollywood is constantly changing and regenerating itself. It anticipates competitive threats and deflects the presences of alternative modes, reducing the chances that it could be replaced by any other film industry in its hegemonic reach. Apart from exporting its movies, Hollywood today is out-sourcing its labour-intensive jobs to foreign countries along the line of a "New International Division of Cultural Labour" (Miller et al, 2005: 111–172). Foreign countries actually compete to host Hollywood's so-called "runaway productions". But such developments serve primarily to strengthen and consolidate Hollywood's hegemony, while it is itself highly protectionist and insular, imposing a "culture blockade" on foreign media and films, even as it aggressively spreads its wings globally (Miller, et al, 2005: 95).

On an aesthetic level, Hollywood today smacks of gigantism, symbolized by such titles as *Jurassic Park* (1993), *Titanic* (1997), *Godzilla* (1998), and *King Kong* (2005). It is driven by huge borrowed capital, the high-concept blockbuster, and global markets. It may be said that Hollywood is too tied to the albatross of state and commercial capitalism to be truly unique and creative. Universality is a burden of high capital, and there are always risks involved, not least box-office failure, economic crisis, and a world depression. In contrast, Asian cinemas have lighter loads to carry, and they are often much more creative. Asian cinema is probably the only viable alternative force to Hollywood: the three major Asian film industries of India, China, and Japan combined produce more films than Hollywood, and constitute a rich and diverse source of creative vitality. It can really only function as an alternative mode to Hollywood.

Globalization may be an ideal that many Asian cinemas aspire to but it could also be a pitfall. Already in the Chinese cinema, the trend towards huge blockbuster production over recent years shows how much it relies on the Hollywood model of huge capital and maximum gloss to pull in the masses, both domestically and globally. The trap here is that creativity will in all probability be distorted by a sense of pandering to clichés and stereotypes as computerized special effects and visual bombast take over the narrative. This has already happened in a film such as Chen Kaige's *The Promise*, and one could see its failure as a cautionary tale against globalization and its blockbuster tendency.

Asian cinema is certainly not immune to the commercialism of big businesses and their global ambitions, and we might return to Bollywood as the metaphor not only for an alternative paradigm but also for vulgar commercialism. Bollywood therefore shares this same space with Hollywood. Perhaps in this space they are equal; but that said, I would like to re-invoke the notion of an alternative cinematic space which is immanent within the Hollywood institutional mode of cinematic representation. Such a space is surely immanent within the "Bollywood" mode of vulgar commercialism, and one should remember that in India, there is the "parallel cinema" that runs alongside the Bollywood cinema as the more socially conscious cinematic expression of Indian filmmakers.

However, Bollywood itself is dynamic enough to contain many spaces and we may ultimately see in it that Asian cinematic space in which cultural specificity and localism serve as foundation stones for the construction of a universal paradigm. Insofar as all filmmakers seek a global market for their products, the principle must be that local culture can be understood globally. On the other hand, local culture is never always local – it is subject to global influences. Here the principle is that global influences are usually localized and are transfigured through transcultural techniques of cinematic practice. Hollywood becomes "Bollywoodized": it is mediated, re-nationalized, transformed, and thus submitted to the global gaze of transnational audiences through the methodology of transcultural film practices. "Bollywood" is itself a process of globalization.

Conclusion

Whereas Hollywood's institutional power and hegemonic reach is a historical reality, the real question as Stanley Aronowitz has posed it adroitly is "the status of film as an object-form of which the entire repertoire of human emotions is the subject-form". With this question, we might say that Hollywood has defined film as an object-form through its institutional mode of representation, packaged it superbly and sold it to the world, but has Hollywood monopolized the entire repertoire of human emotions? Has it got the world in its pocket as a subject-form?

I have raised the possibility of looking at Asian cinemas as constituting an alternative mode of cinematic representation, meaning an alternative object-form for the expression of human emotions. As an alternative mode, Asian cinema – which is far from being a uniform, single entity to begin with – encompasses multiple subject-forms: from Bollywood epic melodramas characterized by song and dance, to Chinese martial arts fantasies such as *Crouching Tiger, Hidden Dragon*, to Japanese home dramas touched by the idiosyncratic hand of a master director like Ozu, to a Thai pastiche of the Cowboy Western and the romantic melodrama such as *Tears of the Black Tiger*. Asian cinema utilizes transcultural techniques of film expression and its films reach audiences globally. However, the transcultural process itself involves vectors of culture and other factors, such as influences from Hollywood that determine the direction and the unique approach of Asian filmmakers. These films demand greater awareness on the part of global audiences of the material content, in particular the local substance which are far less familiar to them. It is in the interchange between the local and the global, between Hollywood and "Bollywood" that film strives to be universal.

References

Aronowitz, Stanley 1979, "Film: The Art Form of Late Capitalism", *Social Text*, 1, pp. 110–129.

Benoit-Levy, Jean 1946, *The Art of the Motion Picture*, trans. Theodore R. Jaeckel, New York: Coward-McCann Inc.

Bloem, Walter S. 1924, *The Soul of the Moving Picture*, trans. by Allen W. Porterfield, New York: E. P. Dutton and Company.

Booth, Gregory D. 1995, "Traditional Content and Narrative Structure in the Hindi Commercial Cinema", *Asian Folklore Studies*, 54: 2, pp. 169–190.

Bordwell, David 1988, *Ozu and the Poetics of Cinema*, London and Princeton: BFI and Princeton University Press.

——1997, *On the History of Film Style*, Cambridge, MA and London: Harvard University Press.

——2002, "Intensified Continuity: Visual Style in Contemporary American Film", *Film Quarterly*, 55: 3, Spring, pp. 16–28.

——2005, "Transcultural Spaces: Towards a Poetics of Chinese Film", in Sheldon Lu and Emilie Yueh-yu Yeh (ed.), *Chinese-Language Film: Historiography, Poetics, Politics*, Honolulu: University of Hawai'i Press, pp. 141–62.

Burch, Noël 1979, "Film's Institutional Mode of Representation and the Soviet Response", *October*, 11, pp. 77–96.

Das Gupta, Chidananda 1980, "New Directions in Indian Cinema", *Film Quarterly*, 34: 1, pp. 32–42.

French, Christopher and Rosencrantz, Linda 1979, *Gone Hollywood*, New York: Doubleday and Company.

Giridharadas, Anand 2007, "Hollywood Starts Making Bollywood Films in India", *New York Times*, 8 August.

Higham, Charles 1972, *Hollywood at Sunset*, New York: Saturday Review Press.

Higson, Andrew 1989, "The Concept of National Cinema", *Screen*, 30: 4, pp. 36–46.

Jacobs, Lewis 1939, *The Rise of the American Film: A Critical History*, New York: Harcourt, Brace and Company.

Lindsay, Vachel 1922, *The Art of the Moving Picture*, New York: Macmillan Company.

Miller, Toby, Govil, Nitin, McMurria, John, Maxwell, Richard, and Wang, Ting 2005, *Global Hollywood 2*, London: British Film Institute.

Monaco, James 1977, *How to Read a Film: The Art, Technology, Language, History, and Theory of Film and Media*, New York: Oxford University Press.

Morcom, Anna 2001, "An Understanding between Bollywood and Hollywood? The Meaning of Hollywood-Style Music in Hindi Films", *British Journal of Ethnomusicology*, 10: 1, pp. 63–84.

Motion Picture Association of America 2007, *Theatrical Market Statistics 2007*, pp. 1–9.

Nayar, Sheila J. 2004, "Invisible Representation: The Oral Contours of a National Popular Cinema", *Film Quarterly*, 57: 3, pp. 13–23.

——2005, "Dis-Orientalizing Bollywood: Incorporating Indian popular cinema into a survey film course", *New Review of Film and Television Studies*, 3: 1, pp. 59–74.

Powdermaker, Hortense 1951, *Hollywood, The Dream Factory*, London: Secker and Warburg.

Rajadhyaksha, Ashish 1987, "The Phalke Era: Conflict of Traditional Form and Modern Technology", *Journal of Arts and Ideas*, 14–15, pp. 47–78.

——1993, "The Epic Melodrama: Themes of Nationality in Indian Cinema", *Journal of Arts and Ideas*, 25–26, pp. 55–70.

Taylor, Richard 1986, "Boris Shumyatsky and the Soviet Cinema in the 1930s: Ideology as Mass Entertainment", *Historical Journal of Film, Radio and Television*, 6: 1: 43–64.

Vasudevan, Ravi S. 2006, "Addressing the Spectator of a 'Third World' National Cinema: The Bombay 'Social' Film of the 1940s and 1950s", in Dimitris Eleftheriotis and Gary Needham (eds), *Asian Cinemas: A Reader and Guide*, Edinburgh: Edinburgh University Press, pp. 295–316.

Wan, Jihong and Kraus, Richard 2002, "Hollywood and China as Adversaries and Allies", *Pacific Affairs*, 75: 3, pp. 419–434.

Yoshimoto, Mitsuhiro 2003, "Hollywood, Americanism and the imperial screen: geopolitics of image and discourse after the end of the Cold War", *Inter-Asia Cultural Studies*, 4: 3, pp. 452–459.

——2006, "The Difficulty of Being Radical: The Discipline of Film Studies and the Post-Colonial World Order", in Dimitris Eleftheriotis and Gary Needham (eds), *Asian Cinemas: A Reader and Guide*, Edinburgh: Edinburgh University Press, pp. 27–40.

22

Global cities

Chris Hudson

Introduction

Much of the research on global cities has given analytic primacy to the socio-economic factors that have engendered urban spatial arrangements, the hierarchy of world cities, and the changing forms of interaction between the structural features of the global, the national, and the local. Cities are also, of course, privileged sites for a global cosmopolitan culture and conduits for a range of powerful forces, not just financial. The global city is a more complex organism than cities in previous eras, more interconnected with other cities and more nebulous. It now demands a range of theoretical perspectives. Amin and Thrift's description of cities as 'relay stations in a world of flows' (Amin and Thrift 2002: 51) is now as important for an understanding of the global city as Friedmann's earlier description of cities as 'basing points for global operations' (1986).

Michael Peter Smith has enculated the problematic of the global city when he states that:

> ... there is no solid object known as the global city appropriate for grounding urban research, only an endless interplay of differently articulated transnational networks and practices best deciphered by studying the agency of the local, regional, national, and transnational actors that shape and sustain these transnational networks and their attendant practices and outcomes ... .
>
> (Smith 1998: 482)

This chapter will examine the global city by considering the ways in which global cities are constituted by their engagement with the universal, but are also enmeshed in an elaborate transnational network operating at multiple levels. While they are at one level basing points for the global economy, they are also sites for the local negotiation of global culture, mediated and acted out in the quotidian world of the locale, the district, the ghetto, the neighbourhood, the *quartier*, the *barrio* – the global city is made up of Appadurai's situated communities of social reproduction (Appadurai 1996: 179). Through nodes of international connectivity, the global is manifested and articulated through the everyday practices of the local. These concepts and their significance for understanding global cities will be the focus of my chapter.

The first three sections provide an overview of the development of thinking about global cities. This chapter cannot, within the limitations of a handbook, attempt to give a comprehensive and definitive history. It will, therefore, engage with what are widely regarded as some of the most important milestones in thinking about global cities in the last few decades, omitting the vast amount of excellent work that has been done to inform each new wave of thinking. The dimensions of the global city that have been identified by Friedmann, Sassen, and Castells will be the theoretical foci of these sections, that is, world/global cities are the 'basing points for global operations' (Friedmann); they can transcend the power of the nation-state (Sassen); they are the spaces of global flows (Castells). These three positions form the basis for the more recent theorizing about transnational cultural practices in global cites. While I have located these general positions in a sequence, it is not intended to promote a crude historicization of what is a complex and diverse tradition of thinking about cities. This structure is merely a shorthand way of understanding developments in thinking about cities. In the last two sections I will consider some of the particular localities that are a feature of global cities and which are imagined, invented, and configured under conditions of powerful globalizing forces.

World cities: basing points for international operations

Lewis Mumford's classic text (1961) is widely considered to be a starting point for thinking about cities. While recognizing the inherent ambiguities and contradictions of urban life, a theme taken up in more depth by later scholars, he argues that in the transformation from village to city the resulting complexity of social life and the enlargement of all the dimensions of life created a higher unity than that found in the village (Mumford 1961: 42). He recognized that the defining features of the city are its constant state of dynamic tension, and that it is a symbol of the possible (Mumford 1961: 42). Later work by Hall (1966) identified cities as centres of national power, the most significant function of which is government. Hall took the term 'world cities' from Scottish geographer Patrick Geddes' (1915) work on cities, and distinguished world cities from other major population centres by, first and foremost, their concentration of political power.

Theorizing about world cities in the last three decades has problematized key features of Hall's and Mumford's analyses. Hall's stress on cities as significant for the national, and Mumford's suggestion that cities should be read as holistic, even unified aggregations have been points of difference. Revision of Mumford and Hall's 1960 works has emerged from examination of the restructuring of the international economy. Later works (to be discussed below) have stressed: firstly, rather than seeing the world city as a conduit for the power of the nation, the increasing power of cities will create a tension between the national and the global. To some extent the major cities have decoupled themselves from their national economies and their interconnections to other global cities are now as important as their relationship to the nation in which they are located; secondly, the image of city as a holistic entity, depicted by Mumford as a bounded space of stability, and a symbol of the possible (1961: 42), is now more often than not conceived of as an amorphous sprawl with porous and ever-shifting boundaries. Mumford's city is a very different place from Sudjic's 100-mile city spreading in every direction (Sudjic 1992), or Davis' mega-cities and their networks of ever expanding slums (2006).

Indeed, Davis (2006) illustrates the difficulty of distinguishing the urban from the rural in some places, and even one city from another, with his description of the mega-sprawl of Jakarta (Davis 2006: 10). When urban slums spread to subsume nearby villages, the notion that urban development is the consequence of movement from the village to the city is also rendered obsolete. The increasing immiseration of millions of people in such megacities reminds us that the city is now also a symbol of the impossible.

Castells (1972) and Harvey (1973), writing in the Marxist tradition, moved the research focus away from a concern with the historical development of forms and functions of cities to an emphasis on social structure, modes of production, and the demands of twentieth century capitalism in general. In pointing out that Mumford used the evolution of spatial forms to classify the stages of universal history (Castells 1977: 7 [first published in French 1972]), Castells shifts the emphasis from history to political economy and outlines his premise that there is a 'relation between productive forces, social classes and cultural forms (including space)' (Castells 1977: 8). Taking the approach that urbanization in the underdeveloped regions of the global South must be understood with reference to the general problematic of underdevelopment and capitalist social relations (Castells 1977: 43), he refocuses the study of urbanization, not on individual countries or cities, but on the economic relations between the imperialist metropolises and the 'underdeveloped' countries (Castells 1977: 43). This dependent urbanization, a feature of the system of production and its accompanying class relations, is expressed in the spatial arrangements of cities.

Harvey's (1973) innovative contribution to the development of the field of urbanism, was to focus on space as an effect of social process (Harvey 1973: 27). Through what he called the 'social-process-spatial-form theme' (Harvey 1973: 14) he transformed thinking about space by arguing that the spatial logic of cities can only be understood with reference to the mode of production: 'Urbanism is a social form, a way of life predicated on, among other things, a certain division of labour and a certain hierarchical ordering of activity which is broadly consistent with the dominant mode of production' (Harvey 1973: 202). Harvey and Castells moved the study of urbanization and the spatial arrangements of cities into the context of a specific mode of production, the division of labour it imposes, and the class relations that arise from it. Whereas Mumford's work focused on cities as a product of time (Mumford 1986 [first published 1938]), subsequent revisions have focused on cities as a product of space. It is now recognized that capitalist development has been driven by a spatio-temporal rhythm, a 'conjunction of periodicity and spatialization' (Soja 1989: 3). As far as Friedmann (1986) is concerned, these early works of Castells and Harvey revolutionized the study of urbanization and paved the way for subsequent developments in thinking about world cities.

Economic developments of the last three decades have resulted in transformations in the spatial organization of capitalism. In turn, these have precipitated a change in the direction of research. Up until the 1970s, the international economy was managed by a monetary order and its accompanying institutions established by the Bretton Woods system in 1945. The international financial system of exchange rates, monetary policies and the determining of the value of currencies rested on the trade between sovereign nations across national borders. As the post-World War Two industrial structure – that precipitated, amongst other developments, the rise of the so-called Asian Tiger economies – was being transformed into a more flexible regime of production and accumulation, certain patterns of urban development were also taking place. The collapse of the Fordist production model and the development of global financial, media, entertainment, information and communication technology industries (amongst others), created the means for more flexible patterns of capitalist accumulation. Restructuring of the economic system was not limited to any specific nation or region, but resulted in a global shift, the chief characteristic of which came to be known as the 'New International Division of Labour'. The multinational corporations were seen as the major agents in this shift, and were widely understood to be capable of transcending national boundaries and state power to further their own ends of capital accumulation through a global reach of corporate power. The multinationals gained greater control over the world's raw materials, penetrated new markets and exploited the cheap labour outside the multinational's home country (King 1990: 15) thereby exporting the capitalist relations of production that Castells and Harvey detailed. Taylor (2004) points out that even though scholars had identified a 'global reach' (Barnett and Muller 1974) and a 'world without borders' (Brown 1973), at this time, the framework for understanding the economic restructuring that was embracing most of the globe was understood to be 'the new international division of labour' rather than globalization (Taylor 2004: 21). Sudjic has described the 1980s as a period of 'explosive dislocation' in which 'the industrial city finally shook off the last traces of its nineteenth-century self and mutated into a completely new species' (Sudjic 1992: 1). Major cities were transformed by the annihilation of traditional industries and the rise of technological innovation and new work patterns. Since the 1980s urban scholars have begun to explore the questions of how global forces and dynamics impact on local and regional spaces. Featherstone et al.'s (1995) volume, for example, is devoted to considering the extent to which the globalization *problématique* represents the spatialization of social theory (1995:1).

Wallerstein's World System Theory (1976) appeared in the 1970s to investigate the nexus between capitalism and the increasingly systematic control of spaces of economic activity. Since the sixteenth century, Wallerstein pointed out, there has been one principal mode of production, or capitalist world economy. The economy of the world can be understood spatially by recognizing three zones, distinguished by their mode of engagement with the world economy, and their stage of economic development. They are: *core* (regions with post-industrial economies and corporate headquarters such as the US, Europe, Japan, Australia), *semi-periphery* (rapidly industrializing areas still dependent on the core, such as Singapore, Mexico, Brazil, Egypt) and the *world periphery* (poor, technologically lagging and politically weak states). He argued that world economy is no longer defined by imperial might, but by transnational capital, spatially articulated through world cities as the control centres of the global economy. World city formation entrenches social class divisions and transnational elites are the dominant class in the world city in which an underclass will be a structural feature (Wallerstein 1976: 1999).

The world city as a research agenda and framework for understanding the dynamics of the international economy was arguably given its greatest fillip with the publication of Friedmann and Wolff's influential paper: *World City Formation: An Agenda for Research and Action* in 1982. They argued that specific modes of their articulation into the global economy give rise to an urban hierarchy of influence and control, at the top of which is a small number of massive urban regions they call 'world cities'. These include Tokyo, Los Angeles, New York, London, Paris, Frankfurt, Cairo, Bangkok, Hong Kong, and so on (Friedmann and Wolff 1982).

The core of their argument, and the point of departure for a research agenda, was that since World War Two, capitalist institutions have increasingly freed themselves from the constraints of national structures and organized global production and markets for their own purposes. Huge megalopolises such as Los Angeles – more an 'urban field' than a city with discernible boundaries – are the material form that this economic restructuring on a global scale assumes. Friedmann and Wolff outlined the historical context from which world cities have emerged, and noted amongst other points that: world cities as an instrument for the control of production and market organization are in a dialectical relationship to the nations in which they are situated; the interests of the nation state and transnational capital are in conflict; the mode of integration of cities into the world system will affect their social, spatial, and political structures, and the specific forms of urbanization; structural instability and class inequality will be a permanent feature of a world city (Friedmann and Wolff 1982). In addition, an important point is that in world cities this class inequality will be reflected spatially: some districts will be characterized by modes of urbanization reminiscent of the Third World (Friedmann and Wolff 1982), while the transnational elite will live in areas that Friedmann and Wolff call 'citadels' (1982). An important feature of the world city is the presence of a globally mobile managerial and entrepreneurial class. Its chief functions are: management, banking and finance, legal services, accounting, technical consulting, telecommunications and computing, international transportation, research and higher education (Friedmann and Wolff 1982: 320).

In his later work, *The World City Hypothesis* (1986), Friedmann emphasized the inherent tension between capitalist production in a global era, and the interests of the nation-state. In the context of the New International Division of Labour that accompanied this, the control of the global economy was shifting from the nation to the city. In this scenario, world cities are 'basing points' in the spatial organization and articulation of production and market, and the location for the concentration for international capital. The resulting linkages make it possible to arrange world cities in a complex spatial hierarchy (Friedmann 1986). Castells (1972) and Harvey (1973), writing in the Marxist tradition, moved the research focus away from a concern with the historical development of forms and functions of cities to an emphasis on social structure, modes of production, and the demands of twentieth century capitalism in general. World city status is not determined by size, but by the concentration of economic and cultural power. A common feature is a 'dichotomized workforce' of professionals carrying out control functions at one end, and manufacturing and service industries at the other (Friedmann 1986).

Studies of the expansion of multinational and transnational corporations and the new international division of labour on which their success was predicated, encouraged the emergence of a new paradigm of conceiving the world economy not so much as international, but as global. In the global economy, a more powerful network of economic and political processes operate globally and have the potential to evade national structures and regulations. World cities are points of control, not only for the global economy, especially since they are the nodes for the movement of global money (Knox 1995), but also for global culture. Since the 1980s the study of the growth of cities has focused on the interconnection between economics and space, in a global economy now acknowledged to be increasingly oblivious to national boundaries (Sassen 2007). Brenner (1998) has argued that post-Fordist global capitalism works through strategies of reterritorialization and the global city is the privileged site for this. World capitalism, once relying on a 'state-centric configuration' (Brenner 1998: 28) embedded in a 'Fordist-Keynsian sociospatial regime' (Brenner 1998: 18), has been spatially transformed. Urban configurations have become disarticulated from the nation and have become nodes of accumulation of global capital and 'sites of reterritorialization for post-Fordist forms of global industrialization'(Brenner 1998: 3). Shifting research foci on the changing functions of cities have roughly paralleled changes in the global economy and concomitant spatial arrangements.

Global cities: command points in the global economy

Cohen (2006 [1981]) was one of the first to describe the emergence of the global city as the site for advanced corporate services and the coordination and control of the new international division of labour (Cohen 2006: 50), but Saskia Sassen probably did more to promote the idea of the global city than anyone else. She argues that with the breakdown of conditions supporting the international regime based largely on the economic dominance of the US, the global economy was transformed. It became simultaneously globally integrated and spatially dispersed (Sassen 1991: 3). It is within the context of this duality that major cities found a new strategic role in global economic affairs, and a new type of city emerged.

The central role of cities in international trade had long been established. An international economic system with its power based in key urban centres, or 'world cities', pre-dates modernity. Robertson and Inglis' (2004) analysis of Rome and the ancient Mediterranean world and Abu-Lughod's (1989) study of the geographically dispersed cities enmeshed in a network of commercial and cultural exchange a thousand years before European hegemony demonstrate this. Now, however, certain cities could be thought of as *global* cities, rather than world cities, because of the new functions they had taken on in this dualized economic environment. Sassen argued that cities were now: first, highly concentrated command points in the organization of the world economy; second, key locations for finance and for specialized service firms, which have replaced manufacturing as the leading economic sectors; third, as sites of production, including the production of innovations, in these leading industries; and fourth, as markets for the products and innovations produced (Sassen 1991: 3–4). Cites are now, more than ever, globally integrated with each other.

Sassen identified New York, London, and Tokyo as the prime examples of a global city. What she found of greatest interest was the fact that these three cities had undergone massive changes in their economic base, spatial organization, and social structure and that although these cities have diverse historical and cultural conditions, the changes seemed to be parallel. The one feature they all share is the continuing increase in the agglomeration of central functions as the economy becomes more globalized. Sassen argues that global cities are different from cities in economic formations that existed prior to the 1970s because there is now a greater need for expanded central control and management. Following on from Friedmann's notion of cities as nodal points for the coordination of processes (Friedmann 1986) she argues that they are also sites for the production of specialized services that globally dispersed capitalist institutions require. Services and processes are now the 'things' the global city makes (Sassen 1991: 5). New York, London, and Tokyo are the prime production sites for financial innovations and centralized marketplaces for these 'products' (1991: 6).

Castells follows Sassen and maintains that these three dominant global nodes operate largely as a unit in the same system of endless transactions, covering the spectrum of time zones for the purpose of financial trading (Castells 1996: 410). Thrift imagines this process as a blizzard of transactions – continuous, never-ending transactions (Thrift 1999: 272). In this way, the global city can overcome the constraints of both time and space. Rather than competing with each other as the centre of rival nations, these cities constitute a system which produces global control for cities, rather than nations. Global control is located in these cities (Sassen 1991: 6) and much of Sassen's more recent work has explored the potential for dislocating the global city from the nation state (2002, 2005, 2007).

Friedmann followed up his two earlier articles mentioned above by revisiting the world city research agenda a decade later (Friedmann 1995). Recognizing the ambiguities that had arisen since the original world city hypothesis, he sought to define the class of cities that had by then come to be commonly termed global or world cities. In the work of Sassen and others, a new type of city had been identified, and Friedmann defines common characteristics of that new type of city. Cities, as spatially organized socio-economic systems, act as centres which articulate larger regional and national economies into the global economy or the *space of global accumulation* (Friedmann's emphasis). This serves the purposes of capital accumulation on a worldwide scale (Friedmann 1995: 22). Cities are urbanized regions defined by forms of interaction, not by political or administrative boundaries. Friedmann cites Sudjik's 'hundred-mile' city as a prime example of this (1995: 23). These cities are the commanding nodes of the global system and can be arranged into a *hierarchy of spatial articulations* (Friedmann's emphasis; 1995: 23). Position in the hierarchy is not only unstable, but is contingent upon fierce inter-city competition (Castells 1996: 414) that can result in fluctuations in fortune due to financial failure. Nevertheless, Friedmann has ranked cities, according to their spatial articulations into the various fields of authority (Friedmann 1995: 24). This is not a measure of size, but a way of defining and evaluating their spheres of influence. He reiterates that those cities identified by Sassen (London, New York, Tokyo) as truly global cities are at the top of the hierarchy because they have established the most powerful global financial articulations. The second tier cities are identified by the level of their multinational articulations. These cities include Miami, Los Angeles, Frankfurt, Amsterdam, and Singapore. A third tier is distinguished by the importance of their national articulations and include Paris, Zurich, Madrid, Sydney, Seoul. Friedmann's final field of articulation is subnational and regional articulations and includes Osaka-Kobe and the Kansai region in Japan, Hong Kong and the Pearl River Delta region in China, amongst others (Friedmann 1995: 24).

It is less important to distinguish conceptually between global cities and world cities than to understand their functions. After all, Friedmann, an important pioneer of work on global cities uses the terms interchangeably (1995: 31) as do Brenner (1998) and others. There is general agreement among observers that London, New York, Tokyo, and Paris are global cities and will appear at the top of most hierarchies of cities through which economic and cultural power flows. Cities below that level, however, are more difficult to classify. Any inventory of cities and their functions will need constantly revising to take account of the changing fortunes of urban fields and their relationship to circuits of cultural and financial power. Sassen points out that global circuits that constitute the networks of global cities are still emerging, and that cities such as Shanghai and Beijing have only recently come onto the circuit (Sassen 2002: 83). Nevertheless, Beaverstock, Taylor, and Smith have produced a roster of world cities in which *global competence* (authors' emphasis) as an indicator of their power is defined in relation to four key services: accounting, advertising, banking, and law (Beaverstock, Taylor, and Smith 1999). Their inventory of world cities – too comprehensive to be reproduced here – is constructed by using the criteria identified by major scholars such as Friedmann, Hall, Thrift, Knox, and Sassen as part of the Globalization and World Cities Research Network (www.lboro.ac.uk/gawc/). The research network ranks cities in groups, with alpha cities heading the list. Their alpha cities are: London, New York, Paris, Tokyo, Chicago, Frankfurt, Hong Kong, Los Angeles, Milan, and Singapore. Comparison of populations gives an idea of the importance of global competence rather than size: London has a population of around 7,662,399, while Singapore as an alpha-ranked global city has a population of only 4,839,000. This is, of course, the total population of the Singapore nation, since Singapore is 100 percent urban. In addition, primate cities such as London often dwarf the next most populous city in the country. Birmingham, Great Britain's second biggest city has a population of around 999,900. It is also important to note the political as well as cultural dominance of global cities within their countries. The position of Mayor of London carries with it so much political influence that Prime Minister Gordon Brown campaigned for Labour candidate Ken Livingstone in the March 2008 elections for Mayor of London, despite ten years of public enmity between him and Livingstone. Former mayor of New York, Rudy Giuliani, was once known as 'America's Mayor', and was named *Time* magazine's Person of the Year for 2001 for his management of the September 11 attacks on the World Trade Centre. His position as mayor, afforded him the legitimacy to run for the Republican Party nomination in the 2008 US presidential election.

Beaverstock, et al., point out that global cities, defined as the most powerful global service centres, are concentrated in certain regions and implicated in forms of uneven globalization (Beaverstock et al 1999: 457). They note that world city formation has primarily taken place in three world regions – North America, Western Europe, and Pacific Asia (Beaverstock et al 1999: 457). It is also important to note that while global cities may be antagonistic to one another (Sudjic 1992: 1), and the competitive *angst* that Friedmann refers to (1995:23) is pervasive, they can also form conglomerates which link regions or extend them. Some time in the not too distant future, Mike Davis predicts, we can expect to see Tokyo-Shanghai world city dipole equal to the New York-London axis in its control of global flows of capital and information (Davis 2006: 7). Castells alludes to the possibility of a Tokyo-Yokohama-Nagoya triad – already functioning as a unit – joining the Osaka-Kobe-Kyoto conurbation, thereby creating the largest metropolitan agglomeration in human history (Castells 1996: 438). On current estimates, the population of Tokyo is around 12 million – some ten percent of the total population of Japan. The urban agglomeration of Tokyo-Yokohama, however, is estimated to be more than thirty-three million. This is thought to be the largest 'city' in the world, followed by Seoul with some 22 million and Mexico City with more than 19 million.

These expanding megalopolises and urban axes across national boundaries substantiate Sassen's proposition that there is in the new world economic order a systemic discontinuity between global cities and their national contexts, while at the same time global cities are systematically linked to each other (Sassen 1991: 8-9). Relations between cities, rather than nation-states is now at the forefront of many new studies and the key research focus of the Globalization and World Cities Research Network. While megacities can transcend the nation as the centres of economic, technological, cultural, and political power globally, their countries' economic fate is still dependent on them (Castells 1996: 440).

Networked cities: relay stations in a world of flows

Theorizing about the nature of cities is more likely now to focus on fluidity rather than the fixity of zones, fragmentation rather than integrity, and extraterritorial rather than intra-national connections in cities. Thinking about cities has reached the point where Amin and Thrift can assert that the city has no centre, no completeness and no fixed parts; it can not even be theorized as a whole (Amin and Thrift 2002: 8). This shift in thinking has paralleled changes in the dominant mode of production described above.

When the information economy replaces the industrial economy as a mode of production, new conceptualizations and alternative paradigms emerge to take account of the effects this will have on urban space. That is why for Castells, it is important to see the global city now in terms of *flows*, and to recognize 'the spatial logic of the new system' (Castells 1996: 417). He follows Sassen's description of the new strategic role for major cities through which they are implicated in a system of spatial dispersal and global integration (see above, Sassen 1991: 3-4). It is the dominant spatial logic of our society because it is the spatial logic of the dominant interests of our society (Castells 1996: 445). The advanced services, which are at the core of global economic processes (finance, insurance, legal, accounting, scientific innovation, and so on), can all ultimately be reduced to knowledge generation and information flows (Castells 1996: 409).

In Castells' account, flows are not merely an aspect of our economic, political, and symbolic lives, but are the processes that dominate it. He defines flows as the 'purposeful, programmable sequences of exchange and interaction between physically disjointed positions held by social actors in the economic, political and symbolic structures of society' (Castells 1996: 442). From this he argues that these flows inhabit a new spatial form: the space of flows (Castells 1996: 442). The space of flows is the material form of support for dominant processes constituted by three layers of material support: circuits of electronic exchanges; nodes and hubs that link up specific places; the spatial organization of the dominant, managerial elite (Castells 1996: 442-5). This networked society has profound implications for conceptualizing the global city. Perhaps one of the most exciting hypotheses to emerge in the new thinking about cities, and which is clearly articulated by Castells, is that the global city is not a place but a process (Castells 1996: 417). The process entails the interconnection of cities as centres of production and consumption of advanced services embedded in a global network. Sassen draws a parallel between the spaces of flows and the fate of the nation: 'these multiple flows and transactions are increasingly producing a cross-border space anchored in cities that to some extent bypass national states' (Sassen 2002: 83). It is the flows of information, of technology, of organizational interaction, images, sounds, and symbols (Castells 1996: 442) that give the global city its power, link it to other cities, and provide the conditions for the diminution of the economic significance of the national hinterland.

Appadurai (1996) has also conceptualized global interactions as a series of flows. He problematizes the centre-periphery model for understanding the spatial arrangements of the international division of labour made popular by Wallerstein (1976, 1999) and others associated with the Marxist tradition, arguing that the global cultural economy can be conceptualised as a series of global cultural flows. These flows are: *ethnoscapes* (the landscape of mobile people such as tourists, immigrants, refugees, exiles, guest workers, and so on); *mediascapes* (the flow of images as an interconnected repertoire of print, celluloid, electronic screens and billboards which present accounts of reality); *technoscapes* (the global dispersal of technology); *financescapes* (the disposition of global capital through currency markets, stock exchanges, commodity speculations, and so on); *ideoscapes* (the landscape of images and ideas that are often associated with the ideologies of states and state power) (Appadurai 1996: 32-36). These landscapes of flows are important for an understanding of the global city for two reasons: firstly, the conduits for these flows are cities, and they are constitutive of a global cosmopolitan culture; and secondly, they are *imagined worlds* (Appadurai's emphasis) 'that is, multiple worlds that are constituted by the historically situated imaginations of persons or groups spread around the globe' (Appadurai 1996: 33). Through these imagined worlds, Appadurai points out, people may be

437

'able to contest and sometimes even subvert the imagined worlds of the official mind ...' (Appadurai 1996: 33). In other words, they may offer a competing claim on the imagination that could unsettle other affiliations and the imagined communities (Anderson 1991) of the nation. This makes possible the multiple attachments to dispersed places and produces the 'endless interplay' (Smith 1998) of networks that is a feature of global society.

In recent work, Sassen has focused on questions of place and scale in the global system, and on the concept of multiscalar. According to her, there are about forty global cities in the world connected through networks that can bypass national states. These networks are now one of the critical global formations (Sassen 2007: 13), and an indication that the global is partially constituted through the denationalizing of components of the national territory and its institutional domains (Sassen 2007: 14). The subnational is an important arena for theorizing the global city, since practices and conditions at the local scale are articulated with global dynamics (Sassen 2007: 18). For Sassen, 'the crucial conditionality here is the partial embeddedness of the global in the national, of which the global city is perhaps most emblematic' (Sassen, 2007: 22). What is most important for an understanding of the construction of locality in a global city is that, as Sassen states: Global processes do not need to move through the hierarchies of national states; they can directly become articulated with certain kinds of localities and local actors (Sassen 2007: 33). Global cities are now the sites for the playing out of globalizing tendencies that can partially decouple the global from the national. They are the conduits for multiscalar interactions through which the hierarchy of scale – global, national or local – is less important than its multiplicity (Sassen, 2007). These three fields of action operate in various dimensions, on multiple scales, and in multiple and shifting modes of interaction.

Transnational cities: spaces and places

If globalization was once thought of as an all-too-powerful force through which local cultural identities would be subsumed and erased in favour of the global, this notion has been undermined by the extensive works that have been carried out on the relationship between the local and the global (for example, Wilson and Dissanayake's widely cited 1996 text). Robertson (1995) used the term 'glocalization' (now in common use) to denote a situation in which there is neither global homogenization nor heterogenization but an oddly oxymoronic amalgamation of the two; a combining of the universal and the particular in everyday life. He points out that the local does not assert itself *against* the global and that locality should not be cast as a form of opposition to the global (Robertson 1995: 29). If the national and the global are not mutually exclusive (Sassen 2007: 22), neither are the global and the local. The local is constituted through the global via the increasing interconnectedness of cultures and involves the 'invention' of locality, not in opposition to the global, but somehow in the changing context of the global. (Robertson, 1995: 35). Smith (2001) promotes the term 'transnationalism' and argues that the very concept of 'urban' requires 'reconceptualization as a social space that is a cross-roads ... for the interplay of diverse *localizing* (Smith's emphasis) practices of national, transnational or even global-scale actors ... ' (Smith 2001: 27). 'Transnational urbanism' (Smith 2001) is both multiscalar and localizing. The multiplicity of scales on which these actors can operate and the modes of transnational urbanism can be understood with reference to Hannerz's four social categories who have transnational relationships and play a major role in the making of world cities. They are: a highly educated, highly mobile, professionally skilled managerial and entrepreneurial class; semi-skilled and unskilled people from various parts of the Third World who carry out a large amount of the servicing required for the global economy; people involved in 'expressive activities', for example art, film and the entertainment industries; and tourists. Of these categories, the professionals, the transnational elite, are the dominant class (Hannerz 1996: 128–9).

The human and cultural flows of which these people are a part, give the world city its transnational character. Embedded in the global city is a large variety of cultural environments emerging from the formation of transnational identities. These are also a fundamental aspect of globalization (Sassen 1998: xxx) and a constitutive feature of the global city. Immigration, leading to diversifying ethnicity in new locations, might be thought of as 'a set of processes whereby global elements are localized, international labour markets are constituted, and cultures from all over the world are de- and reterritorialized' (Sassen 1998: xxxi). All the sets of actors identified by Hannerz relocate to spaces (even if only temporarily) which become sites of the subnational, and all in some way constitute the denationalization of the global city.

Denationalization, deterritorialization, and the construction of transnational identities means that the local, or the *place* of this construction is now central to the global economy. A deeper understanding of the local can be read through Castells' supposition that the space of flows does not permeate to every level of urban environment and the places of cultural practice. Most people live in a place which might be understood in the anthropological sense as relational, historical, and concerned with identity (Augé 1995: 79). George Ritzer (2007) has distinguished between place as 'unique settings characterised by deep ties to the locale's history' and spaces, defined by flows which are 'generic, lack geographic ties and have a "time-free quality"' (Ritzer 2007: 61).

Castells distinction between the spaces of flows – hollow spaces not anchored in a given nation or community – and spaces of place can be roughly translated into a global space/local place polarization. This has been judged by some scholars to be too simplistic a polarization (Hubbard 2006: 177). Recent thinking, particularly postmodern accounts of urban geography (Soja 1989; Dear 2000), have stressed that urban spatial configurations and the locales embedded within them are mutable, permeable, and multilayered. The now widespread use of the metaphor 'flow' is an indication of how amorphous urban geographers and cultural theorists consider global interactions at all levels and in all modes to be. The global or world city – the location of spaces and places – should be thought of less in terms of the integrity described by Mumford, and more in terms of Amin and Thrift's city as an 'amalgam of often disjointed processes and social heterogeneity, a place of near and far connections' (Amin and Thrift 2002: 8). This requires an acceptance of the fluid, amorphous, and ephemeral relations between the local, the national and the global, and an understanding of Sassen's central premise that global processes operate on multiple scales, some deep within the nation (2007). Castells' distinction is nevertheless a useful tool for considering the difference between the spaces of flows in a global city, and transnational cultural practices at the local level, if only because the modes of transnational connection encompassed by these conceptualizations are different.

While it is clear that class and ethnic concentration in districts, ghettos, and quarters has always been a feature of cities, Marcuse and van Kempen (2000) maintain that global cities now encompass intensified spatial concentrations of poverty at one end of the economic spectrum, and the space for protected enclaves for the rich, cosmopolitan class at the other. They are structurally integrated but socially fragmented. One way to consider the global city is to think of it as a postmodern congeries of fragmented, disconnected, and socially differentiated enclaves (Soja 1989; Dear 2000) of which Los Angeles is often the prime example; another is as a series of urban villages, or quarters, each offering a distinctive cultural timbre (Bell and Jayne, 2004). Whichever way it is imagined, the point to be made is that globalization has increased the mobility of both cosmopolitan elites and labour immigrants, and has created what Beck has called 'transnational social spaces' (Beck, 2000). They operate on subnational scales – the spaces of denationalized global classes (Sassen 2007, 164–189) or deterritorialized immigrants (Appadurai 1996, 37–38).

It is clear, in a world in which for the first time in human history the urban population of the earth will soon outnumber the rural (Davis 2006: 1), that the dominant culture of the world is *cosmopolitan* (Friedmann 1995: 23). Like Hannerz (1996), Sklair has identified the new controllers of this dominant culture as the 'transnational capitalist class' (Sklair 2001), a strata of people more or less in control of the processes of globalization, not unlike Tom Wolfe's New York bond trading fictional 'Masters of the Universe' (Wolfe 1987). Sudjic sums up the transnational cosmopolitan capitalist class: 'In Knightsbridge and Beverly Hills the dentists and tax lawyers lead similar kinds of lives, protected by the same burglar alarms, driving back and forth in the same late-model Mercedes' (Sudjic 1992: 5). One could also add here that in the twenty-first century the tax lawyers and dentists (or bond traders and IT specialists) protecting themselves with the burglar alarms and driving the latest Mercedes also inhabit the 'exclusionary enclaves' (Marcuse and van Kempen 2000: 4) of the high earning, mobile elites to be found in Asian global cities such as Shanghai, Beijing, Tokyo, Singapore, and Seoul, or the more recently emerged second or third tier global cities of Mumbai and Kuala Lumpur. A saunter through the Takashimaya Centre in Orchard Road, Singapore, or the KL City Centre in Kuala Lumpur, or a stroll down Nanjing Road, Shanghai will reveal the availability of universal elite brands of clothing, cars, cosmetics, and so on from Japan, the US, and Europe. The spaces of global elites are characterized by a certain sameness, anonymity, and blandness in a continuum with a universal set of 'nullities' (Ritzer 2007). They are, if you will, spaces of flows consistent with Castells proposition that the global city is not a place but a process (1996: 417) entailing the interconnection of global cities as centres of production and consumption of advanced services embedded in a global network of flows. There is any number of examples of communities of transnational elites – generally known in the English vernacular as 'expats' – all over the world in global cities. In many cases, such as in Dubai, parallel universes of expats are created where schools, shopping complexes, doctors, dentists and so on, not accessed by the local population can be found. These are, of course, places of denationalization and deterritorialization, in Sassen's terms.

Deterritorialized cities: globurbs and ethnoburbs

The global, the national and the subnational should not be understood as discrete fields, but as overlapping, and unstable in their modes of engagement with each other. Similarly Hannerz's social categories, the actors in these fields, may also need to be reconceptualized to account for slippage in the categories and the possibility for overlap, modifications over time and the ability to move between categories. In addition to Hannerz's four transnational categories, I suggest two sub-groups that are a feature of global cities. They are implicated in the processes which take place in national and local settings but are still part of globalization since they involve: 'transboundary networks and formations connecting or articulating multiple local or "national" processes and actors' (Sassen 2005:

156). These two categories of people are the inhabitants of places that are partially denationalized, while at the same time embedded within the nation. One is the 'local transnational elites'; the other is a permanently settled but ethnically differentiated sub-national group with both national and transnational connections. Both these groups have created specific places that reflect the sense of belonging to multiple worlds spread across the globe portrayed by Appadurai (1996: 33). These microcosms are the locations of competing claims on the imagination.

Mike Davis has identified enclaves for communities of local transnational elites. As 'parallel worlds', they are often gated communities for the wealthy, and usually some distance from the host city. A defining characteristic is that they are in some ways disconnected from the local culture in its chaotic richness, while at the same time connected to a global commodified culture through which the status attached to the consumption of luxury and the public endorsement of their privileged position is produced. Davis describes 'Orange County' as 'a gated estate of sprawling million-dollar California-style homes, designed by a Newport Beach architect and with Martha Stewart décor, on the Northern outskirts of Beijing ... ' (Davis 2006: 115). He reports that in China people feel Orange County is a brand name, like Giorgio Armani (Davis 2006: 115). Giroir's (2006) version of this is the 'Purple Jade Villas' community, another upmarket private residential estate outside Beijing. It represents not just 'socio-spatial differentation' (Giroir 2006: 143) from the rest of Beijing, but also a sort of niche world in which the economy runs on the US dollar. Everyday spending is done with yuan (with prices determined by yuan-dollar parity), but all other expenditure (rental payments, club memberships, and so on) is in dollars (Giroir 2006: 149). A microcosmic political economy of luxury is embedded in an economy operating at the national scale, while at the same time integrally connected to the global scale economically and culturally. As Sassen has emphasized, the local scale can be articulated with global dynamics (Sassen 2007: 18), and can bypass the nation, in this case, even the national economy.

King (2004) points out that asipring global cities often define themselves in the context of other world cities. In advertising, Beijing's new developments are compared with those at Tokyo's Ginza, New York's Manhattan, and London's Canary Wharf. He has dubbed these communities of 'newly affluent locals' (King 2004: 120) and transnational elites, *globurbs*. His neologism is a way of discussing new forms of territoriality and new classes of city dwellers, and to counter the impression that all manifestations of globalization are high-rise office towers, international banks, and corporations located in the CBDs and downtowns of major cities (King 2004: 98). The globurb is a settlement on the outskirts of a city, the origins of which 'are generated less by developments inside the city, or even inside the country, and more by external forces beyond its boundaries' (King 2004: 103).

The global cities of India also have their spaces for local elite that reference global cultural standards and announce their connection with places outside the national or local cultural milieu. One Indian globurb is Gurgaon, a satellite suburb of Delhi. An article in the New York Times describes Gurgaon as: 'A beacon of India's red-hot economy ... an island of air conditioned malls and roaring, round-the-clock office towers ... ' (Sengupta 2008). Gurgaon is an example of what Davis – using the terminology of Ridley Scott's *Blade Runner* – calls 'off-worlds' (Davis 2006: 115), parallel universes geographically and culturally separated from their host cities and even host nations. While Gurgaon, which calls itself 'The Millenium City' (http://gurgaon.nic.in/), is a brightly lit boomtown, the rest of the country is a 'vast nation of darkness and cow-dung-fuelled stoves' (Sengupta 2008). Gurgaon is a space of transnational culture (King, 2004) and, in a reversal of the

441

usual diasporic flows of people, hopes to be a mecca for what is commonly known in India as the NRI – Non-Resident Indian. While the NRIs act out the culture of global success, others are excluded from the 'constructed dream' (King, 2004: 129). Some people work in the Gurgaons of the New India but live in villages such as Chakai Haat, Bihar, which has no access to the electricity grid. Somini Sengupta cites one such worker, Muhamammad Mumtaz Alam, who encompasses the divide between the global city and the space of the nation when he says: 'There, we live in light. Here, we live in darkness' (Sengupta 2008). Gurgoan offers the location for a community of NRIs, in which the shared category of Indian-ness may be less important than the shared category of affluent, mobile, outwardly oriented agents of global capitalism. Their participation as actors in the global economic system may be more important than their participation in the local or national economy. In some cases their status as NRIs is certainly more important than their status as Indian nationals. King points out that some of the new globurbs in India offer 'world class homes' built to 'global specifications', that are 'exclusively for the Non-Resident Indians' (2004: 132–3). The Gurgaon phenomenon is consistent with Wallerstein's view that world city formation entrenches social class divisions (Wallerstein 1976: 1999) and that this will be reflected spatially by modes of differential urbanization (Friedmann and Wolff 1982). Sassen has identified this as a 'new geography of centrality and marginality' (Sassen 1998: xxv) in the development of global cities.

The second transnational sub-category is people who have once been part of the shifting, mobile world, but who have since created stable communities in a new location. The Chinatowns of many global cities are the result of nineteenth-century diasporic flows of people, and are not the result of the transformation of the global economy in the 1970s. Where they once housed a concentration of low-skilled immigrant labour, they are no longer the polar opposite of the 'exclusionary enclaves', or citadels for the transnational elite. The thriving 'Little Saigons' of Melbourne and Sydney, for example, are the result of refugee flows from the end of the Vietnam War. While these communities may be stable, Appadurai believes that ' … the warp of these stabilities is everywhere shot through with the woof of human emotion … ' (Appadurai 1996: 33–4). They live in multiple imaginary worlds connecting the 'life-worlds constituted by relatively stable associations, by relatively known and shared histories' (Appadurai 1996: 191) to geo-graphically separate emotional 'homelands'. For Appadurai, these life-worlds are funda-mentally opposed to the imaginary of the nation-state (Appadurai 1996: 191). It is perhaps more accurate to say that in particular neighbourhoods in global cities, more than one imaginary, and more than one mode of engagement with the local, the national, and the global is possible.

In his study of the Chinese communities in California, Li (1998) has identified a similar transnational urban concentration of a diasporized ethnic group. He calls this an *ethnoburb*. The ethnoburb is characterized by vibrant communities dominated by a single ethnic group, and, significantly, by strong ties to the global economy. The ethnoburb has two salient features: firstly, it is a community which shares language, food, family, and other networks, as well as television, radio, and vernacular newspapers focused on news from the former homeland. This 'makes people feel at home' (Li 1998) when 'home' is in more than one location; and secondly, it has substantial ties to the global economy through the business activities, mobility, and extensive networks of its inhabitants. Li describes it as 'an integrated business and residential outpost designed to serve globalized capital' (Li 1998). It might be more useful, however, to see these ethnoburbs not as 'outposts', but as a part of a circuit in the global economy, as described by Sassen, and as a constitutive feature of the global city. Such communities represent one level of Sassen's subnational scales and spaces of denationalized global classes (Sassen 2007, 164–189) and are much more significant in the global economy than 'outposts'. They are an example of the ways in which the 'contemporary local-global interplay' (Brenner 1998: 3) is manifested in multiple spatial scales.

Hannerz (1996) has described the production of 'habitats of meaning', lived spaces in which inhabitants create and manage meaning in their everyday lives. This is related to the concept of place, as Augé uses it, that is, it is concerned with human connection and identity (Augé 1995: 79). Whereas the ethnoburb or the transnational social space represents a form of deterritorialization from a home country, it also offers a form of reterritorialization and the possibility for the creation of habitats of meaning in one location overlapping with distant spaces, also saturated with meaning. Shukla (2003) writes of the creation of forms of global belonging in Little Indias around the world. London's Southall is the location of modes of transnational urbanism and an example of transnational place-making (Smith 2001) where the local and the global intersect and operate on multiscalar circuits. Southall, the home of London's Punjabi community is one such Little India which creates a habitat of meaning for a transcultural citizen, or what Smith calls 'positioned subjects occupying multiple social locations … ' (Smith 2001: 6), in which the practices of everyday life in the global city encompass both a national and a transnational imaginary. Southall has a gurdwara (Sikh temple) and is crowded with Indian grocers, Indian restaurants, shops specializing in Indian clothes. It has Indian travel agents, Indian banks, cinemas devoted to Bollywood movies, bhangra (Indian dance music) clubs, a Punjabi radio station, and so on. The sign for Southall Railway Station is in two languages. Ethnoburbs such as Southall represent a deterritorialization since it is a displaced world, but also a reterritorialization through the creation of a new habitat of meaning for Indians. The Indian diaspora, generally thought to number about twenty million, maintains transnational circuits on subnational scales. The transnational Indian family has resulted in the development of transnational family money, with remittances to India estimated to be around US$ 21.7 billion annually (Singh 2006). The sourcing of marriage partners from India is a commonplace transnational practice that links the local with other locals and is contingent upon a flexible, transnational imaginary.

While neighbourhoods may be in perpetual struggle against the competing discourses of the nation, as Appadurai has asserted (1996: 189), there are also many examples of vibrant neighbourhoods, or ethnoburbs, in global cities all over the world, whose structure of feeling and properties of social life (Appadurai 1996, 189) are manifestly robust. The continuing existence of the Little India, Little Italy, Little Saigon, Koreatown, and the ubiquitous Chinatown in locations in global cities everywhere is an indication that although none is immutable, nor impervious to change, they survive as denationalized enclaves embedded in the cultural and economic landscape of the nation.

Conclusion

Global restructuring and the emergence of post–Fordist regimes of capital accumulation have reconfigured global socio-spatial arrangements. For Brenner, a key point about globalization is that it must be understood as the re-scaling of the global social space but this does not necessarily entail the subordination of localities to the deterritorializing and placeless dynamic of Castells' 'space of flows' (Brenner, 1998: 27). The creation of *locales* or habitats of meaning at the local level is a result of what is perhaps one of the most significant points to note about the formation of global cities, that is, the globalization of urbanization. Brenner (1998) points out that until the late 1960s, the national scale was assumed to be the *sine qua non* condition for the accumulation of capital. With extensive studies of the mobility of capital and people, global cultural flows, the emergence of hybrid cultural and political identities, the expansion of the imagination of place and belonging, and the varieties of urbanization which have grown out of these transformations, this assumption has been undermined.

It seems that global cities are now a long way from Mumford's historical city with a higher unity than that found in the village and Hall's city as the point of concentration of national power. Generally speaking, the key features of the global cities, articulated by a range of scholars, but most notably by Friedmann, Sassen, and Castells are: they are now interconnected in a global network more securely imbricated than in the international economy; they can transcend the state and pose a challenge to the nation; and their spatial logic can be understood as a series of powerful flows taking up real or metaphorical space in the global city. Nineteenth-century London was a spatial expression of the power of the British nation in a system of global imperialism and a geographically dispersed division of labour. In the context of the British Empire and rivalry for European hegemony it would have been unimaginable to think of London as transcending the nation, the Crown or the British Empire. If London was once a primate city representing the nation as a global power at the pinnacle of nineteenth-century modernity, it is now a global city in Sassen's terms – it is transnational and characterized by flows of economic and technological power in which the interests of global capital, rather than the nation, determine its spatial organization. Toulouse says of London that: 'The City is now a global stage located in Britain rather than a British stage in the global arena' (Toulouse 1991: 62). London is also the location at the local level of transnational urban practices which bypass the nation and encourage the development of multiple economic, cultural, and political affiliations. These, in turn, are contingent upon a transnational imaginary.

In a spatialized, rather than historical, paradigm the global city is where the myth of globalization as the triumph of culturally homogenizing forces may be dispelled (Robertson 1995). The global city is also the locus of the transition from the national to the global. Beck makes the point that in all the theorizing about late modernity and globalization the one constant feature is the reaffirmation of the notion that we do not live in self-enclosed spaces of national states and societies (Beck 2000: 20). A sophisticated understanding of global cities, particularly in the context of debates about globalization, now demands that we recognize that the city is 'a shifting set of conceptual possibilities' (Amin and Thrift 2002: 14).

References

Abu-Lughod, J. (1989). *Before European Hegemony. The World System, A.D. 1250–1350*. Oxford: Oxford University Press.

Allen, J., Massey, D. and Pryke, M. (eds) (1999). *Unsettling Cities: Movement/Settlement*. London and New York: Routledge.

Amin, A. and Thrift, N. (2002). *Cities: Reimagining the Urban*. Cambridge: Polity.

Anderson, B. (1991). *Imagined Communities: Reflections on the Origin and Spread of Nationalism*. London: Verso.

444

Appadurai, A. (1996). Disjuncture and difference in the global cultural economy. In A. Appadurai (ed.), *Modernity at Large: Cultural Dimensions of Globalization* (pp. 27–47). Minneapolis, London: University of Minnesota Press.

Appadurai, A. (ed.) (1996). *Modernity at Large: Cultural Dimensions of Globalization*. Minneapolis, London: University of Minnesota Press.

Augé, M. (1995). *Non-places: Introduction to an Anthropology of Supermodernity*. New York, London: Verso.

Barnett, R. J. and Muller, R. E. (1974). *Global Reach*. New York: Simon and Schuster.

Beaverstock, J. V., Taylor, P. J. and Smith, R. G. (1999). A roster of world cities. *Cities, 16*(6), 445–458.

Beck, U. (2000). *What is Globalization?* Cambridge, UK: Polity Press.

Bell, D. and Jayne, M. (eds) (2004). *City of Quarters: Urban Villages in the Contemporary City*. Aldershot: Ashgate.

Brenner, N. (1998). Global cities, glocal states: global city formation and state territorial restructuring in contemporary Europe. *Review of International Political Economy, 5*(1 Spring), 1–37.

Brown, L. R. (1973). *World Without Borders*. New York: Vintage.

Castells, M. (1977 [1972]). *The Urban Question. A Marxist Approach*. London: Edward Arnold.

——(1996). *The Rise of the Network Society*. Oxford: Blackwell.

Cohen, R. (2006 [1981]). The new international division of labor, multinational corporations and urban hierarchy. In N. Brenner and R. Keil (eds), *The Global Cities Reader* (pp. 49–66). London: Routledge.

Davis, M. (2006). *Planet of Slums*. London: Verso.

Dear, M. (2000). *The Postmodern Urban Condition*. Oxford: Blackwell.

Featherstone, M., Lash, S. and Robertson, R. (eds). (1995). *Global Modernities*. London: Sage.

Friedmann, J. (1986). The world city hypothesis. *Development and Change, 17*, 69–84.

——(1995). Where we stand: a decade of world city research. In P. L. Knox and P. J. Taylor (eds), *World Cities in a world-system* (pp. 21–47). Cambridge: Cambridge University Press.

Friedmann, J. and Wolff, G. (1982). World city formation: an agenda for research and action. *International Journal of Urban and Regional Research, 6*(3), 309–344.

Geddes, Patrick (1915). *Cities in Evolution*. London: Williams and Norgate.

Giroir, G. (2006). The Purple Jade Villas (Beijing): a golden ghetto in red China. In G. Glasze, C. Webster and K. Frantz (eds), *Private Cities: Global and Local Perspectives* (pp. 153–169). London and New York: Routledge.

Glasze, G., Webster, C. and Frantz, K. (eds). (2006). *Private Cities: Global and Local Perspectives*. London and New York: Routledge.

Hall, P. (1966). *The World Cities*. London: Weidenfeld and Nicholson.

Hannerz, U. (1996). *Transnational Connections: Culture, People, Places*. London and New York: Routledge.

Harvey, D. (1973). *Social Justice and the City*. London: Edward Arnold.

Hubbard, P. (2006). *City*. New York: Routledge.

King, A. D. (1990). *Global Cities: Post-Imperialism and the Internationalization of London*. London: Routledge.

——(2004). *Spaces of Global Cultures: Architecture urbanism identity*. London and New York: Routledge.

Knox, P. L. (1995). World cities in a world–system. In P. L. Knox and P. J. Taylor (eds), *World Cities in a World-system* (pp. 3–20). Cambridge: Cambridge University Press.

Knox, P. L. and Taylor, P. J. (eds). (1995). *World Cities in a World-system*. Cambridge: Cambridge University Press.

Li, W. (1998). 'Anatomy of new ethnic settlement: The Chinese "ethnoburb" in Los Angeles'. *Urban Studies, 35*(3), 479–501.

Marcuse, P. and van Kempen, R. (eds). (2000). *Globalizing Cities. A New Spatial Order?* Oxford: Blackwell.

Miller, D. E. (ed.) (1986). *The Lewis Mumford Reader*. New York: Pantheon.

Mumford, L. (1961). *The City in History: Its Origins its Transformations, and its Prospects*. London: Penguin.

——(1986). What is a city? In *The Lewis Mumford Reader* (pp. 104–107). New York: Pantheon.

Ritzer, G. (2007). *The Globalization of Nothing?* Thousand Oaks: Pine Forge Press.

Robertson, R. (1995). Glocalization: time–space and homogeneity–heterogeneity. In M. Featherstone, S. Lash and R. Robertson (eds), *Global Modernities* (pp. 25–44). London: Sage.

Robertson, R. and Inglis, D. (2004). The global *animus*: In the tracks of world consciousness. *Globalizations*, 1(1), 38–49.

Sassen, S. (1991). *The Global City: New York, Paris, London*. Princeton, New Jersey: Princeton University Press.

——(1998). *Globalization and its Discontents*. New York: The New York Press.

——(2002). Cities and globalization: The present and future of urban space. *Harvard Asia Pacific Review*, 6(2), 83–86.

Sassen, S. (ed.). (2002). *Global Networks: Linked Cities*. New York and London: Routledge.

Sassen, S. (2002). Locating cities on global circuits. In S. Sassen (ed.), *Global Network. Linked Cities* (pp. 1–36). New York and London: Routledge.

——(2005). The many scales of the global: implications for theory and for politics. In R. P. Appelbaum and W. I. Robinson (eds), *Critical Globalization Studies* (pp. 155–166). New York and London: Routledge.

——(2007). *A Sociology of Globalization*. New York and London: W. W. Norton and Company.

Sengupta, S. (2008). Thirsting for Eneregy in India's Boomotowns and Beyond. *New York Times*, 2 March.

Shukla, S. (2003). *India Abroad: Diasporic cultures of postwar America and England*. Princeton, NJ: Princeton University Press.

Singh, S. (2006). Towards a sociology of money and the family in the Indian diaspora. *Contributions to Indian Sociology*, 40(3), 375–398.

Sklair, L. (2001). *The Transnational Capitalist Class*. Oxford: Blackwell.

Smith, M. P. (1998). The global city – whose social construct is it anyway? *Urban Affairs Review*, 33(4), 482.

——(2001). *Transnational Urbanism: Locating Globalization*. Oxford: Blackwell.

Soja, E. (1989). *Postmodern Geographies: The Reassertion of Space in Critical Social Theory*. London and New York: Verso.

——(2000). *Postmetropolis: Critical Studies of Cities and Regions*. Oxford: Basil Blackwell.

Sudjic, D. (1992). *The 100 Mile City*. London: Andre Deutsch.

Taylor, P. J. (2004). *World City Network: A Global Urban Analysis*. London: New York.

Thrift, N. (1999). Cities and economic change. In J. Allen, D. Massey and M. Pryke (eds), *Unsettling Cities: Movement/Settlement* (pp. 271–320). London and New York: Routledge.

Toulouse, C. (1991). Thatcherism, class politics and urban development in London. *Critical Sociology*, 81(1), 55–76.

Wallerstein, I. (1976). *Modern World-system: Capitalist Agriculture and the Origins of the European World-economy in the Sixteenth Century*. New York: Academic Press.

——(1999). *The Capitalist World Economy*. Cambridge: Cambridge University Press.

Wilson, R. and Dissanayake, W. (eds). (1996). *Global/Local: Cultural Production and the Transnational Imaginary*. Durham and London: Duke University Press.

Wolfe, T. (1987). *The Bonfire of the Vanities*. New York: Farrar, Straus & Giroux.

23

Crossing divides

Consumption and globalization in history

Frank Trentmann

Introduction

The world is a big place. Our knowledge of the material lives of its inhabitants is patchy and fragmented. This is, perhaps, no more apparent than in our highly uneven under-standing of consumption in different cultures in the new era of globalization that fol-lowed on the age of exploration five centuries ago. While we know in fine detail the precise number of porcelain cups, knives and forks, books, furniture and gowns owned by merchants, lawyers, and even some artisans in eighteenth-century England and Spain (Brewer and Porter 1993; Weatherill 1996; Torras and Yun 1999) we know virtually nothing about the possession let alone use of things by hundreds of millions of Chinese people in the same period, other than estimates of their overall standard of living (Pomeranz 2005). Yet, our historical understanding has suffered as much from an excess of knowledge as from its deficit. As scholarship on particular areas and problems has deepened, new divides have opened up, between periods, disciplines, and indeed about the very stuff of consumption.

Three projects currently co-exist which are characterized by different vantage points, global goods, and moralities. First, for the seventeenth and eighteenth century, a fresh interest in the global history of consumption has reintegrated the Indian Ocean and China into a history of material culture previously monopolized by Britain and Holland. The career of Indian cottons is symbolic of this more interactive understanding of the entanglement between East and West.

If we fast forward to the twentieth century, it is as if the world has shrunk. Historical accounts are overwhelmingly of individual nations, cities, even districts and particular shops; comparative studies are few and far between (Haupt 2002; Capuzzo 2006). With some notable exceptions (Burke 1996), the central axis for transnational flows in this second group is that between the United States and Europe, the story of an "Irresistible Empire: America's Advance through 20th-century Europe" (de Grazia 2005), sym-bolized by Hollywood and the supermarket. Whereas recent accounts of the eighteenth century emphasize mutual entanglements – with Britain as much in the role of follower as leader – the multi-directional flow of consumer cultures, and dispersed centres of technologies and creativity, the Americanization story remains overwhelmingly a one-way street.

A third narrative is that of consumerism as a new lifestyle, the defining mode of contemporary society where consumption is crucial for self-fashioning and lifestyle, the actualization of the self, and the rise of a consumer-citizen. While it has been connected to competing social theories (late modernity, postmodernity, liquid society, governmentality), this story remains the shared orthodoxy for most in the social science community today (Giddens 1991; Baudrillard 1970/98; Featherstone 1991; Bauman 2007; Miller and Rose 1997). This literature presumes a sharp break between contemporary consumer society and earlier histories. With a few notable exceptions (Fine 2002; Sassatelli 2004), the past is primarily held up as a stylized model of standardized mass production and class cultures in contrast to more fluid, reflexive contemporary consumer culture.

Americanization and global consumerism are not necessarily the same; anthropologists and geographers in particular have emphasized how local cultures play an active role in shaping the global (Wilk 2006, Miller 1995b, Watson 1997, Massey 1994). Still, rather than tracing hybridity or glocalization, the few historians who have linked past and present directly have tended to do so via a stage model where Americanization launches an unsustainable global consumerism based on fossil fuel, cars, and an addiction to shopping (Mazlish 2005; Stearns 1997; Stearns 2001). Consumerism, in this view, is characterized by "unlimited material desire," no longer balanced by other values (Mazlish 2005: 132). Consumerism has tended to be upheld as an ideal type, even historical telos, associated with Western excess and selfish materialism, against which all kinds of other commercial cultures are judged.

The problem is that consumerism is a slippery, morally charged category rather than a tight, historically helpful term of analysis. It rose to prominence during the Cold War and expressed the anxieties of observers about the pathologies of consumer society rather than the realities of how people lived their lives in affluent societies. Various scholars have cautioned against the arbitrary and moralistic portrayal of consumerism, stressing instead the ongoing centrality of family, sociality, routines, and politics (Douglas and Isherwood 1996; Miller 2001; Gronow and Warde 2001; Soper and Trentmann 2007). But it is this "consumerist" approach that is amongst the very few treatments of the subject that has made it into global history readers and surveys and continues to inform public commentary, a fact worth recognizing at the outset of our inquiry. One reason for this mismatch lies in the continuing gulf between different disciplines. Where many social scientists continue to invoke a model of modern mass society that no longer commands consent amongst historians, historians of twentieth-century globalization now run the risk of working with a model of "consumerism" that many anthropologists, sociologists, and geographers have similarly discarded. Genuine multidisciplinary work remains the exception (Appadurai 1986; Miller 1995a; Brewer and Trentmann 2006).

These approaches to consumption express more general differences about the genealogy of modernity and about the practice of history itself. The recent turn to a global history of consumption in the seventeenth and eighteenth centuries has been part of a more general effort to move beyond Eurocentric narratives of modernity. European modernity was not the *sui generis* result of a unique meeting of scientific mentality and the rule of law (Weber). Nor was it primarily the product of capitalist exploitation of other lands (Marx). Rather it was a transnational achievement which mobilized non-European knowledge, goods, technology, and labour and resources – some of it through trade (like Indian textiles), some of it through coercion (slave plantations) (Berg 2004b;

Pomeranz 2000). By contrast, the interest in Americanization and its twin "global consumerism" continues to treat the United States as origin and centre. It is a self-critical inversion of the "Rise of the West", which replaces the positive telos of liberty, law, and commerce with a negative one of unbounded materialism.

Decentring the Anglo-American story of consumer society has implications well beyond the eighteenth century. It raises questions about the "modern" qualities of consumption, its origins, dynamics, and consequences, with implications for the geographic distribution of agency, ethics, and political responsibility. If many regions and traditions have shaped the world of goods, it may be too simple to view "consumerism" as an alien import or to focus on the ethical responsibility of affluent consumers in the North.

This chapter, then, is an invitation to cross several divides at once: between East and West, between the eighteenth and twentieth centuries, and between history and the social sciences. In their seminal essay, Glennie and Thrift already challenged the association between "modern" consumer society and industrialized mass-production, drawing on research on urbanization and the slow, piecemeal nature of industrialization in eighteenth-century Britain. Consumption, they pointed out, expanded in an artisanal setting, driven by people's need to communicate identities in increasingly complex urban environments, rather than by emulation (Glennie and Thrift 1992). This essay adds a global dimension to the critique of the "modern" model, and its intellectual twin, late modern consumer culture. I want to place the parallel narratives of global consumption alongside each other to show how new research on the seventeenth and eighteenth centuries further undermines the conventional link between consumer society, modernity, and industrial mass production. Far from being new, signs of late modern consumerism, creolization, self-fashioning, and diversity were already integral to this earlier global moment. This, in turn, raises questions about the role assigned to markets, commodification and individual choice in the spread of consumption, relative to the role of empire, social networks, and politics.

Multiple modernities: global networks of consumption before European hegemony

Ideas of a distinctly Western form of modernity have long shaped views of consumer culture. F.W. Hegel imagined fashion to be a monopoly of the West. In the course of the nineteenth century, the difference in development between Europe and China became so vast that it encouraged a search for unique endowments that favoured modernization in Europe. Marx traced the rise of the West to the accumulation of profit via exploitation of the rest. This idea was given a new lease of life in the late twentieth century by "world systems" with its account of a European core and a dependent non-European periphery (Wallerstein 1974; Wallerstein 1980; Wallerstein 1989).

Recent research has effectively overturned these meta-narratives (O'Brien 2001; Frank 1998). Transnational economic systems did not have to wait for European genius or industry. The Indian Ocean was an integrated world system by the tenth century at the latest. Already in the eleventh century, dyed and block-printed cottons went from India via Cairo to East Africa, finding their way into clothes, beddings, and curtains, for poorer as well as richer people (Barnes 1997). From Bengal and the Coromandel coast, Indian cotton and textiles went to Southeast Asia and China (Crill 2006). When European explorers and trading companies entered these parts, they found vibrant commercial networks that were not easily taken over. In 1600, over a century after da Gama's voyage, only one quarter of Asian pepper and spices went to Europe (Findlay and O'Rourke 2007: 157). As late as the eighteenth century, it is difficult to decide which was core and which periphery. Asian silks were already invading European markets in the fifteenth century. When Indian cottons began to spread in the late seventeenth century, English producers felt they were being swamped by superior, colourful goods and agitated (successfully) for a prohibition on the import of calicoes (1701, 1721). For most of the eighteenth century, British imitators found it impossible to match the dyeing and printing techniques of Indian artisans. Their eventual success was not the result of some national genius for science but of competitive emulation, learning, and transnational technological rivalry (Parthasarathi and Riello 2008). Nor did the eventual triumph of cotton factories in Britain lead to wholesale de-industrialization in India; while spinning was crushed, handloom cloth production survived.

The model of "modern mass consumption" has encouraged the idea that the mass market and shopping were spawned by industrial mass production, and that prior to the late nineteenth century, most people lived in a world without things or shops; at best, they had a few kitchen utensils, a shirt or a dress, obtained through barter or self-production (Williams 1982: 2–3; Richards 1990). This is fiction, not history. Shops, shop-windows, and shopping as a pastime were well established by the eighteenth century (Walsh 2006; Welch 2005). The poor, even slaves, frequented shops. The pauper did not live like a king, but the poor, too, had more and more access to the conveniences and goods associated with a polite, consuming society, including teakettles, soft furnishings (curtains, quilts, pillows), and mirrors (Styles 2007; Vickery and Styles 2006).

Spices and silk were early examples of global consumer goods. Cotton took such exchanges to a new level. Cotton textiles were as successful, fashionable, and desirable in the late seventeenth and eighteenth centuries as jeans have been since the 1950s. An average of 682,235 pieces of Indian textiles were imported a year into England in the 1680s. Floral patterned and in bright, fast colours, "checks" and other cottons found growing use in soft furnishings and curtains. Chintzes (painted or printed cottons) quickly became popular. In 1690 they still made up only 10 per cent of total textile imports. By 1700, they had reached 40 per cent, before becoming the target of prohibitive legislation the following year (Aiolfi 1987: 217 and Tables 8–9; Chaudhuri 1978). In the course of the eighteenth century, cotton gowns, stockings, handkerchiefs, sheets, and towels became part of the wardrobe of most people in England and France, including artisans, servants, and the poor. In England in 1777 a servant girl reported the theft of "one pink and black Manchester gown, lined with green stuff; one garnett stuff gown; one striped and flowered cotton; one flowered cotton go[w]n; one coloured quilted stuff coat" (Lemire 1991: 97). As far away as backcountry Virginia, slaves, too, bought textiles, hats, and ribbons – sometimes selling cotton seed or the chicken they raised in exchange (Smart Martin 2008).

On the eve of the French Revolution, cotton made up one third of all clothing. People did not overnight adopt underwear and nightclothes, but the advance is impressive nonetheless. In 1700 only 5 per cent of artisans and 30 per cent of shopkeepers had nightclothes, by 1798 it was 87 per cent and 97 per cent (Roche 1994 (1989): 138, 163–7). A new market emerged for ready-made clothing. The number of fashion plates increased five-fold, helped by innovations in printing. The cotton craze was not necessarily driven by price; curtains made of cotton, for example, were not cheaper than worsteds or linen ones (Styles 2006: 74). Rather the appeal was aesthetic and practical.

Cottons were colourful, comfortable, and convenient – the fabric kept colour better and could be cleaned more easily than wool or linen. They were also light, thus requiring additional layers of clothing, and more consumption. Contemporaries noted that people were replacing their clothes more often, searching for novelty.

Thanks to European inventories, and the sheer volume and painstaking research that grew out of the "birth of consumer society" project, we now have a more detailed picture of the spread of goods in Europe than ever before. It would be erroneous, however, to presume that the disproportionate mountain of articles and monographs on Europe necessarily reflects the stasis of consumer culture elsewhere. When they turned East, European traders found demanding consumers. In 1617, for example, the director general of the Dutch VOC (Verenigde Oost-Indische Compagnie) urged that "only the best quality goulongs and tapi-sarassas were procured for Java since these people were very particular about the quality and ... would pay a very good price for the right kind of textiles"; goulongs had gold thread (Prakash 2008). Here is a good example of how, in the early modern world, trade and the global demand for luxuries boosted the role of extra-European societies as consumers: the high price of pepper had increased people's purchasing power in Java.

Nor did fashion come only out of Paris or European courts, as commonly assumed in accounts of the rise of capitalism, luxury, and modernity in the West since F. W. Hegel and Werner Sombart. Elaborate designs and changing specifications about style, colour, and patterns can just as well be found in the order books of European companies trading with the East. Excessive consumption and the velocity with which styles were changing were a frequent target in late Ming China. Rural villages as well as cities were subject to growing commercialization. Young men in their villages, so the scholar Chen Yao complained in the 1570s, were no longer content with the customary light silk gauze but now lusted for Suzhou embroideries. "Long skirts and wide collars, broad belts and narrow pleats – they change without warning." They were all after "the look of the moment" (*shiyang*) (Brook 1998: 220; see also Finnane 2003 for early Qing). The more fashionable, the better. In East Africa, too, European merchants encountered demanding consumers and changing fashions for beads and other goods (Presthold 2003). Instead of a highly localized Western birth of consumer society, such studies suggest a transnational space for diverse yet expanding cultures of consumption that shared an impulse for self-fashioning and had points of contact, exchange, incorporation and emulation.

We know far less about the flow of goods from West to East than vice versa, but it is worth emphasizing that the East were not just producers: they were consumers of things and images as well, including European ones. In early Qing China this included English wool used in fashionable clothes. The import and cultivation of tobacco was followed by a range of fancy tobacco receptacles not perhaps so different from the craze for novelties and gadgets sparked by exotic goods in Europe. Some experts have provocatively invoked an "early modernity" for late Ming China (Clunas 1991). There was certainly a rich visual engagement with material objects. Where later nineteenth-century commentators only saw fundamental differences between Europe and China, seventeenth- and eighteenth-century travellers were still able to see many parallels between their material cultures. Late Ming fashion prized imported novelties, from porcelain with Arabic script and European books to the well-rubbed tombstone of the Jesuit missionary Matteo Ricci (d. 1610) which carried Latin as well as Chinese inscription (Clunas 2007: 100–3). Ricci himself noted the large concentration of cotton production in Nankin province ("they say there are two hundred thousand weavers here") and how elsewhere, the Chinese, "now weave a cloth made entirely of silk", "in imitation of European products". Instead of difference, he was struck by "the similarity of customs … Their use of tables, chairs, and beds is wholly unknown to any of the peoples of the states that border on China … there are numerous points of advantageous contact between ourselves and the Chinese people" (Ricci 1583–1610/1953: 13, 25, 550).

The chronology of consumer culture has expanded with its geography. The authenticity of "consumer society's" eighteenth-century "birth" (McKendrick et al. 1982) has been questioned by a number of authors. Luxury trades have been found thriving in seventeenth-century England, unperturbed by the upheaval of the civil war (Peck 2005). Some Italian Renaissance towns already matched the number of shops in Georgian England (Welch 2005). Such has been the number of competing claims for the birth of "consumer society", that it may be sensible to suspend the concept altogether, not least in recognition of its own problematic roots in a post-1945 telos of modernization and growth (Brewer June 2004). A simple, linear periodiziation probably does more harm than good. As cultures of consumption are diverse (within societies as well as across them), the quest for a biological birth moment is flawed. It would be easy, for example, to play the periodization game and emphasize the flow of Indian textiles to the Horn of Africa in the eleventh century or the use of cotton cloth in the Niger region in the same period. There was a good deal of shopping and spending in ancient Athens and Rome. Such individual instances, however, must not be confused with an argument about consumer culture as a whole network of values, spaces, and practices that assumes critical importance in the life of people and society as a whole.

If the global broadening of consumer culture has challenged the direct trajectory from eighteenth-century England to twentieth-century models of development, it also indicates what sets the seventeenth and eighteenth centuries apart from earlier periods. There was a deepening and broadening of consumption. Expanding trading networks between Europe and Asia, on the one hand, and the establishment of slave-based plantations in the New World, on the other, left their mark. Exotic luxuries like tea, sugar, and tobacco became popular necessities. Their prices fell rapidly. Sugar consumption in Britain, for example, increased six-fold in the eighteenth century to 24 pounds per person (Berg 2004a). People not only wore more cotton. They wore more diverse clothes, using a greater range of goods and mixes of fabrics, pattern, and colour, ranging from "bull's blood" to "goose shit" (Roche 1994 [1989]). In the "luxury debates", new consumption habits and desires became tied to questions of national development as well as individual morals. Above all, goods played an ever more important function as social positioning devices in increasingly complex, growing urban environments.

The original error was to tie the story of consumption causally to the story of industrial modernity. Ken Pomeranz' seminal *The Great Divergence* made the important argument that people in China were just as well off as people in Britain in the eighteenth century, certainly in advanced areas like the Yangzi delta. In other words, it was misguided to trace the contrast in their respective development by the late nineteenth century to some unique, earlier take-off in Britain as a consumer society. Instead, it was Europe's ability to break through resource constraints – access to coal underground and, through colonialism and forced slavery, to cheap labour and land in the New World – that made Europe, not China, the first industrial society (Pomeranz 2000). Clearly, without the slave trade it would have taken a long time to extract as much cotton, tobacco, and sugar from the New World, and European levels of consumption would consequently have been lower. It is debatable, however, how much slavery helps to explain industrialization, which primarily benefited from technological innovation (not profit or exploitation) and resources and demand internal to Europe. Overseas trade did, however, enable Europe to reap the full benefits of technological changes by escaping from resource constraints and offering a cushion of added markets and security (Findlay and O'Rourke 2007: ch. 6). Recent estimates have widened the gap in the standard of living once more. Already by the middle of the eighteenth century, the North West of Europe was more urbanized and workers had a lead over those in Beijing. In terms of their standard of living, people in the Yangzi delta were closer to the bottom than the top of Europe (Allen et al. 2005; Broadberry and Gupta 2005). Industrialization sharpened the divergence between East and West: it did not initiate it.

On the eve of industrialization, the world contained several, connected societies with dynamic, mainly urban cores of consumption. What set Britain and Holland apart from China was not some unique presence of these centres as such, but their relative scope and density.

Compared to twentieth-century consumer societies, eighteenth-century Britain was distinguished by constant purchasing power (until c. 1820) even as the ownership and consumption of things was rising. The principal attempt to resolve this conundrum has been the thesis of the "industrious revolution" (deVries 1994). Households, in this view, began to work harder to support a more consumption-intensive lifestyle. Instead of making things for themselves, they sold more of their labour in the marketplace so they could buy more goods from the market. They became more commercial and less self-sufficient. The Industrial Revolution, a supply-side phenomenon, was preceded in this view by a paradigmatic shift in demand, the result of "changes in taste", and a willingness to work harder, "emanating to a substantial degree from the aspirations of the family" (deVries 1994: 256).

It is debatable whether families work and live as in this application of Becker's econ-omistic model of household utility maximization. It is also unclear why the arrival of new goods and tastes should have motivated one people at one time in history to intensify and commodify – not other societies at other times. Nor do new tastes and preferences spread automatically – or easily. Exotic goods like tobacco and coffee were initially rejected in Europe as vile, dangerous, and barbarian. The career of hot, caffei-nated beverages was a global one, never just the success story of a new modern Western habitus.[1] More generally, similarly advanced industrializing regions like Catalonia show no sign that producers were selling more of their labour to fund more consumption (Marfany). Research on British households certainly cautions against seeing direct con-sumption and consumption via the market as mutually exclusive. Many families simul-taneously produced more for their own use and bought more (Overton et al. 2004). Above all, when and whether Britons started to work more remains a subject of debate (Voth 2001; Clark and Werf 1998). Instead of new tastes tempting people into the market, it might have been hard times that pushed them there. A more commodified world of goods may have been effect rather than cause.

There are moral-ideological histories hidden in the Anglo-centric story of the "industrious revolution". It has its roots in a material civilizing project dating back to the very period it is seeking to explain. In the late seventeenth century, writers like Nicholas Barbon and John Cary presented a new, optimistic view of popular consumption. New goods and desires were a good thing, and ordinary people should be encouraged to pursue them, not condemned. Their desire for more goods would make them work harder. Idleness would give way to enterprise and initiative. Wealth, manners, and civilization would all improve. This was always a prescriptive discourse. In the British Empire, too, the "civilizing" mission of commerce sought to instil in the native the habitus of acquisitiveness. Early nineteenth-century missionaries and colonizers in Southern Africa believed that the sight of a shop on mission ground would "rout superstition, slavery, [and] sloth" (Philip 1828 cited in Comaroff and Comaroff 2005: 157). For vassals and some subordinate groups, the new markets of goods could be empowering. For others it brought brandy and other unsettling temptations. That the arrival of foreign goods was a mixed blessing was already apparent before the "new imperialism" led to a more intense phase of capitalist extraction and exploitation.

Consuming empires: diversity, hybridity, and self-fashioning

The global expansion of consumption took place in the context of empire. The role of imperial power and culture for the flow and appropriation of goods and tastes has received particular attention for the seventeenth and eighteenth centuries. An influential model is Chris Bayly's distinction between archaic globalization, proto-globalization, and modern globalization. Instead of seeing present globalization just as a bigger version of the past, these ideal types point to ruptures and highlight the different ways in which cultural and political systems have stimulated global consumption. Instead of a clean succession of stages, Bayly presents these systems as overlapping. Archaic and proto-global systems were subordinated and redirected in the mid-nineteenth century by an emerging modern system shaped by new ideologies of industrial capitalism, the nation-state, and consumerism.

In archaic globalization (thirteenth–eighteenth centuries), the flow of goods between Eurasia and northern Africa was connected to a shared idea of cosmic kingship, which, in turn, created a distinct logic of trade and consumption. The Chinese, the Mughal, and the Ottoman empires lived out a sense that they had a historic title to global dominion. The divine message had been dispersed across the globe and could be accessed through its many material forms. Aggregating the world of goods in all its diversity was part of what made a king a universal over-lord. This exotic impulse stimulated long-distance trade and gift-exchange, moulding a highly discriminating elite culture that cherished diversity. It was this cosmic logic, Bayly points out, that explains why otter furs from Bangladesh found their way into northern China in the seventeenth century, or why precious books and religious objects from the Middle East made it to India and Southeast Asia (Bayly 2002: 51–2).

With plantations and American slavery, the European empires introduced a new logic. Where previously goods had been agents of globalization because they were prized for their geographic specificity, now they were diffused. The cultivation of coffee and cotton was globalized. At the same time, there was an initial symbiosis between new "proto-global" forces and the "archaic" elite-based ideology of consumption. Drinking coffee or chocolate were aspects of elite sociability, not yet of mass consumption.

The consumption regimes of these systems of globalization were tied to different production regimes. The exotic orientation of "archaic globalization" "involved the use of rare embodied labour skills, knowledge and reputation, which could not easily be reproduced" (Bayly 2002: 55). Together with the shift from cosmic kingship to territorially bounded nation-states, Bayly has argued, the "modern" pattern of globalization shifts production from locally specific artistic production to standardized "consumerism".

If the collection of things was in part inspired by visions of cosmic kingship, it was reinforced by imperial rivalries, especially between Britain and France in India and Egypt. Collecting shares many attributes more conventionally associated with consumerism in late modernity, such as self-fashioning, the hybridity of styles, and the creation of new polyglot cultures of consumption. Robert Clive, "Clive of India" and the nabob par excellence, chose goods from the East to refashion himself as an aristocratic connoisseur. He accumulated Mughal elite objects, from filigree boxes to betel-nutcrackers in an attempt to disguise the commercial origins of his wealth. Lucknow in the late eighteenth century has been described as a place where "diversity was a way of life" (Jasanoff 2005: 58). Persian, Muslim, Hindu, and European styles were fused. Empires collected things and cultures as well as territories. They were fluid, hybrid, and unstable, lubricating the global exchange of goods and cultures. Together with evidence we have of the intensely fashion conscious and reflexive outlook in some texts from early Qing China – where English cloth played an important role for selfhood (Finnane 2003) – these accounts suggest that a reflexive interest in other cultures and in fusing material reference points is much older than tends to be recognized.

The "archaic" type of globalization derives part of its appeal from its stark and not exactly charitable portrayal of its "modern" successor associated with standardized uniformity. "Whereas modern complexity demands the uniformity of Levis and trainers, the archaic simplicity of everyday life demanded that great men prized difference in goods. ... In one sense archaic lords and rural leaders were collectors, rather than consumers" (Bayly 2002: 52). The realm of the spirit, of elites versed in exotic languages and cultures, and appreciative of the local expertise and materials that went into the making, say, of a particular Kashmir shawl or a handsome book from the Middle East, gives way to standardized, mass produced, soulless goods. Some of this echoes older stories of the disenchantment and loss of authenticity resulting from industrialism, mechanical reproduction, and mass consumer culture (for critiques: Slater 1997; Miller 1987; Zelizer 2005a).

The almost Weberian ideal-type of archaic globalization, with its focus on elite-based connoisseur collecting, misses more popular dynamics of consumption at play already in this early phase. Equally significantly, it tends to project a stylized version of modern "consumerism" onto modern globalization that obscures how older practices have survived, adapted, and evolved to the present. "Consumerism" appears in such unflattering, monolithic light because it appears as a terminal point of industrial capitalism with little cultural or political autonomy of its own. Inevitably, this view is at loggerheads with work in the social sciences that has stressed the diversity of the material world and of consumption practices today, and the need to appreciate their own logics instead of seeing them as the products of nation or production and its social formations (Miller 1995a; Appadurai 2005).

Collecting, diversity, and hybridity have not all suffered a shared fate in "modern globalization". They were reshaped by the nation-state, industrial capitalism, and democracy, not destroyed by them. The spread of more rigid, hierarchial forms of racial knowledge and politics in the nineteenth century put an end to the mixing of Indian and British consumption styles amongst the colonial elite. But racism and the more territorially-bounded project of national identity did not stop the collection of material culture. Rather, diversity was reclassified according to a more linear vision of progress. Royal and elite collections were superseded by private and public museums, international exhibitions, and travelling shows of exotic objects and peoples – the Paris exposition of 1878 included native villages. Museums, fairs, and department stores were successors to the early modern *Wunderkammern*. Indian styles continued to find their way into shop-design, fashion, and the interior.

Collecting and consuming are not competing, successive tropes. They feed off each other. Almost a third of all people in the United States today have their own collections. In the 1980s, 230 museums opened each year in the United States, while in Britain a new museum sprang up every fortnight. If consumer society is defined as a way of viewing "an increasing profusion of both natural and human-produced things as objects to be desired, acquired, savored, and possessed", then, Belk has argued, "the proliferation of individual and institutional collections" might be recognized as "the most prominent manifestation of such consumerism" (Belk 2001: 1). Of course, some people just go to a museum to shop. Yet, many collectors take pride in participating in a global project of preserving knowledge and the richness of the past. It may be rare beer-cans or discontinued toys rather than finely hand-made books or exotic furs, but the quest for diversity and local specificity remains alive and well – too much so, in the eyes of some family members who have to live with collectors. Mickey, the 50-year old wife of an American stockbroker, for instance, carefully notes the origin, from East Africa to Germany, on the bottom of each of her nutcrackers (Belk 2001: 84). Without the sense of acquiring a slice of authenticity from a distant culture it would be difficult to explain the range of trinkets that find their way into tourists' luggage and into their vitrines and living rooms. Whereas a production perspective highlights modern capitalism's imperative for uniformity, a consumption perspective reveals how globalization involves, perhaps even requires, local value and distinction. Where commercial consumer culture has made a difference is in terminating the exclusive hold of a small elite. Everyone can be a collector, just as every customer is king. Cosmic kingship has been democratized: anyone can play the role of conservator and guardian of things facing extinction.

Modern ideologies further complicate the thesis that the transition from archaic to modern globalization involved a change from a "transcendent" ideal to one where goods are simply "self-referential to themselves and to the markets that create demand for them" (Bayly 2002: 52). Some scholars have diagnosed a secular individualizing shift from religious salvation to self-realization in the United States in the late nineteenth century (Lears, 1983), but the trend has not been all in one direction. Collective political projects and social movements have continued to link consumption to transcendent ideals – all the way to ethical consumerism today. British Free Trade played the role of a commercial-imperial successor to cosmic kingship: surely, God had created diverse climates and continents because he wanted people to trade freely and enjoy all the fruits of his creation. Nationalism and imperialism, in East and West, also tried to co-opt consumption for their own ends. These were directed against the global diversity and free flow of goods, but they, too, set goods and tastes within transcendent ideologies. In early twentieth-century China, the national products movement organized mass boycotts of foreign goods in the hope that national clothes would make strong citizens (Gerth 2003). In India, Gandhi led the campaign for *swadeshi* and local products. Transcendent ideologies of consumption also continued in the most advanced capitalist societies. In inter-war Britain, hundreds of thousands of Conservative women were involved in Empire shopping weeks where consumers were urged to pay a bit extra to help their white brother-and-sister producers in the colonies – a kind of imperial racist precursor to fair trade (Trentmann 2008a).

Instead of moving from diversity/transcendence to uniformity/self-reference, then, the ideologies of nation-state and empire ensured that the global integration of the commodity trade saw a collision between fluid, diversifying ideals of consumption and more rigid, uniform ones. This makes it unhelpful to periodize or measure the degree of globalization in terms of price convergence in wheat or the flow of investments. Globalization is not of one piece – cultural, political, and economic processes of integration and divergence cut across each other. The global integration of commodity trade in the nineteenth century heightened the concern for the local. Locally specific goods became charged as symbolic carriers of difference, be it Indian and Chinese cloth or an Empire pudding.

Colonies were more than passive by-standers responding to a globalizing dynamic pouring forth from an advanced imperial core. Conceptually, there are parallels here between geographers' emphasis on the relational production of space and place (Massey 1994) and the new imperial history with its emphasis that ideas and practices flow from colony to metropole as well as the other way around (Hall and Rose 2006; Burton 2003). For consumption, the process of "globalization at the margins" has been especially illuminated by anthropologists and geographers (Wilk 2006: 63; see also Miller 1995b; Miller 1998; Foster, 2006). In the case of British Honduras (Belize), it was the hunger of pirates, settlers, and merchants for British foods that helped create a system where, instead of developing its own agriculture and food industry, the colony exported logs of mahogany and tortoise shell to import pickled Bristol tripe, smoked tongues, brandy, and imperial citronade. The story of Belize shows the tremendous importance of where things come from in a global economy. Place of origin did not become irrelevant. People in Belize wanted ham and punch from Britain, not a local variant. It was colonial tastes as much as imperial design that made Belize a dependent consumer economy. Time and again, the metropole tried to make the colony import less food – in vain.

The contradictory workings of imperial globalization considerably complicate analytical categories like agency, power, and resistance. On the one hand, food preferences were not freely chosen. The empire established a hierarchical system of distinction that made those in the colony recycle metropolitan tastes and habits. Emulation and distinction is an imperial as much as a social-class practice. On the other hand, over time these preferences developed a power of their own. This was not just a matter of the colonial elite demonstrating their superiority. It also included the people of Belize more generally, including slaves. By "mixing up their cuisines and eating European foods", Wilk argues, "local people were breaking through these [racial] barriers and boundaries, and achieving a kind of categorical equality with the British" (Wilk 2006: 70). At the end of the year, slaves indulged in general binges, experiencing a sense of choice and dignity from consuming like their masters. Wilk stresses how preference for European meats and processed foods ultimately reinforced Belize's colonial dependence. But we could also argue that, in the long term, cultural-dietary resilience helped undermine the imperial project; Belize's heavy food imports were a drain on Westminster. Colonialism, even as it helped to globalize foods like sugar and coffee through its plantation systems and forced labour, was an inherently unsustainable cultural system, as people in the colonies refused to be just consumers of local goods and producers of global ones.

Americanization revisited

Such perspectives from the margins of globalization point to the limitations of a simple binary between the local (authentic; diverse; free) and the global (artificial; standardized; imposed). Their implications are not limited to European empires. Victoria de Grazia has placed consumption at the centre of her account of the United States as a hegemonic "market empire" after World War Two (de Grazia 2005). While the choice of analytical categories has been criticized (Sassatelli 2007), de Grazia's story is significant for returning older concerns of political economy to the study of material culture. Commercial culture is shaped by political institutions, norms, and values. The US government backed social networks, like the Rotary Clubs, and a world view of peace, democracy and best practice that were important in spreading American material civilization. American consumer culture, with its limitless territorial and social ambition, is contrasted with "old bourgeois" Europe, bounded by class and nation. Inevitably, this approach highlights a clash between material civilizations rather than affinities or continuities. Yet European societies were diverse and had their own dynamics like music halls, dance clubs, advertising, and tourism. Contemporaries were struck by the similarities between Berlin and Chicago. Cultural transfer was never a one-way street (Haupt and Nolte 2008). Americanization, too, occurred at the margins and took hybrid forms, as Europeans picked certain aspects and fused them with their inherited traditions. Exhibits of the "American way of life" had different receptions in France, Germany, and Britain (Kroen 2006).[2]

How the American empire of goods fits into a longer history of empire and consumption deserves further exploration. The American idea of creating peace by going out and selling goods went one step further than the British imperial mission of spreading civilization through commerce. Advertisers and businessmen continued where missionaries and Free Traders had been before. Best practice and material comfort replaced the gospel and the promise of atonement, but the global mission of leading people up the ladder of consumption to a higher plane continued. Class cultures were, perhaps, more entrenched in Europe than in the United States (McKibbin 1998) but divisions across race, income, and region never lay far from the surface of the idealized American way of life either (Cohen 2003). Notwithstanding its more inclusive, democratic ambition, the American vision of a consumer society had precursors. The turn to the consumer as a universal or public interest was well under way in Britain before World War One (Trentmann 2006c). Suspicion of unbridled materialism was strong amongst European elites (though not absent in the United States), but equally important perhaps is that by the 1930s, dreams of a better material life were circulating within Europe. These would be reaped in the affluent Fifties and Sixties, and reinforced by American consumer culture, but they were not solely a foreign import. Thus, the Nazi regime and business together created anticipatory desires for a world of material comfort that outlived war and destruction and that families took with them into the post-war years (Wiesen 2007).

Looking back at Europe in the twentieth century, what is striking is the ongoing diversity, not some drift towards monoculture. The post-war decades saw the American expansion of the Hollywood star-system, the self-service supermarket, and corporate advertising. Advertising and the rationalization of retail systems, however, also had endogenous roots. How Europeans consume remains distinctive across nations, even regions. As late as the early 1980s, Italians and the French bought only 2 per cent and 14 per cent of their food in supermarkets; compared to 32 per cent in Germany and 70 per cent in the United States. People from Scandinavia and the Mediterranean tend to holiday in their home country, while the Irish, Germans, and Austrians prefer to go abroad (Trentmann 2006a). Recent sociologists who have compared practices (like eating and reading) across affluent countries, have found no overall convergence. In the last thirty years, the time spent by Britons and Americans eating out has significantly increased, but not amongst Norwegians. French people continue to eat leisurely at home

(96 minutes on average) – Americans don't (42 minutes). The same practices carry different statuses in these countries, and they are unevenly distributed within them. One suggestion is that the United States (followed by Britain) is becoming more diversified and specialized, whereas countries like Holland and Norway show greater homogeneity. (Warde et al. 2007; Gronow and Southerton forthcoming). Ironically, it is the society most often seen as promoting a global mono-culture (the United States) that appears to have the largest internal degree of diversification.[3]

What is impressive is the very different outcome of local-global exchanges in different fields of consumer culture. In contrast to movies, music shows the creative encounter of national music styles with American pop-music and its diverse and pluralistic consequences. In Italy in the Fifties, for example, singers were turning to American crooners as they tried to move away from the routinized form of Italian song. The emerging *urlatori* or screamers paved the way for the novel *cantautore*, the singer songwriters of the 1960s–1970s. Instead of standardization, the outcome was diversification, with new styles and rhythms, new social themes, and new types of producers, performances, and audiences. The emergence of politically engaged singers out of this new wave shows the fallacy of equating commercialized modes of mechanical reproduction with alienation and a loss of critical reason. American influences were absorbed selectively and creatively; Adriano Celentano, the rock-and-roll teen-idol amongst the *urlatori*, blended in jazz but ignored the blues. American music was always only one influence amongst others. Songs, composers, and styles travelled between Italy and Brazil (bossa nova), and between Italy and France (the chanson), as well as between Europe and the United States (Labianca 2007; Gundle 2006; Santoro and Solaroli 2007).

Commodification reassesed: gifts, politics, agency

The stylistic and social diversity of popular music points to more general questions about the role of commodification. In models of modern mass consumption, consumption has often been collapsed with commodification, which, in turn, was tied to standardized or Fordist mass production. Commodification is seen to unmoor things from time and place, making them exchangeable and universal.

This line of reasoning has flaws on the production side as well as the consumption side. Modern production methods have been and remain diverse. Factory tooling matters for some things (the can opener; the washing machine), much less so for others (furniture, software, clothes), where small producers can more easily attain equipment and skills (Molotch 2005). Consumption, moreover, is not the same as commodification. It concerns use and practices (Warde 2005). How jeans are personalized by their wearers is just one example. The diversification of goods is as much an in-built part of modern capitalism as is the standardized, mass-manufactured product. Once again, revisionist work has turned in different directions in neighbouring disciplines. Thus, historians have mainly challenged the commodification paradigm for the period prior to industrial capitalism. The new anthropology of consumption, by contrast, has stressed how goods have played similar social functions across time (Douglas and Isherwood 1996) and how, instead of a linear progression, they pass through cycles of commodification and decommodification (Appadurai 1986). Material culture scholars in particular have shown how, instead of prompting alienation, goods, provisioning, and commercial services continue to be part of social relationships, a source of identity, morality, and communication (Miller 1998;

Buchli 2002; see also Zelizer 2005b). Recognition of people's creative appropriation of goods in the process of consumption, has stripped away much of the dehumanizing weight previously placed on the commodity fetishism. Conversely, scholars working on the South, have emphasized that commodification is not a preserve of the developed North (van Binsbergen and Geschiere 2005). Put alongside each other, these perspectives amount to a critique of a meta-narrative of modernization where the spread of commodity culture signalled a shift from a traditional social world of gift exchange and community to a modern system of markets and individualism.

In social theory, it is possible to contrast ideal types of community/gift exchange and market society/commodification, but in history, these mostly overlapped.[4] Households have long relied on a mix of provisioning systems (and continue to do so, in some respects). Earlier eras of expanding global consumption are no exception. Kinship networks and gift exchange played an important part in the "emotional economy" of Anglo-Indian society in the late eighteenth and early nineteenth centuries (Finn 2006), features at odds with the thesis of a new more hedonistic consumer (Campbell 2005 (1987)). To function, empire needed to create and maintain relations between members of its imperial family separated by space. Goods and gifts fulfilled that function, carrying with them feelings, obligations, and assertions of power and connections. In turn, these imperial exchanges lubricated the circulation of Indian-inspired fashionable goods and floral patterns within the British market and added to their desirability amongst families without direct imperial connection.

The mixture of market and gift-exchange in this moment shows the danger of tracing expanding cultures of consumption back to a particular type of the "modern" individual. For some anthropologists, the circulation of things reveals larger conceptions of personhood. Marilyn Strathern thus aligned exchange with individuality and contrasted it with the "dividuality" of gift-giving in Melanesia, where persons exist as part of relationships (Strathern 1988). Such juxtapositions carry echoes of older contrasts between *Gemeinschaft* und *Gesellschaft*. There is no need, however, to turn them into historically sequential types – in fact, F. Tönnies stressed that they were always simultaneous, although with changing form and power (Harris 2001). People in contemporary societies continue to display individual and "dividual" characteristics: consumers are also members of a family, a club, or a community. Applied to the history of consumption, the task is not to ignore commercial networks and commodification, but to recognize the contribution of dividual forms and of national, imperial, and other forms of power for the circulation and quest for goods. Consumption has fired on more than one piston in the modern world.

I want to briefly point to three additional approaches with which historians have contributed to our understanding of the "politics of value" so crucial to Appadurai's initial "social life of things" (Appadurai 1986). These concern practices, knowledge, and the agency and ethics of consumers.

The "circuits of culture" approach developed by geographers emphasizes the variety of practices and knowledges at play between producers, merchants, and consumers of a particular good (Cook 2004). The emphasis here is on segmentation and contestation – a flower, a chicken, or a papaya mean different things to different people in the commodity chain. What deserves equal attention is that practices have the power of integration and interaction, stabilizing meaning and creating shared forms of use and reception. One way forward, therefore, may be to focus even more on the practices and the synergies and networks between them. An illustration is Bob Batchelor's comparison of porcelain in northwestern Europe and Asia in the seventeenth and eighteenth centuries (Batchelor 2006). Batchelor emphasizes how consumption practices were tied to different geographic regimes of production and communication. A porcelain bowl was read as well as a container for eating or drinking. Practices were mutually constitutive. Porcelain had performative powers, and these were shaped by different regional networks of print and production – the typographic regime of the Atlantic world centred on London and Amsterdam, the calligraphic regime in Southeast Asia and old Islamic trading networks, and the xylographic network of coastal China. In all these regions, porcelain circulated ever more freely. But what we see here is ultimately not a story of the same article reaching ever more consumers across the world. Rather it is about the diverse genres of representations, systems of production, and habits of reading through which porcelain passed in each of these regimes. Speaking more generally, the global history of consumption involves the coming together, interweaving and unravelling of clusters of practices.

Globalization involves the encounter between established bundles of practices and creates openings for their transfer, domestication or extermination. In anthropology and geography, the thrust of research has been to question the hegemonic power of global goods and brands and to reclaim the active role of local consumers in domesticating Barbie, Coca Cola or McDonalds (MacDougall 2003; Howes 1996; Watson 1997; Miller 1995b). In historical research, by contrast, the opposite direction has received more attention, especially regarding the transfer of exotic foods and beverages from the new world to the old. How to account for the revolution in taste and lifestyle, from the initial repulsion in the seventeenth century to their ever more popular adoption in the following century? One recent attempt to reclaim Indian agency has stressed how Spanish missionaries acquired new tastes through a proximity with Indian cultural milieus. Rather than manipulating local food and custom to suit their own imperial identity, they internalized the Indigenous social aesthetics and habits of drinking chocolate in New Spain, including frothing and the use of honey and special receptacles (Norton 2006). Spanish missionaries acted as ambassadors of chocolate in the old word, though it is debatable whether they alone would have been able to initiate its popular triumph which took over a century.

To recognize that taste has some autonomous force need not mean that it was not also tied to a politics of value and social hierarchies that legitimated, prized, and channelled taste. Before new forms of sociability (the chocolatada, the tea-party) and new quotidian routines (hot breakfast drinks) could evolve around these exotic goods, they had to be domesticated. The Galenic theory of humours helped by assigning exotic foods and beverages specific medicinal benefits. Equally important for the dietary transformation of taste was, arguably, the prior, more general upgrading of taste in systems of knowledge. Botanists, explorers, scholars and doctors in seventeenth century Holland accorded taste a central role in their investigations. Instead of abstractions or discourse, they prized "tasteful objectivity" as a key to understanding the world, acquired through practical acquaintance, exploration, and demonstration (Cook 2007: 41; Cowan 2007). This involved the collecting and cultivation of exotic goods in Europe, and an analysis of their beneficial properties. Exotic goods like nutmeg and tea acquired their status within this scientific-cultural hierarchy of taste and knowledge.

A growing number of geographers and anthropologists have explored the active role played by local consumers in globalization. This retrieval of agency has mainly focused on how local people appropriate global goods, fitting them into local values and practices (Foster 2006 for an overview). Meanwhile, a contemporary interest in caring and the

461

ethics of consumption has led to calls for a "new moral political economy" where consumers in the North mobilize their agency to help distant producers (for critical discussion, see Trentmann 2007). For all their insights, both of these approaches tend to picture consumers as outside the centres of political economy, perhaps with enough agency to domesticate a Barbie doll, stripping it of its exported corporate meaning, or to buy Fairtrade products, but nonetheless at one remove from the mainsprings of globalization associated with trade, capital, and multinational corporations. Yet, globalization was not simply a process steered by capitalists and imperialists. Consumers played an active role in it, not only as beneficiaries of cheaper goods but as political groups and social movements, most notably in the popular support in Britain for Free Trade a century ago (Trentmann 2008a).

Globalization and consumers therefore have entwined histories. Conversely, the consumer as a public actor and social identity would not have evolved the way it did without globalization and the conflicts to which it gave rise. The identity of the consumer as a public interest was moulded in campaigns against slavery and for Free Trade and has continued to evolve in more recent campaigns in the international consumer movement over world food security, trade policy, and health and safety (Sussman 2000; Trentmann 2006b; Hilton 2007). Globalization placed new moral burdens on consumers, sharpening a sense of the conflicting obligations between caring for distant others and for those near at home. This tension has an intellectual history that reaches back to Adam Smith's thoughts on sympathy and that has been well explored in the history of ideas. It is worth emphasizing that ordinary consumers, too, have ideas about the world and their place in it, which has affected the course of globalization.[5] The current interest in ethical consumption and FairTrade should therefore be viewed less as a contemporary innovation and break, than an evolving story, steeped in earlier imperial as well as international traditions that helped to shape the global world we live in.

Outlook

Globalization is more than financial flows and commodity trade. It involves human actors whose ideas, identities, anxieties, and power can facilitate, manipulate or contain global exchanges. Consumption has been a decisive arena in global encounters, precisely because many of the things consumed are central to life, identity, and social order. Globalization therefore is not all about integration. It has come with conflicting modes of imperialism, nationalism, and internationalism. Tensions about what and how to consume reached new levels in the late nineteenth and early twentieth century just as global markets became fully integrated. Consumers played an active role in this process. Their role in these earlier conflicts deserves recognition, not least since "the consumer" is today easily imagined to be a new product of late modernity or "advanced liberal" governmentality. A more historical engagement with the entangled stories of consumption and globalization is helpful not so much because it identifies precursors ("we have seen it all before") or because it creates symmetrical connections between equals (present globalization is just a bigger version of the past). Rather it provides perspective on the quite different constellations of power and ideas which have shaped globalization over time. Globalization and its politics has a history that bears the marks of these earlier developments.

Placing "consumerism" in a global historical perspective offers a critical space for reflecting on several core assumptions in the contemporary debate. The focus on the "dark side of consumerism" (Mazlish, 2005) echoes the still heavily moralistic suspicion of consumption amongst American and European commentators as dangerous, selfish, and addictive, the enemy of community and citizenship. This critique has a long history (Horowitz 1992; Horowitz 2004; Davidson 1999; Hilton 2004). Significantly, the closer scholars move to the present, the darker the image of consumption. The bright picture of new textiles in brilliant colours and new tastes and freedoms that dazzled people in the late seventeenth and eighteenth centuries is replaced by a bleak image of contemporary shopping addicts who are selling their souls on an ever-faster hedonistic treadmill (Schor 1999; Frank 1999; Schwartz 2005; Offer 2006). An emphasis on diversity, novelty, and new freedoms gives way to one on uniformity, stress, and the tyranny of choice.

In our understanding of the global history of consumption, we have reached a point where the conventional chronological markers of tradition, modernity, and late modernity have lost their fixed positions. Similar suspicions and anxieties about feverish consumption and materialist habits were heard in eighteenth century Europe and late Ming China. Researchers should look back past the 1960s, which currently still stands like a temporal wall in the head of the social science community. A more global view of consumption holds out a profound challenge to a simple binary between modernity associated with the West (individualism, markets, science, dynamism) and tradition associated with the East (community, gift, religion, stasis). The period since the sixteenth century saw a rapid expansion of the world of goods in many parts of the globe. Its flow and appropriation was not the preserve of the West, nor was it simply steered by individualism and markets. Self-fashioning, a reflexive interest in other cultures, care, and hybridity have a longer past than accounts of contemporary "consumerism" tend to recognize. Community, politics, and social mobilization have continued to envelop the global flow of commodities.

Acknowledgement

This chapter draws on a longer version published in the *Journal of Consumer Culture*, 2009, vol. 9.

Notes

1 For a critique of Schivelbusch's (1992) association of hot beverages with a modern bourgeois West, see Clarence-Smith, 2008 and Norton, 2006. In Asia, the stimulating properties of tea were valued in Buddhism as an aid to meditation, not industriousness. The relation of alcaloids to addiction, social customs, and behaviour change is complex and variable across the world (Clarence-Smith 2008; Anderson et al. 2007).

2 De-centring the role of the United States in global histories of consumption also points to the role of other transnational networks and relations. In the case of Japan, which did not receive Marshall Plan aid, links with Europe were especially important for savings policy which shaped the country's post-war dynamics of expanding consumption; see Garon 2006; Garon and Maclachlan 2006.

3 Diversity reaches all the way into everyday life, not least in the side-by-side of old and new technologies, old and new routines, and so forth. Consumers lived in multiple time zones, as the Lynds found in their pioneering study of Middletown in 1929:

> A single home may be operated in the twentieth century when it comes to ownership of automobile and vacuum cleaner, while its lack of a bath tub may throw it back into another

era and its lack of sewer connection and custom of pumping drinking-water from a well in the same back yard with the family 'privy' put it on par with life in the Middle Ages.

(Lynd and Lynd 1929: 175)

For the ongoing diversity and disruption of everyday life and technologies, see Lefebvre 2002 (1961); Trentmann, 2008b; Edgerton, 2006.

4 The simultaneity of different systems of provision in a given society may be one reason why historians, keen on integrating groups, practices, and ideas in a given period, have been less inclined to pursue individual commodity biographies which became a prominent genre in anthropology and geography in the 1980s and 1990s as a way of connecting producers and consumers across space and for tracking the "politics of value" over time (Appadurai, 1986; Mintz 1985; for recent discussion see Foster 2006; Nuetzenadel and Trentmann 2008).

5 The importance of imperial and internationalist ideas for consumers and other social movements is now well-established for Britain and the British Empire. Research on post-war Europe has only recently begun to explore how responses to consumption were informed by theories of imperialism, focusing especially on violent critics like the Red Army Faction (Mausbach 2006; Poiger 2006). We still need to know more about how the people who did the consuming viewed the world.

References

Aiolfi, Sergio. 1987. *Calicos und gedrucktes Zeug: Die Entwicklung der englischen Textilveredelung und der Tuchhandel der East India Company 1650–1750* Stuttgart.

Allen, Robert C., Jean-Pascal Bassino, Debin Ma, Christine Moll-Murata and Jan Luiten van Zanden. 2005. "Wages, Prices, and Living Standards in China, Japan, and Europe." GPIH Working Paper No. 1, Version: October: http://gpih.ucdavis.edu/Papers.htm#1.

Anderson, David, Susan Beckerleg, Degol Hailu, and Axel Klein. 2007. *The Khat Controversy: Stimulating the Debate on Drugs*. Oxford: Berg.

Appadurai, Arjun, ed. 1986. *The Social Life of Things: Commodities in Cultural Perspective*. Cambridge: Cambridge University Press.

——2005. "Materiality in the Future of Anthropology." In *Commodification: Things, Agency, and Identities (The Social Life of Things revisited)*, eds. Wim van Binsbergen and Peter L. Geschiere. Brunswick: Transaction: 55–62.

Barnes, Ruth. 1997. *Indian Block-Printed Textiles In Egypt: The Newberry Collection in the Ashmolean Museum*. Oxford: Oxford University Press.

Batchelor, Robert. 2006. "On the Movement of Porcelains: Rethinking the Birth of the Consumer Society as Interactions of Exchange Networks, China and Britain, 1600–1750." In *Consuming Cultures, Global Perspectives*, ed. John Brewer and Frank Trentmann. Oxford: Berg.

Baudrillard, Jean. 1970/98. *Société de Consommation English – The Consumer Society: Myths and Structures*. London: Sage.

Bauman, Zygmunt. 2007. *Consuming Life*: Cambridge: Polity.

Bayly, C.A. 2002. "'Archaic' and 'Modern' Globalization in the Eurasian and African Arena, ca. 1750–1850." In *Globalization in World History*. London: 45–72.

Belk, Russell W. 2001. *Collecting in a Consumer Society*. London and New York: Routledge.

Berg, Maxine. 2004a. "Consumption in Eighteenth- and Early Nineteenth-Century Britain." In *The Cambridge Economic History of Modern Britain: Volume 1: Industrialisation, 1700–1860*, ed. Roderick Floud and Paul Johnson. Cambridge Cambridge University Press: 357–387.

——2004b. "In Pursuit of Luxury: Global History and British Consumer Goods in the Eighteenth Century", *Past and Present* 182(1): 85–142.

Brewer, John. 2004. "The Error of Our Ways: Historians and the Birth of Consumer Society": www.consume.bbk.ac.uk, working paper no. 012, June.

Brewer, John and Roy Porter, eds. 1993. *Consumption and the World of Goods*. London and New York: Routledge.

Brewer, John and Frank Trentmann, eds. 2006. *Consuming Cultures, Global Perspectives*. Oxford: Berg.

Broadberry, Stephen and Bishnupriya Gupta. 2005. "The Early Modern Great Divergence: Wages, Prices and Economic Development in Europe and Asia, 1500–1800." Warwick: University of Warwick.

Brook, Timothy. 1998. *The Confusions of Pleasure: Commerce and Culture in Ming China*. Berkeley: University of California Press.

Buchli, Victor, ed. 2002. *The Material Culture Reader*. Oxford and New York: Berg.

Burke, Timothy. 1996. *Lifebuoy Men, Lux Women: Commodification, Consumption, and Cleanliness in Modern Zimbabwe*. Durham, NC: Duke University Press.

Burton, Antoinette, ed. 2003. *After the Imperial Turn: Thinking with and through the Nation*. Durham, NC: Duke University Press.

Campbell, Colin. 2005 (1987). *The Romantic Ethic and the Spirit of Modern Consumerism*. Third edition. London: Alcuin Academics.

Capuzzo, Paolo. 2006. *Culture del consumo*. Bologna: Il Mulino.

Chaudhuri, Kirti N. 1978. *The Trading World of Asia and the East India Company: 1660–1760*. Cambridge: Cambridge University Press.

Clarence-Smith, William Gervase. 2008. "The Global Consumption of Hot Beverages, c. 1500 to c. 1900." In *Food and Globalization*, ed. Alexander Nuetzenadel and Frank Trentmann. Oxford: Berg: 37–56.

Clark, Gregory and Ysbrand Van Der Werf. 1998. "Work in Progress? The Industrious Revolution." *Journal of Economic History* 58(3): 830–843.

Clunas, Craig. 1991. *Superfluous Things: Material Culture and Social Status in Early Modern China*. Chicago: University of Illinois Press.

——2007. *Empire of Great Brightness: Visual and Material Cultures of Ming China, 1368–1644* London: Reaction Books.

Cohen, Lizabeth. 2003. *A Consumer's Republic: The Politics of Mass Consumption in Postwar America*. New York: Alfred A. Knopf.

Comaroff, Jean and John Comaroff. 2005. "Colonizing Currencies: Beasts, Banknotes, and the Colour of Money in South Africa." In *Commodification: Things, Agency, and Identities (The Social Life of Things revisited)*, ed. Wim van Binsbergen and Peter L. Geschiere. New Brunswick and London: Transaction.

Cook, Harold J. 2007. *Matters of Exchange: Commerce, Medicine, and Science in the Dutch Golden Age*. New Haven, CT: Yale University Press.

Cook, Ian. 2004. "Follow the Thing: Papaya." *Antipode* 36(4): 642–664.

Cowan, Brian. 2007. "New Worlds, New Tastes: Food Fashions After the Renaissance." In *Food: The History of Taste*, ed. Paul Freedman. Berkeley, CA: University of California Press: 196–231.

Crill, Rosemary. 2006. *Textiles from India: The Global Trade*. Calcutta: Seagull.

Davidson, James. 1999. *Courtesans and Fishcakes: The Consuming Passions of Classical Athens*. New York: HarperPerennial.

de Grazia, Victoria. 2005. *Irresistible Empire: America's Advance through 20th-Century Europe*. Cambridge, MA: Belknapp Press.

Douglas, Mary and Baron Isherwood. 1996. *The World of Goods: Towards an Anthropology of Consumerism*. 2nd edition. London: Routledge.

Edgerton, David. 2006. *The Shock of the Old: Technology and Global History since 1900*. London: Profile Books.

Featherstone, Mike. 1991. *Consumer Culture and Postmodernism*. London: Sage.

Findlay, Ronald and Kevin H. O'Rourke. 2007. *Power and Plenty: Trade, War, and the World Economy in the Second Millenium*. Princeton, NJ: Princeton University Press.

Fine, Ben. 2002. *The World of Consumption: The Material and Cultural Revisited*. London: Routledge.

Finn, Margot C. 2006. "Colonial Gifts: Family Politics and the Exchange of Goods in British India." *Modern Asian Studies* 40(1): 203–231.

Finnane, Antonia. 2003. "Yangzhou's 'Mondernity': Fashion And Consumption In The Early Nineteenth Century." *Positions: East Asia Cultures Critique* 11(2): 395–425.

Foster, Robert J. 2006. "Tracking Globalization: Commodities and Value in Motion." In *Handbook of Material Culture*, ed. Christopher Tilley, Webb Keane, Susanne Küchler, Michael Rowlands and Patricia Spyer. London: Sage.

465

Frank, Andre Gunder. 1998. *ReOrient: Global Economy in the Asian Age*. Berkeley: University of California Press.

Frank, Robert H. 1999. *Luxury Fever: Money and Happiness in an Era of Excess*. Princeton, NJ: Princeton University Press.

Garon, Sheldon. 2006. "Japan's Post-war 'Consumer Revolution', or Striking a 'Balance' between Consumption and Saving." In *Consuming Cultures, Global Perspectives*, ed. John Brewer and Frank Trentmann. Oxford: Berg.

Garon, Sheldon and Patricia L. Maclachlan eds. 2006. *The Ambivalent Consumer: Questioning Consumption in East Asia and the West*. Ithaca, NY: Cornell University Press.

Gerth, Karl. 2003. *China Made: Consumer Culture and the Creation of the Nation*. Cambridge, MA: Harvard University Asia Centre.

Giddens, Anthony. 1991. *Modernity and Self–Identity*. Cambridge: Polity.

Glennie, P. D. and N. J. Thrift. 1992. "Modernity, Urbanism, and Modern Consumption." *Environment and Planning D: Society and Space* 10: 423–443.

Gronow, Jukka and Dale Southerton, forthcoming. "Consumption and Leisure in Europe." In *Handbook of European Societies*, ed. G. Therborn and S. Immerfell. London: Springer.

Gronow, Jukka and Alan Warde eds. 2001. *Ordinary Consumption*. London: Routledge.

Gundle, Stephen. 2006. "Adriano Celentano and the Origins of Rock and Roll in Italy." *Journal of Modern Italian Studies* 11(3): 367–386.

Hall, Catherine and Sonya O Rose eds. 2006. *At Home with the Empire*. Cambridge: Cambridge University Press.

Harris, Jose ed. 2001. *Tönnies: Community and Civil Society* Cambridge: Cambridge University Press.

Haupt, Heinz-Gerhard. 2002. *Konsum und Handel: Europa im 19. und 20. Jahrhundert*. Göttingen: Vandenhoeck & Ruprecht.

Haupt, Heinz–Gerhard and Paul Nolte. 2008. "Konsum und Marktgesellschaft: Deutschland und die USA." In *Wettlauf um die Moderne: Die USA und Deutschland seit 1890,* eds. Christof Mauch and Kiran Klaus Patel. Munich: Pantheon.

Hilton, Matthew. 2004. "The Legacy of Luxury: Moralities of Consumption Since the Eighteenth Century." *Journal of Consumer Culture* 4(1): 101–123.

——2007. "The Banality of Consumption." In *Citizenship and Consumption*, ed. Kate Soper and Frank Trentmann: Palgrave Macmillan.

Horowitz, Daniel. 1992. *The Morality of Spending: Attitudes Towards the Consumer Society in America, 1875–1940*. Chicago: Ivan R. Dee.

Horowitz, Daniel. 2004. *The Anxieties of Affluence: Critiques of American Consumer Culture, 1939–1979*. Amherst, MA: University of Massachusetts Press.

Howes, David, ed. 1996. *Cross-Cultural Consumption: Global Markets, Local Realities*. London: Routledge.

Jasanoff, Maya. 2005. *Edge of Empire: Lives, Culture, and Conquest in the East 1750–1850*. New York: Vintage Books.

Kroen, Sheryl. 2006. "Renegotiating the Social Contract in Post–War Europe: The American Marshall Plan and Consumer Democracy", ed. John Brewer and Frank Trentmann. Oxford: Berg.

Labianca, Ermanno. 2007. *Canzone Per Te: Appunti di Musica Leggera (1957–2007)*. Rome: Arcana.

Lears, Jackson. (1983) "From Salvation to Self-Realization: Advertising and the Therapeutic Roots of Consumer Culture, 1880–1930." In *Culture of Consumption*, ed. Richard Wightman Fox and Jackson Lears. New York: Pantheon Books.

Lefebvre, Henri. 2002 (1961). *Critique of Everyday Life: Foundations for a Sociology of the Everyday, Volume II*. London: Verso.

Lemire, Beverly. 1991. *Fashion's Favourite: the Cotton Trade and the Consumer in Britain, 1660–1800*. Oxford: Oxford University Press.

Lynd, Robert S. and Helen Merrell Lynd. 1929. *Middletown: A Study in Modern American Culture*. New York: Harcourt, Brace and Co.

MacDougall, J. P. 2003. "Transnational Commodities as Local Cultural Icons: Barbie Dolls in Mexico." *Journal of Popular Culture* 37(2): 257–275.

MacKendrick, Neil, John Brewer, and J. H. Plumb. 1982. *The Birth of a Consumer Society: The Commercialization of Eighteenth-Century England*. Bloomington: Indiana University Press.

MacKibbin, Ross. 1998. *Classes and Cultures: England 1918–1951*. Oxford: Oxford University Press.

Marfany, Julie. 2002. "Consumer Revolution or Industrious Revolution? Consumption and Material Culture in Eighteenth-Century Catalonia." Seminar at the Institute of Historical Research, 19 January 2007.

Massey, Doreen. 1994. "A Global Sense of Place." In *Space, Place and Gender*, ed. Doreen Massey. Cambridge: Polity Press: 146–156.

Mausbach, Wilfried. 2006. "Burn, ware-house, burn! Modernity, Counterculture, and the Vietnam War in West Germany." In *Between Marx and Coca-Cola: Youth Cultures in Changing European Societies, 1960–1980*, ed. Axel Schildt and Detlef Siegfried. New York: Berghahn Books: 175–202.

Mazlish, Bruce. 2005. "Consumerism in the Context of the Global Ecumene." In *The Global History Reader* eds. Bruce Mazlish and Akira Iriye. New York: Routledge: 125–132.

Miller, Daniel. 1987. *Material Culture and Mass Consumption*. Oxford: Basil Blackwell Ltd.

Miller, Daniel, ed. 1995a. *Acknowledging Consumption: A Review of New Studies*. London: Routledge.

——1995b. *Worlds Apart: Modernity through the Prism of the Local*. London: Routledge.

——1998. *Material Cultures: Why Some Things Matter*. London: University College London Press.

Miller, Daniel. 2001. *The Dialectics of Shopping*. Chicago: University of Chicago Press.

Miller, Peter and Nikolas Rose. 1997. "Mobilizing the Consumer: Assembling the Subject of Consumption." *Theory, Culture and Society* 14(1): 1–36.

Mintz, Sidney. 1985. *Sweetness and Power: The Place of Sugar in Modern History*. New York: Penguin.

Molotch, Harvey. 2005. *Where Stuff Comes From: How Toasters, Toilets, Cars, Computers, and Many Other Things Come to Be as They Are*. New York: Routledge.

Nuetzenadel, Alexander and Frank Trentmann eds. 2008. *Food and Globalization*. Oxford: Berg.

Norton, Marcy. 2006. "Tasting Empire: Chocolate and the European Internalization of Mesoamerican Aesthetics." *American Historial Review* 111(3): 660–691.

O'Brien, Patrick K. 2001. "Metanarratives in Global Histories of Material Progress." *The International History Review* XXIII(2): 345–367.

Offer, Avner. 2006. *The Challenge of Affluence: Self-Control and Well-Being in the United States and Britain since 1950*. Oxford: Oxford University Press.

Overton, Mark, Jane Whittle, Darron Dean, and Andrew Hann. 2004. *Production and Consumption in English Households 1600–1750*. London: Routledge.

Parthasarathi, Prasannan and Giorgio Riello, eds. 2008. *The Spinning World: A Global History of Cotton Textiles, 1200–1850*. Oxford: Oxford University Press.

Peck, Linda Levy. 2005. *Consuming Splendor: Society and Culture in Seventeenth-Century England*. Cambridge: Cambridge University Press.

Poiger, Uta G. 2006. "Imperialism and Consumption: Two Tropes in West German Radicalism." In *Between Marx and Coca-Cola*, ed. Axel Schildt and Detlef Siegfried. New York: Berghahn Books: 161–174.

Pomeranz, Kenneth. 2000. *The Great Divergence: China, Europe, and the Making of the Modern World Economy*. Princeton, NJ: Princeton University Press.

——2005. "Standards of Living in 18th Century China: Regional Differences, Temporal Trends, and Incomplete Evidence." In *Standards of Living and Mortality in Pre-Industrial Times*, ed. Robert Allen, Tommy Bengtsson and Martin Dribe. Oxford: Oxford University Press: 23–54.

Prakash, Om. 2008. "India and the Indian Ocean in Textile Trade." In *The Spinning World: A Global History of Cotton Textiles, 1200–1850*, ed. Prasannan Parthasarathi and Giorgio Riello. Oxford: Oxford University Press.

Presthold, Jeremy. 2003. "East African Consumerism and the Genealogies of Globalization." PhD Thesis. NorthWestern University. Evanston, IL.

Ricci, Matteo. 1583–1610/1953. *China in the Sixteenth Century: The Journals of Matthew Ricci: 1583–1610*, transl from the Latin by Louis J. Gallagher. New York: Random House.

Richards, Thomas. 1990. *The Commodity Culture of Victorian England: Advertising and Spectacle, 1851–1914*. Stanford, CA: Stanford University Press.

Roche, Daniel. 1994 (1989). *The Culture of Clothing: Dress and Fashion in the "Ancien Régime".* Cambridge: Cambridge University Press.

Santoro, Marco and Marco Solaroli. 2007. "Authors and Rappers: Italian Hip Hop and the Shifting Boundaries of *Canzone d'Autore.*" *Popular Music* 26(3): 463–488.

Sassatelli, Roberta. 2004. *Consumo, Cultura e Società.* Bologna: Universale Paperbacks Il Mulino.

——2007. "Impero o mercato? Americanizzazione e regimi di consumo in Europa." *Stato e Mercato* 80, August: 309–23.

Schivelbusch, Wolfgang. 1992. *Tastes of Paradise: A Social History of Spices, Stimulants and Intoxicants.* New York: Pantheon Books.

Schor, Juliet B. 1999. *The Overspent American: Why We Want What We Don't Need.* New York: Harper-Perennial.

Schwartz, Barry. 2005. *The Paradox of Choice: Why More is Less.* New York: HarperCollins.

Slater, Don. 1997. *Consumer Culture and Modernity.* Cambridge: Polity.

Smart Martin, Ann. 2008. *Buying into the World of Goods: Early Consumers in Backcountry Virginia.* Baltimore: Johns Hopkins University Press.

Soper, Kate and Frank Trentmann eds. 2007. *Citizenship and Consumption*: Palgrave Macmillan.

Stearns, Peter. 1997. "Stages of Consumerism: Recent Work on the Issues of Periodization (Review article)." *Journal of Modern History* 69(March): 102–117.

Stearns, Peter N. 2001. *Consumerism in World History: The Global Transformation of Desire.* London: Routledge.

Strathern, Marilyn. 1988. *The Gender of the Gift: Problems with Women and Problems with Society in Melanesia.* Berkeley, CA: California University Press.

Styles, John. 2006. "Lodging at the Old Bailey: Lodgings and their Furnishing in Eighteenth–Century London." In *Gender, Taste and Material Culture in Britain and North America, 1700–1830,* ed. John Styles and Amanda Vickery. New Haven, CT: Yale University Press.

——2007. *The Dress of the People: Everyday Fashion in Eighteenth-Century England.* New Haven, CT: Yale University Press.

Sussman, Charlotte. 2000. *Consuming Anxieties: Consumer Protest, Gender and British Slavery, 1713–1833.* Stanford, CA: Stanford University Press.

Torras, J. and B. Yun eds. 1999. *Consumo, Condiciones de Vida y Comercialización: Cataluña y Castilla, siglos XVII–XIX.* Castille and León: Junta de Castilla y León, Consejería de Educación y Cultura.

Trentmann, Frank. 2006a. "Consumption." In *Europe since 1914: Encyclopaedia of the Age of War and Reconstruction (volume 2),* ed. John Merriman and Jay Winter. Detroit: Charles Scribners Sons.

——2006b. "Coping with Shortage: The Problem of Food Security and Global Visions of Coordination, c. 1890s–1950." In *Food and Conflict in Europe in the Age of the Two World Wars,* ed. Frank Trentmann and Flemming Just. Basingstoke: Palgrave Macmillan: 13–48.

——2006c. "The Modern Genealogy of the Consumer: Meanings, Knowledge, and Identities." In *Consuming Cultures, Global Perspectives: Historical Trajectories, Transnational Exchanges,* ed. John Brewer and Frank Trentmann. Oxford and New York: Berg: 19–69.

——2007. "Before 'Fair Trade': Empire, Free Trade, and the Moral Economies of Food in the Modern World." *Environment and Planning D* 25(6): 1079–1102.

——2008a. *Free Trade Nation: Commerce, Consumption, and Civil Society in Modern Britain.* Oxford: Oxford University Press.

——2008b. "Kurze Unterbrechung – Bitte entschuldigen Sie die Störung – Zusammenbruch, Zäsur und Zeitlichkeit als Perspektiven einer europäischen Konsumgeschichte." In *Unterwegs in Europa: Beiträge zu einer vergleichenden Sozial- und Kulturgeschichte* ed. Sven Oliver Müller Christina Benninghaus, Jörg Requate, Charlotte Tacke. Frankfurt/M: Campus: 219–246.

van Binsbergen, Wim M.J. and Peter L. Geschiere eds. 2005. *Commodification: Things, Agency, and Identities (The Social Life of Things Revisited).* Münster: LIT Verlag.

Vickery, Amanda and John Styles eds. 2006. *Gender, Taste, and Material Culture in Britain and North America, 1700–1830.* New Haven, CT: Yale University Press.

Voth, Hans-Joachim. 2001. *Time and Work in England, 1750–1830.* Oxford: Clarendon Press.

Vries, Jan De. 1994. "The Industrial Revolution and the Industrious Revolution." *Journal of Economic History* 54(2): 249–270.

Wallerstein, Immanuel. 1974. *The Modern World–System, vol. I: Capitalist Agriculture and the Origins of the European World-Economy in the Sixteenth Century.* New York: Academic Press.

——1980. *The Modern World–System, vol. II: Mercantilism and the Consolidation of the European World–Economy, 1600–1750.* New York: Academic Press.

——1989. *The Modern World-System, vol. III: The Second Great Expansion of the Capitalist World–Economy, 1730–1840s.* San Diego: Academic Press.

Walsh, Claire. 2006. "Shops, Shoppping, and the Art of Decision Making in Eighteenth–Century England." In *Gender, Taste, and Material Culture in Britain and North America, 1700–1830,* ed. John Styles and Amanda Vickery. New Haven, CT: Yale University Press.

Warde, Alan. 2005. "Consumption and Theories of Practice." *Journal of Consumer Culture* 5(2): 131–153.

Warde, Alan, Dale Southerton, Shu-Li Cheng and Wendy Olsen. 2007. "Changes in the Practice of Eating: A Comparative Analysis of Time-Use." *Acta Sociologica* 50(4): 363–385.

Watson, James L., ed. 1997. *Golden Arches East: McDonald's in East Asia.* Stanford, CA: Stanford University Press.

Weatherill, Lorna. 1996. *Consumer Behaviour and Material Culture in Britain 1660–1760.* Second edition. London: Routledge.

Welch, Evelyn. 2005. *Shopping in the Renaissance: Consumer Cultures in Italy 1400–1600.* New Haven, CT: Yale University Press.

Wiesen, S. Jonathan. 2007. "Creating the Nazi Marketplace: Public Relations and Consumer Citizenship in the Third Reich." In *Citizenship and National Identity in Twentieth-Century Germany,* ed. Geoff Eley and Jan Palmowski. Stanford, CA: Stanford University Press.

Wilk, Richard. 2006. *Home Cooking in the Global Village: Caribbean Food from Buccaneers to Ecotourists.* Oxford and New York: Berg.

Williams, Rosalind H. 1982. *Dream Worlds: Mass Consumption in Late Nineteenth-Century France.* Berkeley, CA: University of California Press.

Zelizer, Viviana, A. 2005a. "Culture and Consumption." In *The Handbook of Economic Sociology,* ed. Neil J. Smelser and Richard Swedberg. Princeton, NJ: Princeton University Press.

——2005b. *The Purchase of Intimacy.* Princeton, NJ: Princeton University Press.

24

Pluralism, globalization, and the "modernization" of gender and sexual relations in Asia

Michael G. Peletz

Much of the literature concerning the reproduction and transformation of kinship, marriage, and household organization in modern Asian societies focuses on cross-cultural variation in hegemonic expressions of gender and sexuality that are commonly referred to as "heteronormative." This term is typically intended to emphasize the heterosexual relations and desires that are normative in the sense that they are: (a) enjoined upon most (if not all) members of society by means of institutionalized moral expectations that are internalized (more often than not unconsciously) as sentiments, dispositions, and embodied practices through socialization processes and the structures and lived experiences of everyday life; and (b) statistically prevalent throughout society. Gender and sexual diversity does of course exist within—and not merely across—Asian societies, including societies characterized by one or another form of heteronormativity. This chapter engages that diversity, focusing mainly on same-sex relations, transgender practices and identities, and the ways these and attendant phenomena have been informed by different kinds of globalizing forces. We shall see that there is considerable variation in Asian societies with respect to the conceptualization of non-normative expressions of gender and sexuality, that the relative status (prestige/stigma) accorded individuals involved in same-sex relations and/or transgender practice varies a great deal from one society to the next, and, more generally, that in some societies, sentiments and dispositions bearing on gender and sexuality are relatively pluralistic, whereas in others this is decidedly not the case. More broadly, we shall see that the emergence of new ("modern") subject positions and sex/gender subjectivities in many parts of Asia has involved processes that appropriate global terms, styles, and overall identities but usually do so in ways that are heavily informed by Indigenous categories and their interrelations, key features of which continue to serve as templates for the localization of things global with respect to form and content alike.

Especially in recent years, scholars have spilled much ink on the pros and cons of the various terminologies used to designate institutionalized roles and identities that involve one or another type of departure from gender normativity. Along with other scholars, I use the umbrella term "transgender" for this purpose, even though the term is employed by different scholars in different ways. Concerning the prefix "trans," Aihwa Ong (1999: 4) writes that it "denotes both moving through space or across lines, as well as changing the nature of something"—as in transformation or transfiguration—or going beyond it—as in transcend—be it a bounded entity or process, or a relationship between two or more phenomena. As for "transgender," Riki Wilchins (1997: 15–16) observes that it "began its life as a name for those folks who identified neither as crossdressers nor as transsexuals—primarily people who changed their gender but not their genitals. ... The term gradually mutated to include any genderqueers who didn't actually change their genitals: [such as] crossdressers, ... stone butches, and hermaphrodites; ... [and] people began using it to refer to transsexuals [some of whom do change their genitals] as well." Evelyn Blackwood's (2005) conceptualization of transgender builds on Wilchins' definition, although she also employs the term transgendered in its broadest sense to designate anyone who is "transgressively gendered," to borrow Kate Bornstein's (1995: 134–135) phrase.

Many scholars underscore that in some Western contexts these umbrella terms have certain meanings and connotations that are of questionable relevance elsewhere. Such meanings and connotations include the empirically erroneous idea that all variants of transgendering necessarily entail same-sex relations, and vice versa. They also include the equally problematic notion that behavioral transgressions, even in the straightforward definitional sense of practices that transcend or cross boundaries, are typically stigmatized. More generally, even cautious and qualified usages of terms such as "transgender" have their limitations, which is why some scholars prefer to avoid them altogether. Towle and Morgan (2002), for example, contend that "transgender" is a trendy signifier that is too encompassing to allow for the kinds of fine-grain distinctions called for in particular ethnographic and historical contexts, and that its utilization in Western writings (especially in semi-popular accounts) is often heavily freighted with nostalgia for a romanticized past, exemplified by contemporary non-Western Others and their forebears, that may have never existed. Arguably more relevant is that the last two to three decades have seen a dizzying succession of terminologies utilized in scholarly writings dealing with what Manalansan (2003) glosses as "gender insubordinate subjects," and that so too in all likelihood will the next few.

A final set of introductory remarks has to do with the term "pluralism," I use this term to refer to social fields, cultural domains, and more encompassing systems in which two or more principles, categories, groups, sources of authority, or ways of being in the world are not only present, tolerated, and accommodated, but also accorded legitimacy in Max Weber's sense. Legitimacy—however much contested and in flux for reasons delineated by Antonio Gramsci—is thus a sine qua non for pluralism, which means by definition that pluralism is a feature of fields, domains, and systems in which diversity is ascribed legitimacy, and, conversely, that diversity without legitimacy is not pluralism.

Pluralism in gendered fields or domains, here abbreviated as "gender pluralism," includes pluralistic sensibilities and dispositions regarding bodily practices (adornment, dress, mannerisms) and embodied desires, as well as social roles, sexual relationships, and overall ways of being that bear on or are otherwise linked with local conceptions of femininity, masculinity, androgyny, intersexuality (hermaphroditism), etc. Particularly in gendered fields and domains, pluralism transcends and must be distinguished from dualism inasmuch as more than two principles, categories, groups, etc. are usually at stake and accorded legitimacy (e.g., not simply principles constituting categories of heteronormative female-bodied individuals and their male-bodied counterparts). By this definition, sexual pluralism, premised minimally on a concept of relatively "benign sexual variation" (Rubin 1984: 283), is included under the more encompassing rubric of gender pluralism.

"Neither man nor woman": India's *hijras* in comparative perspective

South Asia, like Southeast Asia and Native North America, is one of many world areas with long-established traditions of ritual specialists who engage in transgender practices. These individuals either assume the attire, occupations, demeanor, and (sometimes) the erotic orientations of members of the "opposite" sex, or engage in practices that result in their being considered by others in the society as a "third sex" or "third gender" (and sometimes, as in the case of female-bodied transgenderists in certain Native American societies, a "fourth gender"). In pre-contact Native North America, for example, there appear to have been more than 155 distinct societies with these traditions (Roscoe 1998: 7). In most of those societies, the "two-spirit people" or *berdache*, as they are sometimes called, were male-bodied individuals—although in roughly a third of these societies two-spirit roles existed for phenotypic females as well—who were held to have unique spiritual powers that provided them with an important source of prestige in their communities. As for their domestic arrangements and erotic orientations, a two-spirit person typically engaged in sexual relations and marriage perhaps best summarized as both homosexual and heterogender: a male-bodied two-spirit, for example, typically married and had sexual relations with another person having male genitals who was gendered male, unlike the two-spirit, who was regarded not as a male (despite having male genitals) but as a "woman-man" or "man-woman" and hence a third gender. These relations were thus homosexual from the (culturally muted) anatomical point of view but heterogender in terms of the way the individuals involved were gendered.

Broadly similar ritual roles keyed to homosexual/heterogender matrices have existed in Southeast Asia for many centuries (e.g., among Bugis, Iban, Ngaju Dayak, Javanese, Filipinos, Burmese, and many others (Peletz 2009)). In these Southeast Asian cases, the ritual specialists in question combined elements from and simultaneously transcended the male–female duality that helped structure and animate the universe in its entirety and simultaneously symbolized wholeness, purity, and gender totality, and thus the unfractured universe posited to exist before the advent of humanity and difference (L. Andaya 2000). In many of the cosmologies of the region, important spirits and deities were depicted as exhibiting various degrees of androgyny or as existing in male–female pairs. Ritual specialists exhibiting androgyny were ideally situated both to communicate and successfully negotiate with these spirits and deities, and to personify them.

In South Asia, the best-documented examples of what many scholars and local populations alike consider a "third sex" are known as *hijras*. This term refers to caste-like groups of ritual specialists composed of hermaphrodites as well as males who have had their penis and testes sacrificially excised and have thus become eunuchs, the latter making up the *hijra* majority. (Transgender practices involving female-bodied individuals exist in India as well but are not "as widespread … or prominent as the *hijras*" (Nanda 2000: 40).) *Hijras* dress and adorn themselves as women, adopt stereotypically (often exaggerated) female hand gestures and overall demeanor, engage in female domestic activities such as cooking and sewing, and behave like women in various other ways, though they also have a reputation for being louder and more verbally aggressive than ordinary women. For at least a thousand years, *hijras* have existed in Hindu communities in India and since the sixteenth century if not earlier among Muslims as well, performing sacred roles that have included maintaining temples devoted to deities associated with the Mother Goddess as well as dancing, playing music, and conducting ritual services at weddings and the births of male children, events that are among the most significant ceremonial occasions for Hindus and Muslims throughout India and South Asia as a whole.

The role and social standing of *hijras* in contemporary India is complex and fraught, as are the quotidian negotiations of *hijra* identity both within their own communities and in relation to the larger society. British colonial policies informed by a potent mélange of Victorian-era Protestantism and high-modern capitalism bear some responsibility for this situation in that they criminalized castration, defined eunuchs as dangerous threats to person and property, and otherwise denigrated the role. So too does the fact that many *hijras* no longer maintain the celibacy and asceticism that were long seen as defining features of their identities (Reddy 2005: 26–28). In many cases, moreover, impoverished *hijras* have turned to prostitution with (non-*hijra*, sometimes heterosexually-identified, married) males to support themselves, contributing to dissension and strife among *hijras* as to the proper ways to comport oneself, and adding to the ambivalence with which they are viewed by the general public. *Hijras* are nonetheless accorded an important degree of legitimacy and sanctity by society at large. This is because of the valuable rituals they perform as well as their identification in India's public culture both with "Bahuchara Mata, one of the many versions of the Mother Goddess worshipped throughout India," and with a strongly androgynous if not bisexual form of "the sexually ambivalent Siva" (Nanda 1993: 373, 375).

To understand how the Hindu majority conceptualize *hijras* and their spiritual powers, we need to bear in mind four sets of issues. First, in Hinduism "'male' and 'female' are seen as natural categories in complementary opposition," each of which is "naturally" associated with "different sexual characteristics and reproductive organs, ... different sexual natures ... , and ... different, and complementary, roles in marriage, sexual relations and reproduction" (374). Second, the female principle, which is "more immanent and active" than the male principle, "has a positive, creative, life-giving aspect and a destructive life-destroying aspect." In numerous contexts, "the erotic aspect of female power is dangerous unless it is controlled by the male principle," which is why many (but not all) Hindus and scholars of Hinduism believe that "powerful women, whether deities or humans, must be restrained by male authority. Thus, the Hindu goddess subordinated to her male consort is beneficent, but when dominant the goddess" may be "aggressive, devouring and destructive" (ibid.), at least with respect to demonic enemies, in which case she may still be a savior of humans and male deities. Third, just as many Hindu deities are "sexually ambiguous," often being depicted in myth and iconography in androgynous or dual-gendered forms, so too do many of them change over time, from largely male to predominantly female, and vice versa, for instance, and/or from one to many and back again. The fourth, most general point (which follows partly from the others) is that spiritual salvation presupposes transcendence and change, and that Hinduism's doctrinal emphasis on rebirth, variability, and multiplicity serves both to valorize mutability and transformation and to underscore their intrinsic connections with spiritual potency.

As for issues of identity and subjectivity, most individuals who become *hijras* do so through surgical removal of the penis and testes—which in the case of effeminate boys encouraged by their parents to join the ranks of *hijras*, may occur while they are in their early teens—not because they were born intersexed. Partly for this reason, even when they view themselves as "neither man nor woman" or as "man plus woman," *hijras* sometimes consider themselves as more male than female. Because *hijras* lack male sexual organs as well as sexual desires for women, in some contexts they think of themselves as "not male," "less than male" or as "incomplete males." And because they are not endowed with female sexual organs or the capacity to bear children but dress and adorn themselves like women and perform various female tasks, in other contexts they regard themselves as "incomplete women" rather than in terms of one or another category defined in relation to masculinity or its lack (e.g., "not male," "less than male").

It is important to underscore that these identities, all of which bear on ostensibly bedrock "sexual(ized) difference," are not necessarily the most personally or culturally salient identities negotiated by *hijras*. As with those of other Hindus and Muslims in modern India, *hijras*' subjectivities and senses of self are informed in complex, sometimes contradictory ways by a panoply of factors. These include: their religious affiliations, relative piety, and place of birth; the linguistic communities to which they belong; their past and present involvement in networks of kinship, romance, and desire; the extent to which they honor vows of asceticism or world renunciation; their ritual and artistic specializations, educational attainment, occupational activities, employment status, and overall socio-economic standing; and, last but not least, their familiarity with, and, where relevant, their self-positioning in relation to Indian-inflected global discourses bearing on the meaning of terms such as *gay*, *homosex*, and the like (Reddy 2005: 74–76 passim), which are widely utilized throughout India and other regions of Asia, their meanings and connotations varying according to locale and socio-linguistic context and overlapping to some degree (but not being identical) with their usage in English-language settings. (In some circumstances, Hindi- and other Asian-language usages of *gay* refer primarily to certain categories of phenotypic males—e.g., male-bodied transsexuals and their effeminate male-identified counterparts—who are assumed to have sex exclusively with other males; in many perhaps most others, the term has broader meanings, denoting any male- or female-bodied individual erotically oriented toward same-sex relations, who may or may not engage in heterosexual relations including conventional marriage.)[1]

Indian conceptualizations of *hijras* along with the entailments of the *hijra* role make clear that some Asian societies regard sexuality and gender as fluid, permeable, even hybrid categories that are contextually-specific and subject to combination, flux, and change. The *hijra* example also illustrates that some Asian societies do not insist that at birth every individual be assigned a life-long sexual designation or gender role; and, more generally, that not all societies operate with a binary system based on two sexes or genders. More broadly, while modern-day *hijras* tend to be viewed by normative Hindus and Muslims with ambivalence, and are in some instances less revered than feared (owing to their spiritual potency and tendencies to threaten with misfortune those who cross them), they differ from their gender-transgressive counterparts in the West in that they are accorded a meaningful and seemingly fulfilling role that is both legitimate and in some ways sanctified—unless they are identified as *gay*, in which case they are likely to be denied legitimacy, stigmatized, and viewed in overwhelmingly negative terms for partaking in "Western-style" decadence and perversion that highlights and thus over-emphasizes sexuality, and homoerotic preferences in particular, in personal identity.

In this connection it warrants remark that in recent years a number of "traditional" *hijras* have mounted successful electoral campaigns and have assumed political office in what is frequently touted as "the world's largest democracy," foregrounding (among other things) their claims to inclusion in national narratives bearing on India's past, present, and future. These *hijras*' negotiation of variegated universal(zing) narratives of rights, justice, and democratic process indicate that in some contexts globally inflected discourses are aligned in rather surprising ways and that in certain cases it is exceedingly difficult (and perhaps fruitless if not misguided to attempt) to meaningfully distinguish between local, autochthonous, and/or "traditional" subjectivities on the one hand, and their global, cosmopolitan, and/or "modern" counterparts on the other.

Tom, *dee*, and gender transgression in Thailand and elsewhere in Southeast Asia

Transgender practices and same-sex relations in Thailand, Indonesia, the Philippines, and other regions of Southeast Asia tend to be accorded more legitimacy and are in other respects different from their counterparts in South Asian as well as East Asian settings. The greater degree of legitimacy they enjoy is in keeping with the fact that, broadly speaking, Southeast Asian societies have long evinced less patriarchy and more pluralism with respect to gender and sexuality than neighboring world areas. It is beyond the scope of this discussion to explain why this is so but relevant factors include: the bilateral systems of descent and inheritance coupled with matrifocal ("mother-centered") emphases and matrilocal/neolocal post-marital residence patterns characteristic of Southeast Asia, as distinct from the patrilineal/patrifocal/patrilocal traditions prevalent in South Asia and East Asia; the relatively lower population densities and more favorable distributions of resources long typical of Southeast Asia; the relatively weaker state structures documented for Southeast Asia during the early modern period (and before); differences in systems of production, exchange, and personhood; and last but not least the salience of Indicized but uniquely Southeast Asian mythologies and cosmologies in providing templates for gender and sexuality throughout the region. Many Southeast Asian systems of myth, ritual, and cosmology encourage imaginative play conducive to the creation of implicit cultural models valorizing relativism, pluralism, and different ways of being in the world that allow for a variety of "potential[ly] erotic enterprises" (Butler 1993: 110).

Some argue that what sets Southeast Asia apart from South and East Asia and many other places, and simultaneously renders it broadly analogous to certain regions of Native North America in former times, is not that gender-transgressive practices were construed as legitimate in particular contexts; for such phenomena have long been evident in many world areas and they continue to exist in the contemporary US (e.g., in Ivy League clubs and northern California's infamous Bohemian Grove). Rather, what is distinctive about Southeast Asia is that compared to other world areas the pluralism-friendly dynamics in question were *not* bracketed exceptions to the prevailing hegemonies, which were characterized by a broadly diffused ethos of pluralism. This pluralism (in sentiments, dispositions, etc.) was variably informed by sexual and gendered symbols and practices in ritual domains; by long-term historical dynamics discussed elsewhere (Peletz 2009); and by a nexus of domestic and social structural variables of the sort identified by Beatty (2002) for late twentieth-century Java (widespread fosterage and adoption, high rates of divorce, terminological usages including teknonymy, birth-order names, etc.), which give rise to relationality, temporal flux, and reversal, and otherwise encourage conceptual and moral relativism.

Clifford Geertz (2006: 327) has suggested that in relation to its counterparts in most other world areas, "gender difference" in regions of Southeast Asia such as Java and Bali "is conceived as a derivative, essentially secondary, diffuse, and muted phenomenon." Ironically, it may be in no small measure because gender has tended to be relatively

475

muted and unmarked in comparison to other, culturally elaborated axes of difference and inequality (e.g., descent, age, birth-order, and, in recent times, social class) that many societies in Southeast Asia have long accommodated and accorded value to degrees and expressions of gender and sexual diversity which have been actualized to a lesser degree (or generally fared less well) elsewhere and which, as a consequence, have helped mark the region as distinctive.

The early modern era, commonly defined as the period stretching roughly from the fifteenth through the eighteenth centuries, provides clear evidence of gender pluralism in many parts of Southeast Asia. This was a period in Southeast Asia's history characterized by relatively egalitarian relations between males and females, by a good deal of female autonomy and social control, by considerable fluidity and permeability in gender roles, and by relative tolerance and indulgence with respect to things erotic and sexual, at least for the commoner majority (though this is not to suggest a reigning ethos of "anything goes," particularly since certain incestuous and adulterous offenses could meet with capital punishment) (B. Andaya 2006; Peletz 2009). Portuguese observers of the sixteenth century reported that the predominantly Muslim Malays were "fond of music and given to love," the broader themes being that "pre-marital sexual relations were regarded indulgently, and [that] virginity at marriage was not expected of either party" (Reid 1988: 153). Chinese, Europeans, and others emphasized similar patterns when writing about Thais, Javanese, Filipinos, and Burmese. They also make clear that throughout this period women assumed important roles in politics, trade, and diplomacy, and were rarely secluded or veiled, except in the case of elites. Women also predominated in a good many ritual contexts, associated with agriculture, birth, death, and healing, perhaps because their reproductive capacities were seen as giving them regenerative and spiritual powers that men could not match (Reid 1988: 146).

In light of these patterns it should not be surprising that in the early modern period (and in earlier times as well) many communities of Southeast Asians accorded enormous prestige to male-bodied individuals who dressed in female (or dual-gendered) attire both while performing certain rituals (associated with royal regalia, births, weddings, and the agricultural cycle) and in non-ritual everyday contexts as well, and commonly took normatively gendered males as their husbands. These transgendered ritual specialists, along with female-bodied ritualists who sometimes engaged in transgendered behavior and same-sex relations (but appear to have done so in fewer societies than their male-bodied counterparts), served as sacred mediators between males and females, and between the spheres of humans and the domains of spirits and nature.

Much has obviously changed in Southeast Asia since early modern times, but many aspects of the pluralistic ethos of the early modern period remain alive and well. The strongly Islamic Bugis of South Sulawesi, Indonesia, for instance, not only recognize the existence of five distinctively gendered subject positions—normatively gendered males (*lelaki*), normatively gendered females (*perempuan*), feminine males (*calabai*), masculine females (*calalai*), and androgynous ritual specialists (*bissu*)—they also accord legitimacy and respect to people identified with each of these positions (assuming they uphold basic community norms bearing on good citizenship and the like), even in the case of those who (like *calabai*, *calalai*, and some *bissu*) engage in same-sex relations. Dynamics contributing to the fall of Indonesian President Suharto in 1998 have in fact led to something of a "*bissu* renaissance" and a florescence of variably gendered subjectivities (Davies 2007). This is partly because *bissu* have long been core symbols of the cultural traditions that many Bugis currently seek to revive, and partly because increasing numbers of Bugis travel widely and otherwise engage the discourses of Jakarta-based Muslim feminists and transnationally connected lesbians who embrace and seek to enhance the gendered subject positions and subjectivities that *bissu* are taken to represent.

A broadly analogous situation obtains in present-day, predominantly Buddhist Thailand, where gender-transgressive males known as *kathoey*—who probably performed important ritual services in royal palaces in times past and are actively involved in spirit mediumship—are typically accorded far more legitimacy and respect than their gender-transgressive counterparts in the West. This despite the fact that they sometimes meet with discriminatory state policies and are sometimes derided for behavior that is seen as "unmanly" or "unThai." The term *kathoey* appears originally to have referred to hermaphrodites. At present, however, it is most commonly used to designate a male-bodied individual who either walks, talks, or dresses like a woman, spends "too much" time with women, is involved in stereotypically female pastimes or occupations (hairdressing, fashion design), or behaves like a women in other ways, such as by having sex (in the receptor mode) with men (Morris 1994; Jackson 1997). One of the interesting features of the term and its deployment by Thai speakers is that it does not distinguish among effeminacy, transvestism, transsexualism, and homosexuality. One's erotic orientation, toward someone of the same or "opposite" sex, moreover, is not a primary marker of *kathoey*-ness, the more fundamental issue being that the term refers primarily to gender transgression rather than sexual transgression. These generalizations apply to analogous terms in many other Southeast Asian languages, such as the Indonesian *waria* and *banci* as well as the terms *bakla* and *bantut*, which are utilized in the northern/Christian Philippines and the Muslim south, respectively (see, e.g., Oetomo 1996; Johnson 1997).

Noteworthy as well is that it is by no means uncommon for a normatively gendered Southeast Asian male to have one or more sexual encounters with a gender-transgressive male (e.g., a *kathoey*, *waria*, or *bakla*) prior to or even during his (heterosexual) marriage. As in India and many other regions of Asia (and beyond), such an encounter, if made public, does not result in the male losing his claim to normativity or being considered homosexual or *gay*. Nor would it—or an ongoing relationship with such an individual—feminize him, as would typically occur in the West. Conversely, especially in Java and elsewhere in Indonesia, males who participate in same-sex relations and identify as *gay* tend to be involved in (or plan to enter into) heterosexual marriage leading to procreation, thus fulfilling normative expectations that are in many ways far more weighty than those specifying that sexuality be confined to heterosexual relationships (Boellstorff 1999). In short, as with their counterparts in Thailand, the Philippines, Malaysia, Burma, Vietnam, and other parts of Asia, these men fashion identities and strategies for survival that entail "drawing variously on endogenous traditions and identities as well as exogenous concepts and practices, combining and recombining them, and at the same time contesting both cultural conventions that would condemn homosexuality as incompatible with filial piety and metropolitan notions that would insist there is only one way to be authentically gay" (Proschan 1998: 3).

In this context I want to address a set of issues having to do with the proliferation of sexual and gender diversity that has occurred in the postcolonial era and the last few decades in particular owing largely to massive urbanization and the growth of new middle classes and urban subcultures engaged with transnational media, tourism, and globalizing discourses on sex, gender, and modernity that have helped foster new languages of gender, sexuality, and identity, and new ways of being in the world. At the most general and abstract level the issues involve a loosening of the hegemonic "deep structure" that long informed subjectivities as well as the directionality and the embodiment of erotic activities. I use the term "loosening" here partly because we are not dealing with the shattering of a hegemony in a Gramscian (1971) sense, nor with an epistemic rupture or succession à la Foucault (1978) or Altman (1996, 2001). The evidence for this loosening, which comes from Burma, Thailand, Malaysia, Indonesia, and many other nations of Asia, includes the emergence in the past few decades of (at least) two newly delineated classes of individuals. One is composed of male–identified men who are erotically involved with other men and are endeavoring to create subcultures focused around gay masculinities that are defined to some degree in opposition to the feminized subject positions (such as *kathoey*) long available to phenotypic males. What is new and distinctive about the men involved in these subcultures is that their subject positions and subjectivities are defined not only by their male gender but also by their sexual orientation as gays or men who have sex with men.

The other newly designated group consists of female–identified women who are erotically drawn to other women. What is historically novel and unique about these women is that their subject positions and subjectivities are informed not simply by their female gender but also by their sexual orientation as lesbians or women who engage in sex with women. Consider in the latter connection the referents and meanings of the terms *tom* and *dee*. These terms (and variations like *T*, *T-bird*, *tibo*, and so on) derive from the English "tomboy" and "lady," respectively, and are commonly used in Indonesia, Thailand, the Philippines, and elsewhere in Southeast Asia and beyond to designate female-bodied individuals who engage in same-sex relations, one or another form of transgenderism, or both. There are important variations in the ways these terms are used (and the specific meanings they convey) from one national context to the next—and within these contexts as well—and I thus focus here on Thailand, specifically the Bangkok region as described by Megan Sinnott (2004), who has produced the most sophisticated study of *tom* (masculine females) and *dee* (feminine females involved with *tom*) to date.

The emergence in Bangkok in the past few decades of *dee* identities and subjectivities is highly revealing of both the scope and limits of changes occurring in Thailand and elsewhere in Southeast Asia. What separates *dee* from normative Thai women is not their gender identities or styles of dress or comportment, all of which are broadly congruent with the contours of Thai femininity, but their sexual orientation: the fact that they are attracted to, desirous of, and erotically involved with women rather than men. To reiterate a point made earlier, what is new and distinctive about these women is that their subject positions and subjectivities are defined not only by their female gender but also by their sexual orientation as women who engage in erotic activities with other women. Partly because gender identities in Southeast Asia have always subsumed and largely defined sexual orientations, scholars like Dennis Altman (1996, 2001) see in these kinds of developments (including those involving gay men) evidence of the ways that "Asian homosexualities" are being "Americanized," "Westernized," or otherwise reconfigured by transnational, globalizing developments (see also Morris 1994).

In my view, however, these shifts are not as dramatic as they may appear at first glance. I say this partly because in Thailand and elsewhere in Southeast Asia feminine-identified *dee* tend to form erotic relationships exclusively with masculine-identified *tom*, in contrast to masculine-identified *gay* men whose sexual relationships do not necessarily involve feminized *gay* men, though they sometimes—perhaps typically—do. These relationships, though (homo-)sexualized, are still heterogender as far as most of the participants and others are concerned. As such, they fit comfortably within the heterogender matrix that has long been a central component of sex/gender systems throughout Southeast Asia. For these and other reasons I regard the emergence of new subject positions and sexual subjectivities in Southeast Asia as involving processes that while commonly appropriating global terms, styles, and identities, frequently do so in ways that are informed by Indigenous categories and their interrelations, core elements of which continue to serve as the basis of templates for the localization of things global with respect to form and content alike, much as Marshall Sahlins (1981, 2004) has observed for other processes of historical change in the Pacific and far beyond.

If on the other hand the new subject positions and subjectivities documented for Bangkok involved relationships that were simultaneously homosexual *and* homogender (i.e., of the same sex and similarly or identically gendered) they could pose truly serious challenges to the locally prevalent cultural hegemony. Note though that it would not be the *sexual* patterning—the homosexuality—of these relationships that would raise the specter of subversion via-à-vis local taxonomies and hierarchies and the values and interests they serve. Rather, the real threat of subversion would come from the way they are *gendered*—the fact that they would be homogender. Note too that eroticized homogender relationships between female-bodied individuals reportedly strike the majority of Thais and other Southeast Asian women involved in transgender practices, same-sex relations, or both, as aesthetically and morally offensive, a view shared by their more normatively oriented sisters. Their counterparts however—eroticized homogender relationships involving phenotypic males—do no necessarily evoke negative sentiments among male-bodied persons involved in transgender practices and/or same-sex relations, though they apparently offend most male-bodied individuals in society at large. There are, to repeat, burgeoning subcultures growing up around these latter (male-bodied/homogender) relations in Burma, Thailand, Malaysia, and other nations in Asia. As in other contexts discussed in this essay and elsewhere, male-bodied individuals, however gendered, continue to enjoy an appreciably broader range of experiences and opportunities than their female-bodied counterparts in terms of the directionality and embodiment of potentially erotic enterprises (and much else).

Emerging lesbian desires and youth culture in China

Material from Thailand and other areas of Southeast Asia is profitably viewed in relation to Tze-Lan Sang's *The Emerging Lesbian: Female Same-Sex Desire in Modern China* (2003). This fascinating study of literary and other sources traces the vicissitudes of same-sex desire among Chinese women from late imperial times (especially the eighteenth and nineteenth centuries) through the republican era (1912–1949) and the decades of Maoist rule (1949–1978) to the present-day post-Mao period both on the mainland and in neighboring Taiwan. The focus is less on sexual relations per se than on sisterhood and friendship among women, their feelings and fantasies, their "longing[s], … intimacy, … and gender subordination" (Sang 2003: 42).

In late imperial China (c. 1600–1911), as in most other parts of Asia during this period, transgender practices and same-sex relations were accorded legitimacy in certain (particularly palace and ritual) contexts, at least if they involved male-bodied individuals. Little is known about women involved in transgender practices or same-sex relations, but it appears that same-sex relations between Chinese women were less prohibited or criminalized than denigrated, belittled, and trivialized. Unlike the Christian West, however, imperial-era Chinese "never expressed ... a tangible abomination specifically for the sex act between women as unclean, unnatural, a sin, or a crime" (64). What mattered more than a woman's erotic involvement with other women was that she conform to the expectations enjoining her to enter into a legitimate marriage with a man of appropriate genealogy and social standing, that she produce children, especially male heirs, for that man and his patrilineage, and that she remain faithful to him in the sense that she not participate in inappropriate intimacies with other men. "Therefore, it may be said that *compulsory marriage, compulsory sexual service, compulsory reproduction,* and *compulsory chastity* are more apt than *compulsory heterosexuality* as descriptions of women's fate at the hands of traditional Chinese patriarchy" (92; emphasis in original). Elaborating on the theme that during this time, "intimacies with women" are ultimately "inconsequential," Sang advances a compelling argument that is relevant far beyond late imperial China and may be a general characteristic across Asia: "What determines a woman's gender conformity or non-conformity is first and foremost her relations with men, *not* her relations with women. Female-female desire does not ... make her a gender outcast as long as it cooperates with the imperative of cross-sex marriage. *In sum, female-female desire by itself is not taboo; marriage resistance is*" (93; emphasis added).

Much of the situation described here changed in the early twentieth century, due to globally far-reaching geopolitical developments, including the spread of European colonialism, print capitalism, and Western scientific discourses that congealed in a field that came to be known as "sexual science" or "sexology." During the late nineteenth and early twentieth centuries in particular, European and American scientists and scholars such as Sigmund Freud, Magnus Hirschfeld, and Havelock Ellis developed a corpus of scholarship on the anatomy, physiology, evolution, sociology, and folklore of sexuality that was widely disseminated throughout the world. Most of this scholarship defined transgender practices and same-sex relations as pathological, requiring cure via medical or psychiatric treatment, although some of the literature promoted more positive views of these phenomena. Of broader relevance is that transgender practices, same-sex relations, and what came to be defined as "normal" sex/gender practices and subjectivities were for the first time subject to intense scientific and public scrutiny, having been effectively created as a legitimate object of scientific study and public debate. The military prowess of Western nations in the early twentieth century, when most of Africa, Asia, and the Pacific were subject to Western colonial rule, helped insure that Western scientific discourses, including sexology, were accorded tremendous prestige throughout the world.

In China, for example, nationalistic intellectuals who sought to break with their feudal past were often inspired by Western models of modernity and progress and thus commonly embraced Western notions of race and evolution along with attendant concepts of racial hierarchies and racial degeneration, some of which were yoked to sexology. Put differently, "the scientism of Western-oriented May Fourth [early twentieth-century] intellectuals was assisted by their anxiety over the weakness and regression of the Chinese race, which made them susceptible to the sway of late-nineteenth- and early-twentieth-century European sexology, which claimed to discover hereditary degeneracy, male effeminacy, and female masculinity in homosexuality" (16). In China, Japan, and elsewhere in Asia, these developments gave birth to binary notions of sexuality, sexual "essences," and sexual types ("heterosexuality" vs. "homosexuality," "the heterosexual," "the homosexual," etc.) and a host of other Western-origin concepts that had no local counterparts. At the same time, they contributed to "the sexological abnormalization of same-sex intimacy ... in many Asian societies" as also occurred more or less concurrently in the West (7).

One of the defining characteristics of the May Fourth era in China was the existence of a cultural-political climate conducive to the expression of a wide diversity of views and broad-ranging debates concerning the role and status of women in the family and in society at large, and whether expressions of their sexuality ought to be limited to the institution of (theoretically) monogamous marriage or could involve pre-and extra-marital heterosexual relations and same-sex desire. Unfortunately, this climate of open intellectual exchange did not last for long. "As Japanese military aggression escalated in China during the 1930s, growing Chinese nationalism and the leftists' zealous call for socially engaged literature ... [appear to] have cast an unflattering light on female-female romantic love (as well as heterosexual love), making it seem self-indulgent and irrelevant to the crisis at hand." Similarly, in the wake of Mao Zedong's rise to power and the formation of the People's Republic of China (PRC) in 1949, there occurred a "complete effacement of female same-sex love" and other forms of non-normative erotics as "topic[s] for public debate and artistic representation" (156, 163).

In later years the Chinese Communist Party (CCP) "harshly denounce[d] homo-sexuality either as a Western capitalist corruption or as a heinous feudalist crime," declaring as well (in categorical terms of the sort favored by Iran's current leadership) that there were no instances of homosexuality anywhere in the nation (106). The latter declarations sat uneasily with the public punishment meted out to those suspected of homosexual activity, who were typically charged with "hooliganism" and paraded through the streets carrying signs proclaiming their crimes (167 passim). For the most part, debates about same-sex relations did not reemerge in the public spheres of the PRC until after Mao's death in 1976 and Deng Xiaoping's 1978 proclamations that the CCP would reassess its commitment to a purely socialist path of development and opt for development strategies entailing an "opening" (*kaifang*) of China to global market forces.

These policy shifts helped set the stage for "the resurgence of liberal feminism in the late 1980s and the 1990s" (125, 167). They have also had momentous consequences for kinship and gender relations, household dynamics, consumer and "lifestyle" choices, and understandings and experiences of bodies and selves, particularly in rapidly expanding urban areas. Judith Farquhar describes the situation well. I quote her at length:

> Beginning in the mid-1980s, Chinese modernity began to look a lot more sexy. Several distinct literatures on sex—pornographic novels and magazines, family sexual hygiene manuals, medical sexology, respectable erotic fiction, translations of sexology classics like Havelock's Ellis's *Sexual Psychology* and the Kinsey Report, scholarship on ancient Chinese ars erotica, and a new subdiscipline of traditional medicine called *nanke*, "men's medicine"—emerged and flourished in a book market that was no longer directly controlled by the state. Gender differentiation in the surfaces of everyday life ... became extreme for a while, particularly among the young, with rococo assemblages of ruffles, ... sequins, and satins mostly on women and leather jackets, cowboy gear, and motorcycle boots mostly on men. In many cities, shops opened where white-coated clerks sell birth-control supplies, condoms, herbal aphrodisiacs, skimpy leather clothing, and sexual aids in a matter-of-fact clinical manner. By the late 1990s, Chinese-made movies had begun to include explicitly filmed sex scenes as a matter of routine.
>
> (Farquhar 2002: 211)

481

The proliferation of a number of separate and distinct discourses on sex—some ostensibly "ancient" and "authentically Chinese," others deriving prestige from their association with or definition as "modern science"—has helped fuel the "sexual revolution" in China's urban areas. This is nowhere more apparent than in Shanghai, a megacity with some 20 million residents that has experienced a spectacular economic boom, with growth rates for per capita disposable income more than doubling from 1995 to 2005 and those for gross domestic product quadrupling during the same period. James Farrer's (2002) sociological study of youth sex culture and market reform in Shanghai documents the far-ranging effects of what many in China speak of as *kaifang*. The latter term, which means "opening" or "opening up", refers to China's increased responsiveness and greater vulnerability both to global capitalism and to the attendant temptations and seductions of Western-style consumer culture, including the cult of the materialistic, pleasure-seeking, narcissistic individual that consumer cultures both target and create. For people in Shanghai, especially youth, this trajectory has brought not only radically increased living standards but also unprecedented personal freedom and choice in the realms of dating, leisure, and consumption, although many in Shanghai and elsewhere would say too much freedom and too many choices.

Developments in Shanghai and other parts of China in the past few decades have simultaneously given rise to a critical range of uncertainties, insecurities, and ambivalences as well, as has also occurred in socialist Vietnam since the onset of Doi Moi (Renovation) in 1986. Particularly in China, some of the most unsettling insecurities are material. As capitalist market forces, premised on a logic of supply and demand, replace or supersede centralized state control over the economy, young Chinese no longer enjoy the job or overall economic security they once did. Overcrowded and ever more congested urban areas, coupled with the scarcity and expense of urban housing and the premium placed on geographic and social mobility geared toward the attainment of "success" (which guarantees continued migration from rural to urban locales), all contribute to the undermining of extended family ties, hence the erosion of networks of social security to which one could formerly turn in times of economic need. New and old rationales for gender discrimination in wages, work conditions, and retrenchment exacerbate the situation for female factory workers and other women involved in capitalist production for export. Circumstances such as these encourage women to view dance-hall encounters and dating as opportunities to improve their short- and long-term material standing, just as they give rise to discourses on "greedy Shanghai girls" obsessed with fashion and appearance, and the "weak Shanghai men" who succumb to their superficial—if only because ephemeral, easily transferable—"charms" (affections, loyalties, sexual services).

One indication of the incredibly rapid growth of Shanghai's middle classes and the striking transformations in their modes of consumption is the twenty-five fold increase that occurred from the mid-1980s to the mid-1990s in the number of commercial dance halls ("discos"). Discos numbered a mere 52 in 1985 and an astounding (if only in comparative terms) 1,347 in 1996 (Farrer 2002: 291). The spread of disco culture helped "normalize—actually glorified—sexual voyeurism and display. Young women who would have been careful not to show themselves as 'loose' in daily life could dance with wild pelvic thrusts or snuggle up to a stranger in a slow two-step" and "all could [later] be forgotten as a passing silliness" or "just fooling around" (301). "Mistrust was the ideology of dance, but curious interaction was the practice", especially since for some patrons "it was a chance to find casual sexual partners" (305). Interestingly, while many of the icons of chic in the early years of the disco scene hailed from America, by 1999

Japan had superseded America as the preeminent source of fashion (though American styles were still to be found, along with those from Hong Kong and Korea)—a critically important reminder that many transnational flows do not originate in the West and, more generally, that transnationalism and globalization should not be equated with Americanization or Westernization. Farrer notes, for example, that in 1999 "the youth at Buff [a popular Shanghai disco] ... sported fashion elements ... from the pages of Japanese styles manuals I saw youth perusing in Shanghai: punky orange hair, platform boots, little black party dresses, pigtails shooting out sideways ... , the stocking cap of Tokyo rappers, thick-rimmed glasses, and glitter eye shadow." By the following year, however, Japanese and other "foreigners were no longer the models of style and behavior they used to be," having been replaced by locals (311, 322). The more general points here are that the globalization of sex styles and consumption are intimately intertwined; that the interrelationships are sometimes unexpected; and that they draw on local historical and cultural traditions and in so doing give particular meanings to these circulations.

The sexual revolution that has occurred most dramatically in Shanghai and to a lesser extent in other urban areas of China clearly has a downside, including a "surge in divorce, premarital sex, extramarital affairs, ... new type[s] of financially motivated pragmatism in marriage," and the "reemergence of concubinage" and polygyny among the wealthy (133, 144). The 1990s also witnessed a sharp rise in rates of sexually transmitted diseases (STDs) in Shanghai. National-level data likewise saw startling increases in the reports of STDs, which grew from "1,000 per year in 1983 to over 300,000 per year in 1994. ... Most men were contracting STDs from commercial sex, while women were likely contracting STDs from their regular partners who visited prostitutes" (359–360 n. 15). China's current HIV/AIDS epidemic is particularly grim, on the order of one million cases (perhaps far more).

Not surprisingly, the scarring via STDs of bodies, relationships, psyches, and senses of self that has occurred due to market reform and globalization has gone hand in hand with the development of a widespread cynicism about "the possibility of romance" and the "purity of purpose or motive." Women often suspect the behavior of men due to men's media-hyped desire to appear to be "playboys" or "(cool) players" in games of sexual conquest. Men, for their part, are often suspicious of the comportment of women for reasons noted earlier: because "at heart, they're all 'gold-diggers'" and because virginity, which is still highly valued in a potential wife, is an increasingly uncommon attribute of young women. As laden with ambivalence as they are, such are the facts of life in a consumer culture that engenders heavy anxiety about performance in the rough and tumble of bedroom, boardroom, and back alley.

Contexts such as these help explain the enormous popularity in the Chinese-speaking world, and in East Asia and the Chinese diaspora generally, of films stars like Bruce Lee, Jackie Chan, and Chow Yun Fat. These megastars, along with the martial arts, action films, and video games with which they are iconically associated, offer compelling alternatives to the discourses on "weak, effeminate Chinese men" that circulated in Shanghai and elsewhere at various points in the mid-twentieth century and in earlier times, repeatedly singling out the crisis of (Chinese) masculinity as the primary cause of China's poor showing, both politically and economically, on the world stage. China's early-to-mid-twentieth-century reputation in the West as "the sick man of Asia," which is still bitterly recalled, is clearly relevant in this context. The films and other media products at issue here engage Hollywood constructions of masculinity. But they also glorify the cultivation of self-control and refinement through martial arts and other regimes of discipline that promote physical strength, military prowess, homosocial bonding, and heterosexual abstinence or at least careful regulation of sexual and emotionally deep relations with women. These themes resonate with Confucian and other Chinese ethics emphasizing that control of the self is a prerequisite for rising to positions of power and prestige that involve control over others. It is revealing in this connection that "in the 1990s, immensely popular television soap operas such as *Beijingers in New York* and *Foreign Babes in Beijing* unambiguously correlated sexual 'conquest' of white women with national revival," such that "the victory that Chinese men ... score with foreign women symbolizes not only the resurrection of Chinese masculinity but also a triumph of the Chinese nation itself" (Louie 2002: 75; Lu 2000: 37). It remains to underscore the broader theme, that mass media with global reach can play an active role in challenging gender and sexual codes just as they can be (and perhaps more typically are) deeply complicit in their reproduction.

Popular culture and sexual politics in Taiwan and Japan

The contemporary contours of youth culture in Shanghai cannot be taken as typifying mainland China, let alone the Greater China of the numerous and far-flung diaspora. But analogous phenomena have been reported for other large cities of China and may well be a harbinger of national trends. This seems all the more likely in light of China's intense drive to industrialize its economy, eliminate rural poverty, and create a largely urban workforce. Developments in popular culture and sexual politics on the other side of the Taiwan Strait are relevant here inasmuch as they suggest one of several possible futures that might unfold on the mainland. They do in any event merit consideration in their own right, as do comparisons involving popular culture and sexual politics in Taiwan and Japan, each of which has embraced capitalism and globalizing forces with a vengeance and has developed its own distinct vision of modernity.

Many of the sexual and gender dynamics occurring in Shanghai and other highly urban areas of China in recent years bear a close resemblance to developments in Taiwan over the past few decades. Major differences also exist due to historical and geopolitical factors whose influence continues to be strongly felt. Unlike the situation in China, for example, American political and military institutions played a key role in Taiwan's development since 1949 (when Chiang Kai-shek suffered defeat at the hands of Mao's revolutionary forces, fled the mainland of China with his Kuomintang army, and with massive US assistance established a government across the strait in Taiwan). From the outset, Taiwan's American-backed military rulers and the institutions through which they governed embodied and disseminated a broad range of beliefs and practices associated with American capitalism and Western culture in general, although they did not give priority to American-style democracy. Political repression under martial law (which prevailed through 1987) spawned opposition movements of various stripes, many of which drew inspiration from American writings on freedom, justice, and equality. American cultural influences are also strikingly evident on university campuses, in intellectual circles beyond academia, in journalism and other mass media, in the arts, in feminist movements, and in the realms of lesbian and gay activism. This is not to suggest that such influences have supplanted Chinese culture in these or other areas. It is rather a relative point, underscoring differences between Taiwan and mainland China, where such influences are far less evident.

In Taiwan, as in many parts of the world, popular culture is heavily influenced and in some respects created by an increasingly internationalized media driven by a combination of home-grown and transnational corporate capitalisms. The media in Taiwan seek to capture the hearts and minds both of consumers charged with household provisioning and "status production work" (who, as elsewhere, are generally women) and of others in various niche markets. Here too feminism sells, as does the marshalling via television talk shows and other media outlets of popular opinion arrayed against it. So increasingly do media and commercial products geared toward the burgeoning lesbian and gay sub-cultures that exist in Taiwan and Hong Kong but not yet on any comparable scale elsewhere in China. Mass media might give the impression of a comfortable or mutually supportive relationship in Taiwan between feminism and lesbian (and gay) activism but "in actual political practice, even feminists in the most radical women's organization have questioned the legitimacy of lesbian agendas in the women's movement" (Sang 2003: 237). Lesbians tend to find their concerns marginalized or ignored by the women's movement though the situation may be changing. Further complicating the prospects for cooperation, according to Yuxuan Aji, is that "some lesbians (esp. Ts …) resist female identity," having "always fought against … the institutional violence of heterosexuality"; hence their difficulties embracing a basic principle of feminism: that "women identify with women" (cited in ibid., 242).

In her discussion of mass media and the commercialization of homosexuality, Sang underscores that Taiwanese, like people in most countries, receive the bulk of their knowledge about the world from the media, and that media organizations such as Tai-wan's, while generally conservative, present their readers and viewers with coverage of Western events that is often relatively positive though simultaneously sensationalistic and full of negative stereotypes. These generalizations are germane to the coverage afforded dynamics of sexual culture in America, especially gay pride parades, the ravages and scope of the AIDS epidemic, the development of AIDS activism, gay and lesbian marriage, and other aspects of same-sex sexuality. In treating these topics and their Taiwanese coun-terparts, the media endeavor to titillate and shock their audiences with dramas of sexual escapades and criminality via "story after story about lesbian/gay promiscuity, sexual techniques, cruising parks and bars, crimes, murders, and suicides"; some of these accounts are "voyeuristic," others "plainly fantastic" (247).

The media's excitement over its "discovery" of lesbians in the early 1990s raises some potentially unsettling questions that are also worth raising in other contexts, including the United States: "If homosexuality has become one of the most trendy and best-selling topics in Taiwan, is it because lesbians and gays have become such a distinctive and powerful consumer group that their emotional needs and erotic interests must be catered to?" Or, does the recent development of "lesbian/gay chic" reflect the fact that "lesbian/gay sexualities have been domesticated and turned into curiosities that … [a rapidly expanding middle class] audience that considers itself normal will find entertaining?" (248–249). From Sang's perspective, the dynamic suggested by each of these questions helps explain current trends in media and popular culture in Taiwan, as does the fact that openly gay media tend to embrace middle class consumerism and many of the underlying values (individualism, materialism, etc.) it reinforces.

In Taiwan the internet has become not only an integral component of the commer-cialization and mass mediation of same-sex sexuality but also a powerful technology deployed to resist commercialization and mass mediation as well as the panoply of forces that seek to silence local gay and lesbian voices. One of the signature features of the internet is the near instantaneous global connectedness it provides its users. In Taiwan as elsewhere, the internet has made locally available information concerning Western sexual cultures, as is true to a lesser extent of other media. "The rise in Taiwan during the last decade of novels and whole collections dealing with the subject of lesbian eroticism and lesbian subjectivity ... occurred amid a burgeoning lesbian and gay identity politics and the general proliferation of queer discourses" that "swept through the island during the early to mid-1990s" (256, 258). Just as some local academic critics "tirelessly cite Western queer theory," certain "local queer theorists ... have become media celebrities." Deeply ambivalent about such developments, Sang contends that an "uncritical parroting of the latest trends in First World queer theory is quite the opposite of being queer. ... and might mean misdirecting valuable resources away from, rather than toward, the really challenging problems of local sexual and gender politics" (258, 260, 261). More importantly in the larger scheme of things, "the internet has emerged as a powerful new public medium and forum. ... [and] has proved remarkably effective in supporting non-profit feminist and antihomophobic publishing as well as open, well-circulated discussion under relatively safe and anonymous conditions. Such decentralization of mass communication greatly contributes to the proliferation of lifestyles, and vice versa" (231).

Despite the heightened visibility of lesbian and gay communities in recent years, Taiwanese society as a whole by no means embraces either lesbians or gay men. In addition to having to battle the powerful but conservative media which simultaneously stereotypes them but also uses them as marketing tools to "pry into and capitalize on the eroticism of a formative urban lesbian scene," lesbians in particular must contend with "the Confucian patriarchal family transfigured by the influence of the modern nuclear family [which] continues to prescribe and privilege a particular alignment between biological sex, culturally defined gender behavior, and romantic/erotic desire" (228, 232). Bolstered and legitimized by a conservative medical profession, "this regime of gender and sexuality dictates that, to be considered normal, a woman [must] accept a male spouse, join his family, and fulfill her reproductive destiny." As in the PRC, "the modern heterosexual regime works against women's same-sex desire, not only by denouncing and prohibiting it, but also by silencing it, erasing it, rendering it unthinkable, invisible, and insignificant," just as the "typical family," when forced to react, moves to disavow, punish, or "fix" the errant female (232).

While Taiwan's lesbian movement is more robust than its counterparts in other Chinese-speaking societies (e.g., in the PRC, Hong Kong, and Singapore), it differs in significant ways from the local movement centered around gay men, a contrast that also exists in other Chinese-speaking contexts, and, indeed, in much of the world. One of the most revealing differences is that lesbians in Taiwan cannot readily draw upon a historical past to help provide legitimacy for their practices and identities, even though scholars have documented scattered (regionally-specific) traditions of marriage resistance and female same-sex sexuality that existed in Greater China in earlier times. The relative absence (except in literary sources) of such traditions helps clarify two sets of issues. The first has to do with why discourses of Western origin have been of such importance in Taiwan and in many other parts of Asia throughout the twentieth century and into the new millennium. The second concerns why, despite terms of Indigenous origin such as *tongzhi* (comrade, cadre), which was appropriated from the Maoist period and is utilized in Hong Kong and the PRC, many of the terms utilized by Taiwanese and other Asian women attracted to women involve borrowings from the West (for instance, *tomboy*). Gay men, in contrast, can—and do—point to well-known historical traditions that involved male–male sexuality (such as those that existed in imperial circles) as a way both to legitimize their subject positions and subjectivities and to counter state-sanctioned ideologies that portray them as unacceptable local parodies of Western perversion. As Sang (54) puts it, albeit somewhat dismissively for the males to whom she refers, "the sense of not having a usable Chinese past distinguishes the experience of many ethnic Chinese lesbians from that of the many gay men who cling to the fantasy of belonging to a great homosexual tradition in China."

A proliferation of sexual subcultures has also occurred in Japan, where non-normative sex sells and sells big. Since the early decades of the twentieth century state-sponsored corporate capitalists have conjured all varieties of erotic imagery in the service of creating and aggressively marketing a broad range of media products aimed at titillating, seducing, and otherwise captivating customers, and thus giving rise to and (ideally) capturing increasingly lucrative market shares. At present, such imagery includes depictions of scantily clad teen-aged girls and women, cross-dressing actors, and androgynous "She-Male" figures who abound "in ordinary and pornographic comic books alike, … [in] fantastical, exotic, intersexed, androgynous bodies, most typically portrayed in the form of a figure with breasts and a penis" (Robertson 1998: 201). The term "New Half" (*nyu hafu*) is sometimes used to refer to these comics as well as the members of the youth subcultures who consume them, including, most notably, the growing numbers of males who in niche clubs and other contexts attire themselves in female clothing, emulating the "fictive men (in comic books, for example) who cross-dress in the much fetishized style of Lolitas, or sexually precocious, cute teenage girls" (ibid.). As anthropologist Jennifer Robertson explains, the root-term "half" (*hafu*) is often used as a derogatory gloss for locals of ethnically mixed parentage, and the designation "New Half" thus reflects the Japanese sense that gender and sexual ambiguity entail ethnic (or "racial") ambiguity, and vice versa.

The mutually constitutive nature of these ambiguities—and of the ambivalences associated with them—is clear from the history of Japan's famous Takarazuka Revue, the brainchild of legendary Japanese venture-capitalist and cabinet minister Kobayashi Ichizo (1873–1957). The all-female members of this theatrical troupe (founded in 1913) frequently engage both in cross-dressing and "cross-ethnicking"—portraying members of other ethnic groups, particularly those colonized by Japan during World War II—and thus constitute "exoticized hybrids" par excellence (ibid.). The Revue, though both innovative and more or less acceptably transgressive, builds on earlier traditions of gender and sexuality in Japan, including those that prevailed during the Edo (or Tokugawa) period (1603–1867), during which time bisexuality tended to be the norm for males (but not females) and male homoeroticism was privileged over eroticism of all other varieties, much as in ancient Greece (Louie 2002: 24; cf. Pflugfelder 1999: 5 passim). Ironically, the erotics and cultural politics of the Revue are simultaneously informed by the ethos of the Meiji Restoration (dating from1868), which gave rise to a greater formalization of gender roles in line with increasingly Western-inflected and dichotomized understandings of gender and sexuality, including the imposition of new and more restrictive legal codes premised on the idea that ambiguity involving gender and sexuality is conducive to widely redounding social disorder. Thus targeted was (*inter alia*) much of the homoeroticism and same-sex sexuality that prevailed among *samurai* during the preceding Tokugawa period, as famously (and scandalously) depicted in Nagisa Oshima's 1999 film "Gohatto" (glossed as "Taboo" in English-speaking venues), which is something of a cult classic among contemporary Japanese males involved in same-sex relations.

487

Referring to the "recent fascination in Japanese popular culture with androgyny and cross-dressing," Robertson makes clear that "androgyny is big business. New Half comic books and animations, transvestite clubs for males, Miss Dandy clubs for females, clothing fashions, cross-dressed celebrities, and of course the perennially popular Takarazuka Revue, enjoying an all-time high number of applicants to the Academy, are all part of the powerful and metaphoric—if ambivalent—salience of androgyny" (205). So too are the comic books aimed at women that "specialize in the homoerotic adventures of *bishonen* or 'beautiful boys'. ... [whose] forbidden and often tragic love ... is [seen as] somehow more 'pure' and more 'equal' than that which exists between men and women, constrained as they are by the reproductive demands of the family system" (McLelland 2002: 7).

Also relevant in this context is Gao, "a Japanese version of the gender-bending Canadian popular singer k.d. lang. The Japanese pop icon was discovered—or rather, invented—in 1993. Her public relations campaign capitalizes on and commodifies the image of the androgyne" as is evident from some of the English-language publicity statements aimed at Japanese consumers: "How does Gao spend her one-day-of-the-year? That voice, that prescence, that style—A man? Or is it a woman? ... What's her true sexuality? A million possibilities surface, but if we look at her, none seem to fit. She's unlike anyone else. She's Gao!" (Robertson 1998: 205). It is important to bear in mind that Gao's persona is "the creation not of some radical queer underground but of a powerful corporation (in this case, Victor Entertainment)," much like the Takarazuka Revue, "a component of the giant Hankyu Group of companies" (207).

As might be expected, the aggressive marketing in Japan of things sexual and the extensive flows throughout Japan of increasingly global discourses on sex, gender, and romance have helped bring about an explicitly lesbian movement and a "gay boom," just as they have given rise to the inclusion in everyday spoken Japanese of English-origin loan words such as "gay pride" (*gei puraido*), "coming out" (*kamingu auto*), "homophobia" (*homofobia*), and the like. One should not assume, however, that Western and other global influences in Japan are evident only in arenas of gender and sexuality that are to one or another degree marginal with respect to "mainstream" (normative) Japanese culture. Much as in Korea, Christian/Western-style weddings for heterosexual couples now predominate in Japan, with some three-quarters of all weddings involving quintessentially Western attire, ministers, and music such as "Ave Maria," despite the fact that less than two percent of Japan's population of 127 million people is Christian. Traditional Shinto marriage ceremonies have lost favor due to their association with what are increasingly seen as conservative gender roles, just as Christian/Western-style weddings offered by corporate bridal companies are all the rage both on grounds of fashion and because of the greater degree of equality between husband and wife and the relative autonomy of the bridal couple vis-à-vis encompassing networks of kin they are taken to symbolize. Some elders see much cause for alarm in these and related trends involving a rejection of long sanctified tradition, particularly since they are occurring in a climate characterized by falling birth rates, a rise in divorce, and growing cultural emphases on individualism, materialism, and immediate (hedonistic) gratification. The larger issue for many in Japan and elsewhere in Asia is what current trends portend for the future and whether (as advertised) globalizing forces will enhance the quality of their lives or—as seems more likely—will lead instead to a constriction of life options and further commercialization of their variably embodied experiences.

Some comparative and conceptual implications

By way of conclusion I want to emphasize that from a comparative-historical perspective, the most deeply rooted and widely ramifying taboo throughout the broad swath of Asia addressed in this essay has never been "about" engaging in transgender practices or enacting same-sex desires. Such practices and desires have long been perfectly legitimate if they occurred in certain contexts and involved bonds that were conceptualized in relation to heterogender (but not necessarily heterosexual) marriage. Indeed, heterogender marriage of one sort or another has long been enjoined on everyone, with the notable exception of Buddhist monks and Hindu and other ascetics (including *hijra*) who undertook religious vows requiring celibacy. Hence the most deeply rooted and widely ramifying taboo in question involved resistance to marriage, albeit marriage involving heterogender relationships that were variably embodied and sexed.

The salience of one or another form of marriage in this formulation may seem reminiscent of the West in the last millennium or two, but the apparent commonalities should not obscure the equally striking differences. The latter include both a wider berth for marriage in Asia (allowing for heterosexual unions as well as same-sex marriages in certain contexts as long as they were heterogender); and, related, the existence in Asia of marital institutions and systems of kinship and gender that were in some sense less restrictive, exclusive, and all-encompassing insofar as husbands in particular could—and for the most part still can—engage in same-sex relations without necessarily calling into question their loyalties to their wives, their commitments to matrimony, or their masculinity. Although I cannot explore the issue here it merits remark that from a broadly comparative (global) perspective, the West, not Asia, is anomalous in these areas, and that the anomalies are probably best explained by the peculiar development of the Church in the West and the ways that Church policy helped shape Western institutions of kinship, marriage, gender, and sexuality over the last millennium. Weber (1922[1963]: 239) summed up some of the key contrasts in his comparative-historical observation that the teachings of Christianity, with their "demand of absolute and indissoluble monogamy, went beyond all other religions in the limitations imposed upon permissible and legitimate sexuality." It remains to add that important "East–West" contrasts of the sort at issue here are elided and obscured by uncritical usage of terms like "heteronormative" that unwittingly (or otherwise) so privilege sexuality over gender that they fail to distinguish between culturally salient and analytically relevant categories of relations, such as those that are heterosexual as distinct from those that are heterogender (and may involve same-sex erotics). It is deeply ironic that one of the more enduring legacies of globalizing processes—and of the colonial and immediate postcolonial eras that preceded them—may well be the (further) suppression of culturally meaningful differences even at the hands of those who have helped develop language intended to lay bare and critique various kinds of normalizing discourses and institutions.

Acknowledgments

This essay contains substantially revised material adapted from Peletz (2007: Chap. 3). I am grateful to Carla Freeman for comments on an earlier version of this essay and to Stephanie Loo for research assistance.

Note

1 I use terms such as "gay" (and "lesbian") when I seek to emphasize one or another Asian identity or Asian-language usage. I use regular font when deploying the terms to convey their now conventional English-language meanings (e.g., a person inclined toward erotic relations with others of the same sex). When quoting published material, I retain the author's conventions.

References

Altman, D. (1996) "Rupture or Continuity? The Internationalization of Gay Identities." *Social Text* 48: 77–94.

——(2001) *Global Sex*. Chicago: University of Chicago Press.

Andaya, B. (2006) *The Flaming Womb: Repositioning Women in Early Modern Southeast Asia*. Hawaii: University of Hawaii Press.

Andaya, L. (2000) "The Bissu: Study of a Third Gender in Indonesia." In *Other Pasts*, B. Andaya, ed. Honolulu: Center for SE Asian Studies, University of Hawaii.

Beatty, A. (2002) "Changing Places: Relatives and Relativism in Java." *Journal of the Royal Anthropological Institute*, 8: 469–491.

Blackwood, E. (2005) "Gender Transgression in Colonial and Post-Colonial Indonesia." *Journal of Asian Studies* 64: 849–880.

Boellstorff, T. (1999) "The Perfect Path: Gay Men, Marriage, Indonesia." *QLQ* 5(4): 475–510.

Bornstein, K. (1995) *Gender Outlaw: On Men, Women, and the Rest of Us*. New York: Vintage.

Butler, J. (1993) *Bodies That Matter: On the Discursive Limits of "Sex."* New York: Routledge.

Davies, S. (2007) *Challenging Gender Norms: Five Genders Among the Bugis*. Belmont, CA: Wadsworth.

Farquhar, J. (2002) *Appetites: Food and Sex in Post-Socialist China*. Durham: Duke University Press.

Farrer, J. (2002) *Opening Up: Youth Sex Culture and Market Reform in Shanghai*. Chicago: University of Chicago Press.

Foucault, M. (1978) *The History of Sexuality, Vol. I*. New York: Vintage.

Geertz, C. (2006) "Comment." *Current Anthropology* 47(2): 327–328.

Gramsci, A. (1971) *Selections from the Prison Notebooks of Antonio Gramsci*, ed. and trans. by Q. Hoare and G. Smith. New York: International Publishers.

Jackson, P. (1997) "Kathoey Gay Man: The Historical Emergence of Gay Male Identity in Thailand." In *Sites of Desire, Economies of Pleasure: Sexualities in Asia and the Pacific*. L. Manderson and M. Jolly, eds. Chicago: University of Chicago Press.

Johnson, M. (1997) *Beauty and Power: Transgendering and Cultural Transformation in the Southern Philippines*. Oxford: Berg.

Louie, K. (2002) *Theorising Chinese Masculinity: Society and Gender in China*. Cambridge: Cambridge University Press.

Lu, S. (2000) "Soap Opera in China: The Transnational Politics of Visuality, Sexuality, and Masculinity," *Cinema Journal* 40(1): 25–47.

Manalansan, M. (2003) *Global Divas: Filipino Gay Men in the Diaspora*. Durham: Duke University Press.

McLelland, M. (2002) "Kamingu Auto: Homosexuality and Popular Culture in Japan." *IIAS [International Institute for Asian Studies] Newsletter* 29: 7.

Morris, R. (1994) "Three Sexes and Four Sexualities: Redressing the Discourses on Gender and Sexuality in Contemporary Thailand." *Positions* 2(1): 15–43.

Nanda, S. (1993) "Hijras: An Alternative Sex and Gender Role in India." In *Third Sex, Third Gender: Beyond Sexual Dimorphism in Culture and History*. G. Herdt, ed. New York: Zone Books.

——(2000) *Gender Diversity: Cross-Cultural Variations*. Long Grove, IL: Waveland.

Ong, A. (1999) *Flexible Citizenship: The Cultural Logics of Transnationality*. Durham: Duke University Press.

Oetomo, D. (1996) "Gender and Sexual Orientation in Indonesia." In *Fantasizing the Feminine in Indonesia*. L. Sears, ed. Durham: Duke University Press.

Peletz, M. (2007) *Gender, Sexuality, and Body Politics in Modern Asia*. Ann Arbor: Association for Asian Studies.

——(2009) *Gender Pluralism: Southeast Asia Since Early Modern Times*. New York: Routledge. Pflug-felder, G. (1999) *Cartographies of Desire: Male-Male Sexualities in Japanese Discourse, 1600–1950*. Berkeley: University of California Press.

Proschan, F. (1998) "Filial Piety and Non-Procreative Male-to-Male Sex Among Vietnamese," Paper presented at the Annual Meeting of the American Anthropological Association, Philadelphia, December 2–6.

Reddy, G. (2005) *With Respect to Sex: Negotiating Hijra Identity in South India*. Chicago: University of Chicago Press.

Reid, A. (1988) *Southeast Asia in the Age of Commerce, 1450–1680, Vol. I*. New Haven: Yale University Press.

Robertson, J. (1998) *Takarazuka: Sexual Politics and Popular Culture in Modern Japan*. Berkeley: University of California Press.

Roscoe, W. (1998) *Changing Ones: Third and Fourth Genders in Native North America*. New York: St. Martin's Press.

Rubin, G. (1984) "Thinking Sex: Notes for a Radical Theory of the Politics of Sexuality." In *Pleasure and Danger: Exploring Female Sexuality*. C. Vance, ed. Boston: Routledge & Kegan Paul.

Sahlins, M. (1981) *Historical Metaphors and Mythical Realities: Structure in the Early History of the Sandwich Islands Kingdom*. Ann Arbor: University of Michigan Press.

——(2004) *Apologies to Thucydides: History as Culture and Vice Versa*. Chicago: University of Chicago Press.

Sang, T. (2003) *The Emerging Lesbian: Female Same-Sex Desire in Modern China*. Chicago: University of Chicago Press.

Sinnott, M. (2004) *Toms and Dees: Transgender Identity and Female Same-Sex Relationships in Thailand*. Honolulu: University of Hawai'i Press.

Towle, E. and L. Morgan. (2002) "Romancing the Transgender Native: Rethinking the Use of the 'Third Gender' Concept." *GLQ* 8(4): 469–497.

Weber, M. (1922 [1963]) *The Sociology of Religion*. Boston: Beacon.

Wilchins, R. (1997) *Read My Lips: Sexual Subversion and the End of Gender*. Ithaca: Firebrand Books.

25

Globalization and food

The dialectics of globality and locality

David Inglis

Tell me what thou eatest, and I will tell thee who thou art.

(Alexis Soyer)

The destiny of nations depends on the manner in which they are fed.

(Jean-Anthelme Brillat-Savarin)

It hadn't been a great year for wild sockeye, prices were up at the market and farmed Chilean salmon finally made it into the seafood risotto. It didn't taste bad, exactly; it just didn't taste *right*. ... A fish pen up the coast from Santiago might as well be up the coast from Osaka or Vladivostock or Campbell River. The fish in such a pen lived independent of geography, food chain or ecosystem. These salmon were perfectly commodified as a result, immune to the restrictions of place. There was no *where* that these fish were *from*. And to what end had he made this critical sacrifice, made this culinary homeless risotto that no amount of saffron butter would resurrect?

(Taylor, 2001: 171)

Introduction

The great nineteenth-century gourmet Brillat-Savarin, quoted above, lived in a period where confident assertions about the cultural 'purity' of national cuisines and foodways could be agreed to by all persons of good sense. French cuisine seemed to be as markedly different from its Anglo-Saxon and Germanic neighbours as it was from the cooking of Japan and China, a view shared by people all across Europe. Thus when searching for a way in *Ecce Homo* to describe the cultural essence of the Germans, Nietzsche's (1967: 238) mind seemed naturally to turn to matters of cuisine:

[As to] German cuisine quite generally – what doesn't it have on its conscience! Soup before the meal ... overcooked meats, vegetables cooked with fat and flour; the degeneration of pastries and puddings into paperweights! Add to this the virtually bestial prandial drinking habits of the ancient, and by no means only the ancient, Germans, and you will understand the origin of the German spirit – from distressed intestines.

For those living in the late Victorian period, one could be pretty certain that the world was like a culinary mosaic, made up of various national or regional pieces which were relatively incommensurate with each other, each possessed of its own distinctive alimentary *Volksgeist*.

The world in the present day may well continue to be 'torn and rent by varying views on nutriment', but not in the same ways, and not for the same reasons, as the writers of the late nineteenth-century imagined. This is for a range of reasons, which this chapter will outline and explore. The contemporary world condition of food and cuisine differs from that which pertained a century ago in many ways, the main ones being: (a) a globe-spanning (but certainly not fully integrated) system of food production and distribution has developed over time, especially since the end of World War II; (b) this system, once relatively unchallenged and hidden from the view of most people, has become a source of very public problems, crises, and contestations, especially those centred on the 'health' of both humans, animals, and plant-life across the planet; (c) present-day food and cuisine exhibit a range of markedly homogenizing tendencies, such that 'global McDonaldization' has become one central way in which social actors, of various political hues and dispositions, can imagine and reflect upon contemporary social conditions; (d) relatedly, opposition and hostility to perceived global food homogenization increasingly takes the form of the invention of culinary traditions and the alleged 'rediscovery' of 'real' and 'authentic' ingredients and modes of food preparation and consumption.

In these various ways, then, food today is not only structured by both 'globalizing' and 'localizing' social, political, economic, and cultural forces; it also very often figures as a symbol of these forces, as a crucial stake and resource in the struggles they both express and compel, and as a means by which they are enacted and performed. As Georg Simmel (1997) noted a century ago, food is not just an absolutely essential component of any social order's material functioning; it is also – once transformed by cultural processing into 'cuisine' – a key means of both expressing and regulating sociality. Of all possible sets of phenomena that can symbolize particular epochs of human history, it seems that food and cuisine are particularly able to represent the tendencies of an age, its hopes and fears, its sense of what the 'good life' is and which forces threaten to destroy the latter altogether. Food thus can figure as both *promesse de bonheur* and as the index of approaching apocalypse. In an age of endemic globalization and globality, food both symbolically expresses and is materially constituted in ways that make it a quintessential aspect of the contemporary social order, for it is wholly caught up within the dialectics of globality and locality, of placelessness and situatedness, of brave new worlds and fear-ridden nostalgias.

The salmon used unwillingly by the fictional Vancouver chef in Timothy Taylor's novel cited above, very well embody many of these elements. Reared in a Chilean salmon farm such that they 'lived independent of geography, food chain or ecosystem' and were thus 'immune to the restrictions of place', they seem to be globalized commodities of the first order, the piscine equivalents of the Big Mac and the bottle of Coca-Cola. They point to the dynamics of globalized capitalist agri-business, the tentacles of which reach out all across the planet, traducing apparently age old ecosystems and culinary cultures alike. They also point to endemic factory farming on a massive scale, and to burgeoning fears of what effects genetically-modified creatures and crops will have on the bio-systems of the planet in the medium- and long-terms. But their radically un-situated, hyper-commodified nature – so unsettling because so apparently 'unnatural' – also indicates senses of nostalgia as to biotic conditions and culinary traditions apparently lost forever that goes together with such developments, such sensibilities generating attempts to recapture rooted feelings of history and tradition in and through food. The dialectics of globality and locality in food keep generating ever more senses of crisis and loss, which in turn are productive of projects to create feelings of stability, security, and sense of place in culinary terms.

In a recent book on the subject of food globalization, Nutzenadel and Trentmann (2008: 1) argue, 'in much of the literature on globalization food has played little more than a Cinderella role, marginalized and subordinated to the leading cast of financial markets, migration, communication and transnational political cooperation'. This is true to a certain extent, as in the plethora of work on globalization that has appeared in the last fifteen years or so, food has not figured as a major point of focus or interest. However, this situation varies from one academic discipline to another, with a lot of research on globalized (or localized) foodways being carried out, as we will see below, in anthropology in particular, and also in the sorts of sociology closely related to the latter. Such studies tend – by dint of the ethnographic method they generally employ – to be focused on micro-level processes, while studies of global food systems and regimes have been carried out more by political economists, often those of a radical hue. In this chapter, we will examine the results of both sorts of work, as well as the valuable contributions of historians, which have amply demonstrated both that contemporary food globalization is not wholly historically unprecedented, and that present-day developments have to be contextualized within the broader dynamics of world history.

Histories of food globalization

While the globalization of food and cuisine is arguably particularly a phenomenon of the twentieth century and after, there have been discernible trends towards the 'proto-globalization' of food production, distribution and consumption in earlier historical periods. For the historical anthropologist Jack Goody (1982), the main impetus behind such trends for most of human history has involved the desires of elite groups in certain societies for ingredients and tastes that were considered 'exotic', and which could be deployed as means of class distinction. In all societies possessed of a complex enough division of labour and social structure to allow strong differentiation of the lifestyles of elites and lower groups, there exists a cuisine of the elite and a cuisine 'of the people'. While the latter is characterized by the geographical proximity of its staple ingredients to the places of habitation of peasants and urban lower orders, elite cuisine is often marked by the fact that at least some of its ingredients come from places that are (or are regarded as being) far-flung and distant. This is especially the case with spices and other products used to flavour foodstuffs that may well be more 'local' in origin, spices and suchlike being relatively easy to transport in storage over long distances. Thus for Goody, while peasant cuisine speaks of *terroir* and (enforced) locality, elite cuisine always has a potentially more 'global' element, involving the use of non-Indigenous materials to produce new, more hybrid food forms.

A good case in point concerns the elite foodways of the Roman empire, the latter being a socio-political social order that bears certain similarities to present-day conditions of globality (Robertson and Inglis, 2004). At the peak of their empire's power and geographical reach, the Romans had fairly extensive trading links with south-east Africa, India, Malaysia, and even China. Although such trade was generally operated by Indian and Parthian middlemen, rather than by direct contact between Rome and these locales, nonetheless there was a steady movement of goods, both more mundane and more luxurious, including spices and other kinds of foodstuff that could be kept for several months (Curtin, 1998). Such trade both made possible and further stimulated Roman elites' appetites for the exotic in food tastes. Culinary fashion among the upper classes was pithily characterized by the satirist Petronius (1996: 89) in this manner: 'Far-out and foreign win/What's out-of-bounds is in'. In like fashion, the philosopher Seneca (1889: 334–5) castigated those of his contemporaries 'whose luxury transcends the bounds of an empire which is already perilously wide'. Seneca went on to deride those who would only eat shell-fish if they knew it came 'from the unknown shore of the farthest sea', that is to say Britain, one of the ends of the earth in the Roman imagination. Such finicky epicures demanded that there be brought

> ... from all regions everything, known or unknown, to tempt their fastidious palate: food, which their stomach, worn out with delicacies, can scarcely retain, is brought from the most distant ocean ... they do not even deign to digest the banquets which they ransack the globe to obtain ... they wander through all countries, cross the seas and excite at a great cost the hunger which they might allay at a small one.
>
> (Seneca, 1889: 334–5)

From this point of view, elite Roman epicures and gastronomes had gone too far, in both geographical, moral and gustatory terms, in search of exquisite sweetmeats from every conceivable part of the world (Miller, 1969), the edible and the moral having a strong connection in this culture as in many (perhaps all) others throughout history (see Levi-Strauss, 1965, Korsmeyer, 1999).

The search for ample sources of spices was not restricted to the Romans of the imperial period. The cuisine of Medieval European elites was also heavily spice-driven, with both sweet and savoury tastes being based around the judicious spicing of particular dishes. In a medieval aristocratic feast, one might find such flavours as 'grains of paradise' (*Aframomum melegueta*, of the cardamom family) from Africa, nutmeg and cloves from the Moluccas, cinnamon from Ceylon, ginger from China and pepper from southern India (Colquhoun, 2007; Turner, 2005). By the thirteenth century, sugar began to appear in Europe from the Middle East, and had started to replace honey as a sweetener in the elite diets. As Colquhoun (2007: 54) notes, by the time such products arrived in Western Europe, 'they had passed through so many traders' hands that few really knew where they came from'. But despite the lack of knowledge as to the places of origin of such flavourings, they remained central to the taste culture of elites, the latter involving 'a juxtaposition of the piquant with sweet fruits, nuts and sugars' (Colquhoun, 2007: 54). While the advent of 'fusion' cuisines is sometimes presented as a development in the West of very recent provenance (James, 1996), medieval elite cooking stands as testament to a period prior to the construction of allegedly pure and exclusive 'national' cuisines, a time when food tastes were shared by elites across large swathes of Europe, and when the use of 'exotic' ingredients was as much the norm as it is in the period of, for example, the 'Pacific Rim' hybrid cuisine to be found in the restaurants of present-day Sydney and San Francisco (Gallegos, 2005).

Processes to do with what we today call globalization have arguably been going on since the dawn of humanity, when early humans slowly spread out from their originary location in East Africa throughout all the continents. Likewise, the cultivation of grains,

495

one of the basic foodstuffs that underpins human existence in most parts of the planet, stretches back to the start of settled agriculture in the Tigris and Euphrates valleys c. 7000 BCE. By around 5000 BCE, wheat and barley had spread into Africa and by 4000 BCE into Europe, widespread cultivation of grains leading to major deforestation between 3500 and 3000 BCE – an indication that human agricultural practices have been having major impacts on the natural environment for a very considerable period (Atkin, 1992). For much of human history, however, grains were not transported very far from their original place of production – for example, as recently as the sixteenth century CE, only 1 per cent of the total grain produced in the Mediterranean world was transported internationally (Braudel, 1982). Internationalized, and then globalized, grain production and distribution is primarily a product of the nineteenth century, stimulated at first by the repeal of the protectionist Corn Laws in the United Kingdom in the 1840s, with first the USA and Canada, then Australia, India, and Argentina becoming major grain exporting countries to many parts of the world in the latter half of the nineteenth century (Atkin, 1992: 18). The current global food crisis (see below) is in many ways structured by developments towards 'grain globalization' that occurred in the later Victorian period.

In many accounts of 'modern' globalization – globalization 'proper', as it were – the European 'discovery' of the Americas stands as the point at which the whole planet starts to become 'one place', even if such a place is characterized by fragmentation and centrifugal forces as much as by integration and centripetal tendencies (Scholte, 2000). In terms of the globalization of food, it is certainly possible to claim not only that the trans-Atlantic food transactions attendant upon the European colonization of the Americas marks the beginning of modern food globalization, but also that the 'Columbian' movement of foodstuffs, animals, plant-life, and people between the old world and the new world stands as one of the two most significant material and economic developments within modern food globalization, its consequences as wide-ranging and as disruptive of previous patterns of food cultivation, distribution, and consumption as are the effects of the globalized food regimes of the later twentieth century (Mintz, 2008). Many of the ingredients and tastes that have characterized European food cultures over the last five centuries originated in the Americas and were wholly unknown to Europeans before the conquerors brought them back to their mother countries. Without the expansion of the Spanish empire throughout the sixteenth century, we would not today be familiar with the tastes of either chocolate or peanuts, crops that are now grown in other parts of the world but which were once available only in the Americas (Rebora, 2001). Even more peculiar is the thought that the potato would probably not play such an important role in north European food cultures if it had not been brought back from South America by the means of European conquest (Fernandez-Armesto, 2001). In subsequent European history, allegedly 'national' food cultures were made possible by a collective forgetting of the originally non-Indigenous origins of certain foodstuffs. Thus nothing seems more essentially 'Italian' than the tomato, but it first came from the Americas, along with gnocchi (made from potatoes) and polenta (made from maize, another South American staple). In the same vein, one today associates chilli with the cooking of India and certain Far Eastern countries, yet they too are Indigenous to South America. A converse process of trans-Atlantic movement in foodstuffs also occurred in the post-Columbian period: from Europe and Africa to the Americas and the Caribbean came crops such as rice and bananas, and animals such as beef cattle. Nothing sounds more quintessentially 'Mexican' than chilli con carne, but as it involves either beef or rice, it is using ingredients that came to the Americas only in the last few hundred years.

The vast biotic movements of the post-Columbian period pay testament to the strongly globalizing tendencies of food production and consumption in the early modern period, making it possible to argue that early modernity was quite as 'globalizing' in this regard as was the twentieth century, and as is the twenty-first (Jardine, 1997). But arguably a key difference between early modern and late modern food globalization is that in the former, consciousness of novelty and exoticism in cuisine was soon replaced by processes of normalization, rendering the previously exotic into the known, the taken-for-granted and thus often part of supposedly 'national' cuisines; but in late modern conditions, novelty and exoticism are much more than hitherto more self-consciously imagined, reflected upon and deployed, as are their antitheses, locality, stability, and *terroir*. Early moderns did not subject foodstuffs and their alleged social consequences to the same degree of reflection, reflexivity, and contestation as do their late modern successors (Beck, 1992). Yet it remains the case that the Columbian transfusion of both things and ideas haunts the contemporary landscape of food, precisely insofar as late modern attempts to root the rootless, and to create ontologically secure horizons of consumption, are generally compelled to forget that what is represented – if not indeed fetishized – as truly 'local', 'regional' or 'national' is in fact the product of long-term processes of inter-continental movement, mobility and exchange, driven first by the forces of colonialism (Mintz, 1986) and then by those of corporate agri-capitalism, the latter being the very forces that advocates of locality in food see themselves as struggling against (Leitch, 2003).[1]

Food globalization and risk society

Food globalization processes of the twentieth and twenty-first centuries can only be properly understood if set against the background of the development of the industrialized agri-capitalist food system that has appeared over the last century or so (Friedmann, 1994). From the later nineteenth century onwards, this system has become ever more globe-spanning in reach, although its development in different parts of the world has been uneven and its effects far from being totally homogeneous (Watts and Goodman, 1997). In terms of the ongoing development of this system, key features include massive and rapid urbanization in Europe and North America, leading to large urban populations needing to be fed; the diminishing social role of the peasantry; the transformation of farms into ever larger production units; the development of mass-market oriented agricultural and livestock production systems, tending towards the factory farm model; the application of innovative scientific knowledge, produced and utilized by new sorts of professional cadres, to both animals and crops, especially in terms of producing species that were particularly conducive to rapid and easily manipulated growth; the massification and rationalization of animal breeding techniques and slaughtering systems; the consolidation of nation-wide, and international, transportation systems, such as the development of globally standardized freight and cargo systems (Levinson, 2008); and the development of new modes of packing and preservation, such as industrial freezer systems, and large-scale canning operations (for an overview, see Sorj and Wilkinson, 1985).

All of these innovations, mostly pioneered in Europe and North America, have come to have increasingly world-level ramifications and consequences, such that agriculture world-wide, in one way or another, has come to be affected and restructured in light of the dynamics of globalized agri-capitalism (Friedmann, 1994). At the very least, one can note that agriculture in the present day involves a globalized division of agricultural labour and trans-national chains of production, distribution, and consumption, with the effect that crises in one part of the system can have huge consequences for other parts (Daviron and Ponte, 2005) – such a situation being one of the most important indices of an intricately connected system, as Durkheim (1964 [1893]) recognized more than a hundred years ago. While for most of the twentieth century, this world-spanning industrialized food system operated in relatively unreported ways, turning out its factory-farmed meats and mass-produced cereals in manners relatively closed to controversy, by the later twentieth century one of its key features seemed to be its crisis-prone tendencies, these latter being very much reported upon by the media (Fischler, 1999).

Thus at the time of writing (mid-2008), newspapers are full of reports of a 'global food crisis', this nomenclature itself capturing the manner in which in the present day it seems to be impossible to talk about food outside the terms set by discourses centred around notions of globalization and globality. The current crisis is depicted (see for example *The Economist*, 2008) as resulting from 'butterfly effects' in certain parts of the system that then have uncontrollable unintended consequences in other, geographically disparate, parts of the network. Thus, for example, food riots in countries all around the equator are said to be consequent on shortages in rice, cereals, and other basic foodstuffs; these shortages are in part due to such factors as rising demand in the developed world for certain crops, hitherto used primarily for human food consumption, to be used in bio-fuels, that have themselves been created to ease pressure on an ever more imperilled biosphere. Thus measures intended to resolve one set of problems – in this case, carbon emissions and global warming – in turn create other serious dilemmas, here hunger, deprivation and attendant political unrest, a situation of domino effects utterly characteristic of 'risk society' (Beck, 1992). Likewise, pressure is put on global food systems as living standards in countries such as China, India, and Brazil rise due to rapid industrialization, the latter itself being seen to contribute massively to the environmental woes of the planet. As newly eco-nomically-enfranchised groups in such places demand what they think of as richer and more varied diets, further pressure is put on cereal crops, these now being diverted to the purpose of feeding intensively farmed animals, such cereals being the very crops that are now in short supply in some of the world's poorest regions. Thus as the diets of some 'improve', the access of others to basic foodstuffs goes into freefall. A further factor here is that the gases created by the intensive farming of animals such as cows and pigs are seen to contribute to global warming, such that the increased appetite for meat amongst the planet's 'new middle classes' is seen to be helping to undermine the very biosphere on which all life across the planet depends. Irony piles upon irony, as the material con-ditions of globalized agriculture seem to exhibit ever more contradictory impulses and tendencies, the future outcomes of these being easily susceptible to being represented by concerned (primarily Western) commentators in increasingly apocalyptic terms (e.g. Kimbrell, 2002).

One feature of the world agri-capitalist system that makes it particularly open to being analyzed as part of 'risk society' is that, as it ever more displays – and crucially, is *perceived* by a wide range of different actors and groups as featuring – crisis tendencies, it also seems to be unable to correct itself and to resolve the problems generated by the very nature of its own functioning. According to Ulrich Beck (1992), an essential corollary of a risk society situation is when the institutions of (industrialized, nation-state-centred) 'first modernity' produce consequences – such as environmental degradation and food shortages – that they cannot themselves deal with. While food production and con-sumption have never been more regulated than in the present day (Kjaernes et al., 2007), the manners in which they are regulated are multiple, complex, overlapping, and often contradictory. Various types and levels of regulation, and the bodies that produce and (try to) enforce these, accompanied the development of large-scale food systems throughout the twentieth century. These include national governmental regulations; rules created by agri-capitalist organizations themselves in attempts to 'self-police' (or be seen so to do); international (and putatively 'global') agreements and treaties associated with organizations such as, in world trade, the WTO and GATT, and in international food policy, the UN's Food and Agricultural Organization; the morally-informed standards promoted by non-governmental, campaigning, and charitable organizations, such as Compassion in World Farming; and the procedures of trans-national economic-political bodies, the most wide-ranging to date being those of the European Union (Friedmann, 1994).

Because of the multifarious, multi-level nature of all these different regulative bodies and their respective codes, the world in the present day is far from having a unitary system of regulations and procedures in the realm of food. Consequently, when crises (are seen to) arise, the lack of coordination in both diagnoses of the problems and ways of dealing with them, is very marked. For example, the effects of recent outbreaks of avian flu on the world-wide chicken-rearing industry are potentially disastrous, but it is difficult to coordinate efforts to deal with the problem when, just at the level of state-based institutions, different national governments are members of different, rival trading blocs. As Beck (1998) himself has noted, institutions of 'first modernity' such as national governments are ill-equipped to deal with problems that are by their very nature trans-national and are no respecter of state boundaries. Even institutions that are putatively more geared towards dealing with trans-national problems in food, health, and related matters, such as the EU or UN, are often sclerotic and confused in their responses, in part because they are hamstrung by inter-governmental bickering and the pursuit of naked national self-interest, and by the recalcitrance of agri-business in the face of the prospect of falling profits.

In essence, the contemporary global food system is a quintessential feature of 'risk society' conditions because its industrialized methods of production and distribution are both seen to create a whole series of problems, environmental, moral and otherwise, as well as being highly susceptible to troubles – avian flu, 'mad cow disease', etc. – that are themselves always potentially 'global' in reach, as the dangers they create spiral uncontrollably down the networks of the globalized division of labour (Fischler, 1999). Moreover, as this system itself has both produced and has been subjected to an equally spiralling set of regulatory instruments, problems keep proliferating, not only because the regulative bodies struggle to regulate what they are supposed to regulate, and are very bad at coordinating their responses to crises, but also because – in Niklas Luhmann's (1996) terms – the more ways that exist of categorizing certain phenomena as problems, the more problems come to 'exist' that have to be dealt with. For example, thirty years ago, concerns about intensive factory farming were not a major factor for agri-business to deal with, as such practices very much occurred 'behind the scenes' and out of public view. But due to the successful moral-political entrepreneurship of animal rights groups in the developed world, such issues are now very much in the discursive terrain that shapes perceptions of, and increasingly forms part of, globalized systems of food production, with practices hitherto deemed unproblematic – such as keeping large numbers of animals in very small spaces – now regarded as deeply problematic (Nibert, 2002). As animal rights discourses, and analogous concerns about the ethics and social and biotic consequences of genetic modification of plant and animal life, have become part of the

499

discursive elements of globalized food production, new problems have proliferated, as reality has been reconfigured in light of new sensibilities and moral concerns (Macnaghten, 2004).

It is also worth noting in this regard that not only do such problematizing discourses now exist in, and help to structure, world-level discursive space (Lechner and Boli, 2005), this being sphere of so-called 'global civil society' (Keane, 2003) that agri-business increasingly has to respond to and to at least pay lip-service to; but it is also the case that animal rights and anti-biotechnology groups have themselves become trans-national in their practices and modes of organization. For example, Lien (2004) has shown how trans-nationally active campaign groups have successfully created new food taboos, encouraging people in different countries to reject the attempted defining by the meat industry of certain animals, such as kangaroos, as fit for human consumption. Just as food production systems have become more trans-nationalized, so too have certain food prohibitions, the latter now longer the preserve of the anthropologist who studies food avoidances within, and solely as the products of, the tight-knit confines of small-scale communities (Douglas, 1966; Levi-Strauss, 1965). Thus food taboos have 'gone global' at the same time as a globalized food industry tries to serve up ever new forms of commodifiable comestible on the dining tables of the world.

Under risk society conditions, one would not only expect contestation by various social groups of industrial-capitalist practices, one would also expect the undermining of the bases of scientific authority, perhaps especially – given the moral freightedness of food noted above – in the realm of eating. It is not just the food industry which has experienced severe knocks in the developed world after such recent food chain crises as BSE ('mad cow disease'), foot-and-mouth outbreaks, and the reportedly carcinogenic nature of farmed salmon (Brown and Scott, 2004). It is also the claims to truth of scientists, both those working for governments and for private interests that have taken a battering in recent years. While the levels of public distrust in both the food industry and in food scientists varies from one national context to another (Kjaernes et al., 2007), it is certainly the case that scientific truth claims in the realm of food have never been more opened up to questioning than in the present day. Not only has there been an erosion of scientific authority, there is also a proliferation of different sorts of authorities, each clamouring for public recognition and attention. Different kinds of scientists each have their own sorts of claims, which may be contradictory of each other; different and changing forms of scientific advice are constantly appearing in the public arena; and other sorts of 'experts', among them those drawn from social movement organizations, pressure groups, corporate interests, and even celebrity culture (in the guise of celebrity chefs) all competing for air-time and recognition (Kjaernes et al., 2007).

This pluralization of food expertise certainly can undermine scientific authority in certain areas. For example, while the advocates of genetically modified (GM) crops such as spokespeople for the Monsanto company might have had in the 1970s a relatively easy time convincing public opinion as to the famine-eliminating capacities of this technology, their task in this regard is much more difficult in the present day, because increasing public skepticism towards, and uneasiness about, scientific claims, means that the views of anti-biotech campaigners may well be taken as seriously, if not more so, than those of industry representatives or those seen to be in the pay of corporate vested interests (Charles, 2001). Claims that GM foods, far from 'saving the planet' from the spectre of wide-spread famine in the developing world, in fact promote a corporate strangle-hold over world farmers in the developing world, by compelling them to buy seeds from monopoly-holding corporations that hold lucrative patents on whole strains of plants and crops, may well be appealing to developed world publics that conceive of themselves as 'responsible' consumers and ethically-informed 'global citizens'. Given the hold of these sorts of globally-oriented imaginaries on economically influential middle class groupings, the case of GM foodstuffs is particularly exemplary, insofar as while agri-business continues enthusiastically to embrace the 'scientization' of agriculture, such a process has now been subjected to deep and divisive contestation, with the eventual outcome of public debates on such matters being far from certain.

Certainly the whole arena of the globalized food system is nowadays best characterized by contradictions, paradoxes, and unintentional consequences with far-reaching and difficult-to-control effects, rather than any sense of smooth-running, uncontested operation. This can be seen in the fact that challenges to the scientization of industrialized food production, and thus to the knowledge base of global agri-business, themselves often have outcomes completely unintended by their advocates. Indeed, attempts to make the system both more 'ethical' and more centred around the production of 'healthy' food (as opposed to 'junk food', the new demon of global food imaginaries), may rebound on their progenitors. Thus as Clover (2006) reports, the high praise heaped on the health-giving properties of fish by nutritional scientists and various kinds of dietary entrepreneur, simultaneously encourages developed world consumers to shun apparently health threatening products like industrially-produced hamburgers, while pushing up consumption of a 'virtuous' (i.e. both health-giving and 'slimming') foodstuff like fish. But increased fish consumption is made possible by environmentally-damaging industrialized fishing, which damages ecosystems, threatens to wipe out certain piscine species, and which increasingly is based in the waters of poorer nations (e.g. on the west coast of Africa) whose governments are happy to take the money offered for fishing concessions by the EU and other developed world bodies, despite the environmental havoc that is wreaked on local fishing industries, and thus on local and national food systems more generally. Thus those products and practices that seem to developed world consumers to be environmentally sound may well be based on activities that are very far from being so – but what counts as environmentally sound is also a point of debate and dispute in the first place. If developed world consumers start to go beyond the pleasant-sounding rhetoric of 'organic' and Fairtrade food production, they may well find that the virtuous 'food chain' they thought they were part of is in fact a much more ambivalent phenomenon than they had thought, bearing more resemblance to the 'mainstream' agri-business practices they had thought they were rejecting and avoiding (Wright and Madrid, 2007). Middle class western consumers are now very much enamoured of the notion of 'organic' farming, but the actual practices of organic farmers are ambivalent, for as Guthman (2004) has shown there are many diverse motivations among farmers who participate in organic practices, ranging from environmental philosophy through to regarding organic production purely as a money-spinning enterprise. What may seem at first blush to be ethically progressive practices can be revealed to be more complex and multitudinous than one may have imagined. If any one phrase can be said to depict world food systems under conditions of globalization and endemic risk-generation, then that phrase is most likely 'deep ambivalence'.

McDonaldization and its others

A very simplistic account of food globalization would have it that this process involved solely the world-wide spread of the great American food brands – Coca-Cola, Pepsi,

Kentucky Fried Chicken, Burger King and so on – which allegedly totally eliminate 'local' cuisines and foodways in their all-conquering path. Of all of these brands, none has been subjected to more critique in academic circles, and vilification in activist circles than the hamburger chain McDonald's. Growing from one single outlet in San Bernardino, California in 1948, it had spread to 117 countries world-wide, with a new branch opening somewhere in the world in the mid-1990s *every eight hours* (although this boom had subsided by the first few years of the 21st century – see Watson and Caldwell, 2005: 2). Just as certain foodstuffs can take on great symbolic valence in certain socio-cultural contexts, so too has McDonald's been defined as the great symbol of American-led cultural globalization, going hand in hand with the other products of American 'cultural imperialism', such as Hollywood films and television, and Nike sports-gear (Tomlinson, 1997). Symptomatic of such trends is the great success and widespread dissemination of the argument of the American author Benjamin Barber (1992) that the early twenty-first century is characterized by an epic clash between 'Jihad' (localizing religious and ethnic fundamentalism and separatisms) on the one side, and McWorld (the globalizing institutions of Western corporate capitalism) on the other. That McDonald's can seem plausibly to lend its name to a whole 'world' – or, more specifically, a whole world-view - speaks for its great symbolic power in the present day. Future historians may well look back in some wonderment at how widespread in our own epoch the association was between fears as to the damage wrought by a certain kind of cultural globalization on the one hand, and, of all things, a particular chain of fast-food outlets on the other.

In addition to Barber's ideas, one of the most influential contributions to the defining of McDonald's as somehow emblematic of present-day world-wide social, cultural, and economic conditions, is the work of the American sociologist George Ritzer.[2] For Ritzer (2000), the four cardinal features of the McDonald's approach to food production, preparation and serving are *efficiency, calculation, predictability*, and *control*. Every single aspect of food consumption is strictly regulated according to fine-grained calibrations, from the weight and size of the burgers (wholly standardized), to the methods of assembling them in restaurants (according to the same principles as the Fordist production line), to the regulation of staff (all having been trained in exactly the same manner) and the control of the customers (uncomfortable seating in the restaurants being deliberately designed to prevent consumers from lingering, freeing up space for the next wave of customers). Ritzer defines the process of McDonaldization as 'the process by which the principles of the fast-food restaurant are coming to dominate more and more sectors of American society as well as the rest of the world' (2000: 1). Thus the definition implies not only that the four cardinal principles come to effect how things are organized in ever more sectors of the developed world (for example labour in call-centres), but also that in the sector of food production and consumption, those principles will become ever more important in all parts of the globe. Even if it is not the McDonald's brand itself which is the avatar of such developments, nonetheless it is these principles that are very likely to structure increasingly food production and consumption world-wide.

In this sense, the symbolic efficacy of McDonald's rests particularly in the fact that it has provided a template for hyper-rationalization that is alleged to be geographically and culturally unstoppable. In later work, Ritzer (2004) has argued that globalization processes are in essence the world-wide spreading of 'culturally weightless' products, such as credit cards. These sorts of products have no specific cultural designations, and are thus easily transported and introduced into any milieu as they do not really 'mean' anything. This raises an important issue relating to the products of McDonald's. Should they be seen primarily as culinary embodiments of 'American culture' (a problematic term in its own right) or as devoid of any specific cultural colouring and connotations? This is not just an analytic issue, it is a political one too, for deciding one way or the other in this regard is very much implicated in broader decisions as to what one's orientations towards globalization processes *are*. If one thinks that McDonald's is primarily a symbol of American-led cultural imperialism, then one is committing oneself, at least implicitly, to a certain kind of 'anti-globalization' politics. One of the contemporary hero figures of this kind of politics, possessed of a media profile now stretching far beyond the borders of his homeland, is the French farmer José Bové, who famously bulldozed a branch of McDonald's France in protest at what he saw as the degradation of French culture in general, and food culture in particular, by creeping Americanization (Bové et al., 2002). Conversely, if one regards McDonald's as signifying and representing precisely (in Ritzer's phrasing) 'nothing', then McDonaldization is certainly not equivalent to Americanization, cultural imperialism or the destruction of allegedly 'traditional' and ancient foodways. Rather, it can be seen as a rationalization process – or set of processes – the results of which on particular socio-cultural contexts are open-ended and contingent, rather than wholly predictable and set in stone.

Much of the academic discussion on such matters has focused on the spaces within the McDonald's restaurants themselves. Such locales are very easily placed under the rubric of what the French anthropologist Marc Augé (1995) calls 'non-places', that is decontextualized and deterritorialized locales like the international hotel conference suite and the departure lounges and duty-free stores of large airports world-wide. After all, a McDonald's restaurant in Dayton, Ohio, has – or is supposed to have – the same sort of layout as an equivalent outlet in Frankfurt, Mumbai, and Taipei. If looking at such matters through the lens of cultural imperialism, then such locales are construable as places where the local people, especially the youth, are inculcated into a 'foreign' food culture that weans them away from 'Indigenous' foodways.

Much the same could be said of another phenomenon of the last fifteen years or so, namely the spread of American or American-style coffee shop chains, the foremost amongst which is Starbucks, to many of the more wealthy countries of the world, being enthusiastically embraced in particular by younger, socially aspirant groups. A recent noteworthy issue here is the increasing popularity of Starbucks amongst younger socially mobile groups in the People's Republic of China, 'hanging out' in Starbucks being regarded locally as a very cool thing to do (Harrison et al., 2005). Simpson's (2008) study of the development of Starbucks and similar chains in Macau after the Portugese handing back that territory to the Chinese government in 1999, suggests that over time more collectivist modes of drinking and eating were significantly eroded as more and more middle class people started to structure their daily routines around coffee shops, and more individualistic practices were encouraged, especially those centred around a display of lifestyle aspirations.

Such studies do indeed suggest that quotidian routines can be restructured by restaurant and coffee shop spaces, with concomitant effects on identities and performances of self. However, if one looks at the themes raised by Augé (1995) in a different way, and regards both the space of the burger restaurant or coffee shop itself and the products purveyed within it, as being without any intrinsic meaning in and of themselves, as relatively blank backdrops against which the activities of everyday life are played out, then other possibilities open up. Regarded in this manner, it is possible either that eating at McDonald's or drinking at Starbucks have little or no effects on 'local' cultural practices, or conversely that the literally meaningless space and foodstuffs can be semiotically colonized by 'local' cultural practices themselves (bearing in mind that 'local' can only ever be a very relative term, especially under conditions of endemic globality).

A great deal of ethnographic work was carried out by anthropologists and cognate others in the 1990s, against the background of the spread of McDonald's, Kentucky Fried Chicken and other such outlets to the former Soviet Bloc and a China rapidly embracing a capitalist economy (Watson, 1997; Miller, 1998; Caldwell, 2004; Lozado, 2005). One of the key animating reasons behind such work was to subject to criticism what these authors took to be the often glib assertions, unencumbered by much in the way of empirical evidence, of authors writing within the cultural imperialism tradition (see e.g. Miller, 1998). Ethnographic studies of customer activities within McDonald's and similar locations in places like Moscow and Beijing stressed that far from funda-mentally restructuring symbolic and material practices, once fast food restaurants had lost the glitter of novelty and had become part of everyday life, they were wholly appro-priated into the patterns of quotidian existence that had existed before their arrival on the social scene. Tomlinson (1997: 87) summarizes these claims thus:

> In everyday activities like working, eating or shopping, people are likely to be concerned with their immediate needs – their state of health, their family and personal relations, their finances and so on. In these circumstances the cultural sig-nificance of working for a multinational, eating lunch at McDonald's, shopping for Levis, is unlikely to be interpreted as a threat to national identity, but how these mesh with the meaningful realm of the private: McDonald's as convenient for the children's birthday party; jeans as a dress code for leisure-time activities [and so on].

Thus on this view, apocalyptic and unsubstantiated claims as to the fundamental restruc-turing of symbolic systems and modes of action by 'McDonaldization' and related phenomena have to be dropped in favour of studies of really occurring practices within fast-food locales.

The ethnographic studies mentioned above are themselves not above criticism. They sometimes exhibit tendencies towards assuming that 'local' and 'national' food-related habits and ways of thinking, as enacted in everyday contexts and locations, not only are relatively homogeneous in the first place, but are sufficiently robust to 'withstand' any alleged colonization by Western fast food influences. Thus just as cultural imperialism arguments tend to assume the 'destructive', disenchanting effects of McDonaldization and related processes, some of the ethnographic writings are suffused with romanticizing assumptions about the homogeneity and ongoing vitality of what are taken to be local and national ways of eating. Both positions are open to question, precisely insofar as tacit *a priori* value-orientations are unreflectively incorporated into the analyses being proffered.

Where ethnographic critics of cultural imperialism arguments are on stronger ground concerns their scepticism towards the latter's framing of food globalization issues such that local and national foodways are seen to be under wholly unprecedented threat in the present day by the forces of global food homogenization. Consideration of historical sources reveals that fears as to the adulteration, if not downright destruction, of national and local cuisines by non-Indigenous influences have been around for at least a century in western countries themselves. Thus in George Gissing's novel of 1903 *The Private Papers of Henry Ryecroft*, nothing upsets the eponymous hero more than the sight of for-eign butter in English shop windows. 'This is the kind of thing that makes one gloom over the prospects of England. The deterioration of English butter is one of the worst signs of the moral state of our people' (Gissing, 1987: 152). Just as at a later date Roland Barthes (1993 [1957]) noticed the huge significance that beef-steak could have for symbolizing healthy and vigorous Frenchness, so here does butter take on the burden of signifying both Englishness and threats to the moral and spiritual health of the nation. Likewise, across the Channel after World War I

> ... Frenchmen began to feel that the unprecedented influx of foreign tourists hurrying through the country in fast cars, Riviera or Biarritz bound, not caring what they ate or drank so long as they were not delayed on their way, was threatening the character of their cookery far more than had the shortages and privations of war. Soon, they felt, the old inns and country restaurants would disappear and there would be only modern hotels serving mass produced, impersonal food which could be put before the customers at a moment's notice, devoured, paid for, and instantly forgotten.
>
> (David, 1970 [1960]: 6)

Thus worries as to the advent of 'mass produced, impersonal food' served in hyper-modern non-spaces are not just a feature of contemporary France, but have been around in that country for some time (Fantasia, 1995). While the French intelligentsia may fret about what they see as the disastrous overturning of national culinary patrimony by the forces of American-led globalization, they seem to have forgotten that they are playing out a script which was written at least ninety years before, and which has been a recurring feature of French engagements with (perceived) modernity (Ross, 1996).

Lest it be thought that such matters are peculiar to France, it is worth noting that the same notions have haunted the imaginations of other European elites over the same period. Thus at the very same time, the mid-1920s, that the first pan-Greek cookery books were being written, which codified for the first time what were to be taken as quintessentially 'Greek' ingredients, flavours and means of preparation, it was also the case that Greek intellectuals depicted foodways as a key area of Greek culture that was 'in danger of being swept away by the onslaught of a cosmopolitan modernity' (Peckham, 1998: 173; see also Appadurai, 1988, for the creation in the mid-1980s of the first 'Indian' cookbooks in India). The two processes mentioned here are intimately connected: perceived threats to what are taken as 'authentically national' food habits – in this case, the threats posed by the first appearance in Greece of American- and British-style canned foods – compel authors to compile what is presented as the national culinary heritage; but once that heritage has been identified, the apparent threats to it loom ever larger in the collective imaginary, provoking further, ever more fraught attempts to freeze in time what is taken as the 'pure essence' of national food culture.

Given the rather fraught and febrile relationships that can pertain between particular national intelligentsias on the one hand, and both imagined 'national' and perceived 'global' food cultures on the other, it comes as little surprise to find that the cultural criticism and social theory that flows from the pens of intellectuals should often embody and express the kinds of fears as to culinary adulteration mentioned above. In a now famous passage from the late 1950s, the English cultural critic (and foundational figure in cultural studies) Richard Hoggart (1962 [1957]) took the new methods of serving milk to youth (in the 'non-spaces' of the new, self-consciously US-style 'milk bars') as a telling index of the alleged Americanization of Britain. Drawing an explicit comparison with the 'traditional' space and associated mores of the 'local pub', Hoggart (1962 [1957]: 248) presents the milk bar in this way:

Compared with the pub around the corner, this is all a peculiarly thin and pallid form of dissipation, a sort of spiritual dry-rot amid the odour of boiled milk. Many of the customers – their clothes, their hair-styles, their facial expressions all indicate – are living to a large extent in a myth world compounded of a few simple elements which they take to be those of American life.

Reading Hoggart's text more than fifty years after its writing, the nostalgic yearning for the past expressed within it is quite obvious, the 'pub around the corner' taken as the hallmark of a life-world vanishing before one's eyes. But the nostalgia was very likely not apparent to Hoggart at the time, or the many members of the English intelligentsia of the period who shared similar sorts of feelings, and who would also have taken food and drink as a key barometer of the kinds of social and cultural changes they feared and despised (Williams, 1958). Writings of the present day that see McDonaldization and related phenomena in a wholly hostile light risk smuggling into their analyses of contemporary conditions the sorts of nostalgia that we can now see having underpinned, and in some ways having undercut, the writings of Hoggart and his contemporaries. But equally well, accounts which stress the apparent robustness of local and national food habits in the face of putatively globally homogenizing culinary forces, risk indulging in a glib denial of the ways in which the latter may well be restructuring, albeit in indirect and subtle fashions, how and why people in different parts of the world eat as they do, and how they think about such practices.

Towards heterogenization?

However debates about McDonaldization and related matters play out in the future, it is clear that the globalization of food in the present day has to be construed in terms of dialectical, contradictory relationships between forces of homogenization (or forces that are perceived to be such by specific groups of actors) and forces of heterogenization (or forces that are also perceived as such by actors). Any adequate account of food globalization must take on board the fact that when particular phenomena are perceived as both homogenizing, threatening and potentially destructive by certain groups of people, those people may very likely engage in projects, that may be more or less self-conscious in nature, which stress the values either of cultural heterogeneity or of cultural purity. As Manuel Castells (1997: 2) argues, when people in particular parts of the world feel threatened by the apparently homogenizing forces of (what is taken as) 'globalization', they may well turn towards 'expressions of collective identity that challenge globalization ... on behalf of cultural singularity and people's control over their lives and environment[s]'. Far from destroying more local and specific senses of belonging, identity and affiliation, globalization processes may actually help not only to reinvigorate these, but in actual fact to create them.

Both of the possibilities just mentioned – the assertion either of cultural heterogeneity against perceived global homogenization, or of cultural purity against the eradication of perceived national and local cultures – can be identified in the case of food and foodways. In both cases, when actors in the developed world cast the role of the villains in their dramas of contemporary culinary purity and impurity, they tend to select McDonald's and other global fast food chains on the one hand, and the large supermarket companies on the other, with capitalist agri-business as another nefarious entity lurking in the background (Blythman, 2005). McDonald's and similar corporations stand charged with various sins, from their complicity in ethically-dubious factory farming practices, through to the severe exploitation of employees and the promotion of unhealthy, obesity-inducing diets among the population at large, especially children (Brook, 2005). Likewise, the large supermarket groups like Tesco and Wal-Mart are accused of promoting unsustainable agricultural practices, of holding farmers in many different countries to ransom through the means of their de facto monopolies in various markets, and of being wholly environmentally unsound, through means such as using unnecessary and un-recyclable packaging, and distributing food by plane transport which helps to increase world carbon emissions (Murray, 2007).

Particularly in the last decade or so, a notable feature of public discourse about food in the developed world has been the rise and subsequent ubiquity of critiques of fast food outlets and supermarkets, both in book form (for example Schlosser, 2001; Blythman, 2005) and in cinema-released documentaries (for example Spurlock, 2004). Thus critique of alleged food homogenization, and the claimed deleterious social, cultural, and medical effects thereof, has become an important element of the food system itself, insofar as the various large corporations that are under attack have had to deal with the barrage of criticisms in various ways, either in terms of public relations campaigns and rebranding exercises, or more substantively in terms of changes in the nature of the actual goods being offered for consumption. The recent, rather fraught attempts by McDonald's to present itself as being an enemy of childhood obesity and a friend of healthy diets is a good case in point, increasing claims as to the company being in significant part responsible for obesity in children not only in the developed world but also in new markets like China, forcing company executives to try to take fast remedial action (Cheng, 2004). While relatively uncommon as late as the 1980s (Humphery, 1998), bad publicity and taking action to deal with it, is now as much a part of globalized food systems as are advertising campaigns and customer promotions.

A further effect of the plethora of critical books, articles, television programmes, and films indicting the fast food companies, supermarkets, and agribusiness that have appeared in recent years, is to put into broad public circulation the sorts of fears as to the homogenization of food and the loss of national and local food habits, that hitherto have often been mainly the province of relatively small intellectual and elite groups. For example, a substantial part of prime-time programming on the UK's mainstream commercial television channel Channel 4 in 2007 was devoted to polemical documentaries indicting such phenomena as childhood obesity, unethical factory farming, and exploitation of developing world workers by the large fast food and supermarket corporations, to the extent that it sometimes seemed as if a certain wing of television production was waging systematic rhetorical warfare against the latter. Within such a mediated cultural climate, it is likely that a much wider demographic spread of people, beyond the confines of the intelligentsia, will increasingly be influenced by ways of thinking that stress the threats of supposed food homogenization and degradation. This in turn increases the likelihood of a proliferation of projects to promote either heterogenization or alleged cultural purity in food (Boyle, 2004).

Yet various ironies are at play here. One is that it is the large supermarkets themselves which have to a large extent been responsible for certain types of culinary heterogenization in the countries of the developed world. In the terms set out by Allison James (1996), one notable feature of food globalization in a country such as contemporary Britain is the *mass production of 'foreign' food*. In the 1950s, the food writer Elizabeth David encountered great resistance to her attempts to introduce 'Mediterranean' textures and flavours into the domestic repertoire of British cookery (McLean, 2004). Yet now what are taken to be 'typically' southern Italian, southern French, Spanish, Greek, Indian, Mexican, Chinese, and Thai ingredients and recipes are available in every supermarket, as well as on every high street (Warde et al., 1999). As the large supermarket chains from the 1960s onwards both reflected, and themselves cultivated, changing public attitudes towards food, more and more items that had previously been regarded as queer and exotic became indigenized and familiar. A report published in 2004 by the major UK supermarket chain Sainsbury's indicated that while sales of 'traditional British' dishes such as shepherd's pie and chicken casserole were in terminal decline, there seemed to be an undimmed appetite among consumers of all classes for meals that are presented as Indian and Chinese in origin, with Mexican food coming in close behind. The report concluded that by the year 2034, it was unlikely that more than one out of four meals eaten in Britain would involve 'traditionally British' dishes like steak and kidney pie or sausages and mash. Instead, the supermarket's researchers concluded that flavours and ingredients from as far afield as Japan, North Africa, and Peru would by that time have become familiar parts of the British culinary scene (Sayid, 2004). The lesson to be drawn here is that supermarkets are very happy to promote apparent heterogenization in tastes, even if the underlying material substructure of production and distribution that they have developed is best understood as primarily homogenizing in nature.

A further irony emerges if we consider the development of another, related phenomenon, namely what James dubs the *connoisseurship of national cuisines*. Involving in an often relatively self-conscious manner the threats of homogenization posed by fast food companies and supermarkets, are counter-trends towards defining and defending the parameters of particular 'national' and 'regional' cuisines. In these cases, certain interested parties claim to have found the essence of a particular cuisine, be it associated with a nation, a region, or a particular ethnic or other sort of group. A whole sub-field of the publishing industry has sprung up to cater for this market, selling cookbooks that claim to present the 'real Andalucia' or the 'true taste of Provence' (Boyle, 2004). Here there is a concerted effort not only to capture the 'essence' of each particular cuisine, the culinary *Volksgeist* assumed by nineteenth century commentators, but also to police what are acceptable or unacceptable versions of particular dishes. In the present day, a whole series of culinary entrepreneurs – cookbook authors, food journalists, television food programme hosts, and so on – are all concerned to dictate what is 'authentic' in a cuisine and what is not, even if such authenticity is 'performed' rather than 'real' in the manner its advocates claim (Lu and Fine, 1995). A particularly striking example of these trends is the 'Slow Food' movement, which sprang up in northern Italy in the 1980s as a social movement of the intelligentsia, dedicated to 'saving' both local cuisine and eating habits from the perceived destructive effects of food globalization (Leitch, 2003). Ironically, given the success of the movement amongst a primarily middle class audience in Italy and beyond, the movement is now itself trans-national, having active branches across the developed world including the 'great Satan' of food homogenization itself, the USA. This situation presents the paradoxical sight of a movement dedicated to the preservation of the so-called 'national' and 'local' in food that is itself trans-national in reach and organization. This mirrors the trans-nationalization of groups dedicated to other related causes such as organic food production (itself imbued with various romantic discourses concerned with locality) and Fair Trade distribution (Wright and Madrid, 2007). The apparently 'local' struggles against the negatively-conceived 'global' in food terms have themselves become in significant part globalized, paying testimony to the spiralling ironies that have become inherent in this sphere of human affairs (Leitch, 2003).

A further irony worth mentioning here is that in France, one of the territories most open to the ideas associated with 'Slow Food' ideas, politicians are keen to pay lip service to the need to protect small farmers – and by extension, the culture of *la France profonde* – against the perceived ravages of large-scale agri-capitalism and its avatars, such as the use of genetically-modified crops. However, France is not only one of the world's leading countries for agri-business, being the second largest food exporter in the world (after the USA) and producing almost as much wheat as both Australia and Canada together (Lichfield, 1999); it also has had successive governments that have been very friendly both to agri-business and the genetic modification of crops (Kurzer and Cooper, 2007), even if the domestic media representation of such matters tends to suggest the opposite (Rosenthal, 2008). While French consumers may still pretend that they rarely or never eat in McDonald's and suchlike outlets (Rifkind, 2008), it remains the case that the material sub-structure of French farming has relatively little to do with the kinds of practices associated with Slow Food, such that the latter can be regarded as a comforting patina of nostalgia placed on top of a highly rationalized, globally important agricultural economy.

Within the rhetoric of the Slow Food movement and related groups, 'hybrid' culinary forms are often disparaged, with trendy fusion cuisines particularly held up to ridicule (Petrini, 2003). But what this sort of culinary policing conveniently forgets is that, as we saw above in the case of post-Columbian movements of people, animals, and plant species, many of the cuisines that have apparently been untouched since the mists of time are themselves hybrids, created as the result of long-term processes of migration and trade. Up until the later nineteenth century, the period of the beginnings of world-level systems of food production and distribution, there were few compelling reasons to focus upon the 'purity' or otherwise of a given cuisine. But in the present time, characterized by public discourses focused around the alleged cultural and health disasters attendant upon food homogenization, there exists more and more need to draw demarcation lines around 'true' expressions of a food culture, and to identify and condemn what are seen as mere ersatz imitations of them and as hybridized deviations from the alleged norm. The *reclaiming* of the 'local' or 'regional' in food as often as not involves actually *reinventing* it. One might, for example, think that artisanally produced (that is non-mass production) pasta is a key part of ancient southern Italian food culture. But pasta only became widespread in the region in the eighteenth century, hardly a period long enough away from our own to count as 'ancient' (Serventi and Sabban, 2003). In a world-condition character-ized for many people by perceived flux, movement, and uncertainty, cultures that seem authentic can be a source of much comfort, of much-needed ontological security in a universe of endless contingency (Giddens, 1991). If that is so, then the taste of a 'tradi-tional dish', served in a comfortingly 'local' milieu, accompanied by the signifiers of hundreds of years of culinary heritage, the latter itself both embedded within and pointing towards a broader history of social and cultural continuity rather than change, can provide powerful symbolic resources in a world highly globalizing and globalized, beliefs in tradition and heritage, in cuisine as in anything else, being perhaps a socially necessary form of individual and collective self-delusion at the present time (Ray, 2004).

Conclusion

At the beginning of the twenty-first century, the dictum of the nineteenth-century chef and food writer Alexis Soyer – 'tell me what thou eatest, and I will tell thee who thou

509

art' – remains true, but not necessarily in the ways that Soyer had in mind nearly a hundred and fifty years ago. As we have seen, at that point in time, the world seemed naturally to resemble a culinary mosaic, even if that mosaic had in part been created by large-scale processes of migration and trade, and the post-Columbian transmission of food products and ideas across large stretches of the globe. Analogous forms of forgetting the trans-national social and historical origins of cuisines pertains in the present day, but the effects of today's culinary amnesias are much more politicized and fraught than they were in Soyer's time. Today globalized and crisis-ridden industrialized food systems, and key actors within them such as supermarkets and fast food chains, stimulate a range of responses to their perceived homogenizing effects, ranging from environmental and ethical protests, to the creation of new forms of culinary 'tradition' and the expression of claims to authenticity and purity in cuisine. Food globalization processes are simultaneously deeply material and highly symbolic, involving and generating a range of forms of action, thought and imagination that are simultaneously 'local' and 'global' in nature. The dynamics of food globalization are not only intricate and often unpredictable, they also point to – and in fact, create – many of the contradictions of an epoch in human affairs marked by endemic globality. For that reason alone, they should be given more serious attention in 'mainstream' literature and debates on globalization matters than they have perhaps hitherto enjoyed.

Notes

1 This is a point already made by Marx, in the context of his critique of Feuerbach in *The German Ideology*. Feuerbach's materialism had given the example of a cherry tree in a garden as something essentially 'real', the kind of real object that the idealising philosophy of the time could not grasp in its essential materiality. But Marx argues that Feuerbach

> … does not see that the sensory world which surrounds him is not something immediately given from eternity, something always the same, but the product of industry and the social situation, in the sense that it is an historical product, the result of the activity of a whole series of generations, each one standing on the shoulders of those preceding it, developing previous industry and forms of social intercourse, and changing their social order in accordance with changed needs. Even the objects of the simplest 'sensory certainty' are given through social development, industry and commercial relations. The cherry tree like almost all fruit trees was transplanted to our zone, as is well known, through *commerce*; it was only *by virtue of* this action of a determinate society at a determinate time that it was gives to 'the sensory certainty' of Feuerbach.
>
> (Marx and Engels, 1975 [1845]: 39–40)

This is not a point that would appeal very much to advocates of 'local authenticity' in cuisine such as those associated with the 'Slow Food' movement.

2 Indeed one may note that it is probably significant that it has been two American authors who have been most prominent in diagnosing the alleged cultural consequences of the globalization processes associated with the trans-nationalization of their own country's cultural habits.

References

Appadurai, Arjun, 'How To Make a National Cuisine: Cookbooks in Contemporary India', *Comparative Studies of Society and History*, 31, 1, 1988, pp. 3–24.

Atkin, Michael, *The International Grain Trade* (Cambridge: Woodhead, 1992).

Augé, Marc, *Non-places: Introduction to an Anthropology of Supermodernity* (London: Verso, 1995).

Barber, Benjamin, 'Jihad Vs. McWorld', *The Atlantic Monthly*, 269, 3, 1992, pp. 53–65.

Barthes, Roland, 'Steak and Chips' in *Mythologies* (London: Vintage, 1993 [1957]), pp. 62–64.

Beck, Ulrich, *Risk Society: Towards a New Modernity* (London: Sage, 1992).

——*World Risk Society*, (Cambridge: Polity Press, 1998).

Blythman, Joanna, *Shopped: The Shocking Power of British Supermarkets* (London: HarperPerennial, 2005).

Bové, José et al., *The World Is Not For Sale: Farmers Against Junk Food* (London: Verso, 2002).

Boyle, David, *Authenticity: Brands, Fakes and the Lust For Real Life* (London: HarperPerennial, 2004).

Braudel, Fernand, *Civilization and Capitalism, 15th–18th Centuries, Volume 2, The Wheels of Commerce* (New York: Harper and Row, 1982).

Brook, Stephen, 'McDonald's: "We May Not Win Obesity Debate"', *Guardian*, Friday February 11, 2005, www.guardian.co.uk/media/2005/feb/11/advertising4.

Brown, Paul and Scott, Kirsty, 'Cancer Warning over Scottish Farmed Salmon', *Guardian*, Friday January 9, 2004, www.guardian.co.uk/environment/2004/jan/09/fish.food.

Caldwell, Melissa L., 'Domesticating the French Fry: McDonald's and Consumerism in Moscow', *Journal of Consumer Culture*, 4, 2004, pp. 5–26.

Castells, Manuel, *The Power of Identity, The Information Age: Economy, Society and Culture*. Vol. 2 (Oxford: Blackwell, 1997).

Charles, Daniel, *Lords of the Harvest: Biotech, Big Money and the Future of Food* (Cambridge, MA: Perseus, 2001).

Cheng, Tsung O., 'Childhood Obesity in China', *Health & Place*, 10, 4, 2004, pp. 395–396.

Clover, Charles, *The End of the Line: How Overfishing is Changing The World and What We Eat* (New York, The New Press, 2006).

Colquhoun, Kate, *Taste: The Story of Britain Through its Food* (London: Bloomsbury, 2007).

Curtin, Philip D. *Cross–Cultural Trade in World History* (Cambridge: Cambridge University Press, 1998).

David, Elizabeth, *French Provincial Cooking* (Harmondsworth: Penguin, 1970 [1960]).

Daviron, Benoit and Ponte, Stefano, *The Coffee Paradox: Commodity Trade and the Elusive Promise of Development* (London: Zed Books, 2005).

Douglas, Mary, *Purity and Danger: An Analysis of the Concepts of Pollution and Taboo* (London and New York: Routledge, 1966).

Durkheim, Emile, *The Division of Labour in Society* (New York: Free Press, 1964 [1893]).

Economist, The, 'The Silent Tsunami: The Food Crisis and How To Solve It', April 19–25, 2008.

Fantasia, Rick, 'Fast Food in France', *Theory and Society*, 24, 2, April, 1995, pp. 201–243.

Fernandez-Armesto, Felipe, *Food: A History* (Basingstoke: Macmillan, 2001).

Fischler, Claude, 'The "Mad-Cow" Crisis: A Global Perspective', in Grew, Raymond. (ed.) *Food in Global History* (Boulder: Westview Press, 1999), pp. 207–231.

Friedmann, Harriet, 'The International Relations of Food: The Unfolding Crisis of National Regulation', in Harriss-White, B. and Hoffenberg, R. (eds) *Food: Multidisciplinary Perspectives* (Cambridge: Basil Blackwell, 1994), pp. 174–204.

Gallegos, Danielle, 'Pastes, Powders, and Potions: the Development of an Eclectic Australian Palate', *Food, Culture and Society*, 8, 1, June 2005, pp. 39–46.

Giddens, Anthony, *Modernity and Self-Identity* (Cambridge: Polity, 1991).

Gissing, George, *The Private Papers of Henry Ryecroft* (Oxford: Oxford University Press, 1987).

Goody, Jack, *Cooking, Cuisine and Class: A Study of Comparative Sociology* (Cambridge and New York: Cambridge University Press, 1982).

Guthman, Julie, *Agrarian Dreams: The Paradox of Organic Farming in California* (Berkeley: University of California Press, 2004).

Harrison, Jeffrey S. et al., 'Exporting A North American Concept to Asia: Starbucks in China', *Cornell Hotel and Restaurant Administration Quarterly*, 46, 2, 2005, pp. 275–283.

Hoggart, Richard, *The Uses of Literacy*, (Harmondsworth: Penguin, 1962 [1957]).

Humphery, Kim, *Shelf Life: Supermarkets and the Changing Cultures of Consumption* (Cambridge: Cambridge University Press, 1998), pp. 39 –58.

511

James, Allison, 'Cooking the Books: Global or Local Identities in Contemporary British Food Cultures?', in Howes, David (ed.) *Cross-Cultural Consumption: Global Markets, Local Realities* (London: Routledge, 1996), pp. 77 – 93.

Jardine, Lisa, *Worldly Goods: A New History of the Renaissance* (Basingstoke: Macmillan, 1997).

Keane, John, *Global Civil Society?* (Cambridge: Cambridge University Press, 2003).

Kimbrell, Andrew (ed.) *The Fatal Harvest Reader: The Tragedy of Industrial Agriculture* (Sausalito: Foundation for Deep Ecology, 2002).

Kjaernes, Unni et al., *Trust in Food: A Comparative and Institutional Analysis* (Basingstoke: Palgrave, 2007).

Korsmeyer, Carolyn, *Making Sense of Taste: Food and Philosophy* (Ithaca: Cornell University Press, 1999).

Kurzer, Paulette and Cooper, Alice, 'What's For Dinner? European Farming and Food Traditions Confront American Biotechnology', *Comparative Political Studies*, 40, 9, 2007, pp. 1035–1058.

Lechner, Frank and Boli, John, *World Culture: Origins and Consequences* (Oxford: Blackwell, 2005).

Leitch, Alison, 'Slow Food and the Politics of Pork Fat: Italian Food and European Identity', *Ethnos*, 68, 4, 2003, pp. 437–462.

Levinson, Marc, *The Box: How the Shipping Container Made the World Smaller and the World Economy Bigger* (Princeton: Princeton University Press, 2008).

Levi-Strauss, Claude, 'The Culinary Triangle', *Partisan Review*, 33, 1965, pp. 586–595.

Lichfield, John, 'French Small Farmers Head for Extinction', *Independent*, 10 October, 1999 www.hartford–hwp.com/archives/61/124.html.

Lien, Marianne Elisabeth, 'Dogs, Whales and Kangaroos: Transnational Activism and Food Taboos', in Lien, Marianne Elisabeth and Nerlich, Brigitte (eds), *The Politics of Food* (Oxford and New York, Berg, 2004), pp. 179–197.

Lozado, Eriberto P. Jr., 'Globalized Childhood? Kentucky Fried Chicken in Beijing', in Watson, James L. and Caldwell, Melissa L. (eds) *The Cultural Politics of Food and Eating: A Reader* (Oxford, Blackwell, 2005).

Lu, Shun and Fine, Gary Alan, 'The Presentation of Ethnic Authenticity: Chinese Food as a Social Accomplishment', *The Sociological Quarterly*, 36, 3, June, 1995, pp. 535–553.

Luhmann, Niklas, *Social Systems* (Stanford: Stanford University Press, 1996).

Macnaghten, Phil, 'Animals in their Nature: A Case Study on Public Attitudes to Animals, Genetic Modification and Nature', *Sociology*, 38, 3, 2004, pp. 533–551.

Marx, K and Engels, F. (1975 [1845]) *The German Ideology*, in *Marx–Engels Collected Works*, Vol. 5, London: Lawrence and Wishart, pp. 19–539.

Miller, Daniel, *Material Cultures: Why Some Things Matter* (Chicago: University of Chicago Press, 1998).

Miller, J. Innes (1969) *The Spice Trade of the Roman Empire* (Oxford: Clarendon Press).

McLean, Alice, 'Tasting Language: The Aesthetic Pleasures of Elizabeth David', *Food, Culture and Society*, 7, 1, 2004, pp. 37–46.

Mintz, Sidney W., *Sweetness and Power: The Place of Sugar in Modern History* (Harmondsworth: Penguin, 1986).

——'Food, Culture and Energy' in Nutzenadel, Alexander and Trentmann, Frank, *Food and Globalization* (Oxford: Berg, 2008).

Murray, Sarah, *Moveable Feasts: The Incredible Journeys of the Things We Eat* (London, Aurum, 2007).

Nibert, David, *Animal Rights/Human Rights: Entanglements of Oppression and Liberation* (Lanham: Rowman and Littlefield Publishers Inc, 2002), pp. 195–235.

Nietzsche, Friedrich, 'Ecce Homo' in *On The Genealogy of Morals and Ecce Home*, in W. Kaufmann (ed.) (New York: Vintage, 1967).

Nutzenadel, Alexander and Trentmann, Frank, *Food and Globalization* (Oxford: Berg, 2008).

Peckham, Shannan, 'Consuming Nations' in Griffiths, Sian and Wallace, Jennifer (eds), *Consuming Passions* (London: Times Higher Education Supplement, 1998).

Petrini, Carlo, *Slow Food: The Case for Taste* (New York, Columbia University Press, 2003).

Petronius *Satyrica*, R. Bracht Branham and Daniel Kinney (ed. and trans.) (London: Everyman/J. M. Dent, (1996).

Ray, Krishnendu, *The Migrants' Table* (Philadelphia: Temple University Press, 2004).

Rebora, Giovanni, *Culture of the Fork: A Brief History of Food in Europe* (New York: Columbia University Press, 2001).

512

Rifkind, Hugo, 'Je t'aime', *The Times* (London), Times 2 section, 19 August, 2008, pp. 2–4.

Ritzer, George, *The McDonaldization of Society* (Thousand Oaks, Pine Forge Press, 2000).

——*The Globalization of Nothing* (London: Sage, 2004).

Roberts, J. A. G., *China To Chinatown: Chinese Food in the West* (London: Reaktion Books, 2002), pp. 204–228.

Robertson, Roland and Inglis, David (2004) 'The Global *Animus*: In the Tracks of World–Consciousness', *Globalizations*, 1, 1, pp. 38–49.

Rosenthal, John, 'Militant "Farmer" and French Government Make Common Cause in GM Crop Ban', *World Politics Review*, 18 January, 2008 www.worldpoliticsreview.com/Article.aspx?id=1512.

Ross, Kristen, *Fast Cars, Clean Bodies: Decolonization and the Reordering of French Culture* (Cambridge, MA: MIT Press, 1996).

Sayid, R. 'Will Traditional British Grub Soon Be A Thing of the Pasta?', *Daily Mirror*, Friday, October 29, 2004, p. 38.

Schlosser, Eric, *Fast Food Nation: The Dark Side of the All American Meal* (New York, Houghton Mifflin, 2001).

Scholte, Jan Aart *Globalization: A Critical Introduction*, Basingstoke: Palgrave, 2000).

Seneca 'Consolatio Ad Helvia / Addressed to His Mother Helvia: Of Consolation' in *L. Annaeus Seneca: minor dialogues*, Aubrey Stewart (trans.) (London: George Bell and Sons, 1889).

Serventi, Silvano and Sabban, Francoise, *Pasta: The Story of a Universal Food* (New York: Columbia University Press, 2003).

Simmel, Georg, 'The Sociology of the Meal', in Frisby, D. and Featherstone, M. (eds) *Simmel on Culture: Selected Writings* (London and New York: Sage, 1997), pp. 130–135.

Simpson, Tim, 'The Commercialization of Macau's Cafés', *Ethnography*, 9, 2, 2008, pp. 197–234.

Sorj, Nernardo and Wilkinson, John, 'Modern Food Technology: Industrialising Nature', *International Social Science Journal*, 37, 3, 1985, pp. 301–14.

Taylor, Timothy, *Stanley Park* (Toronto: Vintage Canada, 2001).

Tomlinson, John, *Cultural Imperialism: A Critical Introduction* (London: Pinter, 1997).

Turner, Jack, *Spice: The History of a Temptation* (London: HarperPerennial, 2005).

Warde, Alan., Marten, Lydia and Olsen, Wendy, 'Consumption and The Problem of Variety: Cultural Omnivorousness, Social Distinction and Dining Out', *Sociology*, 33, 1999, pp. 105–127.

Watson, James L. in Watson, James L. (ed.), 'Transnationalism, Localization and Fast Foods in East Asia' in *Golden Arches East: McDonald's in East Asia* (Stanford: Stanford University Press, 1997), pp. 1–38.

Watson, James L. and Caldwell, Melissa L., 'Introduction' in Watson, James L. and Caldwell, Melissa L. (eds) *The Cultural Politics of Food and Eating: A Reader* (Oxford, Blackwell, 2005).

Watts, Michael and Goodman, David, 'Agrarian Questions: Global Appetite, Local Metabolism' in Goodman, David and Watts, Michael, *Globalising Food: Agrarian Questions and Global Restructuring* (London: Routledge, 1997).

Williams, Raymond, *Culture and Society 1780–1950* (London: Chatto and Windus, 1958).

Wright, Caroline, and Madrid Gilma, 'Contesting Ethical Trade in Colombia's Cut-Flower Industry: A Case of Cultural and Economic Injustice', *Cultural Sociology*, 1, 2, (2007), pp. 255–75.

Film

Spurlock, Morgan, *Super Size Me* (Showtime Networks Inc., 2004).

26

Borders, passports, and the global mobility

Mark B. Salter

Introduction

Mobility is one of the distinguishing characters of modern globalization, demonstrated in dramatically increased empirical flows of capital, information, and people. The border has become one of the dominant spatio-legal metaphors of contemporary politics, either in their purported disappearance, rearticulation, or surprising persistence. Michele Acuto says "borders have to be measured for their presence, or absence, and the role they play in constructing social relations" (Acuto 2008: 1). Manuel Castells, Zygmunt Bauman, and John Urry use metaphors of flow, liquidity or fluidity to describe the essence of globalization; the character of these movements is determined by the porosity of borders. In Castells' terms, borders can be understood the "hubs and nodes" that determine the speed, direction, and composition of the "space of flows" (Castells 2000: 443). Within this global network society, routing and identification become key vectors of control. Bauman cautions that mobility should not be over-estimated, arguing that 98 percent of all people are immobile. Borders must be examined in concert with mobility because, as Mimi Sheller and Urry argue, "the study of mobility also involves those immobile infrastructures that organise the intermittent flow of people, information, and image, as well as the borders or 'gates' that limit, channel, and regulate movement or anticipated movement" (Sheller and Urry 2006: 212). Even as mobility becomes one of the primary axes of global inequality, "the map image of the borders of the state still exercises a major influence on the territorial imagination of whose security is at stake, and who most threatens it" (Agnew 2007: 300). Globalization studies, not to mention sociology, and geography, political science, international relations, and anthropology, bring different perspectives to the study of borders.

There are two broad perspectives on borders: difference machines vs. "good fences make good neighbors." From the universalist, solidarist or cosmopolitan perspective, the innate worth of individuals and communities is harmed by their division into us/them, self/other, inside/outside. These binary (or multiple) identities lead, necessarily, to the validation of the self through the denigration of the other, "the consolidation of identity through the constitution of difference. The self-reassurance of identity through the construction of otherness (Connolly 1991: 9). Borders are necessarily undemocratic, divisive, and should be undone, subverted, or revealed to be constructed (rather than natural). From a particularist, pluralist, or civilizational perspective, identities and cultures are like scientific paradigms that are incommensurable, and the value choices that underpin these borders are irreconcilable. Borders that provide a functional way for those identities, cultures, and communities to regulate their limits (and their population) therefore decrease conflict or at least render the political choices of conflict clear.

Borders are particularly important because they are one of the key institutions of the sovereign state. They represent the limit of the state, the space of law, authority, and responsibility. Highly militarized borders are organized around the exclusion of others, whereas internal borders, such as in Europe, are constructed around a different management problem. Borders have evolved, along with other institutions of the modern state system, as a way of answering the governmental problems of security, population management, economic circulation, and identity. Borders define clearly what space needs to be protected, and where citizens may seek refuge (although this was quickly undone with the invention of the airplane, aerial bombing, and missile technologies). Borders are the primary membrane of the traveling population, and determine who gets in and who stays out. Borders inscribe a particular set of economic relations through taxes, duties, and regulation—including the regulation of copyright, technologies, and expertise (although this is undone with globalized commodity chains). Borders are symbolically important for the assertion of a unique identity (even as the importance of physical boundaries is diminished by the ease of global communications).

Borders are limits, zones, points, or lines between different communities that have functional effects, such as legal jurisdiction, social rules or norms, economic regulations, cultural identity, or imaginary differentiation. They are proliferating as the discriminatory effect of the border to exclude or to include is dispersed throughout global space: bordering occurs as much at the fenced and secured physical frontier between nations as at the visa window of an embassy, at UNHCR offices, at the airport, and even virtually in remote databases. There is an important analytical distinction to be made between borders, which have particular effects of exclusion and inclusion in the sovereign community of a state, and boundaries, which have more general effects of exclusion and inclusion in other kinds of communities (Paasi 1998). The bordering function is present whenever inclusion/exclusion is defined: as Connal Parsley argues "as a judgment is performed ... so the border is augured into being" (Parsley 2003: 55). Chris Rumford highlights this change in the discriminatory geopolitical function of borders: "borders are now less important in terms of military defence and coercive control, and are notable for their (selective) permeability to human mobility" (Rumford 2006: 159). Borders always involve the limit of a sovereign state's legal jurisdiction, whereas boundaries exist in many social and political settings. For this article, we focus on the border as a crucial (if dispersed or deterritorialized) site of decision.

Étienne Balibar characterizes borders as overdetermined, polysemic, and heterogenous. Borders are overdetermined because each border represents overlapping political, economic, linguistic, social, and cultural boundaries: they are "world-configuring," and not simply territorial (Balibar 2002: 79). Identities are created and reified by borders, which become heavy with social, cultural, and political meaning. Borders are polysemic, that is to say that borders "do not have the same meaning for everyone ... Today's borders are, to some extent, designed ... not merely to give individuals from different social classes different experiences of the law, the civil administration, the police and elementary rights, such as the freedom of circulation and freedom of enterprise, but actively to *differentiate* between individuals in terms of social class" (Balibar 2002: 81–82). Borders are experientially different for the so-called "kinetic elite," the stationary underclass, and "deportation class" who are moved against their will (Walters 2002). Bauman makes a similar point: "Ability or disability to move divides the world into the globalized and the localized ... some inhabit the globe; others are chained to their place" (Bauman 2000: 21). Finally, Balibar argues, borders are heterogenous: "some borders are not situated at the borders at all, in the geographical-politico-administrative sense of the term. They are in fact elsewhere, wherever selective controls are to be found, such as, for example, health or security checks" (Balibar 2002: 84). These selective controls dovetail with the polysemic nature of borders: dissimilar classes of individuals (refugees, asylum seekers, citizens) will experience these checks differently. However, just because borders are elsewhere, it does not mean that borders are everywhere. The bordering function is defined as the expression of inclusion or exclusion from the jurisdiction of the sovereign state (as opposed to a boundary function which can express the limits of many different kinds of social groups or communities).

Recent writings by Giorgio Agamben on the ban highlight this discriminatory function of borders. Agamben's analysis of the "state of exception" paints the decision as the determinative characteristic of sovereign power; that is, the authority to decide if the law applies because a situation is normal or if the law must be suspended because a situation is an exception or an emergency. The border is a permanent state of exception, because the decision to admit an individual into the community or exile that individual from the protection of the sovereign is at root a political decision (Salter 2008). Agamben continues that "the originary relation of law to life is not application (of the law) but *abandonment* (from the law)" (29). There is no greater power than the sovereign to accept its own citizens—thus, every border encounter is a new act of political formation and community definition. The social contract is made anew with each entry. The fundamental power of the sovereign is to decide the limit of what life may be treated as political and what life treated as purely biological. The clearest example of this bordering function is in the determination of the status of refugees. A refugee claimant arrives at the border (wherever geographically located) and appeals to the sovereign that he/she cannot accept or call upon the protection or jurisdiction of another sovereign, because of a "reasonable fear of persecution." If the "reasonable fear" is accepted by a state authority (border guard or immigration judge for example), then the claimant is treated as a political refugee; if that state authority determines that there is no ground for a "reasonable fear," then the life is treated as biological (because even when being deported, the body is clothed, fed, and sheltered). Every claim and every individual is unique, and the administrative decision to admit or exile is at the limit of the law, a decision about whether the law will apply to that case. The border function, then, is to determine the political nature of the life that engages it and to contain a particular idea of the international. The border is a site of raw sovereign power. At root, "there is no general right for an alien to obtain entry into another country. If he is escaping persecution, he has the right to seek asylum; but no state is obliged to give it to him" (Higgins 1973: 344). The state may even refuse to accept its own citizens (e.g., expelled Ugandan Asians). Certainly, a passport does not guarantee entry into the issuing state—and indeed the modern passport is a twentieth-century invention (Salter 2003). As such, the border decision reenacts the sovereign authority to define and to protect a national "population."

Borders are one of the key sites at which and through which the global mobility regime is structured. Separate from the transportation grids that make mobility possible, it is passports and visas, the documents of mobility and their examination at the frontier, that determine the speed or facility of particular vectors of motion. The bordering function—that is the inclusion or exclusion of an individual in the political life of the community—is structured by the *prima facie* ideology of citizenship. Following Barry Hindess, citizenship is the primary tool for the management in "a dispersed system of governing a large, culturally diverse, and interdependent world population and that it operates by dividing that population into a series of discrete subpopulations and setting them against each other" (Hindess 2000: 1495). Citizenship, in other words, allows for and mandates for a particularist, statist discrimination of outsiders. Nevzat Soguk, Peter Nyers, and William Walters, in slightly different ways, make similar points about the necessary constitution of outsiders: refugees, aliens, and the "deportable" in order to maintain the fiction of a functioning citizenship system. Soguk argues that the figure of the refugee "affords opportunities for participants in practices of statecraft. The practical force of their presence at the juncture of identity boundaries is negotiated, mediated, co-opted, and deployed as a referential resource useful in the production and empowerment of symbolic, metaphorical, formal, and institutional resources (along racial, social, cultural, and economic lines) to which states turn for anchor and for their own empowerment" (Soguk 1999: 16). Following Hannah Arendt's line of argument, the very discourse of human rights is rooted in the authority of the sovereign state. For refugees, their *human* rights are only authorized once recognized by a state (Nyers 2006: 17). This is not to say that the sovereign state has not contracted out the international policing of populations, as Walters (2002) demonstrates so clearly. It is to say that the very notion that citizenship, and the examination of citizenship at the border, structures what mobilities are problematic and what mobilities are encouraged. The polysemic experience of borders are structured by the fundamental ideology of citizenship that "promises the poorest of the world's citizens that, if only they could stay at home and behave themselves, they too could be citizens like us" (Hindess 2000: 1496). Michel Foucault uses the term "technology of the self" to identify those tools of governance "through some political technology of individuals, we have been led to recognize ourselves as a society, as part of a social entity, as part of a nation or of a state" (Foucault 2000: 404). Citizenship, and its marker the passport, is one of these political technologies of the international self: the suite of documents, such as the passport, the visa, the refugee status, the national identity card, lead us to recognize ourselves as part of a subpopulation, to responsibilize a sovereign state for our security and protection, to structure our mobility and (dis)placement. John Torpey views the evolution of the passport from a national-statist perspective, starting with the French Revolution, as the "monopoly on the means of legitimate movement," similar to the Weberian monopoly of legitimate violence and the Marxist monopoly of the means of production (Torpey 2000: 4). The invention and consolidation of the modern passport, which began after the First World War and became an international standard only in 1922, arose with the rise of the bureaucratic state and in many ways defined the liberal individual as a possessor of a unique identity and status that could be triangulated amongst various government databases. As we see in the current global scene, this identity is being both written on the body through the integration of biometric technologies into passports, visas, and border policing regimes, and also constructed internationally through the integration of national databases into a loose assemblage of global "risk" assessments (Amoore 2006). Ronen Shamir argues "the global mobility regime is predicated, first, on the classification of individuals and groups according to principles of perceived threats and risks, and, second, on an emergent technology of intervention that provides the technical/

statistical means for creating elaborate forms of such social distinctions" (Shamir 2005: 200). Thus, globalization involves not only the liberation of flows and conduits for mobility, but also "closure, entrapment, and containment" (Shamir 2005: 199). While passport and visa agencies have long held risk categories that determined the admissibility of an application, the rise of information and communication technologies and the global dominance of the discourse of the war on terror have both led to quicker, faster, and more international constructions of risk categories. In addition to being heterogeneous and polysemic, borders are becoming increasingly virtual. Didier Bigo continues, "police practice is directed at the surveillance of foreigners or poor ethnic minorities and extends its reach beyond its prior limits of criminal investigation, through pro-active actions that enable the police to pinpoint groups that would be 'predisposed to criminality' according to sociological knowledge" (Bigo 2006: 21). We see this in the sharing of data between the United States and its partners (through PNR or passenger name record data, API or advanced passenger information, and "no-fly" lists). Thus, if a traveler is prohibited from boarding a plane because of membership on a no-fly list, even if by an airline employee, that person has experienced the exclusion of a border. Incarceration and containment occur not simply at the border (though it does), but also preemptively, at a distance, and by "remote-control" (Guiraudon and Lahav 2000).

The border examination is crucial for understanding the porosity of borders and the viscosity of the global mobility regime, because it is at the border that the claims to citizenship, entry, or asylum are adjudicated. The discriminatory or discretionary function of the border is to adjudicate the claims to political life. The passport itself is no guarantee of entry—even to one's own country—and must often be supplemented with a verbal cross-examination for one's own country and a visa for other countries. As Bryan Turner writes, in the age of "new xenophobia" "as the 'friendly stranger' has become the 'hostile stranger', every citizen has become a potential enemy within" (Turner 2007: 300). The efficacy of the border examination depends upon the confessionary complex, the acceptance of the authority of the agent of customs and borders to ask questions of us and the obligation to tell the truth. While Foucault discusses other truth-machines, such as the legal court, the medical clinic, and the prison, the border examination resembles quite clearly these other institutions that are authorized to produce a political truth about an individual (their citizenship, their "reasonable fear," their suitability for entry). The sovereign state has appropriated not simply the natural mobility rights of individuals, but also the rights of individuals to decide their own identity, belonging, and community. This appropriation is clearest in the practices of exclusion at the border, or the "politics of immobility" or as Bigo puts it, "the paradoxical liberty 'to go anywhere except where one wants to go'" (2007: 26). Interesting analyses of these sites of immobility, such as waiting zones or detention centers, should be considered (Johns 2005; Makaremi 2008; Salter 2007; Turner 2007).

Guide to disciplinary border studies

The study of globalization is by its nature multi- and inter-disciplinary, and so this chapter includes a brief map of how important different fields study borders. We find in this overview a number of persistent themes, precisely because these fields cross-pollinate: the relation between the border and the exception or the limit, the constitution of identities and differences through bordering practices, and a sensitivity to the spatial dynamics of that border function.

Law and society

The border has always been a place where law was in play, because it is by definition the limit of national jurisdiction. At this site of territoriality, sovereign power, and administrative decision, the border itself occupies a liminal role in critical legal studies, most often reflected upon as an instance of citizenship and immigration law or national security. Pioneering work by Janet Gilboy examined the administrative processes of immigration inspectors at a US airport, with some very interesting conclusions about the politics of discretion (Gilboy 1991). She concludes that informal communication of experiences and folklore were as influential as official policy guidelines in structuring the decisions of immigration inspectors. Genevieve Bouchard and Barbara Wake-Carroll further parse the complexities of administrative discretion, using immigration inspectors (Bouchard and Wake-Carroll 2002). Miriam Ticktin applies a more legal-ethnographic approach to the study of those moments of decision and discretion in the detention centers of France. She argues that "sovereignty is always established upon a border and exercised in the imposition of the borders; the border is precisely the site where the controls and guarantees of the 'normal' juridical order are suspended" (Ticktin 2005: 349). The *zones d'attentes* are outside the normal juridical order, outside even the laws governing the normal border. Taylor uses the Australian example to make a wider point, again using Agamben's notion of the exception: "at the border, the Australian government conduct is mostly ungoverned by statute and, therefore, almost ungovernable by the courts" (Agamben 1998: 75–76). Consequently, the analysis of law at the borders reveals the interface of international law and norms, domestic or national law, and the staging of multiple identities. Nancy Wonders argues that individuals and state agents each perform their identities: "borders are socially constructed via the performance of various state actors in an elaborate dance with ordinary people who seek freedom of movement and identification. The choreography for this dance is shaped by state policies and laws, but it is increasingly shaped by larger global forces as well" (Wonders 2006: 64–65). This supra-legal identity function of the border is highlighted by Alison Kesby: "the border implicates the political, the social and the racial. It is not simply a matter of geography, but an 'institution' and a process tracing the political sphere and constructing identity" (Kesby 2007: 112). The border, then, represents a test case for the critical limits of law, sovereign jurisdiction, and population.

Anthropology

Following an ethnographic methodology, anthropological studies of borders and borderlands focus on the lived experiences of crossing the border. "too often, in the other social sciences, the cultural constructions which symbolize the boundaries between communities, and between nations, are lost in the midst of the 'big picture' of 'national' and 'international' relations ... border societies may be just as important in the creation of nations and states are their so-called core or capital areas" (Donnan and Wilson 1993: 10). Marc Augé defined the border as a "non-place" and particularly "the traveller's space" (Augé 1995: 86), emblematic of supemodernity: "the passenger through non-places retrives his identity only at Customs, at the tollbooth, at the check-out counter. The space of the non-place creates neither singular identity nor relations; only solitude and similitude" (Augé 1995: 103). However, not all anthropologists support this empty description of spaces of transit. Chowra Makaremi, with others, has examined the

519

particular dynamics of power and culture embedded within airports, trainstations, networks of CCTV (closed-circuit television) systems, and other "non-places" to find that identities are performed in many different ways (Makaremi 2008). Orvar Löfgren suggests it is precisely because of the emptiness of such places that the state tries to make the space "pedagogical": "the fascination or strength of border crossings, which still exists in a world of deterritorialization and deregulation, has to do with the fact that in a world where fewer and fewer identities are based on the clear-cut pedagogy of space, the nation state still tries to provide an absolute space: Sweden or the USA starts here!" (Löfgren 1999: 25). A leader in this field, Josiah Heyman has provided a firm empirical grounding for the "bureaucratic thought-work" of border guards determining admission or exclusion at the US–Mexico border by applying legal policies and informal "knowledge" (Heyman 1995). He suggests that immigration officers "subtly classify immigrants perceived by 'moral worth,' distributed on a bipolar axis between the 'hard-working immigrant dream' and the 'criminal' figure from marginal society and economy ... and national origins stereotypes (not the official national origins quota)" (Heyman 2001: 131). Though applying a slightly different methodology than Gilboy (including more political economy and ethnography), Heyman describes exactly how border officers make those crucial, political decisions of inclusion and exclusion (and, indeed, demonstrates that at the US–Mexican border, it is not a binary choice). Similarly, other anthropologists examine the constitution of borderland communities. Gilberto Rosas, for example, using the same site as Heyman, argues that the "borderlands condition, or the coupling of exceptionality and political imaginaries [of race, immigration, and national identity] no longer necessarily remains geographically fixed in the southwestern United States" (Rosas 2006: 336). Between Augé's non-places and Rosas' borderlands condition, the anthropology of globalized borders has been pushed forward particularly by Arjun Appadurai, who has argued for a "postnational geography." He argues that these borderlands, or rather these dispersed sites where the border function is experienced, "create complex conditions for the production and reproduction of locality, in which the ties of marriage, work, business, and leisure weave together various circulating populations with various kinds of 'locals' to create localities that belong in one sense to a particular nation-state but are, from another point of view, what we might call *translocalities*" (Appadurai 1996: 44). The globalized sense of translocality leads to a consideration of other geographical imaginaries of borders.

Geography

Space is at the heart of the geographical study of borders, and particularly the way that space and meaning are co-constituted, the so-called "mobility-turn" in the social sciences originated in geography (Urry 2003). Three core concerns for human and cultural geographers are: mobilities and immobilities, sites and spaces, geospatial imaginations. A set of physical geographers who are primarily interested in the actual demarcation of international borders and boundaries is not studied here (see for example the work of the International Boundaries Research Unit). Economic and political geographers have also engaged with the construction of cross-border areas, fostered particularly in Europe, and the effect of borders on community definition. Of the theoretical concerns, geographers are tackling the concept of mobility and particular kinds mobility germane to borders such as urban and aeromobility. Stephen Graham argues, "Contemporary cities can be understood as socio-technical constructions supporting mobilities and flow to more or less distant elsewheres: flows of people, goods, services, information, capital, waste, water, meaning ... A logic of intense geographical differentiation is underway, within which people and places are enrolled in very different ways into the broadening circuits of economic and technological exchange. Networked infrastructures are actually being organized to exploit differences between places within ever-more sophisticated spatial divisions of labor" (Graham 2002: 1). Similarly Peter Adey adds "we need to consider mobilities in differential and relational ways ... to do this we can build upon conceptions of movement that revolve around a body of work known as the 'politics of mobility'" (Adey 2006: 83). Michael Crang argues, with Urry above, that any serious analysis of mobility must involve "liminal or threshold spaces," such as borders. He continues, they are not "simply places of homogenised commodified experience; nor just the rationality of scheduling and 'flow management', though they rely on both ... they are places of fantasy and desire, places of inclusion and exclusion, and social milieux for different groups of people" (Crang 2002: 573). Thus, the very topography of the spaces of flows is determined by the geography of borders. As with anthropology, geographers are also engaged in studying borderlands, frontiers, and the construction of borders as spaces of meeting or cooperation (Kaplan and Häkli 2002; van Houtum 2000). These questions are also studied by political science.

Political science

As a policy-oriented social science, the vast majority of political studies of the globalization of borders occur within comparative analyses of citizenship and immigration policies or cross-border environmental, economic, or management regimes. Borders present a unique realm for bi- and multi-lateral relations, balancing economic, military, and social security. There is a renewed concern over migration controls in the era of globalization, which often intersects with security studies or political economy. Peter Andreas argues that "borders are not eroding or remaining unchanged, but are being recrafted through ambitious and innovative state efforts to territorially exclude [clandestine transnational actors] while assuring territorial access for 'desireable' entries" (Andreas 2003a:80). Illegal migrants, for example, are increasingly criminalized and militarized. Europe is a test case for these controls; with Schengen, the internal borders of EU countries were dissolved as the external borders were hardened. Although Tim Cresswell points out, "the Schengen accords were represented as the abolition of borders, but they can also be seen as a multiplication of borders and the production of new kinds of borders. Just as the borders were being created, so were the mobilities" (Cresswell 2006: 234). The ongoing evolution of Justice and Home Affairs, and the network of police/intelligence/immigration information sharing and safe-third country agreements, alongside the expansion of the EU, means that Europe is a laboratory for border policies. The connection of EU accession with stronger border controls and safe-third country agreements has also brought the questions of economic development, human trafficking, migration, and asylum to the fore. As a problem for international relations and diplomacy, cross-border cooperation becomes a key problematic. However, some analysts argue that the territorial line is less important than the management of population flows. Bigo, for example, highlights how the actual practices of border policing exceed the control of a territorial line. He concludes: "internal and external security (traditionally two separate domains that were essentially the concern of different institutions, the police and the army), now appear to be converging regarding border, order, and the possible threats to identity ...

521

security is not only a state affair, it is a boundary function" (Bigo 2001: 91). This boundary function, Bigo avers, concerns the constitution of the national self/other through the surveillance, policing, and control of particular groups rather than territories. As Walters avers, "borders are becoming more and more important not as military or economic practices but as spaces and instruments for the policing of a variety of actors, objects and processes whose common denominator is their 'mobility', or more specifically, the forms of social and political insecurity that have come to be discursively attached to these mobilities" (Walters 2006: 187). Within the field of international relations, two chief routes of inquiry have been followed. The very definition of *international* relations depends on a primary border between "inside" and "outside"—the state realm in which the good life might be achieved and the anarchical realm of interstate relations in which all politics are zero-sum and dominated by violence and deception (Walker 1993). The fiction of the sovereign state, therefore, has profound implications for the limits of ethical responsibility: we owe care to those inside and fear the danger from outside. The first is a traditional analysis of the characteristic of the modern Westphalian state-system, and the relation of territorial states to those anarchical relations. Andreas and others examine how border policing and state security are related in both policy and theoretical terms. Mark Zacher describes a norm of "territorial integrity" that emerges over the course of the past 100 years: "Boundaries have not been frozen, but states have been effectively proscribed from altering them by force" (Zacher 2001: 246). This norm is particularly salient in conflict zones and areas of ethnic violence. The border between Israel and the Occupied Palestinian Territories (not to mention the Israeli settlements) is a hotly contested geo-political issue and requires a serious consideration of how the construction of the Separation Barrier (Weizman 2007). The other international norms of non–intervention in the sovereign affairs of other states and the discourses of failed states are both under-pinned by geopolitical assumptions and undermined by territorial facts. How else to explain the paradoxes of military occupation without war or the persistence of states with no effective government without conquest (e.g. Somalia, Rwanda, Congo)? A similar critical approach links "identities, borders, and orders" to better understand the complex and interdependent socio-economic and political relations. Yosef Lapid argues "Processes of collective identity formation invariably involve complex bordering issues. Likewise, acts of bordering invariably carry momentous ramification for political ordering at all levels of analysis. Processes of identity, border, and order construction are therefore mutually self-constituting" (Lapid 2001: 7). A further approach foregrounds "transvers-ality" as a remedy for state-centric thinking. While "most International Relations dis-course would read the transit area (spaces of movement) as an exception that resides either inside or outside the territorial logical of the state," whereas Soguk and Geoffrey Whitehall suggest that "the transit zone exists because of the sovereign logic of the modern state ... in its hybridity, it is a space which is closely patrolled, regimented, and made possible by the fictions of interstate performances" (Soguk and Whitehall 1999: 678). This application of transversality as a key concept draws our attention to cultural and postcolonial studies.

Cultural studies and postcolonial studies

Borders and the identities they represent are a key focus of cultural and postcolonial studies, particular those writing on belonging, race, nationality, and imperialism (Mignolo and

Tlostanova 2006). Because these studies (like anthropology) are more situated, analysis in these fields most often involves the application of identity theory onto particular social-economic-political boundaries, paying close attention to distributions of discursive, imperial, and cultural power. In particular, the third wave of postcolonialism, championed by Homi Bhabha among others argues that "what is theoretically innovative, and politically crucial, is the necessity of thinking beyond initial categories and initiatory subjects and focusing on those *interstitial* moments or processes that are produced in the articulations of 'differences'" (Bhabha 1994a: 269). Mark Salter argued that the truth-producing technology of the border examination was dependent on the predisposition to confession that forms a central part of contemporary, Western society (Salter 2007: 57–59). Against this assumption of anxiety and obedience at the border, Bhabha discusses the inherent paradoxes within the assertion of authority: "in the native refusal to satisfy the colonizer's narrative demand … the natives' resistance represents a frustration of that nineteenth-century tactic of surveillance, the *confession*, which seeks to dominate the 'calculable' individual by positing the truth that the subject *has* but does not *now*" (Bhabha 1994b: 99). In every border examination, there are moments of resistance, mimicry, and refusal that fundamentally demonstrate the gap in the authority of the state to know, to define, and to control the individual. Because these are the kinds of institutional processes through which the sovereign (colonial) state imposes and reenacts national identity, they reveal the fundamental "slipperyness" of power and discourse. This is reinforced by a focus on the migrant, the refugee, or the nomad as determinant figures in postcolonial and cultural studies (Okoye 2004). Borders are everywhere contested and resisted.

Area studies

In addition to these critical studies of the border, we can highlight some empirically "heavy" borders and border disputes that dominate the academic and policy discussion. The changing nature of European borders, particularly with the Schengen Acquis, meant that intra-Schengen and extra-Schengen frontier controls are remarkably different (Bigo and Guild 2005). Even if, as Alexandre Dumas put it, "Africa begins at the Pyrenees," with the end of the Cold War, even NATO moved to secure the "Southern Flank" and the militarization of the Mediterranean must be seen as a border security operation. Questions of border control persist across many frontiers: Iraq/Turkey through Kurdistan; Israel/Lebanon; South Africa/Zimbabwe, Guatamala/Mexico. From a global strategic point-of-view, those unpoliced areas in the Golden Triangle (between Myanmar (Burma), Laos, Vietnam, and Thailand), the Triborder Region (between Paraguay, Argentina, and Brazil near Ciudad del Este), or the Tribal Areas (Pakistan and Afghanistan), yield opportunities for criminal activities precisely because of the presence of the border and impossibility of control. There are also a number of active border conflicts, such as the India/Pakistan struggle over Kashmir or the South Ossetian question between Russia and Georgia. In short, borders are often a locus for conflict (and study). Here are two brief important case studies: USA and Israel.

Case study: borders of the United States of America

The United States of America shares land borders with two countries that are well-established by treaty, over 8,800 km with Canada and over 3,000 km with Mexico;

however, other ports of entry are also dispersed throughout American in airports and seaports. While the Canada–US border was presented as the "longest undefended border in the world" for many years, this perception has changed since the 9/11 attacks and the attempted attack of Ahmed Ressam, the Millennium Bomber in 2000. Without fortification, and with several "gaps" in the border policing regime (notably First Nations tribal lands that straddle the border and un-staffed remote crossings), moves have been made since 2001 to implement a "Smart Border Agreement" that increases security without impeding flows. This involves the familiar tactics of risk management: adding biometric and security measures to passports and visas, the harmonization of no-fly lists, bilateral policing groups (Integrated Border Enforcement Teams), and investments in infrastructure. The recent Western Hemisphere Travel Initiative requires Canadians to present passports at borders, although they are not subject to biometric capture through US-VISIT. The US–Mexico border is in some ways more important—economically and strategically. Maquiladora, or export processing zones, allows American firms to take advantage of low labor prices in Mexico (although there is a great deal of human rights and environmental concerns about these industries), while exporting the finished goods to the US without import duties. The US–Mexico border sees enormous influx of legal crossings (250 million per year) and illegal crossings (500,000 per year, estimated). There is a fundamental dilemma: certain sectors of the US economy depend on illegal migrant labor, but the US political scene also requires the presentation of an image of control of the border. This leads to what Andreas usefully termed "politically successful policy failures" (Andreas 2003b: 3)—wherein the amount of policing increased and the representation of dominance was received, but the policy did not actually seal-off access to a cheap labor pool. In the aftermath of 9/11, domestic pressures to "seal off the borders" intensified—although most thoughtful observers argue that a solution to the problems of illegal migration can only be achieved with comprehensive immigration reform (more than 40% of all illegal migrants overstay a perfectly valid travel document). Two important trends in recent border policing are increasing militarization and technologization. Military tactics, personnel, and technologies are being used to shore up the American southern border, including remote sensing equipment, unmanned aerial vehicles, and military intelligence. The construction of a border fence has had the effect of pushing illegal migrants and smugglers away from metropolitan or urban areas into remote areas, leading to a increased number of deaths. Following the general trend of neoliberalism, certain parts of American border security have been outsourced to private firms. Boeing was awarded a large contract to construct a "Smart Border Initiative," which was an integrated system for border control, but this pilot was largely unsuccessful. The construction of the physical fence, however, is seen as more reliable. America also has a high number of delocalized international border posts, at airports throughout the country, and present a particular vulnerability revealed by the 9/11 attacks. The US–VISIT program captures biometric, personal, and encounter data for every foreign national entering airports or sea ports of entry. This biometric and personal data is then compared with US terrorist and criminal watch-lists, provided by the Terrorism Screening Center. However, the risk assessment that informs these watch-lists is provided by a private consulting firm, Accenture (Amoore 2006). Though the US–VISIT empowering legislation requires the registration of the exit of foreigners, this has proven unfeasible and been delayed. The American border thus displays both old methods of exclusion and modern methods of biopolitical control.

Case study: Israel

Israel shares borders with Lebanon, Syria, Jordan, and Egypt, and these borders have been heavily contested in war. The borders between Jordan and Egypt were negotiated along cease-fire lines in 1949. The Green Line refers to the borders of the armistice line established after the 1948 Arab-Israeli war, which has undergone only minor territorial revisions, although the border itself is not a clear indicator of sovereignty or control. To the north, the Lebanon-Israel border has been a site of tension and conflict; Israel occupied southern Lebanon in 1982 during the First Lebanon War and stayed until 2000, though the "Blue Line" itself was relatively settled by the United Nations. The Syrian border is not settled; Israel occupied the Golan Heights (a strategic plateau above the settlements around the Sea of Galilee) during the Six Day War in 1967. The West Bank was occupied by Jordan until the Six-Day War, when Israel captured the West Bank, the Gaza Strip, and the Sinai Peninsula (which was returned to Egypt in 1982). The Israeli–Palestinian border is also of great importance and interest, particularly since the erection of the security barrier/separation wall, the era of settlements and its attendant system of bypass roads, and the closure regime. During the Israeli occupation of the West Bank, nearly 500,000 Israelis established themselves in 120 settlements, and nearly 100 unrecognized settlements or outposts. Official settlements are supported by the Israeli government and protected by the Israeli military, although the legal basis for these settlements is disputed. Israeli forces also occupied East Jerusalem during the Six Day War, and an undivided Jerusalem is seen as a *sine qua non* for a peace agreement—by both Israelis and Palestinians. While cooperation on urban infrastructure is sometimes lauded by optimists, the extension of Israeli building into Palestinian neighborhoods and the expansion of the Jerusalem municipal boundaries across the Green Line into formerly Palestinian territory sound notes of pessimism. The Oslo Accords (1993) set out three areas in the West Bank with varying degrees of Palestinian and Israeli control; however this fragmented sovereignty was dramatically undermined after the start of the Second Intifada, which started in 2000. As part of the closure regime, Palestinians require Israeli-issued identity cards and movement permits—and are still restricted from entering settlements, driving on Israeli settler roads and in some cases entering Israel proper (Parsons and Salter 2009). Because the space of the Occupied Palestinian Territories have been fractured and splintered by settlements, by-pass roads, and interrupted through checkpoints and closure, the question of borders takes a fundamentally post-sovereign turn: there is no "there" there, no contiguous or continually-inhabited territory. The Occupied Palestinian Territories are essentially an archipelago. The route and architecture of the separation barrier echo older notions of territorial protection and also newer anxieties about the control of population (Weizman 2007). Israeli borders demonstrate both the persistence of hard, military, exclusive territorial borders and also the biopolitical control of populations through identity cards, movement permits, censuses, and surveillance.

Borders and passports

In analyzing the role and function of borders, we can identify a number of important governmental tactics of control: identification and documentation, examination, and risk management. The essence of the border as a semi-permeable limit of the state's population is the decision. Within 30–60 seconds, a border guard, customs or immigration official (or sometimes airline agent or security screener) makes a judgment that the individual may enter the state's jurisdiction. Proliferating and overlapping borders means that these decisions can take place in any number of real and virtual sites, often distant from the actual territorial frontier of the state. In making and adjudicating this primary claim to entry, three processes are engaged: the monopoly of identification by the state; the ability of the state to examine and the obedience of the individual to accept the authority of the state to decide; and the discretionary evaluation of the individual based not only on legal status but a host of other social, political, economic, and cultural scripts. Gérard Noiriel discusses the "revolution identificatoire" that characterizes the evaluation of the modern state through its consolidation of identity (Noiriel 1996). At this time, the passport and the national identity card connect a certifiable identity with a set of bureaucratic institutions. None of these documents are proof, in themselves, of status, such citizenship, legitimate visitor, or a "deserving" refugee. The examination connects what individuals have such as documents with what individuals are such as biometrics and data. Louise Amoore then discusses the integration of this risk management framework within the architecture of border policing: "the turn to digital technologies, data integration and managerial expertise in the politics of border management; and the exercise of biopower such that the body itself is inscribed with, and demarcates, a continual crossing of multiple encoded borders—social, legal, gendered, racialized and so on" (Amoore 2006: 337). Thus, borders are differentially porous, easy or difficult to traverse, based on a set of both national and global social, cultural, political, economic, and legal scripts. The globalization of the substructure of these scripts can be seen in the harmonization of "no-fly" or terrorist watch-lists. In effect, it is not only individuals of certain nationalities or socioeconomic classes that are targeted for examination and expulsion, but sophisticated risk profiling is engaged to compile a "data-double" of the border crosser based on past travel patterns, age, race, gender, national origin, meal preferences and routing, and so on. The border has always been a paradox, undemocratically limiting the democratic political community, but this tension is amplified when the locus of decision is obscure, diffuse, or invisible. It is important to contextualize, in Shamir's terms, the "paradigm of suspicion" that characterizes the global mobility regime with the actual mechanisms of discretion (Shamir 2005: 200). Turner goes further to say that "governments and other agencies seek to regulate spaces and, where necessary, to immobilize flows of people, goods, and services. These sequestrations, exclusions and closures are: (1) military-political; (2) social and cultural; and (3) biological" (Turner 2007: 290). Borders are similar to other exceptional, interstitial places of international politics, where the distinction between force and law is blurry (Salter 2008). This brings the question of hospitality to the fore, which Derrida examines: the foreigner "has to ask for hospitality in a language which by definition is not his won, the one imposed by the master of the house, the host, the king, the lord, the authorities, the nation, the State, the father, etc." (Derrida 2000: 15). We have seen a sea-change in the host ethic that seems in direct proportion to the finitude of borders: when borders or *limes* were zones of indistinction between sovereigns, the host assumed the moral and legal responsibility for the basic care of the visitor (evidenced in the dominance of hospitality themes within the Iliad and the Odyssey), underpinned by a cosmopolitan view of a shared humanity. As borders were concretized, systematized, and all the world's peoples given places, (if not safe places) the host ethic became an ethic of security for particular communities and specific populations. As a consequence, the studies of border ethics are seen in the exceptions: refugees, detention camps, *sans-papiers*, illegal and migrant labour, airports, *zones d'attentes*, and enclaves, etc.

Lines of flight

Borders are one of the most persistent institutions of contemporary political life, given social, cultural, economic, and anthropological meaning by their observance, reinstitution and transcendence. New research on borders is occurring in three areas: the transformation of borders; the construction of new borders; and bordering practices themselves. The old Westphalian border that represented a military, economic, social, and political limit is fundamentally changing. Military strategies and operations are not based on a geometric, Clausewitzian domination of productive territories, but rather a monopoly over the "battle-space," which includes the production of knowledge about the enemy. Economic policies are increasingly drafted by a transnational elite of risk managers, international bureaucrats, and enterprise consultants. Social groups are able to organize and self-conceptualize their community largely independent of national barriers, except in those cases where the lines of communication are state-controlled. In these situations, the social border is over-coded by the digital divide and economic (under)development. Thus, while the physical or juridical borders between states are remarkably stable, the functional borders that individual travelers encounter have multiplied and dispersed: not simply at the border checkpoint or port of entry, but at the visa office, the passport queue, the airport, the airline check-in counter, the database. The dispersion of the bordering function to private as well as state agents requires more investigation. All of these transformations are not homogenous, and we should strike a warning note: borders are not the same across the globe. More and more researchers are using a Deleuzian frame of analysis (Walters 2006). Rather than examine the vertically structured control strategies of the sovereign state, scholars are using a horizontal, rhizomatic model of control: in this view, a varied and multiple set of actors (state, social, and private) may each inscribe, police, use, and subvert borders—without coordination—that has the effect of restraining (unevenly) the freedom of mobility. While it is clear that capital and knowledge enjoy far greater freedom of movement than does labour, this kind of analysis examines how the global mobility system operates in the absence of a sovereign organizer. Bordering practices—social sorting, risk assessment, examination, passport and national identity certification, rejection, detention and removal—shed new light on inclusion/exclusion and the definition of populations on the move. Every border creates a dynamic, suggests certain limits and presents particular opportunities for subversion. What we can say is that, in sum, borders have ceased to be monolithic, in their construction, their maintenance, or their meaning. Borders are multiple and multiplicitous.

References

Acuto, Michele (2008) "Edges of the Conflict: A Three-fold Conceptualization of National Borders," *borderlands e-journal* 7(1).

Adey, Peter (2006) "If Mobility is Everything Then it is Nothing: Towards a Relational Politics of (Im) Mobilities," *Mobilities* 1(1): 75–94.

Agamben, Giorgio (1998) *Homo Sacer: Sovereign Power and Bare Life*, trans. by Daniel Heller-Roazen, Stanford: Stanford University Press.

Agnew, John (2007) "Contributions to the Forum," *International Political Sociology* 1(3): 300.

Amoore, Louise (2006) "Biometric Borders: Governing Mobilities in the War on Terror," *Political Geography* 25(3): 336–351.

Andreas, Peter (2003a) "Redrawing the Line: Borders and Security in the Twenty-first Century," *International Security* 28(2): 78–111.

——(2003b) "A Tale of Two Borders: The US–Canada and US–Mexico Lines after 9-11," in Peter Andreas and Thomas J. Biersteker eds., *The Rebordering of North America*, 1–23, London: Routledge.

Appadurai, Arjun (1996) "Sovereignty without Territoriality: Notes for a Postnational Geography," in Patricia Yaeger ed., *Geography of Identity*, 40–58, Ann Arbor: University of Michigan Press.

Augé, Marc (1995) *Non-places: An introduction to an Anthropology of Supermodernity*, trans. John Howe, London: Verso.

Balibar, Étienne (2002) "What is a Border?" in *Politics and the Other Scene*, 75–86, London: Verso.

Bauman, Zygmunt (2000) "Tourists and Vagabonds: Or, Living in Postmodern Times," in Joseph E. Davis, ed. *Identity and Social Change*, 13–26, New Brunswick, NJ: Transaction.

——(2003) "Utopia with no *Topos*," *History of the Human Sciences* 16(1): 11–25.

Bhabha, Homi (1994a) "Frontlines/Borderposts," in Angelika Bammer ed., *Displacements: Cultural Identities in Question*, 269–272, Indianapolis: Indiana University Press.

——(1994b) "Sly Civility," in *Location of Culture*, 93–101, London: Routledge.

Bigo, Didier (2001) "The Möbius Ribbon of Internal and External Security(ies)," in Mathias Albert, David Jacobson, and Yosef Lapid eds., *Identities, Borders, Orders: Rethinking International Relations Theory*, 91–116, Minneapolis: University of Minnesota Press.

——(2006) "Globalized (In)Security: the Field and the Banopticon," in Anna Tsoukala and Didier Bigo eds., *Illiberal Practices of Liberal Regimes: the (in)security games*, 5–49, Paris: L'Harmattan.

——(2007) "Detention of Foreigners, States of Exception, and the Social Practices of Control of the Banopticon," in Prem Kumar Rajaram and Carl Gruny-Warr eds., *Borderscapes: Hidden Geographies and Politics at Territory's Edge*, 3–33, Minneapolis: University of Minnesota Press.

Bigo, Didier and Elspeth Guild, eds. (2005) *Controlling Frontiers: Free Movement into and within Europe* Aldershot: Ashgate.

Bouchard, Geneviève and Barbara Wake Carroll (2002) "Policy-making and Administrative Discretion: The Case of Immigration in Canada," *Canadian Public Administration* 45(2): 239–257.

Castells, Manuel (2000) *Rise of the Network Society*, Oxford: Blackwell.

Connolly, William E. (1991) *Identity\Difference: Democratic Negotiations of Political Paradox*, Ithaca: Cornell University Press.

Crang, Michael (2002) "Between Places: Producing Hubs, Flows, and Networks," *Environment and Planning A* 34(4): 569–574.

Cresswell, Tim (2006) *On the Move: Mobility in the Modern Western World*, London: Routledge.

Derrida, Jacques (2000) "The Foreigner Question", in Jacques Derrida and Anne Dufoumantelle eds., *Of Hospitality*, trans. Rachel Bowlby, Stanford: Stanford University Press.

Donnan, Hastings and Thomas M. Wilson (1993) "An Anthropology of Frontiers," in Hastings Donnan and Thomas M. Wilson, eds., *Border Approaches: Anthropological Perspectives on Frontiers*, 1–14, New York: University Press of America.

Foucault, Michel (2000) "The Political Technology of Individuals," in Graham Burchill ed., *Power: The Essential Works of Foucault, 1954–1984*, 403–417, New York: New Press.

Gilboy, Janet A. (1991) "Deciding Who Gets In: Decisionmaking by Immigration Inspectors," *Law and Society Review* 25(3): 571–599.

Graham, Stephen S. (2002) "FlowCity: Networked Mobilities and the Contemporary Metropolis," *Journal of Urban Technology* 9(1): 1–20.

Guiraudon, Virginie and Gallya Lahav (2000) "Reappraisal of the State Sovereignty Debate: The Case of Migration Control," *Comparative Political Studies* 33(2): 163–195.

Heyman, Josiah McC. (1995) "Putting Power in the Anthropology of Bureaucracy; The Immigration and Naturalization Service at the Mexico-United States Border," *Current Anthropology* 36(2): 261–287.

——(2001) "Class and Classification at the US-Mexico Border," *Human Organization* 60(2): 128–140.

Higgins, Rosalyn (1973) "The Right in International Law of an Individual to Enter, Stay In and Leave a Country," *International Affairs* 49(3): 341–357.

Hindess, Barry (2000) "Citizenship in the International Management of Populations," *American Behavioral Scientist* 43(9): 1486–1497.

Johns, Fleur (2005) "Guantánamo Bay and the Annihilation of the Exception," *European Journal of International Law* 16(4): 613–635.

Kaplan, David H. and Häkli, Jouni, eds. (2002) *Boundaries and Place: EuropeaN Borderlands in Geographical Context*, Oxford: Rowman and Littlefield Publishers.

Kesby, Alison (2007) "The Shifting and Multiple Border and International Law," *Oxford Journal of Legal Studies* 27(1): 101–119.

Lapid, Yosef (2001) "Identities, Borders, Orders: Nudging International Relations Theory in a New Direction," in Mathias Albert, David Jacobson, and Yosef Lapid eds., *Identities, Borders, Orders: Rethinking International Relations Theory*, 1–20, Minneapolis: University of Minnesota Press.

Löfgren, Orvar (1999) "Crossing Borders: The Nationalization of Anxiety," *Enthologia Scandinavica* 29: 5–27.

Makaremi, Chowra (2008) "Border Detention in Europe: Violence and the Law," paper presented at the annual meeting of the International Studies Association's 49th Annual Convention, San Francisco.

Mignolo, Walter D. and Madina V. Tlostanova (2006) "Theorizing from Borders: Shifting to geo- and body-politics of knowledge," *European Journal of Social Theory* 9(2): 205–221.

Noiriel, Gérard (1996) *The French Melting Pot: Immigration, Citizenship, and National Identity*, trans. Geoffroy de Laforcade, Minneapolis: University of Minnesota Press.

Nyers, Peter (2006) *Rethinking Refugees: Beyond States of Emergency*, London: Routledge.

Okoye, Ikem Stanley (2004) "Rending the 'Nomad'," *Interventions: International Journal of Postcolonial Studies* 6(2): 180–200.

Paasi, Anssi (1998) "Boundaries as Social Processes: Territoriality in the World of Flows," *Geopolitics* 3(1): 69–88.

Parsley, Connal (2003) "Performing the Border: Australia's Judgment of 'Unauthorized Arrivals' at the Airport," *Australian Feminist Law Journal* 18; 55–75.

Parsons, Nigel and Mark B. Salter (2009) "Israeli Biopolitics: Closure, Territorialization and Governmentality in the Occupied Palestinian Territories," *Geopolitics* 13(4): 701–723.

Rosas, Gilberto (2006) "The Thickening Borderlands; Diffused Exceptionality and 'Immigrant' Social Struggles during the 'War on Terror'," *Cultural Dynamics* 18(3): 335–349.

Rumford, Chris (2006) "Theorising Borders," *European Journal of Social Theory* 9(2): 155–169.

Salter, Mark B. (2003) *Rights of Passage: The Passport in International Relations*, Boulder: Lynne Rienner.

——(2007) "Governmentalities of an Airport: Heterotopia and Confession," *International Political Sociology* 1(1): 49–67.

Shamir, Ronen (2005) "Without Borders? Notes on Globalization as a Mobility Regime," *Sociological Theory* 23(2): 197–217.

Sheller, Mimi and John Urry (2006) "The New Mobilities Paradigm," *Environment and Planning A* 38 (2): 207–226.

Soguk, Nevzat (1999) *States and Strangers: Refugees and Displacements of Statecraft*, Minneapolis: University of Minnesota Press.

Soguk, Nevzat and Geoffrey Whitehall (1999) "Wandering Grounds: Transversality, Identity, Territoriality, and Movement," *Millennium: Journal of International Studies* 28(3): 675–698.

Taylor, Savitri (2005) "Sovereign Power at the Border," *Public Law Review* 16(55): 55–77.

Ticktin, Miriam (2005) "Policing and Humanitarianism in France: Immigration and the Turn to Law as State of Exception," *Interventions: The International Journal of Postcolonial Studies* (7)3: 347–368.

Torpey, John (2000) *The Invention of the Passport: Surveillance, Citizenship, and the State*, Cambridge: Cambridge University Press.

Turner, Bryan S. (2007) "The Enclave Society: Towards a Sociology of Immobility," *European Journal of Social Theory* 10(2): 287–303.

Urry, John (2003) "Social Networks, Travel and Talk," *British Journal of Sociology* 54(2): 155–175.

van Houtum, Henk (2000) "An Overview of European Geographical Research on Borders and Border Regions," *Journal of Borderland Studies* 15(1): 57–83.

Walker, R.B.J. (1993) *Inside/Outside: International Relations as Political Theory* Cambridge: Cambridge University Press.

529

Walters, William (2002) "Deportation, Expulsion and the International Policing of Aliens," *Citizenship Studies* 6(3): 265–292.

——(2006) "Border/Control," *European Journal of Social Theory* 9(2): 187–203.

Wonders, Nancy A. (2006) "Global Flows, Semi-Permeable Borders and New Channels of Inequality: Border Crossers and Border Performativity," in Sharon Pickering and Leanne Weber, eds., *Borders, Mobility and Technologies of Control*, 63–86, Dordrecht, The Netherlands: Springer.

Weizman, Eyal (2007) *Hollow Land: Israel's Architecture of Occupation*, London: Verso.

Zacher, Mark (2001) "The Territorial Integrity Norm: International Boundaries and the Use of Force," *International Organization* 55(2): 215–250.

27

Globalization of space

From the global to the galactic

Peter Dickens and James S. Ormrod

There is no longer an outside to capital.

Hardt and Negri (2000: 102)

In the past patriots fought to establish political and economic conditions of free exchange and private property rights. These conditions opened commercial frontiers on Earth and allowed us to create material wealth and technical capacities never dreamed of. By establishing these conditions throughout the solar system, we will open boundless new commercial frontiers.

Hudgins (2002: xxv)

There is a danger in treating our contemporary global society as though it were the final accomplishment of the globalizing process. In this chapter we explore the ways in which globalization has already extended its reaches beyond the globe and into outer space, and we look to the likely future of the humanization of the rest of the galaxy and beyond. Global capitalism's Earthly empire continues to be subject to crises of economic, social, and political sorts, and here we point to capital's attempts to evade implosion by switching and migrating from one domain to the next – in this instance into the rest of the galaxy. Such an extension of globalization to the galactic scale is actively promoted by 'pro-space' advocates who fail to examine critically its implications (e.g. Zubrin 1999). Extending and consolidating control of space (in its broadest sense) continues to be of utmost importance in the maintenance of Earthly power relations, and this now includes places beyond Earth itself.

Space technology and global society

The humanization of outer space is, of course, well under way. In the decade up to 2003, space activities had generated over $1 trillion. And by the end of that period, one hundred million satellite terminals on Earth were capable of receiving transmissions from outer space (Pelton et al. 2004). Revenues from the space industry have been exceptionally high right up until 2008, and 'in a business climate full of uncertainty and cutbacks, all sectors of space continue to grow and provide value to the global economy'

(Space Foundation 2008). Total revenue in 2007 was $252.6 billion (up 11 per cent on the previous year), broken down as follows:

Revenue from spending from US government space budgets	25%
From spending by international government budgets	6%
Purchase for commercial infrastructure (ground equipment, etc.)	14%
Revenue from space tourism	1%
Direct to Home television	26%
GPS (for industry, in-car navigation, chips to detect stolen items)	22%
'Other'	7%

According to the United Nations Office of Outer Space Affairs, which registers all launches made by member states, as of July 2008, 3,270 once functional objects remained in Earth's orbit, of which (based on approximations from official and unofficial information) just over 950 remain functional. Indeed, such is the extent of the humanization of near-Earth space in recent decades that it has become incredibly crowded (see Figure 27.1). This has caused problems both in terms of competition for satellite operating bandwidths (see Dickens and Ormrod 2007: 107–8) and the danger posed to active satellites, space stations, and space vehicles of collision with space debris or junk (ibid: 153–4).

Figure 27.1 Computer-generated image of trackable objects in orbit around Earth (colours inverted – the Middle East can just be made out in black in the top left of the globe).
Source: European Space Agency.

Note: Artist's impression; size of debris exaggerated as compared to Earth.

There is no shortage of accounts praising the role that satellites play as providers of services within our global society. Many point to the sheer popularity of satellite services as evidence of their value. Satellites play a key role in enabling the transmission of data crucial to the information society (Lyon 1988), the economy of which relies on the efficient processing of information (Castells 2004). Equally, they allow the rapid switching of finance capital between investments which is crucial to the liquid economy, and captured in Appadurai's (1990) concept of 'finanscapes'. Much of this switching occurs through Electronic Fund Transfers or EFTs, in which no physical currency is actually exchanged. At any given time, satellites can process $400 trillion in such transactions (Pelton et al. 2004: xiv).

Many accounts of postmodern life focus on the social freedoms network technology has provided its users, opening up new opportunities for education, identity play, and work and sexual relationships. It is often now argued, for example, that the internet is allowing new forms of interaction and decentralized and fluid forms of community using blogs, discussion groups and so on (Benkler 2006). Although terrestrial fibre-optics carry most internet traffic on a local level, only half the world's countries are connected together in this way, the rest relying on bouncing signals off satellites, bypassing in most instances the problems caused by huge distances and impassable terrain. Satellites support internet connections to countries that do not have fibre-optic connectivity and within countries that do not have a terrestrial internet network. This is very much the case in many African and Asian countries.

Although there has been some general disinvestment from satellites in recent years (a possible indicator of overinvestment), the rise of digital entertainment has enhanced their perceived value. Satellite television certainly gives the impression of proliferating choice and pushing back the boundaries of parochialism. Raymond Williams (1974) noted the potential of satellite television. Penetrating beyond national boundaries and control by elites, it could result in an international democratic sharing of information. The fall of the USSR has been attributed in part to satellite television and radio revealing life beyond its limits (Pelton 2004: 270). This is not the whole story for Williams, however, and we return to him later. But the potential for satellites to bring television and internet to the most remote and rural locations in the developing world, and with them increased education and health (and, via remote-sensing, local knowledge), has certainly enhanced the image of the benefits of satellite technology.

It is, however, vital that we think critically about all these perceived benefits. The liquid nature of finance capital has not increased financial security for the billions of people ultimately affected by transfers of funds taking place thousands of kilometres above their heads. Communication through networks divorced from face-to-face contact and the realities of time and space has been found to foster 'mirage' fantasy relationships (Gergen 1991: 164) and paradoxically correlate with alienation and attempts to restore identity based on primary identities based on history and geography (Castells 2004: 22). Serious mental health issues associated with networks are just beginning to come to light (Pelton 2004). Because, as Williams (1974) feared, control of the satellite media lies largely in the hands of the media oligopolies (Steven 2003), neoliberal ideology becomes as apparent as the propaganda of state-sponsored stations. The US army 'Psyops' programme actively promotes pro-US propaganda towards 'enemy' countries, using commercial companies such as CNN as a means of influencing local populations and winning wars by persuasion (see Robinson 2002). Furthermore, the 24-hour preponderance of repetitive, commercial-driven, substance-less satellite television which has numbed the channel-hopping MTV generation would only have amplified Theodore Adorno's (1941) concerns of half a century ago. His argument was that in a capitalist society, entertainment fulfils the worker's simultaneous needs for stimulation and relaxation, with the result that popular culture demands no work from the viewer to appreciate it (and certainly no critical reflection) whilst still superficially providing a stimulating sensory experience. The satellite television generation is one of consumers bombarded with rapidly changing images vying for attention, the result of which is superficial involvement with all of them (Pelton 2004, echoing Simmel).

Satellites circling, capital circulating

If not serving social functions, the question then remains one of why the humanization of outer space has preceded as it has in recent decades and why this looks set to continue. Our answer is rooted in the economic structure of capitalism. It is here that David Harvey's work first becomes useful. Harvey starts his analysis with the 'primary circuit' of capital in which money is invested in machinery, raw materials, and labour power, producing commodities. This commodity is sold and the proceeds are either reinvested or enjoyed by capitalists and their investors. Developing Marx's account, however, Harvey (1982) emphasizes the conditions of overaccumulation of capital that are endemic to the primary circuit and the resultant devaluation of capital and labour. It is from this point that Harvey (2003) outlines two further circuits which involve absorbing surplus capital in longer-term investment. In a 'secondary' circuit surplus capital is re-circulated via the capital market into fixed capital, producer durables, and the built environment. (This secondary circuit also includes a consumption fund for consumer durables, especially housing). Excess capital (and labour) can be expended in the creation of fixed assets. These assets tie-up capital in the short-term, taking 'many years to return their value to circulation through the productive activity they support' (Harvey 2003: 88.) Private investment in satellites is a way of cycling capital through the secondary circuit. As 'producers' durables', they represent sources for further realization of profit for media corporations and other members of the capitalist class. After a relatively large initial investment (JSAT offer satellites for around 20–30 billion yen), it is hoped that such investments will turn a profit as satellite services are leased and sold to consumers who have invested themselves in the equipment necessary to consume them. In a sense they become a new 'landscape for purposes of production, circulation, exchange and consumption' (Harvey 2005: 113). This hope is even more apparent in real-estate developer Chuck Lauer's plans to build 'space business parks' in orbit with modules to rent out to scientists, businesses and tourists (Zubrin 1999: 65).

Space tourism

Satellites are one way in which space has already been invested in as a solution to over-accumulation. Ferrying wealthy tourists into outer space is a much more spectacular example of a similar thing, and quite likely a precursor to a more extensive form of humanization as we discuss later. Space tourism is now a relatively well-established phenomenon. After a number of abortive attempts to create this new industry, the American company Space Adventures has sold a number of flights on-board a Russian Soyuz rocket to the International Space Station. Each flight costs $20 million, the first being that of the millionaire Dennis Tito in 2001. It has currently (mid–2008) sent five tourists into outer space. Such consumption is a development of earlier well-established forms of conspicuous consumption (Veblen 1963), a means by which wealthy individuals can establish their identities. Outer space is the new means by which elites can escape the herds of people who have discovered other previously exclusive locales (Urry 2002).

Space Adventures now reports some two hundred potential space tourists have signed up for suborbital flights, the total deposits being around $3 million. Furthermore, the company has been heavily invested in by Sergey Brin, the founder of the internet search giant, Google. He and five further founders of an 'Orbital Mission Explorers Circle' have each contributed $5 million to Space Adventures with the aim of the company launching a private mission to the International Space Station (Leonard 2008).

A number of companies are now competing in the space tourism business, the aim being to launch exceptionally wealthy people (and in due course somewhat less wealthy people) into the nearby galaxy. These companies concerned include SpaceEx, Xcor, Blue Origin, Armadillo, Space Dev and Scaled Composites. Following the pattern familiar to competitive capitalism, we can expect some of these companies to succeed while others go out of business. Scaled Composites looks like it is particularly likely to succeed since it has been bought out by Northrop-Grumman, one of the leading US defence contractors and the manufacturer of a large range of military surveillance vehicles deployed in outer space. Virgin Galactic is currently, however, the largest company selling vacations in space. This is a collaboration between Richard Branson (head of the Virgin group of companies), Paul Allen (Microsoft co-founder), Burt Rutan (a developer of spacecraft) and Philippe Stark (a design guru). The switches of capital from potentially declining investments into space humanization are extremely noticeable. Not only have Branson and Allen withdrawn capital from their other interests, but PayPal founder Elon Musk has invested in SpaceX and Amazon.com entrepreneur Jeff Bezos has done the same with Blue Origin.

Projections for the future of privately financed space tourism are ambitious (see Figure 27.2). Spencer and Rugg (2004) make the analogy between the early growth of luxury cruising on the oceans and that in space. They argue that Tito's flight was a 'pioneering phase'. It is estimated that in approximately ten years the International Space Station will have been converted into the first 'private orbital yacht' and around one thousand citizens will have travelled 'off world'. In the next 'exclusive' phase, wealthy individuals and corporations will be engaging in orbital yacht racing. The 'mature phase' will be one in which cruise ships seating one hundred persons and offering a range of recreational facilities will be available. By 2050, one million people will be touring off-world and 'the year 2075 could see 3000 to 5000 tourists and sports fans going every day' (Spencer and Rugg 2004: 52).

Even greater 'maturity' is promised with the creation of 'orbital hotels', destinations more akin to earth-bound tourism than the cramped International Space Station. As long ago as 1967 Barron Hilton, president of Hilton Hotels assured the American Astronautical Society that 'when space scientists make it physically feasible to establish hotels in space, the hotel industry will meet the challenge' (Billings 2006: 162). If orbital hotels sound like something fantastical for a distant future, it must be remembered that design and research work is already under way. Bigelow Aerospace, the leading contender, have already tested unmanned habitats and plan to launch a manned version, 'Sundancer', early in the next decade.

These investments are again absorbing surplus capital through the building of an infrastructure for space tourism. Burt Rutan won the $10 million Ansari X-Prize for flight-testing a space tourism vehicle but spent several times that developing Space-ShipOne without immediate hope of return on the investment. Investments have also been made in a number of new 'spaceports' in the southern United States, such as Rutan's Mojave Spaceport, many taking the place of small airfields. For Lefebvre (1976), the making of new, or rehabilitated, forms of physical space on Earth as sites for consumption and tourism has now been made the main way in which the primary circuit of capital escapes from crisis and declining profits.

As Harvey argues, investments in this secondary circuit will be made via increasingly important mediating institutions. They are able to provide, for example, the kind of 'fictitious capital' necessary for such major investment. Declan O'Donnell and his United Societies in Space organization of space lawyers have attempted to establish an International Space Development Authority Corporation, not dissimilar in function to the World Bank, which would act as a space bank for investment in a space colonization programme. Harvey (2003: 117–19) offers a convincing critique of such lending.

In addition to the secondary circuit, a 'tertiary' circuit is concerned with the relation between the primary circuit and state functions. Surpluses are extracted from the primary circuit, this time via taxes, and circulated into developing technological and scientific innovation. The tertiary circuit also includes investment (again via governments) into social expenditures such as education, surveillance, and the military. It is not only private companies that are humanizing the galaxy. States have siphoned off money to invest in space assets as well. These may be used to stimulate further productivity. The spin-off technologies and scientific discoveries from government investment in space are often cited. Whilst some hold out hope for the private sector to colonize space on its own (e.g. Hudgins 2002), many commentators believe that governments will have to pave the way, with entrepreneurs following in their wake (Zubrin 1999: 75–6). But the tertiary circuit also serves important state functions. Space technology is central to both the geopolitics practiced by states through military force and the micro-politics through which populations are ordered and managed on a more day-to-day basis.

Geopolitics, the state, and war

Virilio (1997, 1998) uses the word 'dromology' (derived from the Greek *dromos*, meaning 'racecourse') to enculate the significance of speed and time–space compression in the modern era of military conquest. The history of civilization is not only the history of wealth acquisition but the history of powerful institutions having access to technologies of speed. With speed comes the control of place. Hostilities can now be conducted instantaneously and at great distances. What Virilio calls a 'military class' surveys and pursues enemies throughout the globe by electronic means whilst remaining well out of harm's way. The result, in principle, is a 'pure war' (Virilio and Lotringer 1998): one conducted invisibly by a relatively small number of electronics engineers, software programmers, aerospace engineers, and military strategists in the most powerful societies. President Reagan's Strategic Defense Initiative proposed in 1983, which included space-based interceptors (known as 'Bright Eyes' and 'Brilliant Pebbles') to detect and destroy incoming missiles, was perhaps the most spectacular attempt to make war 'pure': a global conflict without conventional soldiers.

The reality of outer space militarization, as distinct from its weaponization (Deblois 2003) – the placing of weapons in space, which we return to later on – has become surprisingly banal. It is simply a means by which hostilities are conducted on Earth. But the fact that outer space is integral to contemporary 'everyday' warfare makes it even more important to understand. Using outer space to dominate society on Earth is a fundamental principle of military strategy, especially US military strategy, today.

Loring Wirbel (2004: xv) draws attention to the routine use of satellite-guided attacks in the Middle East, defining these as attacks by space weapons. Control over space-based intelligence has also become increasingly important to secure and the US has enlisted the private sector in this. Mean and Wilsdon (2004: 31–2) report that for the duration of the Afghanistan war, the Pentagon paid Space Imaging $2 million a month for the monopoly on its one-meter resolution images of the country, excluding humanitarian groups from using them to assist refugees. Furthermore, satellite communications links are also essential to troops on the ground. Encouraged by the private sector, the US military are planning towards the development of a new form of 'net-centric' warfare. This is a totally new kind of war in which, via a secure internet accessible to every member of the military, intelligence and military activities would be fused and machines would communicate with one another. The resulting perspective on the battlefield would give soldiers a 'God's eye view' according to Lockheed Martin chief executive Robert J. Stevens. 'That's real power', he adds (Weiner 2004). The image of an omniscient and punishing God in the heavens is alive and well, orchestrated by the US military.

In contemporary warfare, missiles surgically guided by satellites are supposed to not only annihilate an enemy but reduce the surviving population into stunned submission. Military proponents of 'shock and awe' tactics make clear that the purpose of speed on a global and now galactic scale is not necessarily to kill large numbers of people, but to shock wider populations into mental defeat through unrelenting attacks on simultaneous targets. This type of 'shock and awe' war has been simultaneously made part of the 'society of the spectacle', one in which massive public events are commodified in the form of live television broadcasts via satellite to a global audience (Debord 1994; Retort 2005; Baudrillard 1995).

The question remains of what ultimate end is being served by the development of space technology to fight Earthly wars. It has been understood for some time that state extraction of capital for the financing of large-scale military and space projects (which usually share common contractors; Dickens 2009) serves important regulatory economic functions. But more than this, in the era of neo-liberalism, military expenditure (including military expenditure in space) is needed to oversee the processes of capitalist imperialism.

Harvey can help us understand how the militarization of space helps establish empires on Earth via imperialism at a distance or 'at arm's length'. The primary goal of this is the opening up investment opportunities for corporations (Foster 2006: 145), an idea to which we return later when discussing galactic imperialism. Retaining our focus on Earthly wars and imperialism for the moment, Harvey is able to offer an explanation for why military space technology is so necessary, invoking what he calls 'a simple rule' that 'those who command space can always control the politics of place even though, and this is a vital corollary, it takes control of some place to command space in the first place' (Harvey 1989: 234). And the strategic importance of control of outer space, often referred to as 'the new high ground', in controlling places on Earth cannot be over-estimated. As President Lyndon B. Johnson argued in 1958:

> There is something more important than the ultimate weapon. That is the ultimate position – the position of total control over the Earth that lies somewhere out in space. That is [...] the distant future, though not so distant as we may have

thought. Whoever gains that position gains control, total control, over Earth, for the purposes of tyranny or for the service of freedom.

(Cited in Air Force 2006)

Unfortunately, those states monopolizing the use of outer space are those attempting to control Earthly social relations in their own interests.

Micro-politics and surveillance

Hopefully our preceding discussion makes it clear that we reject the decentring of power characteristic of post-structuralist theory, but we do believe Foucault's focus on micro-politics highlights other levels at which power can be manifested. Foucault (1977) famously presented Bentham's panopticon as a metaphor for the means by which power is exerted in modern society. He argued that because the prisoners (or others in need of reformation) were never aware if they were being watched, it was not even necessary for the governor to be there at all for them to *feel* as though they were being observed and to regulate their own behaviour, making themselves productive parts of the social order. In a more general sense, 'governmentality' is Foucault's term for the way in which modern individuals are produced and become self-governing, at the same time as being managed as populations.

It has been argued that the whole of our globalized society has now become a 'pla-netary panopticon' (Whitaker 2000) or super-panopticon (Poster 1995; Lyon 2001). Quite apart from the proliferation of closed circuit television cameras at the local level, digital information on people is held in databases and readily transferred around the world. Biometrics (fingerprints, iris scans, and genetic sequences), medical details (including predispositions to certain diseases) information about a person's job and leisure habits, taxation, and social security history are amongst the many pieces of valuable per-sonalized information now being actively amassed (Lyon and Zureik 1994; Garfinkel 2000). But more than this, our argument is that direct surveillance of people from orbiting panoptical satellites represents a much more literal translation of Bentham's design to the galactic scale. Both involve a watchtower up on high that observes 'deviant' populations, and in neither case do the monitored have any knowledge of whether or not they are being watched. Earth-imaging satellites, satellite positioning systems such as GPS, and systems which eavesdrop on satellite communication 'chatter' work to ensure order is maintained, even though authority figures are rarely visible. The super-panopticon is less intrusive than Bentham's model and its inmates are not restricted, but it is no less efficient for this (Poster 1995: 69).

What Gramsci retained, but Foucault subsequently rejected, is a notion of the interests according to which a docile population is managed. What, in more concrete terms, is the planetary panopticon actually regulating? To an increasing extent systems like GPS are being used by the private sector to regulate work life. In *Capital, vol. 1*, Marx laid out the historical process by which labour has been subsumed, or incorporated, by capital to the extent that workers lose their autonomy and become part of the capitalist's machine. Control is exercised through rigid timekeeping, for example. Warehouse workers are now being tagged, and their work monitored by satellite to improve efficiency (Dickens and Ormrod 2007: 119). This tagging, like that of delivery drivers, parallels in the population at large the tagging of offenders released from prison. This latter practice also works in the interests of capital as private companies are being employed by the state to create these hi-tech solutions to social problems (ibid.: 120).

Powerful states are also using such measures to ensure their own real or imagined 'security' from threats to the neoliberal order. Echelon, launched in the 1970s to spy on Soviet satellite communications and now run by the National Security Agency, conducts massive automated searches of all forms of communication, including those by satellite. One commentator, an ex-employee of the US State Department, describes Echelon graphically as sucking up all communications 'like a mammoth vacuum cleaner in the sky' (Blum 2005: 271). His book has been cited by Osama Bin Laden. Yet it is not only the threat of Al Qaeda and the like which has prompted satellite surveillance, but other social movements, including anti-globalization activists, and even members of the Global Network Against Weapons and Nuclear Power in Space, to which we return later.

According to Hardt and Negri (2000), the old model of imperialism, one in which there was a radical distinction between an imperializing inside and an outside to be controlled or exploited has now gone, there being no 'outside' left in our globalized society. For them, a diverse revolutionary 'multitude' is emerging within the new 'smooth space of Empire'. The multitude is constituted from all those who work under the rule of capital. These people constitute the very body of global capitalism, without which it would cease to exist. Such resistance from within has even made use of satellite technology (Lucas and Wallner 1993), though for Harvey (2003) resistance is nothing like as uniform as Hardt and Negri believe. Capital, of course, is not static in all of this as is perhaps implied by Hardt and Negri's assertion of the end of imperialism. Just as its Earthly empire is being contested, it is making plans to resolve elsewhere the contradictions which seem on the brink of imploding. These plans revolve around the seed of possibility which the development of existing space technology has planted in the minds of the global elite – the possibility of a new, galactic, imperialism.

From Earthly empire to galactic imperialism

So far, we have charted ways in which global capitalism has already been shifting capital into space as a means of resolving crises and utilizing the privileged position of Earth's orbit to consolidate Earthly social relations. Ultimately, however, control of outer space will be necessary to any capitalist bloc wishing to forestall crises within its region, and this will necessitate a new era of galactic imperialism in which outer space is brought more fully 'inside' the capitalist system.

Between 1880 and 1914 most of the globe outside Europe was formally partitioned by a small number of states; primarily Great Britain, France, Germany, Italy, the Netherlands, Belgium, the USA, and Japan (Hobsbawm 1987). Now some of the most powerful societies within the globe are on the brink of starting a similar imperializing process, this time extending to the solar system. Furthermore, very similar social, economic, and political processes underpin this new form of galactic imperialism.

Luxemburg – extending capitalist social relations

In the early decades of the twentieth century Rosa Luxemburg (2003) suggested that capitalism always needs an 'outside', a zone of non-capitalism it can exploit. Imperialism, according to Luxemburg, is the competitive struggle between capitalist nations for what remains of the non-capitalist outside. She offered two possible explanations for the necessity of this expansionary dynamic (Brewer 1990). The first is capitalism's tendency towards crises of 'under-consumption'. There are not sufficient markets for products within the capitalist region, and so it must seek new markets elsewhere. Marx and Engels outline in *The Communist Manifesto* the extent to which this expansion-process entails the colonization of non-capitalist societies in the hope of selling products to the middle classes in these regions. 'The need for a constantly expanding market chases the bour-geoisie over the whole surface of the globe. It must nestle everywhere, settle everywhere, establish connections everywhere' (cited by Brewer 1990: 42). And yet, Luxemburg also argued, there is a fundamental contradiction, one ultimately leading to capitalism's collapse. As it increasingly draws its 'outside' into itself capitalism also destroys the very demand it needs for its products.

This model holds out little hope for capitalism resolving its crises through expansion into outer space. At the heart of Luxemburg's understanding is the observation that capitalism is a set of social relations. Once all people become embroiled in the capitalist system, under-consumption is the only possible outcome. Through what Marx called 'the annihilation of space through time', space technology has assisted capitalism in bringing more and more of the world's population into the capitalist economic system, as workers (through practices such as teleworking), consumers (through teleshopping as well as the consumption of media already discussed), and producers (even Samoan islanders have been using satellite communications to negotiate the best prices for their products, Pelton et al. 2004: 22). But there are no people living outside the capitalist system in outer space, who can be brought inside capitalist social relations as a market for its products. There is an idea that a rapidly reproducing human population sent to space from Earth might fuel economic growth. But in itself this would do little but displace the problem, and is only likely to exacerbate contradictions.

The second theory advanced by Luxemburg, with which Brewer has more truck and with which Harvey fails to credit her, is that expansion occurs as part of a search for cheap supplies of labour and raw materials. Searching for the former in outer space is as hopeless as the attempt to find markets. The prospect of utilizing alien (as opposed to alienated!) labour may have been explored by science fiction writers, but for the time being we are happy to leave this aside. The latter, on the other hand appears to offer more of a glimmer of hope. It also maps onto the ideas of contemporary Marxists and space entrepreneurs alike. Neil Smith, a close collaborator of Harvey, has argued that:

> The reproduction of material life is wholly dependent on the production and reproduction of surplus value. To this end, capital stalks the Earth in search of material resources; nature becomes a universal means of production in the sense that it not only provides the subjects, objects and instruments of production, but is also in its totality an appendage to the production process ... no part of the Earth's surface, the atmosphere, the oceans, the geological substratum or the biological superstratum are immune from transformation by capital.
>
> (Smith 1984: 49 and 56)

We would add outer space to Smith's list.

O'Connor – resolving the second contradiction of capitalism

O'Connor (1996) and others have also drawn on Marx to argue that capitalism creates a 'second contradiction' in which 'the natural or external conditions of production' are systematically degraded. (This is in addition to the more familiar first contradiction in Marx between the forces and relations of production.) The second contradiction is seen as an inevitable tendency to capitalist growth.

Outer space is seen by many as a major potential source of new resources and materials. These may in due course be incorporated into production processes on earth and in space. Private companies have been established which are now working on research and design for asteroidal and lunar mines (Lewis 1996; Zubrin 1999; Hudgins 2002). The Moon might seem an obvious first target for the mining of resources but asteroids are currently envisaged as a better bet thanks to their metallic density. They have three hundred times as much free metal as an equal mass taken from the Moon. In the mid-1990s the market value of metals in the smallest known asteroid, known as 3554 Amun, was about $20 trillion. This included $8 trillion worth of iron and nickel, $6 trillion worth of cobalt, and about $6 trillion in platinum-group metals (Lewis 1996). Extracting valuable helium-3 from the Moon is another possibility, one metric ton of helium-3 being worth of $3 million and one million tons being obtainable from the Moon.

Outer space is now also widely envisaged as an unlimited source of solar energy for industrial and domestic production, even though there are serious questions about the profitability of electricity from outer space, at least in the short to medium term (Macauley 2000). Solar panels on the Moon and in space as a whole are never obstructed by weather conditions and benefit from the greater intensity of the Sun outside Earth's atmosphere. Solar panels are already allowing electricity to be generated in outer space. The International Space Station currently provides itself with around 80 kilowatts continuously from an acre of solar panels. The principle can in theory be extended to cover much larger satellites generating huge amounts of electrical power (Macauley and Davis 2002). This could in principle be converted to microwaves and beamed to Earth via laser beams, producing electricity with no greenhouse gas emissions or toxic waste of any kind. A long-standing dream is for Earth's power to be projected directly from space, 'simultaneously providing a large profitable business and dramatically reducing pollution on Earth' (Globus 2005). In the context of present and future demands for electricity, energy companies could stand to make substantial profits; the station on Earth receiving the laser beam from outer space would become the new Middle East.

As an infinite outside array of resources, space appears to have the distinct advantage of not being owned, politically controlled or used by any pre-existing society. Unlike earlier forms of imperialism it does not seem to require dispossession by military means. Bringing this outside zone into capitalism at first seemed wholly benign and beneficial to everyone (Ehricke 1972). But this scenario is almost certainly not so trouble-free as may at first seem. Exploiting space resources, colonizing outer space again does little in terms of addressing the long-run tendency of capitalism to increase the contradiction between its destruction of its material base and social relations. Those consigned to Earth's increasingly degraded environment and wishing to consume the resources of outer space will either be priced out of the market altogether or will have to pay those investing now extortionately for the privilege of 'their' resources. At the same time, space resources are likely to be fought over as have Earthly supplies, and left in a similar state once capital has moved on.

David Harvey – the outer spatial fix

Many Marxists now argue that, while crises of under-consumption are important, crises stemming from overaccumulation of capital and the need for 'outside' regions in which to invest are even more significant as regards further expansion (Brewer 1990). One Marxist taking this position is David Harvey, and his work is particularly useful for understanding the capitalist development of outer space.

Harvey envisages territorial acquisition and control as the central means by which capital accumulation is maintained. These are what Harvey terms 'spatial fixes'. These are literally ways in which capital becomes fixed in space (now including, we argue, *outer* space) and 'fixes' in a more metaphorical sense; hoped-for solutions to capitalism's problems of overaccumulation and declining profitability. Spatial switches of capital, in addition to temporal ones, are outlets for overaccumulated capital and, more than just opening up markets, they provide the cheap supplies of resources and labour possibilities necessary for new rounds of accumulation. The capitalist landscape is never fixed for long, however, as capital constantly reconfigures space to its current advantage (Harvey 2003: 101). In terms of the humanization of outer space we could conclude from Harvey that the universe might offer a series of temporary 'fixes' to the central crisis of capital's overaccumulation.

From tourism to colonization

As Figure 27.2 suggests, space tourism could prefigure a more general colonization of outer space. Space colonization was popularized by science fiction writing in the 1940s and 1950s. It was then taken up by Gerard O'Neill in the 1970s and 1980s, using ideas first created by Bernal and others earlier in the century. O'Neill's idea for 'Island One' proposed space colonies accommodating twenty to thirty thousand inhabitants (O'Neill 1989). They would be located at points where the Earth and Moon's gravitation fields interact in such a way as the colony would remain stable and they would be based on solar energy. Behind such schemes lay the apparent threat of 'limits to growth' on Earth, with population-growth, the over-consumption of resources and widescale pollution making life on Earth intolerable and dangerous (Meadows et al. 1972, 2005). Writer Trudy Bell (1981: 54) echoes the pro-space solution to supposed limits to growth, arguing that 'space industrialization does not fly in the face of the "limits to growth"; it makes them obsolete'. As Kilgore (2003) points out, O'Neill's proposal for colonizing outer space is firmly rooted in an ideal American life which 'could only be guaranteed by plenty of elbow room' (2003: 159). It is a way of life for the wealthy and one based as much on intolerance of others as on universal 'freedom'.

In terms of an economic fix, Harvey (2003: 119) believes that creating new colonies can have a longer-term 'fixing' effect than other reconfigurations of capital. They create their own 'centres of accumulation' and it typically takes time for these to overaccumulate themselves. Getting rid of surplus capital and labour to found these new centres can in the long-term increase demand for goods produced in the original region. Newly created space colonies would likely create demand for goods and labour from Earth for some time at least, but they cannot permanently resolve the central contradictions of its economy.

Colonization is a technological solution to a socio-economic problem, which does not address the underlying dynamic at work. A similar point could be made regarding another kind of proposed colonization seen as a 'solution' to Earthly problems. This is 'terra-forming', in which a planet such as Mars is modified in such a way as to support human life (for a more detailed discussion see Dickens and Ormrod 2007: 148–51 and 157–8). Crises on Earth would again be ignored while at the same time, and as suggested by Beck's (1992) notion of 'risk society', a technical fix (favoured by capital) to solve a socially made problem on Earth only creates new risks which need addressing by yet

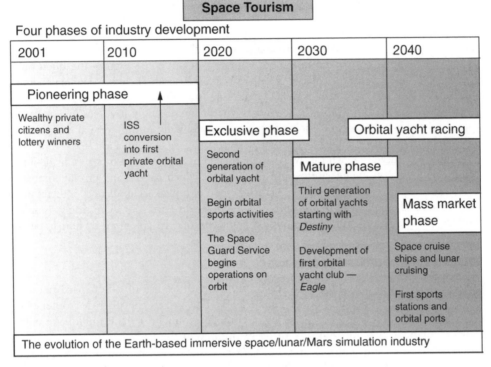

Space Tourism

Four phases of industry development

2001	2010	2020	2030	2040

Pioneering phase

Wealthy private citizens and lottery winners

ISS conversion into first private orbital yacht

Exclusive phase

Second generation of orbital yacht

Begin orbital sports activities

The Space Guard Service begins operations on orbit

Orbital yacht racing

Mature phase

Third generation of orbital yachts starting with *Destiny*

Development of first orbital yacht club — *Eagle*

Mass market phase

Space cruise ships and lunar cruising

First sports stations and orbital ports

The evolution of the Earth-based immersive space/lunar/Mars simulation industry

Figure 27.2 Four phases in the development of space tourism.
Source: Spencer and Rugg (2004).

more technologies. Space technology is a new stage in what Beck calls the 'chain of problem production and problem solution' (ibid.: 178).

A galactic mode of accumulation

Using Marx's concept of 'primitive accumulation', Harvey argues that the dominant contemporary form of attempted crisis resolution has been 'accumulation by dispossession' – a process by which those in power accumulate wealth not by productive activity but by dispossessing others of their rights to their own resources and sources of wealth (Harvey 2006). Attempted resolutions to crisis are forged by privatizing, commodifying, and marketing a previously non-capitalist 'outside'. Overaccumulated capital is capable of turning newly acquired resources and labour to profitable use where previously it had sat idle. With financial capital and institutions such as the International Money Fund to the fore, capitalism's outside has been thoroughly brought inside.

Whilst there may be no people currently living in space and working with its resources who might be dispossessed by this imperialism, it is, in David Harvey's terms, still an example of accumulation by dispossession. The United Nations Outer Space Treaty of 1967, to which we return later, confirmed an international consensus that outer space is 'the province of all mankind' and stated that 'outer space, including the Moon and other celestial bodies, is not subject to national appropriation by means of use or occupation, or by any other means'. All subsequent attempts to appropriate outer space are therefore

543

acts of dispossession. And there are signs that these are giving rise to new inter-imperial rivalries. That capital has turned its sights to the heavens is indication of its ongoing crises. Just as they have done in the past, these crises necessitate spatial fixes, or in this case 'outer spatial' fixes (Harvey's term adapted in Dickens and Ormrod 2007).

Our central point is that the imminent conquest of outer space raises the question of 'outside' and 'inside' yet again. Harvey's 'tertiary' circuit has long included state expenditures being channelled into fixes such as military hardware, surveillance satellites, and the International Space Station. But Harvey's 'secondary circuit' increasingly involves investment in a previously non-capitalist 'outside'; a zone, and a potentially infinite one at that, waiting to be exploited in a new phase of industrial production. Capitalism, in short, has the universe in its sights; an 'outside' which can be privately owned or appropriated by states, made into a commodity for use in manufacturing and an entity for which nations and private companies can compete. What might be termed a 'galactic mode of capital accumulation' is therefore in prospect; one still exploiting populations and resources on Earth but increasingly using the resources of outer space. And in due course the universe may be colonized by human beings.

Galactic commodification and space law

The overall position regarding both space tourism and the use of outer space resources can be summarized with the aid of Figure 27.3. This shows the plans for outer-space exploitation by one company, SpaceDev, a company founded by the millionaire entrepreneur Jim Benson who originally made his money in the early computer industry. It indicates the ambitions and the time-horizons envisaged by this kind of sector, starting with the satellites already sold, continuing with space resource extraction in about five years time, a space tourism station in about 6 years and, around 2020, self-sustaining settlements in orbit and on planets around 2020.

But such plans are now generating major debates over property-relations in outer space and the relations between governments and private capital. As Harvey (2003: 91) argues, capital prefers to work within a state framework which safeguards their activities by law, and only if necessary by force. The most optimistic proponents of space exploitation argue that space resources are infinite and there will be enough for all nations to own plenty of space. Considering the immensity of space as a whole, this is obviously true. But it is the nearer parts of space that will be the most profitable and viable to exploit (Hulstroj 2002). This is now leading to increasing pressure for private ownership to replace the public ownership stance of the United Nations.

There are two UN outer space treaties. The 1967 Treaty (usually referred to as 'The Outer Space Treaty') is the principle basis for most international space law. It was negotiated by the United States and the Soviet Union as a means of arresting the militarization of outer space and it proposes that national sovereignty over any part of outer space cannot be asserted by any nation. Although the sentiment of the Treaty was to prevent the commodification of the nearby universe the wording was left unclear. This led to lawyers and politicians in the US arguing that, firstly, although private property in outer space was not allowed, resources found there could be claimed. This was upheld by the UN. Furthermore, the 1979 'Moon Agreement' explicitly stated that space resources could be appropriated by states, but that the benefits of doing so must be equitably shared amongst all countries, with special consideration for the needs and interests of developing countries. This Treaty was not, however, signed up to by the USSR, the UK, and the United States (see Gorove 1991; Hulstroj 2002).

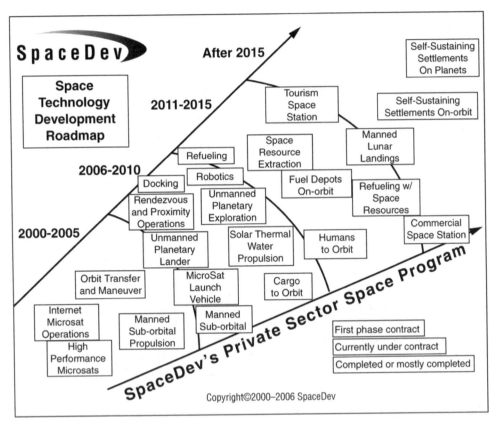

Figure 27.3 SpaceDev's space technology development roadmap.
Source: SpaceDev Inc.

Secondly, it was argued that the Outer Space Treaty only prohibited claims by states, not by private companies (see Pop 2000 for a discussion). Most recently, expert legal opinion sympathetic to the commercialization of outer space has been arguing that the 1967 Treaty does in fact allow for private property rights on the Moon, Mars, and other celestial entities (Wasser and Jobes 2008; Space Settlement Institute 2008). In short, neoliberalist 'accumulation by dispossession' strategies should now, according to the increasing number of individuals and organizations promoting imperialism in outer space, be extended into the galaxy. Those pressing for the commercialization of outer space are also pressing for legislative changes (especially changes by the US government) conferring property titles in outer space without requiring people or their equipment to be physically located there. One recent suggestion is that 'reasonable' claims would be of 600,000 square miles around an initial permanent base. Such a claim would be for an area approximately the size of Alaska (Wasser and Jobes 2008).

Such galactic neoliberalism would be a clear logical next step to the investment of surplus capital on a merely global scale. But who is most likely to benefit? The proponents of outer space commercialization usually celebrate the benefits accruing to hard working, self-improving property-owners similar to those celebrated by Enlightenment philosophers such as John Locke. In practice it is more likely that powerful individuals and corporations would gain most. Analogies between the mythical smallholders celebrated by eighteenth-century philosophers and Jim Benson and Richard Branson (multimillionaires switching surplus cash from other enterprises) are clearly far-fetched.

Wars, property, and power blocs in capitalism's outside

Harvey notes a tension between 'capitalistic' and 'territorial' logics. Whilst a portion of capital remains necessarily fixed in space, it otherwise operates in a fluid way and on a global scale. Yet within particular 'regions', spatial configurations of capital become relatively stabilized (2003: 101). Governments, reflecting local social relations, can operate in ways which are uncongenial to fluid, global capital. At this point the stage is set for inter-bloc competition and even war. War is the ultimate form of capital devaluation and it can create undreamt-of scope for yet more capital investment.

As part of the outer spatial fixes under development, military space technology is now being developed for two main reasons (as acknowledged by Bruce Gagnon of the Global Network, see Dickens and Ormrod, 2007: 88). One is to give competing nations the ability to control accumulation by dispossession on Earth via space, as discussed earlier. The second is securing property and resources in outer space itself. This is actually pre-figured by the *Star Trek* science fiction series in which the primary role of 'the Federation' is the protection of capitalist mining colonies (Goulding 1985). The use of military means to protect private assets and conduct war in outer space has not yet occurred. But the means for doing so are already under active development by global society's main regional power-blocs: the USA, Europe, and China (Khanna 2008).

The USA: 'full spectrum dominance'

The binding purpose of US aerospace corporations and military strategists is complete social, military, and political power not only over the globe but throughout outer space. (Dennis 2008). As early as 1992 the then Undersecretary of Defence, Paul Wolfowitz, stated that the United States must 'prevent any hostile power from dominating a region whose resources would, under consolidated control, be sufficient to generate global power'. This is a clear demonstration of the way in which the great monopoly capitalist powers strive for hegemonic control. By 2001, and now as Deputy Secretary of Defense, Wolfowitz confirmed that this understanding of 'Pax Americana' had become main-stream strategic thinking and that access to the seas, to the air and to outer space would indeed all be governed by US authority. 'To control space', the US Space Command now argues, 'in order to protect US interests and investments', force will be projected 'in space, from space and into space' (cited in Global Network 2006). The European Commission's Galileo satellite navigation system, still in development, was intended to safeguard against the monopoly held by the US GPS system, but this threat has provoked suspicion and threats of attack from the US (Mean and Wilsdon 2004; Xinhua News Agency 2004). There is every possibility of US 'full spectrum dominance' in space, as well as on Earth, achieving quite the opposite results to those intended, sparking off resistances from other states and coalitions of states also attempting to protect *their* territories and resources in outer space. Underlining Harvey's point about the fluidity of capital, however, American-based armaments and space companies including Boeing and Northrop-Grumman are also actively lobbying for business in Brussels.

Europe: 'new things to chew on'

In Europe there are close working connections between political leaders and those with economic power, as have been recognized in the US for a long time under the label of the military-industrial (or military-space-industrial) complex. For example, one of the largest industrial groupings in Europe is the European Aeronautic Defence and Space Company (EADS), formed in 2000 as a merger between Daimler/Chrysler Aerospace, Aerospatiale and Construcciones Aeronauticas. Making both civil and military equipment including satellites and space vehicles, it has exercised considerable influence on the European Commission's thinking. As an EADS director put it in 2001, 'industry cannot put forward institutional or policy changes, of course, but it can give EU and national politicians new things to chew on' (Slijper 2005: 22).

One of the 'new things to chew on' is the supposed growing need for an aerospace industry focused on defence and military programmes at the expense of the civil sector. Though the European outer space sector industrial remains more focused on civil applications than that in the US (Mean and Wilsdon 2004), this has indeed been the way in which European space policy has developed since 2001 (Slijper 2005).

China: Star Wars in the east

The imperialisms of the United States and Russia were originally the chief generators of the state-driven Chinese space program in the 1950s. Nuclear armed ballistic missiles were seen by the Chinese authorities as the way to counter both the American threat in Taiwan and the supposed threat from the Soviet Union (Dellios 2005). China now possesses what one commentator calls 'one of the oldest, largest, and most diversified military-industrial complexes in the world', consisting of some 300,000 engineers and technicians working in about 1,000 enterprises employing a total of three million workers. It is now attempting to open up private sector competition for contracts through new 'defense industry enterprise groups' (Bitzinger 2005). Despite its supposedly primitive form, China's military power in space is growing (David 2006). One indicator is their recent destruction of one of their old weather satellites with a ground-based missile, which sent shockwaves round the Western world (Kaufman and Linzer 2007). This development can be seen as part of an embryonic Chinese 'star wars' programme. As such, it has triggered alarm in the Pentagon and was followed soon afterwards by a missile from US Navy vessel destroying an inoperable spy satellite.

Such are the key power-bloc rivals, each seeking to imperialize by making spatial fixes either on Earth or, in due course, in outer space. As outlined earlier, these territorial rivalries, orchestrated by national and regional politicians, are essential to the competitive industrial and financial system operating at a global scale. As such, they form an important part of regional spatial (and, increasingly, outer spatial) 'fixes'. Yet they are, potentially at least, profoundly destructive. The competition for resources combined with the intensification of military production could well turn into outright armed wars, especially if US-style unilateralism prevails.

Legitimation and power in outer space

The use of public funds to promote economic and political growth into outer space as described above needs to be legitimated. As Marx pointed out, capitalism survives largely because capitalist states' practices are couched in terms of general, universal values rather than in terms of the factional interests and struggles of which a capitalist economy is composed. Different groups within the imperializing powers engage in a range of universalizing practices.

Firstly, the massive military space investments benefitting large corporations have also started to utilize a more innocuous discourse in talking about 'defence' rather than conquest. Arms lobbyists have recently been recommended by the European Space Agency to use 'civil society language'. 'Protecting civil society and the freedom of citizens' is deemed a better alternative to 'macho ads with missiles and fighter planes' (Slijper 2005: xx). Indeed the Missile Defense Advocacy Alliance in the US use the slogan 'protecting our world, our nation, our families, our way of life'.

Second, there is considerable emphasis on the 'pure', universal, scientific knowledge to be supposedly gained by outer space exploration. The latest dramatic pictures of asteroids, the Moon, and Mars are used by NASA as a means of capturing the public imagination. Pro-space organizations such as Carl Sagan's Planetary Society support exploration in the name of science, though less keen on development and colonization. Even the space tourism industry has suggested its clients will be able to conduct scientific experiments for the good of humanity.

Thirdly, there is considerable stress on the benefits of outer spatial fixes to the global environment and to the world population. The European Space Agency (2000), for example, emphasizes the monitoring of ecological conditions by satellite in the context of 'the challenge to the planetary environment.' The Google Earth Outreach programme uses satellite pictures of the Earth to aid a number of non-profit causes, and made the news recently as its pictures are being used to track deforestation in the Amazon and to help the Surui tribe in particular to defend their traditional way of life using modern technology. Intelsat's Satellites for Rural Health and Education programme in the 1980s in another seeming positive application. The UN Moon Agreement proposed that developing countries should receive share of the economic benefits of space exploitation, but, when it was not ratified, projects which supplied services from which it was thought the third world could benefit were promoted instead (for example by the UN Programme on Space Applications). These examples suggest that it is not only the West that benefits from satellite services.

A fourth discourse, which is used by governments and pro-space groups alike (e.g. the Mars Society) hinges around humanity's innate need to explore. In 1961, for example, NASA asserted 'man's questing spirit' as a rationale for visiting the moon. More recently, the European Union has talked of 'the timeless thirst for exploration and discovery' in justifying space exploration (ESA 2000: 18). Questionable sociobiological arguments are drawn on by pro-space activists to support a theory that curiosity and a desire to explore are genetically determined either in individuals, particular species or in organisms in general (see Dickens and Ormrod 2007: 169–172). Although not always recognized as such, this is quite different from the argument that exploration of the frontier is a fundamental part of the American national character, promoting an individualist survivalism. This argument was first outlined in regard to the Western frontier by Frederick Jackson Turner and utilized most recently by George W. Bush when announcing his Moon–Mars Initiative in 2004. Gerard O'Neill entitled his 1984 book *The High Frontier*, an idea that has very much stuck in pro-space circles.

Leading on from this, there has been a movement in pro-space circles (which used to include far more activists from different political persuasions) towards a libertarian discourse which fits more directly with the increasing privatization of space activity. This ideology often originates with observations about the limits to growth faced by the global economy. But it couches the problem predominantly in terms of the constraints this is starting to place on the ability of Western consumers to consume as much as they would like. This they claim to be a curtailing of their freedom, and they see expansion into space and the only was of achieving the unlimited growth necessary for them to prosper as individuals. Furthermore, they see this dream as necessary in inspiring disillusioned young people (see Dickens and Ormrod 2007: 165–9).

From a global to a true cosmopolitanism

Our argument has major implications for social identity and the politics of outer space. Addressing recent sociological literature on cosmopolitanism is a good way to restate our argument and some political implications (e.g. Beck and Sznaider 2005; Beck 2006; Turner 2006). Current developments such as environmental crises, terrorism, and Earthly conflicts of many kinds all militate, it is argued, for a 'cosmopolitan' citizenship and identity. This recognizes global society as a single moral community while simultaneously recognizing 'difference' and 'otherness' within that community. This version of cosmopolitanism echoes the argument discussed earlier, that 'the outside' is now fully 'inside'. As Beck and Sznaider (2005: 160) put it, 'rooted cosmopolitanism points out that in a postcolonial world, there is no pure, precolonized nation to go back to.'

But in light of our argument that outer space is capitalism's new outside, we suggest that the concept of 'cosmopolitanism' should again be revisited. It is useful to recall the kind of cosmopolitanism developed by Ancient Greek philosophers from the Stoic and Cynic traditions. The cosmos, rather than the immediate locality in which people lived, was seen by these Ancients as the common denominator affecting literally everyone's lives. It, rather than the city and its artificial laws, is the true home of humanity. The emancipatory aim of the Stoic and Cynic philosophers such as Diogenes and Zeno was to enable everyone to become a cosmic citizen, sharing a common existence within a set of laws literally affecting everyone.

What, according to these Ancients, should relations with the cosmos be? According to the Stoics and Cynics, it was to be an undivided, commonly-possessed, entity. Within such an entity wise cosmic 'sages' should 'graze' like herd animals over common pasture. Contemporary philosophers such as Gilles Deleuze and Felix Guatari share the Cynics' and Stoics' relative indifference to the city or region where one happened to have been born. They too promote the idea of an undivided cosmos available for all people to traverse like 'nomads' (Deleuze and Guatari 1987; Sellars 2007).

The vision of cosmopolitanism offered by Cynic–Stoic philosophers also entails a radically different vision of human 'freedom' from that now being offered and pursued in the cosmos as it is 'opened for business'. Contemporary ideals of 'freedom' are often couched in terms of the individual freedom to consume. And it is indeed this kind of freedom that is now being pursued by the vast majority of pro-space activists, including those promoting space travel. As we have elsewhere outlined in detail, such activists tend to be possessed of a psychology in which using outer space in accordance with their own personal desires and fantasies plays a central part (Ormrod 2007; Dickens and Ormrod 2007). It is above all a form of narcissism, one in which adults have not fully surrendered their childhood self and its expectation that the world, and now the cosmos, is simply out there to be controlled and consumed to satisfy human wants. The social implications of such 'freedom' are manifold. It is a freedom sometimes enjoyed by elites but with the great mass of people not being able to realize such freedoms, even if granted them in principle.

The alternative view of freedom implied in the writings of the Cynics and Stoics is a corrective to possessive individualism and to the entrepreneurs and the many pro-space

549

activists hoping to extend the 'free market' vision of freedom out into the solar system. The cosmopolitanism outlined by them suggests an alternative kind of undivided space outside of the state's division and allocation of land. Instead of just incorporating this outside within capitalist social relations, there is now an opportunity to use it for the enhancement of all. Fulfilment is more likely to be found through social interaction and interaction with the cosmos in a commonly-held space rather than through continued acquisition of private property for individual consumption. The coming humanization of the cosmos therefore offers the opportunity for making our cosmic society very different from that on Earth.

Aspirations and visions of this kind will need new alliances and political practices. One suggestive example comes in the form of the Global Network Against Weapons and Nuclear Power in Space. As this movement asserts, there are many pressing issues to be confronted down here on Earth, not least the conversion of armaments-production into institutions aimed at directly fulfilling many human needs. Owning and controlling parts of the universe will lead to yet more inequalities and potential dangers not only on Earth but now in outer space. From within the Earthly 'empire' of capitalism comes resistance to continued imperialism as it threatens to dispossess the world of its cosmos; a cosmos to which activists ascribe meaning and value.

Given an ideal of cosmic cosmopolitanism and alternative social and political coalitions, the original intentions of the 1967 Outer Space Treaty could be revived with a much more explicit ban on private property in outer space. Humanizing the cosmos does not have to be imperialistic, warlike and dominated by the economically and politically powerful. Popular control over space-humanization could lead to the creation of alternative social, environmental, and political priorities.

Popular culture: towards a cosmic mode of production

One way of envisaging, developing, and promoting such alternatives is via science fiction. Science fiction can mount a radical critique, offering not only escapism but fictions which can be learnt from and which suggest alternative futures (Parker et al. 2007). A case of popular culture posing critique comes from George Lucas, the director of the *Star Wars* Films. As an anti-war propagandist he offers a commentary on the greed, aggressiveness, hatred, and fear underlying war (Lancashire 2002). Still more relevant to this chapter, he attacks the greedy corporations whose interests are served by war. The parallel with American society is made clearer in the prequels to the initial trilogy, in which we witness the formation of the Empire. Here Lucas is deliberately critical of American society, represented by the Republic, which turns its back on democracy to become the Empire. Separatists work a deal with corporations (the Trade Federation) to destroy the Republic, bringing 'profits beyond your wildest imagination'. The Republic, motivated by fear, is manipulated by greedy and ambitious rulers into investing in the development of immense military power. In the later films the Empire will ironically be defeated by distinctly American rebels seeking freedom. Such, for Lancashire, is Lucas's portrayal of the cycle of empire.

An example contemplating alternative forms of society in space is Kim Stanley Robinson's trilogy of books on a Martian mining colony, exploring the ethics of exporting capitalism to the rest of the solar system. In the first book, 'Red Mars', groups of Martian settlers break away from the capitalist mining operations to establish their own social orders based on socialist, environmentalist, and even nudist principles.

Science fiction literature and film can condense and project a vision for a new kind of cosmic society, one with major implications for how Earthly society may be re-organized.

On the other hand, they are often detached from harsh contemporary realities. They describe conditions in galaxies 'far, far away' and do little to critique the contemporary power-relations underlying cosmic expansion. This work must be left to less glamorous contemporary politicians and activists.

A more progressive cosmic mode of production could conceivably emerge out of the increasingly divisive, unequal and dangerous capitalist mode which has spawned the humanization of outer space. Science fiction, combined with the kinds of philosophy offered by the Cynics and Stoics two thousand years ago, offers a vision of what a true cosmopolitanism could look like.

Acknowledgements

We wish to thank the European Space Agency, Apogee Books, and SpaceDev Inc. for permission to reproduce the images in Figures 27.1, 27.2 and 27.3, respectively.

References

Adorno, T. (2002 [1941]) 'On popular music', in Leppert, C. (ed.) *Essays on Music*, Berkeley: University of California Press: 437–69.

Air Force (2006) 'Air Force Doctrine 2–2'. Online. Available HTTP: www.fas.org/irp/doddin/usaf/afddz_z.pdr (accessed 19 July 2007).

Appadurai, A. (1990) 'Disjuncture and difference in the global cultural economy', in M. Featherstone (ed.) *Global Culture*, London: Sage.

Baudrillard, J. (1995) *The Gulf War Did Not Take Place*, Bloomington, IN: Indiana University Press.

Beck, U. (1992) *The Risk Society*, London: Sage.

——(2006) *Cosmopolitan Vision*, Oxford: Polity.

Beck, U. and Sznaider, N. (2005) 'Cosmopolitan sociology' in Ritzer, G. (ed.) *Encyclopaedia of Social Theory*, Thousand Oaks: Sage.

Bell, T. E. (1981) 'Space activism', *Omni*, Februrary: 50–4 and 90–4.

Benkler, J. (2006) *The Wealth of Networks*, New Haven, CT: Yale University Press.

Billings, L. (2006) 'Exploration for the masses? Or joyrides for the ultra rich? Prospects for space tourism', *Space Policy*, 22: 162–4.

Bitzinger, R. (2005) 'The PRC's defense industry: reform without improvement'. Online. Available HTTP: www.jamestown.org/publications_details.php?volume_id=&issue_id=3263&article_id=2369416 (accessed 12 May 2008).

Blum, T. (2005) *Rogue State*, London: Zed.

Brewer, A. (1990) *Marxist Theories of Imperialism (2nd edn)*, London: Routledge.

Castells, M. (2004 [1996]) *The Information Age (Vol. 1): The Rise of the Network Society*, Oxford: Blackwell.

David, L. (2006) 'China's military space power growing'. Online. Available HTTP: www.space4peace.org/gnbot.htm (accessed 23 June 2008).

Deblois, B. (2003) 'The advent of space weapons', *Astropolitics*, 1(1): 29–53.

Debord, G. (1994 [1967]) *The Society of the Spectacle*, New York: Rebel Press.

Deleuze, G. and Guattari, F. (1987) *A Thousand Plateaux*, London: Continuum.

Dellios, R. (2005) 'China's space program: a strategic and political analysis'. *Culture Mandala,* Vol. 7 (1). Online. Available HTTP: www.international-relations.com/CM7-1WB/ChinasSpaceWB.htm (accessed 10 May 2008).

Dennis, K. (2008) 'Global gridlock: how the US military-industrial complex seeks to contain and control the Earth and Its eco-system', Online. Available HTTP: www.globalresearch.ca/index.php?context=va&aid=8499 (accessed 12 May 2008).

Dickens, P. (2009) 'The cosmos as capitalism's outside', in Parker, M. and Lee, D. (eds) *Cultures of Space Travel*, London: Blackwell.

Dickens, P. and Ormrod, J. (2007). *Cosmic Society: towards a sociology of the universe*, London: Routledge.

Ehricke, K. A. (1972) 'In-depth exploration of the solar system and its utilization for the benefit of Earth', *Annals of the New York Academy of Sciences*, 187(1): 427–56.

European Space Agency (2000) *Investing in Space: the challenge for Europe*, Report by Long-Term Space Policy Committee. Online. Available HTTP: www.esa.int/esapub/sp/sp2000/sp2000.pdf (accessed 14 August 2008).

Foster, J. B. (2006) *Naked Imperialism: the US pursuit of global dominance*, New York: Monthly Review Press.

Foucault, M. (1977) *Discipline and Punish*, trans. A. Sheridan, New York: Vintage.

Garfinkel, S. (2000) *Database Nation: the death of privacy in the 21st century*, Sebastopol, CA: O'Reilly.

Gergen, K. (1991) *The Saturated Self*, New York: Basic Books.

Global Network Against Weapons and Nuclear Power in Space (2006) 'War from space'. Video of workshop at World Peace Forum, Vancouver, Canada, June 2006. Available HTTP: www.space4peace.org/ (accessed 17 February 2007).

Globus, A. (2005) 'Space settlement basics'. Online. Available HTTP: http:www.nas.nasa.gov/About/ Education/SpaceSettlement/Basics/www.html (accessed 10 April 2007).

Gorove, S. (1991) *Developments in Space Law*, Dordrecht: Martinus Nijhoff.

Goulding, J. (1985) *Empire, Aliens and Conquest*, Toronto: Sisyphus.

Hardt, M. and Negri, A. (2000) *Empire*, Cambridge, MA: Harvard University Press.

——(2006) *Multitude*, Harmondsworth: Penguin.

Harvey, D. (1982) *The Limits to Capital*, Oxford: Basil Blackwell.

——(1989) *The Condition of Postmodernity*, Oxford: Blackwell.

——(2003) *The New Imperialism*, Oxford University Press.

——(2005) 'The Urban Process Under Capitalism' in Fyfe N. R. and Kenny, J. T. (eds) *The Urban Geography Reader*, London: Routledge.

——(2006) 'A Conversation with David Harvey', *Logos*, 5(1). Online. Available HTTP: www.logosjournal. com/issue_5.1/harvey.htm (accessed 29 July 2008).

Hobsbawm, E. (1987) *The Age of Empire*, London: Weidenfeld.

Hudgins, E. (2002) (ed.) *Space: The Free Market Frontier*, Washington DC: Cato Institute.

Hulstroj, P. (2002) 'Beyond global: the international imperative of space', *Space Policy*, 18(2): 107–16.

Kaufman, M. and Linzer, D. (2007) 'China criticized for anti-satellite missile test', *Washington Post*, 19 January.

Khanna, P. (2008) *The Second World*, Harmondsworth: Allen Lane.

Kilgore, D. (2003) *Astrofuturism: Science, Race and Visions of Utopia in Space*, Philadelphia, PA: University of Pennsylvania Press.

Lancashire, S. (2002) 'Attack of the Clones and the politics of *Star Wars*', *Dalhousie Review*, 82(2): 235–53.

Lefebvre, H. (1976) *The Survival of Capitalism: Reproduction of the Relations of Production*, New York: St. Martin's Press.

Lenin, V. (2004 [1939]) *Imperialism: The Highest Stage of Capitalism*, New York: International Publishers.

Leonard, T. (2008) 'Google's founder books his space seat' *Daily Telegraph*, 12 June.

Lewis, J. (1996) *Mining the Sky*, Reading, MA: Addison-Wesley.

Lucas, M. and Wallner, M. (1993) 'Resistance by satellite', in T. Dowmunt (ed.) *Channels of Resistance*, London: British Film Institute and Channel 4 TV.

Luxemburg, R. (2003 [1913]) *The Accumulation of Capital*, London: Routledge.

Lyon, D. (1988) *The Information Society*, Cambridge: Polity.

——(2001) *Surveillance Society: The Monitoring of Everyday Life*, Buckingham: Open University Press.

Lyon, D. and Zureik, E. (eds) (1994) *Computers, Surveillance and Privacy*, Minneapolis, MN: University of Minnesota.

Macauley, M. (2000) 'Can power from space compete?' *Space Policy*, 16: 283–5.

Macauley, M. and Davis, J. (2002) 'An economic assessment of space solar power as a source of electricity for space-based activities', *Space Policy*, 18: 45–55.

Meadows, D., Radners, J. and Meadows, D. (1972) *The Limits to Growth*, New York: Earth Island.

——(2005) *Limits to Growth: The 30-year Update*, London: Earthscan.

Mean, M. and Wilsdon, J. (2004) *Masters of the Universe: Politics and the New Space Race*, London: Demos.

NASA (2008). 'America Starts for the Moon: 1957–1963', Online. Available HTTP: http://history. nasa.gov/SP-4214/ch1-3.html (accessed 15 July 2008).

O'Connor, J. (1996) 'The second contradiction of capitalism', in T. Benton (ed.) *The Greening of Marxism*, New York: Guilford.

O'Neill, G. K. (1989) *The High Frontier: Human Colonies in Space*, Burlington, Ontario: Collector's Guide Publishing.

Ormrod, J. S. (2007) 'Pro-space activism and narcissistic phantasy', *Psychoanalysis, Culture and Society*, 12(3): 260–78.

Parker, M., Fournier, V., Reedy, P. (eds) (2007) *The Dictionary of Alternatives: utopianism and organization*, London: Zed Books.

Pelton, J. N. (2004) 'New opportunities and threats for 21st century life' in J. N. Pelton, R. J. Oslund and P. Marshall (eds) *Communications Satellites: Global Change Agents*. Mahwah, NJ: Lawrence Erlbaum Associates.

Pelton, J. N., Oslund, R. J. and Marshall, P. (eds) (2004) *Communications Satellites: Global Change Agents*, Mahwah, NJ: Lawrence Erlbaum Associates.

Pop, V. (2000) 'Appropriation in outer space: the relationship between land ownership and sovereignty on the celestial bodies', *Space Policy*, 16: 275–82.

Poster, M. (1995) *The Second Media Age*, Cambridge: Polity.

Retort (2005) *Afflicted Powers: Capital and Spectacle in a New Age of War*, London: Verso.

Robinson, P. (2002) *The CNN Effect: The Myth of News, Foreign Policy and Intervention*, London: Routledge.

Sellars, J. (2007) 'Deleuze and cosmopolitanism', *Radical Philosophy*, 142: 30–37.

Simons, B., Lartey, E. and Cudjoe, F. (2007) 'One thing China can't offer Africa.' *Asia Times,* 1 February.

Slijper, F. (2005) *The emerging EU Military-Industrial Complex: Arms Industry Lobbying in Brussels*, Transnational Institute Briefing Series 2005/1.

Smith, N. (1984) *Uneven Development: Nature, Capital and the Production of Space*, Oxford: Blackwell.

Space Settlement Institute (2008) 'The Space Settlement Initiative', Online. Available HTTP: www. spacesettlement.org/ (accessed 20 June 2008).

Space Foundation (2008) 'Space report'. Online. Available HTTP: www.thespacereport.org (accessed 24 June 2008).

Spencer, J. and Rugg, K. (2004) *Space Tourism: Do You Want To Go?* Burlington, Ontario: Apogee.

Steven, P. (2003) *Global Media*, London: Verso.

Turner, B. (2006) 'Classical sociology and cosmopolitanism: a critical defence of the social', *British Journal of Sociology*, 57 (1): 131–151.

Urry, J. (2002) *The Tourist Gaze*, London: Sage.

Veblen, T. (1963) *The Theory of the Leisure Class*, New York: New American Library.

Virilio, P. (1997) *Open Sky*, London: Verso.

——(1998) 'Military space', in J. Der Derian (ed.) *The Virilio Reader*, Oxford: Blackwell.

Virilio, P. and Lotringer, S. (1998) *Pure War*, New York: Columbia University.

Wasser, A. and Jobes, D. (2008) 'Space settlements, property rights and international law: could a lunar settlement claim the lunar real estate it needs to survive?' *Journal of Air Law and Commerce*, 73 (1): 38–73.

Weinberg, S. (2007) 'Nobel Laureate Disses NASA's Manned Space Flight', Online. Available HTTP: www.space.com/news/070918_weinberg_critique.html (accessed 9 May 2008).

Weiner, T. (2004) 'Pentagon envisaging a costly internet for war', *New York Times*, 13 November.

Whitaker, R. (2000) *The End of Privacy: How Total Surveillance is Becoming a Reality*, Melbourne: Scribe.

Williams, R. (1974) *Television: Technology and Cultural Form*, London: Fontana.

Wirbel, L. (2004) *Star Wars: US Tools of Space Supremacy*, London: Pluto.

Xinhua News Agency (2004) 'Earth must resist US monopoly of space'. Online. Available HTTP: www.spacedaily.com/news/china-04zzv.html (accessed 1 April 2007).

Zubrin, R. (1999) *Entering Space: Creating a Spacefaring Civilization*, New York: Tarcher.

28

Globalization and Americanization

Stephen Mennell

'Nothing is more fruitless, when dealing with long-term social processes', remarked Norbert Elias (2006: 249), 'than to attempt to locate an absolute beginning.' Many years ago, I pointed out that even globalization, which is so often seen as something that began in the 1990s, or perhaps after the Second World War, in fact has no meaningful starting point (Mennell, 1990). At most, one can say that the survival groups on which most people depend for the basic requirements of their lives have, over many millennia, grown larger and fewer in number; and that the chains of interdependence that link survival units to each other have become more numerous and tighter. Such chains include bonds of rivalry, hostility, and violence as well as of collaboration, amity, and peaceful coexistence. Viewed in this long-term perspective, globalization has been driven as much by war as by the expansion of trade and contact between cultures.

But, in a more conventional perspective, the term globalization is often used almost as a synonym for Americanization – for the rise to military, economic, financial, and cultural dominance of the United States of America, since 1990 the self-proclaimed sole super-power. The period 1945–90, when the USA and the USSR, with their respective networks of allies, confronted each other across the planet, was a key precursor period. Such bipolar figurations had existed before, but they had been regional rather than global in scope, with the result that the victor in each contest was sooner or later confronted by opponents with roughly equivalent or greater power potential. What was different about the Cold War, Elias (2007: 154, but writing in 1980–81) pointed out, was that 'in the present phase of the millennial elimination struggle, all possible actors are already on stage'. In another essay, he foresaw the collapse of one of the rival parties to the conflict as one possible outcome, in which 'unification of the world under a central monopoly would be brought about – a world state under the leadership of one of the two hegemonic powers' (Elias, 2008a: 103), but did not live quite long enough to witness the formal dissolution of the Soviet Union or the USA's more or less conscious and intentional attempt to fulfil his prophecy.

Both globalization and Americanization need to be studied in long-term perspective, but not as two separate things: to assume that, because two words exist, there must be two separate processes is to fall into the fallacy of misplaced concreteness. Nevertheless, the period of American supremacy – brief as it may prove to have been[1] – is of peculiar interest. It is tempting to interpret the phase of American world dominance as only one more manifestation of the cyclical rise and fall of great powers (Kennedy, 1988), and that may indeed prove to be the correct interpretation. Yet the absence of a major rival since the fall of Communism has given the power of the USA unparalleled reach. Its power has had military, economic, and cultural components, not existing in separate 'spheres', but inextricably (if incoherently) interwoven with each other (Mann, 2003). I have found that Elias's theory of civilizing and decivilizing processes helpful in exploring this tangled web (Mennell, 2007). On the model of his most famous book (Elias, 2000 [1939]), I shall begin by discussing the shaping of American social habitus.

Americanization of habitus

In one respect, Elias was wrong: there *is* an absolute beginning for Americanization, even if by sociologists' usual standards it is a long time ago. For, I would argue, the central experience shaping Americans' social habitus is of becoming ever more powerful in relation to their neighbours, and that process began almost immediately after the first European settlements in North America in the early sixteenth century.

At first glance, that seems to be at odds with the popular perception of the social character of Americans, whose manners are generally seen to reflect the egalitarian character of American society. The truth is a little more complicated than that.

In the earliest days of English settlement in North America, society was indeed relatively flat. The settlers included very few members of the upper class of the parent society in England – no aristocrats or members of the gentry to speak of. The early elite consisted of university-educated clerics and lawyers, along with merchants – people who would have perhaps been considered prosperous middle class at home. But equally, few members of the very poorest strata made the journey across the Atlantic. In spite of that, the settlers did bring with them the acute status-consciousness of English society, and in the course of the later seventeenth and eighteenth centuries a fairly considerable colonial gentry emerged, consciously modelling itself on the English gentry. After Independence, this gentry was largely eclipsed – except in the slave-owning South, of course. The agrarian republic that Alexis de Tocqueville visited in the early 1830s represented American society in its most egalitarian phase, the age of Jacksonian Democracy. Tocqueville pictured at length the relatively easy and informal manners to be seen in the relations between men and women, masters and servants, even officers and other ranks in the army. In a telling comparison with Britain, he wrote:

> In America, where the privileges of birth never existed and where riches confer no peculiar rights on their possessors, men unacquainted with each other are very ready to frequent the same places, and find neither peril nor advantage in the free interchange of their thoughts. ... their manner is therefore natural, frank and open.
>
> (Tocqueville, 1961 [1835–40]: I, 202–30)

In contrast, English people encountering each other by chance were typically reserved, from fear that a casual acquaintance – struck up when travelling abroad for instance – would prove an embarrassment when they returned to the rigidly demarcated social boundaries at home.

Yet the later nineteenth century, the Gilded Age of rapid industrial growth and the formation of vast fortunes, was in America too a period of intense social competition, as waves of *nouveaux riches* battered down the gates of the old social elites. This is well depicted in the novels of Edith Wharton. Status distinctions became more marked, manners books sold in large numbers to people who wanted to emulate not just the ways of the old upper classes America, but also the manners of the European upper classes (Schlesinger, 1947). There were even attempts to introduce the practice of chaperoning, though not with much success – egalitarian traditions still retained some force.

This period may seem an aberration. With some fluctuations, the twentieth century saw the trend reversed, and 'informalization' became dominant (Wouters, 2007). It is not just a matter of easy 'have a nice day' manners; it also extends to relations between the sexes (Wouters, 2004).

It is important to stress that, although the connection is no doubt indirect and complicated, this trend of informalization ran broadly parallel to trends in the distribution of income and wealth in American society which, from 1913 until the last decades of the twentieth century and with some fluctuations, became relatively flatter compared with the Gilded Age. Today, however, we are living in a new Gilded Age, when in America (and to a lesser extent in Britain) the income and wealth of the top one per cent in particular has increased astronomically, while the poor are becoming poorer and the standard of living even of what the Americans call 'the middle class' (which includes skilled manual workers in steady employment) is static or falling.[2] Nor are rates of social mobility as great as is commonly believed: a recent study shows them to be lower in the USA (and in the UK) than in Canada, Germany, and the four Scandinavian countries (Blanden et al., 2005). I have spoken of the disparity between perception and reality as 'the curse of the American Dream' (Mennell, 2007: 249–65).

I cannot point to any evidence that the factually gross inequality of American society is yet reflected in a distancing in everyday manners. In the long term, manners tend to reflect the power ratios between people, and more egalitarian manners are generally taken as an index of a widening circle of 'mutual identification' (De Swaan, 1995; Mennell, 1994). But the late Leona Helmsley's notorious comment, that 'paying taxes is for little people', is only one bit of the abundant evidence of a callous disregard by the American rich for the welfare of the poor and middling sort of people. What prevails may not be a widening circle of mutual identification among all strata of the American people, but rather a kind of '*upwards* identification':[3] the American myth-dream of equality is actively promoted through the fostering of 'patriotism' – meaning American nationalism – among the middling and lower strata, but uncaring attitudes prevail among the holders of power to the large numbers of disadvantaged people. Their lot is still seen as being 'their own fault' – those in need are viewed, in an attitude that we used to consider characteristic of the nineteenth century, as 'the undeserving poor'.

Egalitarian manners in the contemporary USA are perhaps becoming an instance of what Marxists call 'false consciousness'. An alternative interpretation may, however, be derived from Cas Wouters's explanation of the apparent egalitarianism of manners *within* the British upper class at the end of the nineteenth century. The British elite tended to look askance at the apparent boastfulness and overt status striving of their American counterparts. Wouters argues that the boundaries of the British elite, especially those of London 'Society', were so clearly defined and universally recognized that those who belonged to it had no need to assert either their standing among fellow members or their superiority over those who did not. Such clear boundaries were absent in America: the

USA differs historically from many countries in Western Europe in that it never had a single national model-setting class that succeeded in monopolizing the moulding of manners and habitus. Today, however, the irony is that Americans today form a clearly defined elite for the world as a whole, and that their strong we-feelings as members of that elite diminishes the need for overt expressions of 'superiorism' *within* the USA. If that is indeed one consequence of a common American 'patriotism', it is not without precedent. At the height of British world power, Benjamin Disraeli (1872) looked to the working class for the preservation of the British empire: 'the people of England, and especially the working classes of England, are proud of belonging to a great country, and wish to maintain its greatness – that they are proud of belonging to an Imperial country, and are resolved to maintain, if they can, the empire … '.

A smouldering ember: the legacy of the south

America never had a nobility, but it had in effect several competing aristocracies. Among these, Massachusetts, with a passing footnote to Quaker Philadelphia, still looms too large in Europeans' perception of what shaped American social character. In New England, certainly, there took shape something like the German *Bildungsbürgertum*, an elite of educated professionals and merchants. To them, and to the pressures of commercial and professional life, can be attributed to a certain extent the egalitarian strain in American habitus, not showing open disdain towards their fellow citizens, even if they were inwardly confident of their superior education, understanding, and feeling. Visiting the USA in the 1830s, not long after Tocqueville, Harriet Martineau (1837: I, 10) commented upon the great cautiousness that was entrenched early and deeply in Northern people; she described as 'fear of opinion' something very similar to what Elias (2000: 70) termed the habitual 'checking of behaviour' in anticipation of what others would think. She thought she could distinguish Northern from Southern members of Congress simply by the way they walked:

> It is in Washington that varieties of manners are conspicuous. There the Southerners appear at most advantage, and the New Englanders to the least; the ease and frank courtesy of the gentry of the South (with an occasional touch of arrogance, however), contrasting with the cautious, somewhat *gauche*, and too deferential air of the members from the North. One fancies one can tell a New England member in the open air by his deprecatory walk. He seems to bear in mind perpetually that he cannot fight a duel, while other people can.
>
> (Martineau, 1837: I, 145)

Which brings us to the other great rival aristocracy, that of the slave-owning South. From the Constitution's coming into force until the Civil War, Southerners held the lion's share of political power in the Union.[4] The reference to duelling among them is highly significant. As Norbert Elias (1996: 44–119) argued, in nineteenth-century Germany the quality of *Satisfaktionsfähigkeit* – being judged worthy to give satisfaction in a duel – became a principal criterion for membership of the German upper class. And although the greatest plantation owners may have been more conscious of looking towards their counterparts in England or France, the more appropriate comparison is between them and the Prussian *Junkers* (Bowman: 1993). One similarity is that they both

557

provided a large part of the officer corps of the national army. At home, they both ruled autocratically over a *Privatrechtstaat* – they had the right to adjudicate and enforce their judgements on their own estates, with little or no interference by agencies of the government. State authorities did not intervene in relations between white masters and blacks, whether during slavery in the antebellum period or during the long decades of the Jim Crow laws and lynching between the end of Reconstruction (in 1876) and the interwar period. Nor did they intervene in what is now called 'black on black' violence. This absence has cast a long cultural shadow to the present day.[5]

But neither were white-on-white quarrels very much the business of state authorities. The social arrangements of the Old South were also associated with the prevalent code of 'honour', and questions of honour were commonly settled by the duel (Wyatt-Brown, 1982). Many European travellers, from Harriet Martineau to the great geologist Sir Charles Lyell, were astonished by its prevalence: it was remarked that in New Orleans alone, someone died in a duel on average every day (Nevins, 1948). The code of 'honour', in its various forms in Europe and America, has been widely discussed. Roger Lane (1997: 85–86) contrasts the Southern 'man of honour' with the New England 'man of dignity', who would very likely take a quarrel to court rather than fight a duel. The propensity to litigation through the legal apparatus of the state is a function not only – not mainly, indeed – of culturally conditioned individual dispositions, but also of the degree of internal pacification and the effectiveness of the state monopoly of the legitimate use of violence in a given territory. Yet the difference between the codes of 'honour' and 'dignity' *is* associated with different personal and emotional styles: the Southerner, like the *Satisfaktionsfähig* gentleman of the *Kaiserreich*, displayed a 'hard', unemotional style; it has been suggested that a legacy of this can be seen in the hard, speak-your-weight-machine delivery of many American military spokesmen today.

Other competing elites deserve to be mentioned – the relatively autonomous social elites of many American cities in the past, the plutocracy that arose after the Civil War and today exercises overwhelming economic and political power. Perhaps we should also mention the significance of Hollywood and the heroes and heroines of popular culture. But I want simply to return to the point that in our perceptions of America past and present, the New England model plays too large a part, and its rival from the South far too little – something that is of great importance given the massive shift in the power ratio in favour of the South since about 1970.

And there remains one great irony about American manners and habitus. If the USA has not, to the same extent as many countries of Western Europe, witnessed the formation of a monopolistic model-setting upper class, it can also be said that today America and Americans serve as just such an upper class for the rest of the world, including Europe. It was not always so. As Allan Nevins pointed out, until around 1825 British visitors to the USA were mainly working and middle class people, especially businessmen, who tended to speak with respect of the manners of the social equals they met. After 1825, however, more upper class and professional visitors arrived from Britain, and there is in general a more marked note of condescension in their reports about what they saw and the people they met. Subsequently, this trick of perspective was further complicated by the changing balance of power between Britain and America. By the inter-war years of the twentieth century,

> For the first time, the great majority of British visitors showed themselves distinctly respectful of the rich, powerful, and exceedingly complex nation beyond the seas.

During the period we have described as one of Tory condescension [1825–45], the travellers have tended to look down on the Americans; during the later period we have described as one of analysis [1870–1922], they tended to look at the United States with level gaze; but now they frequently tended to look up at America!

(Nevins, 1948: 403)

Today, some Americans think of the widespread appeal of American popular culture, and the constant emulation of American styles – from clothes to food to speech – as a form of 'soft power' wielded in the American interest. It may be as well to remember, though, that the *ancien régime* bourgeoisie desperately aped the courtiers – but that did not prevent them resenting the aristocracy. Nor did it prevent the French Revolution.

The formation of the American state and empire

There is a tendency – especially among Americans – to think about the United States as if it were an emanation of the human spirit, as if its existence and its constitutional arrangements were a bloodless product of the Enlightenment, John Locke, the genius of the Founding Fathers, and the pure democratic spirit of 'No taxation without representation!'.

In fact, the formation of the territorial unit that we now know as the USA was a bloody business, not at all dissimilar to the formation of states in Western Europe. If we look back a thousand years, Western Europe was fragmented into numerous tiny territories, each ruled – that is, protected *and* exploited – by some local warlord. Thinking of Afghanistan after the tender loving care of numerous foreign interventions is perhaps the closest present-day equivalent. Out of the patchwork, over a period of many centuries there gradually emerged a smaller number of larger territories. It was a violent 'elimination contest' (Elias, 2000: 263–78). It is a mistake to see the process as driven by 'aggression', as if the personality traits of individual warriors were the determining force. That would be to fall into the same trap of a one-sided cultural explanation as the 'pure Enlightenment' account of the USA's origins. In an age when the control of land was the principle basis of power, a peace-loving local magnate could not sit idly by while his neighbours slugged it out: the winner, who gained control over a larger territory, would then be able to gobble up the little peace-loving neighbour. War and 'aggression' thus had a survival value. The process was Janus-faced: as larger territories became *internally* pacified, the wars *between* territories came to be fought on a steadily larger scale.

In fact Elias hit the nail on the head when he drew a humorous comparison between medieval Europe and westward expansion in nineteenth-century USA: 'To some extent the same is true of the French kings and their representatives as was once said of the American pioneer: "He didn't want all the land; he just wanted the land next to his"' (Elias, 2000: 312). One difference between the two continents is that the struggle for territory after the beginnings of European settlement was initially driven exogenously by conflicts between the great powers back in Europe, as much as by rivalries endogenous to North America. In the early stages, the process somewhat resembled the struggle for territory in nineteenth-century Africa. Most of the early wars there were branches of contemporaneous wars in Europe, whether the Anglo-Dutch wars, the War of the Spanish Succession, the Seven Years War or whatever. Through these contests, first the Swedish colonies and then the Dutch were eliminated, and later French and Spanish power was broken. The various Indian tribes were also involved in these struggles as

559

allies of the European powers, and were simultaneously engaged in an elimination contest amongst themselves. Gradually, however, the struggles came to be shaped much more by endogenous forces, and especially by the logic of 'wanting the land next to his'.

This is not the place to retell the story of how American Independence came about, except to say that the taxation to which the settlers did not wish to contribute without representation arose from the costs of military control over a much larger territory after the effective elimination of the French from Canada and the trans-Appalachian region. But there is another side to the story besides this familiar one. The British had intended to reserve the Ohio Valley for their Iroquois allies, but settlers were already pressing westwards. As has been recognized at least since Theodore Roosevelt wrote *The Winning of the West* (1889–99), the War of Independence was also a war over the control of conquests. The colonials were also colonizers.

I shall not dwell upon what has been called the American Holocaust (Stannard, 1992), save to say that westward expansion at the expense of the Native Americans was driven by the pressure of land-hungry migrants pushing forward in advance of effective federal government control of the territory, in contrast with policies followed in the settlement of Canada and Siberia. The scenes with which we are familiar from the Western movies are a glamorized version of a process of conquest and internal pacification.

Americans are fond of pointing out that they *bought* much of their territory rather than conquering it by force of arms. That is certainly true of the Louisiana Purchase, which in 1803 doubled the federal territory. It arose, however, out of a particularly favourable conjunction in European power politics, when it suited Napoleon to be rid of extraneous responsibilities. It is also true that another huge acquisition of land took place when the United States paid Mexico for a vast swathe of territory. But that was only after it had impressed upon Mexico that this was an offer it could not refuse, by invading that unfortunate country and sacking its capital city. 'Poor Mexico! So far from God and so close to the United States', as President Porfirio Diáz later remarked. Ulysses Grant, who served as a young officer in the Mexican War, regarded the war as 'one of the most unjust ever waged by a stronger against a weaker nation. It was an instance of a republic following the bad example of European monarchies, in not considering justice in their desire to acquire additional territory' (Grant, 1994 [1885]: 37).

There is no point in moralizing about this and many other episodes. My point is not to denounce 'bad men' for what happened; that would be to fall into the same trap of individualism that infected the Bush regime's view of the world. My point is rather that American development was as a whole a relatively unplanned long-term social process. It is one instance of what Norbert Elias (1991: 64) enculated in his couplet

> From plans arising, yet unplanned
> By purpose moved, yet purposeless

On the other hand, the balance between the 'accidental' and the 'intended' tilts towards the planned pole as one party gains a great power advantage within a power ratio (Elias, 1978: 71–103). The interplay between the two can be seen in the acquisition of the first United States Empire in 1898, which followed neatly on from the 'closing of the frontier' declared in the 1891 census. It was not an accident that the completion of westward expansion led smoothly into the acquisition of overseas territories, including the Philippines, Hawaii, Puerto Rico, and, for a time, Cuba (Zimmerman, 2002). They marked America's re-entry into world politics. The United States invaded the Philippines, with

British support – the American fleet sailed from Hong Kong – because both powers feared that either Germany or Japan would do so if the USA did not. In a sense the wheel had turned full circle: the expansion of British North America had begun with wars that were overseas branches of European wars. But it was a really a spiral, not a circle, because now the wars were beyond the contiguous territory of the United States.

The Monroe Doctrine of American overlordship in the western hemisphere is a similar story. In 1819, the British proposed a joint declaration to oppose Spanish recolonization of South America. In the event, John Quincy Adams, as Secretary of State, insisted on its being in America's name alone. But there was no question of its applying to Britain's subsequent seizure of the Falkland Islands – the USA did not then have the power to prevent it. By the early twentieth century its power had greatly increased, and the Roosevelt Corollary to the Monroe Doctrine was used in justifying numerous American military interventions in Latin America throughout that century. By the early twenty-first, what I have called the 'Dubya Addendum' (Mennell, 2007: 211–12), propounded in the 2002 *National Security Strategy of the United States*, declared that the USA had the right to intervene against its opponents anywhere in the globe, and came very close to claiming for the American government a monopoly of the legitimate use of force throughout the world. In other words, in terms of Max Weber's definition of a state, the present regime has come close to declaring the USA a world state. In some ways, indeed, the USA does now act as a world government (Mandelbaum, 2006). It claims extra-territorial jurisdiction for its own laws in many fields, while itself refusing to be bound by the corpus of international law that most other countries accept. Its military expenditure is now as large as that of all the other countries in the world combined. It has in effect garrisoned the planet, dividing the entire globe into US military commands.[6] It now has military bases in two-thirds of the countries of the world, including much of the former Soviet Union.[7]

Yet there is another side to the coin. Historically, the USA always had what was in international terms a low 'military participation ratio' (Andreski, 1968) – in other words, it normally had a very small army in relation to its population (Mennell, 2007: 240–44). After each war – in the War of 1812, the Mexican war, the Civil War, the war with Spain, the First World War – its military establishment fell back to very low peacetime levels. But, for the first time, that did not happen after the Second World War. By 1961, in his famous farewell address to the nation, President Eisenhower (1961) warned his fellow Americans against what he christened 'the military–industrial complex'. His warning was not heeded. In effect, America has, ever since the Second World War, fought a series of 'splendid little wars'[8] that have had the latent function of keeping its economy going and feeding the congressional pork-barrel process.

Functional de-democratization and diminishing foresight

Pork-barrel politics remind us of the continuing populist 'pressure from below' within American society, but also of the inextricable entanglement of military and economic power. One of the most complex and apparently self-contradictory trends within glo-balization is that the pork-barrel process – defenders of which see it as a key component of democratic politics – is entirely compatible with very greatly increasing inequalities in the key power ratios both within the USA and between the USA and the rest of the world. 'Pressure from below' works effectively when it is also aligned with the economic, political or other interests of powerful players on a higher tier of the American political game.[9] Whether responsiveness to local interests within America is entirely appropriate when the US government claims to be acting in many respects as a *world* government is questionable: what about responsiveness to the interests of the rest of the world? Sooner or later, the rest of the world may begin to articulate a modern version of 'No taxation without representation', or to echo Bertolt Brecht's ironic remark, 'The people have failed; we must elect a new people'. More generally, I want to argue that increasingly unequal power ratios tend to promote shortsightedness in economic and political policy-making.

A key component of a civilizing process, according to Elias, is the spreading social pressure on people habitually to exercise foresight. This arose out of what he referred to as 'functional democratization', which he viewed as a dominant trend in increasingly complex and more closely integrated societies. His assumption seems to have been that, others things being equal, longer 'chains of interdependence' would involve relatively more equal power ratios between each link in the chain. Corresponding to the integration of more and more people into an ever more widespread worldwide network of interdependence was 'the necessity for an attunement of human conduct over wider areas and over longer chains of action than ever before', with commensurate standards of self-constraint (2000: 379). In order to play their part at their own node in a nexus of inter-dependences, individual people have acquired the social skills to anticipate all sorts of dangers, from breaches of social codes that cause embarrassment, through the dangers of economic risk, all the way to dangers to life and limb. The effective exercise of foresight involves trying to anticipate the unanticipated, foresee the unforeseen to deal with the side effects or unintended consequences of intended actions.

Processes of functional democratization were certainly a marked feature of the twentieth century, which witnesses an astonishing sequence of emancipation struggles: of workers, of colonial people, of ethic groups, of women, of homosexuals, of students, and so on. But what if, while the 'horizontal' expansion of chains of interdependence is marked by functional democratization, at the same time there is a growth of (so to speak) 'vertical' chains marked by *increasingly unequal* power ratios between the links? What if, in other words, there is also a trend towards functional *de*-democratization, with greater con-centrations of power in the higher reaches of American society, and in the higher reaches of the world hierarchy of states? Is it not likely that the result will be *diminishing foresight*?

Examples are not hard to find. America's invasion of Iraq in 2003 will doubtless go down in history as one of the most spectacular and counterproductive instances of lack of foresight. It is not merely that the American government invaded because it had the military means to do so, but that its policy making was infected by a high level of fantasy, and its military power advantage meant that there was inadequate pressure to test its assumptions in advance against reality, to make them more 'reality congruent' in Elias's phrase. Power, as Karl Deutsch (1963: 111) remarked, is 'the ability to talk instead of listen [and] the ability to afford not to learn'.

In the case of economic power, the problem is often that the 'externalities' of eco-nomic decisions are foreseen, but that corporations have the power to ignore them (Mennell, 2007: 114–17, 307–10): instances such as the effects of drilling for oil or of logging in forests upon local populations (and the environment) come to mind. The problem of global warming is the most serious illustration of this principle; for most of its existence, the regime of the second President Bush more or less denied the existence of the problem, and the USA, with five per cent of the world's population but producing about a quarter of its emissions of carbon dioxide, played the part on the world stage of an individual or company that denies any responsibility for the external costs it imposes on others. Not that the whole blame can be placed on the USA – action on global warming is a classic instance of an international oligopolistic deadlock – but the problem certainly cannot be taken in hand without the active involvement of the world's self-proclaimed most powerful nation. Until recently, the dominance in America and in global financial markets of what the Nobel prize-winning economist Joseph Stiglitz (2002) called *market fundamentalism* has tended to absolve individuals, organizations, and governments from wider ethical considerations regarding the consequences of their actions. The financial crash of 2008 may mark the end of all that – but it is too early to say.

Conclusion: America through the one-way mirror

If I am right in arguing that the central experience running right through American history is of the power ratios between the Americans and their neighbours swinging steadily in America's favour, there are important consequences.

When some people have a large power advantage, the experience affects in quite specific ways how they perceive themselves and others. This can be seen at every level from the microcosm of the partners in a marriage, for instance – right up to the macrocosm of international relations. The principle can be derived from Hegel's (1977: 111) discussion of the master–slave relationship, but its relevance struck me through the findings of a study of a Dutch refuge for battered women and of their violent partners. These were marital relationships with a very unequal power balance, and the authors (Van Stolk and Wouters, 1987) found that the women took much more notice of their men than the men did of the women, and the women were much more attuned to their men's wishes and needs than the men were to theirs. When the women were asked to give a character sketch of their partner, they could do so with considerable precision, nuance, and insight, while the men could not describe their wives except in terms of clichés applicable to women in general. It appears to be a general characteristic of the unequal power ratios in established outsiders relations that the outsiders 'understand' the established better than the established do the outsiders. This appears to apply to the grandest-scale established–outsider relation of all, between the US superpower and the rest of the world. Billions of educated people outside the USA know an immense amount about America, its constitution, its politics, its manners and culture; all these are extremely vizable to the rest of the world. But it is as if they were looking through a one-way mirror:[10] they cannot see the observers behind the mirror, and when they look in that direction they see only their own reflection. A mass of survey evidence suggests that Americans do not see out at all clearly, and tend to think about the 'outside world' if at all in stereotypical and indeed Manichean terms. (As always, there are of course large numbers of Americans of whom this is not true: we are speaking of general tendencies and differences in averages between Americans and, in particular, Europeans.) They tend to think and talk about themselves in terms of a national narrative based on the 'minority of the best'. That is sometimes coupled with an account of the rest of the world derived from a 'minority of the worst': there is always 'a horrendous foreign enemy at hand to blow us up in the night out of hatred of our Goodness and rosy plumpness' (Vidal, 2004: 6).[11] And perceptions matter: 'if men define situations as real, they are real in their consequences', as William Isaac Thomas famously remarked.

The financial crisis of 2008, which is in spectacular progress as I write, *may* prove to be an historical turning point. It looks as though it may carry away not just 'casino capitalism' but the ideology of market fundamentalism too. Somewhat more definitely, it is likely to mark a stage in the decline of the USA as a world power *relative* to a number of other countries. Western banks have been rescued from the consequences of their unfettered greed by those of countries that adhered to more traditional banking practices, and by the sovereign wealth funds of countries such as China and the Gulf states. Thomas Friedman of the *New York Times*, one of the great champions of globalization, stated his expectation that the same would go for manufacturing corporations during the coming recession. And,

> once the smoke clears, I suspect we will find ourselves living in a world of globalization on steroids – a world in which key global economies are more intimately tied together than ever before.
>
> It will be a world in which America will not be able to scratch its ear, let alone roll over in bed, without thinking about the impact on other countries and economies. And it will be a world in which multilateral diplomacy and regulation will no longer be a choice. It will be a reality and a necessity. We are all partners now.
>
> (Friedman, 2008)

This prediction seems to presage a return to dominance of the trend towards functional democratization, at least in relations between America and the wider world. Even if that proves to be the case, it is not without dangers. Because of people's strong emotional identification with their country – Americans' we-feelings appear to be especially strong– national decline may produce 'complex symptoms of disturbance … which are scarcely less in strength and in capacity to cause suffering than the individual neuroses' (Elias, 1996: 19). This may have alarming consequences. Examples of 'national hubris' in the past have included Germans' reactions to defeat in the First World War and the Anglo-French invasion of Egypt in the Suez crizas of 1956, and as long ago as 1960 Elias spoke of the growing hubris of the great powers even then (Elias, 2008b: 239–42, 249). The military supremacy of the USA will no doubt endure for another generation, and its power position in the world has enabled it in certain respects to continue to live in the 1890s. But that makes it especially dangerous now that in many other ways its relative power is declining. Its behaviour since the humiliation of the attacks on New York and Washington on 11 September 2001 is a good example of what Thomas Scheff (1994) calls a 'shame–rage spiral'. If decline brings with it further humiliations, triggering further twists of the shame–rage spiral, the USA will become a rogue state that the world has to manage. And a final thought: perhaps the cultural legacy of the South, the smouldering ember of the code of 'honour', will make that more likely.

Notes

1 I am writing this essay in late September and early October 2008, when the world financial crisis brought on by unregulated American 'casino capitalism' is leading many commentators to suggest that this will mark the end of American dominance as much as 1990 marked the end of Soviet dominance in a large segment of the world. But, especially for an advocate of long-term perspectives, it is too early to be confident that that is the correct inference.

2 The work of the French economist Thomas Piketty and his collaborators – see, for example, A. B. Atkinson and Thomas Piketty, 2007 – has been especially valuable in shedding light on long-term trends in the distribution of income and wealth in Europe and the USA. See the fuller discussion in Mennell, 2007: 249–65.

3 My thanks are due to Johan Goudsblom for suggesting that term.

4 For more than three quarters of that period of 72 years, the President had been a slaveholding southerner; after the war, no southern resident was elected President until Lyndon Johnson in 1964. In Congress, 23 of the 36 Speakers of the House and 24 of the 36 Presidents Pro Tempore of the Senate had been southerners; for half a century after the war, none was. Before the war, 20 of the 35 Justices of Supreme Court had been southerners, and they had been in a majority throughout the period; only five of the 26 justices appointed in the five decades after the war were from the South. See McPherson, 1990: 12–13.

5 Lynching, mainly of African American men, declined after the 1920s, but did not die out until the 1960s; county by county in the South, there is a high correlation between the incidence of lynching in the past and that of homicide at the present day (Messner et al., 2005: 633–55). It is significant that by far the greatest use of the death penalty occurs in those states and counties where vigilante activity and lynchings were most common in the past, and a very disproportionate fraction of those executed are African Americans.

6 For their boundaries, see the maps in the endpapers of Kaplan (2005). They have since been modified to create a new US Africa Command.

7 In 2004, it had bases in 130 out of 194 countries; see Johnson, 2004.

8 The phrase 'splendid little war' was used by John Hay (subsequently US Secretary of State) to describe the Spanish–American War of 1898. In a letter to his friend Theodore Roosevelt, he wrote:

> It has been a splendid little war; begun with the highest motives, carried on with magnificent intelligence and spirit, favoured by the fortune which loves the brave. It is now to be concluded, I hope, with that firm good nature which is after all the distinguishing trait of our American character.
>
> (Quoted in Thomas, 1971: 404).

9 See Elias's 'Game Models' (1978: 71–103).

10 For the analogy of a one-way mirror, I am indebted to Goudsblom (1989).

11 The terms 'minority of the worst' and 'minority of the best' are taken from Elias's classic discussion of the social functions of gossip (Elias and Scotson, 2008).

References

Andreski, Stanislav (1968) *Military Organization and Society*, 2nd edn. London: Routledge.

Atkinson, A. B. and Thomas Piketty (2007) *Top Incomes over the Twentieth Century: A Contrast between English-speaking and European Countries*. Oxford: Oxford University Press.

Blanden, J., P. Gregg, and S. Machin (2005) *Intergenerational Mobility in Europe and North America: A Report supported by the Sutton Trust*. London: Centre for Economic Performance, London School of Economics.

Bowman, Shearer Davis (1993) *Masters and Lords: Mid-Nineteenth Century United States Planters and Prussian Junkers*. New York: Oxford University Press, 1993.

Deutsch, Karl W. (1963) *The Nerves of Government: Models of Political Communication and Control*. New York: Free Press.

Disraeli, Benjamin (1872) 'Speech to the National Union of Conservative and Constitutional Associations at the Crystal Palace' (24 June).

Eisenhower, Dwight D. (1961) 'Farewell Address to the Nation', 17 January 1961, in *Public Papers of the Presidents of the United States*, pp. 1035–40. Washington, DC: United States General Printing Office.

Elias, Norbert (1978) *What is Sociology?* London: Hutchinson [Collected Works, vol. 5, forthcoming from UCD Press].

——(1991) *The Society of Individuals*. Oxford: Blackwell [Collected Works, vol. 10, forthcoming from UCD Press].

——(1996) *The Germans*. Cambridge: Polity Press [*Studies on the Germans*, Collected Works, vol. 11, forthcoming from UCD Press].

——(2000) *The Civilizing Process*, rev. edn. Oxford: Blackwell [*On the Process of Civilisation*, Collected Works, vol. 3, forthcoming from UCD Press].

——(2006) *The Court Society*. Dublin: UCD Press [Collected Works, vol. 2].

——(2007) *Involvement and Detachment*. Dublin: UCD Press [Collected Works, vol. 8].

——(2008a) 'Power and Civilisation', in *Essays III: On Civilising Processes, State Formation and National Identity*. Dublin: UCD Press [Collected Works, vol. 15], pp. 93–104.

——(2008b) 'National Peculiarities of British Public Opinion', in *Essays III: On Civilising Processes, State Formation and National Identity*. Dublin: UCD Press [Collected Works, vol. 15], pp. 230–55.

Elias, Norbert and John L. Scotson (2008), *The Established and the Outsiders*. Dublin: UCD Press [Collected Works, vol. 4].

Friedman, Thomas (2008), 'The Great Iceland Meltdown', *New York Times*, 19 October.

Goudsblom, Johan (1989) 'Stijlen en beschaving', *De Gids*, 152: 720–22.

Grant, Ulysses S. (1994) *Personal Memoirs of U. S. Grant*. New York: Smithmark.

Hegel, G. W. F. (1977) *Phenomenology of Spirit*. Oxford: Clarendon Press.

Johnson, Chalmers (2004) *The Sorrows of Empire: Militarism, Secrecy, and the End of the Republic*. London: Verso.

Kaplan, Robert D. (2005) *Imperial Grunts: the American Military on the Ground*. New York: Random House.

Kennedy, Paul (1988) *The Rise and Fall of the Great Powers: Economic Change and Military Conflict from 1500 to 2000*. London: Unwin Hyman.

Lane, Roger, *Murder in America: A History* (1977) Columbus, OH: Ohio State University Press.

McPherson, James M. (1990) *Abraham Lincoln and the Second American Revolution*. New York: Oxford University Press.

Mandelbaum, Michael (2006) *The Case for Goliath: How America acts as the World's Government in the Twenty-First Century*. New York: Public Affairs.

Mann, Michael (2003) *Incoherent Empire*. London: Verso.

Martineau, Harriet (1837) *Society in America*, 3 vols. London: Saunders & Otley.

Mennell, Stephen (1990) 'The Globalization of Human Society as a Very Long-term Social Process: Elias's Theory', *Theory, Culture and Society*, 7 (3): 359–71.

——(1994) 'The Formation of We-Images: A Process Theory', in Craig Calhoun, ed., *Social Theory and the Politics of Identity*. Oxford: Blackwell, pp. 175–97.

——(2007) *The American Civilizing Process*. Cambridge: Polity Press.

Messner, Steven F., Robert D. Baller, and Matthew P. Zevenbergen (2005) 'The Legacy of Lynching and Southern Homicide' *American Sociological Review*, 70 (4): 633–55.

Nevins, Allan, ed. (1948) *America through British Eyes*. New York: Oxford University Press.

Roosevelt, Theodore (1995) *The Winning of the West*, 4 vols. Lincoln: Nebraska University Press.

Scheff, Thomas J. (1994) *Bloody Revenge: Emotions, Nationalism and War*. Boulder, CO: Westview.

Schlesinger, Arthur M. Sr (1947) *Learning How to Behave: A Historical Study of American Etiquette Books*. New York: Macmillan.

Stannard, David E. (1992) *American Holocaust: Columbus and the Conquest of the New World*. New York: Oxford University Press.

Stiglitz, Joseph (2002) *Globalization and its Discontents*. London: Allen Lane.

Stolk, Bram van and Cas Wouters (1987) 'Power changes and self-respect: a comparison of two cases of established–outsiders relations', *Theory, Culture and Society*, 4 (2–3): 477–88.

Swaan, Abram de (1995) 'Widening Circles of Identification: Emotional Concerns in Sociogenetic Perspective', *Theory, Culture and Society*, 12 (2): 25–39.

Thomas, Hugh (1971) *Cuba or the Pursuit of Freedom*. London: Eyre & Spottiswoode.

Tocqueville, Alexis de (1961) *Democracy in America*, 2 vols. New York: Schocken. 1961.

United States Government (2002) 'The National Security Strategy of the United States of America'. Washington, DC: US Government Printing Office.

Vidal, Gore (2004) *Imperial America: Reflections on the United States of Amnesia*. London: Clairview.

Wouters, Cas (2004) *Sex and Manners: Female Emancipation in the West, 1890–2000*. London: Sage.

——(2007) *Informalization: Manners and Emotions since 1890*. London: Sage.

Wyatt-Brown, Bertram (1982) *Southern Honor: Ethics and Behavior in the Old South*. New York: Oxford University Press.

Zimmerman, Warren (2002) *First Great Triumph: How Five Great Americans Made Their Country a World Power*. New York: Farrar, Straus & Giroux.

Part IV

Critical solutions

29

Globalization and labour

Putting the ILO in its place

Anthony Woodiwiss

Introduction

Whereas universal and lasting peace can be established only if it is based upon social justice. And whereas conditions of labour exist involving such injustice, hardship and privation to large numbers of people as to produce unrest so great that the peace and harmony of the world are imperilled; and an improvement in those conditions is urgently required; as, for example, by the regulation of the hours of work, including the establishment of the maximum working day and week, the regulation of the labour supply, the prevention of unemployment, the provision of an adequate living wage, the protection of the worker against sickness, disease and injury arising out of his employment, the protection of children, young persons and women, provision for old age and injury, protection of the interests of workers when employed in countries other than their own, recognition of the principle of equal remuneration for work equal value, recognition of the principle of freedom of association, the organisation of vocational and technical education and other measures; Whereas also the failure of any nation to adopt humane conditions of labour is an obstacle in the way of other nations which desire to improve the conditions in their own countries ...

(Preamble to the Constitution of the International Labour Organization).

When asked to consider labour rights in the context of globalization, and putting to one side the multiple issues relating to migration, a conventional response would be simply to outline the role, history, texts, and politics of and around the International Labour Organization (ILO). Indeed all of this is part of the story, and moreover the ILO is one of the oldest properly global institutions and certainly the most visible of the many 'standard setting' bodies that preceded and have survived alongside it (Murphy, 1994). However, for a sociologist the study of institutional life is only a part of the story and neither the most interesting part nor a sufficient condition for understanding (Berman, 2005; Helfer, 2006). This is because, for the sociologist, institutional life must be somehow not so much located in a wider social context, to use the gestural term of friendly non-sociologists, as located in actual social places and so understood as a 'natural product, like organisms or plants, which are born, which grow and develop through some natural necessity' (Emile Durkheim, quoted in Traugott 1978: 44–5).

When I use the term 'actual social places' I do not mean simply actual territorial spaces so much as such spaces understood sociologically, that is understood in terms of socio-logical concepts. Rather than spend any time trying to explain what this might mean abstractly (but see Woodiwiss, 2001), I will now simply move on to talking about the ILO in such terms. Perhaps the best way to characterize the ILO sociologically is to understand it, like the wider international human rights system and indeed like much of the international legal system, as located somewhere between the social domain in general and the more specific formation that we term 'the legal' (for an excellent and concise survey of the development of social theory in this area, see Tomlins, 2007). The legal sphere proper is populated, one realizes once one suspends one's taken-for-granted assumptions, by a mysterious set of institutions and discourses. At its core it is simply a collection of words, concepts, and statements and yet these linguistic artefacts have a special status and therefore power in that violating them can result in fines, confinement, and killing. For the most part international legal institutions and discourses do not have such powerful disciplinary effects, however, just as we try to understand the mysteries of our universe by probing ever deeper into space, so we can discover much about our present systems of domestic law through investigating the, at first sight at least, less tightly structured realm of international law. Thus by pondering this realm we can gain both insights into the origins of the law and pre-figurative knowledge of its future. For all the law's con-temporary doctrinal refinement, it is the more brutal aspects (intellectual as well as physical and political) of today's struggles that remind us of its origins and will determine its future. In the arena of international politics when the sovereign is challenged, effective-ness and the control of territory are the most important prerequisites for legal standing, for the possession of rights. Thus challenging groups that are the effective controllers of territory are called 'insurgents' whereas those who have no such control are called 'ter-rorists' (Cassese, 2001). In other words and in the end, the most significant difference between governments, insurgents, and terrorists – between law makers and law break-ers – is how much territory they control or how much power they have. Although the terrain of struggle in the ILO is purely a matter of discourse and although one is there-fore only ever talking of a war of words, it is the same in the ILO in that neither the location of the sovereign nor the extent of its writ in the senses of discursive dominance and the extent of its enforceability respectively are ever unchallenged or certain (for an argument that the ILO has a better enforcement record than is commonly understood, see Douglas et al., 2004). Today what might be termed the sovereign discourse projected by the ILO still owes much to Western influences. However, ideas of, for example, Asian provenance that were as beyond the pale as the ideas of any group of terrorists have come to occupy wider and wider swathes of discursive space within the ILO with the result that they now qualify as insurgent ideas. Accordingly, it is not at all surprising that today the discourse of international labour rights like that of international law in general is both a deeply suspect enterprise and the world's last great hope.

International law in general is deeply suspect because it has long been characterized by the pre-emption of the possibility of a global consensus by the prior formation of a Western one. Thus, although in theory the most venerable source of international law is 'international custom' or the ways in which states customarily relate to one another, in practice the states whose interaction is regarded as defining has most often been limited to Western or Western-like states. Thus, in the nineteenth century, the 'unequal treaties' between various Western and non-colonized Asian states that, amongst other things, denied these Asian states jurisdiction over their Western residents even in the case of very serious crimes were justified by reference to the customary 'law of nations' which pro-hibited any interference with trade and communication between nations. Indeed many Western nations considered themselves to have been rather generous in drawing up such treaties since they harboured serious doubts about whether or not non-Western nations were covered by international law because of the Asian states' non-Christian character. Moreover, the issue was only 'settled' in 1874, when the Paris Institute of International Law decided that non-Western nations could claim legal equality with their Western equivalents under international law provided they conformed to what the West defined as the 'universal principles of civilization'. Hence the necessity of establishing a Western-style Constitution such as Japan's Meiji Constitution (1890) and the accompanying set of legal Codes before such 'unequal treaties' could be renegotiated. Today international law is much more than simply a prejudiced commentary on the purportedly customary nature of international intercourse. It comprises two major and in some senses highly developed bodies of law. The first is public international law, which primarily concerns state to state relations around issues such as the recognition of governments, the use of force, and the treatment of prisoners of war, but has more recently come to encompass certain aspects of states' relations to individuals through international human rights law. The second is private international law which primarily concerns family and economic issues where they have an international dimension. It is, then, because international law embodies more than a hundred years of effort on the part of the international commu-nity to distil the 'universal principles of civilization' as they apply to these basic issues that it carries the hopes of the world, especially now that there is only one superpower. But how universal are these principles even today, and even in relation to labour rights?

In the West domestic law is commonly understood to derive its power from its role as the symbol and indeed the major structural guarantor of fairness, consistency, and justice – to the degree that societies without law or within which the law plays a relatively small role in social life are generally considered to lack something very important, to be intrinsically unfair, arbitrary, unjust, and therefore to be inferior. When viewed histori-cally and sociologically, however, Western domestic law may be seen to have in fact initially derived its power from its role in ensuring fairness, consistency, and justice for a very small group of people. These were people who wished firstly to benefit personally from their possession of land and/or other factors of production, and secondly to be excused both the payment of feudal tithes and any broader responsibility to their employees than the payment of wages, and thirdly to appropriate for themselves any surplus produced through their cooperation with others. By the end of the eighteenth century these privileges had been broadened to include a second order of entitlements that allowed the beneficiaries of the first order to speak up for, and organize themselves politically in defence of, the same privileges.

The statements in which the courts defined both the first and second-order privileges eventually came to be known as civil and political rights. As the beneficiaries of these privileges prospered, multiplied, amassed fortunes, and gained control of states, their rights came to be seen as both sources and instruments of power. Moreover, these civil rights soon came to be regarded as universal not because everyone actually enjoyed them, but because they were available to all property owners and it had become possible for anyone to be a property owner. Thus it was not surprising that when the Western European nations began their colonization of the rest of the world they took their law with them thinking it to be beneficial both to themselves and the benighted peoples of other lands.

The reason why the few rather than the many actually enjoyed their rights was because, at the same time as the arrival of capitalism freed the few from economic subordination, it also deprived the many of economic security and therefore of any realistic possibility of owning their own productive property. In other words, economic freedom came at a price: the right of the few to own property required that the many sacrifice the fruits of their labour in the interests of the few. In time, of course, the propertyless won the rights to vote and stand for election and succeeded in achieving a certain amelioration of the sacrifices demanded of them. Thus tithes returned in the form of taxes and the state took responsibility for the general welfare by creating certain economic and social rights.

In the course of the Second World War and led by the United States, the Allied Western Powers achieved a consensus around this individual-centred complex of rights and subsequently succeeded in having it adopted by the newly formed United Nations in 1948 as the Universal Declaration of Human Rights. These rights are more or less deeply embedded in the social routines of Western societies and are therefore widely respected. Despite or because of the spread of capitalism, these rights are neither so deeply embedded nor so widely respected in the rest of the world. Is this really because the rest of the world is less civilized than the West? Or might this be yet another case of the preemption of the possibility of a global consensus by the prior formation of a Western one? Is an unalloyed individualism in fact the only basis upon which a discourse of respect for the other may be constructed? Why is it so hard for us to see that most of the world's population still depends on the virtuous behaviour of superiors for any protection it possesses? Why is it that evil can be prohibited but goodness cannot be required? Why not make virtue, duty, or benevolence legally enforceable? (see also Kuper, 2005).

The social clause and the problem of justiciability

Elsewhere, I and others (Woodiwiss, 2003: ch. 4; 2008; Udombana, 2006) have argued for the domestic justiciability, more general enforceability and the effectiveness of economic and social rights in the form of 'claims' and 'powers.' Here I will seek to develop these ideas by arguing for their international justiciability. At first sight it might seem that merely to mention labour rights in this connection closes the discussion in favour of their international justiciability. As mentioned above this is because the international repository of labour rights, the ILO, is the oldest institution in the UN family and has long exercised the same semi-judicial role as the human rights committees of the UN. Unfortunately, things are not so simple and largely because something very similar to the differentiation of justiciable from supposedly non-justiciable rights has happened with respect to international labour rights as has happened in the case of international human rights and indeed international law more generally. And the result may yet be another twist of the double bind that currently afflicts many millions of people in the less developed societies. In this case the differentiation has taken the form of the singling out of seven core conventions as part of the recent, failed attempt by some Western governments led by the Clinton Administration to insert a Social Clause into the protocols of the World Trade Organization (WTO). The seven conventions concern: (i) freedom of association and protection of the right to organize; (ii) the right to organization and collective bargaining; (iii) forced labour; (iv) abolition of forced labour; (v) discrimination in employment; (vi) equal remuneration; and (vii) the establishment of minimum age for employment.

The argument that follows is divided into two parts. The first argues that these core conventions, which are intended to ensure that competition in the rapidly emerging global economy takes place on a level playing field that allows respect for the fundamental rights of labour, is in fact biased in favour of the West in general and the United States in particular. The second begins by outlining the current state of play in the debate over what role, if any, labour standards should play in the global trading regime. It then moves on to explain why the current core set should be augmented and indicates how this might be done in a way that is more sensitive to social differences and would therefore enhance not just the chances of success of any future effort to achieve a Social Clause but also the more general enforceability of economic and social rights.

The bias that I am concerned with is evidenced by the fact that it would be much easier for Northern governments to ratify and locally enact the core standards than it would be for Southern governments. This automatically, and I am sure unintentionally, presents many Southern societies in a bad light that is not warranted if one takes into account their achievements across the full range of labour standards. That is, most Northern governments have little trouble agreeing that, for example, child labour, gender or racial discrimination in employment, and limitations on freedom of association, are bad things that something can be done about because of the existence of powerful or at least well-organized pressure groups within Northern countries. By contrast, in many Southern societies not simply the absence of such groups but also sometimes the presence of antithetical but nevertheless valued cultural preferences make it very difficult to agree that such practices are bad, let alone that something should be done about them.

As I will explain in more detail below, what perhaps makes it especially galling for some Pacific-Asian nations, and indeed employers, to see themselves rhetorically disadvantaged in this way is the fact that the current core standards exclude the possibility of any reference to their achievements with respect to other standards outside of the core. These latter are standards that are consistent with their values, supported by their social-structural arrangements and generally mitigate the consequences of any derelictions with respect to the existing core. It is therefore unsurprising to me that the majority of Southern nations should have rejected the American-led effort to have the present set of core labour standards included within the protocols of the WTO. However, this rejection was not couched in terms of cultural bias. This also is unsurprising since, whatever may be the balance of domestic opinion, few nations are prepared to risk being branded in international fora as enemies of freedom, oppressors of children, women and ethnic minorities, or as proponents of slavery and the banning of mother's apple pie. Indeed it is precisely in producing this risk that the discriminatory rhetorical power of the present core shows itself. Instead, the opponents of the Social Clause stressed their fear that it might be invoked for protectionist purposes or in order to justify interference in their domestic affairs. Unfortunately, this tack only made it seem that they had something to hide. In my view, because of the biased nature of the proposal, the fear of domestic interference was better grounded than the fear of protectionism. The fear of protectionism could be easily assuaged through the setting up of a properly representative, multilateral sanctions committee − such a committee would surely be more alert to the dangers of protectionism than those operating within the context of the present, unilateral Generalized Systems of Preferences (GSPs) of the United States and the European Union. However, if the core had been approved it would have been very difficult both to change it subsequently as well as to resist the intrusions of WTO emissaries intent on enforcing it and unable to accept mitigating arguments based upon achievements with respect to other standards because they were outside their remit.

575

On the other side of the debate, it seems to me that the International Confederation of Free Trade Unions (ICFTU) were equally ill-advised in their support for the proposed core. In their case, they were seduced by both its apparently common-sense or apple-pie character and, very understandably, by the fact that it protected their role. As Stephen Pursey (2003), formerly of the ICFTU has put it, the unions saw the core as supportable because in protecting their role it was enabling in that it allowed for local and future improvements in labour's rights. However, for reasons that will be outlined shortly, it is sometimes very difficult for unions to turn formal enablement into actual achievements and very often unions have to depend upon sympathetic and/or politically dependent governments to secure improvements in labour's rights by improved claims and enhanced powers. In sum, then, it seems to me that the trade-union side has reason to be grateful that the draft Social Clause was rejected, since it would have severely limited its strategic options in seeking to improve labour conditions.

The construction of an Ameri-centric core

In order to justify my point concerning the biased nature of the existing set of core labour standards, I will now provide a very short historical account of how they came to be so designated. Although the Preamble to the Constitution of the ILO was drafted by a commission presided over by the then President of the American Federation of Labor, Samuel Gompers, it more accurately reflected the consensus between Western European employers, employees, and politicians than between their American equivalents. This was because there was no consensus as regards the labour question on the American side, as became very clear when President Wilson lost the election of 1920 and the new Republican Administration refused to seek ILO membership. This also explains why all but one of the 86 ILO Conventions adopted prior to 1948, which was when the Convention on Freedom of Association was adopted, related to the protective measures or claims sanctioned by the communitarian values that comprised the Western-European consensus.

Although freedom of association had been included in the Preamble as a means of alleviating injustice, hardship, and privation and was strongly desired by the trade unions, it was given no special status vis à vis the protective claims either through its position in the listing of preferred means or through any textual gloss where it does appear. This changed in 1946 when the ILO adopted a new constitution that incorporated just such a gloss through its inclusion as an annex to the Declaration of Philadelphia, which had been agreed by the 1944 ILO Conference. By this time the United States had been a member for ten years and, not surprisingly given its role as the arsenal of the free world, its influence is very much in evidence throughout the Declaration. Amongst the most obvious signs of this influence are the identity and ordering of the fundamental principles contained within the Declaration, which privilege the post New Deal American consensus by deriving labour's case for special consideration from what has always seemed to me to be the curiously romantic – but because of the Sherman Anti-Trust Act of 1890 – legally necessary American statutory declaration (Clayton Act, 1914) that labour is not a commodity. Labour is bought and sold which makes it manifestly a commodity. Moreover, it has also always seemed to me that Karl Marx was much closer to the mark when he argued that what he termed 'labour power' rather than 'labour' was not only a commodity under capitalist conditions but one that it was particularly unfortunate to be dependent upon since its exchange value was basically determined by its reproduction costs rather than by the prices its products could command.

Be that as it may, the Declaration of Philadelphia then moves on to state, in the manner of the National Labour Relations Act (NLRA) or Wagner Act of 1935, that freedom of expression and of association are essential to sustained progress. Again it is perhaps worth repeating why the Wagner Act so emphasized freedom of association, since such a stress is uniquely American. Despite the fact that the United States had been a British colony and had maintained its commitment to the Common Law after achieving its independence, the British route to the legal empowerment of labour did not turn out to be available in the United States. This was not so much because there was no electoral majority for it but more because in the latter half of the nineteenth century the Supreme Court managed to read laissez faire into the Constitution and so was hostile to any form of collective action that might interfere with freedom of contract (Woodiwiss, 1990b: ch. 5). By the 1930s, this hostility had lessened somewhat but was still strong enough to make the framers of the NLRA aware that they had to ground it in a constitutional principle of greater venerability and cultural resonance than the antagonistic, judge-made one of laissez-faire. Although it was much less obvious that this should be the case in the 1930s than it seems today, they found this alternative principle in the First Amendment to the Constitution which includes freedom of association, and indeed it proved to be of great help to the lawyers who had to defend the constitutionality of the act when it was indeed challenged.

Other obvious textual signs of American influence in the Declaration of Philadelphia are the stressing of individual equality of opportunity when the Western European states were domestically stressing what might be termed collective equality of opportunity, and the requirement, anticipating the 1947 additions to the preamble to the amended NLRA, that the ILO should consider all relevant economic and financial factors before making its decisions and recommendations. Of course, much of the rest of the Declaration makes it clear that the European protective agenda was still in place and indeed had been broadened to include the social-democratic aspiration to achieve the extension of social security measures to provide a basic income to all in need and comprehensive medical care. In sum, what the passing of the Philadelphia Declaration 1944 meant was that, long before the rise of the neo-liberalism associated with Reaganism, the actual social space that governed the ILO's judgments was thenceforth no longer simply the communitarianism of Western European societies wherein labour was relatively powerful, but also the only slightly qualified individualism of an American society that tended to regard powerful trade unions as a mark of a social and economic failure to modernize (Woodiwiss, 1990b). Hence the United States government's difficulties in accepting the bone fides of Soviet and East European employers' representatives during the 1950s and 1960s. Hence too its related withdrawal from the ILO between 1977 and 1980 because of what it saw as the ILO's excessive partiality towards the labour interest. And hence, finally, it is understandable and not at all disingenuous singling out of the seven Core Conventions when it made its Social Clause proposal at the WTO.

The primacy of the ethical dimension

The first thing to say about the debate provoked by the Clinton proposal is that it is in a sense a re-run of an earlier debate that took place in the course of the discussions that led to the formation of the ILO in 1919. The 1919 debate, like the current one, essentially related to the issue of enforcement and turned on whether or not International Labour Conference resolutions and especially Conventions should be obligatory on members and therefore have superior legal status to national legislation. Support for the granting of supranational legislative powers to the Conference came from the French and Italian delegations as well as the union delegates. In the event, however, the majority of delegates decided to limit the obligations incumbent upon member states to consideration by their legislatures of whether or not to ratify and locally enact the Conventions passed by the Conference. Rather obviously, then, if still rather surprisingly given the recent hegemony of neo-liberal ideas in the United States, the current debate arises out of the Western nations, dissatisfaction with this rather reserved exercise of international legislative power and the consequently similarly reserved mode of enforcement: members who fail to enact Conventions have simply to provide their reasons and members who fail to fulfil their obligations under Conventions that they have ratified merely risk having to respond to a negative ILO report (Johnston, 1970: 97–106).

The current Western view is that, in the interests of fair competition, both entry into and participation in the WTO system of tariff management and reduction should be conditional upon ratification and enactment of the Core ILO standards and any violations should be punished by trade sanctions. The majority Pacific-Asian and Southern view, on the part of employers and governments if not unions (Ago, 1995), is that the imposition of such standards would be both inappropriate because of these nations' lower level of development, and unfair because it would deprive them of their major comparative advantage, namely their relatively low labour costs. In sum, on the one hand, Western governments see a strengthened system of international labour standards as a universal benefit in that it should lead to both an improvement in the conditions of labour in the South and the prevention of the race to the bottom in terms of wages and conditions that their own electorates fear may be the consequence of globalization. On the other hand, their opponents see any such strengthening of labour standards as something that would serve only selfish, Western political and economic interests.

Drawing on the work of other scholars (Bhagwati and Hudec, 1996; Freeman, 1994; Golub, 1997; Krugman, 1997; OECD, 1996; Rodrik, 1995), Eddy Lee (1997) has recently shown with particular clarity that the jury is still out on the merits of the economic cases made by the two sides. Not being an economist, I am in no position to disagree with this judgment. The result is that, like Lee, I believe that, in the absence of strong economic arguments either way, the more purely moral dimension of the debate becomes the most salient one (see also, Sen, 1999). At this level Western governments argue that there can be no problem since the standards at issue are universal, not only because they were promulgated by the internationally representative International Labour Conference but also because they have in all cases been repeated in the various global human rights texts. Two main points are or could be made by the opponents of the clause. First, the real rather than formal representativeness of the Conference has always been questionable, given the different levels of financial clout possessed by the various delegations. Second, to invoke human rights, especially civil and political rights such as freedom of association, is to compound the problem since the pre-eminence accorded such rights over social, economic, and cultural rights represents an instance of Western cultural imperialism.

The result of this impasse was that the WTO referred back the labour standards issue to the ILO at its 1996 ministerial meeting in Singapore. The ILO's response has been to mount a very energetic and partially successful campaign to have the core ratified by more member states and to gain the ILO Conference's support for a new Declaration on Fundamental Principles which again stresses the core. Beneficial though these efforts undoubtedly are, the fact remains that international labour standards still lack the teeth that their inclusion in a WTO Social Clause would give them, and which unfortunately are still necessary given the activities of those unscrupulous employers and governments who seek a competitive advantage by abusing the human rights of their employees no matter what form these rights take. Moreover, 43 ILO member states from the South and Pacific Asia chose to abstain rather than support the new Declaration. Thus it has always seemed to me that if the abstainers' concerns could be assuaged it would not only be worth trying again for a Social Clause but there would also be a good chance of its successful adoption. In the event and as of October 2008 no effort to assuage the abstainers concerns has been made with the result being that the debate remains stuck where it was in the 1990s (see Trachtman, 2006) which is why the present argument retains its pertinence.

Towards a hybrid core

At this point I would like to draw again on the work (Woodiwiss, 1998) informing the ideas set out in the preceding chapters, since these ideas suggest some ways in which the global appropriateness of any Social Clause might be better assured. This work convinced me that, as in the case of human rights more generally, neither side in the debate has thought hard enough – more specifically, sociologically hard enough – about the issues involved. Moreover, it is my view that had those involved in the debate thought socio-logically harder, they would have discovered that the difference between the two sides is a lot smaller than they currently imagine. My reasons for saying this are twofold. First, ironically, the cultural differences between Western and non-Western societies, whilst considerable in respects that have been neglected, are far less marked as regards the features that have been focused upon in the debate. Second, if we assume, as I think we must, that the desire for social justice is equally strong on both sides, then when the full range, rather than the so-called core, of ILO Conventions is considered they provide an excellent basis upon which any remaining differences, and there are some, may be reconciled.

As regards the first point, my principal argument is that the present appearance of great cultural differences is an artefact of the highly generalized, stereotypical models that have been used when, for example, Western and Pacific-Asian values have been compared. That is, typically Western values have been represented as strongly individualistic and liberal, whilst their Pacific-Asian equivalents have been represented as communitarian and state-centred if not downright illiberal or authoritarian. Now, the first representation seems to me to be far closer to the value reality of the United States than that of Western Europe, which has long been communitarian, statist and rights-based, whilst, on the other hand, individualism and liberalism and therefore rights discourse represent a far more influential dimension of non-Western values than some non-Western business and political leaders have been prepared to acknowledge so far.

As has been explained elsewhere (Woodiwiss, 2003: ch. 4; 2005: 148–151), the social differences that nevertheless remain have to do with the much stronger resonance that familial values have in the routines of Pacific-Asian societies on both sides of the labour contract. What this means on the good employers' side is a deep fear of disorder, and even a sense of personal failure to fulfil ones social obligations, that the occurrence of a strike, for example, might produce. What it means on the labour side is an equally pro-found reticence when it comes to taking action that might be construed as disloyal to a respected superior. The result is that the less scrupulous, culturally opportunistic gov-ernments and employers have had some success in branding the proposed core labour standards as an alien cultural intrusion. As significantly, the post-colonial histories that I have looked at in other work (Woodiwiss, 1998) suggest that, even where labour has been granted the core rights, it has not been able to make much use of them. Thus unions have not developed in step with the economy. Of course, there are many other reasons for the failure of unions to develop apart from these inhibiting political and cultural factors. These include the still very large rural surplus populations in many Southern and Pacific-Asian societies, and most pertinently in the current context, the fact that it is very difficult to bring local collective bargaining to a successful conclusion where companies participate in the earlier and simpler links of global commodity chains, whether these are buyer-driven as in much of the apparel industry, or producer-driven as in the electronics industry. This point is reinforced once one notes that, for example, a substantial amount of industrial production in the ASEAN countries takes place in Export Processing Zones where, amongst many other advantages, Western and Japanese multinational producers especially benefit from the suspension of numerous domestic labour laws.

Turning now to my second and more positive point concerning the advantages of thinking in terms of the full range of labour standards rather than the core if one wishes to overcome the problems created by the cultural differences indicated by the greater resonance of familialism in Southern and Pacific-Asian societies. Here my thinking was strongly affected by the discovery reported in my book *Globalisation, Human Rights and Labour Law in Pacific Asia* (1998) that, although the core freedom to associate as well as that to organize and bargain have been greatly restricted in many non-Western societies, there have been compensations through the enhancement of protective standards and the development of social policy, at least where democracy and the rule of law have been in place. In Japan these take the form of the Labour Standards Law and a legally developed right to lifetime employment. In Hong Kong and Singapore, they take the form of very good individual contracts of employment that incorporate many elements derived from the more protective ILO Conventions and, especially in the case of Singapore, very sub-stantial citizenship rights with respect to housing and education. Even in the benighted Philippines, strenuous and largely successful efforts were made by a badly under-resourced Department of Labour and the trades unions to enforce a minimum wage between the mid-1950s and the declaration of martial law in 1972.[1]

It is also the case, again to repeat, that it is the form that the non-Western restrictions to freedom of association take – a preference for enterprise unions, for example - that has troubled many in the West rather than their existence as such. This, of course, is because restrictions on the freedoms to associate, organize, and bargain have also been imposed in the West and sometimes for the same ILO-sanctioned reasons (see the *Preamble* repro-duced at the head of this chapter), namely the prevention of economic and social dis-order. Examples of such restrictions include: closed shop and/or union no-poaching agreements, the prohibition of communist-led organizations, excessively weak recogni-tion procedures, the absence of employer obligations to bargain, the prohibition of sec-ondary actions, strict limitations on picketing, and requirements both to hold secret ballots and give notice before strikes. Moreover, in all Western countries save the United States such restrictions have been compensated for in very similar if, unsurprisingly, most often more generous ways. Finally, it should be noted that the society that has the best safeguards in place with respect to the problem of enterprise unions abusing their posi-tions is Japan (Woodiwiss, 1992: 138). This is because the constitutional right to freedom of association is so unambiguously defined as an individual right rather than a trade-union right that alternative and minority unions have successfully sustained themselves against many legal challenges. In other words, Japanese labour law suggests how freedom of association should perhaps be reconfigured in a world where individual employment contracts are becoming more important than collective ones and where co-operation between labour and capital has become more and more necessary, whether in the form of enterprise unionism or co-determination structures. In such a world individual employees need to feel both that they can have access to union support regardless of whether their colleagues are unionized, and to be sure that in a unionized workplace a co-operative union does not become a sweetheart union. In sum, then, in order to be globally pertinent, freedom of association should be reconfigured so as to protect indi-vidual employees against potentially oppressive unions as well as against potentially oppressive employers, even though this challenges the union movement's well estab-lished and, I have to say, historically well grounded antipathy towards dual unionism. Within this conception, then, state-guaranteed individual employment contracts represent enabling conditions since they enhance employee confidence and so make employees more likely to feel able to engage in collective action for redistributive purposes if they consider this necessary.

What, several years later, finally enabled me to 'cash in', so to speak, such local knowledge and argue that the Japanese system of industrial justice was part of a distinctive human rights regime was the realization that the anti-naturalistic and pluralistic conception of juridical or legal relations set out in Wesley Hohfeld's classic text, *Fundamental Legal Conceptions*, could be used sociologically to distinguish and therefore, by implication, to design human rights discourses that could achieve the same protective aims in the diverse ways appropriate to different social contexts. According to Hohfeld, and I have changed his nomenclature slightly, rights may be understood as discursively defined clusters of: 'liberties' to perform certain actions; 'claims' or expectations vis-à-vis specified others; 'powers' that allow legal subjects to assume certain specified roles and change certain social relations; and 'immunities' against prosecution and/or civil suit when pursuing ends that are otherwise defined as illegal.

What this suggested to me was that, provided democracy and the rule of law are present, human rights may be effective policy instruments despite, or indeed because of, their uneven development along one or more of these dimensions. That is, given the mutually implicatory character of the different dimensions of rights and the similarity of the protective outcomes that can be achieved, and although liberties and so forth are ultimately irreducible to one another, the more, so to speak, there is of one, the less need there is for the others. To elaborate, if liberties are clearly and broadly defined, there is less need for their implications in terms of claims or whatever to be spelt out, since the existence of the latter is juridically and socially implied, albeit as a last resort in order to enable people to exercise their liberties. Thus even the ultra liberal United States has some sort of social safety net. Likewise, if claims, for example, are clearly and broadly defined, there is less need for their implications in terms of liberties or whatever to be spelt out, since acceptance of the existence of claims against another juridically and socially implies acceptance of one's liberty to require their satisfaction, albeit again as a last resort as seems to be the case in Japan. Neither the institutions through which claims are delivered nor the social behaviours directly protected as claims are the same as those

581

that deliver, and are protected as, liberties but a similar protective effect is achieved – for example, in the case of the Japanese as opposed to the American industrial relations system, enterprise rather than craft or industrial unions represent employees and conflicts are more often resolved by mediation or conciliation than by strikes or lockouts.

The similarity of protective effects occurs because, whereas liberties allow one to try to force a limitation on the freedom of the more powerful, claims achieve the same limitation on the powerful by imposing a prior duty or obligation on them. Given the particular cultural and social-structural circumstances obtaining in Japan, notably the continuing importance and widespread acceptance of the hierarchical principle, the latter mode of limitation is one that is much more widely supported, and indeed more safely insisted upon, than might be the case if employees had only their liberties to rely on.

It is, then, because of the realization of the sociological pertinence of this system of differences in how rights may be written and the equivalencies in the outcomes that can nevertheless be achieved that I regard international human rights discourse as in fact far richer and more open-ended than is conventionally supposed. That is, what the equivalencies with regard to protective outcomes allow are translations between differently configured and institutionalized discourses of rights. More specifically still what, in turn, these equivalencies allow – provided again that democracy and the rule of law are present – is that a discourse that was originally configured in terms of the liberties that have proved to be reasonably effective in protecting Americans in a society where individualism dominates the value system and there is ready access to the court system may be translated into discourses configured in terms that stress claims, powers or immunities where other values are dominant and non-legal institutions more salient in terms of providing means of enforcement.

I will now briefly outline some of the legal/social ideal types that make such translations possible.

Systems configured in terms that stress claims appear to be particularly appropriate, albeit for rather different reasons and with different institutional consequences, not only in developed hierarchical societies such as Japan where the dominant value is 'familialism' and the company is the key social institution, as we have seen, but also in Western European social democracies where the dominant value is social partnership and there is a solidaristic welfare state.

Systems configured in terms that stress immunities appear to be particularly appropriate in societies where particular social groups are otherwise totally dominant as in Britain in the late nineteenth century where these dominant values were nevertheless contested and the legislature consequently became the critical social institution.

And finally, systems configured in terms that stress powers may in time prove to be particularly appropriate in states, as in much of Sub-Saharan Africa, where collectivist values and kinship relations retain their importance.

In sum, the differences between different rights regimes are neither accurately nor most usefully thought of in terms of the relative importance of different kinds of rights (that is, civil and political or economic and social) but instead are best understood in terms of different forms of discourse and their modes of institutionalization. Thus the normative choice one is confronted with when considering how to go about localizing labour rights as with human rights more generally is not between two kinds of rights but rather between different ways of writing and institutionalizing both kinds of rights. The challenge, then, is to discover or invent ways in which rights originally written and institutionally delivered as liberties may be rewritten and institutionally delivered as claims or whatever. Fortunately, human social inventiveness is such that we already have available a huge inventory, drawn from the past as well as the present, of statutory forms and institutional modalities to refer to. Clearly, the ideal types I have just outlined need to be refined and developed before they can effectively guide any such rewriting and institutionalizing, but not much since what one would be looking for would be sources of suggestive insights rather than off-the-peg solutions.

The advantages, then, of thinking in terms of the full range of standards rather than the Core are numerous. First, it provides a set of internationally legitimate means with which to reconcile cultural differences. Second, these means appear to be culturally acceptable to the better Pacific-Asian employers and thus call the cultural bluff of their less scrupulous colleagues, since these standards involve no direct challenge to their cultural prerogative as the sources of benevolence. Third, although the compensations I have described have only been obtained where, for a variety of reasons, the labour movement has been relatively strong, the fact that they have proved to be acceptable to employers in the most successful economies of the region ought to reduce the strength of any objections to their being enjoyed by more reticent or less circumstantially advantaged employees. Fourth, the level playing field argument deployed by Western governments becomes usable within the South in general and not simply between it and the West. And, finally, multinationals would be both less able to force a race to the bottom and spared the considerable effort and costs involved in sustaining the Corporate Codes of Conduct, best exemplified by that of the Nike Corporation, necessary to assuage the fears and consciences of their metropolitan consumers (Gibbons, 1998; Murphy, 2005).

The case for adding just and favourable conditions at work to the core

At least three questions still require answers, however: (1) Which of the more than 180 protective ILO Conventions presently in force should be selected for inclusion in an augmented but still manageable new Social Clause? (2) What would the compensatory algorithm, so to speak, look like that would enable one to determine whether a particular set of trade-offs had passed the compliance threshold? (3) How legitimate or legally safe would the operation of such a algorithm be in the light of the principles of international human rights law?

Concerning the first question, an obvious principle of selection suggests itself, namely that, like the existing Core, the additional Conventions should be those that embody human rights (Leary, 1996), specifically the economic and social rights – to work, just and favourable conditions, health, and an adequate standard of living – in order to balance the current emphasis on civil and political rights. All of these rights overlap with the remit of the ILO. However, Article 7 of the Convention on Social and Economic Rights – just and favourable conditions of work – and, as a self-evident corollary, ILO Convention 81 on Labour Inspection, seem to be a particularly strong candidates to play a critical role in the construction of any compensatory algorithm for reasons that will be specified below. Article 7 reads as follows:

> The States Parties to the present Covenant recognize the right of everyone to the enjoyment of just and favourable conditions of work, which ensure in particular:

(a) Remuneration which provides all workers, as a minimum with:
  (i) fair wages and equal remuneration for work of equal value without distinction of any kind, in particular women being guaranteed conditions of work not inferior to those enjoyed by men, with equal pay for equal work;
  (ii) a decent living for themselves and their families in accordance with the provisions of the present covenant;
(b) Safe and healthy working conditions;
(c) Equal opportunity for everyone to be promoted in his employment to an appropriate higher level, subject to no consideration other than those of seniority and competence;
(d) Rest, leisure, and reasonable limitation of working hours and periodic holidays with pay, as well as remuneration for public holidays.

As regards the second question, in my view only derelictions with respect to the Forced Labour Conventions could not be translated into any alternative entitlements. The Minimum Age Convention is anyway very flexible (Servais, 1986: 195–196), and the most obvious reason why Article 7 might be expected to play a critical role in the construction of any compensatory algorithm is the fact that it repeats two of the existing Core Standards, those requiring the elimination of discrimination in employment. This leaves in need of translation only derelictions with respect to the freedoms to associate, organize, and bargain. Here what also recommends Article 7 as the critical principle of selection is that its requirements are much more specific than the others, with the result that measuring compliance and therefore compensatory effectiveness would be relatively easy. Almost all the paragraphs simply require contractual or procedural safeguards to be in place which are reasonably precisely specifiable and hence readily justiciable and add little to the costs of employers, if not governments. The latter would clearly have to increase their expenditures on Labour Departments, inspectorates, employment tribunals and such like but not hugely. Another feature that would reduce still further the possible costs involved is that the language used in Article 7 and indeed the cognate ILO Conventions features terms such as fair wages and decent living which clearly imply local rather than international points of comparison.

The final reason for regarding Article 7 as critical is politics. Without Article 7's inclusion in a revised Social Clause, any judgement of labour standards in the non-West is likely to be negative. However, with it not only would some countries in Pacific Asia in particular look better and others may be made to live up to their own self-chosen standards, but also some Western societies, notably the United States, would look worse. It may surprise some readers to learn that one of the societies that would have most to compensate for under Paragraph (d) of Article 7 would be the United States where individual employment contracts are legally largely unregulated in this respect (Summers and Grodin, 1993, p. 184). Thus, from the point of view of the South and Pacific-Asia, the augmentation of the Core would be attractive not simply in acknowledging their cultural particularity but also by posing a balancing challenge to the United States, albeit a small one.

Finally, turning to the third question, pertaining to the legal legitimacy of the operation of any compensatory algorithm, I will simply make two points. The translating of the freedoms to associate, organize, and bargain into contractual and welfare enhancements has long been accepted as politically and culturally legitimate in Western Europe. Second, the development and deployment by the European Court of Human Rights of the doctrines known as the margin of appreciation and the effectiveness principle both suggest that such exchanges could be seen as acceptable when judged against the principles of international human rights law (Woodiwiss, 2003: 5, 80).

Conclusion

In conclusion, then, the Clinton Administration deserves full credit for having insisted that any new global trading regime should be premised upon respect for labour's human rights even though it was unaware of the partial nature of its conception of what these might be. However, and whatever their given and indeed non-given reasons, many of the Southern objectors to a Social Clause, and indeed to the ILO Declaration on Fundamental Principles, also deserve credit rather than obloquy for at least four reasons. First, global institutions like the WTO and the ILO should not privilege one set of values over another but should instead be leaders in the formation of a new, plurally defined global ethic. Second, continued debate over a possible Social Clause provides an excellent opportunity to demonstrate that such an ethic need be neither non-justiciable nor in any strong sense culturally relativistic since a more plurally defined set of core standards chosen from the existing array of 180 or so would be both legally binding and enforceable as well as represent a more truly universal standard. Third, the effectiveness of the initial draft of the Social Clause in enhancing the human rights of Southern employees would have been minimal, since such enhancement depends not a jot on formal governmental ratification but instead upon its provisions being embeddable and therefore enforceable within local social conditions which the draft provisions manifestly were not. Finally, several of the objectors to both the draft clause and indeed the Declaration could have supported them in far better faith than many who did but either had no intention of being bound by them or more often had little hope of enforcing them because of the weakness of their state institutions. Such objectors in particular deserve credit for risking the wrath of – or in some ways worse being patronized by – Western governments for whom the rights and wrongs of the issue appeared to be disturbingly clear.

The present Core Labour Standards are the product of a particular history and their recent rejection as an element in the global trading regime suggests not so much that there is no place for them but, rather, that it is time to take that history one step further and reconstruct the Core on a still justiciable but more equal civilizational basis. Encouragingly, not only is there strong evidence that the preparation for such a reconstruction is underway (cf. Hahn, 2007), but remarkably the sites where this preparatory activity has been and continues to be undertaken are the very bilateral, Free Trade Agreements that the US government has signed with other governments in order to try to ensure that progress towards global free trade should continue despite the difficulties inherent in the WTO process. Thus, beginning with the first of the present wave of FTAs which was that with Jordan in 2001, the sections on labour have always included the following provision relating to the 'application and enforcement' of the law:

> Parties recognize that that each party retains the right to exercise discretion with respect to investigatory, prosecutorial, regulatory, and compliance matters and to make decisions regarding the allocation of resources to enforcement with respect to other labour matters determined to have higher priorities. Accordingly, the Parties understand that a party is in compliance ... where a course of action or inaction reflects a reasonable exercise of such discretion, or results from a bona fide decision regarding the allocation of resources.

Moreover, the texts also always go on to include and give equal status to the following 'internationally recognized labor right': 'Acceptable conditions of work with respect to minimum wages, hours of work, and occupational health and safety.' Of course, 'acceptable conditions of work' are not the same as 'just and favourable conditions of work' neither in their general tone nor in their specifics, but the former is a minimalist version of the latter and when read within the context of the 'right to exercise discretion', creates the possibility that labour's rights may eventually be as effectively protected in places where kin, community, and heteronomy are more important values than individual autonomy.

Reflection on the story that has just been told prompts a more general conclusion too. This is that, counter-intuitively, the very process of seeking global agreement may turn out to be an inherently self-limiting one in that it places enormous pressures on states' parties to reach agreements based on universalistic rather than cosmopolitan principles, and therefore to deny social difference when it would be more just as well as more effective to acknowledge such difference. Bilateral negotiations, by contrast, create similarly intense pressures on states parties to acknowledge social differences and make effectiveness rather than doctrinal consistency the critical basis for judgement since without such an acknowledgement very few agreements will be possible. It could well be, then, that in the end the debate over the Social Clause, and the resulting recognition that bilateral as well as multilateral negotiations (cf. Blum, 2008; Hassel, 2008) have a role to play in securing globally effective treaties and agreements, will be regarded as a positive rather than a negative event in what I hope will be the story of the creation of a truly cosmopolitan world order.

Acknowledgements

The discussion of international law with which this chapter begins is derived from Woodiwiss (2006). The earliest version of the remainder of this chapter was delivered at a conference on Labour Relations in Asia and Europe organized by the Asia-Europe Foundation (ASEF), the International Institute for Social History, the International Institute for Asian Studies, and the Nordic Institute for Asian Studies. It was held at the Dutch Foreign Ministry in The Hague in October 1998. I am very grateful to my fellow conference participants for their many useful comments. The papers from the conference were published in Koh and van der Linden (2000). A later version was published as Chapter 5 in Woodiwiss (2003). My knowledge of the history of the ILO is largely derived from the following sources: Cassese, 1990; Charnovitz, 1987; Johnston, 1970; Murphy, 1994; Osieke, 1985.

Note

1 In making this point, I am not of course saying that these exchanges are necessarily adequate nor that more should not be done to secure freedom of association (see the discussions of Hong Kong, Singapore and the Philippines in Woodiwiss, 1998), but only that the overall balances of imperfections in at least some of these labour rights regimes are not qualitatively worse than those in many Western societies, notably those in Britain (Ewing, 1994) and the United States where, in particular, the process of union recognition leaves much to be desired (Weiler, 1990).

References

Ago, S. (1995) 'The Social Clause as Understood in Asia', Kyushu University, Department of Law, mimeo,

Berman, P. S. (2005) 'From International Law to Law and Globalization', *Columbia Journal of International Law*, 43, 2: 485–556.

Bhagwati, J. and Hudec, R. (eds) (1996) *Fair Trade and Harmonisation: Prerequisites for Free Trade?* Vol. 2, Cambridge: MIT Press.

Blum, G. (2008) 'Bilateralism, Multilateralism, and the Architecture o International Law', *Harvard International Law Journal*, 49, 2: 323–379.

Cassese, A. (2001) *International Law*, Oxford: Oxford University Press.

——(1990) *Human Rights in a Changing World*, Cambridge: Polity.

Charnovitz, S. (1987) 'The Influence of International Labor Standards on the World Trading Regimes: A Historical Overview', *International Labour Review*, vol. 126, no. 5, pp. 565–584.

Compa, L. and Diamond, S. (eds) (1996) *Human Rights, Labor Rights and International Trade*, Philadelphia: University of Pennsylvania Press.

Douglas, W. A., Ferguson, J. P., Klett, E. (2004) 'An Effective Confluence of Forces in Support of Workers' Rights: ILO Standards, US Trade laws, Unions and NGOs', *Human Rights Quarterly*, 26, 2: 273–299.

Ehrenberg, R. (ed.) *Labor Markets and Integrating National Economies*, Washington: The Brookings Institution.

Elias, J. (2007) 'Women Workers and Labour Standards: the Problem of Human Rights,' *Review of International Studies*, 33, 1: 45–57.

Ewing, K. (1994) *Britain and the ILO*, 2nd edn, London: The Institute of Employment Rights.

Freeman, R. (1994)'Comments' in Ehreberg, R. (ed.) *Labor Markets and Integrating National Economies*, Washington: The Brookings Institution.

Gibbons, S. (1998) *International Labour Rights – New Methods of Enforcement*, London: Institute of Employment Rights.

Golub, S. (1997) 'International Labor Standards and International Trade', Washington. mimeo, IMF.

Hahn, M. (2007) 'The Convention on Cultural Diversity and International Economic Law', *Asian Journal of WTO and International Health Law and Policy*, 2, 2: 229–265.

Hassel, A. (2008) 'The Evolution of the Global Labor Governance Regime', *Governance: an International Journal of Policy and Administration*, 21, 2: 323–379.

Helfer, L. R. (2006) 'Understanding Change in International Organisations: Globalization and Innovation in the ILO', *Vanderbilt Law Review*, 69, 3: 649.

Hughes, S. and Wilkinson, R. (1998) 'International Labour Standards and World Trade: No Role for the World Trade Oganization?', *New Political Economy*, 3, 3: 375–389.

Johnston, G. A. (1970) *The International Labour Organisation: Its Work for Social and Economic Progress*, London: Europa Publications.

Krugman, P. (1997) 'What Should Trade Negotiators Negotiate About?', *Journal of Economic Literature*, 35: 113–120.

Kuper, A. (ed.) (2005) *Global Responsibilities: Who Must Deliver?* London: Routledge.

Lee, E. (1997) 'Globalization and Labour Standards: a Review of the Issues, *International Labour Review*, 136, 2, 173–189.

Levine, M. J. (1997) *Worker Rights and Labor Standards in Asias Four New Tigers: A Comparative Perspective*, New York: Plenum Press.

Merrils, J. (1988) *The Development of International Law by the European Court of Human Rights*, Manchester: Manchester University Press.

Murphy, C. (1994) *International Organization and Industrial Change*, Cambridge: Polity.

Murphy, S. D. (2005) 'Taking Multinational Corporate Codes of Conduct to the Next Level', *Columbia Journal of International Law*, 43, 2: 389–433.

OECD (1996) *Trade Employment and Labour Standards: A Study of Core Workers Rights and International Trade*, Paris: OECD.

Pursey, S. (2003) 'Trade Unions and Global Governance: The Debate on the Social Clause', *British Journal of Industrial Relations*, 41, 4, 789–795.

Rodrik, D. (1995) 'Labor Standards and International Trade: Moving Beyond the Rhetoric,' Washington, mimeo, Overseas Development Council.

Sen, A. (1999) *Development as Freedom*, Oxford: Oxford University Press.

Servais, J. M. (1986) 'Flexibility and Rigidity in International Labour Standards', *International Labour Review*, 125, 2: 193–208.

Tomlins, C. (2007) 'How Autnomous is Law?', *Annual Review of Law and Social Science*, 3, 45–68.

Trachtman, J. (ed.) (2006) *Cornell International Law Journal*, 'Special Issue on Global Justice: Poverty, Human Rights and Responsibilities', 39, 3.

Traugott, M. (1978) *Emile Durkheim on Institutional Analysis*, Chicago: Chicago University Press.

Udombana, N. J. (2006) 'Social Rights are Human Rights: Actualizing the Rights to Work and Social Security in Africa', *Cornell International Law Journal*, 39, 2: 181–242.

Weiler, P. (1990) *Governing the Workplace: The Future of Labor and Employment Law*, Cambridge, MA: Harvard University Press.

Wilkinson, R. (1999) 'Labour and Trade-Related Regulation: Beyond the Trade-Labour Standards Debate?', *British Journal of Politics and International Relations*, 1, 2: 165–191.

Wilkinson, R. and Hughes, S. (1999) 'Labor Standards and Global Governance: Examining the Dimensions of Institutional Engagement', mimeo, Department of Government, Manchester University.

Woodiwiss, A. (1990a) *Social Theory After Postmodernism: Rethinking Production, Law and Class*, London: Pluto.

——(1990b) *Rights v. Conspiracy: A Sociological Essay on the Development of Labour Law in the United States*, Oxford: Berg.

——(1998) *Globalisation, Human Rights and Labour Law in Pacific Asia*, Cambridge, Cambridge University Press.

——(2001) *The Visual in Social Theory*, London: Continuum.

——(2006) 'International Law,' *Theory, Culture and Society*, 23, 2–3: 524–5.

30

The globalization of human rights

Thomas Cushman

Introduction

The terms "globalization" and "human rights" enculate two of the most prominent areas of concern across a wide terrain of disciplines and perspectives in the social sciences and the humanities. The term "globalization" generally refers to the expansion of global capitalism, a process which began with the imperial expansion of Europe, accelerated with the Industrial Revolution, and developed in the twentieth century in a variety of new forms, such as the transnational corporation. At the most basic level, one might speak of globalization as the increasing diffusion of what Max Weber called instrumental rationality, both in terms of degree and intensity, across time and space into virtually every geographical area on the planet. Yet the exact nature of this process and its effects are highly contested, with some seeing globalization as an expansion of freedom and opportunity (Bhagwati, 2004) and others seeing it as an intensification of the more negative aspects of capitalism first diagnosed by Marx and intensified in the process capitalist expansion (Falk, 1999; Harvey, 2006). In general, it would be safe to say that globalization is almost always considered in terms of its human outcomes, that it is to say, its effects on human agency, and, in particular, on the well-being of human beings as they experience globalization.

Globalization cannot be seen purely in economic terms, though the ability to measure concrete economic outcomes facilitates this (see, for instance, Joyce, 2009). Empirical measures of global inequality, for instance, allow us to look concretely at the effects of capitalist expansion in various locales and measure the effects of this expansion in terms of the relative economic status of nations to each other or a sociological approach sees the overall process of globalization as consisting of a variety of other processes. Globalization is characterized by the expansion of media and communication technologies that enhance the interconnectedness of human beings on a global scale, allowing people to communicate and interact instantaneously across time and space on a historically unprecedented scale (Albrow, 1997). Another central aspect of globalization is the accelerating and expansive migration of peoples across national boundaries and population transfers (including ones that are forced and involuntary). Transnational migration is, of course, driven by capitalist labor markets, but such flows of people also being new cultural forms as migrants fuse their cultures of origin with their host cultures, producing new, and hybrid forms of culture (Levitt, 2001). Another aspect of globalization is the process of the global diffusion of culture across national boundaries. Globalization entails the "dislocation" of cultural meanings from particular locales with the effect that a new, virtually infinite, universe of cultural exchanges take place "outside" of traditional boundaries that contained and protected local cultures prior to the advent of modernity.

In this essay, I would like to argue that human rights is also part of the process of globalization. In another work, I have defined human rights as socially constructed ideals of freedom and human well-being (Cushman, 2006). On this definition, all societies have norms, values, and ideals which might be labeled as "human rights" that guide human action. Yet the term is generally used to describe ideals of freedom that are universal, which all humans have as a consequence of simply being human. Human rights are, by their very nature and in their very language, global rights. In what follows, I would like to outline the process of the globalization of human rights in a variety of ways. First, I will consider the successive development of different conceptions of rights from early modernity to the present. The focus here is in showing how competing definitions of human rights evolved historically so that when we look at the world today we find the major conceptions of human rights, conceptions which, however, are not necessarily commensurate with one another and exist in tension. The second part of this essay examines the globalization of rights as a process that involves the movement of universal ideas of human rights into new cultural locales and spaces. This is a process that is fraught with tension and conflict, as universal ideas of human freedom and well-being clash with local conceptions of right and wrong. The third and final part of this essay examines the emergence of new institutional and organizational forms that are based on the idea of human rights and that function to foster human rights in a global context. These new forms are often said to constitute something called "global civil society" or "transnational cosmopolitanism." As with the other sections, I will critically examine this concept and raise the question: has globalization led to the emergence of global civil society, and if so, what is the nature of this new entity?

There are no doubt many other processes which could be examined in an analysis of the globalization of human rights, but the three I have outlined here are ones which constitute the main processes of the globalization of human rights. Generally, discussions of globalization and human rights focus on another set of questions. How do the structural processes of globalization—especially economic, political, and legal structures which constitute globalization as a process—affect human rights? Does globalization lead to an advance of human freedom and thriving and social justice? Does globalization advance human rights? Or, is globalization a "dark" force, a process of hypermodernity that has brought on new forms of domination and new patterns of social suffering? These questions are not of central concern in this essay, though they will be raised in conjunction with the discussion of the main questions about the globalization of human rights. Looking at the globalization *of* human rights is not the same as looking at how globalization has *affected* human rights. The latter question will be explored only insofar as we must take note of the fact that a large part of the literature on globalization and human rights attempts to assess the impact of the former on the latter. To foreshadow my argument a bit, I want to argue there can be no valid empirical or ontological measure of the effects of globalization of human rights. The conceptions of human rights are so varied that what constitutes the freedom or the protection afforded by rights for one individual might be seen as subjugation and domination for others.

Generations of rights

Scholars of human rights have generally considered the emergence of human rights in modernity as the process of the successive development of different ideas of rights as ideals of human freedom and as protections against particular kinds of human vulnerability (Turner, 2006). Generally, these are referred to as *generations of rights*. The first generation of rights began with the American and French Revolutions. The revolutions were based on a conception of human rights as the civil and political rights of individuals over and against forms of state power and tyrannical rule. In both of these revolutions, individual rights were specified primarily as "negative rights", or ideals that aimed to negate the power of the state or the sovereign (in these cases, the King of England and the King of France) over supposedly free individuals. Most of the rights in the American Bill of Rights are specified in this negative language: the First Amendment, for instance, states that: "Congress shall make *no* law respecting an establishment of religion, or prohibiting the free exercise thereof; or abridging the freedom of speech, or of the press; or the right of the people peaceably to assemble, and to petition the Government for a redress of grievances."

These rights were specified as "natural and inalienable" and were held to be superior and peremptory to what were considered unjust laws and political practices. They specified ideas about the liberty of individuals *from* external forms of power. It is especially important to underscore here the fact that the rights which underpinned these revolutions were negative, because later conceptions of human rights—and especially those which are very prevalent in present-day global world-system—conceived of human rights in terms of the obligations of states to foster human thriving and alleviate vulnerability by specifying what states should or ought to do *for* individuals, or groups of specifically vulnerable individuals.

The American Revolution was quite limited in its geographic scope, even if the ideals of human rights in which it was grounded were specified in universal language. The French Revolution is generally considered to be the first major revolution which, in addition to redressing intrusions on human freedom in France, aspired to be universal (see Hunt, 2007). The French Revolution was a model for successive revolutionary movements, in that it specified a central body of core "rights of man and the citizen," which presented themselves as sacred ideas that various groups of disenfranchised individuals could then aspire to acquire (Hunt, 1996). In this sense, the French Revolution established citizenship as a kind of status, with human rights as its central cultural capital. Citizenship entailed the recognition that one had certain rights, and many of the struggles of the French Revolution were about which groups of individuals ought to "possess" these rights, and by virtue of this enhance their freedoms and guard against vulnerability.

One way to conceptualize the model of the French Revolution is to imagine human rights as the central normative core of a society. People who are peripheral in the society, and therefore "unprotected" or vulnerable, aspire to move from the periphery to the core. The reason this model is important for the discussion of the globalization of human rights is that it has been followed historically in various struggles for human rights from the time of the French Revolution to the present. Western movements for women's human rights relied fundamentally on this idea that human rights were a sacred core of protection, and the social movements for women's rights aimed to move women into the protective realm of that core. The contemporary movement for the rights of gay and lesbian people to marry has relied on a strategy of claiming that this right is a "human right," which all citizens enjoy and which gay and lesbian people deserve as citizens. The

591

model of the French Revolution, then, is an important benchmark for understanding the more general sociological process of how vulnerable or disenfranchised people seek to achieve the status of citizenship and thereby enjoy the protection of rights.

The French Revolution was important in other ways, since it served as the inspiration for major critiques of human rights, which themselves have inspired critiques of human rights into the present day (Waldron, 1987). Jeremy Bentham's vicious critique of the French Revolution became the foundation for contemporary utilitarian critiques of human rights, which argue that what ought to be done for the good of society should not be measured by some abstract ideal or standard, but by considerations of what is practical for the happiness or good of the many. Edmund Burke's critique of human rights, which focused on the importance of national traditions in determining what is best for societies and individuals, was a template for defenses of national cultures and sovereign traditions over and against the abstract, transnational, universalizing ideas of human rights. Bentham and Burke could be seen as precursor critiques of the "globalization of human rights," Bentham arguing for the universal principle of utility in social planning and Burke arguing against the trumping of national traditions and rights of cultures over and against abstract, universal ideas which would, in his view, sow disorder and chaos in societies. Their basic logic is present in the modern world among those who argue that one can seek improvements to society without any recourse to the language of human rights (see, for instance, Singer, 2004) or that universal human rights are a threat to the national cultures and values that best serve people within their own nation states.

Yet in terms of thinking about globalization—and especially the economic aspects of globalization that are so important to modern debates—it was Marx's famous critique of the French Revolution, put forth in his "The Jewish Question," which has been most decisive. Marx argued that the French Revolution, with its model of disenfranchised individuals and groups aspiring to acquire citizenship based on rights, was an illusory form of liberation and freedom. For Marx, the Revolution served mainly to foster the freedom of individuals or members of groups to be granted civil and political rights for themselves. This social movement, then, while appearing quite radical, was merely a half-measure which occluded his utopian dream of abolishing capitalism and unifying people across classes and groups into a whole united by what he referred to as the spirit of "species-being." Marx originated the idea that it is not individuals, per se, who are oppressed, but social classes and groups, and the specific source of this oppression is capitalism. The "real" revolution in human rights would occur only when capitalism had been overthrown.

Marx's argument against individual rights and his argument that freedom could only be achieved through the abolition of capitalism is the groundwork of what are called *second generation rights*. Second generation rights are social and economic rights that are necessary to protect individuals from the particular vulnerabilities inflicted by capitalism. In contrast to first generation rights, social and economic rights conceive of freedom as fostering and ensuring the physical (and by way of that the mental) well-being of human beings. The aim of these rights is to alleviate human vulnerability through interventions, especially by the state, to provide basic necessities of human life such things as food, shelter, and health care. Historically, this generation of rights proceeded not so much on the exact revolutionary logic of Marx for the complete abolition of capitalism (though the Soviet Union and China, as communist societies, attempted to do so with quite drastic human costs), but on the idea that capitalism was a force which by its very nature (diagnosed so astutely by Marx) violated human dignity and created specific forms of protracted human suffering. Social and economic rights such as "the right to food," or the "right to housing" aim to "tame" capitalism's excesses by specifying that something ought to be done *for* individuals to alleviate their capitalist-induced vulnerabilities.

The idea of social and economic rights became more and more prominent in Western capitalist societies in the twentieth century in the development of the welfare state and the ideology of democratic socialism. For purposes of discussing the process of the globalization of human rights, it is important to underscore that the idea of social and economic rights exists in tension to the overtly individualistic and libertarian ideals of the first generation of individual rights. Many of the debates about the effects of globalization have to do with what individuals have the right to do in terms of pursuing self-interest in a global capitalist society versus what other individuals, classes, or groups have to suffer as a result of the expansion of capitalism on a global scale. Contemporary debates on human rights proceed primarily between proponents of first and second generation rights, with proponents of individual rights stressing such things as economic freedom and civil and political rights and proponents of social and economic rights arguing for the fundamental necessity to protect against human vulnerability. The process of the globalization of human rights has produced a global situation which is, in fact, quite tense, since the very idea of freedom embodied in different conceptions is highly contested. The tensions between Europe and the United States, for instance, are often about the fact that Europeans have strongly adopted the imperative of social and economic rights as centrally in their societies, while Americans continue to guided by libertarian ideas of rights (though periodically, the United States has its own tensions between libertarianism and socialist ideals).

Increasingly in the twentieth century, new kinds of rights claims began to emerge in addition to these first two generations of human rights. This so-called *third generation* of rights is based on the idea that groups and cultures, as collective entities, have specific rights (Kymlicka, 1989). The logic underlying this perspective is similar to the Marxian logic that the proletariat is oppressed as a group by bourgeois capitalists, but extends that logic to include a wider variety of groups such as oppressed minorities or Indigenous cultures. These new kinds of group or cultural rights have been referred to as *third generation rights*. These rights are based on the conception that people are more or less vulnerable depending on the group or culture to which they belong, or to which they are seen by the dominant society as belonging. Because groups or cultures are made vulnerable *as* members of groups or cultures, the alleviation of that vulnerability involves the articulation of the rights of particularly vulnerable groups or cultures. In this conception of rights, mobilization for human rights proceeds not by claiming individual rights, or even social and economic rights (though these claims can be made for members of these groups), but by seeking special protections and rights for groups or cultures that have special kinds vulnerabilities by virtue of their position in the dominant society.

The emergence of third generation rights is important in relation to globalization, since globalization is a process that is seen as having particular consequences (usually negative) for particular vulnerable groups. Thus, while lower class members of a particular society might make claims for social and economic rights in the face of economic vulnerability, these very same members might make a further set of claims for further specific or special rights by virtue of their membership in a minority group or culture. For instance, a member of an Indigenous culture might receive substantial advantage of social and economic rights provided by the state, but might make further claims for special rights such as unlimited land use or fishing, the practice of their religion, or the right to be educated in their own language. Group rights put specific demands on members

593

of groups to follow group norms and thus can be quite at odds with individual rights. A member of a group, for instance, might desire to exercise the right of freedom of association or the right to choose a marital partner, but these acts could violate the central norms of what the group or culture has defined as "right" and "wrong."

This brief elaboration of the successive generations of rights is important, because many of the contemporary debates about globalization center around what kinds of rights are primary. We can conceive of the globalization of human rights as a process of the successive emergence of different kinds of normative ideals in modernity, each with its particular origins and logic, but now coexisting at the same moment in dialectical tension with each other. The process of the globalization of human rights might be conceived as a process of the competition of different sets of ideas about what constitutes the main source of domination and vulnerability of human beings and how the latter can be alleviated. For purposes of understanding the central debates about the relation between globalization and human rights, it is the tension between social and economic rights, on the one hand, and individual rights, which is most instructive.

Debates about globalization and its consequences

As noted earlier, the main debates about globalization have been about the nature and effects of global capitalism. In globalization studies, these debates are quite protracted and seemingly intractable, with scholars looking at the very same kinds of processes and seeing very different outcomes. In studies of globalization, there is a tendency to consider the effects of globalization in economic terms. This is driven by the fact that there is a firm methodological and empirical basis for measuring such things as economic inequality both between and within nations. Another characteristic of studies of globalization, however, is ideological: in focusing on capitalism's negative effects many analysts of globalization are grounded in a Marxian theoretical logic that vilifies capitalism and stresses the primacy of social and economic rights. Various works attach metaphors to the process of globalization that indicate a negative appraisal of its overall effects. Anthony Giddens (2002) for instance, sees globalization as a juggernaut which destroys everything in its path. Richard Falk (1999) refers to globalization as "predatory," and outlines its devastating effects. David Harvey (2006) sees globalization in the modern world as the fulfillment of Marx's prediction of the forward march of capitalism and the expansion of capitalist exploitation on a global scale. Blau and Moncada (2006), have simply argued that individual rights are not human rights at all and that the only "authentic" human rights are social and economic rights, and that as a result, the global expansion of capitalism demands the expansion of the social and economic rights in all spheres of social life.

Very often, the process of capitalist globalization is referred to with the ideological label "neoliberalism," which opens up vast new opportunities for capitalist exploitation on a global scale. Oftentimes neoliberalism is conceived of as a dangerous and threatening ideology that is the grounding for a new, and even more potently destructive, form of globalized capitalism (Harvey, 2005). The point here is to stress that discussions of the effects of globalization are often starkly politicized and ideological and that they very often proceed on the basis that the idea of social and economic rights are, *in fact,* the most important kinds of rights and that the outcomes of globalization must be measured in terms of the advancement of social and economic rights.

Much of the debate about globalization has to do with how globalization is defined and how human rights is seen in relation to the process. Thus Bhagwati (2004), in defining human freedom (and therefore human rights) as the expansion of individual freedom, sees globalization as a process that facilitates individual rights, especially to economic freedom and opportunity that were previously closed off to economically vulnerable individuals. Modern critics of globalization argue that it has increased inequality and social suffering, and have taken a more or less socialist approach in arguing against "neoliberalist capitalism" and in favor of the expansion of state power to provide "positive rights" to vulnerable individuals. In the social science literature, there are very few defenses of globalization as a progressive process: for the most part, nearly all of the major works in the field are highly critical of globalization and consider it a negative and destructive process, much the same as Marx saw capitalism as a force under which "all that is solid melts into air."

Globalization and the incommensurability of conceptions of human rights

The question of the relationship between globalization and human rights cannot be answered decisively because there is no one standard by which one can measure human rights. Since I have defined human rights as ideas about freedom, the idea of what constitutes freedom is of necessity highly subjective, or at least prone to being defined in ideological terms so that one form of freedom can be seen by someone else as a form of domination or subjugation and vice versa. The freedom of the disenfranchised worker who is able, through the acquisition of capital from some source, to advance his own well-being comes at the expense of the subjugation of the person he employs. Heavy taxation and the expropriation of resources to provide for the well-being of others (and therefore their potential for freedom) violates the idea of freedom of control over one's own property. The point to be made here is that when we are considering both the process of the globalization of human rights and the effects of globalization of human rights, it is impossible to develop a standard—as so many analysts of globalization have tried to do—as to what constitutes the "best" measure of human rights. That is because the successive generations of rights, in terms of how they understand human vulnerability and freedom, are incommensurate and in tension with each other. The best we can do from a strictly sociological point of view is to understand the globalization of human rights as a process of the evolution of conflicting definitions of vulnerability and freedom and to examine movements in relation to the efforts of actors or institutions to advance this or that conception.

The example of the Soviet Union and Eastern Europe is instructive here. Under the domination of the Soviet Union, Eastern Europeans experienced an almost complete obliteration of individual political and civil rights. The legitimating ideology of the Soviet Union was grounded in rigid ideology of social and economic rights, which argued that the rights of individuals must be abrogated in order to protect the state, which provided social and economic rights. Notwithstanding the actual provision of such rights, it is hard to see the experiences of citizens of these countries as freedom, if we consider freedom in the negative sense, as the absence of state intrusion and the facilitation of civil and political rights, individual liberty, and the free exercise of human agency. The downfall of the Soviet empire opened the way for rapid intrusion of capitalism into these formerly communist societies. Clearly, new forms of capitalism had tremendous influences on these types of societies (as indicated by the use of the term "shock therapy" to describe the process). And clearly, as one would expect in any capitalist society, new forms of inequality and vulnerability emerged within these societies.

Yet, from the point of view of citizens of formerly communist countries, the negative valences of capitalism were not always experienced as forms of domination, but as new forms of opportunity, both for individuals and for the nations in which they lived. Capitalism was clearly a structural force that enhanced individual freedom, especially in the economic sphere, in spite of its negative effects. It also enabled freedom of choice in the political sphere, which enabled the formerly communist countries to enter rather rapidly into the global political and economic world-system. Consider that many of the nations of the former Soviet bloc are now members, or candidate members, of the European Union, which allows for a hitherto unprecedented degree of financial possibility, freedom of association to create new political parties, and freedom of movement to pursue new economic opportunities. To point out these "positive" outcomes in human rights is not to gloss over the very real effects of capitalism or the fact of new forms of economic exploitation in this area of the world. But is it to note that the downfall of communism and the rise of capitalism offered an unprecedented opportunity for millions of people to claim a set of human rights that were unimaginable under Soviet domination. In most of the social science literature on globalization, such experiences of freedom are generally elided as theorists derive their conceptions of globalization from Marxian conceptions of capitalism, and because of that, capitalism becomes the major source of negative social outcomes. To be sure, to describe the experience of global capitalism purely as "freedom" would be naïve in the extreme; it would surely only parrot the ideologies of capitalists and leaders of capitalist states. Yet on the other hand, to consider globalization as a process that is inherently destructive is to miss the experience of freedom that for many actors is an authentic and valuable experience of freedom.

Globalization as the intersection between global human rights and local cultures

One of the major issues in the study of the globalization of human rights is the ways in which universal ideas of human rights intersect with particular, or local ideas of rights (Appadurai, 1996; Robertson, 1992; Merry, 2006). Because so many rights are specified in universal terms, they have served as templates for actors who wish to assist other vulnerable individuals and groups and as cultural tools for the latter in their own struggles for freedom and well-being. Globalization accelerates the process of cultural diffusion, and one of the central ideas that has been diffused is the idea of human rights.

This issue has been conditioned by the long-standing debates in human rights about universalism and relativism. When the Universal Declaration of Human Rights (UDHR) was ratified by the United Nations in 1948, it provoked a sharp critical response by anthropologists, who argued that there could be no conception of human rights that would be valid across the wide diversity of global cultures (Engle, 2001). While not specifically couched in the language of relativism, what many anthropologists were arguing is that there could be no such thing as rights *outside* of particular cultures and that Western ideas of human rights represented a form of cultural imperialism. The anthropological critique of rights echoed many of the sentiments that had been expressed in the drafting of the UDHR. The UDHR was a product of a tense and conflictual process of dialogue and debate among representatives of different types of conceptions of rights and religious traditions (Glendon, 2001). Representatives of Western democracies argued for civil and political rights, while communist representatives argued for social and economic rights. Representatives of world religions such as Islam and Confucianism found the freedoms of individual rights contrary and even hostile to the duties specified in their religious traditions. Nonetheless, such differences were put aside and those who drafted and put forth the declaration did so with a certain degree of "bad faith" in the sense that they not only disagreed with many of the rights in it, but knew the Declaration would not challenge the power, say, of the Soviet Union's conceptions of rights, or the obdurate power of Islamic traditions in Muslim societies.

So even though the UDHR emerged as an "objective" set of rights that was valid for all people on a global scale, it did not have the power of authentic, collective agreement and consensus behind it. The problem of the incommensurability of rights noted above is one which is embodied in the UDHR. Though the rights specified in it are presumably universal, it is quite clear that the vast majority of human beings on the planet do not enjoy the full protection of these rights and it is probably safe to say that the majority of human beings do not enjoy many if not most of these rights. Yet many have argued that the document is important, since it serves as a normative template by which the ideas of human rights can proceed and *possibly* be achieved on a more global scale. The globalization of human rights is based not on the actuality of rights, but on an aspiration that they might be generalized as widely as possible.

Human rights culture has diffused into local contexts some actors (to be discussed below) who have perceived or defined "violations" of human rights. Detecting such violations, however, means that there is some ontologically valid standard by which violations can be measured. Generally, that standard has been the various ideas of human rights that can be found in the UDHR or some conception of freedom and vulnerability derived from philosophical principles of justice and rights (usually of Western origin). Yet these conceptions often conflict with the norms and values in various locales, and so the fundamental character of the intersection of a universalizing human rights culture and local culture is one of tension. Outside elites who come into a society with human rights language threaten traditional order and the position of elites who justify their power through the language of tradition. Human rights culture offers the possibility of freedom and agency to people who live in societies in which freedom and agency are deliberately suppressed in the name of tradition and order. The globalization of human rights has often been seen as a form of cultural imperialism, since it represents an alternative model of existence which often stands in stark contrast to many enduring and obdurate cultural traditions (Mutua, 2002). Human rights are clearly "from away" and clearly are "out of place" in local cultures, and clearly threaten the autonomous culture of societies. Regardless of whether or not the globalization of human rights represents "imperialism", however, the fact is that the world is now characterized by the *presence* of human rights culture in virtually every geographical locale around the globe. The question is thus not so much whether human rights are present in the globalized world, but how rights and local cultures interact with each other.

Scholar and practitioners of human rights have tried to escape the dualism of the universalism–relativism dichotomy by recreating the project of human rights as a dialogic one (see, for instance, Cowan et al., 2001). A dialogic approach is one in which advocates of universal human rights recognize the social constructedness of their own conceptions of human rights as they attempt to assist vulnerable individuals in other locales. Human rights are not seen as a naturalized, essentialized forms of truth, but as a conceptions that offer alternatives to damaging cultural practices. Human rights are seen by those who believe in them as forms of culture not to be imposed on others, but to be introduced to them in a way that respects local customs and tries to "work within" cultures to effect changes that reduce harm and foster well-being.

One example of this dialogic process might be illustrated with the case of female genital circumcision, often referred to as female genital mutilation. The very use of the term mutilation conceives of the process of clitorectomy in negative terms, naming a specific kind of vulnerability inflicted on young women as part of their normal socialization in the cultures in which they live. There are a variety of forms and degrees of female circumcision, but there is some sense in which, from the standpoint of universal human rights, the practice is a fundamental violation of the bodily integrity of women and their rights to exercise control over their own sexuality. Yet, as Billet (2007) notes, the practice serves a variety of social functions in the societies in which it occurs. It serves as a marker of status, representing the transition into adulthood. It has utility in marriage markets where circumcised women are more valuable to men, and where uncircumcised women have less value, thus profoundly affecting the life chances of women. To forego the process is to risk social marginalization and enhance economic risk: circumcision is a necessary part of maximizing women's chances in a society that values this social practice.

The idea of the right of a woman to choose what happens to her body is thus threatening to women, on the one hand, and to the social order in which the practice has value, on the other. A dialogic perspective would approach the problem as a "negotiation" in which, say, the human rights advocate would suggest that an alternative, less invasive, and less harmful practice could be substituted for the original practice. One might suggest, for instance, a ritual circumcision, in which a ceremony occurs and a symbolic act is performed on the genitalia that involves perhaps a slight drawing of blood that leaves no permanent damage. The ritual would serve the dual function of maintaining this important symbolic marker of womanhood, but alleviate the marked vulnerability of women to a dangerous procedure. This solution would not be easy, since one would have to negotiate with and persuade the members of the culture that this new practice would have the authenticity and sacred meaning of the actual practice.

This dialogic practice of human rights, or human rights as a negotiation with local cultures, is a significant new facet of the contemporary globalization of human rights. It proceeds with an understanding on the part of the human rights practitioner of the power and limitations of her own cultural ideals, a respect for the ideals of others, and the possibility of protecting the vulnerable by producing new hybrid practices. It also recognizes, as Dembour (2001) has argued, that pure relativism—in this case simply deciding that the practice of female circumcision is valid on its own terms in the cultures in which it exists—leads to indifference and acquiescence. From a purely relativistic position, one would not be in a position to do anything, since any action would be considered an intrusion on other peoples' cultures. The real quandary of the globalization of human rights is how to avoid imposing human rights as a form of cultural imperialism, on the one hand, and how to avoid the indifference that would result if one simply decided that all cultures are valid. In the former case, human rights becomes domination, in the latter case, there simply is no basis for arguing that human rights have any special value, and therefore, there can be no universalizing project of human rights on a global scale.

It is hard to know the extent to which such dialogic practices are at work in the world today, or how effective they are, although it is clear that human rights practitioners are aware of the dangerousness of an unchecked human rights universalism. Dialogic approaches represent a new facet of the process of globalization in which the advocates of human rights denaturalize their own conceptions of rights and accept the validity of other culture practices. Also, for those advocates of human rights, the idea is not to colonize local cultures, but to enhance the thriving of individuals by offering them alternatives. In many cases, this simply means establishing a *presence* in another society and through that presence, to make vulnerable individuals aware of other options for self-reclamation should they choose (or be able to choose) to avail themselves of them. This dialogic practice is also at work in the attempts by people in other cultures who wish to mobilize in order to alleviate their own vulnerability. Activists in Indigenous movements for rights, for instance, are in increasing contact with global representatives of human rights culture, and learn how to frame their causes in the language of human rights and get assistance from the variety of human rights activists increasingly present in the world (Bob, 2005).

Among certain writers on human rights (Walzer, 1994; Ignatieff, 2001), the quest to foster a wide body of rights across cultures has been abandoned. The focus here is on developing a body of the most fundamental, basic rights—a "minimal morality"—on which a large number of societies can agree. This movement represents a scaling back of the aspirations of universal human rights, a humility in the face of recognition that some types of cultural practices, while violating the norms of universal human rights, are not as bad as others. In this view, the focus is on the most egregious violations of human rights such as torture, genocide, infanticide, or sex trafficking. Such dialogic and consensual approaches to human rights represent a significant scaling back of the imperial aspirations sometimes attributed to the Western project of human rights and are a recognition of the limitations of Western ideas outside of their Western contexts.

The dialogic approach has not solved the problem of relativism, nor does it completely exculpate human rights advocates from the charge of cultural imperialism. By their very nature, universalized notions of human rights exert force in locales simply by their mere presence. The reality of globalization means that human rights are "here to stay." They are borne into other cultures by human rights activists, and people who are vulnerable seek them out as models for the alleviation of vulnerability.

Globalization and the rise of global civil society

I have spoken so far of the globalization of human rights primarily in terms of cultural diffusion of human rights and the intersections of universalizing conceptions of rights and local cultures. The last question to address in this globalization process is the organizational and institutional forms by which human rights culture is spread on a global scale. For the most part, attention here has been paid to the rise of non-governmental organizations, consisting of human rights activists, which have human right agendas in various areas of the world. Keck and Sikkink (1998) have referred to this movement as one of "activists beyond borders."

It is hard to characterize NGOs in terms of any one overall project; they range from those that are primarily autarkic in dealing with problems within their own societies, to those that are purposely global in their aspirations. Some NGOs, such as Human Rights Watch or Amnesty International, aim to document human rights violations around the globe and to call attention to these as a way to provide the impetus for political action on the part of other NGOs. Other NGOs are advocacy organizations that focus on mobilizing to prevent and ameliorate human rights violations that occur around the world. Often, these NGOs are "cause driven" and reactive, that is, they are oriented toward a particular cause, such as the prevention of genocide or torture. Examples of the causes that drive NGOs might be the various organizations that emerge to respond to particularly egregious violations of human rights such as genocide in Darfur, or the banning of landmines on a global scale.

In spite of the diversity of types of NGOS, they can, as a whole, be conceptualized as a very important new structural force in modernity. Their significance lies in the fact that they challenge the traditional Westphalian idea that what states do within their own borders is their own business and that "outsiders" have no right to intervene. The globalization of NGOs represents a movement toward considering human beings as having universal rights outside of their states and conceiving of state borders as artificial and, in most cases, detrimental to the advancement of human rights on a global scale. In this sense, the collective of global NGOs poses a considerable challenge to the traditional idea of state sovereignty in global affairs. Human rights activists, especially those with considerable resources and political connections, have considerable potential to force states to comply with various human rights treaties and in many cases, pose significant challenges to those states that violate human rights under the protection of state boundaries and the principle of non-intervention.

One paradox of the current system of global governance represented by the United Nations is that the Universal Declaration of Human Rights articulates a very clear and powerful objective set of substantive human rights, rights that all humans regardless of their geographical location have by virtue of being human, while at the same time, specifies in its charter the principle of non-intervention in the affairs of other states (at least for the purposes of redressing human rights violations). Thus, the globalization of human rights, as a system of ethics, is challenged by the limitations of what is allowable under international law. For purposes of understanding the reality of the global system of human rights and international law, it is useful to stress that human rights and international law are not necessarily the same thing (Cushman, 2005). What can be completely legitimate in terms of the UDHR—ensuring that all people enjoy human rights—can be completely illegitimate according to international law. An example of this is the United Nations Convention Against Genocide, ratified in 1948. This treaty specifies that in situations where genocide is present, states have an obligation to intervene to stop it. Yet, because of the enduring power of the principle of non-intervention, which is specified in the United Nations Charter as being only allowed in cases of self-defense, the treaty has never been invoked and there have been no specific cases in which states have intervened to stop genocide (with the possible exception of the NATO intervention in Kosovo, though that intervention was grounded in the logic of security, rather than the international law against genocide or the advancement of human rights). The major point here is the intervention by states in the name of stopping human rights violations is not a major aspect of the process of the globalization of human rights. Indeed, one of the central questions in discussions of human rights is whether and when states should intervene to prevent gross violations of human rights and the debate on this issue is tense and unresolved.

Because of the dominance of the principle of non-intervention, much of the work of intervention in the name of human rights has fallen to NGOS. Their prevalence in the global landscape is so widespread that many scholars have come to refer to them collectively as constituting a *global civil society*. Kaldor, Anheler, and Glasius (2004/2005) have defined global civil society as a "sphere of ideas, values, institutions, organizations, networks, and individuals located between the family, the state, and the market and operating beyond the confines of national societies, polities and economics." This rather amorphous definition contains a virtual infinitude of human action, but suggests that globalization has brought on a discernible new social formation that consists of both culture and forms that stand outside of the state and aim, as a whole, to advance the agenda of human rights. Unlike most definitions of society, which rely on some idea of geographical boundaries and borders, this definition locates global civil society as existing somewhere outside of the time and space of the "normal" configuration of states and societies. In the terms of this definition, it is hard to conceive of limitations as to who or what might be a "member" of global civil society. An organization can specify that it is part of this entity and once many organizations do this, one does see a new social formation that the actors involved consider to be part of global civil society. It is harder to imagine what it might mean for a person to say, "I am a member of global civil society," except if we define membership as normative action outside of traditional boundaries of politics of national societies, polities, and economics. Such a person, however, would still be a citizen of a specific country and enjoy the rights and privileges of such citizenship, even though they are a new type of actor in the global world-system. In many ways, the concept of global civil society is a reified one which aims to describe the very real new global patterns of normative, organizational engagement in the world. It is at once an analytical construct, but also a highly idealized and utopian idea. It might be said that global civil society is a social imaginary, or in Benedict Anderson's (1991) terms, an imagined community, an idealized conception that describes what citizens of global civil society *think* they are doing, rather than what they actually are doing.

This conception of civil society has been subject to a rather pointed critique by Rieff and Anderson (2004/2005), which does not accept the idealized image of global civil society as either a useful analytical concept or a utopian ideal. Rieff and Anderson argue that "the global civil society movement might better be understood as imagining itself as the bearer of universal values, both operating in the teeth of globalisation and yet simultaneously using globalisation as its vehicle for disseminating universal values. It may be seen better understood as a movement seeking to universalize the ultimately parochial model of European Union Integration." Rieff and Anderson go on to say that global civil society is a collection of undemocratic and unaccountable "social movement missionaries." While this is a rather caustic view, it does articulate a salient sociological critique of the idea of global civil society. NGOs are, first and foremost, social organizations, and, as such, they have their own interests, values, norms, procedures, and social hierarchies. They are not, in a sense, democratic institutions, since in general they rely on hierarchies of administration and membership that are not elected by a polity. A human rights representative to another from the United States government would be a representative of an elected government and accountable to that government, while an NGO actor would be a representative of his or her organization, and accountable solely to that organization.

In this sense, it is important to throw into relief the idea that, while the NGOs that constitute this supposed global civil society are to be oriented toward the protection of the vulnerable, this global civil society, if it exists at all, is a new constellation of power. It is beyond the scope of this essay to consider the implications of this observation in the manner which they deserve. The important point is that in speaking about the globalization of human rights, one has to be very careful in confusing analytical concepts with idealistic and utopian ones. There is no doubt that a formidable phalanx of global NGOs exist in the global world-system, and there is no doubt that they have made significant advances in fostering their conceptions of human rights. Yet at the same time, as part of the process of globalization, global civil society, either as an idealized conception needs to be considered critically in the same way that we would consider other processes of globalization such as capitalism.

Conclusion

The topic of the globalization of human rights is rather a large one, and in this essay, I have tried to outline the overall process in terms of three central subprocesses. These by no means exhaust the possibilities of what is mean by the globalization of human rights. Conceiving of human rights as a form of culture is paramount in importance, since it constantly reminds us that human rights are social constructions. Conceiving of human rights as socially constructed ideas about what constitutes freedom and human vulnerability and how to alleviate that vulnerability and promote freedom is an important new analytical strategy for understanding what we mean by human rights in the modern world. By understanding human rights as generations of rights that are incommensurate, we can understand the process of advancing human rights as a conflictual one, not only in terms of conflicts between human rights activists and states who violate human rights, but also among human rights proponents with different conceptions of what human rights ideas are. By understanding the reality of the present day situation of human rights as an intersection between the universal and the particular, we can understand both the limitations and the possibilities of human rights that are inherent in the dialogic approach to human rights, which, in my opinion, is one of the more positive aspects of human rights. Finally, by understanding that the constructions that human rights activists use to describe and conceptualize what it is they are doing, we stress the globalization of human rights is not simply about looking at how human rights have advanced (or not), but also about reflexively examining the actors and institutions who act in the name of human rights. The idealism that has always been the foundation of human rights must also be tempered by the necessity to understand and rethink what it means to act in the world on behalf of the other, and what the limitations of such action are in the face of the grim realities that still characterize much of the world.

References

Cowan, Jane K., Marie-Bénédicte Dembour, and Richard A. Wilson. Eds. 2001. *Culture and Rights: Anthropological Perspectives* (Cambridge and New York: Cambridge University Press).

Cushman, Thomas. 2006. "Rights, Human." Pp. 517–23 in Bryan S. Turner, ed., *The Cambridge Dictionary of Sociology* (Cambridge: Cambridge University Press).

——2005. " The Conflict of the Rationalities: International Law, Human Rights, and the War in Iraq." *Deakin Law Review.* Vol. 10, No. 2, pp. 546–571.

Dembour, Marie-Bénédicte. 2001. "Following the Movement of a Pendulum: Between Universalism and Relativism." In Jane Cowan, Marie-Bénédicte Dembour, and Richard A. Wilson, eds., *Culture and Rights: Anthropological Perspectives* (Cambridge and New York: Cambridge University Press).

Engle, Karen. 2001. "From Skepticism to Embrace: Human Rights and the American Anthropological Association." *Human Rights Quarterly*, Vol. 23, No. 3, pp. 536–59.

Falk, Richard. 1999. *Predatory Globalization: A Critique* (Cambridge: Polity Press).

Giddens, Anthony. 2002. *Runaway World: How Globalisation is Reshaping Our Lives* (London: Profile).

Glendon, Mary Ann. 2001. *A World Made New: Eleanor Roosevelt and the Universal Declaration of Human Rights* (New York: Random House).

Harvey, David. 2005. *A Brief History of Neoliberalism* (New York: Oxford University Press).

——2006. *Spaces of Global Capitalism* (London: New York: Verso).

Hunt, Lynn Avery. 2007. *Inventing Human Rights: A History.* (New York: W.W. Norton).

Hunt, Lynn, ed. 1996. *The French Revolution and Human Rights: A Brief Documentary History* (Boston, MA: Bedford Books of St. Martin's Press).

Ignatieff, Michael. 2001. *Human Rights as Politics and Idolatry* (Princeton, NJ: Princeton University Press).

Joyce, Joseph. 2009. "Globalization and Inequality Among Nations," in Sisay Asefa (ed.), *Economic Globalization and Development: Critical Issues of the 21st Century* (Kalamazoo, MI: W.E. Upjohn Institute for Employment Research).

Kaldor, Mary, Helmut Anheier and Marlies Glasius. 2004/2005. "Introduction", Global Civil Society Yearbook at: www.lse.ac.uk/Depts/global/yearbook04chapters.htm#part1.

Keck, Margaret E. and Kathryn Sikkink. 1998. *Activists Beyond Borders: Advocacy Networks in International Politics* (Ithaca, NY: Cornell University Press).

Kymlicka, Will. 1989. *Liberalism, Community, and Culture* (Oxford: Clarendon Press).

Levitt, Peggy. 2001. *The Transnational Villagers* (Berkeley, CA: University of California Press).

Merry, Sally Engle. 2006. *Human Rights and Gender Violence: Translating International Law into Local Justice* (Chicago, IL: University of Chicago Press).

Mutua, Makau. 2002. *Human Rights: A Political and Cultural Critique* (Philadelphia, PA: University of Pennsylvania Press).

Rieff, David and Kenneth Anderson. 2004/2005. "Global Civil Society: A Skeptical View," Global Civil Society Yearbook at: www.lse.ac.uk/Depts/global/yearbook04chapters.htm#part1.

Robertson, Roland. 1992. *Globalization: Social Theory and Global Culture* (London; Thousand Oaks, CA: Sage, 1992).

Singer, Peter. 2004. "Outsiders: Our Obligations to Those Outside Our Borders." pp. 11–32 in Deen K. Chaterjee, ed., *The Ethics of Assistance: Morality and the Distant Needy* (Cambridge: Cambridge University Press).

Turner, Bryan. 2006. *Vulnerability and Human Rights* (University Park, PA: Pennsylvania State University Press).

Waldron, Jeremy. 1987. *Nonsense Upon Stilts: Bentham, Burke, and Marx on the Rights of Man* (London and New York: Methuen).

Walzer, Michael. 1994. *Thick and Thin: Moral Argument at Home and Abroad* (Notre Dame, IN: University of Notre Dame Press).

603

31

Global civil society and the World Social Forum

Kadambari Anantram, Christopher Chase-Dunn, and Ellen Reese

This chapter reviews recent research on global civil society and the global public sphere in world historical context, with particular attention to transnational social movements and their relationship to the globalization of economic and political institutions. Following Kaldor (2003: 44–45) we define civil society broadly as "the medium through which one or many social contracts between individuals, both women and men, and the political and economic centers of power are negotiated and reproduced." The concept refers to the domestic realm of institutions, such as private schools and families, as well as non-governmental organizations (NGOs), business firms, informal networks, social clubs, non-state religious organizations, unions, and social movement organizations (SMOs). This is true regardless of the content of the political orientation of such institutions and organizations. Civil society thus includes corporate-sponsored think tanks, conservative churches, fascist and racist organizations, as well as more politically moderate and progressive types of social and political groups. Because they are uncivil in their tactics, terrorist and other armed political groups and actors are excluded from the concept of "civil society," however.

For the purpose of this essay, we use the term global (or transnational) civil society very broadly to refer to civil society institutions and organizations that cross one or more national boundaries, even if they are not fully global in their reach. This concept includes such conservative and elite-dominated institutions as the World Economic Forum and the Catholic Church and purportedly neutral international organizations, such as international charities. For interests of space, our essay here reviews only on the recent, and burgeoning, scholarship on the progressive and left wings of transnational civil society, and their relationship to the World Social Forum. Since its first meeting in 2001, the World Social Forum has quickly become the largest international gathering of social justice activists affiliated with a family of progressive and left-wing social movements, or a "movement of movements" associated with the global justice movement.

We begin by reviewing the historical development and scholarly contentions regarding the concepts of "civil society" and "global" or "transnational" civil society. We then review the empirical research on international social movement organizations (INGOs), transnational social movements, transnational advocacy networks, and the rise of the

World Social Forum. We end this essay by considering the relevance of these various kinds of transnational actors, movements, and institutions to the historical and possible future development of global governance and global democracy.

Conceptual foundations: "civil society," the market, and the state

The concept of "civil society," which had its roots in early modern European thought, was revived following the events of Central and Eastern Europe, and democratization within other parts of the world. Subsequently, the notion has traveled across the globe, through intellectual discourse, activist exchange, and the official policies of development donors and politicians (Anheier et al. 2001; Kaviraj and Khilnani 2001; Kaldor 2003). From being an area of interest to historians and political scientists, "civil society" now straddles the boundaries of academy, policy-making, and advocacy, and is one of the most ubiquitous concepts employed in social science today. Often viewed as an "arena" which nurtures people's participation in struggles for democracy, autonomy, self-determination, justice and social change, it is claimed that civil society institutions are a key locus for social transformation. Yet as Kaviraj and Khilnani (2001: 1) state, " ... such diverse popularity itself creates a problem of indeterminacy." The export of various "civil society projects" in Eastern Europe and the South can be understood as a neo-imperialist project of imposing Western hegemony. Yet, the meaning of civil society, and grassroots efforts to promote it, do vary considerably across different political and cultural contexts. Moreover, "the meaning attributed to the concept [of civil society] has shifted within traditions of thought, as well as between traditions" (Chandhoke 1995: 76).

The usage of the term "civil society" ebbed in the mid-nineteenth century, but bounced back into fashion in the twentieth century through the writings of Antonio Gramsci. Gramsci shifted the focus of attention from the material relations of society, which Marx and Engels (1973) emphasized, to the cultural and religious agencies that shaped collective consciousness of individuals. In this broad sense, "civil society" was not peculiar to bourgeois society, and existed in the Middle Ages, where the "church was civil society" (Gramsci 1972: 170). He viewed civil society as "between the economic structure and the state" (ibid.: 170). Civil society was the realm of free associational activity, and included the family, universities, the press, trade unions, cultural institutions, publishing houses, and the like. Unlike the state, which exercised direct domination over society, the dominant classes used the institutions of civil society to mobilize popular consent in favor of the prevailing economic order and to establish "hegemony" (ibid.: 125). Working classes and their organic intellectuals needed to contest this. The Gramscian vision of the classless communist society was very similar to Marx. The people would reclaim the power they had hitherto abdicated to the state, and all social institutions, and the state would be run democratically. "Coercive elements of the state would wither away by degrees" (ibid.: 263) and free, equal, and socially conscious individuals, would carry out the laws they had given themselves, and the external discipline of law would be replaced by the internal pressure of morality. Gramsci distinguished between hegemony, based on consent, and domination, based on coercion.

In the 1990s, civil society became the new buzzword. The global trend towards democracy opened up space for "civil society" in erstwhile dictatorial nations. In the US and Europe, public disillusionment with party systems ignited interest in civil society. The current usage of the term draws heavily not only on the European discourse, but also on the Tocquevillian account of the vital role of voluntary associations. For Tocqueville, American democracy was dominated by the idea of equality, which had its great virtues but also the tendency to isolate and atomize individuals. The only way to ensure social cohesion was to create an extensive network of voluntary associations. Putnam (2000) draws on this, and stresses the importance of building trust, social capital, and solidarity. Walzer (1995: 7) defines "civil society" as " ... the space of uncoerced human association and also the set of relational networks—formed for the sake of family, faith, interest and ideology—that fill this space." The notion of "identity" is defined through different forms of membership in society. For example, a Marxist paradigm defines membership through the class system, a liberal approach locates it in the marketplace, and a nationalist paradigm views it in terms of some ethnic or national grouping, and so on. Walzer's list can be extended to include religious, communitarian, and gender identities. Clearly, these memberships are not water-tight compartments; most individuals have cross-cutting loyalties, their magnitude differing under differing circumstances. Deakin (2001: 7), extending Walzer's analysis, suggests it is useful to concentrate on the idea of civil society as an "arena," "in which the various activities that take place are informed by the different values determined by different perspectives Walzer describes. The various institutions that operate there will do so on the basis of different priorities, influenced by these perspectives. Individuals do so on the basis of values indicated through their background, education and experience."

Various scholars claim that "civil society" possesses a distinct raison d'etre compared to the the state and the market and thus it is seen as an alternative to both. It emerges as a "third sphere of collective life" (Chandhoke 2002: 36). The discourse on "civil society" discussed above displays a remarkable consistency. It presupposes a rational thinking individual, who is aware that individual self-interest can be realized in the common good of society. It refers to an area of associative freedom—the freedom of individuals to enter into relations with others and pursue common purposes. The reference here is not to freedom per se, but the active exercise of freedom in forming networks of social relations.[1] It involves a rule-governed society, based on the consent of individuals, or a society based on social contract of individuals. The changing definitions of civil society reflect ways in which consent was generated in different periods given the salient issues of the time. The underlying idea is that of a "process" through which individuals negotiate, argue, and struggle with each other and with the centers of economic and political authority. Hence, the basic idea behind "civil society" is maximization of associative freedom and minimization of coercion—by the state, political society, or the dominant class. Liberal theory for instance, considers "civil society" to be the property of democratic states (Chandhoke 1995).

While the concepts of civil society, the market, and the state may be analytically distinct, actual civil society organizations, states, and markets frequently interact and shape each other. Civil society is not only constituted by the state and the market, but is also permeated by the same logic that underpins these two spheres; it came into being through the same historical processes that generated the other two spheres. Even as modern life witnesses an escalating rise of social interaction in the public sphere, this interaction is permeated by the ethos of the capitalist system and instrumental action. Fukuyama (1995) in *Trust: The Social Virtues and Creation of Prosperity* asserts that capitalist accumulation requires trust—a "social capital" that can buttress economic transactions. Civil society and the market are dependent on each other, and do not provide an alternative to each other.

The values frequently associated with "civil society" are those of accountability of the state, and limits to state power. On the other hand, it is important to keep in mind that a state has functions that extend much beyond coercion. Civil society actors need states and their institutions to substantiate and codify their demands in law. For example, women's groups cannot expect justice without corresponding demand for state protection of women's rights. Or in the fight against violations of civil liberties, there is a need for states to punish offenders, to set up "rights commissions," etc. This is analogous to Hegel's idea of the state, including and transcending civil society. "Civil society" envelops the three inter-related aspects of Civil Society Organizations (CSOs); values, norms and aspirations of society governed by civil processes (such as tolerance, cooperation, and inclusion); and the provision of spheres for public discourse on issues and ideas (Batliwala and Brown 2006: 2–6).

The public sphere is sandwiched between the power of the state and particularistic discourses, such as ethnic nationalism or racism. This is precisely the reason why classical political theory, as espoused by Hegel, was dubious about a society based on the primacy of self-interested individuals pursuing their own interests; and therefore the need for the state to provide a framework for civil society to function. But using the Hegelian argument, an individual in the absence of collective consciousness and collective interest is vulnerable to both the depredations of the state and of power of the majority. Moreover, the balance between the state and "civil society" has very little margin for error. As Brown (2000: 8) states, " ... if the state is too extensive, it will strangle civil society at birth, too weak and private institutions will compete for its role as provider of order; if people are too involved in each other's lives then they will lose the sense of distance needed to preserve civility, too little involved and they become part of an atomized 'mass society.'"

Across theoretical traditions, civil society is portrayed as an important source of political transformation and liberation. Marxism, while critiquing the notion of the state acting "autonomously," free from the grasp of the dominant classes, insisted that the state could be transformed. But this transformation cannot take place without collective projects. "Emancipation" needed a public sphere, where the practices of the dominant classes (majority) and the state could be challenged. Liberalism, as a strand of modern theory is sensitive to the overwhelming power of the state. Tocqueville, for example, sought to construct civil society as an associational sphere, which would generate a discourse on the common good.

Since different societies have varied histories, the idea of civil society plays a distinct role and acquires different degrees of urgency in each society. In the former communist countries, the state was an overarching presence and while it safeguarded citizens' rights to employment, income, and other services, it stifled many areas of life. When communism collapsed, the demand for the long-suppressed associative freedom dominated popular consciousness. In developing countries, after independence, the idea of civil society did not dominate the landscape, but the focus was on organization of political life, so that the state could pursue developmental goals and remain accountable to the people. In deeply religious societies, economic life is regulated by moral and religious norms. Likewise, impediments to associative freedom could range from the caste system, to tribes, to religion. Therefore, thinking that civil society should have the same shape and form world over, or that institutions that form part of civil society in one nation, must also form part of it in another is taking a myopic view. It is important not to universalize Western history and Western models of civil society and expect all others to conform to it; else this would reiterate hegemonic Western thinking—placing the non-capitalist world on the capitalist grid. It is self-contradictory, to take a monistic view of an area of life that is by definition expected to be home of plurality.

The idea of "civil society" cannot be dismissed as having little meaning outside its Western origins; but neither can it be simply exported by Western donors into the global South, and used as a package for "good governance." The potential usefulness can be analyzed across two dimensions: it is "useful to act with," and it is "useful to think with." "Civil society" is flanked by the domain of individualistic, identity-forming loyalties, and the state. It is an enormously complex arena, housing rights-bearing individuals, associative life, and moving towards the construction of a critical discourse on modes of social and political organization. While, its existence is not a sufficient condition for democracy, it is essential for democratic life.

The notion of "transnational" or "global civil society"

The effort to systematically study global civil society is a recent growth industry (e.g. Anheier et al. 2001; Anheier and Katz 2003). In the 1990s, theories of global system of states and markets began to hypothesize a "third sphere"—"global civil society." Shaw (1994) espouses that civil society has become global to the extent societies increasingly represent themselves "globally"—across nation-state boundaries, through the formation of "global institutions." These may be "formal organizations" (that link national institutions such as parties, churches, unions, professional associations, or media organizations), "informal networks and movements" (such as the women's or peace movements) and "globalist organizations" (such as Amnesty International or Greenpeace). These latter organizations are established with a specifically global orientation, global membership, and their activities take on a global scope. The plurality of actors and agencies are armed with the view of reshaping the architecture of international politics, representing a "third sector"—an alternative to state-centric international order and networks of global markets.[2]

Amoore and Langley (2004) refute the idea of a clearly identifiable GCS sphere, distinct from the state and the market, and instead focus on particular uses of the concept as it is deployed to legitimate and challenge the discourse and practice of global governance. They view GCS as a bounded space, comprising voluntary associations, and as an agent of empowerment and resistance. This is in contrast with policy prescriptions and international organizations that have tended to view GCS as a neutral space, and academics which have emphasized its potential to transform society. Recognizing that the term "global civil society" is a contested concept, the editors of the *Global Civil Society* yearbook define it as "the realm of non-coercive collective action around shared interests and values that operates beyond the boundaries of nation states" (Glasius et al. 2006: v).

The rise of the GCS is seen largely within the framework of "globalization." The alleged pernicious consequences of "globalization"—escalating inequalities, re-colonization, ecological crises, and lack of "real" democracy—have generated calls for resistance to reverse, or shape the trends in less destructive ways. For many, globalization implies withering away of the national state: of state sovereignty, state structures, and national identities and commitments (Halperin and Laxer 2003: 1). This idea has led several analysts and activists to argue that resistance to globalized finance capital and rule by multinational corporations calls for strengthening "global civil society" and "global citizenship." Yet, as Sassen (2006) and Robinson (2004) contend, national states have not so much withered as become reconfigured to be institutions that support the operation of a global capitalist world economy in the interests of a transnational capitalist class.

It is important to make a distinction between globalization and globalism. The former is generally viewed as a growing and intensifying network of connections of organizations and people across national, geographic and cultural borders. It refers to increasing global connectivity, integration, and interdependence in the economic, social, technological, cultural, political, and ecological spheres.[3] So globalization is an increase in connectivity, and in this sense it has been going on for millennia. But quantitative research has shown that globalization in the nineteenth and twentieth centuries has occurred in waves that have been separated by periods of deglobalization in which connectivity has decreased (Chase-Dunn et al. 2000; O'Rourke and Williamson 1999).

Halperin and Laxer (2003: 3) define "globalism" or the Washington Consensus as, "an overarching ideology of governance that combines neo-liberalism with an insistence and faith that global integration is inevitable and good."[4] Globalism dons several facades— "structural adjustment programs," "new world order," "shock therapy," etc. Hence it is often not useful to employ the language of "anti-globalization," since what is being rejected or contested by GCS are the neoliberal policies bundled along with "globalization as integration"—privatization of public enterprises, deregulating businesses, reduction in public spending and corporate taxes, and international free trade agreements. This is what Klein (2004: 226) calls "McGovernment." On the other hand, many participants in the global justice movement do want to deglobalize and strengthen the autonomy of local communities. In this sense, some elements of global civil society really are anti-globalizationists. But, a number of others want to pursue "globalization from below" or "alterglobalization," a different kind of integration based on cooperation, equality, and democracy. These alterglobalists often call for the democratization of institutions of global governance and seek to make alliances with those who are pursuing local or national self-reliance.

Because links between civil society organizations are frequently regionally concentrated or bi-national, some scholars prefer to use the term "trans-national civil society" (TCS). The prefix "trans" here has the connotation of "across" or "beyond" the national, and also "surpassing" or "transcending" it (Halperin and Laxer 2003: 7). This is distinct from "inter-national" referring to "between," or "forming alliances with" representatives of distinct nation-states. This is also distinct from the term "global", which tends to connote linkages that are evenly distributed across the globe.

Appadurai (2006: xi–xiii) in defining TCS states that it should not be viewed as formed, fixed and institutionalized. It is (a) a process of network building, alliance formation, and advocacy networks, which enhance transnational exchange across sites, movements, and organizations with the common aim of affecting transnational governance decisions and organizations (some visible and permanent, such as the WTO and IMF, and some covert, such as those involved in the illegal trafficking of women or weapons, etc); and (b) a space, running counter to the commonsense geographies of nations, that people envisage, and is interstitial, overlapping, and uneven. Drawing on Hirschman's (1970) categorization of political and economic attachments as falling into three categories (loyalty, exit, and voice), Appadurai states that the main purpose of TCS is to strengthen the voice approach to shape "globalization."[5]

TCS helps to fulfill a number of goals associated with democracy: the identification of issues and articulation of value implications, mobilization of concerned citizens, balancing of power differences, creation of transnational social capital, exerting influence on decision makers and policies, and monitoring enforcement and compliance. TCS faces several challenges, to achieve the above: scale and levels of problems, and diversity of actors that must be engaged; differences in resources, power, culture, language, and the expectations to reach agreements on values and strategies across many countries. Also, since many efforts of these movements are ad-hoc, unstructured, spontaneous, and sporadic, they face the danger of becoming hierarchical, bureaucratized, slow, and conservative as they become better networked, supported, and institutionalized.[6]

Globalism (the neoliberal globalization project) has strongly challenged the democracies and welfare state institutions that had developed in the core regions of the world-system since World War II. Markoff (2006) contends that the attack on organized labor, especially in the United States, has been made possible by Reagan–Thatcher policies and by new technologies that make it easier for firms to relocate in order to avoid or undercut strong labor unions. Silver (2003) has analyzed this process of job blackmail and capital flight that has repeatedly occurred since the nineteenth century. The bad news is that capital flight does undermine democracy and working class power in the places that are abandoned, but in the new locations of production, workers usually organize effective labor unions and have important effects on democratizing the newly industrializing countries. Thus the "spatial fix" only resolves some of the contradictions of capitalism temporarily. The long-term answer is for workers to organize globally so that they can contend with global firms. Of course the labor movement has a long history of internationalism, and some of the structures that were created in earlier eras now act as obstacles to new efforts to engage in cross-border organizing and to create global unions (Harrod and O'Brien 2002). But renewed efforts to create a relevant global approach for labor in the twenty-first century are under way (see Waterman 2006).

International Non-Governmental Organizations (INGOs)

Since the 1990s, the concept of "global civil society" (GCS) has been the focus of a great deal of research and criticism (Colas 2002; Drainville 1998; Lipschutz 1992; Pasha and Blaney 1998; Walzer 1995). Largely addressed within the context of "globalization," the corpus of literature on GCS has produced rich empirical studies on the efflorescence of transnational activism, networks, movements and volunteerism; and on the dynamic processes and constituent mechanisms that facilitate actors to operate transnationally (Glasius et al. 2004).

Many scholars associate GCS with the activities of progressive international non-governmental organizations (INGOs) that create networks across national borders and create a new space for solidarity within the world-system (Chandhoke 2005). The idea that people across the world were united by common concerns; and since no one group of citizens could tackle these problems in isolation, the need for common strategies and cooperation formed the *first plank* of INGO agendas. The *second plank* of the agenda was the inequitable nature of the global political economy and the mobilization against multilateral institutions in particular.

It is important to mention here, that the emergence of the NGO in general is linked to (a) "neoliberal globalization"—the rolling back of the state to allow for the unhindered growth of the market, cleared a space where NGOs emerged to take over the functions hitherto reserved for the state (health, education, income-generation, etc.), i.e. NGOs were transformed into the guardians of civil society; and (b) the "post-Washington consensus"—in the mid 1990s, emphasis shifted from an unfettered market to an idea that the processes of "globalization" had to be governed. There was a replacement of the language of the market by that of "governance," "accountability," "transparency," and "democracy." NGOs were "consultants" in decision-making activities of international organizations such as the World Bank in the latter's "development" programs (infrastructure, rural poverty alleviation, and the like).

The *third plank* was that of "norm setting." INGOs are said to have established norms on how governments should behave towards their citizens, and have hence inaugurated a "normative" turn in world politics. Chandhoke (2005: 359) writes, "they possess moral authority which is absolutely essential for ethical political intervention, ... because they claim to represent the public or the general interest against the power-driven interests of the state and the profit driven interests of the economy." Likewise, Naidoo (2006: 57) argues:

> What these groups and movements have come to represent for many people around the world are spaces where the voices of average citizens are heard in discussions on social, political and economic justice. They are venues where people and groups who feel increasingly alienated from the prevailing political system can join to explore alternative visions for a more ethical form of governance that works for the benefit of average people.

Given the increasing "democracy deficit"—when lives and well-being of people lie increasingly with supranational institutions, which are not directly accountable to citizens, and when many poorer states, such as those required to adopt structural adjustment programs by international financial institutions, have no choice but to hand over substantive decision-making power to these institutions—INGOs fill in this gap, according to Naidoo. How much power has shifted to supranational bodies, the degree of roll-back of the state, and whether these shifts have produced shifts in contentious politics "from below," and the sources and extent of INGOs' "moral authority" are empirical questions, and should be addressed *in situ*.

The issue of "representation" and "accountability" of INGOs looms large. The notion of local movements uniting globally to fight against the injustices of neoliberal globalization, with the aim of forging an "alternative" world order is appealing. The idea that groups across the world have equal access and equal voice in GCS is unrealistic and misleading however. The sphere is dominated by groups, who possess the correct vocabulary (spokespersons), logistics and funds, and the correct networks. The majority of the world's people, for example, are not connected via internet or telephone, but are connected to distant others only through unidirectional media, such as through commodity chains that operate within hierarchies of class, gender, and race. GCS can hence be exclusive and exclusionary, empowering for some and disempowering for many. There is an imminent danger for political agency here—"ordinary" human beings who have suffered injustices in their lives, are denied the opportunity to frame responses in their own terms. "Visible" NGOs have their own programs, their own ideas of what is wrong, and how the situation can be remedied; and are often incomprehensible for the inhabitants who they "represent" (Reitan 2006; Chandhoke 2005; Sundstrom 2003).

Moreover, most INGOs are situated in the Western hemisphere, and transnational solidarity networks are characterized by sharp divisions in life-worlds, economic advantages and cultural differences. Those in the North are embroiled in a system reliant on appropriation of cheap labor and environmental degradation in the South, and often lack the "reflexivity" to see this. They may engage in "small acts of kindness" as a substitution for more radical redistribution, which may perpetuate inequalities. Moreover, with GCS, INGOs are unelected, and are often accountable to those who fund them. Critics of INGOs raise concerns both about the politics of representation within these organizations and the extent to which INGOs may discourage rather than enhance ordinary citizens' capacities to mobilize to preserve old customs or forge new rights (Reitan 2006; Chandhoke 2005).

Transnational social movements and campaigns

It would be convenient to assume that transnational social movements are entirely a phenomenon of the recent past, but this is decidedly not true. The unique aspects of contemporary movements can only be specified accurately by comparing these with earlier transnational social movements (e.g., Keck and Sikkink 1998: Chapter 2; Chase-Dunn and Reese 2007). A world historical approach suggests that both contemporary movements and the current situation can best be comprehended in terms of a series of "world revolutions" that have played an important part in the evolution of institutions of global governance for centuries (Chase-Dunn 2007).

Keck and Sikkink (1998: 219–20) distinguish between "transnational social movements" (TSMs) and "transnational advocacy networks" (TANs). TSMs require regular cross-national interactions, mass mobilizations, shared understandings of issues, a common form of political discourse, and a collective identity based shared communication, experience, and history. Often, movements that appear to be transnational are actually nationally rooted and directed movements that coordinate transnationally (Halperin and Laxer 2003: 6). Coordination beyond the nation does not make a movement transnational; only regular, frequent, long-term interaction across nations, coupled with similar framing issues, and mass mobilizations, make movements transnational. TANs are communicative structures for political exchange that are ephemeral and highly mobile. They are a "set of relevant organizations working internationally with shared values, a common discourse, and dense exchanges of information" (ibid.: 236–37). It is indispensable to discern between TSMs and TANs. Transnational social movement organizations (TSMOs) refer to a subset of INGOs that were "explicitly founded to promote some social or political change" (Smith and Wiest 2005: 622).

While transnational social movements date back to at least the Protestant Reformation, the scope and scale of international ties among social activists have risen dramatically over the past few decades, as they have increasingly shared information, conceptual frameworks, and other resources, and coordinated actions across borders and continents. In the 1980s and 1990s, the number of formal TSMOs rose by nearly 200 percent. The number of TSMOs with multi-issue agendas also increased significantly, from 43 in 1983 to 161 in 2000. TSMOs are still largely housed in the global North. Of the 25 countries with the greatest number of TSMOs, 19 are located in the North. Yet, a rising portion is located in, and has ties to, the global South, and regional TSMOs based in the South have more cross-regional ties than those located in the North (Smith 2004a: 6–7, Smith 2004b: 266; Smith and Wiest 2005: 623; Wiest and Smith 2007: 138). Quantitative analyses reveal that, controlling for other factors, "countries with stronger democratic traditions were better represented in transnational social movement organizations" (Smith and Wiest 2005: 637). Their analyses also shows that TSMOs are greater in countries that participate in intergovernmental organizations and that ratify human rights treaties, while regional TSMOs are more prevalent where states participate in regional intergovernmental organizations and regional treaty ratification (Smith and Wiest 2005; Wiest and Smith 2007).

This rise in transnational organizing contributed to, and helped to produce, the global justice movement. The *global justice movement* is a "movement of movements," that includes all those who are engaged in sustained and contentious challenges to neoliberal global capitalism, propose alternative political and economic structures, and mobilize poor and relatively powerless peoples. While this movement resorts to non-institutional forms of collective action, it often collaborates with institutional "insiders," such as NGOs that lobby and provide services to people, as well as policy-makers (Reitan 2006; Tarrow 2005).

Tarrow and McAdam (2004) claim that, although transnational contention has some distinct properties not found in domestic movements, local and national movements provide a battery of insights that help us to understand transnational movements. They also emphasize the continuing significance of national politics to the dynamics and impacts of social movements. Along the lines of Halperin and Laxer (2003: 122), the authors declare, " ... much that passes for 'global' in the study of transnational contention actually takes the form of 'internationalization' (e.g., domestic claims-making against international or foreign targets), or what we would call 'global framing' (e.g., mounting of domestic disputes in the language of globalization)." Mobilization of actors and key relationships in transnational contention start within the national arena, and transnationalization leads to a "transposition, not liquidation of local and national movements" (ibid.: 123).

Scholars have begun to study the conditions under which, and processes through which, activists "go global" and shift the scales of contention upward. In *Dynamics of Contention* (2001: 331), McAdam et al. define the process of "scale shift" as "a change in the number and level of coordinated contentious actions leading to broader contention involving a wider range of actors and bridging their claims and identities." The basic proposition is that "localized collective action spawns broader contention when information concerning initial action reaches a distant group, which, having defined itself as sufficiently similar to the initial insurgents (attribution of similarity) engages in similar action (emulation), leading ultimately to coordinated action between the two sites" (Tarrow and McAdam 2004: 127). They posit thee analytically distinct routes which aid in the spread of contention beyond its localized origins: "non-relational diffusion" (transfer of information by means of impersonal carriers, e.g., media), "relational diffusion" (transfer of information along established lines of interaction), and "brokerage" (information transfer dependent upon linkages between two or more previously unconnected sites) (ibid.: 127).

Reitan's (2006) research tells the story of several different transnational social movement networks affiliated with the broader global justice movement. She analyzes the conditions under which these movement networks have "gone global"—scaled up their organizational efforts to involve transnational collaborations and mobilizations. Reitan's main idea is that neoliberalism, or "the globalization project," has been the main stimulus promoting popular social movements to scale up. Her close studies of Via Campesina, Jubilee 2000, Jubilee South, and the Global Call to Action, and Peoples' Global Action are exciting stories that demonstrate the trials and tribulations of trying to confront the powers that be on a global scale.

The challenges of "going global" are, of course, enormous and myriad. Activists must overcome many challenges, including "the tyranny of distance," cultural and linguistic differences, as well as the usual challenges confronting inter-organizational alliances, such as political and ideological differences. Especially when they involve North-South alliances, transnational movements and campaigns confront resource inequalities among their constituent groups. Such inequalities, along with contradictory interests and conflicting perspectives arising from broader global inequalities as well as distinct historical experiences and political and cultural contexts, frequently give rise to internal power relations and struggles within TSMOs, transnational campaigns, and transnationally funded NGOs (Sundstrom 2003; Bandy and Smith 2005).

Hardt and Negri (2004) suggest that social movements don't always have to "go global" to challenge global forces. Seeking to overcome the shortcomings of earlier Marxist approaches, they conceive the emergent agents that challenge the logic of global capital as the "multitude." Their writings have a huge following, especially among young European "autonomists" and other kinds of "horizontalists" in the global justice movement. Hardt and Negri (2004) emphasize how the forces of empire are diffused and multidimensional, operating like a multi-headed hydra, and that even local-level resistance movements have global significance. They suggest that, even through seemingly uncoordinated local-level acts of defiance, the "multitude" can weaken the forces of empire, popping up like many moles through a matrix of inter-connected subterranean tunnels to surprise and disarm the hydra.

The rise of the World Social Forum

The social forum process is an important initiative to expand and strengthen the progressive wing of global civil society, or what de Sousa Santos (2006) refers to as the "global left." The World Social Forum was organized as the popular alternative to the World Economic Forum. The WEF was established in 1971 as a non-partisan independent international organization committed to improving the state of the world by engaging leaders in partnerships to shape global, regional and industry agendas. The WEF maintains a headquarters in Geneva and usually holds its annual meeting in Davos, Switzerland. The WEF invites discussion among corporate and political leaders who want to help cope with problems that are exacerbated, or not resolved, by corporate globalization. They are concerned about the environment and poverty in less developed countries and about corporate social responsibility.

The WSF was established in 2001 as a counter-hegemonic popular project focusing on issues of global justice and democracy and it represents a rather different slice of global civil society. Initially organized by the Brazilian labor movement and the landless peasant movement, the WSF was intended to be a forum for the participants in, and supporters of, grassroots movements from all over the world rather than a conference of representatives of political parties or governments. Nevertheless, the WSF has been supported by the Brazilian Workers Party, and has been most frequently held in Porto Alegre, Brazil, a traditional stronghold of that party. The Chavez government in Venezuela also played an important role in sponsoring the 2006 polycentric WSF meeting in Venezuela. Both Hugo Chavez, president of Venezuela, and Lula de Silva, president of Brazil, were also featured as speakers at WSF meetings (Smith et al. 2008).

Since its inception, the WSF has quickly become the largest international gathering of participants in the global justice movement and their allies. According to the official website for the WSF, the first meeting of the WSF, held in Porto Alegre, Brazil, in 2001 reportedly drew 20,000 registered participants from 117 countries and subsequent meetings grew in size. After several more meetings held in Porto Alegre, the WSF moved to Mumbai, India in 2004. In 2006, "polycentric" meetings were held in three locations. As of 2008, the 2005 meeting in Porto Alegre was the largest social forum, drawing 155,000 registered participants from 135 countries. The 2007 WSF meeting in Nairobi, Kenya drew less than half this number of participants (74,000), but its size was still impressive considering that this was the first WSF ever held in this nation, a highly impoverished country (Reese et al. 2008; Smith et al. 2008).

In opposition to Margaret Thatcher who declared that, "there is no alternative" to neoliberal globalization, WSF participants proclaim that "another world is possible." The WSF is both an institution—with its own leadership, mission, and structure—and an "open space" where a variety of social actors—activists, policy experts, students, intellectuals, journalists, and artists—from around the world can meet, exchange ideas, participate in multi-cultural events, and coordinate actions. The WSF is open to all those opposed to neoliberal globalization, but excludes groups advocating armed resistance. Since its inception, the WSF has inspired the spread of hundreds of local, national, regional, and thematic social forums which have varied considerably in their size, composition, and focus. While these have been most widespread in Western Europe and Latin America, social forums have taken place within North America, Asia, and Africa (della Porta 2005b; Patomaki and Teivainen 2004; Smith et al. 2008).

The vast majority of activities occurring within the WSF are workshops that are self-organized by participants and range in size from 10 to several hundred people. Large plenary events, drawing tens of thousands, feature famous politicians, intellectuals, writers, and social justice activists. Cultural activities also abound, including musical and dance performances. The WSF opens with an "opening march" that highlights the myriad of social justice causes, organizations, and countries with which participants are affiliated. Founders of the WSF designed it to be an "open space" where individual participants and groups can speak, issue declarations, and coordinate actions. According to its original charter, the WSF itself was not supposed to act as a representative body, issue statements, or coordinate actions. Some participants have become critical of the limits of this "open space" and seek to transform it into something more than merely a "talk shop." Such criticisms gave rise to the Assembly of Social Movements. At this Assembly, calls to action for the coming year are made by participants involved in a variety of movements (Smith et al. 2008). The social forum process has been credited with helping to organize and coordinate the international actions against the US invasion of Iraq on February 15, 2003, in which 30 to 60 million people participated in over 100 countries (Reitan 2006: 15). Participants at the WSF have also issued various manifestos, the most well-known of which were the "Porto Alegre Consensus," issued by the "Group of 19," and the "Bamako Appeal" (Smith et al. 2008). Other critics of social forums, such as those affiliated with autonomous and anarchist movements, claim they are overly reformist and overly controlled by leaders of centralized SMOs, NGOs, and union federations. Such criticisms gave rise to the development of "autonomous spaces" by "horizontalists," who advocate horizontal network forms of organization (Smith et al. 2008).

While some WSF participants are long-time veterans of transnational campaigns and organizations, others are involved in local and national campaigns. Surveys of WSF participants at the 2005 and 2007 meetings reveal that most participants are social movement activists. The majority participated in at least two protests in the past year and were actively involved in at least two types of social movements. More than 80% were affiliated with some sort of organization, most commonly with a social movement organization or NGO. Most respondents came from the local area surrounding the meeting site; North Americans and Western Europeans are also over-represented. Most respondents were young (below the age of 36). They were also highly educated, with most respondents claiming to have 16 years or more of education and the ability to speak two or more languages (Reese et al. 2007; Reese et al. 2008; Smith et al. 2008).

The finding that most participants come from the country hosting the WSF is consistent with Tarrow's (2005) claim that transnational activists are mainly "rooted cosmopolitans" (i.e., locally based activists working on "global" issues). In line with this, Fisher et al. (2005) found, in their surveys of participants in five global protest events in North America and Europe, that 95% or more of all respondents were from the country where the protest took place.

While WSF participants are united in their opposition to neoliberal global capitalism and imperialist wars, they are politically divided about how much change they seek in the current global political economy in the long-run. While some participants seek to abolish the major institutions structuring the global economy, including capitalism, the International Monetary Fund, and the World Trade Organization, others seek to reform them or to replace existing global governance structures with more democratic ones. Research suggests that the prevalence of these political orientations varies considerably across WSF gatherings. Most WSF participants surveyed in 2005, when the meeting was held in Brazil, favored abolishing or replacing capitalism, the IMF and the WTO in 2005 rather than reforming these institutions. In contrast, most WSF participants surveyed in 2007, when the meeting was held in Kenya, were in favor of reforming these institutions.

The somewhat less radical responses from attendees of the WSF 2007 meeting likely reflects, in part, the rather different sponsorship context of the 2005 and the 2007 meetings. Porto Alegre had been a stronghold of the Brazilian Workers Party and that leftist party strongly supported the founding of the WSF and the meetings held there. In contrast, the President of Kenya was a centrist and the meeting did not get much financial support from the Kenyan government, which saw it mainly as an opportunity to promote tourism. This rather different form of official sponsorship, differences in the political orientation of the local 2005 and 2007 Organizing Committees, and broader contrasts in Brazil's and Kenya's political cultures that such differences reflect, are probably each important factors behind the somewhat less radical nature of the attendees in Nairobi compared with Porto Alegre. The contrast in these two WSF meetings and their attendees suggests that, even within "global" civil society, local context matters (Reese et al. 2008).

GCS, global governance, and global democracy

Global governance is often understood to refer to contests among contemporary international organizations, national states, transnational firms, and NGOs. Our world historical and structuralist approach looks at the long-term evolution of the institutions of global governance. We note the continuing importance of the Westphalian interstate system of competing and allying national states that was extended to the periphery of the world-system in a series of waves of decolonization that began in the eighteenth century. The main form of power in this system has consisted of a series of hegemonies in which strong and wealthy capitalist core states have provided a semblance of global order while yet maintaining the multicentric form of the interstate system (Arrighi 1994).

The contemporary period is well understood by noting that the US economic hegemony has been declining for the last several decades with new centers of power emerging in Europe and Asia. The situation is similar in many respects to the period of British hegemonic decline in the last decades of the nineteenth century and the early decades of the twentieth century. We also note that international organizations and incipient global state formation have been emerging since the Concert of Europe after the Napoleonic Wars. This adds a growing layer of institutions over the top of the interstate system. Thus the global polity is an interstate system with cycles of the rise and fall of hegemons and a growing layer of political globalization in the form of international organizations.

The institutions of global governance are not very democratic, even by the taken-for-granted standards that have become accepted in the dominant discourse. Rule by a hegemon may involve polyarchic elections, but only the citizens of the hegemon itself are allowed to vote. The United Nations Security Council, dominated by the winners of World War II, has the right to veto any legal effort to significantly devolve its powers, or to open it up to broader participation. The UN is understood by most of the people of the world (who have heard of it) as a puppet of the United States. And the international financial institutions (International Monetary Fund, the World Trade Organization, the World Bank) are also seen in much the same light. Thus the existing institutions of global governance are not legitimate in terms of the most institutionalized set of ideals in the world—the notion of democracy. Democracy is most usually understood as a variable characteristic of national states. But global activists seek global democracy, and their main consensus is that there is a serious "democratic deficit."

Arguably, a variety of phenomena are straining the traditional state-centric system, from above and below. These include international organizations such as the UN and the European Union; multinational corporations such as Shell and General Motors; national separatist movements in places such as Sri Lanka; international terrorist organizations and international NGOs such as Greenpeace. The latter has extended the range of citizen action beyond institutional parameters of the sovereign state.

Turner (1998) highlights several cases where GCS challenges the state's monopoly of authority by redefining the nature of legitimacy. As legitimacy is a function of public perception, the state's monopoly of authority is increasingly strained by a diverse and active global citizenry. Furthermore, this proactive citizenry coordinates its activities through information media and communication technologies that transcend national boundaries of states. For example, international networking was pivotal in the World Bank's cancellation of the Narmada dam project in India. A number of groups formed the *Narmada Bachao Andolan* (Save the Narmada), which forged links with a variety of Indian groups and international organisations such as Environmental Defense Fund in Washington DC, Survival International in London, and Friends of the Earth, Tokyo.

The declaration of the withering away of the state, in light of globalization, is a tad premature. States are not ceding power when it comes to matters that are crucial. In the aforementioned example of the Narmada Dam, despite local, national, and international pressure, the government decided to go ahead with raising the height of the dam; the decision based on keeping "development" priorities of India in mind. Moreover, the state has been a fundamental constitutive element in globalizing capital. The fact that capital and corporations are not limited to the territory of a single state, does not mean that they are not linked to states. In fact, every transnational corporation (TNC) has a national base that depends on it to sustain its viability; and on other states to allow it

617

access to other markets and human capital. Hence states remain a central locus of political power and strategic sites of conflict. States hence drive and regulate "globalism."

Often, states are forced to succumb to allow access to local markets and resources to TNCs, highlighting the issue of "power differentials" between states. Deflecting energies away from the national arena, to "globalize resistance," may prove counter-productive, by diverting attention from struggles for democratic control of the state. There is a need for political engagement within countries where laws are made and mass mobilizations occur.

This is not to say that transnational campaigns are never fruitful. The "International Baby Food Campaign" provides one example of an effective transnational campaign.[7] The Campaign mobilized diverse associations (churches, unions, NGOs, citizen initiatives) to challenge Nestlé's products and to build a social consensus on appropriate marketing practices across national boundaries (Batliwala and Brown 2006). Various international antisweatshop campaigns have helped workers in various countries to secure better wages, working conditions, and the right to collective bargaining (Armbruster-Sandoval 2005). The antidebt movement managed to gain support from various national governments for relieving poor nations of their international debt (Reitan 2006). Transnational feminist movements have helped to secure support for national and international policies supporting women's rights (Moghadam 2005). Local activists have also made human rights gains through the "boomerang strategy," through which international allies and international governance institutions and treaties are used to increase pressure on national governments (Keck and Sikkink 1998).

Conclusion

While it is common to conceive of global civil society as a sphere distinct from multinational corporations and inter-governmental organizations, it is interconnected with it. Research by Smith and Wiest (2005) and Wiest and Smith (2007) suggest that nation-states' participation in intergovernmental organizations and their ratification of international treaties stimulates the formation of transnational social movement organizations as it legitimates democratic norms and opens international channels for political influence. Likewise, the structural violence associated with neoliberal globalization and the practices of multinational corporations has stimulated the development of various transnational social movement networks (Reitan 2006). We should, of course, not romanticize the progressive wing of global civil society, which is dominated by groups that are relatively privileged, such as actors from the global North and those with high levels of education. Nor should we underestimate the external and internal challenges it faces. Nevertheless, the rise of the global justice movement, the WSF, TSMOs, and TANs have helped to highlight unmet demands for a more democratic global order, while various transnational campaigns have managed to challenge some of the more exploitative and oppressive practices around the world.

Notes

1 Coercion of any kind violates dignity, and rational nature of the individual, and is hence undesirable and should be avoided. However, since human beings fail to act rationally, coercion becomes necessary. However, this should be minimized, placed in the hands of a legitimate public authority and exercised according to clearly stated and rationally defensible laws.

2 Colas (2002) argues that this civil society is "international" and corresponds to the state system and its national states, while Shaw (2000) posits that the emergence of the "global state" enveloping the heartland of the West, which may offer the political framework for GCS.

3 Chase-Dunn (2006) calls this increasing global integration "structural globalization" and distinguishes between economic, political, and cultural globalization.

4 Chase-Dunn (2006) and McMichael (2004) call this the "globalization project" or Reaganism-Thatcherism.

5 Loyalty refers to followers, adherents to a product, party or movement, fully committed to its virtues. Exit refers to those who have moved into the anti-globalization camp. Voice refers to those who have stayed committed to a party, product, nation, or cause, but who voice their criticism of it.

6 A parallel can be drawn here to the Weberian notion of "charismatic authority." As the "have-nots" seize power and legitimacy, bureaucratization/routinization sets in, in the forms of rules, etc.

7 In the 1970s, news began to leak that Nestlé was using some questionable marketing practices to promote sales of baby-food formula in developing countries. Nestlé had recruited hospital personnel to recommend new mothers that the feed their infants with the company's tinned formula. However, when mixed with unpotable water, it caused dysentery. European Civil Society Organizations published the study under the title, "Nestlé kills babies.". Nestlé instituted a libel suit, and the ensuing trial initiated widespread public debate on corporate responsibilities. The Campaign eventually produced a Code of Conduct for TNCs operating in the developing world, which was adopted by the UN.

References

Amoore, L. and Langely, P. (2004) "Ambiguities of Global Civil Society," *Review of International Studies*, 30: 89–110.

Anheier, H. K, Glasius, M. and Kaldor, M. (2001) "Introducing Global Civil Society," in H.K.Anheier, M. Glasius, and M. Kaldor (eds.) *Global Civil Society 2001*, Oxford: Oxford University Press.

Appadurai, A. (2006) "Foreword" in S. Batliwala and L.D. Brown (eds.) *Transnational Civil Society, An Introduction*, Sterling, VA: Kumarian Press.

Armbruster-Sandoval, R. (2005) *Globalization and Cross-Border Labor Solidarity in the Americas: The Anti-Sweatshop Movement and the Struggle for Social Justice*, New York: Routledge.

Arrighi, G. (1994) *The Long Twentieth Century*. London: Verso.

Bandy, J. and Smith, J. (eds.) (2004) *Coalitions Across Borders: Transnational Protest and the Neoliberal Order*, Lanham, MD: Rowman and Littlefield Publishers.

Batliwala, S. and Brown, L. D. (eds.) (2006) *Transnational Civil Society: An Introduction*, Sterling, VA: Kumarian Press.

Brown, C. (2000) "Cosmopolitanism, world citizenship and civil society," *Critical Review of International Social and Political Philosophy*, 3(1):7–27.

Chandhoke, N. (1995) *State and Civil Society, Explorations in Political Theory*, New Delhi, Thousand Oaks, CA, London: Sage Publications.

——(2002) "*The Limits of Global Civil Society*," in H. Anheier, M. Glasius and M. Kaldor (eds.) (2003) *Global Civil Society 2002*, Oxford: Oxford University Press.

——(2005) "How Global is Global Civil Society," *Journal of World-systems Research*, XI (2): 355–71.

Chase-Dunn, C. (2006) "Globalization: A World-Systems Perspective," in C. Chase-Dunn and S. Babones (eds.) *Global Social Change*, Baltimore, MD: Johns Hopkins University Press.

——(2007) "The world revolution of 20xx," in J. Harris (ed.) *Contested Terrains of Globalization*. Chicago, IL: Global Studies Association.

Chase-Dunn, C., Kawano, Y. and Brewer, B. (2000) "Trade globalization since 1795: waves of integration in the world-system," *American Sociological Review*, 65: 77–95.

Chase-Dunn, C. and Reese, E. (2007) "The World Social Forum—a global party in the making?" in K. Sehm-Patomaki and M. Ulvila (eds.) *Global Political Parties*, London: Zed Press.

Colas, A.(2002) *International Civil Society*, Cambridge: Polity Press.

619

della Porta, D. (2005a) "Multiple Belongings, Tolerant Identities, and the Construction of 'Another Politics': Between the European Social Forum and the Local Social For a," in *Transnational Protest and Global Activism*, D. Della Porta and S. Tarrow (eds.), Lanham, MD: Rowman & Littlefield Publishers, Inc.

——(2005b) "Making the Polis: Social Forums and Democracy in the Global Justice Movement," *Mobilization,* 10(1): 73–94.

della Porta, D., Garza, R. I., Juris, J. S., Mosca, L., Reese, E., Smith, P. and Vázquez, R. (2008) *Global Democracy and the World Social Forums*, Boulder, CO, and London: Paradigm Publishers.

Deakin, N. (2001) *In Search of Civil Society*, Basingstoke, Hampshire: Palgrave.

Drainville, A. (1998) "The Fetishism of Global Civil Society: Global Governance, Guarzino (eds.) *Transnationalism from Below*, New Brunswick, NJ: Transaction. Transnational Urbanism and Sustainable Capitalism in the World Economy," in M. P. Smith and L. E.

Fisher, Dana R. Kevin Stanley, David Beerman, and Gina Neff (2005) "How Do Organizations Matter? Mobilization and Support for Participants at Five Globalization Protests," *Social Problems,* 52: 102–21.

Fukuyama, F. (1995) *Trust: The Social Virtues and Creation of Prosperity*, New York: Free Press.

Glasius, M., Kaldor, M. and Anheier, H. (eds.) (2006) *Global Civil Society 2006/7*. London: Sage Publications.

Glasius, M., Lewis, D and Seckinelgin, H. (eds.) (2004) *Exploring Civil Society, Political and Cultural Contexts*, London and New York: Routledge.

Gramsci, A., 1972, *Selections from the Prison Notebooks of Antonio Gramsci*, ed. Q. Hoare and G.N. Smith, London: Lawrence and Wishart.

Halperin, S. and Laxer, G. (2003) "Introduction: Effective Resistance to Corporate Globalization," in Laxer, G. and Halperin, S. (eds.) *Global Civil Society and Its Limits*, Basingstoke, NY: Palgrave Macmillan.

Harrod, J. and O'Brien, R. (2002) *Global Unions? Theory and Strategies of Organized Labour in the Global Political Economy*. London: Routledge.

Hardt, M. and Negri, A. (2004) *Multitude: War and Democracy in the Age of Empire*. New York: Penguin.

Hirschman, A. (1970) *Exit, Voice and Loyalty*, Cambridge: Cambridge University Press.

Kaldor, M. (2003) *Global Civil Society*, London: Polity Press.

Kaviraj, S. and S. Khilnani. (eds.) (2001) *Civil Society: History and Possibilities*, Cambridge: Cambridge University Press.

Keck, M.E. and Sikkink, K. (eds.) (1998) *Activists Beyond Borders: Advocacy Networks in International Politics*, Ithaca, NY: Cornell University Press.

Klein, N. (2004) "Reclaiming the Commons," in T. Mertes (ed.) *A Movement of Movements: Is Another World Really Possible?* London and New York: Verso.

Laxer, G. and Halperin, S. (eds.) (2003) *Global Civil Society and Its Limits*, Basingstoke, NY: Palgrave Macmillan.

Lipschutz, R. (1992) "Reconstructing World Politics: The Emergence of Global Civil Society", *Millennium: Journal of International Studies*, 21: 328–420.

Markoff, J. (2006) "Globalization and the future of democracy" in C. Chase-Dunn and S. Babones (eds.) *Global Social Change*, Baltimore, MD: Johns Hopkins University Press.

Marx, K. and Engels, F., 1973, *Selected Works, Vol. 1*, Moscow: Progress Publishers.

McAdam, D., Tarrow, S. and Tilly, C. (2001) *Dynamics of Contention*, New York: Cambridge University Press.

McMichael, P. (2004) *Development and Social Change: A Global Perspective*. Thousand Oaks, CA: Pine Forge Press.

Moghadam, V. M. (2005) *Globalizing Women: Transnational Feminist Networks*, Baltimore, MD: John Hopkins University Press.

Naidoo, K. (2006) "Claiming Global Power: Transnational Civil Society and Global Governance" in S. Batliwala and L. D. Brown (eds.) *Transnational Civil Society: An Introduction*, Sterling, VA: Kumarian Press.

O'Rourke, K. H. and Williamson, J. G. (1999) *Globalization and History: The Evolution of a 19th Century Atlantic Economy*, Cambridge, MA: MIT Press.

Pasha, M. K. and Blaney, D. (1998) "Elusive Paradise: The Promise and Peril of Global Civil Society," *Alternatives*, 23: 417–50.

Patomaki, H. and Teivainen, T. (2004) "The World Social Forum: an open space or a movement of movements," *Theory, Culture and Society*, 21(6): 145–54.

Putnam, R. (2000) *Bowling Alone: The Collapse and Revival of American Community*, New York: Simon and Schuster.

Reese, E. and Christopher C.-D. (2007) "Do Organizational Affiliations Shape Political Views? Evidence from the World Social Forum Surveys." Paper presented at the workshop organized by the Collective Behavior and Social Movements Section of the American Sociological Association at Hofstra University.

Reese, E., C. Chase-Dunn, K. Anantram, G. Coyne, M. Kaneshiro, A. N. Koda, R. Kwon, and P. Saxena (2008) "Place and Base: The Public Sphere in the Social Forum Process." Working Paper #45. Institute for Research on World Systems. http://irows.ucr.edu/papers/irows45/irows45.htm (retrieved July 24, 2008).

Reitan, R. (2006) *Global Activism*, London: Routledge.

Robinson, W.I. (2004) *A Theory of Global Capitalism*, Baltimore, MD: Johns Hopkins University Press.

Santos, Bonaventura de Sousa (2006) *The Rise of the Global Left*, New York: Palgrave Macmillan.

Sassen, S. (2006) *Territory-Authority-Rights: From Medieval to Global Assemblages*, Princeton, NJ: Princeton University Press.

Shaw, M. (1994) "Civil Society and Global Politics: Beyond a Social Movements Approach," *Millennium: Journal of International Studies*, 23 (3): 647–67.

Silver, B. (2003) *Forces of Labor*, Cambridge: Cambridge University Press.

Smith, J. (2004a) "Social Movements and Multilateralism: Moving from the 20th to 21st Century," Visiting Scholar, Institute on Globalization and the Human Condition McMasters University.

——(2004b) "Exploring the Connections Between Global Integration and Political Mobilization," *Journal of World Systems Research*, 10(1): 255–85.

——(2004c) "The World Social Forum and the challenges of global democracy," *Global Networks*, 4(4): 413–21.

——(2004d) "Transnational Processes and Movements," in D. A. Snow, S. A. Soule, and H. Kriesi (eds.), *The Blackwell Companion to Social Movements*. Oxford: Blackwell Publishers.

Smith, J. and D. Wiest (2005) "The Uneven Geography of Global Civil Society: National and Global Influences on Transnational Association," *Social Forces*, 84 (2): 621–52.

Smith, J., M. Karides, M. Becker, D. Brunelle, C. Chase-Dunn, D. della Porta, R. Icaza Garza, J. S. Juris, L. Mosca, E. Reese, P. J. Smith, and R. Vázquez (2008) *Global Democracy and the World Social Forums*, Boulder, CO, and London: Paradigm Publishers.

Sundstrom, L. M. (2003) "Transnational Assistance to Russian NGO Development," in Laxer, G. and Halperin, S. (eds.) *Global Civil Society and its Limits*, Basingstoke, NY: Palgrave MacMillan.

Tarrow, S. (2005) *The New Transnational Activism*, New York: Cambridge University Press.

Tarrow, S. and McAdam, D. (2004) "Scale Shift in Transnational Contention," in D. Della Porta and S. Tarrow (eds.) *Transnational Protest and Global Activism*, Lanham, MD: Rowman and Littlefield Publishers.

Turner, S. (1998) "Global Civil Society, Anarchy and Governance: Assessing an Emerging Paradigm," *Journal of Peace Research*, 35 (1): 25–42.

Walzer, M. (ed.) (1995) *Toward a Global Civil Society*, Providence MA and Oxford: Berghahn Books.

Waterman, P. (2006) "Toward a Global Labor Charter Movement?" Online Available HTTP: http://wsfworkshop.openspaceforum.net/twiki/tiki-read_article.php?articleId=6 (accessed June 5, 2008).

Wiest, D. and Smith, J. (2007) "Explaining Participation in Regional Transnational Social Movement Organizations," *International Journal of Comparative Sociology*, 48(2–3): 137–66.

32

Muslim cosmopolitanism

Contemporary practice and social theory

Humeira Iqtidar

> I met this woman from a peasant family in Sargodha here. I think they have a small piece of land that they till. And she had gone to Indonesia for tabligh. She didn't understand their language and they didn't understand hers. But she went and she learnt about another world. When I saw her, I thought if she can do this then why can't I? After all I am educated, a doctor, with income to spare.

> I feel I have wasted money and time previously when I travelled to the US for 'ser' [leisure/tourism]. I used to travel without really meeting anybody in the countries I went to.

As I listened to women from fairly diverse class and ethnic backgrounds speak about their experiences with the *tablighi jama'at* at their headquarters in Lahore, Pakistan, I was struck by the fact that current theoretical understandings of cosmopolitanism do not allow for accidental and incidental formulations of the 'ironic' distance (Turner, 2002) that characterize cosmopolitanism in practice. The women quoted above who are members of the religious organization Tablighi Jama'at did not set out to seek and learn from difference. If anything their impulse was to homogenize religious practice. The focus of Tablighi Jama'at proselytizing are other Muslims. The idea is to bring them to the path of 'correct' practice and belief, and in the process of doing so learn and improve one's own life too. The instruction by Maulana Ilyas, its founder, for 'Muslims [to] become [true] Muslims' is a product of the context in which it was founded. Christian and later Hindu proselytizing missions had begun making inroads into a community close to present day Delhi that was nominally Muslim. Tablighi Jama'at was created as a response to their activities (Metcalf, 1994, 2002; Sikand, 2000; Masud, 2000). Yet, in the process they were exposed to ways of life, modes of interaction, and manners of being that helped them think about their own lives more critically. Are people who live cosmopolitanism, only cosmopolites if there is a plan or conscious action on their part?

In contemporary political and social theory, cosmopolitanism is a project as much as a concept. Archibugi and Held (1995) for instance, propose a program of 'cosmopolitan democracy' which would involve a global governance structure, as yet undefined, to allow for greater interaction for people and as a counterbalance to the far superior mobility afforded to capital today. In laying out their program they (Archibugi and Held 1995: 13) clarify:

The term *cosmopolitan* is used to indicate a model of political organization in which citizens, wherever they are located in the world, have a voice, input, and political representation in international affairs, in parallel with and independently of their own governments. The conception of *democracy* deployed here is one that entails a substantive process rather than merely a set of guiding rules, transforming politics from a mode of domination to a mode of service.

Yet it is precisely how these politics are to be transformed that remains under-conceptualised.

Since the fall of the Soviet Union and the ensuing ideological disarray, the intensification of neo-liberal globalization and increased migration (legal and illegal) of humans, but more so of capital, cosmopolitanism has emerged as an important concept and project. In this context, cosmopolitanism has been regarded by some as a project with the potential to harness some positive potential out of this latest form of globalization. It is useful to remind ourselves here that while something is definitely new and different about globalization today, there are also strong parallels with times past. Andre Gunder Frank (1998) points out that contrary to the rhetoric of this round of globalization heralding a brand new era of international economic linkages, globalization in terms of trade and economic flows is not new. For instance, in 1997 world trade as a percentage of total population had only just reached the level of pre-World War I years (Frank 1998). Perhaps it is no coincidence that the years preceding the World War I also comprise the period we associate today with the high point of colonial extraction.

In the context of a world beset with increasing economic dependence and not just interaction, ethnic warfare and forced migrations, illegal workers and legal migrants making claims of citizenship in different countries, global hotel chains providing 'authentic' local food, brands dictating fashion in disparate parts of the world, but primarily in a world dealing with one superpower, cosmopolitanism emerged as a liberating concept for many liberals and radicals alike. From claiming it integral to life (Appiah, 2006) to supporting it as a remedial measure in a particular national context (Nussbaum, 1996) to promoting an agenda for world governance (Archibuggi and Held, 1995) cosmopolitanism has offered a middle way between xenophobic nationalism/patriotism and unfettered globalization. At the same time, the impulse to define a set of basic normative values for engagement, such as that present in the work of Nussbaum (1996; 1999) brings its own dangers. A conversation tilted heavily towards the interests and values of one party often ends up in a monologue rather than a dialogue.

Whether the hopes associated with cosmopolitanism as a project are justified remains to be seen. One important avenue for exploring concrete manifestations of its limitations and possibilities is through a closer look at contemporary Muslim cosmopolitanism. My attempt here is twofold. First, I try to provide an overview of themes in the academic literature on cosmopolitanism in the context of contemporary Muslim societies. Second, I attempt to provide a window into actually existing practices within these societies. In the process of doing so I hope to be able to tease out some of the limitations of current formulations of both the concept and the project of contemporary cosmopolitanism.

The making and unmaking of 'muslim cosmopolitanism'

The association of cosmopolitanism with Muslims and predominantly Muslim societies is shot through with the ambivalence that characterizes much debate and discussion about

623

Muslims in the current political context. On the one hand there is the recognition that Muslim societies were cosmopolitan in the past, and on the other a sense that somehow these societies have lost precisely that quality in the contemporary context. There is an increasing body of literature that reminds us that Ottoman cities, Mughal courts, African and Indonesian ports, many with either large Muslims populations or under Muslim rulers or both, were centres of multi-religious, multi-ethnic, multi-lingual diversity (Karen Barkey, 2008; Fawaz and Bayly, 2002; Engseng Ho, 2006; Hobson, 2004; Subrahmanyam and Alam, 2000). In fact, this diversity was not just limited to the great cities and ports but, as a new body of literature points out, very much part of the fabric of rural and small town life as well (Lawrence and Gilmartin, 2000; Asher and Talbot, 2006; Mallampali, n.d. in the case of India). This diversity was not without its tensions and occasional violence, yet layers of interaction and co-existence allowed greater room for negotiation. Implicit in some of this is a sense that by taking a detailed look at what these societies were 'then' it would be possible to imagine what they can be in the future. Even if sometimes a silent presence in these discussions, the concern is very much with the 'now', which is seen as problematic. The very absences by which contemporary Muslim societies are defined mark their shortcomings (Turner, 1974). The 'now' remains problematic, suspended in perpetual contrast to the past and the imagined future.

Some scholars are not afraid to verbalize this relationship of absence. Meijer (1999: 1–2) in his introduction to the volume on 'Cosmopolitanism, Identity and Authenticity in the Middle East' that he edited, makes an unabashed case:

> The attainment of a cosmopolitan attitude is more difficult for some regions than others. The Middle East in particular is a region where an open attitude has become problematic. During the Ottoman period, the Middle East was an open undefined territory in which groups of different religious and ethnic backgrounds intermingled and exchanged ideas and lifestyles. European imperialism led to demise of cosmopolitanism in Middle East but nationalist revolutions, in particular, sounded the death knell of cosmopolitanism in the name of 'authentic' Arab Indigenous values. After the fall of the cosmopolitan elite and the exodus of Greeks, Italians, Syrians and Jews, who were accused of collaborating with the Western colonial powers, the cosmopolitan freehavens were absorbed again into the hinterland.

What such a formulation of the problem and its manifestation in the Middle East does not seem to account for is the diversity that exists within even the 'Arab' and/or 'Muslim' identity, the fissures along classes, gender roles, linguistic, religious, and ethnic divisions that continue to exist and are overcome in new ways. My argument here then is not that there was no change, but that these societies did not move suddenly from being diverse, multi-coloured rainbows to monochromatic dredges. Instead new lines of identity and difference had to be negotiated; new ways of being cosmopolitan learned. There is no denying a reduction in some types of diversity. The type of reduction in diversity that Meijer seems to be thinking of has been a phenomenon in the global south as new states were created, their boundaries solidified and nations created to fit within those boundaries. For instance, the formation of Pakistan meant that Lahore, a city that had a majority population of Hindus and Sikhs living alongside Muslims, suddenly became an overwhelmingly Muslim city. Everyday encounters with other ways of believing, worshipping, and practicing a faith became extinct. As the generation that had experienced such encounters dies, the vast majority of the city's inhabitants do not have any memory of such co-existence.

At the same time, it is useful to remind ourselves that diversity is not necessarily the same thing as cosmopolitanism (Breckenbridge and Appudarai, 2002; Rajan and Sharma, 2006). Nor is it the same as internationalism, even though the vast majority of contemporary literature is concerned with precisely the interaction across nations and nationalities (see Brennan, 1997; Vertovec and Cohen, 2002 for representative writings as well as a critique). One of the key aspects of difference that notions of cosmopolitanism do not seem to take adequately on board regard the differentials in social, economic, and cultural locations. Path dependencies induced by such differences may lead to very different life-worlds, such that those going through the highly stratified education system in Pakistan may indeed by classified as 'denizens of alien worlds' (Rahman, 2004).

In critiquing the cosmopolitanism of 'frequent travellers', Calhoun (2002: 875) raises the possibility that such elite formulations of 'cosmopolitan ideals of global civil society can sound uncomfortably like those of the civilizing mission behind colonialism'. Similarly, Baubock (2002: 113) asks whether 'any cosmopolitan project [can] ever be anything other than an inherently hegemonic and violent undertaking?' What does cosmopolitanism lived and experienced within contemporary Muslim societies look like? An emerging stream of literature is beginning to move beyond defining these societies by the absences and pay closer attention to processes on the ground. In the following sections I will take a look at mass media, pilgrimages, and proselytizing movements as they mediate identities and forms of associating beyond the familiar. The aim here is not to provide a comprehensive or schematic overview of the various avenues of 'being cosmopolitan' in contemporary Muslims societies. Nor am I interested in providing a catalogue of all the particular and peculiar ways in which Muslims may be cosmopolitan. Rather it is to highlight what Bayat (2008) has quite rightly pointed out is the contradictory process of living cosmopolitanism, particularly in urban contexts. He shows through a close look at the lower middle class neighbourhood of Shubra in Cairo where Muslims and Christians live together that:

> a modern city like Cairo tends, on the one hand, to differentiate, fragment and break down the traditional face-to-face ethnic or religious-based communities by facilitating the experience of sharing with other cultural-religious groupings. At the same time, however, religious–ethnic identities may persist or get reinvented not necessarily through face-to-face interactions, but through the construction of imaginary or 'distanced' communities.
>
> (Bayat, 2008: 181)

Thus, Bayat alerts us to the possibility that an interest and engagement with the other goes hand in hand with increased awareness of, and 'exaggerated emphasis' (p. 198) on boundaries, demarcation, and difference. Echoes of this can also be found in Kaviraj's (forthcoming 2009) formulation of 'thick' and 'thin' religion in the South Asian context. Through a focus on his personal and familial experience he contrasts the differences between thick religious identities that are bound together in a limited geographical and temporal zone through daily interaction (for instance within a neighbourhood) and 'thin' ones that are spread out over a wider geographical and temporal zone (for instance, the outrage expressed by individuals in one part of the country/world over the treatment of co-religionists in a different part of the country or the world). That this awareness and emphasis lends itself periodically to violence should not draw attention from the fact that the violence is the anomaly, and that the interaction for the most part is characterized by peaceful co-existence.

Mass media

One important mechanism for gaining an 'ironic' distance (Turner, 2002) from one's immediate context that was not available to the Greek philosophers who still influence academic understanding of cosmopolitanism today, is modern mass media. Indeed it allows a window into other ways of being without travelling. Travelling, of course, has been imagined as a key constitutive element of cosmopolitanism. From mass education and print media, to television, radio, VCRs, DVD players, satellite channels, and the internet, technologies of mass communication have had a profound influence on every-day conceptions of a how a life is to be lived. Earlier media of mass communication such as pamphlets and books depended heavily upon mass education. Dale Eickelman's seminal study (1992) on the impact of mass high education in Muslim societies particu-larly Oman and North Africa has focused on the 'objectification' of religious practices. He contends that this opened the way for thinking about religion in a systematic manner, prompting questions such as: 'What is my religion? Why is it important in my life? How do my beliefs guide my conduct?' (Eickelman, 1992: 643). The intimate connection between mass education and Islamist organization has lent further impetus to the process of objectification (Iqtidar, 2007). However, a new social imaginary due to oral and communal consumption of print precedes mass education in most Muslim societies (Edwards 1995; Francis Robinson, 1996). Oral traditions were not simply replaced by print media but in fact not only shaped the contours of dialogue in print but also facilitated the reach and impact of the printed word. Finally, the impact of mass and new media, such as the internet, in Muslim societies is beginning to receive some academic attention (Eickelman and Anderson, 2003)

Here I wish to use Lila Abu-Lughod's perceptive analysis of consumption and pro-duction of television soap operas in rural Egypt to destabilize understandings of cosmo-politanism predicated on the interaction of one bounded 'national' culture with another. The wide variety of 'cultures' that exist within the same village and beyond that within Egypt allow us to think about variegated interaction within and beyond the 'community' facilitated by television. Abu-Lughod (1997: 127) details the interaction of three women within 'an agricultural village in the heart of the tourist industry in a disadvantaged region in Egypt in the 1990s'. The first one is an uneducated peasant woman, Zaynab, who nevertheless has over the years interacted with and hosted many foreign researchers. The second is a relatively wealthy and younger woman Fayruz leading a more comfortable but confined life within a joint family. The third one is Zaynab's young daughter, Sumaya, more educated than both the others but lacking Fayruz's access to material resources. By paying close attention to the particular configurations of power, education, and wealth in their specific context Abu-Lughod shows how the desires, imaginaries, and aspirations cultivated by television vary widely for all three women. Moreover, television productions, even though 'Egyptian', speak of and to a different world than the one these women inhabit. Writer of television dramas Al-'Assal – urban, educated, and a feminist – is staunchly opposed to veiling. Yet the very imagery produced within her dramas allows Fayruz, the relatively well off village woman, to place herself in a middle-class moral world symbolized by veiling, when she visits Cairo. The creator and the consumer of the TV drama inhabit different Egypts, so to speak, and their interaction with each other's worlds proceeds in a non-linear manner. Critically, for our purposes here, Abu-Lughod's study destablises the commonly held notion of cosmopolitanism that does not pay close enough attention to variations in class and social position.

Class, gender, national, ethnic, and sectarian differences are often glossed over when talking of the 'Muslim'. Such presumption of internal coherence has created its own dynamics. Even as the category 'Muslim' remains internally riven and stratified, since 2001, the US led invasions of Afghanistan and Iraq and critically media conflation of Muslim and terrorist (Mamdani, 2005; Iqtidar, 2008), the external modalities of a Muslim identity have undergone a subtle shift: it has become a much more politicized category. This is particularly the case in the 'cosmopolitan' centres of Europe. Public association with this identity through dress, speech or other means, has become a political as much as personal matter. The introduction in UK of video games such as 'Muslim Massacare' that urge players to 'wipe out the Muslim race with an arsenal of the world's most destructive weapons' to ensure that 'no Muslim man or woman is left alive' and whose creators describe it as 'fun and funny', would be unthinkable about any other religious identity in the current context.[1] The imposition of a religious identity among populations that may have previously identified themselves primarily through ideological, national or linguistic affiliations has generated significant resistance amongst some Muslims (see, for instance, Begum and Eade, 2005 in the case of Bangladeshi community in London).

Travel and pilgrimages

Travel is intricately linked to notions of cosmopolitanism. The 'frequent traveller' then epitomizes a higher level of cosmopolitan sophistication (Calhoun, 2002). A form of travel compulsory for all practising Muslims who can afford it is the Hajj. The Hajj is an annual pilgrimage to the city of Mohammed's birth and initiation into divine revelation, Mecca in Saudi Arabia. While shorter versions of the Hajj, called Umra, are performed through out the year, the Hajj can only be performed on specific dates in the last month of the Islamic calendar. Since the Islamic calendar is lunar, the dates for the Hajj shift by about 11 days every year, and is thus performed in different seasons over the years. Every year more than 2 million pilgrims from over 70 different countries perform the Hajj.[2]

This coming together of citizens of many different countries, with different languages, modes of habitation and thought is mediated by a common and standardized ritual of worship at the Grand Mosque in Mecca. In itself, the Hajj affords as many opportunities as limits for interaction with the unknown. On the one hand the vast majority of pilgrims move in small groups of their co-nationalists and often close friends or family. On the other hand, the process of travelling from their homes to what is for most of the participants a distant land, and once there, sharing the space of worship with Muslims from all over the world opens many new opportunities for interaction and experience. In a recent study assessing the impact of Hajj the authors concluded that Hajj increases tolerance of other religious and ethnic groups among the Hajjis (people who have performed Hajj) (Clingingsmith et al., 2008). They point out that as the pilgrims accounts stress a feeling of unity with fellow Muslims, outsiders fear that this is could be accompanied by feelings of anti-pathy towards non-Muslims. However, they find that increased feeling of association with other Muslims is part of a broader increase in the belief in peace and harmony across religious, sectarian, and ethnic divides.[3] The study is primarily quantitative and does not set out to provide adequate explanations for why this might be the case. Nevertheless, the study provides some preliminary information about the impact of Hajj, a process that millions of Muslims go through every year.

For the large majority of Muslims in different parts of the world though, pilgrimages to local shrines and places of worship are in some ways a substitute of the Hajj. The overwhelming majority of studies conducted on these pilgrimages from Palestine to India, Indonesia, and Morocco comment on the hybridity of practices and motives that characterize these. In addition, these pilgrimages seem to be venues of interfaith mingling and interaction. Bowman (1993) discusses the case of Mar Elyas, a Greek Orthodox shrine frequented by both Muslims and Christians near Bethlehem. He shows that attendance at the shrine and related festivals by both Muslims (Shias and Sunnis) and Christians (Orthodox, Catholic, and others) is mediated by a range of motives and interests. The miraculous power seen to be resident at the shrine is seen as a general and broad pretext for getting together. Some are motivated by specific religious strictures, others by seeking cures for ailments. Still others are looking for avenues of conviviality and interaction, while there were those who expected to profit from such gatherings through sales of their products and services. Most significantly Bowman detected a relative fluidity to notions of belonging and association. Incoming pilgrims introduced themselves through their villages and places of origins, professions, religion or family name but not necessarily exclusively through religion. Similar, fluidity of identity and interaction is noted by others working in the South and South East-Asian context, particularly regarding the shrines of Sufi saints (van der Veer, 1992 and 1994; Eaton, 1978; Hayden, 2002, Bayly, 1989; McDonnell, 1990; Tapper, 1990). Moreover, pilgrimages are particularly important for decentring the focus on urban centres as the locus of cosmpolitanism. Many Sufi shrines tend to be located in cities but just as frequently they are located in semi-urban or rural areas. More significantly, those undertaking the pilgrimages often travel from and across rural areas. Emerging work on cosmopolitanism within the rural context (for Pakistan, Marsden, 2008) is important for highlighting channels of interaction and travel that allow for an expanded imaginary.

Proselytizing movements

While movements of renewal and reform have been an integral part of the Muslim history (Esposito 1999: 645), the modern proselytizing movement is a significantly different phenomenon that is only now beginning to receive some academic attention. In the context of Christian evangelical movements in North and South America as well as Europe, the importance of education, travel facilities, and mass media has been highlighted (e.g. Lehmann, 1996). An important proselytizing movement of the Muslim world is the Tablighi Jama'at. Its annual gathering in Raiwind, Pakistan and Dhaka, Bangladesh attract more participants than the Hajj. These meetings draw members of the Tablighi Jama'at from all over the world including a significant presence of Africans and South East Asians.

The movement originated in the last years of colonial rule in India. Its founder Maulana Ilyas articulated a vision of change at the individual level which is the inverse of the more overtly political conception put forward by his contemporary Abul A'ala Maududi. D'awa or the call to the truth is a central act of worship that believers must carry out on a daily basis to ensure a place in heaven in the after life. Typically, members are inducted into more rigorous proselytizing missions by travelling outside their region for a three-day, three-week, three-month and eventually six-month period. Women were discouraged from participating in d'awa missions in the early years of the TJ's existence, but increasingly they are coming to play a more active role. The TJ prides itself in its low profile and the official dictum of *naa parcha, naa charcha, naa kharcha* – no publication, no fame, no expenditure (Sikand, 2000) – seems to still be quite ingrained in the workings of groups in different parts of the world. At the same time, several high profile converts to the TJ cause have highlighted its reach within different segments of Pakistani society. These TJ members and associates include famous cricketers, rock stars, and politicians including a former president.

In 2005, I conducted interviews with women members of the Tablighi Jama'at in Lahore, Pakistan. In addition, I attended weekly dars sessions carried out at the homes of some TJ members. A wide variety of pedagogical exercises are carried out under the banner of *dars,* including lectures to large audiences in the thousands to two others, cassette sermons, mosque addresses following prayers, discussions of exegetical issues in private homes, and sermons at marriage and death ceremonies. The content of the *dars* may also vary as might the teaching methodology from a Socratic conversation to a lecture. One of the weekly dars groups met at the home of a wealthy businessman's daughter-in-law in an expensive locality of Lahore. The women assembled belonged to the upper and upper middle class of Pakistan. Of the approximately 40 women, close to 70 per cent were university educated, either in Pakistan or in the US or Europe. A significant proportion, approximately 35 per cent, were professionals working as doctors, teachers, or civil servants. Another 20 per cent owned and operated their own business, typically designing and assembling wedding dresses[4] at workshops set up in their own homes. The rest tended to be housewives or young women waiting to be married off.

Many of the women had travelled outside of Pakistan to visit family, perform the Hajj and/or umra, and for tourism. A few had travelled for work as well. In discussing their experiences of travelling for other reasons and travelling for d'awa, those who had gone on such excursions expressed a clear sense of difference. Noreen (names changed in accordance to norms of anthropological research), a middle aged doctor, had travelled extensively in the US and Europe. Her two sons were studying in the US, and she visited them every year until her involvement with the TJ. With the TJ she had most recently undertaken a d'awa trip to South Africa. D'awa groups, especially those including women, are mobilized on the invitation of locals from a destination. In this case, the host families were primarily Muslims of Gujrati Indian descent who had settled in South Africa several generations ago The hosts then undertake to provide food and housing for the group, particularly for the women. Men and women, even if from the same family, tend to stay in different homes. The men might even stay in the local mosque. Noreen had stayed with four different families in the course of her week-long stay in South Africa. As is the norm for such visits, the host families had invited their friends and family to come and meet the visiting women. Noreen explained:

We were busy from morning till night with people who just came to speak to us. Most of them could only understand a little bit of Urdu. Some were not able to speak much English either. On our side too, not all the women could speak English and of course, we did not know Gujrati or any of their local languages. Still we read the Quran to them in its universal language of love. And then they would talk to us separately or sometimes in groups. Some of them just wanted to talk about the problems in their lives, with their children or their husbands or their health. Others were looking to quench a spiritual thirst. In such a short time I was able to understand how people live there, how they organise their homes and what kind of problems they face ... *I feel I have wasted money and time previously when I travelled to the US for 'ser' [leisure/tourism]. I used to travel without really meeting anybody in the countries I went to.*

Noreen's description of her trip, substantiated by many others who had either gone on similar trips or on the same trip with her, highlight the non-linearity of cosmopolitan experience. At the end of each mission, the women were expected to hold *dars* meetings at their homes or at least in one of the homes, and talk about their experiences with those who had not gone on the mission. In part this was a recruitment drive for volunteers both to go to a new place and proselytize and to host incoming groups in their homes. This was a more structured and predictable part of the meeting. Speakers, often women who had been involved in TJ for some time or those who had just gone on the mission, would speak about their personal experiences a little bit, emphasizing the spiritual peace and satisfaction (*sakoon*) they had gained from the mission. They would then go on to extol other women to go on missions. Typically they would list all the reasons women are reluctant to commit to a mission. Apart from financial difficulties and husband's consent, both of which were not discussed in much detail, the speakers would focus on the psychological barrier that women had in leaving their homes:

> Some women say they can't go because their children are taking their exams and it is a difficult time to leave them. But what about the bigger exam that we will all face when we have to account for our deeds on this earth? They say our children are sick we can't go now. Do they think they are the ones to cure their children? Do they think they control decisions of life, death and disease? They say we don't know the people we are going to stay with. Well that is true, but they become like our family when we do meet them. When we live in their homes for a while how can we not come to some understanding of different kinds of lives, different ways of thinking and different reasons that people may or may not come to the right path?

The more interesting part of the meetings, though, was the informal part when women would typically sit in smaller groups or move from one to the next. Those who had just been to on a mission would talk in more detail about particular people they met there, the kinds of problems they discussed, the way their houses are organized differently, recipes, and general observations about the country. One young woman who had recently been on a mission to the UK said:

> I was quite worried. We hear so much about the way Muslims are perceived and treated in the UK. I thought this is going to be a horrible experience. Yet, I went because the more difficult the mission, the more *sawab* we earn. I was so surprised by the way we were treated in the UK. I realise that some Muslims do have a very bad experience, particularly the ones who live there. But my own experience was very good.

I am not suggesting here that all of the women who embark upon d'awa transform into cosmopolites. Rather, I want to emphasize the fragility of cosmopolitanism as a project. The project of fostering cosmopolitanism such as that envisioned by many radicals and liberals must allow for non-linear interactions and unintended consequences. My suggestion here is precisely that even though these women did not set out explicitly, or at least only, to engage with some 'other', the very structure of their interaction fostered some understanding of different ways of being. For the project of cosmopolitanism it might be more productive to focus on creating structures that are conducive to long term interaction rather than focusing on the normative strictures of engagement.

Conclusion

The two competing strands of argument within this paper may seem to be contradicting each other. On the one hand I have tried to open up the categories 'Cosmopolitanism' and 'Muslim' separately, and suggested that given the immense variation within the category 'Muslim' it is not entirely feasible to conceive of a coherent and stable phenomenon called 'Muslim Cosmopolitanism'. At the same time, I have tried to show through a focus on particular locations and contexts the forms that contemporary practices take in predominantly Muslim societies. Through the consumption of media in Egypt, the practice of pilgrimage in Palestine and the involvement in a proselytizing movement in Pakistan I have attempted to show the diversity of ways in which an ironic distance from the self, an engagement with another way of being – a cosmopolitanism if you will – is practiced in contemporary Muslim societies. These sections are not intended to give a comprehensive survey of contemporary Muslim practice with regards to cosmopolitanism. Rather my intention has been to look at some of the important ways in which these societies maintain their engagement with the new and the different. More critically, I have tried to raise questions about our association of cosmopolitanism with a particular kind of liberal subjectivity and selfhood.

Critically, a characteristic that many pre-dominantly Muslim societies share with many other non-Muslim global south societies is the critical self-examination that they have already embarked upon as a result of what Asad (1973, 1991) has called the 'colonial encounter'. As Marshall Hodgson observed at the end of his three volume study of Islam, Western societies have managed to retain a deeper and more continuous link with their past. This is particularly true in terms of a philosophical dialogue that continues today to rely upon the same philosophers, religious references and texts that it has for several hundreds of years. 'Western' societies can be seen to be far more traditional than Muslims ones in this context. The break with their past, whether it is in forms of knowledge, modes of habitation or philosophical traditions, for many Muslim societies has been immense and has led to a wide variety of responses (Iqtidar, 2009). It has already produced a certain sense of 'ironic distance'. Over the last century and a half in particular, prominent philosophers, writers, and political personalities have articulated variant and at times contradictory visions of what the Muslim 'self' might consist of and the various ways in which it has to change. The cacophony of options and views is actually a testimony to a wide ranging conversation that is inflected with a critical distance to what is familiar.

Acknowledgements

I am grateful to Bryan Turner for his encouragement and patience; to Kamran Asdar Ali for critical feedback and for raising more questions than I could answer; and to Asef Bayat for discussions and ideas.

Notes

1 'Muslim Massacre' Game Assailed, Dawn, September 13, 2008 at http://www.dawn.com/2008/09/13/top18.htm last accessed 13.09.08.
2 Ministry of hajj kingdom of Saudi Arabia website http://www.hajinformation.com/main/l.htm, http://edition.cnn.com/SPECIALS/2006/hajj/. Both sites accessed last on July 31, 2008
3 The results of the study are based on a 2006 survey of more than 1600 Sunni Muslims in Pakistan who applied to the Hajj visa allocation lottery. Saudi Arabia limits the number of pilgrims to a certain quota for each country every year for logistical and safety reasons. Pakistani government allocates the vast majority of its quota through a lottery. The study compared successful applicants with unsuccessful ones to assess changes in attitudes. The study found that Hajjis are 22 percent more likely to declare that people of different religions are equal and 11 percent more likely to state the people of different religions can live in harmony (Clingingsmith et al. 2008: 2). For a review of autobiographical accounts of Hajjis from South Asia from late 1800 to the 1980s, often stressing increased feelings of peace and harmony towards mankind generally, see Metcalfe, 1990.
4 The wedding dress market is one of the most resilient in Pakistan. Wedding dresses include not just the dress worn by the bride on the two main days of wedding celebrations, but also the heavily worked dresses for use in these and other functions by the guests at the wedding. Given the social requirements for involvement and participation in weddings, most upper middle class women prepare at least five or six such suits every year.

References

Abu-Lughod, Lila, 'The Interpretation of Culture(s) After Television', *Representations*, 59, Summer, 109–34, 1997.

Appiah, Anthony, *Cosmopolitanism: Ethics in a World of Strangers*, New York: W.W. Norton, 2006.

Archibugi, Daniele and David Held, *Cosmopolitan Democracy: An Agenda for a New World Order*, Cambridge: Polity Press, 1995.

Asad, Talal, *Anthropology and the Colonial Encounter*, London: Ithaca Press, 1973.

——'From the history of colonial anthropology to the anthropology of Western hegemon' in G. Stocking, ed., *Colonial Situations*, Madison: University of Wisconsin Press, 1991.

Asher, Katherine, and Talbot, Cynthia, *India Before Europe*, Cambridge: Cambridge University Press, 2006.

Barkey, Karen, *Empire of Difference: The Ottomans in Comparative Perspective*, New York: Cambridge University Press, 2008.

Baubock, Rainer, 'Political Community Beyond the Sovereign State. Supranational Federalism and Transnational Minorities' in Robin Cohen and Steven Vertovec, ed., *Conceiving Cosmopolitanism: Theory, Context and Practice*, Oxford: Oxford University Press, 2002.

Bayat, Asef, 'Cairo Cosmopolitanism: Living Together through the Communal Divide, Almost' in Shail Mayaram, ed., *The Other Global City*, London, Routledge, 2008.

Bayly, Susan, *Saints, Goddesses and Kings: Muslims and Christians in South Indian Society 1700–1900*, Cambridge: Cambridge University Press, 1989.

Begum, H. and Eade, J. *All Quiet on the Eastern Front? Bangladeshi reactions in Tower Hamlets*, in T. Abbas, ed., *Muslim Britain Communities under Pressure*, London/New York: Zed Press, 179–93, 2005.

Bowman, Glenn, 'Nationalising the Sacred: Shrines and Shifting Identities in Israeli Occupied Territories', *Man* 28: 431–60, 1993.

Breckenbridge, Carol and Appudarai, Arjun, *Cosmopolitanism*, Durham, NC; London: Duke University Press, 2002.

Brennan, Timothy, *At Home in the World: Cosmopolitanism Now*, Cambridge: Harvard University Press, 1997.

Calhoun, Craig, 'The Class Consciousness of Frequent Travellers: Toward a Critique of Actually Existing Cosmopolitanism', *The South Atlantic Quarterly*, 101, 4: 869–97, Fall 2002.

Clingingsmith, Khawaja and Kremer, 'Estimating the Impact of the Hajj: Religion and Tolerance in Islam's Global Gathering', Harvard University Working Paper Series, April 2008.

Eaton, Richard, *Sufis of Bijapur*, Princeton: Princeton University Press, 1978.

Edwards, David B., 'Anthropological Analysis and Islamic Texts', *Anthropological Quarterly*, 68/3: 171–84, July 1995.

Eickelman, Dale, *Moroccon Islam: Tradition and society in a pilgrimage centre*, Austin: University of Texas Press, 1976.

——'Mass higher education and the religious imagination in contemporary Arab Societies', *American Ethnologist*, 19/4: 643–55, November 1992.

Eickelman, Dale and Jon Anderson, eds, *New Media inthe Muslim World*, Bloomington, IN: Indiana University Press, 2003.

Esposito, John, 'Contemporary Islam: Reformation or Revolution?' in John Esposito, ed., *The Oxford History of Islam*, Oxford University Press, 1999.

Fawaz, Leila and Chris Bayly, *Modernity and Culture from the Mediterranean to the Indian Ocean*, New York: Columbia University Press, 2002.

Frank, Andre Gunder, *ReOrient: Global Economy in an Asian Age*, Berkeley, CA: California University Press, 1998.

Hayden, Richard, 'Antagonistic Tolerance: Competitive Sharing of Religious Sites in South Asia and the Balkans', *Current Anthropology*, 43/2, 205–19, 2002.

Hefner, Robert, 'Print Islam: Mass Media and Ideological Rivalries among Indonesian Muslims', *Indonesia* 64: 77–103, Oct. 1997.

Ho, Enseng, *The Graves of Tarim, Genealogy and Mobility Across the Indian Ocean*, Berkeley: University of California Press, 2006.

Hobson, John, *The Eastern Origins of Western Civilization*, Cambridge: University of Cambridge Press, 2004.

Iqtidar, Humeira, Changes in the Role of 'Muslim Fundamentalists' in Pakistan, unpublished PhD thesis, University of Cambridge, 2007.

——Terrorism and Islamism: Differences, Dynamics and Dilemmas' in special issue on 'Terrorism, Security and Business', *Global Business and Economic Review*, 10/2, 2008.

——'Colonial Secularism and the Genesis of Islamism in North India' in Gareth Stedman-Jones and Ira Katznelson, ed., *Religion and the Political Imagination*, Cambridge University Press, forthcoming 2009.

Kaviraj, Sudipta, 'On Thick and Thin Religion', in Gareth Stedman Jones and Ira Katznelson eds., *Religion and the Political Imagination*, Cambridge University Press, forthcoming 2009.

Lawrence, Bruce and David Gilmartin, *Beyond Turk and Hindu: Rethinking Religious Identities in Islamicate South Asia*, Gainseville: University of Florida Press, 2000.

Lehmann, David, *Struggle for the Spirit: Religious Transformation and Popular Culture in Brazil and Latin America*, Cambridge: Polity Press, 1996.

McDonnell, Mary Bryne, 'Patterns of Mulsim pilgrimage from Malaysia, 1885–1985' in Eickelman and Piscatori, ed., *Muslim Travellers: Pilgrimage, Migration and the Religious Imagination*, London: Routledge: 1990.

Mallampali, Chandra, 'Cosmopolitanism in the Hinterland? Bellary Distinct through Fresh Lenses, 1800–840', unpublished paper.

Mamdani, Mahmood, *Good Muslim, Bad Muslim: America, the Cold War, and the Roots of Terror*, New York: Three Leaves Press, 2005.

Marsden, Magnus, 'Muslim cosmopolitans? Transnational Life in northern Pakistan', Journal of Asian Studies, 67/1: 213–48, 2008.

Masud, Mohammed Khalid, ed., *Travellers in Faith: Studies of the Tablighi Jama'at as a transnational Islamic Movement for Faith Renewal*, Lieden: Brill, 2000.

Meijer, Roel, *Cosmopolitanism, Identity and Authenticity in the Middle East*, Richmond, Surrey: Curzon, 1999.

Metcalf, Barbara D., 'The Pilgrimage Remembered: South Asian Accounts of the *Hajj*', in Eickelman and Piscatori, ed., *Muslim Travellers: Pilgrimage, migration and the religious imagination*, London: Routledge: 1990.

——'Remaking Ourselves: Islamic Self-Fashioning in a Global Movement of Spiritual Renewal', in Marty, M. and Appleby, R.S., ed., *Accounting for Fundamentalisms: The Dynamic Character of Movements*, University of Chicago Press, 1994.

——'Traditionalist Islamic Activism: Deoband, Tablighis and Taliban', *International Institute for the Study of Islam in the Modern World (ISIM) Paper*, 2002.

Nussbaum, Martha, 'Patriotism and Cosmopolitanism' in Joshua Cohen, ed., *For Love of Country?* Boston: Beacon Press, 1996.

——*Sex and Social Justice*, New York: Oxford University Press, 1999.

Rahman, Tariq *Denizens of Alien Worlds: A Study of Education, Inequality and Polarization in Pakistan*, Karachi: Oxford University Press, 2004.

Rajan, Gita and Shailaja Sharma, *New cosmopolitanisms: South Asians in the US*, Stanford, CA: Stanford University Press, 2006.

Robinson, Francis, 'Islam and the Impact of Print in South Asia', in Nigel Crook, ed., *The Transmission of Knowledge in South Asia: Essays on Education, Religion, History and Politics*, Delhi: Oxford University Press, 1996.

Sikand, Yoginder, *The Origins and Development of the Tablighi Jam'aat, 1920–2000: A Cross-country Comparative Study*, New Delhi: Orient Longman, 2000.

Subrahmanyam, Sanjay and Alam, Muzaffar, *The Mughal State 1526–1750*, New Delhi, Oxford: Oxford University Press, 2000.

Tapper, Nancy, 'Ziyaret: gender, movement and exchange in a Turkish community' in Eickelman and Piscatori, ed., *Muslim Travellers: Pilgrimage, migration and the religious imagination*, London: Routledge: 1990.

Turner, Bryan, *Weber and Islam: A Critical Study*, London: Routledge, 1974.

——'Cosmopolitan Virtue, Globalization and Patriotism' *Theory Culture & Society*, 19, 1/2: 45–63, 2002.

van der Veer, Peter, Playing or Praying: A sufi saint's day in Surat, *Journal of Asian Studies*, 51: 545–64, 1992.

——*Religious Nationalism: Hindus and Muslims in India*, Berkeley: University of California Press, 1994.

Vertovec, Steven and Robin Cohen, eds. *Conceiving Cosmopolitanism: Theory, Context and Practice*, Oxford: Oxford University Press, 2002.

33

New cosmopolitanism in the social sciences

Ulrich Beck and Natan Sznaider

Introduction: why is there a need for a cosmopolitan social and political theory?

At the beginning of the twenty-first century we have to redefine and reinvent the social sciences and humanities for the global world. This is a double challenge: first to discover and criticize how sociology, political science, history and other fields are still prisoners of the nation-state and give birth to a historically mistaken national imagination. Second, how to redefine trans-nationally the basic theoretical concepts and units of empirical research like politics, society, identity, state, history, class, law, democracy, community, solidarity, justice, mobility, military, household, and other institutions in a cosmopolitan perspective. This calls for a paradigm shift. It is also a Cosmopolitan Manifesto for the social sciences not only to renew their scientific standing and public claims but bring the social sciences back on the public agenda.

The classics of sociology are so thoroughly pervaded with a spatially fixed understanding of culture that is rarely remarked upon. It is a conception that goes back to sociology's birth amidst the nineteenth-century formation of nation-states. The territorial conception of culture and society – the idea of culture as 'rooted' and 'limited', constituted through the opposition of the 'We' and 'Them' – was itself a reaction to the enormous changes that were going on as that century turned into the twentieth. It was a conscious attempt to provide a solution to the uprooting of local cultures that the formation of nation states necessarily involved. Sociology understood the new symbols and common values above all as means of integration into a new unity. The triumph of this national imagination can be seen in the way the nation-state has ceased to appear as a project and a construct and has become instead widely regarded as something natural and the opposition national and international the internalized compass of the Social Sciences. A cosmopolitan sociology is posing a challenge to this idea that binding history and borders tightly together is the only possible means of social and symbolic integration. This also means that sociological perspectives are geared to and organized in terms of the nation-state. All the traditional fields of the social sciences (like the sociology of inequality, of the family, of politics, of mobility and class and so on) are still being researched pretty much in the nation state (or international) tradition. The concept of 'cosmopolitanization', by contrast, is an explicit attempt to overcome this 'methodological (inter-)nationalism' and produce concepts capable of reflecting a newly transnational world. It consciously develops a new methodology: 'methodological cosmopolitanism'. None of this will make ethno-nationalism go away, of course. It is here to stay and even if we as moral philosophers are more inclined to believe in cosmopolitan values than in group values, as social scientists we need to establish the reality of cosmopolitanization – not as dream but as empirical reality.

Globalization versus cosmopolitanization

How can we understand the difference between the discourse of 'globalization' and the new code word 'cosmopolitanization' or 'cosmopolitanism'? Are the latter just another example of the 'newspeak' (Orwell) in the social sciences? Not at all: the more we reflect on what 'globalization' means for the social sciences, the more the new cosmopolitanism wins its distinct meaning and importance.

We can distinguish four phases in how the word 'globalization' has been used in the social sciences: first, denial, second, conceptual refinement and empirical research, third, 'cosmopolitanization' and fourth, epistemological shift. The first reaction of the mainstream was to deny the reality or relevance of (economic) globalization and to declare that nothing that fell under the heading 'globalization' on the social scientific agenda was historically new. This explanation of the phenomenon began to lose credibility in the second phase when social scientists in the most diverse disciplines began to subject phenomena of globalization to conceptual analysis and to situate them in the theoretical and empirical semantics of the social sciences (for example, Held et al. 1999). Through this sophistication it came to mind that a new landscape of societies is in the making. Its dominant features include interrelatedness and interdependence of people across the globe; growing inequalities in a global dimension; emergence of new supra-national organizations in the area of economy (transnational co-operations), politics (non-state actors such as International Monetary Fund, World Bank, the World Trade Organization, the International Court of Justice), and civil society (advocacy social movements of global scope such as Amnesty International, Greenpeace, feminist organizations, Attac); new normative precepts like human rights, new types and profiles of global risks (climate change, financial threats, and turbulences), new forms of warfare, global organized crime and terrorism.

In the third phase important social scientific consequences of this came to mind, the common denominator being 'cosmopolitanization'. How can this key concept be defined? 'Cosmopolitanization' means (a) the erosion of clear borders, separating markets, states, civilizations, religions, cultures, life-worlds of common people which (b) implies the involuntary confrontation with the alien other all over the globe. The world has certainly not become borderless, but the boundaries are becoming blurred and indistinct, becoming permeable to flows of information, capital, and risk. This does, of course, not mean that everybody is becoming a 'cosmopolitan'. Even – as Steffen Mau et al. (2008) show (on the basis of a representative survey of German citizens carried out in 2006) – people with border crossing experiences and transnational social relations are more likely to adopt cosmopolitan attitudes with respect to foreigners and global governance. Often the opposite seems to be the case: a wave of re-nationalization and re-ethnification in many parts of the world. But at the same time it does mean that there is a new need for a hermeneutics of the alien other in order to live and work in a world in which violent division and unprecedented intermingling coexists, and danger and opportunity vie. This may influence human identity construction, which need no longer be shaped by the opposition to others, in the negative, confrontational dichotomy of 'we' and 'them'.

In the books of Ulrich Beck (for example *Power in the Global Age*, 2005; *The Cosmopolitan Vision*, 2006 and *A God of One's Own*, 2009) it is emphasized that cosmopolitanization does not operate somewhere in the abstract, in the external macro-sphere, somewhere above human heads, but is internal to everyday life of people ('mundane cosmopolitanism'). This mundane cosmopolitanism is not only to be found in people's heads (even though not a bad place to be), but can be found foremost in people's hearts. That means that cosmopolitanism is as much a reasonable option as it is a sentiment. This is also shown in Natan Sznaider's book *Memory-Scape Europe* (2008), which takes the history of the Jews as an example. The same is true for the internal operation of politics, which at all levels, even the domestic level, has to become global, taking into account the global scale of dependencies, flows, links, and threats ('global domestic politics'). The awareness of these changes lags behind objective reality, because people are still thinking in terms of the 'national outlook' which suggests the nation-states as the universal and most important 'containers' within which human life is spent. Similarly, most of sociology is still applying the rules of 'methodological nationalism', treating societies confined in the borders of nation-states as natural units of data collections and analyses. But this is a blind avenue: just as nation-based economics has come to a dead end, so too has nation-state sociology.

In the growing discourse on cosmopolitanism there is a danger of fusing the ideal with the real. What cosmopolitanism *is* cannot ultimately be separated from what cosmopolitanism *should be*. But the same is true of nationalism. The small, but important, difference is that in the case of nationalism the value judgment of the social scientists goes unnoticed because methodological nationalism includes a naturalized conception of nations as real communities. In the case of the cosmopolitan '*Wertbeziehung*' (Max Weber, value relation), by contrast, this silent commitment to a nation-state centred outlook of sociology appears problematic. What is at stake here? Whereas in the case of the nation-state centred perspective there is a historical correspondence between normative and methodological nationalism (and for this reason this correspondence has mainly remained latent), this does not hold for the relationship between normative and methodological cosmopolitanism. In fact, the opposite is true: even the re-nationalization or re-ethnification of minds, culture, and institutions has to be analyzed within a cosmopolitan frame of reference.

Cosmopolitan social science entails the systematic breaking up of the process through which the national perspective of politics and society, as well as the methodological nationalism of political science, sociology, history, and law, confirm and strengthen each other in their definitions of reality. Thus it also tackles (what had previously been *analytically* excluded as a sort of conspiracy of silence of conflicting basic convictions) the various developmental versions of de-bounded politics and society, corresponding research questions and programmes, the strategic expansions of the national and international political fields, as well as basic transformations in the domains of state, politics, and society.

And this is why a new cosmopolitanism is in the air: through criticism, the concept has been rediscovered and reinvented. Over the last years or so there has been a sharp increase in the literature that attempts to relate the discourse on globalization (in cultural and political terms) to a redefinition of cosmopolitanism for the global age.

Thus, cosmopolitanism relates to a pre-modern ambivalence towards a dual identity and a dual loyalty. Every human being is rooted by birth in two worlds, two communities – in the cosmos (that is nature) and in the polis (that is the city-state).

637

To be more precise: individuals are rooted in one cosmos but in different cities-territories-ethnicities-hierarchies-nations-religions and other settings at the same time. This creates not exclusivity, but an inclusive plural membership. Being part of the cosmos means that every man and every woman are equal by nature, yet being part of different states organized into territorial units (polis). 'Cosmopolitanism' ignores the 'either or' principle and embodies 'this or that' principle. These are ancient hybrid – melange-scale – flow concepts. Thus, cosmopolitanism generates a logic of non-exclusive oppositions, creating 'patriots' of two worlds who are at the same time equal and different.

To the extent that this has been reflected, the fourth phase witnesses an epistemological shift. This insight began to gain ground when the unit of research of the respective social scientific discipline became arbitrary, when the distinction between internal and external, national and international, local and global, lose their sharp contours. The question for sociological research following the epistemological turn is: what happens when the premises and boundaries that define these units disintegrate? My answer is that the whole conceptual world of the 'national outlook' becomes disenchanted; that is, de-ontologized, historicized, and stripped of its inner necessity. However, it is possible only to justify this and think through its consequences within the framework of an interpretative alternative which replaces ontology with methodology, that is, the currently prevailing ontology and imaginary of the nation-state with what I propose to call 'methodological cosmopolitanism'. But in order to develop this we want to position this project in a long tradition of cosmopolitan thinking in the Social Sciences.

Cosmopolitan traditions

If we ask who are the intellectual progenitors of this internal cosmopolitanization of national societies, Adam Smith, Alexis de Tocqueville, and John Dewey come to mind, as well as such classical German thinkers as Kant, Goethe, Herder, Humbt, Nietzsche, Marx and Simmel. All of them construed the modern period as a transition from early conditions of relatively closed societies to 'universal eras' (Goethe) of interdependent societies, a transition that essentially involved the expansion of commerce and the dissemination of the principle of republicanism. For Kant, even more so for Marx, and in different ways also for Adam Smith and Georg Simmel, the dissolution of small territorial communities and the spread of universal social and economic interdependence (though not yet the associated risks) was the essential mark, and even the law, of world history. Their preoccupation with long lines of historical development made them sceptical towards the idea that state and society in their nationally homogenous manifestations could constitute the end point of world history. Cosmopolitanization indicates: there is simply no way of turning the clock back to a world of sovereign nation-states and national societies. Therefore we need a cosmopolitan sociology – even to understand why anti-cosmopolitan movements actually influence, and in the future maybe even dominate, the world.

Different ways of dealing with cultural difference

So far, the understanding of cosmopolitanism has been primarily normative and philosophical. We want to define the concept in a new way – namely, as a *social scientific* concept – and for quite specific social facts – namely, a specific way of socially dealing with cultural difference (see also Kurasawa 2004). The concept of cosmopolitanism can thereby be distinguished in an ideal type manner from a number of other social ways of dealing with difference, in particular, hierarchical subordination (racism), universalistic and nationalistic sameness and postmodern particularism. The predicament with this universalistic account of cosmopolitanism is not only that it carries a Eurocentric bias and that it operates with thin conceptions of identity. Its central shortcoming, politically and analytically, is that it operates with an a-historical notion of history that seeks to mould (and freeze) particular memories of the past into universal standards for the future. In doing so it fails to recognize the persistence of particularism and exclusion as central features. It simplifies the complex relationship between nationalism and cosmopolitanism. On the one hand nationalism and especially ethno-nationalism may be considered the enemies of cosmo-politanism and something to be overcome (Calhoun 2002), while on the other hand cosmopolitanism prepoposes nationalism (Beck and Grande 2007).

In the first place, cosmopolitanism differs fundamentally from all forms of vertical dif-ferentiation that seek to bring social difference into a hierarchical relation of *superiority and subordination*. Typical here is that one denies 'the others' the status of sameness and equality and perceives them in a relation of hierarchical subordination or inferiority. At the extreme, the others count as 'barbarians' devoid of rights.

Second, there is universalism that is the *dissolution of differences* which represents the countervailing principle to hierarchical subordination. Universalism obliges us to respect others as equals in principle, yet for that very reason it neglects what makes others different. On the contrary, the particularity of others is sacrificed to an assumed universal equality which denies its own origins and interests. Universalism thereby becomes two-faced: respect and hegemony. Often it is a contextual universalism. Then it means *European* universalism. An African universalism would mean: the real European does have a black soul.

From this we have – third – to distinguish nationalism. *Nationalism* standardizes dif-ferences while at the same time demarcating them in accordance with national oppositions. As a strategy of dealing with difference, it too follows an either/or logic, though instead of the distinction between higher and lower it operates with the distinction between internal and external. Nationalism has two sides: one directed inwards, the other out-wards. Towards the inside, nationalism aims to dissolve differences and promote uniform norms. It has this in common with universalism. In this sense, nationalism dissolves differ-ences internally while at the same time producing and stabilising it towards the outside.

Cosmopolitanism differs from all of the previously mentioned forms in that here the *recognition of difference* becomes a maxim of thought, social life, and practice, both internally and towards the outside. It neither orders differences hierarchically nor dis-solves them, but accepts them as such, indeed invests them with a positive value. It is sensitive to historic cultural particularities, asking for the specific dignity and burden of a group, a people, a culture, a religion. Cosmopolitanism affirms what is excluded both by hierarchical difference and by universal equality, namely, preceding others as different *and* at the same time equal.

Whereas universalism and nationalism are based on the either/or principle, cosmopo-litanism rests on the 'both/and' principle. The foreign is not experienced and assessed as dangerous, disintegrating, and fragmenting but as enriching. My curiosity about myself and about difference makes others irreplaceable for me. There is also an egoism of cos-mopolitan interest. Those who integrate the perspective of others into their own lives learn more about themselves *as well as* others. Hence cosmopolitanism calls for new concepts of integration and identity that facilitate and affirm coexistence across borders, without requiring that distinctiveness and difference be sacrificed on the altar of supposed (national) equality. 'Identity' and 'integration' are then nothing more than different words for hegemony over the other or others, of the majority over minorities. Cosmopolitanism accepts difference but does not absolutize it; rather, it seeks out ways for rendering it universally tolerable. In this, it relies on a framework of uniting and universally binding norms that should prevent deviation into postmodern particularism.

Hellenism might be a good starting point for current cosmopolitan sensibilities. Besides claiming it as the first golden age of cosmopolitanism, many of the principles that underlie our current theories and practices of cosmopolitanism derive as much from this period as from the cosmopolitan golden age of the Enlightenment. Historically, there are many things we can learn from this period that are often obscured when we study Enlightenment cosmopolitanism alone. The first thing that is obvious when we look at the Hellenistic period is that the rise and spread of cosmopolitan ideas always has a social and political underpinning. The Hellenistic period can also teach us about the connections between cosmopolitanism and empire, which is today part of the new discourse. This is often less obvious when we concentrate on the abstract philosophy of the Enlightenment. In the Hellenistic period (as opposed to the Enlightenment), cosmopolitan ideas spread among people at all levels of society. And part of the reason it did so is because philosophy became religion, specifically the syncretistic religions that are still considered one of the prime characteristics of specifically Hellenistic culture. It presents, therefore, the clearest historical example of what actually happens when universalistic philosophy and particularistic local cultures exist side by side for centuries: they mix and produce new forms of both. They produce new forms of rooted cosmopolitanism, and they produce new forms of localism that are open to the world. By 'rooted cosmopolitanism', we mean universal values that are emotionally engaging, that descend from the level of pure abstract philosophy and into the emotions of people's everyday lives. It is by becoming symbols of people's personal identities that cosmopolitan philosophy becomes a political and social force. And it is by embodying philosophy in rituals that such identities are created, reinforced, and integrated into communities. This is what happened in the transition from Greek philosophy to syncretistic religions. Because the most important syncretistic religion to grow out of the Hellenistic period was Christianity, a clear combination of universalistic, Hellenistic Greek philosophy (especially stoicism and neo-Platonism) with local religious beliefs (most notably Jewish Messianism). Together it changed the elite ethos of stoicism into the mass religion of Christianity. But what difference does it make for the spread of cosmopolitan ideas? Because calling it a secularized religion rather than an abstracted philosophy emphasizes the centrality of emotional engagement and social integration. And it emphasizes that both are bound up with symbol and ritual, and not just with spoken ideas. It is symbol and ritual that makes philosophy into personal and social identity. And for a cosmopolitan sociology, this is a central point distinguishing it form abstract cosmopolitan ideas.

But more is at stake here. Following the historical route of the cosmopolitan tradition from Hellenism via Christianity to the modern Western world makes the idea of cosmopolitanism open to criticism from outside the Western traditions. In order to avoid that pitfall, researchers have done well by going outside philosophy and history and by finding new paths to Non-Western forms of cosmopolitanism. Anthropological research can open ways to find Muslim cosmopolitanism (see for instance Marsden 2008) by looking at ways for real people to negotiate their particular identities in specific settings. This kind of research is about cosmopolitans and not cosmopolitanism (for Chinese cosmopolitans see Strassler 2008). In addition, Sheldon Pollock (2000) draws our attention to the Sanskrit cosmopolis and relates it as well to social action and literary critic. Mufti (2007) compares Muslim and Jewish particularism within the framework of cosmopolitanism in India. Chang Kyung-sub (1999) demonstrates how the 'compressed modernity' produces a specific border interacting Korean society in transition. These studies drawing on anthropological and literature criticism demonstrate quite clearly that even if the concept and the tradition of cosmopolitanism originates in the Western tradition it can be cosmopolitanized from without (for more relevant literature see Beck and Sznaider 2006b).

Moral cosmopolitanism

For example, one of the leading modern cosmopolitan ideas today is expressed in the concept of human rights. The text most people think of as the founding text of modern human rights campaigning is Kant's *On Perpetual Peace*. But Kant's idea was that a stable and peaceful political order could be constructed only out of nation states that made mutually supportive vows of non-intervention. This view was embodied to a large degree in the League of Nations and the original UN charter, and can be considered in many ways to be the beginning of the idea of modern international law, an essential cosmopolitan idea. But there is no escaping that Kant's project regards the sovereignty of nation-states as sacrosanct. However, modern cosmopolitan politics begins with the principle that sovereignty is not the highest principle and is not sacrosanct. Rather the highest principle is human dignity and well-being, and the duty to prevent suffering wherever it occurs. And for cosmopolitanism to spread widely among the world's population, and become the basis of political mobilization, it needs to be embodied in symbols and rituals so that it can become the basis of personal identity. Thus cosmopolitan attitudes can be learned through transnational social practices (Mau et al. 2008). This last point is important because this is finally the ultimate political foundation of cosmopolitanism: the feeling of individuals that they are doing something wrong by ignoring suffering. Properly mobilized, this is what creates the new political facts that enable cosmopolitan political action. However, not only morality is at stake here. The new political facts that enable cosmopolitan action create at the same time new inequalities which have to be thought *Beyond Class and Nation* (Beck 2007).

Beyond class and nation: The radicalization of social inequalities and the resistance against globalization

But sociological realism tells us the opposite story: globalization is striking back. Today re-nationalization and re-ethnification are powerful reactions towards Europeanization. What are the social consequences of globalization? Especially in relation to social structures, to inequality on a national as well as on a global scale.

From the massive wave of re-nationalization taking place in Russia to the success of the populists in Latin America and Eastern Europe, untrammelled capitalism is generating fears and defensive reactions that are unprecedented in comparison to anything we have experienced since the fall of the Berlin Wall. Resistance is growing as the middle sections of global society begin to realize that they have no share in the benefits generated by the current period of economic growth – indeed, that their slice of the cake may even be getting smaller. Ordinary middle class workers – whether they live in Manchester, the

641

American Midwest, the de-industrialized Ruhr area of Germany, France, Latin America or Eastern Europe – find themselves left out. 'When the local bakery increased the price of a baguette for the third time in six months in 2007, Anne-Laure Renard and Guy Talpot invested in a bread-baking machine. When gasoline became their single biggest monthly expense in January, they decided to sell one of their two cars. Now, as everything from baby milk to chocolate desserts drives up their living costs, Renard, a teacher, and Talpot, a mailman, are planning their most radical lifestyle change yet: They are getting married to reduce their tax bill. "I never thought I would be in this position, counting every cent," Renard said one recent evening: "I mean, I am a teacher. If I can't get by, how do others manage?"' (*Herald Tribune*, 30 April 2008, p. 1). Across Europe, people in the middle layer of the labour force – from office workers to low-level managers – are coping with a growing sense that they are being pushed to the margins like never before. The phenomenon is similar wherever you look: the rates of growth of average family incomes are far lower than productivity growth rates, and have been so for years. Economic globalization is giving rise to new forms of inequality which, increasingly, will have to be tackled *trans*nationally, or even globally.

It is therefore necessary to reframe the social inequalities beyond methodological nationalism, which includes three crucial points:

- class being but one of historical forms of inequality;
- nation-state is one of its historical frames, and
- 'the end of national class society' is not 'the end of social inequality' but just the opposite: the radicalization of inequalities, nationally and transnationally.

(Beck 2007)

What we are witnessing here at the beginning of the twenty-first century is a kind of repetition of the process, which Max Weber had in mind when he analyzed the origins of modern capitalism. The difference is that now we have it on a planetary scale. He said we have to look at the separation of business from household – in other words the emancipation of business interests. Today we have to look at the emancipation of business interests from the national institutions of control and supervision. What this means (in 'the second stage modernity') is the *separation of power (Herrschaft) from politics*.

In the first stage of modernity it was the emerging modern nation-state that managed to develop the institutions of politics and governance to limit the social and cultural damages of the modern industrial economy. It was done within the territorial borders of the nation-state and it was a kind of marriage between power and politics which now is ending in divorce. In the second stage of modernity power is partly being extrapolated and distributed into cyber space, into markets and mobile capital, and partly even into the life-politics of individualized individuals, who now have to cope with the risks that are being produced. And, actually, now there is no equivalent in sight to the sovereign state, which can give the answers to basic questions of the world society of risk. And because of this globalization produces huge inequalities and separation between winners and losers of globalization. The winners of globalization are the global elites, which aren't acting and living solely in national spaces anymore, but are highly mobile. They are living a trans-national life, and also parts of the middle class, especially the younger generations trans-nationalize themselves through education, friendships, though the internet, and all kinds of communication. But the most powerful groups in modern society so far are the losers of globalization – this is the rest of the middle class and the lower classes, who still keep to national and territorial identities and who need the shelter of the nation-state.

We have to look at the prime stratification factor in the global age, which is about the facility or the capacity of interaction between borders – which, of course, includes all kinds of resources, passports, education, language, money – and on the other side those who haven't got the capacities and facilities of movement and who define themselves in terms of an existentially threatened, territorially defined nationality. Here the reason for re-nationalization is to be found. In these parts of the population people experience themselves as losers of globalization (and Europeanization).

Elements of a social theory of cosmopolitan modernity

Today's world is full of challenges that do not belong to a single state. Those challenges are the product of *radicalized* modernization on a global scale, they are not 'crises' (in the old meaning), but consequences of the *victory* of industrial modernization which undermine basic institutions of first nation-state modernity. They constitute what we call 'world risk society'. These 'manufactured risks without passports' can only be addressed by collective action. No individual government, no matter how powerful, can solve them. And they are as urgent as they are numerous. The latest is the potentially global financial crisis. This world-wide-web of shared challenges encircles and connects involuntarily north and south, developed and developing, rich and poor, and will only yield to a shared response. From this paradoxically the 'cosmopolitan moment' of world risk society arises. But then we have to ask: how can we understand cosmopolitanism in terms of social theory?

Thus, we need a new sociological starting-point, one which continues the sociological tradition, but also one which recreates it and understands its newness. And when talking about morality – sociology is after all a moral science – then we should start with the well understood point that *morality is based on particularity*. It is based on being able to look ourselves in the mirror and say that we have fulfilled the moral obligations that make us who we are. And that includes above all the special responsibilities we have to particular others who have been attached to us by accidents of history and birth. To ignore all that – to pretend we don't show preference to our friends – or to pretend there is something wrong with that – that morality should be based on ideas and not on feeling – is to misunderstand the basis of morality. Morality is based on moral convictions. This idea of the basis of morality in identity, and the basis of identity in collective identity – or overlapping collective identities – this could be the cosmopolitan answer to what it means to maintain a tension between the universal and the particular (see Sznaider 2007, 2008). Our argument is far more fundamental, namely that universalism is an inadequate response to particularism and no less dangerous. It leads to the belief – superficially compelling but quite false – that there is only one truth about the essential of the human condition, and it holds true for all people at all times. If I am right, your are wrong. If what I believe is the truth, then your belief, which differs from mine, must be an error from which you must be converted, cured, and saved. From this flowed some of the great crimes of history, some under religious auspices, others under the banner of secular philosophies. Only cosmopolitanism, rooted in particular identity gives us moral motivation, because it's the basis of our passions and our self. Universal maxims, like 'we should help the poor' or 'we should save the innocent,' because they contain no personal element, are merely pious maxims that no one acts on – until they are mixed with the passion of identity, the feeling that you just can't look yourself in the face if you allow this to happen without doing something. Pure reasoning is indifferent to its ends. It is determined by our starting points, which reason does not supply. Real convictions are emotional convictions a point Kant and modern Kantian cosmopolitans have a tendency to overlook. And the ultimate basis of our emotional convictions is our identity: what we can't imagine ourselves doing. We think that this is the starting point of modern cosmopolitanism. Squaring the circle between the universal and the particular is no easy task but it is a sociological attempt which also requires squaring the circle between thought and feeling, morality and identity, and the Ought and the Is. It's not an easy path. But it's the only way not to get stuck in the trap of universalism where identity doesn't matter – and cosmopolitanism doesn't exist.

Towards a cosmopolitan social science

This is what makes cosmopolitanism so interesting for social and political theory of modern societies, namely the thinking and living in terms of inclusive oppositions. Nature is associated with society, the object is part of subjectivity, otherness of the other is included in one's own self-identity, and self-definition, and the logic of exclusive oppositions is rejected. Nature is no longer separated from national or international society, either as a subject or object. 'We' are not opposed to the 'Them'. Particularism and universalism are not moral choices, but sociological categories which need to be conceptualized together. This has clear methodological consequences. We argue, therefore, that in the social sciences, 'methodological cosmopolitanism' is opposed to 'methodological nationalism,' rejecting the state-centred perspective and sociological (lack of) imagination. It attempts to overcome the naive universalism of early Western sociology. Methodological cosmopolitanism implies becoming sensitive and open to the many universalisms, the conflicting contextual universalisms for example of the post-colonial experience, critique and imagination. Methodological cosmopolitanism also means including other ('native') sociologies – the sociologies of and about African, Asian, and South-American experiences of 'entangled modernities' (Randeira). 'Entangled modernities' replace the dualism of the modern and the traditional, pointing to and again creating the image of a deterritorialized melange of conflicting contextual modernities in their economic, cultural, and political dimensions. All of our existing political categories presume the nation-state as the ultimate political reality, and this methodological nationalism is clearly at work in our conviction that the way to clarify any mixture is to segregate out which nation is the influencer and which one is the influence. The world is generating a growing number of such mixed cases, which make less sense according to the 'either/or' logic of nationality than to the 'this-as-well-as-that' logic of transnationality.

Institutionalized cosmopolitanism

The First Modern world was a national world. There was a clear division between inner and outer, between domestic and foreign. In that world, the nation state was the principle of order. Politics were national politics, culture was national culture, labour, and class formation and class conflict were all primarily features of the nation state. International politics was a multiplication of nation states, each defining each other's borders and mirroring each other's essential categories. National and international were two sides of an interdependent whole. It was as impossible to conceive of a nation–state in isolation as to imagine an inner without an outer. Rooted cosmopolitanism, on the other hand, is defined against the two extremes of being at home everywhere and being at home nowhere. It means to be engaged in the local and the global at the same time. It is opposed to ethnocentrism but also to universalism, whether from the Left or the Right. When it comes to the critique of imperialism, rooted cosmopolitanism points out that in a postcolonial world, there is no pure, pre-colonized nation to go back to.

Cosmopolitan sentiments or a cosmopolitan common sense has to be distinguished from *institutionalized cosmopolitanism* through legal institutions like the International Criminal Court, the Human Rights regime codified in Conventions and courts and multi-lateral agreements. The European Union and its 'cosmopolitan entrepreneurs' the European Commission, Court, and Parliament appear to incorporate some answers not only to the horrors of the twentieth century, but to the increasing loss of state sovereignty.

A 'cosmopolitan state' not only separating nation and state but acting trans-nationally seems to be the next stage in an institutionalized cosmopolitanism (Beck 2005). Cosmopolitan states connect self-determination with responsibility for those who are not part of the nation-state. And this becomes institutionalized through the Human Rights Regime which will find a way to civilize a global risk society. And it should not be confused with a 'false cosmopolitanism' or global unilateralism, which means nothing but the pursuit of national interest in the name of cosmopolitan values. Another side of 'institutionalized cosmopolitanism' is through individualism or internalized cosmopolitanism. Issues of global concerns are becoming part of one's moral life-worlds, no matter if people are for or against it. The cosmopolitan horizon becomes institutionalized in our own subjective lives. A cosmopolitan sociology therefore, brings the subject back into the social sciences after system theory and post-structuralist theories have tried to construct a social science without subjects.

Cosmopolitanism and universalism: the case of religion and world risk society

Cosmopolitanism diverges from universalism in that it assumes that there is not one language of cosmopolitanism, but many languages, tongues, grammars. Cosmopolitanism means also disputing about its consequences. This paradigmatic reconstruction of social science from a national to a cosmopolitan perspective can be understood and explained as a 'positive problem shift' (Lakatos 1970). Previously, the national cosmos could be decomposed into a clear distinction between inside and outside. Between the two, the nation-state governed and order was established. Thus, there is a strong and hidden relationship between universalism and nationalism. In the inner space of the nation-state, the central themes of sociology like work, politics, law, social inequality, justice, and cultural identity were negotiated against the background of the action. And even here, the national/international distinction always represented a permanent self-affirming prophecy. Against the background of a cosmopolitan social science it becomes suddenly obvious that it is neither possible to distinguish clearly between the national and the international, nor, in a similar way, to contrast homogenous units. National spaces have become de-nationalized, so that the national is no longer national, just as the international is no longer international. And therefore, the universalism of social and political theory collapses as well. Let's take religion and especially Christianity as an example of these processes.

Religion

For religion one feature is absolute: faith – measured against it all other social differences and oppositions are unimportant. The New Testament says: 'All men are equal before God.' This equality, this annulment of the boundaries separating people, groups, classes, nations, societies, cultures is the social foundation of (Christian) religion. As it is written in Galatians 3:28: '*There is neither Jew nor Greek, there is neither slave nor free man, there is neither male nor female; for you are all one in Christ Jesus.*' A further consequence, however, is this: a new fundamental distinction and hierarchy is established in the world with the same absoluteness that social and political distinctions were annulled: the distinction between *believers* and *non-believers*, then we are only one in Christ Jesus. The non-believers (likewise in accordance with the logic of this duality) are denied the equality and dignity of human beings. Religions can build bridges between people where hierarchies and borders exist; at the same time they create new religion-determined chasms where there were none before. Thus cosmopolitanism is not only about 'Eternal Peace' but also about 'Eternal Fear' and 'Eternal Risk'. Which empirical indicators speak for it and which against it? Is it pure cynicism to attempt to seek a final spark of hope in the collective distress over uncertainty? Is this merely wishful thinking? We will try to counter this well-founded scepticism by means of six conceptual components that constitute the 'cosmopolitan moment' of world risk society (Beck 2008), namely, enforced enlightenment, communication across all divides and boundaries, the political power of catharsis, enforced cosmopolitanism, risks as a wake-up call in the face of the failure of governments and the possibility of alternative forms of governance in a globalized world. In what follows we employ two concepts of cosmopolitanism, a narrower and a broader one. In the broader sense, we speak of the 'cosmopolitan moment' of world risk society, in the narrower of 'enforced cosmopolitanization'.

Of course, there is a world of difference between cosmopolitanism as 'reality' and as 'maxim'. In the normative sense (of 'maxim'), cosmopolitanism means *recognition* of cultural otherness, both internally and externally. Differences are neither hierarchically ordered nor dissolved but are accepted as such, and even viewed positively. However, nowhere in the world at the beginning of the twenty-first century are such conditions anywhere near being accepted. But what can unite human beings of different skin colour, religion, nationality, location, pasts and futures if not recognition? The answer proposed by the theory of world risk society is: by the traumatic experiences of the enforced community of global risks that threaten everyone's existence. However, the recognition of the reality of the threat by no means includes the recognition of otherness.

Hence, we must make a clear distinction between a world in which the plurality of others is denied, ignored or condemned, even though it can no longer be expunged from the world, and a world in which this plurality is *recognized* and in which all share in the commonality of difference. The 'cosmopolitan moment' of world risk society means, first, the *conditio humana* of the irreversible non-excludability of those who are culturally different. We are all trapped in a shared global space of threats – without exit. This may inspire highly conflicting responses, to which re-nationalization and xenophobia also belong. *One* of them incorporates the *recognition* of others as equal *and* different, namely, normative cosmopolitanism.

Enforced enlightenment: danger and representation

It is a commonplace that the Greek *polis* only knew face-to-face communication and that it was both elitist and exclusive because it excluded women, slaves, and the underprivileged.

Danger globalized via the mass media can lend the poor, the marginalized and minorities a voice in the global public arena. Hurricane Katrina was a horrifying act of nature. As a global media event, it also performed an involuntary and unintended *enlightening function*. What no social movement, no political party, and certainly no sociological analysis, no matter how brilliant and well-founded, could ever have achieved occurred within the space of a couple of days: America and the world were confronted with the voices and images of the repressed *other* America, the racist face of poverty in the sole remaining superpower. American television does not care for images of poor people but they were ubiquitous during the coverage of Katrina. The whole world saw and heard that the black districts of New Orleans were destroyed by the storm tides because of their social vulnerability. The hurricane was a natural occurrence. Thus it does not seem to fit with the conceptual scheme that attributes catastrophes to human decisions rather than to nature. In fact, however, the scale of events such as the 2004 tsunami rests on social differences and previous developments. Thus the lack of information and early warning systems contributed to the monstrous abruptness of the tidal wave. This also led to many people losing their lives because they ran helplessly in the wrong direction. The deforestation of the islands and beaches and deficiencies in the location and construction of hotels, and slums contributed to aggravating the threat posed by tidal waves. Is climate change already reflected in the rise of the sea level, so that the force of the 'giant wave' and the defencelessness of the population were further magnified by the effects of civilization? In this sense, 'pure' natural occurrences are also 'risks', because decision-making in world risk society ensures that nature and society are intermeshed.

Thus, the television images of the tsunami disaster brought the first law of world risk society – namely, that *the risk of catastrophes haunts the poor* – into every living room. Global risks have two sides, namely, the probability of possible catastrophes and the social vulnerability as a consequence of catastrophes. There are good grounds for the prediction that climate change will cause devastation especially in the poor regions of the world, where the problems of high population growth, poverty, water and air pollution, inequalities between classes and genders, AIDS epidemics and corrupt, authoritarian governments all overlap.

A further aspect of the ambivalence of risk, however, is that with the globalization of compassion – as reflected in the unprecedented willingness to donate to the relief effort – the tsunami victims were simultaneously categorized, and became the focus of political debates, in accordance with their *nationality*. Compassion involves an active moral impetus to address others' suffering. Directed toward those outside the scope of personal knowledge, it becomes public compassion, shaping moral obligations to strangers in public arenas. This is the foundation for the recognition of human rights. Like 'human rights,' compassion expresses a strong belief in universal benevolence, optimism, and the idea that happiness can be achieved in this life on earth (Sznaider 2001, Levy and Sznaider 2005). Moreover, the many other catastrophes that go completely unreported, or are only fleetingly reported, in the West are indicative of the egoistic selectivity with which the West responds to the threats of world risk society.

Which moments or principles of publicity are operative here? And which theoretical proposals can help us to understand them? We just mentioned one principle: there is an imperative which creates an at least fleeting 'voting right', not necessarily in their municipalities but in national and global media publics, especially for the underprivileged and the excluded 'regardless of status and class'. Of course, this should not be idealized. The mass media do not follow the principles of enlightenment but those of market rationality and profit. There are also good reasons for doubting whether the voice of the voiceless really acquires argumentative and political influence and shapes judgements and decisions. And yet the individualized and anonymous individual destinies are bundled in a powerful way through the dangers and harms that blamelessly befall them in the exemplary stories of suffering narrated by television images and reports (which used to be possible only through protest marches) and in this way they are forged into a political event that cries out for identifying those responsible, for rethinking and for policy changes. Culture can no longer be understood as a closed national space, because it now competes constantly with other spaces. Transnational media and mass culture such as film and music loosen the national framework without abandoning it entirely. The globalization of communication technologies challenges national identities by confronting the viewer with the presence of others. In the process, conceptions and ideas about the world come into conflict with conceptions and ideas about the nation. Even television viewers who never leave their hometown must integrate global value systems that are produced elsewhere into their national frame of reference. The rise of rapid, electronically based communication has led to an interlocked system without national borders. The immediate speed and imagery of the new global communications facilitate a shared consciousness and cosmopolitan memories that span territorial and linguistic borders.

The principle of almost *boundless inclusion*, both as regards groups and topics, is reminiscent of analyses of the public sphere such as those offered by Hannah Arendt, Jürgen Habermas, and most recently Roger Silverstone (2006). Interestingly, this cosmopolitan moment engages with the social hierarchy both towards the top and towards the bottom: not only the voiceless but also powerful people who do not vote are included and called to account. Correspondingly, with the declaration 'imminent danger' the light of publicity is shone, irrespective of topic, into even the darkest corners of power and the most hermetic spaces of decision. The media are also undergoing cosmopolitanization. Human Rights politics is put into action when the sight of suffering leads to political action intended to lessen the suffering of others. This is only possible when a language is shared which makes the suffering of others understandable. The current suffering of others must be made comprehensible, however; it must be integrated into a cognitive structure that is connected to the 'memory' of other people's suffering. In this way, earlier catastrophes become relevant in the present and can determine a future that is articulated outside the parameters of the nation-state. However, there are communal boundaries to this globalized compassion. The recognition that compassion and rights are bound to communities and the needs of people in concrete settings is the starting point for a cosmopolitan methodology (Levy and Sznaider, forthcoming).

However, global risk public spheres have a completely different structure from the 'public sphere' explored by Jürgen Habermas. Habermas's public sphere presupposes that all concerned have equal chances to participate and that they share a commitment to the principles of rational discourse. The threat to the public sphere is founded on involuntariness and is emotionally and existentially determined. Here it is terror that breaks through the armour of anonymity and indifference, even if for most people it is images of terror that become the source of terror. This is as little a matter of commitment as it is of rationality. Potential bearers of responsibility who hide behind 'systemic constraints' are hauled before the court of global public opinion via the media. Without mercy and without regard for their social status, they are confronted with objections and are convicted of self-contradiction. The images of horror do not produce cool heads but they do give rise to cross-border compassion. False alarms, misunderstandings, and condemnations are

part of the story. In these risk public spheres, too, the pressure reaches volcanic proportions. Threat publics are impure, they distort, they are selective and stir up emotions and
anger. They make possible more, and at the same time less, than the public sphere
described by Habermas. They resemble more the picture of 'Mediapolis' so minutely and
sensitively painted by Roger Silverstone (2006) and the picture sketched by John Dewey
in *The Public and Its Problems* (1954). There Dewey defends the thesis that it is not actions
but their *consequences* that lie at the heart of politics. Although he was not thinking of
global warming, BSE or terrorist attacks, his theory can be applied perfectly to world risk
society. A global public discourse does *not* arise out of a consensus on decisions, but
rather out of *disagreement* over the *consequences* of decisions. Modern risk crises are constructed out of just such controversies over consequences. Although some insist on seeing
an overreaction to risk, risk conflicts do indeed have an enlightening function. They
destabilize the existing order but can also be seen as a vital step towards the construction
of new institutions. Global risk has the power to confuse the mechanisms of organized
irresponsibility and even to open them up for political action.

Conclusion: cosmopolitanism, globalization, and the Christian moment

Let us come full circle. As already mentioned above, it was Paul, a Hellenistic Jew who,
more than any other figure in the Jesus movement, turned Christianity from a Jewish
sect into a global religious force with a universalistic vision. He pulled down the walls:
'There is neither Jew nor Greek, there is neither bond nor free, there is neither male nor
female' (Galatians 3:28). The humanitarian universalism of believers is based on the
identification with God – and on a demonization of the opponents of God who, as Paul
and Luther put it, are 'servants of Satan'. This ambivalence of tolerance and violence can
be broken down into three elements: World religions overcome given hierarchies and
boundaries between nations and ethnic groups; they are in a position to do so, to the
extent that they create a religious universalism, in the face of which all national and social
barriers become less important; there simultaneously arises, however, the danger that
instead of ethnic, national, and class barriers, barricades are now raised between believers
in the right faith on the one hand and believers in the wrong faith and non-believers on
the other. Since this moment, particularism has been discredited.

The history of European colonization is of course the primary historical example of
how the category of unbelievers, who were to be converted for the sake of the salvation
of their own souls, permitted unimaginable atrocities and acts of violence and cruelty to
be carried out and 'legitimated'. Columbus expressed it with quite undisguised brutality.
To him the spreading of the faith 'and the enslavement of the non-believers were
indissolubly linked'. But the demonization of the religious other can also be effectively
illustrated by the 'mixed marriages war' between Catholic and Protestant Christians
which raged in the long nineteenth century and into the twentieth century. With the
establishment of national equality the boundary of hate and contempt between Catholic
and Protestant Christians of the same nationality – who, contrary to all declarations of
love within marriage, family, parenthood, attacked and excluded one another as 'false
faith communities of heretics' – had again and again to be proclaimed with fiery words
and actions. In particular, it appeared to both Catholic and Protestant churchmen a
betrayal of their own religion to abandon the education of children to the other religion:

'Whoever does not merely have the name of a Protestant Christian, but also that Protestant faith, for whose sake thousands once suffered a martyr's death, he also knows, what this faith is worth (…). Whoever, whether out of indifference or to gain some kind of worldly good, abandons his children to the Catholic Church, not only sins most gravely against their souls, but himself also ceases to be a Protestant Christian, he may no longer allow God's Word to dwell in his house, he may no longer with his family worship his God and Saviour in spirit and in truth.' The historian Tilmann Bendikowski has reconstructed many such stories, at whose core is the message: 'So heed this, dear Christian – beware of mixed marriage!' What unites both churches is that by condemning and combating mixed marriage they have erected and maintained a 'confessional apartheid'.

This confessional fundamentalism which refuses to see and acknowledge the other Christian in the 'other believer' is increasingly being rejected, not least by active believers. Here, as Hans Joas has written, a 'reversal of the burden of proof' (Daniel Deckers) has taken place with respect to ecumenical co-operation: 'What increasingly has to be justified is its absence, not its occurrence'.

Even the question 'What is religion?' displays a European bias. Because religion is understood as a substantive, by which a clearly defined social set of symbols and practices is assumed, constituting a monotheistic either/or – one can only either believe in it or not believe it, and one cannot, if one is a member of one church, simultaneously belong to another. It is, therefore, useful and necessary to introduce a distinction between 'religion' and 'religious' as substantive and as adjective.

The substantive 'religion' organizes the religious field in accordance with an either/or logic. The adjective 'religious', on the other hand, organizes it in accordance with a both/ and logic. To be religious is not based on adherence or non-adherence to a particular group or organisation; it defines, rather, a particular attitude to the existential questions concerning the position and the understanding of self of human beings in the world. That raises the question: Is it primarily 'religion' which displays the Janus face of brotherly love and deadly enmity, but perhaps not 'religious'? Can the violence-laden, monotheistic either/or be relativized, undermined, defused by the syncretic tolerance of both/and?

The authority in principle of revived faith is the sovereign self, which assembles a 'god of its own'. What is emerging as a result is certainly not the end of religion, but the advent of a new kind of subjective faith anarchy transcending all religious boundaries, which less and less fits inside the dogmatic frameworks which the institutionalized religions provide. The unity of religion and religious is breaking up. Indeed, religion and religious are coming into conflict. In Western societies, which have internalized the autonomy of the individual, human beings are creating ever more independently those little narratives of belief – 'the god of one's own' – which fit one's 'own' life and 'own' horizon of experience. This 'god of one's own', however, is no longer the One God, dictating salvation by appropriating (hi)story and authorizing intolerance and force. The principle of the religious melange is accompanied by the principle of a subjective polytheism. The blurred forms of faith of a 'god of one's own' could (to borrow and adapt a formulation of Odo Marquard) give rise to a subjectively willed and realized division of powers even 'within the absolute', directed against the sole claim of the monotheistic religions. Are we seeing a regression of the monotheism of religion to a polytheism of the religious governed by the principle of 'a god of one's own'?

This brings us back to our earlier points about Hellenism and the Hellenistic Empire. The syncretic tolerance is not only spreading in the sphere of detached religiosity, but can also be practised quite naturally in institutional forms, as can be observed, for example, in Japan. People there don't regard it as a problem to visit a Shinto shrine at certain times of the year, to arrange a marriage in accordance with Christian ceremonies and to be buried by a Buddhist monk. The disbelieving astonishment at that comes from within a monotheistic horizon of God monogamy ('Thou shalt have no other gods before me!'), which is quite foreign to Japanese eclecticism with respect to religions, but also generally in East Asia, including China. Peter L. Berger, the sociologist of religion, quotes the summing-up of the Japanese philosopher Nakamura: 'The West is responsible for two fundamental errors. One is monotheism – there is only one god, and the other is the Aristotelian principle of opposition – something is either A or not-A. Every intelligent person in Asia knows that there are many gods and that things can be both A and not-A at the same time.' We have arrived at the Cosmopolitan Moment. Now we need to wait for the social sciences to follow the moment and arrive as well.

References

Beck, Ulrich (2005) *Power in the Global Age*. Cambridge: Polity Press.
——(2006) *The Cosmopolitan Vision*. Cambridge: Polity Press.
——(2008) *World at Risk*. Cambridge: Polity Press.
——(2009) *A God of Its Own*. Cambridge: Polity Press.
Beck, Ulrich and Edgar Grande (2007) *The Cosmopolitan Europe*. Cambridge: Polity Press.
Beck, Ulrich and Natan Sznaider (2006a) 'Unpacking Cosmopolitanism for the Social Sciences: A Research Agenda'. *British Journal of Sociology*, 57 (1): 1–23.
——(2006b) 'A Literature on Cosmopolitanism: An Overview'. *British Journal of Sociology*, 57 (1): 153–64.
Berger, Peter L. (1979) *The Heretical Imperative: Contemporary Possibilities of Religious Affirmation*. Garden City, NY: Anchor Press/Doubleday.
Calhoun, Craig (2002) 'Imagining Solidarity: Cosmopolitanism, Constitutional Patriotism, and the Public Sphere'. *Public Culture*, 14 (1): 147–71.
Chang, Kyung-sub (1999) 'Compressed Modernity. South Korean society in transition'. *Economy and Society*, 28 (1): 33–55.
Dewey, John (1954) *The Public and its Problems*. Denver: Swallow.
Held, David et al. (1999) *Global Transformations*. Cambridge: Polity Press.
Joas, Hans (2007) 'Die Zukunft des Christentums'. *Blätter für deutsche und internationale Politik*, 8: 976–84.
Kurasawa, Fuyuki (2004) *The Ecological Imagination – A Cross-Cultural Critique of Modernity*. Minneapolis: University of Minnesota Press.
Lakatos, Imre (1970) 'Falsification and the Methodology of Scientific Research Programs'. In I. Lakatos and A. Musgrave (eds), *Criticism and the Growth of Knowledge*. Cambridge: Cambridge University Press.
Levy, Daniel and Natan Sznaider (2005) *The Holocaust and Memory in the Global Age*. Philadelphia: Temple University Press.
——(forthcoming) *Memory and Human Rights*. Penn.: Penn State University Press.
Marquard, Odo (1995) 'Lob des Polytheismus'. In *Abschied vom Prinzipiellen*. Stuttgart. Reclam.
Marsden, Magnus (2008) 'Muslim Cosmopolitans? Transnational Life in Northern Pakistan', Journal of Asian Studies, 67 (1): 213–48.
Mau, Steffen et al. (2008) 'Cosmopolitan Attitudes through Transnational Social Practices'. *Global Networks* 8 (1): 1–24.
Mufti, Amir (2007) *Enlightenment in the Colony. The Jewish Question and the Crisis of Postcolonial Culture*. Princeton: Princeton University Press.
Pollock, Sheldon (2000) 'Cosmopolitan and Vernacular in History'. *Public Culture*, 12 (3): 591–625.
Silverstone, Rogers (2006) *Media and Morality: On the Rise of the Mediapolis*. Cambridge: Polity Press.

Strassler, Karen (2008) 'Cosmopolitan Visions: Ethnic Chinese and the Photographic Imagining of Indonesia in the Late Colonial and Early Postcolonial Periods'. Journal of Asian Studies, 67 (2): 395–432.

Sznaider, Natan (2001) *The Compassionate Temperament: Care and Cruelty in Modern Society*. Bolder, CO: Rowman & Littlefield.

——(2007) 'Hannah Arendt's Jewish Cosmopolitanism: Between the Universal and the Particular'. *European Journal of Social Theory*, 10 (1): 113–23.

——(2008) *Gedächtnisraum Europa: Kosmopolitismus: Jüdische Erfahrung und Europäische Vision*, Bielefeld: transcript.

34

Globalization and its possible futures

Bryan S. Turner

Introduction: eleven theses on globalization

Conclusions are best when they are short and sharp rather than protracted and prolonged. The key issue that emerges from this collection is whether globalization will
corrode culture and community on the one hand or whether it will sustain and enlarge
democracy on the other. Can we draw an optimistic conclusion that globalization may
create conditions for the emergence of both wholly new communities and a cosmopolitan consciousness? Will globalization destroy the underlying foundations of solidarity
and conviviality that make life tolerable if not enjoyable? Will globalization foster and
expand the opportunities for friendship, sociability, and intimacy? Some commentators
see globalization as the religion of a new economic god dominating our lives and the
driving force behind the capitalist destruction of the world. Thus

> [t]he priests in globalization (the small group of families with disproportionate pri-
> vate ownership and distribution power of the world's wealth) and those who
> accept the leadership of this 'clergy' act as if concentrated monopoly, finance
> capitalist wealth is a god ... Globalization is a religious system of capitalist wealth
> concentration on a global scale, rapidly pursuing its object of faith – an indefinite
> increased concentration.
>
> (Hopkins, 2001: 19)

This pessimistic view was reinforced by the financial crisis of 2008–9 which convinced
many social sciences that we now need a new paradigm for globalization studies. Although
globalization presents the world with many pressing dangers, a religious framework is not
helpful in dealing with these problems because it reduces these global difficulties to the
motivation of a few bankers, but equally the complexity of the global world cannot be
reduced simply to economic forces. We do however need to attend to the negative
dimensions of globalization with some degree of political urgency. What are these?

In a concluding contribution to George Ritzer's edited work *The Blackwell Companion
to Globalization* I outlined eleven theses about the possible future direction of globalization

processes (Turner, 2007a). These theses were obviously an attempt to mimic Karl Marx's eleven theses, many of which pointed in his estimation to the need to change the world. While philosophers had interpreted the world, Marx called upon his generation to change it. My theses were by contrast largely negative in their assessment of our collective futures. In editing this book on globalization studies at the beginning of 2009, the future of globalization looks deeply problematic. In fact our prospects look bleaker now than when Ritzer's book was published in 2007. The prospects of a continuing world recession are very real and the response of many governments to this crisis may well include a return to protectionism, namely a step back from existing commitments to free trade, economic de-regulation and the globalization of labour markets. There were other worrying signs of social closure in early 2009 such as wild cat strikes in the United Kingdom against foreign workers and the desire on the part of some Republican senators to re-open the debate about illegal migration and to urge companies who are faced with 'down-sizing' to ensure that foreign workers go first.

My predominantly negative theses in the Ritzer collection on globalization included the following.

(1) The globalization of terrorism will persist as a problematic feature of modern politics, despite President Obama's apparently 'softer' more inclusive approach to foreign policy. It is also probable that increased securitization in the West will continue in response to 'new wars', 'warlordism', and the rise of the 'narco-state', namely the dominance of a drug economy, while failed states will continue to present major issues for world governance. In more specific terms, there are strong indications that America and its allies will not be successful in Afghanistan and that the border regions of Pakistan, given the volatility of Pakistani politics, will remain areas of recruitment for *jihadist* groups. At the same time, the growth of authoritarianism in Russia will make the search for a settlement with Iran and for political stability in Ukraine and Georgia problematic and uncertain. These global conflicts are merely the obverse side of the issue of empire as an outcome of further globalization. These threats will ensure that national boundaries are well policed and the porosity of state borders will be highly limited. In short, predictions about the decline of the nation state have been premature to say the least.

(2) Paradoxically such conflicts will create the conditions for a further development of the juridical revolution, the globalization of human rights and the quest for the rule of law as responses to these growing social conflicts. The instability in relations between states will make the role of the UN or similar global institutions more important and urgent. Faced with growing civil conflict in Africa (especially in the Congo and Zimbabwe), there will be an enhanced need for the establishment of the rule of law and human rights to provide some minimal protection to vulnerable social groups and political minorities. Rising political powers tend to create powerful navies, which is exactly what we have seen in the case of India and China. We can envisage growing tension with the emerging power of the Chinese navy in the South China seas around the Spratly and Paracel Islands. While these sites of tension call for legal restraint and diplomatic engagement, we also know from recent experiences that human rights conventions can also be used by powerful states to intervene militarily beyond their own borders, thereby exacerbating existing conflicts in the shape of human rights wars. There is a desperate need for better legal and political regulation of scarce resources, but it is clearly difficult for states to embrace such

constraints when their own electorates in the West expect for example to continue to enjoy private vehicle transport.

(3) These conflicts can be seen as a continuation of the 'clash of civilizations' thesis (Huntington, 1993 and 1996), in which it is claimed that the future of political globalization will continue to revolve around further conflicts over the sacred and political sovereignty. This thesis has been subject to a good deal of criticism. For example, the world is not divided simply into Christianity versus the rest since there is for example considerable conflict between Sunni and Shi'ite communities in the Middle East and Asia. However, as a general argument, we need to take note of the growth of religious fundamentalism and revivalism that have been important if unanticipated aspects of cultural globalization. One consequence has been the disappearance of the secularization thesis from academic debate, and modernization is no longer seen as inevitably producing the demise of the sacred. In recent years, sociologists have been more inclined to talk about the 'de-secularization' of social reality than about secularization (Berger, 1999). Transnationalism and diasporic cultures will continue to result in ethno-religious conflict and at the same time the crisis of liberal multiculturalism will continue while governments search for a political solution to a post-secular environment. Further globalization will see an increasing presence of extreme cults, and modern millenarian movements in response to ongoing social disruption and cultural change. The Sarin nerve gas attack by a Japanese religious cult killing twelve and injuring five thousand in Tokyo's underground some six years ago is one bizarre example.

(4) A neglected feature of the Huntington thesis was its underlying Malthusian assumptions. With improvements in public health, health care, and education, there was in the post-war period a rapid global demographic growth. Improvements in educational provision which many governments have seen an important key to economic development have played an important role in improving the status of women in developing societies and this change in gender status has been associated with health improvement. However, with the failure of economic growth in many nationalist and socialist regimes (such as Egypt, Iran, and eastern Europe) in the post-war period, radical generations of over-educated and under-employed youth emerged around the world, and these 'lost generations' became the breeding ground for radical groups, both religious and political. If 1968 symbolized the presence of radical middle class youth in western consumer society, the militant groups of the Third World in the late twentieth century represent a new breed of post-communist political mobilization. These radicalized youth have been referred to in the literature of modern conflict as 'overpopulation warriors' (Diessenbacher, 1998). Al Qa'ida can be regarded as a diverse generational cohort arising from such societies as Algeria and Afghanistan with these population characteristics. In the contemporary context, the credit crunch of 2008–9 threatens severely to contract the labour market in China with the possibility of bringing thousands of unemployed and alienated youth on to the streets of Shanghai and Beijing. The speed of the downturn in 2009 may well create the conditions for the alienation of youth and their recruitment into radical political movements with extremist ideologies.

(5) A further aspect of this Malthusian dimension to globalization is the ageing of the globe's population. It is very clear that North America and Europe have ageing populations that are placing serious economic burdens on their future economic growth, and there is generally a crisis around the provision of pensions for the

elderly. It is probably instructive to pause for a while over the Japanese case, because ageing in Japanese society is often quoted as the example of extremely rapid demographic change. The population over the age of 65 will rise from its 1988 figure of 11.0 per cent to 23.6 per cent by 2021 and Japanese women in particular are surviving in significant numbers into deep old age. In 2008, average life expectancy for Japanese women was already 85 years and it is predicted to rise to 97 years by 2050. In Okinawa 600 people out of a population of 1.3 million are centenarians – the highest density of centenarians in the world. Looking at the statistics on centenarians, in 2007 the United States had 55,000 people of that age, while Japan had 30,000. It is estimated that by 2050 the United States will have 834,000 centenarians and the Social Security Administration has raised the prediction of life expectancy to 119 years of age. These increases in the number of centenarians are a reflection of the general rise in life expectancy and they illustrated significant improvements in hygiene, health care, and medical advances. Ageing populations will have important consequences for the labour market, for consumption, for pensions and for life styles. The growth of gated communities will become a significant industry for countries such as Thailand and Malaysia as destinations for Japanese and other geriatric migrants.

(6) There is a crisis of multiculturalism. Liberal sociologists have frequently championed the possibility of an ethical cosmopolitanism, but conservative critics argue that multiculturalism is no longer sustainable. If commitment to multiculturalism as a public policy fails or is abandoned, we can expect a crisis of multiculturalism and further developments in the clash of civilizations, ethnic conflict, and religious wars. In addition to a crisis of multiculturalism, there is a parallel erosion of citizenship. There is ample evidence that the liberal and social frameworks of citizenship are in crisis. Liberal capitalist societies have created a set of conditions that has produced an erosion of citizenship (Turner, 2001). Participation in the market is obviously important and the idea of the worker-citizen has been a foundational aspect of modern society. However, there are clearly problems with this foundation, especially where there is profound casualization of labour, under-employment, early retirement and flexible hours of work. As Richard Sennet (1998) has argued, the modern market creates part-time, short-term, and ad hoc working conditions, resulting in what he calls a corrosion of character. In the case of the United States, Judith Shklar (1991) emphasized the centrality of earning a wage to the original American notion of citizenship. The sharp down turn in the labour market in the United States with the financial crisis is thus a further erosion of citizenship.

While national forms of citizenship appear to be in crisis, there is considerable interest in the possibility of global citizenship. The notion that there could be a 'citizen of the world' has long been part of the utopian imaginary of the democratic tradition. It was implicit in Augustine's idea of the City of God within which the legacy of Roman global society would be perfected. It was part of Kant's vision of a 'perpetual peace' (Kant, 1983) in which the Enlightenment dream of a world free from irrational prejudice could be realized. It was also part of Goethe's cosmopolitan idea of world society that would transcend the narrow limitations of emerging German militarism.

(7) There will be a globalization of the medical utopia. Thomas Malthus (1970) in his famous *Essay on the principle of population as it affects the future improvement of society* proposed that population will outstrip the food supply because cultivatable land is fixed while sexual appetite is not. One response to Malthusian pessimism was that

technology can make the food supply more efficient and help to control the consequences of the sexual drive through contraception and induced abortion. What is the likely impact of medical technology on this Malthusian problem? In the short term, stem cell research will help people in rich countries to live longer – indeed 'live for ever'. This technical possibility of longevity will seriously exacerbate the problem of scarcity of resources.

One aspect of these medical developments has been the emergence of a global market for organs and in particular there is a demand for 'fresh organs', that is organs from living bodies, because recipients tend not to want to receive organs that have been taken from cadavers. Nancy Scheper-Hughes controversially calls this global harvesting of organs a form of neo-cannibalism in which there a fetishization of the body in a diversified market for skin, bone, marrow (Scheper-Hughes and Wacquant, 2003). There is also 'biopiracy' from the Third World which offers fresh stocks of generic material for organ brokers.

(8) The balance between scarcity and pollution is an important aspect of the Malthusian conundrum. Optimistic theories of international trade from Adam Smith onwards have however not taken the problem of waste and scarcity seriously. One further dimension of globalization will be the long-term exhaustion of the world's resources especially oil and gas. This crisis will continue to fuel anti-globalization, and many anti-globalization movements will become increasingly violent resulting in eco-terrorism, because national governments will find it difficult to handle their own waste issues. Environmental damage, population explosions, and civil unrest will result in conflicts over scarce resources resulting in 'water wars' and a scramble for basic energy supplies leading to a new round of geo-politics in the Arctic, Central Africa, and the South China Sea.

One feature of recent economic globalization has been the extreme volatility in commodity prices. Of course volatility is not a new phenomenon, but with a global economy the effects are felt worldwide. For example at the beginning of 2008, there was a huge increase in oil and wheat prices, but by the end of 2008 and into 2009 there was a global slump in basic commodity prices. For example soybean prices have plunged by around forty percent between July 2008 and February 2009. In Argentina where soybean production had become a successful component of agricultural exports, there had been several years of good harvests and rising prices between 2003 and 2008. The growth rate in Argentina had been on average around five percent, creating the basis for significant foreign investment but the collapse in prices was accompanied by the worst drought in seventy years. The collapse in soybean prices has been followed by copper and oil, bringing about a sudden closure of economic development. This combination of environmental disaster – in this case drought – and problematic price volatility is likely to remain a feature of developmental problems for the foreseeable future.

(9) One consequence of globalization, which has been somewhat neglected in mainstream sociology, has been the globalization of health and illness. A major feature of modern globalization has been the spread of communicable disease. The HIV/AIDS epidemic was a major feature of contemporary globalization, but new additions to the list of threatening conditions such as SARS will have serious economic consequences and put constraints on global travel and migration. In a period of global communication and transport, disease does not recognize national borders. The 2003 outbreak of SARS that spread rapidly from Beijing to Toronto is a classic example.

The spread of infectious disease is also closely associated with the global conduct of war. The deadly disease Ebola has been carried through central Africa by guerrilla troops for example by the Lord's Resistance Army, a messianic rebel army that blends Christianity and Islam, passing between southern Sudan and Uganda in 2003. The global spread of narcotics also has an important impact on national health through their negative effect on individual health behaviours. The domestic politics of Columbia have a major outcome on health behaviour in New York, because the supply of drugs can be easily disrupted by domestic conflicts in South America. For similar economic and political reasons, the collection of the opium crop in Afghanistan has a direct impact on health and lifestyle in London and Sydney. The rapid spread of crack cocaine as a lifestyle drug among young people, sex workers, and ethnic minority groups in inner city areas in the last fifteen years has had detrimental consequences for health, especially in terms of enhanced HIV risk.

(10)   Social and political crises will produce cultural and psychological responses, such as new theodicies and cosmologies. The Black Death in European societies produced millenarian religious movements. The tsunami of December 2004 produced fundamentalist cosmologies that attribute causal responsibility to this Asian disaster to the tourist industries of Thailand, the youth cultures of consumerism and soft drugs, and tourist sex industries. The global crises of pollution and population will result in bizarre planetary cosmologies. The internet facilitates the spread of these millenarian ideologies which resemble the cargo cults of anthropological research and with the emergence of virtual realities the division between fact and fantasy becomes blurred. While we may hope to see the emergence of cosmopolitan mentalities, there will be other more problematic and challenging forms of consciousness emerging with globalization that will not sit comfortably with a liberal, multicultural world. Roland Robertson (1992) pointed to the role of religion in shaping the early development of globalization and if we are moving into a post-secular environment it invokes a question about the possibilities of future forms of religious consciousness. What form can a dark eschatology for the planet assume?

(11)   Environmental crises can perhaps be seen as the most serious consequence of global industrialization especially in societies such as China and India. One possible response to the earth's environmental crisis is for governments to consider exploiting extra-terrestrial resources through space exploration and colonization. There will therefore be the rise of global interplanetary societies. Since the development of rocket warfare in the Second World War, planetary exploration has been an important feature of scientific exploration and development. So far these investments have been primarily for military purposes, but with the degradation of resources on earth these explorations of outer space will become increasingly significant for sustaining earth's economic system, and for future opportunities for human colonization.

Globalizing democracy

The tone and intent of these eleven theses is essentially pessimistic. We do not have adequate solutions to the problems raised by globalization and therefore the real issue behind any possible future is the question of democracy. The feasibility of any future social life will probably hinge on the tensions between the opportunities for further democratization versus the need for greater security. A common theme of much contemporary literature is the question of renewing community and reviving the public sphere in the current context of what may prove to be a turning point in neo-conservative politics and neo-liberal economics.

We are familiar with the argument closely associated with Jürgen Habermas (1989) that the civil sphere created by bourgeois society has been severely compromised by the commercialization of the media, the concentration of media ownership, and the consequent trivialization of information circulating to the public. This Habermasian interpretation of communication is part of a larger contemporary debate in which it is asserted that the whole edifice of 'the social' has been challenged and corroded by neo-liberal economic orthodoxy which privileged markets over social relations, praised individual entrepreneurship over community responsibility, and installed a radical policy of downsizing, privatizing, and out-sourcing that stripped social life of its foundations. This whole development was epitomized by Margaret Thatcher's infamous statement during an interview in 1987 with *Woman's Own* magazine that 'there is no such thing as society, only individuals and their families'. Critical responses to the contemporary crisis in the financial markets suggests that faith in the neo-liberal creed has been severely damaged, and financial gurus in Wall Street and the City have been roundly condemned for their destructive greed. One obvious response is to suggest that a return to some form of Keynesianism might be the principal solution for rebuilding the social fabric. One other argument is that after the destructive phase of market-driven relationships internet networks can create new global communities within which citizens can once more become actors within a reconstituted public sphere.

In thinking about the possibility of new communalism, I shall initially organize these reflections around Daniel Drache's *Defiant Publics* (2008). Against Habermas's pessimistic view that the re-feudalization of the public sphere means that the bureaucracy has trapped the citizen in a client relationship, Drache claims that the new communication technologies have extended and enhanced the access points to public discourse. Just as print was constitutive of modern forms of national identity within imagined communities, so the hypertext has given rise to the global citizen who is connected to other citizens through networked public spaces. However according to Drache, the global citizen is disgruntled with the Washington Consensus, globalization, predatory corporations, unregulated free trade and rampant consumerism, and this disenchantment is producing criticism, debate, and protest – the stuff of democratic politics. Disgruntled voters are punishing neo-liberal governments and programs, because they have produced demonstrably disastrous results. These deregulated economies gave rise to Enron, Worldcom, the Hollinger newspaper empire, the credit crunch of 2008–9 and disreputable characters like Bernie Madoff. These alienated voters are likely to elect coalition governments that can put a brake on neo-liberal policies such as privatization. While the current financial crisis may not prove to be long-lasting, the growing economic inequality appears to be a more generic feature of globalization itself. Economic globalization produced increasing income inequality. Taking a long term perspective, in 1870 the world's average per capita income was $873 while the income of rich countries was $2,419. In the poor countries, which meant primarily African societies, it was $500 or a ratio of 5:1. By 1950 income of the rich had risen to $9,268 and the poor to $890 and the ratio was 13:1. In 2003, in rich countries the average income had grown to $28,039 and the poor countries it was $1,549. In 2006 the Congo had a per capita income of $649 and in France it was $28,877 or a ratio of 40:1.

However, these negative economic dimensions of neo-liberal globalization may be quite separate from the question of democracy, which depends to some extent on viable civil societies and robust communities (Held et al., 1999; Keane, 2003). The new internet communities are very different publics from the past, because they are to a large extent post-national and typically ephemeral. They also operate outside the spatial territories of the national state. Insofar as there is global citizenship, the citizen now belongs to groups who organize and communicate beyond the fixed boundaries of the state. In a period when trust in major institutions – corporations, states, and professional bodies – is declining, citizens have, it is argued, found new ways of belonging together through file-sharing, blogging, and texting. Furthermore the digital divide is contracting with the shrinking cost of technology and as a result of programs such as One Laptop per Child.

Network society has grown at a startling pace. In the G8 countries, the number of people using the internet exploded from around seven and a half million in 1993 to 297 million by 2001, and in the same period the number of internet users in the G20 countries rose from 430,000 people to 25 million. By the year 2007, there were one billion people on line. In tandem with this network society, NGOS have also increased dramatically. Since 1950 the number of NGOs which are active internationally (that is with memberships in three or more countries) has grown from 1,000 to 25,000. These developments can become part of the larger framework of debate and dissent.

Drache suggests that modern dissent is articulated around four large themes or clusters of concern. The first issue concerns social inclusion and is directed towards the homeless, the illegal migrant, the stateless refugees and asylum seekers, and the mass of people who are generally drifting and disrupted. The second cluster is engaged with trust and human security, thereby incorporating a large contingent of activists who are potentially carriers of a cosmopolitan hope. The institutional expression of these global concerns is to be found in such organizations as Medecins Sans Frontieres, OneWorld, ActionAid and the Global Development Network. The third configuration of concern is centred on the question of individual freedom. This is a libertarian cluster that addresses questions of recognition and the protection of minorities. This dimension is represented by such activist groups as ACT UP, Global AIDS Alliance, and Health Global Alliance Project (GAP). The final cluster is the project of building political community. These are the micro-activists who develop networks and enhance the social power of the public such as Habitat for Humanity providing homes for the homeless and support for low-income groups. These micro-activists often organize highly visible campaigns from the cancellation of Third World Debt to the protection of workers in the sex trade. The diverse nature of these clusters suggests that modern dissent is ideological fluid and no longer tied to orthodox Marxism or doctrinaire socialism. The new dissenters move easily and rapidly between clusters and social movements, employing modern communication technology to mobilize globally in cycles of political rebellion and nonconformity that cut across age, gender, ethnic, and class barriers. The mentality of the disgruntled citizen is primarily one of scepticism in expressing disbelief in official information and public pronouncements. Distrustful of official news sources, these dissenting groups use various internet sources to counter and contradict official stories and justifications.

In Marxism, the political vision of a monolithic, emancipated, and disciplined public is no longer relevant to modern forms of organization, dissent, and opposition. Like the world of which it is critical, modern dissent is fragmented, mobile, and diverse. In fact we can longer speak of 'the public' in the singular, but of a multitude of publics. If there is anything that holds these publics together, it is 'fright at the excesses of corporate greed and the absence of responsible governance practices' (Drache, 2008: 146). The hope of progressive politics is that this multitude can act as an inclusive movement in bringing about social and political change.

Of course publics in the past were also built by states creating public utilities such as drainage systems, sewerage, roads, street lighting, public toilets, and civic buildings through the taxation of its citizens. Will the modern state with a shrinking taxation base be able to maintain existing public works let alone build new utilities? One problem with the modern state is that in following neo-liberal economics most of our public utilities are in need of costly repair and with privatization many public utilities have simply ceased to be public. The other problem is that a large proportion of taxes goes into military expenditure and governments have used the defence budget as a means of job creation. It is estimated that over the next fifteen to twenty-five years the US government will spend $238 billion on the National Missile Defence System in a society where forty-seven million citizens have no health care protection. In short how do we reconcile the need for taxation and accountable governments with the sprawling mobile communities that lie beyond the state?

There are at least two (probably fatal) criticisms of these optimistic interpretations of global communication. First, in addition to its democratic possibilities, the internet is also a conduit for gambling, pornography, hacking, and sleaze as well as fraud, blackmail, and corruption. We may also wonder whether useful information competes successfully with the daily wave of spam and junk mail? Of course nobody can give an entirely plausible answer to this question, but we do need to know what safeguards can be built into the new publics to protect them from these undesirable aspects? Perhaps more importantly we need to recognize that the web facilitates democracy but equally it permits the mobilization of fascism, racism, and other extreme ideologies. The second problem is a version of the first issue. In the general literature on alternative politics, the disgruntled citizen is seen to be basically a concerned, responsible, and caring social actor. These assumptions look naïve. Disgruntled citizens may also decide to plant bombs in government buildings, mail anthrax to politicians and sabotage public spaces. Timothy McVeigh, the so-called Oklahoma Bomber, was a disgruntled citizen who was opposed to what he thought was a tyrannical federal government. McVeigh had become a disgruntled and alienated citizen while serving as an American soldier. He was horrified by the slaughter of Iraqi soldiers on the road out of Kuwait in the Gulf War. Although his act of revenge was criminal, resulting in a terrible and tragic loss of life, McVeigh was not a monster and his criticisms of American central government received a sympathetic analysis in Gore Vidal's *Perpetual War for Perpetual Peace* (2002).

Community and globalization

The term 'community' has proved to be as problematic as 'society' in the history of the social sciences (Brydon and Coleman, 2009). The conventional and minimal view in sociology has been that community involves a residential dimension, the propinquity of its members (for example in a face-to-face community), and shared values and customs that exercise moral control over its constituent members. Sociologists, having regularly presided over the decline of community under the pressure of urbanization, have more

661

recently turned to the corrosive consequences of globalization. Equally sociologists keep rediscovering community for example in the classical study of working-class communities in Young and Willmott's *Family and Kinship in East London* (1957). Conceptualizing 'community' in relation to the local and the global is problematic, but one solution is to think of communities as being 'nested' in different scales and operating across the global. Clearly the existence of global communities must at some stage become connected with new types of consciousness such as environmentalism or cosmopolitanism (Beck, 2000). It is important in any discussion of the global not to lose sight of the importance of place. It is well recognized that the new media offer opportunities for constructing innovative forms of belonging through networking and 'netweaving' that can pull together a diverse concatenation of places. Although most pessimistic visions of globalization treat globalization as standardization resulting in conformity, it is possible to show how global mobility might for example enhance the capabilities of women to gain a greater degree of autonomy. Finally, it is all too easy to idealize the notion of 'community' which as a moral form can exert power, even authoritarian power, over personal autonomy.

It appears that there is no consistent pattern in relationships between local communities and global social structures. Many communities are fragile and may well disappear under the impact of globalization, whereas other communities are surviving as a collection of dispersed places held together by the internet. We may also reasonably hope there will be communities of the future. Similarly some global processes appear to erode individual autonomy, while other processes appear through the use of modern communications technology to enhance autonomy. Given these unpredictable outcomes, two forms of community are important. Firstly global communications have greatly enhanced the ability of people with disability to form supportive communities thereby to some extent overcoming the physical immobility that often plagues people with such crippling impairments. If any collection of individuals has become a global community, then it is the community of the disabled, which is held together on and by the internet. Modern technologies have also greatly enhanced their autonomy and mobility. Secondly some of the most prominent examples of communities existing across space are provided by religion. The modern Islamic *ummah* is probably the primary example of a community that has in recent years come into existence largely through the internet (Mandaville, 2001). Similar examples could be taken from other world religions and with the growth of religious diasporas as a consequence of global migration an important illustration of communal survival could be taken from various communities of Filipino maids (often connected with the El Shaddai movement) or the global Chinese diasporic communities (Ong, 1999).

Should one be optimistic or pessimistic about such 'defiant publics' and the rise of new communities? While there is plenty of room for optimism, especially regarding the communities of the sick and the disabled, there is also cause for alarm. One needs to take the security issue seriously. While many social scientists in the final decade of the last century predicted the end of the state and celebrated the porous boundaries between societies, 9/11 and other terrorist acts changed the mood of globalization studies and there has been, if anything, a return of the state (Calhoun, 2007). The building of walls at frontiers, the increasing level of surveillance at all boundaries, the creation of gated communities, bio-profiling and the securitization of societies has resulted in the 'enclave society' in which communities are bounded and gated, and the individual's autonomy is premised on an extensive network of controls and surveillance. In this context, global 'network power' will continue to have a social dynamic that nation states cannot easily control and hence the globalization process does not lend itself to any steering mechanism (Grewal, 2008).

Enclave societies and global security

In the euphoric *fin-de-siecle* of the last century, the possibility of peaceful globalization and expanding democratization had never looked more promising. In response to these political changes, there was a general sense that political borders and cultural boundaries were disappearing. This view of modern societies is closely associated with the work of sociologists such as Zygmunt Bauman, Ulrich Beck, Anthony Giddens, and John Urry who have often criticized mainstream sociology for its alleged focus on nation–states as its central topic. This optimistic vision of a changing social world was widely shared in the late 1990s. For example the notion of a network society was developed to replace existing conceptions of national capitalism (Castells, 1996) as a framework for understanding the globalization of the economy.

With the development of more intensive forms of securitization after 9/11, there have been a growing number of restrictions on migration and a greater emphasis on the management of borders. I have elsewhere developed a critique of the idea that modern globalization has created a world of porous boundaries and these criticisms of the general idea of flows, networks and mobility can be captured in the idea of an emerging 'enclave society' (Turner, 2007b). In such an enclosed society, states and their agencies seek to regulate spaces and where necessary to contain and immobilize flows of people, goods and services (Shamir, 2005). These closures can assume various forms such as the military-political, the social and cultural, and finally the biological. I propose to coin a new term 'enclavement' to describe these strategies, tactics, and technologies for both domestic and international regulation. Enclavement describes these processes that seek to install governmentality, often in extreme form, over populations by enclosure, bureaucratic barriers, legal exclusions, and classification. Rather than increasing mobility, we have witnessed emergence of an immobility regime of gated communities, racial ghettoes, and mass prisons. Alongside these institutions, there are related practices such as the tagging of criminals, misfits, and deviants. There is also increasingly a public-health need for quarantine to ensure biological closure against the resurgence of established diseases such as tuberculosis, venereal disease and HIV/AIDS, the recent advance of contagious outbreaks such as SARS, and the growing prospect of a catastrophic pandemic of avian influenza in Asia and beyond.

Whereas religious enclavement in medieval times served important demographic functions in creating influential roles and cultures niches for (aristocratic) women in medieval society (Laven, 2002), modern forms of enclavement have very different causes and consequences. They are less benign in purpose and more closely associated with regulation and surveillance of alien, undesirable or socially marginal populations. The sequestration of populations could be regarded as the most elementary form of social regulation with the aim of protecting host populations from infectious disease or from dangerous persons who are regarded as morally or biologically undesirable. In the inter-war years European campaigns to achieve 'racial hygiene' promoted the idea of national fitness and national eugenics strategies included negative measures such as sterilization of the biologically unfit. In the 1930s and 1940s negative eugenics, being obsessed by the prospect of biological degeneration, became preoccupied with the problem of the mentally ill. These measures were not only part of fascist ideologies but were also embraced by social democracies as necessary aspects of public health policies. Such practices that sequester special sections of the population may be regarded as essentially illustrations of what Max Weber understood as a process of rationalization applied to the management of populations. By contrast, the creation of gated communities to protect the elderly or the vulnerable is designed, not to exclude threats from the outside, but to protect local communities from internal dangers including self harm. With the rapid ageing of the populations of the developed world, declining fertility and increasing life expectancy, multiple strategies to manage the elderly have emerged, including the construction of overseas retirement villages, homes for the elderly and luxury cruise ships for rich geriatric strata. Because it is unlikely that the deeply aged will ever actively and voluntarily return to the formal labour market, such strategies of governmentality are best conceptualized as a response to the growth of 'social waste' that is to sections of the population who are unlikely to benefit from the interventions of an administrative state. Such forms of enclavement can be treated as examples of 'social storage'.

Global cities, punk and urban tribes

Whereas Durkheim had developed an image of mechanical solidarity in *The Elementary Forms* (2001) as a society based on commonalities, collective rituals and shared emotions, the social world of the post-war period gave rise to very different images and theories. With the growth of world-wide urbanization and the rise of global mega-cities, social life is thought to be increasingly fragmented, giving rise to urban ghettoes, alienated minorities, the inner-city no-go areas and violent youth subcultures. The idea of the 'lonely crowd' and the 'inner-directed personality' paints a picture of passive and isolated urban dwellers glued to their TVs.

It was claimed that from 1950 onwards, there were new youth subcultures associated with a growing consumerism. Ethan Watters (2003) in *Urban Tribes* suggested that these new social groups were composed of 'never-marrieds' between the ages of 25 and 45 years who formed common but ephemeral interest groups. Their new life styles were constituted by shifting forms of identification within these fragmented groups. Dick Hebdige (1979) wrote a classic account of these developments in his *Subculture: The Meaning of Style* to describe the oppositional movements that followed 'rock n roll' such as punk, Goths and other rave cultures. These studies had in fact been preceded by Michel Maffesoli's *The Time of the Tribes* in 1996. The subtitle of this work in its English translation of 1988 was *The Decline of Individualism in Mass Society*. Maffesoli argued that various micro-groups were emerging in modern society who shared a common but shallow informal culture. Although these 'tribes' were fleeting, their members shared a common emotional bond that was very different from the cold, bureaucratic ties of formal organizations. Punks were probably the classical illustration of such youth interest groups.

In 1967 Guy Debord published his *The Society of the Spectacle* in which he developed Marx's theories of alienation to argue that modern society was further alienated by the impact of the mass media. Everyday life had been colonized by commodities producing what Marx had called the fetish of commodities. We can only experience our world through this mediation – being had become merely appearing and the relations between people had become a spectacular world of appearances and commodities. Debord's work on a spectacular society was the ideological foundation of the movement (mainly among students) of the Situationist International. Debord encouraged events and demonstrations as a protest against the alienation of a media–dominated world and his ideas had a profound effect on the student protests of 1968.

These ideas about the media and alienation became part of postmodern theory. Although Baudrillard came to be seen as a leading figure of postmodern theory, he can also be interpreted as a major critic of postmodern consumer society. He was influenced by Marshall McLuhan and Karl Marx, but criticized Marxism as a theory of production for neglecting consumption (Rojek and Turner, 1993). In any case Marx could not have anticipated the growth of media. Baudrillard, who emphasized the ways in which reality and fiction, substance and appearance had merged, became a well-known writer for his *The System of Objects* (1968/1996), *The Mirror of Production* (1973/1975), and *Simulation and Simulcra* (1981/1996), but he gained world-wide notoriety for his argument in 1991 that the Gulf War was a TV spectacular in *The Gulf War Did Not Take Place* (1995). He was mistakenly criticized for claiming that there was no such war whereas his argument was about the media construction of the war. However, this accusation of trivializing the conflict stayed with him.

These ideas about social fragmentation, liquid modernity, and representation began simultaneously to influence science fiction and social theory around the themes of cyberspace and cyberpunk. The works of William Gibson such as the *Neuromancer* 1984 were said to give expression to a new community of hackers and the technologically literate who were socially disaffected and searching for social forms that could express the connectivity made possible by computerization. The new possibilities might overcome the 'electronic industrial ghettoes' (Stone, 1991: 95) that characterized modern society. Some social theorists began to speculate about 'cybersociety' as a more accurate description or alternative to the idea of the information city (Jones 1994). These theories also celebrated the merging of fiction and social science writing arguing that traditional social sciences had no chance of capturing even the basic features of the information age. One example is Davis's *Beyond Blade Runner: Urban Control – the Ecology of Fear* (1992).

These ideas which can be dated from the publication of J.-F. Lyotard's *The Postmodern Condition* (1979/1984) are still influential, but the debate has moved on to the study of globalization. Interestingly globalization theory rarely engages with this literature that was so popular and influential in the 1960s and 1970s. While globalization studies have been overwhelmingly concerned with the impact of the internet on global transactions, they have been less concerned with claims about the end of grand narratives – in part because globalization is itself a grand narrative. The debate about cyberspace, cyborgs, and postmodern culture was, we might suggest, concerned with two questions – is society changing and do we need new methods and epistemologies to capture those changes? In its bleakest moments, globalization theory asks not what type of society might exist, but whether society is possible at all in a world without water and a serious decline in basic commodities (such as oil, rice and soyabean). If there are not enough resources to support existing populations, the outcome will be 'new wars' or low intensity wars about borders and water, or hot wars around access to oil (such as the emerging conflict around oil deposits in the South China Sea). The war on terrorism has diverted attention away from discussions of simulation and representation to a focus on borders, border conflict, refugees, and fundamentalism. One does not hear too frequently the claim that the wars in Iraq and Afghanistan are simply media events. However, there may be an argument to suggest that the underlying issues of much postmodern debate – has the modernization project failed and what type of society or societies might emerge with modern technologies? – remain.

665

Conclusion: democracy and cosmopolitanism

One can predict without much anxiety of being contradicted that the credit crunch of 2008–9 and the growing liquidity crisis will produce a new paradigm shift. Although some may be tempted to think up new concepts that predict the end of globalization such as post-globalization, such a development appears to be unlikely. While there may be some degree of de-coupling where some societies attempt to isolate themselves from global process and while many governments may be tempted to experiment with pro-tectionism, globalization appears to be more deeply entrenched than such anti-globalization strategies imply. It is unlikely that internet use will decline or the Indian farmers will give up their cell phones or that enthusiasm for English football clubs in Asia will decline. It is also unlikely that the threat of global epidemics from infectious diseases will decline or that the current wave of urban terrorism will suddenly evaporate. We can expect eco-nomic turbulence to continue. Price instability is likely to increase the income inequalities that are such a central feature of neo-liberal globalization.

The real question remains – what of the prospect of global democracy? Everything in this collection points to the growing weakness of civilties, the social fabric, and com-munal bonds. The punk studies of earlier postmodern theory adequately captured the instabilities and incivilities of modern urban life. Internet communities are unlikely to replace the communities that survived the early stages of capitalist development. This urban instability exists alongside the more disturbing developments described by Mary Kaldor and others as 'new wars'. It is for these reasons that securitization appears to be a continuing trend with globalization and it is for this reason that I am inclined to see modern developments in terms of the enclave society. The moral programme for a per-petual peace which Kant (1992) designed in 1795 continues to be an impossible dream.

Will there be a new paradigm for globalization studies? The answer is affirmative in the sense that we can expect studies that emphasize the uneven nature of globalization, the fragility of financial markets in such a context, the growing problem of youth unemployment as a consequence of economic uncertainties, and the growth of genera-tional and class conflicts over scarce resources. The years of prosperity and boom that we saw with the Clinton administration are over for the immediate future. As China and India continue nevertheless to grow and expand, the policeman role of the United States as the global policeman can no longer be sustained.

The two promising aspirations of globalization studies are the building of new internet communities which may provide support for a revival of civil society and the evolution of cosmopolitanism both as an ideology and as an attitude towards diversity, resulting eventually in a new type of consciousness. The prospects of global citizenship are limited as are the prospects of further democratization. We may be forced to hope for small steps towards local democratic experiments and small steps towards cosmopolitan virtue.

References

Baudrillard, Jean (1968) *The System of Objects*, London: Verso.
——(1975) *The Mirror of Production*, New York: Telos Press.
——(1995) *The Gulf War Did Not Take Place*, Bloomington, IN: Indiana University Press.
——(1996) *Simulation and Simulacra*, Ann Arbor, MI: University of Michigan Press.
Beck, Ulrich (2000) *What is Globalization?* Cambridge: Polity Press.

Berger, Peter L. (ed.) (1999) *The Desecularization of the World: Resurgent Religion and World Politics*, Grand Rapids: Eerdmans.

Beyer, P. (1994) *Religion and Globalization*, London: Sage.

Brydon, Diana and Coleman, William D. (eds) (2009) *Renegotiating Community: Interdisciplinary Perspectives, Global Contexts*, Vancouver, Toronto: UBC Press.

Calhoun, Craig (2007) *Nations Matter: Culture, History, and the Cosmopolitan Dream*, London: Routledge.

Castells, Manuel (1996) *The Rise of Network Society*, Cambridge, MA: Harvard University Press.

Davis, M. (1992) *Beyond Blade Runner: Urban Control – the Ecology of Fear*, Westfield: Open Media.

DeBord, Guy (1967) *La société du spectacle*, Paris: Buchet-Chastel.

Diessenbacher, H. (1998) *Kriege der Zukunft: Die Bevölkerungsexplosion gefährdet den Frieden*, Munich: Hanser.

Drache, Daniel (with Marc D. Froese) (2008) *Defiant Publics: The Unprecedented Reach of the Global Citizen*, Cambridge: Polity Press.

Durkheim, Emile (2001) *The Elementary Forms of the Religious Life*, Oxford: World Classics.

Gibson, William (1984) *Neuromancer*, New York: Ace Books.

Grewal, David Singh (2008) *Network Power: The Social Dynamics of Globalization*, New Haven, CT: Yale University Press.

Habermas, Jürgen (1989) *The Structural Transformation of the Public Sphere*, Cambridge: Polity Press.

Hebdige, Dick (1979) *Subculture: The Meaning of Style*, London: Methuen.

Held, David, McGrew, Anthony, Goldblatt, David and Perraton, Jonathan (1999) *Global Transformations: Politics, Economics and Culture*, Cambridge: Polity Press.

Hopkins, Dwight N. (2001) 'The Religion of Globalization' in Dwight N. Hopkins, Lois Ann Lorentzen, Eduardo Mendieta and David Batstone (eds) *Religions/Globalizations: Theories and Cases*, Durham, NC: Duke University Press, pp. 7–32.

Huntington, S. (1993) 'The Clash of Civilizations', *Foreign Affairs* 72(3): 22–48.

——(1996) *The Clash of Civilizations: Remaking of World Order*, New York: Touchstone.

Jones, S. (ed.) (1994) *Cybersociety*, London: Sage.

Kant, Immanuel (1992) *Perpetual Peace: A Philosophical Sketch*, London: Thoemmes Press.

Keane, John (2003) *Global Civil Society?* Cambridge, Cambridge University Press.

Laven, Mary (2002) *Virgins of Venice: Enclosed Lives and Broken Vows in the Renaissance Convent*, London: Viking Books.

Lyotard, J.-F. (1984) *The Postmodern Condition: A Report on Knowledge*, Manchester: Manchester University Press.

Malthus, Thomas (1970) *Essay on the principle of population as it affects the future improvement of society*, Harmondsworth: Penguin.

Mandaville, Peter (2001) *Transnational Muslim Politics: Reimagining the Umma*, London: Routledge.

Ong, Aihwa (1999) *Flexible Citizenship: The Cultural Logics of Transnationality*, Durham, NC: Duke University Press.

Robertson, Roland (1992) *Globalization: Social Theory and Global Culture*, London: Sage.

Rojek, Chris and Turner, Bryan S. (eds) (1993) *Forget Baudrillard?* London: Routledge.

Scheper-Hughes, Nancy and Wacquant, Loic (eds) (2003) *Commodifying Bodies*, London: Sage.

Sennet, Richard (1998) *The Corrosion of Character: The Personal Consequences of Work in the New Capitalism*, New York: W.W.Norton.

Shamir, Ronen (2005) 'Without Borders? Notes on Globalization as a Mobility Regime', *Sociological Theory* 23 (2): 197–217.

Shklar. Judith N. (1991) *American Citizenship: The Quest for Inclusion*, Cambridge: Harvard University Press.

Stone, A. R. (1991) 'Will the Real Body Please Stand Up? Boundary Stories about Virtual Cultures' in M. Benedikt (ed.) *Cyberspace: First Steps*, London: MIT Press.

Turner, Bryan S. (2001)'The Erosion of Citizenship', *British Journal of Sociology* 52 (2): 189–209.

——(2007a) 'The Futures of Globalization' in George Ritzer (ed.) *The Blackwell Companion to Globalization*, Oxford: Blackwell, pp. 675–92.

——(2007b) 'The Enclave Society: Towards a Sociology of Immobility', *European Journal of Social Theory* 10 (2): 287–303.

Turner, Bryan S. and Rojek, Chris (2001) *Society & Culture: Principles of Scarcity and Solidarity*, London: Sage.

Vidal, Gore (2002) *Perpetual War for Perpetual Peace*, Los Angeles: Thunder's Mouth Press.

Walker, James W. St. G. and Andrew S. Thompson (eds) (2009) *Critical Mass: The Emergence of Global Civil Society*, Wilfred Laurier University Press.

Watters, Ethan (2003) *Urban Tribes: A Generation Redefines Friendship, Family and Commitment*, London: Bloomsbury.

Wise, J. McGregor (2009) *Cultural Globalization: A User's Guide*, Oxford: Wiley-Blackwell.

Young, Michael and Willmott, Peter (1957) *Family and Kinship in East London*, London: Routledge.

Index

Abdel-Malek, Kamal 275
Abduh, Muhammad 272
Abercrombie, N. and Longhurst, B. 404
Abu-Lughod, Janet L. 434
Abu-Lughod, Lila 626
accumulation 15, 47, 546; capitalist
  accumulation 156, 370, 372, 432–33, 435,
  443–44, 542, 544, 606–7; centers of 542; by
  dispossession 107, 543, 545; galactic mode of
  543–44; inequalities of 177; overaccumulation
  of capital 534, 541–42; primitive accumulation
  543
ACT UP 660
Action Aid 85, 660
activism: Direct Action Network 80; global
  justice movement (GJM), analysis and 84–86;
  indigenous artists, activism of 295; People's
  Global Action (PGA) 79, 80; Rainforest
  Action Network 80; Seattle, anti globalization
  activism in 80–81; transnational collective
  action 69–70, 77
Acuto, Michele 514
Adam, D. 188
Adams, John Quincy 561
Adey, Peter 521
Adler, F., Mueller, G.O.W. and Laufer, W.S.
  245
Adorno, Theodore 534
al-Afghani, Jamal al-din 272
Afghanistan 16–17, 82, 96, 107, 119, 150, 241,
  261, 265, 341, 356, 537, 559, 627, 654, 655,
  658
Africa: Christian missions in 272; conflict in 654;
  Ebola in 658; genocide in 320–22; Kalahari
  Peoples Fund (FPF) 299; Lord's Resistance

Army in 658; migration within 164–65; Pan-
  Africanism 77; Sub-Saharan Africa 119, 120,
  149, 150, 151, 152, 154, 582; Working
  Group of Indigenous Minorities in Southern
  Africa (WIMSA) 299–300
Agamben, Giorgio 516, 519
ageing world: commodification of pensions in
  367–68; globalization and population in 655–56
agency: of Asian migrants 172; consumption and
  globalization in history 459–62; globalization,
  effects on human agency 589–90, 595, 597;
  modern risk, product of human agency 230,
  231; political agency, autonomy and 340, 611;
  power, resistance and 457; of Sikhs in
  suppression of fundamentalism 280–81; world
  risk society and 128–29, 131
Agnew, John 514
Agnoletto, Vittioro 85
Ago, S. 578
agri-business, dynamics of 493–94
Ahmad, N. and Wyckoff, A. 190
Aiolfi, Sergio 450
Aji, Yuxuan 485–86
Al Qa'ida 265, 539, 655
Alam, Muhamammad Mumtaz 442
Alamgir, Mohiuddin 234
Albert, Michel 84
Albrow, Martin 8, 9, 589
Algeria 655
Ali, Kamran Asdar 631
Aliber, R. and Kindleberger, C.P. 58
Alison, J. 305–6n21
Allbright, Madeleine 357
Allen, B. 251
Allen, Paul 535

eBooks – at www.eBookstore.tandf.co.uk

A library at your fingertips!

eBooks are electronic versions of printed books. You can store them on your PC/laptop or browse them online.

They have advantages for anyone needing rapid access to a wide variety of published, copyright information.

eBooks can help your research by enabling you to bookmark chapters, annotate text and use instant searches to find specific words or phrases. Several eBook files would fit on even a small laptop or PDA.

NEW: Save money by eSubscribing: cheap, online access to any eBook for as long as you need it.

Annual subscription packages

We now offer special low-cost bulk subscriptions to packages of eBooks in certain subject areas. These are available to libraries or to individuals.

For more information please contact webmaster.ebooks@tandf.co.uk

We're continually developing the eBook concept, so keep up to date by visiting the website.

www.eBookstore.tandf.co.uk